GUINNESS BOOK OF RECORDS

EDITORS AND COMPILERS
NORRIS AND ROSS McWHIRTER

SPORTS EDITOR
SUZI BIGGAR

FOR SUPERLATIVE ACHIEVEMENT

Standard Book Number ISBN: 0 900424 26 5
Standard Book Number ISBN: 0 900424 27 3
(Australian Edition)
Copyright © 1975 Guinness Superlatives Ltd
& Norris & Ross McWhirter
World Copyright Reserved
Twenty-Second Edition

Note
In keeping with the standardization sought by the Booksellers' Association, The Library Association and The Publishers' Association, editions have been designated thus:

Edition	Published	Edition	Published
First Edition	October 1955	Twelfth Edition	November 1965
Second Edition	October 1955	Thirteenth Edition	October 1966
Third Edition	November 1955	Fourteenth Edition	October 1967
Fourth Edition	January 1956	Fifteenth Edition	October 1968
Fifth Edition	October 1956	Sixteenth Edition	October 1969
Sixth Edition	December 1956	Seventeenth Edition	October 1970
Seventh Edition	November 1958	Eighteenth Edition	October 1971
Eighth Edition	November 1960	Nineteenth Edition	October 1972
Ninth Edition	April 1961	Twentieth Edition	October 1973
Tenth Edition	November 1962	Twenty First Edition	October 1974
Eleventh Edition	November 1964	Twenty Second Edition	October 1975

Note
No back numbers are now available. Orders for current editions published overseas will willingly be passed on to the publishers concerned.

OVERSEAS AND FOREIGN LANGUAGE EDITIONS
Dates refer to the latest available year of publication in the country concerned

Guinness Book of World Records, 1975, Casebound, U.S.A., Sterling Publishing Co. Inc., New York
Guinness Book of World Records 1974, Paperback, U.S.A., Bantam Books Inc., New York
Le Livre des Records, 1975, Casebound, French Editions Denoel, Paris
Guinness Rekord bog Først og Størst Sidst og Mindst, 1975, Casebound, Danish Politikens Forlag, Copenhagen Denmark
Guinness Lexikon Der Superlative, 1975, Paperback, German Bertelsmann Lexikon-Verlag, Gütersloh, W. Germany
Guinness Rekordboken Først og Størst Sist og Minst, 1973, Casebound, Norwegian Chr. Schibsteds Forlag, Oslo
Guinness Korega Sekai Ichi, 1975, Casebound, Japanese Kodan Sha Ltd., Tokyo, Japan
Enciclopedia Guinness de Superlativos Mundiales 1975, Paperback Spanish (American), Editors Press Service Inc., New York
Il Guinness dei Primati, 1975, Paperback, Italian Arnoldo Mondadori Editore, Milan, Italy
Guinness Suuri Ennätys Kirja, 1974, Casebound, Finnish Sanoma Osakeyhtio, Helsinki, Finland
Guinness Rekord bok Först och Störst 1974, Casebound, Swedish Bokforlaget Forum AB, Stockholm, Sweden
Guinness Groot Record Boek 1976, Casebound, Uitgeberij Luitingh BV, Laren, Holland
Guinness Livro dos Recordes, 1974, Casebound, Portuguese Editora Abril, São Paulo, Brazil
Note: Czechoslovak, Serbo-Croatian and Spanish (European) editions have been contracted for publication shortly

OVERSEAS DISTRIBUTORS AND AGENTS

AUSTRALIA Collins Leutenegger Pty. Ltd. in Brisbane and Sydney; Collins Forlib Pty. Ltd. in Burwood, Victoria; Marley, W.A. and Forest Ville, S.A.

CANADA Hurtig Publishing 10,560 105th St., Edmonton, Alberta

CHANNEL ISLANDS L.S.T., 9 Patriotic Street, St. Helier, Jersey

EUROPEAN D. Richard Bowen, Post Box 30037, S-200 61, Malmö 30, Sweden

INDIA Allied Publishers Private Ltd., 15 Graham Road, Ballard Estate, Bombay

JAMAICA Sangsters Book Stores Ltd., P.O. Box 366, 97 Harbour Street, Kingston

MALTA Agius & Agius Ltd., 42a South Street, Valletta

MIDDLE EAST Nigel M. Ealand, Ealand Enterprises, Agios Vlasios, Platanidia, Volos, Greece

NEW ZEALAND Whitcoulls, Private Bag, Christchurch

SOUTH AFRICA P. B. Mayer, 902 Norwich House, Heerengracht, Cape Town

SOUTH EAST ASIA Times Distributors, Rivery Valley Rd., Singapore 9

Artwork by DON ROBERTS
Layout by FLAX & KINGSWORTH and DAVID ROBERTS

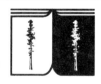

Made and produced in Great Britain by
REDWOOD BURN LIMITED
Trowbridge & Esher

GUINNESS SUPERLATIVES LIMITED
2 CECIL COURT, LONDON ROAD, ENFIELD, MIDDLESEX, ENGLAND

FOREWORD

By the Rt. Hon. The Earl of Iveagh

Chairman Arthur Guinness Son & Co Ltd, St James's Gate and Park Royal Breweries

When we first brought out this book, twenty years ago, we did so in the hope of providing a means for peaceful settling of arguments about record performances in this record-breaking world in which we live. We realise, of course, that much joy lies in the argument, but how exasperating it can be if there is no final means of finding the answer.

In the event, we have found that the interest aroused by this book has exceeded our wildest expectations. We are now obliged to include the gratifying entry that in November 1974 with sales of 23,950,000 our title qualified as the world's all-time best seller among commercially sold books.

Whether the discussion concerns the highest that any man has jumped over his own height, the greatest weight lifted by a woman, the nationality of the first woman to climb Everest, or—an old bone of contention—the longest time to become a Saint, I can but quote the words used in introducing the first edition, "How much heat these innocent questions can raise: Guinness, in producing this book, hopes that it may assist in resolving many such disputes, and may, we hope, turn heat into light".

Iveagh

October 1975

PREFACE

This 22nd Edition has been completely revised, and re-illustrated throughout.

In this edition references to places in Scotland conform to the 12 regional and island authorities (see page 61) which became operative on 16 May 1975.

There has been in recent months a marked increase in efforts to establish records for sheer endurance in many activities. In the very nature of record-breaking the duration of such 'marathons' will tend to be pushed to greater and greater extremes and it should be stressed that marathon attempts are not without possible dangers. Organizers of such events would be well counselled to seek medical advice before and surveillance during marathons which involve extended periods without sleep.

NOTES ON ACCEPTABILITY OF RECORDS

We are likely to publish only those records which improve upon previous records or which are newly significant in having become the subject of widespread and preferably international competitiveness.

It should be stressed that unique occurrences and interesting peculiarities are not in themselves necessarily records. Records which are *qualified* in some way, for example, by age, day of the week, county, etc cannot be accommodated in a reference work so general as *The Guinness Book of Records*.

Claimants should send independent corroboration in the form of local or national newspaper cuttings, radio or TV coverage reports and signed authentication by independent adult witnesses or representatives of organisations of standing in their community. Signed log books should show there has been unremitting surveillance in the case of endurance events. Five minutes rest intervals (optional but aggregate) must be *permitted* after each completed hour even in "non-stop" marathon events.

If an activity is one controlled by a recognised world or national governing body that body should be consulted and involved in ratifying it.

The publishers do *not* normally supply personnel to invigilate record attempts but reserve the right to do so.

If there are discrepencies between entries in one edition and another, it may be generally assumed that the *later* entry is the product of the more up to date research.

Finally the editorial office, which is concerned with maintaining and improving the quality of each succeeding edition, is unable to perform also the function of a free general information bureau for quiz competitions and the like, by telephone or by correspondence.

Editors and compilers

Norris McWhirter

Ross McWhirter

October 1975   Guinness Superlatives Limited, 2 Cecil Court, London Road, Enfield, Middlesex

CONTENTS

1. DIMENSIONS

TALLEST GIANTS

The height of human giants is a subject on which accurate information is frequently obscured by exaggeration and commercial dishonesty. The only admissible evidence on the true height of giants is that collected in the last 100 years under impartial medical supervision.

The assertion that Goliath of Gath (*c.* 1060 B.C.) stood 6 cubits and a span (9 ft 6½ in [*290 cm*]) suggests a confusion of units or some over-zealous exaggeration by the Hebrew chroniclers. The Jewish historian Flavius Josephus (born A.D. 37 or 38, died *post* A.D. 93) and some of the manuscripts of the Septuagint (the earliest Greek translation of the Old Testament) attribute to Goliath the more credible height of 4 Greek cubits and a span (6 ft 10 in [*208 cm*]).

Extreme mediaeval data, taken from bone measurements, invariably refer to specimens of extinct whale, giant cave bear, mastodon, woolly rhinoceros or other prehistoric non-human remains.

Circus giants and others who are exhibited are normally under contract not to be measured and are, almost traditionally, billed by their promoters at heights up to 18 in *45 cm* in excess of their true heights. There are many notable examples of this, and 23 instances were listed in the *Guinness Book of Records* (14th edition). The acromegalic giant Eddie Carmel (b. Tel Aviv, Israel, 1938), formerly "The Tallest Man on Earth" of Ringling Bros. and Barnum & Bailey's Circus (1961–68) was allegedly 9 ft 0⅝ in *275 cm* tall (weighing 38 st. 3 lb. [*242 kg*]), but photographic evidence suggests that his true height was about 7 ft 6⅝ in *229,6 cm*. He died in New York City on 14 Aug. 1972 when his standing height due to severe kyphoscoliosis, was *c.* 7 ft *212 cm*.

An extreme case of exaggeration concerned Siah Khān ibn Kashmir Khān (b. 1913) of Bushehr (Bushire), Iran. Prof. D. H. Fuchs showed photographs of him at a meeting of the Society of Physicians in Vienna, Austria, in January 1935, claiming that he was 320 cm *10 ft 6 in* tall. Later, when Siah Khān entered the Imperial Hospital in Teheran for an operation, it was revealed that his actual height was a full metre less at 220 cm *7 ft 2.6 in.*

World Modern opinion is that the tallest recorded man of whom there is irrefutable evidence was Robert Pershing Wadlow, born at 6.30 a.m. on 22 Feb. 1918 in Alton, Illinois, U.S.A. Weighing 8½ lb. *3 kg 860* at birth, his abnormal growth began almost immediately. His height progressed as follows:

Age in Years	Height		Weight in lb.	kg	Age in Years	Height		Weight in lb.	kg
5	5'4"	*163 cm*	105	*48*	15	7'8"	*234 cm*	355	*161*
8	6'0"	*183 cm*	169	*77*	16	7'10½"	*240 cm*	374	*170*
9	6'2½"	*189 cm*	180	*82*	17	8'0½"	*245 cm*	315[1]	*143*
10	6'5"	*196 cm*	210	*95*	18	8'3½"	*253 cm*	—	
11	6'7"	*200 cm*	—		19	8'5½"	*258 cm*	480	*218*
12	6'10½"	*210 cm*	—		20	8'6⅔"	*261 cm*	—	
13	7'1¾"	*218 cm*	255	*116*	21	8'8½"	*265 cm*	491	*223*
14	7'5"	*226 cm*	301	*137*	22.4[2]	8'11"	*272 cm*	439	*199*

[1] *Following severe influenza and infection of the foot.*
[2] *Wadlow was still growing during his terminal illness.*

THE HUMAN BEING

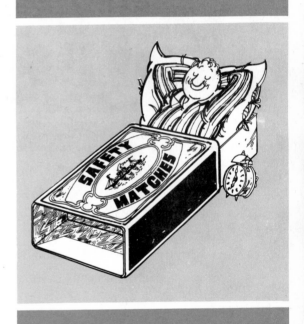

Dr. C. M. Charles, Associate Professor of Anatomy at Washington University's School of Medicine in St. Louis, Missouri, measured Robert Wadlow at 272 cm *8 ft 11.1 in* in St. Louis on 27 June 1940. Wadlow died 18 days later, at 1.30 a.m. on 15 July 1940, in Manistee, Michigan, as a result of cellulitis of the feet aggravated by a poorly fitted brace.

He was buried in Oakwood Cemetery, Alton, Illinois in a coffin measuring 10 ft 9 in *328 cm* in length, 32 in *81 cm* wide and 30 in *76 cm* deep. His greatest recorded weight was 35 st. 1 lb. *222 kg 710*, on his 21st birthday. He weighed 31 st. 5 lb. *199 kg* at the time of his death. His shoes were size 37AA (18½ in *47 cm* long) and his hands measured 12¾ in *32 cm* from the wrist to the tip of the middle finger (c.f. the depth of this page at 11¼ in *28,6 cm*).

The only other men for whom heights of 8 ft *244 cm* or more have been reliably reported are the seven listed below. In each case gigantism was followed by acromegaly, a disorder which causes an enlargement of the nose, lips, tongue, lower jaw, hands and feet,

The world's tallest ever man Robert Wadlow with his brother—Robert is the one wearing glasses (see page 7)

due to renewed activity by an already swollen pituitary gland, which is located at the base of the brain.

John F. Carroll (1932–69) of Buffalo, New York State, U.S.A. (a) 8 ft 7¾ in *263,5 cm*.

John William Rogan (1871–1905), a Negro of Gallatin, Tennessee, U.S.A. (b) 8 ft 6 in *259,1 cm*.

Unnamed pituitary giant (*fl.* 1966) Kenya 8 ft 3 in *251,4 cm*.

Don Koehler (b. 1925-*fl.* 1974) of Denton, Montana, U.S.A. (c) 8 ft 2 in *248,9 cm*, now lives in Chicago.

Väinö Myllyrinne (1909–63) of Helsinki, Finland (d) 8 ft 1.2 in *247 cm*.

"Constantine" (1872–1902) of Reutlingen, West Germany (e) 8 ft 0.8 in *246 cm*.

Sulaimān 'Alī Nashnush (b. 1943) of Tripoli, Libya (f) 8 ft 0.4 in *245 cm*.

(a) *Severe kypho-scoliosis (two dimensional spinal curvature). The figure represents his height with assumed normal spinal curvature, calculated from a standing height of 8 ft 0 in 244 cm, measured on 14 Oct. 1959. His standing height was 7 ft 8¼ in 234 cm shortly before his death.*

(b) *Measured in a sitting position. Unable to stand owing to ankylosis (stiffening of the joints through the formation of adhesions) of the knees and hips.*

(c) *Same spinal curvature. Present standing height c.7 ft 10 in 238, 4cm. He has a twin sister who is 5 ft 9 in 175 cm tall. His father was 6 ft 2 in 1,87 m and his mother 5 ft 10 in 1,77 m.*

(d) *Stood 7 ft 3½ in 222 cm at the age of 21 years. Experienced a second phase of growth in his late thirties and may have stood 8 ft 3 in 251 cm at one time.*

(e) *Height estimated, as both legs were amputated after they turned gangrenous. He claimed a height of 259 cm 8 ft 6 in.*

(f) *Operation to correct abnormal growth in Rome in 1960 was successful.*

A table of the tallest giants of all-time in the 31 countries with men taller than 7 ft 4 in *223,5 cm* was listed in the 15th edition of the *Guinness Book of Records* (1968) at page 9.

Gabriel Estevão Monjane (b. 1944) of Monjacaze, Mozambique has been credited with heights up to 8 ft 6 in *259 cm*. This eunuchoid-infantile giant has not however grown since he was anthropometrically assessed by Dr. Manuel Simoes Alberto in Lourenço Marques in Dec. 1965, when his standing height was *238,5 cm* 7 ft 10 in.

England The tallest Englishman ever recorded was William Bradley (1788–1820), born in Market Weighton,

Humberside. He stood 7 ft 9 in *236 cm*. John Middleton (1578–1623), the famous Childe of Hale, from near Liverpool, was credited with a height of 9 ft 3 in *282 cm* but a life-size impression of his right hand (length 11½ in *29,2 cm* c.f. Wadlow's 12¾ in *32,4 cm*) painted on a panel in Brasenose College, Oxford indicates his true stature was nearer 7 ft 8 in *233,3 cm*. James Toller (1795–1819) of St. Neots, Cambridgeshire was alleged to be 8 ft 6 in *259 cm* but was actually 7 ft 6 in *229 cm*. Albert Brough (1871–1919), a publican of Nottingham, reached a height of 7 ft 7½ in *232 cm*. Frederick Kempster (1889–1918) of Bayswater, London, was reported to have measured 8 ft 4½ in *255 cm* at the time of his death, but photographic evidence suggests that his height was 7 ft 8½ in *235 cm*. He measured 234 cm *7 ft 8.1 in* in 1913. Henry Daglish, who stood 7 ft 7 in *231 cm*, died in Upper Stratton, Wiltshire, on 16 March 1951, aged 25. The much-publicized Edward (Ted) Evans (1924–58) of Englefield Green, Surrey, was reputed to be 9 ft 3 in *282 cm* but actually stood 7 ft 8½ in *235 cm*. The tallest fully mobile man now living in Great Britain is Christopher Paul Greener (b. New Brighton, Merseyside, 21 Nov. 1943) of Hayes, Kent, who measures 7 ft 5¼ in *226,6 cm*. Terence Keenan (b. 1942) of Rock Ferry, Merseyside measures 7 ft 6 in *229 cm*, but is unable to stand erect owing to a leg condition. His abnormal growth began at the age of 17 when he was only 5 ft 4 in *163 cm* tall.

Scotland The tallest Scotsman, and the tallest recorded "true" (non-pathological) giant, was Angus Macaskill (1825–63), born on the island of Berneray, in the Sound of Harris, in the Western Isles. He stood 7 ft 9 in *236 cm* and died in St. Ann's, on Cape Breton Island, Nova Scotia, Canada. Lambert Quételet (1796–1874), a Belgian anthropometrist, considered that a Scotsman named MacQuail, known as "the Scotch Giant", stood 8 ft 3 in *251 cm*. He served in the famous regiment of giants of Frederick William I (1688–1740), King of Prussia. His skeleton, now in the Staatliche Museum zu Berlin, East Germany, measures 220 cm *7 ft 2.6 in*. Sam McDonald (1762–1802) of Lairg in Sutherland, was reputed to be 8 ft *244 cm* tall but actually stood 6 ft 10 in *208 cm*. The tallest Scotsman now living is George Gracie (b. 1938) of Forth, Strathclyde. He stands 7 ft 3 in *221 cm* and weighs 28 st. *178 kg*. His brother Hugh (b. 1941) is 7 ft 0½ in *215 cm*.

Wales The tallest Welshman ever recorded was George Auger (1886–1922), born in Cardiff, South Glamorgan. He stood 7 ft 5 in *226 cm* and died in New York City, N.Y., U.S.A.

Ireland The tallest Irishman was Patrick Cotter O'Brian (1760–1806), born in Kinsale, County Cork. He died at Hotwells, Clifton, Avon. He said that he was 8 ft 7¾ in *264 cm* at the age of 26, but his actual living height was 7 ft 10.86 in *241 cm*, calculated from measurements of his long bones made by Dr. Edward Fawcett, Professor of Anatomy at University College, Bristol, on 3 March 1906, after his coffin had been accidentally exposed during excavation work.

The tallest Irishman now living is believed to be Jim Cully (b. 1926) of Tipperary, a former boxer and wrestler. He stands 7 ft 2 in *218 cm*.

TALLEST GIANTESSES

World Giantesses are rarer than giants but their heights are
All-time still spectacular. The tallest woman in medical history was the acromegalic giantess Jane ("Ginny") Bunford, born on 26 July 1895 at Bartley Green, Northfield, West Midlands. Her abnormal growth started at the age of 11 following a head injury, and on her 13th birthday she measured 6 ft 6 in *198 cm*. Shortly before her death on 1 April 1922 she stood 7 ft 7 in *231 cm* tall, but she had a severe curvature of

THE HUMAN BEING

the spine and would have measured about 7 ft 11 in *241 cm* with assumed normal curvature. Her skeleton, now preserved in the Anatomical Museum in the Medical School at Birmingham University, has a mounted height of 7 ft 4 in *229 cm*. It was announced on 10 Feb. 1972 that the skeleton of a mediaeval giantess measuring 8 ft 3 in *251 cm* had been found in the Laga mountains near Abruzzi, Italy by archaeologists but this was a hoax. Anna Hanen Swan (1846–88) of Nova Scotia, Canada, was billed at 8 ft 1 in *246 cm* but actually measured 7 ft 5½ in *227 cm*. In London on 17 June 1871 she married Martin van Buren Bates (1845–1919) of Whitesburg, Letcher County Kentucky, U.S.A., who stood 7 ft 2½ in *220 cm*. Ella Ewing (b. Mar. 1872) of Gorin, Missouri, U.S.A., was billed at 8 ft 2 in *249 cm* and reputedly measured 6 ft 9 in *206 cm* at the age of 10 (*cf.* 6 ft 5 in [*196 cm*] for Robert Wadlow at this age). She measured 7 ft 4½ in *225 cm* at the age of 23 and may have attained 7 ft 6 in *229 cm* before her death in January 1913.

Living The tallest living woman is Sandy Allen (b. 18 June 1955) of Chicago, Illinois U.S.A. and now living in Shelbyville, Indiana. In September 1974 she was measured to be 7 ft 5 5/16 in *226,7 cm* in height and is still growing. A 6½ lb. *2,910 kg* baby, her abnormal growth began soon after birth. She now weighs 30 st. 1 lb. *191 kg* and takes a 16EEE size shoe and 6 yds *5,48 m* of material for a dress.

SHORTEST DWARFS

The strictures which apply to giants apply equally to dwarfs, except that exaggeration gives way to understatement. In the same way as 9 ft *274 cm* may be regarded as the limit towards which the tallest giants tend, so 23 in *58 cm* must be regarded as the limit towards which the shortest mature dwarfs tend (*cf.* the average length of new-born babies is 18–20 in [*46–50 cm*]). In the case of child dwarfs the *age* is often enhanced by their agents or managers.

There are many form of dwarfism. Ateleiotic dwarfs, known as midgets, who suffer from growth hormone deficiency, are usually well proportioned. Such dwarfs tended to be even shorter when human stature was generally shorter due to lower nutritional standards. The dwarfs of shortest stature are currently found among forms of chrondrodystrophic or skeletal dwarfs such as those who have cartilage-hair hypophasia or pseudoachrondrophasia.

The most famous midget in history was Charles Sherwood Stratton, *alias* "General Tom Thumb", born on 11 Jan. 1832 in Bridgeport, Connecticut, U.S.A. He measured 25 in *64 cm* at the age of 5 months and grew to only 70 cm *27.6 in* by the age of 13½. He was 30½ in *77 cm* tall at the age of 18 and 35 in *89 cm* at 30. He stood 40 in *102 cm* tall at the time of his death from apoplexy on 15 July 1883.

Another celebrated midget was Józef ('Count') Boruwalaski (b. November 1739) of Poland. He measured only 8 in *20 cm* long at birth, growing to 14 in *36 cm* at the age of one year. He stood 17 in *43 cm* at 6 years, 21 in *53 cm* at 10, 25 in *64 cm* at 15, 35 in *89 cm* at 25 and 39 in *99 cm* at 30. He died near Durham, England, on 5 Sept. 1837, aged 97.

World The shortest mature human of whom there is independent evidence was Pauline Musters ('Princess Pauline'), a Dutch midget. She was born at Ossendrecht, on 26 Feb. 1876 and measured 12 in *30 cm* at birth. At the age of 9 she was 55 cm *21.65 in* tall and weighed only 1 kg 50 *3 lb. 5 oz.* She died, at the age of 19, of pneumonia, with meningitis, her heart weakened from alcoholic excesses, on 1 March 1895 in New York City, N.Y., U.S.A. Although she was billed at 19 in *48 cm*, she was found to be 59 cm *23.2 in* tall. A *post mortem* examination showed her to be exactly 24 in *61 cm* (her body was slightly elongated after death).

The 19th Century's most celebrated Midget General Tom Thumb with his wife (see Col 1)

Peter van Oosten

Her mature weight varied from 7½ lb. to 9 lb. *3 kg 40–4 kg* and her "vital statistics" were 18½-19-17 *47-48-43 cm*.

The Italian girl Caroline Crachami, born in Palermo, Sicily, in 1815, was only 20.2 in *51.3 cm* tall when she died in London in 1824, aged 9. At birth she measured 7 in *18 cm* long and weighed 1 lb. *450 g*. Her skeleton, measuring 19.8 in *50,3 cm*, is now part of the Hunterian collection in the Museum of the Royal College of Surgeons, London.

Male The shortest recorded adult male dwarf was Calvin Phillips, born on 14 Jan. 1791 in Bridgewater, Massachusetts, U.S.A. He weighed 2 lb. *0 kg 910* at birth and stopped growing at the age of 5. When he was 19 he measured 26½ in *67 cm* tall and weighed 12 lb. *5 kg 40* with his clothes on. He died two years later, in April 1812, from progeria, a rare disorder characterised by dwarfism and premature senility.

William E. Jackson, *alias* "Major Mite", born on 2 Oct. 1864 in Dunedin, New Zealand, measured 9 in *23 cm* long and weighed 12 oz. *0 kg 34* at birth. In November 1880 he stood 21 in *53 cm* and weighed 9 lb. *4 kg*. He died in New York City, N.Y., U.S.A., on 9 Dec. 1900, when he measured 27 in *70 cm*.

The world's shortest living mature human reported is Nruturam (b. 28 May 1929) a rachitic dwarf in Naydwar, India, who measures 28 in *71 cm*. The more famous circus midget Mihaly Meszaros (b. Hungary, 1 Oct. 1939), currently billed as the "Smallest Man on Earth" stands 83 cm *32⅝ in* tall. On first meeting Don Koehler (page 9) in New York on 5 Apr. 1974 in the TV. Show "David Frost Presents the Guinness Book of World Records" he uttered his only word of English —"Jesus".

United The shortest mature human ever recorded in Britain
Kingdom was Miss Joyce Carpenter (b. 21 Dec. 1929), a rachitic dwarf of Charford, Hereford and Worcester, who

stood 29 in *74 cm* tall and weighed 30 lb. *13 kg 600*. She died on 7 Aug. 1973 aged 43. Hopkins Hopkins (1737–54) of Llantrisant, Mid Glamorgan was 31 in *79 cm*. Hopkins, who died from progeria (see above) weighed 19 lb. *8 kg 620* at the age of 7 and 13 lb. *6 kg* at the time of his death. There are an estimated 2,000 people of severely restricted growth i.e. under 4 ft 8 in *142 cm* living in Britain today.

The famous "Sir" Geoffrey Hudson (b. 1619) of Oakham, Leicestershire, was reputedly 18 in *46 cm* tall at the age of 30, but this extreme measurement is not borne out in portraits which show he was then about 3 ft 6 in *107 cm*. At the time of his death in London in 1682 he measured 3 ft 9 in *114 cm*.

Ireland The shortest recorded Irish adult dwarf was Mrs. Catherine Kelly (b. in August 1756), known as "the Irish fairy", who stood 34 in *86 cm* tall and weighed 22 lb. *10 kg*. She died in Norwich, Norfolk, on 15 Oct. 1785. David Jones (b. 28 April 1903) of Lisburn, County Antrim, Northern Ireland, reputedly measured 26 in *66 cm* at the time of his death on 1 April 1970 aged 66. But as he weighed 4 st. *25 kg*, his height was probably nearer 36 in *91 cm*.

Most variable stature Adam Rainer, born in Graz, Austria, in 1899, measured 1,18 m *3 ft 10.45 in* at the age of 21. But then he suddenly started growing upwards at a rapid rate, and by 1931 he had reached 2,18 m *7 ft 1¾ in*. He became so weak as a result that he was bed-ridden for the rest of his life. He died on 4 March 1950 aged 51.

RACES

Tallest The tallest race in the world is the Tutsi (also called Batutsi, Watutsi, or Watussi), Nilotic herdsmen of Rwanda and Burundi, Central Africa whose males average 6 ft 1 in *185 cm*, with a maximum of 7 ft 6 in *229 cm*. The Tehuelches of Patagonia, long regarded as of gigantic stature (*i.e.* 7 to 8 ft [*213 to 244 cm*]), have in fact an average height (males) of 5 ft 10 in *178 cm* with a maximum of just over 2 m *6 ft 6¾ in*. A tribe with an average height of more than 6 ft was discovered in the inland region of Passis Manua of New Britain in December 1956. In December 1967 the inhabitants of Barbuda, Leeward Islands were reported to have an average height in excess of 6 ft *183 cm*. The tallest people in Europe are the Montenegrins of Yugoslavia, with a male average of 5 ft 10 in *178 cm* (in the town of Trebinje the average height is 6 ft [*183 cm*]), compared with the men of Sutherland, at 5 ft 9½ in *176,5 cm*. In 1912 the average height of the men living in Balmaclellan, Kirkcudbrightshire was reported to be 179 cm *5 ft 10.4 in*.

Shortest The world's shortest known race is the negrito Onge tribe, of whom only 22 (12 men, 10 women) survived on Little Andaman Island in the Indian Ocean by May 1956. Few were much more than 4 ft *122 cm*. The smallest pygmies are the Mbuti, with an average height of 4 ft 6 in *137 cm* for men and 4 ft 5 in *135 cm* for women, with some groups averaging only 4 ft 4 in *132 cm* for men and 4 ft 1 in *124 cm* for women. They live in the forests near the river Ituri in the Congo (Kinshasa), Africa. In June 1936 there was a report, not subsequently substantiated, that there was a village of dwarfs numbering about 800 in the Hu bei (Hupeh) province of Central China between Wu han and Lishan in which the men were all less than 4 ft *122 cm* tall and the women slightly taller.

WEIGHT

Heaviest heavy-weights World Men The greatest weight ever attributed to a human has been 84 st. 11 lb. (1,187 lb.) *538 kg* in the case of Francis John Lang (b. 1934) *alias* Michael Walker of Clinton, Iowa, U.S.A. He could not be admitted for treatment for inflammation of the gall bladder in the Veteran's Administration Hospital, Houston, Texas U.S.A. because of the impossibility of getting him through the doors. He was treated in a caravan in the car park and

discharged on 5 Jan. 1972 unweighed but estimated to be between 900 and 1,000 lb. *408–453 kg*. The more precise weight above was claimed for him, while suffering from drug-induced bulimia, in the summer of 1971 when he was working with the Christian Farms of Killeen, Texas. There is, however, no independent corroboration for this precise upper weight quoted.

The highest undisputed weight for a human remains 76 st 5 lb. (1,069 lb.) *485 kg* for Robert Earl Hughes (b. 1926) buried in a piano case-sized coffin in Binville Cemetery, Illinois, U.S.A. on 10 July 1958.

The only other men for whom weights of more than 55 stone (770 lb.) or 350 kg have been reliably reported are the nine listed below:

	Stone	lb.	kg
Mills Darden (1798–1857) U.S.A. (7 ft 6 in [*2,29 m*])	72	12	*463*
John Hanson Craig (1856–94) U.S.A. (6 ft 5 in [*1,95 m*])[1]	64	11	*411*
Arthur Knorr (1914–60) U.S.A. (6 ft 1 in [*1,85 m*])[2]	64	4	*408*
Toubi (b. 1946) Cameroon	61	3½	*389*
T. A. Valenzuela (1895–1937) Mexico (5 ft 11 in [*1,80 m*])	60	10	*386*
David Maquire (1904–*fl.* 1935) U.S.A. (5 ft 10 in [*1,78 m*])	57	12	*367*
William J. Cobb (b. 1926) U.S.A. (6 ft 0 in [*1,83 m*])[3]	57	4	*364*
Unnamed Patient (b. 1936) Richmond, Virginia, U.S.A. Aug. 1973	57	2¼	*363*
Smith Poti (1900–1942) South Africa (5 ft 6 in [*1,67 m*])	55	10	*355*

[1] *Won $1,000 in a "Bonny Baby" contest in New York City in 1858.*
[2] *Gained 300 lb. 136 kg in the last 6 months of his life.*
[3] *Reduced to 16 st. 8 lb. 105 kg by July 1965.*

Women The heaviest woman ever recorded was the late Mrs. Percy Pearl Washington, 46 who died in a hospital in Milwaukee, on 9 Oct. 1972. The hospital scales registered only up to 800 lb. (57 st. 2 lb.) *362 kg 80* but she was believed to weigh about 880 lb. (62 st. 12 lb.) *399 kg 10*. The previous feminine weight record had been set 84 years earlier at 850 lb. *386 kg* although an unsubstantiated report exists of a woman Mrs Ida Maitland (1898–1932) of Springfield Mississippi, U.S.A., who reputedly weighed 65 st. 1 lb. (911 lb. *413 kg 200*). She was said to have died endeavouring to pick a four leaf clover. The local press and hospitals are unable to trace her existence.

A more reliable and better documented case was that of Mrs. Flora Mae Jackson (*née* King), a 5 ft 9 in *175 cm* negress born in 1930 at Shugualak, Mississippi, U.S.A. She weighed 10 lb. *4 kg 50* at birth, 19 st. 1 lb. *121 kg* at the age of 11, 44 st. 5 lb. *282 kg* at 25 and 60 st. *381 kg* shortly before her death in Meridian, Mississippi, on 9 Dec. 1965. She was known in show business as "Baby Flo".

Great Britain Men The heaviest recorded man in Great Britain was William Campbell, who was born in Glasgow in 1856 and died on 16 June 1878, when a publican at High Bridge, Newcastle upon Tyne, Tyne and Wear. He was 6 ft 3 in *191 cm* tall and weighed 53 st. 8 lb. *340 kg* with an 85-in *216 cm* waist and a 96-in *244 cm* chest. His coffin weighed 1,500 lb *680 kg*. He was "a man of considerable intelligence and humour". The only other British man with a recorded weight of more than 50 st. *317 kg 50* was the celebrated Daniel Lambert (1770–1809) of Leicester. He stood 5 ft 11 in *180 cm* tall, weighed 52 st. 11 lb. *335 kg* shortly before his death and had a girth of more than 92 in *234 cm*.

The highest weight attained by any man living in Britain today was that of Eric Keeling (born 1933) of Islington, Greater London who scaled 47 st. *299 kg* in mid-1971. An 11 lb. *5 kg* baby he weighed 18 st. *114 kg 500* at the age of 13. By November 1973 he had reduced by dieting (600 calories per day) to 33 st. *210 kg*. He is 6 ft 5 in *195,5 cm* tall.

The world's heaviest twins Benny and Billy McCreary who weigh well over ¼ ton *250 kg* each (see below)

Keystone

George MacAree (b. 24 Dec. 1923) of Newham, London, who scaled 39½ st. *251 kg* in March 1975 is now the heaviest man in Britain. He is 5 ft 10½ in *179 cm* tall and has vital statistics of 75-73-82 *190-185-208 cm*.

Ireland The heaviest Irishman is reputed to have been Roger Byrne, who was buried in Rosenallis, County Laoighis (Leix), on 14 March 1804. He died in his 54th year and his coffin and its contents weighed 52 st. *330 kg*. Another Irish heavyweight was Lovelace Love (1731–66), born in Brook Hill, County Mayo. He weighed "upward of 40 st. *254 kg*" at the time of his death.

Women The heaviest recorded woman in Great Britain was Nellie Ensall (*née* Lambert) (b. 3 April 1894) of Leicester and later Birmingham who weighed 40 st. 3 lb. *255 kg* at the age of 19. She stood 5 ft 3 in *160 cm* tall, with a waist of 88 in *224 cm* and a 26 in *66 cm* upper arm. She claimed to be a great-great-granddaughter of Daniel Lambert (see above). The heaviest weight of a woman living in Britain today was that of Miss Jean Renwick (b. 1939) of Brixton, London, who weighed 40 st. 2 lb. *254 kg* (height 5 ft 3½ in [*161 cm*]) in January 1972 before she joined the Weight Watchers. By dieting she had reduced to 25 st. *159 kg* by March 1975.

Greatest Differential The greatest weight differential recorded for a married couple is 65 st. 12 lb. *419 kg* in the case of Mills Darden (72 st. 12 lb. *463 kg*—see col. 1) and his wife Mary (7 st. 12 lb. *44;5 kg*). Despite her diminutiveness, however, Mrs. Darden bore her husband three children before her death in 1837.

Heaviest twins The heaviest twins in the world are the wrestlers Billy and Benny McCreary *alias* Doug and Billy McGuire (b. 1948) of Hendersonville, North Carolina, U.S.A., who in March 1970 weighed 47 st. 2 lb. *299 kg* and 45 st. 10 lb. *290 kg*. Since becoming professional wrestlers they have been billed at weights up to 770 lb. (55 st.) *349 kg 250*. They married Canadian sisters Danielle (115 lb. *52 kg*) and Maryce (130 lb. [*59 kg*]). "I married the fat one", commented the fatter twin Benny.

Lightest lightweights
World The lightest adult human on record was Lucia Zarate (b. San Carlos, Mexico 2 Jan. 1863, d. October 1889), an emaciated Mexican ateleiotic dwarf of 26½ in *67 cm*, who weighed 2 kg 125 *4.7 lb.* at the age of 17. She "fattened up" to 13 lb. *5 kg 90* by her 20th birthday. At birth she weighed 2½ lb. *1 kg 10*. The lightest adult ever recorded in the United Kingdom was Hopkins Hopkins (Shortest dwarfs, see p. 18).

The thinnest recorded adults of normal height are those suffering from Simmonds' Disease (Hypophyseal cachexia). Losses up to 65 per cent of the original body-weight have been recorded in females, with a "low" of 3 st. 3 lb. *20 kg* in the case of Emma Shaller (b. St. Louis, Missouri 8 July 1868—d. 4 Oct. 1890), who stood 5 ft 2 in *1,57 m*. In cases of anorexia nervosa, weights of under 5 st. *32 kg* have been reported. Edward C. Hagner (1892–1962), *alias* Eddie Masher (U.S.A.) is alleged to have weighed only 3 st. 6 lb. *22 kg* at a height of 5 ft 7 in *170 cm*. He was also known as "the Skeleton Dude". In August 1825 the biceps measurement of Claude-Ambroise Seurat (b. 10 April 1797, d. 6 April 1826) of Troyes, France was 4 in *10 cm* and the distance between his back and his chest was less than 3 in *8 cm*. According to one report he stood 5 ft 7½ in *171 cm* and weighed 5 st. 8 lb. *35 kg*, but in another account was described as 5 ft 4 in *163 cm* and only 2 st. 8 lb. *16 kg*. It was recorded that the American exhibitionist Rosa Lee Plemons (b. 1873) weighed 27 lb. *12 kg* at the age of 18.

Great Britain Robert Thorn (b. 1842) of March, Cambridgeshire weighed 49 lb. *22 kg* at the age of 32. He was 4 ft 6 in *137 cm* tall and had a 27 in *68 cm* chest (expanded) and 4½ in *11 cm* biceps.

Slimming The greatest recorded slimming feat was that of William J. Cobb (b. 1926), *alias* "Happy Humphrey", a professional wrestler of Macon, Georgia, U.S.A. It was reported in July 1965 that he had reduced from 57 st. 4 lb. *364 kg* to 16 st. 8 lb. *105 kg*, a loss of 40 st. 10 lb. *259 kg* in 3 years. His waist measurement declined from 101 in to 44 in *257 cm* to *112 cm*. In October 1973 it was reported the "Happy" was back to his normal weight of 46½ st. or 650 lb. *295 kg*.

11

The U.S. circus fat lady Mrs. Celesta Geyer (b. 1901), *alias* Dolly Dimples, reduced from 553 lb. *251 kg* to 152 lb. *69 kg* in 1950–51, a loss of 401 lb. *182 kg* in 14 months. Her vital statistics diminished *pari passu* from 79-84-84 *200-213-213 cm* to a *svelte* 34-28-36 *86-71-91 cm*. Her book "How I lost 400 lbs." was not a best-seller because of the difficulty of would-be readers identifying themselves with the dressmaking problems of losing more than 28 st. *178 kg* when 4 ft 11 in *150 cm* tall. In December 1967 she was reportedly down to 7 st. 12 lb. *50 kg*. The speed record for slimming was established by Paul M. Kimelman, 21, of Pittsburgh, Pennsylvania, U.S.A., who from 25 Dec. 1966 to August 1967 went on a crash diet of 300 to 600 calories per day to reduce from 487 lb. (34 st. 11 lb.) *215,9 kg* to 130 lb. (9 st. 4 lb.) *59 kg*—a total loss of 357 lb. (25 st. 7 lb.) *156,9 kg*. He has now stabilised at 175 lb. (12 st. 7 lb.) *79 kg*. On 4–8 February 1951 Mrs. Gertrude Levandowski (b. 1893) of Burnips, Michigan, U.S.A. successfully underwent a series of operations to reduce her weight from 44 st. *280 kg* to 22 st. *140 kg*.

Arthur Armitage (born a 5 lb. *2 kg 300* baby on 28 June 1929) of Knottingley, North Yorkshire, reportedly lost 12 st. *76 kg* in 6 weeks in November-December 1970 when reducing from 40 st. *254 kg* towards his target of 16 st. *102 kg*. Claude Halls (b. 1937) of Sible Hedingham, Essex reduced from 33 st. 6¾ lb. to 12 st. 10 lb.—a loss of 20 st. 10¾ lb. *131,8 kg* in the 14 months January 1974 to March 1975.

The feminine Weight Watchers champion in Britain was Mrs. Dolly Wager (b. 1933) of Charlton, London who, between Sept. 1971 and 22 May 1973 reduced from 31 st. 7 lb. *197 kg* to 11 st. *69 kg 853* so losing 20 st. 0½ lb. *127 kg*.

Weight gaining A probable record for gaining weight was set by Arthur Knorr (b. 17 May 1914), who died on 7 July 1960, aged 46, in Reseda, California, U.S.A. He gained 21 st. 6 lb. *136 kg* in the last 6 months of his life and weighed 64 st. 4 lb. *408 kg* when he died. Miss Doris James of San Francisco, California, U.S.A. is alleged to have gained 23 st. 3 lb. *147 kg* in the 12 months before her death in August 1965, aged 38, at a weight of 48 st. 3 lb. *306 kg*. She was only 5 ft 2 in *157 cm* tall.

2. ORIGINS

EARLIEST MAN
SCALE OF TIME
If the age of the Earth-Moon system (latest estimate at least 4,700 million years) is likened to a single year, Handy Man appeared on the scene at about 8.35 p.m. on 31 December, Britain's earliest known inhabitants arrived at about 11.32 p.m., the Christian era began about 13 sec before midnight and the life span of a 113-year-old woman (page 14) would be about three-quarters of a second. Present calculations indicate that the Sun's increased heat, as it becomes a "red giant", will make life insupportable on Earth in about 10,000 million years. Meanwhile there may well be colder epicycles. The period of 1,000 million years is sometimes referred to as an aeon.

Man (Homo sapiens) is a species in the sub-family Homininae of the family Hominidae of the super-family Hominoidea of the sub-order Simiae (or Anthropoidea) of the order Primates of the infra-class Eutheria of the sub-class Theria of the class Mammalia of the sub-phylum Vertebrata (Craniata) of the phylum Chordata of the sub-kingdom Metazoa of the animal kingdom.

World The earliest known primates appeared in the Palaeocene period of about 70,000,000 years ago. The sub-order of higher primates, called Simiae (or Anthropoidea), evolved from the catarrhine or old-world sect nearly 30,000,000 years later in the Lower Oligocene period. During the Middle and Upper Oligocene the super-family Hominoidea emerged. This contains three accepted families, *viz* Hominidae (bipedal, ground-dwelling man or near man), Pongidae (brachiating forest apes) and Oreopithecidae, which includes *Apidium* of the Oligocene and

Oreopithecus of the early Pliocene. Opinion is divided on whether to treat gibbons and their ancestors as a fourth full family (Hylobatidae) or as a sub-family (Hylobatinae) within the Pongidae. Some consider that Proconsulidae should also comprise a family, although others regard the genus *Proconsul*, who lived on the open savannah, as part of another sub-family of the Pongidae.

Earliest Hominid There is a conflict of evidence on the time during which true but primitive Hominidae were evolving. Fossil evidence indicates that it was some time during the Upper Miocene (about 10,000,000 to 12,000,000 years ago). The characteristics of the Hominidae, such as a large brain, very fully distinguish them from any of the other Hominoidea. Evidence published in August 1969 indicated that the line of descent of *Ramapithecus*, from the north-eastern Indian subcontinent, was not less than 10,000,000 years old and that of *Australopithecus*, from Eastern Africa 5,500,000 years old.

Earliest Genus Homo The earliest known true member of the genus *Homo* was found to the east of Lake Rudolf in Northern Kenya by Bernard Ngeneo and announced on 9 Nov. 1972 by Richard Leakey, Director of the Kenya National Museum's Centre for Pre-History and Palaeontology. In addition to an almost complete skull, pieced together by Dr. Maeve Leakey, femur, tibia and fibula leg bones were also found. The cranial capacity was about 800 cm³ compared to less than 500 cm³ of *Australopithecus*. The remains, known as No. 1470, have been dated to 2,800,000 years ago. Richard Leakey is the son of the late Louis Leakey (1903–72).

The greatest age attributed to fossils of the genus *Homo* is for remains discovered on 17 and 18 Oct. 1974 near the Hadar, a tributary of the Awash River, north-eastern Ethiopia by Alemeyn Asfew. The deposit was at a stratigraphic level *below* a volcanic basalt dated to 3.25 million years by the potassium-argon method.

Earliest Homo sapiens The earliest recorded remains of the species *Homo sapiens*, variously dated from 300,000 to 450,000 years ago in the Middle Pleistocene, were discovered on 24 Aug. 1965 by Dr. Lászlo Vértes in a limestone quarry at Vértesszöllös, about 30 miles west of Budapest, Hungary. The remains, designated *Homo sapiens palaeo-hungaricus*, comprised an almost complete occipital bone, part of a skull with an estimated cranial capacity of nearly 1 400 cm³ *85 in³*.

Earliest man in the Americas date from at least 50,000 B.C. and "more probably 100,000 B.C." according to the late Dr. Leakey after the examination of some hearth stones found in the Mojave Desert, California and announced in October 1970. The earliest human relic is a skull found in the area of Los Angeles, California dated in December 1970 to be from 22,000 B.C.

Great Britain The earliest firm evidence able to be established for human occupation in Great Britain dates from the time of the Hoxian interglacial (200,000–250,000 B.C.) named from the Hoxne site in Suffolk, where hand axes were found in 1797. The earlier part of this period between the earlier Anglian and the later Wolstonian glaciations was characterised by Clactonian assemblages of chopping and pebble tools known only from the sites of Clacton-on-Sea, Essex, the lower deposits in the Barnfield Pit, Swanscombe, Kent in August 1969 and Barnham St. Gregory, Suffolk. Two seemingly pre-Hoxian sites, dating possibly from a warmer interstadial of the Anglian glaciation (250,000 350,000 B.C.) are at Fordwich, Kent and Kent's Cavern, Torquay, Devon. The oldest human remains ever found in Britain are pieces of a brain case from a specimen of *Homo sapiens fossils*, believed to be a woman, recovered in June 1935 and March 1936 by

Dr. Alvan T. Marston from the Boyn Hill terrace in the Barnfield Pit, near Swanscombe, northern Kent, This find is attributed to Acheulian man, type *III* or *IV*, dating from the warm Hoxnian interglacial period, of about 200,000 to 250,000 years ago.

3. LONGEVITY

No single subject is more obscured by vanity, deceit, falsehood and deliberate fraud than the extremes of human longevity. Extreme claims are generally made on behalf of the very aged rather than by them.

Many hundreds of claims throughout history have been made for persons living well into their second century and some, insulting to the intelligence, for people living even into their third. Centenarians surviving beyond their 110th year are in fact of the extremest rarity and the present absolute proven limit of human longevity does not yet admit of anyone living to celebrate a 114th birthday.

It is highly significant that in Sweden, where alone proper and thorough official investigations follow the death of every allegedly very aged citizen, none has been found to have surpassed 110 years. The most reliably pedigreed large group of people in the world, the British peerage, has, after ten centuries, produced only two centenarian peers but neither reached their 101st birthdays. However, this is possibly not unconnected with the extreme draughtiness of many of their residences.

Scientific research into extreme old age reveals that the correlation between the claimed density of centenarians in a country and its regional illiteracy is 0.83 ± 0.03. In late life, very old people often tend to advance their ages at the rate of about 17 years per decade. This was nicely corroborated by a cross analysis of the 1901 and 1911 censuses of England and Wales. Early claims must necessarily be without the elementary corroboration of birth dates. England was among the earliest of all countries to introduce compulsory local registers (Sept. 1538) and official birth registration (1 July 1837) which was made fully compulsory only in 1874. Even in the United States, where in 1971 there were reputed to be 12,642 centenarians, 45 per cent of births occurring between 1890 and 1920 were unregistered.

Several celebrated super-centenarians are believed to have been double lives (father and son, brothers with the same names or successive bearers of a title). The most famous example is Christian Jakobsen Drackenberg allegedly born in Stavanger, Norway on 18 Nov. 1626 and died in Aarhus, Denmark aged seemingly 145 years 326 days on 9 Oct. 1772. A number of instances have been commercially sponsored, while a fourth category of recent claims are those made for political ends, such as the 100 citizens of the Russian Soviet Federative Socialist Republic (population about 132,000,000 at mid-1967) claimed in March 1960 to be between 120 and 156. From data on documented centenarians, actuaries have shown that only one 115-year life can be expected in 2,100 million lives (*cf.* world population was estimated to be 4,025 million at mid-1975).

The height of credulity was reached on 5 May 1933, when a newsagency solemnly filed a story from China with a Peking date-line that Li Chung-yun, the "oldest man on Earth", born in 1680, had just died aged 256 years (*sic*). Recently the most extreme case of longevity claimed in the U.S.S.R. has been 168 years for Shirali "Baba" Mislimov of Barzavu, Azerbaijan, who died on 2 Sept. 1973 and was reputedly born on 26 Mar. 1805. No interview of this man has ever been permitted to any Western journalist or scientist. He was said to have celebrated the 100th birthday of his third wife

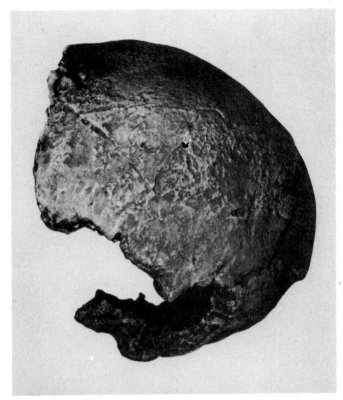

The oldest human remains in Britain were found by a dentist 40 years ago in Kent. The jawless Swanscombe skull may be 250,000 years old

Hartun, in 1966, and that of one of his grandchildren in August 1973. It was reported in 1954 that in the Abkhasian Republic of Georgia, U.S.S.R., 2.58 per cent of the population was aged over 90—25 times the proportion in the U.S.A.

Dr. Zhores A. Medvedev, the expelled Soviet gerontologist, in Washington D.C., on 30 Apr. 1974 referring to U.S.S.R. claims stated "The whole phenomenon looks like a falsification" adding "He (Stalin) liked the idea that (other) Georgians lived to be a 100 or more". "Local officials tried hard to find more and more cases for Stalin". He points out that (a) the *average* life span in the regions claiming the highest incidence of centenarians is lower than the U.S.S.R. average and (b) the number of centenarians claimed in the Caucasus has declined rapidly from 8,000 in 1950 to 4,500 in 1970 Dr. I. M. Spector, of the Institute of Traumatology, Kazan, U.S.S.R. quoted the maximum life-span of man in Apr. 1974 as "110–115 years".

The Andean valley of Vilcabamba in Ecuador became the source of reports of extreme longevity after the 1971 census in which 9 of the 819 inhabitants were returned at ages of more than 100, of whom 3 were listed as over 120. The two oldest claims were for Miguel Carpio Mendreta or Mendieta and José David Toledo, who were reputedly 122 and 140. Dr. David Davies of University College, London supports the claim of Francisco Camacho of Sacapalka as his best candidate for the title of the world's oldest living man with a baptismal registration on 19 Apr. 1847.

Charlie Smith of Bartow, Florida, U.S.A. obtained a Social Security card in 1955 when claiming to be born on 4 July 1842 in Liberia. The U.S. Department of Health, Education and Welfare state that they are "unable to disclose the type of evidence used" to determine Mr. Smith's age because such disclosure "would infringe on the confidentiality of the individual's record". The *essential* data on the ages entered for him in any of the 10 censuses from 1860 to 1950 remains undisclosed. He has a son born in 1902.

Mrs Delina Filkins (1815-1928), who made the closest proven approach yet to celebrating a 114th birthday

Miss Rose Heeley, now the oldest of Britain's 2,430 centenarians, when only 105

Courtesy of Distressed Gentlefolk's Aid Association

Oldest authentic centenarian **World** The greatest authenticated age to which a human has ever lived is 113 years 214 days in the case of Mrs. Delina Filkins *née* Ecker who was born at Stark, Herkimer County, New York on 4 May 1815 and died at Richfield Springs, New York on 4 Dec. 1928. She never wore spectacles. The following national records can be taken as authentic:

AUTHENTICATED NATIONAL LONGEVITY RECORDS

	Years	Days		Born		Died	
United States[1]	113	214	Delina Filkins (*née* Ecker)	4 May	1815	4 Dec.	1928
Canada[2]	113	124	Pierre Joubert	15 July	1701	16 Nov.	1814
Morocco	>112		El Hadj Mohammed el Mokri (Grand Vizier)		1844	16 Sept.	1957
Japan[4]	112	100	Mito Umeta (Mrs.)	27 Mar.	1863	*fl.* July	1975
United Kingdom[3]	112	39	Alice Stevenson	10 July	1861	18 Aug.	1973
Ireland	111	327	The Hon. Katherine Plunket	22 Nov.	1820	14 Oct.	1932
South Africa[5]	111	151	Johanna Booyson	17 Jan.	1857	16 June	1968
Czechoslovakia	111	+	Marie Bernatkova	22 Oct.	1857	*fl.* Oct.	1968
Channel Islands	110	321	Margaret Ann Neve (*née* Harvey)	18 May	1792	4 April	1903
Northern Ireland	110	234	Elizabeth Watkins (Mrs.)	10 Mar.	1863	31 Oct.	1973
Yugoslavia	110	150+	Demitrius Philipovitch	9 Mar.	1818	*fl.* Aug.	1928
Australia[6]	110	39	Ada Sharp (Mrs.)	6 April	1861	15 May	1971
U.S.S.R.[7]	110	+	Khasako Dzugayev	7 Aug.	1860	*fl.* Aug.	1970
Netherlands	110	5	Baks Karnebeek (Mrs.)	2 Oct.	1849	7 Oct.	1959
France	109	309	Marie Philoméne Flassayer	13 June	1844	18 April	1954
Italy	109	179	Rosalia Spoto	25 Aug.	1847	20 Feb.	1957
Scotland	109	14	Rachel MacArthur (Mrs.)	26 Nov.	1827	10 Dec.	1936
Norway	109	+	Marie Olsen (Mrs.)	1 May	1850	*fl.* May	1959
Tasmania (State of)	109	+	Mary Ann Crow (Mrs.)	2 Feb.	1836		1945
Germany[8]	108	128	Luise Schwatz	27 Sept.	1849	2 Feb.	1958
Portugal[9]	108	+	Maria Luisa Jorge	7 June	1859	*fl.* July	1967
Sweden	108	+	Anna Johansson		1865	21 Nov.	1973
Finland	107	+	Marie Anderson	3 Jan.	1829		1936
Belgium	106	267	Marie-Joseph Purnode (Mrs.)	17 April	1843	9 Nov.	1949
Austria	106	231	Anna Migschitz	3 Feb.	1850	1 Nov.	1956
Spain[10]	106	14	Jose Palido	15 Mar.	1866	29 Mar.	1972
Malaysia	106	+	Hassan Bin Yusoff	14 Aug.	1865	*fl.* Jan.	1972
Isle of Man	105	221	John Kneen	12 Nov.	1852	9 June	1958

[1] *The U.S. Veterans Administration was in March 1974 paying pensions to 272 women attested to be widows of veterans of the Civil War (1860-65), the last soldier having died 15 years earlier in 1959. The oldest of these is Angela Felicia Virginia Davalos (Mrs. Harry Harrison Moran), who filed a claim dated 1928 with a baptismal certificate showing 17 May 1856 in Morelia, Mexico as her date and place of birth.*

[2] *Mrs. Ellen Carroll died in North River, Newfoundland, Canada on 8 December 1943, reputedly aged 115 years 49 days.*

[3] *A man named Nakamura of Kamaishi, northern Japan, was reported to have died on 4 May 1969 aged 116 years 329 days.*

[4] *London-born Miss Isabella Shepheard was allegedly 115 years old when she died at St. Asaph, Clwyd, North Wales, on 20 Nov. 1948, but her actual age was believed to have been 109 years 90 days. Charles Alfred Nunez Arnold died in Liverpool on 15 Sept. 1941 reputedly aged 112 years 66 days based on a baptismal claim (London, 10 Nov. 1829).*

[5] *Mrs. Susan Johanna Deporter of Port Elizabeth, South Africa, was reputedly 114 years old when she died on 4 August 1954. Mrs. Sarah Lawrence, Cape Town, South Africa was reputedly 112 on 3 June 1968.*

[6] *Reginald Beck of Sydney, New South Wales, Australia was allegedly 111 years old when he died om 13 April 1928.*

[7] *There are allegedly 21,700 centenarians in U.S.S.R. (c.f. 7,000 in U.S.A.). Of these 21,000 are ascribed to the Georgian S.S.R. i.e. one in every 232. In July 1962 it was reported 128, mostly male, were in the one village of Medini.*

[8] *Friedrich Sadowski of Heidelberg reputedly celebrated his 111th birthday on 31 October 1936. Franz Joseph Eder d. Spitzburg 3 May 1911 allegedly aged 116.*

[9] *Senhora Jesuina da Conceicao of Lisbon was reputedly 113 years when she died on 10 June 1965.*

[10] *Juana Ortega Villarin, Madrid, Spain, was allegedly 112 in February 1962. Ana Maria Parraga of Murcia was reportedly 107 in Nov. 1969.*

In the face of the above data the claim published in the April 1961 issue of the Soviet Union's *Vestnik Statistiki* ("Statistical Herald") that there were 224 male and 368 female Soviet citizens aged in excess of 120 recorded at the census of 15 Jan. 1959, indicates a reliance on hearsay rather than evidence. Official Soviet insistence on the unrivalled longevity of the country's citizenry is curious in view of the fact that the 592 persons in their unique "over 120" category must have spent at least the first 78 years of their prolonged lives under Tsarism. It has recently been suggested that the extreme ages claimed by some men in Georgia, U.S.S.R., are the result of attempts to avoid military service when they were younger, by assuming the identities of older men.

Great Britain The oldest living Briton among an estimated population of 2,900 (2,360 women and 540 men) centenarians is Miss Rose Adelaide Heeley (b. Ladywood, Birmingham on 25 Aug. 1864) of the Distressed Gentlefolk's Aid Associations nursing home at Rashwood, Droitwich, Worcestershire was aged 110 years 309 days on 1 July 1975. The oldest reported man is Richard Southey who had a 110th birthday party at Somertrees Old People's Home, Lewisham, Greater London on 17 Mar. 1975. His claim to have been born in Burma on 17 Mar. 1865 is however unsupported by a birth certificate. The number of centenarians reported in Britain was only 140 in 1951, but 520 in 1961 and 2,430 in the 1971 census.

Most reigns The greatest number of reigns during which any English subject could have lived is ten. A person born on the day (11 April) that Henry VI was deposed in 1471 had to live to only the comparatively modest age of 87 years 7 months and 6 days to see the accession of Elizabeth I on 17 Nov. 1558. Such a person could have been Thomas Carn of London, born 1471 and died 28 Jan. 1578 in his 107th year.

4. REPRODUCTIVITY

MOTHERHOOD

Most children *World* The greatest number of children produced by a mother in an independently attested case is 69 by the first wife of Fyodor Vassilet, a peasant of the Moscow Jurisdiction, Russia, who, in 27 confinements, gave birth to 16 pairs of twins, 7 sets of triplets and 4 sets of quadruplets. Most of the children attained their majority. Mme. Vassilet (1816–72) became so renowned that she was presented at the court of Tsar Alexander II.

Currently the highest reported figure is a 32nd child born to Raimundo Carnauba, and his wife Madalena of Ceilandia, Brazil. She was married at 13 and has had 24 sons and 8 daughters. The mother in May 1972 said "They have given us a lot of work and worry but they are worth it", and the father "I don't know why people make such a fuss". The above figures are tentative since no two published interviews with this family seem to produce entirely consistent data.

Great Britain The British record is probably held by Mrs. Elizabeth Greenhille (d. 1681) of Abbot's Langley, Hertfordshire. It is alleged that she gave birth to 39 children (32 daughters and 7 sons), all of whom attained their majority. She was married at 16, had a world record 38 confinements and died reputedly aged 64. Her last son Thomas (d. c. 1740) became surgeon to the 10th Duke of Norfolk and was the author of the "Art of Embalming" (1705). According to an inscription on a gravestone in Conway Church cemetery, Gwynedd, North Wales, Nicholas Hookes (d. 27 March 1637) was the 41st child of his mother Alice Hookes, but further details are lacking. It was reported in December 1634 that the wife of a Scottish weaver living in Newcastle upon Tyne had borne her husband 62 children. It has not been possible to corroborate or refute this

report. The highest recent reported figure is 24 children born to Mrs. Emily Jane Lucas (b. 1881) of Tonbridge, Kent who died in July 1967.

Great Britain's champion mothers of today are believed to be Mrs. Margaret McNaught, (b. 1923) of Balsall Heath, Birmingham (12 boys and 10 girls, all single births) and Mrs. Mabel Constable (b. 1920), of Long Itchington, Warwickshire who also has had 22 children including a set of triplets and two sets of twins.

Oldest mother *World* Medical literature contains extreme but unauthenticated cases of septuagenarian mothers, such as Mrs. Ellen Ellis, aged 72, of Four Crosses, Clwyd, who allegedly produced a still-born 13th child on 15 May 1776 in her 46th year of marriage. Many cases are cover-ups for illegitimate grandchildren. The oldest recorded mother of whom there is certain evidence is Mrs. Ruth Alice Kistler (*née* Taylor), formerly Mrs. Shepard, of Portland, Oregon, U.S.A. She was born at Wakefield, Massachusetts, on 11 June 1899 and gave birth to a daughter, Suzan, at Glendale, near Los Angeles, California, on 18 Oct. 1956, when her age was 57 years 129 days. The incidence of quinguagenarian births varies widely with the highest purported rate being in Albania (with nearly 5,500 per million) compared with 2 per million in England & Wales.

Great Britain The oldest British mother reliably recorded is Mrs. Winifred Wilson (*née* Stanley) of Eccles, Greater Manchester. She was born in Wolverhampton on 11 Nov. 1881 or 1882 and had her tenth child, a daughter Shirley, on Nov. 14 1936, when aged 54 or 55 years and 3 days. She died aged 91 or 92 in January 1974. At Southampton on 10 Feb. 1916, Mrs. Elizabeth Pearce gave birth to a son when aged 54 years 40 days.

Ireland The oldest Irish mother recorded was Mrs. Mary Higgins of Cork, County Cork (b. 7 Jan. 1876) who gave birth to a daughter, Patricia, on 17 March 1931 when aged 55 years 69 days.

Descendants In polygamous countries, the number of a person's descendants can become incalculable. The last Sharifian Emperor of Morocco, Moulay Ismail (1672–1727), known as "The Bloodthirsty", was reputed to have fathered a total of 548 sons and 340 daughters.

Capt. Wilson Kettle (b. 1860) of Grand Bay, Port aux Basques, Newfoundland, Canada, died on 25 Jan. 1963, aged 102, leaving 11 children by two wives, 65 grandchildren, 201 great-grandchildren and 305 great-great-grandchildren, a total of 582 living descendants. Mrs. Johanna Booyson (see page 14), of Belfast, Transvaal, was estimated to have 600 living descendants in South Africa in January 1968.

Mrs. Sarah Crawshaw (d. 25 Dec. 1844) left 397 descendants, according to her gravestone in Stones Church, Ripponden, Halifax, West Yorkshire.

Multiple great-grandparents Theoretically a great-great-great-great-grandparent is a possibility, though in practice countries in which young mothers are common generally have a low expectation of life. The case of an 97 year old woman in the U.S.A. was reported in June 1973 who had four great-great-great-grandchildren among her 67 living descendants, while Hon. General Walter Washington Williams (1855–1959) of Houston, Texas, U.S.A., was reportedly several times a great-great-great-grandfather. Mrs. Alice Jones Miller Eierdam (b. 15 Dec. 1875) of St. Maries, Idaho, U.S.A. held her granddaughter's great-grandchild Shasta (b. 18 Nov. 1973) in her arms. Similarly in 1973 Mrs. Alvena Dan Liming (b. 3 Jan. 1877) sat in a 6 generation photograph with her great-great-great-granddaughter Mollie Marie Rettinger (b. 8 Oct. 1972).

MULTIPLE BIRTHS

Quinde-caplets It was announced by Dr. Gennaro Montanino of Rome that he had removed the foetuses of 10 girls and 5 boys from the womb of a 35-year-old housewife on 22 July 1971. A fertility drug was responsible for this unique and unsurpassed instance of quindecaplets.

Triplets
Oldest The longest lived triplets on record were Faith, Hope and Charity Caughlin born at Marlboro, Massachusetts, U.S.A. on 27 Mar. 1868. The first to die was Mrs. (Ellen) Hope Daniels aged 93 on 2 Mar. 1962.

Fastest The fastest recorded natural birth of triplets was of Angela (1.25 p.m.); Lorna (1.28 p.m.) and Karen (1.30 p.m.) born to Mrs. Mary Helena Richardson *née* Edwards of Stonehouse, Strathclyde, Scotland on 21 Sept. 1973.

Twins The chances of identical twins both reaching 100 are said to be one in 700 million. The oldest recorded twins were Gulbrand and Bernt Morterud, born at Nord Odal, Norway, on 20 Dec. 1858. Bernt died on 1 Aug. 1960 in Chicago, Illinois, U.S.A. aged 101, and his brother died at Nord Odal on 12 Jan. 1964, aged 105. Twin sisters, Mrs. Vassilka Dermendjhieva and Mrs. Vassila Yapourdjieva of Sofia, Bulgaria allegedly celebrated their joint 104th birthday on 27 Sept. 1966.

Oldest The oldest twins on record in Great Britain have been the Bean twins Robert, of Birkenhead, Merseyside and Mary (now Mrs. Simpson) of Etton, Cambridgeshire who celebrated their 100th birthday on 19 Oct. 1973.

Lightest The lightest recorded birthweight for a pair of surviving twins has been 2 lb. 3 oz. *992 g* in the case of Mary 16 oz. *453 g* and Margaret 19 oz. *538 g* born to Mrs. Florence Stimson, Queens Road, Old Fletton, Peterborough, England, delivered by Dr. Macaulay on 16 Aug. 1931. Margaret is now Mrs. M. J. Hurst

MULTIPLE BIRTHS

	World	United Kingdom
Highest number reported at single birth	10 (decaplets) (2 male, 8 female) Bacacay, Brazil 22 Apr. 1946 (also report from Spain, 1924 and China 12 May 1936)	—
Highest number medically recorded	9 (nonuplets) (5 male, 4 female) to Mrs. Geraldine Broderick at Royal Hospital, Sydney, Australia on 13 June 1971. 2 males stillborn. Richard (12 oz. [*340 g*]) survived 6 days 9 (all also died) to patient at University of Pennsylvania, Philadelphia 29 May 1972	6 (sextuplets) (2 male, 4 female) to Mrs. Sheila Ann Thorns (*née* Manning) at New Birmingham Maternity Hospital on 2 Oct. 1968. Three survive 6 (1 male, 5 female) to Mrs. Rosemary Letts (*née* Egerton) at University College Hospital, Greater London on 15 Dec. 1969. One boy and 4 girls survive
Highest number surviving	6 out of 6 (3 males, 3 females) to Mrs. Susan Jane Rosenkowitz *née* Scoones, later Pelly-Fry (b. Colombo, Sri Lanka, 28 Oct. 1947) at Mowbray, Cape Town, South Africa on 11 Jan. 1974 In order of birth they were: David, Nicolette, Jason, Emma, Grant and Elizabeth. They totalled 24 lb. 1 oz. *10,915 kg*.	5 out of 6 (as above) and also 5 out of 5 (5 females) to Mrs. Irene Mary Hanson (*née* Brown) at Queen Charlotte's Hospital, London on 13 Nov. 1969 and 5 out of 5 (1 male, 4 females) to Mrs. James Bostock of Armadale, Lothian, Scotland (no use of fertility drugs) on 14 Apr. 1972
	Heaviest	**Most Sets**
Quintuplets *World*	25 lb. *11,350 kg* Mrs. Lui Saulien, Chekiang, China 7 June 1953 25 lb. *11,350 kg* Mrs. Kamalammal Pondicherry, India, 30 Dec. 1956	No recorded case of more than a single set
Quadruplets *World and U.K.*	21 lb. 5 oz. *9,665 kg* Mrs. Penny McPherson, Liverpool Maternity Hospital, England 8 July 1972	4 Mde. Fyodor Vassilet, Moscow Jurisdiction, Russia (d. 1872)
Triplets *World*	26 lb. 6 oz. *11,960 kg* (unconfirmed) Iranian case (2 male, 1 female) 18 Mar. 1968	15 Maddalena Granata (1839–*fl* 1886)
U.K.	22 lb. 8 oz. *10,205 kg* Mrs. Elizabeth Parker, Stepping Hill Hospital, Stockport, Greater Manchester 21 Feb. 1972	
Twins *World*	35 lb. 8 oz. *16,100 kg* (liveborn) Warren's case (2 males) reported in *The Lancet* from Derbyshire, England on 6 Dec. 1884 27 lb. 12 oz. *12,590 kg* (surviving) Mrs. J. P. Haskin, Fort Smith, Arkansas, U.S.A. 20 Feb. 1924	16 Mde. Vassilet (see above). Mrs. Barbara Zulu of Barberton, South Africa bore 3 sets of girls and 3 mixed sets in 7 years (1967–73) 15 Mrs. Mary Jones of Chester (d. 4 Dec. 1899)—all sets were boy and girl

"Siamese" Conjoined twins derived the name "Siamese" from the celebrated Chang and Eng Bunker (known in Thailand as Chan and In) born at Maklong, on 11 May 1811. They were joined by a cartilaginous band at the chest and married in April 1843 the Misses Sarah and Adelaide Yates and fathered ten and twelve children respectively. They died within three hours of each other on 17 Jan. 1874, aged 62. There is no genealogical evidence for the existence of the much-publicized Chalkhurst twins, Mary and Aliza, of Biddenden, Kent, allegedly born in *c.* 1550 (not 1100). The earliest certain record is one of 26 Apr. 1618 from Long Melford, Suffolk, England when conjoined twins were born to Mrs. Rose Sheapherd. The earliest successful separation of Siamese twins was performed on Prisna and Napit Atkinson (b. May 1953 in Thailand) by Dr. Dragstedt at the University of Chicago on 29 March 1955.

The rarest form of conjoined twins is Dicephales tetrabrachius dipus (two heads, four arms and two legs) of which only two examples are known to exist today—in Russia and Brazil. In the Brazilian case the girls, Juraci and Nadir Climerio de Oliveira, born in the interior of Bahia State in 1962 and now living permanently at the Climerio de Oliveira Maternity Hospital in Salvador, share one intestinal and renal system. The Russian pair Masha and Dasha were born on 4 Jan. 1950.

BABIES

Largest
World
The heaviest normal new-born child recorded in modern times was a boy weighing 11 kg *24 lb. 4 oz.*, born on 3 June 1961 to Mrs. Saadat Cor of Cegham, Southern Turkey. A report from Dezful, S.W. Iran, that Mrs. Massoumeh Valizadeh or Valli-Ullah 32, had given birth to a 12 kg *26 lb. 6½ oz.* boy on 7 Feb. 1972, was later officially stated to be incorrect. There is also an unconfirmed report of a woman giving birth to a 27 lb. *12,25 kg* baby in Essonnes, a suburb of Corbeil, central France, in June 1929. A deformed baby weighing 29¼ lb. *13,28 kg* was born in May 1939 in a hospital at Effingham, Illinois, U.S.A., but only lived for 2 hours.

United
Kingdom
The greatest recorded live birth weight in the United Kingdom is 21 lb. *9,53 kg* for a child born on Christmas Day, 1852. It was reported in a letter to the *British Medical Journal* (1 Feb. 1879) from a doctor in Torpoint, Cornwall. The only other reported birth weight in excess of 20 lb. *9,07 kg* is 20 lb. 2 oz. *9,13 kg* for a boy born to a 33-year-old schoolmistress in Crewe, Cheshire, on 12 Nov. 1884 with a 14½ in *36,8 cm* chest. A baby of 33 lb. *14,97 kg* was reportedly born to a Mrs. Lambert of Wandsworth Road, London *c.* 1930 but its measurements indicate a weight of about 17 lb. *7,7 kg*.

Most
Bouncing
Baby
The most bouncing baby on record was probably James Weir (1819–1821) who, according to his headstone in Cambushnethan, Old Parish Cemetary, Wishaw, Strathclyde, Scotland was 8 st. or 112 lb. *50,8 kg* at 13 month, 3 ft. 4 in *1,01 m* in height and 39 in *99 cm* in girth.

Therese Parentean, who died in Rouyn, Quebec, Canada on 11 May 1936 aged 9 years, weighed 24 st. 4 lb. *154 kg*.

Smallest
The lowest birth weight for a surviving infant, of which there is definite evidence, is 10 oz. *283 g* in the case of Marion Chapman, born on 5 June 1938 in South Shields, Tyne and Wear. She was 12¼ in *31 cm* long. By her first birthday her weight had increased to 13 lb. 14 oz. *6 kg 290*. She was born unattended and was nursed by Dr. D. A. Shearer, who fed her hourly through a fountain pen filler. Her weight on her 21st birthday was 7 st. 8 lb. *48 kg 080*. The smallest viable baby reported from the United States has been Jacqueline Benson born at Palatine, Illinois on 20 Feb. 1936, weighing 12 oz. *340 g*.

A weight of 8 oz. *227 g* was reported on 20 March 1938 for a baby born prematurely to Mrs. John Womack, after she had been knocked down by a lorry in East Louis, Illinois, U.S.A. The baby was taken alive to St. Mary's Hospital, but further information is lacking. On 23 Feb. 1952 it was reported that a 6 oz. *170 g* baby only 6½ in *17 cm* long lived for 12 hours in a hospital in Indianapolis, Indiana, U.S.A. A twin was still-born.

Longest
pregnancy
The longest medically unrefuted pregnancy for a live-born baby was one of 398 days in the case of Mrs. Jacqueline Haddock of Albrighton, Salop, England ending on 23 Mar. 1975. The baby, Sarah Jane, weighed only 3 lb. *1,360 kg*. English law has accepted pregnancies with extremes of 174 days (*Clark* v. *Clark*), 1939) and only 349 days (*Hadlum* v. *Hadlum*, 1949).

Coincident
Birthdates
The only verified example of a family producing children with coincident birthdays on four occasions (involving 5 children, because of a twin birth) is that of Lynn Marie (1966); Timothy Edward (1967); twins Jerry Paul and John Peter (1969) and Daniel Joseph (1972), born to Mr and Mrs. Edward Herbert Petritz of Butte, Montana U.S.A. all on 15 April. The odds are calculable at about 3,900 million to 1 against which closely coincides with the world population.

The first birthday party of the world's only surviving set of sextuplets with their parents Susan and Colin Rosenkowitz (see page 16)

5. PHYSIOLOGY AND ANATOMY

A U.S. scientific publication in 1975 set the value of the raw materials in a 150 lb. 68 kg human body at $5.60. It may be a commentary on world inflation that a 1936 figure was 98 U.S. cents, then 4s 10d. (24p). Hydrogen (63%) and oxygen (25.5%) constitute the commonest of the 24 elements in the human body. In 1972 four more trace elements were added—fluorine. silicon, tin and vanadium. The "essentially" of nickel is now being studied.

BONES

Longest
The thigh bone or *femur* is the longest of the 206 bones in the human body. It constitutes usually 27½ per cent of a person's stature, and may be expected to be 19¾ in *50 cm* long in a 6-ft *183 cm* -tall man. The longest recorded bone was the femur of the German giant Constantine, who died in Mons, Belgium, on 30 March 1902, aged 30 (see page 16). It measured 76 cm *29.9 in*. The femur of Robert Wadlow, the tallest man ever recorded, measured approximately 29½ in *75 cm*.

Smallest
The *stapes* or stirrup bone, one of the three auditory ossicles in the middle ear, is the smallest human bone, measuring from 2,6 to 3,4 mm *0.10 to 0.17 in.* in length and weighing from 2,0 to 4,3 mg *0.03 to 0.065 gr*. Sesamoids are not included among human bones.

MUSCLES

Largest
Muscles normally account for 40 per cent of the body weight and the bulkiest of the 639 muscles in the human body is the *gluteus maximus* or buttock muscle, which extends the thigh.

Smallest
The smallest muscle is the *stapedius*, which controls the *stapes* (see above), an auditory ossicle in the middle ear, and which is less than 1/20th of an inch *0,127 cm* long.

Smallest
waists
Queen Catherine de Medici (1519–89) decreed a waist measurement of 13 in *33 cm* for ladies of the French court. This was at a time when females were more diminutive. The smallest recorded waist among women of normal stature in the 20th century is a reputed 13 in *33 cm* in the case of the French actress Mlle. Polaire (1881–1939) and Mrs. Ethel Granger (b. 12 April 1905) of Peterborough who reduced from a natural 22 in *56 cm* over the period 1929–1939.

Largest chest measurements The largest chest measurements are among endomorphs (those with a tendency toward globularity). In the extreme case of Hughes (see page 18) this was reportedly 124 in *315 cm* but in the light of his known height and weight a figure of 104 in *264 cm* would be more supportable. George MacAree (see Britain's heaviest man) has a chest measurement of 75 in *190 cm*. Among muscular subjects (mesomorphs), chest measurements above 56 in *142 cm* are extremely rare. The largest such chest measurement ever recorded was that of Angus Macaskill (1825–63) of Berneray, Western Isles (see page 8), who may well have been the strongest man who ever lived. His chest measured 65 in *165 cm* at his top weight of 37½ st. *235 kg*.

Longest necks The maximum measured extension of the neck by the successive fitting of copper coils, as practised by the Padaung or Karen people of Burma, is 15¾ in *40 cm*.

From the male viewpoint the practice serves the dual purpose of enhancing the beauty of the female and ensuring fidelity. The neck muscles can become so atrophied that the removal of the support of the coils can produce asphyxiation.

BRAIN AND BRAIN POWER

Largest The brain has 10×10^{10} nerve cells or neurons interconnected by dendrites or filaments and 10×10^{11} glia. Some of the brain's chemical reactions require only one millionth of a second. After the age of 18 the brain loses some 10^3 cells per day. The brain of an average adult male (*i.e.* 30–59 years) weighs 1 410 g *3 lb. 1.73 oz.* falling to 1 030 g *2 lb. 4.31 oz.* The heaviest brain ever recorded was that of Ivan Sergeyvich Turgenev (1818–83), the Russian author. His brain weighed 2 012 g *4 lb. 6.96 oz.* The brain of Oliver Cromwell (1599–1658) reputedly weighed 2 222 g *4 lb. 14.8 oz.*, but the size of his head in portraits does not support this extreme figure. The brain of Lord Byron, who died in Greece in 1824 aged 36, reportedly weighed 6 Neopolitan pounds (1 924 g or *4 lb. 3.86 oz.*, but this also included a certain amount of blood. In January 1891 the *Edinburgh Medical Journal* reported the case of a 75-year-old man in the Royal Edinburgh Asylum whose brain weighed 1 829 g *4 lb. 0.5 oz.*

Smallest The brain of Anatole France (1844–1924), the French writer, weighed only 1 017 g *2 lb. 4 oz.* without the membrane, but there was some shrinkage due to old age. His brain probably weighed *c.* 1 130 g *2 lb. 7.78 oz.* at its heaviest.

Brains in extreme cases of microcephaly may weigh as little as 300 g *10.6 oz.* (*cf.* 20 oz. *[567 g]* for the adult male gorilla, and 16–20 oz. *[454–567 g]* for other anthropoid apes).

Highest I.Q. On the Terman index for Intelligence Quotients, 150 represents "genius" level. The indices are sometimes held to be immeasurable above a level of 200 but a figure of 210 has been attributed to Kim Ung-Yong of Seoul, South Korea (b. 7 March 1963). He composed poetry and spoke four languages (Korean, English, German and Japanese), and performed integral calculus at the age of 4 years 8 months on television in Tokyo on "The World Surprise Show" on 2 Nov. 1967. Both his parents, Dr. and Mrs. Kim Soo Sun, are University professors and were both born at 11 a.m. on 23 May 1934. Research into past geniuses at Stanford University, California, U.S.A., has produced a figure of "over 200" for John Stuart Mill (United Kingdom) (1806–73), who began to learn ancient Greek at the age of three. A similar rating has also been attributed to Emanuel Swedenborg (1688–1772) and Johann Wolfgang von Geothe (1749–1832). More than 20 per cent of the 22,000 members of the International Mensa society have an I.Q. of 161 or above on the Cattell index which is equivalent to 142 on the Terman index.

The new champion for memorizing π Michael Poulteney, who could not remember the 3,026th place. This is, of course, zero

Human Computer The fastest time that anyone has succeeded by purely mental process in extracting a 23rd root from a 200 digit number is 10 min 30 secs achieved by Willem Klein (Netherlands) at Lycée Mixte Nationalisé, Lyon, France on 5 Mar. 1975. Baron Herbert de Grote (b. 9 July 1892) of Mexico City, Mexico extracted a 9 digit root from a 300 digit number on 15 May 1975.

Human memory Mehmed Ali Halici of Ankara, Turkey on 14 Oct. 1967 recited 6,666 verses of the Koran from memory in six hours. The recitation was followed by six Koran scholars. Rare instances of eidetic memory—the ability to re-project and hence "visually" recall material—are known to science.

The greatest number of places of π The greatest number of places to which Pi (ratio of circles' circumference to diameter) has been memorised is 3,025 by Michael John Poultney B.A. (Oxon) (b. 15 Dec. 1950) of Bede Sixth Form College, Billingham, Cleveland, England in 25 minutes on 15 Oct. 1974 before an audience of 200 including a reporter from the *Evening Gazette* and recordist from Radio Cleveland. Note: The approximation of π at 22/7 recurrs after its sixth decimal place and can, of course, be recited *ad nauseam*.

HANDS AND HAIR

Touch sensitivity The extreme sensitivity of the fingers is such that a vibration with a movement of 0.02 of a micron can be detected. On 12 Jan. 1963 the Soviet newspaper *Izvestiya* reported the case of a totally blindfolded girl, Rosa Kulgeshova, who was able to identify colours by touch alone. Later reports in 1970 completely refuted this claim.

Most fingers In 1938 the extreme case of a baby girl with 14 fingers and 12 toes was reported from St. George's Hospital, Hyde Park, Greater London.

Longest finger nails The longest recorded finger nails were reported from Shanghai in 1910, in the case of a Chinese priest who took 27 years to achieve nails up to 22¾ in *58 cm* in length. Probably the longest nail now grown is one of 15 in *38 cm* grown by Ramesh Sharma of Delhi after 12 years. The 5 nails on the left hand of Murari Mohan Aditya of Calcutta had, by July 1975, grown to a total of 61 in *154 cm* since March 1962.

Longest hair The longest recorded hair was that of Swami Pandarasannadhi, the head of the Thiruvadu Thurai monastery in India. His hair was reported in 1949 to be 26 ft *7,93 m* in length, and being matted he was doubtless suffering from the disease Plica caudiformis. The hair of Jane Bunford (see p. 8–9) which she wore in two plaits, reached down to her ankles, indicating a length in excess of 8 ft *2,43 m*.

Longest beard The longest beard preserved was that of Hans N. Langseth (b. 1846 in Norway) which measured 17½ ft *5,33 m* at the time of his death in 1927 after 15 years residence in the United States. The beard was presented to the Smithsonian Institution, Washington, D.C. in 1967. Richard Latter (b. Pembury, Kent, 1831) of Tunbridge Wells, Kent, who died in 1914 aged 83, reputedly had a beard 16 ft *4,87 m* long but contemporary independent corroboration is lacking and photographic evidence indicates this figure was exaggerated. The beard of the bearded lady Janice Deveree (b. Bracken Co., Kentucky, U.S.A., 1842) was measured at 14 in *36 cm* in 1884.

Longest moustache The longest moustache on record is that of Masuriya Din (b. 1908), a Brahmin of the Partabgarh district in Uttar Pradesh, India. It grew to an extended span of 8 ft 6 in *2,59 m* between 1949 and 1962, and costs £13 per annum in upkeep. The longest moustache in Great Britain is that of Mr. John Roy (b. 14 Jan. 1910), licensee of the "Cock Inn" at Beazely End, near Braintree, Essex. It attained a span of 60½ in *153 cm* between 1939 and when last measured by his local police Superintendent in 1975.

ILLNESS AND DISEASE

Commonest illness The commonest illness in the world is coryza (acute nasopharyngitis) or the common cold. Only 2,820,000 working days were reportedly lost as a result of this illness in Great Britain between mid 1971 and mid 1972, since absences of less than three days are not reported. The greatest reported loss of working time in Britain is from bronchitis, which accounted for 30,570,000, or 9.96 per cent, of the total of 306,710,000 working days lost in the same period.

The most resistant recorded case to being infected at the Medical Research Council Common Cold Unit, Salisbury, Wiltshire is J. Brophy, who has had one mild reaction in 24 visits.

Earliest influenza An epidemic bearing symptoms akin to influenza was first recorded in 412 B.C. by Hippocrates (*c. 460-c. 375* B.C.). The earliest description of an epidemic in Great Britain was in the *Chronicle of Melrose* in 1173, although the term influenza was not introduced until 1743 by John Huxham (1692–1768) of Plymouth, Devon.

Earliest slipped disc The earliest description of a prolapsed intervertebral cartilage was by George S. Middleton and John H. Teacher of Glasgow, Scotland, in 1911.

Commonest disease The commonest disease in the world is dental caries or tooth decay. In Great Britain 13 per cent of people have lost all their teeth before they are 21 years old. During their lifetime few completely escape its effects. Infestation with pinworm (*Enterobius vermicularis*) approaches 100 per cent in some areas of the world.

Rarest disease Medical literature periodically records hitherto undescribed diseases. A disease as yet undescribed but predicted is podocytoma of the kidney—a tumor of the epithelial cells lining the glomerulus of the kidney.

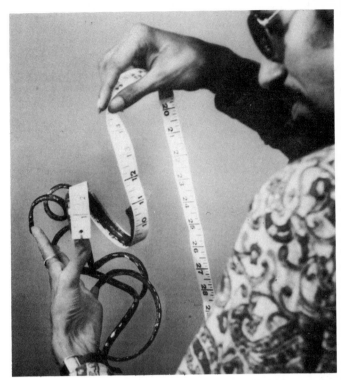

Mohan Aditya of Calcutta, India. The nails on his left hand were in March 1975 ½ in *1,27 cm* short of five feet *152,4 cm*

Of once common diseases, rabies (hydrophobia) was unreported in Britain from 1922 until a field case reported in Kent in 1969 due to a dog imported from India despite 6 months quarantine. Kuru, or laughing sickness, afflicts only the Fore tribe of eastern New Guinea and is 100 per cent fatal. It is transmitted by the cannibalistic practice of eating human brains. The rarest fatal diseases in England and Wales have been those from which the last deaths (all males) were all recorded more than 40 years ago—yellow fever (1930), cholera nostras (1928) and bubonic plague (1926).

Most and least infectious disease The most infectious of all diseases is the pneumonic form of plague, with a mortality rate of about 99.99 per cent. Leprosy transmitted by *Mycobacterium leprae* is the least infectious of communicable diseases.

Highest morbidity Rabies in humans has been regarded as uniformly fatal when associated with the hydrophobia symptom. A 25-year-old woman Candida de Sousa Barbosa of Rio de Janeiro, Brazil, was believed to be the first ever survivor of the disease in November 1968, though some sources give priority to Matthew Winkler, 6, in 1970.

Most notorious carrier The most notorious of all typhoid carriers has been Mary Mallon, known as Typhoid Mary, of New York City, N.Y., U.S.A. She was the source of the 1903 outbreak, with 1,300 cases. Because of her refusal to leave employment, often under assumed names, involving the handling of food, she was placed under permanent detention from 1915 until her death in 1938.

BLOOD

Blood groups The preponderance of one blood group varies greatly from one locality to another. On a world basis Group O is the most common (46 per cent), but in some areas, for example London and Norway, Group A predominates.

The full description of the commonest sub-group in Britain is O MsNs, P+, Rr, Lu(a−), K−, Le(a−b+), Fy(a+b+), Jk(a+b+), which occurs in one in every 270 people.

The rarest blood group on the ABO system, one of nine systems, is AB, which occurs in less than three per cent of persons in the British Isles. The rarest type in the world is a type of Bombay blood (sub-type A-h) found so far only in a Czechoslovak nurse in 1961 and in a brother and sister in New Jersey, U.S.A. reported in February 1968. The American male has started a blood bank for himself.

Richest Natural Resources Joe Thomas of Detroit, Michigan, U.S.A. was reported in August 1970 to have the highest known count of Anti-Lewis B, the rare blood antibody. A U.S. biological supply firm pays him $1,500 per quart—an income of $12,000 (£5,000) per annum. The Internal Revenue regard this income as a taxable liquid asset.

Champion blood donor Joseph Elmaleh (b. 10 Aug. 1915) of Marseilles, France, made his 629th donation since 1931 in June 1974. He has been awarded 17 medals. A 50-year-old haemophiliac Warren C. Jyrich required 2,400 pt *1 364 litres* of blood when undergoing open heart surgery at the Michael Reese Hospital, Chicago, U.S.A., in December 1970. The most blood got from a Stone is believed to be that from Norman Stone, a regular donor since 1966 and Michael Stone who has to date given 18 pints.

Largest vein The largest vein in the human body is a cardiac vein, known as the *vena cava*, which returns most of the blood from the body below the level of the heart.

Most alcoholic subject It is recorded that a hard drinker named Vanhorn (1750–1811), born in London, averaged more than four bottles of ruby port per day for the 23 years from 1788 to his death aged 61 in 1811. The total of his "empties" was put at 35,688.

The youngest recorded death from alcoholic poisoning was that of an 8 year old boy at Redon, France in Oct. 1965. He worked in his uncle's bar and was addicted to cider.

The United Kingdom's legal limit for motorists is 80 mg of alcohol per 100 ml of blood. The hitherto recorded highest figure in medical literature of 605 mg per 100 ml was submerged when the late Mr. Michael Walker, 22, of Stapleford, Nottinghamshire was found by a pathologist to have a level of 640 m on 14 Aug. 1973.

BODY TEMPERATURE

Highest body temperature In Kalow's case (*Lancet*, 31 Oct. 1970) a woman following halothane anaesthesia ran a temperature of 112° F *44,4° C*. She recovered after a procainamide infusion. Marathon runners in hot weather attain 105.8° F *41° C*.

A temperature of 115° F *46,1° C* was recorded in the case of Christopher Legge in the Hospital for Tropical Diseases, London, on 9 Feb. 1934. A subsequent examination of the thermometer disclosed a flaw in the bulb, but it is regarded as certain that the patient sustained a temperature of more than 110° F *43,3° C*.

Lowest body temperature There are two recorded cases of patients surviving body temperatures as low as 60.8° F *16,0° C* Dorothy Mae Stevens, (1929–74) was found in an alley in Chicago, Illinois on 1 Feb. 1951 and Vickie Mary Davis aged 2 years 1 month in an unheated house in Marshalltown, Iowa on 21 Jan. 1956 both with this temperature.

MEDICAL EXTREMES

Heart stoppage The longest recorded heart stoppage is 3 hours in the case of a Norwegian boy, Roger Arntzen, in April 1962. He was rescued, apparently drowned, after 22 minutes under the waters of the River Nideelv, near Trondheim.

The longest recorded interval in a *post mortem* birth was one of at least 80 minutes in Magnolia, Mississippi, U.S.A. Dr. Robert E. Drake found Fanella Anderson, aged 25, dead in her home at 11.40 p.m. on 15 Oct. 1966 and he delivered her of a son weighing 6 lb. 4 oz. *2 kg 830* by Caesarean operation in the Beacham Memorial Hospital on 16 Oct. 1966.

Longest coma The longest recorded coma is that being undergone of Elaine Esposito (b. 3 Dec. 1934) of Tarpon Springs, Florida, U.S.A. She has never stirred since an appendicectomy on 6 Aug. 1941, when she was six, in Chicago, Illinois, U.S.A. On 6 Dec. 1974 her coma surpassed 33 years 4 months—a third of a century.

Longest Dream Dreaming sleep is characterized by rapid eye movements known as REM. The longest recorded period of REM is one of 2 hours 23 minutes on 15 Feb. 1967 at the Department of Psychology, University of Illinois, Chicago on Bill Carskadon, who had had his previous sleep interrupted.

Pulse Rates A normal adult pulse rate is 70–72 beats per minute at rest for males and 78–82 for females. Rates increase to 180 or more during violent exercise and drop to as low as 12 in the extreme case of Dorothy Mae Stevens (see Lowest temperature above).

Largest stone The largest stone or vesical calculus reported in medical literature was one of 13 lb. 14 oz. *6 294 g* removed from an 80-year-old woman by Dr. Humphrey Arthure at Charing Cross Hospital, London, on 29 Dec. 1952.

Longest in iron lung The longest recorded survival in an iron lung is one since 29 June 1948 by Mrs. Laurel Nisbet of La Crescenta, California. The longest survival in an "iron lung" in Britain is since 5 Oct. 1949 by Mr. Dennis Atkin in Lodge Moor Hospital, Sheffield, South Yorkshire. Paul Bates of Horsham, West Sussex entered his 21st year on a mechanical positive pressure respirator on 13 Aug. 1973. During 20 years he received 148,176,300 respirations into his lungs *via* his trachea.

Fastest reflexes The results of experiments carried out in 1943 have shown that the fastest messages transmitted by the nervous system travel at 265 m.p.h. *426 km/h*. With advancing age impulses are carried 15 per cent more slowly.

Pill-taking It is recorded that among hypochondriacs Samuel Jessup (b. 1752), a wealthy grazier of Heckington, Lincolnshire, has never had a modern rival. His consumption of pills from 1794 to 1816 was 226,934, with a peak annual total of 51,590 in 1814. He is also recorded as having drunk 40,000 bottles of medicine before death overtook him at the surprisingly advanced age of 65.

Most tattoos Vivian "Sailor Joe" Simmons, a Canadian tattoo artist, had 4,831 tattoos on his body. He died in Toronto on 22 Dec. 1965 aged 77. Britain's most tattooed man is George Bone (b. 10 Nov. 1946) of Ealing, Greater London whose last few gaps have been blocked in by the Aldershot tattoo artist Bill Skuse. Britain's most decorated woman is Rusty Field (b. 1944) of Aldershot, Hampshire, who after 12 years under the needle, came within 15 per cent of totality.

Hiccoughing The longest recorded attack of hiccoughs was that afflicting Charles Osborne (b. 1894) of Anthon, Iowa, U.S.A., from 1922 to date. He contracted it when slaughtering a hog. His first wife left him and he is unable to keep in his false teeth. The infirmary at Newcastle upon Tyne is recorded to have admitted a young man from Long Witton, Northumberland on 25 March 1769 suffering from hiccoughs which could be heard at a range of more than a mile.

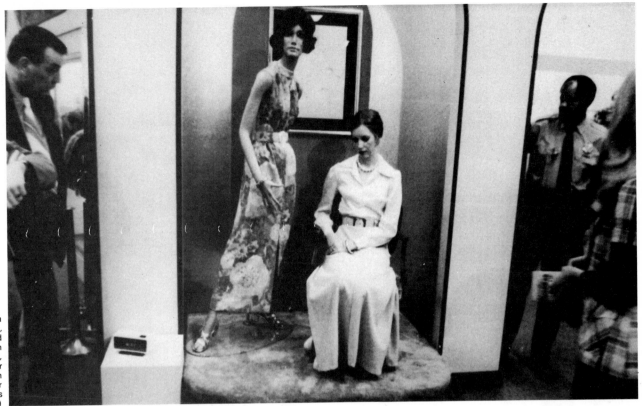

Mardeana Odom (seated), the 16 year old American 'freeze model', setting her world duration record for motionlessness (see below)

Sneezing The most chronic sneezing fit ever recorded was that of June Clark, aged 17, of Miami, Florida, U.S.A. She started sneezing on 4 Jan. 1966, while recovering from a kidney ailment in the James M. Jackson Memorial Hospital, Miami. The sneezing was stopped by electric "aversion" treatment on 8 June 1966, after 155 days. The highest speed at which expelled particles have been measured to travel is 103.6 m.p.h. *167 km/h.*

Snoring Research at the Ear, Nose and Throat Department of
Loudest St. Mary's Hospital, London, published in November 1968, shows that a rasping snore can attain a loudness of 69 decibels (*c.f.* 70–90 for a pneumatic drill).

Yawning In Lee's case, reported in 1888, a fifteen-year-old female patient yawned continuously for a period of five weeks.

Sleepless- Researches indicate that on the Circadian cycle for
ness the majority peak efficiency is attained between 8 p.m. and 9 p.m. and the low point comes at 4 a.m. The longest recorded period for which a person has voluntarily gone without sleep is 288 hr (12 days) by Roger Guy English, 23 in a waterbed showroom in San Diego, California from 10.30 a.m. 20 March to 10.30 a.m. 1 Apr. 1974 without stimulants other than coffee. He has suffered hallucinations following this most ill-advised test.

Motionless- The longest that anyone has voluntarily remained
ness motionless is 5 hr. 32 min by Miss Mardeana Odom, 16, a "freeze model" in a department store in Indianapolis, Indiana on 30 Mar. 1974. The longest recorded case of involuntarily being made to stand to attention was when Staff Sgt. Samuel B. Moody U.S.A.F. was so punished in Narumi prison camp, Nagoya, Japan for 53 hours in spring of 1945. He survived to write *Reprieve from Hell.*

Swallowing The worst reported case of compulsive swallowing was an insane female Mrs. H. aged 42, who complained of a "slight abdominal pain". She proved to have 2,533 objects, including 947 bent pins, in her stomach. These were removed by Drs. Chalk and Foucar in June 1927 at the Ontario Hospital, Canada. The heaviest object extracted from a human stomach has been a 5 lb. 3 oz *2,530 kg* ball of hair in Swain's case from a 20 year female at the South Devon and East Cornwall Hospital England on 20 Mar. 1895.

Sword The longest length of sword able to be "swallowed" by a practised exponent, after a heavy meal, is 27 in *69 cm.* Perhaps the greatest exponent is Alex Linton, born on 25 Oct. 1904 in Boyle, County Roscommon, Ireland. Sandra Dee Reed (Lady Sandra) of Florida has swallowed five 30 in *152,4 cm* blades to two thirds of their length simultaneously.

Fasting Most humans experience considerable discomfort after an abstinance from food for even 12 hr but this often passes off after 24–48 hr. Records claimed without unremitting medical surveillance are of little value.

The longest period for which anyone has gone without food is 382 days by Angus Barbieri (b. 1940) of Tayport, Fife, who lived on tea, coffee, water, soda water and vitamins in Maryfield Hospital, Dundee, Angus, from June 1965 to July 1966. His weight declined from 33 st. 10 lb. *214 kg 10* to 12 st. 10 lb. *80 kg 740.* Dr. Stephen Taylor, 43, of Mount Roskill, New Zealand, fasted 40 days with only a glass of water per day in a political protest in 1970.

Hunger The longest recorded hunger strike was one of 94 days
strike by John and Peter Crowley, Thomas Donovan, Michael Burke, Michael O'Reilly, Christopher Upton, John Power, Joseph Kenny and Seán Hennessy in Cork Prison, Ireland, from 11 Aug. to 12 Nov. 1920. These nine survivors from 12 prisoners owed their lives to expert medical attention and an appeal by Arthur Griffith. The longest recorded hunger strike in a British gaol is 385 days from 28 June 1972 to 18 July 1973 by Denis Galer Goodwin in Wakefield Prison, West Yorkshire protesting his innocence of a rape charge. He was fed by tube orally.

Most Jack Sholomir (G.B.) blew a flame from his mouth
voracious to more than 5 m *16 ft 4¾ in* at Randers, Denmark on
fire eater 6 June 1973.

Komar (Vernon E. Craig) sauntering across a bed of coals measured at 1,183° F 638° C

Human salamanders The highest dry-air temperature endured by naked men in the U.S. Air Force experiments in 1960 was 400° F *204,4° C* and for heavily clothed men 500° F *260° C*. Steaks require only 325° F *162,8° C*. Temperatures of 140° C *284° F* have been found quite bearable in *Sauna* baths.

The highest temperature recorded by pyrometer for the coals in any fire walk was 1,220° F *660° C* for a 25 ft *7,60 m* walk by "Komar" (Vernon E. Craig) of Wooster, Ohio at the Phoenix Psychic Seminar, Arizona, U.S.A. on 7 Mar. 1975.

Underwater The world record for voluntarily staying underwater is 13 min 42.5 sec by Robert Foster, aged 32, an electronics technician of Richmond, California, who stayed under 10 ft *3,05 m* of water in the swimming pool of the Bermuda Palms Motel at San Rafael, California, U.S.A., on 15 March 1959. He hyperventilated with oxygen for 30 min before his descent. The longest unprepared record is 6 min 29.8 sec by Georges Pouliquin in Paris on 3 Nov. 1912. It must be stressed that record-breaking of this kind is *extremely dangerous*.

g forces The acceleration g, due to gravity, is 32 ft 1.05 in per sec per sec *978,02 cm/sec²* at sea-level at the Equator. A *sustained* acceleration of 31 g was withstood for 5 sec by R. Flanagan Gray, 39, at the Johnsville U.S. Naval Air Development Center in Warminster, Pennsylvania, on 5 Dec. 1958. This makes the bodyweight of a 13 st. 3 lb. *83 kg 910* man seem like 2.54 tons *2 585 kg*. The highest value endured in a dry capsule is 25 g. The highest g value endured on a water-braked rocket sled is 82.6 g for 0.04 of a sec by Eli L. Beeding Jr. at Holloman Air Force Base, New Mexico, U.S.A., on 16 May 1958. He was put in hospital for 3 days. A man who fell off a 185 ft *56,39 m* cliff (before 1963) has survived a *momentary* g of 209 in decelerating from 68 m.p.h. *109 km/h* to stationary in 0.015 of a sec.

The land divers of Penecost Island, New Hebrides dive from Platforms 70 ft *21,3 m* high with liana vines attached to their ankles. The jerk can transmit a momentary g force in excess of 100.

Isolation The longest recorded period for which any volunteer has been able to withstand total deprivation of all sensory stimulation (sight, hearing and touch) is 92 hr, recorded in 1962 at Lancaster Moor Hospital, Lancashire.

The farthest that any human has been isolated from all other humans has been the lone pilots of lunar command modules when antipodal to their Apollo missions, two lunar explorers 2,200 miles *3 540 km* distant.

DENTITION

Earliest The first deciduous or milk teeth normally appear in infants at five to eight months, these being the mandibular and maxillary first incisors. There are many records of children born with teeth, the most distinguished example being Prince Louis Dieudonné, later Louis XIV of France, who was born with two teeth on 5 Sept. 1638. Molars usually appear at 24 months, but in Pindborg's case published in Denmark in 1970 a 6 week premature baby was documented with 8 natal teeth of which 4 were in the molar region.

Most Cases of the growth in late life of a third set of teeth have been recorded several times. A reference to an extreme case in France of a fourth dentition, known as Lison's case was published in 1896. A triple row of teeth was noted in 1680 by Albertus Hellwigius.

Most dedicated dentist Brother Giovanni Battista Orsenigo of the Ospedale Fatebenefratelli, Rome, Italy, a religious dentist, conserved all the teeth he extracted in three enormous cases during the time he exercised his profession from 1868 to 1904. In 1903 the number was counted and found to be 2,000,744 teeth.

OPTICS

Smallest visible object The resolving power of the human eye is 0.0003 of a radian or an arc of one minute (1/60th of a degree), which corresponds to 100 microns at 10 in. A micron is a thousandth of a millimetre, hence 100 microns is 0.003937, or less than four thousandths, of an inch. The human eye can, however, detect a bright light source shining through an aperture only 3 to 4 microns across. In Oct. 1972 the University of Stuttgart, West Germany reported that their student Frl. Veronica Seider (b. 1953) possessed a visual acuity 20 times better than average. She could identify people at a distance of more than a mile *1,6 km.*

Colour sensitivity The unaided human eye, under the best possible viewing conditions, comparing large areas of colour, in good illumination, using both eyes, can distinguish 10,000,000 different colour surfaces. The most accurate photo-electric spectrophotometers possess a precision probably only 40 per cent as good as this.

Colour blindness About 7.5% of men and 0.1% of women are colour blind. The most extreme form, monochromatic vision, is very rare. The highest recorded rate of red-green colour blindness is in Czechoslovakia and the lowest rate among Fijians and Brazilian Indians.

VOICE

Highest and lowest The highest and lowest recorded notes attained by the human voice before this century were a C in *alt-altissimo* (c^{iv}) by Lucrezia Agujari (1743–83), noted by the Austrian composer Wolfgang Amadeus Mozart (1756–91) in Parma, northern Italy, in 1770, and an A_1 (55 cycles per sec) by Kaspar Foster (1617–73). Madeleine Marie Robin (1918–1960) the French operatic coloratura could produce and sustain the B♭ above high C in the Lucia mad scene in *Lucia de Lammermoor.* Since 1950 singers have achieved high and low notes far beyond the hitherto accepted extremes. However, notes at the bass and treble extremities of the register tend to lack hormonics and are of little musical value. Frl. Marita Gunther, trained by Alfred Wolfsohn, has covered the range of the piano from the lowest note, A_{11}, to c^v. Of this range of $7\frac{1}{4}$ octaves, six octaves are considered to be of musical value. Mr. Roy Hart, also trained by Wolfsohn, has reached notes below the range of the piano. The highest note being sung by a tenor is g in *alt-altissimo* by Louis Lavelle, coached by Mr. S. Pleeth, in *Lovely Mary Donelly.* The lowest note put into song is a D_{11} by the singer Tom King, of King's Langley, Hertfordshire. The highest note called for in singing was an f^{iv}♯, which occurred twice in Zerbinetta's Recitative and Aria in the first (1912) version of the opera *Ariadne auf Naxos* by Richard Georg Strauss (1864–1949). It was transposed down a tone in 1916.

Greatest range The normal intelligible outdoor range of the male human voice in still air is 200 yd *180 m.* The *silbo*, the whistled language of the Spanish-speaking Canary Island of La Gomera, is intelligible across the valleys, under ideal conditions, at five miles *8 km.* There is a recorded case, under freak acoustic conditions, of the human voice being detectable at a distance of $10\frac{1}{2}$ miles *17 km* across still water at night. It was said that Mills Darden (see page 11) could be heard 6 miles *9 km* away when he shouted at the top of his voice.

At the "World" Shouting Competition at Scarborough, North Yorkshire on 17 Feb. 1973 the title was won by Skipper Kenny Leader with 111 decibels at $2\frac{1}{2}$ metres *8 ft 1¼ in.* Mrs. Margaret Featherstone hit the feminine record of 109.7 decibels on 12 June 1974.

Lowest detectable sound The intensity of noise or sound is measured in terms of pressure. The pressure of the quietest sound that can be detected by a person of normal hearing at the most sensitive frequency of *c.* 2,750 Hz is 2×10^{-5} pascal. One tenth of the logarithm to this standard provides a unit termed a decibel. Prolonged noise above 150 decibels will cause immediate permanent deafness while 200 decibels could be fatal. A noise of 30 decibels is negligible.

'Mado' Robin (1918-1960) the French coloratura who could sustain the B flat above High C

Highest detectable pitch The upper limit of hearing by the human ear has long been regarded as 20,000 Hz (cycles per sec), although children with asthma can often detect a sound of 30,000 cycles per sec. It was announced in February 1964 that experiments in the U.S.S.R. had conclusively proved that oscillations as high as 200,000 cycles per sec can be heard if the oscillator is pressed against the skull.

Fastest talker Few people are able to speak *articulately* at a sustained speed above 300 words per min. The fastest broadcaster has been regarded as Gerry Wilmot (b. Victoria B.C., Canada 6 Oct. 1914) the ice hockey commentator in the post World War II period. Raymond Glendenning (1907–1974), the B.B.C. horseracing commentator, once spoke 176 words in 30 sec while commentating on a greyhound race. In public life the highest speed recorded is a 327 words per min burst in a speech made in December 1961 by John Fitzgerald Kennedy (1917–63), then President of the United States. Tapes of attempts to recite Hamlet's 262 word Soliloquy in under 24 secs (655 w.p.m.) have proved indecipherable.

OPERATIONS

Longest The most protracted operations are those involving brain surgery. Such an operation lasting up to 31 hr was performed on Victor Zazueta, 19, of El Centro at San Diego Hospital, California by Drs. John F. Alksne and Randall Smith on 17–18 Jan. 1972.

Oldest subject The greatest recorded age at which a person has been subjected to an operation is 111 years 105 days in the case of James Henry Brett, Jr. (b. 25 July 1849, d. 10 Feb. 1961) of Houston, Texas, U.S.A. He underwent a hip operation on 7 Nov. 1960. The oldest age established in Britain was the case of Miss Mary Wright (b. 28 Feb. 1862) who died during a thigh operation at Boston, Lincolnshire on 22 April 1971 aged 109 years 53 days.

Youngest subject Babies are now increasingly operated on within minutes of birth so there is no specific record for the youngest subject.

Universal Pictorial Press

Dr Christiaan Barnard, the South African pioneer of heart transplant surgery

Heart The first human heart transplant operation was performed on Louis Washkansky, aged 55, at the Groote Schuur Hospital, Cape Town, South Africa, between 1.00 a.m. and 6 a.m., on 3 Dec. 1967, by a team of 30 headed by Prof. Christiaan Neethling Barnard (b. Beaufort West, South Africa, 8 Oct. 1922). The donor was Miss Denise Ann Darvall, aged 25. Washkansky died on 21 Dec. 1967. The longest surviving heart male transplantee has been the American negro Louis B. Russell, of Indianapolis (b. 1923), who received his replacement heart from Robert Clarence Brown, 17, who had died from gunshot wounds, in Richmond, Virginia on 24 Aug. 1968. He celebrated his sixth re-birthday in 1974 but died on 27 Nov. 1974. Mrs. Betty Anick of Milwaukee, Wisconsin, U.S.A. (*fl.* July 1975) broke the record on 27 Jan. 1975. Britain's longest-surviving heart transplant patient has been Mr. Charles Hendrick who died in Guy's Hospital of a lung infection on 31 Aug. 1969 107 days after his operation.

Laryngectomy On 24 July 1924 John I. Poole of Plymouth, Devon after diagnosis of carcinoma then aged 33 underwent total laryngectomy in Edinburgh. In July 1974 he entered his 51st year as a "neck-breather".

Earliest appendicectomy The earliest recorded successful appendix operation was performed in 1736 by Claudius Amyand (1680–1740). He was Serjeant Surgeon to King George II (reigned 1727–60).

Earliest anaesthesia The earliest recorded operation under general anaesthesia was for the removal of a cyst from the neck of James Venable by Dr. Crawford Williamson Long (1815–78), using diethyl ether ($C_2H_5)_2O$), in Jefferson, Georgia, U.S.A., on 30 March 1842. The earliest use of an anaesthetic in Great Britain was by Dr. James Robinson and Dr. Francis Boott in the latter's surgery in Gower Street, London on 19 Dec. 1846. A tooth was extracted from a Miss Lonsdale.

Fastest amputation The shortest time recorded for a leg amputation in the pre-anaesthetic era was 13 to 15 seconds by Napoleon's chief surgeon Dominique Larrey.

Surgical instruments The largest surgical instruments are robot retractors used in abdominal surgery introduced by Abbey Surgical Instruments of Chingford, Essex in 1968 and weighing 11 lb. *5 kg.* Some bronchoscopic forceps measure 60 cm *23½ in* in length. The smallest are Elliot's eye trephine, which has a blade 0.078 in *0.20 cm* in diameter and "straight" stapes picks with a needle type tip or blade of 0,3 mm *0.013 in* long.

PSYCHIC FORCES

Extra-sensory perception The highest consistent performer in tests to detect powers of extra-sensory perception is Pavel Stepánek (Czechoslovakia) known in parapsychological circles as "P.S.". His performance on nominating hidden white or green cards from May 1967 to March 1968 departed from a chance probability yielding a Chi^2 value corresponding to $P < 10^{-50}$ or odds of more than 100 octillion to one against the achievement being one of chance. One of the two appointed referees recommended that the results should not be published. The highest published scores in any E.S.P. test were those of a 26-year-old female tested by Prof. Bernard F. Reiss of Hunter College, New York in 1936. In 74 runs of 25 guesses each she scored one with 25 all correct, two with 24 and an average of 18.24 instead of the random 5.00. Such a result would depart from chance probability by a factor $> 10^{700}$. This produced the comment from some that there might be a defect in the theory of probability.

Most durable ghosts Ghosts are not immortal and, according to the *Gazeteer of British Ghosts*, seem to deteriorate after 400 years. The most outstanding exception to their normal "half-life" would be the ghosts of Roman soldiers thrice reported still marching through the cellars of the Treasurer's House, York Minister after nearly 19 centuries. The book's author, Peter Underwood, states that Britain has more reported ghosts per square mile than any other country with Borley Rectory near Long Melford, Suffolk the site of unrivalled activity between 1863 and its destruction by fire in 1939.

2 THE ANIMAL AND PLANT KINGDOM

ANIMAL KINGDOM
GENERAL RECORDS

Note—Guinness Superlatives Ltd. has published a specialist volume entitled *The Guinness Book of Animal Facts and Feats*. This work treats the dimensions and performances of all the Classes of the Animal Kingdom in greater detail, giving also the sources and authorities for much of the material in this chapter.

Largest and heaviest The largest and heaviest animal in the world, and probably the biggest creature which has *ever* existed, is the Blue or Sulphur-bottom whale (*Balaenoptera musculus*), also called Sibbald's rorqual. The largest specimen ever recorded was a female landed at the Cia Argentina de Pesca, South Georgia *c.* 1912 which measured 33.58 m *110 ft 2½ in* in length. Another female measuring 96¾ ft *29,48 m* brought into the shore station at Prince Olaf, South Georgia in *c.* 1931 was calculated to have weighed 163.7 tons *166 tonnes*, exclusive of blood and other body fluids, judging by the number of cookers that were filled by the animal's blubber, meat and bones and internal organs. The total weight of this whale was believed to have been 174 tons *177 tonnes*.

In November 1947 a weight of 190 tons *193 tonnes* was reported for a 90¾ ft *27,66 m* Blue whale weighed piecemeal by the Russians during the first cruise of the "Slava" whaling fleet in the Antarctic, but this figure was a misprint and should have read 140 tons *142 tonnes*. On the principle that the weight should vary as the cube of linear dimensions, a 100 ft *30,48 m* Blue whale in good condition should weigh about 160 tons *163 tonnes*, but in the case of pregnant females the weight could be as much as 190–200 tons *193–203 tonnes*—equivalent to 35 adult bull African elephants.

Tallest The tallest living animal is the Giraffe (*Giraffa camelopardalis*), which is now found only in the dry savannah and semi-desert areas of Africa south of the Sahara. The tallest ever recorded was a Masai bull (*G. camelopardalis tippelskirchi*) named "George", received at Chester Zoo, England on 8 Jan. 1959 from Kenya. His head almost touched the roof of the 20 ft *6,09 m* high Giraffe House when he was 9 years old. George died on 22 July 1969. Less credible heights of up to 23 ft *7 m* have been claimed for bulls shot in the field.

The first giraffe ever seen in England was a six-month-old cow of the Nubian race (*G.c. camelopardalis*) presented to George IV (1762–1830) by Mohammed Ali, Pasha of Egypt. The 9 ft 2 in *2,79 m* tall animal arrived in London in August 1827. It was kept at Windsor for 26 months, grew another 18 in *45 cm* and died in Oct. 1829.

Longest The longest animal ever recorded is the giant jellyfish *Cyanaea arctica*, which is found in the north-western Atlantic Ocean. One specimen washed up in Massachusetts Bay, Mass., U.S.A., in *c.* 1865 had a bell diameter of 7½ ft *2,29 m* and tentacles measuring 120 ft *36,5 m*, thus giving a theoretical tentacular span of some 245 ft *75 m*.

Smallest The smallest of all free-living organisms are pleuropneumonia-like organisms (P.P.L.O.) of the *Mycoplasma*. One of these, *Mycoplasma laidlawii*, first discovered in sewage in 1936, has a diameter during its early existence of only 100 millimicrons, or 0.000004 of an in. Examples of the strain known as H.39 have a maximum diameter of 300 millimicrons and weigh an estimated 1.0×10^{-16} of a gramme. Thus a 174 ton *177 tonnes* Blue whale would weigh 1.77×10^{23} or 177,000 trillion times as much.

Longest lived Few non-bacterial creatures live longer than humans. It would appear that tortoises are the longest lived such animals. The greatest authentic age recorded for a tortoise is 152-plus years for a male Marion's tortoise (*Testudo sumeirii*) brought from the Seychelles to Mauritius in 1766 by the Chevalier de Fresne, who presented it to the Port Louis army garrison. This specimen (it went blind in 1908) was accidentally killed in 1918. When the famous Royal Tongan tortoise "Tu'malilia" (believed to be a specimen of *Testudo radiata*) died on 19 May 1966 it was reputed to be over 200 years old, having been presented to the then King of Tonga by Captain James Cook (1728–79) on 22 Oct. 1773, but this record lacks proper documentation.

25

"Discovery" Committee, Colonial Office, London

The largest animal which has ever lived—a Blue Whale. Specimens may range up to 110 ft 2½ in *33,58 m* and 174 tons/*177 tonnes*

The bacteria *Thermoactinomyces vulgaris* has been found alive in cores of mud taken from the bottom of Windermere, Cumbria, England which have been dated to 1,500 yrs before the present.

Fastest The fastest reliably measured speed of any animal is 106.25 m.p.h. *171 km/h* for the Spine-tailed swift (*Chaetura caudacuta*) reported from the U.S.S.R. in 1942. In 1934 ground speeds ranging from 171.8 to 219.5 m.p.h. *276,5–353,3 km/h* were recorded by stop-watch for spine-tailed swifts over a 2-mile *3 km* course in the Cachar Hills of north-eastern India, but scientific tests since have revealed that this species of bird cannot be seen at a distance of 1 mile *1,6 km*, even with a standard binocular. This bird is the fastest moving living creature and has a blood temperature of 112.5° F *44,7° C*. Speeds even higher than a "free fall" maximum of 185 m.p.h. *297 km/h* have been ascribed to the Peregrine falcon (*Falco peregrinus*) in a stoop, but in recent experiments in which miniature air speedometers were fitted, the maximum recorded diving speed was 82 m.p.h. *132 km/h*.

Rarest The best claimant to the title of the world's rarest land animal are those species which are known only from a single (type) specimen. One of these is the tenrec *Dasogale fontoynonti*, which is known only from a specimen collected in eastern Madagascar (Malagasy) and now preserved in the Museum d'Histoire Naturelle, Paris.

Commonest It has been estimated that man shares the earth with about 3,000,000,000,000,000,000,000,000,000,000,000 (3,000 quintillion or 3×10^{33}) other living things. Of these, more than 75 per cent are bacteria, namely 2,200 quintillion or 2.2×10^{33}.

Most valuable The most valuable animals in cash terms are thoroughbred racehorses. *Secretariat* (see Chapter XII, Horse-racing) was sold in February 1973 for $6,080,000 (*then £2,432,000*). The most valuable zoo exhibits is the Giant Panda (*Ailuropoda melanoleuca*) for which $250,000 (*£104,160*) was offered by the San Diego Zoological Gardens for a fertile pair in 1971. The most valuable marine exhibit is the Killer Whale (*Orcinus orca*). Trained specimens such as "Ramu" at the Windsor Safari Park, Berkshire are valued at £35,000.

Fastest growth The fastest growth in the Animal Kingdom is that of the Blue whale calf (see p. 25). A barely visible ovum weighing a fraction of a milligramme (0.000035 of an oz.) grows to a weight of *c.* 26 tons *26 tonnes* in 22¾ months, made up of 10¾ months gestation and the first 12 months of life. This is equivalent to an increase of 30,000 million-fold.

Largest egg The largest egg of any living animal is that of the Whale shark (*Rhiniodon typus*). One egg case measuring 12 in by 5.5 in by 3.5 in *30 × 14 × 9 cm* was picked up by the shrimp trawler "Doris" on 29 June 1953 at a depth of 31 fathoms (186 ft [*56,6 m*]) in the Gulf of Mexico 130 miles *209 km* south of Port Isabel, Texas, U.S.A. The egg contained a perfect embryo of a Whale shark 13.78 in *35 cm* long.

Greatest size difference between sexes The largest female deep-sea angler fish of the species *Ceratias holboelki* on record weighed half a million times as much as the smallest known parasitic male. It has been suggested that this fish would make an appropriate emblem for the Women's Lib. Movement.

Longest gestation The viviparous Alpine black salamander (*Salamandra atra*) has a gestation period of up to 38 months at altitudes above 1 400 m *4,600 ft* in the Swiss Alps, but this drops to 24–26 months at lower altitudes.

Heaviest brain The Sperm whale (*Physeter catodon*) has the heaviest brain of any living animal. The brain of a 49 ft *14,93 m* bull processed in the Japanese factory ship *Nissin Maru No. 1* in the Antarctic on 11 Dec. 1949 weighed 9,2 kg *20.24 lb.* compared with 6,9 kg *15.38 lb.* for a 90 ft *27 m* Blue whale. The heaviest brain recorded for an elephant is 16.5 lb. *7,5 kg* in the case of an Asiatic cow. The normal brain weight for an adult African bull is 12 lb. *5,440 kg*.

Largest eye The giant squid *Architeuthis sp.* has the largest eye of any living animal. The ocular diameter may exceed 38 cm *15 in* compared to 10–12 cm *3.93 to 4.71 in* for the largest Blue whales.

Highest G Force The highest g force encountered in nature is the 400 g endured by the 12 mm *0.47 in* long click beetle *Athous haemorrhoidalis* (a common British species) when jack-knifing into the air to a height of 30 cm *11¾ in* to escape predators. According to Dr. Glyn Evans of Manchester University the parts of the click beetle farthest from its central pivot travel at an even greater acceleration, the brain being subjected to a peak deceleration at the end of the movement of 2000 g.

1. MAMMALS *(Mammalia)*

Largest and heaviest World For details of the Blue whale (*Balaenoptera musculus*) see page 25. Further information: the tongue and heart of a 27.6 m *90 ft 8 in* long female Blue whale taken by the Slava whaling fleet in the Antarctic on 17 March 1947 weighed 4.22 tons *4,29 tonnes* and 1,540 lb. *698 kg 50* respectively.

British waters The largest Blue whale ever recorded in British waters was probably an 88 ft *26,8 m* specimen killed near the Bunaveneader station in Harris in the Western Isles, Scotland in 1904. In Sept. 1750 a Blue whale allegedly measuring 101 ft *30,75 m* in length ran aground in the River Humber estuary. Another specimen stranded on the west coast of Lewis, Western Isles, Scotland in *c.* 1870 was credited with a length of 105 ft *32 m* but the carcase was cut up by the local people before the length could be verified. In both cases the length was probably exaggerated or taken along the curve of the body instead of in a straight line from the tip of the snout to the notch in the flukes. Four Blue whales have been stranded on British coasts since 1913. The last occurrence (*c.* 60 ft

[18 m]) was at Wick, Highland, Scotland on 15 Oct. 1923.

Blue whales inhabit the colder seas and migrate to warmer waters in the winter for breeding. Observations made in the Antarctic in 1947–48 showed that a Blue whale can maintain a speed of 20 knots (23 m.p.h. *[37 km/h]*) for ten minutes when frightened. It has been calculated that a 90 ft *27 m* Blue whale travelling at 20 knots *37 km/h* would develop 520 h.p. *527 c.v.* Newborn calves measure 6,5 to 8,6 m *21 ft 3½ in to 28 ft 6 in* in length and weigh up to 3,000 kg *2.95 tons*.

It has been estimated that there are only *c.* 25,000 Blue whales living throughout the oceans in 1974. The species has been protected *de jure* since 1967.

Deepest dive The greatest *recorded* depth to which a whale has dived is 620 fathoms (3,720 ft *[1,134 m]*) by a 47 ft *14,32 m* bull Sperm whale (*Physeter catodon*) found with its jaw entangled with a submarine cable running between Santa Elena, Ecuador and Chorillos, Peru, on 14 Oct. 1955. At this depth the whale withstood a pressure of 1,680 lb/in² *118 kg.f/cm²* of body surface. On 25 August 1969 a Sperm whale was killed 100 miles *160 km* south of Durban after it had surfaced from a dive lasting 1 hr 52 min, and inside its stomach were found two small sharks which had been swallowed about an hour earlier. These were later identified as *Scymnodon sp.*, a species found only on the sea floor. At this point from land the depth of water is in excess of 1,646 fathoms (10,476 ft *[3 193 m]*) for a radius of 30–40 miles *48–64 km*, which now suggests that the Sperm whale sometimes may descend to a depth of over 10,000 ft *3 000 m* when seeking food.

Largest on land World The largest living land animal is the African bush elephant (*Loxodonta africana africana*). The average adult bull stands 10 ft 6 in *3,20 m* at the shoulder and weighs 5.6 tons *5,7 tonnes*. The largest specimen ever recorded was a bull shot 48 miles *77 km* north-west of Macusso, Angola on 13 Nov. 1955. Lying on its side this elephant measured 13 ft 2 in *4,01 m* in a projected line from the highest point of the shoulder to the base of the forefoot, indicating that its standing height must have been about 12 ft 6 in *3,8 m*. Other measurements included an over-all length of 33 ft 2 in *10,10 m* (tip of extended trunk to tip of extended tail) and a maximum bodily girth of 19 ft 8 in *5,99 m*. The weight was estimated at 24,000 lb. (10.7 tons *[10,9 tonnes]*). On 6 March 1959 the mounted specimen was put on display in the rotunda of the U.S. National Museum in Washington, D.C., U.S.A. (see also Shooting, Chapter 12). Another outsized bull elephant known as "Dhlulamithi" (Taller than the Trees), reputed to stand over 12 ft *3,65 m* at the shoulder, was shot at Fishan, east of the Lundi River, Rhodesia in Aug. 1967 by a South African police officer, after it had strayed outside the Gona-Re-Zhou Reserve.

Britain The largest wild mammal in the British Isles, excluding the wild pony (*Equus caballus*) is the Red deer (*Cervus elephus*). A full-grown stag stands 3 ft 8 in *1,11 m* at the shoulder and weighs 230–250 lb *104–113 kg*. The heaviest ever recorded was probably a stag weighing 462 lb. *209 kg* killed in Glenmore Deer-forest, Highland, Scotland in 1877. The heaviest park Red deer on record was a stag weighing 476 lb. *215 kg 90* (height at shoulder 4 ft 6 in *[1,37 m]*) killed at Woburn, Bedfordshire in 1836. The wild population in 1968 was estimated at 180,000 to 185,000.

The largest ever measured specimen of the largest of all surviving land animals—the stuffed 10.7 ton *10 875 kg* African elephant shot in Angola in 1955

Smithsonian Institute

Tallest The tallest mammal is the Giraffe (*Giraffa camelopardalis*). For details see page 25.

Smallest The smallest recorded mammal is Savi's white-
Land toothed pygmy shrew (*Suncus etruscus*), also called the Etruscan shrew, which is found along the coast of the northern Mediterranean and southwards to Cape Province, South Africa. Mature specimens have a head and body length of 36–52 mm *1.32–2.04 in*, a tail length of 24–29 mm *0.94–1.14 in* and weigh between 1,5 and 2,5 g *0.052 and 0.09 oz*. The smallest mammal found in the British Isles is the European pygmy shrew (*Sorex minutus*). Mature specimens have a head and body length of 43–64 mm *1.69–2.5 in*, a tail length of 31–46 mm *1.22–1.81 in* and weigh between 2,4 and 6,1 g *0.084 and 0.213 oz*.

Marine The smallest totally marine mammal is the Sea otter (*Enhydra lutris*), which is found in coastal waters off California, western Alaska and the Komandorskie and Kurile Islands in the Bering Sea. Adult specimens measure 120–156 cm *47.24–61.5 in* in total length and weigh 25–38,5 kg *55–81.4 lb*.

Rarest The rarest placental mammal in the world is now the fully protected Javan rhinoceros (*Rhinoceros sondaicus*) In May 1973 there were only 44 in the Udjung-Kulon (also called Oedjoeng Kuelon) Reserve of 117 miles² *300 km²* at the tip of western Java, Indonesia, but there may also be a few left in the Tenasserim area on the Thai-Burmese border. Among sub-species, the Bali tiger (*Panthera tigris sondaica*) was believed to have become extinct in 1974 when only a single specimen was reported to have been sighted in 1973. The last Arabian oryx reported in the wild was a male on 20 Oct. 1972 in the Oman desert.

The rarest British land mammal is the Pine marten (*Martes martes*), which is found in the highlands of Scotland, particularly in Coille na Glas, Leitire, Ross and Cromarty, and thinly distributed in North Wales and the Scottish border country. The largest specimens measure up to 34 in *863 mm* from nose to tip of tail (tail 6–9 in [*152–228 mm*]) and weigh up to 4 lb. 6 oz. *1 984 g*.

Fastest The fastest of all land animals over a short distance
World (*i.e.* up to 600 yds [*549 m*]) is the Cheetah or Hunting leopard (*Acinonyx jubatus*) of the open plains of East Africa, Iran, Turkmenia and Afghanistan, with a probable maximum speed of 60–63 m.p.h. *96–101 km/h* over suitably level ground. Speeds of 71, 84 and even 90 m.p.h. *114, 135 and 145 km/h* have been claimed for this animal, but these figures must be considered exaggerated. Tests in London in 1937 showed that on an oval greyhound track over 345 yds *316 m* a female cheetah's average speed over three runs was 43.4 m.p.h. *69,8 km/h* (*cf.* 43.26 m.p.h. [*69,6 km/h*] for the fastest racehorse), but this specimen was not running flat out. The fastest land animal over a sustained distance (*i.e.* 1,000 yds [*914 m*] or more) is the Pronghorn antelope (*Antilocapra americana*) of the western United States. Specimens have been observed to travel at 35 m.p.h. for 4 miles *56 km/h for 6 km*, at 42 m.p.h. for 1 mile *67 km/h for 1,6 km* and 55 m.p.h. for half a mile *88,5 km/h for 0,8 km*. On 14 Aug. 1936 at Spanish Lake, in Lake County, Oregon a hard-pressed buck was timed by a car speedometer at 61 m.p.h. *98 km/h* over 200 yds *183 m*.

Britain The fastest British land mammal over a sustained distance is the Roe deer (*Capreolus capreolus*), which can cruise at 25–30 m.p.h. *40–48 km/h* for more than 20 miles *32 km*, with occasional bursts of up to 40 m.p.h. *64 km/h*. On 19 Oct. 1970 a frightened runaway Red deer (*Cervus elephus*) registered a speed of 42 m.p.h. *67,5 km/h* on a police radar trap as it charged through a street in Stalybridge, Greater Manchester.

Slowest The slowest moving land mammal is the Ai or Three-toed sloth (*Bradypus tridactylus*) of tropical America. The usual ground speed is 6 to 8 ft *c. 2,10 m* a minute (0.068 to 0.098 m.p.h. [*0,109–0,158 km/h*]), but one mother sloth, speeded up by the calls of her infant, was observed to cover 14 ft *4 m* in one minute (0.155 m.p.h. [*0,249 km/h*]). In the trees this speed may be increased to 2 ft *0,61 m* a sec (1.36 m.p.h. [*2,19 km/h*]) (*cf.* these figures with the 0.03 m.p.h. [*0,05 km/h*] of the common garden snail and the 0.17 m.p.h. [*0,27 km/h*] of the giant tortoise).

Longest No mammal can match the extreme proven age of 113
lived years attained by Man (*Homo sapiens*) (see page 14). It is probable that the closest approach is among Blue and Fin whales (*Balaenoptera physalus*) the annual growth layers in the ear plugs of which indicate an age of 90–100 years. A bull Killer whale (*Orcinus orca*) with distinctive physical characteristics known as "Old Tom" was seen every winter from 1843 to 1930 in Twofold Bay, Eden, New South Wales, Australia.

The longest lived land mammal, excluding Man, is the Asiatic elephant (*Elephas maximus*). The greatest age that has been verified with reasonable certainty is an estimated 78 years in the case of "Modoc", a cow exported to the U.S.A. in 1898 as a two year old. She is now retired to the Lion Country Safari, Irvine, South California. An elephant's life span is indicated by the persistence of its teeth, which generally wear out around the 50–55th year.

Highest The highest living wild mammal in the world is
living probably the Yak (*Bos grunniens*), in Tibet and the Szechwanese Alps, China, which occasionally climbs to an altitude of 20,000 ft *6,100 m* when foraging. The Bharal (*Pseudois nayaur*) and the Pika or Mouse hare (*Ochotona thibetana*) may also reach this height in the Himalayas. In 1890 the tracks of an elephant were found at 15,000 ft *4 570 m* on Kilimanjaro, Tanzania.

Largest The largest herds on record were those of the
herds Springbok (*Antidorcas marsupialis*) during migration across the plains of the western parts of southern Africa in the 19th century. In 1849 John Fraser (later Sir John Fraser) saw a *trekbokken* that took three days to pass through the settlement of Beaufort West, Cape Province. Another herd seen moving near Nels Poortje, Cape Province in 1888 was estimated to contain 100,000,000 head.

Longest and The longest of all mammalian gestation periods is that
shortest of the Asiatic elephant (*Elephas maximus*), with an
gestation average of 609 days or just over 20 months and a
periods maximum of 760 days—more than two and a half times that of a human. The gestation period of the American opossum (*Didelphis marsupialis*), also called the Virginian opossum, is normally 12 to 13 days but may be as short as eight days.

The gestation periods of the rare Water opossum or Yapok (*Chironectes minimus*) of Central and northern South America (average 12–13 days) and the Eastern native cat (*Dasyurus viverrinus*) of Australia (average 12 days) may also be as short as 8 days.

Largest The greatest recorded number of young born to a *wild*
litter mammal at a single birth is 32 (not all of which survived) in the case of the Common tenrec (*Centetes ecaudatus*) found in Madagascar and the Comoro Islands. The average litter size is thirteen to fourteen. In March 1961 a litter of 32 was also reported for a House mouse (*Mus musculus*) at the Roswell Park Memorial Institute in Buffalo, N.Y., U.S.A. (average litter size 13–21) (see also Chapter 9 Agriculture, prolificacy records—pigs).

Youngest The Streaked tenrec (*Hemicentetes semispinosus*) of
breeder Madagascar is weaned after only 5 days, and females are capable of breeding 3–4 weeks after birth.

CARNIVORES

Largest
Land
World
The largest living terrestrial carnivore is the Kodiak bear (*Ursus arctos middendorffi*), which is found on Kodiak Island and the adjacent Afognak and Shuyak islands in the Gulf of Alaska, U.S.A. The average adult male has a nose to tail length of 8 ft *2,4 m* (tail about 4 in [*10 cm*]), stands 52 in *132 cm* at the shoulder and weighs between 1,050 and 1,175 lb. *476–533 kg.* In 1894 a weight of 1,656 lb. *751 kg* was recorded for a male shot at English Bay, Kodiak Island, whose *stretched* skin measured 13 ft 6 in *4,11 m* from the tip of the nose to the root of the tail. This weight was exceeded by a male in the Cheyenne Mountain Zoological Park, Colorado Springs, Colorado, U.S.A. which scaled 1,670 lb. *757 kg* at the time of its death on 22 Sept. 1955.

Weights in excess of 1,600 lb. *725 kg* have also been reported for the Polar bear (*Ursus maritimus*), but the average adult male weighs 850–900 lb. *386–408 kg* and measures 7¾ ft *2,4 m* nose to tail. In 1960 a polar bear allegedly weighing 2,210 lb. *1 002 kg* before skinning was shot at the polar entrance to Kotzebue Sound, north-west Alaska. In April 1962 the 11 ft 1½ in *3,39 m* tall mounted specimen was put on display at the Seattle World Fair, Washington. U.S.A.

Britain The largest land carnivore found in Britain is the badger (*Meles meles*). The average adult boar measures 3 ft *90 cm* including a 4 in *10 cm* tail and weighs 27 lb. *12,3 kg* in the early spring and 32 lb. *14,5 kg* at the end of summer when it is in "grease". Weights up to 43 lb. *19,54 kg* have been reliably reported from boars and exceptionally may even exceed 50 lb. *22,72 kg.*

The oldest reported badger is a sow "Tikki" reared by Mrs. Ruth Murray of Okehampton, Devon in 1956 which entered her 19th year in 1974.

Largest
Sea
The largest toothed mammal ever recorded is the Sperm whale (*Physeter catodon*), also called the cachalot. The average adult bull measures 47 ft *14,30 m* in length and weighs about 33 tons *33,5 tonnes.* The largest accurately measured specimen on record was a 67 ft 11 in *20,7 m* bull captured off the Kurile Islands, North-West Pacific, by a U.S.S.R. whaling fleet in the summer of 1950. Twelve cachalots have been stranded on British coasts since 1913. The largest, a bull measuring 61 ft 5 in *19 m* was washed

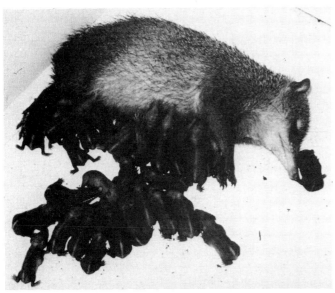

Eddie Schuurling/Frank W. Lane

The most numerous litters of any mammals are those of the tenrec. Thirty young, as here, are not unusual

Smithsonian Institute

Head of the largest tiger ever shot—David Hasinger's 857 lb. *388 kg* trophy

ashore at Birchington, Kent on 18 Oct. 1914. Another bull measuring 60 ft *18 m* was stranded at North Roe, Shetland on 30 May 1958.

Smallest The smallest living carnivore is the Least weasel (*Mustela rixosa*), also called the Dwarf weasel, which is circumpolar in distribution. Four races are recognised, the smallest of which is *M.r. pygmaea* of Siberia. Mature specimens have an overall length of 177–207 mm *6.96–8.14 in* and weigh between 35 and 70 g *1¼ and 2½ oz.*

Largest
feline
The largest member of the cat family (Felidae) is the long-furred Siberian tiger (*Pantheria tigris altaica*), also called the Amur or Manchurian tiger. Adult males average 10 ft 4 in *3,15 m* in length (nose to tip of extended tail), stand 39–42 in *99–107 cm* at the shoulder and weigh about 585 lb. *265 kg.* In November 1967 an Indian tiger (*Panthera tigris*) shot in northern Uttar Pradesh by David J. Hasinger was 857 lb. *388, 7kg* and 10 ft 7 in *3,22 m* between pegs.

The average adult African lion (*Pantheria leo*) measures 9 ft *2,7 m* overall, stands 36–38 in *91–97 cm* at the shoulder and weighs 400–410 lb *181–185 kg.* The heaviest wild specimen on record was one weighing 690 lb. *313 kg* shot by Mr. Lennox Anderson just outside Hectorspruit in the eastern Transvaal, South Africa in 1936. In July 1970 a weight of 826 lb. *375 kg* was reported for an 11-year-old black-maned lion named "Simba" (b. Dublin Zoo, 1959) at Colchester Zoo, Essex. He died on 16 Jan. 1973 at Knaresborough Zoo, North Yorkshire and is now stuffed. In 1953 a weight of 750 lb. *340 kg* was recorded for an 18-year-old male liger (a lion-tigress hybrid) living in Bloemfontein Zoological Gardens, South Africa.

Smallest The smallest member of the cat family is the Rusty-spotted cat (*Felis rubiginosa*) of southern India and Ceylon. The average adult male has an overall length of 25–28 in *64–71 cm* (tail 9–10 in [*23–25 cm*]) and weighs about 3 lb *1 350 kg.*

PINNIPEDS (Seals, Sea-lions and Walruses)

Largest
World
The largest of the 32 known species of pinniped is the Southern elephant seal (*Mirounga leonina*), which inhabits the sub-Antarctic islands. Adult bulls average 16½ ft *5 m* in length (tip of inflated snout to the extremities of the outstretched tail flippers), 12 ft *3,7 m* in maximum bodily girth and weigh about 5,000 lb. (2.18 tons *2 268 kg*). The largest accurately measured

specimen on record was a bull killed in Possession Bay, South Georgia on 28 February 1913 which measured 21 ft 4 in *6,50 m* after flensing (original length about 22½ ft [*6,85 m*]) and probably weighed at least 4 tons/*tonnes*. There are old records of bulls measuring 25, 30 and even 35 ft *10,66 m* but these figures must be considered exaggerated.

British The largest pinniped among British fauna is the Grey seal (*Halichoerus grypus*), also called the Atlantic seal, which is found mainly on the western coasts of Britain. Adult bulls have been recorded up to 9 ft 6 in *2,90 m* in length and 700 lb. *318 kg* in weight.

Smallest The smallest pinniped is the Baikal seal (*Pusa sibrica*) of Lake Baikal, a large freshwater lake in southern Siberia, U.S.S.R. Adult specimens measure about 4 ft 6 in *1,37 m* from nose to tail and weigh 140 lb. *63 kg*.

Fastest and The highest speed recorded for a pinniped is 25 m.p.h.
deepest *40 km/h* for a Californian sea lion (*Zalophus californianus*). The deepest diving pinniped is the Weddell seal (*Leptonychotes weddelli*), which is found along the Antarctic mainland and neighbouring islands. In March 1966 a large bull with a depth-gauge attached to it recorded a dive of 600 m *1,968 ft* in McMurdo Sound. At this depth the seal withstood a pressure of 875 lb./in² *6 033 k Pa* of body area.

Longest A female Grey seal (*Halichoerus grypus*) shot at
lived Shunni Wick in the Shetland Islands on 23 April 1969 was believed to be "at least 46 years old" based on a count of dental annuli.

Rarest The Caribbean or West Indian monk seal (*Monachus tropicalis*) has not been recorded since 1962 when a single specimen was sighted on the beach of Isla Mujueres off the Yucatan Peninsula, Mexico, and the species is now believed to be on the verge of extinction.

BATS
Largest The only flying mammals are bats (order Chiroptera),
World of which there are about 1,000 living species. That with the greatest wing span is the Kalong (*Pteropus vampyrus*), a fruit bat found in Malaysia and Indonesia. It has a wing span of up to 170 cm *5 ft 7 in* and weighs up to 900 g *31.7 oz*.

Britain The largest bat found in Britain is the very rare Large mouse-eared bat (*Myotis myotis*). Mature specimens have a wing span of 355–450 mm *13.97–17.71 in* and weigh up to 45 g *1.58 oz*.

Smallest The smallest known species of bat is the rare Tiny
World pipistrelle (*Pipistrellus nanulus*) found in West Africa. It has a wing span of about 152 mm *6 in* and weighs about 2,5 g *0.088 oz.*, which means it rivals the Etruscan pygmy shrew (*Suncus etruscus*) for the title of "smallest living mammal".

Britain The smallest native British bat is the Pipistrelle (*Pipistrellus pipistrellus*). Mature specimens have a wing span of 200–230 mm *7.87–9.05 in* and weigh between 5,5 and 7,5 g *0.19–0.26 oz.*

Fastest Because of the great practical difficulties little data on bat speeds have been published. The greatest speed attributed to a bat is 32 m.p.h. *51 km/h* in the case of a Free-tailed or Guano bat (*Tadarida mexicana*) which flew 31 miles *50 km* in 58 min. This speed is closely matched by the Noctule bat (*Nyctalus noctula*) and the Long-winged bat (*Miniopterus schreibersi*), both of which have been timed at 31 m.p.h. *50 km/h*.

Rarest The rarest native British bat is Bechstein's bat (*Myotis*
Britain *bechsteini*), which is confined to a small area in southern England, with the New Forest as the main centre of population. There have been about a dozen records since 1900. In January 1965 fifteen specimens

of the Grey long-eared bat (*Plecotus austriacus*) were discovered in the roof of the Nature Conservancy's Research Station at Furzebrook, Dorset. Up to then this species, which is found all over Europe, had only been recorded once in Britain (Hampshire, 1875).

Longest The greatest age reliably reported for a bat is "at least
lived 24 years" for a female Little brown bat (*Myotis lucifugus*) found on 30 April 1960 in a cave on Mount Aeolis, East Dorset, Vermont, U.S.A. It had been banded at a summer colony in Mashpee, Massachusetts on 22 June 1937.

Highest Because of their ultrasonic echolocation bats have the
detectable most acute hearing of any terrestrial animal. Vampire
pitch bats (*Desmodontidae*) and fruit bats (*Pteropodidae*) can hear frequencies as high as 150 k Hz (*cf.* 20 k Hz for the adult human limit but 153 k Hz for the Bottle-nosed dolphin (*Tursiopis truncatus*)).

PRIMATES
Largest The largest living primate is the Eastern lowland gorilla (*Gorilla gorilla grauer*) which inhabits the lowlands of the eastern part of the Upper Congo (now the republic of Zaire) and south-western Uganda. The average adult bull stands 5 ft 9 in *1,75 m* tall (including crest) and measures 58 to 60 in *147–152 cm* round the chest and weighs about 360 lb. *163 kg*. The greatest height (top of crest to heel) recorded for a gorilla is 6 ft 2 in *1,88 m* for a bull of the Mountain race (*Gorilla g. beringei*) shot in the eastern Congo in *c.* 1921.

The heaviest gorilla ever kept in captivity was an Eastern lowland bull named "Mbongo", who died in San Diego Zoological Gardens, California, U.S.A. on 15 March 1942. During an attempt to weigh him shortly before his death the platform scales "fluctuated from 645 pounds to nearly 670 [*293–304 kg*]". This specimen measured 5 ft 7½ in *1,71 m* in height and 69 in *175 cm* around the chest. The heaviest gorilla living in captivity today is the Western lowland (*Gorilla g. gorilla*) bull "Samson" (b. 1949) of Milwaukee County Zoological Park, Wisconsin, U.S.A. He has weighed as much as 658 lb. *299 kg* but now fluctuates between 585 and 605 lb. *266–275 kg*.

Smallest The smallest known primate is the rare Feather-tailed tree shrew (*Ptiolcercus lowii*) of Malaysia. Adult specimens have a total length of 230–330 mm *9–13 in* (head and body 100–140 mm *3.93–5.51 in.*, tail 130–190 mm *5.1–7.5 in*) and weigh between 35 and 50 grammes. The Mouse lemur Microcebus murinus of Madagascar is approximately the same length (274–300 mm *10.8–11.8 in*) but heavier, adults weighing 45–80 grammes.

Longest The greatest irrefutable age reported for a primate
lived (excluding humans) is 50 years 3 months for a male chimpanzee (*Pan troglodytes*) named "Heine" at Lincoln Park Zoological Gardens, Chicago, Illinois, U.S.A. He arrived there on 10 June 1924 when aged about 3 years and died on 10 September 1971.

Rarest The rarest primate is the Hairy-eared mouse lemur (*Cheirogaleus trichotis*) of Madagascar which, until fairly recently, was known only from the type specimen and two skins. In 1966, however, a live example was found on the east coast near Mananara.

Strength In 1924 "Boma", a 165 lb. *74,80 kg* male chimpanzee at Bronx Zoo, New York, N.Y., U.S.A. recorded a right-handed pull (feet braced) of 847 lb. *384 kg* on a dynamometer (*cf.* 210 lb. [*95 kg*] for a man of the same weight). On another occasion an adult female chimpanzee named "Suzette" (estimated weight 135 lb. [*61 kg*]) at the same zoo registered a right-handed pull of 1,260 lb. *572 kg* while in a rage. A record from the U.S.A. of a 100 lb. *45 kg* chimpanzee achieving a two-handed dead lift of 600 lb. *272 kg* with ease suggests that a male gorilla could with training raise 1,800 lb. *816 kg*!

MONKEYS

Largest The largest member of the monkey family is the Mandrill (*Mandrillus sphinx*) of equatorial West Africa. Adult males have an average head and body length of 24–30 in *61–76 cm* and weigh 55–70 lb. *25–32 kg.* The greatest reliable weight recorded for a mandrill is 54 kg *119 lb.* for a specimen which had a head and body length of 36 in *91 cm*, but unconfirmed weights up to 130 lb. *59 kg* have been reported.

Smallest The smallest known monkey is the Pygmy marmoset (*Cebuella pygmaea*) of Ecuador, northern Peru and western Brazil. Mature specimens have a maximum total length of 304 mm *12 in* half of which is tail, and weigh from 49 to 80 g *1.7 to 2.81 oz.*, which means it rivals the mouse lemur for the title of the smallest living primate (see page 30).

Longest lived The greatest reliable age reported for a monkey is *c.* 46 years for a male mandrill (*Mandrillus sphinx*) named "George" of London Zoological Gardens, who died on 14 March 1916. He had originally been imported into Europe in 1869.

Most and least intelligent Of sub-human primates, chimpanzees appear to have the most superior intelligence. Lemurs have less learning ability than any monkey or ape and, in some tests, are inferior to dogs and even pigeons.

RODENTS

Largest The world's largest rodent is the Capybara (*Hydrochoerus hydrochaeris*), also called the Carpincho or Water Hog, which is found in tropical South America. Mature specimens have a head and body length of 3¼ to 4½ ft *0,99–1,4 m* and weigh up to 79 kg *174 lb.* Britain's largest rodent is now the Coypu (*Myocastor coypus*), also known as the Nutria, which was introduced from Argentina by East Anglian fur-breeders in 1927. In 1937 four escaped from a nutria-farm near Ipswich, Suffolk. Adult males measure 30–36 in *76–91 cm* in length (including short tail) and weigh up to 28 lb. *13 kg* in the wild state (40 lb. [*18 kg*] in captivity).

Smallest The smallest rodent is probably the Old World harvest mouse (*Micromys minutus*), of which the British form measures up to 135 mm *5.3 in* in total length and weighs between 4,2 and 10,2 g *0.15 to 0.36 of an oz.* In June 1965 it was announced that an even smaller rodent had been discovered in the Asian part of the U.S.S.R. (probably a more diminutive form of *M. minutus*), but further information is lacking.

Rarest The rarest rodent in the world is believed to be the James Island rice rat (*Oryzomys swarthi*), also called Swarth's rice rat. Four specimens were collected on this island in the Galapagos group in 1906, and it was not heard of again until January 1966 when the skull of a recently dead animal was found.

Fastest Breeder The female Meadow vole (*Microtus agrestis*) found in Britain, can reproduce from the age of 25 days and have up to 17 litters of 6 to 8 young in a year.

Longest lived The greatest reliable age reported for a rodent is 22 years for an Indian crested porcupine (*Hystrix indica*) which died in Trivandrum Zoological Gardens, south-western India in 1942.

INSECTIVORES

Largest The largest insectivore is the Moon rat (*Echinosorex gymnurus*), also known as Raffles' gymnure, which is found in Burma, Thailand, Malaysia, Sumatra and Borneo. Mature specimens have a head and body length of 265–445 mm *10.43–17.52 in*, a tail measuring 200–210 mm *7.87–8.26 in.* and weigh up to 1,400 g *3.08 lb.* Although Anteaters (family Myrmecophagidae) feed on termites and other soft-bodied insects they are not insectivores, but belong to the order Edentata, which means "without teeth".

Norman Zeisloft

Gorillas, the largest of all primates, have chest measurements up to 69 in *175 cm*. There appears to be some doubt as who owns whom between Tommy and Robert Noell

Smallest The smallest insectivore is Savi's white-toothed shrew (see Smallest mammal, page 28).

Longest lived The greatest reliable age recorded for an insectivore is 10½ years for a Hedgehog tenrec (*Setifer setosus*), which died in London Zoo in 1971. There is an unconfirmed record of a Hedgehog (*Erinaceus europaeus*) living for 14 years.

ANTELOPES

Largest The largest of all antelopes is the rare Derby eland (*Taurotragus derbianus*), also called the Giant eland, of West and north-central Africa, which may surpass 2,000 lb. *907 kg.* The Common eland (*T. oryx*) of East and South Africa has the same shoulder height of up to 5 ft 10 in *1,78 m* but is not quite so massive, although there is one record of a 5 ft 5 in *1,65 m* bull shot in Nyasaland (now Malawi) in *c.* 1937 which weighed 2,078 lb. *943 kg.*

Smallest The smallest known antelope is the Royal antelope (*Neotragus pygmaeus*) of West Africa. Mature specimens measure 10–12 in *25–31 cm* at the shoulder and weigh only 7–8 lb. *3–3,6 kg* which is the size of a large Brown hare (*Lepus europaeus*). The slender Swayne's dik-dik (*Madoqua swaynei*) of Somalia, East Africa weighs only 5–6 lb. *2–2,7 kg* when adult, but this species stands about 13 in *33 cm* at the shoulder.

Rarest The rarest antelope is probably Jentink's duiker (*Cephalophus jentinki*), also known as the Black-headed duiker, which is found only in a restricted area of tropical West Africa. Only one, "Alpha" a female born on 1 Dec. 1971, survives in captivity in the Gladys Porter Zoo, Brownsville, Texas, U.S.A.

DEER

Largest The largest deer is the Alaskan moose (*Alces alces gigas*). A bull standing 7 ft 8 in *2,3 m* at the withers and weighing an estimated 1,800 lb. *816 kg* was shot on the Yukon River in the Yukon Territory, Canada in Sept. 1897. Unconfirmed measurements up to 8½ ft *2,59 m* at the withers and estimated weights up to 2,600 lb. *1 180 kg* have been claimed. The record antler span is 78½ in *199 cm*.

Smallest The smallest true deer (family Cervidae) is the pudu (*Pudu mephistophiles*) of Ecuador the male of which stands 13–15 in *33–38 cm* at the shoulder and weighs 18–20 lb. *8–9 kg*. The smallest known ruminant is the Lesser Malayan chevrotain or Mouse deer (*Tragulus javanicus*) of south-eastern Asia. Adult specimens measure 8–10 in *20–25 cm* at the shoulder and weigh 6–7 lb. *2,7–3,2 kg*.

Rarest The rarest deer in the world is Fea's muntjac (*Muntiacus feae*), which is known only from two specimens collected on the borders of Tennasserim, Lower Burma and Thailand.

Oldest The greatest reliable age recorded for a deer is 26 years 6 months 2 days for a Red Deer (*Cervus elephus*) which died in the National Zoological Park, Washington, D.C., U.S.A. on 24 March 1941.

TUSKS

Longest The longest recorded elephant tusks (excluding prehistoric examples) are a pair from the eastern Congo (Zaïre) preserved in the National Collection of Heads and Horns kept by the New York Zoological Society in Bronx Park, New York City, N.Y., U.S.A. The right tusk measures 11 ft 5½ in *3,49 m* along the outside curve and the left 11 ft *3,35 m*. Their combined weight is 293 lb. *133 kg*. A single tusk of 11 ft 6 in *3,50 m* has been reported, but further details are lacking.

Heaviest The heaviest recorded tusks are a pair in the British Museum of Natural History, London which were collected from an aged bull shot at the foot of Mount Kilimanjaro, Kenya in 1897. They were sent to London for auction in 1901. The tusks were measured in 1955, when the first was found to be 10 ft 2½ in *3,11 m* long, weighing 226½ lb. *102,7 kg* and the other 10 ft 5½ in *3,18 m* weighing 214 lb. *97 kg* giving a combined weight of 440½ lb. *199,8 kg*. The tusks, when fresh, were reportedly 236 lb. and 225 lb. *107 and 102 kg* giving a combined weight of 461 lb. *209 kg*. Another pair collected in Dahomey, West Africa exhibited at the Paris Exposition of 1900 allegedly weighed 117 kg *258 lb.* and 97 kg *213 lb.* making a total of 214 kg *471 lb*. All trace of this record pair has now been lost.

HORNS

Longest The longest recorded animal horn was one measuring 81¼ in *206 cm* on the outside curve, with a circumference of 18¼ in *46 cm*, found on a specimen of domestic Ankole cattle (*Bos taurus*) near Lake Ngami, Botswana (formerly Bechuanaland). The largest head (horns measured from tip to tip across the forehead) is one of 13 ft 11 in *4,24 m* for a specimen of wild buffalo (*Bubalus bubalis*) shot in India in 1955. In 1941 a Texas Longhorn steer was recorded to measure 8 ft 7⅜ in *2,62 m* tip to tip.

Rhinoceros The longest recorded anterior horn of a rhinoceros is one of 62¼ in *158 cm* found on a female southern race White rhinoceros (*Ceratotherium simum simum*) shot in South Africa in *c.* 1848. The interior horn measured 22¼ in *57 cm*. There is also an unconfirmed record of an anterior horn measuring 81 in *206 cm*.

Blood tempera- tures The highest mammalian blood temperature is that of the Domestic goat (*Capra hircus*) with an average of 103.8° F *39,9° C*, and a normal range of from 101.7° to 105.3° F *38,7° to 40,7° C*. The lowest mammalian blood temperature is that of the Spiny anteater (*Tachyglossus aculeatus*), a monotreme found in Australia and New Guinea, with a normal range of

72° to 87° F *22,2° to 24,4° C*. The blood temperature of the Golden hamster (*Mesocricetus auratus*) sometimes falls as low as 38.3° F *3,5° C* during hibernation, and an extreme figure of 29.6° F *1,4° C* has been reported for a myotis bat (family Vespertilionidae) during a deep sleep.

Most valuable furs The highest-priced animal pelts are those of the Sea otter (*Enhydra lutris*), also known as the Kamchatka beaver, which fetched up to $2,700 (then £675) before their 55-year-long protection started in 1912. The protection ended in 1967, and at the first legal auction of sea otter pelts at Seattle, Washington, U.S.A. on 31 January 1968 Neiman-Marcus, the famous Dallas department store, paid $9,200 (then £3,832) for four pelts from Alaska. On 30 Jan. 1969 a New York company paid $1,100 £457 for an exceptionally fine pelt from Alaska. On 26 Feb. 1969 forty selected pelts of the mink-sable cross-breed "Kojah" from the Piampiano Fur Ranch, Zion, Illinois, U.S.A. realised $2,700 £1,125 in New York City. In May 1970 a Kojah coat costing $125,000 £52,083 was sold by Neiman-Marcus to Welsh actor Richard Burton for his then wife, Elizabeth Taylor.

Heaviest ambergris The heaviest piece of ambergris (a fatty deposit in the intestine of the Sperm whale) on record was a 1,003 lb. *455 kg* lump recovered from a Sperm whale (*Physeter catodon*) taken in Australian waters on 3 Dec. 1912 by a Norwegian whaling fleet. It was later sold in London for £23,000.

MARSUPIALS

Largest The largest of all marsupials is the Red kangaroo (*Macropus rufa*) of southern and eastern Australia. Adult males or "boomers" stand 6–7 ft *1,83–2,13 m* tall, weigh 150–175 lb. *68–79 kg* and measure up to 8 ft 11 in *2,71 m* in a straight line from the nose to the tip of the extended tail. The Great grey kangaroo (*Macropus giganteus*) of eastern Australia and Tasmania is almost equally as large, and there is an authentic record of a boomer measuring 8 ft 8 in *2,64 m* from nose to tail (9 ft 7 in [*2,92 m*] along the curve of the body) and weighing 200 lb. *90,7 kg*. The skin of this specimen is preserved in the Australian Museum, Sydney, New South Wales.

Smallest The smallest known marsupial is the rare Kimberley planigale or marsupial mouse (*Planigale subtilissima*), which is found only in the Kimberley district of Western Australia. Adult males have a head and body length of 44.5 mm *1.75 in*, a tail length of 51 mm *2 in* and weigh about 4 g *0.141 oz*. Females are smaller than males.

Rarest The rarest marsupial was the sandhill Dunnart, (*Sminthopsis psammophila*) also known as the narrow-footed marsupial mouse, which is known only from the type specimen collected in 1894 near Lake Amadeus, Northern Territory, Australia.

In September 1973 a marsupial "mouse", still unnamed, of hitherto unknown species was trapped in the Billiatt Conservation Park, 100 miles *160 km* east of Adelaide, South Australia.

Highest and longest jumps The greatest measured height cleared by a hunted kangaroo is 10 ft 6 in *3,20 m* over a pile of timber. During the course of a chase in January 1951 a female Red kangaroo (*Macropus rufus*) made a series of bounds which included one of 42 ft *12,80 m*. There is also an unconfirmed report of a Great grey kangaroo (*M. canguru*) jumping nearly 13,5 m *44 ft 8½ in* on the flat.

HORSES AND PONIES

Largest The heaviest horse ever recorded was a 19.2-hand (6 ft 6 in [*1,98 m*]) pure-bred Belgian stallion named "Brooklyn Supreme" (foaled 12 April 1928) owned by Ralph Fogleman of Callender, Iowa, U.S.A. who weighed 3,200 lb. 1.42 tons *1,44 tonnes* shortly before his death on 6 Sept. 1948 aged 20. The same weight was claimed in November 1973 for a 18.2 hand *1,87 m* Belgian mare "Wilma" owned by Mr. John Arden of Reno, Nevada, U.S.A. The heaviest horse ever recorded in Britain was probably the 17.2 hand Shire stallion "Honest Tom" foaled in Littleport, Cambridgeshire in 1884, who weighed 2,912 lb. *1 325 kg* in c. 1890.

Tallest The tallest horse documented was the Percheron-Shire cross "Firpon" (foaled 1959), owned by Julio Falabella which stood 21.1 hands (7 ft 1 in [*2,16 m*]) and weighed 2,976 lb. *1 350 kg.* He died on the Recco de Roca Ranch near Buenos Aires, Argentina on 14 Mar. 1972. A height of 21.1 hands was also claimed for the Clydesdale gelding "Big Jim" (foaled 1950) bred by Lyall M. Anderson of West Broomley, Montrose, Scotland. He died in St. Louis, Missouri in 1957. A claim for 21.2 hands *2,18 m* was made in 1908 for a horse named "Morocco" weighing 2,835 lb. *1 286 kg* in Allentown, Pennsylvania, U.S.A. The tallest horse living in Britain today is the Shire stallion "Ladbrook Invader" (foaled 17 Apr. 1968), owned by Mr. Arthur Lewis of Tamworth, Staffordshire. He stands 19.1½ hands (6 ft 5½ in [*1,97 m*]) and weighs about 22 cwt. (2,464 lb. [*1,120 kg*]). The tallest Hunter is the grey gelding "Lancer", owned by K. Sizer of Muswell Hill, London, who stands 18.2½ hands (6 ft 2½ in [*1,89 m*]).

Smallest The smallest breed of horse are those bred by Julio Falabella (see above). Adult specimens range from under 15–30 in *38–76 cm* at the shoulder and 40–100 lb. *18–45 kg.* The upper accepted limit for the American Miniature Horse Breeders Association is 34 in *86,3 cm.* The smallest breed of pony is the Shetland pony, which usually measures 8–10 hands (32–40 in [*81–102 cm*]) and weighs 275–385 lb. *125–175 kg.* In March 1969 a measurement of 3.2 hands (14 in [*36 cm*]) was reported for a "miniature" but probably not fully grown Shetland pony named "Midnight", owned by Miss Susan Perry of Worths Circus, Melbourne, Victoria, Australia.

Oldest The greatest reliable age recorded for a horse is 62 years in the case of "Old Billy" (foaled 1760), believed to be a cross between a Cleveland and Eastern blood, who was bred by Mr. Edward Robinson of Wild Grave Farm in Woolston, Lancashire. In 1762 or 1763 he was sold to the Mersey and Irwell Navigation Company and remained with them in a working capacity (i.e. marshalling and towing barges) until 1819 when he was retired to a farm at Latchford, near Warrington, where he died on 27 November, 1822. The skull of this horse is preserved in the Manchester Museum, and his stuffed head is now on display in the Bedford Museum. The greatest reliable age recorded for a pony is 54 years for a stallion owned by a farmer in Central France which was still alive in 1919.

Strongest The greatest load hauled by a pair of draught horses
draught (probably Shires) was 50 logs comprising 36,055 board-feet of timber (= 53.8 tons [*55 tonnes*] on a sledge litter across snow at the Nester Estate, Ewen, Ontonagon County, Michigan, U.S.A. in 1893. In a test at Liverpool Road, Islington, Greater London on 25 Feb. 1924 an 8-year-old Shire gelding. "Umber" moved a 2 ton 9½ cwt *2 515 kg* cart carrying 16 tons *16 tonnes* of iron on stone setts.

DOGS

Largest The heaviest breed of domestic dog (*Canis familiaris*) is the St. Bernard. The heaviest recorded example was "Schwarzwald Hof Duke", owned by Dr. A. M. Bruner of Oconomowoc, Wisconsin, U.S.A. He was whelped on 8 Oct. 1964 and weighed 21 st. 1 lb.

Courtesy, Mrs Addison

A horse of unsurpassed stature, the Clydesdale *Big Jim* of 21.1 hands

133 kg 80 on 2 May 1969, dying three months later aged 4 years 10 months. The largest St. Bernard ever weighed in Britain is "Burton Black Magician", also called "Shane" (whelped 11 Jan. 1969), owned by Mr. Derek Roy. In Oct. 1973 he scaled 19 st. 0 lb. 4¾ oz. *120,79 kg.* His weight now fluctuates between 17½ st. and 18 st.

Tallest The world's tallest dog is the Great Dane "Dominic", whelped in 1970 and now 40 in *101 cm* at the shoulder. He is owned by Mrs. Iris Bates of Harlow, Essex, England.

Smallest The world's smallest fully grown dog is a Chihuahua of 10 oz. *283 g* owned by Rodney M. Sprott of Clemson, South Carolina, U.S.A. The same weight was reported in April 1971 for an adult bitch Yorkshire Terrier (Britain's smallest breed) "Sylvia", owned by Mrs. Connie Hutchins of Walthamstow, Greater London.

Oldest Authentic records of dogs living over 20 years are extremely rare, but even 34 years has been accepted by one authority. The greatest reliable age recorded for a dog is 27 years 3 months for a black Labrador gun-dog named "Adjutant", who was whelped on 14 August 1936 and died on 20 Nov. 1963 in the care of his lifetime owner, James Hawkes, a gamekeeper at the Reversby Estate, near Boston, Lincolnshire. Less reliable is a claim of 29 years 5 months for a Queensland "heeler", named "Bluey", who died in Melbourne Australia in February 1940.

Rarest The rarest breed of dog may be the *Shar-pei* or Chinese Fighting Dog, which is, due to restriction on trading and ownership, extinct in China. Only 14 specimens were known to exist in Jan. 1975 in California but there may be others in Korea. The rarest breed recognized by the Kennel Club is the Portuguese Water dog (*Caes de Agua*). There were no more than 50 known to be living anywhere in March 1974.

Fastest The fastest breed of dog (excluding the greyhound or possibly the whippet) is the Saluki, also called the Arabian gazelle hound or Persian greyhound. Speeds up to 43 m.p.h. *69 km/h* have been claimed, but tests in the Netherlands have shown that it is not as fast as the present-day greyhound which has attained a measured speed of 41.7 m.p.h. *67,1 km/h* on a track.

Largest litter The largest recorded litter of puppies is one of 23 thrown on 19 June 1944 by "Lena", a foxhound bitch owned by Commander W. N. Ely of Ambler, Pennsylvania, U.S.A. On 6–7th February 1975 "Careless Ann", a St. Bernard bitch, owned by Robert and Alice Rodden of Lebanon, Missouri, U.S.A. also produced a litter of 23, 14 of which survived. The British record is held by "Settrina Baroness Medina", a Red Setter bitch owned by Mgr. M. J. Buckley, Director of the Wood Hall Centre, Wetherby, West Yorkshire, who gave birth to 22 puppies, 15 of which survived, on 10 January 1974.

Most prolific The greatest sire of all time was the champion greyhound "Low Pressure", nicknamed "Timmy", whelped in September 1957 and owned by Mrs. Bruna Amhurst of Regent's Park, London. From December 1961 until his death on 27 November 1969 he fathered 2,414 registered puppies, with at least 600 others unregistered.

Most popular The breed with the most Kennel Club registrations in 1973 was the Alsatian with 15,185. In 1974, Cruft's Dog Show (founded in 1886 for terriers only) had an entry of 7,877, compared with the record entry of 10,650 dogs in 1936 before entrants were restricted to prize winners.

Most expensive In June 1972 Mrs. Judith Thurlow of Great Ashfield, Suffolk turned down an offer of £14,000 for her champion greyhound "Super Rory" who was whelped in October 1970. The highest price ever paid for a dog is £2,000 by Mrs. A. H. Kempton in December 1929 for the champion greyhound "Mick the Miller" (whelped in Ireland in June 1926 and died 1939). In 1947 a figure of £2,000 was also quoted for a champion English bulldog sold to an American breeder, but further details are lacking.

"Top dog" The greatest altitude attained by a mammal is 1,050 miles *1 690 km* by the Samoyed husky bitch fired as a passenger in Sputnik II on 3 Nov. 1957. The dog was variously named "Kudryavka" (feminine form of "Curly"), "Limonchik" (dimunitive of lemon), "Malyshka", "Zhuchka" or by the Russian breed name for husky, "Laika".

Most Pampered A leading New York dog delicatessen catering for the topmost of the city's 470,000 dogs provides private dining rooms for pets riding up in chauffeured limousines. The menu includes Maryland lump crab-meat at $3.50 per 4 oz. and shrimps at 65 cents a pair. One 'client' with 75 coats has a red satin-lined pearl encrusted cloak and rhinestone-trimmed sunglasses.

Highest and longest jump The canine "high jump" record is held by an Alsatian named "Crumstone Danko" owned by the De Beers mining company, who scaled an 11 ft 3 in *3,43 m* high wall without a springboard in Pretoria, South Africa in May 1942. He was also credited with 16½ ft *5,03 m* off a springboard. The British record is 10 ft 6 in *3,20 m* by the Lancashire Police dog "Lancon Sultan VI", handled by P.C. John Evans at Hutton, near Preston, Lancashire on 8 Aug. 1973. The longest recorded canine long jump was one of 30 ft *9,14 m* by a greyhound named "Bang" made in jumping a gate in coursing a hare at Brecon Lodge, Gloucestershire in 1849.

Strongest The greatest load ever shifted by a dog is 4,400 lb. *1 995 kg* pulled over a 15 ft *4,57 m* dirt course in accordance with Sled Dog Association rules by the champion Newfoundland dog "Barbara-Allen's Bonzo Bear", owned by Elizabeth Stackhouse, at Bothell, Washington, U.S.A. on 28 July 1973. The record time for the annual 1,049 mile *1 680 km* dog sled race from Anchorage to Nome, Alaska is 14 days 14 hrs. 43 min by Emitt Peters in the 1975 race.

Ratting The greatest ratter of all time was Mr. James Searle's bull terrier bitch "Jenny Lind", who killed 500 rats in 1 hr 30 min at "The Beehive", Old Crosshall Street, Liverpool on 12 July 1853. Another bull terrier named "Jacko", owned by Mr. Jemmy Shaw, was credited with killing 1,000 rats in 1 hr 40 min, but the feat was performed over a period of ten weeks in batches of 100 at a time. The last 100 were accounted for in 5 min 28 sec in London on 1 May 1862.

Tracking The greatest tracking feat on record was performed by a Doberman named "Sauer", trained by Detective-Sergeant Herbert Kruger. In 1925 he tracked a stock-thief 100 miles *160 km* across the Great Karroo, South Africa by scent alone. On "Whisky", an 8-year-old miniature fox terrier, lost by his master, truck driver Geoff Hancock at Hayes Creek, 120 miles south of Darwin, Northern Territory, in October 1973, turned up at Mambray Creek, 150 miles north of Adelaide, South Australia on 13 June 1974 having covered 1,700 miles *2 720 km* across Central Australia.

Police Dogs The highest score recorded in the National Police Dog championships is 938½ out of a possible 1,000 points by "Skol of Baswich" near Cheltenham, Gloucestershire on 26–30 May 1963. Obedience, agility, searching, chase and attack tests are included. "Skol" was prepared by Chief Inspector (then Sgt.) J. Howell.

Greatest Dog Funeral The greatest dog funeral on record was for the mongrel dog Lazaras belonging to the eccentric Emperor Norton I of the United States, Protector of Mexico, held in San Francisco, California in 1862 which was attended by an estimated 10,000 people.

CATS

Heaviest The heaviest domestic cat (*Felis catus*) on record was a 9-year-old ginger and white tom named "Spice", owned by Mrs. Loren C. Caddell of Ridgefield, Connecticut, U.S.A. who scaled 43 lb. *19,54 kg* on 26 June 1974. He has since reduced to 35 lb. *15,9 kg*. The British record is held by a female tabby named "Gigi" (1959–72), owned by Miss Ann Clark of Carlisle, Cumbria, who weighed 42 lb. *19 kg* in April 1970. The average weight for an adult cat is 11 lb. *5 kg*.

Oldest Cats are longer-lived animals than dogs and there are a number of authentic records over 20 years. Information on this subject is often obscured by two or more cats bearing the same nickname in succession. The oldest cat ever recorded was probably the tabby "Puss", owned by Mrs. T. Holway of Clayhidon, Devon who celebrated his 36th birthday on 28 November 1939 and died the next day. A more recent and better-documented case was that of the female tabby "Ma", owned by Mrs. Alice St. George Moore of Drewsteignton, Devon. She was put to sleep on 5 Nov. 1957 aged 34. In January 1972 an unconfirmed age of 32 years was reported for a female cat named "Snow" owned by Mrs. Bridget Whidett of Islington, Greater London.

Largest kindle The largest live litter ever recorded was one of 14 kittens born in December 1974 to the Persian cat "Bluebell", owned by Mrs. Elenore Dawson of Wellington, South Africa. On 23 April 1972 a one-year-old seal point Siamese cat named "Seeley", owned by Mrs. Harriet Browne of Southsea, Hants., gave birth to a litter of 13 kittens, 11 of which survived. In July 1970 a litter of 19 kittens (four incompletely formed) was reportedly born by Caesarean section to "Tarawood Antigone", a brown Burmese owned by Mrs. Valerie Gane of Church Westcote, Kingham, Oxfordshire, but this claim has never been fully substantiated.

Most prolific A cat named "Dusty", aged 17, living in Bonham, Texas, U.S.A., gave birth to her 420th kitten on 12 June 1952. A 21-year-old cat "Tippy" living in

Courtesy, Mrs St George Moore
The oldest cat of proven age, the tabby *Ma* of Devon, England who survived her 34th birthday

Kingston-upon-Hull, Humberside gave birth to her 343rd kitten in June 1933.

Greatest On 24 Apr. 1973 a cat named "Quincy" fell from a
Escape 19th storey balcony on Broadway Avenue, Toronto, Canada and was under care of a veterinarian for 7 days. "Paula", an 18 month old part-Persian cat was reported on 25 April 1972 to have made an unwitnessed fall from a locked apartment on a 26th storey in Erskine Avenue, Toronto, Canada. In December 1937 an R.S.P.C.A. inspector rescued a cat which had fallen down a 45 ft *13,7 m* deep quarry shaft on Idle Moor, West Yorkshire, England 18 months earlier.

Richest and Dr. William Grier of San Diego, California, U.S.A.
most died in June 1963 leaving his entire estate of $415,000
valuable to his two 15-year-old cats "Hellcat" and "Brownie". When the cats died in 1965 the money went to the George Washington University in Washington, D.C. In 1967 Miss Elspeth Sellar of Grafham, Surrey turned down an offer of 2,000 guineas (£2,100) from an American breeder for her champion copper-eyed white Persian tom "Coylum Marcus" (b. 28 March 1965).

Rarest breed The rarest of the 72 recognised breeds of cat in Britain is the Red self Persian or Long-haired red self.

Ratting and The greatest ratter on record was probably the female
mousing tabby named "Minnie" who during the six year period 1927 to 1933 killed 12,480 rats at the White City Stadium, London. The greatest mouser on record was a tabby named "Mickey", owned by Shepherd & Sons Ltd. of Burscough, Lancashire which killed more than

22,000 mice during 23 years with the firm. He died in November 1968.

Cat The largest cat population is that of the U.S.A.
population with 30,000,000. Of Britain's cat population of 4,200,000, an estimated 100,000 are "employed" by the Civil Service.

RABBITS

Largest The largest breed of domestic rabbit (*Oryctolagus cuniculus*) is the Flemish giant, which has an average toe to toe length of 36 in *91 cm* when fully extended and weighs 12–14 lb. *5 kg 40–6 kg 30*. The heaviest recorded specimen was a male named "Floppy" who weighed 25 lb. *11 kg 30* shortly before his death in June 1963 aged eight. In May 1971 a weight of 25 lb. *11 kg* was also reported for a four-year-old Norfolk Star named "Chewer", owned by Mr. Edward Williams of Attleborough, Norfolk. The heaviest recorded wild rabbit is one of 5 lb. 8½ oz. *2,50 kg* shot by G. Farrall at Adlington, Cheshire in September 1972.

Oldest The greatest reliable age recorded for a domestic rabbit is 18 years for a doe which was still alive in 1947. A buck rabbit named "Blackie" owned by Mrs. H. H. Chivers of Brixham, Devon died on 13 March 1971 aged 16 years 3 months.

Most The most prolific domestic breed is the Norfolk Star.
prolific Females produce 9 to 10 litters a year, each containing about 10 young (*cf.* five litters and three to seven young for the wild rabbit). "Chewer" (see above) fathered over 40,000 offspring in the period 1968–73 before being retired from stud.

2. BIRDS (*Aves*)

Largest The largest living bird is the North African ostrich
Ratite (*Struthio camelus camelus*), which is found in reduced numbers south of the Atlas Mountains from Upper Senegal and Niger across to the Sudan and central Ethiopia. Male examples of this flightless or ratite sub-species have been recorded up to 9 ft *2,74 m* in height and 345 lb. *156,5 kg* in weight.

Carinate The heaviest flying bird or carinate is the Kori bustard or Paauw (*Otis kori*) of East and South Africa. Weights up to 40 lb. *18 kg* have been reliably reported for cock birds shot in South Africa. The Mute swan (*Cygnus olor*), which is resident in Britain, can also reach 40 lb. *18 kg* on occasion, and there is a record from Poland of a cob weighing *22,5 kg 49.5 lb*, which was probably too heavy to fly. The heaviest bird of prey is the Andean condor (*Vultur gryphus*), adult males averaging 20–25 lb. *9,09–11,30 kg*. An unconfirmed weight of 31 lb. *14,090 kg* has been claimed for a California condor (*Gymnogyphs californianus*) (average weight 20 lb. *9,090 kg*) now preserved in the California Academy of Sciences, Los Angeles.

Largest The Wandering albatross (*Diomedea exulans*) of the
wing span southern oceans has the largest wing span of any living bird, adult males averaging 10 ft 4 in *3,15 m* with wings tightly stretched. The largest recorded specimen was a male measuring 11 ft 10 in *3,60 m* caught by banders in Western Australia in *c*. 1957, but some unmeasured birds may reach or possibly just exceed 13 ft *3,96 m*. The only other bird reliably credited with a wingspread in excess of 11 ft *3,35 m* is the vulture-like Marabou or Adjutant stork (*Leptoptilus crumeniferus*) of Africa and South-East Asia. A measurement of *c*. 12 ft *3,65 m* has been reported for one specimen, and there is an unconfirmed claim of 13 ft 4 in *4,06 m* for another stork shot in Central Africa in the 1930's.

Smallest The smallest bird in the world is Helena's humming-
World bird (*Mellisuga helenae*) of Cuba and the Isle of Pines. An average adult male measures 58 mm *2.28 in* in total length—bill 15 mm *0.59 in*, head and body 15 mm *0.59 in* and tail 28 mm *1.10 in*—and weighs

about 2 g *0.07 oz.*, which means it is lighter than a Sphinx moth (0.08 oz.).

United Kingdom The smallest regularly-breeding British bird is the Goldcrest (*Regulus regulus*), also known as the Golden-crested wren or Kinglet. Adult specimens measure 90 mm *3.5 in* in total length and weigh between 3,8 and 4,5 g *0.108* and *0.127 oz.*

Most abundant **Wild** The most abundant species of wild bird is the Red-billed quelea (*Quelea quelea*) of the drier parts of Africa south of the Sahara with a population estimated at 10,000,000,000 of which a tenth are destroyed each year by pest control units.

Domestic The most abundant species of domesticated bird is the Chicken, the domesticated form of the wild Red jungle fowl (*Gallus gallus*) of south-east Asia. In 1974 there were believed to be about 4,000,000,000 in the world, or about one chicken for every member of the human race. The fowl stock in Britain was estimated at 130,000,000 in 1972, producing 270,000,000 chicks annually. The most abundant sea bird is Wilson's petrel (*Oceanites oceanicus*). No population estimates have been published, but the number runs into hundreds—possibly thousands—of millions. The top-breeding British sea-bird is the Guillemot (*Uria aalge*) with an estimated 577,000 breeding pairs in 1973.

United Kingdom The commonest wild breeding land birds in Great Britain are the blackbird (*Turdus merula*), and the House Sparrow (*Passer domesticus*) both of which have an estimated population of 10,000,000 in early spring. It was estimated in 1967 that 250,000 pigeon fanciers owned an average of 40 racing pigeons per loft, making a population of *c.* 10,000,000 in Great Britain.

Rarest **World** Great practical difficulties attend the identification of the rarest species of bird in the wild. Three of the strongest candidates are (a) a new species of sparrow-sized honeycreeper found on Maui, Hawaiian Islands in late 1973; (b) the Mauritius Kestrel of which 7 survive and (c) Eskimo curlew (*Numenius borealis*) last sighted on 7 Aug. 1972 in Massachusetts, U.S.A.

United Kingdom According to the British Ornithologists Union there are 28 species of birds which have been recorded only once in the British Isles—18 of them since the end of the Second World War in 1945. That which has not recurred for the longest period is the Black-capped petrel (*Pterodroma hasitata*), also known as the "Diablotin". A specimen was caught alive on a heath at Southacre, near Swaffham, Norfolk in March or April 1850. The most tenuously established British bird is the Snowy owl (*Nyctea scandiaca*), with one pair breeding recurringly on Fetlar, Shetland Islands.

Longest lived The greatest irrefutable age reported for any bird is 72+ years in the case of a male Andean condor (*Vultur gryphus*) named "Kuzya", which died in Moskovskii Zoologicheskii Park, Moscow, U.S.S.R. in 1964. This bird had been received as an adult in 1892. The British record is 68+ years in the case of a female European eagle-owl (*Bubo bubo*) which was living in 1899. Other records which are regarded as *probably* reliable include 73 years (1818–91) for a Greater sulphur-crested cockatoo (*Cacatua galerita*); 72 years (1797–1869) for an African grey parrot (*Psittacus erithacus*); 70 years (1770–1840) for a Mute swan (*Cygnus olor*) and 69 years for a Raven (*Corvus corax*). In 1972 a Southern Ostrich (*Struthio camelus australis*) aged 62 years and 3 months was killed in the Ostrich Abbatoir at Oudtshoorn, Cape Province, South Africa.

"Jimmy", a red and green Amazon parrot owned by Mrs. Bella Ludford of Liverpool, England was allegedly hatched in captivity on 3 Dec. 1870 and lived 104 years in his original brass cage dieing on 5 Jan. 1975.

Fastest flying The fastest flying bird is the Spine-tailed swift (*Chaetura caudacuta*). For details see page 26.

The bird which presents the hunter with the greatest difficulty is the Spur-wing goose (*Plectropterus gambiensis*), with a recorded air speed of 60 m.p.h. *96 km/h* in level flight and 88 m.p.h. *141 km/h* in an escape dive.

Fastest and slowest wing beat The fastest recorded wing beat of any bird is that of the hummingbird Heliactin cornuta of tropica South America with a rate of ninety beats a secondl This rate is probably exceeded by the Bee humming-birds Mellisuga helenae and Acestrura bombus but no figures have yet been published. Large vultures (family Vulturidae) can soar for hours without beating their wings, but sometimes exhibit a flapping rate as low as one beat per sec.

Longest flights The greatest distance covered by a ringed bird during migration is 12,000 miles *19 300 km* by an Arctic tern (*Sterna paradisaea*), which was banded as a nestling on 5 July 1955 in the Kandalaksha Sanctuary on the White Sea coast and was captured alive by a fisherman 8 miles *13 km* south of Fremantle, Western Australia on 16 May 1956. The American golden plover (*Pluvialis dominica*), which flies to South America from its breeding grounds in Alaska and the Arctic in the autumn, sometimes gets as far as New Zealand before returning home in the spring. This means it covers a distance of between 15,000 and 17,000 miles *24 000–27 200 km* in just over six months.

Highest flying The celebrated example of a skein of 17 Egyptian geese (*Alopochen aegptiacus*) photographed by an astronomer at Dehra Dun, northern India on 17 Sept. 1919 as they crossed the sun at an estimated height of between 11 and 12 miles (58,080–63,360 ft [*17 700–19 310 m*]), has been discredited by experts.

The highest acceptable altitude recorded for a bird is 8 200 m *26,900 ft* for a small number of Alpine choughs (*Pyrrhocorax graculus*) which followed the British Everest expedition of 1924, but their take-off point may have been as high as 20,000 ft *6 100 m*. On three separate occasions in 1959 a radar station in Norfolk picked up flocks of small passerine night migrants flying in from Scandinavia at heights up to 21,000 ft *6 400 m*. They were probably Warblers (*Sylviidae*), Chats (*Turnidae*) and Flycatchers (*Muscicapidae*).

Most airborne The most aerial of all birds is the Sooty tern (*Sterna fuscata*) which, after leaving the nesting grounds, remains continuously aloft for three or four years before returning to the breeding grounds. The most aerial land bird is the Common swift (*Apus apus*) which remains "airborne" for at least 9 months of the year.

Fastest swimmer The fastest swimming bird is the Gentoo penguin (*Pygoscelis papua*). In January 1913 a small group were timed at 10 m a sec *22.3 m.p.h.* under water near the Bay of Isles, South Georgia. This is a respectable flying speed for some birds. The deepest diving bird is the Emperor penguin (*Aptenodytes forsteri*) of the Antarctic which can reach a depth of 265 m *870 ft* and remain submerged for up to 18 minutes.

Most acute vision Tests have shown that under favourable conditions the Long-eared owl (*Asio otus*) and the Barn owl (*Tyto alba*) can swoop on targets from a distance of 6 ft *1,83 m* or more in an illumination of only 0.00000073 of a ft candle (equivalent to the light from a standard candle at a distance of 1,170 ft [*356 m*]). This acuity is 50–100 times as great as that of human night vision. In good light and against a contrasting background a Golden eagle (*Aquila chrysaetos*) can detect an 18 in *46 cm* long hare at a range of 2,150 yds *1 966 m* (possibly even 2 miles [*3,2 km*]).

Eggs
Largest The largest egg produced by any living bird is that of the Ostrich (*Struthio camelus*). The average example measures 6–8 in *15–20 cm* in length, 4 to 6 in *10–15 cm* in diameter and weighs 3.63 to 3.88 lb. *1,65 kg–1,78 kg* (equal to the volume of two dozen hen's eggs). It requires about 40 min for boiling. The shell is one-sixteenth of an in *15,8 mm* thick and can support the weight of a 20 st. *127 kg* man. The largest egg laid by any bird on the British list is that of the Mute swan (*Cygnus olor*), which measures from 4.3 to 4.9 in *109–124 mm* in length and between 2.8 and 3.1 in *71–78,5 mm* in diameter. The weight is 12–13 oz. *340–368 g*.

Smallest The smallest egg laid by any bird is that of the bee hummingbird *Mellisuga helenae*, the world's smallest bird (see page 35). A specimen collected at Boyate, Santiago de Cuba on 8 May 1906 and later presented to the U.S. National Museum, Washington, D.C., U.S.A. measures 11,4 mm *0.45 in* in length, 8 mm *0.32 in* in diameter and weighs 0,5 of a g *0.176 oz*. The smallest egg laid by a bird on the British list is that of the Goldcrest (*Regulus regulus*), which measures 12,2–14,5 mm *0.48–0.57 in* in length and between 9,4 and 9,9 mm *0,37 and 0,39 in* in diameter.

Incubation
Longest and shortest The longest normal incubation period is that of the Wandering albatross (*Diomedea exulans*), with a normal range of 75 days to 82 days. There is a case of an egg of the Mallee fowl (*Leipoa ocellata*) of Australia taking 90 days to hatch against its normal incubation of 62 days. The shortest incubation period is probably that of the Hawfinch (*Coccothraustes coccothraustes*), which is only 9–10 days. The idlest of cock birds include hummingbirds (family Trochilidae), Eider duck (*Somateria mollissima*) and Golden pheasant (*Chrysolophus pictus*) among whom the hen bird does 100 per cent of the incubation, whereas the female Common kiwi (*Apteryx australis*) leaves this entirely to the male for 75 to 80 days.

Feathers
Longest The longest feathers grown by any bird are those of the cock Long-tailed fowl or Onagadori (a strain of *Gallus gallus*) which have been bred in south-western Japan since the mid 17th century. In 1973 a tail covert measuring 10,60 m *34 ft 9½ in* was reported by Masasha Kubota of Kochi, Shikoku.

Most In a series of "feather counts" on various species of bird a Whistling swan (*Cygnus columbianus*) was found to have 25,216 feathers. A Ruby-throated hummingbird (*Archilochus colubris*) had only 940, although hummingbirds have more feathers per area of body surface than any other living bird.

Earliest and latest cuckoo It is unlikely that the Cuckoo (*Cuculus canorus*) has ever been *heard and seen* in Britain earlier than 2 March, on which date one was observed under acceptable conditions by Mr. William A. Haynes of Trinder Road, Wantage, Oxfordshire in 1972. The two latest dates are 16 Dec. 1912 at Anstey's Cove, Torquay, Devon and 26 Dec. 1897 or 1898 in Cheshire.

DOMESTICATED BIRDS

Chicken
Heaviest The heaviest breed of chicken are the cross breed, called White Sully, developed by Mr. Grant Sullens of West Point, California, U.S.A. One monsterous rooster named "Weirdo" reportedly weighed 22 lb. *10 kg* in January 1973 when aged 4 years. "Weirdo" murdered an 18 lb. *8,160 kg* son, crippled a dog, and has so far injured his owner to the extent of 8 stitches besides killing two cats.

Turkey
Heaviest The greatest *live* weight recorded for a Turkey (*Meleagris gallapavo*) is 75 lb. *34 kg 015* reported in December 1973 for a "holiday" turkey reared by Signe Olsen, Salt Lake City, Utah, U.S.A. The U.S. record for a dressed bird is 68½ lb. *31 kg 070* in 1953. The British record for a *frozen oven-ready* turkey is 64 lb. 4 oz. *29 kg 025* for a stag reared by J. P. Wood & Sons of Craven Arms, Shropshire. It's live-weight was more probably nearer to 75 lb. *34 kg 015* rather than 70 lb. *31 kg 750*. Turkeys were introduced into Britain *via* Germany from Mexico in 1549.

Longest lived The longest lived domesticated bird (excluding the Ostrich) is the domestic goose (*Anser anser domesticus*) which normally lives about 25 years. A gander named "George", owned by Mrs. Florence Hull of Thornton, Lancashire celebrated his 48th birthday in 1975. He was hatched out in c. April 1927. The longest lived small cagebird is the Canary (*Serinus carnaria*). It was reported in June 1972 that Mrs. Kathleen Leck, 32, of Hull still had a 31-year-old example bartered by her father, Mr. Ross, in Calabar, Nigeria when she was one. In March 1975 a Budgerigar (*Melopsittacus undulatus*) named "Georgie", owned by Mrs. Elsie Ramshaw of Denaby Main, South Yorkshire, received an award from the Newcastle and Gateshead Budgerigar Society for reaching the ripe old age of 25 years. The largest caged budgerigar (*Melopsittacus undulatus*) population is probably that of the United Kingdom with an estimated 3½–4 million. In 1956 the population was about 7 million. This small parakeet is found wild in Australia.

Most talkative The world's most talkative bird is a male African grey parrot (*Psittacus erythacus*) named "Prudle", owned by Mrs. Lyn Logue of Golders Green, London, which won the "Best talking parrot-like bird" title at the National Cage and Aviary Bird Show held in London each December for ten consecutive years (1965–1974). Prudle was taken from a nest in a tree about to be felled at Jinja, Uganda in 1958.

3. REPTILES (*Reptilia*)
(Crocodiles, snakes, turtles, tortoises and lizards.)

Largest and heaviest The largest reptile in the world is the Estuarine or Salt-water crocodile (*Crocodylus porosus*) of southeast Asia, northern Australia, New Guinea, the Philippines and the Solomon Islands. Adult bulls average 12–14 ft *3,7–4,3 m* in length and scale about 1,100 lb. *499 kg*. In 1823 a notorious man-eater measuring 27 ft *8,23 m* in length and weighing an estimated 2 tons/*tonnes* was shot at Jala Jala on Luzon Island in the Philippines after terrorising the neighbourhood for many years. Its skull, the largest on record if we exclude fossil remains, is now preserved in the Museum of Comparative Zoology at Harvard University, Cambridge, Massachusetts, U.S.A. Another outsized example with a reputed length of 33 ft *10,05 m* and a maximum bodily girth of 13 ft 8 in *4,16 m* was shot in the Bay of Bengal in 1840, but the dimensions of its skull (preserved in the British Museum of Natural History, London) suggest that it must have come from a crocodile measuring about 24 ft *7,31 m*. In July 1957 an unconfirmed length of 28 ft 4 in *8,63 m* was reliably reported for an Estuarine crocodile shot on MacArthur Bank, in the Norman River, north-western Queensland, Australia.

Smallest The smallest known species of reptile is believed to be *Sphaerodactylus parthenopiom*, a tiny gecko found only on the island of Virgin Gorda, one of the British Virgin Islands, in the West Indies. It is known only from 15 specimens, including some gravid females found between 10 and 16 Aug. 1964. The three largest females measured 18 mm *0.71 in* from snout to vent, with a tail of approximately the same length. It is possible that another gecko, *Sphaerodactylus elasmorhynchus*, may be even smaller. The only known specimen was an apparently mature female with a snout-vent length of 17 mm *0.67 in* and a tail the same measurement found on 15 March 1966 among the roots of a tree in the western part of the Massif de la Hotte in Haiti. A species of dwarf chameleon,

Evoluticauda tuberculata found in Madagascar, and known only from a single specimen, has a snout-vent length of 18 mm *0.71 in* and a tail length of 14 mm *0.55 in*. Chameleons, however, are more bulky than geckos, and it is not yet known if this specimen was fully grown.

The smallest reptile found in Britain is the Viviparous or Common lizard (*Lacerta vivipara*). Adult specimens have an overall length of 108–178 mm *4.25–7 in*.

Fastest The highest speed measured for any reptile on land is 18 m.p.h. *29 km/h* for a Six-lined racerunner (*Cnemidophorus sexlineatus*) pursued by a car near McCormick, South Carolina, U.S.A. in 1941. The highest speed claimed for any reptile in water is 22 m.p.h. *35 km/h* by a frightened Pacific leatherback turtle (see below).

Lizards The largest of all lizards is the Komodo monitor or
Largest Ora (*Varanus komodoensis*), a dragonlike reptile found on the Indonesian islands of Komodo, Rintja, Padar and Flores. Adult males average 8 ft *2,43 m* in length and weigh 175–200 lb *79–91 kg*. Lengths up to 23 ft *7,01 m* (*sic*) have been quoted for this species, but the largest specimen to be accurately measured was a male presented to an American zoologist in 1928 by the Sultan of Bima which taped 3,05 m *10 ft 0.8 in*. In 1937 this animal was put on display in St. Louis Zoological Gardens, Missouri, U.S.A. for a short period. It then measured 10 ft 2 in *3,10 m* in length and weighed 365 lb. *166 kg*.

Oldest The greatest age recorded for a lizard is more than 54 years for a male Slow worm (*Anguis fragilis*) kept in the Zoological Museum in Copenhagen, Denmark from 1892 until 1946.

Chelonians The largest of all chelonians is the Pacific leatherback
Largest turtle (*Dermochelys coriacea schlegelii*). The average adult measures 6–7 ft *1,83–2,13 m* in overall length (length of carapace 4–5 ft [*122–152 cm*]) and weighs between 660 and 800 lb. *299–363 kg*. The greatest weight reliably recorded is 1,908 lb. *865 kg* for a specimen captured off Monterey, California, U.S.A. in August 1961 which is now on display at the Wharf Aquarium, Fisherman's Wharf, Monterey. The largest chelonian found in British waters is the Atlantic leatherback turtle (*Dermochelys coriacea coriacea*). One weighing 997 lb. *452 kg* and measuring more than 7 ft *2,13 m* in length was caught by a French fishing trawler in the English Channel on 8 May 1958, and another specimen reportedly weighing 1,345 lb. *610 kg* was caught by a fishing vessel in the North Sea on 6 Oct. 1951.

The largest living tortoise is *Geochelone* (*Testudo*) *gigantea* of the Indian Ocean islands of Aldabra, Mauritius, Réunion and Seychelles (introduced 1874). Adult males sometimes exceed 350 lb. *158 kg* in weight and a specimen weighing 900 lb. *408 kg* was allegedly collected in Aldabra in 1847.

Longest Tortoises are the longest lived of all vertebrates. (See
lived Animal Kingdom Records above.) Other reliable records over 100 years include a Common box tortoise (*Testudo carolina*) of 138 years and a European pond-tortoise (*Emys orbicularis*) of 120+ years. The greatest proven age of a continuously observed tortoise is 116+ years for a Mediterranean spur-thighed tortoise (*Testudo graeca*) which died in Paignton Zoo, Devon in 1957. On 19 May 1966 the death was reported of "Tu'imalilia" or "Tui Malela", the famous but much battered Madagascar radiated tortoise (*Testudo radiata*) reputedly presented to the King of Tonga by Captain James Cook in 1773, but this record lacks proper documentation.

Slowest Tests on a giant tortoise (*Geochelone gigantea*) in
moving Mauritius show that even when hungry and enticed by a cabbage it cannot cover more than 5 yds *4,57 m* in a

min (0.17 m.p.h. [*0,27 km/h*]) on land. Over longer distances its speed is greatly reduced.

SNAKES

Longest The longest (and the heaviest) of all snakes is the
World Anaconda (*Eunectes murinus*) of tropical South America. The largest anaconda on record was probably a specimen shot on the upper Orinoco River, eastern Colombia in 1944 which later recovered and escaped. It had been provisionally measured at 37½ ft *11,43 m*. Another anaconda killed on the lower Rio Guaviare, in south-eastern Colombia in November 1956 reportedly measured 10,25 m *33 ft 7½ in*, but nothing of this snake was preserved. In 1912 a Reticulated python (*Python reticulatus*) measuring 10 m *32 ft 9½ in* was killed near a mining camp on the north coast of Celebes in the Malay Archipelago. An African rock python (*Python sebae*) measuring 9,81 m *32 ft 2¼ in* was killed in the grounds of a school at Bingerville, Ivory Coast in 1932.

In Captivity The longest snake ever kept in a zoo was probably "Colossus", a female Reticulated python (*Python reticulatus*), who died of reptilian tuberculosis on 15 April 1963 in the Highland Park Zoological Gardens, Pittsburgh, Pennsylvania, U.S.A. She measured 28 ft 6 in *8,68 m* on 15 Nov. 1956 and was probably at least 29 ft *8,84 m* at the time of her death. Her maximum girth before a feed was measured at 36 in *91 cm* on 2 March 1955 and she weighed 22 st. 12 lb. *145 kg* on 12 June 1957. A long-standing reward of $5,000 (now £2,000) offered by the New York Zoological Society in Bronx Park, New York City, U.S.A. for a living specimen of any snake measuring more than 30 ft *9,14 m* has never been collected.

The longest snake living in captivity anywhere in the world today is a female Reticulated python named "Cassius" owned by Mr. Adrian Nyoka at Knaresborough Zoo, North Yorkshire. In January 1973 this specimen (collected in Malaysia in 1972) measured 27 ft 4 in *8,33 m* in length and weighed 220 lb. *99 kg*.

British The longest snake found in Britain is the Grass snake (*Natrix natrix*), which is found throughout southern England, parts of Wales and in Dumfries and Galloway Scotland. Adult males average 610 mm *24.01 in* in length and adult females 760 mm *29.92 in*. The longest accurately measured specimen on record was probably a female caught in the New Forest, Hampshire in *c.* 1883 which measured 189 cm *6 ft 2¼ in*.

Shortest The shortest known snake is the thread snake *Leptotyphlops bilineata*, which is found on the islands of Martinique, Barbados and St. Lucia in the West Indies. It has a maximum recorded length of 11,9 cm *4.7 in*.

Heaviest The heaviest snake is the Anaconda (*Eunectes murinus*). The specimen shot in eastern Colombia in 1944 (see above) probably weighed nearly 1,000 lb. *454 kg*. The heaviest venomous snake is the Eastern diamondback rattlesnake (*Crotalus adamanteus*) of the southeastern United States. One specimen measuring 7 ft 9 in *2,36 m* in length weighed 34 lb. *15 kg*. Less reliable lengths up to 8 ft 9 in *2,66 m* and weights up to 40 lb. *18 kg* have been reported. A 15 ft 7 in *4,75 m* King cobra (*Ophiophagus hannah*) captured alive on Singapore Island and presented to Raffles Museum weighed 26½ lb. *12 kg*.

Venomous The longest venomous snake in the world is the King
Longest and cobra (*Ophiophagus hannah*), also called the Hama-
Shortest dryad, of south-east Asia and the Philippines. A specimen collected near Port Dickson in the state of Negri Sembilan, Malaya in April 1937 grew to 18 ft 9 in *5,71 m* in London Zoo. It was destroyed at the outbreak of war in 1939. The shortest venomous snake is probably Peringuey's adder (*Bitis peringueyi*) of south-west Africa which has a maximum recorded length of 12 in *31 cm*.

Amphibians

THE ANIMAL KINGDOM

Oldest The greatest irrefutable age recorded for a snake is 38 years 2 months in the case of a Common boa (*Boa constrictor constrictor*) at Philadelphia Zoological Garden, Philadelphia, Pennsylvania, U.S.A. which was still alive on 1 April 1975.

Fastest moving The fastest moving land snake is probably the slender Black mamba (*Dendroaspis polylepis*). On 23 April 1906 an angry Black mamba was timed at a speed of 7 m.p.h. *11 km/h* over a measured distance of 47 yds *43 m* near Mbuyuni on the Serengeti Plains, Kenya. Stories that Black mambas can overtake galloping horses (maximum speed 43.26 m.p.h. [*69,62 km/h*]) are wild exaggerations, though a speed of 15 m.p.h. *24 km/h* may be possible for short bursts over level ground. The British grass snake (*Natrix natrix*) has a maximum speed of 4.2 m.p.h. *6,8 km/h*.

Most venomous The world's most venomous snake is now believed to be the sea snake *Hydrophis belcheri* which has a venom one hundred times as lethal as that of the Australian taipan (*Oxyuranus scutellatus*). The snake abounds round Ashmore Reef in the Timor Sea, off North West Australia. The most venomous land snake is probably the peninsular tiger snake (*Notechis ater niger*) found on Kangaroo Island and in the Sir Joseph Banks Group in Spencers Gulf, South Australia which grows to a length of 4 to 5 ft *1,22 m– 1,52 m*. The average venom yield is sufficient to kill 300 sheep. It is estimated that between 30,000 and 40,000 people (excluding Chinese and Russians) die from snakebite each year, 75 per cent of them in densely populated India. Burma has the highest mortality rate with 15.4 deaths per 100,000 population per annum.

Britain The only venomous snake in Britain is the Adder (*Vipera berus*). Since 1890 nine people have died after being bitten by this snake, including five children. The most recently recorded death was on 13 May 1957 when a 14-year-old boy was bitten on the right hand at Carey Camp, near Wareham, Dorset and died three hours later. The longest specimen recorded was one of 38 in *9,65 cm* killed on Walberswick Common, Suffolk on 7 July 1971.

Longest fangs The longest fangs of any snake are those of the Gaboon viper (*Bitus gabonica*) of tropical Africa. In a 6 ft *1,83 m* long specimen they measured 50 mm *1.96 in*. On 12 Feb. 1963 a Gaboon viper bit itself to death in the Philadelphia Zoological Gardens, Philadelphia, Pennsylvania, U.S.A. Keepers found the dead snake with its fangs deeply embedded in its own back.

4. AMPHIBIANS (*Amphibia*)

Largest World The largest species of amphibian is the Chinese giant salamander (*Megalobatrachus davidianus*), which lives in the cold mountain streams and marshy areas of north-eastern, central and southern China. The average adult measures 1 m *39,37 in* in total length and weighs 11–13 kg *24.2 to 28.6 lb*. One huge individual collected in Kweichow (Guizhou) Province in southern China in the early 1920s measured 5 ft *1,52 m* in total length and weighed nearly 100 lb. *45 kg*. The Japanese giant salamander (*Megalobatrachus japonicus*) is slightly smaller, but one captive specimen weighed 40 kg *88 lb*. when alive and 45 kg *100 lb*. after death, the body having absorbed water from the aquarium.

Britain The longest British amphibian is the Warty or Great crested newt (*Triturus cristatus*). One specimen collected at Hampton, Greater London measured 162 mm *6.37 in* in total length, and another one collected at Dunbar, Lothian, Scotland weighed 10,6 g *0.37 oz*.

Smallest World The smallest species of amphibian is believed to be the arrow-poison frog *Sminthillus limbatus*, found only

The largest of all amphibians, the Chinese giant salamander which can grow to 5 ft *1,52 m* in length

in Cuba. Adult specimens have a snout-vent length of 8,5–12,4 mm *0.33–0.48 in*.

Britain The smallest amphibian found in Britain is the Palmate newt (*Triturus helveticus*). Adult specimens measure 7,5–9,2 cm *2.95–3.62 in* in total length and weigh up to 2,39 g *0.083 oz*. The Natterjack or Running toad (*Bufo calamita*) has a maximum snout-vent length of only 8 cm *3.14 in*, but it is a bulkier animal.

Longest lived The greatest authentic age recorded for an amphibian is about 55 years for a male Japanese giant salamander (*Megalobatrachus japonicus*) which died in the aquarium at Amsterdam Zoological Gardens on 3 June 1881. It was brought to Holland in 1829, at which time it was estimated to be three years old.

Highest and lowest The greatest altitude at which an amphibian has been found is 8 000 m *26,246 ft* for a Common toad (*Bufo vulgaris*) collected in the Himalayas. This species has also been found at a depth of 340 m *1,115 ft* in a coal mine.

39

Most poisonous The most active known poison is the batrachotoxin derived from the skin secretions of the Kokoi (*Phyllobates latinasus*), an arrow-poison frog found in north-western Colombia, South America. Only about 1/100,000th of a gramme *0.0000004 oz.* is sufficient to kill a man.

Newt
Largest World The largest newt in the world is the Pleurodele or Ribbed newt (*Pleurodeles waltl*), which is found in Morocco and on the Iberian Peninsula. Specimens measuring up to 40 cm *15.74 in* in total length and weighing over 1 lb. *450 g* have been reliably reported.

Smallest The smallest newt in the world is believed to be the Striped newt (*Notophthalmus perstriatus*) of the south-eastern United States. Adult specimens average 51 mm *2.01 in* in total length.

Frog
Largest World The largest known frog is the rare Goliath frog (*Rana goliath*) of Cameroun and Spanish Guinea, West Africa. A female weighing 3 306 g *7 lb. 4.5 oz.* was caught in the rapids of the River Mbia, Spanish Guinea on 23 Aug. 1960. It had a snout-vent length of 34 cm *13.38 in* and measured 81,5 cm *32.08 in* overall with legs extended. In December 1960 another giant frog known locally as "agak" or "carn-pnag" and said to measure 12–15 in *30–38 cm* snout to vent and weigh over 6 lb. *2 kg 70* was reportedly discovered in central New Guinea, but further information is lacking. In 1969 a new species of giant frog was discovered in Sumatra.

Britain The largest frog found in Britain is the *introduced* Marsh frog (*Rana r. ridibunda*). Adult males have been measured up to 96 mm *3.77 in* snout to vent, and adult females up to 133 mm *5.25 in*, the weight ranging from 60 to 95 g *1.7 oz.* to *3 oz.*

Longest jump The record for three consecutive leaps is 32 ft 3 in *9,83 m* by a 2 in *5 cm* long South African sharp-nosed frog (*Rana oxyrhyncha*) named "Leaping Lena" (later discovered to be a male) on Green Point Common, Cape Town on 16 Jan. 1954. At the annual Calaveras County Jumping Frog Jubilee at Angels Camp, California, U.S.A. on 21 May 1973 "Wet Bet" made a *single* leap of 17 ft 4⅜ in *5,29 m* for its owner Leonard Hall.

Tree frog
Largest The largest species of tree frog is *Hyla vasta*, found only on the island of Hispaniola (Haiti and the Dominican Republic) in the West Indies. The average snout-vent length is about 9 cm *3.54 in* but a female collected from the San Juan River, Dominican Republic, in March 1928 measured 14,3 cm *5.63 in*.

Smallest The smallest tree frog in the world is the Least tree frog (*Hyla ocularis*), found in the south-eastern United States. It has a maximum snout-vent length of 15,8 mm *0.62 in*.

Toad
Largest World The most massive toad in the world is probably the Marine toad (*Bufo marinus*) of tropical South America. An enormous female collected on 24 Nov. 1965 at Miraflores Vaupes, Colombia and later exhibited in the Reptile House at Bronx Zoo, New York City, U.S.A. had a snout vent length of 23,8 cm *9.37 in* and weighed 1 302 g *2 lb. 11¼ oz.* at the time of its death in 1967.

The largest toad in the world, the rather unlovely Marine toad of tropical South America

Associated Press

Britain The largest toad and heaviest amphibian found in Britain is the Common toad (*Bufo bufo*). Females of up to 102 mm *3.94 in* in length and 114 g *3.2 oz.* have been recorded.

Smallest The smallest toad in the world is the sub-species *Bufo*
World *taitanus beiranus*, first discovered in *c.* 1906 near Beira, Mozambique, East Africa. Adult specimens have a maximum recorded snout-vent length of 24 mm *0.94 in.*

Salamander The smallest species of salamander is the Pygmy
Smallest salamander (*Desmognathus wrighti*), which is found only in Tennessee, North Carolina and Virginia, U.S.A. Adult specimens measure from 37 to 50,8 mm *1.45 to 2.0 in.* in total length.

5. FISHES (*Pisces, Bradyodonti, Selachii, Marsipoli*)

Largest The largest fish in the world is the rare plankton-
Marine feeding Whale shark (*Rhiniodon typus*), which is
World found in the warmer areas of the Atlantic, Pacific and Indian Oceans. It is not, however, the largest marine animal, since it is smaller than the larger species of whales (mammals). In 1919 a Whale shark measuring 59 ft *18 m* in length and weighing an estimated 42.4 tons *43 tonnes* was trapped in a bamboo stake-trap at Koh Chik, in the Gulf of Siam. The largest carnivorous fish (excluding plankton eaters) is the rare Great white shark (*Carcharodon carcharias*), also called the "Man-eater", which is found mainly in tropical and sub-tropical waters. In June 1930 a specimen measuring 37 ft *11,27 m* in length was found trapped in a herring weir at White Head Island, New Brunswick, Canada. Another Great white shark which ran aground in False Bay, near the Cape of Good Hope, South Africa many years ago reportedly measured 43 ft *13,10 m* but further information is lacking. The longest of the bony or "true" fishes (Pisces) is the Russian sturgeon (*Acipenser huso*), also called the Beluga, which is found in the temperate areas of the Adriatic, Black and Caspian Seas but enters large rivers like the Volga and the Danube for spawning. Lengths up to 8 m *26 ft 3 in* have been reliably reported, and a gravid female taken in the estuary of the Volga in 1827 weighed 1 474 kg 20 *1.44 tons*. The heaviest bony fish in the world is the Ocean sunfish (*Mola mola*), which is found in all tropical, sub-tropical and temperate waters. On 18 Sept. 1908 a huge specimen was accidentally struck by the S.S. *Fiona* off Bird Island about 40 miles *65 km* from Sydney, New South Wales, Australia and towed to Port Jackson. It measured 14 ft *4,26 m* between the anal and dorsal fins and weighed 2.24 tons/*2,28 tonnes*.

Britain The largest fish ever recorded in the waters of the British Isles was a 36 ft 6 in *11,12 m* Basking shark (*Cetorhinus maximus*) washed ashore at Brighton, East Sussex in 1806. It weighed an estimated 8 tons/ *tonnes*. The largest bony fish found in British waters is the Ocean sunfish (*Mola mola*). A specimen measuring 6 ft 6 in *1,98 m* between the anal and dorsal fins and weighing 672 lb. *305 kg* was washed ashore at Kessingland near Lowestoft, Suffolk on 19 Dec. 1948.

Largest The largest fish which spends its whole life in fresh or
Freshwater brackish water is *now* the very rare Pa Beuk (*Pangasia-*
World *nodon gigas*), which is found in the Mekong River of Laos and Thailand. Adult males average 8 ft *2,43 m* in length and weigh about 375 lb. *170 kg*. This size was exceeded by the European catfish or Wels (*Silurus glanis*) in earlier times (in the 19th century lengths up to 15 ft *4,57 m* and weights up to 720 lb. *336,3 kg* were reported for Russian specimens), but today anything over 6 ft *1,83 m* and 200 lb. *91 kg* is considered large. The Arapaima (*Arapaima glanis*), also called the Pirarucu, found in the Amazon and other South American rivers and often claimed to be the

largest freshwater fish, averages 6½ ft *2 m* and 150 lb. *68 kg*. The largest "authentically recorded" measured 8 ft 1½ in *2,48 m* in length and weighed 325 lb. *147 kg*. It was caught in the Rio Negro, Brazil in 1836.

Britain The largest fish ever caught in a British river was a Common sturgeon (*Acipenser sturio*) weighing 460 lb. *208 kg* taken in the Esk, North Yorkshire in 1810. Another one measuring 9 ft *2,74 m* and allegedly weighing "over 500 lb. [*227 kg*]" was caught in the Severn at Lydney, Gloucestershire on 1 June 1937, but further details are lacking. Larger specimens have been taken at sea—notably one weighing 700 lb. *317 kg* and 10 ft 5 in *3,18 m* long netted by the trawler *Ben Urie* off Orkney and landed at Aberdeen on 18 Oct. 1956.

Smallest The smallest recorded marine fishes are the Marshall
Marine Islands goby (*Eviota zonura*) measuring 12 to 16 mm *0.47 to 0.63 in* and *Schindleria praematurus* from Samoa, measuring 12 to 19 mm *0.47 to 0 74 in*, both in the Pacific Ocean. Mature specimens of the latter fish, which was not described until 1940, have been known to weigh only 2 mg, equivalent to 17,750 to the oz—the lightest of all vertebrates and the smallest catch possible for any fisherman. The smallest British marine fish is the Diminutive or Scorpion goby (*Gobios scorpoides*) of the English Channel which measures 20 to 25 mm *0.78 to 0.98 in* in length.

Freshwater The shortest known fish, and the shortest of all vertebrates, is the Dwarf pygmy goby (*Pandaka pygmaea*), a colourless and nearly transparent fish found in the streams and lakes of Luzon in the Philippines. Adult males measures only 7,5 to 9,9 mm *0.28 to 0.38 in* in length and weigh 4 to 5 mg *0.00014 to 0.00017 oz.*

Fastest The Sailfish (*Isiophorus platypterus*) is generally considered to be the fastest species of fish, although the practical difficulties of measurement make data extremely difficult to secure. A figure of 68.1 m.p.h. *109,7 km/h* (100 yds [*91 m*] in 3 sec) has been cited for one off Florida, U.S.A. The Swordfish (*Xiphias gladius*) has also been credited with very high speeds, but the evidence is based mainly on bills that have been found deeply embedded in ships' timbers. A speed of 50 knots (57.6 m.p.h. [*92,7 km/h*]) has been calculated from a penetration of 22 in *56 cm* by a bill into a piece of timber, but 30 to 35 knots (35 to 40 m.p.h. [*56-64 km/h*]) is the most conceded by some experts. Speeds in excess of 35 knots (40 m.p.h. [*64 km/h*]) have also been attributed to the Marlin (*Tetrapturus sp.*), the Wahoo (*Acanthocybium solandri*), the Great blue shark (*Prionace glauca*) and the Bonefish (*Albula vulpes*), and the Bluefin tuna (*Thunnus thynnus*) has been scientifically clocked at 43.4 m.p.h. *69,8 km/h* in a 20 sec dash. The Four-winged flying fish (*Cypselurus heterururs*) may also exceed 40 m.p.h. *64 km/h* during its rapid rush to the surface before take-off (the average speed in the air is about 35 m.p.h. [*56 km/h*]). Record flights of 90 sec, 36 ft *11 m* in altitude and 1 110 m *3,640 ft* length have been recorded in the tropical Atlantic.

Longest Aquaria are of too recent origin to be able to establish
lived with certainty which species of fish can fairly be regarded as the longest lived. A Lake sturgeon 6 ft 9 in *2,05 m* long and weighing 215 lb. *97 kg* caught in the Lake of the Woods Kenora, Ontario, Canada on 15 July 1953 was believed (but not by all authorities) to be 154 years old based on a growth ring. In July 1974 a growth ring count of 228 years was reported for a female Mirror carp (*Cyprinus carpion*) named "Hanako" living in a pond in Higashi Shirakawa, Gifu Prefecture, Japan, but the greatest authoritatively accepted age for this species is "more than 50 years".

Oldest While goldfish (*Carassius auratus*) have been reported
goldfish to live for over 40 years in China, the British record is probably 29 years 10 months 21 days for a specimen

which lived in an aquarium at Woolwich, Greater London and died on 11 Apr. 1883.

Shortest lived The shortest-lived fishes are probably certain species of the sub-order Cyprinodontei (killifish) found in Africa and South America which normally live about eight months in the wild state.

Deepest The greatest depth from which a fish has been recovered is 8 300 m *27,230 ft* in the Puerto Rico Trench (27,488 ft [*8 366 m*]) in the Atlantic by Dr Gilbert L. Voss of the U.S. research vessel *John Elliott* who took a 6½ in *16,5 cm* long *Bassiogigas profundissimus* in April 1970. It was only the fifth such brotulid ever caught. Dr. Jacques Piccard and Lieutenant Don Walsh, U.S. Navy, reported they saw a sole-like fish about 1 ft *33 cm* long (tentatively identified as *Chascanopsetta lugubris*) from the bathyscaphe *Trieste* at a depth of 35,802 ft *10 912 m* in the Challenger Deep (Marianas Trench) in the western Pacific on 24 Jan. 1960. This sighting, however, has been questioned by some authorities, who still regard the brotulids of the genus *Bassogigas* as the deepest-living vertebrates.

Most eggs The Ocean sunfish (*Mola mola*) produces up to 300,000,000 eggs, each of them measuring about 0.05 in *0,127 mm* in diameter. The egg yield of the guppy *Poecilia reticulatus* is usually only 40–50, but these are borne to maturity. A female measuring 1¼ in *31 mm* in length had only four in her ovaries.

Most venomous The most venomous fish in the world are the Stonefish (family Synanceidae) of the tropical waters of the Indo-Pacific. Direct contact with the spines of their fins, which contain a strong neurotoxic poison, often proves fatal.

Most electric The most powerful electric fish is the Electric eel (*Electrophorus electricus*), which is found in the rivers of Brazil, Columbia, Venezuela and Peru. An average sized specimen can discharge 400 volts at 1 ampere, but measurements up to 650 volts have been recorded.

River Thames The first salmon caught in the Thames since June 1833 was taken at West Thurrock Power Station, Essex in November 1974 and weighed 8 lb. 4½ oz. *3,757 kg.*

6. STARFISHES (*Asteroida*)

Largest The largest of the 1,600 known species of starfish in terms of total diameter is the very fragile brisingid *Midgardia xandaros*. A specimen collected by the Texas A & M University research vessel *Alaminos* in the southern part of the Gulf of Mexico in the late summer of 1968, measured 1 380 mm *54.33 in* tip to tip but the diameter of its disc was only 26 mm *1.02 in*. Its dry weight was only 70 g *2.46 oz*. The most massive species of starfish is probably the five-armed *Evasterias echinosoma* of the North Pacific. One specimen collected by a Russian expedition in the flooded crater of a volcano on Broughton Bay, Semushir, one of the Kurile Islands in June 1970 measured 960 mm *37.79 in* in total diameter and weighed more than 5 kg *11 lb*. The largest starfish found in British waters is the fragile seven-armed *Luidia ciliaris* of which the largest accurately measured specimen was one of 599 mm *23½ in* caught by Steven Cox off Fowey, Cornwall on 23 Apr. 1973.

Smallest The smallest recorded starfish is *Marginaster capreenis*, found in the Mediterranean, which has a maximum total diameter of 20 mm *0.78 in*. The smallest starfish found in British waters is the Cushion starfish (*Asterina gibbosa*), which has a maximum total diameter of 60 mm *2.36 in*.

Deepest The greatest depth from which a Starfish has been recovered is 7 584 m *24,880 ft* for a specimen of *Porcellanaster sp.* collected by the U.S.S.R. research ship *Vityaz* in the Marianas Trench, in the Pacific in 1959.

7. ARACHNIDS (*Arachnida*)

SPIDERS (Order Araneae)

Largest World The world's largest known spider is the bird-eating spider *Theraphosa leblondi* of northern South America. A male specimen with a leg span of 10 in *25 cm* when fully extended and a body length of 3½ in *8,9 cm* was collected at Montagne la Gabrielle, French Guiana in April 1925. It weighed nearly 2 oz *56 g*. The heaviest spider ever recorded was a female "tarantula" of the genus *Lasiodora* collected at Manaos, Brazil in 1945. It measured 9½ in *241 mm* across the legs and weighed almost 3 oz *85 g*.

Britain Of the 617 known British species of spider covering an estimated population of over 500,000,000,000,000,000, the Cardinal spider (*Tegenaria parietina*) has the greatest leg span. In 1974 one spanning 5.3 in *134,6 mm* was trapped in a house in Wokingham, Berkshire but later escaped. This spider is found only in southern England. The well-known "Daddy Longlegs" spider (*Pholcus phanlangoides*) rarely exceeds 3 in *75 mm* in leg span, but one outsized specimen collected in England measured 6 in *152 mm* across. The heaviest spider found in Britain is probably the orb weaver *Araneus quadratus* (formerly called *Araneus reaumuri*). An *averaged-sized* specimen collected in October 1943 weighed 1,174 g *0.041 oz.* and measured 15 mm *0.58 in* in body length.

Smallest World The smallest known spider is *Patu marplesi* (family Symphytognathidae) of Western Samoa. Adult males measure 0,43 mm *0.017 in* overall—the size of this full stop . The smallest spider found in Britain is the money spider *Glyphesis cottonae*, which is confined to a swamp near Beaulieu Road Station, New Forest, Hampshire and Thurley Heath, Surrey. Adult specimens of both sexes have a body length of 1 mm *0.039 in*.

Largest webs The largest webs are the aerial ones spun by the tropical orb weavers of the genus *Nephila*, which have been measured up to 18 ft 9¾ in *573 cm* in circumference. The smallest webs are spun by spiders like *Glyphesis cottonae*, etc. which are about the size of a postage stamp.

Most venomous The most venomous spider in the world is probably *Latrodectus mactans* of the Americas, which is better known as the "black widow" in the United States. Females of this species (the much smaller males are harmless) have a bite capable of killing a human being, but deaths are rare. The Funnel web spider (*Atrax robustus*) of Australia, the Jockey spider (*Latrodectus hasseltii*) of Australia and New Zealand, the Button spider (*Latrodectus indistinctus*) of South Africa, the Podadora (*Glyptocranium gasteracanthoides*) of Argentina and the Brown recluse spider (*Loxosceles reclusa*) of the central and southern United States have also been credited with fatalities.

Rarest The most elusive of all spiders are the primitive atypical tarantulas of the genus *Liphistius*, which are found in south-east Asia. The most elusive spider in Britain is the handsome crimson and black Lace web eresus spider (*Eresus niger*), found in Hampshire, Dorset and Cornwall, which is known only from eight specimens (seven males and one female). In the early 1950s a specimen was reportedly seen at Sandown on the Isle of Wight, but it escaped.

Fastest The highest speed recorded for a spider on a level surface is 1.73 ft *53 cm/sec* (1.17 m.p.h. [*1,88 km/h*]) in the case of a specimen of *Tegenaria atrica*.

Longest lived The longest lived of all spiders are the primitive *Mygalomorphae* (tarantulas and allied species). One mature female tarantula collected at Mazatlan, Mexico in 1935 and estimated to be 12 years old at the time, was kept in a laboratory for 16 years, making a total of 28 years. The longest-lived British spider is probably the purse web spider (*Atypus affinis*). One specimen was kept in a greenhouse for nine years.

8. CRUSTACEANS (*Crustacea*)

(Crabs, lobsters, shrimps, prawns, crayfish, barnacles, water fleas, fish lice, woodlice, sandhoppers, krill, etc.)

Largest
World The largest of all crustaceans (although not the heaviest) is the giant spider crab (*Macrocheira kaempferi*), also called the stilt crab, which is found in deep waters off the south-eastern coast of Japan. Mature specimens usually have a 12–14 in *30–35 cm* wide body and a claw-span of 8–9 ft *2,43–2,74 m* but unconfirmed measurements up to 19 ft *5,79 m* have been reported. A specimen with a claw span of 12 ft 1½ in *3,69 m* weighed 14 lb. *6 kg*. The heaviest crab is the *Psuedocarcinus gigas* found in the Bass Strait, Australia, which weighs up to 30 lb. *13,6 kg*.

The largest species of lobster, and the heaviest of all crustaceans, is the American or North Atlantic lobster (*Homarus americanus*). One weighing 42 lb. 7 oz. *19 kg 050* and measuring 4 ft *121 cm* from the end of the tail-fan to the tip of the claw was caught by the smack *Hustler* in a deep-sea trawl off the Virginia Capes, Virginia, U.S.A. in 1934 and is now on display in the Museum of Science, Boston, Massachusetts. Another specimen allegedly weighing 48 lb. *21 kg 772* was caught off Chatham, New England, U.S.A. in 1949.

Britain The largest crustacean found in British waters is the common or European lobster (*Homarus vulgarus*), which averages 2–3 lb. *900–1 360 g* in weight. On 17 Aug. 1967 a lobster weighing 14½ lb. *6,575 kg* was caught by a skin-diver off St. Ann's Head, Dyfed. It is now mounted in the "Coracle Restaurant" at the Glan-y-môr Country Club, Laugharne, Dyfed. The largest crab found in British waters is the Edible or great crab (*Cancer pagurus*). In 1895 a crab measuring 11 in *279 mm* across the shell and weighing 14 lb. *6,35 kg* was caught off the coast of Cornwall.

Smallest The smallest known crustaceans are water fleas of the genus *Alonella*, which may measure less than 0,25 mm *0.0098 in* in length. They are found in British waters. The smallest known lobster is the Cape lobster (*Homarus capensis*) of South Africa which measures 10–12 cm *3.93–4.72 in* in total length. The smallest crabs in the world are the aptly named pea crabs (family Pinnotheridae). Some species have a shell diameter of only 0.25 in *63 mm*, including *Pinnotheres pisum* which is found in British waters.

Longest lived The longest lived of all crustaceans is the American lobster (*Homarus americanus*). Very large specimens may be as much as 50 years old.

Deepest The greatest depth from which a crustacean has been recovered is 9 790 m *32.119 ft* for an amphiopod (order Amphiopoda) collected by the Galathea Deep Sea Expedition in the Philippine Trench in 1951. The marine crab *Ethusina abyssicola* has been taken at a depth of 14,000 ft *4 265 m*.

9. INSECTS (*Insecta*)

Heaviest
World The heaviest insect in the world is the Goliath beetle *Goliathus goliathus* of equatorial Africa. One specimen measuring 148,5 mm *5.85 in* in length (tip of mandible to end of abdomen) and 100 mm *3.93 in* across the back weighed 3.52 oz. *99,8 g*. The longhorn beetles *Titanus giganteus* of South America and *Xinuthrus heros* of the Fiji Islands are also massive insects, and both have been measured up to 150 mm *5.9 in* in length.

Evening Post

Britain's largest beetle, the Stag beetle which can grow to 3 in *77,4 mm* in length

Britain The heaviest beetle found in Britain is the Stag beetle (*Lucanus cervus*) widely distributed over southern England. The largest specimen on record was a male collected at Sheerness, Kent, in 1871 and now preserved in the British Museum (Natural History), London, which measures 77,4 mm *3.04 in* in length (body plus mandibles) and probably weighed over 6,000 mg *0.17 oz*. when alive.

Longest The longest insect in the world is the tropical stick-insect *Pharnacia serratipes*, females of which have been measured up to 33 cm *12.99 in* in body length. The longest known beetle (excluding antenae) is the Hercules beetle (*Dynastes hercules*) of Central and South America, which has been measured up to 18 cm *7.08 in*, but over half of this length is accounted for by the "prong" from the thorax. The longhorn beetle *Batocera wallacei* of New Guinea has been measured up to 26,7 cm *10.5 in*, but 19 cm *7.5 in* of this was antenna.

Smallest
World The smallest insects recorded so far are the "Hairy-winged" beetles of the family Trichopterygidae and the "battledore-wing fairy flies" (parasitic wasps) of the family Mymaridae. They measure only 0,2 mm *0.008 in* in length, and the fairy flies have a wing span of only 1 mm *0.04 in*. This makes them smaller than some of the protozoa (single-celled animals). The male bloodsucking banded louse (*Enderleinellus zonatus*), ungorged, and the parasitic wasp *Caraphractus cinctus* may each weigh as little as 0,005 mg, *or 567,000 to an oz*. The eggs of the latter each weigh 0.0002 mg, *or 14,175,000 to the oz*.

Commonest The most numerous of all insects are the Springtails (Order Collembola), which have a very wide geographical range. It has been calculated that the top 9 in *288 mm* of soil in one acre of grassland contain 230,000,000 springtails or more than 5,000 per square foot.

Fastest flying Experiments have proved that the widely publicised claim by an American entomologist in 1926 that the Deer bot-fly (*Cephenemyia pratti*) could attain a speed of 818 m.p.h. *1 316 km/h* (sic) was wildly exaggerated. Acceptable modern experiments have now established that the highest maintainable air-speed of any insect, including the Deer bot-fly, is 24 m.p.h. *39 km/h*, rising to a maximum of 36 m.p.h. *58 km/h* for short bursts. A relay of bees (maximum speed 11 m.p.h.

[18 km/h]) would use only a gallon of nectar in cruising 4,000,000 miles *6,5 million km* at an average speed of 7 m.p.h. *11 km/h.*

Longest lived The longest-lived insects are queen termites (*Isoptera*), which have been known to lay eggs for up to 50 years.

Loudest The loudest of all insects is the male cicada (family Cicadidae). At 7,400 pulses/min its tymbal organs produce a noise (officially described by the United States Departments of Agriculture as "Tsh-ee-EEEE-e-ou") detectable more than a quarter of a mile *400 m* distant. The only British species is the very rare Mountain cicada (*Cicadetta montana*), which is confined to the New Forest area in Hampshire.

Southern-most The farthest south at which any insect has been found is 77° S (900 miles *[1 450 km]* from the South Pole) in the case of a springtail (order Collembola).

Largest locust swarm The greatest swarm of Desert locusts (*Schistocerea gregaria*) ever recorded was one covering an estimated 2,000 miles² *5 180 km²* observed crossing the Red Sea in 1889. Such a swarm must have contained about 250,000,000,000 insects weighing about 500,000 tons *508 000 tonnes.*

Fastest wing beat The fastest wing beat of any insect under natural conditions is 62,760 a min by a tiny midge of the genus *Forcipomyia*. In experiments with truncated wings at a temperature of 37° C *98.6° F* the rate increased to 133,080 beats/min. The muscular contraction-expansion cycle in 0.00045 or 1/2,218th of a sec, further represents the fastest muscle movement ever measured.

Slowest wing beat The slowest wing beat of any insect is 300 a min by the swallowtail butterfly (*Papilo machaon*). Most butterflies beat their wings at a rate of 460 to 636 a min.

Largest ants The largest ant in the world is the Driver ant (*Dinoponera grandis*) of Africa, workers of which measure up to 33 mm *1.31 in* in length. The largest of the 27 species found in Britain is the Wood ant (*Formica rufa*), males reaching 9 mm *0.35 in* and queens 11 mm *0.43 in*. The smallest is the Thief ant (*Solenopsis fugax*), whose workers measure 1,5–3 mm *0.059–0.18 in.*

Hive record The greatest reported amount of wild honey ever extracted from a single hive is 404 lb. *183,2 kg* recorded by Ormond R. Aebi of Santa Cruz, California on 29 Aug. 1974.

Bush-cricket Largest The bush-cricket with the largest wing span is the New Guinean grasshopper *Siliquofera grandis* with female examples measuring more than 10 in *254 mm*. *Pseudophyllanax imperialis*, found on the island of New Caledonia in the south-western Pacific has antennae measuring up to 8 in *203 mm*. The largest bush-cricket found in Britain is *Tettigonia viridissima*, which normally has a body length of 1¼ in *31,8 mm*. In August 1953 a female measuring 77 mm *3.03 in* in body length (including ovipositor) was caught in a sand pit at Grays, Essex and later presented to London Zoological Gardens. The largest of the 14 true grasshoppers found in Britain is *Mecostethus grossus*, females of which measure up to 39 mm *1.53 in* in body length.

Dragonflies Largest The largest dragonfly in the world is *Tetracanthagyne plagiata* of north-eastern Borneo, which is known only from a single specimen preserved in the British Museum of Natural History, London. This dragonfly has a wing span of 194 mm *7.63 in* and an overall length of 108 mm *4.25 in*. The largest dragonfly found in Britain is the Golden-ringed dragonfly (*Cordulegaster boltoni*), which has been measured up to 84 mm *3.3 in* in overall length and may have a wing span of more than 100 mm *3.93 in*. The smallest British dragonfly is the Scarce ischnura (*Ischnura pumilio*), which has a wing span of 33 mm *1.3 in.*

Flea Largest The largest known flea is *Hystricopsylla schefferi schefferi*, which was described from a single specimen taken from the nest of a Mountain beaver (*Aplodontia rufa*) at Puyallup, Washington, U.S.A. in 1913. Females measure up to 8 mm *0.31 in* in length which is the diameter of a pencil. The largest flea (61 species) found in Britain is the Mole and Vole flea (*H. talpae*), females of which have been measured up to 6 mm *0.23 in.*

Longest jump The champion jumper among fleas is the common flea (*Pulex irritans*). In one American experiment carried out in 1910 a specimen allowed to leap at will performed a long jump of 13 in *330 mm* and a high jump of 7¾ in *197 mm*. In jumping 130 times its own height a flea subjects itself to a force of 200 g. Siphonapterologists recognise 1,830 varieties.

Smallest and largest tick The smallest known tick is a male *Ixodes soricis* from a British Columbian shrew, and the largest an engorged female, *Amblyomma varium* from a Venezuelan sloth.

BUTTERFLIES AND MOTHS (order Lepidoptera)

Largest World The largest known butterfly is the giant birdwing *Troides victoriae* of the Solomon Islands in the south-western Pacific. Females may have a wing span exceeding 12 in *30 cm* and weigh over 5 g *0.176 oz*. The largest moth in the world is the Hercules moth (*Coscinoscera hercules*) of tropical Australia and New Guinea. Females measure up to 10½ in *266 mm* across the outspread wings and have a wing area of up to 40.8 in² *263,2 cm²*. In 1948 an unconfirmed measurement of 360 mm *14.17 in* was reported for a female captured near the post office at the coastal town of Innisfail, Queensland, Australia. The rare Owlet moth (*Thysania agrippina*) of Brazil has been measured up to 30 cm *11.81 in* in wing span, and the Atlas moth (*Attacus atlas*) of south-east Asia up to 28 cm *11.02 in*, but both these species are less bulky than *C. hercules*.

Britain The largest (but not the heaviest) of the 21,000 species of insect found in Britain is the very rare Death's head hawk moth (*Acherontia atropos*), females of which have a body length of 60 mm *2.36 in*, a wing span of up to 133 mm *5.25 in* and weigh about 1,6 g *0.065 oz*. The largest butterfly found in Britain is the Monarch butterfly (*Danaus plexippus*), also called the Milkweek or Black-veined brown butterfly, a rare vagrant which breeds in the southern United States and Central America. It has a wing span of up to 5 in *127 mm* and weighs about 1 g *0.04 oz*. The largest *native* butterfly is the Swallowtail (*Papilo machaon*), females of which have a wing span of 70–100 mm *2.75–3.93 in*. This species is now confined to a small area of the Norfolk Broads.

Smallest World and Britain The smallest of the 140,000 known species of Lepidoptera is the moth *Johanssonia acetosae* (*Stainton*) which has a wing span of *c.* 2 mm *0.08 in* with a similar body length. It is found in Britain on the leaf of the Common Sorrel (*Rumex acetosa*) or Sheep's Sorrel (*R. acetosella*). The world's smallest known butterfly is the Dwarf blue (*Brephidium barberae*) of South Africa. It has a wing span of 14 mm *0.55 in*. The smallest butterfly found in Britain is the Small blue (*Cupido minimus*), which has a wing span of 19–25 mm *0.75–1.0 in.*

Rarest The rarest of all butterflies (and the most valuable) is the giant birdwing *Troides allottei*, which is found only on Bougainville in the Solomon Islands. A specimen was sold for £750 at an auction in Paris on 24 Oct. 1966. The rarest British butterfly is the Large blue (*Maculinea arion*), which is now confined to few localities in north Cornwall. The total population is now so small (estimated at only 100–150 in 1972) that the British Butterfly Conservation Society believe that it would only need poor weather conditions during the flight season for this species to become extinct in Britain. Britain's rarest moth is the Tree-lichen Beauty

(*Briophila algae*), one specimen of which was captured in Greater Manchester in July 1858.

Most acute sense of smell The most acute sense of smell exhibited in nature is that of the male Emperor moth (*Eudia pavonia*) which, according to German experiments in 1961, can detect the sex attractant of the virgin female at the almost unbelievable range of 11 km *6.8 miles* upwind. This scent has been identified as one of the higher alcohols ($C_{16}H_{29}OH$), of which the female carries less than 0.0001 mg.

10. CENTIPEDES (*Chilopoda*)

Longest The longest known species of centipede is a large variant of the widely distributed *Scolopendra morsitans*, found on the Andaman Islands, Bay of Bengal. Specimens have been measured up to 13 in *330 mm* in length and 1½ in *38 mm* in breadth. The longest centipede found in Britain is *Haplophilus subterraneus*, which measures up to 70 mm *2.75 in* in length and 1,4 mm *0,05 in* across the body but on 1 Nov. 1973 Mr Ian Howgate claims to have seen a thin amber-coloured specimen in St. Albans, Herts. measuring at least 4½ in *114 mm*.

Shortest The shortest recorded centipede is an unidentified species which measures only 5 mm *0.19 in*. The shortest centipede found in Britain is *Lithobius dubosequi*, which measures up to 9,5 mm *0.374 in* in length and 1,1 mm *0.043 in* across the body.

Most legs The centipede with the greatest number of legs is *Himantarum gabrielis* of southern Europe which has 171–177 pairs when adult.

Fastest The fastest centipede is probably *Scutiger coleoptrata* of southern Europe which can travel at a rate of 50 cm *19.68 in* a sec or 4.47 m.p.h. *7,19 km/h*.

11. MILLIPEDES (*Dilopoda*)

Longest The longest known species of millipede are *Graphidostreptus gigas* of Africa and *Scaphistostreptus seychellarum* of the Seychelles in the Indian Ocean, both of which have been measured up to 280 mm *11.02 in* in length and 20 mm *0.78 in* in diameter. The longest millipede found in Britain is *Cylindroiulus londinensis* which measures up to 50 mm *1.96 in*.

Shortest The shortest millipede in the world is the British species *Polyxenus lagurus*, which measures 2,1–4,0 mm *0.082–0.15 in* in length.

Most legs The greatest number of legs reported for a millipede is 355 pairs (710 legs) for an unidentified South African species.

12. SEGMENTED WORMS (*Annelida* or *Annulata*)

Longest The longest known species of giant earthworm is *Microchaetus rappi* (=*M. microchaetus*) of South Africa. An average-sized specimen measures 136 cm *4 ft 6 in* in length (65 cm *25½ in* when contracted), but much larger examples have been reliably reported. In *c.* 1937 a giant earthworm measuring 22 ft *6,70 m* in length when naturally extended and 3 in *7,6 cm* diameter was collected in the Transvaal, and in November 1967 another specimen measuring 11 ft *3,35 m* in length and 21 ft *6,40 m* when naturally extended was found reaching over the national road (width 6 m *19 ft 8½ in*) near Debe Nek, eastern Cape Province. The longest segmented worm found in Britain is the King rag worm (*Nereis vireus*). In 1973 a specimen measuring 870 mm *32.3 in* was collected at Berwick on Tweed, Northumberland.

Shortest The shortest known segmented worm is *Chaetogaster annandalei*, which measures less than 0,5 mm *0.019 in* in length.

13. MOLLUSCS (*Mollusca*)
(Squids, octopuses, shellfish, snails, etc.)

Largest squid The heaviest of all invertebrate animals is the Atlantic giant squid (*Architeuthis sp.*). The largest specimen ever recorded was one measuring 55 ft *16,76 m* in total length (head and body 20 ft [*6,09 m*] tentacles 35 ft [*10,66 m*]) captured on 2 Nov. 1878 after it had run aground in Thimble Tickle Bay, Newfoundland, Canada. It weighed an estimated 2 tons/*tonnes*. In October 1887 a giant squid (*Architeuthis longimanus*) measuring 57 ft *17,37 m* in total length was washed up in Lyall Bay, New Zealand, but 49 ft *14,93 m* of this was tentacle. In 1896 Dr. DeWitt Webb recorded the remains of a cephalopod on the beach 12 miles *19,2 km* south of St. Augustine, Florida, U.S.A., which belonged, he believed, to a 6–7 ton giant octopus with a tentacular span of 200 ft *60,9 m*. The largest squid ever recorded in British waters was one found at the head of Whalefirth Voe, Shetland on 2 Oct. 1949 which measured 24 ft *7,31 m* in total length.

Largest octopus The largest known octopus is the Common Pacific octopus (*Octopus apollyon*). On 18 Feb. 1973 skin-diver Donald E. Hagen caught a specimen in Lower

Argosy Magazine

The stranded remains of the world's largest invertebrate the *Architeuthis longimanus* with an estimated weight of 5 tons

Hoods Canal, Puget Sound, Washington, U.S.A. which had a radial spread of 25 ft 7 in *7,79 m* and weighed 118 lb. 10 oz. *53,8 kg*. The octopus was seized at a depth of 60 ft *18 m* and then "wrestled" to the surface single-handed. In 1874 a radial spread of 32 ft *9,75 m* was reported for an octopus (*Octopus hong-kongensis*) speared in Illiuliuk Harbour, Unalaska Island, Alaska, U.S.A., but the body of this animal only measured 12 in *305 mm* in length and it probably weighed less than 20 lb. *9 kg*. The largest octopus found in British waters is the Common octopus (*Octopus vulgaris*), which has been measured up to 7 ft *2,13 m* in radial spread and may weigh more than 10 lb. *4,5 kg*.

Most ancient mollusc The longest existing living creature is *Neopilina galatheae*, a deep-sea worm-snail which had been believed extinct for about 320,000,000 years. In 1952, however, specimens were found at a depth of 11,400 ft *3 470 m* off Costa Rica by the Danish research vessel *Galathea*. Fossils found in New York State, U.S.A., Newfoundland, Canada, and Sweden show that this mollusc was also living about 500,000,000 years ago.

SHELLS

Largest The largest of all existing bivalve shells is the marine Giant clam (*Tridacna derasa*), which is found on the Indo-Pacific coral reefs. A specimen measuring 43 in *109,2 cm* by 29 in *73,6 cm* and weighing 579½ lb. *262 kg 90* (over a quarter of a ton) was collected from the Great Barrier Reef in 1917, and is now preserved in the American Museum of Natural History, New York City, N.Y., U.S.A. Another lighter specimen was measured to be 137 cm *53,9 in* overall. The largest bivalve shell found in British waters is the Fan mussel (*Pinna fragilis*). One specimen found at Tor Bay, Devon measured 37 cm *14.56 in* in length and 20 cm *7.87 in* in breadth at the hind end.

Smallest The smallest bivalve shell found in British waters, and one of the smallest in the world, is *Ammonicera rota*, which measures 0,5 mm *0.02 in* in diameter. *Tornus unisulcatus* measures 0,4 mm by 0,8 mm *0.015 × 0.03 in*.

Rarest The most highly prized of all molluscan shells in the hands of conchologists is the 3 in *7,5 cm* long Whitetooth cowrie (*Cypraea leucodon*), which is found in the deep waters off the Philippines. Only three examples are known, including one in the British Museum of Natural History, London. The highest price ever paid for a sea shell is £1,350 in a sale at Sotheby's, London, on 4 March 1971 for one of the four known examples of *Conus bengalensis*. The 4 in *10 cm* long shell was trawled by fishermen in the Andaman Sea, South East Asia in December 1970.

Longest lived The longest lived mollusc is probably the Freshwater mussel (*Margaritifera margaritifera*) which has been credited with a potential maximum longevity of 100 years. The Giant clam (*Tridacna derasa*) lives about 30 years.

SNAILS

Largest The largest known species of snail is the sea hare *Tethys californicus*, which is found in coastal waters off California, U.S.A. The average weight is 7 to 8 lb. *315–360 g* but one specimen scaled 15 lb. 13 oz. *7 kg 172*. The largest known land snail is the African giant snail (*Achatina fulica*), which has been recorded up to 10¾ in *273 mm* in overall length and 1 lb. 2 oz. *510 g* in weight. The largest land snail found in Britain is the Roman or Edible snail (*Helix pomatia*), which measures up to 4 in *10 cm* in overall length and weighs up to 3 oz. *85 g*. The smallest British land snail is *Punctum pygmaeum*, which has a shell measuring 0.023–0.035 of an in *6–9 mm* by 0.047–0.059 of an in *12–15 mm*.

Speed The fastest-moving species of land snail is probably the common garden snail (*Helix aspersa*). According to tests carried out in the United States of America absolute top speed for *Helix aspersa* is 0.0313 m.p.h. (or 55 yds [*50,3 m*] per hr.) while some species are at full stretch at 0.00036 m.p.h. (or 23 in [*58 cm*] per hr). This snail would thus take over 16 weeks to cover a mile, provided it did not stop for rest or food.

14. RIBBON WORMS (*Nermertina* or *Rhynchopods*)

Longest The longest of the 550 recorded species of ribbon worms, also called nemertines (or nemerteans), is the "Boot-lace worm" (*Lincus longissimus*), which is found in the shallow waters of the North Sea. A specimen washed ashore at St. Andrews, Fife, Scotland in 1864 after a severe storm measured more than 180 ft *55 m* in length, making it easily the longest recorded worm of any variety.

15. JELLYFISHES (*Scyphozoa* or *Scyphomedusia*)

Largest and smallest The largest jellyfish is *Cyanea arctica*. For details see page 25.

The largest coelenterate found in British waters is the rare "Lion's mane" jellyfish (*Cyanea capillata*), which is also known as the Common sea blubber. One specimen measured at St. Andrew's Marine Laboratory, Fife, Scotland had a bell diameter of 91 cm *35.8 in* and tentacles stretching over 45 ft *13,7 m*. Some true jellyfishes have a bell diameter of less than 20 mm *0.78 in*.

Most venomous The most venomous coelenterates are the box jellies of the genera *Chiropsalmus* and *Chironex* of the Indo-Pacific region, which carry a neuro-toxic venom similar in strength to that found in the Asiatic cobra. These jellyfish have caused the deaths of at least 60 people off the coast of Queensland, Australia in the past 25 years. Victims die within 1–3 min. A most effective defence is women's panty hose outsize versions of which are now worn by Queensland life savers at surf carnivals.

16. SPONGES (*Parazoa, Porifera* or *Spongida*)

Largest The largest known sponge is the barrel-shaped Loggerhead sponge (*Spheciospongia vesparium*) of the West Indies and the waters off Florida, U.S.A. Single individuals measure up to 3 ft 6 in *105 cm* in height and 3 ft *91 cm* in diameter. Neptune's cup or goblet (*Poterion patera*) of Indonesia grows to 4 ft *120 cm* in height, but it is a less bulky animal. In 1909 a Wool sponge (*Hippospongia canaliculatta*) measuring 6 ft *183 cm* in circumference was collected off the Bahama Islands. When first taken from the water it weighed between 80 and 90 lb. *36 and 41 kg* but after it had been dried and relieved of all excrescences it scaled 12 lb. *5 kg 440* (this sponge is now preserved in the U.S. National Museum, Washington, D.C., U.S.A.).

Smallest The smallest known sponge is the widely distributed *Leucosolenia blanca*, which measures 3 mm *0.11 in* in height when fully grown.

Deepest Sponges have been recovered from depths of up to 18,500 ft *5 637 m*.

17. EXTINCT ANIMALS

Longest
World The first dinosaur to be scientifically described was *Megalosaurus* ("large lizard"), a 20 ft *6,09 m* long bipedal theropod, in 1824. A lower jaw and other bones of this animal had been found before 1818 in a slate quarry at Stonesfield, near Woodstock, Oxfordshire. It stalked across what is now southern England about 130,000,000 years ago. The word "dinosaur" ("fearfully great lizard") was not used for such reptiles until 1842. The longest recorded dinosaur was *Diplodocus* ("double-beam"), an attenuated sauropod which ranged over western North America about 150,000,000 years ago. A composite skeleton of three individuals excavated near Split Mountain, Utah between 1909 and 1922 and mounted in the Carnegie Museum of the Natural Sciences in Pittsburgh, Pennsylvania measures 87½ ft *26,67 m* in total length (neck 22 ft, body 15 ft, tail 50 ft 6 in [*6,70; 4,57; 15,40 m*])—nearly the length of three London double-decker buses—and 11 ft 9 in *3,6 m* at the pelvis (the highest point on the body). This animal weighed a computed 10,56 metric tons in life.

Britain Britain's longest dinosaur was the sauropod *Cetiosaurus* ("whale lizard"), which lived in what is now England about 165,000,000 years ago. It measured up to 60 ft *18,28 m* in total length and weighed over 15 tons/tonnes. The bones of this dinosaur were first discovered in the No. 1 Brickyard at the New Peterborough Brick Co., Peterborough, Cambridgeshire in May 1898 and subsequently in Oxfordshire.

Heaviest The heaviest of all prehistoric animals, and the heaviest land vertebrate of all time, was probably *Brachiosaurus* ("arm lizard") which lived from 135 to 165,000,000 years ago. Its remains have been found in East Africa (Rhodesia and Tanzania), U.S.A. (Colorado, Oklahoma and Utah) and Europe. A complete skeleton excavated near Tendaguru Hill, southern Tanganyika (Tanzania) in 1909 and now mounted in the Museum für Naturkunde, East Berlin, Germany, measures 74 ft 6 in *22,68 m* in total length and 21 ft *6,40 m* at the shoulder. This reptile weighed a computed 78,26 metric tons in life, but isolated bones have since been discovered in East Africa which indicate that some specimens may have weighed as much as 100 tons *102 tonnes* and measured over 90 ft *27 m* in total length.

In the summer of 1972 the remains of another enormous sauropod, new to science, was discovered in a flood-plain bonejam in Colorado, U.S.A. by an expedition from Brigham Young University, Provo, Utah. Excavations are still continuing, but a study of the incomplete series of cervical vertebrae indicate that this dinosaur must have had a neck length of approximately 39 ft *11,88 m* (compare 22 ft [*6,70 m*] for *diplodocus*) and measured over 100 ft *30,48 m* in total length when alive.

Largest predator It is now known that some carnosaurs were even larger than the 6¾ ton/*tonnes* 47 ft *14,32 m* *Tyrannosaurus*. In 1930 the British Museum Expedition to East Africa dug up the pelvic bones and part of the vertebrae of another huge carnosaur at Tendaguru Hill which must have measured about 54 ft *16,45 m* in total length when alive. During the summers of 1963–65 a Polish-Mongolian expedition discovered the remains of a carnosaur in the Gobi Desert which had 8 ft 6 in *2,59 m* long forelimbs! It is not yet known, however, whether the rest of this dinosaur was built on the same colossal scale.

Most brainless *Stegosaurus* ("plated reptile"), which measured up to 30 ft *9 m* in total length and weighed 1¾ ton/*tonnes*, had a walnut-sized brain weighing only 2½ oz. *70 g*, which represented 0.004 of one per cent of its body weight (*cf.* 0.074 of 1 per cent for an elephant and 1.88 per cent for a human). It roamed widely across the Northern Hemisphere about 150,000,000 years ago.

Largest dinosaur eggs The largest known dinosaur eggs are those of *Hypselosaurus priscus*, a 30 ft *9,14 m* long sauropod which lived about 80,000,000 years ago. Some specimens found in the valley of the Durance near Aix-en-Provence southern France in October 1961 would have had, uncrushed, a length of 12 in *300 mm* and a diameter of 10 in *255 mm*.

Largest flying creature The largest flying creature was a winged reptile (not yet named) of the order Pterosauria which glided over what is now the state of Texas, U.S.A. about 70,000,000 years ago. Partial remains (four wings, a neck, hind legs and mandibles) of three specimens discovered in Big Bend National Park, West Texas recently indicate that this pterosaur must have had a wing span of at least 11 m *36.08 ft* and that the maximum expanse may have been as great as 21 m *68.89 ft* cf. 27 ft [*8,23 m*] for *Pteranodon ingens*.

Largest marine reptile The largest marine reptile ever recorded was *Kronosaurus queenslandicus*, a short-necked pliosaur which swam in the seas around what is now Australia about 100,000,000 years ago. It measured up to 55 ft *16,76 m* in length and had an 11½ ft *3,60 m* long skull. *Stretosaurus macromerus*, another short-necked pliosaur, was also of comparable size. A mandible found in Cumnor, Oxfordshire must have belonged to a reptile measuring at least 50 ft *15,23 m* in length.

Largest crocodile The largest known crocodile was *Deinosuchus riograndensis*, which lived in the lakes and swamps of what is now the state of Texas, U.S.A. about 75,000,000 years. Fragmentary remains discovered in Big Bend National Park, West Texas, indicate it must have measured at least 50 ft *15,24 m* in total length. The less bulky gavial *Rhamphosuchus*, which lived in what is now northern India about 7,000,000 years ago, also reached a length of 50 ft *15,24 m*.

EARLIEST OF THEIR TYPE

Type	Scientific name and year of discovery	Location	Estimated years before present
Ape	*Aegyptopitherus zeuxis* (1966)	Fayum, U.A.R.	28,000,000
Primate	tarsier-like	Indonesia	70,000,000
	lemur	Madagascar	70,000,000
Social insect	*Sphecomyrma freyi* (1967)	New Jersey, U.S.A.	100,000,000
Bird	*Archaeopteryx lithographica* (1861)	Bavaria, W. Germany	140,000,000
Mammal	shrew-like (1966)	Thaba-ea-Litau, Lesotho	190,000,000
Reptiles	*Hylonomus, Archerpeton, Protoclepsybrops, Romericus*	all in Nova Scotia	290,000,000
Amphibian	*Ichthyostega* (first quadruped)	Greenland	350,000,000
Spider	*Palaeostenzia crassipes*	Tayside, Scotland	370,000,000
Insect	*Rhyniella proecursor*	Tayside, Scotland	370,000,000
Vertebrates	Agnathans (Jawless fish)	near Leningrad, U.S.S.R.	480,000,000
Mollusc	*Neophilina galatheae* (1952)	off Costa Rica	500,000,000
Crustacean	*Karagassiema* (12 legged)	Sayan Mts., U.S.S.R.	c. 650,000,000

Largest chelonians The largest prehistoric marine turtle was probably *Archelon ischyros*, which lived in the shallow seas over what are now the states of South Dakota and Kansas, U.S.A. about 80,000,000 years ago. An almost complete skeleton with a carapace (shell) measuring 6 ft 6 in *1,98 m* in length was discovered in August 1895 near the south fork of the Cheyenne River in Custer County, South Dakota. The skeleton, which has an overall length of 11 ft 4 in *3,45 m* (20 ft [*6,09 m*] across the outstretched flippers) is now preserved in the Peabody Museum of Natural History at Yale University, New Haven, Connecticut, U.S.A. This specimen is estimated to have weighed 6,000 lb. (2.7 tons/*tonnes*]) when it was alive. In 1914 the fossil remains of another giant marine turtle (*Cratochelone berneyi*) which must have measured at least 12 ft *3,65 m* in overall length when alive were discovered at Sylvania Station, 20 miles *32 km* west of Hughenden, Queensland, Australia.

Largest tortoise The largest prehistoric tortoise was probably *Colossochelys atlas*, which lived in what is now northern India between 7 and 12,000,000 years ago. The fossil remains of a specimen with a carapace 5 ft 5 in *165 cm* long (7 ft 4 in [*2,23 m*] over the curve) and 2 ft 11 in *89 cm* high were discovered near Chandigarh in the Siwalik Hills in 1923. This animal had a nose to tail length of 8 ft *2,43 m* and is computed to have weighed 2,100 lb. *952 kg* when it was alive. Recently fossil remains of a similarly sized tortoise were reported from Texas, U.S.A.

Longest snake The longest prehistoric snake was the python-like *Gigantophis garstini*, which inhabited what is now Egypt about 50,000,000 years ago. Parts of a spinal column and a small piece of jaw discovered at El Faiyum indicate a length of about 42 ft *12,80 m*.

Largest amphibian The largest amphibian ever recorded was the alligator-like *Eogyrinus* which lived between 280,000,000 and 345,000,000 years ago. It measured nearly 15 ft *4,57 m* in length.

Largest fish No prehistoric fish larger than living species has yet been discovered. The belief that the Great shark (*Carcharodon megalodon*) was 80 ft *24 m* long has recently been shown to be mistaken and 43 ft *13,1 m* is now regarded as more probable.

Largest insect The largest prehistoric insect was the dragonfly *Meganeura monyi*, which lived between 280,000,000 and 325,000,000 years ago. Fossil remains (*i.e.* impressions of wings) discovered at Commentry, central France, indicate that it had a wing span reaching up to 70 cm *27.5 in*.

Most southerly The most southerly creature yet found is a freshwater salamander-like amphibian *Labyrinthodont*, represented by a 2½ in *63,5 mm* piece of jawbone found near Beardmore Glacier, Antarctica, 325 miles *523 km* from the South Pole, dating from the early Jurassic of 200,000,000 years ago. This discovery was made in December 1967.

Largest bird The largest prehistoric bird was the Elephant bird (*Aepyornis maximus*), also known as the "Roc bird", which lived in southern Madagascar. It was a flightless bird standing 9–10 ft *2,74–3,04 m* in height and weighing nearly 1,000 lb. *453 kg*. Aepyornis also had the largest eggs of any known animal. One example preserved in the British Museum (Natural History), London measures 33¾ in *86 cm* round the long axis with a circumference of 28½ in *72 cm* giving a capacity of 2.35 gal *10,68 litres*—seven times that of an ostrich egg. A more cylindrical egg preserved in the Academie des Sciences, Paris, France measures 12⅞ by 15⅜ in *32,7–39 cm* and probably weighed about 27 lb. *12 kg* with its contents. This bird may have survived until *c.* 1660 In 1974 the fossilised remains of a huge emu-like bird were discovered near Alice Springs, central

Australia. The bird, which lived about 10,000,000 years ago, stood more than 10 ft *3,04 m* tall and may have been even heavier than Aepyornis maximus. The flightless moa *Dinornis giganteus* of North Island, New Zealand was even taller, attaining a height of over 13 ft *3,96 m* but it only weighed about 500 lb. *227 kg*.

The largest prehistoric bird actually to fly was probably the condor-like *Teratornis incredibilis* which lived in what is now North America about 100,000,000 years ago. Fossil remains discovered in Smith Creek Cave, Nevada in 1952 indicate it had a wing span of 5 m *16 ft 4¼ in* and weighed nearly 50 lb. *22 kg 50*. A wing span measurement of 5 m *16 ft 4¼ in* has also been reported for another flying bird named *Ornithodesmus latidens*, which flew over what is now Hampshire and the Isle of Wight about 90,000,000 years ago.

Another gigantic flying bird named *Osteodontornis orri*, which lived in what is now the state of California, U.S.A. about 20,000,000 years ago, had a wing span of 16 ft *4,87 m* and was probably even heavier. It was related to the pelicans and storks. The albatross-like *Gigantornis eaglesomei*, which flew over what is now Nigeria between 34,000,000 and 58,000,000 years ago, has been credited with a wing span of 20 ft *6,09 m* on the evidence of a single fossilised breastbone.

Largest mammal The largest prehistoric land mammal ever recorded, was *Baluchitherium* (=*Indricotherium*, *Paraceratherium*, *Aceratherium*, *Thaumastotherium*, *Aralotherium* and *Benaratherium*), a long necked hornless rhinoceros which lived in Europe and central western Asia between 20,000,000 and 40,000,000 years ago. It stood up to 17 ft 9 in *5,41 m* to the top of the shoulder hump (27 ft [*8,23 m*] to the crown of the head), measured 35–37 ft *10,66–11,27 m* in length and probably weighed nearly 20 tons/*tonnes*. The bones of this gigantic browser were first discovered in 1907–1908 in the Bugti Hills in east Baluchistan, Pakistan. The largest known prehistoric marine mammal was Basilosaurus (=Zeuglodon) of 50,000,000 years ago. A specimen from Alabama measured 70 ft *21,33 m* and weighed an estimated 27 tonnes.

Largest mammoth The largest extinct elephant was *Paraelephas trogontherii* which roamed both central Europe and North America a million years ago. A fragmentary skeleton found in Mosbach, West Germany indicates a shoulder height of 4,5 m *14 ft 9 in*.

Tusks **Longest** The longest tusks of any prehistoric animal were those of the straight-tusked elephant *Hesperoloxodon antiquus germanicus*, which lived in what is now northern Germany about 2,000,000 years ago. The

The American Museum of Natural History

The largest prehistoric land mammal was Baluchitherium which was over 17 ft tall, up to 37 ft long and must have weighed nearly 20 tons

average length in adult bulls was 5 m *16 ft 4¾ in.* A single tusk of a woolly mammoth (*Mammonteus primigenius*) preserved in the Franzens Museum at Brno, Czechoslovakia measures 5,02 m *16 ft 5½ in* along the outside curve. In *c*. August 1933, a single tusk of an Imperial mammoth (*Archidiskodon imperator*) measuring 16+ ft *4,87+ m* (anterior end missing) was unearthed near Post, Gorza County, Texas, U.S.A. In 1934 this tusk was presented to the American Museum of Natural History in New York City, N.Y., U.S.A.

Heaviest The heaviest fossil tusk on record is one weighing 330 lb. *149 kg 700* with a maximum circumference of 35 in *89 cm* now preserved in the Museo Civico di Storia Naturale, Milan, Italy. The specimen (in two pieces) measures 11 ft 9 in *3,58 m* in length. The heaviest recorded mammoth tusks are a pair in the University of Nebraska Museum, Lincoln, Nebraska, U.S.A. which have a combined weight of 498 lb. *226 kg* and measure 13 ft 9 in *4,21 m* and 13 ft 7 in *4,16 m* respectively. They were found near Campbell, Nebraska in April 1915.

Horns The prehistoric Giant deer (*Megaceros giganteus*),
Longest which lived in northern Europe and northern Asia as recently as 50,000 B.C., had the longest horns of any known animal. One specimen recovered from an Irish bog had greatly palmated antlers measuring 14 ft *4,3 m* across.

18. PROTISTA AND MICROBES

PROTISTA

Protista were first discovered in 1676 by Anton van Leeuwenhoek of Delft (1632–1723), a Dutch microscopist. Among Protista characteristics common to both plants and animals are exhibited. The more plant-like are termed Protophyta (protophytes) and the more animal-like are placed in the phylum Protozoa (protozoans).

Largest The largest protozoans which are known to have existed were the now extinct Nummulites, which each had a diameter of 0.95 of an in *24,1 mm.* The largest existing protozoan is *Pelomyxa palustris*, which may attain a length of up to 0.6 of an in *15,2 mm.*

Smallest The smallest of all free-living organisms are pleuropneumonia-like organisms (P.P.L.O.) of the *Mycoplasma*. For fuller details see page 25. The smallest of all protophytes is *Micromonas pusilla*, with a diameter of less than 2 microns.

Fastest The protozoan *Monas stigmatica* has been measured
moving to move a distance equivalent to 40 times its own length in a second. No human can cover even seven times his own length in a second.

Fastest The protozoan *Glaucoma*, which reproduces by binary
reproduction fission, divides as frequently as every three hours. Thus in the course of a day it could become a "six greats grandparent" and the progenitor of 510 descendants.

Densest The most densely existing species in the animal kingdom is the sea water dinoflagellate *Gymnodinium breve*, which exists at a density of 240 million/ga. or *52 million/litre* of sea water in certain conditions of salinity and temperature off the coast of Florida, U.S.A.

BACTERIA

Largest The largest of the bacteria is the sulphur bacterium *Beggiatoa mirabilis*, which is from 16 to 45 microns in width and which may form filaments several millimetres long.

Highest In April 1967 the U.S. National Aeronautics and Space Administration reported that bacteria had been recently discovered at an altitude of 135,000 ft (25.56 miles) *41 100 m.*

Longest The oldest deposits from which living bacteria are
lived claimed to have been extracted are salt layers near Irkutsk, U.S.S.R., dating from about 600,000,000 years ago. The discovery was not accepted internationally. The U.S. Dry Valley Drilling Project in Antarctica claimed resuscitated rod-shaped bacteria from caves up to a million years old.

Toughest The bacterium *Micrococcus radiodurans* can withstand atomic radiation of 6.5 million röntgens or 10,000 times that fatal to the average man.

VIRUSES

Largest The largest true viruses are the brick-shaped pox viruses (*e.g.* smallpox, vaccina, orf etc.) measuring *c.* 250 × 300 millimicrons (mμ) or 0.0003 of a mm.

Smallest Of more than 1,000 identified viruses, the smallest is the potato spindle tuber virus measuring less than 20 mμ in diameter.

Sub viral Evidence was announced from the Institute of Re-
infective search on Animal Diseases at Compton, Berkshire,
agents in January 1967 for the existence of a form of life more basic than both the virus and nucleic acid. It was named SF or Scrapie factor, from the sheep disease. If proven this will become the most fundamental replicating particle known. Its diameter is believed to be not more than 7 millionths of a mm. Having now been cultured, it has been allocated back to its former status of an ultra-virus.

19. PLANT KINGDOM (*Plantae*)

PLANTS

Earliest life If one accepts the definition of life as the ability of an
World organism to make replicas of itself by taking as
and United building materials the simpler molecules in the
Kingdom medium around it, life probably appeared on Earth *c.* 3,355 million years ago. This date for the earliest spheroid photosynthesising micro-organisms (7–10 mμ in diameter) from the Lower Onverwacht strata of the South Africa-Swaziland border was announced in January 1973. The oldest known living life-form was announced in December 1970 by Drs. Sanford and Barbara Siegel of Harvard University, U.S.A., to be a microscopic organism, similar in form to an orange slice, first collected near Harlech, Gwynedd, Wales in 1964. It has been named *Kakabekia barghoorniana* and has existed from 2,000 million years ago.

Rarest Plants thought to be extinct are rediscovered each year and there are thus many plants of which specimens are known in but a single locality. The rose purple Alpine coltsfoot (*Homogyne alpina*), recorded by Don prior to 1814 in the mountains of Clova, Tayside, Scotland, was not again confirmed until 1951. The only known location of the adder's-tongue spearwort (*Ranunculus ophioglossifolius*) in the British Isles is the Badgeworth Nature Reserve, Gloucestershire. The Lady's Slipper orchid (*Cypripedium calceolus*) is probably Britain's rarest flowering plant.

Commonest The most widely distributed flowering plant in the
World world is *Cynodon dactylon*, a toothed grass found as far apart as Canada, Argentina, New Zealand, Japan and South Africa.

British The most widely distributed plant in Great Britain appears to be Ribwort plantain.

Northern- The yellow poppy (*Papaver radicatum*) and the Arctic
most willow (*Salix arctica*) survive, the latter in an extremely stunted form, on the northernmost land (83° N).

THE PLANT KINGDOM

Southern-most The most southerly plant life recorded is seven species of lichen found in 1933–34 by the second expedition of Rear-Admiral Richard E. Byrd, U.S. Navy, in latitude 86° 03′ S. in the Queen Maud Mountains, Antarctica. The southernmost recorded flowering plant is the carnation (*Colobanthus crassifolius*), which was found in latitude 67° 15′ S. on Jenny Island, Margaret Bay, Graham Land (Palmer Peninsula), Antarctica.

Highest The greatest altitude at which any flowering plant has been found is 20,130 ft *6 135 m* in the Himalaya for *Stellaria decumbens*.

Deepest roots The greatest reported depth to which roots have penetrated is a calculated 400 ft *120 m* in the case of a wild fig tree at Echo Caves, near Ohrigstad, East Transvaal, South Africa.

Worst weeds The most intransigent weed is the mat-forming water weed *Salvinia auriculata*, found in Africa. It was detected on the filling of Kariba Lake in May 1959 and within 11 months had choked an area of 77 miles² *199 km²* rising by 1963 to 387 miles² *1,002 km²*. The world's worst land weeds are regarded as purple nut sedge, Bermuda grass, barnyard grass, junglerice, goose grass, Johnson grass, Guinea grass, cogon grass and lantana. The most damaging and widespread cereal weeds in Britain are the wild oats *Avena fatua* and *A. ludoviciana*. Their seeds can withstand temperatures of 240° F *115,6° C* for 15 minutes and remain viable.

Most spreading plant The greatest area covered by a single clonal growth is that of the wild box huckleberry (*Gaylussacia brachyera*), a mat-forming evergreen shrub first reported in 1796. A colony covering 8 acres *3,2 hectares* was discovered in 1845 near New Bloomfield, Pennsylvania. Another colony, covering about 100 acres, was "discovered" on 18 July 1920 near the Juniata River, Pennsylvania. It has been estimated that this colony began 13,000 years ago.

Largest aspidistra The aspidistra (*Aspidistra elatior*) was introduced to Britain as a parlour palm from Japan and China in 1822. The biggest aspidistra in the world is one 49¾ in *126 cm* tall and grown by George Munns at Perth University, Western Australia and measured in January 1972.

Largest cactus The largest of all cacti is the saguaro (*Cereus giganteus* or *Carnegieia gigantea*), found in Arizona, New Mexico and California, U.S.A., and Sonora, Mexico. The green fluted column is surmounted by candelabra-like branches rising to a height of 53 ft *16,15 m* in the case of a specimen found in 1950 near Madrona, New Mexico. They have waxy white blooms which are followed by edible crimson fruit. A cardon cactus in Baja California, Mexico was reputed to reach a height of 58 ft *17,67 m* and a weight of 9 tons/*tonnes*.

Tallest hedge World The world's tallest hedge is the Meikleour beech hedge in Perthshire, Scotland. It was planted in 1746 and has now attained a trimmed height of 85 ft *26 m*. It is 600 yds *550 m* long. Some of its trees now exceed 100 ft *30,48 m*.

Yew The tallest yew hedge in the world is in Earl Bathurst's Park, Cirencester, Gloucestershire. It was planted in 1720, runs for 170 yds *155 m* reaches 36 ft *11 m*, is 15 ft *4,57 m* thick at its base and takes 20 man-days to trim.

Box The tallest box hedge is 35 ft *10,7 m* in height at Birr Castle, Offaly, Ireland dating from the 18th century.

Mosses The smallest of mosses is the pygmy moss (*Ephemerum*) and the longest is the brook moss (*Fontinalis*), which forms streamers up to 3 ft *91 cm* long in flowing water.

Longest seaweed Claims made that seaweed off Tierra del Fuego, South America, grows to 600 ft *182,5 m* and even to 1,000 ft 305 m in length have gained currency. More recent and more reliable records indicate that the longest species of seaweed is the Pacific giant kelp (*Macrocystis pyrifera*), which does not exceed 196 ft *60 m* in length. It can grow 45 cm *17¾ in* in a day. The longest of the 700 species of seaweed recognised around the coasts of Britain is the brown seaweed *Chorda filum* which grows up to a length of 20 ft *6,10 m*. The largest British seaweed is *Saccorhiza polyschides* single plants of which may weigh 2 cwt./*100 kg*.

Largest vines The largest recorded grape vine was one planted in 1842 at Carpinteria, California, U.S.A. By 1900 it was yielding more than 9 tons/*tonnes* of grapes in some years, and averaging 7 tons/*tonnes* per year. It died in 1920. Britain's largest vine (1898–1964) was at Kippen, Stirling with a girth, measured in 1956, of 5 ft *1,52 m*. England's largest vine is the Great Vine, planted in 1768 at Hampton Court, Greater London. Its girth is 38 in *96,5 cm* with branches up to 110 ft *33,5 m* long and an average yield of 1,200 lb. *545 kg*.

Most Northerly Vineyard The most northerly vineyard is that at Renishaw Hall, Derbyshire with 260 vines. It lies in Lat. 53° 18′ N.

TREES AND WOOD

Most massive tree The most massive living thing on Earth is the biggest known California big tree (*Sequoiadendron giganteum*) named the "General Sherman", standing 272 ft 4 in *83 m* tall, in the Sequoia National Park, California, U.S.A. It has a true girth of 79.1 ft *24,11 m* (at 5 ft [*1,52 m*] above the ground). The "General Sherman" has been estimated to contain the equivalent of 600,120 board feet of timber, sufficient to make 5,000,000,000 matches. The foliage is blue-green, and the red-brown tan bark may be up to 24 in *61 cm* thick in parts. In 1968 the official published figure for its estimated weight was "2,145 tons" (1,915 long tons [2 030 *tonnes*]).

The seed of a "big tree" weighs only 1/6,000th of an oz. *4,7 mg*. Its growth at maturity may therefore represent an increase in weight of over 250,000 million fold.

Tallest World The world's tallest known species of tree is the coast redwood (*Sequoia sempervirens*), now found growing indigenously only near the coast of California from just across the Oregon border south to Monterey.

The tallest example is now believed to be the Howard Libbey Tree in Redwood Creek Grove, Humboldt County, California announced at 367.8 ft *112,10 m* in 1964 but discovered to have an apparently dead top and re-estimated at 366.2 ft *111,60 m* in 1970. It has a girth of 44 ft *13,41 m*. The nearby tree announced to a Senate Committee by Dr. Rudolf W. Becking on 18 June 1966 to be 385 ft *117,34 m*, proved on re-measurement to be no more than 311.3 ft *94,88 m* tall. The tallest non-sequoia is a Douglas fir at Quinault Lake Park trail, Washington, U.S.A. of c. 310 ft *94,5 m*.

All-time The identity of the tallest tree of all-time has never been satisfactorily resolved. Although there have been claims as high as 525 ft *160 m* (subsequently reduced in May 1889 on re-measurement to 220 ft *67 m*]), the now accepted view is that maximum height recorded by a qualified surveyor was the 375 ft *114,3 m* Cornthwaite Tree (*Eucalyptus regnans*, formerly *E. amygdalina*) in Thorpdale, Gippsland, Victoria in 1880. Claims for a Douglas fir (*Pseudotsuga taxifolia*) of 417 ft *127,10 m* with a 77 ft *23,47 m* circumference felled by George Carey in 1895 in British Columbia have been obscured, though not necessarily invalidated by a falsified photograph. The tallest specimen now known is c. 310 ft *94,5 m* (see above). A coast redwood of 367 ft 8 in *112,06 m* felled in 1873 near Guerneville, California, U.S.A., was thus precisely the same height as the Howard Libbey Tree as originally measured.

TALLEST TREES IN UNITED KINGDOM AND IRELAND — By species

Species	Location	ft	m
Alder (Italian)	Westonbirt, Gloucester	92	28
Alder (Common)	Sandling Park, Kent	85	25
Ash	Chiswick Ho., Greater London	118	36
Beech	Whitfield Ho., Hereford & Wor.	135	41
Birch	Nr. Woburn, Bedfordshire	97	29
Cedar	Petworth House, West Sussex	132	40
Chestnut (Horse)	Petworth House, West Sussex	125	38
Chestnut (Sweet)	Godinton Park, Kent	118	35
Cypress (Lawson)	Endsleigh, Devon	126	38
Cypress (Monterey)	Tregothnan, Cornwall	120	36
Douglas Fir	Powis Castle, Powys	180	54
Elm (Wych)	Rossie Priory, nr. Dundee	128	39
Elm (Jersey)	Wilton, Wiltshire	121	36
Eucalyptus (Blue Gum)	Glengarriff, Co. Cork	140	42
Grand Fir	Leighton Park, Powys	185	56
Ginkgo	Linton Park (Maidstone), Kent	93	28
Hemlock (Western)	Benmore, Strathclyde	157	47
Holly	Staverton Thicks, Suffolk	74	22
Hornbeam	Hutton-in-the-Forest, Cumbria	98	29
Larch (European)	Bonskeid, Tayside	145	44
Larch (Japanese)	Blair Castle, Tayside	121	36
Lime	Duncombe Park, North Yorks.	150	45
Metasequoia	Savill Gardens, Windsor, Berkshire	64	19
Monkey Puzzle	Scorrier House, Cornwall	87	26
Oak (Common)	Fountains Abbey, North Yorks.	120	36
Oak (Sessile)	Whitfield Ho., Hereford & Worcs.	140	42
Oak (Red)	West Dean, East Sussex	115	35
	Cowdray Park, West Sussex	115	35
Pear	Borde Hill, West Sussex	64	19
Pine (Corsican)	Stanage Park, Powys	144	43
Plane	Bryanston, Dorset	145	44
Poplar (Black Italian)	Fairlawne, Kent	140	42
Poplar (Lombardy)	Marble Hill, Twicken'm, G. London	118	35
Redwood (Coast)	Undisclosed site, north Devon	138	42
Silver Fir	Dupplin Castle, Tayside	154	46
Spruce (Sitka)	Murthly, Tayside	174	53
Sycamore	Drumlanrig Castle, Dumfries & Gal.	112	34
Tulip-tree	Taplow House, Buckinghamshire	120	36
Walnut	Mottisfont Abbey, Hampshire	74	22
Wellingtonia	Endsleigh, Devon	165	50
Willow (weeping)	Trinity College, Cambridge	76	23
Yew	Midhurst, West Sussex	85	25

Great Britain The tallest tree in Great Britain is a Grand fir (*Abies grandis*) at Leighton Park, Powys, Wales, now about 185 ft *56,38 m* tall. The tallest in England is a Wellingtonia (*Sequoiadendron giganteum*) measured at 165 ft *50,29 m* in February 1970 at Endsleigh, Devon. The tallest measured in Scotland is the Grand fir (*Abies grandis*) at Strone' Cairndow, Strathclyde, planted in 1876, and 175 ft *53,34 m* when measured in May 1969 and now estimated to be at least 180 ft *54,86 m* tall.

Ireland The tallest tree in Ireland is a Sitka spruce (*Picea sitchensis*) 166 ft *50,59 m* tall at Curraghmore, Waterford, measured in March 1974.

Tallest Christmas Tree The tallest Christmas tree erected in Trafalgar Square, London was a 69 ft *21,03 m* conifer from Norway in 1970.

Greatest girth World The Santa Maria del Tule Tree, in the state of Oaxaca, in Mexico is a Montezuma cypress (*Taxodium mucronatum*) with a girth of 112–113 ft *34,1–34,4 m* (1949) at a height of 5 ft *1,52 m* above the ground. A figure of 167 ft *51 m* in circumference was reported for the pollarded European chestnut (*Castanea sativa*) known as the "Tree of the 100 Horse" (Castagno di Cento Cavalli) on Mount Etna, Sicily, Italy in 1972.

Britain The tree of greatest girth in Britain is a Sweet Chestnut at Canford, Dorset, with a bole 43 ft 9 in *13,33 m* in circumference.

Britain's greatest oaks The largest-girthed living British oak is one at Bowthorpe Farm near Bourne, south Lincolnshire, measured in Sept. 1973 to be 39 ft 1 in *11,91 m*. The largest "maiden" (*i.e.* not pollarded) oak is the Majesty Oak at Fredville, Kent, with a girth of (1973) 38 ft 1 in *11,60 m*.

Oldest tree World The oldest recorded tree is a bristlecone pine (*Pinus longaeva*) designated WPN–114, which grew at 10,750 ft *3 275 m* above sea-level on the north-east face of Wheeler Peak (13,063 ft [*3 981 m*]) in eastern California, U.S.A. During studies in 1963 and 1964 it was found to be about 4,900 years old but was cut down with a chain saw. The oldest known *living* tree is the bristlecone pine named *Methuselah* at 10,000 ft *3 050 m* in the California side of the White Mountains confirmed as 4,600 years old. In March 1974 it was reported that this tree had produced 48 live seedlings. Dendrochronologists estimate the *potential* life-span of a bristlecone pine at nearly 5,500 years, but that of a "Big Tree" at perhaps 6,000 years. Ring count dating extends back to >6,200 B.C. by cross dating living and dead bristlecone pine trunks. Such tree-ring datings have led archaeologists to realize that some radiocarbon datings are 8 centuries or more too young.

Great Britain Of all British trees that with the longest life is the yew (*Taxus baccata*), for which a maximum age well in excess of 1,000 years is usually conceded. The oldest known is the Fortingall Yew near Aberfeldy, Tayside, part of which still grows. In 1777 this tree was over 50 ft *15,24 m* in girth and it cannot be much less than 1,500 years old today.

Earliest species The earliest species of tree still surviving is the maidenhair tree (*Ginkgo biloba*) of Chekiang, China, which first appeared about 160,000,000 years ago, during the Jurassic era. It was "re-discovered" by Kaempfer (Netherlands) in 1690 and reached England *c.* 1754. It has been grown in Japan since *c.* 1100 where it was known as *ginkyō* ("silver apricot") and is now known as *icho*.

Fastest growing Discounting bamboo, which is not botanically classified as a tree, but as a woody grass, the fastest growing tree is *Eucalyptus deglupta*, which has been measured to grow 35 ft *10,66 m* in 15 months in New Guinea. The youngest recorded age for a tree to reach 100 ft *30,48 m* is 7 years for *E. regnans* in Rhodesia and for 200 ft *60,96 m* is 40 years for a Monterey pine in New Zealand.

Slowest growing The speed of growth of trees depends largely upon conditions, although some species, such as box and yew, are always slow-growing. The extreme is represented by a specimen of Sitka spruce which required 98 years to grow to 11 in *28 cm* tall with a diameter of less than 1 in *2,5 cm* on the Arctic tree-line. The growing of miniature trees or *bonsai* is an oriental cult mentioned as early as *c.* 1320.

Remotest The tree remotest from any other tree is believed to be one at an oasis in the Ténéré Desert, Niger Republic. In Feb. 1960 it survived being rammed by a lorry driven by a Frenchman. There are no other trees within 50 km *31 miles*.

Most expensive The highest price ever paid for a tree is $51,000 (then £18,214) for a single Starkspur Golden Delicious apple tree from near Yakuma, Washington, U.S.A., bought by a nursery in Missouri in 1959.

Largest forest World The largest afforested areas in the world are the vast coniferous forests of the northern U.S.S.R., lying mainly between latitude 55° N. and the Arctic Circle. The total wooded areas amount to 2,700,000,000 acres (25 per cent of the world's forests), of which 38 per cent is Siberian larch. The U.S.S.R. is 34 per cent afforested.

Great Britain The largest forest in England is Kielder Forest (72,336 acres [*29 273 ha*]), in Northumberland. The largest forest in Wales is the Coed Morgannwg (Forest of Glamorgan) (42,555 acres [*17 221 ha*]). Scotland's most extensive forest is the Glen Trool Forest (51,376 acres [*20 791 ha*]) in Kirkcudbrightshire. The United Kingdom is 7 per cent afforested.

Wood The heaviest of all woods is black ironwood (*Olea*
Heaviest *laurifolia*), also called South African ironwood, with a specific gravity of up to 1.49, and weighing up to 93 lb./ft³ *1 490 kg/m³*. The heaviest British wood is boxwood (*Buxus sempervivens*) with an extreme of 64 lb./ft³ *1 025 kg/m³*.

Lightest The lightest wood is *Aeschynomene hispida*, found in Cuba, which has a specific gravity of 0.044 and a weight of only 2¾ lb./ft³ *44 kg/m³*. The wood of the balsa tree (*Ochroma pyramidale*) is of very variable density—between 2½ and 24 lb./ft³ *40* and *384 kg/m³* The density of cork is 15 lb./ft³ *240 kg/m³*.

Bamboo The tallest recorded species of bamboo is *Dendro-*
Tallest *calamas giganteus*, native to southern Burma. It was reported in 1904 that there were specimens with a culm-length of 30 to 35 m *100* to *115 ft* in the Botanic Gardens at Peradeniya, Ceylon.

Fastest Some species of the 45 genera of bamboo have
growing attained growth rates of up to 36 in *91 cm* per day (0.00002 m.p.h. [*0,00003 km/h*]), on their way to reaching a height of 100 ft in less than three months.

Earliest The oldest fossil of a flowering plant with palm-like
flower imprints was found in Colorado, U.S.A., in 1953 and dated about 65,000,000 years old.

BLOOMS AND FLOWERS

Largest The mottled orange-brown and white parasitic
bloom stinking corpse lily (*Rafflesia arnoldi*) has the largest
World of all blooms. These attach themselves to the cissus vines of the jungle in south-east Asia and measure up to 3 ft *91 cm* across and ¾ of an in *1,9 cm* thick, and attain a weight of 15 lb. *7 kg*.

The largest known inflorescence is that of *Puya raimondii*, a rare Bolivian plant with an erect panicle (diameter 8 ft [*2,4 m*]) which emerges to a height of 35 ft *10,7 m*. Each of these bears up to 8,000 white blooms (see also Slowest-flowering plant, below).

The world's largest blossoming plant is the giant Chinese wisteria at Sierra Madre, California, U.S.A. It was planted in 1892 and now has branches 500 ft *152 m* long. It covers nearly an acre, weighs 225 tons *228 tonnes* and has an estimated 1,500,000 blossoms during its blossoming period of five weeks, when up to 30,000 people pay admission to visit it.

Great The largest bloom of any indigenous British flowering
Britain plant is that of the wild white water lily (*Nymphaea alba*), which measures 6 in *15 cm* across. Other species bear much larger inflorescences.

Smallest The smallest of all flowering plants are duckweeds,
flowering seen on the surface of ponds. Of these the rootless
plant *Wolffia punctata* has fronds only 1/50th to 1/35th of an in *0,5* to *0,7 mm* long. Another species, *Wolffia arrhiza*, occurs in Great Britain but rarely, if ever, flowers there. The smallest plant regularly flowering in Britain is the chaffweed (*Cetunculus minimus*), a single seed of which weighs 0.00003 of a gramme.

Slowest The slowest flowering of all plants is the rare *Puya*
flowering *raimondii*, the largest of all herbs, discovered in
plant Bolivia in 1870. The panicle emerges after about 150 years of the plant's life. It then dies. (See also above under Largest blooms.)

Largest The largest wreath ever constructed was the wreath
wreath constructed by the Teleflower conference at Rotorua, New Zealand on 27 Feb. 1975. It weighed 1,008 lb. *457 kg* and measured 25 ft 6 in *7,77 m* in diameter.

Longest The longest daisy chain on record is one of 2,500 ft
daisy chain *762 m*, made by the girls of Form IV of King Edward VI Camp Hill School, King's Heath, Birmingham, England on 19 May 1974.

Tallest The tallest reported hollyhock (*Althaea rosea*) is one of
Hollyhock 17 ft 10 in *5,43 m* grown by Mr. Ernest T. Eksten of Bremerton, Washington, U.S.A. measured on 2 Oct. 1973.

Orchid The largest of all orchids is *Grammatophyllum specio-*
Largest *sum*, native to Malaysia. Specimens have been recorded up to 25 ft *7,62 m* in height. The largest orchid flower is that of *Phragmipedium caudatum*, found in tropical areas of America. Its petals are up to 18 in *46 cm* long, giving it a maximum outstretched diameter of 3 ft *91 cm*. The flower is, however, much less bulky than that of the stinking corpse lily (see Largest blooms above.)

Tallest The tallest free standing orchid is the *Grammatophyllum speciosum* (see above), which may grow to more than 20 ft *6,09 m* in height. *Galeola foliata* may attain 49 ft *15 m* on decaying rainforest trees in Queensland, Australia.

Smallest The smallest orchid is *Bulbophyllum minutissimum*, found in Australia. Claims have also been made for *Notylia norae* found in Venezuela. The smallest orchid flowers are borne by *Stelis graminea* being less than 1 mm *0.04 in* long.

Highest The highest price ever paid for an orchid is 1,150
priced guineas (£1,207.50), paid by Baron Schröder to Sanders of St. Albans for an *Odontoglossum crispum* (variety *pittianum*) at an auction by Protheroe & Morris of Bow Lane, London, on 22 March 1906.

Largest The largest species of rhododendron is the scarlet
rhododen- *Rhododendron arboreum*, examples of which reach a
dron height of 60 ft *18,25 m* at Mangalbaré, Nepal. The cross-section of the trunk of a *Rhododendron giganteum*, reputedly 90 ft *27,43 m* high from Yunnan, China is preserved at Inverewe Garden, Ross-shire. The largest in the United Kingdom is one 25 ft *7,60 m* tall and 272 ft *82,90 m* in circumference at Government House, Hillsborough, Co. Down.

Largest A "Lady Banks" rose tree at Tombstone, Arizona,
rose tree U.S.A., has a trunk 40 in *101 cm* thick, stands 9 ft *2,74 m* high and covers an area of 5,380 ft² *499 m²* supported by 68 posts and several thousand feet

Syndication International

The record 5 lb 15¾ oz onion brings tears to the eyes of Ernie Jones but not his brother Edward

RECORD DIMENSIONS AND WEIGHTS FOR FRUIT, VEGETABLES AND FLOWERS GROWN IN THE UNITED KINGDOM

Most data subsequent to 1958 comes from the annual *Garden News* Giant Vegetable and Fruit Contest

Apple	3 lb. 1 oz.	*1,375 kg*	V. Loveridge	Ross-on-Wye, Hereford and Worcester	1965
Artichoke	8 lb.	*3,625 kg*	A. R. Lawson	Tollerton, North Yorkshire	1964
Beetroot	24 lb.	*10,875 kg*	R. G. Arthur	Longlevens, Gloucestershire	1971
Broad Bean	23⅜ in	*59,3 cm*	T. Currie	Jedburgh, Borders	1963
Broccoli	28 lb. 14¾ oz.	*13,100 kg*	J. T. Cooke	Funtington, West Sussex	1964
Brussels Sprout[1]	16 lb. 1 oz.	*7,285 kg*	E. E. Jenkins	Shipston-on-Stour, Warwickshire	1974
Cabbage[2]	96 lb. 0 oz.	*43,525 kg*	C. Bowcock	Willaston, Merseyside	1973
Carrot[3]	7 lb. 5 oz.	*3,300 kg*	R. Clarkson	Freckleton, Lancashire	1970
Cauliflower	52 lb. 11½ oz.	*23,900 kg*	J. T. Cooke	Funtington, West Sussex	1966
Celery	35 lb. 0 oz.	*15,875 kg*	C. Bowcock	Willaston, Merseyside	1973
Cucumber	11 lb. 6 oz. (indoor)	*5,155 kg*	W. J. Smith	St. Ives, Cornwall	1973
	8 lb. 4 oz. (outdoor)	*3,740 kg*	W. J. Smith	St. Ives, Cornwall	1973
Dwarf Bean	17⅛ in	*43,4 cm*	C. Bowcock	Willaston, Merseyside	1973
Gourd	196 lb.	*88,900 kg*	J. Leathes	Herringfleet Hall, Suffolk	1846
Kale	12 ft tall	*3,65 m*	B. T. Newton	Mullion, Cornwall	1950
Leek	9 lb. 5½ oz.	*4,235 kg*	E. E. Jenkins	Shipston-on-Stour, Warwickshire	1968
Lemon[4]	1 lb. 12 oz. (girth 15 in [*38,1 cm*])	*0,775 kg*	T. P. Matthews	Iver Heath, Buckinghamshire	1969
Lettuce	25 lb. 0 oz.	*11,335 kg*	C. Bowcock	Willaston, Merseyside	1974
Lupin*	6 ft 0½ in	*1,84 m*	J. Lawlor	New Maldon, Surrey	1971
Mangold	46 lb.	*20,850 kg*	D. Bolland	Spalding, Lincolnshire	1964
Marrow[5]	60 lb.	*27,200 kg*	A. V. Bishop	Snailwell, Cambridgeshire	1963
Mushroom[6]	54 in circum.	*1,37 m*	—	Hasketon, Suffolk	1957
Onion	5 lb. 15¾ oz.	*2,700 kg*	A. E. Jones	Llanfyllin, Powys	1973
Parsnip[7]	10 lb. 0 oz.	*4,525 kg*	C. Bowcock	Willaston, Merseyside	1973
Pea Pod	10⅛ in	*25,7 cm*	T. Currie	Jedburgh, Borders	1964
Pear	2 lb. 10½ oz.	*1,200 kg*	Mrs. K. Loines	Hythe, Hampshire	1973
Potato[8]	7 lb. 1 oz.	*3,200 kg*	J. H. East	Spalding, Lincolnshire	1963
Pumpkin[9]	204 lb. 8 oz.	*92,750 kg*	F. H. Smith	Coventry, West Midlands	1970
Radish[10]	16 lb. 8 oz.	*7,475 kg*	E. E. Allen	Heston, Hounslow, Greater London	1966
Red Cabbage	33 lb. 2 oz.	*15,025 kg*	A. Bratton	Ryton, Salop	1963
Rhubarb	5 ft 1⅜ in 4 lb. 3½ oz.	*155,2 cm 1,910 kg*	A. C. Setterfield	Englefield, Berkshire	1974
Runner Bean	33¾ in long	*85,7 cm*	A. Bratton	Ryton, Salop	1966
Savoy	38 lb. 8 oz.	*17,450 kg*	W. H. Neil	Retford, Nottinghamshire	1966
Shallot*	1 lb. 10 oz.	*725 g*	C. Bowcock	Willaston, Merseyside	1973
Strawberry	7¼ oz.	*205 g*	E. Oxley	Walton-on-the-Naze, Essex	1972
Sugar Beet[11]	21 lb.	*9,525 kg*	L. Hawcroft	Home-on-Spalding Moor, Humberside	1971
Sunflower*	19 ft 2 in tall	*5,84 m*	E. Purver	Camberley, Surrey	1974
Swede[12]	32 lb. 8 oz.	*14,725 kg*	R. T. Leeson	Irchester, Northamptonshire	1963
Tomato	4 lb. 4 oz.	*1,925 kg*	C. Roberts	Eastbourne, East Sussex	1974
Tomato Plant	20 ft tall, 34 lb. fruit	*6,09 m, 15,400 kg*	—	Southport, Merseyside	1957
Tomato Truss	20 lb. 4 oz.	*9,175 kg*	C. Bowcock	Willaston, Merseyside	1973
Turnip[13]	35 lb. 4 oz.	*15,975 kg*	C. W. Butler	Nafferton, Humberside	1972

1 *A Brussels Sprout plant measuring 10 ft 3½ in* 3,13 m *was grown by G. Mobbs of Leavesden, Hertfordshire in May 1974. A post 1974 Contest claim for 16 lb. 1 oz.* 7,285 kg *was made by E. E. Jenkins of Shipston-on-Stour, Warwickshire.*

2 *The Swalwell, County Durham Red cabbage of 1865 grown by William Collingwood (d. 8 Oct. 1867)* reputedly weighed 123 lb. *55,7 kg* and was 259 in *6,57 m* in circumference.

3 *One of 7 lb. 7 oz.* 3,35 kg (*15 in* [38 cm] *long) reported grown by Police Sgt. Alfred Garwood of Blidworth, Nottinghamshire in November 1970. A specimen of 7 lb. 10 oz.* 3,455 kg *was grown by Roger Bignell in Bothwell, Tasmania in 1973.*

4 *A lemon weighing 2,65 kg* 5 lb. 13¼ oz. *with a 61 cm* 24 in *girth was reported by Mrs Violet Philips of Cordelea, Queensland, Australia in May 1974.*

5 *A 96 lb.* 43,525 kg *marrow has been reported from Suffolk. A 63½ lb.* 28,800 kg *specimen grown by J. C. Lewis of Blackwood, Gwent, won a contest in 1937.*

6 *Same size reported by J. Coombes at Mark, Somerset on 28 July 1965. In Sept. 1968 one weighing 18 lb. 10 oz.* 8,425 kg *was reported from Whidbey Is., Washington, U.S.A. A mushroom with an estimated circumference of 75 in* 190 cm *was reported by the Lulualaba river, Zaire in 1920.*

7 *60 in* 152 cm *long: M. Zaninovich of Wanneroo, Western Australia*

8 *One weighing 18 lb. 4 oz.* 8,275 kg *reported dug up by Thomas Siddal in his garden in Chester on 17 Feb. 1795. A yield of 1,701 lb.* 771,550 kg *from 6 uncut sets reported in Sept 1971 by J. T. Cooke (see Broccoli above).*

9 *A 245 lb.* 111 kg *pumpkin was grown by Edward Concarzi of Wrightstown, New Jersey, U.S.A. in Oct. 1974. A squash* (Cucurbita maxima) *weighing 353 lb.* 160,1 kg *grown by E. Van Wyck of Roland, Manitoba, Canada reported in 1971.*

10 *A Chinese radish of 25 lb.* 11,340 kg *25½ in* 64,5 cm *long was grown by Glen Tucker of Stanbury, South Australia in Aug. 1974.*

11 *One weighing 35 lb.* 15,87 kg *was grown by Fritz Kuhn of Imperial Valley, California in 1973.*

12 *One weighing 39 lb. 8 oz.* 17,9 kg *claimed by E. R. Reay of Gaitsgill Hall, Dalston, Cumbria, 1940 (unratified).*

13 *A 73 lb.* 33,1 kg *turnip was reported in December 1768.*

* *Not in official contest.*

of piping. This enables 150 people to be seated under the arbour. The cutting came from Scotland in 1884.

FRUIT

Most and least nutritive An analysis of the 38 commonly eaten raw (as opposed to dried) fruits shows that the one with the highest with calorific value is avocado (*Persea americana*), with 741 calories per edible lb. or *163 cals* per *100 gr*. That with the lowest value is cucumber with 73 calories per lb. Avocados probably originated in Central and South America and contains also vitamins A, C, and E and 2.2 per cent protein.

Pineapple *Largest* A pineapple weighing 16 lb. 8 oz. *7,485 kg* was reported from a Dole Co. plantation in Mindanao, Philippine Islands in 1967.

FERNS

Largest The largest of all the more than 6,000 species of fern is the tree fern (*Alsophila excelsa*) of Norfolk Island, in the South Pacific, which attains a height of up to 60 ft *18,28 m*.

Smallest The world's smallest ferns are *Hecistopteris pumila*, found in Central America, and *Azolla caroliniana*, which is native to the United States.

GRASSES

Longest The tallest of the 160 grasses found in Great Britain is the common reed (*Phragmites communis*), which reaches a height of 9 ft 9 in *2,97 m*.

Shortest The shortest grass native to Great Britain is the very rare sand bent (*Mibora minima*) from Anglesey, Gwynedd which has a maximum growing height of under 6 in *15 cm*.

Hay fever The highest recorded grass pollen count in Britain was one of 720 (mean number of grains/m³ of air noon to noon) near London on 15–16 June 1964. A figure of 2,160 for plane tree pollen was recorded on 9 May 1971. The lowest counts are nil.

FUNGUS

Largest The largest recorded specimen of the giant puff ball (*Lycoperdon gigantea*) was one 62 in *157 cm* in diameter and 18 in *45,5 cm* high found at Mellor, Derbyshire in 1971. A flatter specimen 64 in *162,5 cm* in diameter was recorded in New York State, U.S.A. in 1877.

The largest officially recorded tree fungus was a specimen of *Oxyporus* (*Fomes*) *nobilissimus*, measuring 56 in *142 cm* by 37 in *94 cm* and weighing at least 300 lb. *136 kg* found by J. Hisey in Washington State, U.S.A., in 1946. The largest recorded in the United Kingdom is an ash fungus (*Fomes fraxineus*) measuring 50 in by 15 in *127 cm* by *38 cm* wide, found by the forester A. D. C. LeSueur on a tree at Waddesdon, Buckinghamshire, in 1954.

Most poisonous toadstool The yellowish-olive death cap (*Amanita phalloides*) is regarded as the world's most poisonous fungus. It is found in England. From six to fifteen hours after tasting, the effects are vomiting, delirium, collapse and death. Among its victims was Cardinal Giulio de' Medici, Pope Clement VII (b. 1478) on 25 Sept. 1534.

The Registrar General's Report states that between 1920 and 1950 there were 39 fatalities from fungus poisoning in the United Kingdom. As the poisonous types are mostly *Amanita* varieties, it is reasonable to assume that the deaths were predominantly due to *Amanita phalloides*. The most recent fatality was probably in 1960.

LEAVES

Largest World The largest leaves of any plant belong to the raffia palm (*Raphia raffia*) of the Mascarene Islands, in the Indian Ocean, and the Amazonian bamboo palm (*R. toedigera*) of South America, whose leaf blades may measure up to 65 ft *19,81 m* in length with petioles up to 13 ft *3,96 m*.

The largest undivided leaf is that of *Alocasia macrorrhiza*, found in Sabah, East Malaysia. One found in 1966 was 9 ft 11 in *3,02 m* long and 6 ft 3½ in *1,92 m* wide, with a unilatral area of 34.2 ft² *3,17 m²*.

Great Britain The largest leaves to be found in outdoor plants in Great Britain are those of *Gunnera manicata* from Brazil with leaves 6 to 10 ft *1,82–3,04 m* across on prickly stems 5 to 8 ft *1,52–2,43 m* long.

Twelve-leafed clover A twelve-leafed clover (*Trifolium pratense*) was found by Miss Constance M. Kelly of Heswell, Wirrall, Merseyside, England on 31 Aug. 1957.

SEEDS

Largest The largest seed in the world is that of the double coconut or Coco de Mer (*Lodoicea seychellarum*), the single-seeded fruit of which may weigh 40 lb. *18 kg.* This grows only in the Seychelles, in the Indian Ocean.

Smallest The smallest seeds are those of *Epiphytic* orchids, at 35,000,000 to the oz. (*cf.* grass pollens at up to 6,000,000,000 grains/oz.). A single plant of the American ragweed can generate 8,000,000,000 pollen grains in five hours.

Most viable The most protracted claim for the viability of seeds are those of the Arctic lupin (*Lupinus arcticus*) found in frozen silt at Miller Creek in the Yukon, Canada in July 1954. They were germinated in 1966 and were dated by the radio carbon method of associated material to at least 8,000 B.C. and more probably to 13,000 B.C.

Most Conquering Conker The highest recorded battle honours for an untreated conker (fruit of the Common horse-chestnut or *Aesculus hippocastanum*) is a "five thousander plus", which won the BBC Conker Conquest in 1954. A professor of botany has however opined that this heroic specimen might well have been a 'ringer', probably an ivory or tagua nut (*Phytelephas macrocarpa*).

20. PARKS, ZOOS, AQUARIA AND OCEANARIA

PARKS

Largest World The world's largest park is the Wood Buffalo National Park in Alberta, Canada (established 1922), which has an area of 11,172,000 acres (17,560 miles² [*45 480 km²*]).

Britain The largest National Park in Great Britain is the Lake District National Park which has an area of 866 miles² *2 240 km².* The largest private park in the United Kingdom is Woburn Park (3,000 acres [*1 200 ha*]), near Woburn Abbey, the seat of the Dukes of Bedford. The largest common in the United Kingdom is Llansantffraed Cwmdauddwr (28,819 acres [*11 662 ha*]) in Powys, Wales.

ZOOS

Largest game reserve It has been estimated that throughout the world there are some 500 zoos with an estimated annual attendance of 330,000,000. The largest zoological preserve in the world has been the Etosha Reserve, South West Africa established in 1907 with an area which grew to 38,427 miles² *99 525 km².*

Largest collection The largest collection in any zoo is that in the Zoological Gardens of West Berlin, Germany. At 1 Jan. 1973 the zoo had a total of 13,373 specimens from 2,409 species. This total included 1,061 mammals (232 species), 2,808 birds (747 species), 623 reptiles (304 species), 307 amphibians (95 species), 2,351 fishes (775 species) and 6,223 invertebrates (256 species).

Oldest The earliest known collection of animals was that set up by Shulgi, a 3rd dynasty ruler of Ur in 2094–2047 B.C. at Puzarish in south-east Iraq. The oldest known zoo is that at Schönbrunn, Vienna, Austria, built in 1752 by the Holy Roman Emperor Franz I for his wife Maria Theresa. The oldest privately owned zoo in the world is that of the Zoological Society of London, founded in 1826. Its collection, housed partly in Regent's Park, London (36 acres [*14,5 ha*]) and partly at Whipsnade Park, Bedfordshire (541 acres [*219 ha*]), opened 22 May 1931 as the most comprehensive in the United Kingdom. At the stocktaking on 1 Jan. 1975 accounted for a total of 10,239 specimens. These comprised 1,828 mammals, 2,199 birds, 590 reptiles and amphibians, an estimated total of 3,018 fish and an estimated total of 2,604 invertibrates. Locusts, ants and bees are excluded from these figures. The record annual attendances are 3,031,571 in 1950 for Regent's Park and 756,758 in 1961 for Whipsnade.

AQUARIA

Largest aquarium The world's largest aquarium, as opposed to fish farm, is the John G. Shedd Aquarium on 12th Street and Grant Park, Chicago, Illinois, U.S.A. completed in November 1929 at a cost of $3,250,000 (now £1,354,166). The total capacity of its display tanks is 375,000 gal. *1,7 million litres* with reservoir tanks holding 1,665,000 gal *7,5 million litres*. Exhibited are 7,500 specimens from 350 species. Salt water is brought in road and rail tankers from Key West, Florida, and a tanker barge from the Gulf of Mexico. The record attendances are 78,658 in a day on 21 May 1931, and 4,689,730 visitors in the single year of 1931.

The largest marine mammal ever held in captivity was a female Pacific grey whale (*Eschrichtius gibbosus*), named "Gigi", who was captured in Scammon's lagoon, Baja California, Mexico, on 13 March 1971 and then transferred to the Sea World Aquarium in Mission Bay, San Diego, California, U.S.A. She measured 18 ft 2 in *5,53 m* in length on arrival, and weighed 4,300 lb. *1 950 kg.* She was released at sea off the San Diego coast on 13 March 1972, after she had grown to an unmanageable 27 ft *8,23 m* and 14,000 lb. *6 350 kg.*

OCEANARIA

Earliest and largest The world's first oceanarium is Marineland of Florida, opened in 1938 at a site 18 miles *29 km* south of St. Augustine, Florida, U.S.A. Up to 5,800,000 gal *26,3 million litres* of sea-water are pumped daily through two major tanks, one rectangular (100 ft [*30,48 m*] long by 40 ft [*12,19 m*] wide by 18 ft [*5,48 m*] deep) containing 375,000 gal *1.7 million litres* and one circular (233 ft [*71 m*] in circumference and 12 ft [*3,65 m*] deep) containing 330,000 gal *1,5 million litres*. The tanks are seascaped, including coral reefs and even a shipwreck. The salt water tank at the Marineland of the Pacific Palos Verdes Peninsula, California, U.S.A. is 251½ ft *76,65 m* in circumference and 22 ft *6,7 m* deep, with a capacity of 530,000 gal *2,4 million litres*. The total capacity of this whole oceanarium is 1,830,000 gal *8,3 million litres*.

THE EARTH

The Earth is not a true sphere, but flattened at the poles and hence an ellipsoid. The polar diameter of the Earth (7,899.809 miles [*12 713,510 km*]) is 26.576 miles *42,770 km* less than the equatorial diameter (7,926.385 miles [*12 756,280 km*]). The Earth also has a slight ellipticity of the equator since its long axis (about longitude 37° W) is 174 yds *159 m* greater than the short axis. The greatest departures from the reference ellipsoid are a protuberance of 244 ft *74 m* in the area of New Guinea and a depression of 354 ft *108 m* south of Sri Lanka, in the Indian Ocean.

The greatest circumference of the Earth, at the equator, is 24,901.47 miles *40 075,03 km*, compared with 24,859.75 miles *40 007,89 km* at the meridian. The area of the surface is estimated to be 196,937,600 miles² *510 066 100 km²*. The period of axial rotation, *i.e.* the true sidereal day, is 23 hrs 56 min 4.0996 sec, mean time.

The mass of the Earth is 5,882,000,000,000,000,000,000 tons *5 976 × 10¹⁸ tonnes* and its density is 5.517 times that of water. The volume is an estimated 259,875,620,000 miles³ *1 083 208 840 000 km³*. The Earth picks up cosmic dust but estimates vary widely with 40,000 tons/*tonnes* a day being the upper limit. Modern theory is that the Earth has an outer shell or lithosphere about 25 miles *40 km* thick, then an outer and inner rock layer or mantle extending 1,800 miles *2 900 km* deep, beneath which there is an iron-nickel core at an estimated temperature of 3 700° C *6,700° F*, and at a pressure of 22,000 tons/*tonnes* per in² or 3,400 kb. If the iron-nickel core theory is correct, iron must be by far the most abundant element in the Earth.

1. NATURAL PHENOMENA

EARTHQUAKES

Greatest
World It is estimated that each year there are some 500,000 detectable seismic or micro-seismic disturbances of which 100,000 can be felt and 1,000 cause damage.

Using the comparative scale of Mantle Wave magnitudes (defined in 1968), the world's largest earthquake since 1930 has been the cataclysmic Alaska, U.S.A., or Prince William Sound earthquake (epicentre Lat. 61° 10′ N., Long. 147° 48′ W.) of 1964 March 28 with a magnitude of 8.9. The Kamchatka, U.S.S.R., earthquake (epicentre Lat. 52° 45′ N., Long. 159° 30′ E.) of 1952 Nov. 4 and the shocks around Lebu, south of Concepción, Chile on 1960 May 22 are both now assessed at a magnitude of 8.8. Formerly the largest earthquake during this period had been regarded as the submarine shock (epicentre Lat. 39° 30′ N., Long. 144° 30′ E.) about 100 miles off the Sanriku coast of north-eastern Honshū, Japan of 1933 March 2 estimated at 8.9 on the Gutenberg-Richter scale (1956). It is possible that the earthquake in Lisbon, Portugal, of 1755 Nov. 1 would have been accorded a magnitude of between 8¾ and 9 if seismographs, invented in 1853, had been available to record traces. The first of the three shocks was at 9.40 a.m. and lasted for between 6 and 7 min. Lakes

in Norway were disturbed. The energy of an earthquake of magnitude 8.9 is about 5.6×10^{24} ergs, which is equivalent to 10,000 megatons—an explosion 100 times greater than the largest nuclear device ever detonated.

Worst
death roll
World The greatest loss of life occurred in the earthquake in Shensi Province, China, of 1556 Jan. 23, when an estimated 830,000 people were killed. The greatest material damage was in the earthquake on the Kwanto plain, Japan, of 1923 Sept. 1 (magnitude 8.2, epicentre in Lat. 35° 15′ N., Long. 139° 30′ E.). In Sagami Bay the sea-bottom in one area sank 400 m *1,310 ft*. The

official total of persons killed and missing in the *Shinsai* or great 'quake and the resultant fires was 142,807. In Tōkyō and Yokohama 575,000 dwellings were destroyed. The cost of the damage was estimated at £1,000 million (now more than £3,000 million).

Great The East Anglian or Colchester earthquake of 1884
Britain April 22 (9.18 a.m.) (epicentres Lat. 51° 48′ N., Long. 0° 53′ E., and Lat. 51° 51′ N., Long. 0° 55′ E.) caused damage estimated at £10,000 to 1,200 buildings, and the death of at least 4 people. Langenhoe Church was wrecked. Windows and doors were rattled over an area of 53,000 miles² *137 250 km²* and the shock was felt in Exeter and Ostend, Belgium. The most marked since 1884 and the worst since instruments have been in use (*i.e.* since 1927) occurred in the Midlands at 3.43 p.m. on 1957 Feb. 11, showing a strength of between five and six on the Davison scale. The strongest Scottish tremor occurred at Inverness at 10.45 p.m. on 1816 Aug. 13, and was felt over an area of 50,000 miles² *130 000 km²*. The strongest Welsh tremor occurred in Swansea at 9.45 a.m. on 1906 June 27 (epicentre Lat. 51° 38′ N., Long 4° W.). It was felt over an area of 37,800 miles² *97 900 km²*.

Ireland No earthquake with its epicentre in Ireland has ever been instrumentally measured, though the effects of remoter shocks have been felt. However, there was a shock in 1734 August which damaged 100 dwellings and five churches.

VOLCANOES

The total number of known active volcanoes in the world is 455 with an estimated 80 more that are submarine. The greatest active concentration is in Indonesia, where 77 of its 167 volcanoes have erupted within historic times. The name volcano derives from the now dormant Vulcano Island in the Aeolian group in the Mediterranean.

Greatest The total volume of matter discharged in the eruption
eruption of Tambora, a volcano on the island of Sumbawa, in Indonesia, 5–7 April 1815, has been estimated at 36.4 miles³ *151,7 km³*. The energy of this eruption was 8.4×10^{26} ergs. The volcano lost about 1 250 m *4,100 ft* in height and a crater seven miles *11 km* in diameter was formed. This compares with a probable 15 miles³ *62,5 km³* ejected by Santorini and 4.3 miles³ *18 km³* ejected by Krakatoa (see below). The internal pressure causing the Tambora eruption has been estimated at 46,500,000 lb./in² or more than 20,000 tons/in² *315 000 kg/cm²*.

Greatest The greatest volcanic explosion in historic times was
explosion the eruption in *c.* 1470 B.C. of Thira (Santorini), a volcanic island in the Aegean Sea. It is highly probable that this explosion destroyed the centres of the Minoan civilization in Crete, about 80 miles *130 km* away, with a *tsunami* 50 m *165 ft* high. Evidence was published in December 1967 of an eruption that spewed lava over 100,000 miles² *260 000 km²* of Oregon, Idaho, Nevada and northern California about 3,000,000 years ago.

The greatest explosion since Santorini occurred at *c.* 10 a.m. (local time), or 3.00 a.m. G.M.T., on 27 Aug. 1883, with an eruption of Krakatoa, an island (then 18 miles² [*47 km²*]) in the Sunda Strait, between Sumatra and Java, in Indonesia. A total of 163 villages were wiped out, and 36,380 people killed by the wave it caused. Rocks were thrown 34 miles *55 km* high and dust fell 3,313 miles *5 330 km* away 10 days later. The explosion was recorded four hours later on the island of Rodrigues, 2,968 miles *4 776 km* away, as "the roar of heavy guns" and was heard over 1/13th part of the surface of the globe. This explosion has been estimated to have had about 26 times the power of the greatest H-bomb test detonation but was still only a fifth part of the Santorini cataclysm.

Highest The highest extinct volcano in the world is Cerro
Extinct Aconcagua (22,834 ft [*6 960 m*]) on the Argentine side of the Andes. It was first climbed on 14 Jan. 1897 and was the highest summit climbed anywhere until 12 June 1907.

Dormant The highest dormant volcano is Volcán Llullaillaco (22,058 ft [*6 723 m*]), on the frontier between Chile and Argentina.

Active The highest volcano regarded as active is Volcán Antofalla (20,013 ft [*6 100 m*]), in Argentina, though a more definite claim is made for Volcán Guayatiri or Guallatiri (19,882 ft [*6 060 m*]), in Chile, which erupted in 1959.

Northern- The northernmost volcano is Beeren Berg (7,470 ft
most and [*2 276 m*]) on the island of Jan Mayen (71° 05′ N.) in
southern- the Greenland Sea. It erupted on 20 Sept. 1970 and the
most island's 39 inhabitants (all male) had to be evacuated. It was possibly discovered by Henry Hudson in 1607 or 1608, but definitely visited by Jan Jacobsz May (Netherlands) in 1614. It was annexed by Norway on 8 May 1929. The Ostenso seamount (5,825 ft [*1 775 m*]) 346 miles *556 km* from the North Pole in Lat. 85° 10′ N. Long 133° W was volcanic. The most southerly known active volcano is Mount Erebus (12,450 ft [*3 795 m*]) on Ross Island (77° 35′ S.), in Antarctica. It was discovered on 28 Jan. 1841 by the expedition of Captain (later Rear-Admiral Sir) James Clark Ross, R.N. (1800–1862), and first climbed at 10 a.m. on 10 March 1908 by a British party of five, led by Professor (later Lieut.-Col. Sir) Tannatt William Edgeworth David (1858–1934).

Largest The world's largest *caldera* or volcano crater is that of
crater Mount Aso (5,223 ft [*1 590 m*]) in Kyūshū, Japan, which measures 17 miles *27 km* north to south, 10 miles *16 km* east to west and 71 miles *114 km* in circumference. The longest lava flows known as *pahoehoe* (twisted cord-like solidifications) are 60 miles *96 km* in length in Iceland.

GEYSERS

World's The Waimangu geyser, in New Zealand, erupted to a
tallest height in excess of 1,500 ft *457 m* in 1904, but has not been active since it erupted violently in 1917. Currently the world's tallest active geyser is the U.S. National Parks' Service Steamboat Geyser, which from 1962–1969 erupted with intervals ranging from 5 days to 10 months to a height of 250–380 ft *76–115 m*. The most frequently erupting geyser is the nearby "Old Faithful", whose 90–180 ft spire rarely varies more than 21 minutes either side of its 66 min. average. The *Geysir* ("gusher") near Mount Hekla in south-central Iceland, from which all others have been named, spurts, on occasions, to 180 ft *55 m*.

2. STRUCTURES AND DIMENSIONS

OCEANS

Largest The area of the Earth covered by sea is estimated to be 139,670,000 miles² *361 740 000 km²* or 70.92 per cent of the total surface. The mean depth of the hydrosphere was once estimated to be 12,450 ft *3 795 m*, but recent surveys suggest a lower estimate, of 11,660 ft *3 554 m*. The total weight of the water is estimated to be 1.3×10^{18} tons, or 0.022 per cent of the Earth's total weight. The volume of the oceans is estimated to be 308,400,000 miles³ *1 285 600 000 km³* compared with only 8,400,000 miles³ *35 000 000 km³* of fresh water.

The largest ocean in the world is the Pacific. Excluding adjacent seas, it represents 45.8 per cent of the world's oceans and is about 63,800,000 miles² *165 250 000 km²* in area. The shortest navigable trans-Pacific distance from Guayaquil, Ecuador to Bangkok, Thailand is 10,905 miles *17 550 km*.

The highest geyser eruption this century the Waimangu, New Zealand which played daily up to 1,000 ft *300 m* in 1902-05

Longest voyage The longest possible great circle sea voyage is one of 19,860 miles *31 960 km* from a point 150 miles *240 km* west of Karachi, Pakistan to a point 200 miles *320 km* north of Uka' Kamchatka *via* the Mozambique Channel, Drake Passage and Bering Sea.

Most southerly The most southerly part of the oceans is 85° 34′ S., 154° W., at the snout of the Robert Scott Glacier, 305 miles *490 km* from the South Pole.

Deepest *World* The deepest part of the ocean was first discovered in 1951 by H.M. Survey Ship *Challenger* in the Marianas Trench in the Pacific Ocean. The depth was measured by sounding and by echo-sounder and published as 5,960 fathoms (35,760 ft [*10 900 m*]). Subsequent visits to the Challenger Deep have resulted in claims by echo-sounder only, culminating in one of 6,033 fathoms (36,198 ft [*11 033 m*]) or 6.85 miles by the U.S.S.R.'s research ship *Vityaz* in March 1959. On 23 Jan. 1960 the U.S. Navy bathyscaphe *Trieste* descended to 35,820 ft *10 917 m*. A metal object, say a pound ball of steel, dropped into water above this trench would take nearly 63 min to fall to the sea-bed 6.85 miles *11,03 km* below. The average depth of the Pacific Ocean is 14,000 ft *4 267 m*.

British waters The deepest point in the territorial waters of the United Kingdom is an area 6 cables (1,200 yds) off the island of Raasay, Highland, in the Inner Sound at Lat 57° 30′ 33″ N, Long. 5° 57′ 27″ W. A depth of 1,038 ft (173 fathoms) was found in Dec. 1959 by H.M.S. *Yarnton* (Lt.-Cdr. A. C. F. David, R.N.).

Sea temperature The temperature of the water at the surface of the sea varies from −2° C (*28.5° F*) in the White Sea to 35.6° C (*96° F*) in the shallow areas of the Persian Gulf in summer. A freak geo-thermal temperature of 56° C (*132.8° F*) was recorded in February 1965 by the survey

ship *Atlantis II* near the bottom of Discovery Deep (7,200 ft [*2 195 m*]) in the Red Sea. Ice-focused solar rays have been known to heat lake water to nearly 80° F *26,6° C*. The normal sea temperature in the area is 22° C (*71.6° F*).

Remotest spot from land The world's most distant point from land is a spot in the South Pacific, approximately 48° 30′ S., 125° 30′ W., which is about 1,660 miles *2 670 km* from the nearest points of land, namely Pitcairn Island, Ducie Island and Cape Dart, Antarctica. Centred on this spot, therefore, is a circle of water with an area of about 8,657,000 miles² *22 421 500 km²*—about 7,000 miles² *18 000 km²* larger than the U.S.S.R., the world's largest country (see Chapter 11).

Largest sea The largest of the world's seas (as opposed to oceans) is the South China Sea, with an area of 1,148,500 miles² *2 974 600 km²*. The Malayan Sea comprising the waters between the Indian Ocean and the South Pacific, south of the Chinese mainland covering 3,144,000 miles² *8 142 900 km²* is not now an entity accepted by the International Hydrographic Bureau.

Largest gulf The largest gulf in the world is the Gulf of Mexico, with an area of 580,000 miles² *1 500 000 km²* and a shoreline of 3,100 miles *4 990 km* from Cape Sable, Florida, U.S.A., to Cabo Catoche, Mexico.

Largest bay The largest bay in the world is the Bay of Bengal, with a shoreline of 2,250 miles *3 620 km* from south-eastern Ceylon to Pagoda Point, Burma. Its mouth measures 1,075 miles *1 730 km* across. Great Britain's largest bay is Cardigan Bay which has a 140 mile *225 km* long shoreline and measures 72 miles *116 km* across from the Lleyn Peninsula, Gwynedd to St. David's Head, Dyfed in Wales.

Highest seamount The highest known submarine mountain, or seamount is one discovered in 1953 near the Tonga Trench, between Samoa and New Zealand. It rises 28,500 ft *8 690 m* from the sea bed, with its summit 1,200 ft *365 m* below the surface.

STRAITS

Longest The longest straits in the world are the Tartarskiy Proliv or Tartar Straits between Sakhalin Island and the U.S.S.R. mainland running from the Sea of Japan to Sakhalinsky Zaliv. This distance is 800 km *497 miles*—thus marginally longer than the Malacca Straits.

Broadest The broadest named straits in the world are the Davis Straits between Greenland and Baffin Island which at one point narrow to 210 miles *338 km*. The Drake Passage between the Diego Ramirez Islands, Chile and the South Shetland Islands is 710 miles *1 140 km* across.

Narrowest The narrowest navigable straits are those between the Aegean island of Euboea and the mainland of Greece.

The gap is only 45 yds *40 m* wide at Chalkis. The Seil Sound, Argyllshire, Scotland, narrows to a point only 20 ft *6 m* wide where a bridge joins the island of Seil to the mainland and is thus said to span the Atlantic.

HIGHEST WAVES

The highest officially recorded sea wave was measured by Lt. Frederic Margraff U.S.N. from the U.S.S. *Ramapo* proceeding from Manila, Philippines, to San Diego, California, U.S.A., on the night of 6–7 Feb. 1933, during a 68-knot (78.3 m.p.h. [*126 km/h*]) gale. The wave was computed to be 112 ft *34 m* from trough to crest. A stereo photograph of a wave calculated to be 24,9 m (*81.7 ft*) high was taken from the U.S.S.R.'s diesel-electric vessel *Ob'* in the South Pacific Ocean, about 600 km *370 miles* south of Macquarie Island, on 2 April 1956. The highest instrumentally measured wave was one 77 ft *23,5 m* high, recorded by the British ship *Weather Adviser* on station Juliette, in the North Atlantic at noon on 17 March 1968. Its length was 1,150 ft *350 m* and its period was 15 sec. It has been calculated on the statistics of the Stationary Random Theory that one wave in more than 300,000 may exceed the average by a factor of 4.

On 9 July 1958 a landslip caused a wave to wash 1,740 ft *530 m* high along the fjord-like Lituya Bay, Alaska, U.S.A.

Seismic wave The highest recorded *tsunami* (often wrongly called a tidal wave), was one of 220 ft *67 m* which appeared off Valdez, south-west Alaska, after the great Prince William Sound earthquake of 28 March 1964. *Tsunami* (a Japanese word which is singular and plural) have been observed to travel at 490 m.p.h. *790 km/h*. Between 479 B.C. and 1967 there were 286 instances of devastating *tsunami*.

CURRENTS

Greatest The greatest current in the oceans of the world is the Antarctic Circumpolar Current or West Wind Drift Current which was measured in 1969 in the Drake Passage between South America and Antarctica to be flowing at a rate of 9,500 million ft³ *270 000 000 m³* per sec—nearly treble that of the Gulf Stream. Its width ranges from 185 to 1,240 miles *300 to 2 000 km* and has a surface flow rate of ¾ of a knot *1,4 km/h*.

Strongest The world's strongest currents are the Saltstraumen in the Satlfjord, near Bodø, Norway, which reach 15.6 knots (18.0 m.p.h. *29 km/h*). The flow rate through the 500-ft *150 m* wide channel surpasses 500,000 cu secs *14 250 m³/sec*. The fastest current in British territorial waters is 10.7 knots *19,8 km/h* in the Pentland Firth between the Orkney Islands and Highland, Scotland's northernmost mainland region.

GREATEST TIDES

Extreme tides are due to lunar and solar gravitational forces affected by their perigee, perihelion and conjunctions. Barometric and wind effects can superimpose an added "Surge" element. Coastal and sea-floor configurations can accentuate these forces.

World The greatest tides in the world occur in the Bay of Fundy, which separates Nova Scotia, Canada, from the United States' north-easternmost state of Maine and the Canadian province of New Brunswick. Burncoat Head in the Minas Basin, Nova Scotia, has the greatest mean spring range with 47.5 ft *14,50 m* and an extreme range of 53.5 ft *16,30 m*.

United Kingdom The place with the greatest mean spring range in Great Britain is Beachley, on the Severn, with a range of 40.7 ft *12,40 m*, compared with the British Isles' average of 15 ft *4,57 m*. Prior to 1933 tides as high as 28.9 ft *8,80 m* above and 22.3 ft *6,80 m* below datum (total range 51.2 ft [*15,60 m*]) were recorded at Avonmouth though an extreme range of 52.2 ft *15,90 m* for Beachley was officially accepted. In 1883 a freak tide of greater range was reported from Chepstow, Gwent.

Ireland The greatest mean spring tidal range in Ireland is 17.3 ft *5,27 m* at Mellon, Limerick, on the banks of the River Shannon.

ICEBERGS

Largest The largest iceberg on record was an Antarctic tabular 'berg of over 12,000 miles² *31 000 km²* (208 miles [*335 km*]) long and 60 miles [*97 km*] wide and thus larger than Belgium) sighted 150 miles *240 km* west of Scott Island, in the South Pacific Ocean, by the U.S.S. *Glacier* on 12 Nov. 1956. The 200-ft *61 m* thick Arctic ice island T.1 (140 miles² [*360 km²*]) was discovered in 1946, and was still being plotted in 1963.

Most southerly Arctic The most southerly Arctic iceberg was sighted in the Atlantic in 30° 50′ N., 45° 06′ W., on 2 June 1934. The tallest on record was one calved off north-west Greenland with 550 ft *165 m* above the surface. The southernmost iceberg reported in British home waters was one sighted 60 miles *96 km* from Smith's Knoll, on the Dogger Bank, in the North Sea.

Most northerly Antarctic The most northerly Antarctic iceberg was a remnant sighted in the Atlantic by the ship *Dochra* in Latitude 26° 30′ S., Longitude 25° 40′ W., on 30 April 1894.

LAND

There is satisfactory evidence that at one time the Earth's land surface comprised a single primeval continent of 80 million miles² *2 × 10⁸ m²*, now termed Pangaea, and that this split about 190,000,000 years ago, during the Jurassic period, into two super-continents, termed Laurasia (Eurasia, Greenland and Northern America) in the north and Gondwanaland (Africa, Arabia, India, South America, Oceania and Antarctica) and named after Gondwana, India. The South Pole was apparently in the area of the Sahara as recently as the Ordovician period of c. 450 million years ago.

ROCKS

The age of the Earth is generally considered to be within the range of 4600 ± 100 million years, by analogy with directly measured ages of meteorites and of the moon. However, no rocks of this great age have yet been found on the Earth since geological processes have presumably destroyed the earliest record.

Oldest World The greatest recorded age for any reliably dated rock is 3,800 ± 100 million years for granite gneiss rock found near Granite Falls in the Minnesota river valley, U.S.A. as measured by the lead-isotope and rubidium-uranium methods by the U.S. Geological Survey and announced on 26 Jan. 1975. These metamorphic samples compare with the Amitsoq gneiss from Godthaab, Greenland assessed at between 3700 and 3750 million years.

Britain A considerable proportion of the Lewisian Complex of north west Highland, Scotland and of the Outer Hebrides has been proved to be 2800–2900 million years old by measurements using the rubidium-strontium and uranium-lead methods.

Largest The largest exposed rocky outcrop is the 1,237-ft *377 m* high Mount Augustus (3,627 ft [*1 105 m*] above sea-level), discovered on 3 June 1858, 200 miles *320 km* east of Carnarvon, Western Australia. It is an up-faulted monoclinal gritty conglomerate 5 miles *8 km* long and 2 miles *3 km* across and thus twice the size of the celebrated monolithic arkose Ayer's Rock (1,100 ft [*335 m*]), 250 miles *400 km* south-west of Alice Springs, in Northern Territory, Australia.

CONTINENTS

Largest Only 29.08 per cent, or an estimated 57,270,000 miles² *148 330 000 km²* of the Earth's surface is land, with a mean height of 2,480 ft *756 m* above sea-level. The Eurasian land mass is the largest, with an area (including islands) of 21,053,000 miles² *54 527 000 km²*.

Smallest The smallest is the Australian mainland, with an area of about 2,940,000 miles² *7 614 500 km²*, which, together with Tasmania, New Zealand, New Guinea and the Pacific Islands, is described sometimes as Oceania. The total area of Oceania is about 3,450,000 miles² *8 935 000 km²* including West Irian (formerly West New Guinea), which is politically in Asia.

Land remotest from the sea *World* There is an as yet unpinpointed spot in the Dzoosotoyn Elisen (desert), northern Sinkiang, China, that is more than 1,500 miles *2 400 km* from the open sea in any direction. The nearest large town to this point is Wulumuchi (Urumchi) to its south.

Great Britain The point furthest from the sea in Great Britain is a point near Meriden, West Midlands, England, which is 72½ miles *117 km* equidistant from the Severn Bridge, the Dee and Mersey estuaries and the Welland estuary in the Wash. The equivalent point in Scotland is in the Forest of Atholl, north west Tayside 40½ miles *65 km* equidistant from the head of Loch Leven, Inverness Firth and the Firth of Tay.

Peninsula The world's largest peninsula is Arabia, with an area of about 1,250,000 miles² *3 250 000 km²*.

ISLANDS

Largest *World* Discounting Australia, which is usually regarded as a continental land mass, the largest island in the world is Greenland (part of the Kingdom of Denmark), with an area of about 840,000 miles² *2 175 000 km²*. There is some evidence that Greenland is in fact several islands overlayed by an ice-cap.

Great Britain The mainland of Great Britain (Scotland, England and Wales) is the eighth largest in the world, with an area of 84,186 miles² *218 041 km²*. It stretches 603½ miles *971 km* from Dunnet Head in the north to Lizard Point in the south and 287½ miles *463 km* across from Porthaflod, Dyfed to Lowestoft, Suffolk. The island of Ireland (32,594 miles² [*84 418 km²*]) is the 20th largest in the world.

Details of the 1,040 British Islands will appear in the forthcoming **Guinness Book of British Islands.**

Freshwater The largest island surrounded by fresh water is the Ilha de Marajó (1,553 miles² [*4 022 km²*]), in the mouth of the River Amazon, Brazil. The world's largest inland island (*i.e.* land surrounded by rivers) is Ilha do Bananal, Brazil. The largest island in a lake is Manitoulin Island (1,068 miles² [*2 766 km²*]) in the Canadian (Ontario) section of Lake Huron. This island itself has on it a lake of 41.09 miles² *106,42 km²* called Manitou Lake, in which there are several islands. The largest lake island in Great Britain is Inchmurrin in Loch Lomond Strathclyde/Central, Scotland with an area of 284 acres *115 ha*.

Remotest *World* *Uninhabited* The remotest island in the world is Bouvet Øya (formerly Liverpool Island), discovered in the South Atlantic by J. B. C. Bouvet de Lozier on 1 Jan. 1739, and first landed on by Capt. George Norris on 16 Dec. 1825. Its position is 54° 26′ S., 3° 24′ E. This uninhabited Norwegian dependency is about 1,050 miles *1 700 km* from the nearest land—the uninhabited Queen Maud Land coast of eastern Antarctica.

Inhabited The remotest inhabited island in the world is Tristan da Cunha, discovered in the South Atlantic by Tristao da Cunha, a Portuguese admiral, in March 1506. It has an area of 38 miles² *98 km²* (habitable area 12 miles² [*31 km²*]) and was annexed by the United Kingdom on 14 Aug. 1816. The island's population was 235 in August 1966. The nearest inhabited land is the island of St. Helena, 1,320 miles *2 120 km* to the north-east. The nearest continent, Africa is 1,700 miles *2 735 km* away.

British The remotest of the British islets is Rockall 191 miles *307 km* west of St. Kilda, allocated to the County of Inverness in 1971. This 70-ft *21 m* high rock measuring 83 ft *25 m* across was not formally annexed until 18 Sept. 1955. The remotest British island which has ever been inhabited is North Rona which is 44 miles *70,8 km* from the next nearest land at Cape Wrath and the Butt of Lewis. It was evacuated c. 1844. Muckle Flugga, off Unst, in the Shetlands, is the

The world's remotest island Bouvet Øya first landed on in 1825

Norsk Polarinstitutt

Geodeatisk Institut

The world's most northerly chip of land discovered in 1921, north of Greenland Kaffeklubben Oyen

northernmost inhabited with a population of 3 (1971) and is in a latitude north of southern Greenland. Just to the north of it is Out Stack.

Newest The world's newest island is a volcanic one about 100 ft *30 m* high, which began forming in 1970 south of Gatukai Island in the British Solomon Islands, southwest Pacific.

Greatest archipelago The world's greatest archipelago is the 3,500-mile *5 600 km* long crescent of more than 13,000 islands which forms Indonesia.

Northern-most land The most northerly land is Kaffeklubben Øyen (Coffee Club Island) off the north-east of Greenland, 440 miles *708 km* from the North Pole, discovered by Dr. Lange Koch in 1921, but determined only in June 1969 to be in Latitude 83° 40′ 6″.

Largest atoll The largest atoll in the world is Kwajalein in the Marshall Islands, in the central Pacific Ocean. Its slender 176-mile *283 km* long coral reef encloses a lagoon of 1,100 miles² *2 850 km²*. The atoll with the largest land area is Christmas Island, in the Line Islands, in the central Pacific Ocean. It has an area of 184 miles² *477 km²*. Its two principal settlements, London and Paris, are 4 miles *6 km* apart.

Longest reef The longest reef is the Great Barrier Reef off Queensland, north-eastern Australia, which is 1,260 geographical miles *2 027 km* in length. Between 1959 and 1971 a large section between Cooktown and Townsville was destroyed by the proliferation of the Crown of Thorns starfish (*Acanthaster planci*).

DEPRESSIONS

Deepest World The deepest depression so far discovered is beneath the Hollick-Kenyon Plateau in Marie Byrd Land, Antarctica, where, at a point 5,900 ft *1 800 m* above sea-level, the ice depth is 14,000 ft *4 267 m*, hence indicating a bed rock depression 8,100 ft *2 468 m* below sea-level. The greatest submarine depression is a large area of the floor of the north west Pacific which has an average depth of 15,000 ft *4 570 m*.

The deepest exposed depression on land is the shore surrounding the Dead Sea, 1,291 ft *393 m* below sea-level. The deepest point on the bed of this lake is 2,600 ft *792 m* below the Mediterranean. The deepest part of the bed of Lake Baykal in Siberia, U.S.S.R., is 4,872 ft *1 484 m* below sea-level.

Great Britain The lowest lying area in Great Britain is in the Holme Fen area of the Great Ouse, in Cambridgeshire, at 9 ft *2,75 m* below sea-level. The deepest depression in England is the bed of part of Windermere, 94 ft *28,65 m* below sea-level, and in Scotland the bed of Loch Morar, Highland 987 ft *300,8 m* below sea-level.

Largest The largest exposed depression in the world is the Caspian Sea basin in the Azerbaydzhani, Russian, Kazakh and Turkmen Republics of the U.S.S.R. and northern Iran (Persia). It is more than 200,000 miles² *518 000 km²* of which 143,550 miles² *371 792 km²* is lake area. The preponderant land area of the depression is the Prikaspiyskaya Nizmennost', lying around the northern third of the lake and stretching inland for a distance of up to 280 miles *450 km*.

CAVES

Longest The most extensive cave system in the world is that under the Mammoth Cave National Park, Kentucky, U.S.A. first discovered in 1799. On 9 Sept. 1972 an exploration group led by Dr. John P. Wilcox completed a connection, pioneered by Mrs. Patricia Crowther on 30 Aug., between the Flint Ridge Cave System and the Mammoth Cave system so making a combined system with a total mapped passageway length of 157 miles *252 km*. The longest cave system in Great Britain is Ogof Ffynnon Ddu, Powys, in which 23.92 miles *38,5 km* of passages have so far been surveyed.

DEEPEST CAVES BY COUNTRIES
These depths are subject to continuous revisions

Ft below Entrance	m		
3,842	1 171	Resea de la Pierre Saint-Martin, Pyrenees	France-Spain
3,743	1 143	Gouffre Berger, Sornin Plateau, Vercors	France
3,018	920	Abisso Michele Gortani	Italy
2,802	854	Grüberhornhöle Dachstein	Austria
2,798	853	Sumidero de Cellagua, Cantabria	Spain
2,651	808	Hölloch, Muotathal, Schwyz	Switzerland
2,467	752	Jaskini Sniezny Tatras	Poland
2,463	751	Ghar Parau, Zagros Mountains	Iran
2,221	676	Kef Toghobeit	Morroco
2,211	674	Poloska Jama	Yugoslavia
2,040	621	Gouffre de Faour Dara	Lebanon
2,009	612	El Sótano de San Agustin*	Mexico
1,885	574	Ragge favreraige	Norway
1,720	524	Arctomys Pot, Mt. Robson, Brit. Columbia	Canada
1,690	515	Anou Boussouil, Djurdjura	Algeria
1,620	493	Bibina Cave, Kundiawa	Papua New Guinea
1,454	443	Epos Cavern	Greece
1,350	411	Oumi Senri	Japan
1,336	407	La Cima de Milpo	Peru
1,312†	400	Schachta Oktjabviskaya, Crimea	U.S.S.R.
1,184	361	Neffs Canyon Cave, Utah	U.S.A.
1,171	356	Harwood Hole	New Zealand
1,115	340	Izvorul Tausoarelor, Rodna	Romania
1,053	321	Khazad-Dum, Tasmania	Australia
1,010	307	Ogof Ffynnon Ddu	Wales
642	196	Oxlow Cavern, Giant's Hole, Derbyshire	England
460	140	Carrowmore, Co. Sligo	Ireland

* This cave has the longest vertical pitch of 410 m 1,345 ft.
† A cave of 750 m 2,460 ft has been reported but not named in the USSR

Longest stalactite The longest known stalactite in the world is a wall-supported column extending 195 ft *59 m* from roof to floor in the Cueva de Nerja, near Málaga, Spain. The rather low tensile strength of calcite (calcium carbonate) precludes very long free-hanging stalactites, but one of 38 ft *11,60 m* exists in the Poll an Ionain cave in County Clare, Ireland.

Tallest stalagmite The tallest known stalagmite in the world is La Grande Stalagmite in the Aren Armand cave, Lozère, France, which has attained a height of 98 ft *29 m* from the cave floor. It was found in September 1897.

MOUNTAINS

Highest World An eastern Himalayan peak of 29,028 ft *8 848 m* above sea-level on the Tibet-Nepal border (in an area first designated Chu-mu-lang-ma on a map of 1717) was discovered to be the world's highest mountain in 1852 by the Survey Department of the Government of India, from theodolite readings taken in 1849 and

HIGHEST POINTS IN THE GEOGRAPHICAL DIVISIONS OF THE UNITED KINGDOM
AND THE REPUBLIC OF IRELAND

Numbers in brackets indicate the order of the divisions with the highest point. New Administration Areas became operative in England and Wales on 1 April 1974 and in Scotland on 16 May 1975.

	Height in ft	Height in m	Location
ENGLAND 46 Geographical counties			
Avon	870	265	Southern boundary
Bedfordshire	798	243	Dunstable Downs
Berkshire	974	296	Walbury Hill
Buckinghamshire	857	261	near Aston Hill
Cambridgeshire	478	145	300 yds 275 m south of the Hall, Great Chishill
Cheshire (10)	1,834	559	Shining Tor
Cleveland	1,078	328	Hob on the Hill
Cornwall	1,377	419	Brown Willy
Cumbria (1)	3,210	978	SCAFELL PIKE
Derbyshire (6)	2,088	636	Kinder Scout
Devon (8)	2,038	621	High Willhays
Dorset	908	276	Pilsdon Pen
Durham (3)	2,591	798	Mickle Fell
East Sussex	813	247	Ditchling Beacon
Essex	480	146	In High Wood, Langley
Gloucestershire	1,083	330	Cleeve Cloud
Greater Manchester	1,774	540	Featherbed Moss
Hampshire	937	285	Pilot Hill
Hereford and Worcester (5)	2,306	702	in Black Mountains
Hertfordshire	802	244	Hastoe
Humberside	807	246	Cot Nab
Isle of Wight	785	239	St. Boniface Down
Kent	824	251	Westerham (old fort trig. point)
Lancashire (7)	2,057	626	Gragareth
Leicestershire	912	277	Bardon Hill
Lincolnshire	550	167	Normanby-le-Wold
London, Greater	809	246	33 yds 30 m S.E. of "Westerham Heights" (a house) on the Kent-G.L.C. boundary
Merseyside	588	179	Billinge Hill
Norfolk	335	102	Sandy Lane, east of Sheringham
Northamptonshire	734	223	Arbury Hill
Northumberland (2)	2,676	815	The Cheviot
North Yorkshire (4)	2,419	737	Whernside
Nottinghamshire	652	198	Herrod's Hill
Oxfordshire	856	260	White Horse Hill
Salop	1,772	540	Brown Clee Hill
Somerset	1,705	519	Dunkery Beacon
Staffordshire	1,684	513	Oliver Hill
South Yorkshire	1,791	545	Margery Hill
Suffolk	420	128	Rede
Surrey	965	294	Leith Hill
Tyne and Wear	851	259	Nr. Chopwell
Warwickshire	854	260	Ilmington Downs
West Midlands	876	267	Turner's Hill
West Sussex	919	280	Blackdown Hill
West Yorkshire (9)	1,908	581	Black Hill
Wiltshire	964	293	Milk Hill and Tan Hill

	Height in ft	Height in m	Location
SCOTLAND 12 Geographical regions (formerly 33 counties)			
Borders	2,756	840	Broad Law
Central (4)	3,852	1 174	Ben More
Dumfries and Galloway (6)	2,770	844	Merrick
Fife	1,713	522	West Lomond

	Height in ft	Height in m	Location
Grampian (2)	4,296	1 309	Ben Macdhui
Highland (1)	4,406	1 342	BEN NEVIS
Lothian	2,137	651	Blackhope Scar
Orkney	1,570	478	Ward Hill, Hoy
Shetland (Zetland)	1,486	452	Ronas Hill, Mainland
Strathclyde (5)	3,766	1 147	Bidean nam Bian
Tayside (3)	3,984	1 214	Ben Lawers
Western Isles	2,622	799	Clisham, Harris

	Height in ft	Height in m	Location
WALES 8 Geographical counties			
Clwyd (3)	2,713	826	Moel Sych
Dwfed (4)	2,500+	762+	Carmarthen Fan Foel
Gwent (5)	2,228	679	Chwarel-y-Fan
Gwynedd (1)	3,560	1 085	SNOWDON (Yr Wyddfa)
Mid Glamorgan (7)	c. 1,920	585	on boundary
Powys (2)	2,907	885	Pen-y-Fan (Cader Arthur)
South Glamorgan (8)	451	137	Nr. St. Hilary
West Glamorgan (6)	1,969	600	Cefnffordd

NORTHERN IRELAND

The former six counties of Northern Ireland have now been divided into 26 Districts. The highest point in Northern Ireland is Slieve Donard (formerly in County Down) at 2,796 ft 852 m.

	Height in ft	Height in m	Location
†REPUBLIC OF IRELAND 26 Geographical counties			
Carlow (6)	2,610	795	Mount Leinster*
Cavan	2,188	666	Cuilcagh
Clare	1,746	532	Glennagalliagh
Cork	2,321	707	Knockboy
Donegal	2,466	751	Errigal
Dublin	2,475	754	Kippure
Galway	2,395	729	Benbaun
Kerry (1)	3,414	1 040	CARRAUNTOOHILL
Kildare	1,248	380	Cupidstown Hill
Kilkenny	1,694	516	Brandon
Leitrim	2,113	644	Truskmore (slopes)
Leix	1,734	528	Arderin*
Limerick (3)	3,018	919	Galtymore*
Longford	916	279	Cornhill
Louth	1,935	589	Slieve Foye
Mayo (5)	2,688	819	Mweelrea
Meath	911	277	Carnbane East
Monaghan	1,250	381	Slieve Beagh (slopes)
Offaly	1,734	528	Arderin*
Roscommon	c. 1,350	411	Corry Mountain (slopes)
Sligo	2,120	646	Truskmore
Tipperary (3)	3,018	919	Galtymore*
Waterford (8)	2,609	795	Knockmealdown
Westmeath	855	260	Mullaghmeen
Wexford (6)	2,610	795	Mount Leinster*
Wicklow (2)	3,039	926	Lugnaquillia

† Relative to the Poolbeg (Dublin) datum.   * Shared point.

1850. In 1860 its height was computed to be 29,002 ft 8 840 m. The 5½ mile 8,85 km peak was named Mount Everest after Sir George Everest, C.B. (1790–1866), formerly Surveyor-General of India. After a total loss of 11 lives since the first reconnaissance in 1921, Everest was finally conquered at 11.30 a.m. on 29 May 1953. (For details of ascents, see under Mountaineering in Chapter 12.) The mountain whose summit is farthest from the Earth's centre is the Andean peak of Chimborazo (20,561 ft [6 267 m]), 98 miles 158 km south of the equator in Ecuador, South America. Its summit is 7,057 ft 2 150 m further from the Earth's centre than the summit of Mt. Everest. The highest mountain on the equator is Volcán Gayambe (19,285 ft [5 878 m]), Ecuador, in Long. 83°.

The highest insular mountain in the world is the unsurveyed Djajatop formerly Mount Sukarno, formerly Carstensz Pyramide in Irian Jaya, Indonesia formerly Netherlands New Guinea. According to cross-checked altimeter estimates, it is 16,500 ft 5 030 m high.

Highest U.K. and Ireland The highest mountain in the United Kingdom is Ben Nevis (4,406 ft [1 343 m] excluding the 12-ft [3,65 m] cairn), 4¼ miles 6,85 km south-east of Fort William, Highland, Scotland. It was climbed before 1720 but was not discovered to be higher than Ben Macdhui (4,300 ft [1 310 m]) until 1870. In 1830 Ben Macdhui and Ben Nevis (Gaelic, Beinn Nibheis) were respectively quoted as 4,418 ft 1 346 m and 4,358 ft 1 328 m.

There is some evidence that, before being ground down by the ice-cap, mountains in the Loch Bà area of the Island of Mull were 15,000 ft 4 575 m above sea-level.

Peaks over 3,000 ft There are 577 peaks and tops over 3,000 ft 915 m in the whole British Isles and 165 peaks and 136 tops in Scotland higher than England's highest point, Scafell Pike. The highest mountain off the mainland is Sgùrr Alasdair (3,309 ft [1 008 m]) on Skye named after Alexander (in Gaelic Alasdair) Nicolson, who made the first ascent in 1873.

Kangbachan (25,925 ft 7 900 m) in the Himalaya, whose 10 year reign as the highest unclimbed mountain was ended in 1974

Highest unclimbed Excluding Gasherbrum III (26,090 ft [7 952 m]) in the Karakoram, the highest unclimbed separate mountain is now Batura Peak (25,540 ft [7 784 m]) in the Karakoram. These rank, respectively, 15th and 30th in height in the world.

Largest The world's tallest mountain measured from its submarine base (3,280 fathoms [6 000 m]) in the Hawaiian Trough to peak is Mauna Kea (Mountain White) on the Island of Hawaii, with a combined height of 33,476 ft 10 203 m of which 13,796 ft 4 205 m are above sea-level. Another mountain whose dimensions, but not height, exceed those of Mount Everest is the Hawaiian peak of Mauna Loa (Mountain Long) at 13,680 ft 4 170 m. The axes of its elliptical base, 16,322 ft 4 975 m below sea-level, have been estimated at 74 miles 119 km and 53 miles 85 km. It should be noted that Cerro Aconcagua (22,834 ft [6 960 m]) is more than 38,800 ft 11 826 m above the 16,000 ft 4 875 m deep Pacific abyssal plain or 42,834 ft 13 055 m above the Peru-Chile Trench which is 180 miles 290 km distant in the South Pacific.

Greatest ranges The world's greatest land mountain range is the Himalaya-Karakoram, which contains 96 of the world's 109 peaks of over 24 000 ft 7 315 m. The greatest of all mountain ranges is, however, the submarine mid-Atlantic Ridge, which is 10,000 miles 16 100 km long and 500 miles 805 km wide, with its highest peak being Mount Pico in the Azores, which rises 23,615 ft 7 198 m from the ocean floor (7,615 ft [2 320 m] above sea-level).

Greatest plateau The most extensive high plateau in the world is the Tibetan Plateau in Central Asia. The average altitude is 16,000 ft 4 875 m and the area is 77,000 miles² 200 000 km².

Sheerest Wall The 3,200 ft 975 m wide northwest face of Half Dome, Yosemite, California U.S.A. is 2,200 ft 670 m high but nowhere departs more than 7 degrees from the vertical.

Highest halites Along the northern shores of the Gulf of Mexico for 725 miles 1 160 km there exist 330 subterranean "mountains" of salt, some of which rise more than 60,000 ft 18 300 m from bed rock and appear as the low salt domes first discovered in 1862.

Largest swamp The world's largest tract of swamp is in the basin of the Pripet or Pripyat River—a tributary of the Dnieper in the U.S.S.R. These swamps cover an estimated area of 18,125 miles² 46 950 km².

Sand dunes The world's highest measured sand dunes are those in the Saharan sand sea of Isaouane-N-Tiferine of east central Algeria in Lat. 26° 42′ N, Long. 6° 43′ E. They have a wavelength of nearly 3 miles 5 km and attain a height of 430 metres [1,410 ft].

62

RIVERS

The river systems of the world are estimated to contain 55,000 miles³ 230 000 km³ of fresh water.

Longest World The two longest rivers in the world are the Amazon (*Amazonas*), flowing into the South Atlantic, and the Nile (*Bahr-el-Nil*) flowing into the Mediterranean. Which is the longer is more a matter of definition than of simple measurement.

The true source of the Amazon was discovered in 1953 to be a stream named Huarco, rising near the summit of Cerro Huagra (17,188 ft [5 238 m]) in Peru. This stream progressively becomes the Toro then the Santiago then the Apurímac, which in turn is known as the Ene and then the Tambo before its confluence with the Amazon prime tributary the Ucayali. The length of the Amazon from this source to the South Atlantic *via* the Canal do Norte was measured in 1969 to be 4,007 miles 6 448 km (usually quoted to the rounded off figure of 4,000 miles [6 437 km]).

If, however, a vessel navigating down the river turns to the south of Ilha de Marajó through the straits of Breves and Boiuci into the Pará, the total length of the watercourse becomes 4,195 miles 6 750 km. The Pará is not however a tributary of the Amazon, being hydrologically part of the basin of the Tocantins.

The length of the Nile watercourse, as surveyed by M. Devroey (Belgium) before the loss of a few miles of meanders due to the formation of Lake Nasser, behind the Aswan High Dam, was 4,145 miles 6 670 km. This course is the hydrologically acceptable one from the source in Ruanda of the Luvironza branch of the Kagera feeder of the Victoria Nyanza *via* the White Nile (*Bahr-el-Jebel*) to the delta.

Ireland The longest river in Ireland is the Shannon, which is longer than any river in Great Britain. It rises 258 ft 78,6 m above sea-level, in County Cavan, and flows through a series of loughs to Limerick. It is 240 miles 386 km long, including the 56 mile 90 km long estuary to Loop Head. The basin area is 6,060 miles² 15 695 km².

Great Britain The longest river in Great Britain is the Severn, which empties into the Bristol Channel and is 220 miles 354 km long. Its basin extends over 4,409 miles² 11 419 km². It rises in south-western Powys and flows through Salop, Hereford and Worcester, Gloucestershire and Avon. The longest river *wholly* in England is the Thames, which is 215 miles 346 km long to the Nore. Its remotest source is at Seven Springs, Gloucestershire shire, whence the River Churn joins the other head waters. The source of the Thames proper is Trewsbury Mead, Coate, Cirencester, Gloucestershire. The basin measures 3,841 miles² 9 948 km². The longest river wholly in Wales is the Towy, with a length of 64 miles 102 km. It rises in Dyfed and flows out into Carmarthen Bay. The longest river in Scotland is the Tay, with Dundee, Tayside, on the shore of the estuary. It is 117 miles 188 km long from the source of its remotest head-stream, the River Tummel, Tayside and has the greatest volume of any river in Great Britain, with a flow of up to 49,000 cusecs 1 387 m³ per sec. Its basin extends over 1,961 miles² 5 078 km².

Shortest river The strongest claimant to the title of the world's shortest river is the D River, Lincoln, Oregon, U.S.A., which connects Devil Lake to the Pacific Ocean and is 440 ft 134 m long at low tide.

Greatest flow The greatest flow of any river in the world is that of the Amazon, which discharges an average of 4,200,000 cusecs 120 000 m³/sec into the Atlantic Ocean, rising to more than 7,000,000 cusecs 200 000 m³/sec in full flood. The lowest 900 miles 1 450 km of the Amazon average 300 ft 90 m in depth.

Structures and Dimensions

Largest basin and longest tributary The largest river basin in the world is that drained by the Amazon (4,007 miles [6 448 km]). It covers about 2,720,000 miles² 7 045 000 km². It has about 15,000 tributaries and subtributaries, of which four are more than 1,000 miles 1 609 km long. These include the Madeira, the longest of all tributaries, with a length of 2,100 miles 3 380 km, which is surpassed by only 14 rivers in the whole world.

Longest sub-tributary The longest sub-tributary is the Pilcomayo (1,000 miles [1 609 km] long) in South America. It is a tributary of the Paraguay (1,500 miles [2 415 km] long), which is itself a tributary of the Paraná (2,500 miles [4 025 km]).

Submarine river In 1952 a submarine river 250 miles 400 km wide, known as the Cromwell current, was discovered flowing eastward 300 ft 90 m below the surface of the Pacific for 3,500 miles 5 625 km along the equator. Its volume is 1,000 times that of the Mississippi.

Sub-terranean river In August 1958 a crypto-river was tracked by radio isotopes flowing under the Nile with a mean annual flow six times greater—560,000 million m³ 20 million million ft³.

Longest estuary The world's longest estuary is that of the Ob', in the northern U.S.S.R., at 450 miles 725 km.

Largest delta The world's largest delta is that created by the Ganga (Ganges) and Brahmaputra in Bangla Desh (formerly East Pakistan) and West Bengal, India. It covers an area of 30,000 miles² 75 000 km².

RIVER BORES

World The bore on the Ch'ient'ang'kian (Hang-chou-fe) in eastern China is the most remarkable in the world. At spring tides the wave attains a height of up to 25 ft 7,5 m and a speed of 13 knots 24 km/h. It is heard advancing at a range of 14 miles 22 km. The bore on the Hooghly branch of the Ganges travels for 70 miles 110 km at more than 15 knots 27 km/h. The annual downstream flood wave on the Mekong sometimes reaches a height of 46 ft 14 m. The greatest volume of any tidal bore is that of the Canal do Norte (10 miles [16 km] wide) in the mouth of the Amazon.

Great Britain The most notable river bore in the United Kingdom is that on the Severn, which attained a measured height of 9¼ ft 2,8 m on 15 Oct. 1966 downstream of Stonebench, and a speed of 13 m.p.h. 20 km/h. It travels as far up as Severn Stoke, Hereford & Worcester.

Fastest rapids The fastest rapids which have ever been navigated are the Lava Falls on the River Colorado, U.S.A. At times of flood these attain a speed of 30 m.p.h. 48 km/h (26 knots) with waves boiling up to 12 ft 3,65 m.

WATERFALLS

Highest The highest waterfall in the world is the Salto Angel in Venezuela, on a branch of the River Carrao, an upper tributary of the Caroni with a total drop of 3,212 ft 979 m—the longest single drop is 2,648 ft 807 m. It was re-discovered by a United States pilot named James (Jimmy) Angel (died 8 Dec. 1956), who crashed nearby on 9 Oct. 1937. The falls, known by the Indians as Cherun-Meru, were first reported by Ernesto Sanchez La Cruz in 1910. The Auyan-Tepui plateau was first climbed on 13 Jan. 1971.

United Kingdom The tallest waterfall in the United Kingdom is Eas a'Chùal Aluinn, from Glas Bheinn (2,541 ft [774 m]), Highland, Scotland, with a drop of 658 ft 200 m. England's highest fall above ground is Caldron (or Cauldron) Snout, on the Tees, with a fall of 200 ft 60 m in 450 ft 135 m of cataracts, but no sheer leap. It is at the junction of Durham, Cumbria and North Yorkshire. The cascade in the Gaping Gill Cave descends 365 ft 111 m. The highest Welsh waterfall is the Pistyll Rhaiadr (240 ft [73 m]), on the River Rhaiadr, in southern Clwyd.

Britain's highest waterfall—Eas a'Chual Aluinn, which drops 658 ft 200 m in the remote north west Highland region of Scotland

J. A. Fielden

Ireland The highest falls in Ireland are the Powerscourt Falls (350 ft [106 m]), on the River Dargle, County Wicklow.

Greatest On the basis of the average annual flow, the greatest waterfall in the world is the Guairá (374 ft [114 m] high), known also as the Salto dos Sete Quedas, on the Alto Paraná River between Brazil and Paraguay. Although attaining an average height of only 110 ft 33,5 m, its estimated annual average flow over the lip (5,300 yds [4 850 m] wide) is 470,000 cusecs 13 300 m³/sec. The amount of water this represents can be imagined by supposing that it was pouring into the dome of St. Paul's Cathedral—it would fill it completely in three-fifths of a sec. It has a peak flow of 1,750,000 ft³/sec 50 000 m³/sec. The seven cataracts of the Stanley Falls in the Congo (Kinshasa) have an average annual flow of 600,000 ft³/sec 17 000 m³/sec.

It has been calculated that, when some 5,500,000 years ago the Mediterranean basins began to be filled from the Atlantic through the Straits of Gibraltar, a waterfall 26 times greater than the Guairá and perhaps 800 m 2,625 ft high was formed.

Widest The widest waterfalls in the world are the Khône Falls (50 to 70 ft [15–21 m] high) in Laos, with a width of 6.7 miles 10,8 km and a flood flow of 1,500,000 cusecs 42 500 m³/sec.

Longest fjords and sea lochs **World** The world's longest fjord is the Nordvest Fjord arm of the Scoresby Sund in eastern Greenland, which extends inland 195 miles 313 km from the sea The longest of Norwegian fjords is the Sogne Fjord, which extends 183 km 113.7 miles inland from Sygnefest to the head of the Lusterfjord arm at Skjolden. It averages barely 3 miles 4,75 km in width and has a deepest point of 4,085 ft 1 245 m. If measured from Huglo along the Bømlafjord to the head of the Sørfjord arm at Odda, the Hardangerfjorden can also be said to extend 183 km 113.7 miles. The longest Danish fjord is the Limfjorden (100 miles [160 km] long).

63

Great Scotland's longest sea loch is Loch Fyne, which
Britain extends 42 miles *67,5 km* inland into Argyllshire.

LAKES AND INLAND SEAS

Largest The largest inland sea or lake in the world is the
World Kaspiskoye More (Caspian Sea) in the southern
U.S.S.R. and Iran (Persia). It is 760 miles *1 225 km*
long and its total area is 143,550 miles² *371 800 km²*.
Of the total area some 55,280 miles² *143 200 km²*
(38.6%) is in Iran, where it is named the Darya-ye-
Khazar. Its maximum depth is 980 m *3,215 ft* and its
surface is 92 ft *28 m* below sea-level. Its estimated
volume is 21,500 miles³ *89 600 km³* of saline water.
Since 1930 it has diminished 15,000 miles² *39 000 km²*
in area with a fall of 62 ft *18,90 m* while the shore line
has retreated more than 10 miles *16 km* in some places.
The U.S.S.R. Government plan to reverse the flow of
the upper Pechora River from flowing north to the
Barents Sea by blasting a 70 mile *112 km* long canal
with nuclear explosives into the south-flowing Kolva
river so that *via* the Kama and Volga rivers the Caspian
will be replenished.

Freshwater The freshwater lake with the greatest surface area is
lake Lake Superior, one of the Great Lakes of North
World America. The total area is 31,800 miles² *82 350 km²*, of
which 20,700 miles² *53 600 km²* are in Minnesota,
Wisconsin and Michigan, U.S.A. and 11,100 miles²
27 750 km² in Ontario, Canda. It is 600 ft *182 m* above
sea-level. The freshwater lake with the greatest volume
is Baykal (see Deepest lake, below) with an estimated
volume of 5,750 miles³ *24 000 km³*.

United The largest lake in the United Kingdom is Lough
Kingdom Neagh (48 ft [*14,60 m*] above sea-level) in Northern
Ireland. It is 18 miles *28,9 km* long and 11 miles *17,7
km* wide and has an area of 147.39 miles² *381,73 km²*.
Its extreme depth is 102 ft *31 m*.

Great The largest lake in Great Britain, and the largest
Britain inland loch in Scotland is Loch Lomond (23 ft [*7,0 m*]
above sea-level), which is 22.64 miles *36,44 km* long
and has a surface area of 27.45 miles² *70,04 km²*.
It is situated in the regions of Strathclyde and Central
and its greatest depth is 623 ft *190 m*. The lake with
the greatest volume is however Loch Ness with
263,162,000,000 ft³ *7 451 920 000 m³*. The longest
lake is Loch Ness which measures 24.23 miles *38,99
km*. The 3 arms of the Y-shaped Loch Awe aggregate
however 25.47 miles *40,99 km*. The largest lake in

England is Windermere, in the county of Cumbria.
It is 10½ miles *17 km* long and has a surface area
of 5.69 miles² *14,74 km²*. Its greatest depth is 219 ft
66,75 m in the northern half. The largest *natural* lake
in Wales is Llyn Tegid, with an area of 1.69 miles²
4,38 km², although it should be noted that the largest
lake in Wales is that formed by the reservoir at Lake
Vyrnwy, where the total surface area is 1,120 acres
453,25 ha.

Largest The largest lagoon in the world is Lagoa dos Patos in
Lagoon southernmost Brazil. It is 158 miles *254 km* long and
extends over 4,110 miles² *10 645 km²*.

Republic of The largest lough in the Republic of Ireland is Lough
Ireland Corrib in the counties of Mayo and Galway. It
measures 27 miles *43,5 km* in length and is 7 miles
11,25 km across at its widest point with a total surface
area of 41,616 acres (65.0 miles² [*168 km²*]).

Lake in The largest lake in a lake is Manitou Lake (41,09 miles²
a lake [*106,42 km²*]) on the world's largest lake island
Manitoulin Island (1,068 miles² [*2 766 km²*]) in the
Canadian part of Lake Huron.

DEEPEST LAKES

World The deepest lake in the world is Ozero (Lake) Baykal
in central Siberia, U.S.S.R. It is 385 miles *620 km* long
and between 20 and 46 miles *32–74 km* wide. In 1957
the Olkhon Crevice was measured to be 1 940 m
6,365 ft deep and hence 1 485 m *4,872 ft* below sea-
level.

Great The deepest lake in Great Britain is the 10.30 mile
Britain *16,57 km* long Loch Morar, in Highland. Its surface
is 30 ft *9 m* above sea-level and its extreme depth
1,017 ft *310 m*. England's deepest lake is Wast Water
(258 ft [*78 m*]), in Cumbria. The lake with the greatest
mean depth is Loch Ness with c. 450 ft *137 m*.

HIGHEST LAKES

World The highest steam-navigated lake in the world is Lago
Titicaca (maximum depth 1,214 ft [*370 m*]), with an
area of about 3,200 miles² *8 285 km²* (1,850 miles²
[*4 790 km²*] in Peru, 1,350 miles² [*3 495 km²*] in
Bolivia), in South America. It is 130 miles *209 km*
long and is situated at 12,506 ft *3 811 m* above
sea-level. There is an unnamed lake 2 miles *3,2 km* long
near Jokpolung, Tibet, which is the true source of the
Sutley River at an elevation of 22,500 ft *6 858 m*.

The bed of
Loch Morar in
the Highland
region of
Scotland
(987 ft *301 m*
below sea
level) is the
deepest
depression in
Great Britain

John Topham Ltd.

64

United The highest lake in the United Kingdom is the 1.9 acre
Kingdom *0,76 ha* Lochan Buidhe at 3,600 ft *1 097 m* above
sea-level in the Cairngorm Mountains, Scotland.
England's highest is Broad Crag Tarn (2,746 ft [*837 m*]
above sea-level) on Scafell Pike Cumbria and the
highest named freshwater in Wales is The Frogs Pool,
a tarn near the summit of Carnedd Llywelyn, Gwynedd
at *c.* 2,725 ft *830 m.*

DESERT

Largest Nearly an eighth of the world's land surface is arid
with a rainfall of less than 25 cm (*9.8 in*) per annum.
The Sahara Desert in N. Africa is the largest in the
world. At its greatest length it is 3,200 miles *5 150 km*
from east to west. From north to south it is between
800 and 1,400 miles *1 275 and 2 250 km.* The area
covered by the desert is about 3,250,000 miles²
8 400 000 km². The land level varies from 436 ft
132 m below sea-level in the Qattâra Depression,
Egypt to the mountain Emi Koussi (11,204 ft [*3 415 m*])
in Chad. The diurnal temperature range in the western
Sahara may be more than 80° F. or *45° C.*

GORGE

Largest The largest gorge in the world is the Grand Canyon on
the Colorado River in north-central Arizona, U.S.A.
It extends from Marble Gorge to the Grand Wash
Cliffs, over a distance of 217 miles *349 km.* It varies in
width from 4 to 13 miles *6 to 20 km* and is up to 7,000
ft *2 133 m* deep.

Deepest The deepest canyon in low relief territory is Hell's
Canyon, dividing Oregon and Idaho, U.S.A. It plunges
7,900 ft *2 400 m* from the Devil Mountain down to the
Snake River. A stretch of the Kali River in central
Nepal flows 18,000 ft *5 485 m* below its flanking
summits of the Dhaulagiri and Annapurna groups. The
deepest submarine canyon yet discovered is one
25 miles *40 km* south of Esperance, Western Australia,
which is 6,000 ft *1 800 m* deep and 20 miles *32 km*
wide.

SEA CLIFFS

Highest The highest sea cliffs yet pinpointed anywhere in the
world are those on the north coast of east Molokai,
Hawaiian near Umilehi Point, which descend 3,300 ft
1 005 m to the sea at an average gradient of >55°.
The highest cliffs in North West Europe are those on
the north coast of Achill Island, in County Mayo,
Ireland, which are 2,192 ft *668 m* sheer above the sea
at Croaghan. The highest cliffs in the United Kingdom
are the 1,300 ft *396 m* Conachair cliffs on St. Kilda,
Western Isles (1,379 ft [*425 m*]). The highest sheer sea
cliffs on the mainland of Great Britain are at Clo Mor,
3 miles *4,8 km* south east of Cape Wrath, Highland,
Scotland which drop 921 ft *280,7 m.* England's highest
cliffs are at Countisbury, north Devon, where they drop
900 ft *274 m.*

NATURAL BRIDGE

Longest The longest natural bridge in the world is the Land-
scape Arch in the Arches and Canyonlands National
Parks, Natural Bridges National Monument, Moab,
Utah, U.S.A. This natural sandstone arch spans 291 ft
88 m and is set about 100 ft *30 m* above the canyon
floor. In one place erosion has narrowed its section to
6 ft *1,82 m.* Larger, however, is the Rainbow Bridge,
Utah discovered on 14 Aug. 1909 with a span of 278 ft
84,7 m and more than 22 ft *7 m* wide.

Highest The highest natural arch is the sandstone arch
25 miles *40 km* WNW of K'ashih, Sinkiang, China,
estimated in 1947 to be nearly 1,000 ft *312 m* tall with a
span of about 150 ft *45 m.*

Longest It is estimated that 6,020,000 miles² *15 600 000 km²*,
glaciers or about 10.4 per cent of the Earth's land surface, is
permanently glaciated. The world's longest known
glacier is the Lambert Glacier, discovered by an

Australian aircraft crew in Australian Antarctic
Territory in 1956–57. It is up to 40 miles *64 km* wide
and, with its upper section, known as the Mellor
Glacier, it measures at least 250 miles *402 km* in
length. With the Fisher Glacier limb, the Lambert
forms a continuous ice passage about 320 miles
514 km long. The longest Himalayan glacier is the
Siachen (47 miles [*75,6 km*]) in the Karakoram range,
though the Hispar and Biafo combine to form an
ice passage 76 miles *122 km* long.

Greatest The greatest avalanches, though rarely observed,
avalanches occur in the Himalaya but no estimates of their volume
have been published. It was estimated that 3,500,000
m³ *120 000 000 ft³* of snow fell in an avalanche in the
Italian Alps in 1885. (See also Disasters, end of
Chapter 10.)

3. WEATHER

The meteorological records given below necessarily
relate largely to the last 125 to 145 years, since data
before that time are both sparse and unreliable.
Reliable registering thermometers were introduced as
recently as *c.* 1820.

Palaeo-entomological evidence is that there was a
southern European climate in England *c.* 90,000 B.C.,
while in *c.* 6,000 B.C. the mean summer temperature
reached 67° F *19,4° C,* or 6 deg F *3,3 deg C* higher than
the present. The earliest authentic British weather
records relate to the period 26–30 Aug. 55 B.C. The
earliest reliably known hot summer was in A.D. 664
during our driest every century and the earliest known
severe winter was that of A.D. 763–4. In 1683–84
there was frost in London from November to April.
Frosts were recorded during August in the period
1668–89.

Progressive The world's extremes of temperature have been noted
extremes progressively thus:

127.4° F	*53,0° C*	Ouargla, Algeria	27 Aug. 1884
130° F	*54,4° C*	Amos, California, U.S.A.	17 Aug. 1885
130° F	*54,4° C*	Mammoth Tank, California, U.S.A.	17 Aug. 1885
134° F	*56,7° C*	Death Valley, California, U.S.A.	10 July 1913
136.4° F	*58,0° C*	Al'Aziziyah (el-Azizia), Libya*	13 Sept. 1922
139° F	*59,4° C*	Insala, Algeria	1973

* Obtained by the U.S. National Geographic Society but not officially recognized by the Libyan Ministry of Communications.

A reading of 140° F 60° C at Delta, Mexico, in August 1953 is not now accepted because of over-exposure to roof radiation. The official Mexican record of 136.4° F 58,0° C at San Luis, Sonora on 11 Aug. 1933 is not internationally accepted.

A freak heat flash reported from Coimbra, Portugal, in September 1933 said to have caused the temperature to rise to 70° C 158° F for 120 seconds is apocryphal.

Lowest Screen Temperatures

—73° F	—58,3° C	Floeberg Bay, Ellesmere Is., Canada	1852
—90.4° F	—68° C	Verkhoyansk, Siberia, U.S.S.R.	3 Jan. 1885
—90.4° F	—68° C	Verkhoyansk, Siberia, U.S.S.R.	5 & 7 Feb. 1892
—90.4° F	—68° C	Oymyakon, Siberia, U.S.S.R.	6 Feb. 1933
—100.4 F	—73,5° C	South Pole, Antarctica	11 May 1957
—102.1° F	—74,5° C	South Pole, Antarctica	17 Sept. 1957
—109.1° F	—78,34° C	Sovietskaya, Antarctica	2 May 1958
—113.3° F	—80,7° C	Vostok, Antarctica	15 June 1958
—114.1° F	—81,2° C	Sovietskaya, Antarctica	19 June 1958
—117.4° F	—83,0° C	Sovietskaya, Antarctica	25 June 1958
—122.4° F	—85,7° C	Vostok, Antarctica	7–8 Aug. 1958
—124.1° F	—86,7° C	Sovietskaya, Antarctica	9 Aug. 1958
—125.3° F	—87,4° C	Vostok, Antarctica	25 Aug. 1958
—126.9° F	—88,3° C	Vostok, Antarctica	24 Aug. 1960

Most The location with the most equable recorded temper-
equable ature over a short period is Garapan, on Saipan, in the
temperature Mariana Islands, Pacific Ocean. During the nine years
from 1927 to 1935, inclusive, the lowest temperature
recorded was 19,6° C *67.3° F* on 30 Jan. 1934 and
the highest was 31,4° C *88.5° F* on 9 Sept. 1931,
giving an extreme range of 11,8 deg C *21.2 deg F.*
Between 1911 and 1966 the Brazilian off-shore island
of Fernando de Noronha had a minimum temperature

THE NATURAL WORLD

of 18,6° C *65.5° F* on 17 Nov. 1913 and a maximum of 32,0° C *89.6° F* on 2 March 1965, an extreme range of 13,4 deg C *24.1 deg F.*

Humidity and discomfort Human comfort or discomfort depends not merely on temperature but on the combination of temperature, humidity, radiation and wind-speed. The United States Weather Bureau uses a Temperature-Humidity Index, which equals two-fifths of the sum of the dry and wet bulb thermometer readings plus 15. When the THI reaches 75 in still air, at least half of the people will be uncomfortable while at 79 few, if any, will be comfortable. A reading of 92 (shade temperature 119° F *[48,3° C]*, relative humidity 22%) was recorded at Yuma, Arizona, U.S.A., on 31 July 1957, but even this will have been surpassed in Death Valley, California, U.S.A.

Greatest temperature ranges The greatest recorded temperature ranges in the world are around the Siberian "cold pole" in the eastern U.S.S.R. Verkhoyansk (67° 33′ N., 133° 23′ E.) has ranged 192 deg F *106,7 deg C* from −94° F *−70° C* (unofficial) to 98° F *36,7° C.*

The greatest temperature variation recorded in a day is 100 deg F *55,5 deg C* (a fall from 44° F *[6,7° C]* to −56° F *[−48,8° C]*) at Browning, Montana, U.S.A., on 23L24 Jan. 1916. The most freakish rise was 49 deg F *27,2 deg C* in 2 min at Spearfish, South Dakota, from −4° F *−20° C* at 7.30 a.m. to 45° F *7,2° C* at 7.32 a.m. on 22 Jan. 1943. The British record is 50.9 deg F *28,3 deg C* (34° F *[1,1° C]* to 84.9° F *[29° C]*) in 9 hrs at Rickmansworth, Hertfordshire, on 29 Aug. 1936.

Longest freeze The longest recorded unremitting freeze (maximum temperature 32° F *[0° C]* and below) in the British Isles was one of 34 days at Moor House, Cumbria, from 23 Dec. 1962 to 25 Jan. 1963. This was almost certainly exceeded at the neighbouring Great Dun Fell, where the screen temperature never rose above freezing during the whole of January 1963. Less rigorous early data includes a frost from 5 Dec. 1607 to 14 Feb. 1608 and a 91 day frost on Dartmoor, Devon in 1854–55. No temperature lower than 34° F *1° C* has ever been recorded on Bishop Rock, Isle of Scilly.

Upper atmosphere The lowest temperature ever recorded in the atmosphere is −143° C *−225.4° F* at an altitude of about 50 to 60 miles *80,5–96,5 km,* during noctilucent cloud research above Kronogård, Sweden, from 27 July to 7 Aug. 1963. A jet stream moving at 408 m.p.h. *656 km/h* at 154,200 ft *47 000 m* (29.2 miles *[46 km]*) was recorded by Skua rocket above South Uist, Outer Hebrides, Scotland on 13 Dec. 1967.

Deepest permafrost The greatest recorded depth of permafrost is 1,5 km *4,920 ft* reported in April 1968 in the basin of the River Lena, Siberia, U.S.S.R.

Most intense rainfall Difficulties attend rainfall readings for very short periods but the figure of 1.23 in *3,12 cm* in 1 min at Unionville, Maryland, U.S.A., at 3.23 p.m. on 4 July 1956, is regarded as the most intense recorded in modern times. The cloudburst of "near 2 ft *[609 mm]* in less than a quarter of half an hour" at Oxford on the afternoon of 31 May (Old Style) 1682 is regarded as unacademically recorded. The most intense rainfall in Britain recorded to modern standards has been 2.0 in *5,08 cm* in 12 min at Wisbech, Cambridgeshire on 28 June 1970.

Falsest St. Swithin's Days The legend that the weather on St. Swithin's Day, celebrated on 15 July since A.D. 912, determines the rainfall for the next 40 days is one which has long persisted. There was a brilliant 13½ hrs sunshine in London on 15 July 1924, but 30 of the next 40 days were wet. On 15 July 1913 there was a 15-hr downpour, yet it rained on only 9 of the subsequent 40 days in London.

The world's biggest rain gauge at the world's wettest weather station —Mt. Wai-'ale-'ale, Hawaii

U.S. Dept. of Commerce

Lightning The visible length of lightning strokes varies greatly. In mountainous regions, when clouds are very low, the flash may be less than 300 ft *91 m* long. In flat country with very high clouds, a cloud-to-earth flash sometimes measures 4 miles *6 km* though in extreme cases such flashes have been measured at 20 miles *32 km.* The intensely bright central core of the lightning channel is extremely narrow. Some authorities suggest that its diameter is as little as half an inch *1,27 cm.* This core is surrounded by a "corona envelope" (glow discharge) which may measure 10 to 20 ft *3–6 m* in diameter.

The speed of a lightning discharge varies from 100 to 1,000 miles/sec *160,9 to 1609 km/sec* for the downward leader track, and reaches up to 87,000 miles/sec *140 012 km/sec* (nearly half the speed of light) for the powerful return stroke. In Britain there is an average of 6 strikes/mile^2 per annum, and an average of 4,200 per annum over Greater London alone. Every few million strokes there is a giant discharge, in which the cloud-to-earth and the return lightning strokes flash from the top of the thunder clouds. In these "positive giants" energy of up to 3,000 million joules (3×10^{16} ergs) is sometimes recorded. The temperature reaches about 30,000° C, which is more than five times greater than that of the surface of the Sun.

Highest waterspout The highest waterspout of which there is a reliable record was one observed on 16 May 1898 off Eden, New South Wales, Australia. A theodolite reading from the shore gave its height as 5,014 ft *1 528 m.* It was about 10 ft *3 m* in diameter. A waterspout moved around Tor Bay, Devon on 17 Sept. 1969 which was according to press estimates 1,000 ft *300 m* in height.

Cloud extremes The highest standard cloud form is cirrus, averaging 27,000 ft *8 250 m* and above, but the rare nacreous or mother-of-pearl formation sometimes reaches nearly 80,000 ft *24 000 m.* The lowest is stratus, below 3,500 ft *1 066 m.* The cloud form with the greatest vertical range is cumulo-nimbus, which has been observed to reach a height of nearly 68,000 ft *20 000 m* in the tropics.

Best and worst British summers According to Prof. Gordon Manley's survey over the period 1728 to 1970 the best (*i.e.* driest and hottest) British summer was that of 1949 and the worst (*i.e.* wettest and coldest) that of 1879. The mean temperature for June, July and August 1911 at Shanklin, Isle of Wight was, however, 2.5 deg F *1,3 deg C* higher than in 1949 at 65.9° F *18,3° C.*

Most recent White Christmas and Frost Fair London has experienced seven "White" Christmas Days since 1900. These have been 1906, 1917 (slight), 1923 (slight), 1927, 1938, 1956 (slight) and 1970. These were more frequent in the 19th century and even more so before the change of calendar in 1752. The last of the nine recorded Frost Fairs held on the Thames was in Dec. 1813 to 26 Jan. 1814.

WEATHER RECORDS

	World Records	**United Kingdom & Ireland**
Highest Shade Temperature:	136.4° F *57,7° C* Al' Aziziyah, Libya, 13.9.1922	100.5° F *38° C*, Tonbridge, Kent, 22.7.1868[1]
Lowest Screen Temperature:	−126.9° F *−88,3° C* Vostok, Antarctica, 24.8.1960[2]	−17° F *−27,2° C*, Braemar, Aberdeenshire, Scotland, 11.2.1895[3]
Greatest Rainfall (24 hours):	73.62 in *1 870 mm*, Cilaos, La Réunion, Indian Ocean, 15–16.3.1952[4]	11.00 in *279 mm*, Martinstown, Dorset, 18–19.7.1955
(Month):	366.14 in *9 299 mm*, Cherrapunji, Assam, India, July 1861	56.54 in *1 436 mm*, Llyn Llydau, Snowdon, Gwynedd, October 1909
(12 Months):	1,041.78 in *26 461 mm*, Cherrapunji, Assam, 1.8.1860–31.7.1861	257.0 in *6 527 mm*, Sprinkling Tarn, Cumbria, in 1954[5]
Greatest Snowfall[6] (12 months):	1,224.5 in *31 102 mm*, Paradise, Mt. Rainer, Washington, U.S.A. 19.2.1971 to 18.2.1972	60 in *1 524 mm*, Upper Teesdale and Denbighshire Hills, 1947
Maximum Sunshine:[7]	97%+ (over 4,300 hours), eastern Sahara, annual average	78.3% (382 hours) Pendennis Castle, Falmouth, Cornwall, June 1925
Minimum Sunshine:	Nil at North Pole—for winter stretches of 186 days	Nil in a month at Westminster, London, in December, 1890[8]
Barometric Pressure (Highest):	1,083.8 mb. (32.00 in), Agata, Siberia, U.S.S.R. (alt. 862 ft [*262 m*]), 31.12.1968	1,054.7 mb. (31.15 in), Aberdeen, 31.1.1902
(Lowest):	877 mb. (25.90 in), about 600 miles *965 km* north-west of Guam, Pacific Ocean, 24.9.1958	925.5 mb. (27.33 in), Ochtertyre, near Crieff, Perthshire, 26.1.1884
Highest Surface Wind-speed:[9]	231 m.p.h. *371 km/h*, Mt. Washington (6,288 ft [*1 916 m*]), New Hampshire, U.S.A., 12.4.1934	144 m.p.h. *231 km/h* (125 knots), Coire Cas ski lift (3,525 ft [*1 074 m*]), Cairn Gorm, Inverness-shire, 6.3.1967[10]
Thunder-Days (Year):[11]	322 days, Bogor (formerly Buitenzorg), Java, Indonesia (average, 1916–19)	38 days, Stonyhurst, Lancashire, 1912 and Huddersfield, West Yorkshire, 1967
Hottest Place (Annual mean):[12]	Dallol, Ethiopia, 94°'F *34,4° C* (1960–66)	Penzance, Cornwall, and Isles of Scilly, both 52.7° F *11,5° C*, average 1931–60
Coldest Place (Annual mean):	Pole of Cold (78° S., 96° E.), Antarctica, −72° F *−57,8° C* (16 deg F [*8,9 deg C*] lower than the Pole)	Braemar, Aberdeenshire, 43.7° F *6,5° C*, average 1931–60
Wettest Place (Annual mean):	Mt. Wai-'ale'ale (5,080 ft [*1 548 m*]), Kauai, Hawaii, 451 in *11 455 mm* (average 1920–72). Up to 350 rainy days per year	Styhead Tarn (1,600 ft [*487 m*]), Cumbria, 172.9 in. *4 391 mm*
Driest Place (Annual mean):	Nil—In the Desierto de Atacama, near Calama, Chile	Great Wakering, Essex 19.2 in *487 mm* (1916–50)[13]
Longest Drought:	c. 400 years to 1971, Desierto de Atacama, Chile	73 days, Mile End, Greater London, 4.3 to 15.5.1893[14]
Most Rainy Days (Year):	Bahía Felix, Chile, 348 days in 1916	Ballynahinch, Galway, 309 days in 1923
Heaviest Hailstones:[15]	1.67 lb. *750 g* (7½ in. [*19 cm*] diameter, 17½ in. [*44,45 cm*] circumference), Coffeyville, Kansas, U.S.A., 3.9.1970	5 oz *141 g*, Horsham, West Sussex, 5.9.1958
Longest Sea Level Fogs (Visibility less than 1,000 yards):	Fogs persist for weeks on the Grand Banks, Newfoundland, Canada, and the average is more than 120 days per year[16]	London, 26.11 to 1.12.1948 (4 days 18 hours). London, 5.12 to 9.12.1952 (4 days 18 hours).
Windiest Place:	The Commonwealth Bay, George V Coast, Antarctica, where gales reach 200 m.p.h. *320 km/h*	Tiree, Argyllshire (89 ft [*27 m*]); annual average 17.4 m.p.h. *28 km/h*

[1] *The shade temperature in London on 8 July 1808 may have reached this figure. The highest temperature recorded in Great Britain in an orthodox Stevenson screen is 98.0° F 36,6° C at Ponders End, Enfield, Greater London on 9 Aug. 1911.*

[2] *Vostok is 11,500 ft 3 505 m above sea-level. The coldest permanently inhabited place is the Siberian village of Oymyakon (63° 16' N., 143° 15' E.), in the U.S.S.R., where the temperature reached −96° F −71,1° C in 1964.*

[3] *The −23° F −30,5° C at Blackadder, Berwickshire on 4 Dec. 1879, and the −20° F −28,9° C at Grantown-on-Spey on 24 Feb. 1955, were not standard exposures. The −11° F −23,9° C reported from Buxton, Derbyshire on 11 Feb. 1895 was not standard. The lowest official temperature in England is −6° F −21,1° C at Bodiam, West Sussex on 20 Jan. 1940, at Ambleside, Cumbria on 21 Jan. 1940 and at Hough-all, Durham on 5 Jan. 1941 and 4 March 1947.*

[4] *This is equal to 7,435 tons 7554 tonnes of rain per acre. Elevation 1 200 m 3,937 ft.*

[5] *The record for Ireland is 145,4 in 3 921 mm near Derriana Lough, County Kerry in 1948.*

[6] *The record for a single snow storm is 175.4 in 4 455 mm at Thompson Pass, Alaska, on 26–31 Dec. 1955, and, for 24 hr, 76 in 1 870 mm at Silver Lake, Colorado, U.S.A. on, 14–15 April 1921. The greatest depth of snow on the ground was 25 ft 5 in 7,74 m at Paradise on 17 Apr. 1972. London's earliest recorded snow was on 25 Sept. 1885, and the latest on 27 May 1821. Less reliable reports suggest snow on 12 Sept. 1658 and on 12 June 1791.*

[7] *St. Petersburg, Florida, U.S.A., recorded 768 consecutive sunny days from 9 Feb. 1967 to 17 March 1969.*

[8] *The south-eastern end of the village of Lochranza, Isle of Arran, Bute is in shadow of mountains from 18 Nov. to 8 Feb. each winter.*

[9] *The highest speed yet measured in a tornado is 280 m.p.h. 450 km/h at Wichita Falls, Texas, U.S.A., on 2 April 1958.*

[10] *The figure of 177.2 m.p.h. 285,2 km/h at R.A.F. Saxa Vord, Unst, in the Shetlands, Scotland, on 16 Feb. 1962, was not recorded with standard equipment. There were gales of great severity on 15 Jan. 1362 and 26 Nov. 1703.*

[11] *Between Lat. 35° N. and 35° S. there are some 3,200 thunderstorms each 12 night-time hrs, some of which can be heard at a range of 18 miles 29 km.*

[12] *In Death Valley, California, U.S.A., maximum temperatures of over 120° F 48,9° C were recorded on 43 consecutive days—6 July to 17 Aug. 1917. At Marble Bar, Western Australia (maximum 121° F [49,4° C]) 160 consecutive days with maximum temperatures of over 100° F 37,8° C were recorded—31 Oct. 1923 to 7 April 1924. At Wyndham, Western Australia, the temperature reached 90° F 32,2° C or more on 333 days in 1946., 1921.*

[13] *The lowest rainfall recorded in a single year was 9.29 in 23,6 cm at one station in Margate, Kent, in 1921.*

[14] *The longest drought in Scotland was one of 38 days at Port William, Wigtownshire on 3 Apr. to 10 May 1938.*

[15] *Much heavier hailstones are sometimes reported. These are usually not single but coalesced stones. An 8½ oz 240 g stone was reported at Bicester, Oxfordshire, on 11 May 1945.*

[16] *Lower visibilities occur at higher altitudes. Ben Nevis is reputedly in cloud 300 days per year.*

The world's hottest place—Dallol, Ethiopia where the temperature averages 94°F *34,4°C* round the clock

D. E. Pedgley

4 THE UNIVERSE AND SPACE

LIGHT-YEAR—that distance travelled by light (speed 186,282.3970 miles/sec or 670,616,629.4 m.p.h. *in vacuo*) in one tropical year (365.24219878 mean solar days at January 0,12 hrs Ephemeris time in A.D. 1900) and is 5,878,499,814,000 miles. The unit was first used in March 1888. In metric terms the speed of light is *299 792,458 km/sec* The light year is *9 460 528 405 000 km*.

MAGNITUDE—a measure of stellar brightness such that the light of a star of any magnitude bears a ratio of 2.511886 to that of a star of the next magnitude. Thus a fifth magnitude star is 2.511886 times as bright, while one of the first magnitude is exactly 100 (or 2.511886[5]) times as bright, as a sixth magnitude star. In the case of such exceptionally bright bodies as Sirius, Venus, the Moon (magnitude—11.2) or the Sun (magnitude —26.7), the magnitude is expressed as a minus quantity.

PROPER MOTION—that component of a star's motion in space which, at right angles to the line of sight, constitutes an apparent change of position of the star in the celestial sphere.

The universe is the entirety of space, matter and anti-matter. An appreciation of its magnitude is best grasped by working outward from the Earth, through the Solar System and our own Milky Way Galaxy, to the remotest extra-galactic nebulae.

METEOROIDS

Meteor shower Meteoroids are mostly of cometary origin. A meteor is the light phenomenon caused by the entry of a meteoroid into the Earth's atmosphere. The greatest meteor "shower" on record occurred on the night of 16–17 Nov. 1966, when the Leonid meteors (which recur every 33¼ years) were visible between western North America and eastern U.S.S.R. It was calculated that meteors passed over Arizona, U.S.A., at a rate of 2,300 per min for a period of 20 min from 5 a.m. on 17 Nov. 1966.

METEORITES

Largest World When a meteoroid penetrates to the Earth's surface, the remnant is described as a meteorite. This occurs about 150 times per year over the whole land surface of the Earth. Although the chances of being struck are deemed negligible, the most anxious time of day for meteorophobes is 3 p.m. The largest known meteorite is one found in 1920 at Hoba West, near Grootfontein in South West Africa. This is a block about 9 ft *2,75 m* long by 8 ft *2,43 m* broad, weighing 132,000 lb. (59 tons/*tonnes*). The largest meteorite exhibited by any museum is the "Tent" meteorite,

weighing 68,085 lb. (30.4 tons [*30 882 kg*]) found in 1897 near Cape York, on the west coast of Greenland, by the expedition of Commander (later Rear-Admiral) Robert Edwin Peary (1856–1920). It was known to the Eskimos as the Abnighito and is now exhibited in the Hayden Planetarium in New York City, N.Y., U.S.A. The largest piece of stony meteorite recovered is a piece of the Norton County meteorite which fell in Nebraska, U.S.A. on 18 Feb. 1948. The greatest amount of material recovered from any non-metallic meteorite is from the Allende fall of more than 1 ton in Chihuahua, Mexico on 8 Feb. 1969. A piece of this has been dated to 4,610 million years—thus is the oldest dated object on Earth.

There was a mysterious explosion of about 35 megatons in Latitude 60° 55′ N., Longitude 101° 57′ E., in the basin of the Podkamennaya Tunguska river, 40 miles north of Vanavara, in Siberia, U.S.S.R., at 00 hrs 17 min 11 sec U.T. on 30 June 1908. The energy of this explosion was about 10^{24} ergs and the cause has been variously attributed to a meteorite (1927), a comet (1930), a nuclear explosion (1961) and to anti-matter (1965). This devastated an area of about 1,500 miles² *3 885 km²* and the shock was felt as far as 1 000 km (more than *600 miles*) away.

United Kingdom and Ireland The heaviest of the 22 meteorites known to have fallen on the British Isles since 1623 was one weighing at least 102 lb. *46 kg 250* (largest piece 17 lb. 6 oz. [*7 kg 880*]), which fell at 4.12 p.m. on 24 Dec. 1965 at Barwell, Leicestershire. Scotland's largest recorded meteorite fell in Strathmore, Tayside on 3 Dec. 1917. It weighed 22¼ lb. *10 kg 090* and was the largest of four stones totalling 29 lb. 6 oz. *13 kg 324*. The largest recorded meteorite to fall in Ireland was the Limerick Stone of 65 lb. *29 kg 50* part of a shower weighing more than 106 lb. *48 kg* which fell near Adare, County Limerick, on 10 Sept. 1813. The larger of the two recorded meteorites to land in Wales was one weighing 28 oz. *794 g* of which a piece weighing 25½ oz. *723 g* went through the roof of the Prince Llewellyn Hotel in Beddgelert, Gwynedd, shortly before 3.15 a.m. on 21 Sept. 1949.

68

Largest craters Aerial surveys in Canada in 1956 and 1957 brought to light a gash, or astrobleme, 8½ miles *13,7 km* across near Deep Bay, Saskatchewan, possibly attributable to a very old and very oblique meteorite. U.S.S.R. scientists reported in Dec. 1970 an astrobleme with a 60 mile *95 km* diameter and a maximum depth of 1,300 ft *400 m* in the basin of the River Popigai. There is a possible crater-like formation 275 miles *442,5 km* in diameter on the eastern shore of the Hudson Bay, where the Nastapoka Islands are just off the coast.

The largest proven crater is the Coon Butte or Barringer crater, discovered in 1891 near Canyon Diablo, Winslow, northern Arizona, U.S.A. It is 4,150 ft *1 265 m* in diameter and now about 575 ft *175 m* deep, with a parapet rising 130 to 155 ft *40–48 m* above the surrounding plain. It has been estimated than an iron-nickel mass with a diameter of 200 to 260 ft *61–79 m* and weighing about 2,000,000 tons/ *tonnes* gouged this crater in *c.* 25,000 B.C., with an impact force equivalent to an explosion of 30,000,000 short tons of trinitrotoluene or T.N.T. ($C_7H_5O_6N_3$).

Evidence was published in 1963 discounting a meteoric origin for the crypto-volcanic Vredefort Ring (diameter 26 miles [*41,8 km*]), to the south-west of Johannesburg, South Africa, but this has now been re-asserted. The New Quebec (formerly the Chubb) "Crater", first sighted on 20 June 1943 in northern Ungava, Canada, is 1,325 ft *404 m* deep and measures 6.8 miles *10,9 km* round its rim.

Tektites The largest tektite of which details have been published has been of 3 kg 20 *7.04 lb* found *c.* 1932 at Muong Nong, Saravane Province, Laos and now in the Paris Museum.

AURORA

Most frequent Polar lights, known as Aurora Borealis or Northern Lights in the northern hemisphere and Aurora Australis in the southern hemisphere, are caused by electrical solar discharges in the upper atmosphere and occur most frequently in high latitudes. Aurorae are visible at some time on every clear dark night in the polar areas within 20 degrees of the magnetic poles. The extreme height of auroras has been measured at 1,000 km *620 miles*, while the lowest may descend to 45 miles *72,5 km*.

Southern-most "Northern Lights" Reliable figures exist only from 1952 since when the record high and low number of nights of auroral displays in Shetland (geomagnetic Lat. 63°) has been 203 (1957) and 58 (1965). On 25 Sept. 1909 a display was witnessed as far south as Singapore (1° 25′ N.). One of the greatest displays on record was that of 1 Sept. 1859 seen even in Honolulu, Hawaiian Islands. The most recent great display in north-west Europe was that of 4-5 Sept. 1958.

Noctilucent Clouds Observations in Western Europe date only from 1964 since when the record high and low number of nights on which these phenomena (at heights of 60 miles [*110 km*]) have been observed have been 33 (1967) and 15 (1970). Observations were made in southern England in 1973.

THE MOON

The Earth's closest neighbour in space and only natural satellite is the Moon, at a mean distance of 238,855 statute miles *384 400 km* centre to centre or 233,812 miles *376 284 km* surface to surface. Its closest approach (perigee) and most extreme distance away (apogee) measured surface to surface are 216,420 and 247,667 miles *348 294 and 398 581 km* respectively or 221,463 and 252,710 miles *356 410/406 697 km* measured centre to centre. It has a diameter of 2,159.6 miles *3 475,6 km* and has a mass of 7.23×10^{19} tons *$7,35 \times 10^{19}$ tonnes* with a mean density of 3.34. The average orbital speed is 2,287 m.p.h. *3 680 km/h.*

The first direct hit on the Moon was achieved at 2 min 24 sec after midnight (Moscow time) on 14 Sept. 1959, by the Soviet space probe *Lunik II* near the *Mare Serenitatis*. The first photographic images of the hidden side were collected by the U.S.S.R.'s *Lunik III* from 6.30 a.m. on 7 Oct. 1959, from a range of up to 43,750 miles *70 400 km* and transmitted to the Earth from a distance of 470 000 km *292,000 miles*. The first "soft" landing was made by the U.S.S.R.'s *Luna IX*, in the area of the Ocean of Storms on 3 Feb. 1966.

"Blue Moon" Owing to sulphur particles in the upper atmosphere from a forest fire covering 250,000 acres *100 000 ha* between Mile 103 and Mile 119 on the Alaska Highway in northern British Columbia, Canada, the Moon took on a bluish colour, as seen from Great Britain, on the night of 26 Sept. 1950. The Moon also appeared blue after the Krakatoa eruption of 27 Aug. 1883 (see page 65) and on other occasions.

Crater *Largest* Only 59 per cent of the Moon's surface is directly visible from the Earth because it is in "captured rotation", *i.e.* the period of revolution is equal to the period of orbit. The largest wholly visible crater is the walled plain Bailly, towards the Moon's South Pole, which is 183 miles *295 km* across, with walls rising to 14,000 ft *4 250 m*. The Orientale Basin, partly on the averted side, measures more than 600 miles *965 km* in diameter.

Deepest The deepest crater is the Newton crater, with a floor estimated to be between 23,000 and 29,000 ft *7 000– 8 850 m* below its rim and 14,000 ft *2 250 m* below the level of the plain outside. The brightest directly visible spot on the Moon is *Aristarchus.*

Highest mountains As there is no water on the Moon, the heights of mountains can be measured only in relation to lower-lying terrain near their bases. The highest lunar mountains were, until 1967, thought to be in the Leibnitz and Doerfel ranges, near the lunar South Pole with a height of some 35,000 ft *10 500 m*. On the discovery from Lunar Orbiter spacecraft of evidence that they were merely crater rims, the names have been withdrawn. It is now established that such an elevation would have been an exaggerated estimate for any feature of the Moon's surface.

Temperature extremes When the Sun is overhead the temperature on the lunar equator reaches 243° F *117,2° C* (31 deg F [*17,2 deg C*] above the boiling point of water). By sunset the temperature is 58° F *14,4° C* but after nightfall it sinks to −261° F *−162,7° C.*

Moon samples The age attributed to the oldest of the moon material brought back to Earth by the *Apollo* programme crews has been soil dated to 4,720 million years. The extreme figure from Apollo 17 samples have been modified to between 4.6 and 4.5 thousand million years due to suspected loss of rubidium.

THE SUN

Distance extremes The Earth's 66,620 m.p.h. *107 220 km/h* orbit of 584,017,800 miles *939 885 500 km* around the Sun is elliptical, hence our distance from the Sun varies. The orbital speed varies between 65,520 m.p.h. *105 450 km/h* (minimum) and 67,750 m.p.h. *109 030 km/h* (maximum). The average distance of the Sun is 1.000 000 230 astronomical units or 92,955,829 miles *149 597 906 km.*

The closest approach (perihelion) is 91,402,000 miles *147 097 000 km* and the farthest departure (aphelion) is 94,510,000 miles *152 099 000 km*. The Solar System is revolving around the centre of the Milky Way once in each 225,000,000 years, at a speed of 481,000 m.p.h. *774 000 km/h* and has a velocity of 42,500 m.p.h. *68 400 km/h* relative to stars in our immediate region such as Vega, towards which it is moving.

The most spectacular of all natural phenomena—a total eclipse of the sun

Temperature and dimensions The Sun has an internal temperature of about 20,000,000 K., a core pressure of 500,000,000 tons/in² and uses up 4,000,000 tons/*tonnes* of hydrogen per sec, thus providing a luminosity of 3×10^{27} candlepower, with an intensity of 1,500,000 candles/in² *1 530 000 candelas*. The Sun has the stellar classification of a "yellow dwarf" and, although its density is only 1.409 times that of water, its mass is 332,946 times as much as that of the Earth. It has a mean diameter of 864,940 miles *1 391 980 km*. The Sun with a mass of 1.958×10^{27} tons *1,989 $\times 10^{27}$ tonnes* represents more than 99 per cent of the total mass of the Solar System.

Sun-spots Largest To be visible to the *protected* naked eye, a Sun-spot must cover about one two-thousandth part of the Sun's hemisphere and thus have an area of about 500,000,000 miles² *1 300 million km²*. The largest recorded Sun-spot occurred in the Sun's southern hemisphere on 8 April 1947. Its area was about 7,000 million miles² *18 000 million km²* with an extreme longitude of 187,000 miles *300 000 km* and an extreme latitude of 90,000 miles *145 000 km*. Sun-spots appear darker because they are more than 1 500 deg C cooler than the rest of the Sun's surface temperature of 5 660° C. The largest observed solar prominence was one measuring 70,000 miles *112 500 km* across its base and protruding 300,000 miles *480 000 km*, observed on 4 June 1946.

Most frequent In October 1957 a smoothed Sun-spot count showed 263, the highest recorded index since records started in 1755 (*cf.* previous record of 239 in May 1778). In 1943 one Sun-spot lasted for 200 days from June to December.

ECLIPSES

Earliest recorded The earliest extrapolated eclipses that have been identified are 1361 B.C. (lunar) and Oct. 2137 B.C. (solar). For the Middle East only, lunar eclipses have been extrapolated to 3450 B.C. and solar ones to 4200 B.C. No centre of the path of totality for a solar eclipse crossed London for the 575 years from 20 March 1140 to 3 May 1715. The next will be on 14 June 2051. The most recent occasion when a line of totality of a solar eclipse crossed Great Britain was on 29 June 1927 for 24.5 secs at 6.23 a.m. at West Hartlepool, Cleveland and the next instance may just clip the Cornish coast on 11 Aug. 1999 and again in 23 Sept. 2090. On 30 June 1954 a total eclipse was witnessed in Unst, Shetland Islands but the line of totality was to the north of territorial waters.

Longest duration The maximum possible duration of an eclipse of the Sun is 7 min 31 sec. The longest actually occurring since 13 June A.D. 717 was on 20 June 1955 (7 min since one of 7 min 15 sec in the Pacific on 13 June A.D. 717 was on 20 June 1955 (7 min 8 sec), seen from the Philippines.One of 7 min 28 sec should occur in the South Atlantic on 16 July 2186. The longest possible in the British Isles is 5½ min. That of 15 June 885

lasted nearly 5 min., as will that of 20 July 2381 also in Scotland. An annular eclipse may last for 12 min 24 sec. The longest totality of any lunar eclipse is 104 min. This has occurred many times.

Most and least frequent The highest number of eclipses possible in a year is seven, as in 1935, when there were five solar and two lunar eclipses; or four solar and three lunar eclipses, as will occur in 1982. The lowest possible number in a year is two, both of which must be solar, as in 1944 and 1969.

COMETS

Earliest recorded The earliest records of comets date from the 7th century B.C. The speeds of the estimated 2,000,000 comets vary from 700 m.p.h. *1 125 km/h* in outer space to 1,250,000 m.p.h. *2 000 000 km/h* when near the Sun. The successive appearances of Halley's Comet have been traced back to 466 B.C. It was first depicted in in the Nuremburg Chronicle of A.D. 684. The first prediction of its return by Edmund Halley (1656–1742) proved true on Christmas Day 1758, 16 years after his death. Its next appearance should be at 9.9 (*viz.* at 9.30 p.m. on the 9th) February 1986, 75.81 years after the last, which was on 19 April 1910.

Closest approach On 1 July 1770, Lexell's Comet, travelling at a speed of 23.9 miles/sec *38,5 km/sec* (relative to the Sun), came within 1,500,000 miles *2 400 000 km* of the Earth. However, the Earth is believed to have passed through the tail of Halley's Comet, most recently on 19 May 1910.

Largest Comets are so tenuous that it has been estimated that even the head of one rarely contains solid matter much more than *c.* 1 km *0.6 miles* in diameter. In the tail 10,000 miles³ contain less than a cubic inch of solid matter (or *2 500 km³* contains less than *1 cm³*). These tails, as in the case of the Great Comet of 1843, may trail for 200,000,000 miles *320 million km*. The head of Holmes Comet of 1892 once measured 1,500,000 miles *2 400 000 km* in diameter.

Comet Bennett which appeared in January 1970 was found to be enveloped in a hydrogen cloud measuring some 8,000,000 miles *12 750 000 km*.

Shortest period Of all the recorded periodic comets (these are members of the Solar System), the one which most frequently returns is Encke's Comet, first identified in 1786. Its period of 1,206 days (3.3 years) is the shortest established. Not one of its 48 returns (up to May 1967) has been missed by astronomers. Now increasingly faint, it is expected to "die" by Feb. 1994. The most frequently observed comets are Schwassmann-Wachmann I, Kopff and Oterma which can be observed every year between Mars and Jupiter.

Longest period At the other extreme is the comet 1910 a, whose path was not accurately determined. It is not expected to return for perhaps 4,000,000 years.

PLANETS

Largest Planets (including the Earth) are bodies within the Solar System and which revolve round the Sun in definite orbits. Jupiter, with an equatorial diameter of 88,070 miles *141 730 km* and a polar diameter of 82,720 miles *133 120 km*, is the largest of the nine major planets, with a mass 317.83 times, and a volume 1,293 times that of the Earth. It also has the shortest period of rotation with a "day" of only 9 hrs 50 min 30.003 sec in the equatorial zone.

Smallest Of the nine major planets, Mercury is the smallest with a diameter of 3,031 ± 1 mile *4 878 ± 2 km* and a mass of 0.055274 Earth masses or 325.1 trillion tons *330,3 $\times 10^{18}$ tonnes*. Mercury, which orbits the Sun at an average distance of 35,983,100 miles *57 909 200 km* has a period of revolution of 87.9686 days so giving the highest average speed in orbit of 107,030 m.p.h. *172 248 km/h*.

Hottest The U.S.S.R. probe *Venera 7* recorded a temperature of 474° C *885° F* on the surface of Venus on 15 Dec. 1970. The surface temperature of Mercury has now been calculated to be 421° C *790° F* on its daylight side at perihelion (28,583,900 miles [*46 001 300 km*]). The planet wih a surface temperatutre closest to Earth's average figure of 59° F *15° C* is Mars with a value of 55° F *12,8° C* for the sub-solar point at a mean solar distance of 141,636,000 miles *227 940 000 km.*

Coldest The coldest planet is, not unnaturally, that which is the remotest from the Sun, namely Pluto, which has an estimated surface temperature of −420° F −251° C (40 deg F [*22 deg C*] above absolute zero). Its mean distance from the Sun is 3,674,488,000 miles *5 913 514 000 km* and its period of revolution is 248.54 years. Its diameter is about 3,400 miles (*c. 5 450 km*) and has a mass about one twentieth of that of the Earth. Pluto was first recorded by Clyde William Tombaugh (b. 4 Feb. 1906) at Lowell Observatory, Flagstaff, Arizona, U.S.A., on 18 Feb. 1930 from photographs taken on 23 and 29 January. Because of its orbital eccentricity Pluto will move closer to the Sun than Neptune between 21 Jan. 1979 and 14 Mar. 1999.

Nearest The fellow planet closest to the Earth is Venus, which is, at times, about 25,700,000 miles *41 360 000 km* inside the Earth's orbit, compared with Mars's closest approach of 34,600,000 miles *55 680 000 km* outside the Earth's orbit. Mars, known since 1965 to be cratered, has temperatures ranging from 85° F *29,4° C* to −190° F *−123° C* but in which infusorians of the *genus* Colpoda *could* survive.

Surface features Mariner 9 photographs have revealed a canyon in the Tithonias Lacus region of Mars which is 62 miles *100 km* wider and 4,000 ft *1 220 m* deeper than the 13 mile *21 km* wide 5,500 ft *1 675 m* deep Grand Canyon on Earth. The volcanic pile Nix Olympica is 305 miles *490 km* across with a 40 mile *64 km* wide crater and rises 79,000 ft *24 000 m* above its surrounding "terrain".

Brightest and faintest Viewed from the Earth, by far the brightest of the five planets visible to the naked eye (Uranus at magnitude 5.7 is only marginally visible) is Venus, with a maximum magnitude of −4.4. The faintest is Pluto, with a magnitude of 14. In April 1972 the existence of a tenth of trans-Plutonian planet more than 6,000 million miles from the Sun with 3 times the mass of Saturn was mooted.

Densest and least dense Earth is the densest planet with an average figure of 5.517 times that of water, whilst Saturn has an average density only about one eighth of this value or 0.705 times that of water.

Conjunc-tions The most dramatic recorded conjunction (coming together) of the other seven principal members of the Solar System (Sun, Moon, Mercury, Venus, Mars, Jupiter and Saturn) occurred on 5 Feb. 1962, when 16° covered all seven during an eclipse in the Pacific area. It is possible that the seven-fold conjunction of September 1186 spanned only 12°. The next notable conjunction will take place on 5 May 2000.

SATELLITES

Most Of the nine major planets, all but Venus, Mercury and Pluto have satellites. The planet with the most is Jupiter, with four large and nine small moons. Jupiter's 13th moon (J-XIII) was first identified by Charles Kowal (U.S.) on 14 Sept. 1974. The Earth is the only planet with a single satellite. The distance of the Solar System's 33 known satellites from their parent planets varies from the 5,828 ± 2 miles *9 380 ± 3 km* of *Phobos* from the centre of Mars to the 14,730,000 miles *23 705 000 km* of Jupiter's ninth satellite (Jupiter IX).

Largest and smallest The most massive satellite is *Ganymede* (Jupiter III) which has a diameter of 3,275 miles *5 570 km*, a mass 2.088 times that of our Moon. The current estimate for the diameter of Saturn's largest moon Titan is 5 000 ± 250 km. The smallest is Mars' outer "moon" *Deimos* discovered on 18 Aug. 1877 by Asaph Hall (U.S.) with an average diameter of 7.8 miles *12,6 km.*

Largest asteroids In the belt which lies between Mars and Jupiter, there are some 45,000 (only 3,100 charted) minor planets or asteroids which are, for the most part, too small to yield to diameter measurement. The largest and first discovered (by Piazzi at Palermo, Sicily on 1 Jan. 1801) of these is *Ceres*, with a diameter of 625 miles *1006 km*. The only one visible to the naked eye is *Vesta* (diameter 315 miles [*507 km*]) discovered on 29 March 1807 by Dr. Heinrich Wilhelm Olbers (1758–1840), a German amateur astronomer. The closest measured approach to the Earth by an asteroid was 485,000 miles *780 000 km* in the case of *Hermes* on 30 Oct. 1937. It was announced in Dec. 1971 that the orbit of *Toro* (disc. 1964), though centered on the Sun, is also in resonance with the Earth-Moon system. Its nearest approach to Earth is 9,600,000 miles *15 450 000 km*. *Amor*, *Eros*, and *Ivar*, are also in resonance.

STARS

Largest and most massive Of those measured, the star with the greatest diameter is believed to be the cold giant star IRS5 in the Perseus spiral arm of the Milky Way with a diameter larger than that of the entire Solar System of 9,200 million miles *15 000 million km*. This was announced in January 1973. The *Alpha Herculis* aggregation, consisting of a main star and a double star companion, is enveloped in a cold gas. This system, visible to the naked eye, has a diameter of 170,000 million miles *275 000 million km*. The fainter component of Plaskett's star discovered by J. S. Plaskett from the Dominion Astrophysical Observatory, Victoria, British Columbia, Canada *c*. 1920 is the most massive star known with a mass *c*. 55 times that of the Sun.

Smallest The smallest known star is LP 327–186, a "white dwarf" with a diameter only half that of the Moon, 100 light-years distant and detected in May 1962 from Minneapolis, Minnesota, U.S.A. The claim that LP 768–500 is even smaller at <1,000 miles *<1 600 km* is not widely accepted. Some pulsars or neutron stars may however have diameters of only 10–20 miles *16–32 km*.

Oldest The Sun is estimated to be about 7,500 million years old but our galaxy is estimated to be between 10,000 million and 12,000 million years old.

Farthest The Solar System, with its Sun, nine principal planets, 32 satellites, asteroids and comets, was discovered in 1921 to be about 27,000 light-years from the centre of the lens-shaped Milky Way galaxy (diameter 100,000 light-years) of about 100,000 million stars. The most distant star in our galaxy is therefore about 75,000 light-years distant.

Nearest Excepting the special case of our own Sun (*q.v.* above) the nearest star is the very faint *Proxima Centauri*, which is 4.3 light-years . (25,000,000,000,000 miles [*40 × 10¹² km*]) away. The nearest star visible to the naked eye is the southern hemisphere star *Alpha Centauri*, or *Rigil Kentaurus* (4.33 light-years), with a magnitude of 0.1.

Brightest Sirius A (*Alpha Canis Majoris*), also known as the Dog Star, is apparently the brightest star of the 5,776 stars visible in the heavens, with an apparent magnitude of −1.58. It is in the constellation *Canis Major* and is visible in the winter months of the northern hemisphere, being due south at midnight on the last day of the year. Sirius A is 8.7 light-years away and has a luminosity 26 times as much as that of the Sun. It has

PROGRESSIVE RECORDS OF THE MOST DISTANT MEASURED HEAVENLY BODIES

The possible existence of galaxies external to our own Milky Way system was mooted in 1789 by Sir William Herschel (1738–1822). These extra-galactic nebulae were first termed "island universes". Sir John Herschel (1792–1871) opined as early as 1835 that some were 48,000 light-years distant. The first direct measurement of any body outside the Solar System was in 1838.

Estimated Distance in Light Years[1]		Object	Method	Astronomer	Observatory	Date
nearly 11 (now 11.08)		61 Cygni	Parallax	F. Bessel	Königsberg, Germany	1838
>20 (now 26)		Vega	Parallax	F. G. W. Struve	Dorpat (now Tartu), Estonia	1840
c. 200		Limit	Parallax			by 1900
750,000 (now 2.2 m)[2]		Galaxy M31	Cepheid variable	E. P. Hubble	Mt. Wilson, Cal., U.S.A.	1923
900,000 (now 2.2 m)[2]		Galaxy M31	Cepheid variable	E. P. Hubble	Mt. Wilson, Cal., U.S.A.	1924

Millions of Light Years*	% of c					
			Red shift[3]			
250 m	2.5	Ursa Major Galaxy		E. P. Hubble	Mt. Wilson, Cal., U.S.A.	by 1934[4]
>350 m	3.6			M. L. Humason	Palomar, Cal., U.S.A.	by 1952
	>10			M. L. Humason	Palomar, Cal., U.S.A.	1954
3,000 m	31	Cluster 1448			Palomar, Cal., U.S.A.	1956
c. 4,500 m	46	3C 295 in Boötes			Palomar, Cal., U.S.A.	June 1960
5,300 m	54.5	QSO 3C 147			Palomar, Cal., U.S.A.	April 1964[5]
8,700 m	80	OSO 3C 9	·	M. Schmidt	Palomar, Cal., U.S.A.	May 1965
c. 10,000 m	81			Mrs. M. Burbidge	Palomar, Cal., U.S.A.	Dec. 1965
	82.2	QSO 1116+12		M. Schmidt	Palomar, Cal., U.S.A.	Jan. 1966
13,000 m	82.4	QSO PKS 0237−23[6]		J. G. Bolton	Parkes, N.S.W.	March 1967
	83.8	QSO 4C 25.5		E. Olsen	Palomar, Cal., U.S.A.	July 1968
	87.5	QSO 4C 05.34			Kitt Peak, Arizona	May 1970
15,000 m	92	QSO OH 471		R. F. Carswell et al.	Steward Observatory, Arizona	March 1973
15,600 m	95	QSO OQ 172		Mrs. M. Burbidge	Lick Observatory, Cal., U.S.A.	April 1973

Note: c is the notation for the speed of light.

[1] Term first utilised in 1888.
[2] Re-estimate by W. Baade in Sept. 1952.
[3] Discovered by V. M. Slipher from Flagstaff, Arizona, U.S.A., 1920.
[4] In this year Hubble opined that the observable horizon would be 3,000 m light-years.

[5] Then said that QSO 3C2 and 286 might be more distant—former even 10,000 m light-years.
[6] The most luminous of all observed heavenly bodies.
* The distances are on a Euclidian model. According to the Sandage model, the maximum possible observable distance of any body before it loses luminosity is 11,400 million light years.

a diameter of 1,500,000 miles *2,4 million km* and a mass of 4,580,000,000,000,000,000,000,000,000,000 tons *4,65 × 10²⁷ tonnes.*

Longest Name The longest name for any star is *Shurnarkabtishashutu,* the Arabic for "under the southern horn of the bull".

Most and least luminous If all stars could be viewed at the same distance, the most luminous would be the apparently faint variable *S. Doradûs,* in the Greater Magellanic Cloud (*Nebecula Major*), which can be 300,000 to 500,000 times brighter than the Sun, and has an absolute magnitude of -8.9. The faintest star detected visually is a very red star 30 light-years distant in *Pisces*, with one two-millionth of the Sun's brightness.

Coolest A 16th magnitude star with a surface temperature of only about 425°C *800°F* was detected in *Cygnus* in 1965.

Densest The limit of stellar density is at the neutron state, when the sub-atomic particles exist in a state in which there is no space between them. Theoretical calculations call for a density of 4.7×10^{15} g/cm³ (*74,400 million tons/in³*) in the innermost core of a pulsar. It has been postulated that a Black Hole (see below) may progress towards a' naked singularity'.

Brightest super-nova Super-novae, or temporary "stars" which flare and then fade, occur perhaps five times in 1,000 years in our galaxy. The brightest "star" ever seen by historic man in believed to be the super-nova close to *Zeta Tauri*, visible by day for 23 days from 4 July 1054. The remains, known as the "Crab" Nebula, now appear to have a diameter of about 3×10^{13} miles *4,8 × 10¹³ km* and are still expanding at a rate of 800 miles/sec *1 275 km/sec* so indicating a diameter of 1.3×10^{14} miles *2,1 × 10¹⁴ km* now. It is about 4,100 light-years away, indicating that the explosion actually occurred in about 3000 B.C.

Constellations The largest of the 89 constellations is *Hydra* (the Sea Serpent), which covers 1,302,844 deg² or 6.3 per cent of the hemisphere and contains at least 68 stars visible to the naked eye (to 5.5 mag.). The constellation *Centaurus* (Centaur), ranking ninth in area embraces however at least 94 such stars. The smallest constellation is *Crux Australis* (Southern Cross) with an area of 68.477 deg² compared with the 41,252.96 deg² of the whole sky.

Stellar planets Planetary companions, with a mass of less than 7 per cent of their parent star, have been reported for 61 *Cygni* (1942), Lalande 21185 (1960) *Krüger 60, Ci 2354, BD + 20° 2465* and one of the two components of 70 Ophiuchi. Barnard's Star's (Munich 15040) "planet" reported in April 1963 was temporarily refuted in Oct. 1973. A planet of 6 times the mass of Jupiter 750 million miles *1 200 million km* from *Epsilon Eridani* (see below) was reported by Peter Van de Kemp in January 1973.

Listening operations ("Project Ozma") on *Tau Ceti* and *Epsilon Eridani* were maintained from 4 April 1960 to March 1961, using an 85-ft *25,90 m* radio telescope at Deer Creek Valley, Green Bank, West Virginia, U.S.A. The apparatus was probably insufficiently sensitive for any signal from a distance of 10.7 light-years to be received. Monitoring has been conducted from Gorkiy, U.S.S.R. since 1969.

Black Holes The first tentative identification of a Black Hole was announced in December 1972 in the binary-star X-ray source Cygnus X-1. This is a small dark companion of some 10 solar masses from which the escape velocity tends to c (the velocity of light). Its diameter is estimated to be 14,7 km *9.1 miles* and density at nearly 160,000 million tons/in³.

THE UNIVERSE

According to Einstein's Special Theory time dilation effect (published in 1905), time slows down on a moving system as measured by the system at rest, according to the Lorentz transformation

$$T = T_0 \sqrt{1 - \frac{v^2}{c^2}}$$

where T_0 = time interval when systems are at rest relatively; c = speed of light constant; v = relative velocity, and T = time measured in one system observing the other moving system.

Outside the Milky Way galaxy, which possibly moves around the centre of the local super-cluster of 2,500 neighbouring galaxies at a speed of 1,350,000 m.p.h. *2 172 500 km/h*, there exist 10,000 million other galaxies. These range in size up to the largest known object in the Universe, the radio galaxy 3C-236 in Leo Minor announced from Westerbork Synthesis Radio Telescope, Netherlands in August 1974, which is 18.6 million light-years across. The nearest heavenly body outside our galaxy is its satellite body the Large Magellanic Cloud near the Southern Cross, at a distance of 160,000 light-years. In 1967 it was suggested

72

by the astronomer G. Idlis (U.S.S.R.) that the Magellanic Clouds were detached from the Milky Way by another colliding galaxy, now in *Sagittarius*, about 3,800,000 years ago.

Farthest visible object The remotest heavenly body visible with the naked eye is the Great Galaxy in *Andromeda* (Mag. 3.47), known as Messier 31. This is a rotating nebula in spiral form, and its distance from the Earth is about 2,200,000 light-years, or about 13,000,000,000,000,000,000 miles 21×10^{18} km. It is just possible however that, under ideal seeing conditions, Messier 33, the Spiral in Triangulum (Mag. 5.79), can be glimpsed by the naked eye of keen-sighted people at a distance of 2,300,000 light-years.

Quasars In November 1962 the existence of quasi-stellar radio sources ("quasars" or QSO's) was established. No satisfactory model has yet been constructed to account for the immensely high luminosity of bodies apparently so distant and of such small diameter. The diameter of 3C 446 is only about 90 light-days, but there are measurable alterations in brightness in less than one day. It is believed to be undergoing the most violent explosion yet detected, since it increased 3.2 magnitudes or 20-fold in less than one year.

"Pulsars" The earliest observation of a pulsating radio source or "pulsar" CP 1919 by Dr. Jocelyn Bell Burnell was announced from the Mullard Radio Astronomy Observatory, Cambridgeshire, England, on 29 Feb. 1968. The 100th was announced from Jodrell Bank in June 1973. The fastest so far discovered is NP 0532 in the Crab Nebula with a pulse of 33 milli-sec. The now accepted model is that they are rotating neutron stars of immense density.

Remotest object The greatest distance yet ascribed to a radio detected and visibly confirmed body is that ascribed to the faint blue quasar QSO OQ172 in Boötes, announced in *Nature* on 7 June 1973. This object was found by Dr. Eleanor Margaret Burbidge F.R.S., Director of the Royal Greenwich Observatory, Herstmonceux Castle, East Sussex with the 120 in *304,8 cm* telescope working at the Lick Observatory, Santa Cruz, California, U.S.A., with Drs. E. J. Wampler, L. B. Robinson and J. B. Baldwin. The object has a stellar magnitude of 17.5 and exhibited a red-shift of $Z = 3.53$, which is consistent on one model with a body receding at 95.5 per cent of the speed of light (177,000 miles/sec [*286 000 km/sec*]) and a distance of 15,600 million light years or 91,700,000,000,000,000,000,000 miles $14,75 \times 10^{22}$ km.

Age of the Universe A reassessment of the three dating methods known, published by David N. Schramm in *Scientific American* in 1973 indicates an age between 10 and 15,000 million years with 20,000 million as an extreme value in one method.

ROCKETRY AND MISSILES

Earliest experiments The origin of the rocket dates from war rockets propelled by a charcoal-saltpetre-sulphur gunpowder, made by the Chinese as early as c. 1100. These early rockets became known in Europe by 1258. The pioneer of military rocketry in Britain was Col. Sir William Congreve, Bt., M.P. (1772–1828), Comptroller of the Royal Laboratory, Woolwich, Greater London and Inspector of Military Machines, whose "six-pound [*2,72 kg*] rocket" was developed to a range of 2,000 yds *1 825 m* by 1805 and used by the Royal Navy against Boulogne, France on 8 Oct. 1806.

The first launching of a liquid-fuelled rocket (patented 14 July 1914) was by Dr. Robert Hutchings Goddard (1882–1945) of the United States, at Auburn, Massachusetts, U.S.A., on 16 March 1926, when his rocket reached an altitude of 41 ft *12,5 m* and travelled a distance of 184 ft *56 m*. The U.S.S.R.'s earliest

rocket was the semi-liquid fuelled GIRD-IX tested on 17 Aug. 1933.

Longest ranges On 16 March 1962, Nikita Khrushchyov, then Prime Minister of the U.S.S.R., claimed in Moscow that the U.S.S.R. possessed a "global rocket" with a range of 30 000 km (*about 19,000 miles*) i.e. more than the Earth's semi-circumference and therefore capable of hitting any target from either direction.

Most powerful World It has been suggested that the U.S.S.R. lunar booster which blew up at Tyuratam in the summer (? July) of 1969 had a thrust of 10 to 14 million lb. *4,5 to 6,35 million kg*. There is some evidence of a launch of a U.S.S.R. "G" class lunar booster, larger than the U.S. Saturn V on 11 May 1973.

The most powerful rocket that has been publicized is the *Saturn V*, used for the Project Apollo and Skylab programmes on which development began in January 1962, at the John F. Kennedy Space Center, Merritt Island, Florida, U.S.A. The rocket is 363 ft 8 in *110,85 m* tall, with a payload of 199,500 lb *90 490 kg* in the case of Skylab I, and gulps 13.4 tons *13,6 tonnes* of propellant per sec for 2½ min (2,005 tons [*2 042 tonnes*]). Stage I (S-IC) is 138 ft *42,06 m* tall and is powered by five Rocketdyne F-1 engines, using liquid oxygen (LOX) and kerosene, each delivering 1,514,000 lb. *686 680 kg* thrust. Stage II (S-II) is powered by five LOX and liquid hydrogen Rocketdyne J-2 engines with a total thrust of 1,141,453 lb. *517 759 kg* while Stage III (designated S-IVB) is powered by a single 228,290 lb. *103 550 kg* thrust J-2 engine. The whole assembly generates 175,600,000 h.p. and weighs up to 7,600,000 lb. (3,393 tons [*3 447 tonnes*]) fully loaded in the case of Apollo 17. It was first launched on 9 Nov. 1967, from Cape Kennedy, Florida.

Highest velocity The first space vehicle to achieve the Third Cosmic velocity sufficient to break out of the Solar System was *Pioneer 10* (see page 74). The Atlas SLV-3C launcher used a modified Centaur D second stage and a Thiokol Te-364-4 third stage left the Earth at an unprecedented 32,114 m.p.h. *51 682 km/h* on 2 March 1972. The highest velocity of any space vehicle has been 107,630 m.p.h. *173 214 km/h* by Pioneer II (now named Pioneer-Saturn) at 1.42 GMT on 2 Dec. 1974 in its fly-by 26,000 miles *41 840 km* distant from Jupiter.

Ion rockets Speeds of up to 100,000 m.p.h. *160 000 km/h* are envisaged for rockets powered by an ion discharge. It was announced on 13 Jan. 1960 that caesium vapour discharge had been maintained for 50 hrs at the Lewis Research Center in Cleveland, Ohio, U.S.A. Ion rockets were first used in flight by NASA's SERT I rocket launched on 20 July 1964.

ARTIFICIAL SATELLITES

The dynamics of artificial satellites were first propounded by Sir Isaac Newton (1642–1727) in his *Philosophiae Naturalis Principia Mathematica* ("Mathematical Principles of Natural Philosophy"), begun in March 1686 and first published in the summmer of 1687. The first artificial satellite was successfully put into orbit at an altitude of 142/588 miles *228,5/946 km* and a velocity of more than 17,750 m.p.h. *28 565 km/h* from Tyuratam, a site located 170 miles *275 km* east of the Aral Sea on the night of 4 Oct. 1957. This spherical satellite *Sputnik* ("Fellow Traveller") *1*, officially designated "Satellite 1957 Alpha 2", weighed 83 kg 60 *184.3 lb.*, with a diameter of 58 cm *22.8 in*, and its lifetime is believed to have been 9 days, ending on 4 Jan. 1958. It was designed under the direction of Dr. Sergey Pavlovich Korolyov (1906–1966).

Up to October 1974 1,718 payloads were launched into space and a further 5,783 objects. The total number which were still in space was 3,244. Of the payloads 10 were British launched.

PROGRESSIVE ROCKET ALTITUDE RECORDS

Height in miles	Height in km	Rocket	Place	Launch Date
0.71	1,14	A 3-in rocket	near London, England	April 1750
1.24	2	Reinhold Tiling[1] (Germany) solid fuel rocket	Osnabruck, Germany	April 1931
3.1	5	GIRD-X liquid fuel (U.S.S.R.)	U.S.S.R.	25 Nov. 1933
8.1	13	U.S.S.R. "Stratosphere" rocket	U.S.S.R.	1935
52.46	84,42	A.4 rocket (Germany)	Peenemünde, Germany	3 Oct. 1942
c. 85	c. 136	A.4 rocket (Germany)	Heidelager, Poland	early 1944
118	190	A.4 rocket (Germany)	Heidelager, Poland	mid 1944
244	392,6	V-2/W.A.C. Corporal (2-stage) Bumber No. 5 (U.S.A.)	White Sands, N.M., U.S.A.	24 Feb. 1949
250	400	M.104 *Raketa* (U.S.S.R.)	? Tyuratam, U.S.S.R.	1954
682	1 097	Jupiter C (U.S.A.)	Cape Canaveral (now Cape Kennedy), Florida, U.S.A.	20 Sept. 1956
>2,700	>74 345	Farside No. 5 (4-stage) (U.S.A.)	Eniwetok Atoll	20 Oct. 1957
70,700	113 770	Pioneer I-B Lunar Probe (U.S.A.)	Cape Canaveral (now Cape Kennedy), Florida, U.S.A.	11 Oct. 1958
215,300,000*	346 480 000	Luna 1 or Mechta (U.S.S.R.)	Tyuratam, U.S.S.R.	2 Jan. 1959
242,000,000*	389 450 000	Mars 1 (U.S.S.R.)	U.S.S.R.	1 Nov. 1962
3,600,000,000[2]	5 800 000 000	Pioneer 10 (U.S.A.) (see page 73)	Cape Kennedy, Florida, U.S.A.	2 Mar. 1972
—[3]	—	Pioneer 11 (U.S.A.)	Cape Kennedy, Florida, U.S.A.	5 Mar. 1973

* *Apogee in solar orbit.*
[1] *There is some evidence that Tiling may shortly after have reached 9,500 m. (5.90 miles) with a solid fuel rocket at Wangerooge, East Friesian Islands, West Germany.*
[2] *This distance will be reached by 1987 on its way to crossing the orbit of Pluto and leaving the Solar System's effective gravitational field.*
[3] *Pioneer 11 will fly-by Saturn on c. 6 Sept. 1979 at 108,000 mph 174 000 km/h and then chase Pioneer 10 in leaving the Solar System for deep space.*

Earliest successful manned satellite The first successful manned space flight began at 9.07 a.m. (Moscow time), or 6.07 a.m. G.M.T., on 12 April 1961. Cosmonaut Flight Major (later Colonel) Yuriy Alekseyevich Gagarin (born 9 March 1934) completed a single orbit of the Earth in 89.34 min in the 4.65 ton *4,72 tonnes* space vehicle *Vostok* ('East') I. The take-off was from Tyuratam in Kazakhstan, and the landing 108 min later near the village of Smelovka, near Engels, in the Saratov region of the U.S.S.R. The maximum speed was 17,560 m.p.h. *28 260 km/h* and the maximum altitude 327 km *203.2 miles* in a flight of 40 868,6 km *25,394.5 miles*. Major Gagarin, invested a Hero of the Soviet Union and awarded the Order of Lenin and the Gold Star Medal, was killed in a jet plane crash near Moscow on 27 March 1968.

First woman in space The first and only woman to orbit the Earth was Junior Lieutenant (now Lieut.-Col.) Valentina Vladimirovna Tereshkova, now Mme. Nikolayev (b. 6 March 1937), who was launched in *Vostok 6* from Tyuratam, U.S.S.R., at 9.30 a.m. G.M.T. on 16 June 1963, and landed at 8.16 a.m. on 19 June, after a flight of 2 days 22 hrs 46 min, during which she completed over 48 orbits (1,225,000 miles [*1 971 000 km*]) and passed momentarily within 3 miles *4,8 km* of *Vostok 5*. She was formerly a textile worker. Her mission was variously reported to be punctuated with pleas to be brought back due to giddiness and of being extended because of her excellent performance.

First in flight fatality Col. Vladimir Mikhailovich Komarov (b. 16 March 1927) was launched in *Soyuz* ("Union") *1* at 00.35 a.m. G.M.T. on 23 April 1967. The spacecraft was in orbit for about 25½ hrs but he impacted on the final descent due to parachute failure and was thus the first man indisputedly known to have died during space flight.

First "walk" in space The first person to leave an artificial satellite during orbit was Lt.-Col. Aleksey Arkhipovich Leonov (b. 30 May 1934), who left the Soviet satellite *Voshkod* ('Sunrise') *2* at about 8.30 a.m. G.M.T. on 18 March 1965. Lt.-Col. Leonov was "in space" for about 20 min, and for 12 min 9 sec he "floated" at the end of a tether 5 m *16 ft* long.

Longest manned space flight The longest time spent in the weightlessness of space has been 84 days 1 hr 15 min 30.8 secs by the third crew to man the U.S. *Skylab* space station; Lt. Col. Gerald Paul Carr U.S.M.C. (b. Denver, Colorado 22 Aug. 1932), Lt-Col. William Reid Pogue U.S.A.F. (b. Okemah, Oklahoma 23 Jan. 1930) and Dr. Edward George Gibson (b. Buffalo, N.Y. 8 Nov. 1936) from 16 Nov. 1973 to 8 Feb. 1974. During this time they became the most travelled humans of all-time with a mileage of 34,469,696 miles *55 474 039 km* *Skylab*

had been launched on 14 May 1973. During the 1,214 orbits with an apogee of 283 miles *455 km* the crew temporarily grew 1 in *2,5 cm* each in stature. No further manned flight is scheduled until July 1975.

Astronaut; Oldest and youngest The oldest of the 73 people in space has been Col. Lev Demin (U.S.S.R.) aboard Soyuz 15, which orbited on 26–28 Aug. 1974. His date of birth was not disclosed but he was said to be a 48 year old grandfather. The youngest was Major (later Col.) Gherman Stepanovich Titov (b. 11 Sept. 1935), who was aged 25 years 329 days when launched in *Vostok 2* on 6 Aug. 1961.

Duration record on the Moon The crew of Apollo XVII collected a record 253 lb. *114,8 kg* of rock and soil during their 22 hrs 5 min "extra-vehicular activity". They were Capt. Eugene A. Cernan, U.S.N. (b. Chicago, 14 Mar. 1934) and Dr. Harrison H. (Jack) Schmitt (b. Santa Rosa, New Mexico 3 July 1935) who became the 12th man on the moon. The crew were on the lunar surface for 74 hrs 59½ min during this longest of lunar missions which took 12 days 13 hrs 51 min on 7–12 Dec. 1972.

Highest Lunar Landing In the absence of a sea level, lunar altitudes are measured relative to a reference sphere of radius 1 738 000 metres or 1,079.9431 miles. *Orion*, the lunar module of the Apollo 16 mission, landed with Cdr John W. Young U.S.N. and Charles M. Duke on the Descartes Highlands at an elevation of 7 830 m or 25,688 ft on 27 April 1972.

First extra-terrestrial vehicle The first wheeled vehicle landed on the Moon was *Lunokhod 1* which began its Earth-controlled travels on 17 Nov. 1970. It moved a total of 10,54 km *6.54 miles* on gradients up to 30 deg in the Mare Imbrium and did not become non-functioning until 4 Oct. 1971. The lunar speed and distance record was set by the Apollo 16 Rover with 11.2 m.p.h. *18 km/h* downhill and 22.4 miles *35,8 km*.

Largest Space Object The heaviest object orbited is the 118 ft *35,96 m* long 12,398 ft[3] U.S. *Skylab* weighing 89.17 tons *90 490 kg* on 14 May 1973. The 442 lb. *200 kg* U.S. R.A.E. (radio astronomy explorer) B or Explorer 49 launched on 10 June 1973 has, however, antennae 1,500 ft *415 m* from tip to tip.

Most expensive project The total cost of the U.S. manned space programme up to and including the lunar mission of *Apollo XVII* has been estimated to be $25,541,400,000 (£9,823,150,000). The estimated cost of the Space Shuttle programme to 1990 will be $42,800 million. The first 15 years of the U.S.S.R. space programme from 1958 to Sept. 1973 has been estimated to have cost $45,000 million.

1. ELEMENTS

All known matter in the Solar System is made up of chemical elements. The total of naturally-occurring elements so far detected is 94, comprising, at ordinary temperature, two liquids, 11 gases and 81 solids. The so-called "fourth state" of matter is plasma, when negatively-charged electrons and positively-charged ions are in flux.

Lightest and heaviest sub-nuclear particles The number of fundamental sub-nuclear particles catered for by the 1964 Unitary Symmetry Theory, or SU(3), was 34. The SU(6) system caters for 91 particles, while the later SU(12) system caters for an infinite number, some of which are expected to be produced by higher and higher energies, but with shorter and shorter lifetimes and weaker and weaker interactions. By November 1973 the existence of 72 resonance *types* was accepted. Of SU(3) particles the one with the highest mass is the omega minus, announced on 24 Feb. 1964 from the Brookhaven National Laboratory, near Upton, Long Island, New York State, U.S.A. It has a mass state of $1,672.2 \pm 0.4$ Mev and a lifetime of 1.3×10^{-10} of a sec. Of all sub-atomic concepts only the neutrino calls for masslessness. There is experimental proof that the mass, if any,

Scene of the discovery of the newest sub-atomic particles—the Stanford Linear Accelerator in California

Lawrence Berkley Laboratory

5

THE SCIENTIFIC WORLD

COMPUTER MK.1

OUT

of an electron neutrino, first observed in June 1956, cannot be greater than one ten-thousandth of that of an electron, which itself has a rest mass of 9.10953 (± 0.00005) $\times 10^{-28}$ g, *i.e.* it has a weight of less than 1.07×10^{-31} g.

Least stable The least stable or shortest lived nuclear particles discovered are the rho prime meson (announced on 29 Jan. 1973) and the 3 baryon resonances N(3030), Δ(2850) and Δ(3230) all 1.6×10^{-24} sec. The discovery of the quork was claimed on 23 May 1973 at Haverah Park near Harrogate, North Yorkshire by researchers from Leeds University but is not internationally accepted.

Newest particles The particles Psi 3105 and Psi 3695 were announced on 16 Nov. and 22 Nov. 1974 from the Stanford Linear Accelerator Center, California. In January 1975 a neutral particle psi 4100 with a lifteime of 10^{-23} sec. was announced.

THE 106 ELEMENTS

There are 94 known naturally occurring elements comprising, at ordinary temperatures, two liquids, 11 gases and 81 solids, of which 72 are metallic. To date a further 12 transuranic elements (Elements 95 to 106) have been synthesized.

Category	Name	Symbol	Discovery of Element	Record
Commonest (lithosphere)	Oxygen	O	1771 Scheele (Germany-Sweden)	46.60% by weight
Commonest (atmosphere)	Nitrogen	N	1772 Priestley (G.B.) et al.	78.09% by volume
Commonest (extra-terrestrial)	Hydrogen	H	1776 Cavendish (G.B.)	90% of all matter
Rarest (of the 94)	Astatine	At	1940 Corson (U.S.) et al.	1/100th oz. in Earth's crust
Lightest	Hydrogen	H	1776 Cavendish (G.B.)	0.005611 lb/ft³ 89,88 mg/l
Lightest (Metal)	Lithium	Li	1817 Afrwedson (Sweden)	33.29 lb/ft³ 0,5333 g/cm³
Densest	Osmium	Os	1804 Tennant (G.B.)	1,410 lb/ft³ 22,59 g/cm³
Heaviest (Gas)	Radon	Em 222	1900 Dorn (Germany)	0.6256 lb/ft³ 10,021 g/l
Newest	Element 106		1974 Ghiorso et al. (U.S.)	announced 9 Sept. 1974
Purest	Germanium	Ge	1886 Winker (Germany)	99.99999999% purity (1967)
Hardest	Carbon	C	— prehistoric	Diamond isotope, Knoop value 8,400
Most Expensive	Californium	Cf	1950 Seaborg et al. (U.S.)	Sold in 1968 for $1000 per µg
Most Stable	Tellerium	Te 130	1782 von Reichenstein (Hung.)	Half life of 2.2 × 10²¹ years.
Least Stable	Helium	He 5	1895 Ramsay (G.B.)	Half-life of 2.4 × 10⁻²¹ sec.
Most Isotopes	Xenon	Xe	1898 Ramsay and Travers (G.B.)	30
Least Isotopes	Hydrogen	H	1776 Cavendish (G.B.)	3 (confirmed)
Most Ductile	Gold	Au	ante 3000 B.C.	1 oz. drawn to 43 miles 1 g/2,4 km
Highest Tensile Strength	Boron	B	1808 Gay-Lussac et al. (France)	3.9 × 10⁶ lb f/in² 2,68 × 10⁷ kPa
Lowest Melting Point	Helium	He	1895 Ramsay (G.B.)	−271,72°C under pressure 26 atmos or 2600 kPa
Highest Melting Point	Tungsten	W	1783 J. J. & F. d'Elhuyar (Spain)	3 417° ± 10 deg C
Most Poisonous	Plutonium	Pu	1940 Seaborg (U.S.) et al.	1 µg or microgramme (1 thirty millionth of an oz.) inhaled or swallowed will cause cancer. With a half-life of 23,640 years, toxicity is retained for a thousand centuries

CHEMICAL COMPOUNDS

It has been estimated that there are more than 4 million described chemical compounds.

Most Refractory	Tantulum Carbide TaC₀.₈₈	Melts at 4 010° ± 75 deg C
Most Refractory (plastics)	Modified polymides	500° C for short periods
Lowest Expansion	Invar metal (Ni-Fe alloy with C and Mn)	2,3 × 10⁻⁶ cm/cm/deg C
Highest Tensile Strength	Sapphire whisker Al₂O₃	6 × 10⁶ lb f/in² 4,27 × 10⁷ kPa
Highest Tensile Strength (plastics)	Polyvinyl alcoholic fibres	1.5 × 10⁵ lb f/in² 10,3 × 10⁵ kPa
Most Magnetic	Cobalt-copper-samarium Co₃Cu₂Sm	10,500 oersted coercive force
Least Magnetic alloy	Copper nickel alloy CuNi	963 parts Cu to 37 parts Ni
Most Pungent	Vanillaldehyde	Detectable at 2 × 10⁻⁸ mg/litre
Sweetest	1n-propoxy-2-amino-4-nitro-benzene	5,600 × as sweet as 1% sucrose
Bitterest	Bitrex or Benzyl diethyl ammonium benzoate	200 × as bitter as quinine sulphate
Most Acidic[1]	Perchloric acid (HClO₄)	pH value of normal solution tends to 0.
Most Alkaline	Caustic soda (NaOH) and potash (KOH) and tetramethylammonium hydroxide (N(CH₃)₄OH)	pH value of normal solution is 14.
Highest Specific Impulse	Hydrogen with liquid fluorine	447 lb f/sec/lb 4382 N/sec/kg
Most Poisonous	Thiopentone (a barbituate)	Intracardiac injection will kill in 1 to 2 secs.

[1] *The most powerful acid, assessed on its power as a hydrogen-ion donor, is a solution of antimony pentafluoride in fluosulphonic acid—SbF₅ + FSO₃H.*

The most expensive substance ever sold—the transuranic element Californium. The price was $1,000 per one millionth of a gram

Oak Ridge National Laboratory

SMELLIEST SUBSTANCE

The most evil smelling substance, of the 17,000 smells so far classified, must be a matter of opinion but ethyl mercaptan (C₂H₅SH) and butyl seleno-mercaptan (C₄H₉SeH), are powerful claimants, each with a smell reminiscent of a combination of rotting cabbage, garlic, onions and sewer gas.

Most expensive perfume The retail prices of the most expensive perfumes tend to be fixed at public relations rather than economic levels. The most expensive ingredient in perfume is pure French middle note jasmine essence at £2,900 per kg or £82.20p per oz.

POISON

Most potent The rikettsial disease, Q-fever can be instituted by a *single* organism but is only fatal in 1 in 1,000 cases. Effectually the most poisonous substance yet discovered is the toxin of the bacterium *Pasteurella tularensis*. About 10 organisms can institute tulaeremia variously called alkali disease, Francis disease or deerfly fever, and this is fatal in 50 to 80 cases in 1,000.

Most powerful nerve gas In the early 1950s substances known as V-agents, notably VX, 300 times more toxic than phosgene (COCl₂) used in World War I, were developed at the Chemical Defence Experimental Establishment, Porton Down, Wiltshire, which are lethal at 1 mg per man. Patents were applied for in 1962 and published in February 1974.

Most powerful drugs The most potent and, to an addict, the most expensive of all naturally-derived drugs is heroin, which is a chemically-processed form of opium from the juice of the unripe seed capsules of the white poppy (*Papaver somniferum*). An oz., which suffices for up to 1,800 hypodermic shots or "fixes", may fetch up to $10,000 (£4,080) in the United States, or a 70,000 per cent profit over the raw material price in Turkey. It has been estimated that an addict who has no income is impelled to steal $50,000 (£20,000) worth of goods per annum to keep him or herself in "fixes". The most powerful synthetically manufactured drug is d-Lysergic Acid Diethylamide tartrate (LSD-25, $C_{20}H_{25}N_3O$) first produced in 1938 for common cold research and as a hallucinogen by Dr. Albert Hoffmann (Swiss) on 16–19 Apr. 1943. The most potent analgesic drug is Etorphine or M-99, announced in June 1963 by Dr. Kenneth W. Bentley (b. 1925) and D. G. Hardy of Reckitt & Sons Ltd. of Hull, Humberside, with almost 10,000 times the potency of morphine.

Most prescribed drug The benzodiazepine group tranquilizing drug Valium discovered by Hoffman-La Roche is the world's most widely used drug. In 1973 there were an estimated 47 million prescriptions in the U.S. alone.

Most absorbant substance The U.S. Department of Agriculture Research Service announced on 18 Aug. 1974 that "H-span" or Super Slurper composed of one half starch derivative and one fourth each of acrylamide and acrylic acid can when treated with iron retain water 1,300 times its own weight.

Finest powder Particulate matter of 25 to 40 Å or $2,564 \times 10^{-6}$ *cm* was reportedly produced by an electron beam evaporation process at the Atomic Energy Establishment, Harwell in October 1972. The paper was published by Dr. P. RamaKrishnan.

2. DRINK

The strength of spirituous liquor is gauged by degrees proof. In the United Kingdom proof spirit is that mixture of ethyl alcohol (C_2H_5OH) and water which at 51° F *10,55° C* weighs 12/13ths of an equal measure of distilled water. Such spirit in fact contains 57.06 per cent alcohol by volume, so that pure or absolute alcohol is 75.254° over proof (O.P.). A "hangover" is due to toxic congenerics such as amyl alcohol ($C_5H_{11}OH$).

Most alcoholic Absolute (or 100%) alcohol is 75.254 degrees over proof (U.K.) or 100° O.P. (U.S.). The strongest alcoholic spirits produced are unmarketable raw rums and vodkas at 97.2% alcohol by volume at 60° F *15,6° C* or 70° O.P. (U.K.) or 194.4 proof (U.S.). Polish White Spirit vodka produced for the Polish State Spirits Monopoly is 79.8% alcohol and 40° O.P. (U.K.) or, 59.9° O.P. (U.S.). Royal Navy rum introduced in 1692, was also 40° O.P. (79.8%) before 1948 but was reduced to 4.5° U.P. (under proof) or 54.7% alcohol by volume, before its abolition on 31 July 1970.

Oldest Vintage The oldest datable vintage of any wine has been a bottle of *Steinwein* 1540 from Wurzburg am Main, West Germany salvaged from the cellars of King Ludwig of Bavaria sold by Ehrmann's of Grafton Street, London and described 420 years later as "dark, feeble but definitely alive".

BEER

Strongest The world's strongest and most expensive beer is EKU Kulminator Urtyp Hell from Kulmbach, West Germany which retails for up to 70p per ½ pint *28,4 cl* bottle. It is 13.2% alcohol by volume at 20° C with an original gravity of 1117.6°.

The strongest beer in Britain is Thomas Hardy's Ale bottled in March 1974 by Dorchester Brewery, Dorset with 10.15 per cent alcohol by weight, 12.58 per cent by volume and an original gravity of 1113.0°. The strongest regularly brewed nationally distributed beer in Britain is Gold Label Barley Wine brewed by Tennant Bros. of Sheffield, a subsidiary of Whitbread & Co. Ltd. It has an alcoholic content of 8.6 per cent by weight, 10.6 per cent by volume and an original gravity of 1098.06°.

Weakest The weakest liquid ever marketed as beer was a sweet ersatz beer which was brewed in Germany by Sunner, Colne-Kalk, in 1918. It had an original gravity of 1,000.96° and a strength 1/30th that of the weakest beer now obtainable in the United Kingdom.

WINE

Most expensive The highest price ever paid for a bottle of wine of any size is 55,000 francs (*then £4,532*) for one of the only 4 known Jeroboams of *Château Mouton* Rothschild 1870 *Pauillac* 2ᵉ Grand Cru Classe red Bordeaux (claret) by Mario Ruspoli (U.S.) in a 'phoned auction bid to Mes. Ader Picard et Tajan of Paris and Sotheby & Co. on 21 Nov. 1972. This bottle contained the equivalent of *five* normal bottles and was thus equivalent to about £150 per glass or £37.75 per fluid oz.

The highest price for a *single* bottle (as opposed to a magnum or above) has been 30,000 French francs (*then £2,470*) for a *Château Ausone* 1900 Saint Emilion les Grand Cru Classé claret auctioned for charity on the same occasion. This was equivalent to £102 90p per fluid oz. (*or 2,84 centilitres*).

Most expensive liqueurs The most expensive liqueur in France is the orange-flavoured *Le Grand Marnier Coronation*. Owing to excise duties, *Elixir Végétale de la Grande Chartreuse* which is 24 degrees O.P. is sold only by special order in miniature bottles of 2.8 fl. oz. *7,95 centilitres* at £1.15 per bottle in the United Kingdom. This liqueur has been produced since 1757, by Carthusian monks from a recipe of 1605, which reputedly contains 130 herbs including *Arnica montana*. Ancient *Chartreuse* (before 1903) has been known to fetch more than £15 per litre bottle *1,76 pints*. An 1878 bottle was sold in 1954 for this price.

Most expensive spirits The most expensive spirit is *Grande Fine Champagne Arbellot* 1749 brandy, retailed at Fauchon, Paris, at 667 francs (*then £48.25*) per bottle. In Britain 50 year old *Remy Martin brandy* retails for £50.50 (including V.A.T.) for a standard bottle.

Largest bottles The largest bottle normally used in the wine and spirit trade is the Jeroboam (equal to 4 bottles of champagne or, rarely, of brandy) and the Double Magnum (equal, since c. 1934, to 6 bottles of claret or, more rarely, red Burgundy). A complete set of Champagne bottles would consist of a ¼ bottle, through the ½ bottle, bottle, magnum, Jeroboam, Rehoboam, Methuselah, Salmanazer and Balthazar, to the Nebuchadnezzar, which has a capacity of 16 litres (*28.16 pt*), and is equivalent to 20 bottles. In May 1958 a 5 ft *152 cm* tall sherry bottle with a capacity of 20½ Imperial gal *93,19 litres* was blown in Stoke-on-Trent, Staffordshire. This bottle, with the capacity of 131 normal bottles, was named an "Adelaide".

Smallest bottles The smallest and meanest bottles of liquor sold are the bottles of Scotch whiskey marketed by The Cumbrae Supply Co. of Glasgow. They contain 24 minims or 1/20 of a fl. oz. *1,42 millilitres* and retailed in 1975 for 25p.

Champagne cork flight The longest distance for a champagne cork to fly from an untreated and unheated bottle 4 ft *1,22 m* from level ground is 94 ft *28,65 m* by David Jon Wiener at San Diego, California on 25 Aug. 1973.

3. GEMS AND OTHER PRECIOUS MATERIALS

Note: The carat was standardised at 205 mg in 1877. The metric carat of 200 mg was introduced in 1913.

PRECIOUS STONE RECORDS

	Largest	Largest Cut Stone	Other records
Diamond (pure crystallised carbon)	3,106 metric carats (over 1¼ lb.) — *The Cullinan,* found by Capt. M. F. Wells 26 Jan. 1905 in the Premier Mine, Pretoria, South Africa. The largest uncut diamond is *The Star of Sierra Leone* found at Kono on 14 Feb. 1972 weighing 969.1 carats. It was sold for an undisclosed amount below its reserve of some $2.6 million in Feb. 1973 to Harry Winston (U.S.).	530.2 metric carats. Cleaved from *The Cullinan* in 1908, in Amsterdam by Jak Asscher and polished by Henri Koe known as *The Star of Africa No. 1* and now in the Royal Sceptre.	Diamond is the *hardest* known naturally-occurring substance, being 90 times as hard as the next hardest mineral, corundum (Al_2O_3). The peak hardness value on the Knoop scale is 8,400 compared with an average diamond of 7,000. The rarest colours for diamond are blue (record—44.4 carat *Hope* diamond) and pink (record—24 carat presented by Dr. John Thoburn Williamson to H.M. The Queen in 1958). Auction record: $1,050,000 (then £437,500) for a 69.42 carat stone bought by Cartier on 13 Oct. 1969 and sold to Richard Burton (at $1,200,000 (then £500,000) for Elizabeth Taylor on 24 Oct. 1969. Tiffany and Co. put a $5 million price on their canary yellow diamond of 1877 for one day on 17 Nov. 1972. Miss Debbie Reynolds (U.S.) wore a tiara owned by Harry Winston, valued at $4,500,000 (£1,875,000) in New York on 25 Sept. 1973.
Emerald (green beryl) [$Be_3Al_2(SiO_3)_6$]	125 lb. *56 kg 70* crystal (up to 15¾ in *[40 cm]* long and 9¾ in *[24,75 cm]* in diameter) from a Ural, U.S.S.R. mine.	2,680 carat unguent jar carved by Dionysio Miseroni in the 17th century owned by the Austrian Government. 1,350 carat of *gem* quality, the *Devonshire* stone from Muso, Columbia.	A necklace of eight major emeralds and one pendant emerald of 75.63 carats with diamonds was sold by Sotheby's in Zurich on 24 Nov. 1971 for £436,550 (then $1,090,000). The Swiss customs at Geneva confirmed on 16th April 1972 the existence of an hexaponal emerald of about 20,000 carats, thus possibly worth more than $100 million.
Sapphire (blue corundum) (Al_2O_3)	2,302 carat stone found at Anakie, Queensland, Australia, in *c.* 1935, now a 1,318 carat head of President Abraham · Lincoln (1809–65).	1,444 carat black star stone carved from 2,097 carats in 1953–1955 into a bust of General Dwight David Eisenhower (1890–1969).	*Note:* both the sapphire busts are in the custody of the Kazanjian Foundation of Los Angeles, California, U.S.A.
Ruby (red corundum) (Al_2O_3)	3,421 carat broken stone reported found in July 1961 (largest piece 750 carats).	1,184 carat natural gem stone of Burmese origin.	Since 1955 rubies have been the world's most precious gem attaining a price of up to £4,000 per carat by 1969. The ability to make corundum prisms for laser technology up to over 12 in *30 cm* in length must now have a bearing on the gem market.

RECORDS FOR OTHER PRECIOUS MATERIALS

	Largest	Where Found	Notes On Present Location, etc.
Pearl (Molluscan concretion)	14 lb. 1 oz. *6 kg 378* 9½ in *24 cm* long by 5½ in *14 cm* in diameter—*Pearl of Lao-tze*	At Palawan, Philippines, 7 May 1934 in shell of giant clam.	In a San Francisco bank vault. It is the property since 1936 of Wilburn Dowell Cobb and was valued at $4,080,000 in July 1971.
Opal ($SiO_2.nH_2O$)	Any stone: 220 troy oz. (yellow-orange). Gem stone: 17,700 carats (*Olympic Australis*)	Andamooka, South Australia Jan. 1970. Coober Pedy, South Australia, Aug. 1956.	The Andamooka specimen was unearthed by a bulldozer.
Crystal (SiO_2)	Any stone: 70 tons/*tonnes* (piezo-quartz crystal). Ball: 106¾ lb. *48 kg 420* 12⅞ in *32,7 cm* diameter, the *Warner* sphere	Kazakhstan, U.S.S.R., Sept. 1958. Burma, (originally a 1,000 lb. *[450 kg]* piece).	Note: There is a single rock crystal of 1,728 lb *783 kg 800* placed in the Ural Geological Museum, Sverdlovsk, U.S.S.R., November 1968. U.S. National Museum, in Washington, D.C.
Topaz [$(Al_2SiO_4)_4(F,OH)_2$]	Any stone: 596 lb. *270 kg* Gem stone: 7,725 carats	Minas Gerais, Brazil.	American Museum of Natural History, New York City, since 1951. Also at the American Museum of Natural History.
Amber (Coniferous fossil resin)	33 lb. 10 oz. *15 kg 250.*	Reputedly from Burma acquired in 1860.	Bought by John Charles Bowring (d. 1893) for £300 in Canton, China. Natural History Museum, London, since 1940.
Jade [$NaAl(Si_2O_6)$]	Sub-marine boulder of 5 short tons *4,53 tonnes* valued at $180,000	Off Monterey, California. Landed 5 June 1971.	Jadeite can be virtually any colour. The less precious nephrite is [$Ca_2(Mg,Fe)_5(OH)_2(Si_4O_{11})_2$]
Marble (Metamorphosed $CaCO_3$)	90 tons/*tonnes* (single slab)	Quarried at Yule, Colorado, U.S.A.	A piece of over 45 tons/*tonnes* was dressed from this slab for the coping stone of the Tomb of the Unknown Soldier in Arlington National Cemetery, Virginia, U.S.A.

RECORDS FOR OTHER PRECIOUS MATERIALS — continued

	Largest	Where Found	Notes on Present Location, etc.
Nuggets— Gold (Au)	7,560 oz. (472½ lb. [214 *kg 318*]) (reef gold) *Holtermann Nugget*	Beyers & Holtermann Star of Hope Gold Mining Co., Hill End, N.S.W., Australia, 19 Oct. 1872	The purest large nugget was the *Welcome Stranger*, found at Tarnagulla, near Moliagul, Victoria, Australia, which yielded 2,248 troy oz. *69 kg 920* of pure gold from 2,280¼ oz. *70 kg 920*.
Silver (Ag)	2,750 lb. troy	Sonora, Mexico	Appropriated by the Spanish Government before 1821.

Other Gems Records:

Largest Stone of Gem Quality:

A 520,000 carat (2 cwt. 5 lb. [*103 kg 800*]) aquamarine ($Be_3Al_2[SiO_3]_6$) found near Marambaia, Brazil in 1910. Yielded over 200,000 carats of gem quality cut stones.

Rarest:

Taaffeite ($Be_4Mg_4Al_{15}O_{32}$) first discovered in Dublin, Ireland, in November 1945. Only two of these pale mauve stones are known—the larger is of 0.84 of a carat.

Densest Gem Mineral:

Stibotantalite [$(SbO)_2(Ta,Nb)_2O_6$] a rare brownish-yellow mineral found in San Diego County, California, has a density of 7.46. The alloy platiniridium has a density of more than 22.0.

The largest cut diamond in the world—the 530.2 carat Stone in the British Royal Sceptre

Eljay Photo Service

4. TELESCOPES

Earliest Although there is evidence that early Arabian scientists understood something of the magnifying power of lenses, their first use to form a telescope has been attributed to Roger Bacon (*c.* 1214–92) in England. The prototype of modern refracting telescopes was that completed by Johannes Lippershey for the Netherlands government on 2 Oct. 1608.

Largest The largest refracting (*i.e.* magnification by lenses)
Refractor telescope in the world is the 62 ft *18,90 m* long 40 in *101,6 cm* telescope completed in 1897 at the Yerkes Observatory, Williams Bay, Wisconsin, and belonging to the University of Chicago, Illinois, U.S.A. In 1900 a 125 cm *49.2 in* refractor 54,85 m *180 ft* in length was built for the Paris Exposition but its optical performance was too poor to justify attempts to use it. The largest in the British Isles is the 28 in *71,1 cm* at the Royal Greenwich Observatory completed in 1894.

Reflector The largest telescope in the world is the 6 m *236.2 in*
World telescope sited on Mount Semirodriki, near Zelenchukskaya in the Caucasus Mountains, U.S.S.R., at an altitude of 6,830 ft *2,080 m*. The mirror, weighing 70 tons/*tonnes* was completed in November 1967, assembled by October 1970 and trials started in November 1974. The overall weight of the 79 m long assembly is 840 tonnes. Being the most powerful of all telescopes its range, which includes the location of objects down to the 25th magnitude, represents the limits of the observable Universe. Its light-gathering power would enable it to detect the light from a candle at a distance of 15,000 miles *24 000 km*.

United The largest reflector in the British Isles is the Isaac
Kingdom Newton 98.2 in *249,4 cm* reflector at the Royal Greenwich Observatory, Herstmonceux Castle, East Sussex. It was built in Newcastle upon Tyne, Tyne and Wear, weighs 92 tons *93,5 tonnes*, cost £641,000 and was inaugurated on 1 Dec. 1967.

Radio The world's largest trainable dish-type radio telescope
Largest is the 100 m *328 ft* diameter, 3,000 ton/*tonnes*
steerable assembly at the Max Planck Institute for Radio
dish Astronomy of Bonn in the Effelsberger Valley, West Germany; it became operative in May 1971. The cost of the installation begun in November 1967 was 36,920,000 DM *£6,150,000*. The earliest fully steerable radio telescope was the 82 ft *25 m* dish at Dwingeloo, The Netherlands completed in May 1956.

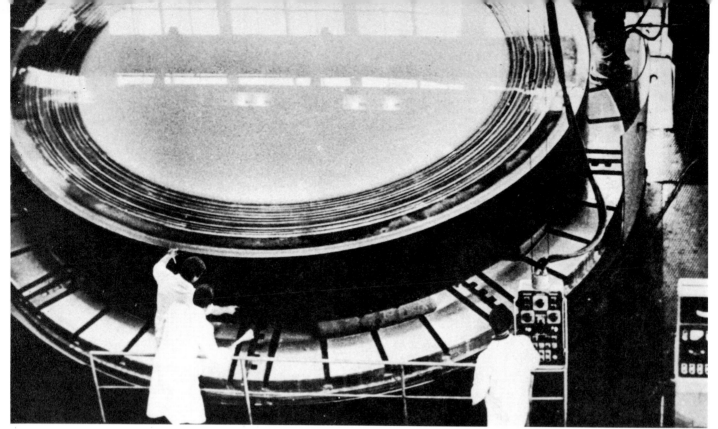

The reflector of the world's largest telescope—the Mt. Semirodriki instrument in the USSR which can detect the light from a candle 15,000 miles *24 000 km* distant

It was announced in June 1974 that the University of Manchester Mark V radio telescope project at Meiford, Powys, Wales, for a 375 ft *120 m* instrument had been abandoned when cost estimates surpassed £17 million.

Largest The world's largest dish radio telescope is the partially-
Dish steerable ionospheric assembly built over a natural bowl at Arecibo, Puerto Rico, completed in November 1963 at a cost of about $9,000,000 (*£3.75 million*). The dish has a diameter of 1,000 ft *304,80 m* and covers 18½ acres *7,28 ha*. Its sensitivity was raised by a factor of 1,000 and its range to the edge of the observable Universe at some 15,000 million light-years by the fitting of new aluminium plates at a cost of $8.8 million. Re-dedication was on 16 Nov. 1974. The RATAN-600 radio telescope being built in the Northern Caucasus, U.S.S.R. will have mirror dishes on a 600 m *1,968.5 ft* perimeter.

Largest The first $3 million instalment for the building of the
World world's largest and most sensitive radio telescope was included by the National Science Foundation in their federal budget for the fiscal year 1973. The instrument termed the VLA (Very Large Array) will be Y-shaped with each arm 13 miles *20,9 km* long with 27 mobile antennae on rails. The site selected will be 50 miles *80 km* west of Socorro in the Plains of San Augustin, New Mexico and the completion date will be 1981 at a cost of $74 million (*now £30.2 million*).

The British Science Research Council 5 Km Radio telescope at Lord's Bridge, Cambridgeshire to be operated by the Mullard Radio Astronomy Observatory of Cambridge University will utilize eight mobile 42 ft *12,80 m* rail-borne computer-controlled dish aerials, which will be equivalent to a single steerable dish 5 km *3 miles 188 yds* in diameter. The project, cost more than £2,100,000 and was completed in 1973.

Solar The world's largest solar telescope is the 480 ft *146,30 m* long McMath telescope at Kitt Peak National Observatory near Tucson, Arizona, U.S.A. It has a focal length of 300 ft *91,44 m* and an 80 in *2,03 m* heliostat mirror. It was completed in 1962 and produces an image measuring 33 in *83,8 cm* in diameter.

Observatory The highest altitude observatory in the world is the
Highest University of Denver's High Altitude Observatory at an altitude of 14,100 ft *4 297 m*, opened in 1973. The principal instrument is an 24 in *60,48 cm* Ealing Beck reflecting telescope.

Oldest The earliest astronomical observatory in the world is the Chomsong-dae built in A.D. 632 in Kyongju, South Korea and still extant.

Planetaria The ancestor of the planetarium is the rotatable
World Gottorp Globe, built by Andreas Busch in Denmark between 1654 and 1664 to the orders of the Duke, Frederick III of Holstein's court mathematician Olearius. It is 34.6 ft *10,54 m* in circumference, weighs nearly 3½ tons/*tonnes* and is now preserved in Leningrad, U.S.S.R. The stars were painted on the inside. The earliest optical installation was not until 1923 in the Deutsches Museum, Munich, by Zeiss of Jena, Germany. The world's largest planetarium, is in Moscow, U.S.S.R., and has a diameter of 82½ ft *25,15 m*.

United The United Kingdom's first planetarium was opened
Kingdom at Madame Tussaud's Marylebone Road, London, on 19 March 1958. Accurate images of 8,900 stars are able to be projected on the 70 ft *21,33 m* high copper dome.

5. PHOTOGRAPHY

CAMERAS

Earliest The earliest photograph was taken in the summer of 1826 by Joseph Nicéphore Niépce (1765–1833), a French physician and scientist. It showed the courtyard of his country house at Gras, near St. Loup-de-Varennes. It probably took eight hours to expose and was taken on a bitumen-coated polished pewter plate measuring 7¾ in by 6½ in *20 × 16,5 cm*. The earliest photograph taken in England was one of a diamond-paned window in Laycock (or Lacock) Abbey, Wiltshire, taken in August 1835 by William Henry Fox Talbot, M.P. (1800–77), the inventor of the negative-positive process. This was bought by the

Photography/Numerology

Product Support Ltd

The world's largest camera—the 27 ton Rolls Royce instrument

Johannesburg City Council for £480 in November 1970. The world's earliest aerial photograph was taken in 1858 by Gaspard Félix Tournachon (1820–1910), *alias* Nadar, from a balloon near Villacoublay, on the outskirts of Paris, France.

Largest The largest camera ever built is the 27 ton Rolls Royce camera built for Product Support (Graphics) Ltd., of Derby, England completed in 1959. It measures 8 ft 10 in *2,69 m* high, 8 ft 3 in *2,51 m* wide and 35 ft *10,66 m* in length. The lens is a 63″ f 15 Cooke Apochromatic. Its value after improvements in 1971 was in excess of £100,000.

Smallest Apart from cameras built for intra-cardiac surgery and espionage, the smallest camera that has been marketed is the circular Japanese "Petal" camera with a diameter of 1.14 in *2,9 cm* and a thickness of 0.65 in *1,65 cm*. It has a focal length of 12 mm *0.47 in.* The B.B.C. T.V. programme *Record Breakers* showed prints from this camera on 3 Dec. 1974.

Fastest In 1972 Prof. Basor of the U.S.S.R. Academy of Sciences published a paper describing an experimental camera with a time resolution of 5×10^{-13} of a sec or $\frac{1}{2}$ a picosec. The fastest production camera in the world is the Imacon 600 manufactured by John Hadland (P.I.) Ltd of Bovingdon, Hertfordshire which is capable of 600 million pictures per sec. Uses include lasar, ballistic, detonic, plasma and corona research.

Most The most expensive range of camera equipment in *expensive* the world is the F-1 35 mm system of Canon Camera Co. Inc. of Tokyo. The 40 lenses offered range from the Fish Eye 7.5 mm F5.6 to the FL 1200 mm F11, while the accessories available number 180. The total cost of the range would exceed £30,000. A Thomas Sutton wet plate camera, *c.* 1865, was sold at auction at Sotheby's for £11,500 on 8 March 1974.

6. NUMEROLOGY

In dealing with large numbers, scientists use the notation of 10 raised to various powers to eliminate a profusion of noughts. For example, 19,160,000,000,000 miles would be written 1.916×10^{13} miles. Similarly, a very small

number, for example 0.0000154324 of a gramme, would be written 1.5432×10^{-5} g. Of the prefixes used before numbers the smallest is "atto-" from the Danish atten for 18, indicating a trillionth part (10^{-18}) of the unit, and the highest is "tera-" (Greek, teras = monster), indicating a billion (10^{12}) fold. The prefix "bronto" has however been proposed for 10^{15}.

NUMBERS

Highest The highest generally accepted named number is the centillion, which is 10 raised to the power 600, or one followed by 600 noughts. Higher numbers are named in linguistic literature the most extreme of which is the milli-millimillillion (10 raised to the power 6,000,000,000) devised by Rudolf Ondrejka. The number Megiston written with symbol ⑩ is a number too great to have any physical meaning. The highest named number outside the decimal notation is the Buddhist *asankhyeya*, which is equal to 10^{140} or 100 tertio-vigintillions (British system) or 100 quinto-quadragintillions (U.S. system).

The number 10^{100} (10,000 sexdecillion (U.K.) or 10 duotrigintillion (U.S.)) is designated a Googol. The term was devised by Dr. Edward Kasner (U.S.) (d. 1955). Ten raised to the power of a Googol is described as a Googolplex. Some conception of the magnitude of such numbers can be gained when it is said that the number of atoms in some models of the observable Universe does not exceed 10^{85}. Factorial 10^{85}, approximates to 10 to the power of $43 + 85 \times 10^{85}$.

Prime A prime number is any positive integer (excluding 1) *numbers* having no integral factors other than itself and unity, *e.g.* 2, 3, 5, 7 or 11. The lowest prime number is thus 2. The highest known prime number is $2^{19937}-1$ (a number of 6,002 digits of which the first five are 43,154 and the last three, 471) received by the American Mathematical Society on 18 March 1971 and calculated on an I.B.M. 360/91 computer in 39 mins. 26.4 sec by Dr. Bryant Tuckerman at Yorktown Heights, New York.

Perfect A number is said to be perfect if it is equal to the sum *numbers* of its divisors other than itself, *e.g.* $1 + 2 + 4 + 7 + 14 = 28$. The lowest perfect number is 6 $(1 + 2 + 3)$. The highest known and the 24th so far discovered, is $(2^{19937} - 1) \times 2^{19936}$ which has 12,003 digits of which

Dr. Tuckerman, discoverer of the highest known prime number—6,002 digits long

IBM

THE SCIENTIFIC WORLD

the first 3 are 931, and the last 3 are 656. It is a consequence of the highest known prime (see above).

Largest Magic Square The largest reported magic square is one which adds vertically, horizontally and diagonally to 578,865 completed in 1975 by Richard Suntag, 13 of Pomona, New York, U.S.A.

Most primitive The most unnumerate people are the Nambiquara of the north west Matto Grosso of Brazil who lack any system of numbers. They do however have a verb which means "they are two alike".

Longest Slide Rule The world's longest slide rule is believed to be one 20 ft *6,10 m* overall weighing 110 lb. *50 kg* constructed in 1973–74 by Ralph Nyberg and members of the Mathematics Club of Roanoke-Benson High School, Illinois, U.S.A.

Most accurate and most inaccurate version of "pi" The greatest number of decimal places to which *pi (π)* has been calculated is 1,000,000 by the French mathematicians Jean Guilloud and Mlle. Martine Bouyer achieved on 24 May 1973 on a CDC 7600 computer but not verified until 3 Sept. 1973. The published value to a million places, in what has been described as the world's most boring 200 page book, was 3.141592653589793 . . . (omitting the next 999,975 places) . . . 5779458151. In 1897 the State legislature of Indiana came within a single vote of declaring that pi should be *de jure* 3.2.

Square root of two The greatest accuracy for √2 is an enumeration to 1,000,082 places by Jacques Dutka of Columbia University, N.Y., U.S.A. announced in Oct. 1971 after a 47½ hour run work on a computer.

Earliest measures The earliest known measure of weight is the *beqa* of the Amratian period of Egyptian civilization *c.* 3,800 B.C. found at Naqada, United Arab Republic. The weights are cylindrical with rounded ends from 188.7 to 211.2 g *6.65 to 7.45 oz*. The unit of length used by the megalithic tomb-builders in Britain *c.* 2300 B.C. appears to have been 2.72±0.003 ft *82,81±82,99 cm*.

TIME MEASURE

Longest The longest measure of time is the *kalpa* in Hindu chronology. It is equivalent to 4,320 million years. In astronomy a cosmic year is the period of rotation of the sun around the centre of the Milky Way galaxy, *i.e.* about 225,000,000 years. In the Late Cretaceous Period of *c.* 85 million years ago the Earth rotated faster so resulting in 370.3 days per year while in Cambrian times some 600 million years ago there is evidence that the year contained 425 days.

Shortest Owing to variations in the length of a day, which is estimated to be increasing irregularly at the average rate of about two milliseconds per century due to the Moon's tidal drag, the second has been redefined. Instead of being 1/86,400th part of a mean solar day, it has, since 1960, been reckoned as 1/31,556,925.9747th part of the solar (or tropical) year at A.D. 1900, January 0 to 12 hrs, Ephemeris time. In 1958 the second of Ephemeris time was computed to be equivalent to 9,192,631,770±20 cycles of the radiation corresponding to the transition of a caesium 133 atom when unperturbed by exterior fields. The greatest diurnal change recorded has been 10 milliseconds on 8 Aug. 1972 due to the most violent solar storm recorded in 370 years of observations. In a nano-second or a milli-micro second (1.0 × 10⁻⁹ of a sec) light travels 11.8 in *29,97 cm*.

SMALLEST UNITS

The shortest unit of length is the atto-metre which is 1.0 × 10⁻¹⁶ of a cm. The smallest unit of area is a "shed", used in sub-atomic physics and first mentioned in 1956. It is 1.0 × 10⁻⁴⁸ of a cm². A "barn" is equal to 10²⁴ "sheds". The reaction of a neutrino occurs over the area of 1 × 10⁻⁴³ of a cm².

82

Numerology/Physical Extremes

7. PHYSICAL EXTREMES (Terrestrial)

TEMPERATURES

Highest The highest man-made temperatures yet attained are those produced in the centre of a thermonuclear fusion bomb, which are of the order of 300,000,000 to 400,000,000° C. Of controllable temperatures, the highest effective laboratory figure reported is 50,000,000°C, for 2/100ths of a second by Prof. Lev A. Artsimovich at Tokamuk in the U.S.S.R. in 1969. At very low particle densities even higher figures are obtainable. Prior to 1963 a figure of 3,000 million ° C. was reportedly achieved in the U.S.S.R. with Ogra injection-mirror equipment.

Lowest The lowest temperature reached is 5 × 10⁻⁷ degree Kelvin, achieved by Professor A. Abragam (b. 1914) in collaboration with M. Chapellier, M. Goldman, and Vu Hoang Chau at the Centre d'Etudes Nucléaires, Saclay, France, in March 1969. Absolute or thermodynamic temperatures are defined in terms of ratios rather than as differences reckoned from the unattainable absolute zero, which on the Kelvin scale is −273,15° C or −459.67° F. Thus the lowest temperature ever attained is 1 in 5.46 × 10⁸ of the melting point of ice (0° C. or 273.15K or 32° F.).

The lowest equilibrium temperature ever attained is 0.0003° K by nuclear refrigeration in a 1,4 kg *3 lb* copper specimen by Prof. Olli V. Lounasmaa (b. 1920) and his team at the Helsinki University of Technology, Otaniemi, Finland, on 17 April 1974.

Solar Power plant The largest solar furnace in the world is the Laboratoire de l'Energie Solaire, at Odeillo, Pyrénées-Orientales, France. It consists of an array of 63 steerable mirrors with a total area of 2 835 m² *30,515 ft²* or seven tenths of an acre which can generate a heat of 3 725° C *6 735° F.*

Claude Gazuit

The Pyrenean solar furnace, which can generate temperatures of 3 725°C *6,735°F*

Highest pressures The highest sustained laboratory pressures yet reported are of 5,000,000 atmospheres or 5,000 kilobars (*7,25 × 10⁷ lbf/in²*), achieved in the U.S.S.R. and announced in October 1958. Using dynamic methods and impact speeds of up to 18,000 m.p.h. *29 000 km/h*, momentary pressures of 75,000,000 atmospheres (490,000 tons/in² [*7 × 10⁹ kPa*]) were reported from the United States in 1958.

Professor Moon with the fastest centrifuge

Birmingham Post & Mail

produced photographs of electron clouds of atoms of neon and argon.

Highest frequency In January 1974 at the U.S. National Bureau of Standards, Boulder, Colorado K. M. Evenson *et al.* attained a frequency of 88,376,245 terahertz (THz) or 8.8×10^{19}Hz with a helium-neon laser emission.

Highest note The highest note yet attained is one of 60,000 megahertz (60 GHz) (60,000 million vibrations/sec), generated by a "laser" beam striking a sapphire crystal at the Massachusetts Institute of Technology in Cambridge, Massachusetts, U.S.A., in September 1964.

Loudest noise The loudest noise created in a laboratory is 210 decibels or 400,000 acoustic watts reported by NASA from a 48 ft *14,63 m* steel and concrete horn at Huntsville, Alabama, U.S.A. in October 1965. Holes can be bored in solid material by this means.

Most powerful sound system The world's most powerful sound system is that installed at the Ontario Motor Speedway, California in July 1970. It has an output of 30,800 watts. connectable to 355 horn speaker assemblies and is thus able to communicate the spoken word to 230,000 people above the noise of 50 screaming racing cars.

Quietest place The "dead room", measuring 35 ft by 28 ft *10,67 × 3,53 m* in the Bell Telephone System laboratory at Murray Hill, New Jersey, U.S.A., is the most anechoic room in the world, eliminating 99.98 per cent of reflected sound.

Highest vacuum The highest (or 'hardest') vacuums obtained in scientific research are of the order of 1.0×10^{-16} of an atmosphere. This compares with an estimated pressure in inter-stellar space of 1.0×10^{-19} of an atmosphere. At sea-level there are 3×10^{19} molecules/cm³ in the atmosphere, but in inter-stellar space there are probably less than 10/cm³.

Fastest centrifuge The highest man-made rotary speed ever achieved and the fastest speed by any earth-bound object is 4,500 m.p.h. *7 250 km/h* by a swirling tapered 6 in *15,2 cm* carbon fibre rod in a vacuum at Birmingham University, England reported on 24 January 1975.

Microscopes Most powerful The world's most powerful microscope was announced by Dr. Lawrence Bartell and Charles Ritz of Michigan University in July 1974 with an image magnification of 260 million fold. It uses an optical laser to decode holograms produced with 40 Kev radiation and has

Finest balance The most accurate balance in the world is the Sartorius Model 4108 manufactured in Göttingen, West Germany, which can weigh objects of up to 0,5 g to an accuracy of 0,01 μg or 0,00000001 g which is equivalent to little more than one sixtieth of the weight of the ink on this full stop .

Lowest viscosity The California Institute of Technology, U.S.A. announced on 1 Dec. 1957 that there was no measurable viscosity, *i.e.* perfect flow, in liquid helium II, which exists only at temperatures close to absolute zero ($-273.15°$ C. or $-459.67°$ F.).

Lowest friction The lowest coefficient of static and dynamic friction of any solid is 0.02, in the case of polytetrafluoroethylene ($[C_2F_4]_n$), called P.T.F.E.—equivalent to wet ice on wet ice. It was first manufactured in quantity by E. I. du Pont de Nemours & Co. Inc. in 1943,

The world's most sensitive balance—able to weigh the ink of a full stop with ease

Scientific Instrument Centre

and is marketed from the U.S.A. as Teflon. In the United Kingdom it is marketed by I.C.I. as Fluon.

At the University of Virginia (see above, Fastest centrifuge) a 30 lb. *13 kg 60* rotor magnetically supported has been spun at 1,000 revs/sec in a vacuum of 10^{-6} mm. of mercury pressure. It loses only one revolution per second per day thus spinning for years.

Most powerful electric current The most powerful electric current generated is that from the Zeus capacitor at the Los Alamos Scientific Laboratory, New Mexico, U.S.A. If fired simultaneously the 4,032 capacitors would produce for a few microseconds twice as much current as that generated elsewhere on Earth.

Most powerful particle accelerator The 1.24 mile *2 km* diameter proton synchrotron at the Fermi National Accelerator Laboratory at Weston Illinois, U.S.A. is the largest and most powerful "atom-smasher" in the world. An energy of 400 GeV was attained on 14 Dec. 1972. Plans to double the energy to nearly 1 Tera electron volts were begun in 1971 by means of a second ring of superconducting magnets but only one sixth of this has so far been authorized.

The £32 million CERN intersecting storage rings (ISR) project near Geneva, Switzerland started on 27 Jan. 1971, using two 28 GeV proton beams, and is designed to yield the equivalent of 1,700 GeV or 1.7 Tev (1.7 million million electron volts) in its centre of mass experiments.

World's largest bubble chamber The largest bubble chamber in the world is the $7 million installation completed in October 1973 at Weston, Illinois (see above). It is 15 ft *4,57 m* in diameter and contains 7,259 gal *33 000 litres* of liquid hydrogen at a temperature of $-247°$ C with a superconductivity magnet of 30,000 gauss.

Strongest magnet The heaviest magnet in the world is one measuring 60 m *196 ft* in diameter, with a weight of 36,000 tons/*tonnes* for the 10 GeV synchrophasotron in the Joint Institute for Nuclear Research at Dubna, near Moscow, U.S.S.R. Intermagnetics General Corporation announced a 165 kilograms superconductive niobium-tin magnet at 3.0 K in September 1973 and plans for a 180 kG vanadium-gallium magnet.

Strongest magnetic field The strongest recorded magnetic fields are ones of 10 megagauss, fleetingly produced by explosive flux compression devices reported in Sept. 1968. The first megagauss field was announced also from the United States in March 1967.

The strongest steady magnetic field yet achieved is one of 255,000 gauss in a cylindrical bore of 1.25 in *3,17 cm* using 10 megawatts of power, called the "1J" magnet designed by D. Bruce Montgomery, which was put into operation at the Francis Bitter National Magnet Laboratory at Massachusetts Institute of Technology in 1964.

The weakest magnetic fields measured is one of 1.6×10^{-10} gauss in the heavily shielded room at the Francis Bitter National Magnet Laboratory, Cambridge, Massachusetts, U.S.A. It is used for research into the very weak magnetic fields generated in the heart and brain.

WIND TUNNELS

World The world's largest wind tunnel is a low-speed tunnel with a 40×80 ft *12,19 $\times$ 24,38 m* test section built in 1944 at the Ames Research Center, Moffett Field, California, U.S.A. The tunnel encloses 800 tons/*tonnes* of air and cost approximately $7,000,000 (*now* £2,916,666). The maximum volume of air that can be moved is 60,000,000 ft³ *1 700 000 m³* per min. On 30 July 1974 NASA announced an intention to increase

it in size to 80×120 ft *24,38 $\times$ 36,57 m* for 345 m.p.h. speeds with a 135,000 h.p. system. The most powerful is the 216,000 h.p. *219 000 c.v.* installation at the Arnold Engineering Test Center at Tullahoma, Tennessee, U.S.A. opened in September 1956. The highest Mach number attained with air is Mach 27 at the works of the Boeing Company in Seattle, Washington State, U.S.A. For periods of micro-seconds, shock Mach numbers of the order of 30 have been attained in impulse tubes at Cornell University, Ithaca, New York State, U.S.A.

United Kingdom The most powerful wind tunnel in the United Kingdom is the intermittent compressed air type installation at the B.A.C. plant at Warton, Lancashire which can be run at Mach 4, which is equivalent to 3,044 m.p.h. *4 898 km/h* at sea level.

Finest cut Biological specimens embedded in epoxy resin can be sectioned by a glass knife microtome under ideal conditions to a thickness of 1/875,000th of an inch or 290 Ångström units.

Sharpest objects The University of California Medical Center, San Francisco announced in July 1974 the ultimate in sharpness—glass electrodes more than 200 times slimmer than a diamond phonograph stylus. These can be used for exploring the cells in the eye. The points are 0.05 μm.

Brightest light The brightest steady artificial light sources are "laser" beams with an intensity exceeding the Sun's 1,500,000 candles/in² *200 000 candelas/cm²* by a factor well in excess of 1,000. In May 1969 the U.S.S.R. Academy of Sciences announced blast waves travelling through a luminous plasma of inert gases heated to 90,000° K. The flare-up for up to 3 microseconds shone at 50,000 times the brightness of the Sun *viz.* 40,000 million candles/in². Of continuously burning sources, the most powerful is a 200 kW high-pressure xenon arc lamp of 600,000 candle-power, reported from the U.S.S.R. in 1965. The most powerful searchlight ever developed was one produced during the 1939–45 war by the General Electric Company Ltd. at the Hirst Research Centre in Wembley, Greater London. It had a consumption of 600 kW and gave an arc luminance of 300,000 candles/in² and a maximum beam intensity of 2,700,000,000 candles from its parabolic mirror (diameter 10 ft *[3,04 m]*).

Shortest wavelength On 15 Apr. 1974 I.B.M. researchers E. Spillar and Armin Segmüller announced that X-rays with a wavelength of only 1.54 Ångstrom units (6,000 millionths of an inch) had been harnessed in a device, which may become a "light pipe" to guide X-rays to required locations.

Most durable light The average bulb lasts for 750 to 1,000 hrs. There is some evidence that a carbide filament bulb burning in the Fire Department, Livermore, South Alameda County, California has been burning since 1901.

Most powerful "laser" beams The first illumination of another celestial body was achieved on 9 May 1962, when a beam of light was successfully reflected from the Moon by the use of an optical "maser" (microwave amplification by stimulated emission of radiation) or "laser" (light amplification by stimulated emission of radiation) attached to a 48-in. *121,9 cm* telescope at Massachusetts Institute of Technology, Cambridge, Massachusetts, U.S.A. The spot was estimated to be 4 miles *6,4 km* in diameter on the Moon. The device was propounded in 1958 by Dr. Charles Hard Townes (born 1915) of the U.S.A. A "maser" light flash is focused into liquid nitrogen-cooled ruby crystal. Its chromium atoms are excited into a high energy state in which they emit a red light which is allowed to escape only in the direction desired. Such a flash for 1/5,000th of a second can bore a hole through a diamond by vaporization at 10,000° C, produced by 2×10^{23} photons.

6 THE ARTS AND ENTERTAIN-MENTS

1. PAINTING

Earliest Evidence of Palaeolithic art was first found in 1834 at Chaffaud, Vienne, France by Brouillet when he recognised an engraving of two deer on a piece of flat bone from the cave, dating to *c.* 20,000 B.C. The number of stratigraphically-dated examples of cave art is very limited. The oldest known dated examples came from La Ferrassie, near Les Eyzies in the Périgord, where large blocks of stone engraved with animal figures and symbols were found in an Aurignacian II layer (*c.* 25,000 B.C.).

LARGEST

World *Panorama of the Mississippi*, completed by John **All time** Banvard (1815–91) in 1846, showing the river for 1,200 miles *1 930 km* in a strip probably 5,000 ft *1 525 m* long and 12 ft *3,65 m* wide, was the largest painting in the world, with an area of more than 1.3 acres *0,52 ha*. The painting is believed to have been destroyed when the rolls of canvas, stored in a barn at Cold Spring Harbor, Long Island, New York State, U.S.A., caught fire shortly before Banvard's death on 16 May 1891.

Existing The largest known painting now in existence is *The Battle of Gettysburg*, completed in 1883, after 2½ yrs of work, by Paul Philippoteaux (France) and 16 assistants. The painting is 410 ft *125 m* long, 70 ft *21,3 m* high and weighs 5.36 tons *5,45 tonnes*. It depicts the climax of the Battle of Gettysburg, in southern Pennsylvania, U.S.A., on 3 July 1863. In 1964 the painting was bought by Joe King of Winston-Salem, North Carolina, U.S.A. after being stored by E. W. McConnell in a Chicago warehouse since 1933.

"Old The largest "Old Master" is *Il Paradiso*, painted *Master"* between 1587 and 1590 by Jacopo Robusti, *alias* Tintoretto (1518–94), and his son Domenico on Wall "E" of the Sala del Maggior Consiglio in the Palazzo Ducale (Doge's Palace) in Venice, Italy. The work is 22 m *72 ft 2 in* long and 7 m *22 ft 11½ in* high and contains more than 100 human figures.

United The largest painting in the United Kingdom is the **Kingdom** giant oval *Triumph of Peace and Liberty* by Sir James Thornhill (1676–1734), on the ceiling of the Painted Hall in the Royal Naval College, Greenwich, Greater London. It measures 106 ft *32,3 m* by 51 ft *15,4 m* and took 20 yrs (1707–1727) to complete.

Smallest The smallest paintings in the world are those executed in oils with a 4 or 5 sable hair brush on pinheads $\frac{1}{32}$ to $\frac{1}{4}$ inch *0,8–6,3 mm* in diameter by Gerard Legare of British Columbia, Canada.

MOST VALUABLE

World The "Mona Lisa" (*La Gioconda*) by Leonardo da Vinci (1452–1519) in the Louvre, Paris, was assessed for insurance purposes at the highest ever figure of $100,000,000 (*then £35.7 million*) for its move for exhibition in Washington, D.C., and New York City, N.Y., U.S.A., from 14 Dec. 1962 to 12 March 1963. However, insurance was not concluded because the cost of the closest security precautions was less than that of the premiums. It was painted in *c.* 1503–07

and measures 77 × 53 cm *30.5 × 20.9 in.* It is believed to portray Mona (short for Madonna) Lisa Gherardini, the wife of Francesco del Giocondo of Florence, who disliked it and refused to pay for it. Francis I, King of France, bought the painting for his bathroom in 1517 for 4,000 gold florins or 492 oz. of gold now worth some £30,000.

HIGHEST PRICE

Auction The highest price ever bid in a public auction for any **price** painting is £2,310,000 for *Portrait of Juan de Pareja*, *World* also known as *The Slave of Velázquez*, painted in Rome in 1649 by Diego Rodríguez de Silva Velázquez (1599–1660) and sold on 27 Nov. 1970 at the salerooms of Christie, Manson & Woods, London to the Wildenstein Gallery, New York. The painting had been sold at Christie's at auction in 1801 for 39 guineas (£40.95) It was in the possession of the Earls of Radnor from May 1811 until 1970.

By British artist The highest auction price for the work of a British artist is the £280,000 paid by Messrs. Colnaghi's at Sotheby's for Thomas Gainsborough's painting of *Mr. and Mrs. Gravenor and their daughters Elizabeth and Dorothea*, from the estate of Major J. Townshend, on 19 July 1972. Executed in *c.* 1748, it measures 35½ in *90 cm* square. It was discovered by Mr. Andrew Festing, a Sotheby expert.

Miniature portrait The highest price ever paid for a portrait miniature is the £65,100 given by an anonymous buyer at a sale held by Christie, Manson and Woods, London on 8 June 1971 for a miniature of Frances Howard, Countess of Essex and Somerset by Isaac Oliver, painted *c.* 1605. This miniature, sent for auction by Lord Derby, measured 5⅛ in *13 cm* in diameter.

New York Metropolitan Museum of Art

Aristotle contemplating the Bust of Homer by Rembrandt—one of only 3 painters to set a world art record at auction

Modern painting The highest price paid for a modern painting is $1,550,000 (*then £645,833*) paid by the Norton Simon Foundation of Los Angeles, California, U.S.A. at the Sotheby-Parke-Bernet Galleries, New York City on 9 Oct. 1968 for *Le Pont des Arts* painted by Pierre Auguste Renoir (1841–1919) of France in 1868. Renoir sold the picture to the Paris dealer Durand-Ruel for about £16.

Living artist World The highest price paid for paintings in the lifetime of the artist is $1,950,000 (*then £812,500*) paid for the two canvases *Two Brothers* (1905) and *Seated Harlequin* (1922) by Pablo Diego José Francisco de Paula Juan Nepomuceno Crispín Crispiano de la Santisima Trinidad Ruiz y Picasso (1881–1973) of Spain. This was paid by the Basle City Government to the Staechelin Foundation to enable the Basle Museum of Arts to retain the painting after an offer of $2,560,000 (*£1,066,666*) had been received from the United States in December 1967.

British and Irish The highest price for any painting by a living United Kingdom born artist is £26,000 for a painting of a Pope in "convulsive hysteria" by Francis Bacon (b. Dublin, Ireland, 1909, then part of the United Kingdom) completed in 1953, sent in anonymously and bought by Lefevre Gallery at auction at Sotheby's in 1970.

Most Prolific Portrait Painter Herman H. Simms (b. Cincinnati, Ohio, 1920), who works at Disneyland, Annaheim, California, painted 9,803 water colour portraits in the year 1973.

Most Prolific Picasso was the most prolific of all painters in a career which lasted 78 years. It has been estimated that Picasso produced about 13,500 paintings or designs, 100,000 prints or engravings, 34,000 book illustrations and 300 sculptures or ceramics. His life-time *oeuvre* has been valued at £300 million.

Drawing The highest price ever attached to any drawing is £804,361 for the cartoon *The Virgin and Child with St. John the Baptist and St. Anne*, measuring 54¼ in by 39¼ in *137 by 100 cm*, drawn in Milan, probably in 1499–1500, by Leonardo da Vinci (1452–1519) of Italy, retained by the National Gallery in 1962. Three United States bids of over $4,000,000 (*then £1,428,570*) were reputed to have been made for the cartoon.

HIGHEST-PRICED PAINTINGS — Progressive records

Price	Equivalent 1975 Value	Painter, title, sold by and sold to	Date
£6,500	£85,300	Antonio Correggio's *The Magdalen Reading* (in fact spurious) to Elector Freidrich Augustus II of Saxony.	1746
£8,500	£111,550	Raphael's *The Sistine Madonna* to Elector Friedrich Augustus II of Saxony.	1759
£16,000	£119,950	Van Eyck's *Adoration of the Lamb*, 6 outer panels of Ghent altarpiece by Edward Solby to the Government of Prussia.	1821
£24,600*	£266,400	Murillo's *The Immaculate Conception* by estate of Marshall Soult to the Louvre (against Czar Nicholas I) in Paris.	1852
£70,000	£918,150	Raphael's *Ansidei Madonna* by the 8th Duke of Marlborough to the National Gallery.	1885
£100,000	£1,312,500	Raphael's *The Colonna Altarpiece* by Sedelmeyer to J. Pierpoint Morgan.	1901
£102,880	£1,351,000	Van Dyck's *Elena Grimaldi-Cattaneo* (portrait) by Knoedler to Peter Widener (1834–1915).	1906
£102,880	£1,116,700	Rembrandt's *The Mill* by 6th Marquess of Lansdowne to Peter Widener.	1911
£116,500	£1,262,000	Raphael's smaller *Panshanger Madonna* by Joseph (later Baron) Duveen (1869–1939) to Peter Widener.	1913
£310,400	£3,363,000	Leonardo da Vinci's *Benois Madonna* to Czar Nicholas II in Paris.	1914
£821,429*	£1,560,000	Rembrandt's *Aristotle Contemplating the Bust of Homer* by estate of Mr. and Mrs. Alfred W. Erickson to New York Metropolitan Museum of Art.	1961
£1,785,714	£3,534,000	Leonardo da Vinci's *Ginevra de' Benci* (portrait) by Prince Franz Josef II of Liechtenstein to National Gallery of Art, Washington, D.C., U.S.A.	1967
£2,310,000*	£3,790,000	Velázquez's *Portrait of Juan de Pareja* by the Earl of Radnor to the Wildenstein Gallery, New York.	1970

*Indicates price at auction, otherwise prices were by private treaty.

Largest gallery The world's largest art gallery is the Winter Palace and the neighbouring Hermitage in Leningrad, U.S.S.R. One has to walk 15 miles *24 km* to visit each of the 322 galleries, which house nearly 3,000,000 works of art and objects of archaeological interest.

Oldest and youngest R.A. The oldest ever Royal Academician has been (Thomas) Sidney Cooper C.V.O., who died on 8 Feb. 1902 aged 98 yrs 136 days, having exhibited 266 paintings over the record span of 69 consecutive years (1833–1902). The youngest ever R.A. has been Mary Moser (1744–1819) (later Mrs. Hugh Lloyd), who was elected on the foundation of the Royal Academy in 1768 when aged 24.

Youngest exhibitor The youngest ever exhibitor at the Royal Academy of Arts Annual Summer Exhibition has been Lewis Melville "Gino" Lyons (b. 30 Apr. 1962). His *Trees and Monkeys* was painted on 4 June 1965, submitted on 17 Mar. 1967 and exhibited to the public on 29 Apr. 1967.

MURALS

Earliest The earliest known murals on man-made walls are those at Catal Hüyük in southern Anatolia, Turkey, dating from *c.* 5850 B.C.

Largest The largest logo and mural painting in the world is the American Revolution Bicentennial symbol, on the curved roof of the Arizona Veterans Memorial Coliseum, Phoenix, Arizona. It occupies 110,000 ft² *10 219 m²* or more than 2½ acres. It will be painted over in 1977. After being outlined by aid of a computer, it took 45 man days to apply the necessary 870 gallons *3 955 l* of patriotic (red, white and blue) paint on 18–26 Aug. 1973.

Largest mosaic The world's largest mosaic is on the walls of the central library of the Universidad Nacional Autónomao de México, Mexico City. There are four walls, the two largest measuring 12,949 ft² *1 203 m²* each representing the pre-Hispanic past.

The largest Roman mosaic in Britain is the Woodchester Pavement, Gloucestershire of *c.* A.D. 325, excavated in 1793, now recovered with protective earth until its 8th showing due in 1983. It measures 48 ft 10 in *14,88 m* square comprising 1½ million tesserae.

MUSEUMS

Oldest The oldest museum in the world is the Ashmolean Museum in Oxford built in 1679.

Largest The largest museum in the world is the American Museum of Natural History on 77th to 81st Streets and Central Park West, New York City, N.Y., U.S.A. Founded in 1874, it comprises 19 interconnected buildings with 23 acres *9 ha* of floor space. The largest museum in the United Kingdom is the British Museum (founded in 1753), which was opened to the public in 1759. The main building in Bloomsbury, London, was built in 1823 and has a total floor area of 17.57 acres *7,11 ha.*

2. SCULPTURE

Earliest World The earliest known examples of sculpture are the so-called Venus figurines from Aurignacian sites, dating to *c.* 25,000–22,000 B.C., *e.g.* the famous Venus of Willendorf from Austria and the Venus of Brassempouy (Landes, France). A piece of ox rib found in 1973 at Pech de l'Aze, Dordogne, France in an early Middle Palaeolithic layer of the Riss glaciation *c.* 105,000 B.C. appears to have several intentional engraved lines on one side.

Britain The earliest British art object is an engraving of a horse's head on a piece of rib-bone from Robin Hood

The world's oldest museum—the Ashmolean at Oxford, England

Cave, Creswell Crag, Derbyshire. It dates from the Upper Palaeolithic period (*c.* 15,000 to 10,000 B.C.). The earliest Scottish rock carving from Lagalochan, Strathclyde dates from *c.* 3,000 B.C.

Most expensive World The highest price ever paid for a sculpture is the $380,000 (£158,333) given at Sotheby's Parke-Bernet New York salerooms, on 5 May 1971 for Edgar Degas' (1834–1917) bronze *Petite Danseuse de Quatorze Ans*, executed in an edition of about 12 casts in 1880.

Ancient The highest price paid for any work of art from any ancient civilization is $260,000 (£140,000) given by the Metropolitan Museum of Art, New York City for the 18th dynasty turquoise glazed Egyptian faience 9⅞ in *24,9 cm* figure of Pharoah Amenhotep III (*c.* 1410–1320 B.C.) at Sotheby Parke-Bernet, New York on 2 May 1972.

Living sculptor The highest price paid for the work of a living sculptor is the $260,000 (£104,000) given at Sotheby's Parke-Bernet Galleries, New York on 1 March 1972 by Fischer Fine Arts of London for the 75 in *189 cm* long wooden carving *Reclining Figure* by Henry Moore, O.M., C.H. (b. Castleford, West Yorkshire, 30 July 1898) sold by Cranbrook Academy, Bloomfield Hills, Michigan, U.S.A.

Largest The world's largest sculptures are the mounted figures of Jefferson Davis (1808–89), Gen. Robert Edward Lee (1807–70) and Gen. Thomas Jonathan ("Stonewall") Jackson (1824–63), covering 1.33 acres *0,5 ha* on the face of Stone Mountain, near Atlanta, Georgia. They are 90 ft *27,4 m* high and took from 1958 to May 1970 to sculpt. When completed the world's largest sculpture will be that of the Indian chief Tashunca-Uitco (*c.* 1849–1877), known as Crazy Horse, of the Oglala tribe of the Dakota or Nadowessioux (Sioux) group. The sculpture was begun on 3 June 1948 near Mount Rushmore, South Dakota, U.S.A. A projected 561 ft *170 m* high and 641 ft *195 m* long, it will require the removal of 5,800,000 tons *5 890 000 tonnes* of stone and is the life work of one man, Korczak Ziolkowski. The work will take until at least 1978.

Ground figures In the Nazca Desert, south of Lima, Peru there are straight lines (one more than 7 miles [*11,2 km*] long), geometric shapes and of plants and animals drawn on the ground sometime between 100 B.C. and A.D. 700 for an uncertain but probably religious or astronomical purpose by a still unknown civilization. They were first detected from the air in *c.* 1928.

Hill figures In August 1968 a 330 ft *100 m* tall figure was found on a hill above Tarapacár, Chile.

The largest human hill carving in Britain is the "Long Man" of Wilmington, East Sussex, 226 ft *68 m* in length. The oldest of all White Horses in Britain is the Uffington White Horse in Oxfordshire, dating from the late Iron Age (*c.* 150 B.C.) and measuring 374 ft *114 m* from nose to tail and 120 ft *36 m* from ear to heel.

Most Massive Mobile The most massive recorded mobile is *Quest* by Jerome Kirk installed at TRW Inc., Redondo Beach, California U.S.A. in Sept. 1968. It is a 32 ft *9,75 m* long wind-driven pivotal mobile weighing 5.35 tons *5,442 kg*. The term mobile was coined to contrast with "stabile" sculpture by Marcel Duchamp in 1932.

3. LANGUAGE

Earliest Anthropologists have evidence that the truncated pharynx of Neanderthal man precluded his speaking anything akin to a modern language any more than an ape or a modern baby. Cro-Magnon man of 40,000 B.C. had however developed an efficient vocal tract. Clay tablets of the neolithic Danubian culture discovered in Dec. 1966 at Tartaria, Moros River, Romania have been dated to the fifth or fourth millennium B.C. The tablets bear symbols of bows and arrows, gates and combs. In 1970 it was announced that writing tablets bearing an early form of the Elamite language dating from 3,500 B.C. had been found in south-eastern Iran. The scientist Alexander Marshack (U.S.) maintains that marked Upper Palaeolithic artifacts, such as a Cro-Magnon bone from 30,000 B.C. in the Musée des Antiquités Nationales, outside Paris with 69 marks with 24 stroke changes, are not random but of possibly lunar or menstrual cycle significance.

Oldest The written language with the longest continuous history is Egyptian from the earliest hieroglyphic inscriptions on the palette of Narmer dated to *c.* 3100 B.C. to Coptic used in churches at the present day more than 5,000 years later. Hieroglyphs were used until A.D. 394 and thus may be overtaken by Chinese characters as the most durable script in the 21st century.

Oldest words in English Recent research indicates that several river names in Britain date from pre-Celtic times (*ante* 550 B.C.). These include Ayr, Hayle and Nairn. This ascendant, Indo-Germanic tongue, which was spoken from *c.* 3000 B.C. on the Great Lowland Plain of Europe, now has only fragments left in Old Lithuanian, from which the modern English word *eland* derives. The word *land* is traceable to the Old Celtic *landa*, a heath and therefore must have been in use on the continent before the Roman Empire grew powerful in the 6th century B.C.

Commonest language Today's world total of languages and dialects still spoken is about 5,000 of which some 845 come from India. The language spoken by more people than any other is Northern Chinese, or Mandarin, by an estimated 68 per cent of the population hence 575 million people in 1975. The so-called national language (*Guóyǔ*) is a standardized form of Northern Chinese (*Běifānghuà*) as spoken in the Peking area. This was alphabetized into *zhuyin zimu* of 39 letters in 1918. In 1958 the *pinyin* system, using a Latin alphabet, was introduced. The next most commonly spoken language and the most widespread is English, by an estimated 360,000,000 in mid-1975. English is spoken by 10 per cent or more of the population in 34 sovereign countries.

In Great Britain and Ireland there are five indigenous tongues: English, Scots Gaelic, Welsh, Irish Gaelic, and Romany (Gipsy). Of these English is, of course,

The memorial to one of the last lifetime speakers of Cornish—Dolly Pentreath who died in 1771

Robert D. Bristow

predominant. Manx followed Cornish (whose last fluent speaker, John Davey, died in 1891) into extinction, when Mr. Edward (Ned) Maddrell (1877–1974) of Glen Chass, Port St. Mary, Isle of Man, died as the last islander whose professed tongue was Manx. In the Channel Islands, apart from Jersey and Guernsey *normand*, there survive words of Sarkese or *Sèrtchais* in which a prayer book was published in 1812, and of which there are very few speakers left.

Most complex The following extremes of complexity have been noted: Chippewa, the North American Indian language of Minnesota, U.S.A., has the most verb forms with up to 6,000; Tillamook, the North American Indian language of Oregon, U.S.A., has the most prefixes with 30; Tabassaran, a language in Daghestan, U.S.S.R., uses the most noun cases with 35, while Eskimaux use 63 forms of the present tense and simple nouns have as many as 252 inflections. In Chinese the *Chung-wên TaTz'ù-tien* dictionary lists 49,905 characters. The fourth tone of "i" has 84 meanings, varying as widely as "dress", "hiccough" and "licentious". The written language provides 92 different characters for "i⁴". The most complex written character in Chinese is that representing the sound of thunder which has 52 strokes and is, somewhat surprisingly, pronounced *ping*. The most complex in current use consists of 36 strokes representing a blocked nose and, less surprisingly, pronounced *nang*.

Rarest and commonest sounds The rarest speech sound is probably the sound written ř in Czech which occurs in very few languages and is the last sound mastered by Czech children. The *l* sound in the Arabic word *Allah*, in some contexts, is pronounced uniquely in that language. The commonest sound is the vowel *a* (as in the English father); no language is known to be without it.

Most and least regular verbs Esperanto was first published by Dr. Ludwig Zamenhof (1859–1917) of Warsaw in 1887 without irregular verbs and is now estimated (by text book sales) to have a million speakers. Swahili has a strict 6-class pattern of verbs and no verbs which are irregular to this pattern. According to the more daunting grammars published in West Germany, English has 194 irregular verbs though there are arguably 214.

Vocabulary The English language contains about 490,000 words plus another 300 000 technical terms, the most in any language, but it is doubtful if any individual uses more than 60,000. Those in Great Britain who have undergone a full 16 years of education use perhaps 5,000 words in speech and up to 10,000 words in written communications.

Greatest linguist According to some uncompleted and hence as yet unpublished researches, the most proficient linguist in history was Sir John Bowring (1792–1872), who was said to be able to read 200 languages and speak 100. The greatest living linguist is probably Georges Schmidt (b. Strasbourg, France in 1915) of the United Nations Translation Department in New York City, U.S.A. who can reputedly speak fluently in 30 languages and has been prepared to embark on the translation of 36 others.

ALPHABET

Oldest The development of the use of an alphabet in place of pictograms occurred in the Sinaitic world between 1700 and 1500 B.C. This western Semitic language developed the consonantal system based on phonetic and syllabic principles.

Longest and shortest The language with most letters is Cambodian with 72 (including useless ones) and Rotokas in central Bougainville Island has least with 11 (just a, b, e, g, i, k, o, p, ř, t and u). Amharic has 231 formations from 33 basic syllabic forms, each of which has seven modifications, so this Ethiopian language cannot be described as alphabetic.

Most and least consonants and vowels The language with most consonantal sounds is the Caucasian language Ubyx, with 80 and that with least is Rotokas, with only 6 consonants. The language with the most vowels is Sedang, a central Vietnamese language with 55 distinguishable vowel sounds and those with the least are the Caucasian languages Abaza and Kabardian with two such. The Hawaiian word for "certified" has 8 consecutive vowels—hooiaioia—while the English record is 5 in queueing. The Estonian word jäääärne, meaning the edge of the ice, has the same 4 consecutively. The Latin genitive for Aeneas's island consists solely of 6 vowels—aeaeae.

Bougainville islanders whose language—Rotakas—manages only 11 letters

Oldest and Youngest Letters The oldest letter is "O", unchanged in shape since its adoption in the Phoenician alphabet c. 1300 B.C. The newest letters in the English alphabet, are "j" and "v" which are of post Shakespearean use c. 1630. There are 65 alphabets now in use.

Largest letter The largest permanent letters in the world are the giant 600 ft *183 m* letters spelling READYMIX on the ground in the Nullarbor near East Balladonia, Western Australia. This was constructed in Dec. 1971. In sky-writing (normally at *c.* 8,000 ft [*2 400 m*]) a seven letter word may stretch for 6 miles *9 km* in length and can be read from 50 miles *80 km*. The world's earliest example was over Epsom racecourse, Surrey on 30 May 1922 when Cyril Turner "spelt out" "London Daily Mail" from an S.E.5A biplane.

WORDS

Longest words World The longest word ever to appear in literature occurs in *The Ecclesiazusae*, a comedy by Aristophanes (448–380 B.C.). In the Greek it is 170 letters long

---

LONGEST WORDS IN VARIOUS LANGUAGES—Only the first 7 are to be found in standard dictionaries

French — Anticonstitutionnellement (25 letters) —anticonstitutionally.

Croatian — Prijestolonasljeduikovice (26 letters) —wife of an heir apparent.

Italian — Precipitevolissimevolmente (26 letters) —as fast as possible

Portuguese — inconstitucionalissimamente (27 letters) —the highest degree of unconstitutionality

Japanese — Ryăgū-no-otohime-no-motoyui-no-kirihazushi (36 letters) —a seaweed, literally of small pieces of the paper hair streamers of the underwater princess.

Russian — ryentgyenoelyektrokardiografichyeskogo (33 Cyrillic letters, transliterating as 38) —of the radioelectrocardiographic.

Hungarian — Engedelmeskedhetetlenségeskedéseitekert (39 letters) —because of your continued disobedience.

Dutch — Rijksluchtvaartdienstweerschepenpersoneel (41 letters) —Government aviation department weather ship personnel.

Turkish — Cekoslovakyalılastıramadıklarımızdanmıymıssınız (47 letters) —"are you not one of that group of persons that we were said to be unable to Czechoslovakanise?"

Mohawk* — tkanuhstsarihsranuhwe'tsraaksahsrakaratattsrayeri' (50 letters) —the praising of the evil of the liking of the finding of the house is right.

German† — Donaudampfschifffahrtselectricitaetenhauptbetriebswerkbauunterbeamtengesellschaft (81 letters) —The club for subordinate officials of the head office management of the Danube steamboat electrical services (Name of a pre-war club in Vienna)

Swedish — Spårvagnsaktiebolagsskensmutsskjutarefackföreningspersonalbeklädnadsmagasinsförrådsförvaltaren (94 letters) —Manager of the depot for the supply of uniforms to the personnel of the track cleaners' union of the tramway company.

* *Mohawk forms words of limitless length. Above is an example.*
† *The longest dictionary word in every day usage is Kraftfahrzeugreparaturwerkstatten (33 letters or 34 if the ä is written as ae) meaning motor vehicle repair shops (or service garages).*

but transliterates into 182 letters in English, thus: lopadotemachoselachogaleokranioleipsanodrimhypotrimmatosilphioparaomelitokatakechymenokichlepikossyphophattoperisteralektryonoptekeph allio kigklopeleiolagoiosiraiobaphetraganopterygon. The term describes a fricassee of 17 sweet and sour ingredients including mullet, brains, honey, vinegar, pickles, marrow and ouzo (a Greek drink laced with anisette).

English The longest word in the Oxford English Dictionary is floccipaucinihilipilification (alternatively spelt in hyphenated form with "n" in seventh place), with 29 letters, meaning "the action of estimating as worthless", first used in 1741, and later by Sir Walter Scott (1771–1832). Webster's Third International Dictionary lists among its 450,000 entries pneumonoultramicroscopicsilicovolcanoconiosis (45 letters), the name of a miners' lung disease.

The nonce word used by Dr. Edward Strother (1675–1737) to describe the spa waters at Bristol was aequeosalinocalcalinoceraceoaluminosocupreovitriolic of 52 letters.

The longest regularly formed English word is praetertranssubstantiationalistically (37 letters), used by Mark McShane in his novel *Untimely Ripped*, published in 1963. The medical term hepaticocholangiocholecystenterostomies (39 letters) refers to the surgical creations of new communications between gallbladders and hepatic ducts and between intestines and gallbladders. The longest word in common use is disproportionableness (21 letters).

Longest The longest known palindromic word is *saippuakaup*
palindromic *pias* (15 letters), the Finnish word for soap-seller. The
words longest in the English language is *redivider* (9 letters), while another nine-letter word, *Malayalam*, is a proper noun given to the language of the Malayali people in Kerala, southern India. The nine letter word ROTAVATOR is a registered trade mark belonging to Rotary Hoes Ltd. The contrived chemical term *detartrated* has 11 letters, as does *kinnikinnik* (sometimes written *kinnik-kinnik*, a 12-letter palindrome), the word for the dried leaf and bark mixture which was smoked by the Cree Indians of North America. Some baptismal fonts in Greece and Turkey bear the circular 25 letter inscription NIΨON ANOMHMATA MH MONAN OΨIN meaning "wash (my) sins not only (my) face". This appears at St. Mary's Church Nottingham, St. Paul's, Woldingham, Surrey and other churches. The longest palindromic composition devised is one of 1,717 words completed by Edward Benbow of Bewdley, Hereford & Worcester, England in March 1975. It begins "Pot no part. Ask Sam to grade Kaffir . . . and hence predictably ends" . . . "if faked argot masks a trap on top".

Most The most over-worked word in English is the word
meanings *set* which has 58 noun uses, 126 verbal uses and 10 as a participial adjective.

Longest The longest chemical term is that describing Bovine
chemical NADP-specific Glutamate Dehydrogenase, which
name contains 500 amino-acids and a resultant name of some 3,600 letters.

Commonest In written English the most frequently used words are
words and in order: the, of, and, to, a, in, that, is, I, it, for *and* as.
letters The most used in conversation is I. The commonest letter is 'e' and the commonest initial letter is 'T'.

Most The most homophonous sound in English is *sōl* which,
Homo- according to the researches of Dora Newhouse of
phones Los Angeles, has 35 meanings with 6 variant spellings *viz* Soal, sol, sole, soul, sowl and the verb sowle, meaning to pull by the ears.

Most Accents were introduced in French in the reign of
accents Louis XIII (1601–43). The word with most accents is *hétérogénéité*, meaning heterogeneity. An atoll in the Pacific Ocean 320 miles *516 km* E.S.E. of Tahiti is named Héréhérétué.

Longest The longest known abbreviation is S.O.M.K.H.P.-
abbreviation B.K.J.C.S.S.D.P.M.W.D.T.B., the initials of the Sharikat Orang-Orang Melayu Kerajaan Hilir Perak Berkerjasama-Serkerjasama Kerana Jimat Chermat Serta Simpanon Dan Pinjam Meminjam Wang Dengan Tanggonnan Berhad. This is the Malay name for the Lower Perak Malay Government Servant's Co-operative Thrift and Loan Society Limited, in Telok Anson, Perak State, West Malaysia (formerly Malaya). The abbreviation for this abbreviation is not recorded.

Longest The longest acronym is ADCOMSUBORDCOM-
Acronym PHIBSPAC (22 letters) used in the U.S. Navy to denote the Administrative Command; Amphibious Forces, Pacific Fleet, Subordinate Command.

Longest The longest non-scientific English words which can
anagrams form anagrams are the 16-letter transpositions "interlaminations" *and* "internationalism" and "conservationists" *and* "conversationists".

Shortest The contrived headline describing the annoyance of
holo- an eccentric in finding inscriptions on the side of a
alphabetic fjord in a rounded valley as "Cwm fjord-bank glyphs
sentence vext quiz" represents the ultimate in containing all 26 letters in 26 letters.

Longest A sentence of 958 words appears in "Cities of the
sentence Plain" by the French author, Marcel Proust (1871– 1922) and one of 3,153 words in *History of the Church of God* composed by Sylvester Hassell of Wilson, North Carolina, U.S.A., *c.* 1884 with 86 semi-colons and 390 commas, while some authors such as James Joyce (1882–1941) appear to eschew punctuation altogether. The Report of the President of Columbia University 1942–43 contained a sentence of 4,284 words. The first 40,000 words of *The Gates of Paradise* by George Andrzeyevski (Panther) appear to lack any punctuation.

PLACE-NAMES

Longest The official name for Bangkok, the capital city of
World Thailand, is Krungtep Mahanakhon. The full name is however: Krungthep Mahanakhon Bovorn Ratanakosin Mahintharayutthaya Mahadilokpop Noparatratchathani Burirom Udomratchanivetmahasathan Amornpiman Avatarnsathit Sakkathattiyavisnukarmprasit (167 letters) which in its most scholarly transliteration emerges with 175 letters. The longest place-name now in use in the world is Taumatawhakatangihangakoauauotamatea(turipukakapikima ungahoronuku)pokaiwhenuakitanatahu, the unofficial 85-letter version of the name of a hill (1,002 ft above sea-level) in the Southern Hawke's Bay district of North Island, New Zealand. This Maori name means "the place where Tamatea, the man with the big knee who slid, climbed and swallowed mountains, known as Traveller (or Land eater) played on his flute to his loved one". The official version has 57 letters (1 to 36 and 65 to 85).

United The longest place-name in the United Kingdom is the
Kingdom concocted 58-letter name Llanfairpwllgwyngyllgogerychwyrndrobwllllantysiliogogogoch, which is translated: "St. Mary's Church in a hollow by the white hazel, close to the rapid whirlpool, by the red cave of St. Tysilio". This is the name used for the reopened (April 1973) village railway station in Anglesey, Gwynedd, Wales, but the *official* name consists of only the first 20 letters of what the Welsh would regard as a 51 letter word since "ll" and "ch" may be regarded as one. The longest genuine Welsh place-name listed

90

in the Ordnance Survey Gazetteer is Lower Llanfihangel-y-Creuddyn (26 letters), a village near Aberystwyth, Dyfed, Wales.

England The longest single word (unhyphenated) place-name in England is Blakehopeburnhaugh, a hamlet between Burness and Rochester in Northumberland, of 18 letters. The hyphenated Sutton-under-Whitestonecliffe, North Yorkshire has 27 letters on the Ordnance Survey but with the insertion of 'the' and the dropping of the final 'e' 29 letters in the Post Office List. The longest multiple name is North Leverton with Habbelsthorpe (30 letters), Nottinghamshire, while the longest parish name is Saint Mary le More and All Hallows with Saint Leonard and Saint Peter, Wallingford (68 letters) in Oxfordshire formed on 5 April 1971.

Scotland The longest single word place-names in Scotland are Claddochknockline, on the island of North Uist, Western Isles and the nearby Claddochbaleshare both with 17 letters. Kirkcudbrightshire (18 letters) became merged into Dumfries and Galloway on 16 May 1975. A 12-acre *5 ha* loch 9 miles *14 km* west of Stornoway on Lewes, Western Isles is named Loch Airidh Mhic Fhionnlaidh Dhuibh (31 letters).

Ireland The longest place-name in Ireland is Muckanaghederdauhaulia (22 letters), 4 miles *6 km* from Costello in Camus Bay, County Galway. The name means "soft place between two seas".

Shortest The shortest place names in the world are the French village of Y (population 143), so named since 1241; the Norwegian village of Å (pronounced "Aw"), U in the Caroline Islands, Pacific Ocean; and the Japanese town of Sosei which is alternatively called Aioi or O-o or even O. There was once a 6 in West Virginia, U.S.A. The shortest place-names in Great Britain are the two-lettered villages of Ae (population 199 in 1961) Dumfries and Galloway; Oa on the island of Islay, Strathclyde and Bu on Wyre, Orkney Islands. In the Shetland Islands there are skerries called Ve and two stacks called Aa. The island of Iona was originally I. The River E flows into the southern end of Loch Mhór, Inverness-shire, and O Brook flows on Dartmoor, Devon. The shortest place-name in Ireland is Ta (or Lady's Island) Lough, a sea-inlet on the coast of County Wexford. Tievelough, in County Donegal, is also called Ea.

Earliest The earliest recorded British place-name is Belerion, the Penwith peninsula of Cornwall, referred to as such by Pytheas of Massalia in *c.* 308 B.C. The name Salakee on St. Mary's, Isles of Scilly is however believed to be pre-Celtic. The earliest distinctive name for what is now Great Britain was Albion by Himilco *c.* 500 B.C. The oldest name among England's 46 counties is Kent, first mentioned in its Roman form of Cantium (from the Celtic *canto*, meaning a rim, *i.e.* a coastal district) from the same circumnavigation by Pytheas. The youngest is Lancashire, first recorded in the 12th century. The earliest mention of England is the form *Angelcynn*, which appeared in the Anglo-Saxon Chronicle in A.D. 880.

PERSONAL NAMES

Earliest The earliest personal name which has survived is possibly N'armer, the father of Men (Menes), the first Egyptian Pharaoh, dating from *ante* 3100 B.C. The earliest known name of any resident of Britain is Divitiacus, King of the Suessones, the Gaulish ruler of the Kent area *c.* 75 B.C. under the name Prydhain. Scotland, unlike England, was never conquered by the Roman occupiers (A.D. 43–410). Calgăcus (b. *c.* A.D. 40), who led this last resistance was the earliest native of Scotland whose name has been recorded.

Longest The only non-Royal English pedigree that can with
Pedigree certainty show a clear pre-Conquest descent is that of the Arden family. It is claimed on behalf of the

Clan Mackay that their clan can be traced to Loarn, the Irish invader of south west Pictland, now Strathclyde, *c.* A.D. 501.

Longest The longest name used by anyone is Adolph Blaine
World Charles David Earl Frederick Gerald Hubert Irvin John Kenneth Lloyd Martin Nero Oliver Paul Quincy Randolph Sherman Thomas Uncas Victor William Xerxes Yancy Zeus Wolfeschlegelsteinhausenbergerdorff, Senior, who was born at Bergedorf, near Hamburg, Germany, on 29 Feb. 1904. On printed forms he uses only his eighth and second Christian names and the first 35 letters of his surname. The full version of the name of 590 letters appeared in the 12th edition of *The Guinness Book of Records*. He now lives in Philadelphia, Pennsylvania, U.S.A., and has shortened his surname to Mr. Wolfe+590, Senior.

The longest Christian or given name on record is Napuamahalaonaonekawehiwehionakuahiweanenawawakehoonkakehoaalekeeaonanainananiakeao'-Hawaiikawao (94 letters) in the case of Miss Dawn N. Lee so named in Honolulu, Hawaii, U.S.A. in February 1967. The name means "The abundant, beautiful blossoms of the mountains and valleys begin to fill the air with their fragrance throughout the length and breadth of Hawaii".

Most The French composer Louis Jullien (1812–1860) had
Christian 36 Christian names because all 36 members of a
names Philharmonic Society insisted on being godfathers.

United The longest surname in the United Kingdom was the
Kingdom six-barrelled one borne by the late Major L.S.D.O.F. (Leone Sextus Denys Oswolf Fraudati filius) Tollemache-Tollemache de Orellana Plantagenet Tollemache Tollemache, who was born in 1884 and died of pneumonia in France on 20 Feb. 1917. Of non-repetitious surnames, the last example of a five-barrelled one was that of the Lady Caroline Jemima Temple-Nugent-Chandos-Brydges-Grenville

Musée Borély Archeologie

Pytheas the first known circumnavigator of Great Britain who recorded Britain's earliest place-names in *c.* 308 B.C.

(1858–1946). The longest single English surname is Featherstonehaugh, correctly pronounced on occasions (but improbably on the correct occasion) Featherstonehaw or Festonhaw or Fessonhay or Freestonhugh or Feerstonhaw or Fanshaw.

Scotland In Scotland the surname nin (feminine of mac) Achinmacdholicachinskerray (29 letters) was recorded in an 18th century parish register.

Shortest The single letter surname O, of which 13 examples appear in the telephone directory in Brussels, besides being the commonest single letter name is the one obviously causing most distress to those concerned with the prevention of cruelty to computers. There are two one-lettered Burmese names E (calm), pronounced aye and U (egg), pronounced Oo. U before the name means 'uncle'. There exist among the 47,000,000 names on the Dept. of Health & Social Security index 5 examples of a one-lettered surname. Their identity has not been disclosed, but they are "A", "B", "J", "N" and "O". Two-letter British surnames include By and On have recently been joined by Oy and Za.

Commonest The commonest surname in the world is the Chinese
World name Chang which is borne according to estimates, by between 9.7% and 12.1% of the Chinese population, so indicating even on the lower estimate that there are at least some 75,000,000 Changs—more than the entire population of all but 7 of the 154 other sovereign countries of the world.

English The commonest surname in the English-speaking world is Smith. There are 671,550 nationally insured Smiths in Great Britain, of whom 7,081 are plain John Smith and another 22,550 are John (plus one or more given names) Smith. Including uninsured persons there are over 800,000 Smiths in England and Wales alone, of whom 90,000 are called A. Smith. There were an estimated 1,678,815 Smiths in the U.S.A. in 1964.

"Macs" There are, however, estimated to be 1,600,000 persons in Britain with M', Mc or Mac (Gaelic "son of") as part of their surnames. The commonest of these is Macdonald which accounts for about 55,000 of the Scottish population.

The most common first or single forenames in England and Wales from Mr. C. V. Appleton's study of a sample of 125,000 (17.3%) from the birth registers at St. Catherines House, Kingsway, London are Sarah/Sara over girls and narrowly Stephen over Paul for boys. In the period 1196–1307 William was the commonest boy's name but since 1340 to recent times this had been John.

Most The palm for the most determined attempt to be last
contrived in the local telephone directory must now be awarded
name to Mr. Zachary Zzzzra of San Francisco, California. He outdid the previous occupant who was a mere Mr. Zeke Zzzypt. In September 1970 Mr. Zero Zzyzz (rhymes with "fizz") was ousted by Mr. Vladimir Zzzyd (rhymes with "outdid") in the Miami directory. In Los Angeles a private enterprise company surpassed all being the ZZZZZZZZ Co. The alpha and omega of Britain's 62 directories are Mr. M. Aab of Hull, Humberside and Mr. F. Zzarino of Waltham Cross, Hertfordshire.

TEXTS AND BOOKS

Oldest The oldest known written text is the pictograph expression of Sumerian speech (see Earliest Language, p. 88). The earliest known vellum document dates from the 2nd century A.D.; it contains paragraphs 10 to 32 of Demosthenes' *De Falsa Legatione*. Demosthenes died in the 4th century B.C.

Oldest The oldest surviving printed work is a Korean scroll or
printed *sutra* from wooden printed blocks found in the foundations of the Pulguk Sa pagoda, Kyongju, Korea, on 14 Oct. 1966. It has been dated no later than A.D. 704. It was claimed in November 1973 that a 28 page book of Tang dynasty poems at Yonsei University, Korea was printed from metal type *c.* 1160.

Oldest It is generally accepted that the earliest mechanically
Mechanic- printed book was the 42-line Gutenberg Bible,
ally printed at Mainz, Germany, in *c.* 1455 by Johann
printed Henne zum Gensfleisch zur Laden, called "zu Gutenberg" (*c.* 1398–*c.* 1468). Recent work on water marks published in 1967 indicates a copy of a surviving printed Latin grammar was made from paper made in

Mansell Collection

William Caxton, the earliest book printer in Britain, shows proofs to King Edward IV in 1473 or 1474

c. 1450. The earliest exactly dated printed work is the Psalter completed on 14 Aug. 1457 by Johann Fust (*c.* 1400–1466) and Peter Schöffer (1425–1502), who had been Gutenberg's chief assistant The earliest printing by William Caxton (*c.* 1422–1491) though undated would appear to be *History of Troy* in late 1473 to spring 1474.

Largest Book The largest book in the world is *The Little Red Elf*, a story in 64 verses by William P. Wood, who designed, constructed and printed the book. It measures 7 ft 2 in *2,2 m* high and 10 ft *3 m* across when open. The book is at present on show in a case at the Red Elf Cave, Ardentinny near Dunoon, Strathclyde.

Smallest Book The smallest book printed in metal type as opposed to any micro-photographic process is one printed for the Gutenberg Museum, Mainz, West Germany. It measures 3.5 mm by 3.5 mm *0.13 of an in square* and consists of the Lord's Prayer in seven languages.

Largest publication The largest publication in the world is the 1,200 volume set of *British Parliamentary Papers* of 1800–1900 by Irish University Press in 1967–1971. A complete set weighs 3¼ tons *3,3 tonnes*, costs £27,000 and would take 6 years to read at 10 hours per day. The production involved the death of 34,000 Indian goats, and the use of £15,000 worth of gold ingots. Further volumes are planned. The total print is 500 sets.

Most valuable Book The most valuable printed books are the three surviving perfect vellum copies of the Gutenberg Bible, printed in Mainz, Germany, in *c.* 1455 by Gutenberg (see above). The United States Library of Congress copy, bound in three volumes, was obtained in 1930 from Dr. Otto Vollbehr, who paid about $330,000 (*then £68,000*) for it. During 1970 a paper edition in the hands of the New York book dealer, Hans Peter Kraus, was privately bought for $2,500,000 (*£1,041,666*).

Broadsheet The highest price ever paid for a broadsheet has been $404,000 (*£168,333*) for one of the 16 known copies of *The Declaration of Independence*, printed in Philadelphia in 1776 by Samuel T. Freeman & Co., and sold to a Texan in May 1969.

Longest novel The longest important novel ever published is *Les hommes de bonne volonté* by Louis Henri Jean Farigoule (b. 26 Aug. 1885), *alias* Jules Romains, of France, in 27 volumes in 1932–46. The English version *Men of Good Will* was published in 14 volumes in 1933–46 as a "novel-cycle". The novel *Tokuga-Wa Ieyasu* by Sohachi Yamaoka has been serialised in Japanese daily newspapers since 1951. When completed it will run to 40 volumes.

Encyclopaedias **Earliest** The earliest known encyclopaedia was compiled by Speusippas (*post* 408–*c.* 388 B.C.) a nephew of Plato, in Athens *c.* 370 B.C. The earliest encyclopaedia compiled by a Briton was *Liber exerptionum* by the Scottish monk Richard (d. 1173) at St. Victor's Abbey, Paris *c.* 1140.

Most comprehensive The most comprehensive present day encyclopaedia is the *Encyclopaedia Britannica*, first published in Edinburgh, Scotland, in Dec. 1768–1771. A group of booksellers in the United States acquired reprint rights in 1898 and completed ownership in 1899. In 1943 the *Britannica* was given to the University of Chicago, Illinois, U.S.A. The current 30-volume 15th edition contains 33,141 pages, and 43,000,000 words from 4,277 contributors. It is now edited in Chicago and in London.

Largest The largest encyclopaedia ever compiled was the *Great Standard Encyclopaedia* of Yung-lo ta tien of 22,937 manuscript chapters (370 still survive), written by 2,000 Chinese scholars in 1403–08.

Largest dictionary The largest dictionary now published is the 12-volume Royal quarto *The Oxford English Dictionary* of 15,487 pages published between 1884 and 1928 with a first supplement of 963 pages in 1933 with a further 3-volume supplement, edited by R. W. Burchfield, in which the second and third volumes covering H to Z will appear in 1975 and 1977. The work contains 414,825 words, 1,827,306 illustrative quotations and reputedly 227,779,589 letters and figures.

Manuscripts **Highest price** The highest value ever paid for any manuscript is £100,000 paid in December 1933 by the British Museum, London to the U.S.S.R Government for parts of the manuscript Bible rescued from a shelf in a monk's cell in the Monastery of St. Catherine below Mount Sinai, Egypt in 1859. The monks had in May 1844 given 43 leaves from the 129, which had been rescued from a waste paper basket there by Lobegott Friedrich Konstantin von Tischendorf (1815–74). These leaves which were part of the Codex Sinaiticus, are in the University Library at Leipzig and are known as the Codex Friderico-Augustanus. Originally the Mss measured 16 × 28 in *40 × 71 cm* before their edges were sheared off to the present size of 15 × 13½–14 in *38 × 34 cm*. The highest price at auction is 1,100,000 Francs (then *£94,933 incl. tax*) paid by H. P. Krauss, the New York dealer, at the salerooms of Rheims et Laurin, Paris on 24 June 1968 for the late 13th-century North Italian illuminated vellum Manuscript of the Apocrypha.

BIBLE

Oldest The oldest known bible is the *Codex Vaticanus* written in Greek *ante* A.D. 350 and preserved in the Vatican Museum, Rome. The earliest Bible printed in English was one edited by Miles Coverdale, Bishop of Exeter (*c.* 1488–1569), printed in 1535 at Marberg in Hesse, Germany. William Tyndale's New Testament in English had, however, been printed in Cologne and in Worms, Germany in 1525.

Longest and shortest books The longest book in the Authorized version of the Bible is the Book of Psalms, while the longest book including prose is the Book of the Prophet Isaiah, with 66 chapters. The shortest is the Third Epistle of John, with 294 words in 14 verses. The Second Epistle of John has only 13 verses but 298 words.

Longest Psalm, verse sentence and name Of the 150 Psalms, the longest is the 119th, with 176 verses, and the shortest is the 117th, with two verses. The shortest verse in the Authorized Version (King James) of the Bible is verse 35 of Chapter XI of the Gospel according to St. John, consisting of the two words "Jesus wept". The longest is verse 9 of Chapter VIII of the Book of Esther, which extends to a 90-word description of the Persian empire. The total number of letters in the Bible is 3,566,480. The total number of words depends on the method of counting hyphenated words, but is usually given as between 773,692 and 773,746. The word "and" according to Colin McKay Wilson of the Salvation Army appears 46,227 times. The longest personal name in the Bible is Maher-shalal-hash-baz, the symbolic name of the second son of Isaiah (Isaiah, Chapter VIII, verses 1 and 3). The caption of Psalm 22, however, contains a Hebrew title sometimes rendered Al-'Ayyeleth Hash-Shahar (20 letters).

MOST PROLIFIC WRITERS

The most prolific writer for whom a word count has been published was Charles Hamilton, *alias* Frank Richards (1875–1961), the Englishman who created Billy Bunter. At his height in 1908 he wrote the whole of the boys' comics *Gem* (founded 1907) and *Magnet* (1908–1940) and most of two others, totalling 80,000 words a week. His lifetime output has been put at 100,000,000 words. He enjoyed the advantages of the use of electric light rather than candlelight and of being unmarried. The champion of the goose quill era was Józef Ignacy Kraszewski (1812–1887) of Poland who produced more than 600 volumes of novels and historical works.

Novels The greatest number of novels published by any author is 904 by Kathleen Lindsay (Mrs. Mary Faulkner) (1903–1973) of Somerset West, Cape Province, South Africa. She wrote under six pen names, two of them masculine. After receiving a probable record 743 rejection slips the British novelist John Creasey M.B.E. (1908–1973), under his own name and 13 *aliases* had 564 books totalling more than 40,000,000 words published from 1932 to his death on 9 June 1973. The British authoress with the greatest total of full length titles is Miss Ursula Harvey Bloom (b. Chelmsford, Essex 1892) (Mrs. A. C. G. Robinson, formerly Mrs. Denham-Cookes), who expects to reach 500 by December 1975, starting in 1924 with *The Great Beginning* and including the best sellers *The Ring Tree* (novel) and *The Rose of Norfolk* (non-fiction). Enid Mary Blyton (1900–68) (Mrs Derrell Waters) completed 600 titles of children's stories many of them brief with 59 in the single year 1955. She was translated into a record 128 languages.

Short stories The highest established count for published short stories is 3,500 in the case of Michael Hervey, M.B.E. (born London, 10 Nov. 1924) of Drummoyne, New South Wales, Australia. Aided by his wife Lilyan Brilliant, he has also turned in 60 detective novels and 80 stage and television plays. The most prolific short story writer in Britain is Herbert Harris (born 1911) of the Isle of Wight, with nearly 3,000 published in Britain and in 28 other countries.

Fastest novelist The world's fastest novelist has been Erle Stanley Gardner (1889–1970) of the U.S.A., the mystery writer who created Perry Mason. He dictated up to 10,000 words per day and worked with his staff on as many as seven novels simultaneously. His sales on 140 titles reached 170 million by his death. The British novelist John Creasey (see above) had an output of 15 to 20 novels per annum, with a record of 22. He once wrote two books in a week with a half-day off.

The English writer and playwright (Richard) Edgar (Horatio) Wallace (1875–1932) began his play *On the Spot* on a Friday and finished it by lunchtime on the following Sunday. This included the stage directions and unusually, after the production the prompt copy was identical to his original. The shortest time in which he wrote a novel was in the case of *The Three Oaks Mystery* which he started on a Tuesday and delivered typed to his publishers on the following Friday.

Highest paid writer The highest rate ever offered to a writer was $30,000 (*then £10,714*) to Ernest Miller Hemingway (1899–1961) for a 2,000-word article on bullfighting by *Sports Illustrated* in January 1960. This was a rate of $15 (*then £5.35*) per word. In 1958 a Mrs. Deborah Schneider of Minneapolis, Minnesota, U.S.A., wrote 25 words to complete a sentence in a competition for the best blurb for Plymouth cars. She won from about 1,400,000 entrants the prize of $500 (*£178*) every month for life. On normal life expectations she would have collected $12,000 (*£4,285*) per word. No known anthology includes Mrs. Schneider's deathless prose.

Top selling author It was announced on 13 March 1953 that 672,058,000 copies of the works of Marshal Iosif Vissarionovich Dzhugashvili, *alias* Stalin (1879–1953), had been sold or distributed in 101 languages.

Among writers of fiction, sales alone of over 300,000,000 have been claimed for Georges Simenon (Belgium) and for the British authoress Dame Agatha Christie (born Agatha Mary Clarissa Miller), now Lady Mallowan (formerly Mrs. Archibald Christie) (b. Torquay, Devon 15 Sept. 1890). Her 80 crime novels have been translated into 103 languages.

Canberra Times

The world's least successful author—William A. Gold of Australia—contemplating

Least Successful Author The world's declared least successful writer is William A. Gold (b. London 29 June 1922). After 18 years unremitting (see photograph) work involving over 3,000,000 words (including 8 full length books written to completion and 7 novels) he struck "pay dirt" with a 50c (28p) remittance from a newspaper in Canberra, Australia on 24 May 1974. Until this bonanza his closest approach to success had been the publication in 1958 of a 150 word book review in the *Workers Education Association Bulletin* in Adelaide on the clearest understanding that it would only be published if it did not attract any fee.

Text Books Britain's most successful writer of text books is the ex-schoolmaster Ronald Ridout (b. 23 July 1916) who between 1948 and May 1975 had 320 titles published with sales of 53,132,000. His *The First English Workbook* has sold 3,776,000 copies.

Oldest authoress The oldest authoress in the world is Mrs. Alice Pollock (*née* Wykeham-Martin, b. 2 July 1868) of Haslemere, Surrey, whose book "Portrait of My Victorian Youth" (Johnson Publications) was published in March 1971 when she was aged 102 years 8 months.

Youngest The youngest recorded commercially-published author is Dorothy Straight (b. 25 May 1958) of Washington D.C., who wrote *How the World Began* in 1962 aged 4 which was published in August 1964 by Pantheon Books, New York.

Longest Literary Gestation The standard German dictionary *Deutsches Wörterbuch*, begun by the brothers Grimm in 1854, was finished in 1971. *Acta Sanctorum* begun by Jean Bolland in 1643, arranged according to saints' days, reached the month of November in 1925 and an introduction for December was published in 1940.

Most Rejections The greatest recorded number of publisher's rejections for a manuscript is 80 for "World Government Crusade" by Gilbert Young (b. 1906). His public meeting in Bath, England in support of his parliamentary candidature as a World Government Candidate, however, drew a crowd of one.

POETS LAUREATE

Youngest and oldest The youngest Poet Laureate was Laurence Eusden (1688–1730), who received the bays on 24 Dec. 1718, at the age of 30 years and 3 months. The greatest age at which a poet has succeeded is 73 in the case of

William Wordsworth (1770–1850) on 6 April 1843. The longest lived Laureate was John Masefield, O.M., who died on 12 May 1967, aged 88 years 345 days. The longest which any poet has worn the laurel is 41 years 322 days, in the case of Alfred (later the 1st Lord) Tennyson (1809–92), who was appointed on 19 Nov. 1850 and died in office on 6 Oct. 1892.

Longest poem The longest poem ever written was the *Mahabharata* which appeared in India in the period *c.* 400 to 150 B.C. It runs to 220,000 lines and nearly 3,000,000 words.

The longest poem ever written in the English language is one on the life of King Alfred by John Fitchett (1766–1838) of Liverpool which ran to 129,807 lines and took 40 years to write. His editor Robert Riscoe added the concluding 2,585 lines.

Most Successful Sloganeer "Think Mink" invented by Jack Gasnick (b. 1910) in 1929 has sold in metal, celluloid and ribbon 50 million since 1950. His *"Cross at the Green . . . not in Between Enterprises"* of New York City has sold 55 million buttons, badges and tabs and 40 million other pieces.

HIGHEST PRINTINGS

World The world's most widely distributed book is the Bible, portions of which have been translated into 1,399 languages. This compares with 222 languages by Lenin. It has been estimated that between 1800 and 1950 some 1,500,000,000 copies were printed of which 1,100,000,000 were handled by Bible Societies. The total distribution of complete Bibles by the United Bible Societies of the United States in the year 1972 was 5,519,909.

It has been reported that 800,000,000 copies of the red-covered booklet *Quotations from the Works of Mao Tse-tung* were sold or distributed between June 1966, when possession became virtually mandatory in China, and Sept. 1971 when their promoter Marshal Lin Piao was killed. The name of Mao Tse-tung (b. 26 Dec. 1893) means literally "Hair Enrich-East".

Non-fiction The total disposal through non-commercial channels by Jehovah's Witnesses of the 190 page hard bound book *The Truth That Leads to Eternal Life* published by the Watchtower Bible and Tract Society of Brooklyn, New York, published on 8 May 1968, reached 74 million in 91 languages by April 1975.

BEST SELLERS

The world's all-time best selling book is *The Guinness Book of Records*, compiled and edited by Norris Dewar and Alan Ross McWhirter (b. 12 Aug. 1925). It was first published from 107, Fleet Street, London, in October 1955 and total sales in 14 languages now running at 60,000 per week, surpassed the 23,916,000 of *The Common Sense Book of Baby and Child Care* by Dr. Benjamin Spock (first published in May 1946) in November 1974.

Fiction The novel with the highest sales has been *Valley of the Dolls* (first published March 1966) by Jacqueline Susann (Mrs. Irving Mansfield) (1921–1974) with a world wide total of 15,800,000 to June 1973. In the first 6 months Bantam sold 6.8 million. In the United Kingdom the highest print order has been 3,000,000 by Penguin Books Ltd. for their paperback edition of *Lady Chatterley's Lover*, by D. H. (David Herbert) Lawrence (1885–1930). The total sales to May 1974 were 3,810,000 copies.

Self-Produced Mrs. Carla Emery of Kendrick, Idaho, U.S.A. has written, printed, published and distributed 30,000 copies of her 628 page *Old Fashioned Recipe Book* ($12.95) up to May 1975.

Slowest seller The accolade for the world's slowest selling book (known in U.S. publishing as slooow-sellers) probably belongs to David Wilkins's Translation of the New Testament from Coptic into Latin published by Oxford University Press in 1716 in 500 copies. Selling an average of one each 139 days it was in print for 191 years.

LARGEST PUBLISHERS

World The largest publisher in the world is the United States Government Printing Office in Washington, D.C., U.S.A. The Superintendents of Documents Division dispatches more than 150,000,000 items every year. The annual list of new titles and annuals is about 6,000.

United Kingdom The U.K. published a record 35,254 book titles in 1973 of which 9,106 were reprints. The highest figure for reprints was 9,977 in 1970.

LARGEST PRINTERS

World The largest printers in the world are R. R. Donnelly & Co. of Chicago, Illinois, U.S.A. The company, founded in 1864, has plants in seven main centres, turning out $200,000,000 (£83,300,000) worth of work per year from 180 presses, 125 composing machines and more than 50 binding lines. Nearly 18,000 tons of inks and 450,000 tons of paper and board are consumed every year.

Print order The print order for the 48th Automobile Association Members' Handbook (1974–75) was 5,300,000 copies. The total print since 1908 has been 64,010,000. It is currently printed by web offset by Petty & Sons of Leeds.

Linotype Operator James Donohue (1884–1974) typeset an estimated 200,000,000 words of *The Anglo-Celt* newspaper in Cavan, Ireland from 1898 to 1967.

Largest cartoon The largest cartoon ever exhibited was one covering five storeys (50 × 150 ft [*15 × 45 m*]) of a University of Arizona building drawn by Dr. Peter A. Kesling for Mom 'n Dad's Day 1954.

Longest lived strip The most durable newspaper comic strip has been the Katzenjammer Kids (Hans and Fritz) created by Rudolph Dirks and first published in the *New York Journal* on 12 Dec. 1897 and currently drawn by Joe Musial. The earliest strip was Little Bear by Jim Lyons (b. 1876) which first appeared in the *San Francisco Examiner* in 1894. The most widely syndicated is *Blondie* appearing in 1600 newspapers in 50 countries.

LETTERS

Longest The longest personal letter based on a word count is one of 720,000 words written in 9 months by Boyd Cabanaw of Bartlesville, Oklahoma to irritate his cousin Andrew L. Cairns in Minnesota on 11 July 1974.

To an editor *Longest* The longest recorded letter to an editor was one of 13,000 words (a third of a modern novel) written to the editor of the *Fishing Gazette* by A.R.I.E.L. and published in 7-point type spread over two issues in 1884.

Most Britain's, and seemingly the world's, most indefatigable writer of letters to the editors of newspapers is Raymond L. Cantwell, 52, of Oxford, who since 1948 has had more than 12,000 letters published in print or on the air. His peak production has been 425 in 36 hours non-stop in aid of charity.

Shortest The shortest correspondence on record was that between Victor Marie Hugo (1802–85) and his publisher Hurst and Blackett in 1862. The author was on holiday and anxious to know how his new novel *Les Misérables* was selling. He wrote "?". The reply was "!".

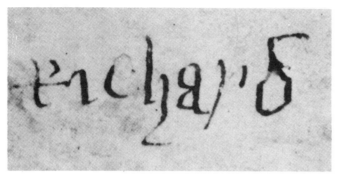

Public Record Office
The earliest surviving signature of an English monarch—Richard II—dated 1386

AUTOGRAPHS AND SIGNATURES

Earliest English Regal The earliest English sovereign whose handwriting is known to have survived is Edward III (1327–1377). The earliest full signature extant is that of Richard II (dated 26 July 1386). The Magna Carta does not bear even the mark of King John (reigned 1199–1216), but carries only his seal. An attested cross of King Cnut (1016–1035) has survived.

Most expensive The highest price ever paid on the open market for a single autograph letter signed is $51,000 (*then £10,500*), paid in 1927 for a letter written by the Gloucestershire-born Button Gwinnett (1732–77), one of the three men from Georgia to sign the United States' Declaration of Independence in Philadelphia on 4 July 1776. Such an item would today probably attract bids of $250,000 (*£100,000*). If one of the six known signatures of William Shakespeare (1564–1616) were to come on the market or a new one was discovered the price would doubtless set a record.

CROSSWORDS

First The earliest crossword was one with 32 clues invented by Arthur Wynne (b. Liverpool, England, d. 1945) and published in the *New York World* on 21 Dec. 1913. The first crossword published in a British newspaper was one furnished by C. W. Shepherd in the *Sunday Express* of 2 Nov. 1924.

Largest The largest crossword ever published is one with 2,007 clues across and 2,008 clues down, compiled by Robert M. Stilgenbauer of Los Angeles in 7½ years of spare time between 15 May 1938 and publication in 1949. Despite the 125,000 copies distributed the best solution so far is one 93.5% complete by Robert L. Vizet of Bayside, New York, U.S.A. The largest crosswords regularly published are "Mammoth" crosswords based on grids of 73 × 73 (5,329) squares with up to 828 clues by First Features Ltd of Hastings, East Sussex since 1 May 1970. Edward Akenhead, Times Crossword Editor, succeeded in 1971 in including in a puzzle the word Honorifieabilitudinitatibus.

Fastest and slowest solution The fastest recorded time for completing *The Times* crossword under test conditions is 3 min 45.0 sec by Roy Dean, 43, of Bromley, Greater London in the B.B.C. "Today" radio studio on 19 Dec. 1970. In May 1966 *The Times* of London received an announcement from a Fijian woman that she had just succeeded in completing their crossword No. 673 in the issue of 4 April 1932. Dr. John Sykes won the Cutty Sark/*Times* championship in 1972-73-74. The only woman to reach a final has been Mrs. Morar Ryton.

Most Durable Compilers Adrian Bell (b. 4 Oct. 1901) of Barsham, Suffolk contributed a record 4,327 crosswords to *The Times* from 2 Jan 1930 to 1 Mar. 1975. R. J. Baddock (b. 30 Oct. 1894) has been a regular contributor to national newspapers since 13 Aug. 1926. Mrs. Phyllis Harvey, 83, of Brighton from December 1924 to December 1974 completed 50 years of contributions to the Evening News Junior Cross Word.

Oldest Map The oldest known map of any kind is a clay tablet depicting the river Euphrates flowing through northern Mesopotamia, Iraq, dated *c.* 3800 B.C. The earliest surviving product of English map-making is the Anglo Saxon *mappa mundi*, known as the Cottonian manuscript from the late 10th century. The earliest printed map of Britain was Ptolemy's outline printed in Bologna, Italy in 1477.

Least Informative Sheet 281 of the 1:2500 scale map of Siteki, published by the Swaziland Government Public Work Department, consists of a single diagonal line. Copies can be obtained from P.O. Box 58, Mbabane.

Birthday Cards The most parsimonious recorded use of a birthday card is a MacGregor card which has shuttled 82 times between C. R. Findley of Vancouver, British Columbia, Canada and Douglas Bohn of Seattle, U.S.A. since November 1933.

Christmas cards The greatest number of personal Christmas cards sent out is believed to be 40,000 in 1969 by former President and Mrs. Nixon to friends and others, some of whom must have been unilateral acquaintances.

LIBRARIES

Largest World The largest library in the world is the United States Library of Congress (founded on 24 April 1800), on Capitol Hill, Washington, D.C. By 1973 it contained more than 72,000,000 items, including 16,000,000 volumes and pamphlets. The buildings contain 35 acres *14,0 ha* of floor space and contain 327 miles *526 km* of book shelves. The tallest library in the world is the University of Massachusetts Library, Amherst, Mass., U.S.A. with 28 storeys and a height of 296 ft 4 in *90,32 m* opened in May 1973.

The Lenin State Library in Moscow, U.S.S.R, claims to house more than 24,000,000 books, but this total is understood to include periodicals.

The largest non-statutory library in the world is the New York Public Library (founded 1895) on Fifth Avenue with a floor space of 525,276 ft² *48 800 m²* and 80 miles *128 km* of shelving. Its collection including 83 branch libraries embraces 8,605,610 volumes 10,683,105 manuscripts and 317,183 maps.

United Kingdom The largest library in the United Kingdom is that in the British Museum, London. It contains more than 9,000,000 books, about 115,000 manuscripts and 101,000 charters on 158 miles *254 km* of shelf. There are spaces for 370 readers in the domed Reading Room, built in 1854. The largest public library in the United Kingdom will be the extended Mitchell Library, North Street, Glasgow with a floor area of 510,000 ft² *47 380 m²* or 11.7 acres *4,7 ha* and an ultimate shelving capacity for 4,000,000 volumes. The oldest public library in Scotland is in Kirkwall, Orkney, founded in 1683.

Overdue books It was reported on 7 Dec. 1968 that a book checked out in 1823 from the University of Cincinnati Medical Library on Febrile Diseases (London, 1805 by Dr. J. Currie) was returned by the borrower's great-grandson Richard Dodd. The fine calculated to be $22,646 (*£9,435*) was waived.

NEWSPAPERS

Most The United States had 1,774 English language daily newspapers at 1 Jan. 1974. They had a combined net paid circulation of 63,147,280 copies per day at 30 Sept. 1973. The peak year for U.S. newspapers was 1910, when there were 2,202. The leading newspaper readers in the world are the people of Sweden, where 515 newspapers were sold for each 1,000 compared with the U.K. figure of 488.

Oldest World The oldest existing newspaper in the world is the Swedish official journal *Post och Inrikes Tidningar*, founded in 1644. It is published by the Royal Swedish Academy of Letters. The oldest existing commercial newspaper is the *Haarlems Dagblad/Oprechte Haarlemsche Courant*, published in Haarlem, in the Netherlands. The *Courant* was first issued as the *Weeckelycke Courante van Europa* on 8 Jan. 1656 and a copy of issue No. 1 survives.

United Kingdom The oldest continuously produced newspaper in the United Kingdom is *Berrow's Worcester Journal* (originally the *Worcester Post Man*), published in Worcester. It was traditionally founded in 1690 and has appeared weekly since June 1709. The oldest newspaper title is that of the *Stamford Mercury* dating back to at least 1714 and traditionally to 1695. The oldest daily newspaper in the United Kingdom is *Lloyd's List*, the shipping intelligence bulletin of Lloyd's, London, established as a weekly in 1726 and as a daily in 1734. The *London Gazette* (originally the *Oxford Gazette*) was first published on 16 Nov. 1665. In November 1845 it became the most expensive daily newspaper ever sold in the United Kingdom, priced at 2s. 8d. per copy. The oldest Sunday newspaper in the United Kingdom is *The Observer*, first issued on 4 Dec. 1791.

Largest and Smallest The most massive single issue of a newspaper was the 7½ lb. *3 kg 40 New York Times* of Sunday 17 Oct. 1965. It comprised 15 sections with a total of 946 pages, including about 1,200,000 lines of advertising. The largest page size ever used has been 51 in by 35 in *130 by 89 cm* for *The Constellation*, printed in 1859 by George Roberts as part of the Fourth of July celebrations in New York City, N.Y., U.S.A. The *Worcestershire Chronicle* was the largest British newpaper. A surviving issue of 16 Feb. 1859 measures 32¼ in by 22½ in *82 by 57 cm*. The smallest recorded page size has been 3½ in by 4½ in *9 by 11 cm* as used in *Diario di Roma*, an issue of which dated 28 Feb. 1829 survives.

HIGHEST CIRCULATION

The first newspaper to achieve a circulation of 1,000,000 was *Le Petit Journal*, published in Paris, France, which reached this figure in 1886, when selling at 5 centimes (*now about ½p*) per copy.

World The claim exercised for the world's highest circulation is that by the *Asahi Shimbun* (founded 1879) of Japan with a figure which attained more than 10,000,000 copies in October 1970. This, however, has been achieved by totalling the figures for editions published in various centres with a morning figure of 6,100,000 and an evening figure of 3,900,000. The highest circulation of any single newspaper in the world is that of the Sunday newspaper *The News of the World*, printed in Bouverie Street, London. Single issues have attained a sale of 9,000,000 copies with an estimated readership of more than 19,000,000. The paper first appeared on 1 Oct. 1843, averaged 12,971 copies per week in its first year and surpassed the million mark in 1905. To provide sufficient pulp for the 1,500 reels used per week, each measuring 5 miles *8 km* long, more than 780,000 trees have to be felled each year. The latest sales figure is 5,775,000 copies per issue (average for 1 July to 31 Dec. 1974), with an estimated readership of 15,594,390.

Daily World The highest circulation of any daily newspaper is that of the U.S.S.R government organ *Izvestia* (founded in Leningrad on 12 March 1917 as a Menshevik news sheet and meaning "Information") with a figure of 8,670,000 in March 1967. The daily tabloid *Pionerskaya Pravda* had an average circulation of 9,181,000 copies per issue in 1966. This is the news organ of the Pioneers, a Communist youth organization founded in 1922.

United Kingdom The highest daily net sale of any newspaper in the United Kingdom is that of *The Daily Mirror*, founded in London in 1903. A print of 7,161,704 was sold out on 3 June 1953. The latest sales figure is 4,205,289 for Jan.–Dec. 1974), with an estimated readership of 13,522,000.

Evening The highest circulation of any evening newspaper is that of *The Evening News*, established in London in 1881. The latest figure is 744,381 copies per issue (average for 1 July to 31 Dec. 1974), with an average readership of 2,314,000.

Most read The newspaper which achieves the closest to a saturation circulation is *The Sunday Post*, established in Glasgow in 1914. In 1973 its total estimated readership of 2,878,000 represented more than 79 per cent of the entire population in Scotland aged 15 and over.

PERIODICALS

Largest circulation World The largest circulations of any weekly periodical is that of *T.V. Guide* which in 1974 became the first magazine in history to sell a billion (1,000 million) copies in a year so averaging more than 19,230,000 per week. In its 30 basic international editions *The Reader's Digest* (established February 1922) circulates 30,500,000 copies monthly in 13 languages, including a United States edition of more than 18,000,000 copies (average for July to December 1974) and a United Kingdom edition (established 1939) of 1,600,000 copies.

Oldest World The oldest continuing perodical in the world is *Philosophical Transactions of the Royal Society*, which first appeared on 6 Mar. 1665.

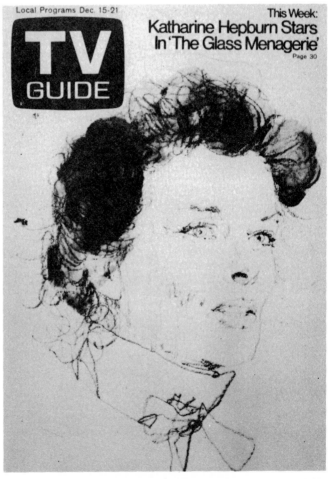

Local Programs Dec. 15-21

TV GUIDE

This Week: **Katharine Hepburn Stars In 'The Glass Menagerie'** Page 30

The front cover of TV Guide the only periodical in history to sell 1,000 million copies in a year. Katharine Hepburn has uniquely won 3 individual Oscars in starring rôles

United Kingdom *The Botanical Magazine* has been in continuous publication since 1787, as several "parts" a year forming a series of continuously numbered volumes. Britain's oldest weekly periodical is *Lancet* first published in 1823. The Scottish monthly *Blackwood's Magazine* has not missed an issue since the first in April 1817. The Editor has always been a Blackwood. Since 1948 it has been Douglas Blackwood great great-grandson of the founder. The *Scots Magazine* began publication in 1739 and ran till 1826, and with three breaks has been produced continuously since 1924.

The highest circulation of any periodical in the United Kingdom is that of the *Radio Times* (instituted on 28 Sept. 1923). The average weekly sale for July-December 1974 was 3,627,361 copies with a readership of 10,609,000. The highest sale of any issue was 9,778,062 copies for the Christmas issue of 1955. *T.V. Times* averaged sales of 3,603,918 in the period Jan.-Sept. 1974 with an estimated readership of 11,408,000.

Annual *Old Moore's Almanack* has been published annually since 1697, when it first appeared as a broadsheet, by Dr. Francis Moore (1657-1715) of Southwark, London to advertise his "physiks". The annual sale certified by its publishers W. Foulsham & Co. Ltd. of Slough England is 1,150,000 copies and its aggregate sale is estimated to be 106 million.

ADVERTISING RATES
The highest ever price for a single page has been $84,100 (*£35,040*) for a four-colour back cover in the now defunct *Life* magazine (circulation 8½ million per week) from Jan. 1969 to Jan. 1971. The current record is $63,320 for a four colour page in *Reader's Digest* in May 1975.

The highest expenditure ever incurred on a single advertisement in a periodical is $950,000 (*then, £395,833*) by Uniroyal Inc. for a 40-page insert in the May 1968 issue of the U.S. edition of *The Reader's Digest*. The British record is some £100,000 for a 20-page colour supplement by Woolworths in the *Radio Times* of 16 Nov. 1972. The colour rate for a single page in the *Radio Times* is £7,400 (since March 1975).

Longest editorship The longest editorship of any national newspaper has been more than 59 years by C. P. Scott (1846-1932) of the (then *Manchester*) *Guardian*, who was appointed aged 25 in 1872 and died on 1 Jan. 1932. John Watson was editor of the South Australian newspaper *The Border Watch* from 1863 to Dec. 1925—a span of 62 years.

Most durable feature The longest lasting feature in the British press from one pen is *Your Stars* by Edward Lyndoe. It has run since 1 Oct. 1933 in *The Sunday People*. C. Gordon Tether (b. 1913) has written the daily Lombard column in *The Financial Times* without intermission since 1955.

4. MUSIC

INSTRUMENTS

Oldest The world's oldest surviving musical notation date from *c.* 1800 B.C. A heptonic scale deciphered from a clay tablet by Dr. Duchesne-Guillemin in 1966-67 was found at a site in Nippur, Sumer, now Iraq. An Assyrian love song also *c.* 1800 B.C. to an Ugarit god from a tablet of notation and lyric was reconstructed for an 11 string lyre at the University of California, Berkeley on 6 Mar. 1974. Musical history is, however, able to be traced back to the 3rd millennium B.C., when the yellow bell (*huang chung*) had a recognised

standard musical tone in Chinese temple music. Whistles and flures made from perforated phalange bones have been found at Upper Palaeolithic sites of the Aurignacian period (*c.* 25,000–22,000 B.C.) *e.g.* at Istallóskö, Hungary and in Molodova, U.S.S.R.

Earliest piano The earliest pianoforte in existence is one built in Florence, Italy, in 1720 by Bartolommeo Cristofori (1655–1731) of Padua, and now preserved in the Metropolitan Museum of Art, New York City.

Organ Largest World The largest and loudest musical instrument ever constructed is the now only partially functional Auditorium Organ in Atlantic City, New Jersey, U.S.A. Completed in 1930, this heroic instrument has two consoles (one with seven manuals and another movable one with five), 1,477 stop controls and 33,112 pipes ranging in tone from $\frac{3}{16}$ of an inch to the 64 ft tone. It is powered with blower motors of 365 horsepower *370 cv*, cost $500,000 (now *£208,333*) and has the volume of 25 brass bands, with a range of seven octaves. The grand organ at Wannamaker's Store, Philadelphia, installed in 1911, was enlarged until by 1930 it had 6 manuals and 30,067 pipes including a 64 ft *19 m* tone Gravissima. The world's largest church organ is that in Passau Cathedral, Germany. It was completed in 1928 by D. F. Steinmeyer & Co. It was built with 16,000 pipes and five manuals. The world's only 5 manual electric organ was installed in the Carnegie Hall, New York City in Sept. 1974.

United Kingdom The largest organ in the United Kingdom is that completed in Liverpool Anglican Cathedral on 18 Oct. 1926, with two five-manual consoles of which only one is now in use, and 9,704 speaking pipes (originally 10,936) ranging from tones of $\frac{3}{4}$ in to 32 feet.

Youngest and Oldest Organists Henry Alban Chambers was appointed organist to Leeds' Cathedral, West Yorkshire in 1913 at the age of 11. The longest recorded reign as an organist has been 67 years in the case of Mr. Reginald Deall of Macclesfield, Cheshire at Bethal and St. George's Street Baptist churches from 1908 to 1975.

Loudest stop The loudest organ stop in the world is the Ophicleide stop of the Grand Great in the Solo Organ in the Atlantic City Auditorium (see above). It is operated by a pressure of 100 in *254 cm* of water (3½ lb./in² *[24 kPa]*) and has a pure trumpet note of ear-splitting

The oldest Surviving piano—the 255 year old Italian made instrument now preserved in the Metropolitan Museum of Art, New York City

volume, more than six times the volume of the loudest locomotive whistles.

Organ marathon The longest church organ recital ever sustained has been 80 hrs 35 min by Vyan Gresty at St. Michael's, Tokyngton, Wembley, England on 27–30 Nov. 1974. The record for playing an electric organ is 143 hrs 37 mins by Steve Gail, 23, in Van Nuys, California, U.S.A., on 30 July–5 Aug. 1974.

Harmonium marathon The longest recorded non-stop harmonium marathon is 72 hrs by Iain Stinson and John Whiteley, both of the Royal Holloway College at Englefield Green, Surrey on 6–9 Feb. 1970.

Accordion marathon Helmut Klug played an electric accordion 52 hrs 8 mins at the Gasthaus Ferstl, Trofaiach, Austria on 7–9 July 1974.

Brass instrument *Largest* The largest recorded brass instrument is a tuba standing 7½ ft *2 m* tall, with 39 ft *12 m* of tubing and a bell 3 ft 4 in *1 m* across. This contrabass tuba was constructed for a world tour by the band of John Philip Sousa (1854–1932), the United States composer, in *c.* 1896–98, and is still in use. This instrument is now owned by a circus promoter in South Africa.

Longest alphorn The longest alphorn is 32 ft 9½ in *10 m* long, reported from Aschau bei Kraiburg, Bavaria, West Germany and requires three blowers.

Stringed instrument *Largest* The largest stringed instrument ever constructed was a pantaleon with 270 strings stretched over 50 ft² *4,6 m²* used by George Noel in 1767. The greatest number of musicians required to operate a single instrument was the six required to play the gigantic orchestrion, known as the Apollonican, built in 1816 and played until 1840.

Largest guitar The largest and presumably also the loudest playable guitar in the world is one 8 ft 10 in *2,6 m* tall, weighing 80 lb. *36 kg* and with a volume of 16,000 in³ *262 200 cm³* (*c.f.* the standard 1,024 in³ *16,780 cm³*) built by The Harmony Company of Chicago and completed in April 1970 and is priced at $15,000 (£6,250).

Largest double bass The largest bass viol ever constructed was an octobass 10 ft *3 m* tall, built in *c.* 1845 by J. B. Vuillaume (1798–1875) of France. Because the stretch was too great for any musician's finger-span, the stopping was effected by foot levers. It was played in London in 1851.

Violin *Most valuable* The highest recorded price for a violin is the $250,000 (£104,166) paid by a private buyer to Harry A. Duffy for the Cessole Stradivarius of 1716 in December 1972. On this valuation the "Messie" Stradivarius in the Ashmolean Museum at Oxford, England, is now worth at least £200,000.

An inventory of 700 known or recorded string instruments made by Antonio Stradivari (1644–1737) is contained in the *Violin Iconography* by Herbert K. Goodkind of which those made between 1720–1730 reached a "tonal zenith".

Underwater Violinist The only violinist to surmount the problems of playing the violin underwater has been Mark Gottlieb. Beneath the Evergreen State College swimming bath in Olympia, Washington, U.S.A. in March 1975 he gave a submarine rendition of Handel's Water Music. He is still working on both his bow speed and his *detaché*.

Largest drum The largest drum in the world is the Disneyland Big Bass Drum with a diameter of 10 ft 6 in *3,2 m* and a weight of 450 lb. *204 kg*. It was built in 1961 by Remo Inc. of North Hollywood, California, U.S.A. and is mounted on wheels and towed by a tractor.

Christian Steiner

Central Park, New York City, during the record 130,000 attendance for any classical concert (see below)

ORCHESTRAS

Largest The vastest orchestra ever recorded were those assembled on Band Day at the University of Michigan, U.S.A. In some years between 1958 and 1965 the total number of instrumentalists reached 13,500. On 17 June 1872, Johann Strauss the younger (1825–99) conducted an orchestra of 2,000, supported by a choir of 20,000, at the World Peace Jubilee in Boston, Massachusetts, U.S.A. The number of violinists was more than 350.

Most Successful Brass band Most British Open Championship titles (inst. 1853) have been won by the Black Dyke Mills Band which has won 21 times from 1862 to 1974 including their 1947–49 and 1972–74 hat tricks.

Marching Band The largest marching band on record was one of 1,976 musicians and 54 drill majors, flag bearers and directors who marched 2 miles down Pennsylvania Avenue in President Nixon's Inaugural Parade on 20 Jan. 1973.

Greatest attendance The greatest attendance at any classical concert has been 130,000 for the New York Philharmonic Orchestra, conducted by Leonard Bernstein, at Sheep Meadow in Central Park, New York City, N.Y., U.S.A., on 6 Aug. 1974.

Pop Festival The greatest claimed attendance at a Pop Festival has been 600,000 for the "Summer Jam" at Watkins Glen, New York, U.S.A., on Sunday 29 July 1973 of whom about 150,000 actually paid. There were 12 "sound towers". The attendance at the third Pop Festival at East Afton Farm, Freshwater, Isle of Wight, England on 30 Aug. 1970 was claimed by its promoters, Fiery Creations, to be 400,000.

Highest and lowest notes The extremes of orchestral instruments (excluding the organ) range between a handbell tuned to g^v (6,272 cycles/sec) and the sub-contrabass clarinet,

99

which can reach C_{11} or 16.4 cycles/sec. The highest note on a standard pianoforte is c^v (4,186 cycles/sec), which is also the violinist's limit. In 1873 a sub double bassoon able to reach $B_{111}\sharp$ or 14.6 cycles/sec was constructed but no surviving specimen is known. The extremes for the organ are g^{vi} (the sixth G above middle c) (12,544 cycles/sec) and C_{111} (8.12 cycles/sec) obtainable from $\frac{3}{4}$-in and 64 ft pipes respectively.

COMPOSERS

Most prolific The most prolific composer of all time was probably Georg Philipp Telemann (1681–1767) of Germany. He composed 12 complete sets of services (one cantata every Sunday) for a year, 78 services for special occasions, 40 operas, 600 to 700 orchestral suites, 44 Passions, plus concertos and chamber music. The most prolific symphonist was Johann Melchior Molter (c. 1695–1765) of Germany who wrote 165. Joseph Haydn (1732–1809) of Austria wrote 104 numbered symphonies some of which are regularly played today.

Most rapid Among composers of the classical period the most prolific was Wolfgang Amadeus Mozart (1756–91) of Austria, who wrote c. 1,000 operas, operettas, symphonies, violin sonatas, divertimenti, serenades, motets, concertos for piano and many other instruments, string quartets, other chamber music, masses and litanies, of which only 70 were published before he died, aged 35. His opera *The Clemency of Titus* (1791) was written in 18 days and three symphonic masterpieces, *Symphony No. 39 in E flat major*, *Symphony in G minor* and the *Jupiter Symphony in C*, were reputedly written in the space of 42 days in 1788. His overture *Don Giovanni* was written in full score at one sitting in Prague in 1787 and finished on the day of its opening performance.

National anthems The oldest national anthem is the *Kimigayo* of Japan, in which the words date from the 9th century. The anthem of Greece constitutes the first four verses of the Solomos poem, which has 158 verses. The shortest anthems are those of Japan, Jordan and San Marino, each with only four lines. The anthems of Bahrain and Qatar have no words at all.

Longest rendering "God Save the King" was played non-stop 16 or 17 times by a German military band on the platform of Rathenau Railway Station, Brandenburg, on the morning of 9 Feb. 1909. The reason was that King Edward VII was struggling inside the train with the uniform of a German Field-Marshal before he could emerge.

Longest symphony The longest of all single classical symphonies is the orchestral symphony No. 3 in D minor by Gustav Mahler (1860–1911) of Austria. This work, composed in 1895, requires a contralto, a women's and a boys' choir and an organ, in addition to a full orchestra. A full performance requires 1 hour 34 min, of which the first movement alone takes 45 min. The Symphony No. 2 (the Gothic, now renumbered as No. 1), composed in 1919–22 by Havergal Brian, has been performed only twice, on 24 June 1961 and 30 Oct. 1966. The total *ensemble* included 55 brass instruments, 31 wood wind, six kettledrummers playing 22 drums, four vocal soloists, four large mixed choruses, a children's chorus and an organ. The symphony is continuous and required, when played as a recording on 27 Nov. 1967, 100 min. Brian wrote an even vaster work based on Shelley's "Prometheus Unbound' lasting 4 hrs 11 min but the full score has been missing since 1961. He wrote 27 symphonies, 4 grand operas and 7 large orchestral works between 1948 when he was 72 and 1968.

The symphony *Victory at Sea* written by Richard Rodgers and arranged by Robert Russell Bennett for N.B.C. T.V. in 1952 lasted for 13 hours.

Longest piano composition The longest continuous non-repetitious piece for piano ever composed has been the Opus Clavicembalisticum by Kaikhosru Shapurji Sorabji (b. 1892). The composer himself gave it its only public performance on 1 Dec. 1930 in Glasgow, Scotland. The work is in 12 movements with a theme and 49 variations and a Passacaglia with 81 and a playing time of $2\frac{3}{4}$ hours.

The longest musical composition of any kind is all 40,320 possible permutations of the C major scale for piano or organ. The score is a computer print out in 16 volumes named *Sadist Factory* by its organiser Philip Crevier. The premiere was in Tritiny College Chapel, Hartford, Connecticut, U.S.A. on 9–13 Aug. 1973 and required 9 players to play for exactly 100 hrs to reach the best part—the end.

Longest silence The most protracted silence in a modern composition is one entitled *4 minutes 33 seconds* in a totally silent *opus* by John Cage (U.S.A.). Commenting on this trend among young composers, Igor Fyodorovich Stravinsky (1882–1971) said that he looked forward to their subsequent compositions being "works of major length".

HIGHEST PAID MUSICIANS

Pianist Liberace (b. West Allis, Wisconsin, U.S.A., 1919) earns more than $2 million each 26 week season with a peak of $138,000 (£60,000) for a single night's performance as a pianist.

The highest paid classical concert pianist was Ignace Jan Paderewski (1860–1941), Prime Minister of Poland from 1919 to 1921, who accumulated a fortune estimated at $5,000,000, of which $500,000 was earned in a single season in 1922–23.

Singers *Most Successful* Of great fortunes earned by singers, the highest on record are those of Enrico Caruso (1873–1921), the Italian tenor, whose estate was about $9,000,000 and the Italian-Spanish coloratura soprano Amelita Galli-Curci (1889–1963), who received about $3,000,000. In 1850, up to $653 was paid for a single seat at the

Radio Times Hulton

Gustav Mahler whose third symphony in D minor ranks as the longest of classical symphonies

Radio Times Hulton

The "Swedish Nightingale", Jenny Lind, for whom people paid over $650 for a seat in 1850, when dollars were gold

concerts given in the United States by Johanna ("Janny") Maria Lind, later Mrs. Otto Goldschmidt (1820–87), the "Swedish Nightingale". She had a range from g to e^{III} of which the middle register is still regarded as unrivalled.

Worst While no agreement exists as to the identity of history's greatest singer, there is unanimity on the worst. The excursions of the soprano Florence Foster Jenkins (1868–1944) into lieder and even high coloratura culminated on 25 Oct. 1944 in her sell-out concert at the Carnegie Hall, New York, U.S.A. The diva's (already high) high F was said to have been made higher in 1943 by a crash in a taxi. It is one of the tragedies of musicology that Madame Jenkins' *Clavelitos*, accompanied by Cosme McMoon, was never recorded for posterity.

Violinist The Austrian-born Fritz Kreisler (1875–1962) is reputed to have received more than £1,000,000 in his career.

Drummer The most highly paid drummer, or indeed "side man" of any kind, is Bernard ("Buddy") Rich (b. 1917) in the band of Harry James, at more than $75,000 (£30,000) per annum.

OPERA

Longest The longest of commonly performed operas is *Die Meistersinger von Nürnberg* by Wilhelm Richard Wagner (1813–83) of Germany. A normal uncut performance of this opera as performed by the Sadler's Wells company between 24 Aug. and 19 Sept. 1968 entailed 5 hrs 15 min of music. An opera *The Life and Times of Joseph Stalin*, performed in 7 acts at the Brooklyn Academy of Music, U.S.A. on 14–15 Dec. 1973 required 13 hrs 25 min. Act 7 was deemed by some to be the best.

Shortest The shortest opera written was *The Deliverance of Theseus* by Darius Milhaud (b. Sept. 1892) first performed in 1928 which lasts for 7 min 27 secs.

Aria The longest single aria, in the sense of an operatic solo, is Brünnhilde's immolation scene in Wagner's *Götterdammerung*. A well-known recording of this has been precisely timed at 14 minutes 46 seconds.

Opera houses The largest opera house in the world is the Metropolitan Opera House, Lincoln Center, New York City, N.Y., U.S.A., completed in September 1966 at a cost of $45,700,000 (*£16,320,000*). It has a capacity of 3,800 seats in an auditorium 451 ft *137 m* deep. The stage is 234 ft *71 m* in width and 146 ft *44,5 m* deep. The tallest opera house is one housed in a 42-storey building on Wacker Drive in Chicago, Illinois, U.S.A.

Largest

Most tiers The Teatro della Scala (La Scala) in Milan, Italy, shares with the Bolshoi Theatre in Moscow, U.S.S.R., the distinction of having the greatest number of tiers. Each has six, with the topmost in Moscow being termed the Galurka.

Opera Singers The youngest opera singer in the world has been Jeanette Gloria La Bianca, born in Buffalo, New York on 12 May 1934, who sang Rosina in *The Barber of Seville* at the Teatro dell'Opera, Rome on 8 May 1950 aged 15 years 361 days, having appeared as Gilda in *Rigoletto* at Velletri 45 days earlier. Ginetta La Bianca was taught by Lucia Carlino and managed by Angelo Carlino. The tenor Giovanni Martinelli sang Emperor Altoum in *Turandot* in Seattle, Washington, U.S.A. on 4 Feb. 1967 when aged 81.

Youngest and Oldest

BELLS

Heaviest World The heaviest bell in the world is the Tsar Kolokol, cast in 1733 in Moscow, U.S.S.R. It weighs 193 tons *196 tonnes* measures 22 ft 8 in *6,9 m* in diameter and over 19 ft *5,8 m* high, and its greatest thickness is 24 in *60 cm*. The bell is cracked, and a fragment, weighing about 11 tons/*tonnes* was broken from it. The bell has stood, unrung, on a platform in the Kremlin, in Moscow, since 1836.

Wilhelm Richard Wagner whose uncut *Meistersingers* requires 5¼ hours to perform

Radio Times Hulton

An artist's impression of the 90 ton Mingun bell in Burma which is rung" by the ramming of a teak boom

The heaviest bell in use is the Mingun bell, weighing 55,555 viss or *90,52 tons* with a diameter of 16 ft 8½ in at the lip, in Mandalay, Burma, which is struck by a teak boom from the outside. It was cast at Mingun late in the reign of King Bodawpaya (1782–1819). The heaviest swinging bell in the world is the Petersglocke in Cologne Cathedral, Germany, cast in 1923 with a diameter of 3,40 m *11 ft 1¾ in* weighing 25.0 tons *25,4 tonnes*.

United Kingdom The heaviest bell hung in the United Kingdom is "Great Paul" in St. Paul's Cathedral, London. It was cast in 1881, weighs 16 tons 14 cwt. 2 qrs. 19 lb. *17 tonnes* and has a diameter of 9 ft 6½ in *2,9 m*. "Big Ben", the hour bell in the clock tower of the House of Commons, was cast in 1858 and weighs 13 tons 10 cwt. 3 qrs. 15 lb. *13 761 kg*.

The heaviest bell ever cast in England and the heaviest tuned bell in the world is the bourdon bell of the Laura Spelman Rockefeller Memorial carillon in Riverside Church, New York City, N.Y., U.S.A. It weighs 18 tons 5 cwt. 1 qr. 18 lb. *18,5 tonnes* and is 10 ft 2 in *3 m* in diameter.

Oldest *World* The oldest bell in the world is reputed to be that found in the Babylonian Palace of Nimrod in 1849 by Mr. (later Sir) Austen Henry Layard (1817–94). It dates from *c*. 1000 B.C.

United Kingdom The oldest *dated* bell in England is one hanging in Lissett church, near Bridlington, Humberside discovered in Oct. 1972 to bear the date MCCLIIII (1254). The oldest inscribed bell is at Caversfield church, Oxfordshire and may be dated *c*. 1210. The uninscribed bell, at the Parish Church of St. Nicholas, Lanark, Strathclyde in daily use was originally founded in 1110 and refounded in 1659, 1740 and 1835.

The heaviest change ringing peal in the world is the ring of 13 bells, cast in 1938–39, weighing 16½ tons *16,7 tonnes*, in Liverpool Anglican Cathedral. The tenor bell, Emmanuel, weighs 82 cwt. 11 lb. *4 170 kg 80*.

CARILLON

Largest The largest carillon in the world is planned for completion in 1976 in a 300 ft *91,4 m* tower on the Cincinnati riverfront Ohio, U.S.A. with 83 bells.

Heaviest The heaviest carillon in the United Kingdom is in St. Nicholas Church, Aberdeen, Scotland. It consists of 48 bells, the total weight of which is 25 tons 8 cwt.

2 qrs. 13 lb. *25 838 kg*. The bourdon bell weighs 4 tons 9 cwt. 3 qrs. 26 lb. *4 571 kg* and the carillon comprises four octaves, less the bottom semi-tone.

BELL RINGING

Eight bells have been rung to their full "extent" (a "Bob Major" of 40,320 changes) only once without relays. This took place in a bell foundry at Loughborough, Leicestershire, beginning at 6.52 a.m. on 27 July 1963 and ending at 00.50 a.m. on 28 July, after 17 hrs 58 min. The peal was composed by Kenneth Lewis of Altrincham, Greater Manchester, and the eight ringers were conducted by Robert B. Smith, aged 25, of Marple, Greater Manchester. Theoretically it would take 37 years 355 days to ring 12 bells (maximus) to their full extent of 479,001,600 changes. The greatest number of peals (minimum of 5,040 changes, all in tower bells) rung in a year is 209 by Mark William Marshall of Ashford, Kent in 1973. The late George E. Fearn rang 2,666 peals from 1928 to May 1974.

SONG

Oldest The oldest known song is the *chadouf* chant, which has been sung since time immemorial by irrigation workers on the man-powered treadwheel Nile water mills (or *saqiyas*) in Egypt (now the United Arab Republic). The English song *Sumer is icumen in* dates from *c*. 1240.

Top songs of all time The most frequently sung songs in English are *Happy Birthday to You* (based on the original *Good morning to all*), by Mildred and Patty S. Hill of New York (published in 1935 and in copyright until 1996); *For He's a Jolly Good Fellow* (originally the French *Malbrouk*), known at least as early as 1781, and *Auld Lang Syne* (originally the Srathspey *I fee'd a Lad at Michaelmass*), some words of which were written by Robert Burns (1759–96). *Happy Birthday* was sung in space by the Apollo IX astronauts on 8 March 1969.

Top selling sheet music Sales of three non-copyright pieces are known to have exceeded 20,000,000 namely *The Old Folks at Home*, *Listen to the Mocking Bird* (1855) and *The Blue Danube* (1867). Of copyright material the two top-sellers are *Let Me Call You Sweetheart* (1910, by Whitson and Friedman) and *Till We Meet Again* (1918, by Egan and Whiting) each with some 6,000,000 by 1967.

Most successful songwriters In terms of sales of single records, the most successful of all song writers have been John Lennon and Paul McCartney (see also Gramophone, Fastest sales, p.

102

107) of the Beatles. Between 1962 and 1 Jan. 1970 they together wrote 30 songs which sold more than 1,000,000 records each.

HYMNS

Earliest There are believed to be more than 500,000 Christian hymns in existence. "Te Deum Laudamus" dates from about the 5th century, but the earliest exactly datable hymn is the French one "Jesus soit en ma teste et mon entendement" from 1490, translated into the well-known "God be in my head" in 1512.

Longest and shortest The longest hymn is "Hora novissima tempora pessima sunt; vigilemus" by Bernard of Cluny (12th century), which runs to 2,966 lines. In English the longest is "The Sands of Time are sinking" by Mrs. Anne Ross Cousin, *née* Cundell (1824–1906), which is in full 152 lines, though only 32 lines in the Methodist Hymn Book. The shortest hymn is the single verse in Long Metre "Be Present at our Table Lord", anonymous but attributed to "J. Leland".

Most prolific hymnists Mrs. Frances (Fanny) Jan Van Alstyne, *née* Crosby (1820–1915), of the U.S.A., wrote more than 8,000 hymns although she had been blinded at the age of 6 weeks. She is reputed to have knocked off one hymn in 15 min. Charles Wesley (1707–88) wrote about 6,000 hymns. In the seventh (1950) edition of *Hymns Ancient and Modern* the works of John Mason Neale (1818–66) appear 56 times.

Longest hymn-in The Cambridge University Student Methodist Society sang through the 984 hymns in the Methodist Hymn Book in 45 hrs 42 min, and completed 1,000 hymns with 16 more requests in 88 min on 7–9 Feb. 1969 in the Wesley Church, Cambridge.

5. THEATRE

Origins Theatre in Europe has its origins in Greek drama performed in honour of a god, usually Dionysus. The earliest amphitheatres date from the 5th century B.C. The largest of all known *orchestras* is one at Megalopolis in central Greece, where the auditorium reached a height of 75 ft *23 m* and had a capacity of 17,000.

Oldest World The oldest indoor theatre in the world is the Teatro Olimpico in Vicenza, Italy. Designed in the Roman style by Andrea di Pietro, *alias* Palladio (1508–80), it was begun three months before his death and finished in 1582 by his pupil Vicenzo Scamozzi (1552–1616). It is preserved today in its original form.

United Kingdom The earliest London theatre was James Burbage's "The Theatre", built in 1576 near Finsbury Fields, London. The oldest theatre still in use in the United Kingdom is the Theatre Royal, Bristol. The foundation stone was laid on 30 Nov. 1764, and the theatre was opened on 30 May 1766 with a "Concert of Music and a Specimen of Rhetorick". The City Varieties Music Hall, Leeds was a singing room in 1762 and so claims to outdate the Theatre Royal. Actors were legally rogues and vagabonds until the passing of an Act (5 Geo. IV c.38) in 1824. The oldest amateur dramatic society is the Amateur Dramatic Society in Cambridge founded by F. C. Burnard in May 1855.

Largest World The world's largest building used for theatre is the National People's Congress Building (*Ren min da hui tang*) on the west side of Tian an men Square, Peking, China. It was completed in 1959 and covers an area of 12.9 acres *5,2 ha*. The theatre seats 10,000 and is occasionally used as such as in 1964 for the play "The East is Red". The largest regular theatre in the world has been Radio City Music Hall in Rockefeller Center, New York City, N.Y., U.S.A. with a seating capacity of more than 6,200 people and thus 8 million per annum. The stage is 144 ft *44 m* wide and 66 ft 6 in *20,26 m* deep, equipped with a revolving turntable 43 ft *13,10 m* in diameter and three elevator sections, each 70 ft *21 m* long.

The greatest seating capacity of any regular theatre in the world is that of the "Chaplin" (formerly the "Blanquita") in Havana, Cuba. It was opened on 30 Dec. 1949 and has 6,500 seats.

United Kingdom The highest capacity theatre is the Odeon, Hammersmith, Greater London, with 3,485 seats in 1975. The largest theatre stage in the United Kingdom is the Opera House in Blackpool, Lancashire. It was re-built in July 1939 and has seats for 2,975 people. Behind the 45 ft *14 m* wide proscenium arch the stage is 110 ft *33 m* high, 60 ft *18 m* deep and 100 ft *30 m* wide, and there is dressing room accommodation for 200 artistes.

Britain's largest open air theatre is at Scarborough, North Yorkshire opened in 1932 with a seating capacity of 7,000 plus standing room for 9,000 and a 182 ft *55 m* long stage.

Smallest The smallest regularly operated professional theatre in Great Britain is the Mull Little Theatre, Tobermory, Isle of Mull, Scotland with a capacity of 36 seats.

Largest amphitheatre The largest amphitheatre ever built is the Flavian amphitheatre or Colosseum of Rome, Italy, completed in A.D. 80. Covering 5 acres *2 ha* and with a capacity of 87,000, it has a maximum length of 612 ft *187 m* and maximum width of 515 ft *157 m*.

Longest runs The longest continuous run of any show in the world is by *The Mousetrap* by Dame Agatha Mary Clarissa Christie, D.B.E. (*née* Miller, now Lady Mallowan) (b. Torquay, Devon, 15 Sept. 1890). This thriller opened on 25 Nov. 1952, at the Ambassadors Theatre (capacity 453) and moved after 8,862 performances 'down the road' to St. Martin's Theatre on 25 Mar. 1974. Its 9,478th performance on 21 Aug. 1975 surpasses even the former composite record of *The Drunkard* in Los Angeles, which ran from 1932–1953, and was revived as a musical.

Revue The greatest number of performances of any theatrical presentation is more than 25,000 in the case of *The Golden Horseshoe Revue*—a show staged at Disneyland Park, Anaheim, California, U.S.A. The show was first put on on 17 July 1955. The three main performers Fulton Burley, Bert Henry and Betty Taylor play as many as five houses a day in a routine lasting 45 minutes. In Britain, the Brighton Corporation's variety show *Tuesday Night at the Dome* reached its 1,385th performance in 29 years on 7 Jan. 1975.

Broadway The Broadway record is 3,242 performances by *Fiddler on the Roof* which closed on 3 July 1972. It had opened on 22 Sept. 1964. Paul Lipson played 1,811 times as Tevye during which time he had ten "wives" and 58 "daughters". The world gross earnings reached $64,300,000 (£25.7 *million*) on an original investment of $375,000. The off-Broadway musical show *The Fantasticks* by Tom Jones and Harvey Schmidt achieved its 6,249th performance as it entered its 16th year at the Sullivan Street Playhouse, Greenwich Village, New York City on 3 May 1975. It has been played in a record 3,788 productions in 55 countries.

Musical shows The longest-running musical show ever performed in Britain was *The Black and White Minstrel Show* later *Magic of the Minstrels*. The aggregate number of performances was 6,187 with a total attendance of 7,466,509. The show opened at the Victoria Palace, London on 25 May 1962 and finally closed on 4 Nov. 1972. One chorus girl claims that a pedometer strapped to her leg registered 6½ miles *10 km* in one night.

One-man shows The longest run of one-man shows is 849 by Victor Borge in his *Comedy in Music* from 2 Oct. 1953 to 21 Jan. 1956 at the Golden Theatre, Broadway, New York City. The world aggregate record for one-man shows is for more than 1,200 performances of *Brief Lives* by Roy Dotrice (b. Guernsey, 5 May 1923) including 400 straight at the Mayfair Theatre, London ending on 20 July 1974. He was on stage for more than 2½ hours per performance of this 17th century monologue.

Most Durable Leading Actress Dame Anna Neagle, D.B.E., played the lead role in *Charlie Girl* at the Adelphi Theatre, London for 2,062 of 2,202 performances between 15 Dec. 1965 and 27 Mar. 1971. She played the role a further 327 times in 327 performances in Australasia.

Shortest runs *World* The shortest run on record was that of *The Intimate Revue* at the Duchess Theatre, London, on 11 March 1930. Anything which could go wrong did. With scene changes taking up to 20 min apiece, the management scrapped seven scenes to get the finale on before midnight. The run was described as "half a performance". In a number of Broadway productions the opening and closing nights have coincided.

Broadway Of the many Broadway shows for which the opening and closing nights coincided, one of the more costly was *Kelly*, a musical costing $700,000 which underwent the double ceremony on 6 Feb. 1965.

Longest play *O'Casey* by Patrick Funge played at the Lantern Theatre, Dublin, lasted 6 hrs 45 min playing time, opening on 24 July 1972 at 3 p.m. and finishing at 11.15 p.m. with a 90 min meal interval. George Begley was never off the stage. The 15th century Cornish Cycle of Mystery Plays was revived in English in July 1969, at the earthwork theatre, St. Piran's Round, Piran, near Perranporth, Cornwall, by the Drama Department of Bristol University. Three parts, *Origo Mundi*, *Passio*, and *Resurrectio*, ran for 12 hrs with two intermissions.

Shakespeare The first all amateur company to have staged all 37 of Shakespeare's plays was The Southsea Shakespeare Actors, Hampshire, England (founded 1947), when in October 1966 they presented *Cymbeline*. The amateur director throughout was Mr. K. Edmonds Gateloy, M.B.E. Nine members of Royal Holloway College, Egham, Surrey, completed a dramatic reading of all the plays, 154 sonnets and five narrative poems in 44 hrs 46 mins on 24–25 Feb. 1974. The longest is *Richard III*.

Longest chorus line The world's longest permanent chorus line was that formed by the Rockettes in the Radio City Music Hall, which opened in December 1932 in New York City, U.S.A. The 36 girls danced precision routines across its 144 ft *43,9 m* wide stage.

Cabaret The highest night club fee in history has been $100,000 (*£40,000*) collected by Liza Minnelli for the New Year's Eve show at the Colonie Hill Club, Long Island, New York on 1 Jan. 1975. Patrons paid $150 per seat.

Ice shows Holiday on Ice Production Inc., founded by Morris Chalfen in 1945, stages the world's most costly live entertainment with up to seven productions playing simultaneously in several of 75 countries drawing 20,000,000 spectators paying $40 million (*£16.6 million*) in a year. The total skating and other staff exceeds 900.

Most Ardent Theatre-goer The highest recorded number of paid theatre attendances in Britain is 2,854 shows in 22 years from 28 Mar. 1953 to 28 Mar. 1975 by John Iles of Salisbury, Wiltshire. He estimates he has travelled 117,050 miles *188,375 km* and spent 7,250 hours in theatres.

104

6. GRAMOPHONE

Origins The gramophone (phonograph) was first *conceived* by Charles Cros (1842–1888) a French poet and scientist, who described his idea in sealed papers deposited in the French Academy of Sciences on the 30th April 1877. However the realisation of a practical device was first *achieved* by Thomas Alva Edison (1847–1931) of the U.S.A. The first successful machine was constructed by his mechanic, John Kruesi on 4-6 Dec. 1877, demonstrated on the 7 Dec. and patented on the 19 Feb. 1878.

The first practical hand cranked, wax coated cylinder phonograph was manufactured in the United States by Chichester Bell and Charles Sumner Tainter in 1886. The forerunner of the modern disc gramophone was patented in 1887 by Emile Berliner (1851–1929), a German immigrant to the U.S.A. Although a toy machine based on his principle was produced in Germany in 1889, the gramophone was not a serious commercial competitor to the cylinder phonograph until 1896.

The country with the greatest number of record players is the United States, with a total of more than 61,200,000 by Dec. 1971. A total of more than half a billion dollars (*now £192 million*) is spent annually on 500,000 juke boxes in the United States.

In the United States retail sales of discs and tapes reached $2,017 million in 1973 which included sales for L.P.'s and for cassettes and cartridges.

OLDEST RECORD
The B.B.C. record library, contains over 750,000 records, including 5,250 with no known matrix. An Edison solid wax cylinder, recorded in Edison's laboratory and dated 26 June 1888 is the oldest record in the library which also contains a collection of early Berliner discs.

Earliest jazz records The earliest jazz record made was *Indiana* and *The Dark Town Strutters Ball*, recorded for the Columbia label in New York City, N.Y., U.S.A., on or about 30 Jan. 1917, by the Original Dixieland Jazz Band, led by Dominick (Nick) James La Rocca (1889–1961). This was released on 31 May 1917. The first jazz record to be released was the O.D.J.B.'s *Livery Stable Blues* (recorded 24 Feb.), backed by *The Dixie Jass Band One-Step* (recorded 26 Feb.), released by Victor on 7 March 1917.

Smallest Record The smallest functional gramophone record is one 1⅜ in *3,5 cm* in diameter of "God Save the King" of which 250 were made by HMV Record Co. in 1924.

Most successful solo recording artist On 9 June 1960 the Hollywood Chamber of Commerce presented Harry Lillis (*alias* Bing) Crosby, Jr. (b. 2 May 1904 at Tacoma, Washington) with a platinum disc to commemorate a sale of 200,000,000 records from the 2,600 singles and 125 albums he had recorded. On 15 Sept. 1970 he received a second platinum disc for selling 300,650,000 discs with Decca. His global life-time sales on 88 labels in 28 countries have totalled, according to his royalty reports, 365,000,000. His first commercial recording was "*I've Got the Girl*" recorded on 18 Oct. 1926 (master number W142785 (Take 3) issued on the Columbia label). The greatest collection of Crosbiana owned by Mr. Bob Roberts of Chatham, Kent includes 1,677 records.

The greatest recorded success in a single year has been the sale of 13.7 million albums in 1966 by the ex-Army trumpeter Herb Alpert (b. Los Angeles, 31 Mar. 1937) with his Tijuana Brass band.

Gramophone

Most successful group The singers with the greatest sales of any group have been the Beatles. This group from Liverpool, Merseyside, comprised George Harrison, M.B.E. (b. 25 Feb. 1943), John Ono (formerly John Winston) Lennon, M.B.E. (b. 9 Oct. 1940), James Paul McCartney, M.B.E. (b. 18 June 1942) and Richard Starkey, M.B.E., *alias* Ringo Starr (b. 7 July 1940). Between February 1963 and June 1972 their group sales were estimated at 545 million in singles' equivalents. This included 85 million albums. The 40,000 strong Beatles Fan Club had been closed down on 31 Mar. 1972.

GOLDEN DISCS

Earliest The earliest recorded piece eventually to aggregate a total sale of a million copies were performances by Enrico Caruso (b. Naples, Italy, 1873, and d. 2 Aug. 1921) of the aria *Vesti la giubba* (*On with the Motley*) from the opera *I Pagliacci* by Ruggiero Leoncavallo (1858–1919), the earliest version of which was recorded with piano on 12 Nov. 1902. The first single recording to surpass the million mark was Alma Gluck's *Carry me back to old Virginny* on the Red Seal Victor label on the 12-inch *30,48 cm* single faced (later backed) record 74420. The first actual golden disc was one sprayed by R.C.A. Victor for presentation to the U.S. trombonist and band-leader Alton 'Glenn' Miller (1904–44) for his *Chattanooga Choo Choo* on 10 Feb. 1942.

Most The only *audited* measure of million-selling records within the United States, is certification by the Recording Industry Association of America introduced 14 Mar. 1958. Out of the 1,540 R.I.A.A. gold record awards made to January 1975, the most have gone to The Beatles with 38 (plus one with Billy Preston) as a group with 8 more awards each to Lennon, McCartney and Starr. The most awards to an individual is 28 to Elvis Aron Presley (b. Tupelo, Mississippi, U.S.A., 8 Jan. 1935) spanning 1958 to 31 Jan. 1975.

Most recorded song Two songs have each been recorded between 900 and 1,000 times in the United States alone—*St. Louis Blues*, written in 1914 by W. C. (William Christopher) Handy (b. Florence, Alabama 1873 and d. 1958), and *Stardust*, written in 1927 by Hoagland ("Hoagy") Carmichael (b. Bloomington, Indiana, 22 Nov. 1899).

Most recordings Miss Lata Mangeshker (b. 1928) between 1948 and 1974 has reportedly recorded not less than 25,000 solo, duet and chorus backed songs in 20 Indian languages. She frequently had 5 sessions in a day and has "backed" 1,800 films to 1974.

Biggest sellers The greatest seller of any gramophone record to date is *White Christmas* by Irving Berlin (b. Israel Bailin, at Tyumen, Russia, 11 May 1888). First recorded in 1941, it reached 135,000,000 by December 1974. The highest claim for any "pop" record is an unaudited 25,000,000 for *Rock Around the Clock*, copyrighted in 1953 by James E. Meyrs under the name Jimmy DeKnight and the late Max C. Freedman and recorded on 12 Apr. 1954 by Bill Haley and the Comets. The top-selling British record of all-time is *I Want to Hold Your Hand* by the Beatles, released in 1963, with world sales of over 13,000,000, including a certified sale of 5,000,000 in the United States by January 1975.

Best-sellers' charts Best sellers' charts were first published in the U.S. periodical *Billboard* on 27 July 1940. The longest stay in the L.P. charts in the U.S.A. has been 490 weeks from late in 1958 to July 1968 by the Columbia album *Johnny's Greatest Hits* (Johnny Mathis). The longest in the U.K. has been *Sound of Music* (sound track) with 362 weeks to April 1973. The longest reign at No. 1 in British charts has been 11 weeks for *Rose Marie* by Slim Whitman in 1955.

Top-selling L.P. The best-selling L.P. is the 20th Century Fox album *Sing We now of Christmas*, issued in 1958 and re-entitled *The Little Drummer Boy* in 1963. Its sales were reported to be more than 14,000,000 by Nov. 1972. The first British L.P. to sell 1,000,000 copies was *With the Beatles* (Parlophone), from November 1963 to January 1964 in the United States and to September 1965 in Britain. The top-selling British L.P. has been the double (4-sided) *Jesus Christ Superstar* by Andrew Lloyd Webber (b. 22 Mar. 1948) and Tim Rice (b. 10 Nov. 1944) released on 10 Oct. 1970. Sales are now approaching 6 million.

Top-selling L.P. sound track The all-time best-seller among long-playing records of musical film shows is *The Sound of Music* sound track album, released by Victor in U.S.A. on 2 March and in Britain on 9 April 1965, with more than 19,000,000 to 1 Jan. 1973. In Britain it was No. 1 in the L.P. Charts for 69 weeks.

Fastest selling L.P.s The fastest selling record of all time is *John Fitzgerald Kennedy—A Memorial Album* (Premium Albums), an L.P. recorded on 22 Nov. 1963, the day of Mr. Kennedy's assassination, which sold 4,000,000 copies at 99 cents (*then 35p*) in six days (7–12 Dec. 1963), thus ironically beating the previous speed record set by the satirical L.P. *The First Family* in 1962–63. The fastest selling British record has been the Beatles' double album *The Beatles* (Parlophone) with "nearly 2 million" in its first week in November 1968.

Advance sales The greatest advance sale was 2,100,000 for *Can't Buy Me Love* by the Beatles, released in the United States on 16 March 1964. The Beatles also equalled their British record of 1,000,000 advance sales, set by *I want to Hold Your Hand* (Parlophone transferred to Apple Aug. 1968) on 29 Nov. 1963, with this same record on 20 March 1964. The U.K. record for advance sales of an L.P. is 750,000 for the Parlophone album *Beatles for Sale* released on 4 Dec. 1964.

Top-selling classical L.P. The first classical long-player to sell a million was a performance featuring the pianist Harvey Lavan (Van) Cliburn, Jr. (b. Kilgore, Texas, 12 July 1934) of the *Piano Concerto No. 1* by Pyotr Ilyich Tchaikovsky (1840–93) (more properly rendered Chaykovskiy) of Russia. This recording was made in 1958 and sales reached 1,000,000 by 1961, 2,000,000 by 1965 and about 2,500,000 by January 1970.

Otis Dewey "Slim" Whitman (b. 20 Jan 1924) who occupied the top spot on the British charts for a record 11 weeks ▸

Longest L.P. set The longest long-playing record is the 137-disc set of the complete works of William Shakespeare (1564–1616). The recordings, which were made in 1957–1964, cost £260.62½ per set, and are by the Argo Record Co. Ltd., London, S.W.3. The Vienna Philharmonic's playing of Wagner's "The Ring" covers 19 L.P.s, was eight years in the making and requires 14½ hrs playing time.

Highest gross and audience The highest gross taking for an individual pop recording group is $309,000 (£123,600) paid by a record 56,800 attenders for the concert by the British group Led Zeppelin at the Tampa Stadium, Florida, U.S.A., on 5 May 1973. There were in addition 6,000 "gate-crashers".

Loudest Pop Group The amplification of *Deep Purple* on a 10,000 watts Marshall P.A. system attained 117 decibels—sufficient in the London Rainbow Theatre in 1972 to render three members of their audience unconscious.

Longest Silence The earliest commercially released silent record was *Three Minutes of Silence* by C.B.S. engineers Hamilton M. O'Hara and Don Foster in 1953. It received rave notices and was rated a "coin grabber" in juke boxes. The longest silent L.P. *Auditory Memory* runs for 52 min 10 sec "recorded" in November 1974 by Jerry Cammarata of Staten Island, N.Y.

7. CINEMA

EARLIEST

Origins The greatest impetus in the development of cinematography came from the inventiveness of Etienne Jules Marey (1830–1903) of France

Earliest silent showings The earliest demonstration of a celluloid cinematograph film was given at Lyon (Lyons), France on 22 March 1895 by Auguste Marie Louis Nicolas Lumière (1862–1954) and Louis Jean Lumière (1864–1948), the French brothers. The first public showing was at the Indian Salon of the Hotel Scribe, on the Boulevard des Capucines, in Paris, on 28 Dec. 1895. The 33 patrons were charged 1 franc each and was ten short films, including *Baby's Breakfast*, *Lunch Hour at the Lumière Factory* and *The Arrival of a Train*. The same programme was shown on 20 Feb. 1896 at the Polytechnic Institute in Regent Street, London.

Earliest 'Talkie' The earliest sound-on-film motion picture was achieved by Eugene Augustin Lauste (b. Paris 17 Jan. 1857) who patented his process on 11 Aug. 1906 and produced a workable system using a string galvanometer in 1910 in London. The event is usually attributed to Dr. Lee de Forest (1873–1961) in New York City, N.Y., U.S.A., on 13 March 1923. The first all-talking picture was *Lights of New York*, shown at The Strand, New York City, on 6 July 1928.

Highest cinema-going The people of Taiwan go to the cinema more often than those of any other country in the world with an average of 66 attendances per person per annum according to the latest data. The Soviet Union has the most cinemas in the world, with 147,200 in 1970 including those projecting only 16 mm film. The number of cinemas in the U.K. declined from 4,542 in 1953 to 1,669 screens in 1975. The average weekly admissions declined from 24,700,000 in 1953 to 3,004,166 in 1974. The most persistent known cinema-goer is Paul Morgan, 92, a retired car paint sprayer. Since 1949 he has attended the Rio Cinema Theatre, Miami, Florida every day including Sundays although the programme is not changed more than thrice weekly. The manager states Mr. Morgan is always "first in line".

Most cinema seats The Falkland Islands and the Cook Islands have more cinema seats per total population than any other country in the world, with 250 seats for each 1,000 inhabitants. The Central African Republic has 2 cinemas and hence one seat for 4,100 people.

CINEMAS

Largest World The largest open-air cinema in the world is in the British Sector of West Berlin, Germany. One end of the Olympic Stadium, converted into an amphitheatre, seats 22,000 people.

United Kingdom The United Kingdom's largest cinema is the Odeon Theatre, Hammersmith, Greater London, with 3,485 seats. The Playhouse, Glasgow had 4,235 seats.

Oldest The earliest cinema was the "Electric Theatre", part of a tented circus in Los Angeles, California, U.S.A. It opened on 2 April 1902. The oldest building designed as a cinema is the Biograph Cinema in Wilton Road, Victoria, London. It was opened in 1905 and originally had seating accommodation for 500 patrons. Its present capacity is 700.

Most expensive film The most expensive film ever made is the 6 hr 13 min long *War and Peace*, the U.S.S.R. government adaptation of the masterpiece of Tolstoy directed by Sergei Bondarchuk (b. 1921) over the period 1962–67. The total cost has been officially stated to be more than £40,000,000. More than 165,000 uniforms had to be made. The re-creation of the Battle of Borodino (7 Sept. 1812) involved 120,000 Red Army "extras" at 3 roubles (£1.38) per month.

Most expensive film rights The highest price ever paid for film rights is $5,500,000, paid on 6 Feb. 1962 by Warner Brothers for *My Fair Lady*, which cost $17,000,000 thus making it the most expensive musical film then made.

Longest film The longest film ever shown is *The Human Condition*, directed in three parts by Masaki Kobayashi of Japan. It lasts 8 hrs 50 min, excluding two breaks of 20 min each. It was shown in Tōkyō in October 1961 at an admission price of 250 yen (24½p). The longest film ever released was **** by Andy Warhol (b. Cleveland, Ohio, 1931) which lasted 24 hrs. It proved, not surprisingly, except reportedly to its creator, a commercial failure and was withdrawn and re-released in 90 min form as *The Loves of Ondine*.

Highest box office gross The film which has had the highest world gross earnings (amount paid by cinema owners) is *The Godfather* (released in March 1972) which reached $155,000,000 (£40 million) world-wide by February 1974.

Highest earnings by an actor The greatest earnings by an actor for one film is a reputed $10,000,000 (£4,160,000) before tax by Marlon Brando from playing the lead rôle in *The Godfather* (see above). Sean Connery, who played James Bond (secret service agent 007) reputedly earned by way of fees and percentage of gross takings $13½ million (£5½ million) for the first five Bond films.

Largest Studios The largest complex of film studios in the world are those at Universal City, South California. The Back Lot contains 561 buildings and there are 34 sound stages.

OSCARS

Most Walter (Walt) Elias Disney (1901–1966) won more "Oscars"—the awards of the United States Academy of Motion Picture Arts and Sciences, instituted on 16 May 1929 for 1927–28—than any other person. His total was 35 from 1931 to 1969. The only actress to win three Oscars in a starring rôle has been Miss Katharine Hepburn, formerly Mrs. Ludlow Ogden Smith (b. Hartford, Conn., 9 Nov. 1909) in *Morning Glory* (1932-3), *Guess Who's Coming to Dinner* (1967) and *The Lion in Winter* (1968). Oscars are named after Mr. Oscar Pierce of Texas, U.S.A. The films with most awards have been *Ben Hur* (1959) with 11, followed by *West Side Story* (1961) with 10. The film with the highest number of nominations was *All About Eve* (1950) with 14. It won four.

Newsreels The world's most durable newsreel commentator has been Bob Danvers-Walker (b. Cheam, Surrey, 11 Oct. 1906), who commentated for Pathé "Gazette" from June 1940 until its demise in February 1970.

8. RADIO BROADCASTING

Origins The earliest description of a radio transmission system was written by Dr. Mahlon Loomis (U.S.A.) (b. Fulton County, N.Y., 21 July 1826) on 21 July 1864 and demonstrated between two kites more than 14 miles *22 km* apart at Bear's Den, Loudoun County, Virginia in October 1866. He received U.S. patent No. 129,971 entitled Improvement in Telegraphing on 20 July 1872. He died in 1886.

Earliest The first patent for a system of communication by
patent means of electro-magnetic waves, numbered No. 12039, was granted on 2 June 1896 to the Italian-Irish Marchese Guglielmo Marconi, G.C.V.O. (Hon.) (1874–1937). A public demonstration of wireless transmission of speech was, however, given in the town square of Murray, Kentucky, U.S.A. in 1892 by Nathan B. Stubblefield. He died destitute on 28 March 1928. The first permanent wireless installation was at The Needles on the Isle of Wight, by Marconi's Wireless Telegraph Co., Ltd., in November 1896.

Earliest The world's first advertised broadcast was made on 24
broadcast Dec. 1906 by the Canadian born Prof. Reginald
World Aubrey Fessenden (1868–1932) from the 420 ft *128 m* mast of the National Electric Signalling Company at Brant Rock, Massachusetts, U.S.A. The transmission included the *Largo* by George Friedrich Händel (1685–1759) of Germany. Fessenden had achieved the broadcast of highly distorted speech as early as November 1900.

United The first experimental broadcasting transmitter in the
Kingdom United Kingdom was set up at the Marconi Works in Chelmsford, Essex, in December 1919, and broadcast a news service in February 1920. The earliest regular broadcast was made from the Marconi transmitter "2 MT" at Writtle, Essex, on 14 Feb. 1922.

Trans- The earliest transatlantic wireless signals (the letter S
atlantic in Morse Code) were received by Marconi and George
trans- Stephen Kemp from a 10 kw station at Poldhu,
missions Cornwall, at Signal Hill, St. John's, Newfoundland, Canada, at 12.30 p.m. on 12 Dec. 1901. Human speech was first heard across the Atlantic in November 1915 when a transmission from the U.S. Navy station at Arlington, Virginia was received by U.S. radio-telephone engineers on the Eiffel Tower.

Earliest The radio-microphone, which was in essence also the
Radio- first 'bug', was devised by Reg. Moores (G.B.) in 1947
Microphones at first used on 76 MHz in the ice show *Aladdin* at Brighton Sports Stadium, East Sussex in Sept. 1949.

Most The country with the greatest number of radio
stations broadcasting stations is the United States, where there were 7,263 authorized broadcast stations in 1973 of which 4,296 were AM (Amplitude modulation) and 2,278 FM (Frequency modulation).

Highest The peak recorded listenership on B.B.C. Radio was
listenership 30,000,000 adults on 6 June 1950 for the boxing fight between Lee Savold (U.S.) and Bruce Woodcock (G.B.).

Longest The longest B.B.C. national broadcast was the reporting of the Coronation of Queen Elizabeth II on 2 June 1953. It began at 10.15 a.m. and finished at 5.30 p.m., after 7 hrs 15 min. The longest local radio transmission has been 9 hrs 55 min by B.B.C. Radio Bristol's programme "Mid Night Rally" on 21–22 Feb. 1975.

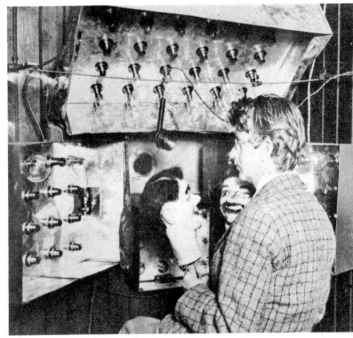

BBC

John Logie Baird, who on 26 Jan. 1926 gave the first public demonstration of Television

The longest continuous broadcast has been one of 208 hrs 32 min by Jim Humphries on WETE Knoxville, Tennessee, U.S.A., on 27 Mar.–5 Apr. 1974.

Most The most durable B.B.C. radio series is *The Week's*
durable *Good Cause* beginning on 24 Jan. 1926. The longest
B.B.C. running record programme is *Desert Island Discs*
programmes which began on 21 Jan. 1942 and on which programme the only guests to be thrice stranded have been Arthur Bowden Askey, O.B.E. (b. 6 June 1900) and Robertson Hare (b. 17 Dec. 1891). The *Desert Island* programme has been presented since its inception by Roy Plomley, who also devised the idea. The longest running solo radio feature is *Letter from America* by (Alfred) Alistair Cooke, Hon. K.B.E. (b. Manchester 20 Nov. 1908), first commissioned as a series of 13 talks on 6 March 1946. The longest running radio serial is *The Archers* which was created by Godfrey Baseley and was first broadcast on 7 June 1950. Up to 1 Jan. 1975 the signature tune *Borwick Green* had been played 27,208 times. The only one of 363 roles which has been played without interruption from the start has been that of Philip Archer by Norman Painting.

Most The highest number of successful requests (up to 1
record Apr. 1975) to play records on national B.B.C. pro-
requests grammes ever claimed is 250 by Mrs. Peggy Wain of Southampton. The record for local radio is 291 by Mrs. Molly Hallgarth of Louth, Lincolnshire. The aggregate record is 319 by Mrs. Wain.

Highest The highest recorded response from a radio show
Response occurred on 27 Nov. 1974 when on a 5 hour talk show on WCAU, Philadelphia, U.S.A., Howard Sheldon, the astrologist registered a call count of 388,299 calls.

9. TELEVISION

Invention The invention of television, the instantaneous viewing of distant objects, was not an act but a process of successive and inter-dependent discoveries. The first commercial cathode ray tube was introduced in 1897 by Karl Ferdinand Braun (1850–1918), but was not linked to "electric vision" until 1907 by Boris Rosing of Russia in St. Petersburg (now Leningrad). The earliest public demonstration of television was given on 26 Jan. 1926 by John Logie Baird (1888–1946) of Scotland, using a development of the mechanical scanning system suggested by Paul Nipkov in 1884. A patent application for the Iconoscope (Number 2,141,059) had been filed on 29 Dec. 1923 by Dr. Vladimir Kosma Zworykin (born in Russia on 30 July 1889, became a U.S. citizen in 1924), and a short range transmission of a model windmill had been made on 13 June 1925 by C. Francis Jenkins in Washington, D.C., U.S.A. The first experimental transmission in Britain was on 30 Sept. 1929. Public transmissions on 30 lines were made from 22 Aug. 1932 until 11 Sept. 1935.

Earliest service The world's first high definition (*i.e.* 405 lines) television broadcasting service was opened from Alexandra Palace, Haringey, Greater London, on 2 Nov. 1936, when there were about 100 sets in the United Kingdom. The Chief Engineer was Mr. Douglas Birkinshaw. A television station in Berlin, Germany, made a low definition (180 line) transmission from 22 March 1935. The transmitter burnt out in Aug. 1935.

Transatlantiu transmission The earliest transatlantic transmission by satellite was achieved at 1 a.m. on 11 July 1962, *via* the active satellite *Telstar I* from Andover, Maine, U.S.A., to Pleumeur Bodou, France. The picture was of Mr. Frederick R. Kappel, chairman of the American Telephone and Telegraph Company, which owned the satellite. The first "live" broadcast was made on 23 July 1962 and the first woman to appear was the *haute couturière*, Ginette Spanier, directrice of Balmain, the next day. On 9 Feb. 1928 the image of J. L. Baird (see above) and of a Mrs. Howe was transmitted from Station 2 KZ at Coulsdon, Surrey, England to Station 2 CVJ, Hartsdale, N.Y., U.S.A.

Most sets In 1971 the total estimated number of television transmitters in use or under construction was 6,400 serving 270,500,000 sets (75 for each 1,000 of the world population). Of these, about 92,700,000 were estimated to be in use in the United States where 96 per cent of the population is reached. The number of colour sets in the U.S.A. has grown from 200,000 in 1960 to 31,300,000 by January 1971. The number of licences current in the United Kingdom was 17,124,619 on 31 March 1973 of which 3,331,996 were for colour sets.

Greatest audience The greatest estimated number of viewers for a televised event is 1,000 million for the live and recorded transmissions of the XXth Olympic Games in Munich, West Germany from 26 Aug. to 11 Sept. 1972.

Largest T.V. prizes World The greatest amount won by an individual in T.V. prizes was $264,000 (*then £94,286*) by Teddy Nadler (b. 1910) of St. Louis, Missouri on quiz programmes in the United States up to September 1958. He reputedly had to pay $155,000 in federal and state taxes and has been unemployed since.

United Kingdom The largest T.V. prize won in the U.K. is £5,580 by Bernard Davis, aged 33, on Granada T.V.'s "Twenty-one" quiz programme, reached on 24 Sept. 1958.

Most successful appeal The greatest amount raised by any Television Appeal has been £1,520,000 raised from an appeal by Jonathan Dimbleby for the Ethiopian and African Drought Appeal on both B.B.C. T.V. and I.B.A. (Thames T.V.) on 30 Oct. 1973.

LARGEST CONTRACTS

World The largest T.V. contract ever signed was one for $34,000,000 (*£14,166,666*) in a three-year no-option contract between Dino Paul Crocetti (b. 7 June 1917) otherwise Dean Martin, and N.B.C.

Dean Martin was acclaimed in September 1968 as the top-earning show-business personality of all-time with $5,000,000 (*over £2 million*) in a year. Currently television's highest-paid performer is Johnny Carson the host of *The Tonight Show*. His current 3 year N.B.C. contract calls for annual payments of some $3,000,000 (*£1,250,000*) for a forty 4 day weeks with 12 weeks' vacation.

United Kingdom The largest contract in British television was one of a reported £9,000,000, inclusive of production expenses, signed by Tom Jones (b. Thomas Jones Woodward, 7 June 1940) of Treforest, Mid Glamorgan, Wales in June 1968 with ABC-TV of the United States and ATV in London for 17 one-hour shows per annum from January 1969 to January 1974.

Hourly The world's highest paid television performer based on an hourly rate has been Perry Como (b. Pierino Como, Canonsburg, Pennsylvania, U.S.A., on 18 May 1912) who began as a barber. In May 1969 he signed a contract with N.B.C. to star in four one-hour video specials at $5,000,000 (*£2,083,333*) or at the rate of £8,680.55 per min. The contract required him to provide supporting artistes.

Longest telecast The longest pre-scheduled telecast on record was a continuous transmission for 163 hours 18 mins by GTV 9 of Melbourne, Australia covering the Apollo XI moon mission on 19–26 July 1969.

Most durable show The world's most durable T.V. show is N.B.C.'s *Meet the Press* first transmitted on 6 Nov. 1947 and weekly since 12 Sept. 1948 originated by Lawrence E. Spivak, who appears weekly as either moderator or panel member.

Most durable B.B.C. programme The longest running T.V. programme on B.B.C. is *Panorama* which was first transmitted, introduced by Patrick Murphy, on 11 Nov. 1953. *Andy Pandy* was first transmitted on 11 July 1950 but consisted of repeats of a cycle of 26 shows until 1970. The seasonal programme *Come Dancing* was first transmitted on 12 Nov. 1951. "The News" started on 23 Mar. 1938.

Earliest T.V. critic The first man in the world appointed to be a T.V. critic and correspondent was Leonard Marsland Gander (b. 27 June 1902) by the London *Daily Telegraph* in 1935—the year before the B.B.C.'s 405 line transmissions. He retired in July 1970 after spanning 35 yrs with T.V. and 44 yrs with radio.

Biggest sale The greatest number of episodes of any T.V. programme ever sold has been 1,144 episodes of "Coronation Street" by Granada Television to CBKST Saskatoon, Saskatchewan, Canada on 31 May 1971. This constituted 20 days 15 hrs 44 min continuous viewing.

Most prolific scriptwriter The most prolific television writer in the world is the Rt. Hon. Lord Willis (b. 13 Jan. 1918), who in the period 1949–74 has created 21 series, including the first seven years and 2,250,000 words of *Dixon of Dock Green* which has been running since 1955, 20 plays and 21 feature films. He has had 18 plays produced. His total output since 1945 can be estimated at 15,000,000 words.

Highest T.V. advertising rates The highest T.V. advertising rate has been $250,000 (*£104,000*) per minute for N.B.C. network prime time during the transmission of Paramount Pictures, *Godfather* bought by the network for $10 million (*£4,166,000*) on 30 July 1974. In Great Britain the I.B.A. peak time weekday network 30 sec spots rate was fixed in Oct. 1974 at £7,736 or £257.86p per sec.

Most takes The highest number of "takes" for a T.V. commercial is 28 in 1973 by Pat Coombs, the commedienne, who has supported Dick Emery on B.B.C.-T.V. Her explanation was "Everytime we came to the punch line I just could not remember the name of the product".

Right: An artist's impression of the world's rarest mammal—the Javan rhinoceros of which no more than 44 are known to survive (see page 28)
World Wildlife Fund

Below: The largest elephant seals may weigh up to 4 tons/tonnes. This bull specimen in Enoshima Marineland, Japan is named Daihichi (see pages 29-30)

Right: Britain's largest and smallest butterflies—the Milkweed (*Danaus plexippus*) and the Small Blue (*Cupida minimus*) (see page 44)
Courtesy Exotic Butterflies

Below Left: The minuscule *Notylia norae*, found in Venezuela. believed to be the smallest member of the orchid family (see page 52)
G. C. K. Dunsterville

Below Right: A demonstration of the strength of the world's largest birds eggs. A 15 stone (*210 lb. 95,25 kg*) man standing on an ostrich egg (see page 37)
G. L. Wood

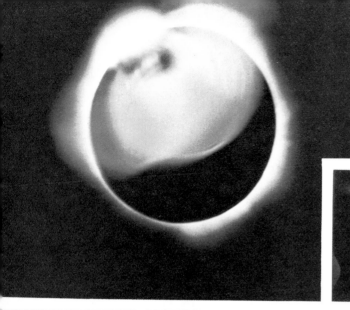

Left: That most spectacular of all natural phenomena—a solar eclipse just after totality (see page 70)

Below: A display of the Northern Lights or Aurora Borealis photographed from northern Canada, where they appear every clear night (see page 69)

THE MILKY WAY GALAXY

ORBITS OF THE PLANETS

THE EARTH AND MOON

Left: The 9 planets of the Solar System with the Sun showing their relative sizes and approximate distances (see pages 69–70)

All illustrations—Ryan Photographic Service Inc.

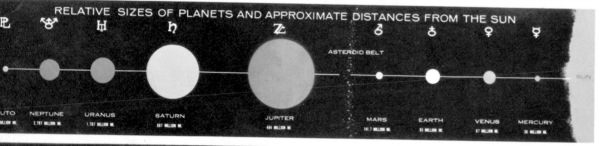

RELATIVE SIZES OF PLANETS AND APPROXIMATE DISTANCES FROM THE SUN

ASTEROID BELT

SUN

| PLUTO | NEPTUNE 2,797 MILLION MI. | URANUS 1,787 MILLION MI. | SATURN 887 MILLION MI. | JUPITER 484 MILLION MI. | MARS 141.7 MILLION MI. | EARTH 93 MILLION MI. | VENUS 67 MILLION MI. | MERCURY 36 MILLION MI. |

MOON

VENUS

MERCURY

EARTH

MARS

SOLAR PROMINENCE

SATURN

JUPITER

URANUS

NEPTUNE

PLUTO

THE SOLAR SYSTEM

AS SEEN LOOKING TOWARD EARTH FROM THE MOON

Below Left: Jupiter—the largest of the 9 planets—317 times more massive than the earth (see page 70)

Below: An artist's impression of the 107,630 mph *173,214 km/h* "fly-by" of Jupiter by the fastest ever man-made object, Pioneer 11 (see page 73)

Right: The largest diamond of the rarest colour—the vivid blue Hope diamond now in Washington DC (see page 78)

Garrard & Co Ltd, Crown Jewellers

Below: Britain's largest Roman mosaic. The 1½ million piece Woodchester Pavement, Gloucestershire (see page 87)

Rev. J. Cull

Right: Leonardo's Ginevra de'Benci (Detail) which set a world art record in 1967 when sold by Prince Franz Josef II of Liechtenstein (see page 86)

Below Right: The world's longest chorus line—the 36 strong Rockettes from Radio City Music Hall, New York City (see Chap. 6)

Radio City

Below: The most massive diamond ever found —an exact replica of the Cullinan against a 10 pence piece (see page 81)

Garrard & Co Ltd, Crown Jewellers

Above: The US Navy's bathyscaph *Trieste*, which descended a record 6.78 miles *10,91 km* in the Marianas Trench in 1960 (see page 57)

US Navy photo

Above left: The world's tallest self-supporting structure, the 1,815 ft 5 in *553,33 m* tall CN Tower in Toronto, Canada (see Chap. 7)

C. N. Tower

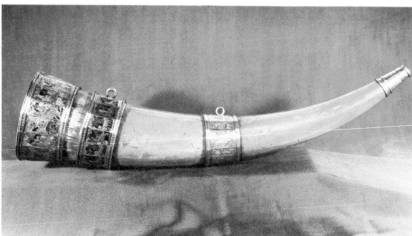

Left: The world's most highly valued piece of silverware—the Savernake Horn, which was sold to the British Museum for £210,000 in December 1974 (see Chap. 9)

S. J. Phillips Ltd

Below left: A US Air Force SR-71 which set the trans Atlantic record of 1 hr 54 min 56.4 sec on 1 Sept 1974 at 1,806.963 mph *2 908,026 km/h* (see Chap. 8)

US Air Force photo

Below: Britain's fastest ever train, the *HST* which ran at 143 mph *230,1 km/h* on 12 June 1973 in North Yorkshire (see Chap. 8)

British Rail

Guinness Superlatives is publishing civil engineering records in greater detail in the more specialist publication "Guinness Book of Structures—Bridges, Towers, Tunnels ..." (price £4.95) obtainable from any good bookshop or, if in difficulties, from the address in the front of this book.

EARLIEST STRUCTURES

World The earliest known human structure is a rough circle of loosely piled lava blocks found in 1960 on the lowest cultural level at the Lower Palaeolithic site at Olduvai Gorge in Tanzania. The structure was associated with artifacts and bones and may represent a work-floor, dating to *circa* 1,750,000 B.C. The oldest free standing structures in the world are now believed to be at the megalithic temples at Mgarr and Skarba in Malta and Ggantija in Gozo dating from *c.* 3,250 B.C. and hence earlier than the Egyptiac at the Sumerian civilisations.

United The rock shelters on Oldbury Hill, ¾ of a mile *1 km*
Kingdom south-west of Ightham, Kent, are believed to have been occupied by the Mousterian people possible during the short Upton Warren interstadial, which has been dated by radio carbon to *c.* 40,000 B.C. The earliest occupation site in Scotland is the mesolithic site at Morton, Fife, announced in 1971, dated by radio carbon to 6100 B.C. ± 150.

Ireland The earliest known structure in Ireland is the very early neolithic site at Ballynagilly, Northern Ireland, announced in 1971. It has been calibrated to 4,580 B.C. and was made of wood.

1. BUILDINGS FOR WORKING

LARGEST BUILDINGS

Commercial The greatest ground area covered by any building in the world is that by the Autolite-Ford Parts Redistribution Center, Brownstown, Michigan, U.S.A. It encloses a floor area of 3,100,000 ft² or 71.16 acres *28,4 ha*. It was opened on 20 May 1971 and employs 1,400 people. The fire control system comprises 70 miles *112 km* of pipelines with 37,000 sprinklers. The building with the largest cubic capacity in the world is the Boeing Company's main assembly plant at Everett, Washington State, U.S.A. completed in 1968 with a capacity of 200 million ft³ *5,6 million m³*.

Scientific The most capacious scientific building in the world is the Vehicle Assembly Building (VAB) at Complex 39, the selected site for the final assembly and launching of the Apollo moon spacecraft on the Saturn V rocket, at the John F. Kennedy Space Center (KSC) on Merritt Island, near Cape Kennedy (formerly Cape Canaveral), Florida, U.S.A. It is a steel-framed building measuring 716 ft *218 m* in length, 518 ft *158 m* in width and 525 ft *160 m* high. The building contains four bays, each with its own door 460 ft *140 m* high. Construction began in April 1963 by the Ursum Consortium. Its floor area is 343,500 ft² (7.87 acres [*3,18 ha*]) and its capacity is 129,482,000 ft³ *3 666 500 m³*. The building was "topped out" on 14 April 1965 at a cost of $108,700,000 (*then £38,8 million*).

7

THE WORLD'S STRUCTURES

Admini- The largest ground area covered by any office building
strative is that of the Pentagon, in Arlington County, Virginia, U.S.A. Built to house the U.S. Defense Department's offices, it was completed on 15 Jan. 1943 and cost an estimated $83,000,000 (*now £34,583,000*). Each of the outermost sides of the Pentagon is 921 ft *281 m* long and the perimeter of the building is about 1,500 yds *1 370 m*. The five storeys of the building enclose a floor area of 6,500,000 ft² *604 000 m²*. During the day 29,000 people work in the building. The telephone system of the building has over 44,000 telephones connected by 160,000 miles *257 500 km* of cable and its 220 staff handle 280,000 calls a day. Two restaurants, six cafeterias and ten snackbars and a staff of 675 form the catering department of the building. The corridors measure 17 miles *27 km* in length and there are 7,748 windows to be cleaned.

The world's tallest inhabited building, the 110 storey Sears Tower at 1,454 ft *443,17 m* dominates the Chicago skyline

Office The largest office buildings in the world are The World Trade Center in New York City, U.S.A. with a total of 4,370,000 ft² (100.32 acres [*40,6 ha*]) of rentable space in each of the twin towers of which the taller is 1,350 ft *411,48 m*.

Single Office
Largest in U.K. The largest single office in the United Kingdom is that of the West Midlands Gas Board at Solihull, West Midlands, built by Spooners (Hull) Ltd. in 1962. It now measures 753 ft by 160 ft *230 by 49 m* (2.77 acres [*1,12 ha*]) in one open plan room accommodating 2,170 clerical and managerial workers.

Britain The largest building in Britain is the Ford Parts Centre at Daventry, Northamptonshire, which measures 1,978 × 780 ft *602 × 237 m* and 1.6 million ft² or 36.7 acres *14,86 ha*. It was opened on 6 Sept. 1972 at a cost of nearly £8 million. It employs 1,600 people and is fitted with 14,000 fluorescent lights.

TALLEST BUILDINGS

World The tallest inhabited building in the world is the Sears Tower, the national headquarters of Sears Roebuck & Co. in Wacker Drive, Chicago, Illinois with 110 storeys rising to 1,454 ft *443 m* and completed in 1974. Its gross area is 4,400,000 ft² (101.0 acres [*40,8 ha*]). It was "topped out" on 4 May 1973. It surpassed the World Trade Center in New York City in height at 2.35 p.m. on 6 March 1973 with the first steel column reaching to the 104th storey. The addition of two T.V. antennae brought the total height to 1,800 ft *548,64 m* The building's population is 16,500 served by 103 elevators and 18 escalators.

Most storeys The project for the 1,610 ft *490 m* Barrington Space Needle, Barrington, Illinois, calls for 120 storeys—10 more than the Sears Tower and the World Trade Center (see above).

United Kingdom The tallest office block in Britain will be The National Westminster tower block in Bishopsgate, City of London due for completion in 1976. It will have 49 storeys and 3 basement levels and will reach a height of 600 ft 4 in *183 m*. The rentable floor area will be 636,373 ft² *59 121 m²*.

HABITATIONS

Greatest altitude The highest inhabited buildings in the world are those in the southern Tibetan herders' settlement of Baruduksum at 21,200 ft *6 460 m*. In April 1961, however, a 3-room dwelling was discovered at 21,650 ft *6 600 m* on Cerro Llullaillaco (22,058 ft [*6 723 m*]), on the Argentine-Chile border, believed to date from the late pre-Columbian period *c.* 1480. The Buddhist monastery at Hanle Kashmir, India at 16,840 ft *5 132 m* is inhabited the year round.

Northernmost The most northerly habitation in the world is the Danish scientific station set up in 1952 in Pearyland, northern Greenland, over 900 miles *1 450 km* north of the Arctic Circle. Eskimo hearths dated to before 1000

B.C. were discovered in Pearyland in 1969. The U.S.S.R. and the United States have maintained research stations on ice floes in the Arctic. The U.S.S.R.'s "North Pole 15", which drifted 1,250 miles *2 000 km*, passed within 1¼ miles *2,8 km* of the North Pole in December 1967.

The most northerly continuously inhabited place is the Canadian Department of National Defence outpost at Alert on Ellesmere Island, Northwest Territories in Lat 82 ° 30′ N. Long. 62 ° W set up in 1950.

Southernmost The most southerly permanent human habitation is the United States' Scott–Amundsen I.G.Y. (International Geophysical Year) base 800 yds *730 m* from the South Pole.

EMBASSIES AND CIVIC BUILDINGS

Largest The largest embassy in the world is the U.S.S.R. embassy on Bei Xiao Jie, Peking, China, in the north-eastern corner of the Northern walled city. The whole 45 acre *18,2 ha* area of the old Orthodox Church mission (established 1728), now known as the *Bei guan*, was handed over to the U.S.S.R. in 1949. The largest in Great Britain is the United States of America Embassy in Grosvenor Square, London. The Chancery Building, completed in 1960, alone has 600 rooms for a staff of 700, on seven floors with a usable floor area of 255,000 ft² (5.85 acres [*2,37 ha*]).

Britain The oldest municipal building in Britain is the Exeter Guildhall first referred to in a deed of 1160. The Tudor front was added in 1593.

INDUSTRIAL STRUCTURES

Tallest chimneys
World The world's tallest chimney is the $5.5 million International Nickel Company's stack 1,245 ft 8 in *379,6 m* tall at Copper Cliff, Sudbury, Ontario, Canada, completed in 1970. It was built by Canadian Kellogg Ltd., in 60 days and the diameter tapers from 116.4 ft *35,5 m* at the base to 51.8 ft *15,8 m* at the top. It weighs 38,390 tons *39 006 tonnes* and became operational in 1971. The world's most massive chimney and Europe's tallest is one of 1,148 ft *350 m* at Puentes, Spain built by M. W. Kellogg Co. It contains 20,600 yd³ *15 750 m³* of concrete and 2.9 million lb. *1 315 tonnes* of steel and has an internal volume of 6.7 million ft³ *189 720 m³*.

Western Times

Britain's oldest municipal building—the new 1593 front of the 800 year old Exeter Town Hall

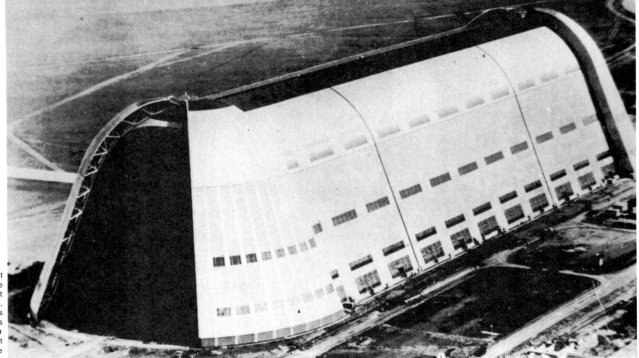

The largest hangar in the world at Akron, U.S.A. which covers over 8 acres *3,23 ha* and was built to house airships

Great The tallest chimney in Great Britain is one of 850 ft
Britain *259 m* at Drax Power Station, North Yorkshire, begun in 1966 and topped out on 16 May 1969. The architects were Clifford Tee & Gale of London. The oldest known industrial chimney in Britain is the Stonedge Chimney, near Chesterfield, Derbyshire built to a height of 55 ft *16,76 m ante* 1771.

Cooling The largest cooling tower in the world is that at the
towers Columbia River Atomic Power Station, near Ranier, Oregon, U.S.A. standing 499 ft *152 m* and completed in 1972 at a cost of $7.8 million. The largest in the United Kingdom are the Ferrybridge "C" power station, West Yorkshire, type measuring 375 ft *114 m* tall and 300 ft *91 m* across the base.

LARGEST HANGARS

World The world's largest hangar is the Goodyear Airship hangar at Akron, Ohio, U.S.A. which measures 1,175 ft *358 m* long, 325 ft *99 m* wide and 200 ft *61 m* high. It covers 364,000 ft² (8.35 acres [*3,38 ha*]) and has a capacity of 55,000,000 ft³ *1,6 million m³*. The world's largest single fixed-wing aircraft hangar is the Lockheed-Georgia engineering test center at Marietta, Georgia measuring 630 ft by 480 ft *192 by 146 m* (6.94 acres [*2,81 ha*]) completed in 1967. The maintenance hangar at Frankfurt/Main Airport, West Germany has a slightly lesser area but a frontage of 902 ft *275 m*. The cable supported roof has a span of 130 m *426.5 ft*. Delta Air Lines' jet base on a 140 acre *56,6 ha* site at Hartsfield International Airport, Atlanta, Georgia, has 36 acres *14,5 ha* under roof.

United The largest hangar building in the United Kingdom is
Kingdom the Britannia Assembly Hall at the former Bristol Aeroplane Company's works at Filton, Avon, now part of the British Aircraft Corporation. The overall width of the Hall is 1,054 ft *321 m* and the overall depth of the centre bay is 420 ft *128 m*. It encloses a floor area of 7½ acres *3,0 ha*. The cubic capacity of the Hall is 33,000,000 ft³ *934 000 m³*. The building was begun in April 1946 and completed by September 1949.

GRAIN ELEVATOR

The world's largest single-unit grain elevator is that operated by the C-G-F-Grain Company at Wichita, Kansas, U.S.A. Consisting of a triple row of storage tanks, 123 on each side of the central loading tower or "head house", the unit is 2,717 ft *828 m* long and 100 ft *30 m* wide. Each tank is 120 ft *37 m* high, with an inside diameter of 30 ft *9 m* giving a total storage capacity of 20,000,000 bushels *7,3 million hl* of wheat

The largest collection of elevators in the world are the 23 at City of Thunder Bay, Ontario, Canada, on Lake Superior with a total capacity of 103.9 million bushels *37,4 million hl*.

GARAGES

Largest The world's largest garage (as opposed to parking lot) is the 100 ft *30,4 m* deep 12 acre *4,85 ha* 6 level subterranean Century City Theme Center garage in Los Angeles, U.S.A. It was opened by Alcoa Properties on 20 July 1972.

The United Kingdom's highest capacity underground car park is that under the Victoria Centre, Nottingham with a capacity of 1,650 cars opened in June 1972.

Private The largest private garage ever built was one for 100 cars at the Long Island, New York mansion of William Kissam Vanderbilt (1849–1920).

Parking The world's largest parking lot is believed to be that
lot at Disneyland, Anaheim, California with a capacity of 12,000 cars.

Filling The largest filling station of 36,000 in the United
station Kingdom is the Esso service area on the M4 at Leigh Delamere, Wiltshire, opened on 3 Jan. 1972. It has 48 petrol and diesel pumps and extends over 43 acres *17,4 ha*. It cost £650,000, has a staff of 280 and can service 2 million vehicles a year.

SEWAGE WORKS

Largest The largest single full treatment sewage works in the
World world is the West-Southwest Treatment Plant, opened in 1940 on a site of 501 acres *203 ha* in Chicago, Illinois, U.S.A. It serves an area containing 2,940,000 people. It treated an average of 685,000,000 gal *3 114 million litres* of wastes per day in 1971. The capacity of its sedimentation and aeration tanks is 1,125,000 m³ *1.4 million yds³*.

United The largest full treatment works in Britain and
Kingdom probably in Europe is the G.L.C. Beckton Works which serves a 2,966,000 population and handles a daily flow of 207 million gal *941 million litres* in a tank capacity of 757,000 ft³ *21 400 m³*.

Glasshouse The largest glasshouse in the United Kingdom is one 826 ft long and 348 ft *252 by 106 m* wide, covering 6.5 acres *2,6 ha* at Brough, Humberside, completed in 1971. A total of 420 tons/*tonnes* of glass was used in glazing it.

115

2. BUILDINGS FOR LIVING

WOODEN BUILDINGS

Oldest The oldest wooden building in the world is the Temple of Horyu (Horyu-ji), built at Nara, Japan, in A.D. 708–715. The largest wooden building in the world, the nearby Daibutsuden, built in 1704–11, measures 285.4 ft long, 167.3 ft wide and 153.3 ft tall *87 × 51 × 46,75 m.*

Largest The world's largest building in timber is the asbestos fibre storage building completed in 1971 at Deception Bay, Quebec Roverie, Canada. It measures 760 ft *231,6 m* long with a clear span of 305 ft *92,96 m* and is 144 ft *43,89 m* high.

CASTLES

Earliest World Castles in the sense of unfortified country houses existed in all the great early civilizations, including that of ancient Egypt from 3,000 B.C. Fortified castles in the more accepted sense only existed much later. The oldest in the world is that at Gomdan, in the Yemen, which originally had 20 storeys and dates from before A.D. 100.

British Isles The oldest stone castle extant in Great Britain is Richmond Castle, Yorkshire, built in *c.* 1075. Iron Age relics from the first century B.C. or A.D. have been found in the lower levels of the Dover Castle site.

Ireland The oldest Irish castle is Ferrycarrig near Wexford dating from *c.* 1180. The oldest castle in Northern Ireland is Carrickfergus Castle, Northern Ireland, which dates from before 1210.

Largest United Kingdom and Ireland The largest inhabited castle in the world is the Royal residence of Windsor Castle at New Windsor, Berkshire. It is primarily of 12th century construction and is in the form of a waisted parallelogram 1,890 ft by 540 ft *576 by 164 m.* The total area of Dover Castle however covers 34 acres *13,75 ha* with a width of 1,100 ft *335,2 m* and a curtain wall of 1,800 ft *550 m* or if underground works are taken in, 2,300 ft *700 m.* The overall dimensions of Carisbrooke Castle (450 ft by 360 ft [*110 by 137 m*]), Isle of Wight, if its earthworks are included, are 1,350 ft by 825 ft *411 by 251 m.* The largest castle in Scotland is Edinburgh Castle with a major axis of 1,320 ft *402 m* and measuring 3,360 ft *1 025 m* along its perimeter wall including the Esplanade. The most capacious of all Irish castles is Carrickfergus (see above) in Antrim but that with the most extensive fortifications is Trim Castle, County Meath, built in *c.* 1205 with a curtain wall 1,455 ft *443 m* long.

The world's largest inhabited castle—Windsor Castle home of Queen Elizabeth II

Forts The largest ancient citadel in the world is the Qila (Citadel) at Halab (Aleppo) in Syria. It is oval in shape and has a surrounding wall 1,230 ft long and 777 ft wide *375 × 237 m.* It dates, in its present form, from the Humanid dynasty of the 10th century A.D. Fort George, Ardersier, Inverness-shire, built in 1748–1769 measures 2,100 ft *640 m* in length and has an average width of 620 ft *189 m.* The total site covers 42½ acres *17,2 ha.*

Thickest walls The walls of Babylon north of Al Hillah, Iraq, built in 600 B.C., were up to 85 ft *26 m* in thickness. The walls of the Great Tower or Donjon of Flint Castle, built in 1277–80 are 23 ft *7,01 m* thick. The largest Norman keep in Britain is that of Colchester Castle measuring 152½ ft *46 m* by 111½ ft *34 m.*

PALACES

Largest World The largest palace in the world is the Imperial Palace (*Gu gong*) in the centre of Peking (*Bei jing*, the northern capital), China, which covers a rectangle 1,050 yds by 820 yds *960 by 750 m* an area of 177.9 acres *72 ha.* The outline survives from the construction of the third Ming Emperor Yong le of 1307–20, but due to constant re-arrangements most of the intra-mural buildings are 18th century. These consist of 5 halls and 17 palaces of which the last occupied by the last Empress was the Palace of Accumulated Elegance (*Chu xia gong*) until 1924.

Residential The largest residential palace in the world is the Vatican Palace, in the Vatican City, an enclave in Rome, Italy. Covering an area of 13½ acres *5,5 ha* it has 1,400 rooms, chapels and halls, of which the oldest date from the 15th century.

United Kingdom The largest palace in the United Kingdom in Royal use is Buckingham Palace, London, so named after its site, bought in 1703 by John Sheffield, the 1st Duke of Buckingham and Normanby (1648–1721). Buckingham House was reconstructed in the Palladian style between 1835 and 1836, following the design of John Nash (1752–1835). The 610 ft *186 m*-long East Front was built in 1846 and refaced in 1912. The Palace, which stands in 39 acres *15,8 ha* of garden, has 600 rooms including a ballroom 111 ft *34 m* long.

The largest ever Royal palace has been Hampton Court Palace, Richmond upon Thames, Greater London, acquired by Henry VIII from Cardinal Wolsey in 1525 and greatly enlarged by the King and later by William III, Anne and George I, whose son George II was its last resident monarch. It covers 4 acres *1,6 ha* of a 669 acre *270,7 ha* site.

Largest moat The world's largest moats are those which surround the Imperial Palace in Peking (see above). From plans drawn by French sources it appears to measure 54 yds *49 m* wide and have a total length of 3,600 yds *3 290 m.*

FLATS

Largest The largest block of private flats in Britain is Dolphin Square, London, covering a site of 7½ acres *3 ha.* The building occupies the four sides of a square enclosing gardens of about three acres *1,2 ha.* Dolphin Square contains 1,220 separate and self-contained flats, an underground garage for 300 cars with filling and service station, a swimming pool, eight squash courts, a tennis court and an indoor shopping centre. It cost £1,750,000 to build in 1936 but was sold to Westminster City Council for £4,500,000 in January 1963. Its nine storeys house 3,000 people.

The Hyde Park development in Sheffield, South Yorkshire, comprises 1,322 dwellings and an estimated population of 4,675 persons. It was built between 1959 and 1966.

Tallest World The tallest block of flats in the world are Lake Point Towers of 70 storeys, and 645 ft *197 m* in Chicago, Illinois, U.S.A.

Building's for Living

Building's for Living

Britain The tallest residential block in the United Kingdom is the Shakespeare Tower in the Barbican in the City of London, which has 116 flats and rises to a height of 419 ft 2⅜ in *127,77 m* above the street. The first of the three towers was "topped out" in May 1971.

HOTELS

Largest The hotel with most rooms in the world is the 12
World storey Hotel Rossiya in Moscow, U.S.S.R., with 3,200 rooms providing accommodation for 5,350 guests opened in 1967. It would thus require more than 8½ years to spend one night in each room. In addition there is a 21 storey "Presidential" tower in the central courtyard. The hotel employs about 3,000 people, and has 93 lifts. The ballroom is reputed to be the world's largest. Muscovites are not permitted as residents while foreigners are charged 16 times more than the very low rate charged to U.S.S.R. officials.

The largest commercial hotel building in the world, is the Waldorf Astoria, on Park Avenue, New York City, N.Y., U.S.A. It occupies a complete block of 81,337 ft² (1.87 acres [*0,75 ha*]) and reaches a maximum height of 625 ft 7 in *191 m*. The Waldorf Astoria has 47 storeys and 1,900 guest rooms and maintains the largest hotel radio receiving system in the world. The Waldorf can accommodate 10,000 people at one time and has a staff of 1,700. The restaurants have catered for parties up to 6,000 at a time. The coffee-makers' daily output reaches 1,000 gal *4 546 litres*. The electricity bill is about $360,000 (£*150,000*) each year. The hotel has housed 6 Heads of States simultaneously and has both a resident gynaecologist and mortician.

United The greatest capacity of any hotel in the United
Kingdom Kingdom is that of the Regent Palace Hotel, Piccadilly Circus, London (opened on 20 May 1915). It has 1,140 rooms accommodating 1,670 guests. The total staff numbers 1,200. The largest hotel is the Grosvenor House Hotel, Park Lane, London, which was opened in 1929. It is of 8 storeys covering 2½ acres *1 ha* and caters for more than 100,000 visitors per year in 470 rooms. The Great Room is the largest hotel room measuring 181 ft by 131 ft *55 by 40 m* with a height of 23 ft *7 m*. Banquets for 1,500 are frequently handled.

Tallest The world's tallest hotel is the 34-storey Ukraina in Moscow, U.S.S.R., which, including its tower, is 650 ft *198 m* tall. The highest hotel rooms in the world are those on the topmost 50th storey of the 509 ft *155 m* tall Americana Hotel, opened on 24 Sept. 1962 on 7th Avenue at 52nd Street, New York City, N.Y., U.S.A. On completion in October 1975 the 1,100 room $50 million Peachtree Plaza Hotel, Atlanta, Georgia, U.S.A. with 70 storeys rising to 700 ft *213 m* will be the world's tallest. Britain's tallest hotel is the 33-storey London Hilton (328 ft [*100 m*]) tall, completed in Park Lane, London, W.1, in 1962. It was opened on 17 April 1963.

Most The world's costliest hotel accommodation is The
expensive Celestial Suite on the ninth floor of the Astroworld Hotel, Houston, Texas which is rented for $2,500 (*£1,000*) a day. It makes the official New York City Presidential Suite in the Waldorf Astoria at $450 (*£180*) a day seem positively middle-class.

The most expensive hotel suites in Britain are the luxury suites in the London Hilton, Park Lane, London, Some suites were £123 27p (incl. service and tax) per night in mid-1975. Breakfast was extra.

SPAS

The largest spa in the world measured by number of available hotel rooms is Vichy, Allier, France, with 14,000 rooms. Spas are named after the watering place in the Liège province of Belgium where hydropathy was developed from 1626. The highest French spa is Baréges, Hautes-Pyrénées, at 4,068 ft *1 240 m* above sea level.

The world's largest hotel, Moscow's Hotel Rossiya of 3,200 rooms

Barracks The oldest purpose built barracks in the world are believed to be Collins Barracks, formerly the Royal Barracks, Dublin, Ireland completed in 1704 and still in use.

HOUSING

Largest The largest housing estate in the United Kingdom is
estate the 1,670-acre *675 ha* Becontree Estate, on a site of 3,000 acres *1 214 ha* in Barking and Redbridge, Greater London, built between 1921 and 1929. The total number of homes is 26,822, with an estimated population of nearly 90,000.

New towns Of the 23 new towns being built in Great Britain that with the largest eventual planned population is Milton Keynes, Buckinghamshire, with 250,000 planned for 1992.

Largest The largest private house in the world is the 250-room
house Biltmore House in Asheville, North Carolina, U.S.A.
World It is owned by George and William Cecil, grandsons of George Washington Vanderbilt II (1862–1914). The house was built between 1890 and 1895 in an estate of 119,000 acres *48 160 ha*, at a cost of $4,100,000 (now £*1,708,333*) and now valued at $55,000,000 with 12,000 acres *4 856 ha*. The most expensive private house ever built is The Hearst Ranch at San Simeon, California, U.S.A. It was built in 1922–39 for William Randolph Hearst (1863–1951), at a total cost of more than $30,000,000 (then £*6,120,000*). It has more than 100 rooms, a 104 ft *32 m* long heated swimming pool, an 83 ft *25 m* long assembly hall and a garage for 25 limousines. The house required 60 servants to maintain it.

United The largest house in the United Kingdom is Went-
Kingdom worth Woodhouse, near Rotherham, South Yorkshire, formerly the seat of the Earls Fitzwilliam. The main part of the house, built over 300 years ago, has more than 240 rooms with over 1,000 windows, and its principal façade is 600 ft *183 m* long. The Royal residence, Sandringham House, Norfolk, has been reported to have 365 rooms. The largest house in Ireland is Castletown in County Kildare, owned by the Hon. Desmond Guinness and is the headquarters of the Irish Georgian Society. Scotland's largest house is Hopetoun House, West Lothian, built between 1696 and 1756 with a west façade 675 ft *206 m* long.

117

THE WORLD'S STRUCTURES

Courtesy Lord Montagu of Beaulieu

Beaulieu, Hampshire—England's most frequented stately home with well over half a million visitors each year

Britain's smallest house presents a 6 ft *1,82 m* frontage onto Conway Quay, Gwynedd, North Wales

J. Chettleburgh

Stately home most visited The most visited stately home, for which figures are published in the United Kingdom, is Beaulieu, Hampshire, owned by Lord Montagu of Beaulieu with 630,212 visitors in 1972. The figures for Woburn Abbey, Bedfordshire, owned by the Duke of Bedford, have not been published since 1963 but reached 470,000 as early as 1961.

Smallest The smallest house in Britain is the 19th century fisherman's cottage on Conway Quay, Gwynedd. It has a 72 in *182 cm* frontage, is 122 in *309 cm* high and has two tiny rooms and a staircase.

Most expensive The Georgian town house in Grafton Street, Mayfair, City of Westminster, formerly the home of Lord Brougham, was sold to the Irish Life Assurance Co. on 28 Aug. 1973 for £3,350,000. It is now let to Mr Henry Ford II.

3. BUILDINGS FOR ENTERTAINMENT

STADIUMS

Largest World The world's largest stadium is the Strahov Stadium in Praha (Prague), Czechoslovakia. It was completed in 1934 and can accommodate 240,000 spectators for mass displays of up to 40,000 Sokol gymnasts.

Football The largest football stadium in the world is the Maracaña Municipal Stadium in Rio de Janeiro, Brazil, where the football ground has a normal capacity of 205,000, of whom 155,000 may be seated. A crowd of 199,854 was accommodated for the World Cup final between Brazil and Uruguay on 16 July 1950. A dry moat, 7 ft *2,10 m* wide and more than 5 ft *1,5 m* deep, protects players from spectators and *vice versa*. Britain's most capacious football stadium is Hampden Park, Glasgow opened on 31 Oct. 1903 and once surveyed to accommodate 184,000 compared with an attendance of 149,547 on 17 Apr. 1937 and the present licensed limit of 135,000.

Covered The Azteca Stadium, Mexico City, Mexico, opened in 1968, has a capacity of 107,000 of whom nearly all are under cover. The largest covered stadium in Britain is the Empire Stadium, Wembley, Brent, Greater London, opened in April 1923. It was the scene of the 1948 Olympic Games and the final of the 1966 World Cup. In 1962–63 the capacity under cover was increased to 100,000 of whom 45,000 may be seated. The original cost was £1,250,000.

Largest Roof The transparent acryl glass "tent" roof over the Munich Olympic Stadium, West Germany measures 914,940 ft² (21.0 acres [*8,5 ha*]) in area resting on a steel net supported by masts. The roof of longest span in the world is the 680 ft *207,2 m* diameter of the Louisiana Superdome (see below). The major axis of the eliptical Texas Stadium completed in 1971 at Irving, Texas is however 240 m *787 ft 4 in.*

Indoor The world's largest indoor stadium is the 13 acre $163.3 million 273 ft *83,2 m* tall Superdome in New Orleans, Louisiana completed in May 1975. Its maximum seating capacity for conventions is 97,365 or 76,791 for football. Box suites rent for $29,000 excluding the price of admission. A gondola with six 312 inch *7,92 m* T.V. screens produces instant replay.

Largest ballroom The largest ballroom in the United Kingdom is the Orchid Ballroom, Purley, Croydon, Greater London. The room is over 200 ft *60 m* long and 117 ft *35,7 m* wide, and has a total floor area of 23,320 ft² *2 170 m²*. When laid out for dance championships, the floor of the Earl's Court Exhibition Hall is 256 ft *78 m* in length.

Amusement resort The world's largest amusement resort is Disney World in 27,443 acres *11 105 ha* of Orange and Osceola counties, 20 miles *32 km* south west of Orlando in central Florida. It was opened on 1 Oct. 1971. This $400 million investment attracted 10,700,000 visitors in its first year. The most attended resort in the world is Disneyland, Anaheim, California where the total number of visitors reached 137,267,000 by 1 Apr. 1975.

Holiday Camps The largest of the 8 major holiday camps in Britain is that at Filey, North Yorkshire opened by Butlins Ltd. It extends over 500 acres *200 ha* and can house 11,000 residents.

RESTAURANTS

Highest The highest restaurant in Great Britain is the Ptarmigan Observation Restaurant at 3,650 ft *1 112 m* above sea-level on Cairngorm (4,084 ft [*1 244 m*]) near Aviemore, Inverness-shire, Scotland.

KITCHEN

Largest The largest kitchen ever set up has been the Indian Government field kitchen set up in April 1973 at Ahmadnagar, Maharashtra in the famine area which daily provides 1.2 million subsistence meals.

NIGHT CLUBS

Oldest The earliest night club (*boite de nuit*) was "Le Bal des Anglais" at 6 Rue des Anglais, Paris, 5e France. It was founded in 1843 but closed *c.* 1960.

Largest The largest night club in the world is that in the Imperial Room of the Concord Hotel in the Catskill Mountains, New York State, U.S.A., with a capacity of 3,000 patrons. In the more classical sense the largest night club in the world is "The Mikado" in the Akasaka district of Tōkyō, Japan, with a seating capacity of 2,000. It is "manned" by 1,250 hostesses, some of whom earn an estimated £4,800 per annum. A binocular is essential to an appreciation of the floor show.

Loftiest The highest night club is Altiteque 727 on the 49th floor of the Royal Bank of Canada Building, Place Ville Marie, Montreal. The height above street level is 617 ft *188 m.*

Lowest The lowest night club is the "Minus 206" in Tiberias, Israel, on the shores of the Sea of Galilee. It is 206 m *676 ft* below sea-level. An alternative candidate is "Outer Limits", opposite the Cow Palace, San Francisco, California which was raided for the 151st time on 1 Aug. 1971. It has been called both "The Most Busted Joint" and "The Slowest to Get the Message".

PLEASURE BEACH

Largest The largest pleasure beach in the world is Virginia Beach, Virginia, U.S.A. It has 28 miles *45 km* of beach front on the Atlantic and 10 miles *16 km* of estuary frontage. The area embraces 255 miles² *660 km²* and 134 hotels and motels.

Longest pleasure pier The longest pleasure pier in the world is Southend Pier at Southend-on-Sea in Essex. It is 1.34 miles *2,15 km* in length. It was first opened in August 1889 with final extensions made in 1929. It is decorated with more than 75,000 lamps. The peak attendance was 5,750,000 in 1949–50.

FAIRS

Earliest The earliest major international fair was the Great Exhibition of 1851 in the Crystal Palace, Hyde Park, City of Westminster, Greater London which in 141 days attracted 6,039,195 admissions.

Largest The largest fair ever held was the New York World's Fair, covering 1,216½ acres *492 ha* of Flushing Meadow Park, Queens Borough, Long Island, New York, U.S.A. The fair was open at times between 20 April 1939 and 21 Oct. 1940 and there were 25,817,265 admissions and an attendance of 51,607,037 for the 1964–65 Fair there.

Record attendance The record attendance for any fair was 65,000,000 for Expo 70 held on an 815-acre *330 ha* site at Osaka, Japan from March to 13 Sept. 1970. It made a profit of more than £11,000,000.

Big Wheel The original Ferris Wheel, named after its constructor, George W. Ferris (1859–96), was erected in 1893 at the Midway, Chicago, Illinois, U.S.A., at a cost of $300,000 (now £125,000). The wheel was 250 ft *76 m* in diameter, 790 ft *240 m* in circumference, weighed 1,070 tons *1 087 tonnes* and carried 36 cars each seating 40 people, making a total of 1,440 passengers. The structure was removed in 1904 to St. Louis, Missouri, and was eventually sold as scrap for $1,800 (now £750). In 1897 a Ferris Wheel with a diameter of 300 ft *91 m* was erected for the Earls Court Exhibition, London. It had ten 1st-class and 30 2nd-class cars. The largest wheel now operating is the Riesenrad in the Prater Park, Vienna, Austria with a diameter of 197 ft *60 m.* It was built by the British engineer Walter Basset in 1896 and carried 15 million people in its first 75 years to 13 June 1971.

Southend-on-Sea Corporation

The world's longest pleasure pier at Southend which takes visitors 1¼ miles *2,01 km* out to sea

Fastest switchback The maximum speeds claimed for switchbacks, scenic railways or roller coasters tend to be exaggerated for commercial reasons. The world's highest is the 110 ft *33,5 m* high "The Racer" in Chapultepec Park, Mexico City. Even the highest of all-time, the 120 ft *36,5 m* now demolished "Blue Streak" in Woodcliffe Pleasure Park, Poughkeepsie, New York, could produce only 57 m.p.h. *91,7 km/h.*

PUBLIC HOUSES

Largest World The largest beer-selling establishment in the world is the Mathäser, Bayerstrasse 5, München (Munich), West Germany, where the daily sale reaches 84,470 pts *48 000 litres.* It was established in 1829, was demolished in World War II and re-built by 1955 and now seats 5,500 people. The through-put at the Dube beer halls in the Bantu township of Soweto, Johannesburg, South Africa may, however, be higher on some Saturdays when the average consumption of 6,000 gal (48,000 pts [*27 280 litres*]) is far exceeded.

United Kingdom The largest public house in the United Kingdom is The Swan at Yardley, West Midlands. It has eight bars with a total drinking area of 13,852 ft² *1 287 m²* with 58 taps and 2 miles *3,2 km* of piping. The sale of beer is equivalent to 31,000 bottles per week. The pub can hold well over 1,000 customers and 320 for banqueting. The permanent staff totals 60 with seven resident. The Swan is owned by Allied Breweries and administered by Ansells Limited.

Smallest The smallest pub in the United Kingdom is the 17th century "The Nutshell", Bury St. Edmunds, Suffolk with maximum dimensions of 15 ft 10 in by 7 ft 6 in *4,82 × 2,28 m.* The runner-up is the "Smiths Arms", Godmanstone, Dorset with a bar area of 11 ft × 19 ft.

Highest The highest public house in the United Kingdom is the Tan Hill Inn in Yorkshire. It is 1,732 ft *528 m* above sea-level, on the moorland road between Reeth, North Yorkshire and Brough, Cumbria. The highest pub open the year round is the Cat and Fiddle in Cheshire, near Buxton, Derbyshire at 1,690 ft *515 m.* The White Lady Restaurant, 2,550 ft *777 m* up on Cairngorm (4,084 ft [*1 244 m*]) near Aviemore, Highland, Scotland is the highest licensed restaurant.

Oldest There are various claimants to the title of the United Kingdom's oldest inn. The foremost claimants include "The Angel and Royal" (*c.* 1450) at Grantham, Lincolnshire, which has cellar masonry dated 1213; the "George" (early 15th century) at Norton St.

119

England's longest named pub (37 letters) in Cabul Road, London SW11

Courtesy The Brewers Society

Philip, Somerset; the oldest Welsh inn the Skirrid Mountain Inn, Llanvihangel Crucorney, Gwent recorded in 1110; "The Trip to Jerusalem" in Nottingham, with foundations believed to date back to 1070; "The Fighting Cocks", St. Albans, Hertfordshire (an 11th century structure on an 8th century site) and the "Godbegot", Winchester, Hampshire dating to 1002. An origin as early as A.D. 560 has been claimed for "Ye Olde Ferry Boat Inn" at Holywell, Cambridgeshire. There is some evidence that it antedates the local church, built in 980, but the earliest documents are not dated earlier than 1100. There is evidence that the "Bingley Arms", Bardsey, near Leeds, West Yorkshire, restored and extended in 1738, existed as the "Priest's Inn" according to Bardsey Church records dated 905.

Longest name The English pub with the longest name was the 39 letter "The Thirteenth Mounted Cheshire Rifleman Inn", at Stalybridge, Greater Manchester. The word "Mounted" is now omitted making "The London, Chatham and Dover Railway Tavern" (37 letters), the champion.

Shortest name There are two public houses in the United Kingdom with a name of only two letters: the "C.B." Hotel Arkengarthdale, near Richmond, North Yorkshire and The H.H. at Cheriton, Hampshire.

Commonest name The commonest pub name in Britain is "Crown", often coupled with the Rose, of which there are some 1,100 examples—more than the total of "Red Lions." of which there are over 900.

Most visits The man who visited most pubs in Britain is Jimmy Young G.M., B.E.M. of "Better Pubs", Crediton, Devon with more than 15,000. Gilbert Lawton of Huddersfield has visited 12,739 to 23 May 1974 since 1956. Mr Stanley House of Totterdown, Bristol, Avon has visited 3,025 pubs with different names by way of public transport only by 21 July 1974.

Longest bars *World* The longest permanent bar with beer pumps is that built in 1938 at the Working Men's Club, Mildura, Victoria, Australia. It has a counter 287 ft *87 m* in length, served by 32 pumps. Temporary bars have been erected of greater length. The Falstaff Brewing Corp. put up a temporary bar 336 ft 5 in *102 m* in length on

Wharf St., St. Louis, Missouri, U.S.A., on 22 June 1970.

United Kingdom and Ireland The longest bar in the United Kingdom with beer pumps is the French Bar (198 ft 5½ in [*60,5 m*]) at Butlin's Holiday Camp, Filey, North Yorkshire. It has 20 beer pumps, 12 tills and stillage for 30 barrels, and is operated by 30 barmaids, 20 floor waiters and 20 other hands. The longest bar in a pub is the 45 ft *13,72 m* counter in Downham Tavern, Bromley, Greater London. The Grand Stand Bar at Galway Racecourse, Ireland completed in 1955, measures 210 ft *64 m*.

Wine cellar The largest wine cellars in the world are at Paarl, those of the Ko-operative Wijnbouwers Vereeniging, known as K.W.V. near Cape Town, in the centre of the winegrowing district of South Africa. They cover an area of 25 acres *10 ha* and have a capacity of 30,000,000 gal *136 million litres*. The largest blending vats have a capacity of 45,700 gal *207 750 litres* and are 17 ft *5 m* high, with a diameter of 26 ft *8 m*.

4. MAJOR CIVIL ENGINEERING STRUCTURES

TALLEST STRUCTURES

World The tallest structure in the world is the guyed Warszawa Radio mast at Konstantynow near Gabin and Płock 60 miles *96 km* north-west of the capital of Poland. It is 2,117 ft 4½ in *645,38 m* tall or more than four tenths of a mile. The mast was completed on 18 May 1974 and put into operation on 22 July 1974. It was designed by Jan Polak and weighs 550 tons/ *tonnes*. The mast is so high that anyone falling off the top would reach their terminal velocity and hence cease to be accelerating before hitting the ground. Work was begun in July 1970 on this tubular steel construction, with its 15 steel guy ropes, It recaptured for Europe a record held in the U.S.A. since the Chrysler Building surpassed the Eiffel Tower in 1929.

United Kingdom The tallest structure in the United Kingdom is the Independent Broadcasting Authority's mast at Belmont, north of Horncastle, Lincolnshire completed in 1965 to a height of 1,265 ft *385 m* with 7 ft *2,13 m* added by meteorological equipment installed in September 1967. It serves Anglia T.V. and weighs 210 tons.

A PROGRESSIVE RECORD OF THE TALLEST STRUCTURES IN THE WORLD

Height in ft	m	Structure	Location	Material	Building or Completion Dates
204	62	Djoser step pyramid (earliest Pyramid)	Saqqâra, Egypt	Tura limestone	c. 2650 B.C.
294	89	Pyramid of Meidun	Meidun, Egypt	Tura limestone	c. 2600 B.C.
c. 336	102	Snefru Bent pyramid	Dahshûr, Egypt	Tura limestone	c. 2600 B.C.
342	104	Snefru North Stone pyramid	Dahshûr, Egypt	Tura limestone	c. 2600 B.C.
480.9[1]	146,5	Great Pyramid of Cheops (Khufu)	El Gizeh, Egypt	Tura limestone	c. 2580 B.C.
525[2]	160	Lincoln Cathedral, Central Tower	Lincoln, England	lead sheathed wood	c. 1307–1548
489[3]	149	St. Paul's Cathedral	City of London, England	lead sheathed wood	1315–1561
465	141	Minster of Notre Dame	Strasbourg, France	Vosges sandstone	1420–1439
502[4]	153	St. Pierre de Beauvais	Beauvais, France	lead sheathed wood	–1568
475	144	St. Nicholas Church	Hamburg, Germany	stone and iron	1846–1847
485	147	Rouen Cathedral	Rouen, France	cast iron	1823–1876
513	156	Köln Cathedral	Cologne, West Germany	stone	–1880
555[5]	169	Washington Memorial	Washington, D.C., U.S.A.	stone	1848–1884
985.9[6]	300,5	Eiffel Tower	Paris, France	iron	1887–1889
1,046	318	Chrysler Building	New York City, U.S.A.	steel and concrete	1929–1930
1,250[7]	381	Empire State Building	New York City, U.S.A.	steel and concrete	1929–1930
1,572	479	KWTV Television Mast	Oklahoma City, U.S.A.	steel	Nov. 1954
1,610[8]	490	KSWS Television Mast	Roswell, New Mexico, U.S.A.	steel	Dec. 1956
1,619	493	WGAN Television Mast	Portland Maine, U.S.A.	steel	Sept. 1959
1,676	510	KFVS Television Mast	Cape Girardeau, Missouri, U.S.A.	steel	June 1960
1,749	533	WTVM & WRBL TV Mast	Columbus, Georgia, U.S.A.	steel	May 1962
1,749	533	WBIR-TV Mast	Knoxville, Tennessee, U.S.A.	steel	Sept. 1963
2,063	628	KTHI-TV Mast	Fargo, North Dakota, U.S.A.	steel	Nov. 1963
2,117.3	645,38	Warszawa Radio Mast	Plock, Poland	galvanised steel	May 1974

[1] *Original height. With loss of pyramidion (topmost stone) height now 449 ft 6 in 137 m.*
[2] *Fell in a storm.*
[3] *Struck by lightning and destroyed 4 June 1561.*
[4] *Fell April 1573, shortly after completion.*
[5] *Sinking at a rate of 0.0047 ft per annum or 5 in 12.7 cm since 1884.*

[6] *Original height. With addition of T.V. antenna in 1957, now 1,052 ft in 320,75 m.*
[7] *Original height. With addition of T.V. tower on 1 May 1951 now 1,472 ft 449 m. On 11 Oct. 1972 it was revealed that the top 15 storeys might be replaced by 33 to give the old champion 113 storeys and a height of 1,494 ft 455,37 m.*
[8] *Fell in gale in 1960.*

TALLEST TOWERS

World The tallest self-supporting tower (as opposed to a guyed mast) in the world is the $44 million CN Tower in Metro Centre, Toronto, Canada, which rises to 1,815 ft 5 in *553,33 m.* Excavation began on 12 Feb. 1973 for the 130,000 ton structure of reinforced, post-tensioned concrete topped out on 2 Apr. 1975. The 400-seat restaurant revolves in the Sky Pod at 1,140 ft *347,5 m* from which the visibility extends to 74½ miles *120 km.*

The tallest tower built before the era of television masts is the Eiffel Tower, in Paris, France, designed by Alexandre Gustav Eiffel (1832–1923) for the Paris exhibition and completed on 31 March 1889. It was 300,51 m *985 ft 11 in* tall, now extended by a T.V. antenna to 1,052 ft 4 in *320,75 m* and weighs 7,224 tons *7 340 tonnes.* The maximum sway in high winds is 5 in *12,7 cm.* The whole iron edifice which has 1,792 steps, took 2 years, 2 months and 2 days to build and cost 7,799,401 francs 31 centimes.

The architects André and Jan Polak put forward a design in February 1969 for a tower 2,378.6 ft *725 m* in height to be erected at La Défense in Paris.

United Kingdom The tallest self-supported tower in the United Kingdom is the 1,080 ft *329,18 m* tall Independent Broadcasting Authority transmitter at Emley Moor, West Yorkshire, completed in September 1971. The structure, which cost £900,000, has an enclosed room at the 865 ft *263,65 m* level and weighs with its foundations more than 15,000 tons/*tonnes.*

5. BRIDGES

OLDEST

World Arch construction was understood by the Sumerians as early as 3200 B.C. and a reference exists to a Nile bridge in 2650 B.C. The oldest surviving dateable bridge in the world is the slab stone single arch bridge over the River Meles in Smyrna (now Izmir), Turkey, which dates from c. 850 B.C.

Britain The clapper bridges of Dartmoor and Exmoor (*e.g.* the Tarr Steps over the River Barle, Exmoor, Somer-

set) are thought to be of prehistoric types although none of the existing examples can be certainly dated. They are made of large slabs of stone placed over boulders. The Romans built stone bridges in England and remains of these have been found at Corbridge (Roman, Corstopitum), Northumberland dating to the 2nd century A.D.; Chester, Northumberland and Willowford, Cumbria. Remains of a very early wooden bridge, have been found at Ardwinkle, Northamptonshire.

LONGEST

Cable suspension World The world's longest single span bridge is the Verrazano-Narrows Bridge stretching across the entrance to New York City harbour from Richmond, Staten Island to Brooklyn. Work on the $305,000,000 (*then £109 million*) project began on 13 Aug. 1959 and the bridge was opened to traffic on 21 Nov. 1964. It measures 6,690 ft *2 039 m* between anchorages and carries two decks, each of six lanes of traffic. The centre span is 4,260 ft *1 298 m* and the tops of the main towers (each 690 ft [*210 m*] tall) are 1⅝ in *4 cm* out of parallel, to allow for the curvature of the Earth.

The world's largest single span bridge, the Verrazano-Narrows. At 4,260 ft it links Staten Island to Brooklyn, New York

Triborough Bridge and Tunnel Authority

THE WORLD'S STRUCTURES

The Mackinac Straits Bridge between Mackinaw City and St. Ignace, Michigan, U.S.A., is the longest suspension bridge in the world measured between anchorages (8,344 ft [2 543 m]) and has an overall length, including viaducts of the bridge proper measured between abutment bearings, of 19,205 ft 4 in *5 853,79 m*. It was opened in Nobember 1957 (dedicated 28 June 1958) at a cost of $100 million (*then £35,700,000*) and has a main span of 3,800 ft *1581 m*.

The main span of the £27.6 million Humber Estuary Bridge, England will be the longest in the world at 4,626 ft *1 410 m* when completed in 1978. Work began on 27 July 1972. Work on the double-deck road-rail Akashi-Kaikyo bridge linking Hinshu and Shikoku, Japan is expected to start in late 1975 for completion in 1988. The main span will be 5,840 ft *1 780 m* in length with an overall suspended length with side spans totalling 11,680 ft *3 560 m*.

United Kingdom The longest span bridge in the United Kingdom is the Firth of Forth Road Bridge with a main channel span of 3,300 ft *1 006 m* and side spans of 1,340 ft *408 m* each, opened on 4 Sept. 1964. The main towers each stand 512 ft *156 m* high. It is the eighth longest span in the world and cost £11,000,000 including the viaducts the approach roads cost £9 million.

Cantilever **World** The Quebec Bridge (Pont de Québec) over the St. Lawrence River in Canada has the longest cantilever truss span of any in the world—1,800 ft *549 m* between the piers and 3,239 ft *987 m* overall. It carries a railway track and 2 carriageways. Begun in 1899, it was finally opened to traffic on 3 Dec. 1917 at a cost of 87 lives, and $Can.22,500,000 (*then £4,623,000*).

United Kingdom The longest cantilever bridge in the United Kingdom is the Forth Bridge. Its two main spans are 1,710 ft *521 m* long. It carries a double railway track over the Firth of Forth 156 ft *47,5 m* above the water level. Work commenced in November 1882 and the first test trains crossed on 22 Jan. 1890 after an expenditure of £3 million. It was officially opened on 4 March 1890. Of the 4,500 workers who built it, 57 were killed in various accidents.

Longest steel arch World The longest steel arch bridge in the world will be the New River Gorge bridge, near Fayettsville, West Virginia, U.S.A., due to be completed in 1976, will have a span of 1,700 ft *518,2 m*.

United Kingdom The longest steel arch bridge in the United Kingdom is the Tyne bridge, Newcastle, Northumberland 531 ft *161,8 m* long opened on 10 Oct. 1930.

Floating bridge **Longest** The longest floating bridge in the world is the Second Lake Washington Bridge, Seattle, Washington State, U.S.A. Its total length is 12,596 ft *3 839 m* and its floating section measures 7,518 ft *2 291 m* (1.42 miles [2,29 km]). It was built at a total cost of $15,000,000 (£6,250,000) and completed in August 1963.

Longest covered bridge The longest covered bridge in the world is that at Hartland, New Brunswick, Canada measuring 1,282 ft *390,8 m* completed in 1899.

Railway bridge **Longest** The longest railway bridge in the world is the Huey P. Long Bridge, Metairie, Louisiana, U.S.A. with a railway section 22,996 ft *7 009 m* (4.35 miles [7 km]) long. It was completed on 16 Dec. 1935 with a longest span of 790 ft *241 m*. It is sometimes claimed that the Yangtse River Bridge, completed in 1968 in Nanking, China is the world's longest railway bridge if the rail deck of *6,7 km* is added to the road deck (4,5 km) to make 11,2 km.

United Kingdom The longest railway bridge in Britain is the second Tay Bridge (11,653 ft [*3 552 m*]), Tayside, Scotland opened on 20 June 1887. Of the 85 spans, 74 (length 10,289 ft [*3 136 m*]) are over the waterway.

Due for completion in 1978, the main span of the Humber Estuary Bridge will be the longest in the world

HIGHEST

World The highest bridge in the world is the bridge over the Royal Gorge of the Arkansas River in Colorado, U.S.A. It is 1,053 ft *321 m* above the water level. It is a suspension bridge with a main span of 880 ft *268 m* and was constructed in 6 months, ending on 6 Dec. 1929. The highest railway bridge in the world is the single track span at Fades, outside Clermont-Ferrand, France, It was built in 1901–09 with a span of 472 ft *144 m* and is 435 ft *132,5 m* above the River Sioule.

United Kingdom The highest railway bridge in the United Kingdom is the Ballochmyle viaduct over the River Ayr, Strathclyde built 169 ft *51,5 m* over the river bed in 1846–48 with the world's longest masonry arch span of 181 ft *55,16 m*.

WIDEST

The world's widest long-span bridge is the 1,650 ft *502,9 m* span Sydney Harbour Bridge, Australia (160 ft [*48 m*] wide). It carries two electric overhead railway tracks. 8 lanes of roadway and a cycle and footway. It was officially opened on 19 Mar. 1932. The Crawford Street Bridge in Providence, Rhode Island, U.S.A., has a width of 1,147 ft *350 m*. The River Roch is bridged for a distance of 1,460 ft *445 m* where the culvert passes through the centre of Rochdale, Greater Manchester and this sometimes claims to be a breadth.

Deepest foundations The deepest foundations of any structure are those of the 3,323 ft *1 013 m* span Ponte de 25 de Abril (formerly Ponte de Salazar), which was opened on 6 Aug. 1966, at a cost of £30,000,000, across the Rio Tejo (the River Tagus), in Portugal. One of the 625 ft *190 m* tall towers extends 260 ft *79 m* down.

Longest bridging The world's longest bridging is the second Lake Pontchartrain Causeway, completed on 23 March 1969, joining Lewisburg and Metairie, Louisiana, U.S.A. It has a length of 126,055 ft *38 422 m* (23.87 miles). It cost $29,900,000 (*£12.45 million*) and is 228 ft *69 m* longer than the adjoining First Causeway completed in 1956. The longest railway viaduct in the world is the rock-filled Great Salt Lake Railroad Trestle, carrying the Southern Pacific Railroad 11.85 miles *19 km* across the Great Salt Lake, Utah, U.S.A. It was opened as a pile and trestle bridge on 8 March 1904, but converted to rock fill in 1955–60.

The longest stone arch bridging in the world is the 3,810 ft *1 161 m* long Rockville Bridge north of Harrisburg, Pennsylvania, U.S.A., with 48 spans containing 196,000 tons/*tonnes* of stone and completed in 1901.

AQUEDUCTS

World longest Ancient The greatest of ancient aqueducts was the Aqueduct of Carthage in Tunisia, which ran 141 km *87.6 miles* from the springs of Zaghouan to Djebel Djougar. It was built by the Romans during the reign of Publius Aelius Hadrianus (A.D. 117–138). By 1895, 344 arches still survived. Its original capacity has been calculated at 7,000,000 gal *31,8 million litres* per day. The triple-tiered aqueduct Pont du Gard, built in A.D. 19 near Nîmes, France, is 160 ft *48 m* high. The tallest of the 14 arches of Aguas Livres Aqueduct, built in Lisbon, Portugal, in 1748 is 213 ft 3 in *65 m*.

Modern The world's longest aqueduct, in the modern sense of a water conduit, is the Colorado River Aqueduct in south-eastern California, U.S.A. The whole system, complete with the aqueduct conduit, tunnels and syphons, is 242 miles *389 km* long and was completed in 1939. The California Aqueduct is 444 miles *714 km* long and was in use in 1973.

United Kingdom The longest aqueduct in the United Kingdom is the Pont Cysylltau in Clwyd on the Frankton to Llantisilio branch of the Shropshire Union Canal. It is 1,007 ft *307 m* long, has 19 arches up to 121 ft *36 m* high above low water on the Dee. It was designed by Thomas Telford (1757–1834) of Scotland, and was opened for use in 1805.

6. CANALS

EARLIEST

World Relics of the oldest canals in the world, dated by archaeologists to 5000 B.C., were discovered near Mandali, Iraq early in 1968.

Britain The first canals in Britain were undoubtedly cut by the Romans. In the Midlands the 11 mile *17 km* long Fossdyke Canal between Lincoln and the River Trent at Torksey was built in about A.D. 65 and was scoured

in 1122. Part of it is still in use today. Though Exeter Canal was cut as early as 1564–68, the first wholly artificial major navigation canal in the United Kingdom was the Bridgewater canal dug in 1759–61. It ran from Worsley, Greater Manchester. Parts of the the Sankey Canal from St. Helens, Merseyside to Widnes, Cheshire, were however, dug before the Bridgewater Canal.

LONGEST

World The longest canalized system in the world is the Volga-Baltic Canal opened in April 1965. It runs 1,850 miles *2 300 km* from Astrakhan up the Volga, *via* Kuybyshev, Gor'kiy and Lake Ladoga, to Leningrad, U.S.S.R. The longest canal of the ancient world has been the Grand Canal of China from Peking to Hangchou. It was begun in 540 B.C. and not completed until 1283 by which time it extended (including canalised river sections) for 1,107 miles *1 781 km.* The estimated work force at one time reached 5,000,000. Having been allowed by 1950 to silt up to the point that it was in no place more than 6 ft *1,8 m* deep, it is now, however, plied by ships of up to 2,000 tons/*tonnes*.

The Beloye More (White Sea) Baltic Canal from Belomorsk to Povenets, in the U.S.S.R., is 141 miles *227 km* long with 19 locks. It was completed with the use of forced labour in 1933 and cannot accommodate ships of more than 16 ft *5 m* in draught.

The world's longest big ship canal is the Suez Canal linking the Red and Mediterranean Seas, opened on 16 Nov. 1869 but inoperative from June 1967 to June 1975. The canal was planned by the French diplomatist Count Ferdinand de Lesseps (1805–94) and work began on 25 April 1859. It is 100.6 miles *161,9 km* in length from Port Said lighthouse to Suez Roads and 60 m *197 ft* wide. The work force was 8,213 men and 368 camels.

The busiest big ship canal is the Panama first transited on 15 Aug. 1914. In 1974 there were a record 14,304 oceangoing transits. The largest liner to transit is *Queen Elizabeth 2* on 25 Mar. 1975 for a toll of $42,077.88. The lowest toll was 36 U.S. cents by the swimmer Richard Halliburton in 1928. The fastest transit has been 4 hr 38 min by the destroyer *U.S.S. Manley.*

Mansell Collection

The original opening of the Suez Canal in 1869 after over 10 heroic years of construction work

United Kingdom Inland Waterways in Great Britain, normally defined as non-tidal (except for a few tidal "links" on the Thames, Trent and Yorkshire Ouse) rivers and canals, consist of 2,390 miles *3 846 km* with 106 miles *170,5 km* being restored. Of this total 2,121 miles *3 413 km* are inter-linked.

The longest possible journey on the system would be one of 408¼ miles *657,0 km* and 153 locks from above Roxton, on the Great Ouse near Bedford to near Ripon, North Yorkshire.

Largest seaway The world's longest artificial seaway is the St. Lawrence Seaway (189 miles [*304 km*] long) along the New York State-Ontario border from Montreal to Lake Ontario, which enables 80 per cent of all ocean-going ships, and bulk carriers with a capacity of 26,000 tons *26 400 tonnes* to sail 2,342 miles *3 769 km* from the North Atlantic, up the St. Lawrence estuary and across the Great Lakes to Duluth, Minnesota, U.S.A., on Lake Superior (602 ft [*183 m*] above sea-level). The project cost $470,000,000 (*then £168 million*) and was opened on 25 April 1959.

Irrigation canal The longest irrigation canal in the world is the Karakumskiy Kanal, stretching 528 miles *850 km* from Haun-Khan to Ashkhabad, Turkmenistan, U.S.S.R. In Sept. 1971 the "navigable" length reached 280 miles *450 km*. The length of the £370 million project will reach 870 miles *1 400 km* by 1975.

LOCKS

Largest World The world's largest single lock is that connecting the Schelde with the Kanaaldok system at Zandvliet, west of Antwerp, Belgium. It is 500 m *1,640 ft* long and 57 m *187 ft* wide and is an entrance to an impounded sheet of water 18 km *11.2 miles* long.

United Kingdom The largest lock on any canal system in the United Kingdom is the Eastham Large Lock, Eastham, Merseyside, on the Manchester Ship Canal. It can handle craft up to 600 ft *182 m* long and 80 ft *24 m* beam.

Deepest The world's deepest lock is the John Day dam lock on the Columbia river, Oregon and Washington, U.S.A. completed in 1968. It can raise or lower barges 108 ft *32,9 m*.

United Kingdom The deepest lock in Britain is the rebuilt Lock 8/9 at Bath on the Kennet and Avon Canal which will lower boats 19½ ft *5,94 m*. In Operation Sealion 120 scouts of the East Reading District traversed their 12 ft 150 lb. boat over 87 miles *140 km* with 105 locks in 46½ hours from Bristol to Reading on 4–6 Oct. 1974.

Longest flight The world's highest lock elevator is at Arzwiller-Saint Louis in France. The lift was completed in 1969 to replace 17 locks on the Marne-Rhine canal system. It drops 146 ft *44,5 m* over a ramp 383.8 ft *116,9 m* long on a 41 degree gradient.

The longest flight of locks in the United Kingdom is on the Worcester and Birmingham Canal at Tardebigge, Hereford and Worcester, where in a 2½ mile *4 km* stretch there are the Tardebigge (30) and Stoke (6) flights which together drop the canal 259 ft *78,9 m*.

Largest cut The Gaillard Cut (known as "the Ditch") on the Panama Canal is 270 ft *82 m* deep between Gold Hill and Contractor's Hill with a bottom width of 500 ft *152 m*. In one day in 1911 as many as 333 dirt trains each carrying 357 tons *363 tonnes* left this site. The total amount of earth excavated for the whole Panama Canal was 8,910,000 tons *9 053 000 tonnes* which total will be raised by the further widening of the Gaillard Cut.

7. DAMS

Earliest The earliest dam ever built was the Sadd al-Kafara, seven miles south-east of Helwan, United Arab Republic. It was built in the period 2950 to 2750 B.C. and had a length of 348 ft *106 m* and a height of 37 ft *11 m*.

Most massive Measured by volume, the largest dam in the world is the Tarbela Dam across the River Indus, in the Hazara District, Pakistan. The total expenditure on the 470 ft *143 m* tall, 9,000 ft *2 743 m* long construction from Dec. 1967 to 1975 surpassed $815 million (*£339.6 million*) including the $623 million contract awarded to the Impregilo Consortium. The total volume of the main dam is 159 million yd³ *121 600 000 m³*.

Largest concrete The world's largest concrete dam, and the largest concrete structure in the world, is the Grand Coulee Dam on the Columbia River, Washington State, U.S.A. Work on the dam was begun in 1933, it began working on 22 March 1941 and was completed in 1942 at a cost of $56 million. It has a crest length of 4,173 ft *1 272 m* and is 550 ft *167 m* high. It contains 10,585,000 yds³ *8 092 000 m³* of concrete and weighs about 19,285,000 tons *19 595 000 tonnes*. The hydro-electric power plant (now being extended) will have a capacity of 9,771,000 kw.

Highest The highest dam in the world is the Grande Dixence in Switzerland, completed in September 1961 at a cost of 1,600 million Swiss francs (*£151,000,000*). It is 932 ft *284 m* from base to rim, 2,296 ft *700 m* long and the total volume of concrete in the dam is 7,792,000 yds³ *5 957 000 m³*. The earth fill Nurek dam on the Vakhsh-Amu Darya river, U.S.S.R. will be 1,017 ft *310 m* high, have a crest length of 2,390 ft *730 m* and a volume of 70,806,000 yds³ *54 million m³*. Work began in 1961 but completion has so far slipped from 1967 to 1979. The concrete Ingurskaya dam in western Georgia, U.S.S.R., was planned to have a final height of 988 ft *301 m*, a crest length of 2,390 ft *728 m* but may be completed only to 892 ft *271 m*.

Under construction the world's highest dam, the 1,017 ft *309.98 m* Nurek Dam, USSR now due for completion in 1979

Novosti

The Akosombo dam in Ghana which made Lake Volta the world's largest artificial lake with a shore line of over 4,500 miles

Longest The longest river dam in the world is the 62 ft *19 m* high Kiev Dam on the river Dnepr, U.S.S.R. which was completed in 1964 to a length of 33.6 miles *54,1 km*. In the early 17th century an impounding dam of moderate height was built in Lake Hungtze, Kiangsu, China to a reputed length of 100 km *62 miles*.

The longest sea dam in the world is the Afsluitdijk stretching 20.195 miles *32,5 km* across the mouth of the Zuider Zee in two sections of 1.553 miles *2,499 km* (mainland of North Holland to the Isle of Wieringen) and 18.641 miles *30 km* from Wieringen to Friesland. It has a sea-level width of 293 ft *89 m* and a height of 24 ft 7 in *7,5 m*.

United Kingdom The most massive (5,630,000 yds³ [*4 304 000 m³*]), the highest (240 ft [*73 m*]) and longest high dam (2,050 ft [*625 m*] crest length) in the United Kingdom is the Scammonden Dam, West Yorkshire, begun in November 1966 and completed in the summer of 1970. This rock fill dam carries the M62 on its crest and was built by Sir Alfred McAlpine's. The cost of the project together with the 6½ miles *10 km* motorway was £8,400,000. There are longer low dams or barrages of the valley cut-off type notably the Hanningfield Dam, Essex, built from July 1952 to August 1956 to a length of 6,850 ft *2 088 m* and a height of 64.5 ft *19,7 m*. The rock fill Llyn Brianne Dam, Dwfed is Britain's highest dam reaching 298½ ft *91 m* in Nov. 1971 and becoming operational on 20 July 1972.

LARGEST RESERVOIR

World The most voluminous man-made is Bratsk reservoir (River Angara) U.S.S.R., with a volume of 137,214,000 acre/ft *169 250 million m³*. The dam was completed in 1964.

The world's largest artificial lake measured by surface area is Lake Volta, formed by the Akosombo dam completed in 1965. By 1969 the lake had filled to an area of 3,275 miles² *8 482 km²* with a shoreline 4,500 miles *7 250 km* in length.

The completion in 1954 of the Owen Falls Dam near Jinja, Uganda, across the northern exit of the White Nile from the Victoria Nyanza marginally raised the level of that *natural* lake by adding 166,000,000

acre/ft *204 750 million m³*, and technically turned it into a reservoir with a surface area of 17,169,920 acres *6,9 million ha* (26,828 miles² [*69 484 km²*]).

United Kingdom The largest wholly artificial reservoir in the United Kingdom is the Queen Mary Reservoir, built from August 1914 to June 1925, at Littleton, near Staines, Surrey, with an available storage capacity of 8,130 million gal. *36 960 million litres* and a water area of 707 acres *286 ha*. The length of the perimeter embankment is 20,766 ft *6 329 m* (3.93 miles [*6,32 km*]). Of valley cut-off type reservoirs the most capacious is Llwyn Celyn, Gwynedd with a capacity of 17,800 million gals *809 million hectolitres*. The capacity of Haweswater Cumbria, was increased by 18,660 million gal *6 786 million litres* by the building in 1929–41 of a 1,540 ft *470 m* long concrete buttress dam 120 ft *36 m* high. The natural surface area was trebled to 1,050 acres *425 ha*. The deepest reservoir in Europe is Loch Morar, Highland, Scotland, with a maximum depth of 1,017 ft *310 m* (see also page 64).

Largest polder The largest of the five great polders in the old Zuider Zee, Netherlands, will be the 149,000 acre *60 300 ha* (232.8 miles² [*602,9 km²*]) Markerwaard. Work on the 66 mile *106 km* long surrounding dyke was begun in 1957. The water area remaining after the erection of the 1927–32 dam (20 miles [*32 km*] in length) is called IJssel Meer, which will have a final area of 487.5 miles² *1 262,6 km²*.

Largest levees The most massive levees ever built are the Mississippi levees begun in 1717 but vastly augmented by the U.S. Federal Government after the disastrous floods of 1927. These extend for 1,732 miles *2 787 km* along the main river from Cape Girardeau, Missouri, to the Gulf of Mexico and comprise more than 1,000 million yds³ *765 million m³* of earthworks. Levees on the tributaries comprise an additional 2,000 miles *3 200 km*.

8. TUNNELS

LONGEST

Water supply World The world's longest tunnel of any kind is the New York City West Delaware water supply tunnel begun in 1937 and completed in 1945. It has a diameter of 13 ft 6 in *4,1 m* and runs for 85.0 miles *136 km* from

The mouth of the 51¼ mile long Orange-Fish Rivers Tunnel, South Africa, which is the longest irrigation tunnel in the world

the Rondout Reservoir into the Hillview Reservoir, in the northern part of Manhattan Island, New York City, N.Y., U.S.A.

United Kingdom The longest water supply tunnel in the United Kingdom is the Thames water tunnel from Hampton-on-Thames to Walthamstow, Greater London, completed in 1960 with a circumference of 26 ft 8 in *8,1 m* and a length of 18.8 miles *30,3 km.*

RAILWAY TUNNELS

World The world's longest main-line tunnel is the Simplon II Tunnel, completed after 4 year's work on 16 Oct. 1922. Linking Switzerland and Italy under the Alps, it is 12 miles 559 yds *19,82 km* long. Over 60 were killed boring this and the Simplon I (1898–1906), which is 22 yds *20 m* shorter. Its greatest depth below the surface is 7,005 ft *2 135 m.*

Sub-aqueous The 33.6 mile *54 km* long Seikan Rail Tunnel, 460 ft *140 m* beneath the sea-bed of the Tsugaru Strait between Tappi Saki, Honshū, and Fukushima, Hokkaidō, Japan, is due to be completed by 1980 at a cost of £240 million. Tests started on the sub-aqueous section (14.5 miles [*23,3 km*]) in 1963 and construction in April 1971 for completion in 1979.

Subway tunnel The world's longest continuous vehicular tunnel is the London Transport Executive underground railway line from Morden to East Finchley, *via* Bank. In use since 1939, it is 17 miles 528 yds *27,8 km* long and the diameter of the tunnel is 12 ft *3,7 m* and the station tunnels 22.2 ft *6,8 m.*

United Kingdom The United Kingdom's longest main-line railway tunnel is the Severn Tunnel (4 miles 628 yds [*6 km*]), linking Avon and Gwent, completed with 76,400,000 bricks between 1873 and 1886.

ROAD TUNNELS

World The longest road tunnel is the tunnel 7.2 miles *11,6 km* long under Mont Blanc (15,771 ft [*4 807 m*] from Pèlerins, near Chamonix, France, to Entrèves, near Courmayeur in Valle d'Aosta, Italy, on which work began on 6 Jan. 1959. The holing through was achieved on 14 Aug. 1962 and it was opened on 16 July 1965, after an expenditure of £22,800,000. The

29½ ft *9 m* high tunnel with its carriage-way of two 12 ft *3,7 m* lanes is expected to carry 600,000 vehicles a year. There were 23 deaths during tunnelling.

Sub-aqueous The world's longest sub-aqueous rail tunnel is the New Kanmon Tunnel, completed in May 1974 which runs 11.6 miles *18,7 km* from Honshū to Kyūshū, Japan.

Channel Tunnel On 8 July 1966 the United Kingdom and French governments reached agreement on a Channel Tunnel for electric trains. It would run in two passages, each of 32.0 miles *51,4 km*, 23 miles *37 km* being sub-aqueous, between Cheriton, near Folkestone, Kent, and Fréthun, Pas de Calais. The project, now known as the "Chunnel", was first mooted in 1802 and was begun on 19 Nov. 1973. Costs were estimated at £1,020 million for completion in 1980. The project was abandoned by the British government on 20 Jan. 1975.

United Kingdom The longest road tunnel in the United Kingdom is the Mersey Tunnel, joining Liverpool and Birkenhead, Merseyside. It is 2.13 miles *3,43 km* long, or 2.87 miles *4,62 km* including branch tunnels. Work was begun in December 1925 and it was opened by H.M. King George V on 18 July 1934. The total cost was £7¾ million. The 36 ft *11 m* wide 4-lane roadway carries nearly 7½ million vehicles a year. The first tube of the second Mersey Tunnel was opened on 24 June 1971.

Largest The largest diameter road tunnel in the world is that blasted through Yerba Buena Island, San Francisco, California, U.S.A. It is 76 ft *23 m* wide, 58 ft *17 m* high and 540 ft *165 m* long. More than 35,000,000 vehicles pass through on its two decks every year.

HYDRO-ELECTRIC OR IRRIGATION TUNNELS

World The longest irrigation tunnel in the world is the 51.5 mile *82,9 km* long Orange-Fish Rivers Tunnel, South Africa, begun in 1967 at an estimated cost of £60 million. The boring was completed in April 1973. The lining to a minimum thickness of 9 inches *23 cm* will give a completed diameter of 17 ft 6 ins *5,33 m.* The total work force was at times more than 5,000. Some of the access shafts in the eight sections descend more than 1,000 feet *305 m.*

United Kingdom The longest in the United Kingdom is that at Ben Nevis, Highland, which has a mean diameter of 15 ft 2 in *4,6 m* and a length of 15 miles *24 km.* It was begun in June 1926 and was holed through into Loch Treig on 3 Jan. 1930 for hydro-electric use. The greatest diameter water tunnel is the 23 ft *7,01 m* tunnel at Clunie, Tayside.

BRIDGE-TUNNEL

The world's longest bridge-tunnel system is the Chesapeake Bay Bridge-Tunnel, extending 17.65 miles *28,40 km* from the Delmarva Peninsula to Norfolk, Virginia, U.S.A. It cost $200,000,000 (*then £71.4 million*) and was completed after 42 months and opened to traffic on 15 April 1964. The longest bridged section is Trestle C (4.56 miles [*7,34 km*] long) and the longer tunnel is the Thimble Shoal Channel Tunnel (1.09 miles [*1,75 km*]).

CANAL TUNNELS

Longest World The world's longest canal tunnel is that on the Rove canal between the port of Marseilles, France and the river Rhône, built in 1912–27. It is 4.53 miles *7,29 km* long, 72 ft *22 m* wide and 50 ft *15 m* high, involving 2¼ million yds³ *1,7 million m³* of excavation.

United Kingdom The longest canal tunnel in the United Kingdom is the Standedge (more properly Stanedge) Tunnel in West Yorkshire on the Huddersfield Narrow Canal built from 1794 to 4 April 1811. It measures 3 miles 418 yds *5,21 km* in length and was closed on 21 Dec.

126

1944. The longest *continuous* tunnel of the 43 still in use is the 3,056 yd *2 794 m* long Blisworth on the Grand Union. The now closed Huddersfield Narrow Canal is also the highest in the United Kingdom, reaching a height at one point of 638 ft *194 m* above sea-level.

Tunnelling record The world's records for rapid tunnelling were set on 18 March 1967 in the 8.6 mile *13,8 km* long Blanco Tunnel, in Southern Colorado when the "mole" (giant boring machine) crew advanced the 10 ft *3 m* diameter heading 375 ft *114 m* in one day and on 26 June 1972 in the 20½ ft *6,95 m* diameter Navajo Tunnel 3 project, New Mexico with an advance of 247 lineal ft *75,28 m.*

9. SPECIALISED STRUCTURES

SEVEN WONDERS OF THE WORLD

The Seven Wonders of the World were first designated by Antipater of Sidon in the 2nd century B.C. They included the Pyramids of Gîza, built by three Fourth Dynasty Egyptian Pharaohs, Hwfw (Khufu or Cheops), Kha-f-Ra (Khafre, Khefren or Chephren) and Menkaure (Mycerinus) near El Gîza (El Gizeh), south-west of El Qâhira (Cairo) in Egypt (now the United Arab Republic). The Great Pyramid ("Horizon of Khufu") was finished c. 2580 B.C. Its original height was 480 ft 11 in *146 m* (now, since the loss of its topmost stone or pyramidion, reduced to 449 ft 6 in [*137 m*]) with a base line of 756 ft *230 m* and thus originally covering slightly more than 13 acres *5 ha.* It has been estimated that a work force of 4,000 required 30 years to manoeuvre into position the 2,300,000 limestone blocks averaging 2½ tons/*tonnes* each, totalling about 5,750,000 tons *5 840 000 tonnes* and a volume of 90,700,000 ft³ *2 568 000 m³.* A costing exercise published in Dec. 1974 indicates that today it would require 405 men 6 years at a cost of $1.13 billion (*£491 million*).

Of the other six wonders only fragments remain of the Temple of Artemis (Diana) of the Ephesians, built in *c.* 350 B.C. at Ephesus, Turkey (destroyed by the Goths in A.D. 262), and of the Tomb of King Mausolus of Caria, built at Halicarnassus, now Bodrum, Turkey, in *c.* 325 B.C. No trace remains of the Hanging Gardens of Semiramis, at Babylon, Iraq (*c.* 600 B.C.); the 40 ft *12 m* tall marble, gold and ivory statue of Zeus (Jupiter), by Phidias (5th century B.C.) at Olympia, Greece (lost in a fire at Istanbul); the 117 ft *35 m* tall statue by Chares of Lindus of the figure of the god Helios (Apollo) called the Colossus of Rhodes (sculptured 292–280 B.C., destroyed by an earthquake in 224 B.C.); or the 400 ft *122 m* tall world's earliest lighthouse built by Sostratus of Cnidus *c.* 270 B.C. (destroyed by earthquake in A.D. 1375) on the island of Pharos (Greek, *pharos* = lighthouse), off the coast of El Iskandarîya (Alexandria), Egypt.

PYRAMIDS

Largest The largest pyramid, and the largest monument ever constructed, is the Quetzalcóatl at Cholula de Rivadahia, 63 miles *101 km* south-east of Mexico City, Mexico. It is 177 ft *54 m* tall and its base covers an area of nearly 45 acres *18,2 ha.* Its total volume has been estimated at 4,300,000 yds³ *3 300 000 m³* compared with 3,360,000 yds³ *2,5 million m³* for the Pyramid of Cheops (see above). The pyramid-building era here was between the 6th and 12th centuries A.D.

Oldest The oldest known pyramid is the Djoser step pyramid at Saqqâra, Egypt constructed to a height of 204 ft *62 m* of Tura limestone in *c.* 2650 B.C. The oldest New World pyramid is that on the island of La Venta in south-eastern Mexico built by the Olmec people *c.* 800 B.C. It stands 100 ft *30 m* tall with a base diameter of 420 ft *128 m.*

TALLEST FLAGSTAFF

World The tallest flagstaff ever erected was that outside the Oregon Building at the 1915 Panama-Pacific International Exposition in San Francisco, California, U.S.A. Trimmed from a Douglas fir, it stood 299 ft 7 in *91 m* in height and weighed 45 tons *47 tonnes.* The tallest unsupported flag pole in the world is a 220 ft *67 m* tall metal pole weighing 28,000 lb. *12 700 kg* erected in 1955 at the U.S. Merchant Marine Academy in King's Point, New York, U.S.A. The pole, built by Kearney-National Inc., tapers from 24 in to 5½ in *61 cm to 14 cm* at the jack.

United Kingdom The tallest flagstaff in the United Kingdom is a 225 ft *68 m* tall Douglas fir staff at Kew, Richmond upon Thames, Greater London. Cut in Canada, it was shipped across the Atlantic and towed up the River Thames on 7 May 1958, to replace the old 214 ft *65 m* tall staff of 1919.

Maypole The tallest reported Maypole erected in England was one of Sitka spruce 105 ft 7 in *32,12 m* tall put up in Pelynt, Cornwall on 1 May 1974.

MONUMENTS

Tallest The world's tallest monument is the stainless steel Gateway to the West Arch in St. Louis, Missouri, U.S.A., completed on 28 Oct. 1965 to commemorate the westward expansion after the Louisiana Purchase of 1803. It is a sweeping arch spanning 630 ft *192 m* and rising to the same height of 630 ft *192 m* and costing $29,000,000 (*£12,083,000*). It was designed in 1947 by Eero Saarinen (died 1961).

The tallest monumental column in the world is that commemorating the battle of San Jacinto (21 April 1836), on the bank of the San Jacinto river near Houston, Texas, U.S.A. General Sam Houston (1793–1863) and his force of 743 Texan troops killed 630 Mexicans (out of a total force of 1,600) and captured 700 others, for the loss of nine men killed and 30 wounded. Constructed in 1936–39, at a cost of $1,500,000 (*now £625,000*), the tapering column is 570 ft *173 m* tall, 47 ft *14 m* square at the base, and 30 ft *9 m* square at the observation tower, which is surmounted by a star weighing 196.4 tons *199,6 tonnes.* It is built of concrete, faced with buff limestone, and weighs 31,384 tons *31 888 tonnes.*

H. H. Seiden

The world's tallest monumental column, the 570 ft edifice at Houston, Texas, which commemorates the nine American soldiers killed at the battle of San Jacinto in 1836

Largest Earthworks

World The largest earthworks in the world carried out prior to the mechanical era were the Linear Earth Boundaries of the Benin Empire in the Mid Western state of Nigeria. These were first reported in 1903 and partially surveyed in 1967. In April 1973 it was estimated by Mr Patrick Darling that the total length of the earthworks was probably between 5,000 and 8,000 miles *8,000–12,800 km* with the total amount of earth moved estimated at from 500 to 600 million yds³ *380–460 million m³*.

Britain The greatest prehistoric earthwork in Britain is Wansdyke, originally Woden's Dyke, which ran 86 miles *138 km* from Portishead, Avon to Inkpen Beacon and Ludgershall, south of Hungerford, Berkshire. It is believed to have been built by the pre-Roman Wessex culture. The most extensive single site earthwork is the Dorset Cursus near Gussage St. Michael, dating from *c.* 1900 B.C. The workings are 6 miles *9,7 km* in length, involving an estimated 250,000 yds³ *191 000 m³* of excavations. The largest of the Celtic hill-forts is that known as Mew Dun, or Maiden Castle, 2 miles *3 km* south-west of Dorchester, Dorset. It covers 115 acres *46,5 ha* and was abandoned shortly after A.D. 43.

Largest mound The largest artificial mound in Europe is Silbury Hill, 6 miles *9,7 km* west of Marlborough, Wiltshire, which involved the moving of an estimated 670,000 tons *681 000 tonnes* of chalk to make a cone 130 ft *39 m* high with a base of 5½ acres *2 ha*. Prof. Richard Atkinson in charge of the 1968 excavations showed that it is based on an innermost central mound, similar to contemporary round barrows, and is now dated to 2,745 ± 185 B.C. The largest long barrow in England is that inside the hill-fort at Maiden Castle (see above). It originally had a length of 1,800 ft *548 m* and had several enigmatic features such as a ritual pit with pottery, limpet shells, and animal bones. The longest long barrow containing a megalithic chamber is that at West Kennet (*c.* 2200 B.C.), near Silbury, measuring 385 ft *117 m* in length.

Henges There are in Britain some 80 henges built *c.* 2500 B.C. of which the largest was Durrington Walls, Wiltshire with an average diameter of 1,550 ft *472 m*. It has been obliterated by road building.

Prehistoric *Largest* Britain's largest megalithic prehistoric monuments are the 28½ acre *11,5 ha* earthworks and stone circles of Avebury, Wiltshire, rediscovered in 1646. The earliest calibrated date in the area of this neolithic site is *c.* 4200 B.C. The whole work is 1,200 ft *365 m* in diameter with a 40 ft *12 m* ditch around the perimeter and required an estimated 15 million man-hours of work. The largest trilithons exist at Stonehenge, to the south of Salisbury Plain, Wiltshire, with single sarsen blocks weighing over 45 tons/tonnes and requiring over 550 men to drag them up a 9° gradient. The calibrated date of the construction of the ditch is 2765 ± 175 B.C. Whether Stonehenge was a lunar calendar or an eclipse-predictor remains debatable.

Youngest ancient monument Of all the ancient monuments scheduled in Great Britain, the youngest is the nickel-steel gun testing shield at Rudder Rock, on the Bristol Channel island of Steep Holm built in 1899.

OBELISKS (Monolithic)

Oldest The longest an obelisk has remained *in situ* is that at Heliopolis, near Aswan, Egypt, erected by Senusret I *c.* 1750 B.C.

Largest The largest standing obelisk in the world is that in the Piazza of St. John in Lateran, Rome, erected in 1588. It came originally from the Circus Maximus (erected A.D. 357) and before that from Heliopolis, Egypt (erected *c.* 1450 B.C.). It is 110 ft *33 m* in length and weighs 450 tons *457 tonnes*. The largest obelisk in the

United Kingdom is Cleopatra's Needle on the Embankment, London, which is 68 ft 5½ in *20 m* tall and weighs 186.36 tons *189,35 tonnes*. It was towed up the Thames from Egypt on 20 Jan. 1878.

Largest tomb The largest tomb in the world is that of Emperor Nintoku (died *c.* A.D. 428) south of Osaka, Japan. It measures 1,594 ft *485 m* long by 1,000 ft *305 m* wide by 150 ft *45 m* high.

Largest ziqqurat The largest surviving ziqqurat (from the verb *zaqaru*, to build high) or stage-tower is the Ziqqurat of Ur (now Muqqayr, Iraq) with a base 200 ft by 150 ft *60 by 45 m* built to at least three storeys of which the first and part of the second now survive to a height of 60 ft *18 m*. It was built by the Akkadian King Ur-Nammu (*c.* 2113–2006 B.C.) to the moon god Nanna covering 30,000 ft² *2 800 m²*.

STATUES

Tallest The tallest free-standing statue in the world is that of "Motherland", an enormous pre-stressed concrete female figure on Mamayev Hill, outside Volgograd, U.S.S.R., designed in 1967 by Yevgenyi Vuchetich, to commemorate victory in the Battle of Stalingrad (1942–43). The statue from its base to the tip of the sword clenched in her right had measures 270 ft *82,30 m*.

The U.S. sculptor Felix de Welton has announced a plan to replicate the Colossus of Rhodes to a height of 308 ft *93,87 m*.

Longest Near Bamiyan, Afghanistan there are the remains of the recumbent Sakya Buddha, built of plastered rubble, which was "about 1,000 ft *305 m*" long and is believed to date from the 3rd or 4th century A.D.

LARGEST DOME

World The world's largest dome is the Louisiana Superdome, New Orleans, U.S.A. It has a diameter of 680 ft *207,26 m*. (See page 118 for further details.) The largest dome of ancient architecture is that of the Pantheon, built in Rome in A.D. 112, with a diameter of 142½ ft *43 m*.

Britain The largest dome in Britain is that of the Bell Sports Centre, Perth, Scotland with a diameter of 222 ft *67 m* designed by D. B. Cockburn and constructed in Baltic whitewood by Muirhead & Sons Ltd. of Grangemouth, Central, Scotland.

Tallest columns The tallest columns (as opposed to obelisks) in the world are the sixteen 82 ft *25 m* tall pillars in the Palace of Labour in Torino (Turin), Italy, for which the architect was Pier Luigi Nervi (born 21 June 1891). They were built of concrete and steel in only 8 days. The tallest load-bearing stone columns in the world are those measuring 69 ft *21 m* in the Hall of Columns

A scale comparison of the Louisiana Superdome (4) compared with the Astrodome (3) and St Peter's, Rome (1) and the Duomo, Florence (2)

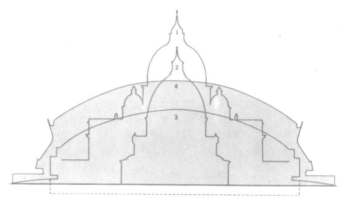

of the Temple of Amun at Al Karnak, the northern part of the ruins of Thebes, the Greek name for the ancient capital of Upper Egypt (now the United Arab Republic). They were built in the 19th dynasty in the reign of Rameses II in *c.* 1270 B.C.

HARBOUR WORKS

Longest jetty The longest deep water jetty in the world is the Quai Hermann du Pasquier at Le Havre, France, with a length of 5,000 ft *1 524 m*. Part of an enclosed basin, it has a constant depth of water of 32 ft *9,8 m* on both sides.

Longest pier
World The world's longest pier is the Damman Pier, Saudi Arabia, on the Persian Gulf. A rock-filled causeway 4.84 miles *7,79 km* long joins the steel trestle pier 1.80 miles *2,90 km* long, which joins the Main Pier (744 ft [*226 m*] long), giving an overall length of 6.79 miles *10,93 km*. The work was begun in July 1948 and completed on 15 March 1950.

United Kingdom The longest pier in Great Britain is the Bee Ness Jetty, completed in 1930, which stretches 8,200 ft *2 500 m* along the west bank of the River Medway, 5 to 6 miles *8 to 9,6 km* below Rochester, at Kingsnorth, Kent.

Longest breakwater
World The world's longest breakwater system is that which protects the Ports of Long Beach and Los Angeles, California, U.S.A. The combined length of the four breakwaters is 43,602 ft (8.26 miles [*13,29 km*]) of which the Long Beach section, built between 1941 and February 1949, is the longest at 13,350 ft (2.53 miles [*4,07 km*]). The North breakwater at Tuticorin, Madras Province, Southern India on which construction began in 1968 extends to 13,589 ft *4,14 km*.

United Kingdom The longest breakwater in the United Kingdom is the North Breakwater at Holyhead, Anglesey, Gwynedd which is 9,860 ft (1.86 miles [*3 005 m*]) in length and was completed in 1873.

LARGEST DRY DOCK

World The world's largest dry dock is the Lisnave dock, Lisbon, Portugal begun in 1969 and completed at a cost of £10,000,000 in 20 months. It measures 1,700 × 318 × 53 ft *518 × 97 × 16,15 m*.

United Kingdom The largest dry dock in the United Kingdom is the Belfast Harbour Commission and Harland and Wolff building dock at Belfast, Northern Ireland. It has been excavated by Wimpey's to a length of 1,825 ft *556 m* and a width of 305 ft *93 m* and can accommodate tankers of 1,000,000 d.w.t. Work was begun on 26 Jan. 1968 and completed on 30 Nov. 1969 and involved the excavation of 400,000 yds³ *306 000 m³*. (See also Largest crane.)

Work started at Nagasaki, Japan on 16 Sept. 1970 on a building dock capable of taking a tanker of 1,200,000 d.w.t. for Mitsubishi Heavy Industries Co. at a cost of £32,000,000.

Dock Gate The world's largest dock gate is that at Nigg Bay, Cromarty Firth, Highland, Scotland first operated in March 1974. It measures 408 ft *124 m* long, 50 ft *15,2 m* high with a 4 ft *1,21 m* thick base, is made of reinforced concrete and weighs 16,000 tons/*tonnes* together with its cill, quoins and roundheads. The builders were Brown and Root-Wimpey Highland Fabricators.

LARGEST FLOATING DOCKS

Sectional The highest capacity floating docks ever constructed are the United States Navy's advanced base sectional docks (A.B.S.D.). These consist of 10 sectional units giving together an effective keel block length of 827 ft *252 m* and clear width of 140 ft *42 m* with a lifting capacity of up to 80,000 tons *81 000 tonnes*. Floating

Portuguese Tourist Office

The world's largest dry dock in Lisbon, Portugal—large enough to lay out 192 doubles tennis courts

Dock No. 2 at Palermo, Sicily, Italy, measures 285 m *936 ft* long and 46 m *151 ft* in the beam.

Single unit The largest single unit floating dock is Admiralty Floating Dock (AFD) 35, which was towed from the Royal Navy's dockyard in Malta to the Cantieri Navali Santa Maria of Genoa, Italy, in May 1965. It has a lifting capacity of 65,000 tons *66 000 tonnes* and an overall length of 857 ft 8 in *261 m*. It had been towed to Malta from Bombay, India, where it was built in 1947.

LIGHTHOUSES

Brightest
World The lighthouse with the most powerful light in the world is Créac'h d'Ouessant lighthouse, established in 1638 and last altered in 1939 on l'Ile d'Ouessant, Finistère, Brittany, France. It is 163 ft *50 m* tall and, in times of fog, has a luminous intensity of up to 500 million candelas *490.5 million candles*.

The lights with the greatest visible range are those 1,092 ft *332 m* above the ground on the Empire State Building, New York City, N.Y., U.S.A. Each of the four-arc mercury bulbs has a rated candlepower of 450,000,000, visible 80 miles *130 km* away on the ground and 300 miles *490 km* away from aircraft. They were switched on on 31 March 1956.

United Kingdom The lighthouse in the United Kingdom with the most powerful light is the shorelight Orfordness, Suffolk. It has an intensity of 7,500,000 candelas. The Irish light with the greatest intensity is Aranmore on Rinrawros Point, County Donegal.

Tallest The world's tallest lighthouse is the steel tower 348 ft *106 m* tall near Yamashita Park in Yokohama, Japan. It has a power of 600,000 candles and a visibility range of 20 miles *32 km*.

Remotest The most remote Trinity House lighthouse is The Smalls, about 16 sea miles (18.4 statute miles [*29,6 km*]) off the Dyfed coast. The most remote Scottish lighthouse is Sule Skerry, 35 miles *56 km* off shore and 45 miles *72 km* north-west of Dunnet Head, Highland. The most remote Irish light is Blackrock, about 9 miles *14 km* off the Mayo coast.

WINDMILLS

Earliest The earliest recorded windmills are those used for grinding corn in Iran (Persia) in the 7th century A.D.

The earliest known in England was the post-mill at Bury St. Edmunds, Suffolk, recorded in 1191. The oldest Dutch mill is the towermill at Zedden, Gelderland built in *c.* 1450. The oldest working mill in

England is the post-mill at Outwood, Surrey, built in 1665, though the Ivinghoe Mill in Pitstone Green Farm, Buckinghamshire, dating from 1627, has been restored.

Largest The largest Dutch windmill is the Dijkpolder in Maasland built in 1718. The sails measure 95¾ ft *29 m* from tip to tip. The tallest windmill in the Netherlands is De Walvisch in Schiedam built to a height of 108 ft *33 m* in 1794. The largest conventional windmill in England is a disused one at Sutton, Norfolk.

WATERWHEEL

Largest The largest waterwheel in the world is the Moham-
World madieh Noria wheel at Hama, Syria with a diameter of 131 ft *40 m* dating from Roman times. The Lady Isabella wheel at Laxey, Isle of Man is the largest in the British Isles and was built for draining a lead mine and completed on 27 Sept. 1854, and dis-used since 1929. It has a circumference of 228 ft *69 m*, a diameter of 72½ ft *22 m* and an axle weighing 9 tons/ *tonnes*. The largest waterwheel in Great Britain is claimed to be the pitch-back indoor wheel of 45 ft *13,70 m* diameter which provided power from 1862– 1932 for the mill of James Wilson & Son Ltd. of Keighley, West Yorkshire.

Barns The largest barn in Britain is one at Manor Farm, Cholsey, near Wallingford, Oxfordshire. It is 303 ft *92 m* in length and 54 ft *16 m* in breadth (16,362 ft² [*1 520 m²*]). The Ipsden Barn, Oxfordshire, is 385½ ft *117 m* long but 30 ft *9 m* wide (11,565 ft² [*1 074 m²*]).

The longest tithe barn in Britain is one measuring 268 ft *81 m* long at Wyke Farm, near Sherborne, Dorset.

NUDIST CAMP

Largest The oldest nudist camp is Der Freilichtpark, Kling-berg, West Germany established in 1903. The largest such camp in the world is Port Nature, west of Marseilles, France with 20,000 *adeptes*.

LONGEST WALL

World The Great Wall of China, completed during the reign of Shih Huang-ti (246–210 B.C.), has main line length of 2,150 miles *3 460 km* with a further 1,780 miles *2 860 km* of branches and spurs, with a height of from 15 to 39 ft *4,5 to 12 m* and up to 32 ft *9,8 m* thick. It runs from Shanhaikuan, on the Gulf of Pohai, to Chiayukuan in Kansu and was kept in repair up to the 16th century.

Britain The longest of the Roman Walls built in Britain was the 15–20 ft *4,5–6 m* tall Hadrian's Wall, built in the period A.D. 122–126. It ran across the Tyne-Solway isthmus for 74½ miles *120 km* from Bowness-on-Solway, Cumbria, to Wallsend-on-Tyne, Tyne and Wear, and was abandoned in A.D. 383.

LONGEST FENCE

The longest fence in the world is the dingo-proof fence enclosing the main sheep areas of Queensland, Australia. The wire fence is 6 ft *1,8 m* high, one foot *30 cm* underground and stretches for 3,437 miles.

DOORS

Largest The largest doors in the world are the four in the
World Vehicle Assembly Building near Cape Kennedy, Florida, with a height of 460 ft *140 m* (see page 113).

The largest doors in the United Kingdom are those to the Britannia Assembly Hall, at Filton, Avon. The doors are 1,035 ft *315 m* in length and 67 ft *20 m* high, divided into three bays each 345 ft *105 m* across. The largest simple hinged door in Britain is that of Ye Old Bull's Head, Beaumaris, Anglesey, Gwynedd, which is 12 ft *3,7 m* wide and 30 ft *9 m* high.

Oldest The oldest doors in Britain are those of Hadstock Church, Essex, which date from *c.* 1040 and exhibit evidence of Danish workmanship.

LARGEST WINDOWS

The largest sheet of glass ever manufactured was one of 50 m² *538.2 ft²*, or 20 m *65 ft 7 in* by 2,5 m *8 ft 2½ in*, exhibited by the Saint Gobian Company in France at the *Journées Internationales de Miroiterie* in March 1958. The largest windows in the world are the three in the Palace of Industry and Technology at Rond-point de la Défense, Paris, with an extreme width of 218 m *715.2 ft* and a maximum height of 50 m *164 ft.*

LONGEST STAIRS

World The world's longest stairs are reputedly at the Mår power station, Øverland, western Norway. Built of wood, these are 4,101 ft *1 250 m* in length, rising in 3,875 steps at an angle of 41 degrees inside the pressure shaft. The length of a very long, now discontinuous, stone stairway in the Rohtang Pass, Manali, Kulu, Northern India, is still under investigation.

Britain The longest stairs in Britain are those from the trans-former gallery to the surface 1,065 ft *324 m* in the Cruachan Power Station, Argyll, Scotland. They have 1,420 steps and the Work Study Dept. allows 27 mins 41.4 sec for the ascent.

TALLEST FIRE ESCAPE

The world's tallest mobile fire escape is a 250 ft *76 m* tall turntable ladder built in 1962 by Magirus, a West German firm.

LARGEST MARQUEE

World The largest tent ever erected was one covering an area of 188,368 ft² (4.32 acres [*17 500 m²*]) put up by the firm of Deuter from Augsburg, West Germany, for the 1958 "Welcome Expo" in Brussels, Belgium.

Britain The largest marquee in Britain is one made by Piggot Brothers in 1951 and used by the Royal Horticultural Society at their annual show (first held in 1913) in the grounds of the Royal Hospital, Kensington and Chel-sea, Greater London. The marquee is 310 ft *94 m* long by 480 ft *146 m* wide and consists of 18¾ miles *30 km* of 36 in *91 cm* wide canvas covering a ground area of 148,800 ft² *13 820 m²*. A tent 390 ft *119 m* long was erected in one lift by the Army for the Colchester Tattoo in Kings Head Meadow with 135 men in July 1970.

LARGEST VATS

The largest vats in the United Kingdom are those used in cider brewing by H. P. Bulmer & Company. Their standard oak vats hold 60,000 gal *272 760 litres* and reinforced concrete vats hold up to 100,000 gal *454 600 litres*. Largest of all is Apollo XI, a lined steel vat with a capacity of 1,100,000 gal *5 million litres* and a diameter of 60 ft *18 m* at Hereford.

The world's largest fermentation vessel is the giant stainless steel container, No. 26M, built by the A.P.V. Co. Ltd. of Crawley, West Sussex, for the Guinness Brewery, St. James's Gate, Dublin, Ireland. This has a nominal capacity of 8,000 standard barrels, or 2,304,000 Imperial pints *1 309 200 litres*, and dimensions of 63 ft *19 m* long by 28 ft 9 in, *8,8 m* wide by 29 ft 7 in *8,9 m* high.

ADVERTISING SIGNS

Largest The greatest advertising sign ever erected was the electric Citroën sign on the Eiffel Tower, Paris. It was switched on on 4 July 1925, and could be seen 24 miles *38 km* away. It was in six colours with 250,000 lamps and 56 miles *90 km* of electric cables. The letter "N" which terminated the name "Citroën" between the second and third levels measured 68 ft 5 in *20,8 m* in height. The whole apparatus was taken down after 11

The Eiffel Tower during the 11 year era of 1925–1936 when it advertized Citroën cars with the world's largest illuminated sign

years in 1936. For the largest ground sign see Chapter 6, page 89—Letters, largest.

The world's largest neon sign was that owned by the Atlantic Coast Line Railroad Company at Port Tampa, Florida, U.S.A. It measured 387 ft 6 in *118 m* long and 76 ft *23 m* high, weighed 175 tons *178 tonnes* and contained about 4,200 ft *1 280 m* of red neon tubing. It was demolished on 19 Feb. 1970. Broadway's largest billboard in New York City is 11,426 ft² *1 062 m²* in area—equivalent to 107 ft *32,6 m* square. Britain's largest illuminated sign is the word PLAYHOUSE extending 90 ft *27 m* across the frontage of the new theatre in Leeds, West Yorkshire opened in 1970.

The world's largest working sign was that in Times Square at 44 & 45th Streets, New York City, U.S.A., in 1966. It showed two 42½ ft *13 m* tall "bottles" of Haig Scotch Whisky and an 80 ft *24 m* long "bottle" of Gordon's Gin being "poured" into a frosted glass. The world's tallest free-standing advertising sign is the 188 ft *57 m* tall, 93 ft *28 m* wide Stardust Hotel sign at Las Vegas, Nevada, U.S.A. completed in February 1968. It uses 25,000 light bulbs and 2,500 ft *762 m* of neon tubing and has letters up to 22 ft *6,7 m* tall.

Highest The highest advertising sign in the world is that atop
World the United California Bank, Los Angeles, California. The building of 62 stories is 858 ft *261,5 m* above street level and bears the initials "UCB".

United The highest advertising sign in the United Kingdom
Kingdom was the revolving name board of the contractors "Peter Lind" on the Post Office Tower, London. The illuminated letters were 12 ft *3,7 m* tall and 563 to 575 ft *171 to 175 m* above the street.

LARGEST GASHOLDER

World The world's largest gasholder is that at Fontaine l'Evêque, Belgium, where disused mines have been adapted to store up to 500 million m³ *17,650 million ft³* of gas at ordinary pressure. Probably the largest conventional gasholder is that at Wein-Simmering, Vienna, Austria, completed in 1968, with a height of 274 ft 8 in *84 m* and a capacity of 10.59 million ft³ *300 000 m³*.

United The largest gasholder ever constructed in the United
Kingdom Kingdom is the East Greenwich Gas Works No. 2 Holder built in 1891 with an original capacity for 12,200,000 ft³ *346 000 m³*. As reconstructed its capacity is 8.9 million ft³ *252 000 m³* with a water tank 303 ft *92 m* in diameter and a full inflated height of 148 ft *45 m*. The No. 1 holder (capacity 8.6 million ft³ [*243 500 m³*]) has a height of 200 ft *61 m*. The River Tees Northern Gas Board's 1,186 ft *361 m* deep underground storage in use since January 1959 has a capacity of 330,000 ft³ *9 300 m³*.

TALLEST FOUNTAIN

World The world's tallest fountain is the Fountain at Fountain Hills, Arizona built at a cost of $1,500,000 for McCulloch Properties Inc. At full pressure of 375 lb./in² *26,3 kg/cm²* and at a rate of 5,828 Imp. gal *26 500 litres/min* the 560 ft *170 m* tall column of water weighs more than 8 tons/*tonnes*. The nozzle speed achieved by the three 600 h.p. pumps is 46.7 m.p.h. *75 km/h.*

United The tallest fountain in the United Kingdom is the
Kingdom Emperor Fountain at Chatsworth, Bakewell, Derbyshire. When first tested on 1 June 1844, it attained the then unprecedented height of 260 ft *79 m*. Since the war it has not been played to more than 250 ft *76 m* and rarely beyond 180 ft *55 m*.

Bonfire The largest recorded bonfire constructed in Britain was
Largest the Coronation bonfire using 600 tons *608 tonnes* of timber and 2,000 gallons of petroleum built to a height of 120 ft *36,6 m* in Whitehaven, Cumbria in 1902.

CEMETERIES

The world's largest cemetery is that in Leningrad, U.S.S.R., which contains over 500,000 of the 1,300,000 victims of the German army's siege of 1941–42. The largest cemetery in the United Kingdom is Brookwood Cemetery, Brookwood, Surrey. It is owned by the London Necropolis Co. and is 500 acres *200 ha* in extent with more than 225,000 interments.

CREMATORIA

Earliest The oldest crematorium in Britain is one built in 1879 at Woking, Surrey. The first cremation took place there on 20 March 1885, the practice having been found legal after the cremation of Iesu Grist Price on Caerlan fields on 13 Jan. 1884.

Largest The largest crematorium in the world is at the Nikolo-Arkhangelskoye Cemetery, East Moscow completed to a British design in March 1972. It has seven twin furnaces and several Halls of Farewell for atheists. Britain's largest is the Enfield Crematorium, Greater London, which extends over 40 acres *16 ha* and in 1973/74 undertook a peak 4,986 cremations.

Tallest A totem pole 173 ft *52,73 m* tall was raised on 6 June
Totem Pole 1973 at Alert Bay, British Columbia, Canada. It tells the story of the Kwakiutl and took 36 man-weeks to carve.

Scaffolding The greatest scaffolding structure ever erected was one comprising 750,000 ft (142 miles [*228,5 km*] of tubing) up to 486 ft *148 m* in height used in the reconstruction of Guy's Hospital, London in 1971.

Tallest The world's tallest barbers pole is one 50 ft 3 in *15,3 m*
Barbers Pole long erected on 1 Nov 1973 on Walker Road, Alexander, New York, U.S.A.

10. BORINGS AND MINES

DEEPEST

World Man's deepest penetration into the Earth's crust is under Rig No 32 gas well at No 1 Bertha Rogers Field, Washita County, Oklahoma, U.S.A. After 503 days drilling the Loffland Brothers Drilling Co. reached

31,441 ft *9 583 m* (5.95 miles [*9,58 km*]) on 3 Apr. 1974. The hole temperature at the bottom was 475° F. *246° C*. A conception of the depth of this $6 million hole can be gained by the realization that it was sufficient in depth to lower the CN Tower down it more than 17 times.

The most recent in a succession of announcements of intentions to drill down 15 km *49,213 ft* from the U.S.S.R was in February 1972 from the Baku Scientific Research Institute. A depth of 21,620 ft *6 590 m* has been reached at the Kura River valley site in Southern Azerbaijan. The target here was announced in August 1974 to be 15 km *49,212 ft*.

Deepest Ocean Drilling The deepest recorded drilling into the sea bed by the *Glomar Challenger* of the U.S. Deep Sea Drilling Project is one of 4,265 ft *1300 m* and the deepest site is one 20,483 ft *6 243 m* below the surface.

PROGRESSIVE RECORDS IN DEEP DRILLING

Depth in ft	m	Location	Date
475	144	Duck Creek, Ohio (brine)	1841
550	167	Perpignan, France (artesian)	1849
5,735	1 748	Schladebach, Germany	1886
6,570	2 002	Schladebach, Germany	1893
7,230	2 203	Schladebach, Germany	1909
8,046	2 452	Olinda, Calif.	1927
8,523	2 597	Big Lake, W. Texas	1928
9,280	2 828	Long Beach, Calif.	1929
9,753	2 972	Midway, Calif.	1930
10,030	3 057	Rinconfield, Calif.	1931
10,585	3 226	Vera Cruz, Mexico	1931
10,944	3 335	Kettleman Hills, Calif.	1933
11,377	3 467	Belridge, Calif.	1934
12,786	3 897	Gulf McElroy, W. Texas	1935
15,004	4 573	Wasco, Calif.	1938
15,279	4 657	Pecos County, W. Texas	1944
16,246	4 951	S. Coles, Levee, Calif.	1944
16,655	5 076	Brazos County, Texas	1945
16,668	5 080	Miramonte, Calif.	1946
17,823	5 432	Caddo County, Oklahoma	1947
18,734	5 710	Ventura County, Calif.	1949
20,521	6 254	Sublette County, Wyoming	1949
21,482	6 547	Bakersfield, Calif.	1953
22,570	6 879	Plaquemines, Louisiana	1956
25,340	7 723	Pecos County, W. Texas	1958
25,600	7 802	St. Bernard Parish, Louisiana	1970
28,500	8 686	Pecos County, W. Texas	1972
30,050	9 159	Beckham County, Oklahoma	1972
31,441	9 583	Washita County, Oklahoma	1974

Courtesy of Loffland Drilling Co.

The Loffland rig which in 503 days drilled 2,413 ft *735,4 m* deeper than Everest is high

OIL FIELDS

The largest oil field in the world is the Ghawar field, Saudi Arabia developed by ARAMCO which measures 150 miles by 22 miles (*240 km by 35 km*). It has been asserted that the Groningen gas field in the Netherlands will prove to be the largest discovered. The area of the designated parts of the U.K. Continental shelf as at 1 Apr. 1975 was 223,550 miles² *579,000 km²* with total recoverable reserves of 3,000 to 4,500 million tons of oil and 44,000,000 million cubic feet of gas. Gas was first discovered in the West Sole Field in October 1965 and oil in the Forties Field in November 1970. The most productive oil field is expected to be Brent (found in July 1971) with 22 million tons per year attainable by 1981.

Greatest gusher The most prolific wildcat recorded is the 1,160 ft *353 m* deep Lucas No. 1, at Spindletop, about 3 miles *4,8 km* south of Beaumont, Texas, U.S.A., on 10 Jan. 1901. The gusher was heard more than a mile away and yielded 800,000 barrels during the 9 days it was uncapped. The surrounding ground subsequently yielded 142,000,000 barrels.

Greatest flare The greatest gas fire was that which burnt at Gassi Touil in the Algerian Sahara from noon on 13 Nov. 1961 to 9.30 a.m. on 28 April 1962. The pillar of flame rose 450 ft *13,7 m* and the smoke 600 ft *182 m*. It was eventually extinguished by Paul Neal ("Red") Adair, aged 47, of Austin, Texas, U.S.A., using 550 lb. *245 kg* of dynamite. His fee was understood to be about $1,000,000 (*then £357,000*).

WATER WELLS

Deepest world The world's deepest water bore is the Stensvad Water Well 11-W1 of 7,320 ft *2 231 m* drilled by the Great Northern Drilling Co. Inc. in Rosebud County, Montana, U.S.A. in October-November 1961. The Thermal Power Co. geothermal steam well begun in Sonora County, California in 1955 is now down to 9,029 ft *2 752 m*.

United Kingdom The deepest well in the United Kingdom is a water table well 2,842 ft *866 m* deep in the Staffordshire coal measures at Smestow. The deepest artesian well in Britain is that at the White Heather Laundry, Stonebridge Park, Brent, Greater London, bored in 1911 to a depth of 2,225 ft *678 m*. The deepest private well is probably that of Friningham Farm, Thurnham, Kent sunk to 415 ft *126,5 m* and deepened by bore to 818 ft *249,3 m* in 1940.

Largest Hand-dug The largest hand-dug well was one 100 ft *30 m* in circumference and 109 ft *33 m* deep dug in 1877–8 at Greensburg, Kansas, U.S.A.

MINES

Earliest The earliest known mining operations were in the Ngwenya Hills of the Hhohho District of northwestern Swaziland where haematite (iron ore) was mined for body paint *c.* 41,000 B.C. The earliest known mines in England are the Neolithic flint mines at Church Hill, Findon, West Sussex dated to 3390 B.C. ± 150.

Deepest World The world's deepest mine is the Western Deep Levels Mine at Carletonville, South Africa. A depth of 12,600 ft *3 840 m* (2.38 miles) was attained by May 1975. At such extreme depths where the rock temperature attains temperatures of 126° F *52,2° C* refrigerated ventilation is necessary. The other great hazard is rock bursts due to the pressures.

United Kingdom The all-time record depth is 4,132 ft *1 259 m* in the Arley Seam of the Parsonage Colliery, Leigh, Greater Manchester in Feb. 1974. The record in Scottish coal-mines was 3,093 ft *942 m* in the Michael Colliery, Barncraig, Fife, reached in August 1939. The deepest present mine workings are the Bickershaw Colliery

Greater Manchester at 3,540 ft *1 079 m*. The deepest in Scotland is the Great Seam at Monkton Hall Colliery, Millerhill, Lothians, at 2,930 ft *893 m*. The deepest ever shaft in England, is that of the Cleveland Potash Ltd. at Boulby, North Yorkshire at 3,754 ft *1 144 m* completed in February 1973 and the deepest in Scotland was Monkton Hall No. 1, Lothians at 3,054 ft *930 m*. The deepest Cornish tin mine was Dolcoath mine, near Camborne, The Williams shaft was completed in 1910 to 550 fathoms (3,300 ft [*1 005 m*]) from adit or approximately 3,600 ft *1 097 m* from the surface.

GOLDMINES

Largest area The largest goldmining area in the world is the Witwatersrand gold field extending 30 miles *48 km* east and west of Johannesburg, South Africa. Gold was discovered there in 1886 by George Harrison and by 1944 more than 45 per cent of the world's gold was mined there by 320,000 Bantu and 44,000 Europeans. Currently 78% of the free world's supply comes from this area whose production reached a peak 999 857 kg *984 tons* in 1970.

Largest World The largest goldmine in area is the East Rand Proprietary Mines Ltd., whose 8,785 claims cover 12,100 acres *4 900 ha*. The largest, measured by volume extracted, is Randfontein Estates Gold Mine Co. Ltd. with 170 million yds³ *129 million m³*—enough to cover Manhattan Island to a depth of 8 ft *2,4 m*. The main tunnels if placed end to end would stretch a distance of 2,600 miles *4 184 km*.

United Kingdom and Ireland The most productive goldmine in Britain was Clogan St. David's, Powys, Wales, in which county gold was discovered in 1836. This mine yielded 120,000 fine oz. in 1854–1914. Alluvial gold deposits are believed to have been worked in the Wicklow Mountains, Ireland, as early as 1800 B.C.

Richest The richest goldmine has been Crown Mines with nearly 45 million ounces *1 275 million g* and still productive. The richest in yield per year was West Driefontein which averaged more than 2½ million oz *71 million g* per year until disrupted in November 1968 by flooding. The only large mine in South Africa yielding more than one ounce per ton *28,8 g/tonne* milled is Free State Geduld.

Iron The world's largest iron-mine is at Lebedinsky, U.S.S.R., in the Kursk Magnetic Anomaly which has altogether an estimated 20,000 million tons *20 320 million tonnes* of rich (45–65 per cent) ore and 10,000,000 million tons *10,16 × 10¹² tonnes* of poorer ore in seams up to 2,000 ft *610 m* thick. The world's greatest reserves

The world's deepest mine at Carletonville, South Africa now 12,600 ft *3 840 m* deep

are, however, those of Brazil, estimated to total 58,000 million tons *58 930 million tonnes* or 35 per cent of the world's total surface stock.

Copper Historically the world's most productive copper mine has been the Bingham Canyon Mine (see below) belonging to the Kennecott Copper Corporation with over 9,000,000 short tons *8 million tonnes* in the 65 years 1904–68. Currently the most productive is the Chuquicamata mine of the Anaconda Company 150 miles *240 km* north of Antofagasta, Chile with more than *300 000 tonnes*.

The world's largest underground copper mine is at El Teniente, 50 miles *80 km* south-east of Santiago, Chile with more than 200 miles *320 km* of underground workings and an annual output of nearly 11,000,000 tons *11 176 000 tonnes* of ore.

Silver, lead and zinc The world's largest lead, zinc and silver mine is the Kidd Creek Mine of Texasgulf Canada Ltd., located at Timmins, British Columbia, Canada. Since 1970 the world's leading lead mine has been the Viburnum Trend, S.E. Missouri, U.S.A. with 489,397 short tons/ *443 700 tonnes* in 1972, from which is extracted some 10 per cent of the world's output of lead. The world's largest zinc smelter is the Cominco Ltd. plant at Trail, British Columbia, Canada which has an annual capacity of 263,000 tons *267 000 tonnes* of zinc and 800 tons *813 tonnes* of cadmium.

Spoil heap The world's largest artificial heap is the sand dump on the Randfontein Estates Gold Mines, South Africa, which comprises 42 million tons *42,6 million tonnes* of crushed ore and rock waste and has a volume six times that of the Great Pyramid. The largest colliery tip in Great Britain covers 114 acres *46 ha* (maximum height 130 ft *40 m*) with 18 million tons *18,3 million tonnes* of slag at Cutacre Clough, Lancashire.

QUARRIES

Largest World The world's largest excavation is the Bingham Canyon Copper Mine, 30 miles *48 km* south of Salt Lake City, Utah, U.S.A. From 1906 to mid-1969 the total excavation has been 2,445 million long tons *2 484 million tonnes* over an area of 2.08 miles² *5,39 km²* to a depth of 2,280 ft *695 m*. This is five times the amount of material moved to build the Panama Canal. Three shifts of 900 men work round the clock with 38 electric shovels, 62 locomotives hauling 1,268 wagons and 18 drilling machines for the 28 tons/*tonnes* of explosive used daily. The average daily extraction is 96,000 tons *97 500 tonnes* of one per cent ore and 225,000 tons *229 000 tonnes* of overburden.

The world's deepest open pit is the Kimberley Open Mine in South Africa, dug over a period of 43 years (1871 to 1914) to a depth of nearly 1,200 ft *365 m* and with a diameter of about 1,500 ft *457 m* and a circumference of nearly a mile, covering an area of 36 acres *14,5 ha*. Three tons/*tonnes* (14,504,566 carats) of diamonds were extracted from the 21,000,000 tons *21 337 000 tonnes* of earth dug out. The inflow of water has now made the depth 845 ft *257 m* to the water surface. The "Big Hole" was dug by pick and shovel.

England The deepest quarry in England is the Old Delabole Slate Quarry, Cornwall, which has been worked since *c.* 1570 and now has a circumference of 1.63 miles *2,6 km* and a depth of 500 ft *152 m*. The largest limestone quarry in Britain is the Imperial Chemical Industries Ltd.'s Tunstead Quarry, near Buxton, Derbyshire. The working face is 1.6 miles *2,57 km* long and up to 180 ft *54,8 m* high. It is producing 6,000,000 long tons of limestone per annum.

Largest stone The largest mined slab of quarried stone on record is one of 1,800 tons of slate from Spouterag Quarry, Larrydale Valley, Cumbria, England in May 1969.

8 THE MECHANICAL WORLD

1. SHIPS

EARLIEST BOATS

Evidence for sea faring between the Greek mainland and Melos to trade obsidian *c.* 7250 B.C. was published in 1971. Oars found in bogs at Magle Mose, Sjaelland, Denmark and Star Carr, Yorkshire, England, have been dated to the eighth millenium B.C.

The oldest surviving boat is the 142 ft *43,4 m* long 40 ton Nile boat buried near the Great Pyramid of Khufu, Egypt *c.* 2515 B.C. and now re-assembled.

Earliest power The earliest experiments with marine steam engines date from those on the river Seine, France, in 1775. Propulsion was first achieved when in 1783 the Marquis Jouffroy d'Abbans ascended a reach of the river Saône near Lyons, France, in the 180 ton *182 tonnes* paddle steamer *Pyroscaphe*.

The tug *Charlotte Dundas* was the first successful power-driven vessel. She was a paddle-wheel steamer built in Scotland in 1801–02 by William Symington (1763–1831), using a double-acting condensing engine constructed by James Watt (1736–1819). The earliest regular steam run was by the paddle-wheeler *Clermont*, built by Robert Fulton (1765–1815), a U.S. engineer, which maintained a service from New York to Albany (150 miles [*240 km*] in 32 hrs) from 17 Aug. 1807.

Oldest Steam vessel The oldest operational steam driven vessel in the world is the 48 ton Bristol dredger *Bertha* of 50 ft *15,42 m* designed by I. K. Brunel in 1844 and afloat at Exeter, Devon, England. Mr. G. H. Pattinson's 40 ft *12,20 m* steam launch, raised from Ullswater, Cumbria, in 1962 and now on Lake Windermere, may date from a year or two earlier. The oldest motor vessel afloat in British waters is the *Prøven* on the run from the Clyde to the Inner Hebrides. She was built in Norway in 1866.

Earliest turbine The first turbine ship was the *Turbinia*, built in 1894 at Wallsend-on-Tyne, Tyne and Wear, to the design of the Hon. Sir Charles Algernon Parsons, O.M., K.C.B. (1854–1931). The *Turbinia* was 100 ft *30,48 m* long and of 44½ tons *45,2 tonnes* displacement with machinery consisting of three steam turbines totalling about 2,000 shaft horsepower. At her first public demonstration in 1897 she reached a speed of 34.5 knots (39.7 m.p.h. [*63,9 km/h*]).

ATLANTIC CROSSINGS

Earliest The earliest crossing of the Atlantic by a power vessel, as opposed to an auxiliary engined sailing ship, was a 22-day voyage begun in April 1827, from Rotterdam, Netherlands, to the West Indies by the *Curaçao*. She was a 127 ft *38,7 m* wooden paddle boat of 438 tons, built in Dundee, Angus, in 1826 and purchased by the Dutch Government for the West Indian mail service. The earliest Atlantic crossing entirely under steam (with intervals for desalting the boilers) was by H.M.S. *Rhadamanthus* from Plymouth to Barbados in 1832. The earliest crossing of the Atlantic under continuous steam power was by the condenser-fitted packet ship *Sirius* (703 tons [*714 tonnes*]) from Queenstown (now Cóbh), Ireland, to Sandy Hook, New Jersey, U.S.A., in 18 days 10 hours on 4–22 April 1838.

The good ship *Bertha* still working after 130 years

The Exeter Maritime Museum

134

Fastest World The fastest Atlantic crossing was made by the *United States* (then, 51,988, now 38,216 gross tons), former flagship of the United States Lines. On her maiden voyage between 3 and 7 July 1952 from New York City, N.Y., U.S.A., to Le Havre, France, and Southampton, England, she averaged 35.59 knots, or 40.98 m.p.h. *65,95 km/h* for 3 days 10 hrs 40 min (6.36 p.m. G.M.T. 3 July to 5.16 a.m. 7 July) on a route of 2,949 nautical miles *5 465 km* from the Ambrose Light Vessel to the Bishop Rock Light, Isles of Scilly, Cornwall. During this run, on 6–7 July 1952, she steamed the greatest distance ever covered by any ship in a day's run (24 hrs)—868 nautical miles *1 609 km*, hence averaging 36.17 knots (41.65 m.p.h. [*67,02 km/h*]). Her maximum speed is 41.75 knots (48 m.h.p. [*77,24 km/h*]) on a full power of 240,000 shaft horse-power.

British The fastest crossing of the Atlantic by a British ship is 3 days 15 hrs 48 min by the Cunard liner *Queen Mary* in September 1946 on a 2,710 mile *4 361 km* voyage from Halifax, Nova Scotia, Canada, to Southampton at an average of 30.86 knots (35.54 m.p.h. [*57,19 km/h*]). On her 2,938-mile *4 728 km* crossing from the Ambrose Light to Bishop Rock on 10–14 Aug. 1938, she averaged 31.69 knots (36.49 m.p.h. [*58,72 km/h*]) for 3 days 20 hrs 42 min.

Most crossings Between 1856 and June 1894 Captain Samuel Brooks (1832–1904) crossed the North Atlantic 690 times—equal to 2,437,712 statute miles *3 923 117 km*. In 1850–51 he had sailed in the brig *Bessie* as an Able Bodied seaman round The Horn to Panama coming home to Liverpool as her master. His life-time sailing distance was at least 2,513,000 miles *4 044 000 km*.

John D. Hunter, Boatswain of the Container Vessel *Sealand McLean* made 45 North Atlantic crossings and steamed 328,500 miles in the year 6 Oct. 1972 to 7 Oct. 1973.

Channel Crossing Bernard Thomas crossed the English Channel from England to France in 13½ hours on 18 July 1974 in a Teifi coracle of willow cane and hazel sapling measuring 4 ft 6 in *1,37 m* long by 3 ft *91 cm* wide.

Pacific crossing The fastest crossing of the Pacific Ocean (Kobe, Japan to Seattle, Washington U.S.A.) is 4 days 21 hrs 24 min (Shionomisaki to Race Rock, B.C.) by the container ship *Sea-Land Commerce* (50,315 tons) on 27 May 1973. On 6 July 1973 she completed the 4,840 nautical miles from Yokohama to Long Beach, California at a higher average of 33.27 knots.

EXTREMITIES REACHED

Northern-most The farthest north ever attained by a surface vessel is 86° 39′ N. in 47° 55′ E. by the drifting U.S.S.R. icebreaker *Sedov* on 29 Aug. 1939. She was locked in the Arctic ice floes from 23 Oct. 1937 until freed on 13 Jan. 1940.

Southern-most The farthest south ever reached by a ship was achieved on 15 Feb. 1913 when the *Fram* reached Lat. 78° 41′ S off the Antarctic coast.

PASSENGER LINERS

Largest Since the laying up of the world's longest (1,035 ft [*315,52 m*]) and largest (66,348 gross tons) liner the *France*, the world's largest active liner has become R.M.S. *Queen Elizabeth 2* of 65,863 gross tons and an overall length of 963 ft *293 m*, completed for the Cunard Line Ltd. in 1969. She set a "turn round" record of 8 hrs 3 min at New York on 17 May 1972. In her 80 day world cruise to 23 ports on five continents 10 Jan. to 31 Mar. 1975 the price of the Trafalgar and Queen Anne suites were $97,035 (£42,189).

Largest ever The R.M.S. *Queen Elizabeth* (finally 82,998 but formerly 83,673 gross tons), of the Cunard fleet, was the largest passenger vessel ever built and had the

The last of a breed—the US Battleship *New Jersey* displaying her 16 inch *40,6 cm* guns in triple turrets

U.S. Navy

largest displacement of any liner in the world. She had an overall length of 1,031 ft *314 m* and was 118 ft 7 in *36 m* in breadth and was powered by steam turbines which developed 168,000 h.p. Her last passenger voyage ended on 15 Nov. 1968. In 1970 she was removed to Hong Kong to serve as a floating marine university and renamed *Seawise University*. On 9 Jan. 1972 she was fired by 3 simultaneous outbreaks and was gutted.

WARSHIPS

Battleships Largest World The largest battleships in the world is now the U.S.S. *New Jersey* with a full load displacement of 59,000 tons and an overall length of 888 ft *270 m*. She was the last fire support ship on active service in the world and was de-commissioned on 17 Dec. 1969.

Largest all-time The Japanese battleships *Yamato* (completed on 16 Dec. 1941 and sunk south west of Kyūshū, Japan, by U.S. planes on 7 April 1945) and *Musashi* (sunk in the Philippine Sea by 11 bombs and 16 torpedoes on 24 Oct. 1944) were the largest battleships ever commissioned, each with a full load displacement of 72,809 tons *73 977 tonnes*. With an overall length of 863 ft *263 m*, a beam of 127 ft *38,7 m* and a full load draught of 35½ ft *10,8 m* they mounted nine 460 mm *18.1 in* guns and three triple turrets. Each gun weighed 162 tons *164,6 tonnes* and was 75 ft *22,8 m* in length, firing a 3,200 lb. *1 451 kg* projectile.

Britain Britain's largest ever and last battleship was H.M.S. *Vanguard* with a full load displacement of 51,420 tons *52 245 tonnes*, overall length 814 ft *248,1 m*, beam 108½ ft *33,07 m*, with a maximum draught of 36 ft *10,9 m*. She mounted eight 15 in *38 cm* and 16 × 5.25 in *13,33 cm* guns. A shaft horse-power of 130,000 gave her a sea speed of 29½ knots (34 m.p.h. [*54 km/h*]). The *Vanguard* was laid down in John Brown & Co. Ltd's yard at Clydebank, Dunbartonshire, on 20 Oct. 1941, launched on 30 Nov. 1944 and completed on 25 April 1946. She was sold in August 1960 for scrap, having cost a total of £14,000,000.

Guns The largest guns ever mounted in any of H.M. ships were the 18 in *45 cm* pieces in the light battle cruiser (later aircraft carrier) H.M.S. *Furious* in 1917. In 1918 they were transferred to the monitors H.M.S. *Lord Clive* and *General Wolfe*. The thickest armour ever carried was in H.M.S. *Inflexible* (completed 1881), measuring 24 in *60 cm*.

AIRCRAFT CARRIERS

Largest World The warship with the largest full load displacement in the world is the $536 million aircraft carrier U.S.S. *Nimitz* at 91,400 tons. She is 1,092 ft *332 m* in length overall and has a speed well in excess of 30 knots

56 km/h. U.S.S. *Enterprise* is, however, 1,123 ft *341,3 m* long and thus still the longest warship ever built. When completed in 1976 the U.S.S. *Dwight D. Eisenhower* will have cost $679 million.

Britain Britain's largest ever aircraft carrier is H.M.S. *Ark Royal*, completed on 25 Feb. 1955, with a full load displacement of 50,786 tons *51 601 tonnes* (previously 53,340 tons *54 196 tonnes*), 845 ft *257,5 m* overall, 166 ft *50,5 m* wide, maximum draught 36 ft *10,9 m*, with a full complement of 2,640 and a capacity of 30 naval jet aircraft and 6 helicopters. Her 152,000 shaft horse-power give her a maximum speed of 31.5 knots (36.27 m.p.h. [*58,37 km/h*]).

Most deck landings The pilot who has made the greatest number of deck landings is Capt. Eric M. Brown, C.B.E., D.S.C., A.F.C., R.N. with 2,407. Capt. Brown (b. Edinburgh, 1919), who retired in 1970, flew a record 325 types of aircraft during his career and also set a world record with 2,721 catapult launchings.

Fastest destroyer The highest speed attained by a destroyer was 45.02 knots (51.84 m.p.h. [*83,42 km/h*]) by the 3,750 ton *3 810 tonnes* French destroyer *Le Terrible* in 1935. She was powered by four Yarrow small tube boilers and two geared turbines giving 100,000 shaft horse-power. She was removed from the active list at the end of 1957.

Fastest warship The world's fastest warship is the 100 ton/*tonne* U.S. Navy test vehicle SES-100B has a design speed of 80 plus knots *148 km/h* and attained more than 70 knots *129 km/h* during a trial on 1 March 1973 on Lake Pontchartrain, Louisiana.

SUBMARINES

Largest The world's largest ever submarine will be the nuclear powered submarine U.S.S. *Trident* (now SSBN 726) due to be commissioned in 1979 with 24 Trident missiles of 6,000 miles *9,650 km* range and a submerged displacement of 15,000 tons. The U.S.S.R. Delta II class submarines first mooted in November 1973 with perhaps 16 missiles may be even larger. The largest submarines ever built for the Royal Navy are the four atomic-powered nuclear missile R class boats with a surface displacement of 7,500 tons *7 620 tonnes* and 8,400 tons *8 534 tonnes* submerged, a length of 425 ft *129,5 m* a beam of 33 ft *10 m* and a draught of 30 ft *9,1 m*.

Fastest The world's fastest submarines are the U.S. Navy's tear-drop hulled nuclear vessels of the Los Angeles class. They have been listed officially as capable of a speed of "30 plus knots" but the true figure is believed to be dramatically higher. The first 4 are to be commissioned in 1975 with a further 19 by 1979.

Deepest The two U.S.N. vessels able to descend 12,000 ft *3650 m* are the 3 man Trieste II (DSV I) of 303 tons recommissioned in November 1973 and the DSV 2 (Deep submergence vessel) U.S.S. *Alvin*. The Trieste II was reconstructed from the record-breaking bathyscaphe Trieste but without the Krupp built sphere, which enabled it to descend to 35,820 ft *10 917 m*. (see Chapter XI).

Largest fleet The largest submarine fleet in the world is that of the U.S.S.R. Navy which numbers 424 boats, of which 117 are nuclear-powered and 307 conventional. The total of nuclear submarines with ballistic missiles is believed to be 69.

TANKERS

Largest The world's largest tanker is the *Globtik London* of 483,939 tonnes deadweight and 1,242 ft 10 in *378,8 m* length overall. She is 203 ft 5 in *62 m* in the beam, draws 92 ft *28 m* and is powered by an I.H.I. turbine set rated at 44,385 s.h.p. She was built by Ishikawa-jima-Harima Heavy Industries Co. Ltd. at Kure, Japan

Aero-Camera

The world's largest car ferry the 12,998 ton/*tonnes Norland* completed in 1974

and was launched in June 1973 and was delivered in October 1973. She is manned by a captain and 37 men and flies the Red Ensign. Her upper deck which is as large as 79 tennis courts or 20 688 m² is equipped to receive helicopters. Shell has a 542,400 tonner *Batilus* (Hull no. B-25) due for launch on 15 Feb. 1976 in St. Nazaire, France. She will measure 1,312.3 ft *400 m* long with a beam of 206.6 ft *63 m* and a draught of 93.5 ft *28,5 m* and capable of a speed of 16.7 knots powered by a 64,800 metric h.p. engine. Her sister ship *Bellaya* (Hull no. X-25) will follow 4 months behind. Some idea of this length can be conveyed by the thought that it would take a golfer standing on the stem, a full-blooded drive and a chip shot to reach the stern.

CARGO VESSELS

Largest The largest vessel in the world capable of carrying dry cargo is the Swedish ore/oil carrier *Svealand* of 278,000 d.wt. tons *152,068 g.r.t.* with a length of 1,108 ft *337,71 m* and a beam of 184 ft *56 m* owned by Angt. A/B. Tirfing completed in 1973. The largest British ore/oil carrier is the P & O's *Lauderdale*, built in Japan in 1972, of 260,424 d.wt. tons, 143,957 g.r.t. and a length of 1,101 ft *335,6 m*.

Fastest built During the Second World War "Liberty ships" of prefabricated welded steel construction were built at seven shipyards on the Pacific coast of the United States, under the management of Henry J. Kaiser (1882–1967). The record time for assembly of one ship of 7,200 gross tons (10,500 tons deadweight) was 4 days 15½ hrs. In January 1968, 900 Liberty ships were still in service.

Largest cable ship The world's largest cable-laying ship is the American Telephone & Telegraph Co.'s German-built *Long Lines* (11,200 gross tons), completed by Deutsche Werft of Hamburg in April 1963, at a cost of £6,800,000. She has a fully-laden displacement of 17,000 tons, measures 511 ft 6 in *156 m* overall and is powered by twin turbine electric engines.

Largest whale factory The largest whale factory ship is the U.S.S.R.'s *Sovietskaya Ukraina* (32,034 gross tons), with a summer deadweight of 46,000 tons *46 738 tonnes* completed in October 1959. She is 714.6 ft *217,8 m* in length and 84 ft 7 in *25,8 m* in the beam.

Most powerful tugs The world's largest and most powerful tug is now the *Smit Rotterdam* rated at 22,000 horse-power and with a bollard pull in excess of 150 tons. She has an overall length of 246 ft *75 m* and a beam of 49 ft 2½ in *15 m*. She was built to handle the largest tankers.

The *Thomas W Lawson* completed in 1902—the only full rigged 7 master ever built

Peabody Museum of Salem

Largest car ferry The world's largest car and passenger ferry is the 502 ft *153 m* long MV *Norland* (12,998 g.r.t.), which made its maiden voyage on 10 June 1974. She can carry 520 cars and has a service speed of 18½ knots and was built by A. G. Weser of Bremerhaven, West Germany.

Largest hydrofoil The world's largest naval hydrofoil is the 212 ft *65 m* long *Plainview* (310 tons [*314 tonnes*] full load), launched by the Lockheed Shipbuilding and Construction Co. at Seattle, Washington, U.S.A., on 28 June 1965. She has a service speed of 50 knots (57 m.p.h. [*92 km/h*]). A larger hydrofoil, carrying 150 passengers and 8 cars at 40 knots *74 km/h* to ply the Göteborg-Ålborg crossing, came into service in June 1968. It was built by Westermoen Hydrofoil Ltd. of Mandal, Norway.

Most powerful icebreaker The world's most powerful icebreaker is the U.S.S.R. atomic powered *Arctika*, able to go through ice 7 ft *2,1 m* thick at 4 knots *7 km/h*. She completed trials in December 1974.

The largest *converted* icebreaker has been the 1,007 ft *306,9 m* long S.S. *Manhattan* (43,000 s.h.p.), which was converted by the Humble Oil Co. into a 150,000 ton *152 407 tonnes* icebreaker with an armoured prow 69 ft 2 in *21,08 m* long. She made a double voyage through the North-West Passage in arctic Canada from 24 Aug. to 12 Nov. 1969. The North-West Passage was first navigated in 1906.

Largest dredger The world's largest dredger is one reported to be operating in the lower Lena basin in May 1967, with a rig more than 100 ft *30 m* tall and a cutting depth of 165 ft *50 m*. The pontoon is 750 ft *228,6 m* long. The largest dredging grabs in the world are those of 635 ft³ *17,98 m³* capacity built in 1965 by Priestman Bros. Ltd. of Hull, Humberside for the dredging pontoon *Biarritz*.

Wooden ship The heaviest wooden ship ever built was the *Richelieu*, 333 ft 8 in *101,70 m* long and of 8,534 tons launched in Toulon, France on 3 Dec. 1873. H.M. Battleship *Lord Warden*, completed 1869, displaced 7,940 tons. The

longest sea-going wooden ship ever built was the New York built *Rochambeau* (1867–1872) formerly *Dunderberg*. She measured 377 ft 4 in *115 m* overall. It should be noted that the biblical length of Noah's Ark was 300 cubits or, at 18 inches *45,7 cm* to a cubit, 450 ft *137 m*.

SAILING SHIPS

Largest The largest sailing vessel ever built was the *France II* (5,806 gross tons), launched at Bordeaux in 1911. The *France II* was a steel-hulled, five-masted barque (square-rigged on four masts and fore and aft rigged on the aftermost mast). Her hull measured 418 ft *127,4 m* overall. Although principally designed as a sailing vessel with a stump topgallant rig, she was also fitted with two steam engines. She was wrecked in 1922. The only seven masted sailing vessel ever built was the 375.6 ft *114,4 m* long *Thomas W. Lawson* (5,218 gross tons) built at Quincy, Massachusetts, U.S.A. in 1902 and was lost in the English Channel on 15 Dec. 1907.

The largest sailing vessel under the Red Ensign is the three-masted topgallant schooner *Captain Scott* of 144 ft *43,8 m* overall and displacing 380 tons completed in September 1971 and based in Loch Eil, Inverness-shire, Scotland.

Largest junks The largest junk on record was the sea-going *Cheng Ho* of *c.* 1420, with a displacement of 3,100 tons *3 150 tonnes* and a length variously estimated at from 300 ft to 440 ft *91 to 134 m*.

A river junk 361 ft *110 m* long, with treadmill-operated paddle-wheels, was recorded in A.D. 1161. In *c.* A.D. 280 a floating fortress 600 ft *182,8 m* square, built by Wang Chün on the Yangtze, took part in the Chin-Wu river war. Modern junks do not, even in the case of the Chiangsu traders, exceed 170 ft *51,8 m* in length.

Longest day's run under sail The longest day's run by any sailing ship was one of 465 nautical miles (535.45 statute miles [*861,72 km*]) by the clipper *Champion of the Seas* (2,722 registered tons) of the Liverpool Black Ball Line running before a

The world's largest propeller of 7½ tons/*tonnes* with seven blades built in Birkenhead, England in 1974

Largest Oil Platforms The largest fixed leg drilling platforms are the two B.P. Forties Field platforms. The overall height from below the mud line to the top of the drilling rig is 686 ft *209 m*. Each weighs 57,000 tons.

The wold's most massive oil platform is Shell-Esso's 230,000 ton deadweight Condeep Brent B Field platform built in Stavanger, Norway and positioned in June 1975. The tallest platform under construction is one 750 ft *228,6 m* in height being built by Redpath Dorman Long for Shell-Esso at Methil, Fife for the Brent Field.

Largest wreck The largest ship ever wrecked has been the *Golar Patricia* of 216,326 deadweight tons (98,894 g.r.t) owned by Olan Oil Ventures of Monróvia, Liberia. She sank after a series of explosions in 55 minutes, 130 miles *210 km* off the Canary Islands on 5 Nov. 1973. The largest vessel ever to be wrecked in British waters has been the 965 ft *294 m* long tanker, *Torrey Canyon*, of 61,275 tons gross and 118,285 tons deadweight, which struck the Pollard Rock of the Seven Stones Reef between the Isles of Scilly and Land's End, Cornwall, England, at 08.50 on 18 March 1967. The resultant oil pollution from some 30,000 tons *30 481 tonnes* of Kuwait crude was "on a scale which had no precedent anywhere in the world". In an attempt to fire the remaining oil, the ship was bombed to virtual destruction on 28–30 March 1967.

Oldest salvaged vessel The oldest wreck to be salvaged has been a 45 ft *13,7 m* merchant vessel, which had sunk in 100 ft *30,5 m* of water off Kyrenia, Cyprus *c* 250 B.C. It was spotted in 1965 and raised after 7 years work.

Greatest Roll The ultimate in rolling was recorded in heavy seas off Coos Bay, Oregon, U.S.A. on 13 Nov. 1971, when the U.S. Coast Guard motor lifeboat *Intrepid* made a 360 degree roll.

2. ROAD VEHICLES

Guinness Superlatives has now published automotive records in greater detail in the more specialist publication "Car Facts and Feats" (price £2.00) and obtainable from any good bookshop or, if in difficulties, from the address in the front of this volume.

COACHING

Before the advent of the McAdam road surfaces in *c.* 1815 coaching was slow and hazardous. The zenith was reached on 13 July 1888 when J. Selby, Esq., drove the "Old Times" coach 108 miles *173 km* from London to Brighton and back with 8 teams and 14 changes in 7 hrs 50 min to average 13.79 m.p.h. *22,19 km/h.* Four-horse carriages could maintain a speed of 21¼ m.p.h. *34 km/h* for nearly an hour. The *Border Union* stage coach, built *c.* 1825, ran 4 in hand from Edinburgh to London (393 miles [*632 km*]). When it ceased in 1842 the allowed schedule was 42 hours 23 mins.

MOTOR CARS

Earliest automobiles Model The earliest automobile of which there is record is a two-foot-long steam-powered model constructed by Ferdinand Verbiest (d. 1687) a Belgian Jesuit priest, and described in his *Astronomia Europaea.* His model of 1668 was possibly inspired either by Giovanni Branca's description of a steam turbine, published in his *La Macchina* in 1629, or by writings on "fire carts" during the Chu dynasty (*c.* 800 B.C.) in the library of the Emperor Khang-hi of China, to whom he was an astronomer during the period *c.* 1665–80. A 3-wheeled model steam locomotive was built at Redruth, Cornwall by William Murdoch (1754–1839) in 1785–6.

north-westerly gale in the south Indian Ocean under the command of Capt. Alex. Newlands. The elapsed time between the fixes was 23 hrs 17 min giving an average of 19,97 knots *37,00 km/h.*

Greatest speed The highest speed by a sailing merchantman is 22 knots (25.3 m.p.h. [*40,7 km/h*]) in 4 consecutive watches, by *Lancing* (ex *La Péreire*) when "running her easting down" on a passage to Melbourne in 1890/91. She was the last 4 masted full-rigged ship (36 sails) and at 405 ft *123,4 m* the longest. Her main and mizzen masts were 203 ft *61,8 m* from keelson to truck with yards 98 ft 9 in *30,09 m* across. In February 1916 she sighted Cape Wrath, Scotland 6 days 18 hrs out of New York.

Largest sails The largest spars ever carried were those in H.M. Battleship *Temeraire*, completed at Chatham, Kent, on 31 Aug. 1877. The fore and main yards measured 115 ft *35 m* in length. The mainsail contained 5,100 ft *1 555 m* of canvas, weighing 2 tons *2,03 tonnes* and the total sail area was 25,000 ft² *2 322 m².*

Largest propeller The largest ship's propellers are ten of 30 ft 9½ in *9,40 m* diameter from blade tip to blade tip and weighing 71¼ tons *72 410 kg* built by Stone Manganese Marine Ltd at Birkenhead, England for the 380,000 ton d.wt. Europa class tankers. The first was dispatched A. G. Weser, Bremen, West Germany on 15 May 1974.

Deepest anchorage The deepest anchorage ever achieved is one of 24,600 ft *7 498 m* in the mid-Atlantic Romanche Trench by Capt. Jacques-Yves Cousteau's research vessel *Calypso*, with a 5¼ mile *8,9 km* long nylon cable, on 29 July 1956.

Road Vehicles

Passenger-carrying The earliest mechanically-propelled passenger vehicle was the first of two military steam tractors, completed at the Paris Arsenal in 1769 by Nicolas-Joseph Cugnot (1725–1804). This reached 2¼ m.p.h. *3,6 km/h* Cugnot's second, larger tractor, completed in May 1771, today survives in the *Conservatoire Nationale des Arts et Métiers* in Paris. Britain's first steam carriage carried eight passengers on 24 Dec. 1801 and was built by Capt. Richard Trevithick (1771–1833).

Internal combustion The first true internal-combustion engined vehicle was that built by the Londoner Samuel Brown (Patent 5350, 25 Apr. 1826) whose 4 h.p. *4,05 c.v.* two cylinder atmospheric gas 88 litre engined carriage climbed Shooters Hill, Blackheath, Kent in May 1826. The first successful petrol-driven car, the Motor-wagen, built by Karl-Friedrich Benz (1844–1929) of Karlsruhe, ran at Mannheim, Germany, in late 1885. It was a 5 cwt. *250 kg* 3-wheeler reaching 8–10 m.p.h. *13–16 km/h.* Its single cylinder 4-stroke chain-drive engine (bore 91.4 mm., stroke 160 mm.) delivered 0.85 h.p. *0,86 c.v.* at 200 r.p.m. It was patented on 29 Jan. 1886. Its first 1 kilometre road test was reported in the local newspaper, the *Neue Badische Landeszeitung,* of 4 June 1886, under the heading "Miscellaneous". Two were built in 1885 of which one has been preserved in "running order" at the Deutsches Museum, Munich.

Earliest British cars In Britain Edward Butler (1863–1940) built a 1,042 c.c. twin-cylinder 2-stroke petrol-engined tricycle at Erith, Kent in 1888 but the earliest successful British built car with an internal combustion engine was the Bremer car built at Walthamstow, Greater London, by the engineer Frederick William Bremer (1872–1941) which first took the road in December 1894 though the body was not completed until the following month. The car has a single cylinder horizontal, water cooled 600 c.c. engine with a two speed chain drive and tiller steering. The maximum speed is about 15 m.p.h. and the car in 1964 completed the London-to-Brighton run. It is now housed in the Vestry House Museum, London E.17. Henry Hewetson drove an imported Benz Velo in the south-eastern suburbs of London in November 1894.

Earliest registrations The world's first plates were probably introduced by the Parisian police in France in 1893. Registration plates were introduced in Britain in 1903. The original A1 plate was secured by the 2nd Earl Russell (1865–1931) for his 12 h.p. *12,1 c.v.* Napier. This plate, willed in September 1950 to Mr. Trevor T. Laker of Leicester, was sold in August 1959 for £2,500 in aid of charity. It was reported in April 1973 that a number plate changed hands for £14,000 in a private deal.

FASTEST CARS

Rocket engined The highest speed attained by any wheeled land vehicle is 631.367 m.p.h. *1 016,086 km/h* over the first measured kilometre by *The Blue Flame,* a rocket powered 4-wheeled vehicle driven by Gary Gabelich on the Bonneville Salt Flats, Utah, on 23 Oct. 1970. Momentarily Gabelich exceeded 650 m.p.h. *1 046 km/h.* The car was powered by a liquid natural gas/hydrogen peroxide rocket engine developing a maximum 22,000 lb.s.t. and thus theoretically capable of 900 m.p.h. *1 448 km/h.* The building of a racing car, the Nikitin *Khadi-9,* by the Institute of Automotive Transport, Khomkov, Ukraine was announced in May 1973 with a design speed of 1200 km/h *745 m.p.h.*

Jet The highest speed attained by any jet-engined car is 613.995 m.p.h. *988,129 km/h* over a flying 666.386 yds *609 342 m* by the 34 ft 7 in *10,5 m* long 9,000 lb. *4 080 kg Spirit of America–Sonic I,* driven by Norman Craig Breedlove (b. 23 March 1938, Los Angeles) on Bonneville Salt Flats, Tooele County, Utah, U.S.A., on 15 Nov. 1965. The car was powered by a General Electric J79 GE-3 jet engine, developing 15,000 lb.s.t. *6 080 kg* at sea-level.

Wheel-driven The highest speed attained by a wheel-driven car is 429.311 m.p.h. *690,909 km/h* over a flying 666.386 yds *609,342 m* by Donald Malcolm Campbell, C.B.E. (1921–67), a British engineer, in the 30 ft *9,10 m* long *Bluebird,* weighing 9,600 lb. *4 354 kg* on the salt flats at Lake Eyre, South Australia, on 17 July 1964. The car was powered by a Bristol-Siddeley Proteus 705 gas-turbine engine developing 4,500 s.h.p. Its *peak* speed was c. 445 m.p.h. *716 km/h.* It was rebuilt in 1962, after a crash at about 360 m.p.h. *579 km/h* on 16 Sept. 1960.

Piston engine The highest speed attained by a piston-engined car is 418.504 m.p.h. *673,516 km/h* over a flying 666.386 yds *609,342 m* by Robert Sherman Summers (born 4 April 1937, Omaha, Nebraska) in *Goldenrod* at Bonneville Salt Flats on 12 Nov. 1965. The car, measuring 32 ft *9,75 m* long and weighing 5,500 lb. *2 494 kg* was powered by four fuel-injected Chrysler Hemi engines (total capacity 27,924 c.c.) developing 2,400 b.h.p.

An intention to attempt to break the sound barrier was announced in 1974 by Sanron Enterprises on an 18 mile *29 km* track at Lake Eyre, South Australia in the 34 ft *10,36 m* long 16 wheeled *Mach 1* driven by Johnny Conway. The car costing $Australian 500,000 was to be powered by 36 engines each of 2.5 litres yielding a total of 14,760 b.h.p.

Fastest racing car The world's fastest racing car yet produced is the Porsche 917/30 Can-Am Car powered by a 5,374 c.c. flat 12 turbo-charged engine developing 1,100 b.h.p. On the Paul Ricard circuit near Toulon, France in Aug. 1973 Mark Donohue (U.S.) took it to 413,6 km/h *257 m.p.h.* The two models existing take 2.1 secs for 0–60 m.p.h., 3.9 secs for 0–100 m.p.h. and 13.4 secs for 0–200 m.p.h. In 1973 the UOP Shadow Can-Am car's 8.1 litre turbo charged Chevrolet V-8 engine developed 1,240 b.h.p.

Production Car The fastest current production car is the Ferrari BB Berlinetta Boxer with a top speed of 188 m.p.h. *302,5 km/h.*

LARGEST

World Of cars produced for private road use, the largest has been the Bugatti "Royale" type 41, known in Britain as the "Golden Bugatti", of which only six (not seven) were made at Molsheim, France by the Italian Ettore Bugatti, and some survive. First built in 1927, this

Gary Gabelich (U.S.) the first man to attain 1 000 kilometres per hour and 650 m.p.h. on land

Associated Press

The 10-door 18 seat U.S. Travelall limousine 25 ft 4½ in 7,70 m in length

machine has an 8-cylinder engine of 12.7 litres capacity, and measures over 22 ft 6,7 m in length. The bonnet is over 7 ft 2 m long. The blood red 1933 Model J Victoria Duesenberg custom-built for Greta Garbo measures 24 ft 7,30 m overall. The longest present-day limousine is the Stageway Coaches Inc. 10 door Travelall 18 seat model measuring 25 ft 4¼ in 7,7 m overall. (For cars not intended for private use, see Largest engines.)

Heaviest The heaviest standard production car is the U.S.S.R.'s Zil 114, which weighs 7,000 lb. 3.12 ton 3 175 kg.

MOST EXPENSIVE

Special The most expensive car to build has been the U.S. Presidential 1969 Lincoln Continental Executive delivered to the U.S. Secret Service on 14 Oct. 1968. It has an overall length of 21 ft 6.3 in 6,56 m with a 13 ft 4 in 4 m wheel-base and with the addition of two tons 2,03 tonnes of armour plate weighs 5.35 tons 5,43 tonnes (12,000 lb. [5 443 kg]). The estimated research, development and manufacture cost was $500,000 (then £208,000) but it is rented at $5,000 (now £1,923) per annum. Even if all four tyres were shot out it can travel at 50 m.p.h. 80 km/h on inner rubber-edged steel discs.

Production The most expensive standard car now available is the Rolls Royce Carmargue, first available in 1975, with coachwork by Mulliner, Park Ward for £29,250 (incl. tax and V.A.T.). The V-8 engine has a capacity of 6,750 cc. The tank holds 24 gallons.

Used The greatest price paid for any used car has been $280,000 (£121,740) for a Rolls Royce Phantom by an undisclosed Kentucky coal merchant from Chas. Schmitt & Co. of St. Louis, Missouri reported on 30 Nov. 1974. The car was "one previous owner, chauffeur driven" and was part of a job lot of seven Rolls Royces. The previous owner was Queen Juliana. The greatest collection of vintage cars is the William F. Harrah Collection of 1,700, estimated to be worth more than $4 million (£1¾ million), at Reno, Nevada, U.S.A. Mr. Harrah is still looking for a Chalmer's Detroit 1909 Tourabout, an Owen car of 1910–12 and a Nevada Truck of 1915.

Most inexpensive The cheapest car of all-time was the 3 h.p. U.S. 1908 Browniekar for children, but designed by the Mora Motor Co. for road use, which sold for $150 (then $30 17s. 3d.). The Kavan of 1905, also of U.S. manufacture, was listed at $200 (then £41 3s.). The early models of the King Midget cars were sold in kit form for self-assembly for as little as $100 (then £24 16s.) as late as 1948.

Longest production The longest any car has been in production is 42 years (1910–52), including wartime interruptions, in the case of the "Flat Twin" engined Jowett produced in Britain. The Ford Model T production record of 15,007,033 cars (1908–1927) was surpassed by the Volkswagen "Beetle" series when their 15,007,034th car since May 1938 came off the production line on 17 Feb. 1972.

LARGEST ENGINES

Cars are compared on the basis of engine capacity. Distinction is made between those designed for normal road use and machines specially built for track racing and outright speed records.

All-time record The world's most powerful piston engine car is "Quad Al." It was designed and built in 1964 by Jim Lytle and was first shown in May 1965 at the Los Angeles Sports Arena. The car featured four Allison V12 aircraft engines with a total of 6840 in³ (112,087 c.c.) displacement and 12,000 h.p. The car has 4-wheel drive, 8 wheels and tyres, and dual six-disc clutch assemblies. The wheelbase is 160 in, and weighs 5,860 lb. 2 658 kg. It has 96 spark plugs and 96 exhaust pipes.

The largest car ever used was the "White Triplex", sponsored by J. H. White of Philadelphia, Pennsylvania, U.S.A. Completed early in 1928, after two year's work, the car weighed about 4 tons 4,06 tonnes and was powered by three Liberty V12 aircraft engines

The mighty 27 litre Merlin engined Rolls Royce which often exceeded 200 m.p.h. 321,8 km/h on continental roads

Associated Newspapers

Road Vehicles

Marconi's Wireless Telegraph Co. Ltd.

The earliest car radio, a 1903 Thornycroft steam bus fitted out by Marconi himself (standing by the rear step)

Longest Tow The longest tow on record was one of 4,759 miles *7 658 km* from Halifax, Nova Scotia to Canada's Pacific Coast, when Frank J. Elliott and George A. Scott of Amherst persuaded 168 passing motorists in 89 days to tow their Model T Ford (in fact engineless) to win a $1,000 bet on 15 Oct. 1927.

Earliest Vehicle Radio The earliest vehicle to carry a radio was the 1901 Thorneycroft steam bus fitted out by Marconi himself (see photograph, standing at rear).

MOTORCYCLES

Earliest The earliest internal combustion-engined motorized bicycle was a wooden-framed machine built at Bad Canstatt in Nov. 1886 by Gottlieb Daimler (1834–1900) of Germany and first ridden by Wilhelm Maybach (1846–1929). It had a top speed of 12 m.p.h. and developed one-half of one horse-power from its single-cylinder 264 c.c. four-stroke engine at 700 r.p.m. The first entirely British motorcycles were the 1,046 c.c. Holden flat-four and the $2\frac{3}{4}$ h.p. Clyde Single both produced in 1898. The earliest factory which made motorcycles in quantity was opened in 1894 by Henry and Wilhelm Hildebrand and Alois Wolfmüller at Munich, West Germany. In its first two years this factory produced over 1,000 machines, each having a water-cooled 1,488 c.c. twin-cylinder four-stroke engine developing about 2.5 b.h.p. at 600 r.p.m.

Fastest road machine The fastest standard motorcycle ever produced is the Dunstall Norton Commando powered by a twin cylinder 850 c.c. engine developing 72 b.h.p. at 7,000 r.p.m. and capable of 140 m.p.h. *225 km/h.*

Fastest racing machine The fastest racing motorcycle ever is the 750 c.c. 117 b.h.p. Suzuki 3-cylinder two-stroke produced in 1974 and capable of 190 m.p.h. *305 km/h* (see also Motorcycle racing, Chapter 12). Of British machines the fastest ever were the 741 c.c. 3-cylinder B.S.A. Rocket 3 and Triumph Trident racers used in the "Daytona 200" on 14 March 1971. They developed 84 b.h.p. and were capable of 170 m.p.h. *273 km/h.*

Largest The largest motorcycle ever put into production was the 1,488 c.c. Hildebrand Wolfmüller (see above). The Huntingdon Park Elks stunt and drill team from California mounted and rode 17 men on a 1200 c.c. Harley Davidson in April 1974.

Most expensive The most expensive road motorcycle in current production is the Italian M.V.-Augusta 750S Sports which retails in the United Kingdom for £2,500 (May 1975). The most expensive British-made motorcycle in current production is the 850 c.c. Dunstall Norton Commando which retailed for up to £1,458 in May 1975.

BICYCLES

Earliest The first design for a machine propelled by cranks and pedals, with connecting rods has been attributed to Leonardo da Vinci (1452–1519) or one of his pupils dated *c* 1493. The earliest such design actually built was in 1839–40 by Kirkpatrick Macmillan (1810–78) of Dumfries, Scotland. It is now in the Science Museum, Kensington and Chelsea, Greater London.

Penny-Farthing record The record for riding from Land's End to John o'Groats on Ordinary Bicycles, more commonly known in the 1870's as Penny-Farthings, is 13 days ($123\frac{1}{2}$ hours riding) by Brian Thompson, 34 in 1970.

Longest The longest tandem "bicycle" ever built is the Farway multipede unveiled at Farway, Devon, England on 26 Aug. 1974. It seats 32 and measures 61 ft 8 ins *18,79 m* in length.

Smallest The world's smallest rideable bicycle is a 3 55/64 in *98 mm* high model with front wheel of $1\frac{1}{4}$ in *32 mm* and a rear wheel $3\frac{3}{4}$ in *95 mm* made and ridden by Peter Gollnow and Rod Bennett at Deakin High School, Australian Capital Territory in 1974.

Largest tricycle The largest tricycle ever made was one manufactured in 1897 for the Woven-Hose and Rubber Company of Boston, Massachusetts, U.S.A. Its side wheels were 11 ft *3,4 m* in diameter and it weighed nearly a ton *1,01 tonnes.* It could carry eight riders.

Tallest unicycle The tallest unicycle ever mastered is one 34 ft 5 in *10,49 m* tall ridden by Daniel K. Haynes, 17 in Hamilton, Ohio, U.S.A. on 22 Aug. 1974. Steve McPeak of Seattle Pacific College, U.S.A. set a duration record when on 26 Nov. 1968 he completed a 2,000 miles *3 218 km* journey from Chicago, Illinois to Las Vegas, Nevada, U.S.A. in 6 weeks on a 13 ft *4 m* unicycle. The unicycle marathon record is 81 miles in 21 hours by Michael Boss, 13, Robert and Richard Nock 12 and 11 of Fairview Park, Ohio on 20–21 Aug. 1974.

The ultimate in small bicycles, Peter Gollnow of Australia riding his minuscule machine (see above)

Canberra Times

LAWN MOWER

Largest The widest gang mower on record is one of 15 over-lapping sections manufactured by Lloyds & Co. of Letchworth Ltd., Hertfordshire, England used by The Jockey Club to mow 2,500 acres *1 011 ha* on Newmarket Heath. Its cutting width is 41 ft 6 in *12,6 m* and has a capacity, with a 15 m.p.h. *24 km/h* tractor, of up to 70 acres *28 ha* per hour.

3. RAILWAYS

Guinness Superlatives has now published railway records in much greater detail in the more specialist publication "Guinness Book of Rail Facts and Feats" (price £2.75) and obtainable from any good bookshop or, if in difficulties, from the address in the front of this volume.

EARLIEST

Railed trucks were used for mining as early as 1550 at Leberthal, Alsace and at the Broseley colliery, Salop in October 1605, but the first self-propelled locomotive ever to run on rails was that built by Richard Trevithick (1771–1833) and demonstrated over 9 miles *14 km* with a 10 ton *10,2 tonnes* load and 70 passengers in Penydarren, Mid Glamorgan, on 21 Feb. 1804. The earliest established railway to have a steam powered locomotive was the Middleton Colliery Railway, set up by an Act of 9 June 1758 running between Middleton Colliery and Leeds Bridge, Yorkshire. This line went over to the use of steam locomotives (gauge 4 ft 1 in) built by Matthew Murray (1765–1826), in 1812. The Stockton and Darlington Railway, Cleveland, which ran from Shildon through Darlington to Stockton, opened on 27 Sept. 1825. The 7 ton *7,1 tonnes Locomotion I* (formerly *Active*) could pull 48 tons *48,7 tonnes* at a speed of 15 m.p.h. *24 km/h*. It was designed and driven by George Stephenson (1781–1848). The first regular steam passenger run was inaugurated over a one mile section (between Bogshole Farm and South Street) on the 6¼ mile *10,05 km* track between Canterbury and Whitstable, Kent, on 3 May 1830 hauled by the engine *Invicta*. The first electric railway was Werner von Siemen's 600 yds *548 m* long Berlin electric tramway opened for the Berlin Trades' Exhibition on 31 May 1879.

George Stephenson (1781–1848) son of the great lighthouse builder who pioneered Britain's railways 150 years ago

FASTEST

Electric The world rail speed record was set by the U.S. Federal Railroad Administration LIMRV (Linear Induction Motor Research Vehicle) built by the Garrett Corporation on the 6.2 mile *9,97 km* long Pueblo test track, Colorado, U.S.A. when a speed of 234.2 m.p.h. *376,9 km/h* was attained on 28 Mar. 1974.

Steam The highest speed ever ratified for a steam loco-motive was 126 m.p.h. *202 km/h* over 440 yds *402 m* by the L.N.E.R. 4-6-2 No. 4468 *Mallard* (later numbered 60022), which hauled seven coaches weighing 240 tons *243 tonnes* gross, down Stoke Bank, near Essendine, between Grantham, Lincolnshire, and Peterborough, Cambridgeshire on 3 July 1938. Driver Joseph Duddington was at the controls with Fireman Thomas Bray. The engine suffered severe damage. On 12 June 1905 a speed of 127.06 m.p.h. *204,48 km/h* was claimed for the "Pennsylvania Special" near Ada, Ohio, U.S.A.

Fastest The fastest point-to-point schedule in the world is **regular run** that of the "New Tokaido" service of the Japanese National Railways from Osaka to Okayama, in-augurated on 15 March 1972. The train covers 99.9 miles *160,7 km* in 58 mins, averaging 103.3 m.p.h. *166,2 km/h*. The peak speed attainable with a 950 ton *965 tonnes* 16 car train is 159 m.p.h. *255,9 km/h*.

The fastest regular run on British Rail is the 65.08 mile *104,73 km* stretch from Rugby to Watford, Hertford-shire in 44 min giving an average of 88.75 m.p.h. *142,82 km/h*. The London–Glasgow record over 401 miles *645 km* was set at 4 hours 58 min by the *Royal Scot* on 6 May 1974. The prototype British Rail 2 unit diesel HST (High Speed Train) attained 143 m.p.h. *230,1 km/h*, driven by James Wilson and Roland Wilson (no kin) between Northallerton, and Thirsk, North Yorkshire on 12 June 1973.

LONGEST NON-STOP

The world's longest daily non-stop run is that on Amtrak's "Silver Meteor" 1,377 miles *2 216 km* from New York City to Miami, Florida. The 659 mile *1 060 km* section between Richmond, Virginia and Jacksonville, Florida is run entirely without stops. The longest run on British Rail without any advertised stop is the Night Motorail Service from Olympia, Kensing-ton and Chelsea, Greater London to Inverness inaugurated in May 1973. The distance is 565 miles *909 km* and the time taken is 13 hours 20 min.

MOST POWERFUL

World The world's most powerful steam locomotive, mea-sured by tractive effort, was No. 700, a triple articulated or triplex 2-8-8-4, the Baldwin Locomotive Co. 6-cylinder engine built in 1916 for the Virginian Railway. It had a tractive force of 166.300 lb. *75 432 kg* working compound and 199,560 lb *90 518 kg* working simple. The greatest horse power generated by an engine was by the Northern Pacific 2-8-8-4 built in 1929 with 45,500 h.p. but a tractive effort of 140,000 lb. *63 500 kg*. Probably the heaviest train ever hauled by a single engine was one of 15,300 tons *15 545 tonnes* made up of 250 freight cars stretching 1.6 miles *2,5 km* by the *Matt H. Shay* (No. 5014), a 2-8-8-8-2 engine which ran on the Erie Railroad from May 1914 until 1929.

PERMANENT WAY

The longest stretch of continuous four track main line in the United Kingdom is between St. Pancras, London, and Glendon North Junction, Northamp-tonshire, and is 75 miles *120 km* in length.

Longest The longest straight in the world is on the Common-**straight** wealth Railways Trans Australian line over the Nullarbor Plain from Mile 496 between Nurina and Loongana, Western Australia, to Mile 793 between

PROGRESSIVE RAILWAY SPEED RECORDS

Speed m.p.h.	km/h	Engine	Place	Date
29.1	46,8	The *Rocket* (Stephenson's and Booth's 0-2-2)	Liverpool—Manchester	8 Oct. 1829
36	58	The *Northumbrian*	from Parkside, Newton-le-Willows	15 Sept. 1830
56¾	91,3	Grand Junction Rly., 2-2-2 *Lucifer*	Madeley Bank, Staffordshire	13 Nov. 1839
c.85[1]	137	Atmospheric railway (Frank Elrington)	Dun Laoghaire-Dalkey, Co. Dublin	19 Aug. 1843
74½	119,5	Great Western Rly., 8 ft *2,4 m* single 4-2-2 *Great Brotain*	Wootton Bassett, Wiltshire	11 May 1845
74½	119,5	Great Western Rly., 8 ft *2,4 m* single 4-2-2 *Great Western*	Wootton Bassett, Wiltshire	1 June 1846
78	125,5	Great Western Rly., 8 ft *2,4 m* single 4-2-2 *Great Britain*	Wootton Bassett, Wiltshire	11 May 1848
81.8	131,6	Bristol & Exeter Rly., 9 ft *2,7 m* single 4-2-4 tank No. 41	Wellington Bank, Somerset	June 1854
89.48	144	Crampton No. 604 engine	Champigny Pont sur Yvonne, France	20 June 1890
98.4[2]	158,4	*Philadelphia & Reading Rly., Engine 206*	*Skillmans to Belle Mead, New Jersey*	*July 1890*
102.8[2]	165,4	*N.Y. Central & Hudson River Rly. Empire State Express No. 999*	Grimesville, N.Y., U.S.A.	9 May 1893
112.5[2][3]	181,1	*N.Y. Central & Hudson River Rly. Empire State Express No. 999*	Crittenden West, N.Y., U.S.A.	11 May 1893
102	164	Pennsylvania Railroad	Landover to Anacosta, U.S.A.	Aug. 1895
90.0	144,8	Midland Rly., 7 ft 9 in *2,4 m* single 4-2-2	Melton Mowbray—Nottingham	Mar. 1897
130[2]	209	*Burlington Route*	*Siding to Arion, Iowa, U.S.A.*	*Jan. 1899*
101.0	162,5	Siemens und Halske Electric	near Berlin	1901
120.0[4]	193,1	Savannah, Florida and Western Rly. mail train No. 111	Screven to Satilla, Florida, U.S.A.	1 Mar. 1901
124.89	200,99	Siemens und Halske Electric	Marienfeld-Zossen, nr. Berlin	6 Oct. 1903
128.43	206,69	Siemens und Halske Electric	Marienfeld-Zossen, nr. Berlin	23 Oct. 1903
130.61	210,19	Siemens und Halske Electric	Marienfeld-Zossen, nr. Berlin	27 Oct. 1903
143.0	230,1	Kruckenberg (propeller-driven)	Karstädt-Cergenthin, Germany	21 June 1931
150.9	242,9	Co-Co S.N.C.F. No. 7121 Electric	Dijon-Beaune, France	21 Feb. 1953
205.6	330,9	Co-Co S.N.C.F. No. 7107 Electric	Facture-Morcenx, France	28 Mar. 1955
205.6	330,9	Bo-Bo S.N.V.F. No. 9004 Electric	Facture-Morcenx, France	29 Mar. 1955
235	378	*L'Aérotrain* (jet aero engines)	Gometz le Chatel-Limours, France	4 Dec. 1967
234.2[5]	376,9	Linear induction motor research vehicle	Pueblo, Colorado, U.S.A.	28 Mar. 1974

[1] *Speed attributed to runaway compressed air train. No independent timings.*
[2] *Not regarded as authentic in Europe.*
[3] *Later alleged to be unable to attain 82 m.p.h. 132 km/h on this track but then hauling 4 coaches.*

[4] *5 miles 8 km in 2½ min alleged but Supt. W. E. Symons stated that watches used were not stop watches.*
[5] *Steel flanged wheels on steel rails, hence a rail record.*

Ooldea and Watson, South Australia, 297 miles *478 km* dead straight although not level. The longest straight on British Rail is the 18 miles *29 km* between Selby, North Yorkshire and Kingston-upon-Hull, Humberside.

Longest line The world's longest run is one of 9 334 km *5,799 miles* on the Trans Siberian line from Moscow to Nakhodka, U.S.S.R. in the Soviet Far East. There are 97 stops.

Widest and Narrowest The widest gauge in standard use is 5 ft 6 in *1,676 m*. This width is used in India, Pakistan, Bangladesh, Sri Lanka (Ceylon), Argentina and Chile. In 1885 there was a lumber railway in Oregon, U.S.A., with a gauge of 8 ft *2,4 m*. The narrowest gauges in use are 1 ft 3 ins *0,381 m* on the Ravenglass & Eskdale Railway, Cumbria (7 jiles *11,2 km*) and the Romney, Hythe & Dymchurch line in Kent (14 miles *22,53 km*).

HIGHEST

World The highest standard gauge (4 ft 8½ in [*1,43 m*]) track in the world is on the Peruvian State Railways at La Cima, on the Morocoha Branch at 15,806 ft *4 817 m* above sea-level. The highest point on the main line is 15,688 ft *4 781 m* in the Galera tunnel.

A Peruvian engine reaching the world's highest point on any rail system in the then Andean air of 15,806 ft *4 817 m*

John Marshall

Great Britain The highest point of the British Rail system is at the pass of Druimnachdar on the Perth-Inverness border, where the track reaches an altitude of 1,484 ft *452 m* above sea-level. The highest railway in Britain is the Snowdon Mountain Railway, which rises from Llanberis, Gwynedd to 3,493 ft *1 064 m* above sea-level, just below the summit of Snowdon (Yr Wyddfa). It has a gauge of 2 ft 7½ in *0,81 m*.

Lowest The lowest point on British Rail is in the Severn Tunnel—144 ft *43,8 m* below sea-level.

STEEPEST GRADIENTS

World The world's steepest standard gauge gradient by adhesion is 1:11. This figure is achieved by the Guatemalan State Electric Railway between the River Samala Bridge and Zunil.

Great Britain The steepest sustained adhesion-worked gradient on main line in the United Kingdom is the two-mile Lickey incline of 1:37.7 in Hereford and Worcester. From the tunnel bottom to James Street, Liverpool, on the former Mersey Railway, there is a stretch of 1:27; and between Folkestone Junction and Harbour a mile *1,6 km* of 1:30.

Shallowest The shallowest gradient posted on the British Rail system is one indicated as 1 in 13,707 between Pirbright Junction and Farnborough, Hampshire. This could, perhaps, also be described as England's most obtuse summit.

BUSIEST

Rail system The world's most crowded rail system is the Japanese National Railways, which in 1971 carried 16,495,000 passengers daily. Professional pushers are employed on the Tōkyō Service to squeeze in passengers before the doors can be closed. Among articles lost in 1970 were 419,929 umbrellas, 172,106 shoes, 250,630 spectacles and hats and also assorted false teeth and artificial eyeballs.

Station The world's busiest station is reputedly the main Moscow Station, U.S.S.R. which in 1972 handled some 2,740,000 passengers daily. The busiest railway junction in Great Britain is Clapham Junction, Wandsworth, Greater London on the Southern Region of British Rail, with over 2,070 trains passing through each 24 hours.

STATIONS

Largest World The world's largest railway station is Grand Central Terminal, Park Avenue and 43rd Street, New York

City, N.Y., U.S.A., built 1903–13. It covers 48 acres *19 ha* on two levels with 41 tracks on the upper level and 26 on the lower. On average more than 550 trains and 180,000 people per day use it, with a peak of 252,288 on 3 July 1947.

United Kingdom The largest railway station in extent on the British Rail system is the 17-platform Clapham Junction, (see above), covering 27¾ acres *11,22 ha* with a total face of 11,185 ft *3 409 m*. The station with the largest number of platforms is Waterloo, London (24½ acres *[9,9 ha]*), with 21 main line and two Waterloo and City Line platforms, with a total face of 15,352 ft *4 679 m*. Victoria Station (21¾ acres *[8,80 ha]*) with 17 platforms has, however, a total face length of 18,412 ft *5 611 m*. The oldest station in Britain is Liverpool Road Station, Greater Manchester, first used on 15 Sept. 1830.

Highest The highest station in the world on standard gauge railways is Condor, Bolivia at 15,705 ft *4 786 m* on the metre gauge Rio Mulato to Potosi line. The highest passenger station on British Rail is Corrour, Highland, at an altitude of 1,347 ft *410,5 m* above sea-level.

Waiting rooms The world's largest waiting rooms are those in Peking Station, Chang'an Boulevard, Peking, China, opened in September 1959, with a capacity of 14,000.

Longest platform The longest railway platform in the world is the Kharagpur platform, West Bengal, India, which measures 2,733 ft *833 m* in length. The State Street Center subway platform staging on "The Loop" in Chicago, Illinois, U.S.A., measures 3,500 ft *1 066 m* in length.

The longest platform in the British Rail system is the 1,981 ft *603,8 m* long platform at Colchester, Essex.

Longest freight train The longest and heaviest freight train on record was one about 4 miles *6 km* in length consisting of 500 coal cars with three 3,600 h.p. diesels pulling and three more pushing on the Iaeger, West Virginia to Portsmouth, Ohio stretch of 157 miles *252 km* on the Norfolk and Western Railway on 15 Nov. 1967. The total weight was nearly 42,000 tons *42 674 tonnes*.

Greatest load The heaviest single piece of freight ever conveyed by rail was a 1,230,000 lb. *557 918 kg* (549.2 ton *[558 tonnes]*) 106 ft *32,3 m* tall hydrocracker reactor which was carried from Birmingham, Alabama, to Toledo, Ohio, U.S.A., on 12 Nov. 1965.

In 1974 a 16th century church at Most, Czechoslovakia weighing 9.980 tons was moved on rails 800 yds *730 m* at 3 cm/min or less than 1/1000th of an m.p.h.

The heaviest load carried by British Rail was a 122 ft *37,1 m* long boiler drum, weighing 275 tons *279 tonnes* which was carried from Immingham Dock to Killinghome, Humberside in September 1968.

Greatest mileage The greatest mileage covered with a weekly roving ticket on British Rail is 9,082 miles *14 616 km* between 3–9 Feb. 1973 by Michael Parker of Leicester.

Season ticket use Mr. Martin Ratcliff (b. 1875) has used a season ticket on Britain's railways since 1891—four years before the first automobile. Since he was 90 he has used a 1st class season ticket presented to him by British Rail.

UNDERGROUND RAILWAYS

Most extensive The most extensive and earliest (opened 10 Jan. 1863) underground or rapid transit railway system of the 67 in the world is that of the London Transport Executive, with 252 miles *405 km* of route, of which 77 miles *1,23 km* is bored tunnel and 22 miles *35 km* is "cut and cover". This whole Tube system is operated by a staff of 18,000 serving 279 stations. The 493

trains comprising 3,523 cars carried 644,000,000 passengers in 1973. The greatest depth is 192 ft *58,5 m* at Hampstead. The record for touring the then 277 stations was 15 hours precisely by Leslie R. V. Burwood on 3 Sept. 1968.

Busiest The busiest subway in the world is the New York City Transit Authority (opened on 27 Oct. 1904) with a total of 230.8 miles *371,4 km* of track and 2,081,810,464 passengers in 1970. The stations are closer set than London's and total 462. The previous peak number carried was 2,051,400,973 in 1947. The record for travelling the whole system is 21 hours 8½ min by Mayer Wiesen and Charles Emerson on 8 Oct. 1973.

MODEL RAILWAYS

Duration Record The non-stop duration record for a model train is 273.84 miles *440,70 km* by a Rovex-Hornby *Princess* hauling 6 bogie coaches over 23,570 circuits at Mevagissey, Cornwall, England, taking 194 hrs 27 mins from 31 July to 8 Aug. 1973. The scale speed was 107 m.p.h. *172,2 km/h*.

TRAMS

Longest tram journey The longest tramway journeys now possible are in the Rhein-Ruhr area of West Germany from Dinslaken to Krefold, a distance of 64 km *40 miles*. The record journeys in the United Kingdom have been by the famous illuminated car from Edgehill Works, Merseyside *via* Knotty Ash, St. Helens, Greater Manchester, Atherton, Leigh, Salford and then branching off to Ashton-under-Lyne on 13 December 1925 and alternatively to Stockport on 14 November 1926. Both journeys were of some 40 miles *64 km* in length.

MONORAIL

Highest Speed The highest speed ever attained on rails is 3,090 m.p.h. *4 972 km/h* (Mach 4.1) by an unmanned rocket-powered sled on the 6.62 mile *10,65 km* long captive track at the U.S. Air Force Missile Development Center at Holloman, New Mexico, U.S.A., on 19 Feb. 1959. The highest speed reached carrying a chimpanzee is 1,295 m.p.h. *2 084 km/h*.

The highest speed attained by a tracked hovercraft is 235 m.p.h. *378 km/h* by the jet-powered *L'Aérotrain*, invented by Jean Bertin (see Progressive speed table page 151).

Speeds as high as Mach 0.8 (608 mp.h. *[978 km/h]*) are planned in 1974 from the Onsoku Kasotai (sonic speed sliding vehicle), a wheeless rocket-powered train running on rollers designed by Prof. H. Ozawa (Japan) and announced in March 1968.

4. AIRCRAFT

Note—The use of the Mach scale for aircraft speeds was introduced by Prof. Acherer of Zürich, Switzerland. The Mach number is the ratio of the velocity of a moving body to the local velocity of sound. This ratio was first employed by Dr. Ernst Mach (1838–1916) of Vienna, Austria in 1887. Thus Mach 1.0 equals 760.98 m.p.h. *1 224,67 km/h* at sea-level at 15° C, and is assumed, for convenience, to fall to a constant 659.78 m.p.h. *1 061,81 km/h* in the stratosphere, i.e. above 11,000 m *36,089 ft*.

EARLIEST FLIGHTS

World The first controlled and sustained power-driven flight occurred near the Kill Devil Hill, Kitty Hawk, North Carolina, U.S.A., at 10.35 a.m. on 17 December 1903, when Orville Wright (1871–1948) flew the 12 h.p. chain-driven *Flyer I* at an airspeed of 30 m.p.h. *48 km/h*, a ground speed of 6.8 m.p.h. *10,9 km/h* and an altitude of 8–12 ft *2,4–3,6 m* for 12 sec covering 120 ft *36,5 m* watched by his brother Wilbur (1867–1912) and three life savers and two others. Both the brothers, from Dayton, Ohio, were bachelors because, as Orville put it, they had not the means to "support a wife as well as an aeroplane". The *Flyer* is now in the Smithsonian Institution, Washington D.C.

Aircraft

Radio Times Hulton

Louis Bleriot minutes after landing from his perilous pioneer Cross-Channel flight at 5.17 a.m. on a summer Sunday morning in 1909

The first man-carrying powered aeroplane to fly, but not entirely under its own power, was the monoplane with a hot-air engine built by Félix Du Temple de la Croix (1823–90), a French naval officer, and piloted by a young sailor who made a short hop after taking off, probably down an incline, at Brest, France, in *c.* 1874. The first hop by a man-carrying aeroplane entirely under its own power was made when Clément Ader (1841–1925) of France flew in his *Eole* for about 50 m *164 ft* at Armainvilliers, France, on 9 Oct. 1890.

British Isles The first officially recognised flight in the British Isles was made by the U.S. citizen Samuel Franklin Cody (1861–1913) who flew 1,390 ft *423 m* in his own biplane at Farnborough, Hampshire, on 16 Oct. 1908. Horatio Frederick Phillips (1845–1924) almost certainly covered 500 ft *152 m* in his Phillips II *"Venetian blind"* aeroplane at Streatham, in 1907. The first resident British citizen to fly in a powered 'plane was Griffith Brewer (1867–1948), as a passenger of Wilbur Wright, on 8 Oct. 1908 at Auvours, France.

Cross-Channel The earliest cross-Channel flight by an aeroplane was made on Sunday, 25 July 1909 when Louis Blériot (1872–1936) of France flew his *Blériot XI* monoplane, powered by a 23 h.p. Anzani engine, 26 miles *41,8 km* from Les Baraques, France, to Northfall Meadow near Dover Castle, England, in 36½ minutes, after taking off at 4.41 a.m.

Jet-engined Proposals for jet propulsion date back to Captain Marconnet (1909) of France, and Henri Coanda (1886–1972) of Romania and to the turbojet proposals of Maxime Guillaume in 1921. The earliest test bed run was that of the British Power Jets Ltd.'s experimental W.U. (Whittle Unit) on 12 April 1937, invented by Flying Officer (now Air Commodore Sir) Frank Whittle (b. Coventry, 1 June 1907), who had applied for a patent on jet propulsion in 1930. The first flight by an aeroplane powered by a turbojet engine was made by the Heinkel He 178, piloted by Flug Kapitan Erich Warsitz, at Marienehe, Germany, on 27 Aug. 1939. It was powered by a Heinkel S3B engine (834 lb. s.t. as installed with long tail-pipe) designed by Dr. Hans 'Pabst' von Ohain and first tested in August 1937.

The first British jet flight occurred when Fl. Lt. P. E' G. "Jerry" Sayer, O.B.E., (k. 1942) flew the Gloster-Whittle E.28/39 (wing span 29 ft [*8,83 m*] length 25 ft 3 in [*7,69 m*]) fitted with a 860 lb. *390 kg* s.t. Whittle W-1 engine for 17 min at Cranwell, Lincolnshire, on 15 May 1941. The maximum speed was *c.* 350 m.p.h. *560 km/h.*

Supersonic flight The first supersonic flight was achieved on 14 Oct. 1947 by Capt. (now Brig.-Gen) Charles ("Chuck") E. Yeager, U.S.A.F. ret' (b. 13 Feb. 1923), over Edwards Air Force Base, Muroc, California, U.S.A., in a U.S. Bell XS-1 rocket plane ("Glamorous Glennis"), with Mach 1.015 (670 m.p.h. [*1 078 km/h*]) at an altitude of 42,000 ft *12 800 m.*

TRANS-ATLANTIC

The first crossing of the North Atlantic by air was made by Lt-Cdr. (later Rear Admiral) Albert Cushing Read (1887-1967) and his crew (Stone, Hinton, Rodd, Rhoads and Breese) in the 84 knot *155 km/h* Curtiss flying-boat NC-4 of the U.S. Navy from Trepassey Harbour, Newfoundland, *via* the Azores, to Lisbon, Portugal, on 16 to 27 May 1919. The whole flight of 4,717 miles *7 591 km* originating from Rockaway Air Station, Long Island, N.Y. on 8 May, required 53 hours 58 min terminating at Plymouth, England, on 31 May.

First non-stop The first non-stop trans-Atlantic flight was achieved from 4.13 p.m. G.M.T. on 14 June 1919, from Lester's Field, St. John's, Newfoundland, 1,960 miles *3 154 km* to Derrygimla bog near Clifden, County Galway, Ireland, at 8.40 a.m. G.M.T., 15 June, when the pilot Capt. John William Alcock, D.S.C. (1892–1919), and the navigator Lt. Arthur Whitten Brown (1886–1948) flew across in a Vickers *Vimy*, powered by two 360 h.p. Rolls-Royce *Eagle VIII* engines. Both men were created K.B.E. on 21 June 1919 when Alcock was aged 26 years 227 days, and won the *Daily Mail* prize of £10,000.

First solo The 79th man to achieve a trans-Atlantic flight but the first to do so solo was Capt. (later Col.) Charles Augustus Lindbergh (1902–1974) who took off in his 220 h.p. Ryan monoplane "Spirit of St. Louis" at 12.52 pm. G.M.T. on 20 May 1927 from Roosevelt Field, Long Island, New York State, U.S.A. He landed at 10.21 pm. G.M.T. on 21 May 1927 at Le Bourget airfield, Paris, France. His flight of 3,610 miles *5 810 km* lasted 33 hours 29½ min and he won a prize of $25,000 (*then £5,300*).

Fastest The trans-Atlantic flight record is 1 hr. 54 min. 56.4 secs. by Major James V. Sullivan, 37 and Major Noel F. Widdifield, 33 flying a Lockheed SR-71A eastwards on 1 Sept. 1974. The average speed, slowed by re-fuelling by a KC-135 tanker aircraft, for the New York–London stage of 3,461.53 miles *5 570,80 km* was 1,806.963 m.p.h. *2 908,026 km/h.*

TRANS-PACIFIC

The first trans-Pacific flight was made from Oakland Field, San Francisco, California to Eagle Farm, Brisbane *via* Honolulu and Suva, Fiji by Capt. Charles Kingsford Smith and C. T. P. Ulm on 31 May–9 June 1928. The flying time for the 7,389 miles *11 891 km* was 83 hr. 38 min.

CIRCUMNAVIGATION

Earliest The earliest flight around the world was completed by two U.S. Army Air Service Douglas aircraft "Chicago" (Lt. Lowell H. Smith and Lt. Leslie P. Arnold) and "New Orleans" (Lt. Erik H. Nelson and Lt. John Harding Jr.) on 28 Sept. 1924 at Seattle, Washington, U.S.A. The 175-day flight of 26,345 miles *42,398 km* began on 6 April 1924 and involved 57 "hops" and a flying time of 363 hours 7 min. These aircraft had inter-changeable wheels and floats. The earliest solo

M. Colomban

The French twin engined aerobatic MC 10 Cricri which weighs under 10 stone *63 kg*

flight round the world was made from 15 to 22 July 1933 by Wiley Hardeman Post (1898–1935) (U.S.A.) in the Lockheed *Vega* "Winnie Mae" starting and finishing at Floyd Bennett Field, New York City, U.S.A. He flew the 15,596 miles *25 099 km* east-about in 7 days 18 hours 49 min—in 10 hops with a flying time of 115 hours 36 min.

Fastest The fastest circumnavigation of the globe was achieved by three U.S.A.F. B-52 *Stratofortresses*, led by Maj.-Gen. Archie J. Old, Jr., chief of the U.S. 15th Air Force. They took off from Castle Air Force Base, Merced, California, at 1 p.m. on 16 Jan. and flew eastwards, arriving 45 hours 19 min later at March Air Force Base, Riverside, California, on 18 Jan. 1957, after a flight of 24,325 miles *39 147 km*. The bombers averaged 525 m.p.h. *844 km/h* and were refuelled four times in flight by KC-97 aerial tankers.

Earliest Solo Cir-cum-polar flight Capt. Elgen M. Long, 44, completed at San Francisco International Airport the first-ever solo polar circumnavigation in his Piper Navajo in 215 hours and 38,896 miles *62 597 km*, flying from 5 Nov. to 3 Dec. 1971. The cabin temperature sank to −40° F. *−40° C.* over Antarctica.

LARGEST AIRCRAFT

Heaviest and Most Powerful The greatest weight at which an aeroplane has taken off is 820,700 lb. *372 263 kg* (366.38 tons/*tonnes*), achieved by the prototype Boeing Model 747-200 (747B) commercial transport at Edwards Air Force Base, California, in November 1970. The basic aeroplane weighed 320,000 lb. (142.9 tons [*145,1 tonnes*]), the remaining weight representing fuel, flight test equipment and an artificial payload of sand and water. The 747B has a wing span of 195 ft 8 in *59,63 m*, is 231 ft 4 in *70,51 m* long. It is structurally capable of accepting 4 Pratt & Whitney JT9D-7W turbofans, giving a total thrust of 188,000 lb. *85 275 kg*.

Largest wing span The aircraft with the largest wing span ever constructed was the $40 million Hughes H.2 *Hercules* flying-boat, which was raised 70 ft *21,3 m* into the air in a test run of 1,000 yds *914 m*, piloted by Howard Hughes, off Long Beach Harbor, California, U.S.A., on 2 Nov. 1947. The eight-engined 190 ton *193 tonnes* aircraft had a wing span of 320 ft *97,53 m* and a length of 219 ft *66,75 m* and never flew again.

Most Powerful The third Boeing E-4A advanced airborne command post version of the Boeing 747B transport flew for the first time on 6 June 1974 powered by 4 General Electric F103-GE-100 turbofan engines with a total thrust of 210,000 lb. *95,250 kg*.

Lightest The lightest aeroplane ever flown is the Whing Ding II, a single seat biplane designed and built by R. W. Hovey of Saugus, California and first flown in Feb. 1971. It has a wing span of 17 ft *5,18 m*, a weight of 123 lb. *55,8 kg* (incl. fuel) empty and 310 lb. *140 kg* fully loaded. It is powered by a 14 h.p. McCulloch Go-Kart engine, driving a pusher propeller and has a maximum speed of 50 m.p.h. *80 km/h* and a range of 20 miles *32 km* on half a gal *2,2 litres* of fuel. The pilot sits on an open seat. At least 200 more Whing Ding IIs were under construction by 1974.

The lightest and smallest twin-engined aeroplane is the MC 10 Cricri single-seat monoplane designed and built by Michel Colomban of Rueil-Malmaison, France, and first flown on 19 July 1973 by 68-year-old Robert Buisson. It has a wing span of 16 ft 4¾ in. *5,00 m*, an empty weight of 139 lb. *63 kg*, and take-off weight of 375 lb. *170 kg*, including pilot. Two 9 h.p. Rowena two-stroke engines give it a maximum speed of 130 m.p.h. *210 km/h* and a range of 248 miles *400 km*. The Cricri is aerobatic.

Smallest The smallest aeroplane ever flown is the Stits *Skybaby* biplane, designed, built and flown by Ray Stits at Riverside, California, U.S.A., in 1952. It was 9 ft 10 in *3 m* long, with a wing span of 7 ft 2 in *2,18 m*, and weighed 452 lb. *205 kg* empty. It was powered by an 85 h.p. Continental C85 engine, giving a top speed of 185 m.p.h. *297 km/h*.

BOMBERS

Heaviest The world's heaviest bomber is the eight-jet swept-wing Boeing B-52H *Stratofortress*, which has a maximum take-off weight of 488,000 lb. (217.86 tons [*221,35 tonnes*]). It has a wing span of 185 ft *56,38 m* and is 157 ft 6¾ in *48,02 m* in length, with a speed of over 650 m.p.h. *1 046 km/h*. The B-52 can carry twelve-750 lb. *340 kg* bombs under each wing and 84 500 lb. *226 kg* bombs in the fuselage, giving a total bomb load of 60,000 lb. *27 215 kg* or 26.78 tons. The ten-engined Convair B-36J, weighing 183 tons *185 tonnes* had a greater wing span, at 230 ft *70,10 m* but it is no longer in service. It had a top speed of 435 m.p.h. *700 km/h*.

Fastest The world's fastest operational bombers are the French Dassault *Mirage IV*, which can fly at Mach 2.2 (1,450 m.p.h. [*2 333 km/h*]) at 36,000 ft *11 000 m*; the American General Dynamics FB-111A, which also flies above Mach 2; and a Soviet swing wing Tupolev bomber known to N.A.T.O. as "Backfire", which has an estimated over-target speed of Mach 2.25–2.5 and a range of up to 6,000 miles *9 650 km*.

Most Expensive Although estimated costs for the U.S. B-1 supersonic Mach 2.2 bomber, rolled out on 26 Oct. 1974, vary widely, it is clearly the most expensive aircraft ever produced. An estimate of $43,900 million for 244 was published a 1970—a cost of $180 million (£78.2 million) for aircraft.

AIRLINERS

Largest World The highest capacity jet airliner is the Boeing 747, "Jumbo Jet", first flown on 9 Feb. 1969, which in November 1970 set a record for gross take-off weight of 820,700 lb. *372 263 kg* (366.38 tons) (see Heaviest aircraft) and has a capacity of from 362 to 500 passengers with a maximum speed of 608 m.p.h. *978 km/h*. Its wing span is 195.7 ft *59,64 m* and its length 231.3 ft *70,50 m*. It entered service on 21 Jan. 1970.

United Kingdom The heaviest United Kingdom airliner in service is the B.A.C. Super VC10, which first flew on 7 May 1964. It weighs 335,000 lb. (149.5 tons) *151,8 tonnes* and is 171.7 ft *52,33 m* long, with a wing span of 146.2 ft *44,56 m*. The largest ever British aircraft was the experimental Bristol Type 167 *Brabazon*, which had a maximum take-off weight of 129.4 tons *131,4 tonnes*, a wing span of 230 ft *70,10 m* and a length of 177 ft *53,94 m*.

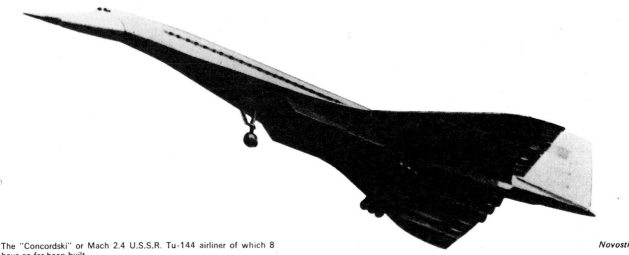

The "Concordski" or Mach 2.4 U.S.S.R. Tu-144 airliner of which 8 have so far been built

Novosti

This eight-engined aircraft first flew on 4 Sept. 1949. The *Concorde* (see below) has a maximum take-off weight of 400,000 lb. *181 435 kg* (178.5 tons).

Largest Cargo Compart-ment The largest cargo compartment of any aircraft is the 39,000 ft³ *1104 m³* of the American Aero Spacelines Guppy-201 which was put into service in Sept. 1971. The compartment is more than 25 ft *7,6 m* in diameter.

Fastest *World* The U.S.S.R.'s Tu-144 supersonic airliner, with a capacity of 140 passengers, first flew on 31 Dec. 1968, with a design ceiling of 65,000 ft *19 812 m*, and it "went" supersonic on 5 June 1969. It first exceeded Mach 2 on 26 May 1970, and attained 1,565.8 m.p.h. *2 519,9 km/h* (Mach 2.37) at 59,000 ft *18 000 m* in late December 1971. During later flight trials it attained Mach 2.4 (1,585 m.p.h. [*2 550 km/h*]) and is expected to enter service in 1976 at an average speed of 1,245 m.p.h. *2 000 km/h*.

Britain The supersonic BAC/Aerospatiale *Concorde*, first flown on 2 March 1969, with a capacity of 128 passengers, is expected to cruise at up to Mach 2.05 (1,355 m.p.h. [*2 180 km/h*]): It flew at Mach 1.05 on 10 Oct. 1969, exceeded Mach 2 for the first time on 4 Nov. 1970 and is expected to enter service in late 1975 or early 1976. In a flight on 13 June 1974 a Concorde flew from Paris to Boston in 3 hrs 9 min.

Scheduled flights *Longest* The longest scheduled non-stop flight is the polar Brussels–Hawaii flight of 7,327 statute miles *11 791 km* inaugurated on 19 June 1974. The Boeing 747C used requires 14 hours and 39,135 gal *177 910 litres* of fuel to make the flight thus requiring a reduction of passenger load from 461 to 200.

Shortest The shortest scheduled flight in the world is that by Loganair between the Orkney Islands of Westray and Papa Westray which has been flown since September

1967. Though scheduled for 2 min, in favourable wind conditions it has been accomplished in 69 secs by Capt. Andrew Alsop.

HIGHEST SPEED

Official record The official air speed record is 2,070.102 m.p.h. *3 331,507 km/h* by Col. Robert L. Stephens and Lt.-Col. Daniel André (both U.S.A.F.) in a Lockheed YF-12A near Edwards Air Force Base, California, U.S.A. over a 15/25 km course on 1 May 1965.

Air-launched record The fastest fixed-wing aircraft in the world was the U.S. North American Aviation X-15A-2, which flew for the first time (after modification) on 28 June 1964 powered by a liquid oxygen and ammonia rocket propulsion system. Ablative materials on the airframe once enabled a temperature of 3,000° F. to be withstood. The landing speed was 210 knots (242 m.p.h. [*389,1 km/h*]) momentarily. The highest speed attained was 4,534 m.p.h. *7 297 km/h* (Mach 6.72) when piloted by Major William J. Knight, U.S.A.F. (b. 1930), on 3 Oct. 1967. An earlier version piloted by Joseph A. Walker (1920–66), reached 354,200 ft *107 960 m* (67.08 miles) also over Edwards Air Force Base, California, U.S.A., on 22 Aug. 1963. The programme was suspended after the final flight of 24 Oct. 1968.

Fastest jet The world's fastest jet aircraft is the U.S.A.F Lockheed SR-71 reconnaissance aircraft (a variant of the YF-12A) which was first flown on 22 Dec. 1964 and is reportedly capable of attaining a speed of 2,200 m.p.h. *3 540 km/h* and an altitude ceiling of close to 100,000 ft *30 480 m*. The SR-71 has a span of 55.6 ft *16,94 m* and a length of 107.4 ft *32,73 m* and weighs 170,000 lb. (75.9 tons [*77,1 tonnes*]) at take-off. Its reported range is 2,982 miles *4 800 km* at Mach 3 at 78,750 ft *24 000 m*. Only 27 are believed to have been built and 9 had been lost by April 1969. The fastest Soviet jet aircraft in

The Mach 3 Lockheed SR-71 which crossed the Atlantic from New York to London in under 2 hours

service is the Mikoyan MiG-25 *alias* E.266 fighter (code name "Foxbat") with a speed of Mach 3.2 (2,110 m.p.h. [*3 395 km/h*]). It is armed with air-to-air missiles.

Fastest biplane The fastest recorded biplane was the Italian Fiat C.R.42B, with a 1,010 h.p. Daimler-Benz DB601A engine, which attained 323 m.p.h. *520 km/h* in 1941. Only one was built.

Fastest piston-engined aircraft The fastest speed at which a piston-engined aeroplane has ever been measured was for a cut-down privately owned Hawker *Sea Fury* which attained 520 m.p.h. *836 km/h* in level flight over Texas, U.S.A., in August 1966 piloted by Mike Carroll (k. 1969) of Los Angeles. The official record for a piston-engined aircraft is 482.462 m.p.h. *776,447 km/h* over Edwards AFB California by Darryl C. Greenamyer, 33, (U.S.) in a modified Grumman F8F-2 *Bearcat* on 16 Aug. 1969.

Fastest propeller-driven aircraft The Soviet Tu-114 turboprop transport is the world's fastest propeller-driven aeroplane. It has achieved average speeds of more than 545 m.p.h. *877 km/h* carrying heavy payloads over measured circuits. It is developed from the Tupolev Tu-95 bomber, known in the West as the "Bear", and has 14,795 h.p. engines. The Republic XF-84H prototype U.S. Navy fighter which flew on 22 July 1955 had a top *design* speed of 670 m.p.h. *1 078 km/h* but was abandoned.

Longest standing record The earliest aeroplane record listed by the Fédération Aéronautique Internationale as still unbeaten is for speed over a 100 km circuit in a piston-engined sea-plane, set up by G. Cassinelli of Italy. He averaged 391.072 m.p.h. *629,370 km/h* in a Macchi C.72 sea-plane with a 2,400 h.p. Fiat AS 6 24-cylinder engine on 8 Oct. 1933.

Largest propeller The largest aircraft propeller ever used was the 22 ft 7½ in *6,89 m* diameter Garuda propeller, fitted to the Linke-Hofmann R II built in Breslau, Germany, which flew in 1919. It was driven by four 260 h.p. Mercédès engines and turned at only 545 r.p.m.

ALTITUDE

Official record The official world altitude record by an aircraft which took off from the ground under its own power is 118,898 ft (22.51 miles [*36,24 km*]) by Aleksandr Fedotov (U.S.S.R.) in a Mikoyan E-266 (MiG-25) aircraft, powered by two turbojet engines on 25 July 1973. *Absolute* altitude records listed progressively are in Chapter XI.

The greatest recorded height by any pilot without a pressure cabin or even a pressure suit has been 49,500 ft *15 085 m* by Sq./Ldr. G. W. H. Reynolds D.F.C. in a Spitfire Mark 5C over Libya in 1942.

DURATION

The flight duration record is 64 days, 22 hours, 19 min and 5 sec, set up by Robert Timm and John Cook in a Cessna 172 "Hacienda". They took off from McCarran Airfield, Las Vegas, Nevada, U.S.A., just before 3.53 p.m. local time on 4 Dec. 1958, and landed at the same airfield just before 2.12 p.m. on 7 Feb. 1959. They covered a distance equivalent to six times around the world with continued refuellings, without landing.

The record for duration without refuelling is 84 hrs 32 min, set by Walter E. Lees and Frederic A. Brossy in a Bellanca monoplane with a 225 h.p. Packard Diesel engine, at Jacksonville, Florida, on 25–28 May 1931.

AIRPORTS

Largest World The world's largest airport is the Dallas/Fort Worth Airport, Texas, U.S.A., which extends over 17,500 acres *7,080 ha* in the Grapevine area, midway between Dallas and Fort Worth. It was opened in January 1974

at an initial cost of $700 million. The present 3 runways and 4 terminal buildings are planned to be extended to 9 runways and 13 terminals with 260 gates with an ultimate capacity for 60 million passengers. The area of the Montreal Airport, Canada will be 18,500 acres *9 000 ha*.

United Kingdom Seventy-two airline companies from 68 countries operate scheduled services into London (Heathrow) Airport (2,721 acres [*1 101 ha*]), and during 1974 there was a total of 288,152 air transport movements handled by a staff of 51,636 employed by the various companies and the British Airports Authority. The total number of passengers, both incoming and outgoing, was 20,415,741. The most flights in a day was 986 on 19 July 1974 and the largest number of passengers yet handled in a day was 85,791 on 1 Sept. 1974. Aircraft fly to over 90 countries.

Busiest The world's busiest airport is the Chicago International Airport, O'Hare Field, Illinois, U.S.A., with a total of 694,674 movements and 37,893,449 passengers in 1974. This represents a take-off or landing every 45.39 seconds round the clock.

The busiest landing area ever has been Bien Hoa Air Base, South Vietnam, which handled more than 1,000,000 take-offs and landings in 1970. The world's largest "helipad" was An Khe, South Vietnam, which serviced U.S. Army and Air Force helicopters.

Highest and lowest The highest airport in the world is El Alto, near La Paz, Bolivia, at 13,599 ft *4 150 m* above sea-level. Ladakh airstrip in Kashmir has, however, an altitude of 14,270 ft *4 349 m*. The highest landing ever made by a fixed-wing 'plane is 6,080 m *19,947 ft* on Dhaulagri, Himalaya by a Pilatus Porter, named *Yeti*, supplying the 1960 Swiss Expedition. The lowest landing field is El Lisan on the east shore of the Dead Sea, 1,180 ft *360 m* below sea-level, but the lowest international airport is Schiphol, Amsterdam, at 13 ft *3,9 m* below sea-level.

LONGEST RUNWAY

World The longest runway in the world is one of 7 miles *11 km* in length (of which 15,000 ft [*4 572 m*] is concreted) at Edwards Air Force Base on the bed of Rogers Dry Lake at Muroc, California, U.S.A. The whole test centre airfield extends over 65 miles² *168 km²*. In an emergency an auxiliary 12 mile *19 km* strip is available along the bed of the Dry Lake. The world's longest civil airport runway is one of 15,502 ft (2.93 miles [*4,72 km*]) at Salisbury, Rhodesia, completed in 1969.

United Kingdom The longest runway available normally to civil aircraft in the United Kingdom is No. 1 at London (Heathrow) Airport, measuring 12,799 ft (2.42 miles [*3,89 km*]).

The world's largest airport between Dallas and Fort Worth, Texas, U.S.A. which will have 260 gates

Bensen Aircraft Corp.

Dr. Igor Bensen aloft in his multi record-breaking open one man Gyro-Copter

HELICOPTERS

Fastest A Bell YUH-1B Model 533 compound research helicopter, boosted by two auxiliary turbojet engines, attained an unofficial speed record of 316.1 m.p.h. *508,7 km/h* over Arlington, Texas, U.S.A., in April 1969. The official world speed record for a pure helicopter is 220.885 m.p.h. *355,485 km/h* by a Sikorsky S-67 Blackhawk, flown by test pilot Kurt Cannon, between Milford and Branford, Connecticut, U.S.A. on 19 Dec. 1970.

Largest The world's largest helicopter is the Soviet Mil *Mi-12* ("Homer"), also known as the V-12, which set up an international record by lifting a payload of 88,636 lb. (39.5 tons [*40,2 tonnes*]) to a height of 7,398 ft *2 255 m* on 6 Aug. 1969. It is powered by four 6,500 h.p. turboshaft engines and has a span of 219 ft 10 in *67 m* over its rotor tips with a fuselage length of 121 ft 4½ in *37,00 m* and weighs 103.3 tons *105 tonnes*.

Highest The altitude record for helicopters is 40,820 ft *12 442 m* by an Aérospatiale SA 315B Lama, over France on 21 June 1972. The highest landing has been at 23,000 ft *7 010 m* below the South-East face of Everest in a rescue sortie in May 1971.

AUTOGYROS

The autogyro or gyroplane, a rotorcraft with an unpowered rotor turned by the airflow in flight, preceded the practical helicopter with engine-driven rotor. Juan de la Cierva (Spain), made the first successful autogyro flight with his model C.4 (commercially named an *Autogiro*) at Getafe, Spain, on 9 Jan. 1923. On 6 Dec. 1955, Dr. Igor B. Bensen (U.S.A.) flew his very simple open-seat Gyro-Copter and then made the design available in kit form to amateur constructor/pilots.

Speed
Altitude
and Distance
Records Dr. Bensen holds the straight-line distance of 82.77 miles *133,2 km* and speed of 79.0 m.p.h. *127,15 km/h* over a 15/25 km course records set in his B.8M Gyro-Copter on 15 May and 15 June 1967 respectively. Wg. Cdr. Kenneth H. Wallis (G.B.) flew his WA-116, with 72 h.p. McCulloch engine, to a record altitude of 15,220 ft *4,639 m* on 11 May 1968, and to a record speed of 111.2 m.p.h. *179 km/h* over a 3 km straight course on 12 May 1969. Awaiting confirmation is his distance record of 416 miles *670 km* over a 100 km closed circuit set in another WA-116 in July 1974.

FLYING-BOAT

The fastest flying-boat ever built has been the Martin XP6M-1 *Seamaster*, the U.S. Navy 4 jet engined minelayer flown in 1955–59 with a top speed of 646 m.p.h. *1 040 km/h*. In Sept. 1946 the Martin *Caroline Mars* flying-boat set a payload record of 68,327 lb. *30 992 kg*.

The official flying-boat speed record is 566.69 m.p.h. *912 km/h*, set up by Niklaai Andrievsky and crew of two in a Soviet Beriev M-10, powered by two AL-7 turbojets, over a 15/25 km course on 7 Aug. 1961. The M-10 holds all 12 records listed for jet-powered flying-boats, including an altitude of 49,088 ft *14 962 m* set by Georgiy Buryanov and crew over the Sea of Azov on 9 Sept. 1961.

AIRSHIPS

Earliest The earliest flight in an airship was by Henri Giffard from Paris in his coal-gas 88,300 ft³ *2 500 m³* 144 ft *43,8 m* long airship on 24 Sept. 1852. The earliest British airship was a 20,000 ft³ *566 m³* 75 ft *22,8 m* long craft built by Stanley Spencer whose maiden flight was from Crystal Palace, Bromley, Greater London on 22 September 1902. The latest large airship to be assembled in Britain is the 202,700 ft³ *5 739 m³* 192½ ft *56,67 m* long *Europa* built at Cardington, Bedfordshire by the Goodyear Tyre & Rubber Co. which first flew on 8 March 1972.

Largest
Rigid The largest rigid airship ever built was the German *Graf Zeppelin II* (LZ 130), with a length of 245 m *803,8 ft* and a capacity of 7,062,100 ft³ *199 977 m³*. She made her maiden flight on 14 Sept. 1938 and in May and August 1939 made radar spying missions in British air space. She was dismantled in April 1940.

British The largest British airship was the R101 built by the Royal Airship Works, Cardington, Bedfordshire, which first flew on 14 Oct. 1929. She was 777 ft *236,8 m* in length and had a capacity of 5,508,800 ft³ *155 992 m³*. She crashed near Beauvais, France, killing 48 aboard on 5 Oct. 1930.

Non-Rigid The largest non-rigid airship ever constructed was the U.S. Navy ZPG 3-W. It had a capacity of 1,516,300 ft³ *42 937 m³*, was 403.4 ft *122,9 m* long and 85.1 ft *25,93 m* in diameter, with a crew of 21. She first flew on 21 July 1958, but crashed into the sea in June 1960.

Greatest
Passenger
Load The most people ever carried in an airship was 207 in the U.S. Navy *Akron* in 1931. The trans-Atlantic record is 117 by the German *Hindenburg* in 1937. The distance record for airships is 3,967.3 miles *6 384,5 km*, set up by the German *Graf Zeppelin*, captained by Dr. Hugo Eckener, between 29 Oct. and 1 Nov. 1928.

BALLOONING

Earliest The earliest recorded balloon was a hot air model invented by Father Bartolomeu de Gusmão (né Lourenço) (b. Santos, Brazil, 1685), which was flown indoors at the Casa da India, Terreiro do Paço, Portugal on 8 Aug. 1709.

Distance
record The record distance travelled is 3 052,7 km *1,896.9 miles* by H. Berliner (Germany) from Bitterfeld,

Walter S. Davies of Hawick who took out his Private Pilot's Licence at the age of 71

Germany, to Kirgishan in the Ural Mountains, Russia, on 8–10 Feb. 1914. Col. Thomas L. Gatch's lost balloon *Light Heart* was sighted some 3,000 miles *4 800 km* from its take-off point at Harrisburg, Pennsylvania, U.S.A. on 19 Feb. 1974. The official duration record is 87 hours by H. Kaulen (Germany) set on 13–17 Dec. 1913.

Highest manned The greatest altitude reached in a manned balloon is the unofficial 123,800 ft (23.45 miles [*37 735 m*]) by Nicholas Piantanida (1933–66) of Bricktown, New Jersey, U.S.A., from Sioux Falls, South Dakota, U.S.A., on 1 Feb. 1966. He landed in a cornfield in Iowa. The official record is 113,740 ft *34 668 m* by Cdr. Malcolm D. Ross, U.S.N.R. and the late Lt.-Cdr. Victor E. Prather, U.S.N. in an ascent from the deck of U.S.S. *Antietam* on 4 May 1961, over the Gulf of Mexico.

The unmanned plastic GHOST balloon launched on 11 Nov. 1971 at Christchurch, New Zealand is presumed to have come down on its 744th day of flight in the South Atlantic.

Largest The largest balloon ever to fly is the 800 ft tall balloon built by G. T. Schjeldahl for the U.S.A.F., first tested on 18 July 1966. It was used for a Martian re-entry experiment by N.A.S.A. 130,000 ft *39 625 m* above Walker AFB, New Mexico, U.S.A., on 30 Aug. 1966. Its capacity is 26 million ft³ *736 237 m³*. The largest hot air balloon in the world is one of 40,000 ft³ *1 132,6 m³* known as *Cumulo Nimbus* built by Mr. Don Cameron in 1972.

Ballooning (Hot-Air) The world's distance record for hot-air ballooning is 337.2 miles *542,7 km* by Matt Wiederkehr, 43, in a Raven S-55A from St. Paul, Minnesota to Butte, Iowa on 7 Mar. 1974. The altitude record is 45,837 ft *13 971 m* by Julian Nott and co-pilot Felix Pole (both G.B.) over Bhopal, India on 25 Jan. 1974 in Daffodil II, the 375,000 ft³ *10618 m³* Cameron A-375 balloon. The largest hot-air balloon ever built is the U.K. Cameron A-500 500,000 ft³ *14158 m³* *Gerard A. Heineken* in 1974. The endurance record is 16 hrs 16 mins by Wiederkehr in making his distance record.

Human-powered flight The greatest distance achieved in human-powered flight is 1,171 yds *1,07 km* in the 80 ft *24,3 m* span *Jupiter* by Flt. Lt. John Potter R.A.F. in 1 min 47.4 sec at R.A.F. Benson, Oxfordshire on 29 June 1972. He achieved 1,355 yds *1,23 km* unofficially in 2 min 15.5 sec on 16 June 1972.

Most Flying Hours Max Conrad, 70 (U.S.A.) between 1928 and mid-1974 totalled 52,929 hr 40 min logged flight—more than 6 years.

Most Landings Tony Cattle and David R. Shevloff in a Cessna 172 took off and landed at 65 airfields in southern England in 16 hrs 19 min in daylight on 19 June 1974 for a British record.

Oldest and Youngest Pilots The youngest age at which anyone has ever qualified as a military pilot is 15 yrs 5 months in the case of Sgt. Thomas Dobney (b. 6 May 1926) of the R.A.F. He had understated his age (14 years) on entry. Miss Betty Bennett took off, flew and landed solo at the age of 10 on 4 Jan. 1952 in Cuba. Anthony Hubbard of St. Athan, South Glamorgan qualified for his P.P.L. (Private Pilots' License) on 13 Oct. 1973 aged 17 years 5 days. The oldest holder of a P.P.L. in Britain is John Noel Gladish of Ripon, North Yorkshire (born 29 Oct. 1898) who is licensed beyond his 77th birthday. Walter S. Davies of Hawick, Roxburghshire took out his P.P.L. in Dec. 1971 aged 71. Mrs. Harry Francklin, 100 took over the controls of a Stinson Voyager light aircraft, piloted by Floyd Johnson over Salem, Oregon, U.S.A. on 23 Mar. 1946 and commented "I get more thrill out of horseback riding".

HOVERCRAFT

Earliest The inventor of the ACV (air-cushion vehicle) is Sir Christopher Sydney Cockerell, C.B.E., F.R.S. (b. 4 June 1910), a British engineer who had the idea in 1954, published his Ripplecraft Report 1/55 on 25 Oct. 1955 and patented it on 12 Dec. 1955. The earliest patent relating to an air-cushion craft was applied for in 1877 by John I. Thornycroft (1843–1928) of Chiswick, London. The first flight by a hovercraft was made by the 4 ton/*tonnes* Saunders-Roe SR-N1 at Cowes on 30 May 1959. With a 1,500 lb. *680 kg* thrust Viper turbojet engine, this craft reached 68 knots *126 km/h* in June 1961. The first hovercraft public service was run across the Dee Estuary by the 60-knot *111 km/h* 24-passenger Vickers-Armstrong's VA-3 between July and September 1962.

Largest The largest is the 200 ton *203 tonne* Westland SR-N4, *Mountbatten*, Mark II. It has a top speed of 77 knots *142 km/h* powered by 4 Bristol Siddeley Marine Proteus engines with 19 ft *5,7 m* propellers. The U.S.N. Bell Aerospace SES (Surface Effect Ship) anti-submarine prototype will be of 1,500 tons *15 023 tonnes* measuring 230 ft × 106 ft *70,1 m × 32,3 m*.

Longest flight The longest hovercraft journey was one of 5,000 miles *8 047 km* through eight West African countries between 15 Oct. 1969 and 3 Jan. 1970 by the British Trans-African Hovercraft Expedition.

Greatest Load The heaviest object moved by "hover floatation" is 600 tons *609 tonnes* by Mears Construction Ltd., in Oct. 1973. Plans to move another storage tank of 1,750 tons *1 776 tonnes* are being made.

MODEL AIRCRAFT

The world record for altitude is 26,929 ft *8 208 m* by Maynard L. Hill (U.S.A.) on 6 Sept. 1970 using a radio-controlled model. The speed record is 213.70 m.p.h. *343,92 km/h* by V. Goukoune and V. Myakinin (both U.S.S.R.) with a radio-controlled model at Klementyeva, U.S.S.R., on 21 Sept. 1971. The record duration flight is one of 25 hrs 44 min 8 sec by Myakinin with a radio controlled glider in Sept–Oct. 1973.

The first cross channel model helicopter flight was achieved by an 11 lb. *5,00 kg* model Bell 212 radio controlled by Dieter Zeigler for 32 miles *52 km* between Ashford, Kent and Ambleteuse, France on 17 July 1974.

Paper Aircraft The flight duration record for a paper aircraft over level ground is 15.0 sec by William Harlan Pryor in the Municipal Auditorium, Nashville, Tennessee, U.S.A. on 26 Mar. 1975. A paper plane was reported to have flown 1,126 yds *1 029 m* by Greg Ruddue, 11 at San Geronimo Valley Elementary School, California on 31 May 1973.

THE WORLD'S LARGEST HYDRO-ELECTRIC GENERATING PLANTS — Progressive List

Kilowattage	First Operational	Location	River
38,400	1898	De Cew Falls No. 1 (old plant)	Welland Canal
132,500	1905	Ontario Power Station	Niagara
403,900	1922	Sir Adam Beck No. 1 (formerly Queenston-Chippawa)	Niagara
1,641,000	1942	Beauharnois, Quebec, Canada	St. Lawrence
2,161,000[1]	1941	Grand Coulee, Washington State, U.S.A.	Columbia
2,100,000	1955	Volga-V.I. Lenin Station, Kuybyshev, U.S.S.R.	Volga
2,543,000	1958	Volga-22nd Congress Station, Volgograd, U.S.S.R.	Volga
4,500,000	1964	Bratsk, U.S.S.R.	Angara
6,096,000	1968	Krasnoyarsk, U.S.S.R.	Yenisey
6,400,000	—	Sayano-Shushensk, U.S.S.R.	Yenisey
10,710,000[2]	—	Itaipu, Brazil–Uruguay	

[1] *Ultimate long-term planned kilowattage will be 9,780,000 kW with the completion of the "Third Powerplant" (capacity 7,200,000 kW).*
[2] *Ultimate kilowattage.*

5. POWER PRODUCERS

LARGEST POWER PLANT

World The world's largest power station is the U.S.S.R.'s hydro-electric station at Krasnoyarsk on the river Yenisey, Siberia, U.S.S.R. with a power of 6,096,000 kW. Its third generator turned in March 1968 and the twelfth became operative in December 1970. The turbine hall, completed in June 1968, is 1,378 ft *420 m* long. The reservoir backed up by the dam was reported in Nov. 1972 to be 240 miles *386 km* in length.

The largest non-hydro-electric generating plant in the world is the 2,500,000 kW Tennessee Valley Authority installation at Paradise, Kentucky, U.S.A. with an annual consumption of 8,150,000 tons *8 280 807 tonnes* of coal. It cost $189,000,000 (*then £78,750,000*).

United Kingdom The power station with the greatest installed capacity in the United Kingdom is Longannet, Fife, Scotland which attained 2,400 MW by Dec. 1972. Ferrybridge "C" near Pontefract, West Yorkshire, reached full power of 2,000 MW in December 1967, and with the Ferrybridge "A" and "B" forms a 2,430 MW complex. At Drax, North Yorkshire, the first stage of 3 × 660 MW sets was completed in 1974 and there is provision, pending Government decision, to double this figure to 3,960 MW. Work has started in the 3,300 MW oil fired installation on the Isle of Grain, Kent.

The largest hydro-electric plant in the United Kingdom is the North of Scotland Hydro-electricity Board's Power Station at Loch Sloy, Central. The installed capacity of this station is 130,450 kW or 175,000 h.p. The Ben Cruachan Pumped Storage Scheme was opened on 15 Oct. 1965 at Loch Awe, Argyll, Scotland. It has a capacity of 400,000 kW and cost £24,000,000. The 1,500–1,800 MW underground pumped storage scheme at Dinorwic, Gwynedd is the largest being built in Europe.

Biggest black-out The greatest power failure in history struck seven north-eastern U.S. States and Ontario, Canada, on 9–10 Nov. 1965. About 30,000,000 people in 80,000 miles[2] *207 200 km[2]* were plunged into darkness. Only two were killed. In New York City the power failed at 5.27 p.m. Supplies were eventually restored by 2 a.m. in Brooklyn, 4.20 a.m. in Queens, 6.58 a.m. in Manhattan and 7 a.m. in the Bronx.

ATOMIC POWER

Earliest The world's first atomic pile was built in a disused squash court at Stagg Field, University of Chicago, Illinois, U.S.A. It went "critical" at 3.25 p.m. on 2 Dec. 1942.

Largest Station The world's largest atomic power station is the Ontario Hydro's Pickering station which in 1973 attained full output of 2,160 Mw.

Largest Reactor The largest single atomic reactor in the world is the 1,098 MW Browns Ferry Unit 1 General Electric boiling water type reactor located on the Wheeler Reservoir, near Decatar, Alabama which became operative in 1973. The Grand Gulf Nuclear Station at Port Gibson, Mississippi will have a capacity of 1,290 MW in 1979.

TIDAL POWER STATION

The world's first major tidal power station is the *Usine marèmotrice de la Rance*, officially opened on 26 Nov. 1966 at the Rance estuary in the Golfe de St. Malo, Brittany, France. It was built in five years at a cost of 420,000,000 francs (*£34,685,000*), and has a net annual output of 544,000,000 kWh. The 880 yd *804 m* barrage contains 24 turbo alternators. This harnessing of the tides has imperceptibly slowed the Earth's rate of revolution. The $1,000 million (*£416 million*) Passamaquoddy project for the Bay of Fundy in Maine, U.S.A., and New Brunswick, Canada, is not expected to be operative before 1978.

Geo-Thermal The world's longest geo-thermal power plant is the Pacific Gas and Electric Co 396,000 kW (1973) plant at Big Geysers Resort, Sonoma County, California.

LARGEST BOILER

The largest boilers ever designed are those ordered in the United States from The Babcock & Wilcox Company (U.S.A.) with a capacity of 1,330 MW so involving the evaporation of 9,330,000 lb. *4 232 000 kg* of steam per hour. The largest boilers now being installed in the United Kingdom are the three 660 MW units for the Drax Power Station (see above) designed and constructed by Babcock & Wilcox Ltd.

LARGEST GENERATOR

Generators in the 2,000,000 kW (or 2,000 Mw) range are now in the planning stages both in the U.K. and the U.S.A. The largest under construction is one of 1,300 Mw by the Brown Boveri Co. of Switzerland for the Tennessee Valley Authority.

LARGEST TURBINES

The largest turbines under construction are those rated at 820,000 h.p. with an overload capacity of 1,000,000 h.p., 32 ft *9,7 m* in diameter with a 401-ton *407 tonnes* runner and a 312½ ton *317,5 tonnes* shaft for the Grand Coulee "Third Powerplant" (see above).

GAS TURBINE

The largest gas turbine in the world is that installed at the Krasnodar thermal power station in August 1969 with a capacity of 100,000 kW. It was built in Leningrad, U.S.S.R.

LARGEST PUMP TURBINE

The world's largest integral reversible pump-turbine is that made by Allis-Chalmers for the $50,000,000

Taum Sauk installation of the Union Electric Co. in St. Louis, Missouri, U.S.A. It has a rating of 240,000 h.p. as a turbine and a capacity of 1,100,000 gallons *5 000 559 litres*/min as a pump. The Tehachapi Pumping Plant, California (1972) pumps 18,300,000 gal/min *83,2 million litres/min* over 1,700 ft *518 m* up.

LARGEST GAS WORKS

The flow of natural gas from the North Sea is diminishing the manufacture of gas by the carbonisation of coal and the re-forming process using petroleum derivatives. Britain's largest ever gasworks 300 acres *120 ha* were at Beckton, Essex. Currently the most productive gasworks are at the oil re-forming plant at Greenwich, Greater London, with an output of 420.5 million ft³ *11 907 298 m³* per day.

Oldest
Steam
Engine The oldest steam engine in working order is the 1812 Boulton & Watt 26 h.p. 42 in bore beam engine on the Kennet & Avon Canal at Great Bedwyn, Wiltshire. It was restored by the Crofton Society in 1971.

6. ENGINEERING

OLDEST MACHINERY

World The earliest machinery still in use is the *dâlu*—a water raising instrument known to have been in use in the Sumerian civilization which originated *c.* 3500 B.C. in Lower Iraq.

Britain The oldest piece of machinery (excluding clocks) operating in the United Kingdom is the snuff mill driven by a water wheel at Messrs. Wilson & Co.'s Sharrow Mill in Sheffield, South Yorkshire. It is known to have been operating in 1797 and more probably since 1730.

LARGEST PRESS

The world's two most powerful production machines are forging presses in the U.S.A. The Loewy closed-die forging press, in a plant leased from the U.S. Air Force by the Wyman-Gordon Company at North Grafton, Massachusetts, U.S.A. weighs 9,469 tons *9 620 tonnes* and stands 114 ft 2 in *34,79 m* high, of which 66 ft *20,1 m* is sunk below the operating floor. It has a rated capacity of 44,600 tons *45 315 tonnes*, and went into operation in October 1955. The other similar press is at the plant of the Aluminium Company of America at Cleveland, Ohio. There has been a report of a press in the U.S.S.R. with a capacity of 75 000 tonnes *73,800 tons* at Novo Kramatorsk. The most powerful press in Great Britain is the closed-die forging and extruding press installed in 1967 at the Cameron Iron Works, Livingston, Lothians. The press is 92 ft *28 m* tall (27 ft *[8,2 m]* below ground) and exerts a force of 30,000 tons *30 481 tonnes*.

Probably 240 years old—Britain's oldest machinery at Shorrow snuff-grinding mill in Sheffield, South Yorkshire

LATHE

The world's largest lathe is the 72 ft *21,9 m* long 385 ton *391 tonnes* giant lathe built by the Dortmunder Rheinstahl firm of Wagner in 1962. The face plate is 15 ft *4,5 m* in diameter and can exert a torque of 289,000 ft/lb. *39 955 m/kg f* when handling objects weighing up to 200 tons *203 tonnes*.

EXCAVATOR

The world's largest excavator is the 33,400 h.p. *33 863 c.v.* Marion 6360 excavator, weighing 12,500 tons *12 700 tonnes*. This vast machine can grab 241 tons *244 tonnes* in a single bite in a bucket of 85 yds³ *65 m³* capacity.

DRAGLINE

World The Ural Engineering Works at Ordzhonikdze, U.S.S.R., completed in March 1962, has a dragline known as the ES-25(100) with a boom of 100 m *328 ft* and a bucket with a capacity of 31.5 yds³ *24 m³*. The world's largest walking dragline is the Bucyrus-Erie 4250W with an all-up weight of 12,000 tons *12 192 tonnes* and a bucket capacity of 220 yds³ *168 m³* on a 310 ft *94,4 m* boom. This machine, the world's largest mobile land machine is now operating on the Central Ohio Coal Company's Muskingum site in Ohio, U.S.A.

United
Kingdom The largest dragline excavator in Britain is "Big Geordie", the Bucyrus-Erie 1550W 6250 gross h.p., weighing 3,000 tons *3 048 tonnes* with a forward mast 160 ft *48,7 m* high. On open-cast coal workings at Widdrington, Northumberland in February 1970, it proved able to strip 100 tons *101 tonnes* of overburden in 65 secs with its 65 yard³ *49,7 m³* bucket on a 265 ft *80,7 m* boom. It is operated by Derek Crouch (Contractors) Ltd. of Peterborough, Cambridgeshire.

BLAST FURNACE

The world's largest blast furnace is one with an inner volume of 5000 m³ *176,570 ft³* at the Krivoi Rog Iron and Steel Works, Ukraine, U.S.S.R. completed in December 1974 with an annual capacity of 4,000,000 tons/*tonnes* per annum.

Largest
forging The largest forging on record is one 53 ft *16,1 m* long weighing 396,000 lb. (176.79 tons *[179,62 tonnes]*) forged by Bethlehem Steel for the Tennessee Valley Authority nuclear power plant at Brown Ferry Alabama, U.S.A. in Nov. 1969.

LONGEST PIPELINES

Oil The longest crude oil pipeline in the world is the Interprovincial Pipe Line Company's installation from Edmonton, Alberta, to Buffalo, New York State, U.S.A., a distance of 1,775 miles *2 856 km*. Along the length of the pipe 13 pumping stations maintain a flow of 6,900,000 gal *31 367 145 litres* of oil per day. In Britain the longest commercial oil pipeline, 242 miles *389 km* from the Thames to the Mersey, is owned by Chevron, Mobil, Petrofina, Shell-Mex and B.P., and Texaco. It was opened on 19 March 1969 at a cost of £8½ million.

The eventual length of the Trans-Siberian Pipeline will be 2,319 miles *3 732 km*, running from Tuimazy through Omsk and Novosibirsk to Irkutsk. The first 30 mile *48 km* section was opened in July 1957.

The world's most expensive pipeline is the Alaska pipeline running 798 miles *1 284 km* Prudhoe Bay to Valdez. By completion in 1977 it will have cost at least $6,000 million (£2,600 million).

Natural gas The longest natural gas pipeline in the world is the TransCanada Pipeline which by 1974 had 5,654 miles *9 099 km* of pipe up to 42 in *106,6 cm* in diameter.

Courtesy of the Ministry of Development, Venezuela

The world's highest ropeway ascending to the summit of Venezuela's 15,629 ft *4 763 m* Pico Espejo

Oil Tank The largest oil tank ever constructed is the Million
Largest Barrel Ekofisk Oil Tank completed in Norway in 1973 and implanted in the North Sea measuring 92 × 92 82 m high (*301.8 ft square and 269 ft high*) and containing 8 000 metric tons *7,873 tons* of steel and 202,000 metric tons *198 809 tons* of concrete. The capacity of 160 000 m³ *209,272 yds³* is equivalent to 1.42 times the amount of oil which escaped from the *Torrey Canyon.*

Largest The world's largest catalyst cracker is the American Oil
Cat Cracker Company's installation at the Texas City Refinery, Texas, U.S.A., with a capacity of 3,322,000 gal *15 101 689 litres* per day.

Largest nut The largest nuts ever made weigh 29.5 cwt. (1.48 tons [*1,50 tonnes*]) each and have an outside diameter of 43½ in *110,5 cm* and a 26 in *66 cm* thread. Known as the Pilgrim Nuts, they are manufactured by Doncaster Moorside Ltd. of Oldham, Greater Manchester, for securing propellers.

Largest The world's largest valve is the 14 ft *4,26 m* diameter
Valve Pratt-Triton XL butterfly valve made in Aurora, Illinois, U.S.A. for water and power systems.

Largest The largest padlock manufacture is ERA No. 1212.
padlock Close shackle 6 lever lock produced by J. E. Reynolds of Willenhall, West Midlands. It weighs 100 lb. *45 kg 30.*

TRANSFORMER

The world's largest single phase transformers are rated at 1,500,000 kVa of which 8 are in service with the American Electric Power Service Corporation. Of these five stepdown from 765 to 345 kV. Britain's largest transformers are those rated at 1,000,000 kVa 400/275 kV built by Hackbridge & Hewittic Co. Ltd., Walton-on-Thames, Surrey first commissioned for the CEGB in Oct 1968.

HIGHEST ROPEWAY OR TELEPHERIQUE

World The highest and longest aerial ropeway in the world is the Teleférico Mérida (Mérida téléphérique) in Venezuela, from Mérida City (5,379 ft [*1 639,5 m*]) to the summit of Pico Espejo (15,629 ft [*4 763,7 m*]), a rise of 10,250 ft *3 124 m.* The ropeway is in four sections, involving 3 car changes in the 8 mile ascent in one hour. The fourth span is 10,070 ft *3 069 m* in length. The two cars work on the pendulum system—the carrier rope is locked and the cars are hauled by means of three pull ropes powered by a 230 h.p. *233 c.v.* motor. They have a maximum capacity of 45 persons and travel at 32 ft *9,7 m* per sec (21.8 m.p.h. [*35,08 km/h*]). The longest single span ropeway is the 13,500 ft *4 114 m* long span from The Coachella Valley to Mt. San Jacinto (10,821 ft [*3 298 m*]), California U.S.A., inaugurated on 12 Sept. 1963.

Great Britain's longest cabin lift is that at Llandudno,
Britain Gwynedd, opened in June 1969. It has 42 cabins with a capacity of 1,000 people per hour and is 5,320 ft *1 621 m* in length.

PASSENGER LIFTS

Fastest The fastest domestic passenger lifts in the world are
World the express lifts to the 103rd floor or 1,340 ft *408 m* level in the 110 storey, Sears Tower in Chicago, Illinois, U.S.A. They operate at a speed of 1,800 ft per min. 20.45 m.p.h. *32,91 km/h.* Much higher speeds are achieved in the winding cages of mine shafts. A hoisting shaft 6,800 ft *2 072 m* deep, owned by Western Deep Levels Ltd. in South Africa, winds at speeds of up to 40.9 m.p.h. *65,8 km/h* (3,595 ft [*1 095 m*] per min).

United The longest lift in the United Kingdom is one 930 ft
Kingdom long inside the B.B.C. T.V. tower at Bilsdale, West Moor, North Yorkshire, built by J. L. Eve Construction Co. Ltd. It runs at 130 ft *39,6 m*/min. The longest fast lifts are the two 15-passenger cars in the Post Office Tower, Maple Street, London W1 which travel 540 ft *164 m* up at up to 1,000 ft *304 m*/min.

LONGEST ESCALATORS

The term was registered in the U.S. on 28 May 1900 but the earliest "Inclined Elevator" was installed by Jesse W. Reno on the pier at Coney Island, New York in 1896. The first installation in Britain was at Harrods, Knightsbridge, London in Nov. 1898. The escalators on the Leningrad Underground, U.S.S.R. have a vertical rise of 195 ft *59,4 m.* The longest escalators in Britain are the four in the Tyne Tunnel, Tyne and Wear installed in 1968. They measure 192 ft 8 in *58,7 m* between combs with a vertical lift of 85 ft *25,9 m* and a step speed of up to 1.7 m.p.h. *2,7 km/h.*

The world's longest "moving sidewalks" are those installed in 1970 in the Neue Messe Centre, Dusseldorf, West Germany measure 225 m *738 ft* between comb plates. The longest in Great Britain is the 375 ft *114,3 m* long Dunlop Starglide at London Airport Terminal 3 installed in March–May 1970.

FASTEST PRINTER

The world's fastest printer is the Radiation Inc. electro-sensitive system at the Lawrence Radiation Laboratory, Livermore, California. High speed recording of up to 30,000 lines each containing 120 alphanumeric characters per minute is attained by controlling electronic pulses through chemically impregnated recording paper which is rapidly moving under closely spaced fixed styli. It can thus print the wordage of the whole Bible (773,692 words) in 65 sec—3,333 times as fast as the world's fastest typist.

TRANSMISSION LINES

Longest The longest span between pylons of any power line in the world is that across the Sogne Fjord, Norway, between Rabnaberg and Flatlberg. Erected in 1955

by the Whitecross Co. Ltd. of Warrington, Cheshire, England as part of the high-tension power cable from Refsdal power station at Vik, it has a span of 16,040 ft *4 888 m* and a weight of 12 tons/*tonnes*. In 1967 two further high tensile steel/aluminium lines 16,006 ft *4 878 m* long, and weighing 33 tons *33,5 tonnes*, manufactured by Whitecross and B.I.C.C. (see below) were erected here. The longest in Britain are the 5,310 ft *1 618 m* lines built by J. L. Eve Co. across the Severn with main towers each 488 ft *148 m* high.

Highest The world's highest are those across the Straits of Messina, with towers of 675 ft *205 m* (Sicily side) and 735 ft *224 m* (Calabria) and 11,900 ft *3 627 m* apart. The highest lines in Britain are those made by British Insulated Callender's Cables Ltd. at West Thurrock, Essex, which cross the Thames estuary suspended from 630 ft *192 m* tall towers at a minimum height of 250 ft *76 m*, with a 130 ton *132 tonnes* breaking load. They are 4,500 ft *1 371 m* in length.

Highest voltages The highest voltages now carried are 800,000 volts from Volgograd to the Donbas basin, U.S.S.R. The Swedish A.S.E.A. Company has been experimenting with possible 1,500,000 volt A.C./D.C. transmission lines.

LONGEST CONVEYOR BELT
The world's longest single flight conveyor belt is one of 9 miles *14 km* installed near Uniontown, Kentucky, U.S.A. by Cable Belt Ltd. of Camberley, Surrey. It has a weekly capacity of 140,000 short tons *142 247 tonnes* of coal on a 42 in *1,06 m* wide 800 ft *243 m*/min belt and forms part of a 12½ mile *20 km* long system. The longest installation in Great Britain is also by Cable Belt Ltd. and of 5½ miles *8,9 km* underground at Longannet Power Station, Fife, Scotland. The world's longest multi-flight conveyor is one of 100 km *62 miles* between the phosphate mine near Bucraa and the port of El Aaiun, Spanish Sahara built by Krupps and completed in 1972. It has 11 flights of between 9 and 11 km *5.6–6.8 miles* and is driven at 4,5 m/sec *10.06 m.p.h.*

LONGEST WIRE ROPE
The longest wire rope ever spun in one piece was one measuring 46.653 ft *14 219 m* (8.83 miles) long and 3⅛ in *7,93 cm* in circumference, with a weight of 28½ tons *28,9 tonnes*, manufactured by British Ropes Ltd. of Doncaster, South Yorkshire. The heaviest reported is one 7 inches *17,8 cm* in circumference 3.94 miles long weighing 81 tons made by Martin–Black & Co. (Wire Ropes) Ltd. at Coatbridge, Strathclyde in 1973.

CLOCKS
Oldest The earliest mechanical clock, that is one with an escapement, was completed in China in A.D. 725 by I Hsing and Liang Ling-tsan.

The oldest surviving working clock in the world is the faceless clock dating from 1386, or possibly earlier, at Salisbury Cathedral, Wiltshire, which was restored in 1956 having struck the hours for 498 years and ticked more than 500 million times. Earlier dates, ranging back to *c.* 1335, have been attributed to the weight-driven clock in Wells Cathedral, Somerset, but only the iron frame is original. A model of Giovanni de Dondi's heptagonal astronomical clock of 1348–64 was completed in 1962.

Largest World The world's most massive clock is the Astronomical Clock in Beauvais Cathedral, France, constructed between 1865 and 1868. It contains 90,000 parts and measures 40 ft *12,1 m* high, 20 ft *6,09 m* wide and 9 ft *2,7 m* deep. The Su Sung clock, built in China at K'aifeng in 1088–92, had a 20-ton *20,3 tonnes* bronze armillary sphere for 1½ tons *1,52 tonnes* of water. It was removed to Peking in 1126 and was last known to be working in its 40 ft *12,1 m* high tower in 1136.

United Kingdom The largest clock in the United Kingdom is that on the Royal Liver Building (built 1908–11) with a dial 25 ft *7,62 m* in diameter with the 4 minute hands each 14 ft *4,26 m* long. The mechanism and dials weigh 22 tons and is 220 ft *67 m* above street level.

Public clocks The largest four-faced clock in the world is that on the building of the Allen-Bradley Company of Milwaukee, Wisconsin, U.S.A. Each face has a diameter of 40 ft 3½ in *12,28 m* with a minute hand 20 ft *6,09 m* in overall length. The tallest four-faced clock in the world is that of the Williamsburgh Savings Bank in Brooklyn, New York City, N.Y., U.S.A. It is 430 ft *131 m* above street level.

Longest stoppage The longest stoppage of Big Ben, Palace of West-minster, London since the first tick on 31 May 1859 has been 8 hours in 1900 due to a snow-storm. In 1945 a host of starlings slowed the minute hand by 5 min.

Most accurate The most accurate and complicated clockwork in the world is the Olsen clock, installed in the Copenhagen Town Hall, Denmark. The clock, which has more than 14,000 units, took 10 years to make and the mechanism of the clock functions in 570,000 different ways. The celestial pole motion of the clock will take 25,753 years to complete a full circle and is the slowest moving designed mechanism in the world. The clock is accurate to 0.5 of a second in 300 years.

Most expensive The highest auction price for any portable English clock is £36,000 for the quarter-repeating ebony bracket clock made by George Graham *c.* 1700, sold at the salerooms of Sotheby & Co., London, to a London dealer on 18 March 1974.

The world's greatest clockwork masterpiece, the Olsen clock in Copenhagen—the only clock to allow for the 25,753 year cycle of celestial pole motion of the Earth

Nordisk Pressefoto

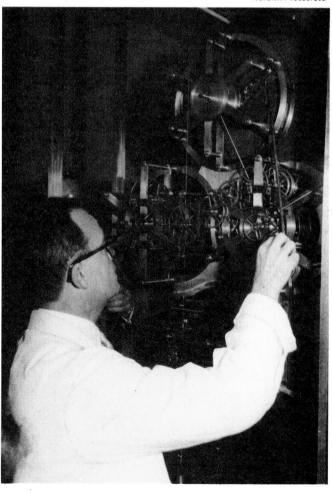

The world's smallest watch weighing less than ¼ oz or *7 grammes* (see below)

WATCHES

Oldest The oldest watch (portable clock-work time-keeper) is one made of iron by Peter Henlein (or Hele) in Nürnberg (Nuremberg), Bavaria, Germany, in *c.* 1504 and now in the Memorial Hall, Philadelphia, Pennsylvania, U.S.A. The earliest wrist watches were those of Jacquet-Droz and Leschot of Geneva, Switzerland, dating from 1790.

Most expensive Excluding watches with jewelled cases, the most expensive standard men's pocket watch is the Swiss *Grande Complication* by Audemars-Piguet which retails for £19,500. On 1 June 1964, a record £27,500 was paid for the Duke of Wellington's watch made in Paris in 1807 by Abraham Louis Bréguet, at the salerooms of Sotheby & Co., London, by the dealers Messrs. Ronald Lee for a Portuguese client.

Smallest The smallest watches in the world are produced by Jaeger Le Coultre of Switzerland. Equipped with a 15-jewelled movement they measure just over half-an-inch *1,2 cm* long and three-sixteenths of an in *0,476 cm* in width. The movement, with its case, weighs under a quarter of an oz. *7 gr.*

TIME MEASURER

Most accurate World The most accurate time-keeping devices are the twin atomic hydrogen masers installed in 1964 in the U.S. Naval Research Laboratory, Washington, D.C. They are based on the frequency of the hydrogen atom's transition period of 1,420,450,751,694 cycles/sec. This enables an accuracy to within one sec/1,700,000 years.

United Kingdom The most accurate measurer in the United Kingdom is the 14 ft *4,2 m* long rubidium resonance Standard Atomic Clock at the National Physical Laboratory, Teddington, Richmond upon Thames, Greater London, devised by Dr. Louis Essen, O.B.E. and Mr. J. V. L. Parry and completed in 1962. It is accurate to within one second in 1,000 years.

RADAR INSTALLATIONS

Largest The largest of the three installations in the U.S. Ballistic Missile Early Warning System (B.M.E.W.S.) is that near Thule, in Greenland, 931 miles *1 498 km* from the North Pole, completed in 1960 at a cost of $500,000,000 (*now £208.3 million*). Its sister stations are one at Cape Clear, Alaska, U.S.A., completed in 1961, and a $115,000,000 (*now £47.9 million*) installation at Fylingdales Moor, North Yorkshire, completed in June 1963. The largest scientific radar installation is the 21 acre *84 000 m²* ground array at Jicamarca, Peru.

Smallest tubing The smallest tubing in the world is made by Accles and Pollock, Ltd. of Warley, West Midlands. It is of pure nickel with an outside diameter of 0.0005 of an in and was announced on 9 Sept. 1963. The average human hair measures from 0.002 to 0.003 of an inch *0,05–0,075 mm* diameter. The tubing, which is stainless, can be used for the artificial insemination of bees and for the medical process of "feeding" nerves, and weighs only 5 oz. *141 gr* per 100 miles *160 km.*

MOST POWERFUL CRANE

World The crane with the world's greatest lifting capacity is that mounted on the craneship *Thor* (ex-super tanker *Veedol*) which lifted a 1,900 ton *1 930 tonne* deck module over its stern in the Forties Field on 14–15 Oct. 1974. *Thor* completed in October 1973 is owned by the Heerema Group, the Netherlands offshore lifting contractors and was built by Boele Bolnef, Netherlands.

Tallest Mobile The tallest mobile crane in the world is the 810 tonnes Rosenkranz K10001 with a lifting capacity of 1 000 tonnes *948 tons*, a combined boom and jib height of 202 m *663 ft*. It is carried on 10 trucks each limited to 75 ft 8 in *23,06 m* and an axle weight of 118 tonnes *116 tons*. It can lift 30 tonnes *29.5 tons* to a height of 160 m *525 ft.*

Greatest Lift The heaviest lifting operation in engineering history was of the 902 ft *274,9 m* long centre span of the Fremont Bridge over the Willamette River, Portland Oregon on 13–15 Mar. 1973. The $1 million hydraulic jacking system raised the 6,000 short tons *5 443 tonne* section at 4 ft *1,21 m* per hour in 42 hours.

COMPUTERS

The modern computer was made possible by the invention of the point-contact transistor by John Bardeen and Walter Brattain announced in July 1948, and the junction transistor by R. L. Wallace, Morgan Sparks and Dr. William Shockley in early 1951.

Most powerful World The world's most powerful computer is the Control Data Corporation CDC 7600 first delivered in January 1969. It can perform 36 million operations in one second and has an access time of 27.5 nano-sec. It has two internal memory cores of 655,360 and 5,242,880 characters (6 bits per character) supplemented by a Model 817 disc file of 800 million characters. The cost is up to $15 million (£6¼ *million*) depending on peripherals. The most capacious storage device is the Ampex Terabit Memory which can store 2.88×10^{12} bits. The Burroughs Corporation $30 million Illiac IV at the NASA Ames Research Center, Moffett Field, California comprises 64 separate computing elements in tandem.

United Kingdom The computer with the largest memory built in the United Kingdom is the International Business Machines' I.B.M. System/370 Model 168 MP which is a multiprocessing computer with 16,777,216 bytes of main storage. A 'byte' is a unit of storage comprising 8 'bits' collectively equivalent to one alphabetic letter or two numerals. This machine is produced at Havant, Hampshire. ICL has proposed a computer with 576 separate streams which would be 50 times faster than ILLIAC IV.

Oldest The oldest operative computer in Britain and probably the world is Witch built at Harwell in 1949–50 and last in service at the Polytechnic, Wolverhampton whence it was transferred in 1973 to the Museum of Science and Industry, Birmingham in full operational condition. It has 827 "Dekatron" cathode tubes.

Fastest Switch An electronic device that can be switched in less than 10 billionth of a second (10^{-11} sec) was announced on 18 Jan. 1973. It utilizes the prediction of the English physicist Brian Josephson (b. 1940) in 1962 that ultra-thin insulators can be made superconductive.

9

THE BUSINESS WORLD

1. COMMERCE

The $(US) has in this chapter been converted at a fixed mean rate of 2.30 to the £ Sterling.

OLDEST INDUSTRY

Agriculture is often described as "the oldest industry in the world", whereas in fact there is no evidence that it was practised before *c.* 11,000 B.C. The oldest known industry is flint knapping, involving the production of chopping tools and hand axes, dating from about 1,750,000 years ago. Salt panning is of comparable antiquity.

OLDEST COMPANY

World The oldest company in the world is the Faversham Oyster Fishery Co., referred to in the Faversham Oyster Fishing Act 1930, as existing "from time immemorial", *i.e.* from before 1189.

158

Britain The Royal Mint has origins going back to A.D. 287. The Whitechapel Bell Foundry of Whitechapel Road, London, E.1, has been in business since 1570. The retail business in Britain with the oldest history is the Cambridge bookshop, which, though under various ownership, has traded from the site of 1 Trinity Street since 1581 and since 1907 under its present title Bowes & Bowes. R. Durtnell & Sons, builders, of Brasted, Kent, has been run by the same family since 1591. The first bill of adventure signed by the English East India Co., was dated 21 March 1601.

GREATEST ASSETS

World The business with the greatest amount in physical assets is the Bell System, which comprises the American Telephone and Telegraph Company, with headquarters at 195 Broadway, New York City, N.Y., U.S.A., and its subsidiaries. The group's total assets on the consolidated balance sheet at 31 Dec. 1973 were valued at $74,047,288,000 (£32,194 million). The plant involved included 117.7 million telephones. The number of employees is approximately 1 million. A total of 20,109 shareholders attended the Annual Meeting in April 1961, thereby setting a world record.

The first company to have assets in excess of $1 billion was the United States Steel Corporation with $1,400 million (*then £287.73 million*) at the time of its creation by merger in 1900.

United Kingdom The enterprise in the United Kingdom, excluding banks, with the greatest capital employed is the Electricity Council and the Electricity Boards in England and Wales with £5,456,100,000 in 1974. This ranks eighth in the western world.

The British private enterprise company with the greatest assets employed is Imperial Chemical Industries Ltd., with £2,412 million, as at 31 Dec. 1974. Its staff and payroll averaged 201,000 during the year. The company, which has 458 U.K. and overseas subsidiaries, was formed on 7 Dec. 1926 by the merger of four concerns—British Dyestuffs Corporation Ltd.; Brunner, Mond & Co. Ltd.; Nobel Industries Ltd. and United Alkali Co. Ltd. The first chairman was Sir Alfred Moritz Mond (1868–1930), later the 1st Lord Melchett.

The net assets of The "Shell" Transport and Trading Company, Ltd., at 31 Dec. 1974 were £2,166,900,000 comprising mainly its 40% share in the net assets of the Royal Dutch/Shell Group of Companies which stood at £5,336 million. Group companies employ 164,000. "Shell" Transport was formed in 1897 by Marcus Samuel (1853–1927), later the 1st Viscount Bearsted.

Greatest sales The first company to surpass the $1 billion (U.S.) mark in annual sales was the United States Steel Corporation in 1917. Now there are 137 corporations with sales exceeding £1,000 million (82 U.S., 42 European, 11 Japanese and 2 Canadian. The list is headed by Exxon of New York with $42,061,336,000 (*£18,287 million*) in 1974.

Greatest profit and loss The greatest net profit ever made by an industrial company in a year is $3,142 million (*£1,366 million*) by Exxon in 1974. The greatest loss ever sustained by a commercial concern in a year is $431.2 million (*£179.6 million*) by Penn Central Transportation Co. in 1970—a rate of $13.67 (*then £5.69*) per second. The top gross profits in the United Kingdom in 1974 were British Petroleum with £2,271.9 million which, after all charges, including £1,747.8 million in overseas tax, resulted in a net profit of £487.4 million. The biggest loss maker in *The Times* Top 1,000 British companies in 1973–74 was Roche Products with £1,824,000.

Most efficient The United Kingdom major company with the highest return on capital in *The Times* 1,000 List (1974–75) is Fluor, the constructional engineers, which showed a pre-tax profit of £972,000 or 123.4% on a capital employed.

Biggest work force The greatest payroll of any single civilian organisation in the world is that of the U.S.S.R. National Railway system with a total work force of 1,996,600. The biggest employer in the United Kingdom is the Post Office with 431,506 employees on 1 Jan. 1975.

Largest Take-Over The largest take-over in commercial history has been the bid of £438,000,000 by Grand Metropolitan Hotels Ltd., for the brewers Watney Mann on 17 June 1972. The value of the consideration was £378.2 million.

Largest Merger The largest merger ever mooted in British business was that of the Hill Samuel Group (£768 million assets) and Slater, Walker Securities (£469 million) in April 1973 with combined assets of £1,237 million. This plan was called off on 19 June 1973.

Biggest Write Off The largest reduction of assets in corporate history was the $800 million *£347 million* write off of Tristar aircraft development costs announced on 23 Nov. 1974.

ADVERTISING AGENTS

The largest international advertising agency in the world is J. Walter Thompson Co., which in 1974 had total world wide billings of $888.3 million (*£386.2 million*). A higher figure of $907 million in 1974 was reported for Dentsu of Japan but is not believed to be comparable since revenues are not wholly derived from agency work.

Biggest advertiser The world's biggest advertiser is Sears Roebuck with $447 million (*£194 million*) in 1974 including $125 million (*£54.3 million*) for its catalogue.

Aircraft manu-facturer The world's largest aircraft manufacturer is the Boeing Company of Seattle, Washington, U.S.A. The corporation's sales totalled $3,730,667,000 (*£1,622 million*) in 1974 and it had 74,400 employees and assets valued at $1,746,314,000 (*£759 million*) at 31 Dec. 1974. Cessna Aircraft Company of Wichita, Kansas, U.S.A., produced 7,187 civil aircraft (40 models) in the year 1974, with total sales of $416 million (*£180.8 million*). The company has produced more than 122,000 aircraft since Clyde's Cessna's first was built in 1911. Their record year was 1965–66 with 7,922 aircraft completed.

AIRLINES

Largest The largest airline in the world is the U.S.S.R. State airline "Aeroflot", so named since 1932. This was instituted on 9 Feb. 1923, with the title of Civil Air Fleet of the Council of Ministers of the U.S.S.R., abbreviated to "Dobrolet". It operates 1,300 aircraft over about 435,000 miles *700 000 km* of routes, employs 400,000 people and carried 90 million passengers in 1974 to 67 countries. The commercial airline carrying the greatest number of passengers in 1974 was United Airlines of Chicago, Illinois, U.S.A. (formed 1931) with 31,510,000 passengers. The company had 49,650 employees and a fleet of 376 jet planes. In March 1975 British Airways were operating a fleet of 226 aircraft, with 20 on order. Staff employed on airline activities totalled 54,437 and nearly 14 million passengers were carried in the year ended 31 March 1975 on a record 461,078 miles *742 033 km* of unduplicated routes.

The world's largest manufacturer of aircraft—Jumbo jets in a giant Boeing hanger designed by the Austin Co. of Cleveland, Ohio

The world's largest cycle factory— Raleigh Industries of Nottingham, England

Keystone

Oldest The oldest existing commercial airline is Koninklijke-Luchtvaart-Maatschappij N.V. (KLM) of the Netherlands, which opened its first scheduled service (Amsterdam-London) on 17 May 1920, having been established in 1919. One of the original constituents of B.O.A.C., Aircraft Transport and Travel Ltd., was founded in 1918 and merged into Imperial Airways in 1924. Delag (Deutsche Luftschiffahrt A.G.) was founded at Frankfurt am Main on 16 Nov. 1909 and started a scheduled airship service in June 1910.

Aluminium The world's largest producer of aluminium is Alcan
producer Aluminium Limited, of Montreal, Quebec, Canada. With its affiliated companies, the company had an output of 2,174,000 short tons *1 972 240 tonnes* and record consolidated revenues of U.S. $2,426,759,000 (*£1,055 million*) in 1974. The company's principal subsidiary, the Aluminum Company of Canada Ltd., owns the largest aluminium smelter in the western world, at Arvida, Quebec, with a capacity of 454,000 short tons *411 866 tonnes* per annum.

Art The largest and oldest firm of art auctioneers in the
auctioneer- world is Sotheby Parke-Bernet of London and New
ing York, founded in 1744. The turnover in 1973–74 was $216,762,480 (*£94.2 million*). The highest total of any single day's sale has been £3,996,933 (*Sw Fr 29.9 million*) for jewels by Christie's of London in Hotel Richemond, Geneva on 21 Nov. 1973.

Largest The largest barbering establishment in the world is
Barbers Norris of Houston, 3200 Audley, Houston, Texas, U.S.A. which employs 60 barbers.

Bicycle The 64-acre *25,9 ha* plant of Raleigh Industries Ltd. at
factory Nottingham is the largest factory in the world producing complete bicycles, components, wheeled toys and prams. The company employs 10,000 and in 1975 has targets to make 850,000 wheeled toys and more than 2 million bicycles.

Book shop The world's largest book shop is that of W. & G. Foyle Ltd., City of Westminster, Greater London. First established in 1904 in a small shop in Islington, the company is now at 119–125 Charing Cross Road. The area on one site is 75,825 ft² *7 044 m²*. The largest single display of books in one room in the world is in the Norrington Room at Blackwell's Bookshop, Broad Street, Oxford. This subterranean adjunct was opened on 16 June 1966 and contains 160,000 volumes on 2½ miles *4 km* of shelving in 10,000 ft² *929 m²* of selling space.

BREWER

Oldest The oldest brewery in the world is the Weihenstephan Brewery, Freising, near Munich, West Germany, founded in A.D. 1040.

Largest The largest single brewer in the world is Anheuser-
World Busch, Inc. in St. Louis, Missouri, U.S.A. in 1973 the company sold 34,097,000 U.S. barrels, equivalent to 7,040 million Imperial pints, the greatest annual volume ever produced by a brewing company. The company's St. Louis plant covers 95 acres *38,4 ha* and has a capacity of 10,500,000 U.S. barrels *2,168 million Imperial pints*. The largest brewery on a single site is Adolph Coors Co. of Golden, Colorado, U.S.A. which is scheduled to produce 13,250,000 U.S. barrels *2,735 million Imperial pints* in 1975.

Europe The largest brewery in Europe is the Guinness Brewery at St. James's Gate, Dublin, Ireland, which extends over 60.44 acres *24,46 ha*. The business was founded in 1759.

United The largest brewing company in the United Kingdom
Kingdom based on its 9,014 public houses, 1,038 off-licenses and 87 hotels, is Bass Charrington Ltd. The company has net assets of £518,300,000, 63,226 employees (including bar-staff) and controls 13 breweries. Their sales figure for the year ending 30 Sept. 1974 was £572,100,000.

160

Greatest The largest exporter of beer, ale and stout in the
exports world is Arthur Guinness, Son & Co. Ltd., of Dublin,
Ireland. Exports of Guinness from the Republic of
Ireland in the 52 weeks ending 15 Mar. 1975 were
1,040,100 bulk barrels (bulk barrel = 36 Imperial
gallons), which is equivalent to 1,645,873 half pint
glasses *1,558,765 thirty centilitre glasses* per day.

Brickworks The largest brickworks in the world is the London
Brick Company plant at Stewartby, Bedfordshire. The
works, established in 1898, now cover 221 acres *90 ha*
and produce 17,000,000 bricks and brick equivalent
every week.

Building The largest construction company in the United King-
contractors dom is George Wimpey & Co. Ltd. (founded 1880),
of London, who undertake building, civil, mechanical,
electrical and chemical engineering work. With gross
assets of £224,998,021 and 26,000 employees, the turnover of work was £380,000,000 in 35 countries in 1974.

Building The biggest building society in the world is the Halifax
societies Building Society of Halifax, West Yorkshire. It was
established in 1853 and has total assets exceeding
£3,700,000,000. It has 6,221 employees and 300
branches and over 1,000 agencies. The oldest building
society in the world is the Chelmsford and Essex
Society, established in July 1845.

Chemist The largest chain of chemist shops in the world is
shop chain Boots The Chemists, which has 1,322 retail branches.
The firm was founded by Jesse Boot (b. Nottingham,
1850), later the 1st Baron Trent, who died in 1931.

Chocolate The world's largest chocolate factory is that built by
factory Hershey Foods Corp. of Hershey, Pennsylvania,
U.S.A., in 1905. It now has 2,000,000 ft² *185,800 m²* of
floor space.

Computer The world's largest computer firm is International
Company Business Machines (IBM) Corporation of New York
which in a 1975 court decision was held to have a
36.7% share in the value of "electronic computers and
peripheral equipment, except parts" based on 1971
shipments. In 1974 assets were $14,027,107,647 and
early in 1975 cash at bank was $3.8 billion.

DEPARTMENT STORES

World The largest department store chain, in terms of number
of stores, is J. C. Penney, Company Inc., founded in
Wyoming, U.S.A., in 1902. The company operates
2,015 retail units in the U.S.A., Belgium and Italy,
with net selling space of 55.8 million ft² *5,17 million m²*.
Its turnover was $6,243,700,000 (£2,601 million) in the
year ending 20 Jan. 1974 the eighteenth consecutive
year of record sales.

United The largest department store in the United Kingdom
Kingdom is Harrods Ltd. of Knightsbridge, City of Westminster,
Greater London named after Henry Charles Harrod,
who opened a grocery in Knightsbridge Village in
1849. It has a total selling floor space of 23 acres
9,3 ha, employs 5,000 people and had a total of
12,600,869 transactions in 1973.

Most The department store with the fastest-moving stock
profitable in the world is the Marks & Spencer premier branch,
known as "Marble Arch" at 458 Oxford Street,
City of Westminster, Greater London. The figure of
£250 worth of goods per square foot of selling space
per year is believed to have become an understatement
when the selling area was raised to 72,000 ft² *6 690 m²*
in October 1970. The Company has 252 branches in
the U.K. and operates on over 5½ million ft² *506 000 m²*
of selling space and now has stores on the Continent
and Canada.

Distillery The world's largest distilling company is Distillers
Corporation-Seagrams Limited of Canada. Its sales
in the year ending 31 July 1974 totalled U.S.

Johnnie Walker,
the world
famous trade
mark of the
top selling
brand of
Scotch whisky,
drawn in 1908

$1,840,986,000 (*£800.4 million,*) of which
$1,560,942,000 (*£678.6 million*) were from sales by
Joseph E. Seagram & Sons, Inc. in the United States.
The group employs about 17,500 people, including
about 12,500 in the United States.

The largest of all Scotch whisky distilleries is Carse-
bridge at Alloa, Clackmannanshire, Scotland, owned
by Scottish Grain Distillers Limited. This distillery is
capable of producing more than 20,000,000 proof
gallons per annum. The largest establishment for
blending and bottling Scotch whisky is owned by
John Walker & Sons Limited at Kilmarnock, Strathclyde with a potential annual output of 151,000,000
bottles. "Johnnie Walker" is the world's largest-
selling brand of Scotch whisky. The largest malt
Scotch whisky distillery is the Tomatin Distillery,
Highland, established at 1,028 ft *313 m* above sea
level in 1897, with an annual capacity 4.75 million
proof gallons. The world's largest-selling brand of gin
is Gordon's.

Largest The largest retailing firm in the world is Sears, Roebuck
retailer and Co. (founded by Richard W. Sears in North
Redwood railway station, Minnesota in 1886) of
Chicago, Illinois, U.S.A. The net sales were
$12,306,229,080 (*£5,127 million*) in the year ending
31 Jan. 1974 when the corporation had 840 retail
stores and 2,785 catalogue, retail and telephone sales
offices and independent catalogue merchants, in
15 countries and total assets valued at $10,427,431,000
(*£4,344 million*).

The world's largest public enterprise merchandiser is
The Defense Logistics Service Center, Battle Creek,
Michigan which sells off surplus U.S. Federal material.

Grocery The largest grocery chain in the world is Safeway
stores Stores Incorporated of Oakland, California, U.S.A.

with sales in 1974 of $8,185,190,000 (*£3,558 million*) and total current assets valued at $816,743,000 as at 28 Dec. 1974. The company has 2,426 stores totalling 50,159,000 ft² *5,403 000 m²*. The total payroll is 121,355.

Largest Hotelier The top revenue-earning hotel business is Holiday Inns Inc., with a 1973 revenue of $885,679,000 (*£369 million*), from 1,591 inns (260,000 rooms) at 31 Dec. 1973 in 40 countries. The business was founded by Charles Kemmons Wilson with his first inn in Summer Avenue, Memphis, Tennessee in 1952.

INSURANCE COMPANIES

World The company with the highest volume of insurance in force in the world is the Prudential Insurance Company of America of Newark, New Jersey with $215,901 billion (*£93,860 million*) which is more than double the U.K. National Debt figure.

United Kingdom The largest insurance company in the United Kingdom is the Prudential Assurance Co. Ltd. At 1 Jan. 1975 the tangible assets were £3,070,000,000 and the total amount assured was £17,599,000,000.

Life policies Largest The largest life assurance policy ever written was one of £10,000,000 $25,000,000 for James Derrick Slater (b. 13 Mar. 1929), Chairman of Slater, Walker Securities, the City of London Investment bankers. The existence of the policy was made known on 3 June 1971.

Highest pay-out The highest pay-out on a single life has been some $14 million (*£5.6 million*) to Mrs. Linda Mullendore, wife of an Oklahoma rancher, reported on 14 Nov. 1970. Her murdered husband had paid $300,000 in premiums in 1969.

Marine insurance The greatest potential insured value of any ship has been £11,054,000 for the tanker *Metula*, owned by a Shell associate, carrying 195,693 tons of crude oil, stranded in the Straits of Magellan on 9 Aug. 1974. The oil slick extended a record 71½ miles *115 km*. The two tankers *Globtik Tokyo* and *Globtik London* are insured for $90 million (*£37.5 million*) each. Some of the largest Liquified Natural Gas container vessels may attract even higher valuations.

Mineral water The world's largest mineral firm is Source Perrier, near Nimes, France with an annual production of more than 1,800,000,000 bottles, of which more than 340,000,000 come from the single spring near Nimes, and 640,000,000 from Contrexeville. The net profits for the year 1974 were 28 555 561 francs (*£3,070,490*) The French drink about 50 litres *88 pts* of mineral water per person per year.

MOTOR CAR MANUFACTURER

The largest manufacturing company in the world is General Motors Corporation of Detroit, Michigan, U.S.A. During its peak year of 1974 world wide sales totalled $31,549,546,126 (*£13,717 million*). Its assets at 31 Dec. 1974 were valued at $20,468,099,914 (*£8,899 million*). Its total 1974 payroll was $9,771,416,000 (*£4,248 million*) to an average of 734,000 employees. The greatest total of dividends ever paid for one year was $1,514,240,066 (*then £630.9 million*) by General Motors for 1973.

The largest British manufacturer was the British Leyland Motor Corporation, with 1,020,000 vehicles produced and a sales turnover of £1,595 million of which 47.1% or £752 million was overseas sales in 180 markets in 1974.

Largest plant The largest single automobile plant in the world is the Volkswagenwerk, Wolfsburg, West Germany, with 40,000 employees and a capacity for 4,000 vehicles daily. The surface area of the factory buildings is 356 acres *144 ha* and that of the whole plant 4,880 acres *1 970 ha* with 45 miles *72 km* of rail sidings.

Salesmanship The all-time record for automobile salesmanship in units sold individually is 1,425 in 1973 by Joe Girard of Detroit, U.S.A., winner of the No. 1 Car Salesman title each year since 1966. His commissions in 1973 totalled $189,000 (*£78,750*). His 1974 total was 1,376.

Oil Company The world's largest oil company is the Exxon Corporation (formerly Standard Oil Company [New Jersey]), with 137,000 employees and assets valued at $25,079,500,000 (*£10,449 million*) on 1 Jan. 1974.

Oil refineries Largest The world's largest refinery is the Pernis refinery in the Netherlands, operated by the Royal Dutch/Shell Group of companies with a capacity of 25,000,000 tons *25,4 million tonnes*. The largest oil refinery in the United Kingdom is the Esso Refinery at Fawley, Hampshire. Opened in 1921 and much expanded in 1951, it has a capacity of 19,000,000 tons *19,3 million tonnes* per year. The total investment on the 1,300 acre *526 ha* site is nearly £150,000,000.

Paper mills The world's largest paper mill is that established in 1936 by the Union Camp Corporation at Savannah, Georgia, U.S.A., with an all-time record output in 1974 of 1,002,967 short tons *909 829 tonnes*. The largest paper mill in the United Kingdom is the Bowater's Kemsley Mill near Sittingbourne, Kent with a complex covering an area of 2,500 acres *1 012 ha* and a capacity in excess of 300,000 tons/*tonnes* a year.

The world's largest car factory, the Volkswagen plant, Wolfsburg, West Germany stretching over 356 acres *144 ha*

Pop-corn plant The largest pop-corn plant in the world is The House of Clarks Ltd. (instituted 1933) of Dagenham, Essex, which in 1974–75 produced 60,000,000 packets of "Butterkist".

Public relations The world's largest public relations firm is Hill and Knowlton, Inc. of 633 Third Avenue, New York City, N.Y., U.S.A. and ten other U.S cities. The firm employs a full-time staff of more than 500 and also maintains offices in 27 overseas cities.

Publishing The publishing company generating most net revenue is Time Inc. of New York City with $825.6 million (£351.3 million) in 1974 of which $124.5 million (£53.0 million) is from *Time* magazine advertising. Britain's largest publisher is Reed Publishing Holdings Ltd. part of the Reed International Group (formerly I.P.C. Ltd.) with a turnover of £247 million in 1974–75. The largest book publishing concern in the world is the Book Division of McGraw-Hill Inc. of New York with sales of $235.9 million (£102.6 million) in 1974.

Restaurateurs The largest restaurant chain in the world is that operated by F. W. Woolworth and Co. with 2,074 throughout six countries. The largest restaurateurs in the United Kingdom are Trust House-Forte who employ up to 48,000 full and part time staff in the U.K. and turned over £303,985,000 in 1973–74.

BANQUETS

Greatest World Outdoors The greatest banquet ever staged was that by President Loubet, President of France, in the gardens of the Tuileries, Paris, on 22 Sept. 1900. He invited every one of the 22,000 mayors in France and their deputies. With the Gallic *penchant* for round numbers, the event has always been referred to as "le banquet des 100,000 maires".

Indoors The largest banquet ever held has been one for 10,158 at a $15 a plate dinner in support of Mayor Richard J. Daley of Chicago at McCormick Place Convention Hall on the Lake, Chicago on 3 March 1971.

Most Expensive The menu for the main $5\frac{1}{3}$ hr banquet at the Imperial Iranian 2500th Anniversary gathering at Persepolis in October 1971 was probably the most expensive ever compiled. It comprised quail eggs stuffed with Iranian caviar, a mousse of crayfish tails in Nantua sauce, stuffed rack of roast lamb, with a main course of roast peacock stuffed with *foie gras*, fig rings and raspberry sweet champagne sherbet, with wines including *Château Lafite-Rothschild* 1945 at £40 per bottle from the cellars of Maxime, Paris.

Shipbuilding In 1974 there were 33,541,289 gross tons of ships, excluding sailing ships, barges and vessels of less than 100 tons, completed throughout the world, excluding the U.S.S.R., Romania and China. Japan completed 16,894,017 gross tons (50.37 per cent of the world total), the greatest tonnage completed in peacetime by any single country. The United Kingdom ranked fifth with 1,198,255 gross tons.

The world's leading shipbuilding firm in 1974 was the Ishikawajima-Harima Heavy Industries Co. of Japan, which launched 43 merchant ships of 2,816,245 gross tons from five shipyards.

Physically the largest shipyard in the United Kingdom is Harland and Wolff Ltd. of Queen's Island, Belfast, which covers some 300 acres *120 ha.*

Shipping line The largest shipping owner and operator in the world is the Royal Dutch/Shell Group (see page 158). The Group on 31 Dec. 1974 owned and managed 187 ships of 12,632,000 deadweight tons and had on charter on the same date a total of 197 ships of 21,179,000 deadweight tons. Additionally the fleet has 8 gas carriers owned or on charter with a combined capacity of 474,739 m³.

Shoe shop The largest shoe shop in the world is that of Lilley & Skinner, Ltd. at 360–366 Oxford Street, City of Westminster, Greater London. The shop has a floor area of 76,000 ft² *7 060 m²* spread over four floors. With a total staff of more than 180 people it offers, in ten departments, a choice of 125,000 pairs of shoes. Every week, on average, over 45,000 people visit this store.

LARGEST SHOPPING CENTRE

The world's largest shopping centre is the Lakewood Center, California with a gross building area of 2,451,438 ft² *227 745 m²* on a 165 acre *66,7 ha* site with parking for 12,500 cars. Britains' largest shopping centre is The Victoria Centre, Nottingham opened in 1972 which extends over 13 acres *5,2 ha.* The world's first was "Suburban Square" in Ardmore, Pennsylvania built in 1928.

Largest store The world's largest store is R. H. Macy & Co. Inc. at Broadway and 34th Street, New York City, N.Y., U.S.A. It covers 50.5 acres *20.3 ha* and employs 11,000 who handle 400,000 items. The sales of the company and its subsidiaries are $1,241,501,000 (£539.7 million). Mr. Rowland Hussey Macy's sales on his first day at his fancy goods store on 6th Avenue, on 27 Oct. 1858, were recorded as $11.06 (*now £4.42*).

Largest supermarket The largest supermarket building in the United Kingdom is the Woolco One-Stop Shopping Centre opened in Bournemouth, Hampshire on 29 Oct. 1968. Currently it has an area of 114,000 ft² *10 590 m²* and parking space for 1,250 cars.

Soft drinks The world's top-selling soft drink is Coca-Cola with over 165,000,000 drinks sold per day at the end of 1974 in more than 130 countries. Coke was invented by Dr. John S. Pemberton of Atlanta, Georgia in 1886 and The Coca-Cola Company was formed in 1892.

STEEL COMPANY

The world's largest producer of steel is Nippon Steel of Tōkyō, Japan which produced 38 480 000 tonnes of steel, steel products and pig iron in 1974. The Fukuyama Works of Nippon Kokan has a capacity of more than 16 000 000 tonnes per annum.

United Kingdom Currently the largest single British plant is the Port Talbot works of the British Steel Corporation, West Glamorgan, which extend for $4\frac{1}{2}$ miles *7,2 km,* with an area of 2,600 acres *1 050 ha.* The total number employed at this plant is 14,000 and its capacity is 3 000 000 tonnes. The £240 million Anchor Complex, Scunthorpe, Humberside, which went into production in 1973 is planned to have a capacity of 5.2 million tonnes.

Tobacco company The world's largest tobacco company is the British American Tobacco Company Ltd. (founded 1902), of London. The group's net assets were £1,442,610,000 at 30 Sept. 1974. Group turnover for 1973–74 was £3,488,000,000. The group has 134 tobacco factories and more than 245,000 employees.

The world's largest cigarette plant is the $200 million Philip Morris plant at Richmond, Virginia, U.S.A. opened in October 1974 with a payroll of 2,700 producing 200 million cigarettes a day.

Toy manufacturer The world's largest toy manufacturer is Mattel Toys of Hawthorne, Los Angeles, U.S.A. founded in 1945. Its 1973 sales were $280,829,000 (£117.0 million).

Toy shop *World* The world's biggest toy store is F.A.O. Schwarz, 745 Fifth Avenue at 58th Street, New York City, N.Y., U.S.A. with 50,000 ft² *4 645 m²* on three floors. Schwarz have 17 branch stores with a further 140,000 ft² *13 006 m²*.

The busiest of the world's stock exchanges, the New York Stock Exchange in Wall Street

United Kingdom Britain's biggest toy shop is that of Hamley of Regent Street Ltd., founded in 1760 in Holborn and removed to Regent Street, London, W.1. in 1901. It has selling space of 24,000 ft² *2 230 m²* on 10 floors, up to 250 employees during the Christmas season and a world-wide mail order catalogue.

Vintners The oldest champagne firm is Ruinart Père et Fils founded in 1729. The oldest cognac firm is Augier Freres & Co., established in 1643.

Fisheries The world's highest recorded catch of fish was 55 790 000 tonnes in 1970. Peru had the largest ever national haul with 12 160 000 tonnes in 1970 comprising mostly anchoveta. The United Kingdom's highest figure was 1 206 000 tonnes in 1948. The world's largest fishmongers are MacFisheries, a subsidiary of Unilever Ltd., with 290 retail outlets as at March 1974.

Largest Net The largest net yet manufactured is one that can fish 6 8 million m³ *8,8 million yd³* per hour announced from West Germany in March 1974.

Landowners The world's largest landowner is the United States Government, with a holding of 760,204,000 acres (1,187,818 miles² [*3,07 million km²*]) which is larger than the area of India. The United Kingdom's greatest ever private landowner was the 3rd Duke of Sutherland, George Granville Sutherland-Leveson-Gower, K.G. (1828–92), who owned 1,358,000 acres *549 560 ha* in 1883. Currently the largest landholder in Great Britain is the Forestry Commission (instituted 1919) with 2,982,158 acres *1 206 818 ha*. The longest tenure is that by St. Paul's Cathedral of land at Tillingham, Essex, given by King Ethelbert before A.D. 616. Currently the landowner with the largest known acreage is the 9th Duke of Buccleuch (b. 1923) with 336,000 acres *136 035 ha*.

LAND VALUES

Highest Currently the most expensive land in the world is that in the City of London. The freehold price on small prime sites reached £1,950/ft² (*£21,230/m²*) in mid 1973. The 600 ft *182,88 m* National Westminster Bank on a 2¼ acre *0,91 ha* site off Bishopsgate has become *pro rata* the world's highest valued building. At rents of £15/ft² on 500,000 net ft² *46 452 m²* and on 18 years purchase, it is worth £135 million. The value of the whole site of 6½ acres *1,6 ha* was £225,000,000. In February 1964 a woman paid $510 (£212.50) for a triangular piece of land measuring 3 by 6½ by 5¾ in, *7,6 × 16,5 × 14,6 cm* at a tax lien auction in North Hollywood, California, U.S.A.—equivalent to $365,182,470 (*£152.1 million*) per acre. The real estate value per square metre of the two topmost French vineyards, Grande and Petite Cognac vineyards in Bordeaux, has not been recently estimated.

Greatest auction The greatest auction was that at Anchorage, Alaska on 11 Sept. 1969 for 179 tracts 450,858 acres *182 455 ha* of the oil-bearing North Slope, Alaska. An all-time record bid of $72,277,133 for a 2,560 acre *1 036 ha* lease was made by the Amerada Hess Corporation—Getty Oil consortium. This £30,115,472 bid indicated a price of $28,233 (*then £11,763*) per acre.

Highest rent The highest recorded rentals in the world are for modern office accommodation in the prime areas of the City of London. In mid-1975 figures of £24/ft² *£304/m²* were reached exclusive of rates and services. For main thoroughfare ground floor banking halls figures up to £46/ft² *£494/m²* were under negotiation.

Companies The number of companies on the register in Great Britain at 1 Jan. 1975 was 598,379 of which 15,553 were public and the balance private companies. The smallest company on the register is Frank Davies Ltd of Hemel Hempstead, Hertfordshire incorporated on 22 Aug. 1924 with a nominal capital of ⅛d divided into two one farthing shares.

Most directorships The record for directorships was set in 1961 by Hugh T. Nicholson, formerly senior partner of Harmond Banner & Co., London who as a liquidating chartered accountant became a director of all 451 companies of the Jasper group in 1961 and had 7 other directorships.

STOCK EXCHANGES

The oldest Stock Exchange in the world is that at Amsterdam, in the Netherlands, founded in 1602. There were 126 throughout the world as of 13 June 1972.

Most markings The highest number of markings received in one day on the London Stock Exchange was 32,665 on 14 Oct. 1959 following the 1959 General Election. The record for a year is 4,396,175 "marks" in the year ending 31 March 1960. There were 9,098 securities (gilt-edged 1,491, company 7,607) quoted at March 1975. Their total nominal value was £69,235 million (gilt-edged £37,751 million, company £31,484 million) and their market value was £210,269 million (gilt-edged £26,892 million, company £183,377 million).

The highest figure of *The Financial Times* Industrial Ordinary share index (1 July 1935 = 100) was 543.6 on 19 May 1972. The lowest figure was 49.4 on 26 June 1940. The greatest rise in a day has been 22.2 points to 339.9 on 17 Apr. 1975, and the greatest fall in a day was 24.0 to 313.8 on 1 March 1974 on the realisation of a fourth post-war Labour government.

Highest and lowest par values The highest denomination of any share quoted in the world is a single share in F. Hoffmann—La Roche of Basel worth £16,825. The record for the London Stock Exchange is £100 for preference shares in Baring Brothers & Co. Ltd., the bankers.

U.S. records The highest index figure on the Dow Jones average (instituted 8 Oct. 1896) of selected industrial stocks at the close of a day's trading was 1,051.70 on 11 Jan. 1973, when the average of the daily "highs" of the 30 component stocks was 1,067.20. The old record trading volume in a day on the New York Stock Exchange of 16,410,030 shares on 29 Oct. 1929, the "Black Tuesday" of the famous "crash" was unsurpassed until April 1968. The Dow Jones industrial average, which had reached 381.17 on 3 Sept. 1929, plunged 30.57 points in the day, on its way to the Depression's lowest point of 41.22 on 8 July 1932. The total lost in security values was $125,000 million (*now £48,076 million*). World trade slumped 57 per cent from 1929 to 1936. The greatest paper loss in a year was $209,957 million (*£91,285 million*) in 1974. The record daily increase of 28.40 on 30 Oct. 1929 was beaten on 16 Aug. 1971, when the index increased 32.93 points to 888.95. The record day's trading was 35,158,320 shares on 13 Feb. 1975. The largest transaction on record "share-wise" was on 14 Mar. 1972 for 5,245,000 shares of American Motors at $7.25 each. The record for one block was $76,135,026 for 730,312 shares of American Standard Class A Preferred shares at $104.25 a share. The largest deal "value-wise" was for two 2,000,000 blocks of Greyhound shares at $20 each sold to Goldman Sachs and Salomon Brothers on 9 Feb. 1971. The highest prices paid for seats on the N.Y. Stock Exchange have been $625,000 (*then £128,600*) in 1929.

Largest equity The greatest aggregate market value of any Corporation is $30.7 billion (*£13,347 million*) assuming a closing price of $206⅝ multiplied by the 148,630,254 shares of I.B.M. extant on 31 Mar. 1975.

Largest new issue The American Telegraph & Telephone Co. offered $1,375 million's worth of shares in a rights offer on 27,500,000 shares of convertible preferred stock on the New York market on 2 June 1971. The largest offering on the London Stock Exchange by a United Kingdom company was the £40 million of loan stock by I.C.I. in December 1970.

Largest investment house The largest investment company in the world, and also once the world's largest partnership (124 partners, 61,200 stockholders at 31 Dec. 1971) is Merrill, Lynch, Pierce, Fenner & Smith Inc. (founded 6 Jan. 1914, went public in 1971) of New York City, U.S.A. It has 18,165 employees, 289 offices and 1,400,000 separate accounts. The firm is referred to in the United States stock exchange circles as "We" or "We, the people" or "The Thundering Herd". The company's assets totalled $4,124,554,000 at 27 Dec. 1974.

Biggest jobber The biggest London Stock Exchange stock and share jobber is Wedd Durlacher Mordaunt Ltd., whose turnover in 1972 (defined as total value of sold bargains) reached £14,300 million and £11,600 million in 1974.

Largest bank The International Bank for Reconstruction and Development (founded 27 Dec. 1945), the United Nations "World Bank" at 1818 H Street N.W., Washington, D.C., U.S.A., has an authorized share capital of $27,000 million (*£10,800 million*). There were 125 members with a subscribed capital of $25,548,900,000 (*£11,108 million*) at 31 Mar. 1975. The International Monetary Fund in Washington, D.C., U.S.A. has 126 members with total quotas of SDR 29,189,400,000 ($36,413 million or £15,176 million) at 31 Mar. 1975.

The private bank with the greatest deposits is the Bank of America National Trust and Savings Association, of San Francisco, California, U.S.A., with $50,662,777,000 at 31 Dec. 1974. Its total resources were $60,376,458,000 (*£25,470 million*). Barclays Bank (with Barclays Bank International and other subsidiary companies) had nearly 5,000 branches in 70 countries (3,075 in the United Kingdom) in December 1974. Deposits totalled £13,287,114,000 and assets £14,198,165,000. The largest bank in the United Kingdom is the National Westminster with total assets of £13,585,672,000 and 3,300 branches as at 1 Jan. 1975.

Largest bank building World The world's tallest bank building is the Bank of Montreal's First Bank Tower, Toronto, Canada which has 72 stories and stands 935 ft *284,98 m*. The largest bank vault in the world, measuring 350 × 100 × 8 ft *106,7 × 30,4 × 2,4 m* and weighing 879 tons *893 tonnes* is in the Chase Manhattan Building, New York City, completed in May 1961. Its six doors weigh up to 40 tons *40,6 tonnes* apiece but each can be closed by the pressure of a forefinger.

2. MANUFACTURED ARTICLES

Guinness Superlatives Ltd. publishes fine art books in colour on English and Irish Glass; Pottery and Porcelain; English Furniture (2 Volumes); Edged Weapons, Militaria and British Gallantry Decorations, obtainable on order from the publishers or from any good book shop.

Antique Largest The largest antique ever sold has been London Bridge in March 1968. The sale was made by Mr. Ivan F. Luckin of the Court of Common Council of the Corporation of London to the McCulloch Oil Corporation of Los Angeles, California, U.S.A. for $2,460,000 (*then £1,029,000*). The 10,000 tons of elevational stonework were re-assembled at a cost of £3 million, at Lake Havasu City, Arizona and "re-dedicated" on 10 Oct. 1971.

Armour The highest price paid for a suit of armour is £25,000, paid in 1924 for the Pembroke suit of armour, made at Greenwich in the 16th century, for the Earl of Pembroke.

Beds Largest In Bruges, Belgium, Philip, Duke of Burgundy had a bed 12½ ft wide and 19 ft long *3,81 × 5,79 m* erected for the perfunctory *coucher officiel* ceremony with Princess Isabella of Portugal in 1430. The largest bed in Great Britain is the Great Bed of Ware, dating from *c.* 1580, from the Crown Inn, Ware, Hertfordshire, now preserved in the Victoria and Albert Museum, London. It is 10 ft 8½ in wide, 11 ft 1 in long and 8 ft 9 in tall *3,26 × 3,37 × 2,66 m*. The largest bed currently marketed in the United Kingdom is the Super Size bed, 9 ft wide by 9 ft long, *2,74 m²* which sells for £1,158 (inc. VAT).

Heaviest The world's most massive bed is the four poster slate bed in Penrhyn Castle, Bangor, Gwynedd, Wales. It measures 7 ft 3 in *2,21 m* long and 6 ft 2 in *1,88 m* wide and weighs 2,070 lb. *938 kg*.

Beer Cans Beer cans date from a test marketting by Krueger Beer of Richmond, Virginia in 1934. The largest collection is claimed by John F. Ahrens of Moorestown, New Jersey with 9,000 *different* cans.

Beer Mats The world's largest collection of beer mats is owned by Leo Pisker of Vienna, who has more than 40,000 different mats. The largest collection of purely British mats is 12,864 by Charles M. Schofield of Glasgow.

CARPETS AND RUGS

Earliest The earliest carpet known is a white bordered black hair pelt from Pazyryk, U.S.S.R. dated to the 5th century B.C. now preserved in Leningrad.

Largest Of ancient carpets the largest on record was the gold-enriched silk carpet of Hashim (dated A.D. 743) of the Abbasid caliphate in Baghdad, Iraq. It is reputed to have measured 180 by 300 ft *54,86 × 91,44 m*.

The world's largest carpet now consists of 88,000 ft² (over two acres *or 0,81 ha*) of maroon carpeting in the Coliseum exhibition hall, Columbus Circle, New York City, N.Y., U.S.A. This was first used for the International Automobile Show on 28 April 1956.

Most expensive The most magnificent carpet ever made was the Spring carpet of Khusraw made for the audience hall of the Sassanian palace at Ctesiphon, Iraq. It was about 7,000 ft² *650 m²* of silk, gold thread and encrusted with emeralds. It was cut up as booty by a Persian army in A.D. 635 and from the known realisation value of the pieces must have had an original value of some £100,000,000. It was reported in March 1968 that a 16th century Persian silk hunting carpet was sold "recently" to an undisclosed U.S. museum by one of the Rothschild family for "about $600,000 (*then £205,000*). The highest price ever paid at auction for a carpet is the $150,000 (*£60,000*) given at Sotheby Parke Bernet, New York City on 9 Dec. 1972 for an early Louis XIV French Savonnerie carpet measuring 18 ft 6 in by 12 ft 7 in *5,63 × 3,83 m* and dating from the third quarter of the 17th century and woven under the administration of Simon Lourdet.

Most finely woven The most finely woven carpet known is one with more than 2,490 knots per in² *386 per cm²* from a fragment of an Imperial Mughal prayer carpet of the 17th century now in the Altman collections in the Metropolitan Museum of Art, New York City.

Ceramics The auction record for any ceramic object is £420,000 for the 16¼ in *41,2 cm* Ming blue and white bottle dated 1403–24 acquired by Mrs. Helen Glatz, a London dealer, at Sotheby, Bernet, London on 2 April 1974. The Greek urn painted by Ueuphromios and potted by Euxitheos in *c.* 530 B.C. was bought by private treaty by the Metropolitan Museum of Art, New York for $1.3 million (*then £541,666*) in August 1972.

Chair
Largest The world's largest chair is claimed to be an American ladderback outside Hayes and Kane furniture store, Bennington, Vermont, U.S.A. 19 ft 1 in *5,81 m* tall and weighing 2,200 lb. *998 kg.*

The most expensive chair in the world—a £34,000 Chippendale made in *c.* 1760

Most Expensive The highest price ever paid for a single chair is $85,000 (*£34,000*) for the John Brown Chippendale mahogany corner chair attributed to John Goddard of Newport, Rhode Island, U.S.A. and made in *c.* 1760. This piece was included in the collection of Mr. Lansdell K. Christie dispersed by Sotheby Parke Bernet, New York on 21 Oct. 1972.

Largest chandelier The largest chandelier is one of Czechoslovak manufacture weighing 7½ tons *7 600 kg* with 936 lights exported to the U.S.S.R. reported in 1973.

CIGARS

Largest The largest cigar in existence is one 5 ft 4½ in *1,63 m* long and 10½ in *26,6 cm* in diameter made by Abraham & Gluckstein, London and now housed at the Northumbrian University Air Squadron. The largest standard cigar in the world is the 9¾ in *24,1 cm* long "Partagas Visible Immensas". The Partagas factory in Havana, Cuba, manufactures special gift cigars 50 cm *19.7 in* long, which retail in Europe for more than £6 each.

Most expensive The most expensive cigar in the world is the Montecristo 'A', which retails in Britain at a suggested £2.69 incl. V.A.T. In Britain tobacco duty is £8 11.05p per lb.

Most voracious smoker The only man to master the esoteric art of smoking 14 full-sized cigars simultaneously whilst whistling, talking or giving bird imitations is Mr. Simon Argevitch of Oakland, California, U.S.A. This he did in New York on 25 Sept. 1973. Scott Case smoked 110 cigarettes simultaneously for 30 secs at the Oddball Olympics in Los Angeles in May 1974.

CIGARETTES

Consumption The heaviest smokers in the world are the people of the United States, where 600,000 million cigarettes (an average of >2,830 per adult) were consumed at a cost of about $13,000 million (*£5,400 million*) in 1974. The peak consumption in the United Kingdom was 3,230 cigarettes per adult in 1973. The peak volume was 243,100,000 lb. *110,2 million kg* in 1961, compared with 225,600,000 lb. *102,3 million kg* in 1974, when 137,000 million cigarettes were sold.

In the United Kingdom 64 per cent of adult men and 44 per cent of adult women smoke. Nicotine releases acetylcholine in the brain, so reducing tension and increasing resolve. It has thus been described as an anodyne to civilization.

Tar/Nicotine Content Of the 109 brands most recently analysed for the Dept. of Health and Social Security the one with highest tar/nicotine content is *Pall Mall King* with 36/3.3 mg per cigarette. *Silk Cut Extra Mild, Embassy Ultra Mild* and *Player's Mild de Luxe Size* with <4/0.3 are at the other end of the league.

Most popular The world's most popular cigarette is "Marlboro", a filter cigarette made by Philip Morris, which sold 82,000 million of them in 1974. The largest selling British cigarette in 1972 was John Player and Sons of Nottingham's "Player's No. 6 Filter". The Wills brand "Passing Cloud" was introduced in 1874.

Longest and shortest The longest cigarettes ever marketed were "Head Plays", each 11 in *27,9 cm* long and sold in packets of 5 in the United States in about 1930, to save tax. The shortest were "Lilliput" cigarettes, each 1¼ in *31,7 mm* long, and ⅛ in *3 mm* in diameter, made in Great Britain in 1956.

Largest collection The world's largest collection of cigarettes is that of Robert E. Kaufman, M.D., of 950 Park Avenue, New York City 28, N.Y., U.S.A. In April 1975 he had

Manufactured Articles

6,705 different kinds of cigarettes from 163 countries. The oldest brand represented is "Lone Jack", made in the U.S.A. in *c*. 1885. Both the longest and shortest (see above) are represented.

Cigarette lighter Most Expensive The most expensive cigarette pocket lighter in the world is made by Alfred Dunhill Ltd. of St. James's, City of Westminster, Greater London and costs £4,543 (incl. V.A.T.). It is a platinum-cased Rollagas lighter with diamond cut crocodile pattern finish mounted with 157 brilliant cut diamonds.

Cigarette packets The world's largest collection of cigarette packets is that of Niels Ventegodt of Frederiksberg Allé 13A, Copenhagen, Denmark. He had 52,021 different packets from 210 countries by March 1974. The countries supplying the largest number were the United Kingdom (6,861) and the United States (3,981) The earliest is the Finnish "Petit Canon" packet for 25, made by Tollander & Klärich in 1860. The rarest is the Latvian 700-year anniversary (1201–1901) Riga packet, believed to be unique.

Cigarette cards The earliest known and most valuable cigarette card is that bearing the portrait of the Marquess of Lorne published in the United States *c*. 1879. The only known specimen is in the Metropolitan Museum of Art, New York City. The earliest British example appeared *c*. 1883 in the form of a calendar issued by Allen & Ginter, of Richmond, Virginia, trading from Holborn Viaduct, City of London. The largest known collection is that of Mr. Edward Wharton-Tigar (b. 1913) of London with a collection of more than 500,000 cigarette and trade cards in about 25,000 sets.

Largest Christmas Cracker The largest cracker ever constructed was one 45 ft *13,71 m* in length and 8 ft *2,43 m* in diameter built for the BBC TV Christmas *Record Breakers* Show transmitted on 27 Dec. 1974.

Credit Card Collection The largest collection of credit cards is one of 537 (all different) by Walter Cavanagh (b. 1943) of Santa Clara, California, U.S.A. The cost of acquisition was nil.

Largest curtain The largest curtain ever built has been the bright orange-red 4-ton 185 ft *56 m* high curtain suspended 1,350 ft *411 m* across the Rifle Gap, Grand Hogback, Colorado, U.S.A. by the Bulgarian-born sculptor Christo, 36 (*né* Javacheff) on 10 Aug. 1971. It blew apart in a 50 m.p.h. *80 km/h* gust 27 hrs later. The total cost involved in displaying this work of art was $750,000 (*£300,000*).

Dinner service The highest price ever paid for a silver dinner service is £207,000 for the Berkeley Louis XV Service of 168 pieces, made by Jacques Roettiers between 1736 and 1738, sold at the salerooms of Sotheby & Co., City of Westminster, Greater London, in June 1960.

Dolls The highest price paid at auction for dolls is £16,000 for a pair of William and Mary painted wooden dolls in original clothes 22 in *55,8 cm* high at Sotheby's on 19 Apr. 1974. After an export license was refused they were purchased, after a public subscription, by Victoria and Albert Museum, London.

Dress Most expensive The most expensive dress ever sold by a Paris fashion house was one by Pierre Balmain (Directrice, Ginette Spanier), to a non-European Royal Personage for £4,500 in 1971.

FABRICS

Most expensive The most expensive fabric obtainable is an evening-wear fabric 40 in *101,6 cm* wide, hand embroidered and sequinned on a pure silk ground in a classical flower pattern. It has 194,400 tiny sequins per yard, and is designed by Alan Hershman of Duke St., London; it cost £165 per meter or £151 per yard in May 1975.

The world's most expensive cigarette lighter, the £4,543 platinum and diamond Dunhill model

Finest cloth The finest of all cloths is Shahtoosh (or Shatusa), a brown-grey wool from the throats of Indian goats. It is sold by Neiman-Marcus of Dallas, Texas, U.S.A., at $18.50 (*£7.71p*) per ft² and is both more expensive and finer than Vicuña. A simple hostess gown in Shahtoosh costs up to $5,000 (*£2,000*). Qiviut, the underwool of a musk ox is about $6.66 per ft².

LARGEST FIREWORK

The most powerful firework obtainable is the Bouquet of Chrysanthemums *hanabi*, marketed by the Marutamaya Ogatsu Fireworks Co. Ltd., of Tōkyō, Japan. It is fired to a height of over 3,000 ft *915 m* from a 36 in *914 mm* calibre mortar. Their chrysanthemum and peony flower shells produce a spherical flower with "twice-thrice changing colours", 2,000 ft *610 m* in diameter. The largest firework produced in Britain is one fired from Brock's 25 in *635 mm*, 22 cwt. *1 117 kg* mortar. The shell weighs 200 lb. *90 kg 70* and is 6½ ft *1,98 m* in circumference and was first used in Lisbon in 1886. The last firing was in London on 8 June 1946 for the World War II Victory Celebration which was the most elaborate show of aerial pyrotechny ever fired. Brock's Fireworks Ltd. of Hemel Hempstead, Hertfordshire was established before 1720.

FLAGS

Oldest The oldest national flag in the world is that of Denmark (a large white cross on a red field), known as the Dannebrog ("Danish Cloth"), dating from 1219, adopted after the Battle of Lindanissa in Estonia, now part of the U.S.S.R. The crest in the centre of the Austrian flag has its origins in the 11th century. The origins of the Iranian flag, with its sword-carrying lion and sun, are obscure but "go beyond the 12th century".

Largest The largest flag in the world is the "Stars and Stripes" displayed annually on the Woodward Avenue side of J. L. Hudson Company store in Detroit, Michigan, U.S.A. The flag 104 by 235 ft *31,69 × 71,62 m* and weighing 1,500 lb. *680 kg* was unfurled on 14 June 1949. The 50 stars are each 5½ ft *1,67 m* high and each stripe is 8 ft *2,43 m* deep. The largest Union Flag (or Union Jack) was one 11,520 ft² (144 by 80 ft [*43,89 × 23,38 m*]) used at a military tattoo in he Olympic Stadium, West Berlin in September 1967. The largest flag *flown* from a public building in Britain is a Union Flag measuring 36 ft *10,97 m* by 18 ft *5,48 m*, flown on occasions from the Victoria Tower of the Palace of Westminster, London. The study of flags is known as vexicollogy.

Largest float The largest float used in any street carnival is the 200 ft *60 m* long dragon *Sun Loong* used in Bendigo, Victoria, Australia. It has 65,000 mirror scales. Six men are needed to carry its head alone.

FURNITURE

Most expensive The highest price ever paid for a single piece of furniture is £240,000 for a French Louis XVI ormolu mounted ebony *bureau plat* and *cartonnier* 5 ft 4½ in *1,63 m* high by 3 ft 1½ in *95 cm* wide at Sotheby Parke Bernet, New Bond Street, London on 13 Dec. 1974.

Oldest British The oldest surviving piece of British furniture is a three-footed tub with metal bands found at Glastonbury, Somerset, and dating from between 300 and 150 B.C.

Largest The largest item of furniture in the world is the Long Sofa—a wooden bench for old seafarers—measuring 72 m *236 ft* in length at Oscarshamn, Sweden.

Glass The most priceless example of the occidental ceramic art is usually regarded as the glass Portland Vase which dates from late in the first century B.C. or 1st century A.D. It was made in Italy and was in the possession of the Barberini family in Rome from at least 1642. It was eventually bought by the Duchess of Portland in 1792 but smashed while in the British Museum in 1847.

Gold plate The world's highest auction price for a single piece of gold plate is £40,000 for a 20 oz. 4 dwt. *628,3 g* George II teapot made by James Ker of Edinburgh for the King's Plate Horse race for 100 guineas at Leith, Scotland in 1736. The sale was by Christie's, City of Westminster, Greater London on 13 Dec. 1967 to a dealer from Boston, Massachusetts, U.S.A.

The gold coffin of the 14th century B.C. Pharaoh Tutankhamun discovered by Howard Carter on 16 Feb. 1923 in Luxor, western Thebes, Egypt weighed 2,448 lb. *1 110 kg*. The exhibition at the British Museum attracted 1,656,151 people (of whom 45.7% bought catalogues) from 30 Mar. to 30 Dec. 1972 resulting in a profit of £657,731.22p.

Gun The highest price ever paid for a single gun is £125,000 given by the London dealers F. Partridge for a French flintlock fowling piece made for Louis XIII, King of France in *c*. 1615 and attributed to Pierre le Bourgeoys of Lisieux, France (d. 1627). This piece was included in the collection of the late William Goodwin Renwick of the United States sold by Sotheby and Co., City of Westminster, Greater London on 21 Nov. 1972.

Hat Most expensive The highest price ever paid for a hat is 165,570 francs (*£14,032*) (inc. tax) by Moët et Chandon at an auction by Maîtres Liery, Rheims et Laurin on 23 April 1970 for one last worn by Emperor Napoleon I (1769–1821) on 1 Jan. 1815.

Jade The highest price ever paid for an item in jade is 1,250,000 Swiss Francs (*£156,250*) for a necklace set with 31 graduated beads of Imperial green jade. This was sold by Christie's at the Hotel Richmond, Geneva, Switzerland, on 9 May 1973. The highest price paid for a single piece of jade sculpture is £71,000 for a massive Ming jade buffalo sold by Sotheby's on 15 March 1973.

Largest jig-saw The largest jig-saw ever made is one 35 ft 11 in × 30 ft 8½ in *10,94 m × 9,35 m* built with 1,020 large pieces for the National Children's Home and first

assembled in Trafalgar Square, London on 31 Mar. 1975. It was cut by fret saw by L/Cpl M. P. J. Marson of the Royal Engineers. The *Festival of Britain* jig-saw by Efroc Ltd., now in Montserrat though of much lesser area contains an estimated 40,000 pieces.

Matchbox labels The oldest match label is that of John Walker, Stockton-on-Tees, Cleveland, England in 1827. Collectors of labels are phillumenists, of bookmatch covers philliberumenists and of matchboxes cumyxaphists. The world's longest set is one of 960 produced by Bouldens Match Co. Ltd. for the Whitbread Brewery, Romsey, Hampshire, in Oct. 1974.

Medal The highest price paid at auction for a British medal or order is £4,200 for a badge of the Royal Order of Victoria and Albert belonging to the late H.R.H. Princess Royal at Sotheby's on 27 June 1973.

Sheerest nylon The lowest denier nylon yarn ever produced is the 6-denier used for stockings exhibited at the Nylon Fair in London in February 1956. The sheerest stockings normally available are 9-denier. An indication of the thinness is that a hair from the average human head is about 50 denier.

Paperweight The highest price ever paid for a paperweight is £8,500 at Sotheby & Co., City of Westminster, Greater London on 16 March 1970 for a 19th century Clichy lily-of-the-valley glass weight. The earliest were made in Italy in the 15th century.

Penknife Most blades The penknife with the greatest number of blades is the Year Knife made by the world's oldest firm of cutlers, Joseph Rodgers & Sons Ltd., of Sheffield, England, whose trade mark was granted in 1682. The knife was built in 1822 with 1,822 blades but now has 1,973 to match the year of the Christian era until A.D. 2000, beyond which there will be no further space. It was acquired by Britain's largest hand tool manufacturers, Stanley Works (Great Britain) Ltd. of Sheffield, South Yorkshire in 1970.

Pens The most expensive writing pens are the 18 carat pair of pens (one fibre-tipped and one ballpoint) capped by diamonds of 3.88 carats sold by Alfred Dunhill (see Cigarette lighter above) for £9,943 the pair (incl. V.A.T.).

Pipe Most expensive The most expensive smoker's pipe is the Charatan *Summa cum Laude* straight-grain briar root pipe available in limited numbers in New York City at $2,500 (*£1,087*).

English Porcelain The highest price ever paid for a single piece of English porcelain is £9,450. This was given for a turquoise ground Worcester bowl 6½ in *16,5 cm* in diameter of the 18th century, dating from the 'Dr Wall' period and decorated in the atelier of James Giles, at Christie's, London on 29 Jan. 1973.

Pistols Most expensive The highest price paid for a pair of pistols at auction is the £78,000 given by the London dealer Howard Ricketts at Sotheby Parke Bernet, London on 17 Dec. 1974 for a pair of English Royal flintlock holster pistols made *c*. 1690–1700 by Pierre Monlong. They were sent for sale by Anne, Duchess of Westminster.

Largest and Longest ropes The largest rope ever made was a coir fibre launching rope with a circumference of 47 in *119 cm* made in 1858 for the British liner *Great Eastern* by John and Edwin Wright of Birmingham. It consisted of four strands, each of 3,780 yarns. The longest fibre rope ever made without a splice was one of 10,000 fathoms or 11.36 miles *18 288 m* of 6½ in *16,5 cm* circumference manila by Frost Brothers (now British Ropes Ltd.) in London in 1874.

Christies

The world's most expensive snuff-box by Messonnier which sold for £89,250 in June 1974

SHOES

Most expensive The most expensive standard shoes obtainable are mink-lined golf shoes with 18 carat gold embellishments and ruby-tipped gold spikes made by Stylo Matchmakers International Ltd., of Northampton, England which retail for £2,700 or $6,426 per pair.

Largest Excluding cases of elephantiasis, the largest shoes ever sold are a pair size 42 built for the giant Harley Davidson of Avon Park, Florida, U.S.A.

Silver The highest price ever paid for a single piece of silver is £210,000 by the British Museum, London to S. J. Phillips of New Bond Street, London in December 1974 for the 11th century Savernake Horn and Harness (see colour illustration page 112).

Most expensive snuff The most expensive snuff obtainable in Britain is "Café Royale" sold by G. Smith and Sons (est. 1869) of 74, Charing Cross Road, City of Westminster, Greater London. It sells at £1.16 per oz.

Snuff Box The highest price ever paid for a snuff box is £89,250 paid by Kenneth Snowman of Wartski's in a sale at Christie's, London on 26 June 1974. This was for the gold and lapis lazuli example uniquely signed by Juste-Oreille Meissonnier (d. 1750) the French master goldsmith and dated Paris 1728. It was made for Marie-Anne de Vaviere-Neubourg, wife of Charles II of Spain. It measures 83 × 57 mm *3¼ × 2¼ in.* It was sent in for sale from the Ortiz-Patino collection.

Apostle spoons The highest price ever paid for a set of 12 apostle spoons is £70,000 paid by Mrs. How in a sale at Christie's, London on 26 June 1974. They are Elizabethan silver-gilt spoons, made by Christopher Wace in 1592, known as the "Tichborne Celebrities".

Stuffed bird The highest price ever paid for a stuffed bird is £9,000. This was given on 4 Mar. 1971 at Messrs Sotheby & Co., London by the Iceland Natural History Museum for a specimen of the Great Auk (*Alca impennis*) in summer plumage, which was taken in Iceland *c.* 1821; this particular specimen stood 22½ in *57 cm* high. The Great Auk was a flightless North Atlantic seabird, which was finally exterminated on Eldey, Iceland in 1844, becoming extinct through hunting. The last British sightings were at Co. Waterford in 1834 and St. Kilda, Inverness-shire *c.* 1840.

Sword The highest price recorded for a European sword is £21,000 paid at Sotheby's on 23 March 1970 for a swept hilt rapier 48½ in *123 cm* long made by Israel Schuech in 1606 probably for Elector Christian II or Duke Johann Georg of Saxony. The hilt is inset with pearls and semi-precious stones. It should be noted that prices as high as £60,000 have been reported in Japan for important swords by master Japanese swordsmiths such as the incomparable 13th century master Masamune.

TAPESTRY

Earliest The earliest known examples of tapestry weaved linen are three pieces from the tomb of Thutmose IV, the Egyptian Pharaoh and dated to 1483–1411 B.C.

Largest The largest single piece of tapestry ever woven is "Christ in His Majesty", measuring 72 ft by 39 ft *21,94 × 11,88 m* designed by Graham Vivian Sutherland O.M. (b. 24 Aug. 1903) for an altar hanging in Coventry Cathedral, West Midlands. It cost £10,500, weighs ¾ ton *760 kg* and was delivered from Pinton Frères of Felletin, France, on 1 March 1962.

Longest Embroidery The longest of all embroideries is the famous Bayeux *Telle du Conquest, dite tapisserie de la reine Mathilde,* a hanging 19½ in *49,5 cm* wide by 231 ft *70,40 m* in length. It depicts events of the period 1064–1066 in 72 scenes and was probably worked in Canterbury, Kent, in *c.* 1086. It was "lost" from 1476 until 1724.

Most expensive The highest price paid for a set of tapestries is £200,000 for four Louis XV pieces at Sotheby & Co., London on 8 Dec. 1967.

Table cloth The world's largest table cloth is one 60 yds *54,8 m* long by 2½ yds *2,28 m* wide woven in linen in Belfast in January 1972 for King Bhumibol of Thailand whose titles include Brother of the Moon and Half-Brother of the Sun.

Earliest tartan The earliest evidence of tartan is the so-called Falkirk tartan, found stuffed in a jar of coins in Bells Meadow, north of Callendar Park, Scotland. It is of a dark and light brown pattern and dates from *c.* A.D. 245. The earliest reference to a specific named tartan has been to a Murray tartan in 1618 although Mackay tartan was probably worn earlier.

Largest wig The largest wig yet made is that by Jean Leonard, owner of a salon in Copenhagen, Denmark. It is intended for bridal occasions, made from 24 tresses, measures nearly 8 ft *2,43 m* in length and costs £416.

Most expensive wreath The most expensive wreath on record was that sent to the funeral of President Kennedy in Washington, D.C. on 25 Nov. 1963 by the civic authority of Paris. It was handled by Interflora Inc. and cost $1,200 (now £460). The only rival was a floral tribute sent to the Mayor of Moscow in 1970 by Umberto Formichello, general manager of Interflora which is never slow to scent an opportunity.

Writing paper The most expensive writing paper in the world is that sold by Cartier Inc. on Fifth Avenue, New York City at $6,000 (£2,608) per 100 sheets with envelopes. It is of hand made paper from Finland with deckle edges and a "personalized" portrait watermark. Second thoughts and mis-spellings are costly.

3. AGRICULTURE

ORIGINS

It has been estimated that only 21 per cent of the world's land surface is cultivable and that of this only two-fifths is cultivated. Evidence adduced in 1971 from Nok Nok Tha and Spirit Cave, Thailand tends to confirm plant cultivation and animal domestication was part of the Hoabinhian culture *c.* 11,000 B.C. Reindeer may have been domesticated as early as *c.* 18,000 B.C. but definite evidence is still lacking.

The earliest attested evidence for the cultivation of grain comes from Ali Kosh, Iran and Jericho, by *c.* 7000 B.C. Goat was domesticated at Asiab, Iran by *c.* 8050 B.C. and dog at Star Carr, North Yorkshire by *c.* 7700 B.C.: the earliest definite date for sheep is *c.* 7200 B.C. at Argissa-Magula, Thessaly, Greece and for pig and cattle *c.* 7000 B.C. at the same site. The earliest date for horse is *c.* 4350 B.C. from Dereivka, Ukraine, U.S.S.R.

FARMS

Earliest The earliest dated British farming site is a neolithic one, enclosed within the Iron Age hill-fort at Hembury, Devon, excavated during 1934–5 and now dated to 3330 B.C. ± 150. Pollen analysis from two sites Oakhanger, Hampshire, and Winfrith Heath, Dorset (Mesolithic *c.* 4300 B.C.) indicates that Mesolithic man may have had herds which were fed on ivy during the winter months.

Largest The largest farms in the world are collective farms in
World the U.S.S.R. These have been reduced in number from 235,500 in 1940 to only 36,000 in 1969 and have been increased in size so that units of over 60,000 acres *25 000 ha* are not uncommon.

Britain The largest farms in the British Isles are Scottish hill farms in the Grampians. The largest arable farm is that of Elveden, Suffolk, farmed by the Earl of Iveagh. Here 11,251½ acres *4 553 ha* are farmed on an estate of 22,918 acres *9 274 ha*, the greater part of which was formerly derelict land. The 1974 production included 1,315,880 gal. *5 981 941 litres* of milk, 2,450 tons/*tonnes* of grain and 4,655 tons *4 731 tonnes* of sugar beet. The livestock includes 4,716 cattle, 1,041 ewes and 4,578 pigs.

Largest The world's largest single wheat field was probably
wheat field one of more than 35,000 acres *14 160 ha* first sown in 1951 near Lethbridge, Alberta, Canada.

Largest The world's largest vineyard is that extending over the
vineyard Mediterranean façade between the Rhône and the Pyrenees in the departments Aude, Hérault Gard and Pyrénées-Orientales in an area of 840 000 ha *2,075,685 acres* of which 52.3% is *monoculture viticole.*

Largest The largest hop field in the world is one of 790 acres
hop field *319 ha* at Toppenish, Washington State, U.S.A. It is owned by John I. Haas, Inc., the world's largest hop growers, with hop farms in British Columbia (Canada), California, Idaho, Oregon and Washington, with a total net area of 3,765 acres *1 522 ha.*

The world's largest hop farm extending over 790 acres *319 ha* at Toppenish, Washington State, U.S.A.

Golding Farms

Cattle The world's largest cattle station is Alexandria
station Station, Northern Territory, Australia, selected in 1873 by Robert Collins, who rode 1,600 miles *2 575 km* to reach it. It has 80 working bores, a staff of 90 and originally extended over 7,207,608 acres *2 916 818 ha*—more than the area of England's four largest counties of North Yorkshire, Cumbria, Devon and Lincoln put together. The present area is 6,500 miles² *16 835 km²* which is stocked with 58,000 shorthorn cattle. Until 1915 the Victoria River Downs Station, Northern Territory, was over three times larger, with an area of 22,400,000 acres (35,000 miles² [*90 650 km²*]).

Sheep The largest sheep station in the world is Common-
station wealth Hill, in the north-west of South Australia. It grazes between 70,000 and 90,000 sheep, *c.* 700 cattle and 25,000 uninvited kangaroos in an area of 4,080 miles² *10 567 km² i.e.* larger than the combined area of Norfolk and Suffolk.

The largest sheep move on record occurred when 27 horsemen moved a mob of 43,000 sheep 40 miles *64 km* from Barealdine to Beaconsfield Station, Queensland, Australia, in 1886.

Mushroom The largest mushroom farm in the world is the Butler
farm County Mushroom Farm, Inc., founded in 1937 in a disused limestone mine near West Winfield, Pennsylvania, U.S.A. It employs 975 in a maze of underground galleries 110 miles *177 km* long, producing 40,000,000 lb. *18 147 tonnes* of mushrooms per year.

Turkey farm The world's largest turkey farm is that of Bernard Matthews Ltd., centred at Weston Longville, Norfolk, with 700 workers tending 3,000,000 turkeys.

Chicken The world's largest chicken ranch is the 600 acre *242 ha*
Ranch "Egg City" Moorpark, California established by Jules Goldman in 1954. Some 2 million eggs are laid daily by 4.5 million chickens. The manure sale totals $72,000 (£28,800) per annum.

CROP YIELDS

Wheat Crop yields for highly tended small areas are of little significance. The British record is 86.10 cwt/acre *10 808 kg/ha* on a field of 28.53 acres *11,54 ha* by Brian Reynolds of Stanaway Farm, Otley, Suffolk in 1974 using Maris Huntsman winter wheat.

Barley A yield of 82.61 cwt./acre *10 371 kg/ha* of Clermont Spring Barley was achieved in 1972 by John Graham of Kirkland Hall, Wigton, Cumbria from a 13.52 acre *5,47 ha* field.

Record Britain's all-time record harvest was achieved in 1972
Harvest with 15,750,000 tons of grain.

Sugar beet The highest recorded yield for sugar beet is 62.4 short tons (55.71 long tons) per acre *1 809 hectolitres/ha* by Andy Christensen and Jon Giannini in the Salinas Valley, California.

DIMENSIONS AND PROLIFICACY

Cattle Of heavyweight cattle the heaviest on record was a Hereford-Shorthorn named "Old Ben", owned by Mike and John Murphy of Miami, Indiana, U.S.A. When he died at the age of 8, in February 1910, he had attained a length of 16 ft 2 in *4,92 m* from nose to tail, a girth of 13 ft 8 in *4,16 m*, a height of 6 ft 4 in *1,93 m* at the forequarters and a weight of 4,720 lb. *2 140 kg.* The stuffed and mounted steer is displayed in Highland Park, Kokomo, Indiana, as proof to all who would otherwise have said "there ain't no such animal". The British record is the 4,480 lb. *2 032 kg* of "The Bradwell Ox" owned by William Spurgin of Bradwell, Essex. He was 15 ft *4,57 m* from nose to tail and had a girth of 11 ft *3,35 m* when 6 years old in 1830. Weights of 4,000 lb. *1 815 kg* are commonplace among Italian Chianina bulls standing 6½ ft *1,98 m* at the shoulder.

The highest recorded birthweight for a calf is 225 lb. *102 kg* from a British Friesian cow at Rockhouse Farm, Bishopston, Swansea, West Glamorgan, in 1961.

On 25 April 1964 it was reported that a cow named "Lyubik" had given birth to seven calves at Mogilev, U.S.S.R. A case of five live calves at one birth was reported in 1928 by T. G. Yarwood of Manchester. The life-time prolificacy record is 30 in the case of a cross-bred cow owned by G. Page of Warren Farm, Wilmington, East Sussex, which died in November 1957, aged 32. A cross-Hereford calved in 1916 and owned by A. J. Thomas of West Hook Farm, Marloes, Dyfed, Wales, produced her 30th calf in May 1955 and died in May 1956, aged 40.

Pigs The heaviest pig ever recorded is "Big Boy", a hog of 1,904 lb. (17 cwt) *863,6 kg* bred by B. Liles and H. A. Sanders of Black Mountain, North Carolina, U.S.A. weighed on 5 Jan. 1939. The British record is a hog of 12 cwt. 66 lb. *639,5 kg* bred by Joseph Lawton of Astbury, Cheshire. In 1774 it stood 4 ft 8½ in *1,43 m* in height and was 9 ft 8 in *2,94 m* long. The highest recorded weight for a piglet at weaning (8 weeks) is 81 lb. *36 kg 70* for a boar, one of nine piglets farrowed on 6 July 1962 by the Landrace gilt "Manorport Ballerina 53rd", *alias* "Mary", and sired by a Large White named "Johnny" at Kettle Lane Farm, West Ashton, Trowbridge, Wiltshire.

The highest recorded number of piglets in one litter is 34, thrown on 25–26 June 1961 by a sow owned by Aksel Egedee of Denmark. In February 1955 a Wessex sow owned by Mrs. E. C. Goodwin of Paul's Farm, Leigh, near Tonbridge, Kent, had a litter of 34, of which 30 were born dead. A litter of 32 piglets (26 live born) was thrown in February 1971 by a British saddleback owned by Mr. R. Spencer of Toddington, Gloucestershire. A sow owned by Mr. L. Witt of Bath, Avon farrowed a litter of 19 (all surviving) on 29 May 1975.

Sheep The highest recorded birthweight for a lamb in Britain is 26 lb. *11 kg 80* in the case of a lamb delivered on 9 Feb. 1967 by Alan F. Baldry from a ewe belonging to J. L. H. Arkwright of Winkleigh, Devon. A case of eight lambs at a birth was reported by D. T. Jones of Priory Farm, Gwent, in June 1956, but none lived. A case of a sheep living to 26 years was recorded in flock book records by H. Poole, Wexford, Ireland.

Egg-laying The highest authenticated rate of egg-laying by a hen is 361 eggs in 364 days by a Black Orpington in an official test at Taranaki, New Zealand, in 1930. The U.K. record is 353 eggs in 365 days in a National Laying Test at Milford, Surrey in 1957 by a Rhode Island Red owned by W. Lawson of Welham Grange, Retford, Nottinghamshire.

The heaviest egg reported is one of 16 oz. *454 g*, with double yolk and double shell, laid by a white Leghorn at Vineland, New Jersey, U.S.A., on 25 Feb. 1956. The largest recorded was one of "nearly 12 oz." for a 5 yolked egg 12¼ in *31 cm* around the long axis and 9 in *22,8 cm* around the shorter axis laid by a Black Minorca at Mr. Stafford's Damsteads Farm, Mellor, Lancashire in 1896.

Most yolks The highest claim for the number of yolks in a chicken's egg is 9 reported by Mrs. Diane Hainsworth of Hainsworth Poultry Farms, Mount Morris, New York, U.S.A. in July 1971.

MILK YIELDS

Cows The world lifetime record yield of milk is 340,578 lb. (152.04 tons [*154 479 kg*]) at 3.3 per cent butter fat by the U.S. Holstein cow "Or-Win Masterpiece Riva"

owned by Willard and Gary Behm at Aprian, Michigan up to 10 Apr. 1975. The greatest yield of any British cow was that given by the British Friesian "Guillyhill Janna 2nd", owned by S. H. West. This cow yielded 330,939 lb. *150 111 kg* up to 1973. The greatest recorded yield for one lactation (365 days) is 50,759 lb. *23 023,8 kg* by "Mowry Prince Corinne" a Holstein at Roaring Springs, Pennsylvania, U.S.A. ending on 8 Dec. 1974. The British and probably world record for milk yield in a day is 198¼ lb. *89 kg 924* by R. A. Pierson's British Friesian "Garsdon Minnie" in 1948.

Hand Milking Andy Faust at Collinsville, Oklahoma, U.S.A. in 1937 achieved 120 U.S. gallons *99.92 U.K. galls* in 12 hours.

Goats The highest recorded milk yield for any goat is 7,546 lb. *3 422 kg* in 365 days by "Waiora Frill Q*" bred by Mr. & Mrs. E. L. Collins of Swanson, Auckland, New Zealand in 1972.

BUTTER FAT

The world record lifetime yield is 13,607 lb. *6 172 kg* from 308,569 lb. *139 964 kg* by the U.S. Brown Swiss cow "Ivetta" (1954–71) in the herd of W. E. Naffziger at Pekin, Illinois, U.S.A. in 4,515 days. The British record butter fat yield in a lifetime is 12,166 lb. *5 518 kg* by the Ayrshire cow "Craighead Welma" owned by W. Watson Steele from 273,072 lb. at 4.45%. The highest recorded lactation (365 days) yield reported is 1,956 lb. *887 kg* from 31,870 lb. *14 455 kg* of milk at 6.14% by Mr. Vincent A. Machin's *Crookgate Aylwinia 7* at Penley, near Wrexham, Clwyd ending on 7 July 1973. This is sufficient to produce 2,386 lb. *1 082,4 kg* of butter. The United Kingdom record for butter fat in one day is 9.30 lb. *4 kg 218* (79 lb. *[35,8 kg]* milk at 11.8 per cent) by Queens Letch Farms' Guernsey Cow "Thisbe's Bronwen of Trewollack".

SHEEP SHEARING

The highest recorded speed for lamb shearing in a working day was that of Steve Morrell who machine-sheared 585 lambs (average 65 per hour) in 9 hrs at Ashburton, New Zealand on 29 Dec. 1971. The blade (*i.e.* hand-shearing) record in a 9 hr working day is 350, set in 1899. The female record is held by Mrs. Pamela Warren, aged 21, who machine-sheared 337 Romney Marsh ewes and lambs at Puketutu, near Piopio, North Island, New Zealand in January 1972.

Britain British records for 9 hrs have been set at 555 by Roger Poyntz-Roberts (300) and John Savery (255) on 9 June 1971 (sheep caught *by* shearers), and 610 by the same pair (sheep caught *for* shearers) in July 1970. In a shearing marathon by the Kingsbridge Young Farmer's Club, four men machine-shore 776 sheep in 24 hrs on 4–5 June 1971.

Lifetime Total The sheep shearer with the largest life-time total is believed to be LaVor Taylor (b. 27 Feb. 1896) of Ephraim, Utah, U.S.A., who with annual totals varying between 8,000 and 22,000 sheep sheared 510,000 head in 60 years.

LIVESTOCK PRICES

Note: Some exceptionally high livestock auction prices are believed to result from collusion between buyer and seller to raise the ostensible price levels of the breed concerned.

Highest Priced Bull The highest price ever paid for a bull is $2,500,000 (£1,087,000) for the beefalo (a ⅜th buffalo, ⅜ charolais, ¼ Hereford) *Joe's Pride* sold by D. C. Basolo of Burlingame, California to the Beefalo Cattle Co. of Canada of Calgary, Alberta Canada on 9 Sept. 1974.

The highest price ever paid for a bull in Britain is 60,000 guineas (£63,000), paid on 5 Feb. 1963 at Perth, Scotland, by James R. Dick (1928–74) co-manager of Black Watch Farms, for "Lindertis

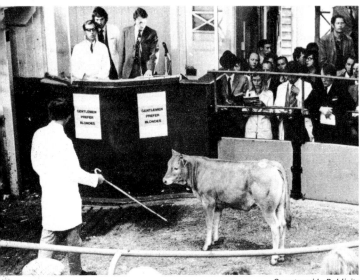

Countrywide Publicity

The cattle auction at Banbury, Oxfordshire at which the Blonde d'Aquitaine heifer West Riddens Juniper set a British record of £14,070

Evulse", an Aberdeen-Angus owned by Sir Torquil and Lady Munro of Lindertis, Kirriemuir, Angus, Scotland. This bull failed a fertility test in August 1963 when 20 months old thus becoming the world's most expensive piece of beef.

Cow The highest price ever paid for a cow is $122,000 (*£50,833*) for the Holstein-Friesian "Tara Hills Pride Lucky Barb" by Pride Barb Syndicate of Ontario at Amenia, N.Y., U.S.A. on 11 Nov. 1972. The British record is £14,070 for "West Riddens Juniper", a 5 month old Blonde d'Aquitaine heifer calf sold to Mr. Keith Johnson of Calgary, Alberta, Canada at Banbury, Oxfordshire on 25 June 1975.

Sheep The highest price ever paid for a sheep is $A36,000 (*£22,000*) for a Merino ram from John Collins & Sons, Mount Bryan, South Australia by Mr. Perce L. Puckridge of White River, Port Lincoln, South Australia at the Royal Adelaide Show on 6 Sept. 1973.

The British auction record is £8,000 paid by A. C. Campbell & Co. of Creetown, Dumfries & Galloway for Hugh Finlays' Scottish Blackface ram lamb on 4 Oct. 1973.

The highest price ever paid for wool is $A46 per kg (*£11.09 per lb.*) for a bale of superfine Merino fleece from the Launceston, Tasmania sales in February 1973 set by Mr. C. Stephen of Mount Morriston estate.

Pig The highest price ever paid for a pig is $38,000 (*£16,520*) for a champion Duroc owned by Forkner Farms, Horton, Missouri by Soga-No-Yo Swine Farms, Hiratsuka, Japan at Austin, Minnesota, U.S.A. on 11 Sept. 1973. The U.K. record is 3,300 guineas (*£3,465*), paid by Malvern Farms for the Swedish Landrace gilt "Bluegate Ally 33rd" owned by Davidson Trust in a draft sale at Reading, Berkshire on 2 March 1955.

Horse The highest price ever given for a farm horse is £9,500, paid for the Clydesdale stallion "Baron of Buchlyvie" by William Dunlop at Ayr, Scotland, in December 1911.

Donkey Perhaps the lowest ever price for livestock was at a sale at Kuruman, Cape Province, South Africa in 1934 where donkeys were sold for less than 2p each.

Turkey The highest price ever paid for a turkey is $990 (*then £353*) for a 33 lb. *15 kg* stag bird bought at the Arkansas State Turkey Show at Springdale, Arkansas, U.S.A. on 3 Dec. 1955.

CHEESE

The most active cheese-eaters are the people of France, with an annual average in 1969 of 29.98 lb. *13 kg 600* per person. The world's biggest producer is the United States with a factory production of 998,800 tons *1 014 827 tonnes* in 1970. The U.K. cheese consumption in 1970 was 11.4 lb. *5 kg 170* per head.

Oldest The oldest and most primitive cheeses are the Arabian *kishk*, made of dried curd of goats' milk. There are today 450 named cheeses of 18 major varieties, but many are merely named after different towns and differ only in shape or the method of packing. France has 240 varieties.

Most expensive The most expensive French cheese in France is the ewe's milk mountain cheese Laruns from the Bearn area of the Pyrenees, France, which is marketed in Paris, at times, for 38 francs per kg (*£1.42 per lb.*). Britain's most costly cheeses are Blue Cheshire and Windsor Red both at 45p per lb. *99p per kg*. In the U.S. Imported Brie from France may cost $5,80 (*£2.32*) per lb. or *£5.11 kg* retail.

Largest The largest cheese ever made was a cheddar of 34,591 lb. *15 190 kg* made in 43 hrs on 20–22 Jan. 1964 by the Wisconsin Cheese Foundation for exhibition at the New York World's Fair, U.S.A. It was transported in a specially designed refrigerated tractor trailer "Cheese Mobile" 45 ft *13,71 m* long.

Longest sausage The longest sausage ever recorded was one 3,124 ft *952 m* long, made on 29 June 1966 by 30 butchers in Scunthorpe, Humberside. It was made from 6½ cwt. *330 kg* of pork and 1½ cwt. *76 kg 20* of cereal and seasoning.

Piggery The world's largest piggery is the Sljeme pig unit in Yugoslavia which is able to process 300,000 pigs in a year. Even larger units may exist in Romania but details are at present lacking.

Cow shed The longest cow shed in Britain is that of the Yorkshire Agricultural Society at Harrogate, North Yorkshire. It is 456 ft *139 m* in length with a capacity of 686 cows. The National Agricultural Centre, Kenilworth, Warwickshire, completed in 1967, has, however, capacity for 782 animals.

Foot-and-mouth disease The worst outbreak of foot-and-mouth disease in Great Britain was that from Salop on 25 Oct. 1967 to 25 June 1968 in which there were 2,364 outbreaks and 429,632 animals slaughtered at a direct and consequential loss of £150,000,000. The outbreak of 1871, when farms were much smaller, affected 42,531 farms. The disease first appeared in Great Britain at Stratford near London in August 1839.

Ploughing The world championship (instituted 1953) has been staged in 17 countries and won by ploughmen of ten nationalities of which the United Kingdom has been most successful with 6 championships. The only man to take the title three times has been Hugh Barr of Northern Ireland in 1954–55–56.

The fastest recorded time for ploughing an acre *0,404 ha* (minimum 32 right-hand turns and depth 9 in [*22 cm*]) is 17 min 52.5 sec by Mervyn Ford using a six-furrow 14 inch Ransomes plough towed by a Roadless 114 four-wheel drive tractor at Bowhay Farm, Ide, Exeter, Devon on 25 Sept. 1970.

The greatest recorded acreage ploughed in 24 hrs is 115 acres *46,53 ha* at North Barn Farm, Dorchester, Dorset on 22–23 Nov. 1971 with a County Eleven Twenty Four tractor with a Bamford Kverneland 7 furrow plough to a depth of 6 in. *15 cm*. John Sephton at Clare Park Farm, Crondall, Hampshire ploughed for 50 hours on 1–3 Nov. 1974.

Above: The fastest humans of all time: the astronauts (l. to r.) Cernan, Young and Stafford, who reached 24,791 m.p.h. *39,897 km/h* in Apollo X on 26 May 1969 (see Table in Chapter XI)

N.A.S.A.

Above: The highest humans of all time: the astronauts (l. to. r.) Haise, Swigert and Lovell who reached 248,655 miles above the Earth's surface in Apollo XIII on 15 Apr. 1970 (see Table in Chapter XI)

N.A.S.A.

Right, From top to bottom: Earliest coin ever minted in Britain, the Westerham gold stater of *c* 95 B.C. of which only 51 examples have ever been found (see Chapter X)

Below: An environmental rendition of Handel's "Water Music" by the world's first underwater violinist (see Chapter VI)

The most coveted academic honour in the world—the gold medal awarded to the Nobel laureates in Sweden each year since 1901
Courtesy Nobel Foundation

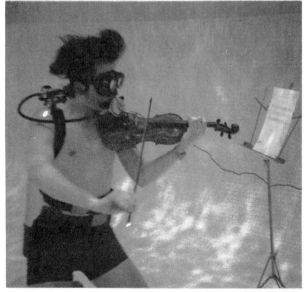

The last gold coin of the Kingdom of Scotland —the gold pistole of King William dated 1701

Holder of British stamp auction record—the 1854 one penny Bermuda "Perot" stamp
Courtesy Stanley Gibbons

Below: The North Pole being visited from beneath the ice-cap by a passing U.S. nuclear submarine

Left: Quintuple Olympic equestrian gold medal winner Hans-Günter Winkler (W. Ger.)

Ed Lacey

Right: Crossbow, the world's fastest yacht which attained a speed of 29.3 knots

Ed Lacey

Below Left: Italy's Giacomo Agostini, winner of most world championship motor cycling titles

Gerry Cranham

Below Centre: James Bolding (USA) the world's record holder for 440 yard hurdles

Ed Lacey

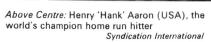

Above Centre: Henry 'Hank' Aaron (USA), the world's champion home run hitter

Syndication International

Above left: Jimmy Connors (U.S.A.), the world's top lawn tennis prize money winner

Tony Duffy

Left: Aleksandr and Irena Zaitsev (*née* Rodnina) (USSR) four times world pairs skating champions. She won two previous titles with Aleksiy Ulanov

Tony Duffy

Right: Bobby Charlton England's top goal scorer in internationals with 49 goals

Syndication International

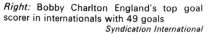

Left: Co-holder of the record of five wins in the *Tour de France*, Eddie Merckx (Belgium)

Colorsport

Right: Liz Allan Shetter (USA), women's world water-ski jump record holder

Below Left: Winner of most major titles, Jack Nicklaus (USA) is the only golfer to win the U.S. Masters 5 times

Colorsport

Above: The world's most successful ever woman skier, Annemarie Moser (*née* Proell) four times winner of the World Cup

Colorsport

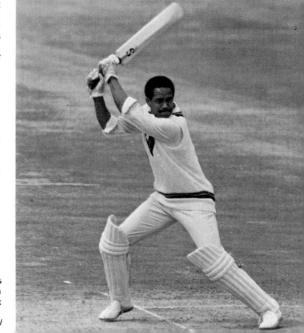

Left: Helena Fibingerova (Czech) holder of the woman's shot putt record

Tony Duffy

Right: Sir Garfield Sobers displaying the style which enabled him to hit six sixes off one over

Sport & General

Above Left: East Germany's multiple world record holder Kornelia Ender

Tony Duffy

Above: Joss Naylor (GB) who traversed the 271½ mile *436,9 km* long Pennine Way in 3 days 4 hr 36 min

Gerry Cranham

Far Left: Arnold Palmer (USA) co-holder of 'The Open' record for the lowest 72-hole aggregate (276)

Gerry Cranham

Centre: Poland's Irena Szewinska, who in 1974 set the world records for 200 and 400 m six years after setting world records in the 100 m and 200 m

Tony Duffy

Below Left: Muhammad Ali Haj (formerly Cassius Clay) (USA) one of only two men to regain a world heavyweight title

Syndication International

Below: Lester Piggott, co-holder of the record of six Derby wins

Gerry Cranham

1. POLITICAL AND SOCIAL

The land area of the Earth is estimated at 57,270,000 miles² *148 270 000 km²* (including inland waters), or 29.08 per cent of the world's surface area.

Largest political division The British Commonwealth of Nations, a free association of 34 independent sovereign states together with their dependencies, covers an area of 13,095,000 miles² *33 915 000 km²* and had a population estimated to be 933 million in 1974.

COUNTRIES

Total The total number of separately administered territories in the world is 221, of which 154 are independent countries. Of these 30 sovereign and 55 non-sovereign are insular countries. Only 29 sovereign and 1 non-sovereign countries are entirely without a seaboard. Territorial waters vary between extremes of 3 miles *4,82 km* (*e.g.* United Kingdom, Australia, France, Ireland and the U.S.A.) up to 200 miles *321,8 km* (*e.g.* Argentina, Ecuador, El Salvador and Panama).

Largest The country with the greatest area is the Union of Soviet Socialist Republics (the Soviet Union), comprising 15 Union (constituent) Republics with a total area of 22 402 000 km² *8,649,500 miles²*, or 15.0 per cent of the world's total land area, and a total coastline (including islands) of 106 360 km *66,090 miles*. The country measures 8 980 km *5,580 miles* from east to west and 4 490 km *2,790 miles* from north to south.

The United Kingdom covers 94,221 miles² *244 030 km²* (including 1,197 miles² [*3 100 km²*] of inland water), or 0.16 per cent of the total land area of the world. Great Britain is the world's eighth largest island, with an area of 84,186 miles² *218 040 km²* and a coastline 5,126 miles *8 249 km* long, of which Scotland accounts for 2,573 miles *4 141 km*, Wales 624 miles *1 004 km* and England 1,929 miles *3 104 km*.

Smallest The smallest independent country in the world is the State of the Vatican City or Holy See (Stato della Città del Vaticano), which was made an enclave within the city of Rome, Italy on 11 Feb. 1929. It has an area of 44 hectares *108.7 acres*. The maritime sovereign country with the shortest coastline is Monaco with 3.49 miles *5,61 km* excluding piers and breakwaters.

The world's smallest republic is Nauru, less than 1 degree south of the equator in the Western Pacific, which became independent on 31 Jan. 1968, has an area of 5,263 acres *2 129 ha* and a population of 7,000 (latest estimate mid-1973).

The smallest colony in the world is Pitcairn Island with an area of 960 acres *388 ha* and a population of 82 (mid-1972).

The official residence, since 1834, of the Grand Master of the Order of the Knights of Malta totalling 3 acres *1,2 ha* and comprising the Villa del Priorato di Malta on the lowest of Rome's seven hills, the 151 ft *46 m* Aventine, retains certain diplomatic privileges

10

THE HUMAN WORLD

and has accredited representatives to foreign governments and is hence sometimes cited as the smallest state in the world.

On 19 Jan. 1972 the two South Pacific atolls of North and South Minerva (400 miles [*640 km*] south of Fiji) were declared to be a sovereign independent Republic under international law by Mr. Michael Oliver formerly of Lithuania.

FRONTIERS

Most The country with the most frontiers is the U.S.S.R., with 13—Norway, Finland, Poland, Czechoslovakia, Hungary, Romania, Turkey, Iran (Persia), Afghanistan Mongolia, People's Republic of China, North Korea and Japan (territorial waters).

177

Longest and Shortest The longest *continuous* frontier in the world is that between Canada and the United States, which (including the Great Lakes boundaries) extends for 3,987 miles *6 416 km* (excluding 1,538 miles [*2 547 km*] with Alaska). The frontier which is crossed most frequently is that between the United States and Mexico. It extends for 1,933 miles *3 110 km* and there are more than 120,000,000 crossings every year. The Sino-Soviet frontier, broken by the Sino-Mongolian border, extends for 4,500 miles *7 240 km* with no reported figure of crossings. The "frontier" of the Holy See in Rome measures 2.53 miles *4,07 km*.

Most impenetrable boundary The "Iron Curtain" (858 miles [*1 380 km*]) dividing the Federal Republican (West) and the Democratic Republican (East) parts of Germany, utilises 2,230,000 land mines and 50,000 miles *80 500 km* of barbed wire, much of it of British manufacture, in addition to many watch-towers containing detection devices. The whole strip of 270 yds *246 m* wide occupies 133 miles² *344 km²* of East German territory.

POPULATIONS

World Estimates of the human population of the world have largely hinged on the accuracy of the component figure for the population of the People's Republic of China, which has published no census since that of 30 June 1953. On 25 Aug. 1974 the Hsinhua Official News Agency announced that the figure was "nearly 800 million"—at least 29 million lower than the U.N. estimate. The world total at mid-1975 can be estimated to be slightly over 4,000 million, giving an average density of 29.5 people per km² *76.5 per mile²* of land (including inland waters). This excludes Antarctica and uninhabited island groups. The daily increase in the world's population was running at 208,000 in 1973–74. It is estimated that about 250 are born and about 101 die every minute in 1973–74. The world's population has doubled in the last 50 years and is expected to double again in the next 35 years. It is now estimated that the world's population in the year 2000 will be more than 6,000 million. The present population "explosion" is of such a magnitude that it has been fancifully calculated that, *if* it were to continue unabated, there would be one person to each square yard by A.D. 2600, and humanity would weigh more than Earth itself by A.D. 3700. It is estimated that 75,000,000,000 humans have been born and died in the last 600,000 years.

WORLD POPULATION —
Progressive mid-year estimates

Date	Millions	Date	Millions
4000 B.C.	85		
A.D. 1	c.300	1960	2,982
1650	c.500–550	1970	3,632
1750	800	1971	3,706
1800	1,000	1972	3,782
1850	1,300	1973	3,860
1900	1,700	1974	3,950
1920	1,862	1975	4,005
1930	2,070	2000	6,493*
1940	2,295	2007	7,600
1950	2,486	2070	25,000†

* U.N. Forecasts made on medium variants.
† Some demographers maintain that the figure will (or must) stabilize at 10 to 15,000 million but above 8,000 million during the 21st century.

Most populous country The largest population of any country is that of the People's Republic of China. For the most recent quasi-official estimate of "nearly 800,000,000" see above. The rate of natural increase is now believed to be 16 per 1,000 or 35,000 per day.

Least populous The independent state with the smallest population is the Vatican City of the Holy See (see Smallest country, page 177), with 880 inhabitants at 1 Jan. 1966.

J. Allan Cash

The world's smallest independent sovereign state, the Holy See in Rome, Italy covering 108 acres *44 ha*

Most densely populated The most densely populated territory in the world is the Portuguese province of Macau (or Macao), on the southern coast of China. It has an estimated population of 262,000 (mid-1973) in an area of 6.2 miles² giving a density of 42,258 per mile² *16 316 per km²*.

The Principality of Monaco, on the south coast of France, has a population of 24,000 (estimated 30 June 1973) in an area of 369.9 acres *149,6 ha* giving a density of 41,500/mile² *16 023/km²*. This is being relieved by marine infilling which will increase her area to 447 acres *180 ha*. Singapore has 2,219,000 (mid-1974 estimate) people in an inhabited area of 73 miles² *189 km²*.

Of territories with an area of more than 200 miles² *518 km²*, Hong Kong (398¼ miles² [*1 031,4 km²*]) contains 4,160,000 (estimated mid-1973), giving the territory a density of 10,440/mile² *4 030/km²*. Hong Kong is now the most populous of all colonies. The transcription of the name is from a local pronunciation of the Peking dialect version of Xiang gang (a port for incense). About 80 per cent of the population lives in the urban areas of Hong Kong island and Kowloon, on the mainland, and the density there is greater than 200,000/mile² *518 000/km²*. At North Point there are 12,400 people living in 6½ acres *2,6 ha* giving an unsurpassed spot density of more than 1,200,000/mile² *463 000/km²*. In 1959 it was reported that in one house designed for 12 people the number of occupants was 459, including 104 in one room and 4 living on the roof.

Of countries over 1,000 miles² *2 589 km²* the most densely populated is Bangladesh with a population of 71,317,000 (March 1974, estimate) living in 55,126 miles² *142 775 km²* at a density of 1,293/mile² *499/km²*. The Indonesian islands of Java and Madura (combined area 51,033 miles² [*132 174 km²*]) had a population of 73,400,000 (estimated for mid-1969), giving a density of 1,438/mile² *555/km²*. The United Kingdom (94,221 miles² [*244 030 km²*]) had an estimated home population of 55,860,000 at 30 June 1974, giving a density of 593.8 people/mile². The projected population figures for 1980 and 2000 are 59,548,000 and 66,100,000. The population density for England alone (50,869 miles²) is 962.7/mile², while that of south-eastern England is more than 1,640/mile².

Most sparsely populated Antarctica became permanently occupied by relays of scientists from October 1956. The population varies seasonally and reaches 1,500 at times.

The least populated territory, apart from Antarctica, is Greenland, with a population of 51,000 (estimated 1 July 1973) in an area of 840,000 miles² *2 175 000 km²* giving a density of one person to every 16.36 miles² *42,4 km²*. The ice-free area of the island is only 132,000 miles² *340 000 km²*.

BRITISH AND IRISH LARGEST AND SMALLEST PRIMARY LOCAL GOVERNMENT AREAS — By size and population

		By Area (in acres/hectares)						By Home Population (estimate 30 June 1973)			
	Largest			Smallest				Most Populous		Least Populous	
England	North Yorkshire	2,055,109	831 661	Isle of Wight	94,141	38 096		Greater London	7,281,800	Isle of Wight[1]	109,806
Wales	Dyfed	1,424,668	576 534	South Glamorgan	102,807	41 604		Mid Glamorgan	536,080[2]	Powys	99,370
Scotland[3]	Highland[4]	6,214,400	2 514 880	Orkney	217,600	88 059		Strathclyde[5]	2,578,000	Orkney	17,500
Northern Ireland[6]	Fermanagh	457,376	185 090	North Down	18,174	7 354		Belfast City	403,900[1]	Moyle	13,979
Republic of Ireland	Cork	1,843,408	745 990	Louth	202,806	82 071		Dublin County	799,048	Longford	28,250

[1] *Figures based on 1971 Census.*
[2] *The most populous town in Wales—the City of Cardiff (pop. 284,012)—is in South Glamorgan.*
[3] *Scotland's 33 Counties were replaced on 16 May 1975 by nine regions and three Island Areas.*
[4] *The inclusion by Act of Parliament on 10 February 1972 of Rockall in the District of Harris in Western Isles put the extremities of that Authority at the record distance apart of 302 miles 486 km.*
[5] *Includes the most populous town in Scotland—the City of Glasgow (pop. 861,898).*
[6] *There are now no counties in Northern Ireland, which is divided only into 26 Districts.*

CITIES

Most populous **World** The most populous city in the world is Shanghai, China with a population in 1971 of 10,820,000 thus surpassing the figure for the 23 wards of Tōkyō, Japan. At the census of 1 Oct. 1970, the "Keihin Metropolitan Area" (Tōkyō-Yokohama Metropolitan Area) of 1,081 miles² *2 800 km²* however contained an estimated 14,034,074 people.

The world's largest city not built by the sea or on a river is Greater Mexico City (Ciudad de Mexico), the capital of Mexico, with a census population of 8,589,630 in 1970.

United Kingdom The largest conurbation in Britain is Greater London (established on 1 April 1965), with a mid-1973 population of 7,281,800. The residential population of the City of London (677.3 acres plus 61.7 acres foreshore) is 4,235 compared with 128,000 in 1801. The peak figure for Greater London was 8,615,050 in 1939.

Largest in area The world's largest town, in area, is Mount Isa Queensland, Australia. The area administered by the City Council is 15,822 miles² *40 978 km²*. The largest city in the United Kingdom is Greater London with an area of 616.4 plus 8.3 miles² foreshore (*1 617,9 km²*).

Smallest town and hamlet The smallest place with a town council is Caerwys, Clwyd, Wales with a population of 801. The town has a charter dated 1284. The only hamlet in Great Britain with an official population of one in the 1961 census was Gallowhill in the parish of Inveravon, Grampian, Scotland. The population (Miss Jessie Ann Stuart) died aged 74 in 1969.

Highest World The highest capital in the world, before the domination of Tibet by China, was Lhasa, at an elevation of 12,087 ft *3 684 m* above sea-level. La Paz, the administrative and *de facto* capital of Bolivia, stands at an altitude of 11,916 ft *3 631 m* above sea-level. The city was founded in 1548 by Capt. Alonso de Mendoza on the site of an Indian village named Chuquiapu. It was originally called Ciudad de Nuestra Señora de La Paz (City of Our Lady of Peace), but in 1825 was renamed La Paz de Ayacucho, its present official name. Sucre, the legal capital of Bolivia, stands at 9,301 ft *2 834 m* above sea-level. The new town of Wenchuan, founded in 1955 on the Chinghai-Tibet road, north of the Tangla range is the highest in the world at 5 100 m *16,732 ft* above sea-level. The highest dwellings in the world are those in Baruduksum, Tibet at 21,000 ft *6 461 m*.

Great Britain The highest village in England is Flash, in northern Staffordshire, at 1,518 ft *462 m* above sea-level. The highest in Scotland is Wanlockhead, in Dumfries-shire at 1,380 ft *420 m* above sea-level.

Lowest The settlement of Ein Bokek, which has a synagogue, on the shores of the Dead Sea is the lowest in the world at 1,299 ft *395,9 m* below sea-level.

Oldest World The oldest known walled town in the world is Arīhā (Jericho). The latest radio-carbon dating on specimens from the lowest levels reached by archaeologists indicate habitation there by perhaps 3,000 people as early as 7800 B.C. The village of Zawi Chemi Shanidar, discovered in 1957 in northern Iraq, has been dated to 8910 B.C. The oldest capital city in the world is Dimashq (Damascus), the capital of Syria. It has been continuously inhabited since *c.* 2500 B.C.

Great Britain The oldest town in Great Britain is often cited as Colchester, the old British Camulodunum, headquarters of Belgic chiefs in the 1st century B.C. However, the place-name Salakee, St. Mary's, Isles of Scilly is believed to be pre-Celtic and hence *ante* 550 B.C.

Northern-most The world's northernmost town with a population of more than 10,000 is the Arctic port of Dikson, U.S.S.R. in 73° 32′ N. The northernmost village is Ny Ålesund (78° 55′ N.), a coalmining settlement on King's Bay, Vest Spitsbergen, in the Norwegian territory of Svalbard, inhabited only during the winter season. The northernmost capital is Reykjavik, the capital of Iceland, in 64° 06′ N. Its population was estimated to be 87,950 in 1973. The northernmost permanent human occupation is the base at Alert (82° 31′ N.), on Dumb Bell Bay, on the north-east coast of Ellesmere Island, northern Canada.

J. Allan Cash

The world's oldest walled city, Jericho, dating from 7,800 BC

179

Southernmost The world's southernmost village is Puerto Williams (population about 350), on the north coast of Isla Navarino, in Tierra del Fuego, Chile, about 680 miles *1 090 km* north of Antarctica. Wellington, North Island, New Zealand is the southernmost capital city on 41° 17′ S. The world's southernmost administrative centre is Port Stanley (51° 43′ S.), in the Falkland Islands, off South America.

Most remote from sea The largest town most remote from the sea is Wulumuch'i (Urumchi) formerly Tihwa, Sinkiang, capital of the Uighur Autonomous Region of China, at a distance of about 1,400 miles *2 250 km* from the nearest coastline. Its population was estimated to be 275,000 at 31 Dec. 1957.

EMIGRATION

More people emigrate from the United Kingdom than from any other country. A total of 255,000 emigrated from the U.K. from mid-1973 to mid-1974. The largest number of emigrants in any one year was 360,000 in 1852, mainly from Ireland in the aftermath of the Great Famine.

IMMIGRATION

The country which regularly receives the most immigrants is the United States, with 400,063 in 1973. It has been estimated that in the period 1820–1973, the U.S.A. has received 46,317,884 immigrants. The peak year for immigration into the United Kingdom was the 12 months from 1 July 1961 to 30 June 1962, when about 430,000 Commonwealth citizens arrived. The number of immigrants for the year ending June 1974 was 182,700.

TOURISM

In 1973 the United Kingdom received a record 7,900,000 visitors, who spent an estimated £835,000,000 excluding fares to British carriers.

BIRTH RATE

Highest and lowest The highest 1965–70 figure is 52.3 for Swaziland. The rate for the whole world was 33 per 1,000 in 1973.

Excluding Vatican City, where the rate is negligible, the lowest recorded rate is 7.6 for Monaco (1973).

The 1974 rate in the United Kingdom was 13.1/1,000 (13.0 in England and Wales, 13.5 in Scotland and 18.7 in Northern Ireland), while the 1973 rate for the Republic of Ireland was 22.5 registered births per 1,000. The highest number of births in England and Wales (since registration in 1837) has been 957,782 in 1920 and the lowest 579,091 in 1941.

DEATH RATE

Highest and lowest The highest of the latest available recorded death rates is 29.9 deaths per each 1,000 of the population in Guinea-Bissau in 1970. The rate for the whole world was 13 per 1,000 in 1973.

The lowest of the latest available recorded rates is 3.2 deaths/1,000 in Tonga in 1971.

The 1974 rate in the United Kingdom was 12.0/1,000 (11.9 in England and Wales, 12.4 in Scotland and 11.1 in Northern Ireland), while the 1972 rate for the Republic of Ireland was 11.3 registered deaths per 1,000. The highest S.M.I. (Standard Mortality Index where the national average is 100) is in Salford, Greater Manchester with a figure of 133.

NATURAL INCREASE

The highest of the latest available recorded rates of natural increase is 38.3 (45.6 − 7.3 in 1970)/1,000 in the U.S. Virgin Island. The rate for the whole world was 33 − 13 = 20 per 1,000 in 1973.

The 1974 rate for the United Kingdom was 1.9/1,000 (1.9 in England and Wales, 1.8 in Scotland and 7.6 in Northern Ireland). The figure for the Republic of Ireland was 10.7/1,000 in 1972. The rate for the first time in the first quarter of 1975 became one of natural decrease.

The lowest rate of natural increase in any major independent country is in East Germany (birth rate 10.6 death rate 13.7) with a negative figure thus of −3.1 per 1,000 for 1973.

Marriage ages The country with the lowest average ages for marriage is India, with 20.0 years for males and 14.5 years for females. At the other extreme is Ireland, with 31.4 for males and 26.5 years for females. In the People's Republic of China the recommended age for marriage for men is 28 and for women 25.

SEX RATIO

The country with the largest recorded shortage of males is the U.S.S.R., with 1,169 females to every 1,000 males at 15 Jan. 1970. The country with the largest recorded woman shortage is Pakistan, with 936 to every 1,000 males in 1972. The figures are, however, probably under-enumerated due to *purdah*. The ratio in the United Kingdom was 1,057.4 females to every 1,000 males at 30 June 1973, and is expected to be 1,014.2/1,000 by A.D. 2000.

INFANT MORTALITY

Based on deaths before one year of age, the lowest of the latest available recorded rates is 9.6 deaths per 1,000 live births in Iceland and in Sweden both in 1973.

The highest recorded infant mortality rate reported has been 195 to 300 for Burma in 1952. Many countries have apparently ceased to make returns. Among these is Ethiopia, where the infant mortality rate was unofficially estimated to be nearly 550/1,000 live births in 1969.

The United Kingdom figure for 1973/74 was 16.8/1,000 live births (England and Wales 16.4, Scotland 19.0, Northern Ireland 20.2). The Republic of Ireland figure for 1972 was 18.0.

LIFE EXPECTATION

There is evidence that life expectation in Britain in the 5th century A.D. was 33 years for males and 27 years for females. In the decade 1890–1900 the expectation of life among the population of India was 23.7 years.

Based on the latest available data, the highest recorded expectation of life at age 12 months is 71.42 years for Norwegian males (1961–65) and 76.7 years for Dutch females (1971).

The lowest recorded expectation of life at birth is 27 years for both sexes in the Vallée du Niger area of Mali in 1957 (sample survey, 1957–58). The figure for males in Gabon was 25 years in 1960–61 but 45 for females. In Guinea-Bissau it averaged 33 years in 1965.

The latest available figures for England and Wales (1969–71) are 69.2 years for males and 75.2 years for females; for Scotland (1968–70) 66.9 years for males and 73.08 years for females; for Northern Ireland (1969–71) 67.9 years for males and 73.7 years for females and for the Republic of Ireland (1960–62) 68.13 years for males and 71.86 years for females. The British figure for 1901–1910 was 48.53 years for males and 52.83 years for females.

STANDARDS OF LIVING

National incomes The country with the highest income per native citizen in 1972 was Nauru, with some £3,400 *$8,500* but with only £1,730 per head. In 1972 the U.S. reached $4,492 *£1,871* per head compared with $2,642 *£1,101* for the U.K. (1973).

HOUSING

For comparison, dwelling units are defined as a structurally separated room or rooms occupied by private households of one or more people and having separate access or a common passageway to the street.

The country with the greatest recorded number of private housing units is India, with 79,193,602 occupied in 1960. These contain 83,523,895 private households.

Great Britain comes fourth among reporting countries, with 18,839,000 dwellings (England 16,076,000, Wales 961,000, Scotland 1,802,000) at June 1971. The 1968 figure for Northern Ireland was 435,000. The Republic of Ireland had 687,304 private households in 1966. The record number of permanent houses built has been 425,800 in 1968.

PHYSICIANS

The country with the most physicians is the U.S.S.R., with 555,400 in 1969, or one to every 433 persons. China has more than a million para-medical personel known as "bare foot doctors". In England and Wales there were 24,775 doctors employed by the National Health Service on 30 Sept. 1970.

The country with the highest proportion of physicians is Israel, where there were 7,281 (one to every 400 inhabitants) in 1970. The country with the lowest recorded proportion is Upper Volta, with 58 physicians (one for every 92,759 people) in 1970.

Dentists The country with the most dentists is the United States, where 119,000 were registered members of the American Dental Association in 1972.

Psychia- trists The country with the most psychiatrists is the United States. The registered membership of the American Psychiatric Association was 20,277 in 1974. The membership of the American Psychological Association was 35,000 in 1974.

HOSPITALS

Largest World The largest medical centre in the world is the District Medical Center in Chicago, Illinois, U.S.A. It covers 478 acres *193 ha* and includes five hospitals, with a total of 5,600 beds, and eight professional schools with more than 3,000 students.

The largest mental hospital in the world is the Pilgrim State Hospital, on Long Island, New York State, U.S.A., with 12,800 beds. It formerly contained 14,200 beds.

The largest maternity hospital in the world is the Kandang Kerbau Government Maternity Hospital in Singapore. It has 239 midwives, 151 beds for gynaecological cases, 388 maternity beds and an output of

The world's most productive maternity hospital which in 1966 reached a peak of one birth each 13 min 11 sec

Emperor Hirohito, the 124th in line from Jimmu Tenno, first Emperor of Japan

31,255 babies in 1969 compared with the record "birthquake" of 39,856 babies (more than 109 per day) in 1966.

United Kingdom The largest hospitals of any kind in the United Kingdom are the Rainhill Hospital near Liverpool, with 2,250 staffed beds, and St. Bernard's Hospital, Southall, Ealing, Greater London, which has 1,785 staffed beds for mental patients.

The largest general hospital in the United Kingdom is the St. James Hospital, Leeds, West Yorkshire, with 1,413 available staffed beds.

The largest maternity hospital in the United Kingdom is the Mill Road Maternity Hospital, Liverpool with 177 staffed beds.

The largest children's hospital in the United Kingdom is Queen Mary's Hospital for Children, at Carshalton, Sutton, Greater London, with 686 staffed beds.

Longest stay in hospital Miss Martha Nelson was admitted to the Columbus State Institute for the Feeble-Minded in Ohio, U.S.A. in 1875. She died in January 1975 aged 103 years 6 months in the Orient State Institution, Ohio after spending 99 years in institutions.

2. ROYALTY AND HEADS OF STATE

Oldest ruling house The Emperor of Japan, Hirohito (born 29 April 1901), is the 124th in line from the first Emperor, Jimmu Tenno or Zinmu, whose reign was traditionally from 660 to 581 B.C., but probably from c. 40 to c. 10 B.C. His Imperial Majesty Muhammad Rizā Shāh Pahlavi of Iran (b. 26 Oct. 1919) claims Cyrus the Great (reigned c. 559–530 B.C.) as an ancestor.

Her Majesty Queen Elizabeth II (b. 21 April 1926) represents dynasties historically traceable at least back until the 5th century A.D.; notably that of Elesa of whom Alfred The Great was a 13 great grandson and the Queen is therefore a 49 great granddaughter.

REIGNS

Longest The longest recorded reign of any monarch is that of Pepi II, a Sixth Dynasty Pharaoh of ancient Egypt. His reign began in c. 2,310 B.C., when he was aged 6, and lasted c. 94 years. Musoma Kanijo, chief of the Nzega district of western Tanganyika (now part of Tanzania), reputedly reigned for more than 98 years from 1864, when aged 8, until his death on 2 Feb. 1963. The 6th Japanese Emperor Koo-an traditionally reigned for 102 years (from 392 to 290 B.C.), but probably his actual reign was from about A.D. 110 to

Mary Evans

England's long-lived Head of State, Richard Cromwell the Lord Protector of 1658-59, who lived to his 86th year

Shortest The shortest recorded reign was that of Jean I, King of France, who was born posthumously on 15 Nov. 1316 and died aged 4 days on 19 Nov. 1316.

Highest post-nominal numbers The highest post-nominal number ever used to designate a member of a Royal House was 75 briefly enjoyed by Count Heinrich LXXV Reuss (1800–1801). All male members of this branch of this German family are called Heinrich and are successively numbered from I upwards *each* century.

The highest British regnal number is 8, used by Henry VIII (1509–1547), who was the first British user of regnal numbers, and by Edward VIII (1936) who died as H.R.H. the Duke of Windsor, K.G., K.T., K.P., G.C.B., G.C.S.I., G.C.M.G., G.C.I.E., G.C.V.O., G.B.E., I.S.O., M.C. on 28 May 1972. Jacobites liked to style Henry Benedict, Cardinal York (born 1725), the grandson of James II, as Henry IX in respect of his "reign' from 1788 to 1807 when he died the last survivor in the male line of the House of Stuart.

Longest lived 'Royals' The longest life among the Blood Royal of Europe is the 96 years 247 days of H.R.H. Princess Anna of Battenberg, daughter of Nicholas I of Montenegro, who was born 18 Aug. 1874 and died in Switzerland 22 April 1971. The greatest age among European Royal Consorts is the 99 years 110 days of H.S.H Princess Marie Felixovna Romanovsky-Krassinsky, who was born 19 Aug. 1872 and died in Paris 7 Dec. 1971. The longest-lived Queen on record has been the Queen Grandmother of Siam, Queen Sawang (b. 10 Sept. 1862), 27th daughter of King Mongkut (Rama IV), who died on 17 Dec. 1955 aged 93 years 3 months.

Roman Occupation During the 369 year long Roman occupation of England, Wales and parts of Scotland there were 40 sole and 27 co-Emperors of Rome. Of these the longest reigning was Constantinus I (The Great) from 31 March 307 to 22 May 337—30 years 2 months.

Head of State oldest and youngest The oldest head of state in the world is Marshal Josip Broz Tito G.C.B.(Hon.) (b. 25 May 1892), President of the Republic of Yugoslavia since 1953. The youngest non-royal head of state is Jean-Claude du Valier, (b. 3 July 1951) President of Haiti.

Youngest King and Queen Of the world's 24 monarchs that with the youngest King is Bhutan where King Jigme Singye Wangchuk was born 11 Nov. 1955. Crowned on 2 June 1974. Queen Alia, third wife of King Hussein I of Jordan became Queen on the eve of her 24th birthday (b. 25 Dec. 1948).

about A.D. 140. The reign of the 11th Emperor Suinin was traditionally from 29 B.C. to A.D. 71 (99 years), but probably from A.D. 259 to 291. The longest reign in European history was that of King Louis XIV of France, who ascended the throne on 14 May 1643, aged 4 years 8 months, and reigned for 72 years 110 days until his death on 1 Sept. 1715, four days before his 77th birthday.

Currently the longest reigning monarch in the world is King Sobhuza II, K.B.E. (b. 4 July 1899), the *Ngwenyama* (Paramount Chief) of Swaziland, under United Kingdom protection since December 1899, and independent since 6 Sept. 1968. Hirohito (see above) has been Emperor in Japan since 25 Dec. 1926.

BRITISH MONARCHY RECORDS

	Kings	Queens Regnant	Queens Consort
Longest Reign or tenure	59 years 96 days[1] George III 1760–1820	63 years 216 days Victoria 1837–1901	57 years 70 days Charlotte 1761–1818 (Consort of George III)
Shortest Reign or tenure	77 days[2] Edward V 1483	13 days Jane, July 1553	154 days Yoleta (1285–1286) (2nd consort of Alexander III)
Longest lived	81 years 239 days[3] George III (b. 1738–d. 1820)	81 years 243 days Victoria (b. 1819–d. 1901)	85 years 303 days Mary of Teck (b. 1867–d. 1953) (Consort of George V)
Most children (legitimate)[4]	18 Edward I 1272–1307	9[5] Victoria (b. 1819–d. 1901)	15 Eleanor (c 1244–1290) and Charlotte (b. 1744–d. 1818)
Oldest to start reign or consortship	64 years 10 months William IV 1830–1837	37 years 5 months Mary I 1553–1558	56 years 53 days Alexandra (b. 1844–d. 1925) (Consort of Edward VII)
Youngest to start reign or consortship	269 days Henry VI in 1422	6 or 7 days Mary, Queen of Scots in 1542	6 years 11 months Isabella (second consort of Richard II in 1396)
Most married	6 times Henry VIII 1509–1547	3 times Mary, Queen of Scots 1542–1567 (executed 1587)	4 times Catharine Parr (b. c. 1512–d. 1548) (sixth consort of Henry VIII)

Notes (*Dates are dates of reigns or tenures unless otherwise indicated*).

[1] *James Francis Edward, the Old Pretender, known to his supporters as James III, styled his reign from 16 Sept. 1701 until his death 1 Jan. 1766 (i.e. 64 years 109 days).*
[2] *There is the probability that in pre-Conquest times Sweyn 'Forkbeard', the Danish King of England, reigned for only 40 days in 1013–1014.*
[3] *Richard Cromwell (b. 4 Oct. 1626), the 2nd Lord Protector from 3 Sept. 1658 until his abdication on 24 May 1659, lived under the alias John Clarke until 12 July 1712 aged 85 years 9 months and was thus the longest lived Head of State.*
[4] *Henry I (1068–1135) in addition to one (possibly two) legitimate sons and a daughter had at least 20 bastard children (9 sons, 11 daughters), and possibly 22, by six mistresses.*
[5] *Queen Anne (b. 1665–d. 1714) had 17 pregnancies, which produced only 5 live births.*

3. LEGISLATURES

PARLIAMENTS

Oldest The oldest legislative body is the *Alpingi* (Althing) of Iceland founded in A.D. 930. This body, which originally comprised 39 local chieftains, was abolished in 1800, but restored by Denmark to a consultative status in 1843 and a legislative status in 1874. The legislative assembly with the oldest continuous history is the Tynwald Court in the Isle of Man, which is believed to have originated more than 1,000 years ago.

Largest The largest legislative assembly in the world is the National People's Congress of the People's Republic of China. The fourth Congress, which met in March 1969, had 3,500 members.

Smallest quorum The House of Lords has the smallest quorum, expressed as a percentage of eligible voters, of any legislative body in the world, namely less than one-third of one per cent. To transact business there must be three peers present, including the Lord Chancellor or his deputy. The House of Commons quorum of 40 M.P.'s, including the Speaker or his deputy, is 20 times as exacting.

Highest paid legislators The most highly paid of all the world's legislators are Senators of the United States who receive a basic annual salary of $42,500 (*£17,000*). Of this, up to $3,000 (*£1,153*) is exempt from taxation. In addition up to $157,092 (*£62,836*) per annum is allowed for office help, with a salary limit of $30,600 (*£12,240*) for any one staff member (limited to 16 in number). Senators also enjoy free travel, telephones, postage, medical care, telegrams, stationery (limited to 480,000 envelopes per year), flowers and haircuts. They also command very low rates for filming, speech and radio transcriptions and, in the case of women senators, beauty treatment. When abroad they have access to "counterpart funds" and on retirement to non-contributory benefits.

Longest membership The longest span as a legislator was 83 years by József Madarász (1814–1915). He first attended the Hungarian Parliament in 1832–36 as *ablegatus absentium* (*i.e.* on behalf of an absent deputy). He was a full member in 1848–50 and from 1861 until his death on 31 Jan. 1915.

Filibusters The longest continuous speech in the history of the United States Senate was that of Senator Wayne Morse of Oregon on 24–25 April 1953, when he spoke on the Tidelands Oil Bill for 22 hrs 26 min without resuming his seat. Interrupted only briefly by the swearing-in of a new senator, Senator Strom Thurmond (South Carolina, Democrat) spoke against the Civil Rights Bill for 24 hrs 19 min on 28–29 Aug. 1957. The United States national record duration for a filibuster is 42 hrs 3 min by Texas State senator Mick McKool in favour of extra expenditure on mental health in June 1972.

ELECTIONS

Largest The largest election ever held was that for the Indian *Lok Sabha* (House of the People) on 1–10 March 1971. About 152,720,000 of the electorate of 272,630,000 chose from 2,785 candidates for 518 seats.

Closest The ultimate in close general elections occurred in Zanzibar (now part of Tanzania) on 18 Jan. 1961, when the Afro-Shirazi Party won by a single seat, after the seat of Chake-Chake on Pemba Island had been gained by a single vote.

Most expensive The cost of the 1972 Presidential election in the United States was estimated at $49.07 million by the Republicans, who won 49 of the 50 States, and $45.0 million by the Democrats.

Most one-sided North Korea recorded a 100 per cent. turn-out of electors and a 100 per cent vote for the Worker's Party of Korea in the general election of 8 Oct. 1962. The previous record had been set in the Albanian election of 4 June 1962, when all but seven of the electorate of 889,875 went to the polls—a 99.9992 per cent turn-out. Of the 889,868 voters, 889,828 voted for the candidates of the Albanian Party of Labour, *i.e.* 99.9955 per cent of the total poll.

Highest personal majority The highest personal majority was 157,692 from 192,909 votes cast, by H. H. Maharani of Jaipur (born 23 May 1919) in the Indian general election of Feb. 1962.

Communist parties The largest national Communist party outside the Soviet Union (14,254,000 members in 1971) and Communist states has been the Partito Communista Italiano (Italian Communist Party), with a membership of 2,300,000 in 1946. The total was 1,500,000 in 1973. The membership in mainland China was estimated to be 17,000,000 in 1970. The Communist Party of Great Britain, formed on 31 July 1920 in Cannon Street Station Hotel, London, attained its peak membership of 56,000 in December 1942, compared with 28,803 in November 1971. (Latest available figure).

Most parties The country with the greatest number of political parties is Italy with 73 registered for the elections of 19 May 1968. These included "Friends of the Moon" with one candidate.

PRIME MINISTERS

Oldest The longest lived Prime Minister of any country is believed to have been Christopher Hornsrud, Prime Minister of Norway from 28 Jan. to 15 Feb. 1928. He was born on 15 Nov. 1859 and died on 13 Dec. 1960, aged 101 years 28 days.

El Hadji Muhammad el Mokri, Grand Vizier of Morocco, died on 16 Sept. 1957, at a reputed age of 116 Muslim (*Hijri*) years, equivalent to 112.5 Gregorian years.

Longest term of office Prof. Dr. António de Oliveirar Salazar, G.C.M.G. (Hon.) (1889–1970) was the President of the Council of Ministers (*i.e.* Prime Minister) of Portugal from 5 July 1932 until 27 Sept. 1968—36 years 84 days. He was superseded 11 days after going into a coma.

UNITED KINGDOM

Parliament Earliest The earliest known use of the term "parliament" in an official English royal document, in the meaning of a summons to the King's council, dates from 19 Dec. 1241.

The Houses of Parliament of the United Kingdom in the Palace of Westminster, London, had 1,709 members (House of Lords 1,074, House of Commons 635) in June 1973.

Longest The longest English Parliament was the "Pensioners" Parliament of Charles II, which lasted from 8 May 1661 to 24 Jan. 1679, a period of 17 years 8 months and 16 days. The longest United Kingdom Parliament was that of George V, Edward VIII and George VI, lasting from 26 Nov. 1935 to 15 June 1945, a span of 9 years 6 months and 20 days.

Shortest The parliament of Edward I, summoned to Westminster for 30 May 1306, lasted only one day. The parliament of Charles II at Oxford from 21–28 March 1681 lasted 7 days. The shortest United Kingdom Parliament was that of George III, lasting from 15 Dec. 1806 to 29 April 1807, a period of only 4 months and 14 days.

Longest sittings The longest sitting in the House of Commons was one of 41½ hrs from 4 p.m. on 31 Jan. 1881 to 9.30 a.m.

on 2 Feb. 1881, on the question of better Protection of Person and Property in Ireland. The longest sitting of the Lords has been 19 hrs 16 min from 2.30 p.m. on 29 Feb. to 9.46 a.m. on 1 March 1968 on the Commonwealth Immigrants Bill (Committee stage).

Most time consuming legislation The most profligate use of parliamentary time was on the Government of Ireland Bill of 1893–4, which required 82 days in the House of Commons of which 46 days was in Committee. The record for a standing committee is 57 sittings (248 hrs and 4,734 Hansard columns) on the Housing Finance Bill between 25 Nov. 1971 and 27 March 1972.

Divisions The record number of divisions in the House of Commons is 43 in the single session of 20–21 March 1907. The largest division was one of 350–310 on a vote of confidence in 1892.

ELECTORATES

Largest and smallest The largest electorate of all time was the estimated 217,900 for Hendon, Barnet, Greater London, prior to the redistribution in 1941. The largest electorate for a seat in Great Britain is 97,364 for Meriden (1974 Register). In Antrim South, Northern Ireland the figure is 117,834. The smallest electorate of all-time was in Old Sarum (number of houses nil, population nil since c. 1540) in Wiltshire, with eight electors who returned two members in 1821, thus being 54,475 times as well represented as the Hendon electorate of 120 years later. There were no contested elections in Old Sarum for the 536 years from 1295 to 1831. The smallest electorate for any seat is Western Isles with 22,432 electors.

Referendum On the Common Market referendum of 5 June 1975 the electorate was 40,086,677 of whom 25,848,654 cast effective votes. The highest "Yes" vote was 76.3% in North Yorkshire and highest "No" vote was 70.5% in the Western Isles. The highest turnout was 75.0% in the Isles of Scilly and the lowest was 47.1% in Shetland.

MAJORITIES

Party The largest party majorities were those of the Liberals, with 307 seats in 1832 and 356 seats in 1906. In 1931 the Coalition of Conservatives, Liberals and National Labour candidates had a majority of 491. The narrowest party majority was that of the Whigs in 1847, with a single seat.

The largest majority on a division was one of 463 (464 votes to 1), on a motion of "no confidence" in the conduct of World War II, on 29 Jan. 1942. Since the war the largest has been one of 461 (487 votes to 26) on 10 May 1967, during the debate on the government's application for Britain to join the European Economic Community (the "Common Market").

Largest personal **All-time** The largest individual majority of any Member of Parliament was the 62,253 of Sir A. Cooper Rawson, M.P. (Conservative) at Brighton in 1931. He polled 75,205 votes against 12,952 votes for his closer opponent the Labour Candidate, Lewis Coleman Cohen, later Lord Cohen of Brighton (1897–1966), from an electorate of 128,779. The largest majority of any woman M.P. was 38,823 in the same General Election by the Countess of Iveagh (née Lady Gwendolen Florence Mary Onslow), C.B.E. (1881–1966), the Conservative member for Southend-on-Sea, Essex, from November 1927 to October 1935.

Current The largest majority in the October 1974 Parliament is 38,432 held by James H. Molyneaux (United Ulster Unionist Council) in Antrim South where he received 48,892 votes. The highest figure for Great Britain is 34,481 by T. Alec. Jones (Lab.) in Rhondda, Wales.

Narrowest personal *All-time* The closest result occurred in the General Election of 1886 at Ashton-under-Lyne, Greater Manchester when the Conservative and Liberal candidates both received

3,049 votes, The Returning Officer, Mr. James Walker, gave his casting vote for John E. W. Addison (Con.), who was duly returned while Alexander B. Rowley (Gladstone-Liberal) was declared unelected. On 13 Oct. 1892 there was a by-election at Cirencester, Gloucestershire, which resulted in an election petition after which the number of votes cast for the Conservative and Liberal were found to have been equal. A new election was ordered.

Two examples of majorities of one have occurred. At Durham in the 1895 General Election, Matthew Fowler (Lib.) with 1,111 votes defeated the Hon. Arthur R. D. Elliott (Liberal-Unionist) (1,110 votes) after a recount. At Exeter in the General Election of December 1910 a Liberal victory over the Conservatives by 4 votes was reversed on an election petition to a Conservative win by H. E. Duke K.C. (later the 1st Lord Merrivale) (Unionist) with 4,777 votes to R. H. St. Maur's (Lib.) 4,776 votes.

The smallest majority since "universal" franchise was one of two votes by Abraham John Flint (b. 1903), the National Labour candidate at Ilkeston, Derbyshire, in the 1931 General Election. He received 17,587 votes, compared with 17,585 for G. H. Oliver, D.C.M. (Labour).

Current The finest economy of effort in getting elected by any member of the present Parliament was a majority of 22 by Mrs. Margaret A. Bain M.P. (Scot. Nat.) with 15,551 votes in Dunbartonshire East over J. S. Barry Henderson (Con.).

Most recounts The greatest recorded number of recounts has been 7 in the case of Brighton, Kemptown on 16 Oct. 1964 when Dennis H. Hobden (Labour) won by 7 votes and at Peterborough on 31 Mar–1 Apr. 1966 when Sir Harmer Nicholls Bt. (Conservative) won by 3 votes. The counts from the point of view of the loser Michael J. Ward (Labour) went +163, +163; +2, −2, −6, +1, −2, −3. Sir Harmer, with a present majority of 22, has suffered 21 counts in only 8 elections.

Most rapid change of fortune On 3 July 1874 Hardinge Stanley Giffard (Con.), later the 1st Earl of Halsbury (1823–1921), received one vote at Launceston, Cornwall. In 1877 he was returned unopposed for the same seat.

Greatest swing The greatest swing, at least since 1832, was at the Dartford, Kent by-election when on 27 March 1920 Labour turned a Coalition majority of 9,370 to a win by 9,048. This represented a swing of 38.7 per cent. compared with the swing of 32.60 per cent at Sutton

Graphic Dumbarton

Mrs. Margaret Bain, the Scottish Nationalist Party M.P., who presently has the narrowest majority in Parliament

Mrs. Helene Hayman, M.P., the youngest Member of the House of Commons

Tom Iremonger, who gained 19,843 votes in February 1974 (elected) and 19,843 in October 1974 (not elected)

and Cheam, Sutton, Greater London on 7 Dec. 1972 to elect the Liberal Graham Tope, 29. In the 1970 General Election an Ulster Unionist majority of 22,986 was turned into a Protestant Unionist majority of 2,679 over the sitting Member by Ian Richard Kyle Paisley (b. 8 Apr. 1926). Since there was no Protestant Unionist candidate in 1966 no swing figure is therefore calculable. He gained 41.3% of the poll.

Electoral Stability In the March and October elections of 1974 Tom L. Iremonger (Con.) in Ilford North received 19,843 votes on both occasions.

Highest poll The highest poll in any constituency since "universal" franchise was 93.42 per cent in Fermanagh and South Tyrone, Northern Ireland, at the General Election of 25 Oct. 1951, when there were 62,799 voters from an electorate of 67,219. The Anti-Partition candidate, Mr. Cahir Healy (1877–1970), was elected with a majority of 2,635 votes. The highest poll in any constituency in the 1974 General Election was 91.2 per cent in Fermanagh and South Tyrone. The highest figure in Great Britain was 87.27 per cent in Manchester-Wynthenshawe.

M.P.s *Youngest* Edmund Waller (1606–1687) was the Member of Parliament for Amersham, Buckinghamshire, in the Parliament of 1621, in which year he was 15. The official returns, however, do not show him as actually having taken his seat until two years later when, in the Parliament of 1623–24, he sat as Member for Ilchester, Somerset. In 1435 Henry Long (1420–1490) was returned for an Old Sarum seat also at the age of 15. His precise date of birth is unknown. Minors were debarred in law in 1695 and in fact in 1832. Since that time the youngest Member of Parliament has been the Hon. Esmond Cecil Harmsworth (now the 2nd Viscount Rothermere) who was elected for the Isle of Thanet, Kent, on 28 Nov. 1919, when 21 years 183 days. The youngest M.P. is now Mrs. Helene V. H. Hayman *née* Middleweek (b. 26 March 1949) (Lab.), member for Welwyn and Hatfield.

Oldest The oldest of all members was Samuel Young (b. 14 Feb. 1822), Nationalist M.P. for East Cavan (1892–1918), who died on 18 April 1918, aged 96 years 63 days. The oldest "Father of the House" in Parliamentary history was the Rt. Hon. Charles Pelham Villiers (b. 3 Jan. 1802), who was the Member for Wolverhampton when he died on 16 Jan. 1898, aged 96 years 13 days. He was a Member of Parliament for 63

years 6 days, having been returned at 16 elections. The longest sitting member in the present Parliament is the Rt. Hon. George Russell Strauss (b. 18 July 1901), Labour member for Lambeth, Vauxhall, who has sat continuously since 1934 and also from 1929–31. He missed election in 1924 by 29 votes. The oldest member is David Weitzman (Labour) (b. 18 June 1898).

Longest span The longest span of service of any M.P., is 63 years 10 months (1 Oct. 1900 to 25 Sept. 1964) by the Rt. Hon. Sir Winston Leonard Spencer-Churchill, K.G., O.M., C.H., T.D. (1874–1965), with a break only from November 1922 to October 1924. The longest unbroken span was that of C. P. Villiers (see below). The longest span in the Palace of Westminster (both Houses of Parliament) has been 73 years by the 10th Earl of Wemyss and March G.C.V.O., who, as Sir Francis Wemyss-Charteris-Douglas, served as M.P. for East Gloucestershire (1841–46) and Haddingtonshire (1847–83) and then took his seat in the House of Lords, dying on 30 June 1914, aged 95 years 330 days.

Earliest women M.P.s The first woman to be elected to the House of Commons was Mme. Constance Georgine Markievicz (*née* Gore Booth). She was elected as member (Sinn Fein) for St. Patrick's Dublin, in December 1918. The first woman to take her seat was the Viscountess Astor, C.H. (1879–1964) (b. Nancy Witcher Langhorne at Danville, Virginia, U.S.A.; formerly Mrs. Robert Gould Shaw), who was elected Unionist member for the Sutton Division of Plymouth, Devon, on 28 Nov. 1919, and took her seat three days later.

Longest Serving The longest serving woman M.P. of all-time has been Dame Irene Mary Bewick Ward C.H., D.B.E., who fought all 12 General elections (1924–1970) and who served as member for Wallsend (1931–45) and for Tynemouth (1950–74). She shared also the 20th century record for introducing 4 Private Members Bills which became Acts with Sir Robert Gower (1880–1953).

HOUSE OF LORDS

Oldest Member The oldest member ever was the Rt. Hon. the 5th Baron Penrhyn, who was born on 21 Nov. 1865 and died on 3 Feb. 1967, aged 101 years 74 days. The oldest now is the Rt. Hon. Walter Egerton George Lucian Keppel, M.C., ninth Earl of Albermarle (b. 28 Feb. 1882). The oldest peer to make a maiden speech was Lord Maenan (1854–1951) aged 94 years 123 days.

Youngest Member The youngest present member of the House of Lords has been H.R.H. the Prince Charles Philip Arthur George, K.G., G.C.B., the Prince of Wales (b. 14 Nov. 1948). All Dukes of Cornwall, of whom Prince Charles is the 24th, are technically eligible to sit, regardless of age—in his case from his succession on 6 Feb. 1952, aged 3. The 20th and 21st holders, later King George IV (b. 1762) and King Edward VII (b. 1841), were technically entitled to sit from birth. The youngest creation of a life peer under the Peerage Act 1958 has been that of Lord Tanlaw, formerly the Hon. Simon Brooke Mackay (b. 30 March 1934) at the age of 37 years 8 days. However Lady Masham (b. 14 April 1935) was created Baroness Masham of Ilton at the age of 34 years 262 days.

Longest speech The longest recorded continuous speech in the House of Commons was that of Henry Peter Brougham (1778–1868) on 7 Feb. 1828, when he spoke for 6 hrs on Law Reform. He ended at 10.40 p.m. and the report of this speech occupied 12 columns of the next day's edition of *The Times*. Brougham, created the 1st Lord Brougham and Vaux on 22 Nov. 1830, also holds the House of Lords record, also with six hours on 7 Oct. 1831, when speaking on the second reading of the Reform Bill. The longest back bench speech since 7 Feb. 1828 has been one of 3 hrs 16 min by Sir Bernard Braine (b. 1914) the Conservative member for Essex, South East concerning Canvey Island on 23–24 July 1974.

The longest speech in Stormont, Northern Ireland was one of 9½ hours by Tommy Henderson M.P. on the Appropriations Bill on 26–27 May 1936.

Greatest parliamentary petition The greatest petition was supposed to be the Great Chartist Petition of 1848 but of the 5,706,000 "signatures" only 1,975,496 were valid. The all time largest was for the abolition of Entertainment Duty with 3,107,080 signatures presented on 5 June 1951.

PREMIERSHIP

Longest term No United Kingdom Prime Minister has yet matched in duration the continuous term of office of Great Britain's first Prime Minister the Rt. Hon. Sir Robert Walpole, K.G., later the 1st Earl of Orford (1676–1745), First Lord of the Treasury and Chancellor, of the Exchequer from 3 April 1721 to 12 Feb. 1742. The office was not, however, officially recognised until 1905, since when the longest tenure has been that of Herbert Henry Asquith, later the 1st Earl of Oxford

Mansell Collection

Harry Brougham, Britain's most locquacious Parliamentarian, who set records in both the Lords and Commons

and Asquith (1852–1928), with 8 years 243 days from 8 April 1908 to 7 Dec. 1916. This was 7 days longer than the three terms of Sir Winston Churchill, between 1940 and 1955.

Shortest term The Rt. Hon. William Pulteney, the Earl of Bath (1684–1764) held office for 3 days from 10–12 Feb. 1746 but was unable to form a ministry. The shortest term of any ministry was that of the 1st Duke of Wellington, K.G., G.C.B., G.C.H. (1769–1852), whose third ministry survived only 22 days from 17 Nov. to 9 Dec. 1834.

Most times The only Prime Minister to have accepted office five times was the Rt. Hon. Stanley Baldwin, later the 1st Earl Baldwin of Bewdley (1867–1947). His ministries were those of 22 May 1923 to 22 Jan. 1924, 4 Nov. 1924 to 5 June 1929, 7 June 1935 to 21 Jan. 1936, from then until the abdication of 12 Dec. 1936 and from then until 28 May 1937.

Longest lived The longest lived Prime Minister of the United Kingdom has been the Rt. Hon. Sir Winston Leonard Spencer-Churchill, K.G., O.M., C.H., T.D., (b. 30 Nov. 1874), who surpassed the age of the Rt. Hon. William Ewart Gladstone (1809–98) on 21 April 1963 and died on 24 Jan. 1965, aged 90 years 55 days. Gladstone's last day in office on 3 Mar. 1894 was when he was 84 years 64 days—having been elected on 18 Aug. 1892.

Youngest The youngest of Great Britain's 49 Prime Ministers has been the Rt. Hon. the Hon. William Pitt (b. 28 May 1759), who accepted the King's invitation to be First Lord of the Treasury on 19 Dec. 1783, aged 24 years 205 days, He had previously declined on 27 Feb. 1783, when aged 23 years 275 days.

CHANCELLORSHIP

Longest and shortest tenures The Rt. Hon. Sir Robert Walpole, K.G., later the 1st Earl of Orford (1676–1745), served 22 years 5 months as Chancellor of the Exchequer, holding office continuously from 12 Oct. 1715 to 12 Feb. 1742, except for the period from 16 April 1717 to 2 April 1721. The briefest tenure of this office was 26 days in the case of the Baron (later the 1st Earl of) Mansfield (1705–93), from 11 Sept. to 6 Oct. 1767. The only man with four terms in this office was the Rt. Hon. William Ewart Gladstone (1809–98) in 1852–55 1859–66, 1873–74 and 1880–82.

FOREIGN SECRETARYSHIP

Longest tenures The longest term of office of any Foreign Secretary has been the 10 years 196 days of the Most Hon. Robert Stewart, Marquis of Londonderry, formerly Viscount Castlereagh (1769–1822) from 4 March 1812 until his suicide on 16 September 1822. The Most Hon. Robert Arthur Talbot Gascoyne-Cecil, Marquis of Salisbury, K.G., G.C.V.O., in two spells in 1887–92 and 1895–1900 aggregated 11 years 87 days in this office. The longest tenure during this century has been 11 years 75 days by the Rt. Hon. Sir (Robert) Anthony Eden, Earl of Avon, K.G., M.C. (b. 12 June 1897) in three spells in 1935–38, 1940–45 and 1951–55.

COLONIAL SECRETARYSHIP

Longest tenures The longest term of office has been 19 years 324 days by the Rt. Hon. Henry Bathurst, Earl Bathurst (1762–1834), who was Secretary of State for the Colonial and War Department from 11 June 1812 to 1 May 1827. The longest tenure this century has been the 5 years 61 days of the Rt. Hon. Alan Tindal Lennox-Boyd, Viscount Boyd of Merton, C.H. (b. 18 Nov. 1904) during 1954 to 1959.

SPEAKERSHIP

Longest Arthur Onslow (1691–1768) was elected Mr. Speaker on 23 Jan. 1728, at the age of 36. He held the position for 33 years 54 days, until 18 March 1761.

Mansell Collection

"Butcher" Cumberland, the King's general in the last battle on English soil

4. MILITARY AND DEFENCE

WAR

Guinness Superlatives Ltd. has published specialist volumes entitled The Guinness History of Land Warfare *(£2.95) by Kenneth Macksey and* History of Sea Warfare *(£4.95) by Gervis Frere-Cook and Macksey. They deal with the subject in greater detail, and are available from all good bookshops, or if in difficulty, direct from the publishers at the address at the front of this volume.*

Longest The longest of history's countless wars was the "Hundred Years War" between England and France, which lasted from 1338 to 1453 (115 years), although it may be said that the Holy War, comprising the nine Crusades from the First (1096–1104) to the Ninth (1270–91), extended over 195 years.

Last battle on British soil The last pitched land battle in Britain was at Culloden Field, Drummossie Moor, Inverness-shire, on 16 April 1746. The last Clan battle in Scotland was between Clan Mackintosh and Clan MacDonald at Mulroy, Inverness-shire, in 1689. The last battle on English soil was the Battle of Sedgemoor, Somerset, on 6 July 1685, when the forces of James II defeated the supporters of Charles II's illegitimate son, James Scott (formerly called Fitzroy or Crofts), the Duke of Monmouth (1649–85). During the Jacobite rising of 1745–46, there was a skirmish at Clifton Moor, Cumbria, on 18 Dec. 1745, when the British forces under Prince William, the Duke of Cumberland (1721–65), brushed with the rebels of Prince Charles Edward Stuart (1720–88) with about 12 killed on the King's side and 5 Highlanders. This was a tactical victory for the Scots under Lord George Murray.

Shortest war The shortest war on record was that between the United Kingdom and Zanzibar (now part of Tanzania) from 9.02 to 9.40 a.m. on 27 Aug. 1896. The U.K. battle fleet under Rear-Admiral (later Admiral Sir) Harry Holdsworth Rawson (1843–1910) delivered an ultimatum to the self-appointed Sultan Sa'id Khalid to evacuate his palace and surrender. This was not forthcoming until after 38 minutes of bombardment. Admiral Rawson received the Brilliant Star of Zanzibar (first class) from the new Sultan Hamud ibn Muhammad. It was proposed at one time that elements of the local populace should be compelled to defray the cost of the ammunition used.

Bloodiest war By far the most costly war in terms of human life was World War II (1939–45), in which the total number of fatalities, including battle deaths and civilians of all countries, is estimated to have been 54,800,000 assuming 25 million U.S.S.R. fatalities and 7,800,000 Chinese civilians killed. The country which suffered most was Poland with 6,028,000 or 22.2 per cent of her population of 27,007,000 killed.

In the case of the United Kingdom, however, the heaviest armed forces fatalities occurred in World War I (1914–18), with 765,399 killed out of 5,500,000 engaged (13.9 per cent), compared with 265,000 out of 5,896,000 engaged (4.49 per cent) in World War II. The total death roll from World War I was only 17.7 per cent of that of World War II, *viz* 9,700,000.

Most costly The material cost of World War II far transcended that of the rest of history's wars put together and has been estimated at $1.3 million million. The total cost to the Soviet Union was estimated semi-officially in May 1959 at 2,500,000,000,000 roubles (£100,000 million) while a figure of $380,000 million has been estimated for the U.S.A. In the case of the United Kingdom the cost of £34,423 million was over five times as great as that of World War I (£6,700 million) and 158.6 times that of the Boer War of 1899–1902 (£217 million).

Bloodiest civil war The bloodiest civil war in history was the T'ai-p'ing ("Peace") rebellion, in which peasant sympathizers of the Southern Ming dynasty fought the Manchu Government troops in China from 1853 to 1864. The rebellion was led by the deranged Hung Hsiu-ch'üan (poisoned himself in June 1864), who imagined himself to be a younger brother of Jesus Christ. His force was named *T'ai-p'ing T'ien Kuo* (Heavenly Kingdom of Great Peace). According to the best estimates, the loss of life was between 20,000,000 and 30,000,000, including more than 100,000 killed by Government forces in the sack of Nanking on 19–21 July 1864.

Bloodiest battle *Modern* The battle with the greatest recorded number of fatalities was the First Battle of the Somme, France from 1 July to 19 Nov. 1916, with more than 1,030,000 —614,105 British and French and *c.* 420,00 (*not* 650,000) German. The gunfire was heard on Hampstead Heath, London. The greatest battle of World War II and the greatest ever conflict of armour was the Battle of Kursk and Oryol which raged for 50 days on 5 July–23 Aug. 1943 on the Eastern front, which involved 1,300,000 Red Army troops with 3,600 tanks, 20,000 guns and 3,130 aircraft in repelling a German Army Group which had 2,700 tanks. The final investment of Berlin by the Red Army on 16 Apr.–2 May 1945 involved 3,500,000 men; 52,000 guns and mortars; 7,750 tanks and 11,000 aircraft on both sides.

Ancient Modern historians give no credence to the casualty figures attached to ancient battles, such as the 250,000 reputedly killed at Plataea (Greeks *v.* Persians) in 479 B.C. or the 200,000 allegedly killed in a single day

British The bloodiest battle fought on British soil was the Battle of Towton, in North Yorkshire, on 29 March 1461, when 36,000 Yorkists defeated 40,000 Lancastrians. The total loss has been estimated at between 28,000 and 38,000 killed. A figure of 80,000 British

187

Mansell Collection

The bloodiest battle fought on British soil at Towton in 1461 at which at least 28,000 were killed

dead was attributed by Tacitus to the battle of A.D. 61 between Queen Boudicca (Boadicea) of the Iceni and the Roman Governor of Britain Suetonius Paulinus, for the loss of 400 Romans in an army of 10,000. The site of the battle is unknown but may have been near Borough Hill, Daventry, Northamptonshire, or more probably near Hampstead Heath, Greater London. It is improbable that, for such a small loss, the Romans could have killed more than 20,000 Britons.

GREATEST INVASION

Seaborne The greatest invasion in military history was the Allied land, air and sea operation against the Normandy coasts of France on D-day, 6 June 1944. Thirty-eight convoys of 745 ships moved in on the first three days, supported by 4,066 landing craft, carrying 185,000 men and 20,000 vehicles, and 347 minesweepers. The air assault comprised 18,000 paratroopers from 1,087 aircraft. The 42 available divisions possessed an air support from 13,175 aircraft. Within a month 1,100,000 troops, 200,000 vehicles and 750,000 tons of stores were landed.

Airborne The largest airborne invasion was the Anglo-American assault of three divisions (34,000 men), with 2,800 aircraft and 1,600 gliders, near Arnhem, in the Netherlands, on 17 Sept. 1944.

Last on the soil of Great Britain The last invasion of Great Britain occurred on 12 Feb. 1797, when the Irish-American adventurer General Tate landed at Carreg Gwastad with 1,400 French troops. They surrendered near Fishguard, Dyfed, to Lord Cawdor's force of the Castlemartin Yeomanry and some local inhabitants armed with pitchforks. The U.K. Crown Dependency of the Channel Islands were occupied by German armed forces from 30 June 1940 to 8 May 1945.

Worst sieges The worst siege in history was the 880-day siege of Leningrad, U.S.S.R. by the German Army from 30 Aug. 1941 until 27 Jan. 1944. The best estimate is that between 1.3 and 1.5 million defenders and citizens died. The longest recorded siege was that of Azotus (now Ashdod), Israel which according to Herodotus was invested by Psamtik I of Egypt for 29 years in the period 664–610 B.C.

LARGEST ARMED FORCES

Numerically, the country with the largest regular armed force is the U.S.S.R., with 3,525,000 at mid-1974 compared with the U.S.A.'s 2,174,000 at the same date. With the end of conscription this is likely

to sink to 1,800,000 later in 1975. The Chinese People's Liberation Army, which includes naval and air services, has 3,000,000 regulars, but there is also a civilian home guard militia once claimed to be 200 million strong but regarded by the Institute of Strategic Studies to have an effective element of not more than 5,000,000.

DEFENCE

The estimated level of spending on armaments throughout the world in 1974 was $225,000 million *£97,825 million*. This represents £24.76p per person per annum, or more than 6 per cent of the world's total production of goods and services. It was estimated in 1974 that there were 15.5 million full-time armed force regulars or conscripts.

The expenditure on defence by the government of the United States in the year ending 30 June 1975 was $85,800 million (*£37,750 million*) or 5.9 per cent of the country's Gross National Product.

The U.S.S.R.'s defence expenditure in 1974 has been estimated to be of the order of $94,000 million and thus markedly higher than the U.S. level. This represents some 15.7 per cent of the Gross National Product.

At the other extreme is Andorra, whose defence budget, voted in 1972, was reduced to £2.00.

NAVIES

Largest The largest navy in the world is the United States Navy, with a manpower of 551,000 and 196,000 Marines in mid-1974. The active strength in 1974 included 15 attack aircraft carriers, 61 attack nuclear submarines and 12 diesel attack submarines, 72 SAM armed ships including 8 cruisers, 29 destroyers and 26 frigates, and 65 amphibious warfare ships.

The strength of the Royal Navy in mid-1974 was an aircraft carrier, 2 commando carriers, 2 assault ships, 2 missile armed cruisers, 9 destroyers with guided missiles, 58 frigates, 8 nuclear (including 4 with *Polaris* missiles) and 22 other submarines and 45 minesweepers. The uniformed strength was 78,100 including Fleet Air Arm and Royal Marines in mid-1974. In 1914 the Royal Navy had 542 warships including 72 capital ships with 16 building.

Greatest naval battle The greatest number of ships and aircraft ever involved in a sea-air action was 231 ships and 1,996 aircraft in the Battle of Leyte Gulf, in the Philippines. It raged from 22 to 27 Oct. 1944, with 166 United States and 65 Japanese warships engaged, of which 26 Japanese and 6 U.S. ships were sunk. In addition 1,280 U.S. and 716 Japanese aircraft were engaged. The greatest naval battle of modern times was the Battle of Jutland on 31 May 1916, in which 151 Royal Navy warships were involved against 101 German warships. The Royal Navy lost 14 ships and 6,097 men and the German fleet 11 ships and 2,545 men. The greatest of ancient naval battles was the Battle of Salamis, Greece on 23 Sept. 480 B.C. There were an estimated 800 vessels in the defeated Persian fleet and 310 in the victorious Greek fleet with a possible involvement of 190,000 men.

Greatest evacuation The greatest evacuation in military history was that carried out by 1,200 Allied naval and civil craft from the beachhead at Dunkerque (Dunkirk), France between 27 May and 4 June 1940. A total of 338,226 British and French troops were taken off.

ARMIES

Largest Numerically, the world's largest army is that of the People's Republic of China, with a total strength of about 2,500,000 in mid-1974. The total size of the U.S.S.R.'s army in mid-1974 was estimated at

1,800,000 men, believed to be organised into about 167 divisions with a maximum strength of 12,000 each. The strength of the British Army was 178,000 in mid-1974.

Oldest The oldest army in the world is the 83-strong Swiss Guard in the Vatican City, with a regular foundation dating back to 21 Jan. 1506. Its origins, however, extend back before 1400.

Oldest and Youngest soldiers The oldest old soldier of all time was probably John B. Salling of the army of the Confederate States of America and the last accepted survivor of the U.S. Civil War (1861–65). He died in Kingsport, Tennessee, U.S.A., on 16 March 1959, aged 113 years 1 day. The oldest Chelsea pensioner, based only on the evidence of his tombstone, was the 111-year-old William Hiseland (b. 6 Aug. 1620, d. 7 Feb. 1732). The longest serving British soldier has been Field Marshall Sir William Maynard Gomm G.C.B. (1784–1875), who was an ensign in 1794 and as Constable of the Tower to his death aged 91. The youngest 20th century British soldier appears to be Pte. Ernest Wilfred Dowson (b. 28 July 1898), who enlisted in the 5th Batn. York & Lancaster Regt. on 27 June 1912—a month before his 14th birthday.

Youngest "Old Contempt- ible" The youngest recorded age of any member of the British Expeditionary Force in France in 1914 (the "Old Contemptibles") is 15 years 193 days in the case of Private (later Lt. Col.) Robert Martin Peachey (b. 5 Feb. 1899) of the 1st Bridging Train, Royal Engineers.

Tallest soldiers The tallest soldier of all time was Väinö Myllyrinne (1909–63) who was inducted into the Finnish Army when he was 7 ft 3 in *2,20 m* and later grew to 8 ft 1¼ in *2,47 m*. The British Army's tallest soldier was Benjamin Crow who was signed on at Litchfield in November 1947 when he was 7 ft 1 in *2,15 m* tall. Edward Evans (1924–58), who later grew to 7 ft 8½ in *2,34 m* was in the Army when he was 6 ft 10 in *2,08 m*.

British regimental records The oldest regular regiment in the British Army is the Royal Scots, raised in French service in 1633, though the Buffs (Royal East Kent Regiment) can trace back their origin to independent companies in Dutch pay as early as 1572. The Coldstream Guards, raised in 1650, were, however, placed on the establishment of the British Army before the Royal Scots and the Buffs. The oldest armed body in the United Kingdom is the Queen's Bodyguard of the Yeoman of the Guard formed in 1495. The Honourable Artillery Company, formed from the Finsbury Archers, received its charter from Henry VIII in 1537 but this lapsed until reformed in 1610. The infantry regiment with most battle honours is The Royal Hampshire Regt. with 153.

The most senior regiment of the Reserve Army is The Royal Monmouthshire Royal Engineers (Militia) formed in 1572 and never disbanded.

TANKS

Note—Guinness Superlatives Ltd. has published a specialist volume entitled The Guinness Book of Tank Facts and Feats *by Kenneth Macksey (£2.75). This work deals with all the aspects of the development and history of the tank and other armoured fighting vehicles in greater detail, and is available from all good bookshops or if in difficulties, direct from the publishers at the address at the front of this volume.*

Earliest The first fighting tank was "Mother" *alias* "Big Willie" built by William Foster & Co. Ltd. of Lincoln, and first tested on 12 Jan. 1916. Tanks were first taken into action by the Machine Gun Corps (Heavy Section), which later became the Royal Tank Corps, at the battle of Flers, in France, on 15 Sept. 1916. The Mark I Male tank, which was armed with a pair of 6-pounders guns and two machine-guns, weighed 28 tons *28,4 tonnes* and was driven by a motor developing 105 horse-power which gave it a maximum road speed of 3 to 4 m.p.h. *4,8–6,4 km/h.*

Heaviest The heaviest tank ever constructed was the German Panzer Kampfwagen Maus II, which weighed 189 tons *192 tonnes*. By 1945 it had reached only the experimental stage and was not proceeded with.

The heaviest operational tank used by any army was the 81.5 ton *82,8 tonnes* 13-man French Char de Rupture 2C bis of 1923. It carried a 155 mm. howitzer and had two 250 h.p. engines giving a maximum speed of 8 m.p.h. *12 km/h.* On 7 Nov. 1957, in the annual military parade in Moscow, U.S.S.R., a Soviet tank possibly heavier than the German Jagd Tiger II (71.7 tons [*72,8 tonnes*]), built by Henschel, and certainly heavier than the Stalin III, was displayed.

The heaviest British tank ever built was the 78-ton *79 tonnes* prototype "Tortoise". With a crew of seven and a designed speed of 12 m.p.h. *19 km/h*, this tank had a width two inches *5 cm* less than that of the one-time operational 65-ton *66 tonnes* "Conqueror". The most heavily armed is the 52-ton *52,8 tonnes* "Chieftain", put into service in November 1966, with a 120 mm gun.

GUNS

Earliest Although it cannot be accepted as proved, the best opinion is that the earliest guns were constructed in North Africa, possibly by Arabs, in *c.* 1250. The earliest representation of an English gun is contained in an illustrated manuscript dated 1326 at Oxford. The earliest anti-aircraft gun was an artillery piece on a high angle mounting used in the Franco-Prussian War of 1870 by the Prussians against French balloons.

Largest The remains of the most massive gun ever constructed were found near Frankfurt am Main, Germany, in 1945. It was the "Schwerer Gustav" or "Dora", which had a barrel 94.7 ft *28,87 m* long, with a calibre of 800 mm (31.5 in), and a breech weighing 108 tons

Field Marshall Sir William Gomm, who served in the British Army for 81 years

109 tonnes. The maximum charge was 2,000 kg *4,409 lb.* of cordite to fire a shell weighing 4,800 kg *4.7 tons* a distance of 55 km *34 miles.* The maximum projectile was one of 7 tons *7,1 tonnes* with a range of 22 miles *35 km.* Each gun with its carriage weighed 1,323 tons *1 344 tonnes* and required a crew of 1,500 men.

During the 1914–18 war the British army used a gun of 18 in *457 mm* calibre. The barrel alone weighed 125 tons *127 tonnes.* In World War II the "Bochebuster", a train-mounted howitzer with a calibre of 18 in *457 mm* firing a 2,500 lb. *1 133 kg* shell to a maximum range of 22,800 yds *20 850 m,* was used from 1940 onwards as part of the Kent coast defences.

Greatest range The greatest range ever attained by a gun was achieved by the H.A.R.P. (High Altitude Research Project) gun consisting of two 16.5 in *419 mm* calibre barrels in tandem in Barbados. In 1968 a 200 lb. *90 kg* projectile was fired to a height of 400,000 ft (75¾ miles [*121,9 km*]). The static V.3 underground firing tubes built in 50 degree shafts near Mimoyecques, near Calais, France to bombard London were never operative due to R.A.F. bombing.

The famous long range guns, which shelled Paris in World War I, was the *Kaiser Wilhelm geschütz* with a calibre of 220 mm (*8.66 in*), a designed range of 79.5 miles *127,9 km* and an achieved range of 76 miles *122 km* from the Forest of Cérpy in March 1918. The Big Berthas were of greater calibre and of lesser range.

Mortars The largest mortars ever constructed were Mallets' mortar (Woolwich Arsenal, London, 1857), and the "Little David" of World War II, made in the U.S.A. Each had a calibre of 36¼ in *920 mm,* but neither was ever used in action.

Largest cannon The highest calibre cannon ever constructed is the *Tsar Puchka* (King of Cannons), now housed in the Kremlin, Moscow, U.S.S.R. It was built in the 16th century with a bore of 36 in *915 mm* and a barrel 17 ft *5,18 m* long. It was designed to fire cannon balls weighing 2 tons but was never used. The Turks fired up to seven shots per day from a bombard 26-ft *7,92 m* long, with an internal calibre of 42 in *1 066 mm* against the walls of Constantinople (now Istanbul) from 12 April to 29 May 1453. It was dragged by 60 oxen and 200 men and fired a stone cannon ball weighing 1,200 lb. *544 kg.*

Military engines The largest military catapults, or onagers, were capable of throwing a missile weighing 60 lb. *27 kg* a distance of 500 yds *457 m.*

Longest march The longest march in military history was the famous Long March by the Chinese Communists in 1934–35. In 368 days, of which 268 days were of movement, from October to October, their force of 90,000 covered 6,000 miles *9 650 km* northward from Kiangis to Yünnan. They crossed 18 mountain ranges and six major rivers and lost all but 22,000 of their force in continual rear-guard actions against Nationalist Kuo-min-tang (K.M.T.) forces.

Most rapid march The most rapid recorded march by foot-soldiers was one of 12 Spanish leagues (42 miles [*67 km*]) in 26 hours on 28–29 July 1809, by the Light Brigade under Brigadier- (later Major-) General Robert Craufurd (1764–1812), coming to the relief of Lieut.-Gen. Sir Arthur Wellesley, later Field Marshall the 1st Duke of Wellington (1769–1852), after the Battle of Talavera (Talavera de la Reina, Toledo, Spain) in the Peninsular War.

The longest recorded march by a body of 60 without any fall-outs was one of 14 hours 23 minutes (13 hours on the march) by the London Rifle Brigade on 18–19 April 1914 from Duke of York Steps, London, to

Brighton Aquarium. On 8 April 1922, two officers and 27 other ranks of the London Scottish Regiment covered the 53 miles *85 km* from London to Brighton in 13 hours 59 minutes, each carrying 46 lb. *20,8 kg* of equipment, but two men failed to finish.

AIR FORCES
The earliest autonomous air force is the Royal Air Force whose origin began with the Royal Flying Corps (created 13 May 1912); the Air Battalion of the Royal Engineers (1 April 1911) and the Corps of Royal Engineers Balloon Section (1878) which was first operational in Bechuanaland (now Botswana) in 1884.

Largest The greatest Air Force of all time was the United States Army Air Force (now called the U.S. Air Force), which had 79,908 aircraft in July 1944 and 2,411,294 personnel in March 1944. The U.S. Air Force including strategic air forces had 645,000 personnel and 5,000 combat aircraft in mid-1974. The U.S.S.R. Air Force, including Air Defence Forces, with about 900,000 men in mid-1974, had 8,000 combat aircraft. In addition, the U.S.S.R.'s Offensive Strategic Rocket Forces had about 350,000 operational personnel in mid-1974. The strength of the Royal Air Force was 98,200 with some 500 combat aircraft in mid 1974.

BOMBS
The heaviest conventional bomb ever used operationally was the Royal Air Force's "Grand Slam", weighing 22,000 lb. *9 975 kg* and measuring 25 ft 5 in *7,74 m* long, dropped on Bielefeld railway viaduct, Germany, on 14 March 1945. In 1949 the United States Air Force tested a bomb weighing 42,000 lb. *19 050 kg* at Muroc Dry Lake, California, U.S.A.

Camera Press

The weapon that has changed human history—the Hiroshima atom bomb of 1945

Atomic The two atom bombs dropped on Japan by the United States in 1945 each had an explosive power equivalent to that of 20,000 short tons *20 kilotons* of trinitrotoluene ($C_7H_5O_6N_3$), called T.N.T. The one dropped on Hiroshima, known as "Little Boy", was 10 ft *3,04 m* long and weighed 9,000 lb. *4 080 kg.* The most powerful thermo-nuclear device so far tested is one with a power equivalent to 57,000,000 short tons of T.N.T., or 57 megatons, detonated by the U.S.S.R. in the Novaya Zemlya area at 8.33 a.m. G.M.T. on 30 Oct. 1961. The shock wave was detected to have circled the world three times, taking 36 hours 27 min for the first circuit. Some estimates put the power of this device at between 62 and 90 megatons. On 9 Aug. 1961, Nikita Khrushchyov, then the Chairman of the Council of Ministers of the U.S.S.R., declared that the Soviet Union was capable of constructing a 100-megaton bomb, and announced the possession of one in East Berlin, Germany, on 16 Jan. 1963. It has been estimated that such a bomb would make a crater 19 miles *30 km* in diameter and would cause serious fires at a range of from 36 to 40 miles *58–64 km.* The atom bomb became inevitable with the meso-thorium experiments of Otto Hahn, Fritz Strassman and Lise Meitner on 17 Dec. 1938. Work started in the U.S.S.R. on atomic bombs in June 1942 although their first chain reaction was not achieved until December 1945 by Dr. Igor Vasilyevich Kurchatov. The patent for the fusion or H bomb was filed in the United States on 26 May 1946 by Dr. Janos (John) von Neumann (1903–57), a Hungarian-born mathematician, and Dr. Klaus Julius Emil Fuchs (born in Germany, 29 Dec. 1911), the defected physicist.

Largest nuclear arsenal The International Institute for Strategic Studies estimate that if 3 of the 4 known new ICBM (Inter-Continental Ballistic Missiles) systems now being developed in the U.S.S.R. are fully deployed their capacity would be to deliver 7,000 separately-targeted nuclear warheads in the megaton range.

No official estimate has been published of the potential power of the device known as Doomsday, but this far surpasses any tested weapon. A 50,000 megaton cobalt-salted device has been mooted which could kill the entire human race except those who were deep underground and who stayed there for more than five years.

Largest "conventional" explosion The largest use of conventional explosive was for the demolition of German U-Boat pens at Heligoland on 18 Apr. 1947. A charge of 3,997 tons *4 061 tonnes* was detonated by E. C. Jellis aboard H.M.S. *Lassoe* lying 9 miles *14,4 km* out to sea.

5. JUDICIAL

LEGISLATION AND LITIGATION

STATUTES

Oldest The earliest known judicial code was that of King Urnammu during the third dynasty of Ur, Iraq, in *c.* 2145 B.C. The oldest English statue in the Statue Book is a section of the Statue of Marlborough of 1267, retitled in 1948 "The Distress Act, 1267". Some statutes enacted by Henry II (d. 1189) and earlier kings are even more durable as they have been assimilated into the Common Law. An extreme example is Ine's Law concerning the administration of shires *c.* 8 A.D.

Longest in the United Kingdom Measured in bulk the longest statute of the United Kingdom, is the Income Tax and Corporation Tax Act, 1970, which runs to 540 sections, 15 schedules and 670 pages. It is 1½ in *37 mm* thick and costs £2.80. However, its 540 sections are surpassed in number by the 748 of the Merchant Shipping Act, 1894.

Of old statutes, 31 George III XIV, the Land Tax Act of 1791, written on parchment, consists of 780 skins forming a roll 1,170 ft *360 m* long.

Shortest The shortest statute is the Parliament (Qualification of Women) Act, 1918, which runs to 27 operative words—"A woman shall not be disqualified by sex or marriage from being elected to or sitting or voting as a Member of the Commons House of Parliament". Section 2 contains a further 14 words giving the short title.

Earliest English patent The earliest of all known English patents was that granted by Henry VI in 1449 to Flemish-born John of Utynam for making the coloured glass required for the windows of Eton College. The peak number of applications for patents filed in the United Kingdom in any one year was 63,614 in 1969. The shortest, concerning a harrow attachment, of 48 words was filed on 14 May 1956 while the longest, comprising 2,318 pages of text and 495 pages of drawings, was filed on 31 Mar. 1965 by I.B.M. to cover a computer.

Most protracted litigation The longest contested law suit ever recorded ended in Poona, India on 28 April 1966, when Balasaheb Patloji Thorat received a favourable judgment on a

Arthur Orton, alias Castro the Tichborne imposter, whose guilt exercised the Courts for 827 days but detained the jury only 30 minutes

Radio Times Hulton

suit filed by his ancestor Maloji Thorat 761 years earlier in 1205. The points at issue were rights of presiding over public functions and precedences at religious festivals.

The dispute over the claim of the Prior and Convent of Durham Cathedral to administer the spiritualities of the diocese during a vacancy in the See grew fierce in 1283. It smouldered until 1939, having flared up in 1672, 1890 and 1920. In 1939 the Archbishop of Canterbury exercised his metropolitan rights and appointed the Dean as guardian of spiritualities of Durham "without prejudice to the general issue", then 656 years old.

Most inexplicable Statute Certain passages in several Acts have always defied interpretation and the most inexplicable must be a matter of opinion. A Judge of the Court of Session of Scotland has sent the Editors his candidate which reads, "In the Nuts (unground), (other than ground nuts) Order, the expression nuts shall have reference to such nuts, other than ground nuts, as would but for this amending Order not qualify as nuts (unground) (other than ground nuts) by reason of their being nuts (unground)."

Longest British trial The longest trial in the annals of British justice was the Tichborne personation case. The civil trial began on 11 May 1871, lasted 103 days and collapsed on 6 March 1872. The criminal trial went on for 188 days, resulting in a sentence on 28 Feb. 1874 for two counts of perjury (14 years imprisonment and hard labour) on the London-born Arthur Orton, *alias* Thomas Castro (1834–98), who claimed to be Roger Charles Tichborne (1829–54), the elder brother of Sir Alfred Joseph Doughty-Tichborne, 11th Bt. (1839–66). The whole case, during which, miraculously, no juryman fell ill, thus spanned 827 days and cost £55,315. The jury were out for only 30 minutes.

The impeachment of Warren Hastings (1732–1818), which began in 1788, dragged on for seven years until 23 April 1795, but the trial lasted only 149 days. He was appointed a member of the Privy Council in 1814.

The longest recent criminal trial was that of four members of "The Angry Brigade" concerning 25 explosions and two shootings between Jan. 1968 and July 1971. It began at the Old Bailey on 30 May 1972 and concluded on the 109th day on 4 Dec. 1972. The cost was estimated at £750,000.

Murder The longest murder trial in Britain was that of Donat Gomez, 23 charged with murdering Mary Ann Armstrong at Stoke-on-Trent in February 1973. This started at Stafford Crown Court on 13 Nov. 1973 and ended with a hung jury on the 45th trial day on 6 Mar. 1974. After an 18 day re-trial in Birmingham, Gomez was found not guilty on the 63rd day on 22 May.

The shortest recorded British murder hearings were *R. v. Murray* on 28 Feb. 1957 and *R. v. Cawley* at Winchester Assizes on 14 Dec. 1959. The proceedings occupied only 30 sec on each occasion.

Divorce The longest trial of a divorce case in Britain was *Gibbons* v. *Gibbons and Roman and Halperin*. On 19 March 1962, after 28 days, Mr. Alfred George Boyd Gibbons was granted a decree *nisi* against his wife Dorothy for adultery with Mr. John Halperin of New York City, N.Y., U.S.A.

Longest The longest address in a British court was in *Globe* **address** *and Phoenix Gold Mining Co. Ltd.* v. *Amalgamated Properties of Rhodesia*. Mr. William Henry Upjohn. K.C. (1853–1941) concluded his speech on 22 Sept, 1916, having addressed the court for 45 days.

Highest bail The highest amount ever demanded as bail was **World** $46,500,000 (*then £16,608,333*) against Antonio De Angelis in a civil damages suit by the Harbor Tank Storage Co. filed in the Superior Court, Jersey City, New Jersey, U.S.A. on 16 Jan. 1964 in the Salad Oil Swindle. He was released on 4 June 1972.

United The highest bail figure in a British court is £250,000 *Kingdom* granted to the former Hong Kong police chief Peter Godber, 52 at Bow Street Court, Greater London on 16 May 1974 when charged with bribery. This consisted of a maximum of four sureties aggregating £200,000 and £50,000 in his own recognisance.

Longest The longest arbitration (under the 1950 Act) on record **arbitration** has been the Royce Arbitration. It lasted 239 days and concerned the Milchell Construction Co and the East Anglian Regional Hospital Board over the building of Peterborough Hospital.

Best The greatest attendance at any trial was that of Major **attended** Jesús Sosa Blanco, aged 51, for an alleged 108 **trial** murders. At one point in the 12½ hr trial (5.30 p.m. to 6 a.m., 22–23 Jan. 1959), 17,000 people were present in the Havana Sports Palace, Cuba.

Greatest The greatest Crown compensation for wrongful **compensa-** imprisonment has been £17,500 paid to Laszlo Virag, **tion** 35, who had been sentenced to 10 years imprisonment at Gloucester assizes in 1969 for theft and shooting and wounding a police officer. His acceptance of this sum was announced on 23 Dec. 1974 after his having been released in April 1974 on grounds of mistaken identification.

GREATEST DAMAGES

Personal The greatest personal injury damages ever awarded **injury** were to Larry Miedema Jr., 3 against Glendora **World** Community Hospital and Dr. Robert Reinke for malpractice resulting in his becoming mentally retarded and a quadraplegic at Pomona, California on 4 June 1973. If he lives to the average expectation of 68 years the payments will total $21 million (*£8¾ million*).

The highest damages ever actually paid have been $14,387,674, following upon the crash of a private aircraft at South Lake, Tahoe, California, U.S.A. on 21 February 1967, to the sole survivor Ray Rosendin, 45, by the Santa Clara Superior Court on 8 March 1972. Rosendin received *inter alia* $1,069,374 for the loss of both legs and disabling arm injuries; $1,213,129 for the loss of his wife and $10,500,000 punitive damages against Avco-Lyconing Corporation which allegedly violated Federal regulations when it rebuilt the aircraft engine owned by Rosendin Corporation.

United The greatest damages ever awarded in a United *Kingdom* Kingdom court for personal injury were £135,500 awarded to Patricia Conway, 16 in the Belfast High Court on 5 June 1974 for injuries including brain damage sustained in a car accident near Conlig, County Down in 1972. The judgement was made against Mr. David Patton, a fitter, the car driver and his mother the car owner.

On 5 Feb. 1960, the Dublin High Court awarded £87,402 damages for motor injuries to Mr. Kevin P. McMorrow, aged 38, of County Leitrim, against his driver Mr. Edward Knott. It is understood that, after an appeal, a settlement was made out of court for £50,000.

Breach of The greatest damages ever awarded for a breach of **contract** contract were £610,392, awarded on 16 July 1930 to the Bank of Portugal against the printers Waterlow & Sons Ltd., of London, arising from their unauthorized printing of 580,000 five-hundred escudo notes in 1925. This award was upheld in the House of Lords on 28 April 1932. One of the perpetrators, Arthur Virgilio Alves Reis, served 16 years (1930–46) in gaol.

Breach of The largest sum involved in a breach of promise suit in **promise** the United Kingdom was £50,000, accepted in 1913 by Miss Daisy Markham, *alias* Mrs. Annie Moss (d. 20 Aug. 1962, aged 76), in settlement against the 6th Marquess of Northampton (b. 6 Aug. 1885).

Defamation A sum of $16,800,000 (*£6,720,000*) was awarded to **World** Dr John J. Wild, 58, at the Hennepin District Court, Minnesota, U.S.A., on 30 Nov. 1972 against The Minnesota Foundation and others for defamation, bad-faith termination of a contract, interference with professional business relationship and $10.8 million in punitive damages. These amounts are unappealed.

The greatest damages for defamation ever awarded in the United Kingdom were £117,000, awarded on 21 July 1961 in *The Rubber Improvement Co. Ltd.* v. *Associated Newspapers Ltd.* for 51 words which appeared in the *Daily Mail* of 23 Dec. 1958. The company was represented by Colin Duncan, M.C. (now a Q.C.) and Mr. (now Sir) Helenus Patrick Joseph Milmo, Q.C. (b. 24 Aug. 1908), who has since become a judge. After appeal proceedings by both sides this action was settled out of court for a substantially smaller amount.

Greatest The highest alimony awarded by a court has been **Alimony** $2,261,000 (*£983,000*) against George Storer Sr., 74, in favour of his third wife Dorothy, 73, in Miami, Florida on 29 Oct. 1974. Mr Storer, a broadcasting executive, was also ordered to pay his ex-wife's attorney $200,000 (*£86,950*) in fees.

Divorce The greatest amount ever paid in a divorce settlement **Settlement** is $9,500,000 (*£3,393,000*) paid by Edward J. **Highest** Hudson to Mrs. Cecil Amelia Blaffer Hudson, aged 43. This award was made on 28 Feb. 1963 at the Domestic Relations Court, Houston, Texas, U.S.A. Mrs. Hudson was, reputedly, already worth $14,000,000 (*£5,000,000*).

Patent case The greatest settlement ever made in a patent infringement suit is $9,250,000 (£3,303,000), paid in April 1952 by the Ford Motor Company to the Ferguson Tractor Co. for a claim filed in January 1948.

Largest Suit The highest amount of damages ever sought is $675,000,000,000,000 (equivalent to the U.S. Government revenue for 3,000 years) in a suit by Mr. I. Walton Bader brought in the U.S. District Court, New York City on 14 April 1971 against General Motors and others for polluting all 50 states.

HIGHEST COSTS

The highest costs in English legal history arose from the alleged infringement of a patent owned by General Tire and Rubber Co. of America by the Firestone Tyre and Rubber Co. The case was heard by 17 judges over 5½ years ending on 16 April 1975 in a reduction of damages for £1,388,000 to £311,000 but costs were an estimated £500,000.

Income tax The greatest amount paid for information concerning **Highest** a case of income tax delinquency was $79,999.93 **reward** (£28,571) paid by the United States Internal Revenue Service to a group of informers. Payments are limited to 10 per cent of the amount recovered as a direct result of information laid. Informants are often low-income accountants or women scorned. The total of payments in 1965 was $597,731 (*then £213,475*).

Greatest lien The greatest lien ever imposed by a court is 40,000 million lire (£27 million) on 9 Apr. 1974 upon Vittorio and Ida Riva in Milan for back taxes allegedly due on a chain of cotton mills around Turin, Italy inherited by their brother Felice (now safe in Beirut) in 1960.

WILLS

Shortest The shortest valid will in the world is "Vše zene", the Czech for "All to wife", written and dated 19 Jan. 1967 by Herr Karl Tausch of Langen, Hesse, Germany. The shortest will contested but subsequently admitted to probate in English law was the case of *Thorn v. Dickens* in 1906. It consisted of the three words "All for Mother".

Longest The longest will on record was that of Mrs. Frederica Cook (U.S.A.), in the early part of the century. It consisted of four bound volumes containing 95,940 words.

JUDGE

Oldest The oldest recorded active judge was Judge Albert R. **World** Alexander (1859–1966) of Plattsburg, Missouri, U.S.A. He was the magistrate and probate judge of Clinton County until his retirement aged 105 years 8 months on 9 July 1965.

Sir James Gowan, who was made a judge 26 days after his 27th birthday and lived for another 66 years

Britain The greatest recorded age at which any British judge has sat on a bench was 93 years 9 months in the case of Sir William Francis Kyffin Taylor, G.B.E., K.C. (later Lord Maenan), who was born on 9 July 1854 and retired as presiding judge of the Liverpool Court of Passage in April 1948, having held that position since 1903. The greatest age at which a House of Lords judgment has been given is 92 in the case of the 1st Earl of Halsbury (b. 3 Sept. 1823) in 1916.

Youngest The youngest certain age at which any English judge has been appointed is 31, in the case of Sir Francis Buller (b. 17 March 1746), who was appointed Second Judge of the County Palatine of Chester on 27 Nov. 1777, and Puisne Judge of the King's Bench on 6 May 1778, aged 32 years 1 month. Hon. Sir James Gowan K.C.M.G. (b. Ireland) (1815–1909)) was appointed a Judge in Canada on 17 Jan. 1843 when aged 27 years 26 days.

Youngest The earliest age at which a barrister has taken silk **English** since 1900 is 33 years 8 months in the case of Mr. **Q.C.** (later the Rt. Hon. Sir) Francis Raymond Evershed (1899–1966) in April 1933. He was later Lord Evershed, a Lord of Appeal in Ordinary.

Highest paid It was estimated that Jerry Giesler (1886–1962), an **lawyer** attorney in Los Angeles, California, U.S.A., averaged $50,000 (*then £17,850*) in fees for each case which he handled during the latter part of his career. Currently, the most highly paid lawyer is generally believed to be Louis Nizer (b. London 6 Feb. 1902) of New York City, N.Y., U.S.A.

Most Sir Lionel Luckhoo K.C.M.G., C.B.E. senior partner **successful** of Luckhoo and Luckhoo of Georgetown, Guyana **advocate** succeeded in getting his 178th successive murder charge acquittal by 7 May 1975.

CRIME AND PUNISHMENT

GREATEST MASS KILLINGS

China The greatest massacre ever imputed by the government of one sovereign nation against the government of another is that of 26,300,000 Chinese during the regime of Mao Tse-tung between 1949 and May 1965. This accusation was made by an agency of the U.S.S.R. Government in a radio broadcast on 7 April 1969. The broadcast broke down the figure into four periods:—2.8 million (1949–52); 3.5 million (1953–57); 6.7 million (1958–60); and 13.3 million (1961–May 1965). The highest reported death figures in single monthly announcements on Peking radio were 1,176,000 in the provinces of Anhwei, Cheki-ang, Kiangsu, and Shantung, and 1,150,000 in the Central South Provinces. Po I-po, Minister of Finance, is alleged to have stated in the organ *For a lasting peace, for a people's democracy* "in the past three years (1950–52) we have liquidated more than 2 million bandits". General Jacques Guillermaz, a French diplomat estimated the total executions between February 1951 and May 1952 at between 1 million and 3 million. In April 1971 the Executive *Yuan* or cabinet of the implacably hostile government of The Republic of China in Taipei, Taiwan announced its official estimate of the mainland death roll in the period 1949–69 as "at least 39,940,000". This figure, however, excluded "tens of thousands" killed in the Great Proletarian Cultural Revolution, which began in late 1966. The Walker Report published by the U.S. Senate Committee of the Judiciary in July 1971 placed the parameters of the total death roll since 1949 between 32.25 and 61.7 million.

U.S.S.R. The total death roll in the Great Purge, or *Yezhovs-hchina*, in the U.S.S.R., in 1936–38 has, not surprisingly, never been published. Evidence of its magnitude may be found in population statistics which show a deficiency of males from before the outbreak of the

1941–45 war. The reign of terror was administered by the *Narodny Kommissariat Vnutrennykh Del* (N.K.V.D.), or People's Commissariat of Internal Affairs, the Soviet security service headed by Nikolay Ivanovich Yezhov (1895–?1939), described by Nikita Khrushchyov in 1956 as "a degenerate". S. V. Utechin, an expert on Soviet affairs, regards estimates of 8,000,000 or 10,000,000 victims as "probably not exaggerations".

Nazi Germany *Obersturmbannführer* (Lt.-Col.) Karl Adolf Eichmann (b. Solingen, West Germany 19 March 1906) of the S.S. was hanged in a small room inside Ramleh Prison, near Tel Aviv, Israel, at just before midnight (local time) on 31 May 1962, for his complicity in the deaths of an indeterminably massive number of Jews during World War II, under the instruction given in April 1941 by Adolf Hitler (1889–1945) for "the Final Solution" (*Endlosung*).

At the S.S (*Schutzstaffel*) extermination camp (*Vernichtungslager*) known as Auschwitz-Birkenau (Oswiecim-Brzezinka), near Oswiecim (Auschwitz), in southern Poland, where a minimum of 920,000 people (Soviet estimate is 4,000,000) were exterminated from 14 June 1940 to 18 Jan. 1945, the greatest number killed in a day was 6,000. The man who operated the release of the "Zyklon B" cyanide pellets into the gas chambers there during this time was Sgt. Major Moll (variously Mold). The Nazi (*Nationalsozialistische Deutsche Arbeiter Partei*) Commandant during the period 1940–43 was Rudolf Franz Ferdinand Höss, who was tried in Warsaw from 11 Mar. to 2 Apr. 1947 and hanged, aged 47, at Oswiecim on 15 Apr. 1947.

Forced Labour No official figures have been published of the death roll in Corrective Labour Camps in the U.S.S.R., first established in 1918. The total number of such camps was known to be more than 200 in 1946 but in 1956 many were converted to less severe Corrective Labour Colonies. An estimate published in the Netherlands puts the death roll between 1921 and 1960 at 19,000,000. The camps were administered by the *Cheka* until 1922, the O.G.P.U. (1922–34), the N.K.V.D. (1934–46), the M.V.D. (1946–53) and the K.G.B. since 1953. Solzhenitsyn's aggregate best estimate is that the number of inmates has been 66 million. In China there are no published official statistics on the numbers undergoing *Lao Jiao* (Education through Labour) nor *Lao Dong Gai Zao* (Reform through manual labour). An estimate published by Bao Ruo-wang, who was released in 1964 due to his father having been a Corsican, was 16,000,000 which approaches 3 per cent of the population.

Largest criminal organization The largest syndicate of organized crime is the Mafia or La Cosa Nostra, which has infiltrated the executive, judiciary and legislature of the United States. It consists of some 3,000 to 5,000 individuals in 24 "families" federated under "The Commission", with an estimated annual turnover in vice, gambling, protection rackets and rigged trading of $30,000 million per annum of which some 25 per cent is profit. The origin in the U.S. dates from the lynching of 11 Mafiosi in New Orleans in 1890 for which a naive U.S. government paid $30,000 compensation to widows which was seized as the initial funding to prime the whole operation. The biggest Mafia (means *swank* from a Sicilian word for beauty or pride) killing was on 11–13 Sept. 1931 when the topmost man Salvatore Maranzano, *Il Capo di Tutti Capi*, and 40 allies were liquidated.

Murder rate **Highest** The country with the highest recorded murder rate is Mexico, with 46.3 registered homicides per each 100,000 of the population in 1970. It has been estimated that the total number of murders in Colombia during *La Violencia* (1945–62) was about 300,000, giving a rate over a 17-year period of more than 48

a day. A total of 592 deaths was attributed to one bandit leader, Teófilo ("Sparks") Rojas, aged 27, between 1948 and his death in an ambush near Armenia on 22 Jan. 1963. Some sources attribute 3,500 slayings to him.

The highest homicide rates recorded in New York City have been 58 in a week in July 1972 and 13 in a day in August 1972. In 1973 the total for Detroit Michigan (pop. 1.5 million) was 751.

Britain In Great Britain the total number of homicides and deaths from injuries purposely inflicted by other persons" in the period mid 1973–mid 1974 was 438. This figure compares with a murder total of 124 in 1937 and 125 in 1958.

Lowest The country with the lowest officially recorded rate in the world is Spain, with 39 murders (a rate of 1.23 per each million of the population) in 1967, or one murder every 9 days. In the Indian protectorate of Sikkim, in the Himalayas, murder is, however, practically unknown, while in the Hunza area of Kashmir, in the Karakoram, only one definite case by a Hunzarwal has been recorded since 1900.

MOST PROLIFIC MURDERER

World It was established at the trial of Buhram, the Indian thug, that he had strangled at least 931 victims with his yellow and white cloth strip or *ruhmal* in the Oudh district between 1790 and 1840. It has been estimated that at least 2,000,000 Indians were strangled by Thugs (*burtotes*) during the reign of the Thugee cult (pronounced tugee) from 1550 until its final supression by the British *raj* in 1852. The greatest number of victims ascribed to a murderess has been 610 in the case of Countess Erszebet Bathory (1560–1614) of Hungary. At her trial which began on 2 Jan. 1611 a witness testified to seeing a list of her victims in her own handwriting totalling this number. All were alleged to be young girls from the neighbourhood of her castle at Csejthe where she died on 21 Aug. 1614. She had been walled up in her room for the 3½ years after being found guilty.

20th century The 20th century's most prolific murderer has been Bruno Lüdke (Germany) (b. 1909), who confessed to 85 murders of women between 1928 and 29 Jan. 1943. He was executed by injection without trial in a hospital in Vienna on 8 April 1944.

Britain The total number of victims of the cannibalistic cave-dwelling Bean family in Galloway, Scotland in the 15th century is not known but may have run as high as 50 per year. Sawney Bean, head of the family, his wife, 8 sons, 6 daughters and 32 grandchildren were taken by an Army detachment to Edinburgh and executed without process.

Six men were each charged with 21 murders at Lancaster Crown Court on 9 June 1975 concerning the bombing of the two Birmingham public houses Mulberry Bush and Tavern in the Tower on 21 Nov. 1974. They were John Walker, Patrick Hill, Robert Hunter, Noel McIlkenny, William Power and Hugh Callaghan.

Judith Theresa Ward, 25 of Stockport, Cheshire was convicted on 11 separate murder charges on 4 Nov. 1974 making 12 in all arising from the explosion in an army coach on the M.62 near Drightlington, West Yorkshire on 4 Feb. 1974. Mary Ann Cotton (*née* Robson) (b. *c.* 1832, County Durham), hanged in Durham Jail in 1873 is believed to have poisoned 14, possibly 20, people.

Gang murders During the period of open gang warfare in Chicago, Illinois, U.S.A., the peak year was 1926, when there were 76 unsolved killings. The 1,000th gang murder

Dr. Joseph Guillotin after whom the decapitation process was named from 1793 to the present day

Radio Times Hulton

in Chicago since 1919 occurred on 1 Feb. 1967. Only 13 cases have ended in convictions.

"Smelling out" The greatest "smelling out" recorded in African history occurred before Shaka (1787–1828) and 30,000 Nguni subjects near the River Umhlatuzana, Zululand (now Natal, South Africa) in March 1824. After 9 hrs, over 300 were "smelt out" as guilty of smearing the Royal *Kraal* with blood, by 150 witch-finders led by the hideous female *isangoma* Nobela. The victims were declared innocent when Shaka admitted to having done the smearing himself to expose the falsity of the power of his diviners. Nobela poisoned herself with atropine ($C_{17}H_{23}NO_3$), but the other 149 witch-finders were thereupon skewered or clubbed to death.

Suicide The estimated daily total of suicides throughout the world surpassed 1,000 in 1965. The country with the highest suicide rate is Hungary, with 33.1 per each 100,000 of the population in 1971. The country with the lowest recorded rate is Jordan with a single case in 1970 and hence a rate of 0.04 per 100,000.

In England and Wales there were 3,930 suicides in 1973–74, or an average of 10.76 per day. In the northern hemisphere April and May tend to be peak months.

CAPITAL PUNISHMENT

Capital punishment was first abolished *de facto* in 1798 in Leichtenstein. The death penalty for murder was formally abolished in Britain on 18 Dec. 1969. Between the 5-4 Supreme Court decision against capital punishment in June 1972 and April 1975, 32 of the 50 States of the U.S.A. voted to restore it.

Capital punishment in the British Isles dates from A.D. 450, but fell into disuse in the 11th century, only to be revived in the Middle Ages, reaching a peak in the reign of Edward VI (1547–1553), when an average of 560 persons were executed annually at Tyburn alone. Even into the 19th century, there were 223 capital crimes, though people were, in practice, hanged for only 25 of these. Between 1830 and 1955 the largest number hanged in a year was 27 (24 men, 3 women) in 1903. The least was 5 in 1854, 1921 and 1930. In 1956 there were no hangings in England, Wales or Scotland, since when the highest number in any year to 1964 was 5.

Largest Hanging The most people hanged from one gallows was 38 Sioux Indians by William J. Duly outside Mankato,

Minnesota, U.S.A. for the murder of unarmed citizens on 26 Dec. 1862.

Last hangings The last public execution in England took place outside Newgate Prison, London at 8 a.m. on 26 May 1868, when Michael Barrett was hanged for his part in the Fenian bomb outrage on 13 Dec. 1867, when 12 were killed outside the Clerkenwell House of Detention, London. The earliest non-public execution was of the murderer Thomas Wells on 13 Aug. 1868. The last public hanging in Scotland was that of the murderer Joe Bell in Perth in 1866. The last in the United States occurred at Owensboro, Kentucky in 1936. The last hangings were those of Peter Anthony Allen (b. 4 Apr. 1943) at Walton Prison, Liverpool, and John Robson Walby (b. 1 April 1940), *alias* Gwynne Owen Evans, at Strangeways Gaol, Manchester both on 13 Aug. 1964. They had been found guilty of the capital murder of John Alan West, on 7 April 1964. The 14th and last woman executed this century was Mrs. Ruth Ellis (*née* Hornby), 28, for the murder of David Blakely, 25, shot outside The Magdala, Hampstead, on 10 Apr. 1955. She was executed on 13 July at Holloway.

Last from yard-arm The last naval execution at the yard-arm was the hanging of Marine John Dalliger aboard H.M.S. *Leven* in the River Yangtze, China, on 13 July 1860. Dalliger had been found guilty of two attempted murders.

Last public guillotining The last person to be publicly guillotined in France was the murderer Eugen Weidmann before a large crowd at Versailles, near Paris, at 4.50 a.m. on 17 June 1939. The last person guillotined in a French prison was the Tunisian child murderer Ali Benyanès, 34 at Marseilles on 12 May 1973. It was the 74 year old executioner's 364th successful execution. Dr. Joseph Ignace Guillotin (1738–1812) died a natural death. He had advocated the use of the machine designed by Dr. Antoine Louis in 1789 in the French constituent assembly.

Youngest Although the hanging of persons under 18 was expressly excluded only in the Children's and Young Person's Act, 1933 (Sec. 33), no person under that age was, in fact executed more recently than 1887. The lowest satisfactorily recorded age was of a boy aged 8 "who had malice, cunning and revenge" in firing two barns and who was hanged at Abingdon, Oxfordshire in the 17th century. The youngest persons hanged since 1900 have been 18 years old:—J. H. Clarkson at Leeds on 29 March 1904; Henry Jacoby on 7 Jan. 1922; Bishop in 1925; another case in 1932; James Farrell on 29 March 1949; and Francis Robert George ("Flossie") Forsyth on 10 Nov. 1960.

Oldest The oldest person hanged in the United Kingdom since 1900 was a man of 71 named Charles Frembd (*sic*) at Chelmsford Gaol on 4 Nov. 1914, for the murder of his wife at Leytonstone, Waltham Forest, Greater London. In 1822 John Smith, said to be 80, of Greenwich, Greater London, was hanged for the murder of a woman.

Most attempts In 1803 it was reported that Joseph Samuels was reprieved in Sydney, Australia after three unsuccessful attempts to hang him in which the rope twice broke.

Death Row Longest Stay The longest stay on "death row" in the United States has been one of more than 14 years by Edgar Labat, aged 44, and Clifton A. Paret, aged 38, in Angola Penitentiary, Louisiana, U.S.A. In March 1953 they were sentenced to death, after being found guilty of rape in 1950. They were released on 5 May 1967, only to be immediately re-arrested on a local jury indictment arising from the original charge. Caryl Whittier Chessman, aged 38 and convicted of 17 felonies, was executed on 2 May 1960 in the gas chamber

195

at the California State Prison, San Quentin, California, U.S.A. In 11 years 10 months and one week on "death row", Chessman had won eight stays.

EXECUTIONER
The longest period of office of a Public Executioner was that of William Calcraft (1800–1879), who was in office from 1828 to 1871 and officiated at nearly every hanging outside and later inside Newgate Prison, London.

BLOODIEST ASSIZES
In the West Country Assizes of 1685 (Winchester to Wells), George Jeffreys, the 1st Baron Jeffreys of Wem (1645–1689), sentenced 330 persons to be hanged, 841 to be transported for periods of ten or more years and larger numbers to be imprisoned and flogged. These sentences followed the Duke of Monmouth's insurrections.

LONGEST SENTENCES
World The longest recorded prison sentence is one of 7,109 years awarded to a pair of confidence tricksters by an Iranian court on 15 June 1969. The duration of sentences are proportional to the amount of the defalcations involved. A sentence of 384,912 years was demanded at the prosecution of Gabriel March Grandos, 22, at Palma de Mallorca, Spain on 11 Mar. 1972 for failing to deliver 42,768 letters.

Juan Corona, a Mexican-American was sentenced to 25 consecutive life terms, for murdering 25 farm workers in 1970–71 around Feather River, Yuba City, California, at Fairfield on 5 Feb. 1973. His U.S. 20th century record for victims was surpassed with the discovery on 13 Aug. 1973 of the body of the 27th victim of the pervert Dean Corll, 33 of Houston, Texas.

United Kingdom Mr. Justice Chapman at Oxford Assizes on 15 Oct. 1971 jailed the police murderer Arthur William Skingle, 25, of London for life with the first recommendation that "life should mean for life".

The longest single period served by a reprieved murderer in Great Britain this century was 40 years 11 months by John Watson Laurie, the Goat Fell or Arran murderer, who was reprieved on the grounds of insanity in November 1889 and who died in Perth Penitentiary on 4 Oct. 1930.

The longest prison sentence ever passed under United Kingdom law was one of three consecutive and two concurrent terms of 14 years, thus totalling 42 years, imposed on 3 May 1961 on George Blake (b. Rotterdam, 11 Nov. 1922 of an Egyptian-born Jewish-British father and a Dutch mother as George Behar), for treachery. Blake, formerly U.K. vice-consul in Seoul, South Korea, had been converted to Communism during 34 months' internment there from 2 July 1950 to April 1953. It had been alleged that his betrayals may have cost the lives of up to 42 United Kingdom agents. He was "sprung" from Wormwood Scrubs Prison, Greater London, on 22 Oct. 1966.

The longest single sentence passed on a woman under United Kingdom law was 20 years for Mrs. Lona Teresa Cohen *née* Petra (b. 1913) at the Old Bailey, City of London on 2 Mar. 1961 for conspiring to commit a breach of the Official Secrets Act, 1911. The sentence of this K.G.B. agent was remitted by the Foreign Secretary on no known lawful authority on 24 July 1969. Ward (see murder above) was sentenced to an aggregate 30 years on 4 Nov. 1974.

Longest Time Served Johnson VanDyke Grigsby, who began serving a life sentence for second degree murder on 5 Aug 1908, was discharged from Indiana State Prison on 9 Dec. 1974 after 66 years 127 days. He believed he was 89 or

90. He complained of the bad language of "modern" prisoners.

Broadmoor The longest period for which any person has been detained in the Broadmoor hospital for the criminally insane, near Crowthorne, Berkshire, is 76 years in the case of William Giles. He was admitted as an insane arsonist at the age of 11 and died there on 10 March 1962, at the age of 87.

The longest escape from Broadmoor was one of 39 years by the Liverpool wife murderer James Kelly, who got away on 28 Jan. 1888, using a pass key made from a corset spring. After an adventurous life in Paris, in New York and at sea he returned in April 1927, to ask for re-admission. After some difficulties this was arranged. He died in 1930.

Oldest prisoner The oldest known prisoner in the United States is John Weber, 95, at the Chillicothe Correctional Institute, Ohio who began his 44th year in prison on 29 Oct. 1970.

Most Appearances There are no collected records on the greatest number of convictions on an individual but the highest recently reported is 1,433 for the gentlemanly but alcoholic Edward Eugene Ebzery, who died in Brisbane Jail, Queensland, Australia on 23 Sept. 1967.

Greatest mass arrest The greatest mass arrest in the United Kingdom occurred on 17 Sept. 1961, when 1,314 demonstrators supporting the unilateral nuclear disarmament of the United Kingdom were arrested for wilfully disregarding the directions of the police and thereby obstructing highways leading to Parliament Square, London, by sitting down. As a consequence of the 1926 General Strike there were 3,149 prosecutions: incitement (1,760) and violence (1,389).

Lynching The worst year in the 20th century for lynchings in the United States has been 1901, with 130 lynchings (105 Negroes, 25 Whites), while the first year with no reported cases was 1952. The last lynching recorded in Britain was that of Panglam Godolan, a Pakistani and a suspected murderer, in London on 27 Oct. 1958. The last case previous to this was of a kidnapping suspect in Glasgow in 1922.

LONGEST PRISON ESCAPES
The longest recorded escape by a recaptured prisoner was that of Leonard T. Fristoe, 77, who escaped from Nevada State Prison, U.S.A., on 15 Dec. 1923 and was turned in by his son on 15 Nov. 1969 at Compton, California. He had had 46 years of freedom under the name Claude R. Willis. He had killed two sheriff's deputies in 1920. The longest period of freedom achieved by a British gaol breaker is more than 15½ years by Irish-born John Patrick Hannan, who escaped from Verne Open Prison at Portland, Dorset, on 22 Dec. 1955 and was still at large in July 1975. He had served only 1 month of a 21-month term for car-stealing and assaulting two policemen.

Greatest gaol break The greatest gaol break in Britain was that from Brixton Prison, Lambeth, Greater London on 30 May 1973 when 20 men got out using a rubbish tipping lorry as a battering ram. Eighteen were captured immediately and one other 5 weeks later, 9 staff were injured.

ROBBERY
Greatest The greatest recorded robbery by market valuation was the removal of 19 paintings, valued at £8,000,000 taken from Russborough House, Blessington, County Wicklow Ireland, the home of Sir Alfred and Lady Beit by 4 men and a woman on 26 Apr. 1974. They included the £3 million Vermeer "Lady Writing a Letter with her maid". The paintings were recovered on 4 May near Glandore, County Cork. Dr. Rose Bridgit

Dugdale (b. 1941) was convicted. It is arguable that the value of the *Mona Lisa* at the time of its theft from The Louvre, Paris on 21 Aug. 1911 was greater than this figure. It was recovered in Italy in 1913 and Vincenzo Perruggia was charged with its theft. On 1 Sept. 1964 antiquities reputedly worth £10,000,000 were recovered from 3 warehouses near the Pyramids, Egypt.

Bank On 20 Oct. 1974, $4,300,000 was removed from the vaults of the Armored Express Co. strongroom in Chicago. Six men were charged including two, Pasquel Marzano, 40 and Luigi Difonzo, 26 who were deported from Grand Cayman on 31 Oct. 1974. On 23 Oct. 1969 it was disclosed that $13,193,000 (*£5,500,000*) of U.S. Treasury bills were inexplicably missing from the Morgan Guaranty Trust, Wall Street, New York City, U.S.A.

Train The greatest recorded train robbery occurred between about 3.03 a.m. and 3.27 a.m. on 8 Aug. 1963, when a General Post Office mail train from Glasgow, Scotland, was ambushed at Sears Crossing and robbed at Bridego Bridge near Mentmore, Buckinghamshire. The gang escaped with about 120 mailbags containing £2,631,784 worth of bank notes being taken to London for destruction. Only £343,448 had been recovered by 9 Dec. 1966.

Jewels The greatest recorded theft of gem stones occurred on 13 Nov. 1969 in Freetown, Sierra Leone, when an armed gang stole diamonds belonging to the Sierra Leone Selection Trust worth £1,500,000. The haul from Carrington & Co. Ltd. of Regent Street, London, on 21 Nov. 1965 was estimated to be £500,000. Jewels are believed to have constituted a major part of the Hotel Pierre "heist" on Fifth Avenue, New York City, U.S.A. on 31 Dec. 1971. An unofficial estimate ran as high as $5,000,000 (*£2,000,000*).

Greatest kidnapping ransom Historically the greatest ransom paid was that for Atahualpa by the Incas to Francisco Pizarro in 1532–33 at Cajamarca, Peru which constituted a hall full of gold and silver worth in modern money some $170 million (*£65 million*).

The greatest ransom ever exported is 1,500 m pesos (25,300,000) for the release of the brothers Jorge Born, 40 and Juan Born, 39 of Bunge and Born paid to the left wing urban guerilla group Montoneros in Buenos Aires, Argentina on 20 June 1975.

The youngest person kidnapped has been Carolyn Wharton born at 12.46 p.m. on 19 Mar. 1955 in the Baptist Hospital, Beaumont, Texas, U.S.A. and kidnapped, by a woman disguised as a nurse, at 1.15 p.m. aged 29 minutes.

Greatest Hijack ransom The highest amount ever paid to hijackers has been £2,000,000 in small denomination notes by the West German government to Popular Front for the Liberation of Palestine representatives 30 miles outside Beirut, Lebanon on 23 Feb. 1972. In return a Lufthansa Boeing 747, hijacked an hour out of New Delhi and bound for Athens which had been forced down at Aden, and its 14 crew members were released.

Largest narcotics haul The heaviest recorded haul of narcotics was made off St. Louis at Rhône, France, where 700 cwt. *35,5 tonnes* of floating bales containing unprocessed morphine, opium, heroin and hashish, worth £30 million on the retail U.S. market were found being loaded into canoes by 3 men on 25 Feb. 1971. The most valuable ever haul was of 937 lb. *425 kg* of pure heroin worth $106¼ million (*£40.8 million*) retail seized aboard the 60 ton shrimp boat *Caprice des Temps* at Marseilles, France on 28 Feb. 1972. The captain, Louis Boucan, 57, who tried to commit suicide was sentenced to 15 years on 5 Jan. 1973.

It was revealed on 31 Jan. 1973 that 398 lb. *180 kg 50* of heroin and cocaine with a street value of $73 million (*£29.2 million*) had been stolen from the New York Police Department—a record for any law enforcement agency.

Penal camps The largest penal camp systems in the world were those near Karaganda and Kolyma, in the U.S.S.R., each with a population estimated in 1958 at between 1,200,000 and 1,500,000. The largest labour camp is now said to be the Dubrovlag Complex of 15 camps centred on Pot'ma, Mordovian A.S.S.R. The official N.A.T.O. estimate for all Soviet camps was "more than one million" in March 1960 compared with a peak of probably 12 million during the Stalinist era.

Devil's Island The largest French penal settlement was that of St. Laurent du Maroni, which comprised the notorious Îles du Diable, Royale and St. Joseph (for incorrigibles) off the coast of French Guiana, in South America. It remained in operation for 99 years from 1854 until the last group of repatriated prisoners, including Théodore Rouselle, who had served 50 years, was returned to Bordeaux on 22 Aug. 1953. It has been estimated that barely 2,000 *bagnard* (ex-convicts) of the 70,000 deportees ever returned. These, however, include the executioner Ladurelle (imprisoned 1921–37), who was murdered in Paris in 1938.

PRISONS
Largest World The largest prison in the world is Kharkov Prison, in the U.S.S.R., which has at times accommodated 40,000 prisoners.

British Isles The largest prison in the United Kingdom is Wormwood Scrubs, West London, with 1,134 cells. The highest prison walls in Great Britain are those of Lancaster Prison measuring 36 to 52 ft *11–15,85 m.*

The largest prison in Scotland is Barlinnie, Glasgow, with 753 single cells. Ireland's largest prison is Mountjoy Prison, Dublin, with 808 cells.

Highest population The peak prison population, including Borstals and detention centres, for England and Wales was the figure for 15 June 1971 of 40,470 compared with 40,075 on 1 June 1975. In Scotland the average prison population was 4,998 and in Northern Ireland 2,406 both in June 1975.

Most secure prison After it became a maximum security Federal prison in 1934, no convict was known to have lived to tell of a successful escape from the prison of Alcatraz ("Pelican") Island in San Francisco Bay, California, U.S.A. A total of 23 men attempted it but 12 were recaptured, 5 shot dead, one drowned and 5 presumed drowned. On 16 Dec. 1962, three months before the prison was closed, one man reached the mainland alive, only to be recaptured on the spot.

Longest Prison Siege The longest prison siege has been one of 10 days 8 hours 58 mins at the Texas State Penitentiary U.S.A. on 24 July–3 Aug. 1974. There were 4 fatalities.

Largest bribe An alleged bribe of £30,000,000 offered to Shaikh Zaid ibn Sultan of Abu Dhabi, Trucial Oman, by a Saudi Arabian official in August 1955, is the highest on record. The affair concerned oil concessions in the disputed territory of Buraimi on the Persian Gulf.

Greatest forgery The greatest recorded forgery was the German Third Reich government's forging operation, code name "Bernhard", engineered by Herr Naujocks in 1940–41. It involved £150,000,000 worth of £5 notes.

Greatest swindle The greatest swindle ever alleged has been that of the Pacific Coast Coin Exchange, known also as Monex International Ltd. run by Louis E. Carabini Jr., who had 25,000 clients buying silver. Money from new "investors" was used to pay off old ones until the latter outnumbered the former. The total discrepancy involved from the 14 regional and 3 international offices was estimated on 12 Dec. 1974 to be "approximately $1 billion" (*£435 million*). In April 1974 preliminary reports of a computer insurance swindle in the U.S. of similar proportions was first suggested.

Biggest fraud The largest amount of money named in a defalcation case has been a gross £33,000,000 at the Lugano branch of Lloyd's Bank International Ltd. in Switzerland on 2 Sept. 1974. Mr. Mark Colombo was arrested pending charges including falsification of foreign currency accounts and suppression of evidence.

Passing bad cheques Mrs. Ann Lorraine Ohlschlager, 54, *alias* Ann Kosak of Los Angeles was charged in January 1974 of writing or "kiting' $37 million (£15.4 million) in bad cheques between January and 24 Oct. 1973 so netting a final $463,000 (£192,916) from the United California Bank.

Welfare swindle The greatest welfare swindle yet worked was that of the gypsy Anthony Moreno on the French Social Security in Marseilles. By forging birth certificates and school registration forms, he invented 197 fictitious families and 3,000 children on which he ·claimed benefits from 1960 to mid-1968. Moreno, nicknamed "El Chorro" (the fountain), was last reported free of extradition worries and living in luxury in his native Spain having absquatulated with an estimated £2,300,000.

FINES

A fine equivalent to £10,686,000 was levied on Jean Pierre Pilato (France) by a court in Valencia, Spain a 6 Feb. 1972 for attempting to smuggle 250 lb *113,6 kg* of heroin worth £16 million from France *via* Spain to the U.S. He was arrested on 5 June 1971 and is serving a 10 year sentence plus 4 years if the fine is unpaid.

Heaviest The heaviest fine ever imposed in the United Kingdom was one of £277,500, plus £3,717 costs, on I. Hennig & Co. Ltd., the London diamond merchants, at Clerkenwell Magistrates' Court, London, on 14 Dec. 1949. The amount was later reduced on appeal.

Rarest prosecution There are a number of crimes in English law for which there have never been prosecutions. Among unique prosecutions are *Rex v. Crook* in 1662 for the praemunire of disputing the King's title and *Rex v. Gregory* for selling honours under the Honours (Prevention of Abuses) Act, 1924, on 18 Feb. 1933. John Maundy Gregory (d. 3 Oct. 1941 in France as "Sir" "Arthur" Gregory) was an honours broker during 6 administrations from 1919 to 1932 and was sentenced to two months in Wormwood Scrubs, London.

6. ECONOMIC

MONETARY AND FINANCE

Largest budget *World* The greatest annual expenditure budgeted by any country has been $349,000 million (*£151,000 million*) by the United States government for the fiscal year ending 30 June 1976. The highest budgeted revenue in the United States has been $280,549 million (*£121,977 million*) in the calander year 1974.

In the United States, the greatest surplus was $8,419,469,844 in 1947–48, and the greatest deficit was $57,420,430,365 in 1942–43.

United Kingdom The greatest budgeted current expenditure of the United Kingdom has been £42,587 million for the fiscal year 1975–76. The highest budgeted current revenue has been £43,778 million after the budget changes of 15 Apr. 1975.

Foreign aid The total net foreign aid given by the United States government between 1 July 1945 and 1 Jan. 1974 was $155,142 million (*£67,453 million*). The country which received most U.S. aid in 1973 was South Vietnam, with $438 million (*£190 million*). U.S. foreign aid began with $50,000 to Venezuela for earthquake relief in 1812.

TAXATION

Most taxed The major national economy with the highest rate of taxation (central and local taxes, plus social security contribution) is that of France with 53.0 per cent of her National Income in 1970 (latest data). The lowest proportion for any advanced national economy in 1973 was 19.5 per cent in Japan, which also enjoyed the highest economic growth rate. In the United Kingdom in 1971 current taxation receipts were 48.7 per cent of G.N.P.

Least taxed There is no income tax paid by residents on Lundy Island off North Devon, England. This 1,062.4 acre *429,9 ha* island issued its own unofficial currency of Puffins and Half Puffins between the Wars for which offence the owner was prosecuted.

Highest Taxation Rates The country with the most confiscatory taxation is Norway where in January 1974 the Labour Party at Socialist Alliance abolished the 80 per cent limit so that some 2,000 citizens have to pay more than 100 per cent of their taxable income. The shipping magnate Hilmar Reksten was assessed at 491 per cent. The highest marginal rate in the United Kingdom, is the 1975–76 rate for taxable incomes over £20,000 at 83 per cent with an additional surcharge on investment income in excess of £2,000 of 15 per cent making a rate of 98 per cent. In 1967–68 a "special charge" of up to 9s. (45p) in the £ additional to surtax brought the top rate to 27s. 3d. (136p) in the £ on investment income. A married man with two children earning £5,000 per year in 1938 would, in June 1975 have to have earned £113,500 to have enjoyed the same standard of living.

Highest and lowest rates in United Kingdom Income tax was introduced in Great Britain in 1799 at the standard rate of 2s. (10p) in the £. It was discontinued in 1815, only to be re-introduced in 1842 at the rate of 7d. (3p) in the £. It was at its lowest at 2d. (0.83p) in the £ in 1875, gradually climbing to 1s. 3d. (6p) by 1913. From April 1941 until 1946 the record peak of 10s. (50p) in the £ was maintained to assist in financing of World War II. Death Duties (introduced in 1894) on millionaire estates began at 8 per cent (1894–1907) and were raised to a peak of 80 per cent by 1949. Capital Transfer Tax rates have yet to be enacted.

NATIONAL DEBT

The largest national debt of any country in the world is that of the United States, where the gross federal public debt of the Federal Government surpassed the half trillion dollar mark in 1975 reaching $509.7 billion (*£221,600 million*) in March 1975. This amount in dollar bills would make a pile 30,174 miles *48,560 km* high, weighing 422,724 tons *429 514 tonnes*.

The United Kingdom National Debt, which became a permanent feature of Britain's economy as early as 1692, was £45,886 million or £820 per person at 31 March 1975. This amount placed in a pile of brand new £1 notes would be 2,820.6 miles *4 539 km* in height.

Gross National Product The estimated world aggregate of Gross National Products in 1971 was about $3,500 billion *£1,400,000 million*. The country with the largest Gross National

Product is the United States, with $1,397. 4 billion in 1974. The estimated G.N.P. of the United Kingdom was £72,953 million for 1974.

National wealth The richest large nation, measured by real Gross National Product per head, is Kuwait with $11,000 (£4,782) per head. The U.S.A. which took the lead in 1910 is now (1974) fifth behind also Switzerland, Sweden and Denmark. The United Kingdom stands 19th with $3,470 (£1,508) per head. It has been estimated that the value of all physical assets in the U.S.A. in 1968 was $3,078,000,000,000 or $15,255 (£6,633) per head. The comparative figure for the United Kingdom is £193,700 million (1972) or £3,472 per head.

Poorest Country According to The World Bank calculations, revised in 1972, the three countries with the lowest annual income per capita are Rwanda, Upper Volta and Burundi each with $60 (£24). The U.N. General Assembly using a "category" system places Rwanda as the least "Least Advanced" nation.

National Savings Mr. Arthur Ellis of Saltergate, Chesterfield between 1958 and his death in June 1971 won one £250, two £100 and 39 £25 premium bond draw prizes. All his winnings were donated to the local parish church.

GOLD RESERVES

The country with the greatest monetary gold reserve is the United States, whose Treasury had $11,652 million (£5,066 million) on hand in January 1975 (if valued at $42.22 per fine oz.). The United States Bullion Depository at Fort Knox, 30 miles south-west of Louisville, Kentucky, U.S.A. is the principal Federal depository of U.S. gold. Gold is stored in standard mint bars of 400 troy ounces 12 kg 441 measuring 7 by 3⅝ by 1⅝ in, 17,7 × 9,2 × 2,8 and each worth $16,888 (£7,342).

The greatest accumulation of the world's central banks' $49,795 million of gold bullion is now in the Federal Reserve Bank at 33 Liberty Street, New York City, N.Y., U.S.A. Some $17,000 million or 14,000 tons is stored 85 ft 25,90 m below street level, in a vault 50 ft 15,24m by 100 ft 30,48m behind a steel door weighing 89 tons.

United Kingdom The lowest published figure for the sterling area's gold and convertible currency reserves was $298,000,000 (then £74 million) on 31 Dec. 1940. The peak figure

A trolly load of gold ingots in the vaults of the U.S. Federal Reserve Bank, New York

was the June 1973 figure of £2,716 million (valued at $2.582 to £ and $42.22 to fine oz.).

MINIMUM LENDING RATE

The highest ever figure for the British bank rate (since 13 Oct. 1972, the Minimum Lending Rate) has been 13% from 13 Nov. 1973 to 4 Jan. 1974. The longest period without a change was the 12 years 13 days from 26 Oct. 1939 to 7 Nov. 1951, during which time the rate stayed at 2 per cent. This record low rate was first attained on 22 Apr. 1852.

BALANCE OF PAYMENTS

The most unfavourable current balance of payments figure for the United Kingdom has been a deficit of £3,828 million in 1974 with the 4th quarter being the worst with £1,075 million. The greatest surplus for a quarter has been £172 million for the 3rd quarter of 1971.

PAPER MONEY

Paper money is an invention of the Chinese and, although the date of 119 B.C. has been suggested, the innovation is believed to date from the T'ang dynasty of the 7th century A.D. The world's earliest bank notes were issued by the Stockholms Banco, Sweden, in July 1661. The oldest surviving banknote is one for 5 dalers dated 6 Dec. 1662. The oldest surviving printed Bank of England note is one for £555 to bearer, dated 19 Dec. 1699 (4½ × 7¾ in [11,4 × 19,6 cm]).

Largest and smallest The largest paper money ever issued was the one kwan note of the Chinese Ming dynasty issue of 1368–99, which measured 9 by 13 in 22,8 × 33,0 cm. The smallest bank note ever issued was the 10 bani note of the Ministry of Finance of Romania, issued in 1917. It measured (printed area) 27,5 mm 1.09 in by 38 mm 1.49 in.

Highest denominations World The highest denomination of paper currency ever authorised in the world are United States gold certificates for $100,000 (£40,000), bearing the head of former President Thomas Woodrow Wilson (1856–1924), issued by the U.S. Treasury in 1934. There also exists in the U.S. Bureau of Engraving and Printing an example of a U.S. Treasury bond for $500,000,000 bearing interest coupons for $15,625,000 each 6 months for 14 years at 6¼ per cent.

The highest denomination notes in circulation are U.S. Federal Reserve Bank notes for $10,000 (£4,166). They bear the head of Salmon Portland Chase (1808–73). None has been printed since July 1944 and the U.S. Treasury announced in 1969 that no further notes higher than $100 would be issued. By 1974 only 400 $10,000 bills were in circulation—reputedly mostly around Christmas time in Texas.

United Kingdom Highest value Two Bank of England notes for £1,000,000 still exist, dated before 1812, but these were used only for internal accounting. The highest issued denominations were £1,000 notes, first printed in 1725, discontinued on 22 Apr. 1943 and withdrawn on 30 April 1945. A total of 62 of these notes were still unaccounted for up to May 1973, of which only 3 are known to be in the hands of collectors.

Lowest denomination The lowest denomination banknote issued is the 1 cent Hong Kong note which is worth 1/12th of one new penny.

Highest circulation The highest ever Bank of England note circulation in the United Kingdom was £5,631 million in December 1974—equivalent to a pile of £1 notes 324.81 miles 522,73 km high.

WORST INFLATION

The world's worst inflation occurred in Hungary in June 1946, when the 1931 gold pengö was valued at

130 trillion (1.3 × 10²⁰) paper pengös. Notes were issued for szazmillio billion (100 trillion or 10²⁰) pengös on 3 June and withdrawn on 11 July 1946. Notes for 1000 trillion or 10²¹ pengös were printed but not circulated. On 6 Nov. 1923 the circulation of Reichsbank marks reached 400,338,326,350,700,000,000. The inflation in Chile from 1950 to 1973 has been 423,100 per cent compared with 199% in Great Britain in the same period.

The United Kingdom's worst rate in a year has been for May 1974 to May 1975 when inflation ran at a rate of 25.00%. The worst single rise in a month was May over April 1975 at 5.4 points to 134.5 (15 Jan. 1974 = 100) or 4.18%.

CHEQUES

Largest The greatest amount paid by a single cheque in the
World history of banking has been one for Rs. 16,64,00,00,000 equivalent to £852,791,660 handed over by Hon. Daniel P. Moynihan, Ambassador of the U.S.A. to India in New Delhi on 18 Feb. 1974. An internal U.S. Treasury check for $4,176,969,623.57 was drawn on 30 June 1954.

United The largest cheque drawn in Britain was one for
Kingdom £119,595,645, drawn on 24 Jan. 1961 by Lazard Brothers & Co. Ltd. and payable to the National Provincial Bank, in connection with the takeover of the British Ford Motor Company.

COINS

Oldest The earliest certainly dated coins are the electrum
World (alloy of gold and silver) staters of Lydia, in Asia Minor (now Turkey), which were coined in the reign of King Gyges (c. 685–652 B.C.). Primitive uninscribed "spade" money of the Chou dynasty of China is now *believed* to date from c. 770 B.C. A discovery at Tappeh Nush-i-jan, Iran of silver ingot currency in 1972 has been dated to as early as 760 B.C. Laos and Paraguay are the only countries today without coins.

British The earliest coins to circulate in Britain were Gallo-Belgic gold imitations of the Macedonian staters of Philip II (359–336 B.C.). The Bellovaci type has been tentatively dated c. 130 B.C. The earliest date attributed to coins minted in Britain is c. 95 B.C. for the Westerham type gold stater of which 51 examples are known

Heaviest A Swedish copper 10 daler coin of 1644 attained a weight of 43 lb 7¼ oz. *19,710 kg.* Of primitive exchange tokens, the most massive are the holed stone discs, or *Fé*, from the Yap Islands, in the western Pacific Ocean, with diameters of up to 12 ft *3,65 m* and weighing up to 185 lb. *84 kg.* A medium-sized one was worth one Yapese wife or an 18 ft *5,18 m* canoe.

Smallest The smallest coins in the world have been the Nepalese ¼ dam or Jawa struck c. 1740 in silver in the reign of Jeya Prakash Malla. The Jawa of between 0.008 and 0.014 g measuring about 2 × 2 mm were sometimes cut into ½ and even ¼ Jawa of 0.002 g or 14,000 to the oz.

Highest The 1654 Indian gold 200 Mohur (£500) coin of the
denomina- Mughal Emperor Khurram Shihāb-ud-dīn Muham-
tion mad, Shāh Jahān (reigned 1628–57), is both the
World highest denomination coin and that of the greatest intrinsic worth ever struck. It weighed 2 177 g *70 troy oz.* and hence has an intrinsic worth of £2,800. It had a diameter of 5⅜ in *136 mm.* The only known example disappeared in Patna, Bihar, India, in c. 1820, but a plaster-cast of this coin exists in the British Museum, London.

British Gold five-guinea pieces were minted from the reign of Charles II (1660–1685) until 1753 in the reign of George II. A pattern 5 guinea piece of George III dated 1777 also exists.

The first meeting of the world's heaviest and lightest coins in Stockholm in 1974. The Swedish 10 daler copper plate weighs 9,855,000 times more than the Nepalese silver ¼ jawa

Svante Palme

Lowest The 5 aurar piece of Iceland, had a face value of
denomina- 0.057 of a penny in 1971. Quarter farthings (sixteen
tion to the penny) were struck in copper at the Royal
World Mint, London, in the Imperial coinage for use in Ceylon, in 1839 and 1851–53.

Rarest There are numerous coins of which but a single
World example is known. An example of a unique coin of threefold rarity is one of the rare admixture of bronze with inlaid gold of Kaleb I of Axum (c. A.D. 500) owned by Richard A. Thorud of Bloomington, Minnesota, U.S.A. Only 700 Axumite coins of any sort are known.

Modern There are known to be unique examples extant of the
British un-issued Edward VIII farthing, halfpenny and penny dated 1937. Only a single example of a 1933 and a 1954 penny is known to be in private hands.

Most The highest price paid at auction for a single coin is
expensive $272,000 (*then £113,000*) or $314,000 inclusive of
World commission for an Athenian silver decadrachm in Zurich, Switzerland on 30 June 1974 by Contantinople Fine Arts Inc. Among the many unique coins that which would attract logically the greatest price on the market would be the unique 1873 dime (U.S. 10 cent piece) with the CC mint mark, since dimes are the most avidly collected series of any coins in the world.

British The highest auction price paid for a British coin is £26,000 for a Queen Anne gold five guineas of 1703 sold by Messrs. Sotheby Parke Bernet of London on 26 Nov. 1974. On 24 Nov. 1972 one of the eight 1933 pennies was auctioned at Sotheby's for £7,000.

Legal tender The oldest legal tender Imperial coins in circulation
coins are the now rare silver shillings (now 5p) and sixpences
Oldest (now 2½p) of the reign of George III, dated 1816. All gold coinage of or above the least current weight dated onward from 1838 is still legal tender. Scotland's separate coinage dates between 1135 and 1709. The last Scottish gold coin was the William II (III of England) pistole of 1701 currently valued at more than £4,000.

Heaviest The gold five-pound (£5) piece or quintuple sovereign
and is both the highest current denomination coin in the
highest United Kingdom and also, at 616.37 grains *1.4066 oz.*
denomina- the heaviest. The most recent specimens available to
tion the public are dated 1937, of which only 5,501 were minted. (See Colour photographs 20th edition).

Lightest and smallest The silver Maundy (new) penny piece is the smallest of the British legal tender coins and, at 7.27 grains (just under 1/60th of an ounce), the lightest. These coins exist for every date since 1822 and are 0.453 in *11,5 mm* in diameter.

Greatest collection It was estimated in November 1967 that the Lilly coin collection of 1,227 U.S. gold pieces now at the Smithsonian Institution, Washington, D.C. U.S.A., had a market value of $5½ million (*£2,290,000*). The greatest single coin collection ever amassed in Britain was that of Richard Cyril Lockett (1873–1950) of Liverpool, Merseyside. The collection realized a record of £387,457.

The greatest hoard of gold of unknown ownership ever recovered is one valued at about $3,000,000 (*£1,070,000*) from the lost £8,000,000 (*£2,860,000*) carried in 10 ships of a Spanish bullion fleet which was sunk by a hurricane off Florida, U.S.A., on 31 July 1715. The biggest single haul was by the diver Kip Wagner on 30 May 1965.

Largest Treasure Trove The largest hoard ever found was one of about 80,000 aurei in Brescello near Modena, Italy in 1814 believed to have been deposited *c.* 37 B.C. The largest hoard of coins ever found in the United Kingdom was the Tutbury hoard, discovered on the bed of the River Dove in Staffordshire in June 1831. It consisted of about 20,000 silver coins of Edward I and Edward II and some of Henry III. The chest is believed to have been deposited in *c.* 1324–25.

Largest mint The largest mint in the world is the U.S. Treasury's mint built in 1965–69 on Independence Mall, Philadelphia, covering 11½ acres *4,65 ha* with an annual capacity on a 3 shift seven day week production of 8,000 million coins. A single stamping machine can produce coins at a rate of 10,000 per minute.

Largest pile The most valuable column of coins amassed for charity was a column totalling £1,100.22 "knocked over" for the Cancer Research Campaign by Henry Cooper in the saloon of "The Black Horse", Rushey Green, Catford, Lewisham, Greater London on 9 Aug. 1973. The first achievement of a kilometre of New Pence was on 19 May 1973 by 112 children from Tattershall C.E. Primary School, Lincolnshire. They used 50,500 coins on a slip road at R.A.F. Coningsby, Lincolnshire.

TRADE UNIONS

Largest World The world's largest union is the Industrie-Gewerkschaft Metall (Metal Workers' Union) of West Germany, with a membership of 2,559,482 on 1 Apr. 1974. The union with the longest name is probably the F.N.O.M.M.C.F.E.T.M.F., the National Federation of Officers, Machinists, Motormen, Drivers, Firemen and Electricians in Sea and River Transportation of Brazil.

Britain The largest union in the United Kingdom is the Transport and General Workers' Union, with 1,872,876 members at 1 Apr. 1975.

Oldest The oldest of the 150 trade unions affiliated to the Trade Union Congress (founded 1868) is the National Society of Brushmakers (current membership 2,700) founded in 1747.

Smallest The smallest affiliated union is the Sheffield Wool Shear Workers' Trade Union with a membership of 19. The unaffiliated London Handforged Spoon and Fork Makers' Society instituted in July 1874, has a last reported membership of 6.

LABOUR DISPUTES

Earliest The earliest recorded strike was one by an orchestra leader from Greece named Aristos in Rome *c.* 309 B.C. The cause was meal breaks.

Largest The most serious single labour dispute in the United Kingdom was the General Strike of 4–12 May 1926, called by the Trades Union Congress in support of the Miners' Federation. During the nine days of the strike 1,580,000 people were involved and 14,500,000 working days were lost.

During the year 1926 a total of 2,750,000 people were involved in 323 different labour disputes and the working days lost during the year amounted to 162,300,000, the highest figure ever recorded. The figure for 1974 was 14,740,000 working days involving 1,601,000 workers.

Longest The world's longest recorded strike ended on 4 Jan. 1961, after 33 years. It concerned the employment of barbers' assistants in Copenhagen, Denmark. The longest recorded major strike was that at the plumbing fixtures factory of the Kohler Co. in Sheboygan, Wisconsin, U.S.A., between April 1954 and October 1962. The strike is alleged to have cost the United Automobile Workers' Union about $12,000,000 (*£4.8 million*) to sustain.

Longest Dispatch to Coventry The longest recorded instance of a worker being "sent to Coventry" by his fellow workers is 4½ years currently being endured by Mr. Tommy Seddon of Droylsden, Greater Manchester since 9 Dec. 1970 at the Wellman Gas Engineering Co.

UNEMPLOYMENT

Highest The highest recorded unemployment in Great Britain was on 23 Jan. 1933, when the total of unemployed persons on the Employment Exchange registers was 2,903,065, representing 22.8 per cent of the insured working population. The highest figure for Wales was 244,579 (39.1 per cent) on 22 Aug. 1932.

Lowest In Switzerland in December 1973 (pop. 6.6 million), the total number of unemployed was reported to be 81. The lowest recorded peace-time level of unemployment was 0.9 per cent on 11 July 1955, when 184,929 persons were registered. The peak figure for the total working population in the United Kingdom has been 26,290,000 in September 1966. The figure for March 1974 was 25,568,000.

Mr. Tommy Seddon in his 54th month of being "in Coventry" for refusing to breech his contract of employment

Manchester Daily Mail

Largest association The largest single association in the world is the Blue Cross, the U.S.-based medical insurance organization with a membership of 87,648,185 on 1 Jan. 1975. Benefits paid out exceeded $5.30 billion (*£2,120 million*). The largest association in the United Kingdom is the Automobile Association (formed 1905) with a membership which reached 5,250,000 on 20 June 1975.

FOOD CONSUMPTION

Calories Of all countries in the world, based on the latest available data, Ireland has the largest available total of calories per person. The net supply averaged 3,450 per day in 1968. The United Kingdom average was 3,180 per day in 1968–69. It has been estimated that Britons eat 7¼ times their own weight in food per annum or 70,000 tons per day. The highest calorific value of any foodstuff is that of pure animal fat, with 930 calories per 100 g *3.5 oz.* Pure alcohol provides 710 calories per 100 g.

Protein Australia and New Zealand have the highest recorded consumption of protein per person, an average of 106 g *3.79 oz.* per day in 1969. The United Kingdom average was 88 g *3.10 oz.* per day in 1968–69.

The lowest *reported* figures are 1,730 calories per day in the Libyan Arab Republic in 1960–62 and 33 g *1.47 oz.* of protein per day in Zaire in 1964–66.

Cereals The greatest consumers of cereal products—flour, milled rice, etc.—are the people of Egypt, with an average of 501 lb. per person *600 g/day* in 1966–67. The United Kingdom average was 160.9 lb. *199 g/day* in 1968–69 and the figure for the Republic of Ireland was 210 lb. *260 g/day* in 1968.

Starch The greatest eaters of starchy food (e.g. bananas, potatoes, etc.) are the people of Gabon, who consumed 4.02 lb. *1 823 g* per head per day in 1964–66. The United Kingdom average was 9.77 oz. *276 g* per day in 1970. The average for Ireland was 12.30 oz. *348 g* in 1968.

Sugar The greatest consumers of sugars are the people of Iceland, with an average of 5.29 oz. *149 g* per person per day in 1964–66. The lowest consumption is 0.70 oz. *19 g* per day in Burundi and Dahomey (both 1964-66). The average was 5.26 oz. *149 g* for Scotland in 1974.

Meat The greatest meat eaters in the world—figures include offal and poultry—are the people of Uruguay, with an average consumption of 10.93 oz. *309 g* per person per day in 1964–66. The lowest consumption is 0.16 oz. *0,45 g* in Sri Lanka (formerly Ceylon) in 1968. The United Kingdom average was 5.60 oz. *158 g* in 1973 and the Irish average was 5.52 oz. *208 g* in 1970.

BEER

Of reporting countries, the nation with the highest beer consumption per person is Western Germany, with 145,4 litres *255,8 pints* per person in 1973. The equivalent figure for the United Kingdom is 114.3 l *25.2 gal* per person. In the Northern Territory of Australia, however, the annual intake has been estimated to be as high as 52 gal *236 l* per person. A society for the prevention of alcoholism in Darwin had to disband in June 1966 for lack of support.

WINE

The consumption of wine in Britain (79.5% imported) in 1974 reached an all-time high of 82.8 million gallons or 11.83 pints per person.

SPIRITS

The U.K. consumption in 1974 of 33.26 million proof gallons at 4.75 pints *8,36 l* per head was however only half the level of gin consumption in 1742.

The mile long banana split—the ultimate in desserts

Prohibition The longest lasting imposition of prohibition has been 26 years in Iceland (1908–34). Other prohibitions have been Russia, later U.S.S.R. (1914–24) and U.S.A. (1920–33). The Faroe Islands have had a public (as opposed to private licensed) prohibition since 1918.

Biggest Round The largest round of drinks ever recorded was one for 1,222 people stood by the *Sunday Sun* and shouted by Jack Amos in Newcastle upon Tyne, England in October 1974 at the conclusion of the Jack o' Clubs road show.

Largest dish The largest menu item in the world is roasted camel, prepared occasionally for Bedouin wedding feasts. Cooked eggs are stuffed in fish, the fish stuffed in cooked chickens, the chickens stuffed into a roasted sheep carcass and the sheep stuffed into a whole camel.

Most expensive food The most expensive food (excluding spices) is white truffle of Alba which fetch, according to seasonal rarity, up to £80 per lb. *£176 per kg* in the market. Truffles in the Périgord district of France require drought between mid-July and mid-August.

Longest Banana Split The longest Banana split ever made was one a mile *1 609 m* in length embracing 10,580 bananas; 33,000 scoops of ice cream; 255 gal of topping, 155 lb *70,33 kg* of chopped nuts and 95 gal of whipped cream at the annual St. Paul Winter Carnival, Minnesota, U.S.A. on 29 Jan. 1973. The calorific value was estimated at 32,670,000.

Largest cake The largest cakes ever baked were a six-sided "birthday" cake weighing 25,000 lb. *11 338 kg*, made in August 1962 by Van de Kemp's Holland Dutch Bakers of Seattle, Washington State, U.S.A., for the Seattle World's Fair (the "Century 21 Exposition"), and a 26 ft *7,92 m* tall creation of the same weight made for the British Columbia Centennial cut on 20 July 1971.

Longest Loaf The longest one-piece loaf ever baked was one of 400 ft 6¾ in *122,09 m* baked by a team of 200 from Boise State University, Idaho, U.S.A. and eaten with a sandwich filling by a crowd of 2,500 at the Bronco Stadium in 40 mins on 19 Apr. 1975.

Largest Easter egg The largest Easter egg yet made was one of 648 lb. *290 kg* made by Darrell Lea Holdings Ltd., of Sydney, Australia weighed on 29 Apr. 1974. It measured 6 ft *1,83 m* in height and 13 ft 3½ in *4,05 m* in girth.

Largest meat pie The largest meat pie ever baked weighed 5¾ tons, measuring 18 × 6 ft and 18 in deep *5,48 × 1,83 × 0,45 m*, the eighth in the series of Denby Dale, West Yorkshire pies, to mark four royal births, baked on 5 Sept. 1964. The first was in 1788 to celebrate King George III's return to sanity but the fourth (Queen Victoria's Jubilee, 1887) went a bit "off" and had to be buried in quick-lime.

Largest Mince Pie The largest mince pie recorded was one of 2,260 lb. *1 025 kg*, 20 × 5 ft *6,09 × 1,52 m*, baked at Ashby-de-la-Zouch, Leicestershire on 15 Oct. 1932.

Largest Omelette The largest omelette made in Britain was one of 1,234 lb. *559,5 kg* made from 5,060 eggs cooked in a 7 × 6 ft *2,13 × 1,83 m* frying tank at the Surrey Agricultural Show, Guildford, Surrey on 28 May 1973. There was a report in February 1954 of a 10,000 egg omelette made in Washington, D.C., U.S.A., but details are lacking.

Largest pizza pie The largest pizza ever baked was one measuring 25 ft 1 in. *7,64 m* in diameter, hence 494 ft² *45,8 m²* in area and 1,200 lb. *544 kg* in weight at the Pizza Inn, Little Rock, Arkansas, U.S.A. on 4 Sept. 1974. It was commissioned by the KARN radio station.

Biggest Salami The largest salami on record was one of 11 ft *3,35 m* long with a circumference of 20 in *58 cm* weighing 142½ lb. *64,6 kg* made at St. Kilda, Melbourne, Australia in November 1974.

Largest sundae The most monstrous ice cream sundae ever concocted is one of 3,956¾ lb. *1 794 kg* by Al Belmont of Farrell's Ice Cream Parlour of Portland, Oregon at McLean, Virginia on 13 July 1975. It comprised 777 gal. of ice cream with 6 gal. of chocolate topping.

Largest beefburger The largest beefburger on record is one of 440 lb. *199,5 kg*, 15 ft *4,57 m* in circumference exhibited by Tiffany Foods Ltd., at the Catering Exhibition, Blackpool, England on 4 Mar. 1975.

Largest Pancake The largest pancake ever flipped intact on any griddle was one of 4 ft 9 in *1,44 m* diameter at the St. Paul Winter Carnival, Minnesota, U.S.A. on 27 Jan. 1974.

Yorkshire Pudding The largest Yorkshire Pudding on record is one measuring 12 ft 8½ in by 3 ft 10 in *3,87 × 1,16 m* baked at Northallerton Rugby Club on 28 Aug. 1972.

Top Selling Sweet The world's top selling sweets (candies) are Life Savers with 25,000 million rolls between 1913 at 14 Nov. 1973. The aggregate depth of the "hole in the middle" exceeds 1,000,000 miles.

Biggest Spit Roast The most monumental barbeque has been one for over 4,000 people at Brisbane, California on 16 Sept. 1973 with a rotissere with 12 ft *3,65 m* spit length impaling 7 buffalo with a dressed weight of 3,755 lb. *1 703 kg*. John De Marco supervised the 26 hour roast.

SPICES

Most expensive The most expensive of all spices is Mediterranean saffron (*Crocus sativus*). It takes 96,000 stigmas and therefore 32,000 flowers to make a pound. Packets of 1.9 grains are retailed in the United Kingdom for 8½p—equivalent to £19.50 per oz. *68p per gramme*.

"Hottest" The hottest of all spices is the capsicum hot pepper known as Tabasco, first reported in 1868 by Mr. Edmund McIlhenny on Avery Island, Louisiana, U.S.A.

Rarest condiment The world's most prized condiment is Cà Cuong, a secretion recovered in minute amounts from beetles in North Vietnam. Owing to war conditions, the price rose to $100 (*now £40*) per ounce *1,41 g* before supplies virtually ceased.

Sweets The biggest sweet eaters in the world are the people of Britain, with 7.8 oz. *221 g* of confectionery per person per week in 1971. The figure for Scotland was more than 9 oz. *255 g* in 1968.

Tea The most expensive tea marketed in the United Kingdom is "Oolong Leaf Bud", specially imported for Fortnum and Mason of Piccadilly, City of Westminster, Greater London, where, in 1974, it retailed for £5.40 per lb. or *£1.19/100 g*. It is blended from very young Formosan leaves. In Britain the *per caput* consumption of tea in 1973 of 114.4 oz. *3 242 g* was overtaken by Ireland.

Coffee The world's greatest coffee drinkers are the people of Finland, who consumed 16,92 kg *37.30 lb.* of coffee per person in 1970. This compared with 1,63 kg *3.59 lb.* for the United Kingdom in 1970. The most expensive coffee is Jamaica Blue Mountain retailed in the U.S. at $5.46 (£2.27) per lb. *£4.78 per kg* in March 1974.

Fresh water The world's greatest consumers of fresh water are the people and industry of the United States, whose average daily consumption reached 317,540 million Imperial gal *14 435 million hectolitres* in 1974 or 1,855 U.S. gal *7 021 litres* per head per day.

Recipe The oldest known surviving written recipe is one dated 1657 handed down from Bernice Bardolf of the Black Horse Tavern, Barnsley, Yorkshire found buried in September 1969 in the yard of the Alhambra Hotel Barnsley. Barnsley Bardolf, a variant, is now on the menu.

ENERGY

To express the various forms of available energy (coal, liquid fuels and water power, etc., but omitting vegetable fuels and peat), it is the practice to convert them all into terms of coal. On this basis the world average consumption was the equivalent of 1 984 kg (*38.9 cwt*) of coal, or its energy equivalents, per person in 1972.

The highest consumption in the world is in the United States, with an average of 11,611 kg *228.4 cwt* per person in 1972. The United Kingdom average was 6 187 kg *121.7 cwt* per person in 1973. The lowest recorded average for 1972 was 10 kg *22 lb.* per person in Burundi.

MASS COMMUNICATIONS

AIRLINES

The country with the busiest airlines system is the United States of America where 161,957,307,000 revenue passenger miles were flown on scheduled domestic and local services in 1973. This was equivalent to an annual trip of 769.3 miles *1 230,4 km* for every one of the inhabitants of the U.S.A. The United Kingdom airlines flew 208,698,000 miles *335 868,000 km* and carried 17,364,000 passengers in 1973.

MERCHANT SHIPPING

The world total of merchant shipping excluding vessels of less than 100 tons gross, sailing vessels and barges was 61,194 vessels of 311,322,626 tons gross on 1 July 1974. The largest merchant fleet in the world as at mid-1974 was that under the flag of Liberia with 2,332 ships of 55,321,641 tons gross. The U.K. figure for mid-1974 was 3,603 ships of 31,566,298 tons gross.

Largest and busiest ports Physically, the largest port in the world is New York Harbor, N.Y., U.S.A. The port has a navigable waterfront of 755 miles *121,5 km* (295 miles *474 km* in New Jersey) stretching over 92 miles² *238 km²*. A total of 261 general cargo berths and 130 other piers give a total berthing capacity of 391 ships at one time.

203

The total warehousing floor space is 422.4 acres *170,9 ha.* The world's busiest port and largest artificial harbour is the Rotterdam-Europoort in the Netherlands which covers 38 miles² *100 km².* It handled 33,296 sea-going vessels and about 300,000 barges in 1974. It is able to handle 310 sea-going vessels simultaneously up to 250,000 tons and 65 ft *19,80 m* draught.

RAILWAYS

The country with the greatest length of railway is the United States, with 202,775 miles *326 334 km* of track at 1 Jan. 1973.

The farthest anyone can get from a railway on the mainland island of Great Britain is 110 miles *177 km* by road in the case of Southend, Mull of Kintyre.

The number of journeys made on British Rail in 1974 was 732,680,000, compared with the peak year of 1957, when 1,101 million journeys (average 20.51 miles) were made.

ROADS

Oldest The oldest trackway yet discovered in the world is the Sweet track, Shapwick, Somerset which has been dated to 4,000 B.C. The first sod on Britain's first motorway, the M6 Preston By-Pass, was cut by bulldozer driver Fred Hackett on 12 June 1956.

The country with the greatest length of road is the United States (all 50 States), with 3,896,713 miles *6 271 151 km* of graded roads at 1 Jan. 1973. Regular driving licences are issuable at 15, without a driver education course only in Hawaii and Mississippi. Thirteen U.S. States issue restricted juvenile licences at 14.

The United Kingdom has 224,281 miles *360 945 km* of road including 1,122 miles *1 805 km* of motorway at 1 April 1973 and 17,394,500 vehicles in Sept. 1973. A total of 23,000,000 vehicles by 1980 has been forecast. The longest of uninterrupted dual carriageway is from Hendon, Barnet, Greater London for more than 425 miles *683 km via* M.1, M.6, A.74, M.74, M.74, to the Stirling by-pass on to the A.9, in Scotland.

Busiest The highest traffic volume of any point in the world is at the Harbor and Santa Monica Freeways interchange in Los Angeles, California, U.S.A. with a 24-hour average on Fridays of 420,000 vehicles in 1970.

The territory with the highest traffic density in the world is Hong Kong. On 31 May 1970 there were 122,274 motor vehicles on 600 miles *965 km* of serviceable roads giving a density of 8.64 yds *7,90 m* per vehicle. The comparative figure for the United Kingdom in 1971 was 24.82 yds *22,69 m.*

The greatest traffic density at any one point in the United Kingdom is at Hyde Park Corner, London. The average daytime 8 a.m.–8 p.m. flow in 1970 (last census) was 164,338 vehicles every 12 hours. The busiest Thames bridge in 1974 was Putney Bridge, with a 24-hour average of 53,213 vehicles. The greatest reported aggregation of London buses was 38, bumper to bumper, along the Vauxhall Bridge Road on 18 Nov. 1965.

Widest The widest street in the world is the Monumental Axis running for 1½ miles *2,4 km* from the Municipal Plaza to the Plaza of the Three Powers in Brasilia, the capital of Brazil. The six-lane Boulevard was opened in April 1960 and is 250 m *273.4 yds* wide. The B Bridge Toll Plaza has 34 lanes (17 in each direction) serving the Bay Bridge, San Francisco, California.

The only instance of 17 carriageway lanes side by side in Britain occurs on the M.61 at Linnyshaw Moss, Worsley, Greater Manchester.

Narrowest The world's narrowest street is St. John's Lane in Rome, with a width of 19 in *48 cm.* The narrowest street in the United Kingdom is Parliament Street, Exeter, Devon, which at one point measures 26 in *66 cm* across.

Longest straight road The longest straight road in the United Kingdom was a stretch of 22¾ miles *33,6 km* between Bailgate in the City of Lincoln and Broughton Village, Lincolnshire. Part of the Roman road Ermine Street, it now comprises sections of Class I (A. 15), Class III and unclassified road, with only two slight deviations of less than 50 ft *15 m* from the true straight line. Part of the road was closed for an airfield, reducing the straight section to 16½ miles *26,5 km.*

Longest World The longest motorable road in the world is the Pan-American Highway, which will stretch 17,018 miles *27 387 km* from North West Alaska, to southernmost Chile. There remains a gap known as the Tapon del Darién, in Panama and the Atrato Swamp, Colombia. This was first traversed by the 1972 British Trans-Americas Expedition, led by Major John Blashford-Snell M.B.E., R.E., which emerged from the Atrato swamp after 99 days. On 9 June 1972 an adapted Range Rover VXC 868K which had made the traverse arrived in Tierra del Fuego, having left Alaska on 3 Dec. 1971.

Most complex interchange The most complex interchange on the British road system is that at Gravelly Hill, north of Birmingham on the Midland Link Motorway section of the M6 opened on 24 May 1972. There are 18 routes on 6 levels together with a diverted canal and river, which consumed 26,000 tons/*tonnes* of steel, 250,000 tons/*tonnes* of concrete, 300,000 tons/*tonnes* of earth and cost £8,200,000.

Longest street This title has been accorded to Figueroa Street which stretches 30 miles *48,2 km* from Pasadena at Colorado Blvd. to the Pacific Coast Highway, Los Angeles, U.S.A.

Britain The longest designated road in Great Britain is the A1 from London to Edinburgh of 404 miles *650 km.* The longest Roman roads were Watling Street, from Dubrae (Dover) 215 miles *346 km* through Londinium (London) to Viroconium (Wroxeter), and Fosse Way, which ran 218 miles *350 km* from Lindum (Lincoln) through Aquae Sulus (Bath) to Isca Dumnoniorum (Exeter). However, a 10-mile *16 km* section of Fosse Way between Ilchester and Seaton remains indistinct. The commonest street name in Greater London is Park Road, of which there are 40.

Shortest The shortest reported measurement of a street in Britain is 58 ft *17,67 m* of Tolbooth Street, Falkirk, Central, Scotland.

Longest hill The longest steep hill on any road in the United Kingdom is on the road westwards from Lochcarron toward Applecross in Ross and Cromarty, Scotland. In 6 miles *9,6 km* this road rises from sea-level to 2,054 ft *626 m* with an average gradient of 1 in 15.4, the steepest part being 1 in 4.

Of the five unclassified roads with 1 in 3 gradients the most severe is Hard Knott Pass between Boot and Ambleside, Cumbria.

Steepest The steepest streets in the world are Filbert Street, Russian Hill and 22nd Street, Doleres Heights, San Francisco with gradients of 31.5% or 1 in 3.17.

Highest World The highest trail in the world is 7 miles *11,2 km* southwest of Barduksum, Tibet which rises to 22,300 ft *6 797 m.* The highest carriageable road in the world is one 1,180 km *733.2 miles* long between Tibet and south western Sinkiang, completed in October 1957, which takes in passes of an altitude up to 18,480 ft *5 632 m* above sea-level. Europe's highest pass (excluding the Caucasian passes) is the Col de Restefond (9,193 ft [*2 082 m*]) completed in 1962 with 21 hairpins between Jausiers and Saint Etienne-de-Tinée, France. It is usually closed between early October and early June. The highest motor road in Europe is the Pico de Veleta in the Sierra Nevada, southern Spain. The shadeless climb of 36 km *22.4 miles* brings the motorist to 11,384 ft *3 469 m* above sea-level and became on completion of a road on its southern side in Summer 1974 originally Europe's highest pass.

United Kingdom The highest road in the United Kingdom is the A6293 tarmac extension at Great Dun Fell, Cumbria, (2,780 ft [*847 m*]) leading to a Ministry of Defence radar installation. A permit is required to use it. The highest classified road in England is the B6293 at Killhope Cross (2,056 ft [*626 m*]) on the Cumbria-Durham border near Nenthead. The highest classified road in Scotland is the A93 road over the Grampians through Cairnwell, a pass between Blairgowrie, Perthshire, and Braemar, Aberdeenshire, which reaches a height of 2,199 ft *670 m*. The highest classified road in Wales is the Rhondda-Afan Inter-Valley road (A4107), which reaches 1,750 ft *533 m* 2½ miles *4 km* east of Abergwynfi, Mid Glamorgan. An estate track exists to the summit of Ben a'Bhuird (3,860 ft [*1 176 m*]) in Aberdeenshire.

Lowest The lowest road in the world is that along the Israeli shores of the Dead Sea, 1,290 ft *393 m* below sea-level. The lowest surface roads in Great Britain are just below sea-level in the Holme Fen area of Cambridgeshire. The world's lowest pass is Rock Reef Pass, Everglades National Park, Florida which is 3 ft *91 cm* above sea-level.

Highest motorway The highest motorway in Great Britain is the trans-Pennine M62, which, at the Windy Hill interchange, reaches an altitude of 1,220 ft *371 m*. Its Dean Head cutting is the deepest roadway cutting in Europe at 183 ft *55,7 m*.

Longest viaduct The longest elevated road viaduct on the British road system is the 2.97 mile *5 730 m* Gravelly Hill to Castle Bromwich section of the M6. It was completed in May 1972.

Biggest square The Tian an men (Gate of Heavenly Peace) Square in Peking, described as the navel of China, extends over 98 acres *39,6 ha*. The Maiden e Shah in Isfahan, Iran extends over 20.1 acres *8,1 ha*. The oldest London square is Bloomsbury Square planned in 1754.

Traffic jams The worst traffic jams in the world are in Tōkyō, Japan. Only 9 per cent of the city area is roadway, compared with London (23 per cent), Paris (25 per cent), New York (35 per cent) and Washington, D.C. (43 per cent). In April 1973 it was stated that there were only 247,000 registered cars in Moscow. The longest traffic jam reported in Britain was one of 35 miles *56 km* out of 42.5 miles *75,6 km* road length between Torquay and Yarcombe, Devon, on 25 July 1964 and 35 miles *56 km* on the A30 between Egham, Surrey and Micheldever, Hampshire on 23 May 1970.

Traffic lights Semaphore-type traffic *signals* had been set up in Parliament Square, London in 1868 with red and green gas lamps for night use. It was not an offence to disobey traffic signals until assent was given to the 1930 Road Traffic Bill. Traffic *lights* were introduced in Great Britain with a one day trial in Wolverhampton on 11 Feb. 1928. They were first permanently operated in Leeds, West Yorkshire on 16 Mar. and in Edinburgh, Scotland on 19 Mar. 1928. The first vehicle-actuated lights were installed at the Cornhill-Gracechurch Junction, City of London in 1932.

Parking meters The earliest parking meters ever installed were those put in the business district of Oklahoma City, Oklahoma, U.S.A., on 19 July 1935. They were the invention of Carl C. Magee (U.S.A.) and reached London in 1958.

Worst driver It was reported that a 75-year-old *male* driver received 10 traffic tickets, drove on the wrong side of the road four times, committed four hit-and-run offences and caused six accidents, all within 20 minutes, in McKinney, Texas, U.S.A., on 15 Oct. 1966.

Milestone Britain's oldest milestone *in situ* is a Roman stone dating from A.D. 150 on the Stanegate, at Chesterholme, near Bardon Mill, Northumberland.

Longest Ford The longest ford in any classified road in England is that at Bilbrook, Old Cleeve parish, Somerset which measures 90 yds *82 m* in width.

TELEPHONES

There were 336,297,000 telephones in the world at 1 Jan. 1974 as estimated by The American Telephone & Telegraph Co. The country with the greatest number was the United States, with 138,286,000 instruments, equivalent to 654.7 for every 1,000 people, compared with the United Kingdom figure of 19,095,317 (third largest in the world to the U.S.A. and Japan), or 340.6 per 1,000 people, at 31 March 1974. The territory with fewest reported telephones is Pitcairn Island with 25.

The country with the most telephones per head of population is Monaco, with 839.3 per 1,000 of the population at 1 Jan. 1974. The country with the least was Bhutan with 0.5 of a telephone per 1,000.

The greatest total of calls made in any country is in the United States, with 188,175 million (894 calls per person) in 1973. The United Kingdom telephone service connected 14,954,111,000 calls in the year 1973–74 an average of 267.3 per person.

The city with most telephones is New York City, N.Y., U.S.A., with 5,952,112 (760 per 1,000 people) at 1 Jan. 1974. In 1972 Washington D.C. reached the level of 1,303 telephones per 1,000 people though in some small areas there are still higher densities such as Beverly Hills, north of Los Angeles with a return of about 1,600 per 1,000.

Busiest Phone The pay phone with the heaviest useage in the world is believed to be 695–9079 on a shelf in the centre of Pennsylvania Station, New York City, which averages 263 calls a day thus used each 5 mins 28 secs round the clock all year.

Longest call The longest telephone connection on record was one of 724 hours 3 mins from 21 Jan. to 20 Fed 1974. between Sigma Nu fraternity and Kappa Delta sority and Morehead State University, Kentucky, U.S.A.

Longest cable The world's longest submarine telephone cable is the Commonwealth Pacific Cable (COMPAC), which runs for more than 9,000 miles *14 480 km* from Australia, *via* Auckland, New Zealand and the Hawaiian Islands to Port Alberni, Canada. It cost about £35,000,000 and was inaugurated on 2 Dec. 1963.

POSTAL SERVICES

The country with the largest mail in the world is the United States, whose population posted 85,187 million letters and packages in 1970 when the U.S. Postal Service employed 715,970 people. The United Kingdom total was 11,010 million letters and 194.9 million parcels in the year ending 31 March 1974.

The United States also takes first place in the average number of letters which each person posts during one year. The figure was 413 in 1970. The United Kingdom figure was 235 per head in 1970–71. Of all countries the greatest discrepancy between incoming and outgoing mail is for the U.S.A. whence in 1970 only 887 million items were mailed in response to 1,477 million items received from foreign sources.

POSTAGE STAMPS

Earliest The earliest adhesive postage stamps in the world were the "Penny Blacks" of the United Kingdom, bearing the head of Queen Victoria, placed on sale on 1 May for use on 6 May 1840. A total of 68,158,080 were printed. The National Postal Museum possesses a unique full proof sheet of 240 stamps, printed in April 1840, before the corner letters, plate numbers or marginal inscriptions were added.

Largest The largest stamps ever issued were the 1913 Express Delivery stamps of China, which measured 9¾ by 2¾ in *247,5 × 69,8 mm*. The largest postage labels ever printed were air mail stamps issued by the former Trucial State of Fujeira (Fujairah) measuring 2⅝ × 4⅛ in *66,6 × 104,7 mm* on 5 Apr. 1972 for the 1972 Olympic Games in which they did not compete. The Universal Postal Union do not regard this as a *bona fide* postal stamp.

Smallest The smallest stamps ever issued were the 10 cents and 1 peso of the Colombian State of Bolívar in 1863–66. They measured 8 mm *0.31 in* by 9,5 mm *0.37 in*. The imperforate 4/4 schilling red of Mecklenburg–Schwerin issued on 1 July 1856 printed in Berlin was divisible into four quarters. Thus a ¼ schilling section measured fractionally over 10 mm² *0.394 in²*.

Highest and lowest denomination The highest denomination stamp ever issued was a red and black stamp for £100, issued in Kenya in 1925–27. Although valid for postage its function was essentially for collection of revenue. The highest denomination postage stamps ever issued in the United Kingdom were the £5 orange Victoria stamp issued on 21 March 1882 and the current £5 orange-yellow and black Post Due issued on 2 Apr. 1973. Owing to inflations it is difficult to determine the lowest denomination stamp but it was probably the 1946 3,000 pengö Hungarian stamp. worth at one time only 6.6×10^{-15}p.

Highest price World The highest price ever paid for a single philatelic item is the $380,000 (*then £158,333*) for two 1d. orange "Post Office" Mauritius stamps of 1847 on a cover bought at H. R. Harmer's Inc., New York City, U.S.A. by Raymond H. Weill Co. of New Orleans, Louisiana for their own account from the Liechtenstein-Dale collection on 21 Oct. 1968. The item was discovered in 1897 in an Indian bazaar by a Mr. Charles Williams who paid less than £1 for it.

The British auction record is £50,000, set at Stanley Gibbons on 4 Oct. 1973, for one of the two known Bermuda Penny "Perot" stamps of 1854 named after William B. Perot the island's post master of 1816–62.

Most valuable World There are a number of stamps of which but a single specimen is known. Of these the most celebrated is the one cent black on magenta issued in British Guiana (now Guyana) in February 1856. It was originally bought for six shillings from L. Vernon Vaughan, a schoolboy, in 1873. This is the world's most renowned stamp, for which £A16,000 (*then £12,774 sterling*) was paid in 1940, when it was sold by Mrs. Arthur Hind. It was insured for £200,000 when it was displayed in 1965 at the Royal Festival Hall, London. It was sold on 24 March 1970 by Frederick T. Small by auction at the Siegal Galleries, New York City, U.S.A. for $280,000 (*then £116,666*) by Irwin Weinberg. It is now "catalogued" at £120,000. It was alleged in October 1938 that Hind had, in 1928, purchased and burned his stamp's twin.

Great Britain The rarest British stamp which is not an error is the King Edward VII 6d. dull purple Inland Revenue

Official stamp issued and withdrawn on 14 May 1904. Only 11 or 12 are known and the only unused example in private hands was from the W. H. Harrison-Cripps collection bought by a Canadian at auction at Stanley Gibbons, London on 27 Oct. 1972 for £10,000. and reputedly re-sold by private treaty in Germany in 1975 for £15,000.

Commonest British stamp The most frequently reproduced United Kingdom stamp has been the definitive Elizabeth II 3d. violet, issued from 1 Oct. 1953 to 17 May 1965, of which 19,920 million were issued.

Largest collection The greatest private stamp collection ever auctioned has been that of Maurice Burrus (d. 1959) of Alsace, France, which realised an estimated £1,500,000.

The largest national collection in the world is that at the British Museum, London, which has had the General Post Office collection on permanent loan since March 1963. The British Royal collection, housed in 400 volumes, is also believed to be worth well in excess of £1,000,000. The collection of the U.P.U. (founded 9 Oct. 1874) in Berne, Switzerland started in 1878 has received 155,000 issued stamps and 2,400 miniature sheets all different from members under Article 7 while the largest international collection open to the public is in the Swiss Postal Museum in Berne.

POSTAL ADDRESSES

Highest numbering The practice of numbering houses began in 1463 on the Pont Notre Dame, Paris, France. The highest numbered house in Britain is No. 2,679 Stratford Road, Hockley Heath, West Midlands, owned since 1964 by Mr. & Mrs. Howard Hughes. The highest numbered house in Scotland is No. 2,629 London Road, Mount Vernon, Glasgow, which is part of the local police station.

Pillar-boxes Pillar-boxes were introduced into Great Britain at the suggestion of the novelist Anthony Trollope (1815–82). The oldest site on which one is still in service is one dating from 8 Feb. 1853 in Union Street, St. Peter Port, Guernsey though the present box is not the original. The oldest original box in Great Britain is another Victorian example at Barnes Cross, Holwell, near Sherborne, Dorset, also dating from probably later in 1853.

Post Offices The Post Office's northernmost post office is at Haroldswick, Unst, Shetland Islands. The most southerly in the British Isles is at Samarès, Jersey. The oldest is at Sanquhar, Dumfriesshire which was first referred to in 1763. In England the Post Office at Shipton-Under-Wychwood, Oxfordshire dates back to April 1845.

TELEGRAMS

The country where most telegrams are sent is the U.S.S.R., whose population sent 365,900,000 telegrams in 1970. The United Kingdom total was 14,361,000 including 7,109,000 sent overseas, in the year ending 31 March 1974.

INLAND WATERWAYS

The country with the greatest length of inland waterways is Finland. The total length of navigable lakes and rivers is about 50,000 km *31,000 miles*. In the United Kingdom the total length of navigable rivers and canals is 3,940 miles *6 340 km*.

Longest navigable river The longest navigable natural waterway in the world is the River Amazon, which sea-going vessels can ascend as far as Iquitos, in Peru, 2,236 miles *3 598 km*

from the Atlantic seaboard. On a National Geographic Society expedition ending on 10 March 1969, Helen and Frank Schreider navigated downstream from San Francisco, Peru, 3,845 miles *6 187 km* up the Amazon, by a balsa raft named *Mamuri* 249 miles *400 km* to Atalaya, thence 356 miles *572 km* to Pucallpa by outboard motor dug-out canoe and thence the last 3,240 miles *5 214 km* towards Belem in the 30 ft *9,14 m* petrol-engined cabin cruiser *Amazon Queen*.

7. EDUCATION

ILLITERACY

Literacy is variously defined as "ability to read simple subjects" and "ability to read and write a simple letter". The looseness of definition and the scarcity of data for many countries preclude anything more than approximations, but the extent of illiteracy among adults (15 years old and over) is estimated to have been 34.7 per cent in 1969. The continent with the greatest proportion of illiterates is Africa, where 81.5 per cent of adults are illiterate. The last published figure for Mali in 1960 showed 97.8% of people over 15 were unable to read.

UNIVERSITIES

World Probably the oldest educational institution in the world is the University of Karueein, founded in A.D. 859 in Fez, Morocco.

United Kingdom The oldest university in the United Kingdom is the University of Oxford, which came into being in *c.* 1167. The oldest of the existing colleges is probably University College (1249), though its foundation is less well documented than that of Merton College in 1264. The earliest college at Cambridge University is Peterhouse, founded in 1284. The largest college at either university is Trinity College, Cambridge. It was founded in 1546. The oldest university in Scotland is the University of St. Andrews, Fife. It was established in 1411.

Greatest enrolment The university with the greatest enrolment in the world is the University of Calcutta (founded 1857) in India, with 178,176 students (internal and external) and 31 professors in 1970–71. Owing to the inadequacy of the buildings and number of lecturers, the students are handled in three shifts per day. The enrolment at all branches of the City University of New York, U.S.A., was 155,414 in 1974 with 11,727 teachers. The University of London had 42,987 students (of whom 35,265 were full-time) as at 1 Jan. 1975.

Largest building The largest university building in the world is the M. V. Lomonosov State University on the Lenin Hills, south of Moscow, U.S.S.R. It stands 240 m *787,4 ft* tall, has 32 storeys and contains 40,000 rooms. It was constructed in 1949–53.

PROFESSORS

Youngest The youngest at which anybody has been elected to a chair in a university is 19 years in the case of Colin MacLaurin (1698–1746), who was admitted to Marischal College, Aberdeen as Professor of Mathematics on 30 Sept. 1717. In 1725 he was made Professor of Mathematics at Edinburgh University on the recommendation of Sir Isaac Newton. In July 1967 Dr. Harvey Friedman, Ph.D., was appointed Assistant Professor of Mathematics at Stanford University, California, U.S.A. aged just 19 years.

Most durable The longest period for which any professorship has been held is 63 years in the case of Thomäs Martyn (1735–1825), Professor of Botany at Cambridge University from 1762 until his death. His father, John Martyn (1699–1768), had occupied the chair from 1733 to 1762.

Dr. Thomas Martyn (1735–1825) the most durable professor, who sat in the Chair of Botany at Cambridge for 63 years

Senior Wranglers Since 1910 the Wranglers (first class honours students in the Cambridge University mathematical Tripos, part 2) have been placed in alphabetical order only. In 1890 Miss P. G. Fawcett of Newnham was placed "above the Senior Wrangler".

Youngest undergraduate The most extreme recorded case of undergraduate juvenility was that of William Thomson (1824–1907), later Lord Kelvin, O.M., G.C.V.O., who entered Glasgow University aged 10 years 4 months in October 1834 and matriculated on 14 Nov. 1834.

SCHOOLS

Largest World The largest school in the world was the De Witt Clinton High School in the Bronx, New York City, N.Y., U.S.A., where the enrolment attained a peak of 12,000 in 1934. It was founded in 1897 and now has an enrolment of 6,000.

United Kingdom The school with the most pupils in Great Britain is Banbury Comprehensive with 2,767 pupils in the 1975 summer term. George Watson's, Colinton Road, Edinburgh with 1,500 boys and 950 girls is the largest school in Scotland. The total in Holy Child School, Belfast, Northern Ireland reached 2,752 in 1973 but has since been split up.

Oldest in Britain The title of the oldest existing school in Britain is contested. It is claimed that King's School in Canterbury, Kent, was a foundation of Saint Augustine, some time between his arrival in Kent in A.D. 597 and his death in *c.* 604. Cor Tewdws (College of Theodosius) at Llantwit Major, South Glamorgan, reputedly burnt down in A.D. 446 was refounded by St. Illtyd in 508 and flourished into the 13th century.

Oldest old school tie The practice of wearing distinctive neckties bearing the colours of registered designs of schools, universities, sports clubs, regiments, etc., appears to date from *c.* 1880. The practice originated in Oxford University, where boater bands were converted into use as "ribbon ties". The earliest definitive evidence stems from an order from Exeter College for college ties, dated 25 June, 1880.

MOST EXPENSIVE

United Kingdom The most expensive school in the United Kingdom is Millfield at Street, Somerset, founded by R. J. O. Meyer in 1937. The terminal fee for boarding entries under 15 including standard extras in the summer term 1975 was £795 indicating an annual rate of some £2,400. The most expensive girl's school in 1974–75 was Benenden, Kent (founded 1924) with annual fees of £1,239.

Most Schools The greatest documented number of schools attended by a pupil is 265 by Wilma Williams, now Mrs. R. J. Horton, from 1933–43 when her parents were in show business.

Most "O" and "A" levels Francis L. Thomason of Cleobury Mortimer, Salop had by August 1974 accumulated 26 "O", 7 "A" and 1 "S" levels making a total of 34. A long-term prisoner in Parkhurst, Isle of Wight, predictably known as "Brains", is expected to boost his total of 32 (8 A's and 24 O's) to at least 36 in late August 1975.

In pre-war days when exemption from metriculation was conditional upon passing all subjects specified, some candidates took subjects semi-annually for several years. In an extreme case D. H. O. John B.Sc. got 37 School Certificate passes and 11 Higher School Certificate passes.

Youngest headmaster The youngest headmaster of a major public school was Henry Montagu Butler (b. 2 July 1833), appointed Headmaster of Harrow School on 16 Nov. 1859, when aged 26 years 137 days. His first term in office began in January 1860.

Most Durable Teachers James Boucher, J. P. (born in Fife, Scotland, 1851) served as a schoolmaster for 72 years from 1866 to January 1939. He began as a pupil teacher in his village school in Ladybank, Fife and ended his career after 50 years, as Headmaster of Garvald Public School from 1884 until 1939. Col. Ernest Achay Loftus C.B.E., T.D. (b. 11 Jan. 1884) served as a teacher over a span of 73 years from Sept. 1901 in York, England until 18 Feb. 1975 in Zambia retiring as the world's oldest civil servant aged 91 years 38 days.

8. RELIGIONS

LARGEST

Religious statistics are necessarily highly approximate. The test of adherence to a religion varies widely in rigour, while many individuals, particularly in the East, belong to two or more religions.

Christianity is the world's prevailing religion, with over 1,025,000,000 adherants in 1975. The Vatican computer reported that for 1971 there were 665,700,000 Roman Catholics. The largest non-Christian religions are Islam (Muslim) and Hindu each with some 535,000,000 followers.

In the United Kingdom the Anglicans comprise members of the Established Church of England, the Dis-established Church in Wales, the Episcopal Church in Scotland and the Church of Ireland. In mid 1970 there were 27,736,000 living persons who had been baptized in Anglican churches in the provinces of Canterbury and York. In the same area it is estimated that there are 9,154,000 persons confirmed, of whom nearly 1,813,892 were Easter communicants in 1970. There were 14,258 parish churches and 17,087 full-time clergymen on 1 Jan. 1972. In Scotland the most numerous group is the Church of Scotland (the Presbyterians), which had 1,133,506 members, apart from adherents.

Largest clergy The world's largest religious organization is the Roman Catholic Church, with 664,388,000 members, 425,000 priests and 900,000 nuns. The total number of cardinals, patriarchs, metropolitans, archbishops, bishops, abbots and superiors is 4,000. There are about 420,000 churches.

Jews The total of world Jewry was estimated to be 15.3 million in 1973. The highest concentration was in the United states, with 6.3 million, of whom 2.8 million were in Greater New York. The total in Israel was 3.24 million. The total of British Jewry is 460,000 of whom 285,000 are in Greater London, and 13,750 in Glasgow. The total in Tōkyō, Japan, is less than 1,000.

Largest Temple The largest religious structure ever built is Angkor Wat (City Temple), enclosing 402 acres *162,6 ha* in Khmer Republic, south-east Asia. It was built to the God Vishnu by the Khmer King Suryavarman II in the period 1113–50. Its curtain wall measures 1,400 by 1,400 yds *1 280 × 1 280 m* and its population before it was abandoned in 1432, was 80,000. The largest Buddhist temple in the world is Borobudur, near Joyjakarta, Indonesia built in the 8th century.

CATHEDRALS

Largest World The world's largest cathedral is the cathedral church of the Diocese of New York, St. John the Divine, with a floor area of 121,000 ft² *11 240 m²* and a volume of 16,822,000 ft³ *476 350 m³*. The corner stone was laid on 27 Dec. 1892, and the Gothic building was still uncompleted in 1975. In New York it is referred to as "Saint John the Unfinished". The nave is the longest in the world, 601 ft *183,18 m* in length, with a vaulting 124 ft *37,79 m* in height.

The cathedral covering the largest area is that of Santa Mariá de la Sede in Sevilla (Seville), Spain. It was built in Spanish Gothic style between 1402 and 1519 and is 414 ft *126,18 m* long, 271 ft *82,60 m* wide and 100 ft *30,48 m* high to the vault of the nave.

United Kingdom The largest cathedral in the British Isles is the Anglican Cathedral of Liverpool. Built in modernized Gothic style, work was begun on 19 July 1904, and when completed will have cost over £3,000,000. The building encloses 100,000 ft² *9 300 m²* and has an overall length of 671 ft *204,52 m*. The Vestey Tower is 331 ft *100,88 m* high.

Smallest The smallest cathedral in the world is the Pro-Cathedral Church of St. John the Baptist, Murray Bridge, South Australia. It was dedicated on 2 Feb. 1887 and has had the cathedra of the Bishop of The Murray since 16 Apr. 1970. It measures 1,025 ft² *95,2 m²* and has a capacity for only 130. The smallest cathedral in use in the United Kingdom (of old foundation) is St. Asaph in Clwyd, Wales. It is 182 ft *55,47 m* long, 68 ft *20,72 m* wide and has a tower 100 ft *30,48 m* high. Oxford Cathedral in Christ Church (College) is 155 ft *47,24 m* long. The nave of the Cathedral of the Isles on the Isle of Cumbrae, Strathclyde measures only 40 × 20 ft *12,19 × 6,09 m*. The total floor area is 2,124 ft² *197,3 m²*.

Longest nave The longest nave in the United Kingdom is that of St. Albans Cathedral, Hertfordshire, which is 285 ft *86,86 m* long compared with 266½ ft *81,22 m* for the nave of Winchester Cathedral, which is of greater overall length.

Largest World The largest church in the world is the basilica of St. Peter, built between 1492 and 1612 in the Vatican City, Rome.

The length of the church, measured from the apse, is 611 ft 4 in *186,33 m*. The area is 18,110 yd² *15 142 m²*. The inner diameter of the famous dome is 137 ft 9 in *41,98 m* and its centre is 119 m *390 ft 5 in* high. The external height is 457 ft 9 in *139,52 m*.

The elliptical Basilique of St. Pie X at Lourdes, France, completed in 1957 at a cost of £2,000,000 has a capacity of 20,000 under its giant span arches and a length of 200 m *656 ft*.

The crypt of the underground Civil War Memorial Church in the Guadarrama Mountains, 45 km *28 miles* from Madrid, Spain, is 260 m *853 ft* in length. It took 21 years (1937–58) to build, at a reported cost of £140,000,000 and is surmounted by a cross 150 m *492 ft* tall.

United Kingdom The largest church in the United Kingdom used as a parish church (since 1548) is the Church of SS John and Martin at Beverley, Humberside, known as Beverley Minister, which is 365 ft *111,25 m* long and 169 ft *51,5 m* across the large transcept with a 64 ft *19,5 m* wide nave and a calculated floor area of 29,840 ft² *2 772 m²*.

Smallest *World* The world's smallest church is the Union Church at Wiscasset, Maine, U.S.A., with a floor area of 31½ ft² *2,92 m²* (7 × 4½ ft [*2,13 × 1,37 m*]). Les Vauxbalets Church in Guernsey has an area of 16 × 12 ft *4,87 × 3,65 m*, room for one priest and a congregation of two.

Britain The smallest church in use in England is Bremilham Church, Cowage Farm, Foxley near Malmesbury, Wiltshire which measures 12 × 12 ft *3,65 × 3,65 m* and is used for service once a year. The smallest completed medieval English church in regular use is that at Culbone, Somerset, which measures 35 × 12 ft *10,66 × 3,65 m*. The smallest Welsh chapel is St. Trillo's Chapel, Rhôs-on-Sea (Llandrillo-yn-Rhos), Clwyd, measuring only 12 × 6 ft *3,65 × 1,83 m*. The smallest chapel in Scotland is St. Margaret's, Edinburgh, measuring 16½ × 10½ ft *5,02 × 3,20 m*, giving a floor area of 173¼ ft² *16,09 m²*.

OLDEST

World The earliest known shrine dates from the proto-neolithic Natufian culture in Jericho, where a site on virgin soil has been dated to the ninth millennium B.C. A simple rectilinear red-plastered room with a niche housing a stone pillar believed to be the shrine of a Pre-Pottery fertility cult dating from *c.* 6500 B.C. was also uncovered in Jericho (now Arīhā) in Jordan. The oldest surviving Christian church in the world is Qal'at es Salihige in eastern Syria, dating from A.D. 232.

United Kingdom The oldest ecclesiastical building in the United Kingdom is a 6th century cell built by St. Brendan in 542 A.D. on Eileachan Naoimh (pronounced Noo), Garvelloch Islands, Argyllshire. The church in the United Kingdom with the oldest origins is St. Martin's Church in Canterbury, Kent. It was built in A.D. 560 on the foundations of a 1st century Roman church. The oldest church in Ireland is the Gallerus Oratory, built in *c.* 750 at Ballyferriter, near Kilmalkedar, County Kerry. Britain's oldest nunnery is St. Peter and Paul Minster, on the Isle of Thanet, Kent. It was founded in *c.* 748 by the Abbess Eadburga of Bugga. The oldest wooden church in Great Britain is St. Andrew's, Greensted, near Ongar, Essex dating to A.D. 835 though some of the timbers date to the original building of *c.* A.D. 650.

TALLEST SPIRES

World The tallest cathedral spire in the world is that of the Protestant Cathedral of Ulm in Germany. The building is early Gothic and was begun in 1377. The tower, in the centre of the west façade, was not finally completed until 1890 and is 160,90 m *528 ft* high. The world's tallest church spire is that of the Chicago Temple of the First Methodist Church on Clark Street, Chicago, Illinois, U.S.A. The building consists of a 22-storey skyscraper (erected in 1924) surmounted by a parsonage at 330 ft *100,5 m*, a "Sky Chapel" at 400 ft *121,92 m* and a steeple cross at 568 ft *173,12 m* above street level.

United Kingdom The highest spire in the United Kingdom is that of the church of St. Mary, called Salisbury Cathedral, Wiltshire. The Lady Chapel was built in the years 1220–25 and the main fabric of the cathedral was finished and consecrated in 1258. The spire was added later, 1334–65, and reaches a height of 404 ft *123,13 m*. The Central Spire of Lincoln Cathedral completed in *c.* 1307 and which fell in 1548 was 525 ft *160,02 m* tall.

D. L. Roberts

Bremilham Church in Wiltshire, the smallest in England

LARGEST SYNAGOGUES

World The largest synagogue in the world is the Temple Emanu-El on Fifth Avenue at 65th Street, New York City, N.Y., U.S.A. The temple, completed in September 1929, has a frontage of 150 ft *45,72 m* on Fifth Avenue and 253 ft *77,11 m* on 65th Street. The Sanctuary proper can accommodate 2,500 people, and the adjoining Beth-El Chapel seats 350. When all the facilities are in use, more than 6,000 people can be accommodated.

Great Britain The largest synagogue in Great Britain is the Edgware Synagogue, Barnet, Greater London, completed in 1959, with a capacity of 1,630 seats.

Largest mosque The largest mosque ever built was the now ruinous al-Malawiya mosque of al-Mutawakil in Samarra, Iraq built in A.D. 842–852 and measuring 9.21 acres *3,72 ha* with dimensions of 784 × 512 ft *238,9 × 156,0 m*. The world's largest mosque in use is the Jama Masjid (1644–58) in Delhi, India, with an area of more than 10,000 ft² *929 m²* and two minarets 108 ft *32,91 m* tall. The largest mosque will be the Merdeka Mosque in Djakarta, Indonesia, which was begun in 1962. The cupola will be 45 m *147.6 ft* in diameter and the capacity in excess of 50,000 people.

Tallest minaret The world's tallest minaret is the Qutb Minar, south of New Delhi, India, built in 1194 to a height of 238 ft *72,54 m*.

Tallest pagoda The world's tallest pagoda is the Shwe Dogon Pagoda in Rangoon, Burma which was increased to its present height of 326 ft *99,36 m* and perimeter of 1,420 ft *432,8 m* by Hsinbyushin, King of Ava (1763–1776). The tallest Chinese temple is the 13-storey Pagoda of the Six Harmonies (*Liu he t'a*) outside Hang-chow. It is "nearly 200 ft [*61 m*] high".

SAINTS

There are 1,848 "registered" saints of whom 628 are Italians, 576 French and 271 from the British Isles. The total includes 15 Popes. The first U.S. born saint is Mother Elizabeth Ann Bayley Seton (1774–1821) canonized 12 Dec. 1974.

Most and least rapidly Canonized The shortest interval that has elapsed between the death of a Saint and his canonization was in the case of St. Anthony of Padua, Italy, who died on 13 June 1251 and was canonized 352 days later on 30 May 1252. The other extreme is represented by St. Bernard

209

of Thiron for 20 years Prior of St. Sabinus, who died in 1117 and was made a Saint in 1861—744 years later. The Italian monk and painter, Fra Giovanni da Fiesole (*né* Guido di Pietro), called *Il Beato* ("The Blessed") Fra Angelico (*c.* 1400–1455), is still in the first stage of canonization.

POPES

Reign
Longest The longest reign of any of the 262 Popes has been that of Pius IX (Giovanni Maria Mastai-Ferretti), who reigned for 31 years 236 days from 16 June 1846 until his death aged 85, on 7 Feb. 1878.

Shortest Pope Stephen II was elected on 24 March 752 and died two days later.

Oldest It is recorded that Pope St. Agatho (reigned 678–681) was elected at the age of 103 and lived to 106, but recent scholars have expressed doubts. The oldest of recent Pontiffs has been Pope Leo XIII (Gioacchino Pecci), who was born on 2 March 1810, elected Pope at the third ballot on 20 Feb. 1878 and died on 20 July 1903, aged 93 years 140 days.

Youngest The youngest of all Popes was Pope Benedict IX (d. 1056) (Theophylact), who has three terms as Pope: in 1032–44; April to May 1045; and 8 Nov. 1047 to 17 July 1048. It would appear that he was aged only 11 or 12 in 1032, though the Catalogue of the Popes admits only to his "extreme youth".

Last non-Italian, ex-Cardinalate and English Popes The last non-Italian Pope was the Utrecht-born Cardinal Priest Adrian Dedel (1459–1523) of the Netherlands. He was elected on 9 Jan. 1522, crowned Pope Adrian VI on 31 Aug. 1522 and died on 14 Sept. 1523. The last Pope elected from outside the College of Cardinals was Bartolomeo Prignano (1318–89), Archbishop of Bari, who was elected Pope Urban VI on 8 April 1378. The only Englishman to be elected Pope was Nicholas Breakspear (born at Abbots Langley, near Watford, Hertfordshire, in *c.* 1100), who, as Cardinal Bishop of Albano, was elected Pope Adrian IV on 4 Dec. 1154, and died on 1 Sept. 1159.

Last married The first 37 Popes had no specific obligation to celibacy. Pope Hormisdas (514–523) was the father of Pope Silverius (536–537). The last married Pope was Adrian II (867–872). Rodrigo Borgia was the father of at least four children before being elected Pope Alexander VI in 1492.

Slowest election After 31 months without declaring *Habemus Papam* ("We have a Pope"), the cardinals were subjected to a bread and water diet and the removal of the roof of their conclave by the Mayor of Viterbo before electing Tebaldo Visconti (*c.* 1210–76), the Archbishop of Liège, as Pope Gregory X on 1 Sept. 1271. The papacy was, however, vacant for at least 3 years 214 days in A.D. 304–308. The shortest conclave was that of 21 Oct. 1503 for the election of Pope Julius II on a first ballot.

BISHOPRIC

Longest tenure The longest tenure of any Church of England bishopric is 57 years in the case of the Rt. Rev. Thomas Wilson, who was consecrated Bishop of Sodor and Man on 16 Jan. 1698 and died in office on 7 March 1755. Of English bishoprics the longest tenure, if one excludes the unsubstantiated case of Aethelwulf, reputedly bishop of Hereford from 937 to 1012, are those of 47 years by Jocelin de Bohun (Salisbury) 1142–1189 and Nathaniel Crew or Crewe (Durham) 1674–1721.

STAINED GLASS

Oldest The oldest stained glass in the world represents the Prophets in a window of the cathedral of Augsburg,

The Bishop of Osnabrück in the fifth year of his bishopric after his appointment at the age of 6 months

Royal Collection

Bavaria, Germany, dating from *c.* 1050. The oldest datable stained glass in the United Kingdom is represented by 12th century fragments in the Tree of Jesse in the north aisle of the nave of York Minster, dated *c.* 1150, and medallions in Rivenhall Church, Essex which appear to date from the first half of that century. Dates late in the previous century have been attributed to glass in a window of the church at Compton, Surrey and a complete window in St. Mary the Virgin, Brabourne, Kent.

Largest The largest stained glass window is the complete mural of The Resurrection Mausoleum in Justice, Illinois, measuring 22,381 ft² *2 079 m²* in 2,448 panels completed in 1971. The largest single stained glass window in Great Britain is the East window in Gloucester Cathedral measuring 72 × 38 ft *21,94 × 11,58 m*, set up to commemorate the Battle of Crécy (1346), while the largest area of stained glass is 125 windows, totalling 25,000 ft² *2 322 m²* in York Minster.

BRASSES

The world's oldest monumental brass is that commemorating Bishop Ysowilpe in St. Andrew's Church, Verden, near Hanover, West Germany, dating from 1231. The oldest in Great Britain is of Sir John D'Abernon at Stoke D'Abernon, near Leatherhead, Surrey, dating from 1277.

CARDINALS

Oldest By 2 February 1973 the Sacred College of Cardinals contained a record 145 declared members compared with 126 in June 1975. The oldest is the 94 year old Cardinal José da Costa Nuñes (born Cardelaria, Portugal, 15 March 1880). The record length of service of any cardinal has been 60 years 10 days by the Cardinal York, a grandson of James VII of Scotland and II of England, from 3 July 1747 to 13 July 1807. The oldest Cardinal of all time was probably Giorgio da Costa (b. Portugal, 1406), who died in Rome on 18 Sept. 1508 aged 102.

Youngest The youngest Cardinal of all time was Luis Antonio de Borbon (b. 25 July 1727) created on 19 Dec. 1735 aged 8 years 147 days. His son Luis was also made a Cardinal but aged 23. The youngest Cardinal is

Antonio Ribeiro, Patriarch of Lisbon, Portugal, who was named on 2 Feb. 1973 aged 45 and elected on 5 Mar. 1973.

BISHOPS

Oldest The oldest serving bishop (excluding Suffragans and Assistants) in the Church of England at 1 July 1975 was the Rt. Rev. John Richard Humpidge Moorman, the 9th Bishop of Ripon, who was born 4 June 1905.

The oldest Roman Catholic bishop in recent years was Mgr. Ernesto Alfonso Carinci (b. 9 Nov. 1862), who was titular Archbishop of Seleucia, in Isauria, from 1945 until his death on 6 Dec. 1963, at the age of 101 years 27 days. He had celebrated Mass about 24,800 times.

Bishop Herbert Welch of the United Methodist Church who was elected a bishop for Japan and Korea in 1916 died on 4 April 1969 aged 106.

Youngest The youngest bishop of all time was H.R.H. The Duke of York and Albany K.G., G.C.B., G.C.H., the second son of George III, who was elected Bishop of Osnabrück, through his father's influence as Elector of Hanover, at the age of 196 days on 27 Feb. 1764. He resigned after 39 years' enjoyment.

The youngest serving bishop (excluding Suffragans and Assistants) in the Church of England at 1 July 1975 was the Rt. Rev. David Stuart Sheppard (b. 6 Mar. 1929), Bishop of Liverpool. He played 22 times for England in test cricket.

Longest incumbency The longest incumbency on record is one of 76 years by the Rev. Bartholomew Edwards, Rector of St. Nicholas, Ashill, Norfolk from 1813 to 1889. There appears to be some doubt as to whether the Rev. Richard Sherinton was installed at Folkestone from 1524 or 1529 to 1601. If the former is correct it would surpass the Norfolk record. The parish of Iden, East Sussex had only two incumbents in the 117-year period from 1807 to 1924.

Longest serving chorister Alfred Ernest Pick (d. 23 Dec. 1973, aged 95) served in the choir of St. Helen's Church, Sandal, Wakefield, West Yorkshire from August 1886 to April 1973—a stretch of 86¾ years.

Oldest parish register The oldest parish registers in England are those of St. James Garlickhythe and St. Mary Bothaw, two old City of London parishes, dating from 1536. Scotland's oldest surviving register is that for Anstruther-Wester, Fife, with burial entries from 1549.

Largest crowd The greatest recorded number of human beings assembled with a common purpose was more than 5,000,000 at the 21-day Hindu festival of Kumbh-Mela, which is held every 12 years at the confluence of the Yamuna (formerly called the Jumna), the Ganges and the invisible "Sarasviti" at Allahabad, Uttar Pradesh, India, on 21 Jan. 1966. According to the Jacobs' Formula for estimating the size of crowds, the allowance of area per person varies from 4 ft² *0,37 m²* (tight) to 9½ ft² *0,88 m²* (loose). Thus such a crowd must have occupied an area of more than 700 acres *283 ha*.

Largest funeral The greatest attendance at any funeral is the estimated 4 million who thronged Cairo, Egypt, for the funeral of President Gamal Abdel Nasser (1918–1970) on 1 Oct. 1970.

Biggest demonstrations A figure of 2.7 million was published from China for the demonstration against the U.S.S.R. in Shanghai on 3–4 April 1969 following the border clashes, and one of 10 million for the May Day celebrations of 1963 in Peking.

The world's worst ever single vehicle road disaster in which only 13 of the 140 passengers survived

U.P.I.

ACCIDENTS AND DISASTERS (Death Tolls)

WORST IN THE WORLD

Category	Description	Death Toll	Date
Pandemic	The Black Death (bubonic, pneumonic and septicaemic plague)	75,000,000	1347–1351
	Influenza	21,640,000	April–Nov. 1918
Famine	Northern China	9,500,000[1]	Feb. 1877–Sept. 1878
Flood	Hwang-ho River, China	3,700,000	Aug. 1931
Circular Storm[2]	Ganges Delta Islands, Bangladesh	1,000,000	12–13 Nov. 1970
Earthquake	Shensi Province, China	830,000	23 Jan. 1556
Landslide	Kansu Province, China	200,000	16 Dec. 1920
Conventional Bombing[3]	Dresden, Germany	135,000	13–15 Feb. 1945
Atomic Bomb	Hiroshima, Japan	91,223[4]	6 Aug. 1945
Marine (single ship)	Wilhelm Gustloff (24,484 tons) German liner torpedoed off Danzig by U.S.S.R. submarine S-13	c. 7,700	30 Jan. 1945
Aluvian Flood	Yungay, Huascarán, Peru	c. 25,000[5]	31 May 1970
Panic	Chungking (Zhong qing) China air raid shelter	c. 4,000	c. 8 June 1941
Dam Burst	South Fork Dam, Johnstown, Pennsylvania	2,209	31 May 1889
Explosion	Halifax, Nova Scotia, Canada	1,963[6]	6 Dec. 1917
Fire[7] (single building)	The Theatre, Canton, China	1,670	May 1845
Mining[8]	Honkeiko Colliery, China (coal dust explosion)	1,572	26 April 1942
Riot	New York City anti-conscription riots	c. 1,200	13–16 July 1863
Crocodiles	Japanese soldiers, Ramree Is., Burma (disputed)	c. 900	19–20 Feb. 1945
Fireworks	Dauphine's Wedding, Seine, Paris	>800	16 May 1770
Tornado	South Central States, U.S.A.	689	18 Mar. 1925
Railway	Modane, France	543[9]	12 Dec. 1917
Man-eating Tigress[10]	Champawat district, India, shot by Col. Jim Corbett	436	1907
Aircraft (Civil)	Turkish Airlines DC-10, Ermenonville Forest, France	346	3 Mar. 1974
Hail	Moradabad, Uttar Pradesh, India	246	20 April 1888
Submarine	U.S.S. Thresher off Cape Cod, Massachusetts, U.S.A.	129	10 April 1963
Road (single vehicle)[11]	Bus crashed into irrigation canal, Egypt	127	9 Aug. 1973
Mountaineering	U.S.S.R. Expedition on Mount Everest	40[12]	Dec. 1952
Space Exploration	Apollo oxygen fire, Cape Kennedy, Fla., U.S.A.	3	27 Jan. 1967
	Soyuz II re-entry over U.S.S.R.	3	29 June 1971

WORST IN THE UNITED KINGDOM

Category	Description	Death Toll	Date
Pandemic	The Black Death (bubonic, pneumonic and septicaemic plague)	800,000	1347–1350
	Influenza	225,000	Sept.–Nov. 1918
Famine	Ireland (famine and typhus)	1,500,000[13]	1846–1851
Flood	Severn Estuary	c. 2,000[14]	20 Jan. 1606
Circular Storm	"The Channel Storm"	c. 8,000	26 Nov. 1703
Earthquake	East Anglian Earthquake	4	22 April 1884
Landslide	Pantglas coal tip No. 7, Aberfan, Mid Glamorgan	144	21 Oct. 1966
Conventional Bombing	London	1,436	10–11 May 1941
Atomic Bomb			
Marine (single ship)	H.M.S. Royal George, off Spithead	c. 800[15]	29 Aug. 1782
Aluvian Flood	Lewes, East Sussex (snowdrifts)	8	27 Dec. 1836
Panic	Victoria Hall, Sunderland, Tyne and Wear	183	16 June 1883
Dam Burst	Bradfield Reservoir, Dale Dyke, near Sheffield South Yorkshire (embankment burst)	250	12 Mar. 1864
Explosion	Chilwell, Notts. (explosives factory)	134[16]	1 July 1918
Fire (single building)	Theatre Royal, Exeter	188[17]	5 Sept. 1887
Mining	Universal Colliery, Senghenydd, Mid Glamorgan	439	14 Oct. 1913
Riot	London anti-Catholic Gordon riots	565 (min.)	2–13 June 1780
Tornado	Widecombe, Devon (casualty figure)	60	21 Oct. 1638
Railway	Triple collision, Quintins Hill, Dumfries & Galloway	227[18]	22 May 1915
Aircraft (Civil)	B.E.A. Trident 1C, Staines, Surrey	118[19]	18 June 1972
Submarine	H.M.S. Thetis, during trials, Liverpool Bay	99	1 June 1939
Road (single vehicle)	Coach crash, River Dibb, North Yorks	32	27 May 1975
Mountaineering	On Cairngorm, Scotland (4,084 ft)	6	21 Nov. 1971

1 In 1770 the great Indian famine carried away a proportion of the population estimated as high as one third, hence a figure of tens of millions. The figure for Bengal alone was also probably about 10 million. It has been estimated that more than 5,000,000 died in the post-World War I famine of 1920–21 in the U.S.S.R. The U.S.S.R. government in July 1923 informed Mr. (later President) Herbert Hoover that the A.R.A. (American Relief Administration) had since August 1921 saved 20,000,000 lives from famine and famine diseases.

2 This figure published in 1972 for the East Pakistan disaster was from Dr. Afzal, Principle Scientific Officer of the Atomic Energy Authority Centre, Dacca. One report asserted that less than half of the population of the 4 islands of Bhola, Charjabbar, Hatia and Ranagati (1961 Census 1.4 million) survived. The most damaging hurricane recorded was the billion dollar Betsy (name now retired) in 1965 with an estimated insurance pay-out of $750 million.

3 The number of civilians killed by the bombing of Germany has been put variously as 593,000 and "over 635,000". A figure of c.140,000 deaths in the U.S.A.F. fire raids on Tokyo of 10 Mar. 1945 has been attributed. United States Casualty Commission figure in 1960 was 79,400, while the Hiroshima Peace Memorial Museum gives a figure of 240,000, excluding later deaths.

5 A total of 10,000 Austrian and Italian troops is reputed to have been lost in the Dolomite valley of Northern Italy on 13 Dec. 1916 in more than 100 snow avalanches. The total is probably exaggerated though bodies were still being found in 1952.
6 Some sources maintain that the final death roll was over 3,000 on 6–7 Dec.
7 Worst ever hotel fire 162 killed. Hotel Taeyonkak, Seoul, South Korea 25 Dec. 1971.
8 The worst gold mining disaster in South Africa was 152 killed due to flooding in the Witwatersrand Gold Mining Co. Gold Mine in 1909.
9 Between 500 and 800 died in the Torro Tunnel, Leon, Spain on 3 Jan. 1944
10 In the period 1941–42 c. 1,500 Kenyans were killed by a pride of 22 man-eating lions. Eighteen of these were shot by a hunter named Rushby.
11 The worst ever years for road deaths in the U.S.A. and the U.K. have been respectively 1969 (56,400) and 1941 (9,169). The U.S.'s 2 millionth victim since 1899 died in Jan. 1973. The world's highest death rate is said to be in Queensland, Australia but global statistics are not available. The greatest pile-up on British roads was on the M6 near Lymm Interchange, near Thelwall, involving 200 vehicles on 13 Sept. 1971 with 11 dead and 60 injured.
12 According to Polish sources, not confirmed by the U.S.S.R., 23 died on Mount Fuji, Japan, after blizzard and avalanche on 20 Mar. 1972.

13 Based on the net rate of natural increase between 1841 and 1851, a supportable case for a loss of population of 3 million can be made out if rates of under-enumeration of 25 per cent (1841) and 10 per cent (1851) are accepted. Potato rot (Phytophthora infestans) was first reported on 13 Sept. 1945.
14 Death rolls of 100,000 were reputed in England and Holland in the floods of 1099, 1421 and 1446.
15 c. 4,000 were lost on H.M. Troopship Lancastria 16,243 tons, off St. Nazaire on 17 June 1941.
16 The Princess Irene blew up at Sherness Kent, on 27 May 1915 killing 346.
17 In July 1212, 3,000 were killed in the crush, burned or drowned when London Bridge caught fire at both ends. The death roll in the Great Fire of London of 1666 was only 8. History's first "fire storm" occurred in the Quebec Yard, Surrey Docks, Southwark, London during the 300-pump fire in the Blitz on 7–8 Sept. 1940. Dockland casualties were 306 killed.
18 The 213 yd long troop train was telescoped to 67 yds. Signalmen Meakin and Tinsley were sentenced for manslaughter.
19 The worst crash by a U.K. operated aircraft was that of the B.O.A.C. Boeing 707 which broke up in mid-air near Mount Fuji, Japan, on 5 March 1966. The crew of 11 and all 113 passengers (total 124) were killed. The cause was violent CAT (Clear Air Turbulence).

HUMAN ACHIEVE-MENTS

1. ENDURANCE AND ENDEAVOUR

LUNAR CONQUEST

Neil Alden Armstrong (b. Wapakoneta, Ohio, U.S.A· of Scoto-Irish and German ancestry, on 5 Aug. 1930), command pilot of the Apollo XI mission, became the first man to set foot on the Moon on the Sea of Tranquillity at 02.56 and 15 sec G.M.T. on 21 July 1969. He was followed out of the Lunar Module *Eagle* by Col. Edwin Eugene Aldrin, Jr. U.S.A.F. (b. Montclair, New Jersey, U.S.A. of Swedish, Dutch and British ancestry, on 20 Jan. 1930), while the Command Module *Columbia* piloted by Lt.-Col. Michael Collins, U.S.A.F. (b. Rome, Italy, of Irish and pre-Revolutionary American ancestry, on 31 Oct. 1930) orbited above. Armstrong is now the Professor of Engineering at the University of Cincinnati, Ohio.

Eagle landed at 20.17 hours 42 sec G.M.T. on 20 July and lifted off at 17.54 G.M.T. on 21 July, after a stay of 21 hours 36 min. The Apollo XI had blasted off from Cape Kennedy, Florida at 13.32 G.M.T. on 16 July and was a culmination of the U.S. space programme, which, at its peak, employed 376,600 people and attained in the year 1966–67 a peak budget of $5,900,000,000 (*then £2,460 million*).

ALTITUDE

Man The greatest altitude attained by man was when the crew of the ill-fated Apollo XIII were at apocynthion (*i.e.* their furthest point) 158 miles *254 km* above the lunar surface and 248,655 miles *400 187 km* above the Earth's surface at 1.21 a.m. B.S.T. on 15 April 1970. The crew were Capt. James Arthur Lovell, U.S.N. (b. Denver, Colorado, 30 Aug. 1931), Frederick Wallace Haise Jr. (b. Cleveland, Ohio, 25 March 1928) and John L. Swigert Jr. (b. Biloxi, Miss. 14 Nov. 1933).

Woman The greatest altitude attained by a woman is 231 km *143.5 miles* by Jnr. Lt. (now Lt. Col.) Valentina Vladimirovna Tereshkova-Nikolayev (b. 6 Mar. 1937) of the U.S.S.R., during her 48-orbit flight in *Vostok 6* on 16 June 1963. The record for an aircraft is 24 336 m *79,842 ft* by Natalia Prokhanova (U.S.S.R.) (b. 1940) in an E-33 jet, on 22 May 1965.

SPEED

Man The fastest speed at which any human has travelled is 24,791 m.p.h. *39 897 km/h* when the Command Module of Apollo X carrying Col. Thomas P. Stafford, U.S.A.F. (b. Weatherford, Okla. 17 Sept. 1930), and Cdrs. Eugene Andrew Cernan (b. Chicago, 14 Mar. 1934) and John Watts Young, U.S.N. (b. San Francisco, 24 Sept. 1930), reached this maximum value at the 400,000 ft *121,9 km* altitude interface on its trans-Earth return flight on 26 May 1969.

Woman The highest speed ever attained by a woman is 28 115 km/h *17,470 m.p.h.* by Jnr. Lt. (now Lt. Col.) Valentina Vladimirovna Tereshkova-Nikolayev (b. 6 March 1937) of the U.S.S.R. in *Vostok 6* on 16 June 1963. The highest speed ever achieved by a woman aircraft pilot is 2 300 km/h *1,429.2 m.p.h.* by Jacqueline Cochran (Mrs. Floyd Bostwick-Odlum) (U.S.A.), in an F-104G1 *Starfighter* jet over Edwards Air Force Base, California, U.S.A., on 11 May 1964.

LAND SPEED

Man The highest speed ever achieved on land is 650 m.p.h. *1 046 km/h* momentarily during the 627.287 m.p.h. *1 009,520 km/h* run of *The Blue Flame* driven by Gary Gabelich (b. San Pedro, California, 29 Aug. 1940) on Bonneville Salt Flats, Utah, U.S.A., on 23 Oct. 1970 (see Mechanical World, page 141). The car built by Reaction Dynamics Inc. of Milwaukee, Wisconsin, is designed to withstand stresses up to 1,000 m.p.h. *1 600 km/h* while the tyres have been tested to speeds of 850 m.p.h. *1 365 km/h*.

Woman The highest land speed recorded by a woman is 539,243 km/h *335.070 m.p.h.* by Mrs Lee Ann Breedlove (*née* Roberts) (born 1937) of Los Angeles, California, U.S.A., driving her husband's *Spirit of America—Sonic I* (see page 141) over the timing kilometre on the Bonneville Salt Flats, Utah, U.S.A., on 3 Nov. 1965.

WATER SPEED

Unofficial The highest speed ever achieved on water is 328 m.p.h. *527,8 km/h* by Donald Malcolm Campbell, C.B.E.

(1921–67) of the U.K., on his last and fatal run in the turbo-jet engined 2¼ ton *2 285 kg Bluebird* K7, on Coniston Water, Lancashire, England, on 4 Jan. 1967.

Official The official record is 285.213 m.p.h. *459,005 km/h* (average of two 1 mile runs) by Lee Taylor, Jr. (b. 1934) of Downey, California, U.S.A., in the hydroplane *Hustler* on Lake Guntersville, Alabama, U.S.A., on 30 June 1967. He is curently experimenting with his 38 ft *11,58 m* jet powered *U.S. Discovery*.

Propeller The world record for propeller-driven craft is 202.42 *driven* m.p.h. *325,76 km/h* set by Larry Hill in his supercharged hydroplane *Mr. Ed* off Long Beach, California. On a one-way run *Climax* recorded 205.19 m.p.h. *330,22 km/h.*

TRAVELLING

Most The man who has visited more countries than anyone **travelled** is Jesse Hart Rosdail (b. 1914) of Elmhurst, Illinois, **man** U.S.A., a teacher of children in the 5th grade. Since 1934 of the 154 sovereign countries and 67 nonsovereign territories of the world making a total of 221 he has visited all but five, namely North Korea, North Vietnam, China, Cuba and French Antarctic Territories. He estimated his mileage as 1,454,587 statute miles *2 340 930 km* at July 1974.

A contemporary print of de Rozier's and the Marquis d'Arlande's first ever flight over Paris on 21 Nov. 1783

PROGRESSIVE ABSOLUTE HUMAN ALTITUDE RECORDS

Ft	m	Pilot	Vehicle	Place	Date
80*	24	Jean Francois Pilâtre de Rozier (France)	Hot Air Balloon (tethered)	Fauxbourg, Paris	15 & 17 Oct. 1783
200	61	J. F. Pilâtre de Rozier (1756–85) (France)	Hot Air Balloon (tethered)	Fauxbourg, Paris	19 Oct. 1783
250	76	J. F. Pilâtre de Rozier (France)	Hot Air Balloon (tethered)	Fauxbourg, Paris	19 Oct. 1783
324	99	de Rozier and Girand de Villette (France)	Hot Air Balloon (tethered)	Fauxbourg, Paris	19 Oct. 1783
c. 330	c. 100	de Rozier and the Marquis Francois-Laurent d'Arlandes (1742–1809) (France)	Hot Air Balloon (free flight)	La Muette, Paris	21 Nov. 1783
c. 3,000	c. 900	Dr. Jacques-Alexander-Cesar Charles (1746–1823) and Ainé Robert (France)	Charlière Hydrogen Balloon	Tuileries, Paris	1 Dec. 1783
c. 9,000	c. 2 750	J.-A.-C. Charles (France)	Hydrogen Balloon	Nesles, France	1 Dec. 1783
c. 13,000	c. 4 000	James Sadler (G.B.)	Hydrogen Balloon	Manchester	May 1785
c. 20,000	c. 6 100	E. G. R. Robertson (U.K.) and Loest (Germany)	Hydrogen Balloon	Hamburg, Germany	18 July 1803
22,965	7 000	Joseph Louis Gay-Lussac (France)	Hydrogen Balloon	Paris	15 Sept. 1804
c. 25,000	c. 7 620	Charles Green, Edward Spencer (G.B.)	Coal Gas Balloon *Nassau*	Vauxhall, London	24 July 1837
25,400[1]	7 740	James Glaisher (1809–1903) (U.K.)	Hydrogen Balloon	Wolverhampton	17 July 1862
27,950	8 520	H. T. Sivel, J. E. Crocé-Spinelli, Gaston Tissandier (only survivor)	Coal Gas Balloon *Zenith*	La Villette, Paris	15 April 1875
31,500	9 615	Prof. A. Berson (Germany)	Hydrogen Balloon *Phoenix*	Strasbourg, France	4 Dec. 1894
35,433	10 800	Prof. Berson and Dr. R. J. Suring (Germany)	Hydrogen Balloon *Preussen*	Berlin, Germany	30 June 1901
36,565	11 145	Sadi Lecointe (France)	Nieuport Aircraft	Issy-les-Moulineaux, France	30 Oct. 1923
42,470[2]	12 945	Capt. Hawthorne C. Gray (U.S.A.)	Hydrogen Balloon	Scott Field, Illinois	4 May 1927
42,470	12 945	Capt. Hawthorne C. Gray (U.S.A.)	Hydrogen Balloon	Scott Field, Illinois	4 Nov. 1927
43,166	13 157	Lt. Apollo Soucek (U.S.A.)	U.S. Navy Wright *Apache*	Washington, D.C.	4 June 1930
51,961	15 837	Prof. Auguste Piccard and Paul Kipfer (Switzerland)	F.N.R.S. I Balloon	Augsburg, Germany	27 May 1931
53,139	16 196	Piccard & Dr. Max Cosyns (Belgium)	F.N.R.S. I Balloon	Dübendorf, nr. Zurich	18 Aug. 1932
60,695[3]	18 500	G. Profkoviev, F. N. Birnbaum and K. D. Godounov (U.S.S.R.)	Army Balloon *U.S.S.R.*	Moscow, U.S.S.R.	30 Sept. 1933
61,237	18 665	Lt.-Cdr. T. G. W. Settle, U.S.N. and Major Chester L. Fordney U.S.M.C.	Hydrogen Balloon *Century of Progress*	Akron, Ohio	20 & 21 Nov. 1933
72, 78[4]	22 000	Raul F. Fedoseyenko, A. B. Vasienko and E. D. Ususkin (U.S.S.R.)	*Osaviakhim* Balloon	Moscow, U.S.S.R.	30 Jan. 1934
72,395	22 066	Capts. Orvill A. Anderson and Albert W. Stevens (U.S. Army Air Corps)	U.S. *Explorer II* Helium Balloon	Rapid City, South Dakota, U.S.A.	11 Nov. 1935
79,600	24 262	William Barton Bridgeman (U.S.A.)	U.S. Douglas D558-II *Skyrocket*	California, U.S.A.	15 Aug. 1951
83,235	25 370	Lt.-Col. Marion E. Carl, (U.S.M.C)	U.S. Douglas D558-II *Skyrocket*	California, U.S.A.	21 Aug. 1953
c. 93,000	c. 28 350	Major Arthur Murray (U.S.A.F.)	U.S. Bell *X-1A* Rocket 'plane	California, U.S.A.	4 June 1954
126,200	38 465	Capt. Iven C. Kincheloe, Jr. (U.S.A.F.)	U.S. Bell *X-2* Rocket 'plane	California, U.S.A.	7 Sept. 1956
136,500	41 605	Major Robert M. White (U.S.A.F.)	U.S. *X-15* Rocket 'plane	California, U.S.A.	12 Aug. 1960
169,600	51 694	Joseph A. Walker (U.S.A.)	U.S. *X-15* Rocket 'plane	California, U.S.A.	30 Mar. 1961

Statute miles	Km				
203.2	327	Flt.-Major Yuriy A. Gagarin (U.S.S.R.)	U.S.S.R. *Vostok I* Capsule	Orbital flight	12 April 1964
253.5	408	Col. Vladimir M. Komarov, Lt. Boris B. Yegorov and Konstantin P. Feoktistov (U.S.S.R.)	U.S.S.R. *Voskhod I* Capsule	Orbital flight	12 Oct. 1961
309.2	497,6	Col. Pavel I. Belayev and Lt -Col. Aleksey A. Leonov (U.S.S.R.)	U.S.S.R. *Voskhod II* Capsule	Orbital flight	18 Mar. 1965
474.4	763,4	Cdr. John Watts Young, U.S.N. and Major Michael Collins U.S.A.F.	U.S. *Gemini X* Capsule	Orbital flight	19 July 1966
850.7	1 369,0	Cdr. Charles Conrad, Jr., U.S.N. and Lt.-Cdr. Richard F. Gordon, Jr., U.S.N.	U.S. *Gemini XI* Capsule	Orbital flight	14 Sept. 1966
234,473	377 347	Col. Frank Borman, U.S.A.F., Capt. James Arthur Lovell, Jr., U.S.N. and Major William A. Anders, U.S.A.F.	U.S. *Apollo VIII* Command Module	Circum-lunar flight	25 Dec. 1968
248,433	399 814	Cdr. Eugene Andrew Gernan U.S.N. and Col. Thomas P. Stafford U.S.A.F.	U.S. *Apollo X* Lunar Module	Circum-lunar flight	22 May 1969
242,285[5]	389 920	Neil Alden Armstrong, Col. Edwin Eugene Aldrin Jr. and Lt.-Col. Michael Collins both U.S.A.F.	U.S. *Apollo XI*	Circum-lunar flight and first MoonLanding	21 & 22 July 1969
248,655	400 187	Capt. James Arthur Lovell Jr. U.S.N., Frederick Wallace Haise Jr. and John L. Swigert Jr.	U.S. *Apollo XIII*	Abortive lunar landing mission	15 April 1970

* *There is some evidence that Father Bartolomeu de Gusmao flew in his hot-air balloon in his 4th experiment post Aug. 1709 in Portugal.*
[1] *Glaisher, with Henry Tracey Coxwell (1819–1900), claimed 37,000 ft 11 275 m from Wolverhampton on 5 Sept. 1862. Some writers accept 30,000 ft 9 145 m.*
[2] *Neither of Gray's altitudes were official records because he had to*

parachute on his first descent and he landed dead from his second ascent to an identical height.
[3] *None survived the ascent.*
[4] *All died on descent.*
[5] *Note. This historic space flight did not establish an altitude record but has been included for reference only.*

PROGRESSIVE ABSOLUTE HUMAN SPEED RECORDS

The progression of the voluntary human speed record is listed below. It is perhaps noteworthy that the petrol-engined car at no time featured in this compilation.

Speed m.p.h.	Km/h	Person and Vehicle	Place	Date
				ante 6500 B.C.
<25	<40	Running	—	*c.* 6500 B.C.
>25	>40	Sledging	Southern-Finland	*c.* 3000 B.C.
>35	>55	Ski-ing	Fenno-Scandia	*c.* 1400 B.C.
>35	>55	Horse-riding	Anatolia, Turkey	A.D. 1609
<50	<80	Ice Yachts (earliest patent)	Netherlands	
56¾	95	Grand Junction Railway 2-2-2 *Lucifer*	Madeley Banks, Staffs., England	13 Nov. 1830
74.5[1]	119	Great Western Railway 4-2-2, 8 ft single *Great Britain*	Wootton Bassett, Wiltshire England	11 May 1846
74.5	119,8	Great Western Railway 2-2-2 8 ft single *Great Western*	Wootton Bassett, Wiltshire, England	1 June 1845
78	125,5	Great Western Railway 4-2-2 8 ft single *Great Britain*	Wootton Bassett, Wiltshire, England	11 May 1848
81.8	131,6	Bristol & Exeter Railway 4-2-4 tank 9 ft single No. 41	Wellington Bank, Somerset, England	June 1854
87.8	141,3	Tommy Todd, downhill skier	La Porte, California, U.S.A.	Mar. 1873
89.48	144	Crampton No. 604 engine	Champigny-Pont sur Yonne, France	20 June 1890
90.0	144,8	Midland Railway 4-2-2 7 ft 9 in single	Ampthill, Bedford, England	Mar. 1897
101.0	162,5	Siemens und Halske electric engine	near, Berlin, Germany	1901
124.89	201	Siemens und Halske electric engine	Marienfeld-Zossen, near Berlin	6 Oct. 1903
128.43	206,7	Siemens und Halske electric engine	Marienfeld-Zossen, near Berlin	23 Oct. 1903
130.61	210,2	Siemens und Halske electric engine	Marienfeld-Zossen, near Berlin	27 Oct. 1903
c. 150	*c.* 257,5	Frederick H. Marriott, (*fl.* 1957) Stanley Steamer *Wogglebug*	Ormond Beach, Florida, U.S.A.	26 Jan. 1907
>210	>338	World War I fighters in dives including Martinsyde F.4's and Nieuport *Nighthawks*	over England and Flanders	1918–19
210.64	339	Sadi Lecointe (France) Nieuport-Delage 29	Villesauvage, France	25 Sept. 1921
211.91	341	Sadi Lecointe (France) Nieuport-Delage 29	Villesauvage, France	21 Sept. 1922
243.94[2]	392,64	Brig-Gen. William Mitchell (U.S. Army) (1879–1936) Curtiss R-6	Detroit, Michigan	18 Oct. 1922
270.5	435,3	Lt. Alford Joseph Williams (U.S.N.) Curtiss R.2 C-1	Mitchel Field, Long Is., N.Y.	4 Nov. 1923
274.2	441,3	Lt. Harold J. Brow (U.S.N.), Curtiss R.2 C-1	Mitchel Field, Long Is., N.Y.	4 Nov. 1923
278.47[3]	448,15	Adj. Chef Florentin Bonnet (France) Bernard-Ferbois V-2	Istres. France	11 Dec. 1927
284	457	Fg. Off. Sidney Norman Webster A.F.C. Supermarine S.5	Calshot, Hampshire	14 July 1924
>300	>482	Flt. Lt. Sidney Norman Webster, A.F.C. Supermarine S.5	Venice, Italy	26 Sept. 1927
313.59	504,67	Col. Mario de Bernardi (Italy) Macchi M-52	Venice, Italy	4 Nov. 1927
322.6[4]	519,1	Lt. Alford J. Williams (U.S.N.) Kirkham-Williams	Mitchell Field, Long Is., N.Y.	7 Nov. 1927
348.6	561	Col. Mario de Bernardi (Italy) Macchi M-52R	Venice, Italy	30 Mar. 1928
362	582	Capt. Guiseppe Motta Macchi 67	Lago di Garda, Italy	22 Aug. 1929
>370	>595,4	Fg. Off. Henry Richard D. Waghorn, A.F.C. and Fg. Off. Richard Llewellyn Roger Atcherley (1904–70) (later Air Marshall Sir, K.B.E., C.B., A.F.C*) Supermarine S.6's	Solent, Hampshire, England	7 Sept. 1929
375	603	Lt. Ariosti Nevi Macchi 72	Desenzano, Italy	July 1931
394	634	Lt. Ariosti Nevi Macchi 72	Desenzano, Italy	Aug. 1931
415.2	668,2	Flt. Lt. (later Wing Cdr.) George Hedley Stainforth A.F.C. Supermarine S 6 B	Lee-on-Solent, England	29 Sept. 1931
430.32[5]	692,529	W.O. Francesco Agelio (Italy) Macchi-Castoldi 72	Lago di Garda, Italy	10 April 1933
>434.96[6]	>700	Col. Mario Bernasconi (I aly) Macchi-Castoldi 72	Desenzano, Italy	18 April 1934
441.22	710,07	Sec. Lt. Francesco Angello (Italy) Macchi-Castoldi 72	Lago di Garda, Italy	23 Oct. 1934
463.94[3]	746,64	Flugkäpitan Hans Dieterle (Germany) Heinkel He. 100 V.8	Oranienburg, E. Germany	30 Mar. 1939
486	782	Flugkäpitan Fritz Wendel (Germany) Messerschmitt Me209 V-1	Augsburg, West Germany	26 April 1939
528	850	Flugkäpitan Heinz Dittmar (Germany) Me163A V-1	Augsburg, West Germany	Spring 1941
571.78	920,2	Flugkäpitan Heinz Dittmar Me. 163V-1	Peenemunde, Germany	July–August 1941
623.85	1 004	Flugkäpitan Heinz Dittmar Me. 163V-1	Peenemunde, Germany	2 Oct. 1941
702[7]	1 130	Rudolf Opitz (Germany) Me 163B V-18 *Komet*	Peenemunde, Germany	6 July 1944
967	1 556	Capt. Charles Elwood Yeager, U.S.A.F., Bel XS-1	Muroc Dry Lake, California	1948
1,135	1 826,6	William Barton Bridgeman, Douglas *Skyrocket* D-558-II	Muroc Dry Lake, California	18 May 1951
1,181	1 900,6	William Barton Bridgeman, Douglas *Skyrocket* D-558-II	Muroc Dry Lake, California	11 June 1951
1,221	1 965,0	William Barton Bridgeman, Douglas *Skyrocket* D-558-II	Muroc Dry Lake, California	23 June 1951
1,238	1 992,3	William Barton Bridgeman, Douglas *Skyrocket* D-558-II	Muroc Dry Lake, California	7 Aug. 1951
1,241	2 013,2	William Barton Bridgeman, Douglas *Skyrocket* D-558-II	Muroc Dry Lake, California	Dec. 1951
1,272	2 047,0	Albert Scott Crossfield, Douglas *Skyrocket* D-558-II	Muroc Dry Lake, California	14 Oct. 1953
1,328	2 137,2	Albert Scott Crossfield, Douglas *Skyrocket* D-558-II	Muroc Dry Lake, California	20 Nov. 1953
1,612	2 594,2	Major Charles Elwood Yeager, Bell X-1A	Muroc Dry Lake, California	12 Dec. 1953
1,934	3 112,4	Lt.Col. Frank K. Everest, Jr. Bell X-2	Muroc Dry Lake, California	23 July 1956
2,094	3 369,9	Capt. Milburn, G. Apt, Bell X-2	Muroc Dry Lake, California	27 Sept. 1956
2,111	3 397,3	Joseph A. Walker, North American X-15	Muroc Dry Lake, California	12 May 1960
2,196	3 534,1	Joseph A. Walker, North American X-15	Muroc Dry Lake, California	4 Aug. 1960
2,275	3 661,1	Major Robert M. White, North American X-15	Muroc Dry Lake, California	7 Feb. 1961
2,905	4 675,1	Major Robert M. White, North American X-15	Muroc Dry Lake, California	7 Mar. 1961
c. 17,560	*c.* 28 260	Flt. Maj. Yuriy Alekseyevich Gargarin, *Vostok I*	Earth orbit	12 April 1961
17,558	28 257	Cdr. Walter Marty Schirra, Jr. U.S.N., *Sigma 7*	Earth orbit	3 Oct. 1962
c. 17,600	*c.* 28 325	Air Eng. Col. Vladimir Mikhaylovich Komarov, Lt. Boris Yegorov and Konstantin Petrovich Feoktistov, *Voskhod I*	Earth orbit	12 Oct. 1964
c. 17,750	*c.* 28 565	Col. Pavel Ivanovich Belyayev and Lt. Col. Aleksey Arkhipovich Leonov, *Voskhod 2*	Earth orbit	18 Mar. 1965
17,943	28 876	Cdr. Charles Conrad Jr., Lt-Cdr. Richard F. Gordon Jr., U.S.N. *Germini XI*	Earth orbit	14 Sept. 1966
24,226	38 988	Col. Frank Borman, U.S.A.F. Capt. James Arthur Lovell, Jr., U.S.N., Major William A. Anders, U.S.A.F. *Apollo VIII*	Trans-lunar injection	21 Dec. 1968
24,572	39 834	Col. Frank Borman. U.S.A.F. Capt. James Arthur Lovell, Jr., U.S.N., Major William A. Anders, U.S.A.F. *Apollo VIII*	Re-entry after lunar orbit	27 Dec. 1968
24,790.8	39 897,0	Cdrs. Eugene Andrew Cernan and John Watts Young, U.S.N. and Col. Thomas P. Stafford, U.S.A.F. *Apollo X*	Re-entry after lunar orbit	26 May 1969

[1] *A speed of 85 m.p.h. 137 km/h was claimed by Frank Elrington in a run-away compressed air railway from Kingstown (now Dun Laoghaire) to Dalkey, County Dublin on 19 Aug. 1843. It was, however, self-timed.*
[2] *Average of 2 runs.*
[3] *Average of 4 runs, individual runs not officially published.*

[4] *Self-timed unofficial run.*
[5] *Earlier runs at 421.58 m.p.h. 678,477 km/h and 424.17 m.p.h. 682,637 km/h.*
[6] *Unofficial single run.*
Marginally sub-sonic at this altitude.

Disabled Person The most countries visited by a disabled person is 119 by Lester Nixon of Sarasota, Florida, U.S.A. who is confined to a wheelchair.

Horesback The most travelled man in the horseback era was probably the Methodist preacher Francis Asbury (b. Birmingham, England), who travelled 264,000 miles *424 850 km* in North America from 1771–1815 preaching 16,000 sermons.

Passport Records The earliest legislation on Passports appears to be an Act of Henry V mentioning safe conducts in 1414. The earliest Passport still extant was one issued on 18 June 1641 and signed by Charles I. The last personally signed Passport by a monarch (George III) was issued in March 1794 to Robert Liston, Esq. Before 1858 British Passports were in French. Photographs were introduced in 1914 and the 32-page Passport came into use in 1921. From 1858 to 1915 Passports cost 10p. The £5 fee was introduced on 16 Nov. 1970. The annual issue first surpassed one million in 1967 with 1,017, 790.

Space The most travelled men in history are the third crew of the U.S. *Skylab* space station with 34,469,696 miles *55 474 039 km* (see details page 74).

215

MARINE CIRCUMNAVIGATION RECORDS (Compiled by Sq. Ldr. D. H. Clarke, D.F.C., A.F.C.)

A true circumnavigation entails passing through two antipodal points (which are at least 12,429 statute miles apart).

CATEGORY	VESSEL	NAME	START PLACE AND DATE	FINISH DATE AND DURATION
Earliest	*Vittoria* Expedition of Fernão de Magalhães, *c.* 1480–1521	Juan Sebastion de Eleano or Del Cano (d. 1526) and 17 crew including Andrews of Bristol (first Briton)	Seville, Spain 20 Sept. 1519	San Lucur, 6 Sept. 1521 30,700 miles *49 400 km*
Earliest British	*Golden Hind* (ex *Pelican*) 100 tons/*tonnes*	Francis Drake (*c.* 1540–1596) (Knighted 4 April 1581)	Plymouth, 13 Dec. 1577	26 Sept. 1580
Earliest Woman	*Etoile*	Crypto-female valet of M. de Commerson, named Baré	St. Malo, 1766	1769
Earliest Solo	*Spray* 36¾ ft *11,20 m* gaff yawl	Capt. Joshua Slocum, 51, (U.S.) (a non-swimmer)	Newport, Rhode Island, U.S.A. *via* Magellan Straits, 24 Apr. 1895	3 July 1898 46,000 miles *74 000 km*
Earliest Solo Eastabout *via* Cape Horn	*Lehg II* 31¼ ft *9,52 m* Bermuda Ketch	Vito Dumas (Argentina)	Buenos Aires, 27 June 1942	7 Sept. 1943 (272 days)
Smallest Boat	*Trekka* 20½ ft *6,25 m* Bermuda Ketch	John Guzzwell (G.B.)	Victoria B.C., 10 Sept. 1955 Westabout *via* Panama	12 Sept. 1959 (4 years 2 days)
Earliest Submerged	*U.S. Submarine Triton*	Capt. Edward L. Beach U.S.N. plus 182 crew	New London, Connecticut 16 Feb. 1960	10 May 1960 30,708 miles *49 422 km*
Earliest Solo with One Stop Over	*Gipsy Moth IV* 53 ft *16,15 m* Bermuda Yawl	Sir Francis Chichester K.B.E. (1901–72)	Plymouth to Sydney 27 Aug. 1966	Sydney to Plymouth 28 May 1967 29,626 miles *47 678 km*
Earliest non-stop Solo (Port to Port)	*Suhaili* 32.4 ft *9,87 m* Bermuda Ketch	Robin Knox-Johnston C.B.E. (b. 1939)	Falmouth, 14 June 1968	22 Apr. 1969 (313 days)
Fastest Solo	*Manureva* (ex *Pen Duick IV*) 70 ft Trimaran	Alain Colas (France)	Saint Malo *via* Sydney	29 Mar. 1974 (167 days)
Fastest	*Great Britain II* 72 ft Ketch	Charles 'Chay' Blyth C.B.E., B.E.M. (b. 1940) and 9 paratroopers (1 lost)	South Sea *via* Sydney 8 Sept. 1973	11 Apr. 1974 (144 days 10 hrs 43 min.)
Fastest Solo Westabout	*Mermaid III* 28 ft *8,80 m* sloop	Kenichi Horie (Japan) (b. 1939)	Osaka 1 Aug. 1973	5 May 1974 (275 days 13 hr)

Round the World The fastest time for a round the world trip on commercial flights for a true circumnavigation is 47 hours 48 mins (flying time) over 25,606 miles *41 208 km* by Victor Kovens (U.S.), 29 and Frank Barbehenn, 43 two T.W.A. employees who passed through the necessary antipodal points near Bangkok, Thailand and Lima, Peru in May 1975.

POLAR CONQUESTS

North Pole The claims of neither of the two U.S. Arctic explorers, Dr. Frederick Albert Cook (1865–1940) nor Cdr. (later Rear Ad.) Robert Edwin Peary, (1856–1920) of the U.S. Naval Civil Engineering branch in reaching the North Pole are subject to positive proof. Cook, accompanied by the Eskimos, Ah-pellah and Etukishook, two sledges and 26 dogs, struck north from a point 60 miles *96,5 km* north of Svartevoeg, on Axel Heibert Is., Canada, 460 miles *740 km* from the Pole on 21 March 1908, allegedly reaching Lat. 89° 31′N on 19 April and the Pole on 21 April. Peary, accompanied by his negro assistant, Matthew Alexander Henson (1866–1955) and the four Eskimos, Ooqueah, Egingwah, Seegloo, and Ootah (1875–1955), struck north from his Camp Bartlett (Lat. 87° 44′ N.) at 5 a.m. on 2 April 1909. After travelling another 134 miles *215 km*, he allegedly established his final camp, Camp Jessup, in the proximity of the Pole at 10 a.m. on 6 April and marched a further 42 miles *67,5 km* quartering the sea-ice before turning south at 4 p.m. on 7 April. On excellent pack ice Herbert's 1968–9 Expedition attained a best day's route mileage of 23 miles *37 km* in 15 hours. Cook claimed 26 miles *41,8 km* twice while Peary claimed a surely unsustainable average of 38 miles *61 km* for 8 consecutive days.

The earliest indisputable attainment of the North Pole over the sea-ice was at 3 p.m. (Central Standard Time) on 19 April 1968 by Ralph Plaisted (U.S.) and three companions after a 42-day trek in four Skidoos (snow-mobiles). Their arrival was indpendently verified 18 hours later by a U.S. Air Force weather aircraft.

Arctic crossing The first crossing of the Arctic sea-ice was achieved by the British Trans-Arctic Expedition which left Point Barrow, Alaska on 21 Feb. 1968 and arrived at the Seven Island Archipelago north-east of Spitzbergen 464 days later on 29 May 1969 after a haul of 2,920 statute miles *4 699 km* and a drift of 700 miles *1 126 km* compared with the straight line distance of 1,662 miles *2 674 km*. The team was Wally Herbert (leader), 34, Major Ken Hedges, 34, R.A.M.C., Allan Gill, 38, and Dr. Roy Koerner, 36 (glaciologist), and 40 huskies. This was the longest sustained journey ever made on polar pack ice and the first indisputable attainment of the North Pole by sledge. Temperatures sank to −47°F *−43,8°C* during the trek.

South Pole The first ship to cross the Antarctic circle (Lat. 66° 30′ S.) was the *Resolution* (462 tons/*tonnes*), under Capt. James Cook (1728–79), on 17 Jan. 1773. The first person to sight the Antarctic *mainland*—on the best available evidence and against claims made for British and Russian explorers—was Nathaniel Brown Palmer (U.S.) (1799–1877). On 17 Nov. 1820 he sighted the Orleans Channel coast of the Palmer Peninsular from his 45 ton/*tonnes* sloop *Hero*.

The South Pole was first reached on 14 Dec. 1911 by a Norwegian party led by Capt. Roald Amundsen (1872–1928), after a 53-day march with dog sledges from the Bay of Whales, to which he had penetrated in the *Fram*. Olav Olavson Bjaaland, the first to arrive, was the last survivor, dying in June 1961, aged 88. The others were the late Helmer Hanssen, Sverre H. Hassell and Oskar Wisting.

Capt. Amundsen (Norway) at the end of his 53 day five-man march to the South Pole in 1911

Women The first woman to set foot on Antarctica was Mrs. Klarius Mikkelsen on 20 Feb. 1935. No woman stood on the South Pole until 11 Nov. 1969. On that day Lois Jones, Kay Lindsay, Eileen McSavenay, Jean Pearson, Tarry Lee Tickhill and Pam Young, all of U.S.A. arrived by air.

Antarctic crossing The first crossing of the Antarctic continent was completed at 1.47 p.m. on 2 March 1958, after a trek of 2,158 miles *3 473 km* lasting 99 days from 24 Nov. 1957, from Shackleton Base to Scott Base *via* the Pole. The crossing party of twelve was led by Dr. (now Sir) Vivian Ernest Fuchs (born 11 Feb. 1908).

Longest sledge journey The longest polar sledge journey was one of 3,720 statute route miles *5 986 km* in 476 days by the British Trans-Arctic Expedition from 21 Feb. 1968 to 10 June 1969 (see above). The longest totally self-supporting Polar sledge journey ever made was one of 1,080 miles *1 738 km* from West to East across Greenland on 18 June to 5 Sept. 1934 by Capt. M. Lindsay (now Sir Martin Lindsay, Bt., C.B.E., D.S.O.); Lt. Arthur S. T. Godfrey, R.E., (later Lt. Col., k. 1942), Andrew N. C. Croft (later Col., D.S.O.) and 49 dogs. The same crossing was first made with man hauled sledges by the inter Services 1974 Trans Greenland Expedition, led by Fl. Llt. D. R. Gleed in 36 days.

MOUNTAINEERING

Highest by man The conquest of the highest point on Earth, Mount Everest (29,028 ft [8 847 m]) was first achieved at 11.30 a.m. on 29 May 1953, by Edmund Percival Hillary (New Zealand) and the Sherpa Tenzing Norkhay, G.M. The female record was set by Mrs. Junko Tabai, 35 (Japan) on Everest's summit on 16 May 1974.

GREATEST OCEAN DESCENT

The record ocean descent was achieved in the Challenger Deep of the Marianas Trench, 250 miles *400 km* south-west of Guam, in the Pacific Ocean, when the Swiss-built U.S. Navy bathyscaphe *Trieste*, manned by Dr. Jacques Piccard (b. 1914) (Switzerland) and Lt. Donald Walsh, U.S.N., reached the ocean bed 35,820 ft (6.78 miles [10 917 m]) down, at 1.10 p.m. on 23 Jan. 1960 (but see also Chapter 3). The pressure of the water was 16,883 lb./in² *1 183 kg f/cm²* and the temperature 37.4° F *3° C*. The descent required 4 hours 48 min and the ascent 3 hours 17 min.

Deep diving records The record depth for the extremely dangerous activity of breath-held diving is 282 ft *86 m* by Jacques Mayol (France) off Elba, Italy on 9 Nov. 1973 for men and 147½ ft *45 m* by Guiliana Treleani (Italy) off Cuba in Sept. 1967 for women. The pressure on Mayol's thorax was 136.5 lb f/in² *9,6 kg/cm²* and his pulse fell to 36. Enzo Maiorca (Italy) surfaced unconscious from a dive of 87 m *285 ft* off Sorento, on 27 Sept. 1974. The record dive with Scuba (self-contained under-water breathing apparatus) is 437 ft *133 m* by John J. Gruener and R. Neal Watson (U.S.A) off Freeport, Grand Bahama on 14 Oct. 1968. The record

TRANS-ATLANTIC MARINE RECORDS (Compiled by Sq. Ldr. D. H. Clarke, D.F.C., A.F.C.)

Earliest Trimaran	John Mikes + 2 crew (U.S.)	*Non Pareil*, 25 ft *7,62 m*	(New York 4 June)	Southampton	43 days	1868
Earliest Solo Sailing	Alfred Johnson (Denmark)	*Centennial* 20 ft *6,09 m*	Nova Scotia	Wales	46 days	1876
Earliest Woman Sailing	Mrs. Joanna Crapo (Scotland)	*New Bedford* 20 ft *6,09 m*	Chatham, Mass.	Newlyn, Cornwall	51 days	1877
Earliest Single-handed race	J. W. Lawlor (U.S.) (winner)	*Sea Serpent* 15 ft *4,57 m*	Boston (17 June)	Coverack, Cornwall	47 days	1891
Earliest Rowing by 2 men	George Harbo and Frank Samuelson (U.S.)	*Richard K. Fox* 18⅓ ft *5,58 m*	New York City (6 June)	Isles of Scilly (1 Aug.)	55 days	1869
Fastest Sailing Ship	Captain and crew	*Lancing* 4 masts	New York	Cape Wrath	6 days 18 hours	1916
Fastest Solo Sailing West-East	J. V. T. McDonald (G.B.)	*Inverarity* 38 ft *11,58 m*	Nova Scotia	Ireland	16 days	1922
Earliest Canoe (with sail)	F. Romer (Germany)	*Deutcher Sport* 19⅓ ft *5,94 m*	Cape St. Vincent (17 Apr.)	St. Thomas, West Indies	58 days	1928
Fastest Solo Sailing East West (Northern)	Cdr. R. D. Graham R.N. (G.B.)	*Emanuel* 30 ft *9,14 m*	Bantry, Ireland	St. John's, Newfoundland	24.35 days	1934
Earliest Woman Solo-Sailing	Mrs. Ann Davison (G.B.)	*Felicity Ann* 23 ft *7,01 m*	Plymouth (18 May 1952)	Miami, Florida (13 Aug. 1953)	454 days	1952 /1953
Smallest	John Riding (G.B.)	*Sjo Ag* 12 ft *3,65 m*	San Diego, 1971	New Zealand, 1973	Lost in Tasman Sea	1971 /1973
Smallest West-East	William Verity (U.S.)	*Nonoalca* 12 ft *3,65 m*	Ft. Lauderdale, Florida	Tralee, Kerry (12 July)	68 days	1966
Earliest Rowing (G.B.)	Capt. John Ridgway M.B.E. Sgt. Charles Blyth B.E.M. (G.B.)	*English Rose III* 22 ft *6,70 m*	Cape Cod (4 June)	Inishmore (3 Sept.)	91 days	1966
Fastest Crossing Sailing (Trimaran)	Eric Tabarly (France) + 2 crew	*Pen Duick IV* 67 ft *20,42 m*	Tenerife	Martinique	251.4 miles *404,5 km*/ day (10 days 12 hours)	1968
Smallest East-West (Southern)	Hugo S. Vihlen (U.S.)	*The April Fool* 5 ft 11½ in *1,81 m*	Casablanca (29 Mar.)	Ft. Lauderdale, Florida (21 June)	85 days	1968
Fastest Solo East-West (Northern)	Geoffrey Williams (G.B.)	*Sir Thomas Lipton* 57 ft *17,37 m*	Plymouth (1 June)	Brenton Reef (27 June)	25.85 days	1968
Fastest Solo Rowing East-West	Sidney Genders, 51 (G.B.)	*Khaggavisana* 19¾ ft *6,02 m*	Sennen Cove, Cornwall	Miami, Florida *via* Antigua (27 June)	37.3 miles *60 km*/day	1970
Earliest Solo Rowing East-West	John Fairfax (G.B.)	*Britannia* 22 ft *6,70 m*	Las Palmas (20 Jan.)	Ft. Lauderdale, Florida (19 July)	180 days	1969
Fastest Solo East-West (Southern)	Sir Francis Chichester K.B.E. (G.B.)	*Gipsy Moth V* 57 ft *17,37 m*	Portuguese Guinea	Nicaragua	179.1 miles *288,2 km*/ day (22.4 days)	1970
Earliest Solo Rowing West-East	Tom McClean (Ireland)	*Super Silver* 20 ft *6,90 m*	St. John's Newfoundland (17 May)	Black Sod Bay, Ireland (27 July)	70.7 days	1969
Fastest Solo East-West (Multi-hull)	Alain Colas (France)	*Pen Duick IV* 70 ft *21,33 m* trimaran	Plymouth (17 June)	Newport, Rhode Is. (7 July)	20½ days	1972

TRANS-PACIFIC MARINE RECORDS

Fastest	Eric Tabarly (France) + 2 crew	*Pen Duick IV* 67 ft *20,42 m* trimaran	Los Angeles, Cal.	Honolulu, Hawaii	8.54 days 260.5 miles *419,2 km*/day	1969
First Solo (Woman)	Sharon Sites Adams	*Sea Sharp II* 31 ft *9,45 m*	Yokohama Japan	San Diego, Cal.	75 days	1969
Earliest Rowing	John Fairfax (G.B.) Sylvia Cook (G.B.)	*Britannia II* 35 ft *10,66 m*	San Francisco, Cal. 26 Apr. 1971	Hayman Is. Australia 22 Apr. 1972	362 days	1971 /1972

N.B.—The earliest single-handed Pacific crossings were achieved East-West by Bernard Gilboy (U.S.) in 1882 in the 18 ft *5,48 m* double-ender *Pacific* and West-East by Fred Rebel (Latvia) in 1932 in the 18 ft *5,48 m Elaine.*

dive utilizing gas mixtures is a simulated dive of 2,001 ft *609 m* in a dry chamber by Patrice Chemin and Robert Gauret (France) at the Comex Chamber, Marseille, France reported in June 1972. Some divers have survived free swimming for short intervals at depths of 1,400 ft *426 m.*

Deepest The deepest underwater rescue achieved was of the
Escape *Pisces III* in which Roger R. Chapman, 28 and Roger Mallinson, 35 were trapped for 76 hours when it sank to 1,575 ft *480 m* 150 miles *240 km* south east of Cork, Ireland on 29 Aug. 1973. She was hauled to the surface by the cable ship *John Cabot* after work by Pisces V, Pisces II and the remote control recovery vessel U.S. C.U.R.V. on 1 Sept. The greatest depth of an actual escape without any equipment has been from 198 ft *60,3 m* by Sub. Lt. W. Morrison, R.N.V.R. and E.R.A. Swatton from H. M. Submarine X.E.11 in Loch Striven, Strathclyde on 6 Mar. 1945.

SALVAGING

Deep sea The world's record depth for a salvage observation
diving chamber is that established by the Admiralty salvage ship *Reclaim* on 28 June 1956, In an observation chamber measuring 7 ft *2,13 m* long and 3 ft *0,91 m* internal diameter, Senior Com. Boatswain (now Lt.-Cdr.) George A. M. Wookey, M.B.E., R.N., descended to a depth of 1,060 ft *323 m* in Oslo Fjord, Norway.

Deepest The greatest depth at which salvage has been achieved is 16,500 ft *5 029 m* by the bathyscaphe *Trieste II* (Lt.-Cdr. Mel Bartels U.S.N.) to attach cables to an "electronic package" on the sea bed 400 miles *645 km* north of Hawaii on 20 May 1972.

Flexible The deepest salvaging operation ever carried out was
dress divers on the wreck of the S.S. *Niagara*, sunk by a mine in 1940, 438 ft *133,5 m* down off Bream Head, Whangarei North Island, New Zealand. All but 6 per cent of the £2,250,000 of gold in her holds was recovered in 7 weeks. The record recovery was that from the White Star Liner *Laurentic*, which was torpedoed in 114 ft *34,7 m* of water off Malin Head, Donegal, Ireland, in 1917, with £5,000,000 of gold ingots in her Second Class baggage room. By 1924, 3,186 of the 3,211 gold bricks had been recovered with immense difficulty.

Largest The largest vessel ever salvaged was the U.S.S.
vessel *Lafayette*, formerly the French liner *Normandie* (83,423 tons), which keeled over during fire-fighting operations at the West 49th Street Pier, New York Harbour, U.S.A., on 9 Feb. 1942. She was righted in October 1943, at a cost of $4,500,000 (*then £1,250,000*) and was broken up at Newark, New Jersey, beginning September 1946.

MINING DEPTHS

Greatest Man's deepest penetration made into the ground is in
penetration the Western Deep Levels Mine at Carltonville, Transvaal, South Africa. By May 1975 a record depth of 12,600 ft *3 840 m* had been attained. The rock temperature at this depth is 52,2° C *126° F.*

Shaft The one month (31 days) world record is 1 251 ft *381,3*
sinking *m* for a standard shaft 26 ft *7,92 m* in diameter at
record Buffelsfontein Mine, Transvaal, South Africa, in March 1962. The British record of 410 ft *124,9 m* of 18 ft 1 in *5,51 m* diameter shaft was set in the Boulby Mine, Whitby, Yorkshire on 18 Jan.–17 Feb. 1971 (30 days). The rock shaft at this potash mine at 3,765 ft *1 147,5 m* is the deepest in Great Britain.

RUNNING

Mensen Ernst (1799–1846) of Norway is reputed to have run from Istanbul, Turkey, to Calcutta, in West Bengal, India, and back in 59 days in 1836, so averaging an improbable 92.4 miles *151,6 km* per day. The greatest non-stop run recorded is 121 miles 440 yds *195,132 km* in 22 hours 27 min by Jared R. Beads, 41, of Westport, Maryland in October 1969. The best distance by a 19th century "wobbler" was 150 miles 395 yds *245,013 km* by Charles Rowell in New York City in February 1882.

Six-day The greatest distance covered by a man in six days
races (*i.e.* the 144 permissible hours between Sundays in Victorian times) was 623¾ miles *1 003,828 km* by George Littlewood (England), who required only 139 hours 1 min for this feat in December 1888 at the old Madison Square Gardens, New York City, U.S.A.

Greatest The greatest life-time mileage recorded by any runner
mileage is 157,295 miles *253 141 km* by Ken Baily of Bournemouth, England up to 19 July 1975. This is more than 6 times round the Equator. When running at night in a luminous track suit he has been attacked by owls.

Longest The longest race ever staged was the 1929 Trans-
running continental Race (3,665 miles [*5 898 km*]) from New
race York City, N.Y., to Los Angeles, California, U.S.A. The Finnish-born Johnny Salo (killed 6 Oct. 1931) was the winner in 79 days, from 31 March to 17 June. His elapsed time of 525 hours 57 min 20 sec gave a running average of 6.97 m.p.h. *11,21 km/h.*

"Go as you The United States coast to coast go as you please (i.e.
Please" running or walking) record is 53 days 7 hrs 45 mins from New York to Los Angeles by E. Gordon Brooks, 28, on 21 June to 13 Aug. 1974.

WALKING

Round the The first person recorded to have "walked round the
World world" is David Kunst, who started with his brother John from Waseca, Minnesota on 10 June 1970. John was killed by Afghani bandits in 1972. David arrived home after walking 17,000 miles *27,360 km* on 5 Oct. 1974. The trans-Asia record is 238 days for 6,800 miles *10 940 km* from Riga, Latvia to Vladivostok, U.S.S.R. by Georgyi Bushuyev, 50 in 1973–74.

Longest Frederick Jago, 38 (G.B.) walked 304.26 miles *483,663*
"marathon" *km* at Vivary Park, Taunton, Devon, England, in 116 hrs 34 mins on 27 Sept.–2 Oct. 1974. He did not permit himself any stops for resting and was moving 97.58% of the time.

Trans The Trans Canada (Halifax to Vancouver) record
Canada walk of 3,764 miles *6 057 km* is 96 days by Clyde McRae, 23 from 1 May to 4 Aug. 1973.

North John Lees, (b. 23 Feb. 1945) of Brighton, England
America between 11 Apr. and 3 June 1972, walked 2,876 miles
coast to *4 628 km* across the U.S.A. from City Hall, Los
coast Angeles to City Hall, New York City in 53 days 12 hours 15 min (average 53.746 miles [*86,495 km*] a day).

Walking The greatest ever exponent of reverse pedestrianism
Backwards has been Plennie L. Wingo (b. 1895) then of Abilene, Texas, who started on his 8,000 mile *12 875 km* transcontinental walks from Santa Monica, California to Istanbul, Turkey, from 15 Apr. 1931 to 24 Oct. 1932. The longest distance reported for walking backwards for 24 hours is 58 miles 167 yds *93,494 km* by Alex James Gear at Lyme Regis, Dorset on 11–12 Aug. 1974.

John Lees (G.B.), the transcontinental walk record holder at 53¾ miles a day, seen campaigning against the dropping of a walking event from future celebrations of the Olympic Games

SWIMMING

The greatest recorded distance ever swum is 1,826 miles *2 938 km* down the Mississippi, U.S.A. by Fred P. Newton, 27 of Clinton, Oklahoma from 6 July to 29 Dec. 1930. He was 742 hours in the water between Ford Dam near Minneapolis and Carrollton Ave., New Orleans, Louisiana. The water temperature fell to 47°F *8,3°C* and Newton used petroleum jelly and axle grease. Mr. Newton, now of Gainesville, Texas became the inventor of the famous Relaxo-Bak support.

Duration The longest duration swim ever achieved was one of 168 continuous hours, ending on 24 Feb. 1941, by the legless Charles Zibbelman, *alias* Zimmy (b. 1894) of the U.S.A., in a pool in Honolulu, Hawaii, U.S.A. The longest duration swim by a woman was 87 hours 27 min in a pool by Mrs. Myrtle Huddleston of New York City, N.Y., U.S.A., in 1931.

The greatest distance covered in a continuous swim is 288 miles *463,5 km* by Clarence Giles from Glendive to Billings, Montana in the Yellowstone River in 71 hours 3 min on 30 June to 3 July 1939.

Longest The longest recorded survival alone on a raft is 133
on a raft days (4½ months) by Second Steward Poon Lim (born Hong Kong) of the U.K. Merchant Navy, whose ship, the S.S. *Ben Lomond*, was torpedoed in the Atlantic 565 miles *910 km* west of St. Paul's Rocks in Lat. 00 30′ N Long. 38° 45′ W at 11.45 a.m. on 23 Nov. 1942. He was picked up by a Brazilian fishing boat off Salinópolis, Brazil, on 5 April 1943 and was able to walk ashore. In July 1943, he was awarded the B.E.M.

Maurice and Maralyn Bailey survived 118¼ days in an inflatable dinghy 4½ ft *1,37 m* in diameter in the north east Pacific from 4 Mar to 30 June 1973.

CYCLING

The duration record for cycling on a track is 168 hours (7 days) by Syed Muhammed Nawab, aged 22, of Lucknow, India, in Addis Ababa, Ethiopia, in 1964. The monocycle duration record is 23 hours 30 min by Steve McReak (U.S.) in 1969 and 17 hours 5 min for a woman by Molly M. Nation at Cheyenne on 1–2 Sept. 1973. The greatest mileage amassed in a cycle tour has been more than 270,000 miles *435 500 km* by the itinerant lecturer Walter Stolle (b. Czechoslovakia) since 24 Jan. 1959. He has covered 140 countries starting from London. He has had 5 bicycles stolen and has suffered 21 other robberies.

Ray Reece, 41, of Alverstoke, Hants., circumnavigated the world (13,000 road miles [*20 900 km*]) between 14 June and 5 Nov. (143 days) in 1971. Paul Cornish of Santa Ana, California rode from Los Angeles to New York City in a record 13 days 5 hrs 20 min on 4–17 Mar. 1973. averaging 225 miles *362 km* a day.

Most on The cyclist troupe from the Chinese Acrobatic Theatre
One Cycle from Shanghai regularly perform tricks involving up to 12 members simultaneously riding one bicycle.

MARRIAGE AND DIVORCE

Most The greatest number of marriages accumulated in the monogamous world is 19 by Glynn de Moss Wolfe (U.S.) (b. 1908) who married for the 19th time since 1931 his 17th wife Gloria, aged 23, on 22 Feb. 1969. His total number of children is, he says 34. He keeps two wedding dresses (different sizes) in his closet for ready use. He has additionally suffered 16 mothers-in-law. The most often marrying millionaire was Thomas F. Manville (1894–1967) who contracted his 13th marriage to his 11th wife Christine Erdlen Popa (1940–71) aged 20, in New York City, U.S.A., on 11 Jan. 1960 when aged 65. His shortest marriage (to his seventh wife) effectively lasted only 7½ hours. His fortune of $20 million came from asbestos, none of which he could take with him.

Mrs. Beverly Nina Avery, then aged 48, a barmaid from Los Angeles, California, U.S.A., set a monogamous world record in October 1957 by obtaining her sixteenth divorce from her fourteenth husband, Gabriel Avery. She alleged outside the court that five of the 14 had broken her nose.

Britain Seven times married individuals in Britain include Sir Francis Ferdinand Maurice Cook, 4th baronet (b. 21 Dec. 1907) and Mr. Lionel Birch.

Oldest Bride The oldest bridegroom on record was Ralph Cam-
and bridge, 105, who married Mrs. Adriana Kapp, 70, at
Bridegroom Knysna, South Africa on 30 Sept. 1971. The British record was set by Edward Reuben Simpson, (1873–1973), who married Mrs. Eva J. Midwinter, 83, at Swindon, Wiltshire, on 8 Dec. 1971 when aged 98 years 10 months.

Dyura Avramovich, 101, married Yula Zhivich, 95, in Belgrade, Yugoslavia in November 1963.

Longest The longest engagement on record is one of 67 years
Engage- between Octavio Guillen, 82 and Adriana Martinez,
ments 82. They finally took the plunge in June 1969 in Mexico City, Mexico.

Longest The longest recorded marriage is one of 86 years
Marriage between Sir Temulji Bhicaji Nariman and Lady
World Nariman from 1853 to 1940 resulting from a cousin marriage when both were five. Sir Temulji (b. 3 Sept. 1848) died, aged 91 years 11 months, in August 1940 at Bombay. The only reliable instance of an 83rd anniversary celebrated by a couple marrying at normal ages is that between the late Edd (105) and Margaret (99) Hollen. who celebrated their 83rd anniversary on 7 May 1972. They were married in Kentucky on 7 May 1889.

219

Britain James Frederick Burgess (born 3 March 1861, died 27 Nov. 1966) and his wife Sarah Ann, *née* Gregory (born 11 July 1865, died 22 June 1965) were married on 21 June 1883 at St. James's, Bermondsey, London, and celebrated their 82nd anniversary in 1965.

Most James and Mary Grady of Illinois, U.S.A. have **married** married each other 27 times as a protest against the existence of divorce in the period 1964–69. They have married in 25 different States, 3 times in a day (16 Dec. 1968), twice in an hour and twice on television.

Mass The largest mass wedding ceremony was one of 1,800 *ceremony* couples officiated over by Sun Myung Moon of the Holy Spirit Association for the Unification of World Christianity in Seoul, South Korea on 14 Feb. 1975. The response to the question "Will you swear to love your spouse for ever?" is "Ye".

Eating out The world champion for eating out is Fred E. Magel of Chicago, Illinois, U.S.A. who since 1928 has dined in 36,000 restaurants in 60 nations as a restaurant grader (to March 1973). He asserts the one serving the largest helpings is Zehnder's Hotel, Frankenmuth, Michigan, U.S.A. Mr. Magel's favourite dishes are South African rock lobster and mousse of fresh English strawberries.

Party The most expensive private party ever thrown was **giving** that of Mr. and Mrs. Bradley Martin of Troy, N.Y., U.S.A. staged at the Waldorf Hotel, Manhattan in February 1897. The cost to the host and hostess was estimated to be $369,200 in the days when dollars were made of gold.

Toast- The Guild of Professional Toastmasters (founded **masters** 1962) has only 12 members. Its founder and President, Ivor Spencer, listened to a speech in excess of 2 hours by the maudlin subject of a retirement luncheon. The Guild also elects the most boring speaker of the year, but for professional reasons, will not publicize the winner's name until A.D. 2000. Red coats were introduced by the pioneer professional, William Knight-Smith (d.1932) *c.* 1900.

Lecture The world's largest lecture agency is the American **Agency** Program Bureau of Boston, Mass., U.S.A., with 400 Personalities on 40 Topics and a turnover of some $5 million. The top rate is $4,000 (*£1,600*) per hour commanded by Ralph Nader (b. Winsted, Connecticut, 27 Feb. 1934). This is $66.66 (*£26.66*) per min.

Working The longest active working week (maximum 168 **week** hours) is up to 139 hours at times by some housemen and registrars in some hospitals. This peak value was alleged by Dr. Adrian Cox at the Norfolk and Norwich Hospital in November 1971.

Working The longest recorded working career in one job in **career** Britain was that of Miss Polly Gadsby who started work with Archibald Turner & Co. of Leicester at the age of 9. In 1932, after 86 years service, she was still at her bench wrapping elastic, aged 95. Mr. Theodore C. Taylor (1850–1952) served 86 years with J. T. & T. Taylor of Batley, West Yorkshire including 56 years as chairman.

Mr. Ernest Turner of Ramsgate, Kent has been working since 1886 (minding sheep at 2s. 6d. a week) and in June 1975 was a canteen cleaner for Volkswagen aged 95. His son, an old age pensioner working part-time, has to get up at 6.30 a.m. every morning to drive 'my dad' to work.

Milkman, Britain's longest serving milkman is Mr. John Baggs **Longest** (b. August 1884) of Horndean, near Portsmouth, **serving** Hampshire, who has been on his round for over 80 years ("I don't like sitting about"). He is assisted by his boy John Baggs Junior, aged 63.

National Dairy Council

Britain's senior milk roundsman, John Baggs, 94, after 80 years on the job. His devotion to delivering is such that he declined to take a day off to collect an award in London

Longest Miss Millicent Barclay, daughter of Col. William **pension** Barclay was born posthumously on 10 July 1872 and became eligible for a Madras Military Fund pension to continue until her marriage. She died unmarried on 26 Oct. 1969 having drawn the pension for every day of her life of 97 years 3 months.

Most jobs The greatest number of different paid jobs recorded in a working life is the 112 accumulated by D. H. "Nobby" Clarke, the yachting author, of Ipswich, Suffolk.

Doctors Dr. Frederick Walter Whitney Dawson (b. 22 Oct. *Oldest* 1876 in Hobsonville, New Zealand) was the first doctor to be registered this century in London on 1 Jan. 1901. He was still practising in April 1975 in his 99th year in Whangarei, New Zealand.

Most in David L. Bernie, M.D. of Dayton, Ohio numbers *a Family* 5 sons and a daughter and 11 other members of his family who are qualified. M.D.'s.

MISCELLANEOUS ENDEAVOURS

Apple The longest single unbroken apple peel on record is **peeling** one of 130 ft 8½ in *39,86 m* peeled by Frank Freer (U.S.) in 8 hours at Wolcott, N.Y., on 17 Oct. 1971. The apple was 15 in *38 cm* in circumference.

Apple The greatest recorded performance is 270 U.S. **picking** bushels (261.6 Imperial bushels [*95,14 hectolitres*]) picked in 8 hours by Harold Oaks, 22, at his father's ranch, Hood River, Oregon, U.S.A. on 30 Sept. 1972.

Bag The record time for the annual "World Coal Carrying **carrying** Championship" over the uphill 1,080 yd *987 m* course at Ossett cum Gawthorpe, West Yorkshire, England with a 112 lb. *50 kg 800* sack is 4 min 36 sec by Tony Nicholson, 26, of Penrith, Cumbria on 3 Apr. 1972. The non-stop distance record carrying 1 cwt. *50,8 kg* of household coal in an open bag is 14 miles

22,53 km from Perranporth to in and around Cambourne, Cornwall by E. John Rapson in 3 hrs 40 min on 4 Apr. 1953.

Bag-pipes The longest duration pipe has been one of 77 hours by Dean Miller, Murray Rogers and Roger and Pete Collins of Broken Hill Cameron Pipe Band, Australia on 29 Nov.–2 Dec. 1974.

Balancing on one foot The longest recorded duration for continuous balancing on one foot is 8 hours 5 min by Alan Maki at Beverly Hills Junior High School, Pennsylvania U.S.A. on 3 Mar. 1975. The disengaged foot may not be rested on the standing foot nor may any sticks be used for support or balance.

The record allowing 5 min rest breaks per hour is 12 hours 14 min by Gordon Clark and John Wheeler in Corsham, Wiltshire on 6 Oct. 1973.

Balloon racing The largest balloon release on record has been one of 100,000 helium balloons at the opening of "Transpo 72" at Dulles Airport, Washington, D.C. on 27 May 1972.

Balloon flights The longest reported toy balloon flight is one of 9,000 miles *14 500 km* from Atherton, California (released by Jane Dorst on 21 May 1972) and found on 10 June at Pietermaritzburg, South Africa. The longest recorded hydrogen-filled balloon flight from the geographical British Isles is one of 5,880 miles *9 460 km* from Jersey which was returned from Camps Bay, Cape Province, South Africa on 28 Apr. 1974, 43 days after release by Gerard Wankling.

Ball punching Ron Renaulf (Australia) equalled his own world duration ball punching record of 125 hours 20 min at 10.20 p.m. on 31 Dec. 1955, at the Esplanade, Southport, Queensland, Australia.

Band marathons The longest recorded "blow-in" is 28 hours 45 min by 30 members of the City of Oxford Youth Band on 26–27 Apr. 1975. Each bandsman was allowed 5 min per hour to regain his wind. The record for a one-man band is 16 hours (no breaks) by Joe Littlefield of McNavy High School, Salem, Oregon on 10 Nov. 1974.

One-Man Band Don Davis of Hollywood, California is the only one-man band able to play 4 melody and 2 percussion instruments simultaneously without electronics.

For his rendition of the 4th movement of Beethoven's Fifth, he utilises his unique 8-prong pendular perpendicular piano pounder and semicircular chromatic radially-operated centrifugally sliding left-handed glockenspiel.

Barrow pushing The heaviest loaded barrow pushed for a minimum 36½ ft *11,13 m* is one loaded with 209 8 lb *3,62 kg* bricks weighing 14 cwt. *711 kg* by Steve Draper, 21 at Wollongong, New South Wales, Australia on 26 Nov. 1974.

Barrel Rolling The record for rolling a 36 gallon metal beer barrel over a measured mile is 12 min 29.5 secs by "The Fletch" A team in Coventry, West Midlands on 13 Oct. 1975.

Barrel jumping The greatest number of barrels jumped by a skater is 17 (total length 28 ft 8 in *[8,73 m]*) by Kenneth LeBel at the Grossinger Country Club, New York State, U.S.A., on 9 Jan. 1965. Roger Wood leapt 29 ft 2 in *8,89 m* on 14 Dec. 1972.

Bath Tub Racing The record for the annual international 36 mile *57,9 km* Nanaimo to Vancouver, British Columbia bath tub race is 1 hr 49 min by David Lyle (Canada) on 23 July 1972. Tubs are limited to 75 in *1,90 m* and 6 h.p. motors. The greatest distance for a hand propelled bath tub in 24 hours is 36 miles 1,072 yds *58,91 km* by 25 Venture scouts at Priory Park, Malvern, Hereford and Worcester on 10–11 May 1975.

Bed making The record time set under the rigorous rules of the Australian Bedmaking Championships is 39.4 secs by Mrs. Kathy Perks of West Pennant Hills, N.S.W., on 28 Apr. 1975.

Bed of nails The duration record for non-stop lying on a bed of nails (needle-sharp 6-inch *[15,2 cm]*; 2 in *[5 cm]* apart) is 25 hours 20 min by Vernon E. Craig (Komar, the Hindu *fakir*) at Wooster, Ohio, U.S.A. 22–23 July 1971. Barrie Walls (El Hakim), 37 endured 26 hr 37 mins with brief rests at Sophia Gardens, Cardiff, Wales on 16–17 Jan. 1975. The feminine record (with 5 min rests per hour) is 25 hrs 30 min by Ruth Marie Porter, 18 at Springfield, Virginia on 13–14 Feb. 1975. Much longer durations are claimed by uninvigilated *fakirs*—the most extreme case being *Silki* who claimed 111 days in São Paulo, Brazil ending on 24 Aug. 1969. The greatest liveweight borne on a bed of nails is also

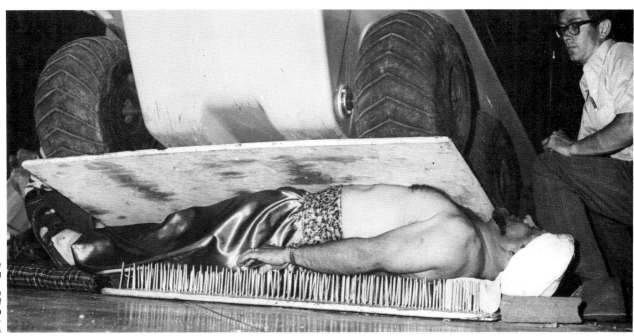

Komar (see also Firewalking in Chapter 1) working out on the bed of nails on which he lay for 25 hours 20 mins

by Komar with 4 persons aggregating 1,142 lb. (81 st. 8 lb. [*518 kg*]) standing on him in Philadelphia, U.S.A. on 26 Mar. 1974.

Bed-pushing The longest recorded push of a normally sessile object is of 1,000 miles *1609,34 km* in the case of a wheeled hospital bed by a team of 9 from Fremont-Newark YMCA, California in 308 hrs on 18–31 Mar. 1975.

Bed race The record time for the annual Knaresborough Bed Race (established 1966) in North Yorkshire is 14 min 9.0 sec for the 2½ mile *4 km* course crossing the River Nidd by the Harrowgate Athletic Club on 14 June 1975.

Beer Label Collecting The greatest collection of British Beer labels is 19,786 different by Keith Osborne, Hon. Sec. of The Labologists Society (founded by Guinness Exports Ltd in 1958). His oldest is a Bass label of 1869.

Best man The world's champion "best man" is Mr. Wally Gant, a bachelor fishmonger from Wakefield, West Yorkshire, who officiated for the 50th time since 1931 in December 1964.

Big Wheel riding The endurance record for riding a Big Wheel is 21 days 3 hours 58 min by the WIXY disc jockey Mike Kelly in Cedar Point Amusement Park, Cleveland, Ohio, U.S.A., on 12 Aug.–2 Sept. 1972. He travelled 11,800 revolutions or 720 miles *1 158 km* with only 15 min allowed off per day.

Billiard table jumping Joe Darby (1861–1937) cleared a full-sized 12 ft *3,65 m* billiard table lengthwise, taking off from a 4 in *10 cm* high solid wooden block, at Wolverhampton, West Midlands on 5 Feb. 1892.

Bomb defusing The highest reported number of unexploded bombs defused by any individual is 8,000 by Werner Stephan in West Berlin, Germany, in the 12 years from 1945 to 1957. He was killed by a small grenade on the Grunewald blasting site on 17 Aug. 1957.

Bond signing The greatest feat of bond signing was that performed by L. E. Chittenden (d. 1902), the Registrar of the United States Treasury. In 48 hours (20–22 March 1863) he signed 12,500 bonds worth $10,000,000 (*now £4 million*), which had to catch a steam packet to England. He suffered years of pain and the bonds were never used.

Boomerang throwing The earliest mention of a word similar to *boomerang* is *wo-mur-rang* in Collins *Acct. N.S. Wales Vocab.* published in 1798. The earliest Australian certain account of a returning boomerang (term established, 1827) was in 1831 by Major (later Sir Thomas) Mitchell.

World championships and codified rules were not established until 1970. Jeff Lewry has won in 1970–71–72–73 and also the Australian title in 1974. The Boomerang Association of Australia's official record for distance reached from the thrower before the boomerang returns is 82 m *89.66 yd* by Jeff Lewry at Albury, N.S.W., on 16 July 1972.

Brick carrying The record for the annual Narrogin Brick Carrying contest in Western Australia (instituted in 1960) is 40.0 miles *64,37 km* by Ronald D. Hamilton on 10 Oct. 1970. The 8 lb. 12 oz. *3 kg 968* wire-cut semi-pressed brick has to be carried in a downward position with a nominated ungloved hand. The feminine record for an 8 lb. 15 oz. *4,05 kg* brick is 4.5 miles *7,24 km* by Debbie Horton at Iowa Wesleyan College, U.S.A. on 13 May 1975. The British record for a 6 lb. *2,72 kg* smooth-sided brick is 2.24 miles *3,60 km* by Mrs. Jane Reynolds of Salisbury, Wiltshire at the B.B.C. T.V. Centre, London on 10 Nov. 1974.

Bricklaying Bill Hardy, 34, formerly of Croydon, England, received the Brick Manufacturers Association Cup at Safety Bay, Western Australia on 28 May 1960 from the previous holder for laying 5,469 rough-pressed bricks in an 8 hour shift supported by a gang of five.

Brick throwing The greatest reported distance for throwing a standard 5 lb. *2 kg 268* building brick is 142 ft 6 in *43,43 m* by Robert Gardner at Stroud, Gloucestershire, England in the 1971 Champion of Champions contest.

Burial alive In June 1951 two men emerged from an underground bunker at Babie Doly, near Gdynia, Poland which had been demolished and blocked by the retreating German army in January 1945. One died immediately.

The longest voluntary burial alive is one of 101 days 37 min by Hendrik Louis Alexander Luypaerts (b. 9 May 1931) at Hechtel, Belgium in a coffin measuring 2 m × 65 cm × 85 cm (*6 ft 6 in × 25½ in × 33½ in*) 3 m *9 ft 10 in* deep on 13 Apr.–23 July 1974. The case of a 119 day claim in 1935 in the United States is however now under investigation.

Car Wrecking The greatest number of cars wrecked in a stunting career is 1,158 to October 1974 by Dick Sheppard of Gloucester, England.

Cat's Cradle Maryann and Rita Di Vona and Geneva Hultenius completed 21,200 cat's cradles in 21 hours at Chula Vista, California on 17–18 Aug. 1974.

Champagne Fountain The tallest successfully filled column of champagne glasses is one 17 high filled from the top by a team of 17 at San Luis Obispo, California, U.S.A. on 9 June 1975.

Clapping The duration record for continuous clapping (sustaining an average of 140 claps per min audible at 100 yd [*91 m*]) is 30 hours by Marie Wagner, Jill Washburn and Kerry Boyce at Denver, Colorado, U.S.A. on 24–25 May 1975.

Club swinging Bill Franks set a world record of 17,280 revolutions (4.8 per sec) in 60 min at Webb's Gymnasium, Newcastle, N.S.W., Australia on 2 Aug. 1934. M. Dobrilla swung continuously for 144 hours at Cobar, N.S.W. finishing on 15 Sept. 1913.

Coal Cutting The first coal mine in Britain to achieve more than 5 tons output per man-shift for a whole year has been Bagworth Colliery, Leicestershire announced on 5 Apr. 1975.

Coal shovelling The record for filling a half-ton *508 kg* hopper with coal is 47.4 sec by R. Hughes of Westport, New Zealand in February 1974.

Coin balancing The greatest recorded feat of coin-balancing is the stacking of 126 coins on top of a silver U.S. dollar on edge by Alex Chervinsky, 65 of Lock Haven, Pennsylvania on 16 Sept. 1971 after 23 years practice.

Coin snatching The greatest number of 10p pieces caught from being flipped from a pile on the back of the forearm is 39 by Chris Redford at the Cardwell Arms, Adlington, Lancashire on 26 Sept. 1973.

Competition Prize The highest value first prize offered in Britain has been a £21,000 cash alternative to a $50,000 New York spending spree offered by Soft Blue Band Luxury Margarine in a contest which closed on 30 Nov. 1971. It was won by Mrs. Susan B. Jenkins of Kirkby, Merseyside, who took the cash.

Competition winnings The largest individual competition prize win on record is $307,500 (*then £109,821*) by Herbert J. Idle, 55, of Chicago in an encyclopaedia contest run by Unicorn Press Inc. on 20 Aug. 1953.

Most successful complainer Ralph Charell (b. 3 Dec. 1929), author of *How I Turn Ordinary Complaints into Thousands of Dollars*, between January 1963 and July 1973 amassed a total of $76,919.31 (£33,443) ranging between $6.95 and $25,000 in refunds and compensations. His latest complaint is against this publication for failing to list his 51 consecutive profitable transactions in "option trading".

Cow Chip tossing The record distance for throwing a dried cow chip is 291 ft *88,69 m* by Carl G. Engel and the feminine record is 115 ft 4 in *35,15 m* by Linda Reece, 17 both made at the 1974 Texas State Championship at Odessa. These increasing distances are anxiously studied by party political campaign managers who are also in support of a rule which precludes the mixing of cement into the cow feed prior to contests.

Crawling The longest crawl (progression with one or other knee in unbroken contact with the ground) on record is 7 miles 803 yd *13,68 km* by Kevin Goodhew and Simon Holmes of Preston Manor High School, Wembley Park, London in 6 hrs 26 min on 10 May 1975.

Crochet The longest recorded crocheted chain is one of 4 ply wool measuring 2.46 miles *3,97 km* completed between 3 Dec. 1974 and 3 May 1975 by Lisa Zwelinski and Chris Kuchalla of Mereden, Connecticut, U.S.A.

Cucumber slicing Norman Johnson of Blackpool College of Art and Technology set a record of 24.2 sec for slicing a 12 in of a 1½ in diameter cucumber at 20 slices to the inch on B.B.C. T.V. 'Record-Breakers' on 28 Sept. 1973.

Custard Pie throwing The most times champion in the annual World Custard Pie Championships at Coxheath, Kent (instituted 1967) have been the "The Birds" and the Coxheath Man each with 3 wins. The target (face) must be 8 ft 3⅞ in *2,53 m* from the thrower who must throw a pie no more than 10¾ in *27,3 cm* in diameter. Six points are scored for a square hit full in the face.

DANCING

Largest Dance The largest dance ever staged was that put on by the Houston Livestock Show at the Astro Hall, Houston, Texas, U.S.A. on 8 Feb. 1969. The attendance was more than 16,500 with 4,000 turned away.

Marathon dancing must be distinguished from dancing mania, which is a pathological condition. The worst outbreak of dancing mania was at Aachen, Germany, in July 1374, when hordes of men and women broke into a frenzied dance in the streets which lasted for hours till injury or complete exhaustion ensued.

The most severe marathon dance staged as a public spectacle in the U.S.A. was one lasting 3,780 hours (22 weeks 3½ days) completed by Callum L. deVillier, (d. June 1973) 24 and Vonny Kuchinski, 20 at Sommerville, Massachusetts, U.S.A. from 28 Dec. 1932 to 3 June 1933. In the last two weeks the rest allowance was cut from 15 min per hour to only 3 min while the last 52½ hours were continuous. The prize of $1,000 was equivalent to less than 26½ cents per hour.

Ballet In the *entrechat* (a vertical spring from the fifth position with the legs extended criss-crossing at the lower calf), the starting and finishing position each count as one such that in an *entrechat douze* there are *five* crossings and uncrossings. This was performed by Wayne Sleep for the B.B.C. *Record Breakers* programme on 7 Jan. 1973. He was in the air for 0.71 of a second.

Most turns The greatest number of spins called for in classical ballet choreography is the 32 *fouettés rond de jambe en tournant* in "Swan Lake" by Pyotr Ilyich Chaykovskiy (Tschaikovsky) (1840–1893). Miss Rowena

A slightly blurred action photograph of the world's most durable belly dancer, "Cyrene"

Jackson (later Chatfield), M.B.E. (b. Invercargill, N.Z., 1926) achieved 121 such turns at her class in Melbourne, Victoria, Australia, in 1940.

Most curtain calls The greatest recorded number of curtain calls ever received by ballet dancers is 89 by Dame Margaret Evelyn Arias, D.B.E. *née* Hookham (born Reigate, Surrey, 18 May 1919), *alias* Margot Fonteyn, and Rudolf Hametovich Nureyev (born on a train near Irkutsk, U.S.S.R., 17 Mar. 1938) after a performance of "Swan Lake" at the Vienna Staatsoper, Austria, in October 1964.

Largest Cast The largest number of ballet dancers used in a production in Britain has been 2,000 in the London Coster Ballet of 1962, directed by Lillian Rowley, at the Royal Albert Hall, London.

Ballroom Marathon The individual continuous world record for ballroom dancing is 106 hours 5 min 10 sec by Carlos Sandrini in Buenos Aires, Argentina, in September 1955. Three girls worked shifts as his partner.

Champions The world's most successful professional ballroom dancing champions have been Bill Irvine, M.B.E. and Bobbie Irvine, M.B.E., who won 13 world titles between 1960 and 1972.

The most consecutive national titles won is 10 in the New Zealand Old Time Championship by Mr. Maurice Fox and his wife Royce (*née* Miles) of Palmerston North in 1959–68.

Belly Dancing The longest recorded belly dance was one of 6 hours (incl. 2 five minute breaks) by Darlene L. Freedman, known as "Cyrene" in San Jose, California on 11 May 1975.

Charleston The Charleston duration record is 30 hours by 15 members of the Grover Cleveland High School, Reseda, California on 24–25 Jan. 1975.

Flamenco The fastest flamenco dancer ever measured is Solero de Jerez aged 17 who in Brisbane, Australia in Sept. 1967 in an electrifying routine attained 16 heel taps per second or a rate of 1,000 a minute.

Go-go The duration record for go-go dancing (Boogoloo or Reggae) is 110 hours (with 5 min breaks each hour) by Patricia Glenister at Bailey's Nightclub, Leicester on 12–16 May 1975.

223

High Kicking The world record for high kicks is 8,005 in 4 hrs 40 min by Veronica Evans (*née* Steen), (b. Liverpool, 20 Feb. 1910) at the Pathétone Studios, Wardour Street, London in summer 1939.

Jiving The duration record for non-stop jiving is 42 hours 30 min by Ken Troy of Winnipeg, Manitoba, Canada on 22–23 May 1975. Breaks of 5 min per hour are permitted for massage.

Limbo The lowest height for a bar under which a limbo dancer has passed under a flaming bar is 6⅛ in *15,5 cm* off the floor by Marlene Raymond, 15 at the Port of Spain Pavilion, Toronto, Canada on 24 June 1973. Strictly no part of the body other than the sole or side of the foot should touch the ground though the brushing of a shoulder blade does not in practice usually result in disqualification.

Modern The longest recorded dancing marathon (50 min per hour) in modern style is one of 114 hours 12½ min by Albert Harding at the Inn Cognitos, Middlesbrough on 17–22 May 1975.

Tap The fastest *rate* ever measured for any tap dancer has been 1,440 taps per min (24 per sec) by Roy Castle on the B.B.C. T.V. *Record Breakers* programme on 14 Jan. 1973.

Twist The duration record for the twist is 102 hours 28 mins 37 sec by Roger Guy English at La Jolla, California, U.S.A., on 11–16 July 1973.

Dance band The most protracted session for a dance band is one of 321 hours (13 days 9 hours) by the Black Brothers of West Germany at Bonn ending on 2 Feb. 1968. Never less than a quartet were in action during the marathon.

Demolition work Fifteen members of the International Budo Association led by Phil Milner (3rd Dan Karate) demolished a 6-roomed early Victorian house at Idle, Bradford, West Yorkshire by head, foot and empty hand in 6 hours on 4 June 1972. On completion they bowed to the rubble.

Disc-jockey The longest continuous period of acting as a disc-jockey is 630 hours by Chris Day at the Club Mon Cheri, Copenhagen, Denmark on 12 Mar.-8 Apr. 1975. L.P.'s are limited to 50% of total playing time.

Drumming The world's duration drumming record is 228 hours by Frans Verbelen of Londerzeel, Belgium on 28 Feb.-10 Mar. 1975 with 5 min breaks per hour.

Ducks and Drakes The best accepted ducks and drakes (stone-skipping) record is 21 skips (including both plinkers and pitty-pats) by Carl Weinoldt (b. 1909) in an international contest in Copenhagen, Denmark in 1957. The modern video-tape verified record is a 19 skipper by David Bogen of Chicago at Mackinac, Michigan, U.S.A., on 5 July 1974.

Egg dropping The greatest height from which fresh eggs have been dropped and remained intact is 600 ft *182 m* by David Donaghue and John Cartwright from a helicopter on 8 Feb. 1974.

Egg and spoon racing Len Dean and Mike O'Kane of Bournemouth College completed a 27 mile *43,45 km* fresh egg and dessert spoon marathon in 5 hours 38 min on 25 Oct. 1972.

Egg-shelling Two kitchen hands, Harold Witcomb and Gerald Harding shelled 1,050 dozen eggs in a 7¼ hour shift at Bowyers, Trowbridge, Wiltshire on 23 Apr. 1971. Both are blind.

Egg throwing The longest recorded distance for throwing a fresh hen's egg without breaking is 316 ft 5¾ in at their 11th

exchange between David Barger and Craig Finley at Lamar High School, Missouri on 2 May 1974.

Escapology The most renowned of all escape artists has been Ehrich Weiss *alias* Harry Houdini (1874–1926), who pioneered underwater escapes from locked, roped and weighted containers while handcuffed and shackled with irons. Shahid Malik performed an escape from a strait jacket when dangling upside down below a helicopter 700 ft *213 m* from the ground over West Yorkshire, England on 27 May 1974.

Reynir Oern Léossen (born 1938) succeeded in breaking out of a cell in Keflavik prison, Iceland on 23 Sept. 1972 from a cell in which he had been locked with three handcuffs behind his back and his hands tied by 5 mm chains each able to withstand a force of 1 270 kg *2,800 lb*. His feet were fastened with footcuffs and he was further loaded with 5 mm and 10 mm (tensile strength 6 050 kg) chains weighing in all 20 kg *44 lb*. Léossen broke out in five hours and 50 min and emerged through a 28 mm *1.1 in* thick 15 cm *5.9 in* wide glass window which he had "extended" by breaking some of the adjoining brickwork. In a laboratory on 24 May 1972 he demonstrated the ability of parting 10 mm *0.4 in* chain which had a tensile strength of 6 100 kg *13,448 lb. or 6.00 tons*.

Fashion Show The longest fashion show ever recorded was one which lasted for 25 hours 37 min in the Peacock Court of the Mark Hopkins Hotel, San Francisco, California, on 14–15 April 1974, staged by Miss Lorraine's Modeling School and Agency, Los Altos, California. John Chaffetz commented throughout while Rita Mason put in 13.06 miles *21,0 km* on the cat walk in 23 hours.

***Faux Pas* Greatest** If measuring by financial consequence, the greatest *faux pas* on record was that of the young multi-millionaire, James Gordon Bennett, committed on 1 Jan. 1877 at the family mansion of his demure fiancée one Caroline May, in Fifth Avenue, New York City. Bennett arrived in a two-horse cutter late and obviously in wine. By dint of intricate footwork, he gained the portals to enter the withdrawing room where he was the cynosure of all eyes. He mistook the fireplace for a plumbing fixture more usually reserved for another purpose. The May family broke the engagement and Bennett (1841–1918) was obliged to spend the rest of his foot-loose and fancy-free life based in Paris with the resultant non-collection of millions of tax dollars by the U.S. Treasury.

Feminine Beauty Female pulchritude being qualitative rather than quantative does not lend itself to records. It has been suggested that, if the face of Helen of Troy (*circa.* 1200 B.C.) was capable of launching 1,000 ships, a unit of beauty sufficient to launch one ship should be a millihelen. The pioneer beauty contest was staged at Atlantic City, New Jersey, U.S.A. in 1921 and was won by a blue-eyed blonde with a 30 in *76,2 cm* chest, Margaret Gorman. The Miss World contest began in London in July 1951. The maximum dimensions of any winner were those of Miss Egypt, Antigone Costanda, in 1954 whose junoesque characteristics were at 40-26-38 in [*101-66-96 cm*] in advance of the classic Western idea of allure. The United Kingdom is the only country to have produced four winners. They were Rosemarie Frankland (1961); Ann Sidney (1964); Lesley Langley (1965) and Helen Morgan (1974).

Fire Pump pulling The longest unaided tow of a fire appliance was one of 18 cwt. *914 kg* for 123.4 miles *198,5 km* on 26–27 July 1974 from Winchester Guildhall, Hampshire to Littlehampton, West Sussex and return by a team 32 Winchester firemen in 24 hours 2 min.

Flute marathon The longest recorded marathon by a flautist is 40 hours by Joe Silmon at Stockport, Cheshire on 5–6 Aug. 1974.

224

Frisbee throwing Competitive Frisbee throwing began in 1958. The longest throw over level ground on record is one of 285 ft *86,86 m* by Robert F. May in San Francisco on 2 July 1971. John Kirkland got off a throw of 326 ft *99,36 m* at Marquette, Michigan on 6 July 1974 downhill with a tail wind. The marathon record is 374 hours 18 min set at Yale University, New Haven, Connecticut, U.S.A., on 26 Mar.–11 Apr. 1974.

Gold panning The fastest time recorded for "panning" a planted gold nugget is 16.4 sec by Jack Roberts of Hacienda Heights, California in the 1974 World Gold Panning Championships held at Taylor, British Columbia on 2 June 1974. Ms Lilly Szcrupa, a school teacher, took the award for the "world's worst gold panner".

Grape catching The largest recorded distance for catching a thrown grape in the mouth is 165 ft *50,29 m* by Dr. Bruce Dobbs outside Parkview Hospital, Philadelphia on 13 June 1974.

Grave digging It is recorded that Johann Heinrich Karl Thieme, sexton of Aldenburg, Germany, dug 23,311 graves during a 50-year career. In 1826 his understudy dug *his* grave.

Guitar playing The longest recorded solo guitar playing marathon is one of 110¼ hours by Dennis Blakey at the WQYK station, Tampa, Florida on 29 July–3 Aug. 1973.

Gum Boot throwing The longest recorded distance (a Size 8 Blue Star Dunlop Boot) for "Wellie wanging" is 144 ft 10 in *44,14 m* by John Hillier at Weston, Hitchin, Hertfordshire on 7 June 1975.

Gun running The record for the Royal Tournament naval gun run competition (instituted 1900, with present rules since 1919) is 2 min 44.7 sec by the Portsmouth 'Pompey' Crew at Earl's Court, Kensington & Chelsea, Greater London in 1973. The barrel alone weighs 8 cwt. *406 kg*. The wall is 5 ft *1,52 m* high and the chasm 28 ft *8,53 m* across. The Portsmouth crew returned 2 min 40.7 sec in a training practice run at Lee-on-Solent, Hampshire in 1972.

Hair Splitting The greatest reported achievement in hair splitting has been that of Alfred West (b. London, 14 Apr. 1901) who has succeeded in splitting a human hair 13 times into 14 parts.

Hair-dressing The world's most expensive men's hairdresser is Tristan of Hollywood, California, U.S.A. who charges any "client" $100 (£40) on their first visit. This consists of a "consultation" followed by "remedial grooming". Louis Sanft of Fall River, Massachusetts, U.S.A. styled, cut and set hair continuously for 120 hrs 3 mins on 4–9 June 1975.

Handbell ringing The longest recorded handbell ringing recital has been one of 24 hrs by 12 members of the Northampton School for Boys Handbell Ringing Guild on 2–3 July 1975.

Hand-shaking A world record for handshaking was set up by Theodore Roosevelt (1858–1919), President of the U.S.A., when he shook hands with 8,513 people at a New Year's Day, White House Presentation in Washington, D.C., U.S.A. on 1 Jan. 1907. Outside public life the record has become meaningless because aspirants merely tend to arrange circular queues and shake the same hands repetitively.

Hand writing The longest recorded hand writing marathon is one of 80 hours by Miss Sara Morris of Dudley College of Education, Hereford and Worcester on 6–9 June 1975. Her highly legible writing was mostly from the Bible.

HIGH DIVING

The highest regularly performed dive is that of professional divers from La Quebrada ("the break in

Fleet Photo. Unit

The record-breaking 1972 Royal Naval gun running crew from *H.M.S. Excellent* at Portsmouth

the rocks") at Acapulco, Mexico, a height of 118 ft *36 m*. The leader of the 27 divers in the exclusive Club de Clavadistas is Raúl Garcia (b. 1928) with more than 35,000 dives. The base rocks, 21 ft *6,40 m* out from the take-off, necessitate a leap of 27 ft *8,22 m* out. The water is 12 ft *3,65 m* deep. The *Wide World of Sports* record is 130 ft 6 in *39,77 m* jointly set by Donnie Vick, Pat Sucher and John Tobler in March 1974.

On 18 May 1885, Sarah Ann Henley, aged 24, jumped from the Clifton Suspension Bridge, which crosses the Avon, England. Her 250 ft *76 m* fall was slightly cushioned by her voluminous dress and petticoat acting as a parachute. She landed, bruised and bedraggled, in the mud on the Gloucestershire bank and was carried to hospital by four policemen. On 11 Feb. 1968 Jeffrey Kramer, 24, leapt off the George Washington Bridge 250 ft *76 m* above the Hudson River, New York City, N.Y. and survived. Of the 511 (to 25 Apr. 1974) people who have made 240 ft *73 m* suicide dives from the Golden Gate Bridge, San Francisco, California, U.S.A. since 1937 seven survived. On 10 July 1921 a stuntman named Terry leapt from a seaplane into the Ohio River at Louisville, Kentucky. The alleged altitude was 310 ft *94,5 m*.

Samuel Scott (U.S.A.) is reputed to have made a dive of 497 ft *151,48 m* at Pattison Fall (now Manitou Falls) in Wisconsin, U.S.A., in 1840, but this would have entailed an entry speed of 86 m.p.h. *138 km/h*. The actual height was probably 165 ft *50,30 m*. Col. Harry A. Froboess, (Switzerland) jumped 110 m *360 ft* into the Bodensee from the airship *Graf Hindenberg* on 22 June 1936.

Highest Shallow Dive Henri La Mothe (b. 1904) set a record by diving 40 ft *12,20 m* into 12½ in *31,7 cm* of water in a child's paddling pool on Broadway, New York City on 5 Apr. 1974.

Hitch-hiking The title of world champion hitch-hiker is claimed by Devon Smith who from 1947 to 1971 thumbed lifts totalling 291,000 miles *468 300 km*. In 1957 he covered all the then 48 U.S. States in 33 days. It was not till his 6,013th 'hitch' that he got a ride in a Rolls-Royce.

The hitch-hiking record for the 873 miles *1 405 km* from Land's End, Cornwall, to John o' Groats, Caithness, Scotland, is 23 hours 50 min by Pam Vere and Georgina Astley both 22 on 27–28 May 1974. The time before the first "hitch" on the first day is excluded. The fastest time recorded for the round trip is 56 hours by Jun. Technician John Frederick Hornsey R.A.F. on 18–20 Sept. 1974, thus overtaking the 57 hrs 8 mins of Peter W. Ford of Cheltenham set in May 1974.

Hoop rolling In 1968 it was reported that Zolilio Diaz (Spain) had rolled a hoop 600 miles *965 km* from Mieres to Madrid and back in 18 days.

Hop Scotch The longest recorded hop scotch marathon is one of 20 hours 16 min by Jeff Meany and Jonathan Skow at Camp Sambica, Washington, U.S.A. on 25–26 Jan. 1975.

Hot Water Bottle Bursting Currently the leading exponents of bursting hot water bottles by lung power are Mel Robson of Sunderland, Tyne & Wear and Stuart Hughes of Durham City. Robson claims a length of 5 ft 6 in *1,67 m* prior to a burst. A blow-off, against the clock, between the two is to be anticipated on television.

House of cards The greatest number of storeys achieved in building houses of cards is 39 in the case of a tower using 1,240 cards by John Wilson, 15, of Port Credit, Ontario, Canada. The highest house with alternate 8 and 6 card storeys is 30 achieved by Julian Bardo in St. John's College, Cambridge on 14 June 1974. He used 4 packs and a plumb-line.

Mr. Joe E. Whitlam of Deborah Scaffolding Ltd, Barnsley, South Yorkshire by exercise of professional expertize built a structure of 73 storeys to a height of 13 ft 10¼ in *4,22 m* with 1,140 cards on 4–5 July 1974. Added strength was given to the structure by dint of bending some cards into angle supports.

Hula hooping The record for sustaining gyrating hoops is 28 set by DeAnn Deluna winning the 1974 U.S. National championship.

Human cannon-ball The record distance for firing a human from a cannon is 175 ft *53,3 m* in the case of Emanuel Zacchini in the Ringling Bros. and Barnum & Bailey Circus, Madison Square Gardens, New York City, U.S.A., in 1940. His muzzle velocity has been estimated at 54 m.p.h. *86,9 km/h*. On his retirement the management were fortunate in finding that his daughter Florinda was of the same calibre.

In the Halifax explosion of 6 Dec. 1917 (see page 214) A. B. William Becker, A.M. (d. 1969) was blown some 1,600 yd *1,46 km* but was found breathing in a tree.

Igloo marathon Jim Randi, 46 entombed himself unclad in an ice igloo under medical surveillance for 43 min 8 sec in Boston, Massachusetts on 31 Aug. 1974.

Ironing The longest recorded ironing marathon was one won by Mrs. J. Maassen, 37 after 89 hours 32 min in Melbourne, Australia on 9 March 1973.

Joke cracking Bal Moane, the Irish comedian, cracked jokes unremittingly at Caesar's Palace, Luton, Bedfordshire for 3 hours 14½ min on 3 Feb. 1975.

Juggling The only juggler in history able to juggle—as opposed to "shower"—10 balls or eight plates was the Italian Enrico Rastelli, who was born in Samara, Russia, on 19 Dec. 1896 and died in Bergamo, Italy, on 13 Dec. 1931.

Jumble Sale The largest known jumble or rummage sale is that staged annually at Rockford, Illinois. In 1974 it used 847 volunteer workers and raised $21,830.23 (*then £9,095*).

Westminster Press Ltd.

Stuart Hughes well on his way to a hot water bottle burst

Kissing The most prolonged osculatory marathon in cinematic history is one of 185 sec by Regis Toomey and Jane Wyman in *You're In the Army Now* released in 1940. In a 'Smoochathon' at Pretoria, South Africa, Inge Ordendaal and Billy Van Der Westhuizen kissed for 119 hours 12 min. Roger Guy English of La Jolla, California claims to have kissed 3,000 girls in 8 hours—a sustained rate of one per 9.6 secs.

Kiss of Life Five St. John's ambulancemen at Gorleston, Norfolk, on 20–21 July 1974 maintained a "Kiss of life" for 24 hours with 14,400 "inflations". The "patient" was a dummy.

Kite Flying *Largest* The largest kite on record was built in Naruto City, Japan in 1936 of 3,100 panes of paper weighing 8½ tons/tonnes. The largest hand-launched kite was one 83 ft *25,3 m* long and of 820 ft² *76 m²* by Robert Bartlett at Grant Park, Chicago, Illinois, U.S.A. on 28 Apr. 1974.

Altitude The greatest reported height attained by kites is 35,530 ft *10 829 m* by a train of 19 flown near Portage by 10 Gary, Indiana high school boys on 13 June 1969. The flight took 7 hours and was assessed by telescopic triangulation using 56,457 ft *17 208 m* of line. The solo record is 22,500 ft (min)–28,000 ft (max) *6 860 to 8 535 m* by Prof. Phillip R. Kunz at Laramie, Wyoming, U.S.A. on 21 Nov. 1967.

Duration The longest recorded flight is one of 168 hours by Walter Scott at Briny Breezes, Florida in 1967 and recorded in the American Kitefliers Association magazine. The most kites flown on a single string is 261 by William R. Bigge at Burtonville, Maryland, U.S.A. on 5 Oct. 1974.

Knitting The world's most prolific hand-knitter of all time has been Mrs. Gwen Matthewman of Featherstone, West Yorkshire, who in 1974 knitted 836 garments involving 9,770 oz. *152,2 kg* of wool (equivalent to the fleece of 79 sheep). She had been timed to average 108 stitches per min in a 30-min test. Her technique has been filmed by the world's only Professor of Knitting—a Japanese. The longest recorded knitting marathon is one of 93 hrs 25 min by Stan Watin of New York (with 5 min time out allowances per hour), on 17–20 Jan. 1975.

Knot-tying The fastest recorded time for tying the six Boy Scout Handbook Knots (square knot, sheet bend, sheep shank, clove hitch, round turn and two half hitches and bowline) on individual ropes is 10.9 secs by Kenneth

L. Purnell, 13 of Calgary, Alberta, Canada on 23 Feb. 1974.

Leap frogging Fourteen members of the Barker Barracks Club, Senne Lager, West Germany covered 236 miles *379,8 km* in 69 hours 12 min on 24–27 May 1974. The participants averaged 176 leaps per mile.

Lecture The longest recorded lecture was one of 50 hours 6 min by Ronald Lackey of Chopticon High School of Morganza, Maryland, U.S.A., on 25–27 Apr. 1974. He took 2 min intervals each two hours.

Life Saving In November 1974 the City of Galveston, Texas and the Noon Optimist Club unveiled a plaque to the deaf-mute lifeguard Leroy Colombo (1905–1974) who saved 907 people from drowning in the waters around Galveston Island from 1917 to his death.

Lightning most times struck The only living man in the world to be struck by lightning 5 times is Park Ranger Roy C. Sullivan (U.S.), the human lightning conductor of Virginia. His attraction for lightning began in 1942 (lost big toe nail), and was resumed in July 1969 (lost eyebrows), in July 1970 (left shoulder seared), on 16 April 1972 (hair set on fire) and, he hopes finally, on 7 Aug. 1973 (new hair refired and legs seared).

Lion-taming The greatest number of lions mastered and fed in a cage by an unaided lion-tamer was 40, by "Captain" Alfred Schneider in 1925. Clyde Raymond Beatty handled more than 40 "cats" (mixed lions and tigers) simultaneously. Beatty (b. Bainbridge, Ohio, 10 June 1903, d. Ventura, California, 19 July 1965) was the featured attraction at every show he appeared with for more than 40 years. He insisted upon being called a lion-trainer. Twenty-one lion-tamers have died of injuries since 1900.

Log rolling The most protracted log rolling contest on record was one in Chequamegon Bay, Ashland, Wisconsin, U.S.A., in 1900, when Allan Stewart dislodged Joe Oliver from a 24 in *60 cm* diameter log after 3 hours 15 min birling.

Message in a bottle The longest recorded interval between drop and pick up is 64 years between 7 Aug. 1910 ("please write to Miss Gladys Potter") in Grand Lake and August 1974 from Lake Huron. Miss Potter was traced as Mrs. Oliver Scheid, 76 of Colombus, Ohio.

Milk Bottle Balancing The greatest distance walked by a person continuously balancing an empty pint milk bottle on the head is

15 miles 1,738 yds. *25,729 km* by William Charlton at Davenport, Tasmania on 4 June 1972.

Morse The highest recorded speed at which anyone has received morse code is 75.2 words per minute—over 17 symbols per second. This was achieved by Ted R. McElroy of the United States in a tournament at Asheville, North Carolina, U.S.A. on 2 July 1939.

Musical Chairs The longest game on record was one starting with 1,006 participants and 800 chairs and ending with Paul Tobyanson on the last chair at the Ulysses S. Grant High School, Van Nuys, California on 18 Apr. 1975.

Needle threading The record number of strands of cotton threaded through a number 13 needle (eye $\frac{1}{2}$ in by $\frac{1}{16}$ of an in *12,7 mm × 1,6 mm*) in 2 hours is 3,795 by Miss Brenda Robinson of the College of Further Education, Chippenham, Wiltshire on 20 March 1971.

Noodle making Stephen Yim (b. Shanghai, China, 1949) made 256 noodle strings (over 5 ft [*1,52 m*]) in 63 sec on the B.B.C T.V. *Record Breakers* programme on 21 Oct. 1973.

Omelette making The greatest number of two-egg omelettes made in 30 min is 105 (26 min 25 sec) by Clement Raphael Freud (later M.P.) (b. 24 Apr. 1924) with a single pan at The Victoria, Nottingham on 15 July 1971.

Pancake tossing Mrs. Sally Cutter at the Island Club, Limassol, Cyprus on Shrove Tuesday, 26 Feb. 1974 achieved 5,010 tosses in 65 min.

Paper Chains The longest recorded paper link chain made in under 24 hours has been one of 8 miles 897 yd *13,71 km* by children at Thorpe-le-Soken Centre, Essex on 24–25 May 1975. They used 125,000 staples.

PARACHUTING

Longest fall without a parachute The greatest altitude from which anyone has bailed out without a parachute and survived is 6 700 m *21,980 ft.* This occurred in January 1942, when Lt. (now Lt.-Col.) I. M. Chisov (U.S.S.R.) fell from an Ilyushin 4 which had been severely damaged. He struck the ground a glancing blow on the edge of a snow-covered ravine and slid to the bottom. He suffered a fractured pelvis and severe spinal damage. It is estimated that the human body reaches 99 per cent of its low level terminal velocity after falling 1,880 ft *573 m* which takes 13 to 14 sec. This is 117–125 m.p.h. *188–201 km/h* at normal atmospheric pressure in a random posture, but up to 185 m.p.h. *298 km/h* in a head down position.

PARACHUTING RECORDS

First from Tower	Sébastian Lenormand	quasi-parachute	Lyons, France	1783
First from Balloon	André-Jacques Garnerin (1769–1823)	2,230 ft *680 m*	Monceau Park, Paris	22 Oct. 1797
First from Aircraft (man)	Capt. Albert Berry	U.S. Army	St. Louis, Missouri	1 Mar. 1912
(woman)	Mrs. Georgina 'Tiny' Broadwick (b. 1893)		Griffith Park, Los Angeles	21 June 1913
	Mrs. Georgina 'Tiny' Broadwick	Pilot Glenn L. Martin	North Island, San Diego, California	13 Sept. 1914
Lowest Escape	S/Ldr. Terence Spencer, R.A.F.	30–40 ft *9–12 m*	Wismer Bay, Baltic	19 April 1945
Longest Duration Fall	Lt. Col. Wm. H. Rankin U.S.M.C.	40 min due to thermals	North Carolina	26 July 1956
Highest Escape	Flt. Lt. J. de Salis and Fg. Off. P. Lowe, R.A.F.	56,000 ft *17 068 m*	Monyash, Derby	9 April 1958
Longest Delayed Drop (man)	Capt. Joseph W. Kittinger[1]	84,700 ft 16.04 miles *25 816 m* from balloon at 102,800 ft *31 333 m*	Tularosa, North Mexico	16 Aug. 1960
(woman)	O. Kommissarova (U.S.S.R.)	14 100 ft *46,250 ft*	over U.S.S.R.	21 Sept. 1965
(civilian)	John Noakes (G.B.)	22,000 ft from 25,000 ft *7 620 m*	Salisbury Plain, Wiltshire	15 May 1973
Most Southerly	T/Sgt. Richard J. Patton (d. 1973)	Operation Deep Freeze	South Pole	25 Nov. 1956
Most Northerly	Ray Munro (Canada)	−39° F (−39,4° C)	In 89° 39′ N	31 Mar. 1969
Career Total	Lt.-Col. Ivan Savkin (U.S.S.R.)	More than 5,000	over U.S.S.R.	12 Aug. 1967
	Patty Wilson	More than 1,000	Elsinore paracenter, California	Nov. 1973
Highest Landing	Ten U.S.S.R. parachutists[2]	23,405 ft *7 133 m*	Lenina Peak	May 1969
Heaviest Load	U.S.A.F. C-130 Hercules	22.52 tons *22,88 tonnes* steel plates 6 parachutes	El Centro, California	28 Jan. 1970
Highest from Bridge	Donald R. Boyle	1,053 ft *320 m*	Royal Gorge, Colorado	7 Sept. 1970
Highest Tower Jump	Herbert Leo Schmidtz (U.S.A.)	KTUL-TV Mast 1,984 ft *604 m*	Tulsa, Oklahoma	4 Oct. 1970
Biggest Star	29 "National Enquirer" Skydiving Team	Connected free fall (3 sec. min)	Zephyr Hill, Florida	25 Mar. 1974
Most Travelled	Kevin Seaman from a Cessna Skylane (pilot Charles E. Merritt)	12,186 miles *19 611 km*	Jumps in all 50 U.S. States	26 July–15 Oct. 1972
Oldest Man	Archie Macfarlane (G.B.)	aged 76 years 6 months	Tilstock, Salop, England	4 Aug. 1974
Woman	Mrs. Cecilia Reeser (U.S.)	aged 62 years	Flint, Michigan, U.S.A.	15 Aug. 1972
24 Hour Total	Jean Pierre Blanchet (Canada)	232 in 24 hrs	Quebec City, Canada	9–10 Sept. 1972

[1] *Maximum speed in rarified air was 614 m.p.h. 988 km/h.*
[2] *Four were killed.*

Vesna Vulovic, 23 a Jugoslavenski Aerotransport hostess, survived when her DC9 blew up at 33,330 ft *10 160 m* over the Czechoslovak village of Ceská Kamenice on 26 Jan. 1972. She fell inside a section of tail unit. She attended hospital for 17 months.

The British record is 18,000 ft *5 485 m* by Flt.-Sgt. Nicholas Stephen Alkemade, aged 21, who jumped from a blazing R.A.F. *Lancaster* bomber over Germany on 23 March 1944. His headlong fall was broken by a fir tree and he landed without a broken bone in a snow bank 18 in *45 cm* deep.

Piano-playing The longest piano-playing marathon has been one of 1,091 hours (45 days 11 hours) playing 22 hours every day from 11 Oct. to 24 Nov. 1970 by James Crowley, Jr., 30 at Scranton, Pennsylvania, U.S.A. The British record is 200 hours 35 mins (with 5 min breaks each hour) set by Michael George of Cheadle Heath, Stockport in a music shop in Edgware Road, London on 12–21 Aug. 1974. The women's world record is 133 hours (5 days 13 hours) by Mrs. Marie Ashton aged 40, in a theatre in Blyth, Northumberland, on 18–23 Aug. 1958.

Piano smashing The record time for demolishing an upright piano and passing the entire wreckage through a circle 9 in *22,8 cm* in diameter is 2 min 26 sec by six men representing Ireland led by Johnny Leydon of Sligo, at Merton, Greater London on 7 Sept. 1968. Messrs Dave Gibbons, Les Hollis and "Ginger" O'Regan smashed a piano with bare hands in 14 minutes in Guernsey on 20 July 1974.

Piano Tuning The record time for pitch raising (almost two semi-tones) and then returning a piano to a musically acceptable quality is 30 mins 9 secs by Steve Fairchild at the Nassau Chapter of the Piano Technicians Guild Inc., New York on 12 Nov. 1974.

Pillar box standing The record number of people to pile on top of a pillar box (oval top of 6 ft² [*0,55 m²*]) is 29, all students of the City of London College, Moorgate, in Finsbury Circus, City of London on 21 Oct. 1971.

Pipe smoking The duration record for keeping a pipe (3.3 g [*0.1 oz*] of tobacco) continuously alight with only an initial match is 253 min 28 sec by Yrjö Pentikäinen of Kuopio, Finland on 15–16 March 1968.

Plate spinning The greatest number of plates spun simultaneously is 44 by Holley Gray, on the *Blue Peter* T.V. show at the B.B.C. T.V. Centre, Hammersmith, Greater London on 18 May 1970.

Pogo Stick Jumping The greatest number of jumps achieved is 40,002 in 6 hr 6 min by Douglas K. Ziegler of Allentown, Pennsylvania, U.S.A. on 5 Oct. 1974.

Pole-squatting Modern records do not, in fact, compare with that of St. Daniel (A.D. 409–493), called Stylites (Greek, *stylos*=pillar), a monk who spent 33 years 3 months on a stone pillar in Syria. This is probably the earliest example of record setting.

There being no international rules, the "standards of living" atop poles vary widely. The record squat is 273 days by Rick Weeks, 43 from 9 Mar. to 7 Dec. 1974 in a camper atop a 32 ft *9,75 m* pole in Augusta, Georgia, U.S.A.

The British record is 32 days 14 hours by John Stokes, aged 32, of Moseley, West Midlands in a barrel on a 45 ft *13,70 m* pole in Birmingham, West Midlands ending on 27 June 1966. This is claimed as a world record for a barrel.

"Pond" baling The record for baling a "village pond" with a No. 1 size sewing thimble is 168 gal *763,7 litres* in 12 hours by 12 children of the Chesterfield Young Oxfam Group on 15 Mar. 1975.

Pop group The duration record for a 4-man pop-playing group is 140 hours 34 min by "The Animation" in St. Andrews Church Hall, Liverpool from 22–28 July 1974. The group at no time sank below a trio.

Pram pushing The greatest distance covered in pushing a pram in 24 hours is 319 miles *513 km* on a track by a 60 strong team from the White Horse Sports and Social Club, Stony Stratford, Buckinghamshire on 19–20 May 1973. A team of 10 with an adult "baby" from "Flore Moderns" covered 226.1 miles *363,8 km* at Flore, Northamptonshire in 24 hours on 28–29 June 1975.

Fastest "psych-iatrist" The world's fastest "psychiatrist" was Dr. Albert L. Weiner of Erlton, New Jersey, U.S.A., who was trained solely in osteopathy but who dealt with up to 50 psychiatric patients a day in four treatment rooms. He relied heavily on narcoanalysis, muscle relaxants and electro-shock treatments. In December 1961 he was found guilty on 12 counts of manslaughter from using unsterilized needles.

Quoit throwing The world's record for rope quoit throwing is an unbroken sequence of 4,002 pegs by Bill Irby, Snr. of Australia in 1968.

Riding in armour The longest recorded ride in full armour is one of 146 miles *234,9 km* from Glasgow to Dumfries *via* Lanark and Peebles, Scotland in 3 days 3 hrs 40 min by Dick Brown, 42 on 12–15 June 1973.

Dick Brown riding through the streets of Dumfries in full armour

Record House, Glasgow

Riveting The world's record for riveting is 11,209 in 9 hours by J. Moir at the Workman Clark Ltd. shipyard, Belfast, Northern Ireland, in June 1918. His peak hour was his seventh with 1,409, an average of nearly 23½ per min.

Rocking chair The longest recorded duration of a "Rockathon" is 320 hrs by Gilbert Nordan at Young Ford Inc. Car Saleroom, Charlotte, North Carolina on 5–18 Apr. 1975.

Rolling pin The record distance for a woman to throw a 2 lb. *907 g* rolling pin is 157 ft 6 in *48,00 m* by Janet Thompson at West London Stadium, Wormwood Scrubs, Greater London on 6 July 1975.

Rope tricks The only man to demonstrate the ability to spin 12 ropes simultaneously has been Roy Vincent (b 1910) of Gloversville, N.Y. in the period 1933–53.

Scooter riding The greatest distance covered by a team of 25 in 24 hours is 326.15 miles *524,88 km* by the Warrack-nabeal High School, Victoria, Australia 16–17 Aug. 1973.

Search **Longest** In October 1972 Frank Jones of Lowestoft, Suffolk ended a 68 year long search by locating his missing brother Arthur Jones.

See-saw The most protracted session for see-sawing is one of 624 hours (26 days) by Greg Fox and Steve Bennett of San Leandro, California, U.S.A. on 18 June–14 July 1974 with only 5 minute breaks per hour.

Sermon The longest sermon on record was delivered by Clinton Locy of West Richland, Washington, U.S.A., in February 1955. It lasted 48 hours 18 min and ranged through texts from every book in the Bible. A congregation of eight was on hand at the close. From 31 May to 10 June 1969 the 14th Dalai Lama (b. 6 July 1934) the exiled ruler of Tibet, completed a sermon on Tantric Buddhism for five to seven hours per day to total 60 hours in India.

Shaving The fastest demon barber on record is Gerry Harley, who shaved 130 men in 60 min with a cut-throat razor at The Plough, Gillingham, Kent on 1 April 1971. In an attempt to set a marathon he ran out of volunteer subjects.

Sheaf tossing The world's best performance for tossing an 8 lb. *3 kg 620* sheaf is 56 ft *17,06 m* by C. R. Wiltshire of Geelong, Victoria, Australia in 1956. Contests date from 1914.

Shoeshine Boys In this category (limited to a team of 4 teenagers; duration of 8 hours; shoes 'on the hoof') the record is 4,314 pairs by the Goscote Boys Club in The Square, Walsall, West Midlands on 20 July 1974.

Fastest shorthand The highest recorded speeds ever attained under championship conditions are: 300 words per min (99.64 per cent accuracy) for five minutes and 350 w.p.m. (99.72 per cent accuracy, that is, two insignificant errors) for two minutes by Nathan Behrin (U.S.A.) in tests in New York in December 1922. Behrin (b. 1887) used the Pitman system invented in 1837. Morris I. Kligman, official court reporter of the U.S. Court House, New York has taken 50,000 words in five hours (a sustained rate of 166.6 w.p.m.). Rates are much dependent upon the nature, complexity and syllabic density of the material. Mr. G. W. Bunbury of Dublin, Ireland held the unique distinction of writing at 250 w.p.m. for 10 min on 23 Jan. 1894.

Currently the fastest shorthand writer in Britain is Mrs. June Meader (*née* Swan) of North Finchley, Barnet, Greater London with a Pitman's Certificate for 230 w.p.m. She demonstrated the ability to write at the *rate of* 260 w.p.m. with a syllabic density of 1.5, on the B.B.C. T.V. Show *Record Breakers* on 31 Dec. 1972.

In Great Britain only four shorthand writers have passed the official Pitman test at 250 w.p.m. for five min:

Miss Edith Ulrica Pearson of London, on 30 June 1927.
Miss Emily Doris Smith of London, on 22 March 1934.
Miss Beatrice W. Solomon of London, in March 1942.
Mrs. Audrey Boyes (*née* Bell) of Finchley, Barnet, Greater London, in 1956.

Shouting The greatest number of wins in the national town criers' contest is eight by Herbert T. Waldron of Great Torrington, Devon. He won every year from 1957 to 1965, except for 1959. (See also Longest-ranged voice, Chapter I.) He retired in Sept. 1971.

Showering The most prolonged continuous shower bath on record is one of 175 hours 7 min by David Foreman at Niagara University, N.Y. U.S.A. on 25 Oct.–2 Nov. 1973. The feminine record is 98 hours 1 min by Paula Glenn, 18 and Margaret Nelson, 20 in Britain on 24 Nov. 1971.

Singing The longest recorded solo singing marathon is one of 105 hours by Eamon McGirr at The Bower Club, Stalybridge, Manchester on 5–10 Aug. 1974. The marathon record for a choir has been 33 hours by the Sixth Form of Bingley Beckfoot Grammar School, Bingley, West Yorkshire on 30 June to 1 July 1975.

The last performance in the now discontinued category of singing without 5 minute breaks per hour was one of 9 hours by Robert Manderson of Great Shalford, Cambridgeshire on 2 Feb. 1975.

Skipping The greatest number of turns ever performed without a break is 43,473 turns in 5 hours by Rabbi Barry Silberg in Milwaukee, Wisconsin on 22 June 1975.

Other records made without a break:

Most turns in one jump	5 by Katsumi Suzuki, Tokyo, early 1968.
Most turns in 1 min	286 by J. Rogers, Melbourne, 10 Nov. 1937.
	and T. Lewis, Melbourne, 16 Sept. 1939.
Most turns in 10 secs	57 by Lu Ann Stolt (U.S.), Bloomer, Wisconsin 1972.
Double turns	2,001 by K. Brooks, Brisbane, Jan. 1955.
Treble turns	70 by J. Rogers, Melbourne, 17 Sept. 1951.
Duration	1,264 miles *2 034 km* by Tom Morris, Brisbane-Cairns, Queensland, 1963.

Slinging The greatest distance recorded for a sling-shot is 1,147 ft 4 in *349,70 m* using a 34 in *86 cm* long sling and a 7½ oz. *212 g* stone by Melvyn Gaylor on Newport Golf Course, Shide, Isle of Wight on 25 Sept. 1970.

Smoke ring blowing The highest recorded number of smoke rings formed from a single pull of a cigarette is 169 rings by Keith Harraway of Harold Hill, Essex on 12 July 1974.

Snakes and Ladders The longest recorded game of Snakes and Ladders has been one of 121 hours by a team of 6 (4 always in play) from Moorside High School, Stoke on Trent on 10–15 Feb. 1975.

Snow Shoeing The fastest time recorded for covering a mile *1 609,34 m* is 5 min 18.6 sec by Clifton Cody (U.S.) at Somersworth, New Haven, on 19 Feb. 1939.

"Space Hopping" The highest "space-hopper" high jump on the BBC T.V. show "Why Don't You" has been one of 30 in *76,2 cm* by Janina Pulaski on 26 May 1975.

Spinning The duration record for spinning a clock balance wheel by hand is 5 min 26.8 sec by Philip Ashley, aged 16, of Leigh, Greater Manchester on 20 May 1968.

Spitting The greatest distance achieved at the annual tobacco spitting classic (instituted 1955) at Raleigh, Mississippi is 27 ft 6 in *8,38 m* by John Raymond Tullos on 28 July 1974. In the 3rd International Spittin', Belchin' and Cussin' Triathlon Harold Fielden reached 34 ft 0¼ in *10,36 m* at Central City, Colorado U.S.A. on 13

July 1973. Distance is dependent on the quality of salivation, absence of cross wind, two finger pressure and the coordination of the quick hip and neck snap. Sprays or wads smaller than a dime are not measured. The record for projecting a melon seed is under WCWSSCA rules is 57 ft 8½ in *17,58 m* by Russ Foster at Weatherford, Oklahoma on 4 Aug. 1973. The highest reported distance for a cherry stone spat from a sitting position is 38 ft 3½ in by Malcolm Dunlop near Harrogate, North Yorkshire on 29 June 1974. Spitters who care about their image wear 12 in *30,4 cm* block-ended boots so practice spits can be measured without a tape.

Standing The longest period on record that anyone has continuously stood is 17 years in the case of Swami Maujgiri Maharij when performing the *Tapasya* or penance from 1955 to November 1973 in Shahjahanpur Uttar Pradesh, India. When sleeping he would lean against a plank.

Stilt-walking The highest stilts ever successfully mastered were more than 21 ft *6,40 m* from the ankle to the ground by Henry Edward Yelding ("Harry Sloan") 1902–1971 of Great Yarmouth, Norfolk. Hop stringers use stilts up to 15 ft *4,57 m*. In 1892 M. Garisoain of Bayonne stilt-walked the last 8 km *4.97 miles* into Biarritz in 42 min to average 11,42 km/h *7.10 m.p.h.* In 1891 Sylvain Dornon stilt-walked from Paris to Moscow *via* Vilno in 50 stages for the 1,830 miles *2 945 km*. Another source gives his time as 58 days.

Stretcher bearing The longest recorded carry of a stretcher case with a 10 st. *63,5 kg* "body" is 62 miles *99,77 km* in 17 hrs 30 mins by two 4 men teams from the St. John's Ambulance Brigade (British Rail Division) at Rugby, England on 29–30 Mar. 1975.

The record limited to Venture Scouts (under 18) and 10 hours carrying is 26 miles *41,8 km* by 8 members of the Churchtown unit, Gloucestershire on 23 Mar. 1974.

String Ball Largest The largest balls of string on record are ones both of 11 ft *3,35 m* in diameter, weighing 4½ tons/*tonnes* amassed by Francis A. Johnson of Darwin, Minnesota, U.S.A., since 1950 and Frank Stoeber of Cawker City, Kansas since at least 1962.

Submergence The longest submergence in a dry suit is 100 hours 3 min by Mrs. Jane Lisle Baldasare, aged 24, at Pensacola, Florida, U.S.A., ending on 24 Jan. 1960. Mrs. Baldasare also holds the feminine underwater distance record at 14 miles *22,5 km*. The record for a wet suit is 88 hours 2 min by Brian Foulds, 23 of the Blackpool & Fylde Sub-Aqua Club at the Imperial Hotel on 4–8 May 1975.

Suggestion boxes The most prolific example on record of the use of any suggestion box scheme is that of John Drayton (b. 13 Sept. 1907) of Pontypool, Gwent who plied British Rail and the companies from which it was formed with a total of 26,500 suggestions since 1924.

Swinging The record duration for continuous swinging is 120 hours by Diane Elin and Dana Calderwood at Indian Hills Swim & Tennis Club, Riverside, California on 15–20 Apr. 1974. Both swung all the time except for one at a time rest-breaks of a maximum 5 min per completed hour.

Switchback riding The world distance record for rides on a roller coaster is 470.9 miles *757,84 km* (728 circuits) on the Kings Island roller, Cincinnati, Ohio, U.S.A. by Ralph Rice, Mike Meier, Joe Hummer and Miss "Corky" Lamb in 36 hours on 31 May–1 June 1974. The endurance record is 52 hr 32 min (764 circuits) at Fun City, Lake of the Ozarks, Missouri by Bob Gibson on 27–29 June 1974.

Tailoring The highest speed in which the making of a 2 piece suit has been made from sheep to finished article is 1 hour 52 min 18.5 sec to the order of Bud Macken of Mascot, N.S.W., Australia on 23 Dec. 1931. The shearing took 35 sec, the carding and teasing 19 min and the weaving 20 min.

Talking The world record for non-stop talking is 138 hours (5 days 18 hours) by Victor Villimas of Cleveland, Ohio, U.S.A. in Leeds, West Yorkshire, England, from 25–31 Oct. 1967. The longest continuous political speech on record was one of 29 hours 5 min by Gerard O'Donnell in Kingston-upon-Hull, Humberside on 23–24 June 1959. The longest recorded lecture was one of 45 hours on "The Christian Faith and its Response" by the Rev. Roger North, 26, at Hartley Victoria Methodist College, Greater Manchester on 15–17 May 1971.

A feminine non-stop talking record was set by Mrs. Mary E. Davis, who on 2–7 Sept. 1958 started at a radio station in Buffalo, New York and did not draw breath until 110 hours 30 min 5 secs later in Tulsa, Oklahoma U.S.A.

The longest after-dinner speech on record is one of 3 hours by the Rev. Henry Whithead (d. March 1896) at the Rainbow Tavern, Fleet Street, London on 16 Jan. 1874.

T-bone dive The so-called T-bone dives or Dive Bomber crash by cars off ramps over and onto parked cars are often measured by the number of cars, but owing to their variable size and that their purpose is purely to cushion the shock, distance is more significant. The longest recorded distance is 176 ft *53,6 m* by Dusty Russell in a 1963 Ford Falcon at Athens, Georgia in April 1973.

Dick Sheppard of the Disaster Squad, Gloucester, England has crashed 1,031 cars to destruction from Dec. 1951 to April 1975.

Ramp Jumping The longest distance claimed for motor cycle long jumping over cars is 171 ft *52,12 m* over 22 cars by Bob Gill (b. St. Peterberg, Florida 26 Sept. 1945) at the Seattle International Raceway, Washington on 17 July 1973. Evel Knievel (b. Robert Craig Knievel, 17 Oct. 1938 at Butte, Montana, U.S.A.) had suffered 433 bone fractures by his 1975 season. His ramp jump of 136 ft *41,4 m* over 12 of the 13 buses provided at Wembley Stadium, London on 26 May 1975 was the longest attempted in Britain. His abortive attempt to cross the Snake River Canyon, Idaho on 8 Sept. 1974 in a rocket reputedly increased his life-time earnings by $6 million (£2½ *million*). The longest car jump recorded is one of 62 metres *203 ft* into water by the stuntman Roland van de Putte (Belgium) in a Volkswagen on 11 Aug. 1968.

Teeth-pulling The man with "the strongest teeth in the world" is "Hercules" John Massis of St. Amandsberg, Belgium, who on 4 Apr. 1974 demonstrated the ability to pull two Long Island railway trucks weighing 80 U.S. tons *72,5 tonnes* along rails with a bit in his teeth.

TIGHTROPE WALKING
The greatest 19th century tightrope walker was Jean François Gravelet, *alias* Charles Blondin (1824–1897), of France, who made the earliest crossing of the Niagara Falls on a 3 in *76 mm* rope, 1,100 ft *335 m* long, 160 ft *48,75 m* above the Falls on 30 July 1855. He also made a crossing with Harry Colcord, pick-a-back on 15 Sept. 1860. Though other artists find it difficult to believe, Colcord was his agent.

Endurance The world tightrope endurance record is 185 days by Henri Rochetain (b. 1926) of France on a wire 394 ft *120 m* long, 82 ft *25 m* above a supermarket in Saint Etienne, France on 28 Mar.–29 Sept. 1973. His ability to sleep on the wire has left doctors puzzled. He walked some 500 km *310 miles* on the wire to keep fit.

Longest The longest walk by any funambulist was achieved by Henri Rochetain (b. 1926) of France on a wire 3,790 yds *3 465 m* long slung across a gorge at Clermont Ferrand, France on 13 July 1969. He required 3 hours 20 min to negotiate the crossing.

The first crossing of the River Thames was achieved by Franz Burbach, 31 on an 800 ft *243 m* wire 55 ft *16,75 m* above the water in 13 min on 25 Aug. 1972.

High-wire act The greatest drop beneath any high wire performance has been from a 140 ft *42,6 m* wire between the 1,350 ft *Highest* *411 m* twin towers of the World Trade Center, New York City by Phillipe Petit, 24 of Nemours, France on 7 Aug. 1974. He was charged with criminal trespass after a 75 minute display of at least 7 crossings. The police psychiatrist opined "Anyone who does this 110 storeys up can't be entirely right".

Treasure Finding The most successful treasure hunter has been C. Fred Ahrendt of Dayton, Ohio, who by Aug. 1974 has found with his metal detector 158 class rings (earliest, 1890) and 149 wedding rings of 14 or more carats. Employees of crematoria are officially excluded from competition.

Tree-climbing The fastest tree-climbing record is one of 36 sec for a 90 ft *27,32 m* pine by Kelly Stanley (Canada) at the Toowoomba Show, Queensland, Australia in 1968.

Tree-sitting The duration record for sitting in a tree is 57 days 20 hrs 53 min by Michael Zeleny, 21 in a red bud at Kingsbury, California from 22 Apr. to 19 June 1974.

Tunnel of fire The significance of the length of a tunnel of fire depends largely upon its dimensions. A height and width of 6 ft 8 in *2,03 m* is now becoming standard. The longest such run is one of 126 ft *38,40 m* by James Dylan at Caenby Corner, Lincolnshire, England on 22 June 1975.

TYPEWRITING

Fastest The highest recorded speeds attained with a ten-word penalty per error on a manual machine are:

One Min: 170 words, Margaret Owen (U.S.A.) (Underwood Standard), New York, 21 Oct. 1918.
One Hour: 147 words (net rate per min) Albert Tangora (U.S.A.) (Underwood Standard), 22 Oct. 1923.

The official hour record on an electric machine is 9,316 words (40 errors) on an I.B.M. machine, giving a net rate of 149 words per min, by Margaret Hamma, now Mrs. Dilmore (U.S.A.), in Brooklyn, New York City, N.Y., U.S.A. on 20 June 1941. Mrs. Barbara Blackburn of Lee's Summit, Missouri has sustained speeds of 170 w.p.m. using the Dvorak Simplified Keyboard (D.S.K.) system.

In an official test in 1946 Stella Pajunas now Mrs. Garnand attained a speed of 216 words in a minute on an I.B.M. machine.

Slowest Chinese typewriters were so complex that even the most skilled operator could not select characters from the 1,500 offered at a rate of more than 11 words a minute. The Hoang typewriter first produced in 1962 now has 5,850 Chinese characters. The keyboard is 2 ft *60 cm* wide and 17 in *43 cm* high.

Longest The world duration record for typewriting on an electric machine is 154 hours 22 mins by Noreen Smith of Benson, Oxfordshire, England on 24–30 June 1974. Mrs. Marva Drew, 51 of Waterloo, Iowa U.S.A. between 1968 and 30 Nov. 1974 typed numbers 1 to 1,000,000 on a manual typewriter on 2,473 pages. Asked why she replied "But I love to type".

The longest duration typing marathon on a manual machine is 120 hours 15 min by Mike Howell, a 23 year-old blind office worker from Greenfield, Oldham, Greater Manchester on 25–30 Nov. 1969 on

The indefatigable Mrs. Marva Drew having typed all the numbers from 1 to a million

Waterloo Courier, Iowa

an Olympia manual typewriter in Liverpool. In aggregating 561,006 strokes he performed a weight movement of 2,482 tons *2 521 tonnes* plus a further 155 tons *157 tonnes* on moving the carriage for line spacing.

Unsupported Circle The highest recorded number of people who have demonstrated the physical paradox of all being seated without a chair is an unsupported circle of 1,306 (variously 1,311) students of Auckland University, New Zealand, organised by Albatross Enterprises, in Albert Park on 6 May 1974.

Walking on hands The duration record for walking on hands is 1 400 km *871 miles* by Johann Hurlinger, of Austria, who in 55 daily 10-hour stints, averaged 1.58 m.p.h. *2,54 km/h* from Vienna to Paris in 1900. Rick Murphy at Weston Michigan University, Kalamazoo U.S.A. on 3 Oct. 1974 completed an inverted 50 yard *45,72 m* sprint in 25.7 secs.

Wall of death The greatest endurance feat on a wall of death was 3 hours 4 min by the motorcyclist Louis W. "Speedy" Babbs on a silo, 32 ft *9,75 m* in diameter refuelling in motion, at the Venice Amusement Pier, California on 11 Oct. 1929. In 1934 Babbs performed 1,003 consecutive loop the loops sitting side-saddle in a globe 18 ft *5,48 m* at Ocean Park Pier, California, U.S.A. In a life of stunting, Babbs, who proclaims "Stuntmen are not fools", has broken 56 bones.

Whip cracking The longest stock whip ever "cracked" (*i.e.* the end made to travel above the speed of sound—760 m.p.h. *1 223 km/h* is one of 80 ft first cracked by Frank Dean (U.S.) at North Dakota State Fair in 1939.

Wood-cutting The earliest competitions date from Tasmania in 1874. The best times ever recorded on Australian hardwoods in competition on 12 in *30,4 cm* logs are thus:

Underhand	20.0 sec	Gus De Blanc	1921
Standing Block	13.7 sec	C. Stewart	1965
Hard Hitting	17 hits	G. Parker and Tom Kirk	1958
Tree Felling	1 min 20.0 sec	Bill Youd	1970

The fastest times ever recorded for double-handed sawing an 18 in *45,7 cm* block of Lombardy poplar is 8.0 sec by Merv. Reed and Nelson Thorburn at Hukerenui, N.Z. on 8 Feb. 1958.

231

Writing under handicap The ultimate feat in "funny writing" would appear to be the ability to write extemporaneously and decipherably backwards, upside down, laterally inverted (mirror-style) while blindfolded with both hands simultaneously. Several close approaches to this are under investigation

Minuscule writing Larry R. Yates of McMinnville, Oregon, U.S.A. has manually engraved the Lord's Prayer within a square millimetre 1/645th in² with a pivot-arm device of his own invention. William R. Woodbridge, 46 of Harrow, England demonstrated in Nov. 1974 the ability without mechanical or optical aid to write the Lord's Prayer 10 times (2,700 words) within the size of a definitive U.K. postage stamp (viz. 0.84 × 0.71 of an inch *21,1 × 18,2 cm*.

Yodelling The most protracted yodel on record was that of Bill Gore, 38 for 5 hrs 3 mins in Birmingham, England on 9 Jan. 1975.

Yo-yo The yo-yo originates from a Filipino jungle fighting weapon recorded in the 16th century weighing 4 lb. with a 20 ft *6 m* cord. The word means "come-come". Though illustrated in a book in 1891 as a bandilore the craze did not begin until it was started by Louis Marx (U.S.A.) in 1929. The most difficult modern yo-yo trick is the double-handed cross-over loop the loop. Sam Konugres achieved 5,753 (consecutive) loop the loops at the Odd Ball Olympics on 5 May 1974. The individual continuous endurance record is 55 hours by

Gary Martin, 14 of Chesapeake, Virginia, U.S.A. on 19–21 July 1974. The highest number of oscillations recorded in 60 min is 4,053 by David Gillibrand at Aberystwyth, Dyfed, Wales on 1 Feb. 1974.

Largest circus The world's largest permanent circus is Circus Circus Las Vegas, Nevada, U.S.A. opened on 18 Oct. 1968 at a cost of $15,000,000 (*then £6,250,000*). It covers an area of 129,000 ft² *11 984 m²* capped by a tent-shaped flexiglass roof 90 ft *27,43 m* high. The new Moscow Circus, completed in 1968, has a seating capacity of 3,200.

WEALTH AND POVERTY

The measurement of extreme personal wealth is beset with intractable difficulties. Quite apart from reticence and the element of approximation in estimating the valuation of assets, as Mr. Getty (see below) once said "if you can count your millions you are not a billionaire". The term millionaire was invented *c.* 1740 and billionaire in 1861. The earliest dollar billionaires were John Davison Rockefeller (1839–1937); Henry Ford (1863–1947) and Andrew William Mellon (1855–1937). In 1937, the last year all 3 were alive, a billion U.S. dollars were worth £205 million but that amount of sterling would today have a purchasing power of in excess £1,400 million.

Living Billionaires There are currently four proclaimed U.S. dollar billionaires (a billion dollars is now £435,000,000);

CIRCUS RECORDS

The following circus acrobatic feats represent the greatest performed, either for the first time or, if marked with an asterisk, uniquely. A "mechanic" is a safety harness.

Flying Trapeze	Earliest Act	Jules Léotard (France)	Circus Napoléon, Paris	12 Nov. 1859
	Double back somersault	Eddie Silbon	Paris Hippodrome	1879
	Triple back somersault (female)	Lena Jordan (Latvia) to Lew Jordan (U.S.A.)	Sydney, Australia	April 1897
	Triple back somersault (male)	Ernest Clarke to Charles Clarke	Publiones Circus, Cuba	1909
	Triple and half back somersault	Tony Steel to Lee Strath Marilees	Durango, Mexico	30 Sept. 1962
	Quadruple back somersault (in practice)	*Ernest Clarke to Charles Clarke	Orrin Bros. Circus, Mexico City, Mexico	1915
	Triple back somersault (bar to bar, practice)	Edmund Ramat and Raoul Monbar	Various	1905–10
	Head to head stand on swinging bar (no holding)	*Ed and Ira Millette (*née* Wolf)	Various	1910–20
Horse back	Running leaps on and off	*26 by "Poodles" Hanneford	New York	1915
	Three-high column without "mechanic"	*Willy, Baby and Rene Fredianis	Nouveau Cirque, Paris	1908
	Double back somersault mounted	(John or Charles) Frederic Clarke	Various	*c.* 1905
	Double back somersault from a 2-high to a trailing horse with "mechanic"	Aleksandr Sergey	Moscow Circus	1956
Fixed Bars	Pass from 1st to 3rd bar with a double back somersault	Phil Shevette, Andres Atayde	Woods Gymnasium, New York, European tours	1925–27
	Triple fly-away to ground (male)	Phil Shevette	Folies Bergere, Paris	May 1896
	Triple fly-away to ground (female)	Loretto Twins, Ora and Pauline	Los Angeles	1914
Giant Spring Board	Running forward triple back somersault	John Cornish Worland, (1855–1933) of the U.S.A.	St. Louis, Missouri	1874
Risley (Human Juggling)	Back somersault feet to feet	Richard Risley Carlisle (1814–74) and son (U.S.A.)	Theatre Royal, Edinburgh	Feb. 1844
Acrobatics	Quadruple back somersault to a chair	Sylvester Mezzetti (voltiger) to Butch Mezzetti (catcher)	New York Hippodrome	1915–17
Aerialist	One arm swings 125 (no net) 32 ft *9,75 m* up	Vicky Unus (La Toria) (U.S.A.)	Ringling Bros., Barnum & Bailey circuit	Nov. 1962
Teeter Board	Seat to seat triple back somersault	The 5 Draytons		1896
Wire-Juggling	16 hoops (hands and feet)	Ala Naito (Japan) (female)	Madison Square Garden, N.Y.	1937
Low Wire (7 ft [*2 m*])	Feet to feet forward somersault	Con Colleano	Empire Theatre, Johannesburg	1923
		Ala Naito (Japan) (female)	Madison Square Garden, N.Y.	1937
High Wire (30–40 ft [*9–12 m*])	Four high column (with mechanic)	*The Solokhin Brothers (U.S.S.R.)	Moscow Circus	1962
	Three layer, 7 man pyramid	Great Wallendas (Germany)	U.S.A.	1961
Ground Acrobatics	Stationary double back somersault	Francois Gouleau (France)		1905
	Four high column	The Picchianis (Italy)		1905
	Five high column	The Yacopis (Argentina) with 3 understanders, 3 second layer understanders, 1 middleman, 1 upper middleman and a top mounter	Ringling Bros., Barnum & Bailey circuit	1941

Mr. Richard Tompkins, Chairman of Green Shield Trading Stamp Co., whose service agreements have made him both the highest salaried executive and the greatest income tax payer in Britain

Jean Paul Getty (b. Minneapolis, Minnesota, 15 Dec. 1892); Howard Robard Hughes (b. Houston, Texas 24 Dec. 1905) now living in London: John Donald MacArthur (b. Pittston, Pennsylvania, 1897); and Daniel K. Ludwig (b. South Haven, Mich., June 1897). H. Ross Perot of Texas (b. Texarkana, Texas, 1930) was in December 1969 worth in excess of a billion dollars on paper.

Fortune Magazine, May 1968 assessed Mr. Getty at $1.338 billion and reassessed Mr. Hughes at $1.200 billion in December 1973. Mr. Ludwig was in January 1972 stated to be richer than either. On proved oil reserve revaluations, however, Mr. Getty would appear to be unsurpassable.

In so far as there are least people with whom to share it the richest oil shekhs are the rulers of Kuwait which in 1974 received $8,000 million in oil export revenues.

Europeans with family assets in excess of the equivalent of a billion dollars, include the Wallenburg family in Sweden. The wealthiest United Kingdom citizen, at the time of his death, was Sir John Reeves Ellerman 2nd Bt. (1909–73), whose fortune was estimated at £600 million (*$1.5 billion*).

Highest The greatest incomes derive from the collection of
Incomes royalties per barrel by rulers of oil-rich sheikhdoms, who have not abrogated personal entitlement. Before his death in 1965, H. H. Sheikh Sir Abdullah as-Salim as-Sabah G.C.M.G., C.I.E. (b. 1895), the 11th Amir of Kuwait was accumulating royalties payable at a rate of £2.6 million per week or £145 million a year.

The highest gross income ever achieved in a single year by a private citizen is an estimated $105,000,000 (*then £21½ million*) in 1927 by the Sicilian born Chicago gangster Alphonse ("Scarface Al") Capone (1899–1947). This was derived from illegal liquor trading and alky-cookers (illicit stills), gambling establishments, dog tracks, dance halls, "protection" rackets and vice. On his business card Capone described himself as a "Second Hand Furniture Dealer".

Proved Wills Sir John Reeves Ellerman, 2nd Bt., (1909–1973) left
and Death £53,238,370 on which all-time record death duties will
Duties be payable. This is the largest will ever proved in the United Kingdom. The greatest will proved in Ireland was that of the 1st Earl of Iveagh (1847–1927), who left £13,486,146.

Million- The world's wealthiest woman was probably Princess
airesses Wilhelmina Helena Pauline Maria of Orange-Nassau (1880–1962), formerly Queen of the Netherlands (from 1890 to her abdication, 4 Sept. 1948), with a fortune which was estimated at over £200 million. The largest amount proved in the will of a woman in the United Kingdom has been the £4,075,550 (duty paid £3,233,454) of Miss Gladys Meryl Yule, daughter of Sir David Yule, Bt. (1858–1928), in August 1957. Mrs. Anna Dodge (later Mrs. Hugh Dillman) who was born in Dundee, Scotland, died on 3 June 1970 in the United States, aged 103, and left an estate of £40,000,000.

Youngest The youngest person ever to accumulate a million dollars was the child film actor Jackie Coogan (b. Los Angeles, 1914) co-star with Sir Charles Chaplin (b. London, 1889) in "The Kid" made in 1920. Shirley Temple (b. Santa Monica, California 23 April 1928), formerly Mrs. John Agar, Jr., now Mrs. Charles Black accumulated wealth exceeded $1,000,000 (*then £209,000* before she was 10. Her child actress career spanned the years 1934–39.

Richest It has been tentatively estimated that the combined
families value of the assets nominally controlled by the du
World Pont family of some 1,600 members may be of the order of $150,000 million. The family arrived penniless in the U.S.A. from France on 1 Jan. 1800.

Britain The largest number of millionaires estates in one family in the British Isles is that of the Wills family of the Imperial Tobacco Company, of whom 14 members have left estates in excess of £1,000,000 since 1910. These totalled £55 million, of which death duties (introduced in 1894) have taken over £27,000,000.

The richest man in Great Britain is reputed to be John Moores, the football pool pioneer in 1923. In 1973 he was estimated to be worth about £400 million. His first job after leaving school at 14 was as a telephone operator. He was born in Eccles, Lancashire in 1896.

Largest The largest recorded dowry was that of Elena Patiño,
dowry daughter of Don Simón Iturbi Patiño (1861–1947), the Bolivian tin millionaire, who in 1929 bestowed £8,000,000 from a fortune at one time estimated to be worth £125,000,000.

Greatest If meanness is measurable as a ratio between expendable
miser assets and expenditure then Henrietta (Hetty) Howland Green (*née* Robinson) (1835–1916), who kept a balance of over $31,400,000 (*then £6.2 million*) in one bank alone, was the all-time world champion. Her son had to have his leg amputated because of her delays in finding a *free* medical clinic. She herself lived off cold porridge because she was too thrifty to heat it and died of apoplexy in an argument over the virtues of skimmed milk. Her estate proved to be of $95 million (*then £19 million [and now worth £170 million]*).

SALARIES AND EARNINGS

Highest The highest salary paid in the United States in 1973
World was to the Chairman of Johnson and Johnson, the drug company with $978,000 (*£407,500*). The United States highest salaried women executive was believed to be Mary Wells Lawrence, Chairman of the advertising firm Wells, Rich, Greene, Inc. of New York, $385,000 (*£160,400*) in 1973. She is the mother of five and has an earning husband—Harding L. Lawrence, chairman of Braniff Airways.

United Britain's highest paid business executive is Mr. Richard
Kingdom Tompkins, Chairman of Green Shield Trading Stamp Company which he founded in 1958. His service agreement entitled him to 15 per cent of profits which for the year ending 31 Oct. 1971 would have earned him £395,000. He waived £135,000. On 1972/73 full standard taxation rates it has been calculated that £185,600 of the £260,000 would be payable in income

233

tax and surtax. His 1973/74 salary is believed to have been less than £100,000 gross.

The highest straight salary paid in British business is the £75,948 payable to the managing director of Shell Trading and Transport, Mr. F. S. McFadzean.

Highest wage The highest recorded wages in Britain are those paid to long haulage lorry drivers and tower crane drivers on bonuses. A specific case of £350 a week has been cited.

Biggest Loss The biggest recorded paper loss in one day was $24,768,630 (£9,907,000) by Arthur Decio, President of Skyline Corporation of Elkhart, Indiana on 26 Dec. 1972 due to share depreciation.

Lowest incomes The poorest people in the world are the Tasaday tribe of cave-dwellers of central Mindanao, Philippines who were "discovered" in 1971 without any domesticated animals, agriculture, pottery, wheels or clothes.

Return of cash The largest amount of *cash* ever found and returned to its owners was $500,000 (U.S.) found by Lowell Elliott, 61 on his farm at Peru, Indiana, U.S.A. It had been dropped in June 1972 by a parachuting hi-jacker.

Greatest bequests The greatest bequest in a life-time of a millionaire were those of the late John Davison Rockefeller (1839–1937), who gave away sums totalling $750,000,000 (*now £312.5 million*). The greatest benefactions of a British millionaire were those of William Richard Morris, later the Viscount Nuffield, G.B.E., C.H. (1877–1963), which totalled more than £30,000,000 between 1926 and his death on 22 Aug. 1963. The Scottish-born U.S. citizen Andrew Carnegie (1835–1919) is estimated to have made benefactions totalling £70 million during the last 18 years of his life. These included 7,689 church organs and 2,811 libraries. He had started life in a bobbin factory at $1.20 per week.

The largest bequest made in the history of philanthropy was the $500,000,000 (£178,570,000) gift, announced on 12 Dec. 1955, to 4,157 educational and other institutions by the Ford Foundation (established 1936) of New York City, N.Y., U.S.A. The assets of the Foundation had a book value of $3,370,521,943 (*now £1,348 million*) in 1971.

GASTRONOMIC RECORDS
Records for eating and drinking by trenchermen do not match those suffering from the rare disease of bulimia (morbid desire to eat) and polydipsia (pathological thirst). Some bulimia patients have to spend 15 hours a day eating, with an extreme consumption of 384 lb. 2 oz. *174 kg 236* of food in six days by Matthew Daking, aged 12, in 1743 (known as Mortimer's case). Some polydipsomaniacs have been said to be unsatisfied by less than 96 pints *54,55 litres* of liquid a day. Miss Helge Andersson (b. 1908) of Lindesberg, Sweden was reported in January 1971 to have been drinking 40 pints *22,73 litres* of water a day since 1922—a total of 87,600 gal *3 982 hectolitres*.

The world's greatest trencherman has been Edward Abraham ("Bozo") Miller (b. 1909) of Oakland, California, U.S.A. He consumed up to 25,000 calories per day or more than 11 times that recommended. He stands 5 ft 7½ in *1,71 m* tall but weighs from 20 to 21½ st. *127–139 kg* with a 57 in *144 cm* waist. He has been undefeated in eating contests since 1931 (see below). The bargees on the Rhine are reputed to be the world's heaviest eaters with 5,200 calories a day. However the New Zealand Sports Federation of Medicine reported in Dec. 1972 that a long-distance road runner consumed 14,321 calories in 24 hours.

While no healthy person has been reported to have succumbed in any contest for eating or drinking

non-alcoholic or non-toxic drinks, such attempts, from a medical point of view, must be regarded as *extremely* inadvisable, particularly among young people. Guinness Superlatives will not list any records involving the consumption of more than 2 litres *3.52 Imperial pints* of beer nor any at all involving spirits. Nor will records for such potentially dangerous categories as live ants, chewing gum, marsh mallow or raw eggs with shells be published.

Specific records have been claimed as follows:

Baked Beans	1,823 cold beans one by one with a cocktail stick in 30 min by Nigel Moore at P.O. Social Club, Manchester on 19 June 1974.
Bananas	63 in 10 min by Michael Gallen, 23 in Cairns, Australia on 11 Oct. 1972.
Beer	Peter G. Dowdeswell (b. London 29 July 1940) of Earls Barton Northamptonshire in 1975 broke all categories:
1 litre	2.0 secs. Romany Hotel, Northants 1 Feb.
2 pints	2.3 secs. Zetters Social Club, Wolverton, Bucks 11 June
2 litres	6.0 secs. Carriage Horse Hotel, Higham Ferrars, Northants 7 Feb.
	Yards of Ale
2½ pints	5.0 secs. R.A.F. Upper Heyford, Oxfordshire 4 May
3 pints	6.0 secs. Dudley Top Rank, Dudley, West Midlands 31 May
	Upsidedown
2 pints	6 4 secs. Top Rank Club, Northants 25 May
Champagne	1,000 bottles per annum by Bobby Acland of the "Black Raven", Bishopsgate, City of London.
Cheese	16 oz. *509 g* of Cheddar in 3 min 32 sec by David Orange in Los Angeles, California, U.S.A. on 27–28 Apr. 1974.
Chicken	27 (2 lb. [*907 g*] pullets) by "Bozo" Miller (see above) at a sitting at Trader Vic's, San Francisco, California, U.S.A. in 1963.
Doughnuts	27 in 7 mins 16 secs by Mike Musselman of Roy, Utah, U.S.A. on 5 Feb. 1975.
Eels	1 lb. *453 g* of elvers (1,300) in 43 sec by Leslie Cole, 37 at Frampton-on-Severn, Gloucestershire on 13 Apr. 1971.
Eggs	(Hard Boiled) 1 dozen in 103 secs by Stanley Judge of Hull, Humberside on 23 Sept. 1974.
	(Soft Boiled) 32 in 130 secs by Douglas L. Burch at Korbets Restaurants, Mobile, Alabama, U.S.A. on 9 May 1975.
Eggs (Raw)	13 in 3.8 sec by James Lindop in Manchester on 29 Sept. 1973.
Fish and Chips	3 lb 11½ oz *1,686 kg* Stewart Milnes, 30 at Fastnet Fish Restaurant, Morley, West Yorkshire on 14 Aug. 1974.
Frankfurters	20 (2 oz. [*56,6 g*]) in 4 min 47 sec by Raymond Kowalski, 21 Hilton Head Island, South Carolina, U.S.A. on 28 Feb. 1974.
Gherkins	1 lb. *453 g* in 1 min 47.5 sec by Peter L. Citron in Omaha, Nebraska, U.S.A. on 20 May 1971.
Grapes	1 lb. *453 g* (unpipped) in 34.6 sec by David Fritzlen at Baker University, Baldwin, Kansas, U.S.A. on 12 Dec. 1973.
Haggis	24 oz. *680 g* in 2 min 42 sec by W. McVeigh at Corby, Northamptonshire on 23 Jan. 1972.
Hamburgers	83 at a 2½ hour sitting by Robert Matern, 21 at University of Rhode Island on 3 May 1973.
Ice Cream	8 lb. (51 2½ oz. [*70 g*] scoops) in 12 min by Ronald C. Long at Friendly's Ice Cream Shop, North Adams, Man. on 2 May 1975.
Kippers	25 (self-filleted) in 60 min by Bob Ibbotson at Scarborough, North Yorkshire on 10 Aug. 1973.
Lemons	12 quarters (3 lemons) whole (including skin and pips) in 55.0 sec by Paul Natschowny at Hatfield Polytechnic, Hertfordshire on 19 Feb. 1975.

Gordon Gustar

William Corfield the champion whelk eater in action

Meat	One whole roast ox in 42 days by Johann Ketzler of Munich, Germany in 1880.
Meat Pies	19.5 oz. *141 g* in a 30 min session by Geoffrey Heenan in Arbroath, Angus Scotland on 25 Oct. 1972.
Milk	2 pt (1 Imperial quart or [*113,5 centilitres*]) in 3.2 sec by Peter Dowdeswell (see above) at Dudley Top Rank Club, West Midlands on 31 May 1975.
Oysters	500 in 60 min by Councillor Peter Jaconelli, Mayor of Scarborough, North Yorkshire at The Castle Hotel (only 48 min 7 sec required) on 27 Apr. 1972. The record for opening oysters is 100 in 3 min 1 sec by Douglas Brown, 26 at Christchurch, New Zealand on 29 Apr. 1974.
Pancakes	(6 in [*15,2 cm*] diameter buttered and with syrup) 61 in 7 min by Mark Mishon, 19 at The Obelix Creperie, Westbourne Grove, London on 11 Feb. 1975.
Peanuts	100 (whole) singly in 59.2 sec by Chris Ambrose in Clerkenwell, City of London on 3 Apr. 1973.
Pickled Onions	66 in 2 min by James Wilson at Ilmington, Warwickshire on 5 May 1973.
Potatoes	3 lb. *1,360 g* in 5 min. 22 sec by Jeffrey Beckett of Harlow, Essex on 9 Nov. 1974.
Potato Crisps	30 2 oz. *56,6 g* bags in 24 min 33.6 sec, without a drink, by Paul G. Tully of Brisbane University in May 1969. The largest single crisp on record is one measured to be 5 in × 3 in *12,7 × 7,6 cm* found at Reeds School, Cobham, Surrey by John Nicol, 16, on 2 Feb. 1971. Another of the same dimensions was reported found by Mr. and Mrs. David J. Buja of Gardner, Massachusetts. on 4 May 1974.
Prunes	130 in 105 sec by Dave Man at Eastbourne on 16 June 1971.
Ravioli	324 (first 250 in 70 min) by "Bozo" Miller (see above) at Rendezvous Room, Oakland, California, U.S.A. in 1963.
Sandwiches	40 in 39 min (jam "butties" 6 × 3¾ × ½ in [*15,2 × 9,5 × 1,2 cm*]) by Steve Street in Edmonton, Greater London on 10 Apr. 1974.
Sausage Meat	89½ Danish 1 oz. *28,3 g* sausages in 6 min by Lee Hang in Hong Kong on 3 May 1972.
Shrimps (Boiled)	3½ lb. *1,585 kg* in 30 min by Larry Sibley (U.S. Coast Guards) Conn Brown Harbor, Texas, U.S.A. on 18 May 1974.
Snails	124 in 15 mins (Moroccan snails) by Mrs. Nicky Bove at 6th Great Escargot Eating Contest, Houston, Texas, U.S.A. 1 Apr. 1974. The style prize was won by Rex Miller.
Spaghetti	100 yds *91,44 m* in 99.3 secs by James Bush at Dubois Park, Florida, U.S.A. on 7 June 1975.
Tortilla	74 by Tom Nall in the 2nd World Championship at Marciano's Mexican Restaurant, Dallas, Texas, U.S.A. on 16 Oct. 1973.
Whelks	81 (unshelled) in 15 min by William Corfield, 35 at the Helyar Arms, East Coker, Somerset on 6 Sept. 1969.

2. HONOURS, DECORATIONS AND AWARDS

Eponymous record The largest object to which a human name is attached is the super cluster of galaxies known as Abell 7, after the astronomer Dr. George O. Abell of the University of California, U.S.A. The group of clusters has an estimated linear dimension of 300,000,000 light years and was announced in 1961. The human who has had most objects named after him is William Prout (1785–1850) who, in 1815 enunciated (the incorrect) Prout's Law that all the atomic weights of all the elements are multiples of the atomic weight of hydrogen. Ernest (later Lord) Rutherford in 1911 named the positively charged nucleous of the atom a Proton (after Prout). It is estimated that there are some 10^{85} protons in the observable universe.

ORDERS AND DECORATIONS

Oldest The earliest of the orders of chivalry is the Venetian order of St. Marc, reputedly founded in A.D. 831. The Castilian order of Calatrava has an established date of foundation in 1158. The prototype of the princely Orders of Chivalry is the Most Noble Order of the Garter founded by King Edward III in *c.* 1348.

Most titles The most titled person in the world is the 18th Duchess of Alba (Albade Termes), Doña María del Rosario Cayetana Fitz-James Stuart y Silva. She is 8 times a duchess, 15 times a marchioness, 21 times a countess and is 19 times a Spanish grandee.

VICTORIA CROSS

Most bars The only three men ever to have been awarded a bar to the Victoria Cross (instituted 1856) are:

Surg.-Capt. (later Lt.-Col.) Arthur Martin-Leake, V.C.*, V.D., R.A.M.C. (1874–1953) (1902 and bar 1915).
Capt. Noel Godfrey Chavasse, V.C.*, M.C., R.A.M.C. (1884–1917) (1916 and bar posthumously 14 Sept. 1917).
Second Lieut. (later Capt.) Charles Hazlett Upham, V.C.*, N.Z.M.F. (born 1911) (1941 and bar 1942).

Youngest The lowest established age for a V.C. is 15 years 100 days for Hospital Apprentice Arthur Fitzgibbon (born at Peteragurh, northern India, 13 May 1845) of the Indian Medical Services for bravery at the Taku Forts in northern China on 21 Aug. 1860. The youngest living V.C. is Lance-Corporal Rambahadur Limbu

Courtesy, Gieves-Hawkes, 1 Saville Row

The maximum permissible regalia of an Admiral of the Fleet, the top rank in the Senior Service, with 4 breast stars and ADC aiguillettes

(b. Nepal, 1939) of the 10th Princess Mary's Own Gurkha Rifles. The award, was for his courage while fighting in the Bau district of Sarawak, East Malaysia, on 21 Nov. 1965.

Longest lived The longest lived of all the 1,349 winners of the Victoria Cross was Captain (later General Sir) Lewis Stratford Tollemache Halliday, V.C., K.C.B., of the Royal Marine Light Infantry. He was born on 14 May 1870, won his V.C. in China in 1900, and died on 9 March 1966, aged 95 years 299 days. The oldest living V.C. is Maj. Gen. Dudley Graham Johnson, V.C., C.B., D.S.O. and bar, M.C. (b. 13 Feb. 1884), who won his decoration at the Sumbre Canal, France on 4 Nov. 1918

Most expensive The highest auction price for any British gallantry decoration is £7,200 for a V.C. group given at Sothebys on 6 Feb. 1975 by J. B. Hayward & Sons for the medals of Lt. Philip E. Curtis V.C. awarded in Korea on 22–23 Apr. 1951.

George Cross The highest award ever given to a woman is the George Cross. The oldest recipient was Miss Emma Josie Townsend (formerly E.G.M.) aged 53 in 1932 and the youngest is Mrs. Doreen Ashburnham-Ruffner (formerly A.M.) aged 11 in 1916.

ORDER OF MERIT

The Order of Merit (instituted on 23 June 1902) is limited to 24 members. Up to 30 June 1974 there have been 124 awards including only 3 women, plus 9 honorary awards to non-British citizens. The longest

The late Field Marshal Lord Roberts V.C. holder of the mention in despatches record at 24 times

lived holder has been the Rt. Hon. Bertrand Arthur William Russell, 3rd Earl Russell, who died on 2 Feb. 1970 aged 97 years 260 days. The oldest recipient was Admiral of the Fleet the Hon. Sir Henry Keppel, G.C.B., O.M. (1809–1904), who received the Order aged 93 years 56 days on 9 Aug. 1902. The youngest recipient has been H.R.H. the Duke of Edinburgh, K.G., K.T., O.M., G.B.E. who was appointed on his 47th birthday on 10 June 1968.

RECORD NUMBER OF BARS (repeat awards) EVER GAZETTED TO BRITISH GALLANTRY DECORATIONS

* = a bar or repeat award

V.C.*	A first bar has been three times awarded to the Victoria Cross (see above).
D.S.O.***	A third bar has been 16 times awarded to the Distinguished Service Order.
R.R.C.*	Over 100 first bars have been awarded to the Royal Red Cross, but of these Dame Sarah Elizabeth Oram, D.B.E., R.R.C.* (1860–1946) uniquely was gazetted *twice* (1896 and 1901) before receiving a bar in 1918, thus indicating 3 awards.
D.S.C.***	A third bar has been uniquely awarded to the Distinguished Service Cross won by Cdr. Norman Eyre Morley, R.N.V.R.
M.C.***	A third bar has been four times awarded to the Military Cross.
D.F.C.**	A second bar has been 54 times awarded to the Distinguished Flying Cross.
A.F.C.**	A second bar has been 12 times awarded to the Air Force Cross.
D.C.M.**	A second bar has been 11 times awarded to the Distinguished Conduct Medal.
C.G.M.*	A first bar has been uniquely awarded to the Conspicuous Gallantry Medal (Naval) won by C.P.O. Arthur Robert Blore, M.M. (1890–1947) and a second medal to Able Seaman D. Barry.
G.M.*	A first bar has been 25 times awarded to the George Medal.
K.P.M.**	A second bar has been uniquely awarded to the King's/Queen's Police Medal for Gallantry won by Supt. Frederick William O'Gorman, C.I.E., O.B.E. (d. 1949).
E.M.*	A first bar has twice been awarded to the Edward Medal (1st Class or in Silver).
D.S.M.***	A third bar has been uniquely awarded to the Distinguished Service Medal won by Petty Officer William Henry Kelly.
M.M.***	A third bar has been uniquely awarded to the Military Medal won by Cpl. Ernest Albert Correy (1888–1972).
D.F.M.**	A second bar has been uniquely awarded to the Distinguished Flying Medal won by Flt.-Sgt. (now Group Capt.) Donald Ernest Kingaby, D.S.O., A.F.C.
A.F.M.*	A first bar has been 8 times awarded to the Air Force Medal.
S.G.M.*	A first bar has been uniquely awarded to the Sea Gallantry Medal won by Chief Officer James Whiteley.
B.E.M.*	A first bar has been 4 times awarded to the British Empire Medal for Gallantry (as instituted in 1957 but abolished in 1974).

No bars have yet been awarded to the George Cross (G.C.), the Conspicuous Gallantry Medal (Flying) (C.G.M.), or the Queen's Gallantry Medal (Q.G.M.). No bars were ever awarded to the now obsolete Albert Medal in Gold (A.M.), the Albert Medal (A.M.), the Edward Medal (in bronze) (E.M.) or the Empire Gallantry Medal (E.G.M.), which have all been superceded by the G.C.

Most mentions in despatches   The record number of "mentions" is 24 by Field Marshal the Rt. Hon. Sir Frederick Sleigh Roberts Bt., the Earl Roberts, V.C., K.G., K.P., G.C.B., O.M., G.C.S.I., G.C.I.E., V.D. (1832–1914).

Most post-nominal letters   Lord Roberts was the only subject with 8 sets of *official* post-nominal letters. Currently the record number is seven by Admiral of the Fleet the Earl Mountbatten of Burma (born 25 June 1900) K.G., G.C.B., O.M., G.C.S.I., G.C.I.E., G.C.V.O., D.S.O.

U.S.S.R.   The U.S.S.R.'s highest award for valour is the Gold Star of a Hero of the Soviet Union. Over 10,000 were awarded in World War II. Among the 109 awards of a second star were those to Marshall Iosif Vissarionovich Dzhugashvili, *alias* Stalin (1879–1953) and Lt.-General Nikita Sergeyevich Khrushchyov (1894–1971). The only war-time triple awards were to Marshal Georgiy Konstantinovich Zhukov, Hon. G.C.B. (1896–1974) (subsequently awarded a fourth Gold Star unique until Mr. Khrushchyov's fourth award) and the leading air aces Guards' Colonel (now Aviation Maj.-Gen.) Aleksandr Ivanovich Polkyrshkin and Aviation Maj.-Gen. Ivan Nikitaevich Kozhedub.

Germany   The only man to be awarded the Knight's Cross of the Iron Cross with swords, diamonds and golden oak-leaves was Col. Hans-Ulrich Rudel.

U.S.A.   The highest U.S. decoration is the Congressional Medal of Honor. Five marines received both the Army and Navy Medals of Honor for the same acts in 1918 and 14 officers and men from 1863 to 1915 have received the medal on two occasions.

Most bemedalled   The most bemedalled chest is that of H.I.M. Field-Marshal Hailé Selassié, K.G., G.C.B. (Hon.), G.C.M.G. (Hon.) (born, as Ras Tafari Makonnen, on 23 July 1892), ex-Emperor of Ethiopia, who has over 50 medal ribbons worn in up to 14 rows.

Emperor Hailé Selassie (b. 1892), who just prior to his being deposed, was having problems in accommodating 14 rows of medal ribbons

Planet News

TOP SCORING AIR ACES (World Wars I and II)

World	80 Rittmeister Manfred, Freiherr (Baron) von Richthofen (Germany). 352[1] Major Erich Hartman (Germany).
United Kingdom	73[2] Capt. (acting Major) Edward Mannock, V.C.[1] D.S.O.**, M.C.*. 38[3] Wg.-Cdr. (now Air Vice Marshal) James Edgar Johnson, C.B. C.B.E., D.S.O.**, D.F.C.*.

A compilation of the top air aces of 13 combatant nations in World War I and of 22 nations in World War II was included in the 13th edition of *The Guinness Book of Records*.

1 *All except one of the aircraft in this unrivalled total were Soviet combat aircraft on the Eastern Front in 1942–45. The German air ace with most victories against the R.A.F. was Oberleutnant Hans-Joachim Marseille (killed 30 Sept. 1942), who, in 388 actions, shot down 158 Allied aircraft, 151 of them over North Africa.*

2 *Recent research suggests that Mannock's total may have been lower than that of Major James Thomas Byford McCudden, V.C., D.S.O.*, M.C.*, M.M. (57 victories).*

3 *The greatest number of successes against flying bombs (V.1's) was by Sqn, Ldr. Joseph Berry, D.F.C.** (b. Nottingham, 1920, killed 2 Oct. 1944). who brought down 60 in 4 months. The most successful R.A.F. fighter pilot was Sqn. Ldr. Marmaduke Thomas St. John Pattle, D.F.C.*, of South Africa, with a known total of at least 40.*

Top jet ace The greatest number of kills in jet to jet battles is 16 by Capt. Joseph Christopher McConnell, Jr., U.S.A.F. (b. Dover, New Hampshire, 30 Jan. 1922) in the Korean war (1950–53). He was killed on 25 Aug. 1954. It is possible that an Israeli ace may have surpassed this total in the period 1967–70 but the identity of pilots is subject to strict security.

Top woman ace The record score for any woman fighter pilot is 12 by Jnr. Lt. Lydia Litvak (U.S.S.R.) (b. 1921) on the Eastern Front between 1941 and 1943. She was killed in action on 1 Aug. 1943.

Anti Tank successes Major Hans-Ulrich Rudel, the German *Stuka* pilot, in 2,530 combat missions destroyed 519 Soviet armoured vehicles and was uniquely awarded the golden oak-leaves to the Knight's Cross of the Iron Cross on 1 Jan. 1945.

Anti-submarine successes The highest number of U-boat kills attributed to one ship in the 1939–45 war was 13 to H.M.S. *Starling* (Capt. Frederick J. Walker, C.B., D.S.O.***, R.N.). Captain Walker was in overall command at the sinking of a total of 25 U-boats between 1941 and the time of his death on 9 July 1944. The U.S. Destroyer Escort *England* sank six Japanese submarines in the Pacific between 18 and 30 May 1944.

Most successful U-boat captain The most successful of all World War II submarine commanders was Korvetten-Kapitän (now Kapitän zur See) Otto Kretschmer (b. 1911), captain of the U.23 and later the U.99. He sank one Allied destroyer and 43 merchantmen totalling 263,682 gross registered tons in 16 patrols before his capture on 17 March 1941. He is a Knight's Cross of the Iron Cross with Oakleaves and Swords. In World War I Kapitän-Leutnant Lothar von Arnauld de la Periere, in the U.35 and U.139, sank 194 allied ships totalling 453,716 gross tons. The most successful boats were U.48, which in World War I sank 54 ships of 90,350 g.r.t. in a single voyage and 535,900 g.r.t. all told, and U.53 which sank 53 ships of 318,111 g.r.t. in World War II.

NOBEL PRIZES

The Nobel Foundation of £3,200,000 was set up under the will of Alfred Bernhard Nobel (1833–96), the unmarried Swedish chemist and chemical engineer, who invented dynamite, in 1866. The Nobel Prizes are presented annually on 10 Dec., the anniversary of Nobel's death and the festival day of the Foundation. Since the first Prizes were awarded in 1901, the highest cash value of the award, in each of the six fields of Physics, Chemistry, Medicine and Physiology, Literature, Peace and Economics was $123,000 (*£53,500*) in 1974.

Most awards by countries The United States has shared in the greatest number of awards (including those made in 1974) with a total of 89 made up of 22 for Physics, 15 for Chemistry, 26 for Medicine-Physiology, 6 for Literature, 15 for Peace and 5 for Economics.

The United Kingdom has shared in 60 awards, comprising 16 for Physics, 16 for Chemistry, 12 for Medicine-Physiology, 6 for Literature, 8 for Peace and 2 for Economics.

By classes, the United States holds the record for Medicine-Physiology with 26, for Physics with 22 and for Peace with 15; Germany for Chemistry with 22; and France for Literature with 12.

Individuals Individually the only person to have won two Prizes outright is Dr. Linus Carl Pauling (b. 28 Feb. 1901), Professor of Chemistry at the California Institute of Technology, Pasadena, California, U.S.A. since 1931. He was awarded the Chemistry Prize for 1954

Rudyard Kipling (1865–1936) the youngest writer ever to win the Nobel Prize for Literature at 41 in 1907

and the Peace Prize for 1962. The only other persons to have won two prizes are Madame Marie Curie (1867–1934), who was born in Poland as Marja Sklodowska. She shared the 1903 Physics Prize with her husband Pierre Curie (1859–1906) and Antoine Henri Becquerel (1852–1908), and won the 1911 Chemistry Prize outright. Professor John Bardeen (b. 23 May 1908) shared the physics prize in 1956 and 1972. The Peace Prize has been awarded three times to the International Committee of the Red Cross (founded 29 Oct. 1863), of Geneva, Switzerland, namely in 1917, 1944 and in 1963, when it was shared with the International League of Red Cross Societies.

Oldest The oldest prizeman has been Professor Francis Peyton Rous (1879–1970) of the United States. He shared the Medicine Prize in 1966, at the age of 87.

Youngest The youngest laureate has been Professor Sir William Lawrence Bragg, C.H., O.B.E., M.C. (1890–1971), of the U.K., who, at the age of 25, shared the 1915 Physics Prize with his father, Sir William Henry Bragg, O.M., K.B.E. (1862–1942), for work on X-rays and crystal structures. Bragg and also Theodore William Richards (1868–1928) of the U.S.A., who won the 1914 Chemistry prize, carried out their prize work when aged 23. The youngest Literature prizeman has been Joseph Rudyard Kipling (1865–1936) at the age of 41 in 1907. The youngest Peace prize-winner has been the Rev. Dr. Martin Luther King, Jr. (1929–68) of the U.S.A., in 1964.

Most statues The world record for raising statues to oneself was set by Generalissimo Dr. Rafael Leónidas Trujillo y Molina (1891–1961), former President of the Dominican Republic. In March 1960 a count showed that there were "over 2,000". The country's highest mountain was named Pico Trujillo (now Pico Duarte). One Province was called Trujillo and another Trujillo Valdez. The capital was named Ciudad Trujillo (Trujillo City) in 1936, but reverted to its old name of Santo Domingo de Guzmán on 23 Nov. 1961. Trujillo was assassinated in a car ambush on 30 May 1961, and 30 May is now celebrated annually as a public holiday. The man to whom most statues have been raised is undoubtedly Vladimir Ilyich Ulyanov, *alias* Lenin (1870–1924), busts of whom have been mass-produced as also in the case of Mao Tse-tung. (b. 26 Dec. 1893) and Hô Chi Minh (1890–1969).

237

PEERAGE

Most ancient The oldest extant peerage is that of the premier Earl of Scotland, the Rt. Hon. Margaret of Mar, the Countess of Mar and 31st holder of this Earldom, b. 19 Sept. 1940, who is the heir-at-law of Roderick or Rothri, 1st Earl (or Mormaer) of Mar, who witnessed a charter in 1114 or 1115 as "Rothri comes".

Oldest creation The greatest age at which any person has been raised to the peerage is 93 years 337 days in the case of Sir William Francis Kyffin Taylor, G.B.E., K.C. (b. 9 July 1854), who was created Baron Maenan of Ellesmere, County Salop (Shropshire), on 10 June 1948, and died, aged 97, on 22 Sept. 1951, when the title became extinct.

Longest lived peer The longest lived peer ever recorded was the Rt. Hon. Frank Douglas-Pennant, the 5th Baron Penrhyn (b. 21 Nov. 1865), who died on 3 Feb. 1967, aged 101 years 74 days. The oldest peeress recorded was the Countess Desmond, who was alleged to be 140 when she died in 1604. This claim is patently exaggerated but it is accepted that she may have been 104. Currently the oldest holder of a peerage, and the oldest Parliamentarian, is the Rt. Hon. Walter Egerton George Lucian Keppal M.C., the 9th Earl of Albemarle who was born on 28 Feb. 1882.

Youngest peers Twelve Dukes of Cornwall became (in accordance with the grant by the Crown in Parliament) peers at birth as the eldest son of a Sovereign; and the 9th Earl of Chichester posthumously inherited his father's (killed 54 days previously) earldom at his birth on 14 April 1944.

The youngest age at which a person has had a peerage conferred on them is 7 days old in the case of the Earldom of Chester on H.R.H. the Prince George (later George IV) on 19 Aug. 1762.

Longest and shortest peerages The peer who has sat longest in the House of Lords was Lt.-Col. Charles Henry FitzRoy, O.B.E., the 4th Baron Southampton (b. 11 May 1867), who succeeded to his father's title on 16 July 1872, took his seat on 23 Jan. 1891, 18 months before Mr. W. E. Gladstone's fourth administration began, and died, aged 91, on 7 Dec. 1958, having held the title for 86 years 144 days.

The shortest enjoyment of a peerage was the "split second" by which the law assumes that the Hon. Wilfrid Carlyle Stamp (b. 28 Oct. 1904), the 2nd Baron Stamp, survived his father, Sir Josiah Charles Stamp, G.C.B., G.B.E., the 1st Baron Stamp, when both were killed as a result of German bombing of London on 16 April 1941. Apart from this legal fiction, the shortest recorded peerage was one of 30 minutes in the case of Sir Charles Brandon, K.B., the 3rd Duke of Suffolk, who died, aged 13 or 14, just after succeeding his brother, Sir Henry, the 2nd Duke, when both were suffering a fatal illness, at Buckden, Cambridgeshire, on 14 July 1551.

Highest numbering The highest succession number borne by any peer is that of the present 35th Baron Kingsale (John de Courcy, b. 27 Jan. 1941), who succeeded to the 746-year-old Barony on 7 Nov. 1969.

Most creations The largest number of new hereditary peerages created in any year was the 54 in 1296. The record for all peerages (including 40 life peerages) is 55 in 1964. The greatest number of extinctions in a year was 16 in 1923 and the greatest number of deaths was 44 in 1935.

Most prolific The most prolific peers of all time are believed to be the 1st Earl Ferrers (1650–1717) and the 3rd Earl of Winchelsea (c. 1620–1689) each with 27 legitimate children. In addition, the former reputedly fathered 30 illegitimate children. Currently the peer with the largest family is the Rt. Hon. Bryan Walter Guinness, 2nd Baron Moyne (b. 27 Oct. 1905) with 6 sons and 5 daughters.

The most prolific peeress is believed to be Elizabeth (née Barnard), who bore 22 children to her husband Lord Chandos of Sudeley (1642–1714).

BARONETS

Oldest The greatest age to which a baronet has lived is 101 years 188 days, in the case of Sir Fitzroy Donald Maclean, 10th Bt., K.C.B., (1835–1936). He was the last survivor of the Charge of the Light Brigade at Balaclava in the Crimea, Russia, on 25 Oct. 1854.

Most and least creations The largest number of creations this century was 51 in 1919. There were none in 1940 and none have been created since 1965.

KNIGHTS

Youngest and oldest The youngest age for the conferment of a knighthood is 29 days for H.R.H. the Prince Albert Edward (b. 9 Nov. 1841) (later Edward VII) by virtue of his *ex officio* membership of the Order of the Garter (K.G.) consequent upon his creation as Prince of Wales on 8 Dec. 1841. The greatest age for the conferment of a knighthood is 98 years 167 days in the case of Sir Alfred Hamish Reed, C.B.E., born Hayes, Kent 30 Dec. 1875, the author-explorer who lives in New Zealand whose knight bachelorhood was announced 15 June 1974.

Queen's Award to Industry The record number of awards (instituted in 1966) for export achievement in their sole right is six by Glaxo Laboratories Ltd. (1967 to 1972). The record number of awards for technological innovation in their sole right is three by Decca Radar Ltd. (1968–71–72) and the Kelvin Hughes division of Smiths Industries (1967–68–75).

Most freedoms Probably the greatest number of freedoms ever conferred on any man was 57 in the case of Andrew Carnegie (1835–1919), who was born in Dunfermline, Fife but emigrated to the United States in 1848. The most freedoms conferred upon any citizen of the United Kingdom is 42, in the case of the Rt. Hon. Sir Winston Leonard Spencer Churchill, K.G., O.M., C.H., T.D. (1874–1965).

Most honorary degrees The greatest number of honorary degrees awarded to any individual is 89, given to Herbert Clark Hoover (1874–1964), former President of the United States (1929–33).

Greatest vote The largest monetary vote made by Parliament to a subject was the £400,000 given to the 1st Duke of Wellington (1769–1852) on 12 April 1814. He received in all £864,000. The total received by the 1st, 2nd and 3rd Dukes to January 1900 was £1,052,000.

Who's Who The longest entry in *Who's Who* (founded 1848) was that of the Rt. Hon. Sir Winston Leonard Spencer Churchill, K.G., O.M., C.H., T.D. (1874–1965), who had 211 lines in the 1965 edition. Apart from those who qualify for inclusion by hereditary title, the youngest entry has been Yehudi Menuhin, Hon. K.B.E. (b. New York City, U.S.A. 22 April 1916), the concert violinist, who first appeared in the 1932 edition. The longest entry of the 66,000 entries in *Who's Who in America* is that of Prof. Richard Buckminster Fuller, Jr. (b. 12 July 1895) whose all-time record of 139 lines compares with the 23 line sketch on President Nixon.

Most brothers The most brothers having entries in Who's Who is five in the case of the Barrington-Wards: Frederick Temple (1880–1938), Sir Lancelot (1884–1953), Sir Michael (1887–1972), Robert McGowan (1891–1948) and John Grosvenor (1894–1946). Their father Canon Mark James (died 1924) of Duloe, Cornwall was himself in Who's Who.

ALL SPORTS

Earliest The origins of sport stem from the time when self-preservation ceased to be the all-consuming human preoccupation. Archery was a hunting skill in mesolithic times (by *c.* 8000 B.C.), but did not become an organized sport until *c.* A.D. 300, among the Genoese. The earliest dated evidence for sport is *c.* 2450 B.C. for fowling with throwing sticks, similar to return boomerangs and hunting. Ball games by girls depicted on Middle Kingdom murals at Ben Hasan, Egypt have been dated to *c.* 2050 B.C.

Fastest The governing body for aviation, *La Fédération Aéronautique Internationale*, records maximum speeds in lunar flight of up to 24,791 m.p.h. *39 897 km/h.* However, these achievements, like all air speed records since 1923, have been para-military rather than sporting. The highest speed reached in a non-mechanical sport is in sky-diving, in which a speed of 185 m.p.h. *295 km/h* is attained in a head-down free falling position, even in the lower atmosphere. In delayed drops a speed of 614 m.p.h. *988 km/h* has been recorded at high rarefied altitudes. The highest projectile speed in any moving ball game is *c.* 160 m.p.h. *260 km/h* in pelota. This compares with 170 m.p.h. *273 km/h* (electronically-timed) for a golf ball driven off a tee.

Slowest In wrestling, before the rules were modified towards "brighter wrestling", contestants could be locked in holds for so long that single bouts could last for 11 hrs 40 min. In the extreme case of the 2 hrs 41 min pull in the regimental tug o' war in Jubbulpore, India, on 12 Aug. 1889, the winning team moved a net distance of 12 ft *3,6 m* at an average speed of 0.00084 m.p.h. *0,000135 km/h.*

Longest The most protracted sporting test was an automobile duration test of 222,618 miles *358 268 km* by Appaurchaux and others in a Ford Taunus. This was contested over 142 days in 1963. The distance was equivalent to 8.93 times around the equator.

The most protracted non-mechanical sporting event is the *Tour de France* cycling race. In 1926 this was over 3,569 miles *5 743 km* lasting 29 days. The total damage to the French national economy of this annual event, now reduced to 23 days, is immense. If it is assumed that one-third of the total working population works for only two-thirds of the time during the currency of *Le Tour* this would account for a loss of more than three-quarters of one per cent of the nation's annual Gross National Product. In 1975 this loss would have been in excess of £1,000,000,000.

Most expensive The most expensive of all sports is the racing of large yachts—"J" type boats, last built in 1937, and International 12-metre boats. The owning and racing of these is beyond the means of individual millionaires and is confined to multi-millionaires or syndicates.

Largest crowd The greatest number of live spectators for any sporting spectacle is the estimated 1,000,000 (more than 20 per cent of the population) who line the route of the annual San Sylvestre road race of 8 600 m *5 miles 605 yd* through the streets of São Paulo, Brazil, on New Year's night. However, spread over 23 days, it is estimated that more than 10,000,000 see the annual *Tour de France* along the route (see also above).

12
SPORTS, GAMES AND PASTIMES

The largest crowd travelling to any sporting venue is "more than 400,000" for the annual *Grand Prix d'Endurance* motor race on the Sarthe circuit near Le Mans, France. The record stadium crowd was one of 199,854 for the Brazil *v.* Uruguay match in the Maracaña Municipal Stadium, Rio de Janeiro, Brazil, on 16 July 1950.

Largest field The largest pitch of any ball game is that of polo, with 12.4 acres *5,0 ha*, or a maximum length of 300 yd *274 m* and a width, without side boards, of 200 yd *182 m.*

Most participants The annual Nijmegen Vierdaagse march in the Netherlands over distances up to 50 km *31 miles 120 yd* attracted 16,667 participants in 1968. The Vasa ski race in Sweden attracted 9,051 starters in 1975 of whom 8,812 finished.

Heaviest sportsmen The heaviest sportsman of all-time was the wrestler William J. Cobb of Macon, Georgia, U.S.A., who in 1962 was billed as the 802 lb. (57 st. 4 lb. *[363 kg]*)

Ice skater Janet Lynn (U.S.A.) the highest ever paid woman in sport, who earned £325,000 in 1974

"Happy Humphrey". The heaviest player of a ball-game has been Bob Pointer, the U.S. Football tackle formerly on the 1967 Santa Barbara High School Team California, U.S.A. and still playing in 1972 at 480 lb. (34 st. 4 lb. [*217 kg*]).

Worst disasters The worst sports disaster in recent history was when an estimated 604 were killed after some stands at the Hong Kong Jockey Club racecourse collapsed and caught fire on 26 Feb. 1918. During the reign of Antoninus Pius (A.D. 138–161) the upper wooden tiers in the Circus Maximus, Rome collapsed during a gladiatorial combat killing some 1,112 spectators. Britain's worst sports disaster was when 66 were killed and 145 injured at the Rangers v. Celtic football match at Exit 13 of Ibrox Park stadium, Glasgow on 2 Jan. 1971.

Youngest world record breakers The youngest age at which any person has broken a world record is 12 years 328 days in the case of Karen Yvette Muir (born 16 Sept. 1952) of Kimberley, South Africa, who broke the women's 110 yds backstroke world record with 1 min 08.7 sec at Blackpool on 10 Aug. 1965.

Youngest and oldest inter-nationals The youngest age at which any person has won international honours is 8 years in the case of Miss Joy Foster, the Jamaican singles and mixed doubles table tennis champion in 1958. It would appear that the greatest age at which anyone has actively competed for his country was 72 years 280 days in the case of Oscar G. Swahn (Sweden) (b. 20 Oct. 1847) who won a silver medal for shooting in the Olympic Games at Antwerp on 26 July 1920.

Youngest and oldest champions The youngest successful competitor in a world title event was a French boy, whose name is not recorded, who coxed the Netherlands' Olympic pair at Paris on 26 Aug. 1900. He was not more than 10 and may have been as young as seven. The youngest individual Olympic winner was Miss Marjorie Gestring (U.S.A.), who took the springboard diving title at the age of 13 years 9 months at the Olympic Games in Berlin in 1936.

Longest reign The longest reign as a world champion is 27 years (1928–1955) by Pierre Etchbaster (b. France, 1893) who retired as undefeated world real tennis champion aged 62.

The longest reign as a British champion is 41 years by the archer Miss Alice Blanche Legh (1855–1948) who first won the Championship in 1881 and for the 23rd and final time in 1922 aged 67.

Greatest earnings The greatest fortune amassed by an individual in sport is an estimated £17,000,000 by the late Sonja Henie of Norway (1912–1969), the triple Olympic figure skating champion (1928–32–36), when later (1936–56) a professional ice skating promoter starring in her own ice shows and 11 films. The highest paid woman athlete in the world is ice skater Janet Lynn (U.S.A.) (b. 6 April 1953), who in, 1974, signed a $1.5 million (*£652,000*) three year contract. In 1974 she earned more than $750,000 (*£325,000*). The highest mooted earnings for a single sports contest is a £3.7 million purse reportedly negotiated from the promoters of the world heavyweight title fight in Manila, Philippines due on 1 Oct. 1975, between Muhammad Ali Haj (U.S.) and Joe Frazier (U.S.). (For Ali's career total see p. 252)

Largest following The sport with most participants in Britain is swimming with 6¾ million. The highest number of paid admissions is 7¾ million for Association Football, which also attracts more than 21 million T.V. viewers.

Best attended sporting funeral A crowd estimated between 60 and 70,000 people attended the funeral of the 1960 and 1964 Olympic marathon champion Abebe Bikila (Ethopia) at Addis Ababa in October 1973.

Most sportsmen According to a report issued in April 1971, 28,400,000 men and 15,200,000 women are actively involved in 209,000 physical culture and sports groups in the U.S.S.R. where there are 6.1 million track athletes, 5.6 million volleyball players, 3.9 million footballers and 891,000 weightlifters. The report lists 2,918 stadiums, 430 indoor and 475 outdoor swimming pools for 791,000 swimmers.

ANGLING

LARGEST SINGLE CATCH

The largest fish ever caught on a rod is an officially ratified man-eating great white shark (*Carcharodon carcharias*) weighing 2,664 lb. *1 208 kg* and measuring 16 ft 10 in *5,13 m* long, caught on a 130 lb. *58 kg* test line by Alf Dean at Denial Bay, near Ceduna, South Australia, on 21 April 1959. Capt. Frank Mundus (U.S.A.) harpooned a 17 ft *5,18 m* long 4,500 lb. *2 040 kg* white shark after a 5-hour battle, off Montauk Point, New York, U.S.A., in 1964.

The largest marine animal ever killed by *hand* harpoon was a blue whale 97 ft *29,56 m* in length, killed by Archer Davidson in Twofold Bay, New South Wales, Australia, in 1910. Its tail flukes measured 20 ft *6,09 m* across and its jaw bone 23 ft 4 in *7,11 m*. To date this has provided the ultimate in "fishing stories".

SMALLEST CATCH

The smallest full-grown fish ever caught is the *Schindleria praematurus*, weighing 1/14,000 of an oz. *0,002 g* (see page 41) found in Samoa, in the Pacific.

Spear fishing The largest fish ever taken underwater was an 804 lb. *364 kg* Giant Black Grouper or Jewfish by Don Pinder of the Miami Triton Club, Florida, U.S.A., in 1955. The British spearfishing record is 89 lb. 0 oz. *40 kg 30* for an angler fish by J. Brown (Weymouth Association Divers) in 1969.

Casting record The longest freshwater cast ratified under I.C.F. (International Casting Federation) rules is 175,01 m *574 ft 2 in* by Walter Kummerow (West Germany), for the Bait Distance Double-Handed 30 g event held at Lenzerheide, Switzerland in the 1968 Championships. The British National record is 148,78 m *488 ft 1 in* by A. Dickison on the same occasion.

Longest fight The longest recorded individual fight with a fish is 32 hrs 5 min by Donal Heatley (b. 1938) (New Zealand) with a broadbill (estimated length 20 ft *6,09 m* and weight 1,500 lb. *680 kg*) off Mayor Island off Tauranga, North Island on 21–22 Jan. 1968. It towed the 12 ton/*tonnes* launch 50 miles *80 km* before breaking the line.

Rarest fish The burbot or eel-pout, the rarest British freshwater fish, is "almost extinct", so it has been agreed that no record for this species should be published, at least until Nov. 1974, in the interests of conservation.

Angling marathon Roy Wyeth of Kingsland, Southampton, Hampshire fished for 336 hrs on 3–16 May 1975.

Championship Records *World* The *Confederation Internationale de la Pêche Sportive* Championships were inaugurated in 1954. France has won 7 times between 1956 and 1972 and Robert Tesse (France) the individual title in 1959–60–65.

British The National Angling Championship (instituted 1906) has been won seven times by Leeds (1909–10–14–28–48–49–52). Only James H. R. Bazley (Leeds) has ever won the individual title twice (1909–1927). The record catch is 76 lb. 9 oz. *34 kg 720* by David Burr (Rugby) in the Huntspill, Somerset in 1965. The team record is 136 lb. 15¼ oz. *62 kg 120* by Sheffield Amalgamated also in the Huntspill in 1955.

Right: The All Tackle world's weight record Blue Marlin at 1,142 lb. This half ton monster was caught by Jack Harrington (left) of Allison Park, Pennsylvania off Nags Head, North Carolina, U.S.A. on 26 July 1974. On the right is Harry Baum captain of the cruiser *Jo Bay* from which the catch was made.

Aycock Brown

WORLD RECORDS (All Tackle)
(Sea fish as ratified by the International Game Fish Association to 1 Jan. 1975. Freshwater fish, ratified by "*Field & Stream*", are marked*)

Species	Weight lb. oz.	kg/g	Name of Angler	Location	Date
Amberjack	149 0	67,585	Peter Simons	Bermuda	21 June 1964
Barracuda	83 0	37,648	K. J. W. Hackett	Lagos, Nigeria	13 Jan. 1952
Bass (Giant Sea)	563 8	255,599	James D. McAdam	Anacapa Is., California, U.S.A.	20 Aug. 1968
*Carp[1]	55 5	25,089	Frank J. Ledwein	Clearwater Lake, Minnesota, U.S.A.	10 July 1952
Cod	98 12	44,792	Alphonse J. Bielevich	Isle of Shoals, Massachusetts, U.S.A.	8 June 1969
Marlin (Black)	1,560 0	707,604	Alfred C. Glassell, Jr.	Cabo Blanco, Peru	4 Aug. 1953
Marlin (Blue)	1,142 0	518,002	Jack Herrington	Nags Head, North Carolina, U.S.A.	26 July 1974
Marlin (Pacific Blue)	1,153 0	522,992	Greg D. Perez	Ritidian Point, Guam	21 Aug. 1969
Marlin (Striped)	415 0	188,240	B. C. Bain	Cape Brett, New Zealand	31 Mar. 1964
Marlin (White)	159 8	72,347	W. E. Johnson	Pompano Beach, Florida, U.S.A.	25 April 1953
*Pike (Northern)	46 2	20,921	Peter Dubuc	Sacandaga Reservoir, N.Y., U.S.A.	15 Sept. 1940
Sailfish (Atlantic)	128 1	58,088	Harm Steyn	Luanda, Angola	27 Mar. 1974
Sailfish (Pacific)	221 0	100,243	C. W. Stewart	Santa Cruz Is., Galapagos Is.	12 Feb. 1947
*Salmon (Chinook)[2]	92 0	41,730	Heinz Wichmann	Skeena River, British Columbia, Canada	19 July 1959
Shark (Blue)	410 0	185,972	Richard C. Webster	Rockport, Massachusetts, U.S.A.	1 Sept. 1960
	410 0	185,972	Martha C. Webster	Rockport, Massachusetts, U.S.A.	17 Aug. 1967
Shark (Shortfin Mako)[3]	1,061 0	481,261	James B. Penwarden	Mayor Island, New Zealand	17 Feb. 1970
Shark (White or Man-eating)	2,664 0	1 208,370	Alfred Dean	Denial Bay, Ceduna, South Australia	21 April 1959
Shark (Porbeagle)	430 0	195,044	Desmond Bougourd	South of Jersey, C.I.	29 June 1969
Shark (Thresher)[4]	729 0	330,668	Mrs. V. Brown	Mayor Island, New Zealand	3 June 1959
Shark (Tiger)	1,780 0	807,394	Walter Maxwell	Cherry Grove, South Carolina, U.S.A.	14 June 1964
*Sturgeon (White)	360 0	163,293	Willard Cravens	Snake River, Idaho, U.S.A.	24 April 1956
Swordfish	1,182 0	536,146	L. E. Marron	Iquique, Chile	7 May 1953
Tarpon	283 0	128,366	M. Salazar	Lago de Maracaibo, Venezuela	19 Mar. 1956
*Trout (Lake)[5]	Record being reviewed.				
Tuna (Allison or Yellowfin)	308 0	139,706	Harold J. Tolson	San Benedicto Is, Mexico	18 Jan. 1973
Tuna (Atlantic Big-eyed)	321 12	145,943	Vito Locaputo	Hudson Canyon, New York, U.S.A.	19 Aug. 1972
Tuna (Pacific Big-eyed)	435 0	197,312	Dr. Russel V. A. Lee	Cabo Blanco, Peru	17 April 1957
Tuna (Bluefin)	1,120 0	508,023	Lee Coffin	North Lake, Prince Edward Island, Canada	19 Oct. 1973
Wahoo	149 0	67,585	John Pirovano	Cat Cay, Bahamas	15 June 1962

[1] *A carp weighing 83 lb. 8 oz. 37 kg 874 was taken (not by rod) near Pretoria South Africa.*
[2] *A salmon weighing 126 lb. 8 oz. 57 kg 379 was taken (not by rod) near Petersburg, Alaska, U.S.A.*
[3] *A 1,295 lb. 587 kg specimen was taken by two anglers off Natal, South Africa on 17 March 1939 and a 1,500 lb. 680 kg specimen harpooned inside Durban Harbour, South Africa in 1933.*
[4] *W. W. Dowding caught one of 922 lb. 418 kg in 1937 on an untested line.*
[5] *A 102 lb. 46 kg 266 trout was taken from Lake Athabasca, northern Saskatchewan, Canada, on 8 Aug. 1961.*

BRITISH ROD-CAUGHT RECORDS
(as ratified by the British Record [rod-caught] Fish Committee of the National Anglers' Council)

(Selected from the complete list of about 100 species)

Species	Weight lb. oz.		kg/g	Name of Angler	Location	Year
Angler Fish	74	8	33,792	J. J. McVicar	S.W. Eddystone Lighthouse	1972
Bass	18	2	8,221	F. C. Borley	Felixstowe Beach, Suffolk	1943
Black Bream	6	7¾	2,927	J. L. D. Atkins	Off Eastern Blackstone Rocks, Devon	1973
Red Bream	9	8¾	4,330	B. H. Reynolds	Mevagissy, Cornwall	1974
Brill	16	0	7,257	A. H. Fisher	Derby Haven, Isle of Man	1950
Bull Huss (Greater Spotted Dogfish)	21	3	9,610	J. Holmes	Hat Rock, Cornwall	1955
Coalfish	30	12	13,947	A. F. Harris	S. of Eddystone	1973
Cod	53	0	24,040	G. Martin	Off Start Point, Devon	1972
Conger	102	8	46,491	R. B. Thomson	Mevagissey, Cornwall	1974
Dab	2	10¾	1,211	A. B. Hare	The Skerries, Dartmouth	1968
Dogfish (Lesser Spotted)	4	8	2,041	J. Beattie	Off Ayr Pier, Strathclyde	1969
Dogfish (Spur)	20	3	9,156	J. Newman	Off Needles Lighthouse	1972
Flounder	5	11½	2,593	A. G. L. Cobbledick	Fowey, Cornwall	1956
Garfish	2	13¾	1,296	Stephen Claeskens	Off Newton Ferrers, Devon	1971
Gurnard	11	7¼	5,195	C. W. King	Wallasey, Merseyside	1952
Gurnard (Red)	5	0	2,267	B. D. Critchley	Off Rhyl, Clwyd, Wales	1973
Haddock	12	10	5,726	Sub. Lt. K. P. White	Falmouth Bay, Cornwall	1975
Hake	25	5½	11,495	Herbert W. Steele	Belfast Lough	1962
Halibut	196	0	88,904	J. T. Newman	Off Dunnet Head, Highland	1974
John Dory	10	12	4,876	B. Perry	Porthallow, Cornwall	1963
Ling	50	8	22,906	B. M. Coppen	Off Eddystone Lighthouse	1974
Lumpsucker	14	3	6,435	W. J. Burgess	Felixstowe Beach, Suffolk	1970
Mackerel	5	6½	2,452	S. Beasley	N. of Eddystone Lighthouse	1969
Megrim	3	10	1,644	D. DiCicco	Ullapool, Highland	1966
Monkfish	66	0	29,937	G. C. Chalk	Shoreham, West Sussex	1965
Mullet (Grey)	10	1	4,564	P/O. P. C. Libby	Portland, Dorset	1952
Mullet (Red)	3	10	1,644	John E. Martel	St. Martin's, Guernsey	1967
Plaice	7	15	3,600	Ian B. Brodie	Salcombe, Devon	1964
Pollack	25	0	11,339	R. J. Hosking	Off Eddystone Lighthouse	1972
Pouting	5	8	2,494	R. S. Armstrong	Off Berry Head, Devon	1969
Ray (Spotted)	16	3	7,342	E. Lockwood	Lerwick Harbour, Shetland	1970
Ray (Thornback)	38	0	17,236	J. Patterson	Rustington, East Sussex	1935
Scad	3	4½	1,488	D. O. Cooke	Mewstone, Plymouth	1971
Allis Shad	3	4½	1,488	Bernard H. Sloane	Torquay, Devon	1964
Twaite Shad	3	2	1,417	T. Hayward	Deal, Kent	1949
	3	2	1,417	S. Jenkins	Tor Bay, Devon	1954
Shark (Blue)	218	0	98,883	N. Sutcliffe	Looe, Cornwall	1959
Shark (Mako)	500	0	226,796	Mrs. J. Yallop	Eddystone Lighthouse	1971
Shark (Porbeagle)	430	0	195,044	see world record list		
Shark (Thresher)	280	0	127,005	H. A. Kelly	Dungeness, Kent	1933
Skate (Common)	226	8	102,738	R. S. Macpherson	Dury Voe, Shetland	1970
Sole	4	3½	1,913	R. Wells	Off Redcliffe Beach, Dorset	1974
Sting Ray	59	0	26,761	J. M. Buckley	Clacton-on-Sea, Essex	1952
Three-bearded Rockling	2	14¼	1,311	S. F. Bealing	Poole Bay, Dorset	1972
Tope	74	11	33,877	A. B. Harries	Caldy Island, Dyfed, Wales	1964
Tunny	851	0	386,007	L. Mitchell-Henry	Whitby, North Yorkshire	1933
Turbot	31	4	14,174	Paul Hutchings	Off Eddystone Lighthouse	1972
Greater Weever	2	4	1,020	P. Ainslie	Brighton, East Sussex	1927
Whiting	6	3	2,811	Mrs. R. Barrett	Rame Head, Cornwall	1971
Wrasse (Ballan)	7	10⅞	3,485	B. K. Lawrence	Trevose Head, Cornwall	1970

FRESHWATER FISH

It will be noted that seven former "records" achieved between 1923 and 1955 have been discarded because they cannot be substantiated under the existing rules. These are noted as being "open to claim" if a specimen comes up to or over the "minimum qualifying standard".

Species	Weight lb. oz.		kg/g	Name of Angler	Location	Year
Barbel	13	12	6,236	J. Day	Royalty Fishery, Christchurch, Hampshire	1962
Bleak	0	3⅞	0,109	D. Pollard	Staythorpe, Nottinghamshire	1971
Bream (Common)	12	14	5,840	G. J. Harper	Stour, Great Cornard, Suffolk	1971
Bream (Silver)	record open to claim (over 1 lb. 8 oz. 680 g)					
Carp	44	0	19,958	Richard Walker	Redmire Pool, Hereford and Worcester	1952
Chub	7	6	3,345	W. L. Warren	River Avon, Hampshire	1957
Crucian Carp	4	15½	2,253	J. Johnstone	Johnsons Lake, New Hythe, Kent	1972
Dace	1	4¼	0,574	J. L. Gasson	Little Ouse, Thetford, Norfolk	1960
Eel	8	10	3,912	A. Dart	Hunstrete Lake, Somerset	1969
Grayling	record open to claim (over 3 lb. 1 kg 360)			M. Morris	Susworth Roach Ponds, Lincolnshire	1971
Gudgeon	0	4	0,113			
Gwyniad (Whitefish)	1	4	0,566	J. R. Williams	Llyn Tegid, Gwynedd	1965
Loch Lomond Powan	1	7	0,651	J. M. Ryder	Loch Lomond, Strathclyde/Central	1972
Perch	4	12	2,154	S. F. Baker	Oulton Broad, Suffolk	1962
Pike[1]	43	0	19,504	Roy R. Whitehall	Lockwood Reservoir, Walthamstow	1975
Roach	3	14	1,757	W. Penney	Lambeth Reservoir, Molesey, Surrey	1938
	3	14	1,757	A. Brown	A pit, near Stamford, Lincolnshire	1964
Rudd	4	8	2,041	Rev. E. C. Alston	Mere, near Thetford, Norfolk	1933
"Ruffe"	0	4	0,113	B. B. Poyner	River Stour, Warwickshire	1969
Salmon[2]	64	0	29,029	Miss G. W. Ballantyne	River Tay, Tayside	1922
Tench	9	1	4,110	John Salisbury	Hemingford Grey, Cambridgeshire	1963
Trout (Brown)[3]	19	4½	8,745	T. Chartres	Lower Lough, Erne	1974
Trout (Rainbow)	13	2	5,953	Dr. W. J. Drummond	Avon tributory, Hampshire	1974
Trout (Sea)	record open to claim					

[1] A Pike of allegedly 52 lb. 23 kg was recovered when Whittlesea Mere, Cambridgeshire was drained in 1851. A pike of reputedly 72 lb. 32,65 kg was landed from Loch Ken, Dumfries and Galloway, by John Murray in 1777.
[2] The 8th Earl of Home is recorded as having caught a 69¾ lb. 31 kg 638 specimen in the River Tweed in 1730. J. Wallace claimed a 67-pounder 30 kg at Barjarg, Dumfries and Galloway in 1812.
[3] In 1866 W. C. Muir is reputed to have caught a 39½ lb. 17 kg 916 specimen in Loch Awe, Strathclyde and in 1816 a 36 lb. 16 kg specimen was reported from the R. Colne, near Watford, Hertfordshire.

IRISH ANGLING RECORDS (as ratified by the Irish Specimen Fish Committee)

(Selected from the complete list of 45 species)

Species	Weight lb. oz.		kg/g	Name of Angler	Location	Date
SEA FISH						
Angler Fish	71	8	32,431	Michael Fitzgerald	Cork (Cóbh) Harbour	5 July 1964
Bass	16	6	7,427	James McClelland	Causeway Coast	13 Nov. 1972
Sea Bream (Red)	9	6	4,252	P. Maguire	Valentia, Kerry	24 Aug. 1963
Coalfish	24	7	11,084	J. E. Hornibrook	Kinsale, Cork	26 Aug. 1967

Cod	42	0	*19,050*	I. L. Stewart	Ballycotton, Cork	1921
Conger	72	0	*32,658*	J. Greene	Valentia, Kerry	June 1914
Dab	1	12½	*0,807*	Ian V. Kerr	Kinsale, Cork	10 Sept. 1963
Dogfish (Greater Spotted)	20	4	*9,185*	James Monaghan	Dunmore East	29 July 1973
Dogfish (Spur)	16	4	*7,370*	Crawford McIvor	Strangford Lough, Co. Down	20 June 1969
Flounder	4	3	*1,899*	J. L. McMonagle	Killala Bay, Co. Mayo	5 Aug. 1963
Garfish	3	10¼	*1,651*	Evan G. Bazzard	Kinsale, Cork	16 Sept. 1967
Gurnard (Grey)	3	1	*1,389*	Brendan Walsh	Rosslare Bay	21 Sept. 1967
Gurnard (Red)	3	9½	*1,630*	James Prescott	Belmullet, Co. Mayo	17 July 1968
Gurnard (Tub)	12	3½	*5,542*	Robert J. Seaman	Achill, Co. Mayo	8 Aug. 1973
Haddock	10	13½	*4,918*	F. A. E. Bull	Kinsale, Cork	15 July 1964
Hake	25	5½	*11,495*	Herbert W. Steele	Belfast Lough	28 April 1962
Halibut	156	0	*70,760*	Frank Brogan	Belmullet, Co. Mayo	23 July 1972
John Dory	7	1	*3,203*	Stanley Morrow	Tory Island, Co. Donegal	6 Sept. 1970
Ling	46	8	*21,092*	Andrew J. C. Bull	Kinsale, Cork	26 July 1965
Mackerel	3	8	*1,587*	Roger Ryan	Clogherhead Pier, Co. Louth	1 July 1972
Monkfish	69	0	*31,297*	Mons. Michael Fuchs	Westport, Co. Mayo	1 July 1958
Mullet (Grey)	7	10	*3,458*	Kevin Boyle	Killybegs Pier, Donegal	8 June 1972
Plaice	10	8	*4,762*	James Stafford	Achill, Co. Mayo	5 Sept. 1973
Pollack	19	3	*8,703*	J. N. Hearne	Ballycotton, Cork	1904
Pouting	4	10	*2,097*	W. G. Pales	Ballycotton, Cork	1937
Ray (Blonde)	36	8	*16,556*	D. Minchin	Cork (Cóbh) Harbour	9 Sept. 1964
Ray (Thornback)	37	0	*16,782*	M. J. Fitzgerald	Kinsale, Cork	28 May 1961
Shark (Blue)	206	0	*93,440*	J. L. McMonagle	Achill, Co. Mayo	7 Oct. 1959
Shark (Porbeagle)	365	0	*165,561*	Dr. M. O'Donel Browne	Keem Bay, Achill, Co. Mayo	28 Sept. 1932
Skate (Common)	221	0	*100,243*	T. Tucker	Ballycotton, Cork	1913
Skate (White)	165	0	*74,842*	Jack Stack	Clew Bay, Westport, Co. Mayo	7 Aug. 1966
Sting Ray	51	0	*23,133*	John K. White	Kilfenora Strand, Fenet	8 Aug. 1970
Tope	60	12	*27,555*	Crawford McIvor	Strangford Lough, Co. Down	12 Sept. 1968
Turbot	26	8	*12,020*	J. F. Eldridge	Valentia, Kerry	1915
Whiting	4	8½	*2,055*	Eddie Boyle	Kinsale, Cork	4 Aug. 1969
Wrasse (Ballan)	7	6	*3,345*	Anthony J. King	Killybegs, Donegal	26 July 1964
FRESHWATER FISH						
Bream	11	12	*5,329*	A. Pike	River Blackwater, Co. Monaghan	July 1882
Carp	18	12	*8,504*	John Roberts	Abbey Lake	6 June 1958
Dace	1	2	*0,510*	John T. Henry	River Blackwater, Cappoquin	8 Aug. 1966
Eel (River)	5	15	*2,693*	Edmund Hawksworth	River Shannon, Clondra	25 Sept. 1968
Perch	5	8	*2,494*	S. Drum	Lough Erne	1946
Pike (River)	42	0[1]	*19,050*	M. Watkins	River Barrow	22 Mar. 1964
Roach	2	13½	*1,289*	Lawrie Robinson	River Blackwater, Cappoquin	11 Aug. 1970
	2	13½	*1,289*	Ronald Frost	River Blackwater, Cappoquin	29 Aug. 1972
Rudd	3	1	*1,389*	A. E. Biddlecombe	Kilglass Lake	27 June 1959
Rudd-Bream hybrid	5	5	*2,409*	W. Walker	Coosan Lough, Garnafailagh, Athlone	5 June 1963
Salmon	57	0[2]	*25,854*	M. Maher	River Suir	1874
Tench	7	13¼	*3,550*	R. Webb	River Shannon, Lanesboro	25 May 1971
Brown Trout (Lake)	26	2[3]	*11,850*	William Meares	Lough Ennell	15 July 1894
Brown Trout (River)	20	0	*9,071*	Major Hugh Ll. Place	River Shannon, Corbally	22 Feb. 1957
Sea Trout	14	3	*6,435*	Dr. Eoin Bresnihan	Dooagh Beach, Achill	8 June 1973

[1] *A Pike in excess of 92 lb.* 41 kg *is reputed to have been landed from the Shannon at Portumna, County Galway, in c. 1796.*

[2] *A 58 lb.* 26 kg *Salmon was reported from the River Shannon in 1872 while one of 62 lb.* 28 kg *was taken in a net on the lower Shannon on 27 March 1925.*

[3] *A 35½ lb.* 16 kg 102 *Brown Trout is reputed to have been caught at Turlaghvan, near Tuam, in August 1738. "Pepper's Ghost", the 30 lb. 8 oz.* 13 kg 834 *fish caught by J. W. Pepper in Lough Derg in 1860 has now been shown to have been a salmon.*

ARCHERY

Earliest references The discovery of stone arrow heads at Border Cave, Northern Natal, South Africa in deposits exceeding the Carbon 14 dating limit indicates the invention of the bow as *ante* 46,000 B.C. Archery developed as an organized sport at least as early as the 4th century A.D. The oldest archery body in the British Isles is the Royal Company of Archers, the Sovereign's bodyguard for Scotland, dating from 1676, though the Ancient Scorton Arrow meeting in North Yorkshire was first staged in 1673. The world governing body is the *Fédération Internationale de Tir à l'Arc* (FITA), founded in 1931.

World records The world records for a single FITA Round are: men 1,291 points (possible 1,440) by Darrell Pace (U.S.A.) at Oxford, Ohio on 6–7 Aug. 1974, and women 1,249 points (possible 1,440) by Lena Sjoholm (Sweden) at Moscow on 1 June 1975.

Highest Championship scores There are no world records for Double FITA Rounds but the highest scores achieved in either a world or Olympic championship were at the 1975 World Championships in Interlaken, Switzerland: men, 2,548 points (possible 2,880) by Darrell Pace (U.S.A.) and women, 2,465 points by Zebiniso Rustamova (U.S.S.R.) on 25–28 June 1975.

British York Round (6 dozen at 100 yds, 4 dozen at 80 yds and 2 dozen at 60 yds)—possible 1,296 pts.
Single Round, 1,097 J. Ian Dixon at Oxford, on 4 July 1968.
Double Round, 2,138 Roy Derek Matthews at Oxford on 3–4 July 1968.
Hereford (Women) (6 dozen at 80 yds, 4 dozen at 60 yds and 2 dozen at 50 yds)—possible 1,296 pts.
Single Round, 1,118 Miss Pauline M. Edwards at London on 26 Aug. 1973.
Double Round, 2,200 Miss Pauline M. Edwards at Oxford, 27–28 June 1973.
FITA Round (Men) (3 dozen each at 90, 70, 50 and 30 m).

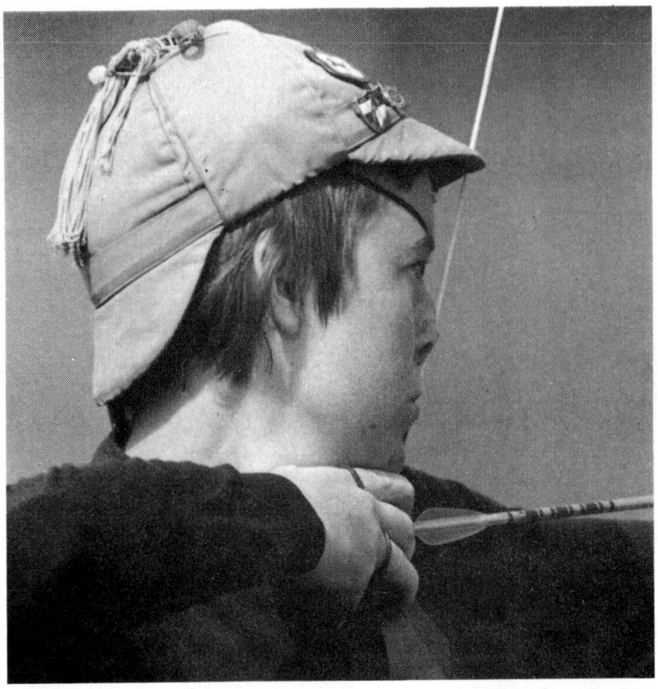

Gerry Cranham

The archer Pauline Edwards, who holds the Hereford Round records

Single Round, 1,219 Roy D. Matthews at Windermere, Cumbria, 7–8 June 1973.
Double Round, 2,386 Roy D. Matthews at Windermere, Cumbria, 7–8 June 1973.
FITA Round (Women's) (3 dozen each at 70, 60, 50 and 30 m).
Single Round, 1,218, Mrs. Barbara A. Gould at Zagreb, Yugoslavia 24–25 Aug. 1974.
Double Round, 2,313 Mrs. Lynne A. Evans (*née* Thomas) at Munich, West Germany, 7–10 Sept. 1972.

Most titles The greatest number of world titles (instituted 1931) ever won by a man is four by H. Deutgen (Sweden) in 1947–48–49–50. The greatest number won by a woman is seven by Mrs. Janina Spychajowa-Kurkowska (Poland) in 1931–32–33–34, 1936, 1939 and 1947. Oscar Kessels (Belgium) participated in 21 world championships since 1931.

Flight shooting Sultan Selim III shot 1,400 Turkish *Pikes* or *gez* near Istanbul, Turkey in 1798. The equivalent is arguably between 953–972 yd *871–888 m*. The longest recorded distance ever shot is 1 mile 268 yd *1 854,40 m* in the unlimited footbow class by the professional Harry Drake of Lakeside, California, U.S.A. at Ivanpah Dry Lake, California on 24 Oct. 1971. Drake also holds the flight records for the handbow at 856 yds 1 ft 8 in

783,23 m and the crossbow at 1,359 yds 2 ft 5 in *1 243,4 m* both at Ivanpah Dry Lake on 14–15 Oct. 1967.

The British record (Men) is 695 yd 2½ in *635,57 m* by Alan Webster at York on 21 April 1974 and (Women) 408 yd 2 ft 9½ in *373,92 m* by Miss Jo Rodwell at York on 29 April 1973.

The greatest number of British Championships is 12 by Horace A. Ford (1822–1880) in 1849–59 and 1867, and 23 by Miss Alice Blanche Legh (1855–1948) in 1881, 1886–87–88–89–90–91–92, 1895, 1898–99–1900, 1902–03–04–05–06–07–08–09, 1913 and 1921–22. Miss Legh was inhibited from winning between 1882 to 1885—because her mother Mrs. Piers Legh was Champion and also for four further years 1915 to 1918 because there were no Championships held owing to the first World War.

Marathon The highest recorded score over 24 hours by a pair of archers is 45,454 during 42 Portsmouth Rounds (60 arrows at 20 yds *18,28 m* with a 2 in *5 cm* diameter 10 ring) shot by Stan Kiehl and Greg Shumaker at the S. & R. Sports Haven, Greentown, Ohio, U.S.A. on 21–22 June 1975.

For **ATHLETICS** *see Track and Field Athletics.*

BADMINTON

Origins The game was devised *c.* 1863 at Badminton Hall in Avon, the seat of the Dukes of Beaufort. The oldest club is the Newcastle Badminton Club formed as the Armstrong College Club on 24 Jan. 1900.

Thomas Cup The International Championship or Thomas Cup (instituted 1948) has been won 5 times by Indonesia in 1957–58, 1960–61, 1963–64, 1970–71 and 1972–73.

The Ladies International Championship or Uber Cup (instituted 1956) has been most often won by Japan with 4 wins (1966–69–72–75).

Inter County Championships The most successful county has been Surrey with 19 wins between 1955 and 1975. The championships were instituted on 30 Oct. 1930.

Longest hit Frank Rugani drove a shuttlecock 79 ft 8½ in *24,29 m* in tests at San Jose, California, U.S.A., on 29 Feb. 1964.

Longest games The longest recorded game has been one of 291 hrs by 5 boys from Kirkham Grammar School, Lancs. from 7 July to 19 July 1972, who maintained continuous singles. The longest doubles marathon has been one of 318 hrs maintained by 8 players from Muslim Youth Association between 18 and 30 July 1974 at the Mill Lane Youth Centre, Newcastle-upon-Tyne, Tyne and Wear.

Rudy Hartono (Indonesia), co-holder of the record number of men's singles wins in the All England Championships with 7

Associated Press

Shortest Game In the 1969 Uber Cup in Jakarta, Indonesia, Miss N. Takagi (Japan) beat Miss P. Tumengkol in 9 min.

Most titles Most wins in the All-England Championships (instituted 1899):

Event	Times	Holder	Dates
Men's Singles	7	Erland Kops (Denmark)	1958, 1960–63, 1965, 1967
	7	Rudy Hartono (Indonesia)	1968–74
Women's Singles	10	Mrs. G. C. K. Hashman (*née* Judy Devlin) (U.S.A.)	1954, 1957–58, 1960–64, 1966–67

Most titles (*i.e.* including doubles):

	Times	Holder	Dates
Men	21	G. A. Thomas (later Sir George Thomas, Bt. d. 1972)	from 1903 to 1928
Women	17	Miss M. Lucas (U.K.)	from 1899 to 1910
	17	Mrs. G. C. K. Hashman (*née* Judy Devlin) (U.S.A.)	from 1954 to 1967

Most internationals Most international appearances:

	Times	Men	Times	Women
England	100	A. D. Jordan, M.B.E., 1951 to 1970	52	Mrs. W. C. E. Rogers (*née* Cooley), 1955 to 1969
Ireland	45	K. Carlisle, 1954 to 1970	54	Miss Y. Kelly, 1955 to 1973
Scotland	65	R. S. McCoig, 1956 to 1975	31	Mrs. Helen McIntosh (*née* Kelly), 1968–75
Wales	38	David Colmer, 1964 to 1975	38	Mrs. Angela Dickson, 1964 to 1975

BASEBALL

Earliest game A woodcut of "Base-Ball" of English provenance dated 1744 is the earliest known reference. On 4 Feb. 1962, it was claimed in *Nedelya*, the weekly supplement to the Soviet newspaper *Izvestiya*, that "Beizbol" was an old Russian game. The earliest baseball game under the Cartwright rules was at Hoboken, New Jersey, U.S.A., on 19 June 1846, with the New York Nine beating the Knickerbockers 23–1 in 4 innings.

Highest batting average The highest average in a career is .367 by Tyrus Raymond Cobb (1886–1961), the "Georgia Peach" of Augusta, Anniston, Detroit (1905–26) and Philadelphia (1927–28). During his career Ty Cobb made a record 2,244 runs from a record 4,191 hits made during a record 11,429 times at bat in a record 3,033 major league games. Lin Wen-Nsiung (Taiwan) is reported to have an average of .727.

HOME RUNS

Most Henry 'Hank' Aaron (Atlanta Braves) surpassed the career home run record of George Herman ("Babe") Ruth (1895–1948) when he struck his 715th homer at the Atlanta, Georgia stadium on 15 Apr. 1974. Babe Ruth's major league record for home runs in one year is 60 in 154 games between 15 April and 30 Sept. 1927. Roger Maris (b. 1935) (New York Yankees) hit 61 homers in a 162-game schedule in 1961. Josh Gibson (1912–1947) of Homestead Grays, a Negro League club, achieved a career total of 800 homers and 84 in one season, and in 1972 was elected to the Hall of Fame.

Longest The longest home run ever measured was one of 188,4 m *618 ft* by Roy Edward Carlyle in a minor league game at Emeryville Ball Park, California, U.S.A., on 4 July 1929. In 1919 "Babe" Ruth hit a 178,9 m *587 ft* homer in a Boston Red Sox *v.* New York Giants match at Tampa, Florida, U.S.A. The longest throw (ball weighs between 141 and 148 g *5 and 5¼ oz.* is 135,88 m *445 ft* 10 in by Glen Gorbaus on 1 Aug. 1957. The longest throw by a woman is 90,2 m *296 ft* by Miss Mildred "Babe" Didrikson (later Mrs. George Zaharis) (U.S.) (1914–56) at Jersey City, New Jersey, U.S.A. on 25 July 1931. The fastest time for circling bases is 13.3 sec by Evar Swanson at Columbus, Ohio, in 1932.

Pitching The first "perfect game" (no hits, no runs, no walks) pitched in a World Series was by Don Larsen (New York Yankees) with 97 pitches (71 in the strike zone) against Brooklyn Dodgers on 8 Oct. 1956.

Fastest Pitcher The fastest pitcher in the world is Nolan Ryan (California Angels) who, on 20 Aug. 1974 at Anaheim Stadium, Calif., U.S.A. was measured to pitch at 100.9 m.p.h. *162,3 km/h.*

Highest earnings The greatest earnings of a baseball player is $1,091,477 amassed by "Babe" Ruth between 1914 and 1938.

Baseball Hall of Fame

The once little known John Gibson, who died in 1947 aged 35, having achieved 800 home runs in his career

Record attendances and receipts The World Series record attendance is 420,784 (6 games with total receipts of $2,626,973.44) when the Los Angeles (ex-Brooklyn) Dodgers beat the Chicago White Sox 4–2 on 1–8 Oct. 1959. The single game record is 92,706 for the fifth game (receipts $552,774.77) at the Memorial Coliseum, Los Angeles, California, on 6 Oct. 1959. The record net receipts for a series has been $3,954,542 from a paid attendance of 363,149 who saw the Oakland A's beat the Cincinnati Reds 4–3 on 14–22 Oct. 1972. The highest seating capacity in a baseball stadium is 76,977 in the Cleveland Municipal Stadium, Ohio, U.S.A.

The all-time season record for attendances for both leagues has been 29,193,417 in 1971.

Highest catch Joe Sprinz (b. 1902), a former Cleveland player, caught a baseball at the fifth attempt dropped from an airship at about 800 ft *243 m* over Treasure Island, San Francisco, U.S.A. on 3 Aug. 1939. He lost 4 front teeth.

Great Britain The England *v* Wales series began in 1908. Up to 1973 Wales have won 35 and England 12 with one game abandoned. The most capped players have been Arthur Rice (England) with 18 and Tom Denning (Wales) with 12 caps.

BASKETBALL

Origins The game of "Pok-ta-Pok" was played in the 7th century B.C., by the Mayas in Mexico, and closely resembled basketball in its concept. "Ollamalitzli" was a variation of this game, played by the Aztecs in Mexico as late as the 16th century. If the solid rubber ball was put through a fixed stone ring the player was entitled to the clothing of all the spectators. Modern basketball was devised by the Canadian-born Dr. James A. Naismith (1861–1939) at the Training School of the International Y.M.C.A. College at Springfield, Massachusetts, U.S.A., in mid-December

1891. The first game played under modified rules was on 20 Jan. 1892. The game is now a global activity. The International Amateur Basketball Federation (F.I.B.A.) was founded in 1932, and the Amateur Basket Ball Association, the governing body for the game in England, was founded in 1936.

Olympic Champions The U.S.A. won all seven Olympic titles from the time the sport was introduced to the Games in 1936 until 1968, without losing a single match. In 1972 in Munich their run of 64 consecutive victories in matches in the Olympic Games was broken when they lost 50–51 to the U.S.S.R. in the Final match.

World Champions Brazil and the U.S.S.R. are the only countries to win the World Championship (instituted 1950) on more than one occasion. Brazil won in 1959 and 1963, the U.S.S.R. in 1967 and 1974.

British Champion-ship England and Scotland have each won 5 British Championship titles, out of the 12 competitions (now biennial) since the tournament was introduced in 1960.

American Professional titles The most National Basketball Association titles (instituted 1947), played for between the leading professional teams in the United States, have been won by the Boston Celtics with 11 victories.

English National Champions The most English National Championship Cup wins (instituted 1936) have been by London Central Y.M.C.A., with eight wins in 1957, 58, 60, 62, 63, 64, 1967 and 69. On 6 Apr. 1974 Sutton and Crystal Palace beat Embassy All Stars in a record score for the final of 120–100.

English Women's titles Most English Women's titles (instituted 1965) have been won by the Malory Club of South London, with 4 wins.

Highest score The highest final aggregate score recorded in any match is 395 by the Nottingham YMCA Falcons v Mansfield Pirates (250–145) at Nottingham, England on 18 June 1974. This was, however, in a handicap competition and Mansfield received 120 points to start.

Highest aggregate The highest aggregate score in an NBA match is 316 in a match between the Philadelphia Warriors (169 points) and the New York Knickerbockers (147 points) at Hershey, Pennsylvania on 2 March 1962.

Inter-national matches The highest score recorded in an international match is 164 by Romania against Wales (50) on 15 May, 1975 in the European Men's Championship at Hagen, West Germany. The highest by a women's team is 153 by U.S.S.R. against Switzerland (25) on 4 June 1956 in the European Championships. The highest in a British Championship is 116 by England when beating Wales (60) on 29 March 1975.

Highest Individual score Mats Wermelin, 13, (Sweden) scored all 272 points in a 272–0 win in a regional boy's tournament in Stockholm, Sweden on 5 Feb. 1974.

The highest individual score in a British National League or Cup match is 51 points by Peter Sprogis (London Latvians) at Swiss Cottage, Greater London on 17 Feb. 1973 in a record scoring 113–108 win.

Most points in career Wilton Norman Chamberlain (b. 21 Aug. 1936), reached a total of 30,003 points in N.B.A. matches on 16 Feb. 1972, in his 941st match. The record for the most points scored in a season, is 4,065 by Travis Grant for Kentucky State in 1971–72.

Tallest players The tallest player of all time has been Emili Rached of Brazil, who competed in the 1971 Pan American Games when measuring 233 cm *7 ft 7⅝ in.* The tallest woman player is Gwendalin Bachman of Englewood, California at 7 ft 0¼ in *213 cm.* The tallest British player has been the 7 ft 5¼ in *226,6 cm* tall Christopher Greener (see p. 8) of London Latvians whose International debut for England was v. France on 17 Dec. 1969.

Most expensive In Aug. 1974 Moses Malone, 19, of the University of Maryland signed a 7 year contract with Utah Stars for a reported $3 million (*£1,300,000*).

Most accurate The greatest goal shooting demonstration has been by Ted St. Martin of Jacksonville, Florida, who, on 28 Feb. 1975, scored 1,704 consecutive free throws.

The world's most famous basketball team The Harlem Globetrotters formed in 1927 and winners of 9,000 victories in 87 countries.

In a 24 hour period, 31 May to 1 June 1975 Fred L. Newman of San José, California, U.S.A. scored 12,874 baskets out of 13,116 throws (98.15% accuracy). John T. Sebastian holds the record for consecutive blindfold free throws with 63 straight at Maine Township High School East, Park Ridge, Illinois on 18 May 1972.

Longest recorded goal The longest recorded field goal in a match is 84 ft 11 in *25,88 m* by George Line, aged 20, of the University of Alabama against University of North Carolina at Tuscaloosa, Alabama, in January 1955. In practice in 1953, Larry Slinkard at Arlington Heights High School, Illinois, scored with a shot from 88 ft *26,82 m.*

Most travelled team The Harlem Globetrotters have travelled over 5,000,000 miles *8 000 000 km*, visited 87 countries on six continents, and have been watched by an estimated 53,000,000. The team was founded by the London-born Abraham M. Saperstein (1903–66) of Chicago, Illinois, U.S.A., and their first game was played at Hinckley, Illinois on 7 Jan. 1927. The team have recorded over 9,000 victories, with fewer than 400 defeats, but they have been entertainers rather than competitive players for much of their existence.

Largest ever gate The Harlem Globetrotters (U.S.A.) played an exhibition in front of 75,000 in the Olympic Stadium, West Berlin, Germany, in 1951. The largest indoor basketball attendance was at the Astrodome, Houston, Texas, U.S.A., where 52,693 watched the match between University of Houston and University of California at Los Angeles (U.C.L.A.), on 20 Jan. 1968.

Marathon records The longest recorded basketball marathon with 24 players (substitutes permitted) is 200 hours by school teams at Christies Beach High School, South Australia ending on 10 Dec. 1974. This time was also played by school teams from Sandwich Secondary School, Ontario, Canada ending on 23 March, 1975. This category is now discontinued.

246

BILLIARDS

Earliest mention The earliest recorded mention of billiards was in France in 1429, and it was mentioned in England in 1588 in inventories of the Duke of Norfolk's Howard House and the Earl of Leicester's property at Wanstead House, Essex. The first recorded public billiards room in England was the Piazza, Covent Garden, London, in the early part of the 19th century. Rubber cushions were introduced in 1835 and slate beds in 1836.

The longest recorded marathon played to F.I.B.A. rules (10 min. half-time intervals permitted) is 56 hrs 1 min by two teams of five players (no substitutes) from St. Mary's High School, Pennsylvania, U.S.A., on 24–26 June 1975.

Highest breaks Tom Reece (1873–1953) made an unfinished break of 499,135, including 249,152 cradle cannons (2 points each), in 85 hrs 49 min against Joe Chapman at Burroughes' Hall, Soho Square, London, between 3 June and 6 July 1907. This was not recognized because press and public were not continuously present. The highest certified break made by the anchor cannon is 42,746 by W. Cook (England) from 29 May to 7 June 1907. The official world record under the then baulk-line rule is 1,784 by Joe Davis, O.B.E. (b. 15 April 1901) in the United Kingdom Championship on 29 May 1936. Walter Lindrum (Australia) made an official break of 4,137 in 2 hrs 55 min against Joe Davis at Thurston's on 19–20 Jan. 1932, before the baulk-line rule was in force. Davis has an unofficial personal best of 2,502 (mostly pendulum cannons) in a match against Tom Newman (1894–1943) (England) in Manchester in 1930. The amateur record is 859 by Mohammed Lafir (Sri Lanka) in the world amateur championships in Bombay, India on 5 Dec. 1973.

Fastest century Walter Lindrum, M.B.E. (1898–1960) of Australia made an unofficial 100 break in 27.5 sec in Australia on 10 Oct. 1952. His official record is 100 in 46.0 sec set in Sydney in 1941.

Most world titles The greatest number of world championship titles (instituted 1870) won by one player is eight by John Roberts, Jnr. (England) in 1870 (twice), 1871, 1875 (twice), 1877 and 1885 (twice). The greatest number of United Kingdom titles (instituted 1934) won by any player is seven (1934–39 and 1947) by Joe Davis (England), who also won four world titles (1928–30 and 1932) before the series was discontinued in 1934. Willie Hoppe (U.S.A.) won 51 "world" titles in the United States variants of the game between 1906 and 1952.

Most amateur titles The record for world amateur titles is four by Robert Marshall (Australia) in 1936–38–51–62. The greatest number of English Amateur Championships (instituted 1888) ever won is eight by Sidney H. Fry (1893 to 1925) A. Leslie Driffield (1952–54, 1957–59, 1962 and 1967) and Norman Dagley (1965–6, 1970–5). The record

Mrs. Maureen Baynton holder of the record number of 9 England Women's Amateur Billiards Championships

Gerry Cranham

number of women's titles is 9 by Maureen Baynton (*née* Barrett) between 1955 and 1968.

Bar billiards The duration record for bar billiards is 216 hours by a team of five from St. Ives, Cornwall ending on 21 Dec. 1974. Thomas Morrison Clayton of Earlsfield, Greater London scored 11,700 in 10 min at the Greyhound, Battersea High Street on 18 June 1974. On 6 Nov. 1974 Norman Day of St. Helier, Jersey, Channel Islands scored 14,130 in 15 min at the Castle Green Hotel, Gorey, Jersey.

POOL

Pool or championship pocket billiards with numbered balls began to become standardised *c.* 1890. The greatest exponents were Ralph Greenleaf (U.S.A.) (b. 1899 d. 15 Mar. 1950) won the "world" professional title 19 times (1919–1937) and William Mosconi (U.S.A.) who dominated the game from 1941–1957.

The greatest number of balls pocketed in 24 hours is 5,688 (a rate of 1 per 15.19 secs) by Bruce Christopher at the Charles Monaco Broadway Billiard Lounge, New York City, on 12–13 Sept. 1974.

The longest recorded game by four players is one of 200 hours in Los Angeles, California on 21–29 Mar. 1975.

3 CUSHION

This pocketless variation dates back to 1878. The world governing body, the *Union Mondiale de Billiard* (UMB) was formed in 1928. The most successful exponent spanning the pre and post international era from 1906–1952 was William F. Hoppe (b. 11 Oct. 1887, Cornwall on Hudson, NY d. 1 Feb. 1959) who won 51 billiards championships in all forms. Most UMB titles have been won by Raymond Ceulemans (Belgium) with 11 consecutive (1963–73) with a peak average of 1.479 in 1973.

BOBSLEIGH

Origins The oldest known sledge is dated *c.* 6500 B.C. and came from Heinola, southern Finland. The word toboggan comes from the Micmac American Indian word *tobaakan*. The oldest bobsleigh club in the world is St. Moritz Tobogganing Club, home of the Cresta Run, founded in 1887. Modern world championships were inaugurated 1924. Four-man bobs were included in the first Winter Olympic Games at Chamonix in 1924 and two-man boblets from the third Games at Lake Placid, U.S.A., in 1932.

Olympic and world titles The Olympic four-man bob title has been won four times by Switzerland (1924–36–56–72). The U.S.A. (1932, 1936), Italy (1956, 1968) and Germany (1952 and (West) 1972) have won the Olympic boblet event twice.

The world four-man bob title has been won eleven times by Switzerland (1924–36–39–47–54–55–56–57–1971–72–73). Italy won the two-man title 13 times (1954, 1956–63, 1966, 1968–9 and 1971). Eugenio Monti (Italy) (b. 23 Jan. 1928) has been a member of eleven world championship crews.

TOBOGGANING

Cresta Run The skeleton one-man toboggan dates, in its present form, from 1892. On the 1,325 yds *1 211 m* long Cresta Run at St. Moritz, Switzerland, dating from 1884, the record from the Junction (2,868 ft [*875 m*]) is 42.96 secs (av. 63.08 m.p.h. [*101,52 km/h*]) by Polid Birchtold of Switzerland in Jan. 1975. The record from Top is 53.24 sec also by Birchtold in Jan. 1975. Momentary speeds of 85 m.p.h. *135 km/h* are attained.

The greatest number of wins in the Cresta Run Grand National (inst. 1885) is eight by the 1948 Olympic champion Nino Bibbia (Italy) (b. 9 Sept 1924) in 1960–61–62–63–64–66–68–73. The greatest number of wins in the Cresta Run Curzon Cup (inst. in 1910) is eight by Bibbia in 1950–57–58–60–62–63–64–69 who hence won the Double in 1960–62–63–64. The greatest number of descents made in a season is 7,749 during the 65 racing days of 1975.

LUGEING

In lugeing the rider adopts a sitting, as opposed to a prone position. It was largely developed by British tourists at Klosters, Switzerland, from 1883. The first European championships were at Reichenberg, East Germany, in 1914 and the first world championships at Oslo, Norway, in 1953. The International Luge Federation was formed in 1957. Lugeing became an Olympic sport in 1964.

Most world and Olympic titles The most successful rider in the world championships is Thomas Köhler (East Germany) (b. 25 June 1940), the only double Olympic gold medallist, who won the single-seater title in 1962, 1964 (Olympic), and 1967 and shared the two-seater title in 1967 and 1968 (Olympic). In the women's championship Otrun Enderlein (East Germany) (b. 12 Jan. 1943) has won thrice, 1964 (Olympic), 1965 and 1967.

Nino Bibbia (Italy) who won his eighth Cresta Run Grand National In 1973 aged 49

Highest speed The fastest luge run is at Krynica, Poland, where speeds of more than 80 m.p.h. *128 km/h* have been recorded.

BOWLING (TENPIN)

Origins The ancient German game of nine-pins was exported to the United States in the early 17th century. In about 1845 the Connecticut and New Haven State Legislatures prohibited the game so a tenth pin was added to evade the ban; but there is some evidence of 10 pins being used in Suffolk about 300 years ago.

In the United States there were 8,922 bowling establishments with 139,483 bowling lanes and 29,500,000 bowlers in 1970–71. The world's largest bowling centre is the Tōkyō World Lanes Centre, Japan with 252 lanes. The largest in Europe is the Excel Bowl at Nottingham, England, where the game was introduced in 1960, with 48 lanes on two floors (24 on each floor).

Highest scores World The highest individual score for three sanctioned games (possible 900) is 886 by Albert (Allie) Brandt of Lockport, New York, U.S.A., on 25 Oct. 1939. The record for consecutive strikes in sanctioned match play is 29 by Frank Caruana at Buffalo, New York, on 5 Mar. 1924, and 29 by Max Stein at Los Angeles, California, on 8 Oct. 1939. The highest number of sanctioned 300 games is 24 (till July 1973) by Elvin Mesger of Sullivan, Missouri, U.S.A. The maximum 900 for a three-game series has been recorded three times in unsanctioned games—by Leo Bentley at Lorain, Ohio, U.S.A., on 26 March 1931; by Joe Sargent at Rochester, New York State, U.S.A., in

1934, and by Jim Margie in Philadelphia, Pennsylvania, U.S.A., on 4 Feb. 1937. Such series must have consisted of 36 consecutive strikes (*i.e.* all pins down with one ball).

United Kingdom The United Kingdom record for a three-game series is 775 by Geoffrey Liddiard at Harrow, Greater London on 3 Oct. 1971. The record score for a single game is 300, first achieved by Albert Kirkham, aged 34, of Burslem, Staffordshire, on 5 Dec. 1965, which has since been equalled on several occasions. The 3 game series record for a woman player is 724 by Mrs. Joyce Presland at the Humber Bowl, Ilkeston, Derby on 8 Oct. 1974.

World championships The world championships were instituted in 1954. The highest pinfall in the individual men's event is 5,963 (in 28 games) by Ed. Luther (U.S.) at Milwaukee, Wisconsin, in 1971.

Marathon Thomas Mogavero (U.S.A.) bowled for 124 hours at Le Roy Serviceman's Club, New York ending on 4 May 1975. He bowled 788 games.

SKITTLES

The duration record for knocking down skittles (9-pins) is 91 hrs (89,786 pins down) by seven skittlers from Truro Garages Social Club, Truro, Cornwall ending on 23 May, 1975. The highest score in 24 hrs is 97,643 pins by 12 players from The Plough Inn Everden, Northamptonshire, on 7–8 July 1972.

BOWLS

OUTDOOR

Origins Bowls can be traced back to at least the 13th century in England. The Southampton Town Bowling was

formed in 1299. After falling into disrepute, the game was rescued by the bowlers of Scotland, headed by W. W. Mitchell, framed the modern rules in 1848–49.

World title In the inaugural World Championship held in Sydney, Australia in October 1966 the Singles Title was won by David John Bryant (b. 1931) (England) and the team title (Leonard Cup) by Australia. In the second Championships at Worthing in 1972 the singles was won by Malwyn Evans (Wales) and Scotland won the Leonard Cup.

Most title wins In the annual International Championships (instituted 1903) Scotland have won 31 times to England's 19. The most consecutive wins are 11 by Scotland from 1965 to 1975.

English titles The record number of English Bowls Association championships is 13 won or shared by David Bryant, M.B.E., of Clevedon, Somerset including five singles three Pairs wins (1965, 1969 and 1974), a Triples win (1966) and uniquely is involved in all four titles with four Rinks or Fours championships (1957, 1968, 1969 and 1971). He has also won 6 British Isles titles (4 singles, 1 pairs, 1 fours) in the period 1957–74.

Oldest Player Tom Fatherson (Long Beach Club) was still playing daily in California after his 103rd birthday in October 1973.

Most internationals The greatest number of international appearances by any bowler is 78 reached by Syd Thompson for Ireland in 1973.

Marathon The most protracted bowls marathon has been one of 24 hours 20 min by triples teams at Hanger Hill B.C., Ealing, London on 1–2 June 1975.

INDOOR

The English Indoor Bowling Association became an autonomous body in 1971. Prior to that it was part of the English Bowling Association.

Most titles The four-corner international championship was first held in 1936. England have won most titles with 16 wins. The National Singles title (inst. 1960) has been won most often by David Bryant (see above) with 6 wins (1963–4, 1966, 1968, 1970–1).

Highest score The highest score in a British International match is 52 by Scotland *v* Wales (3) at Teeside in 1972.

Marathon Two teams of four from Henderson, Auckland, New Zealand, played for 54 hours 33 min ending on 16 Dec. 1974.

BOXING

Earliest references Boxing with gloves was depicted on a fresco from the Isle of Thera, Greece which has been dated 1520 B.C. The earliest prize-ring code of rules was formulated in England on 16 Aug. 1743 by the champion pugilist Jack Broughton (1704–89), who reigned from 1729 to 1750. Boxing, which had, in 1867, come under the Queensberry Rules formulated for John Sholto Douglas, 9th Marquess of Queensberry, was not established as a legal sport in Britain until after the ruling R. *v.* Roberts and others of Mr. Justice Grantham, following the death of Billy Smith (Murray Livingstone) as the result of a fight on 24 April 1901.

Longest fight The longest recorded fight with gloves was between Andy Bowen of New Orleans (k. 1894) and Jack Burke in New Orleans, Louisiana, U.S.A., on 6–7 April 1893. The fight lasted 110 rounds and 7 hr 19 min from 9.15 p.m. to 4.34 a.m., but was declared a no contest when both men were unable to continue. The longest recorded bare knuckle fight was one of 6 hr 15 min between James Kelly and Jack Smith at Fiery Creek, Dalesford, Victoria, Australia on 3 Dec. 1855. The longest bare knuckle fight in Britain was one of 6 hr 3 min (185 rounds) between Bill Hayes and Mike Madden at Edenbridge, Kent, on 17 July 1849. The greatest recorded number of rounds is 278 in 4 hr 30 min when Jack Jones beat Patsy Tunney in Cheshire in 1825.

Shortest fight There is a distinction between the quickest knock-out and the shortest fight. A knock out in $10\frac{1}{2}$ sec (including a 10 sec count) occurred on 26 Sept. 1946, when Al Couture struck Ralph Walton while the latter was adjusting a gum shield in his corner at Lewiston, Maine, U.S.A. If the time was accurately taken it is clear that Couture must have been more than half-way across the ring from his own corner at the opening bell. The shortest fight on record appears to be one at Palmerston, New Zealand on 8 July 1952 when Ross Cleverly (R.N.Z.A.F.) floored D. Emerson (Pahiatua) with the first punch and the referee stopped the contest, without a count, 7 sec after the bell.

The fastest officially timed knock-out in British boxing is 11 sec (including a doubtless fast 10 sec count) when

The Most Hon. Sir John Sholto Douglas Bt., 9th Marquess of Queensberry, who gave his name to the Rules that allowed Boxing to be accepted as a sport

Radio Times Hulton

Jack Cain beat Harry Deamer, both of Notting Hill, Greater London at the National Sporting Club on 20 Feb. 1922.

The shortest world heavyweight title fight occurred when Tommy Burns (b. 17 June 1881 d. 10 May 1955) (*née* Noah Brusso) of Canada knocked out Jem Roche in 1 min 28 sec in Dublin, Ireland, on 17 March 1908. The duration of the Clay *v.* Liston fight at Lewiston, Maine, U.S.A., on 25 May 1965 was 1 min 52 sec (including the count) as timed from the video tape recordings, despite a ringside announcement giving a time of 1 min. Charles "Sonny" Liston (b. 8 May 1932) died 30 Dec. 1970. The shortest world title fight was when Al McCoy knocked out George Chip in 45 sec for the middleweight crown in New York on 7 April 1914. The shortest ever British title fight was one of 40 sec (including the count), when Dave Charnley knocked out David "Darkie" Hughes in a lightweight championship defence in Nottingham on 20 Nov. 1961.

Tallest The tallest boxer to fight professionally was Gogea Mitu (b. 1914) of Romania in 1935. He was 7 ft 4 in *223 cm* and weighed 23 st. 5 lb. *148 kg* (327 lb.). John Rankin, who won a fight in New Orleans, Louisiana, U.S.A., in November 1967, was reputedly also 7 ft 4 in *223 cm*.

WORLD HEAVYWEIGHT CHAMPIONS

Longest and shortest reigns The longest reign of any world heavyweight champion is 11 years 8 months and 7 days by Joe Louis (born Joseph Louis Barrow, Lafayette, Alabama, 13 May 1914), from 22 June 1937, when he knocked out James J. Braddock in the eighth round at Chicago, Illinois, U.S.A., until announcing his retirement on 1 March 1949. During his reign Louis made a record 25 defences of his title. The shortest reign was by Primo Carnera (Italy) for 350 days from 29 June 1933 to 14 June 1934. However, if the disputed title claim of Marvin Hart is allowed, his reign from 3 July 1905 to 23 Feb. 1906 was only 235 days.

Heaviest and lightest The heaviest world champion was Primo Carnera (1906–67) of Italy, the "Ambling Alp", who won the title from Jack Sharkey in 6 rounds in New York City, N.Y., U.S.A., on 29 June 1933. He scaled 267 lb. (19 st. 1 lb. *[121 kg]*) for this fight but his peak weight was 270 lb. *122 kg*. He had an expanded chest measurement of 53 in *134 cm*, the longest reach at 85½ in *217 cm* (finger tip to finger tip) and also the largest fists with a 14¾ in. *37 cm* circumference. The lightest champion was Robert Prometheus Fitzsimmons (1862–1917), who was born at Helston, Cornwall, and at a weight of 167 lb. (11 st. 13 lb. *[75 kg]*), won the title by knocking out James J. Corbett in 14 rounds at Carson City, Nevada, U.S.A., on 17 March 1897.

The greatest differential in a world title fight was 86 lb. *39 kg* between Carnera (270 lb. or 19 st. 4 lb. *[122 kg]*) and Tommy Loughran (184 lb. or 13 st. 2 lb. *[83 kg]*) of the U.S.A., when the former won on points at Miami, Florida, U.S.A., on 1 March 1934.

Tallest and shortest The tallest world champion according to measurements by the Physical Education Director of the Hemingway Gymnasium, Harvard University, was Carnera at 6 ft 5.4 in *196,59 cm* although he was widely reported and believed to be up to 6 ft 8½ in *204 cm*. Jess Willard (1881–1968), who won the title in 1915, often stated to be 6 ft 6¼ in *199 cm* was in fact 6 ft 5.25 in *196,21 cm*. The shortest was Tommy Burns (1881–1955) of Canada, world champion from 23 Feb. 1906 to 26 Dec. 1908, who stood 5 ft 7 in *170 cm* and weighed 12 st 11 lb. *81 kg*.

Oldest and youngest The oldest man to win the heavyweight crown was Jersey Joe Walcott (b. Arnold Raymond Cream, 31 Jan. 1914 at Merchantville, New Jersey, U.S.A.) who knocked out Ezzard Charles on 18 July 1951 in Pittsburgh, Pennsylvania, when aged 37 years 168 days. Walcott was the oldest holder at 38 years 7 months 23 days losing his title to Marciano on 23 Sept. 1952. The youngest age at which the world title has been won is 21 years 331 days by Floyd Patterson (b. Waco, North Carolina, 4 Jan. 1935) of the U.S.A. After the retirement of Marciano, Patterson won the vacant title by beating Archie Moore in 5 rounds in Chicago, Illinois, U.S.A., on 30 Nov. 1956. Patterson and

Muhammad Ali Haj (formerly Cassius Clay 7th) (b. Louisville, Kentucky, U.S.A. 17 Jan 1942) are the only two men to regain the heavyweight championship. Patterson defeated Ingemar Johansson (Sweden) on 20 June, 1960 having lost to him on 26 June 1959. Muhammad Ali defeated George Foreman on 30 Oct. 1974 having lost his title to Joe Frazier on 8 March, 1971.

Longest lived The longest lived of any heavyweight champion of the world has been Jess Willard (U.S.A.), who was born 29 Dec. 1881 at St. Clere, Kansas, and died 15 Dec. 1968 at Pacoima, California aged 86 years 351 days.

Earliest title fight The first world heavyweight title fight, with gloves and 3 min rounds, was that between John Lawrence Sullivan (b. 15 Oct. 1858 d. 2 Feb. 1918) and "Gentleman" James J. Corbett (b. 1 Sept. 1866 d. 18 Feb. 1933) in New Orleans, Louisiana, U.S.A., on 7 Sept. 1892. Corbett won in 21 rounds.

Undefeated Only James Joseph (Gene) Tunney (b. Greenwich Village, New York City, 25 May 1898) (1926–1928) and Rocky Marciano (1952–56) *finally* retired as champions, undefeated in the heavyweight division.

WORLD CHAMPIONS (any weight)

Longest and shortest reign Joe Louis's heavyweight duration record of 11 years 252 days stands for all divisions. The shortest reign has been 54 days by the French featherweight Eugène Criqui from 2 June to 26 July 1923. The disputed flyweight champion Emile Pladner (France) reigned only 47 days from 2 March to 18 April 1929, as did also the disputed featherweight champion Dave Sullivan, from 26 Sept. to 11 Nov. 1898.

Youngest and oldest The youngest age at which any world championship has been claimed is 19 years 6 days by Pedlar Palmer (b. 19 Nov. 1876), who won the disputed bantamweight title in London on 25 Nov. 1895. Willie Pep (b. William Papaleo, 20 Nov. 1922), of the U.S.A., won the featherweight crown in New York on his 20th birthday, 22 Nov. 1942. After Young Corbett knocked out Terry McGovern (b. 9 Mar. 1880 d. 26 Feb. 1918) in two rounds at Hartford, Connecticut, U.S.A., on 28 Nov. 1901, neither was able to get his weight down to nine stone, and the featherweight title was claimed by Abe Attell, when aged only 17 years 25! days. The oldest world champion was Archie Moore (b. Archibald Lee Wright, Collinsville, Illinois on either 13 Dec. 1913 or 1916) (U.S.A.) who

Pedlar Palmer, who was proclaimed world bantamweight champion in London in 1895 only 6 days after his 19th birthday

Muhammad Ali (right) disposes of George Foreman in Kinshasa, Zaire in which fight the purse was £2.2 million each

was recognized as a light heavyweight champion up to 10 Feb. 1962 when his title was removed. He was then believed to be between 45 and 48. Bob Fitzsimmons (1862–1917) had the longest career of any official world titleholder with over 32 years from 1882 to 1914. He won his last world title aged 41 years 174 days in San Francisco, California on 25 Nov. 1903. He was an amateur from 1880 to 1882.

Longest The longest world title fight (under Queensberry
fight Rules) was that between the lightweights Joe Gans (b. 25 Nov. 1874 d. 10 Aug. 1910), of the U.S.A., and Oscar Matthew "Battling" Nelson (b. 5 June 1882, d. 7 Feb. 1954), the "Durable Dane", at Goldfield, Nevada, U.S.A., on 3 Sept. 1906. It was terminated in the 42nd round when Gans was declared the winner on a foul.

Most The only boxer to win a world title five times at one
recaptures weight is "Sugar" Ray Robinson (b. Walker Smith, Jr., in Detroit, 3 May 1920) of the U.S.A., who beat Carmen Basilio (U.S.A.) in the Chicago Stadium on 25 March 1958, to regain the world middleweight title for the fourth time. The other title wins were over Jake LaMotta (U.S.A.) in Chicago on 14 Feb. 1951, Randolph Turpin (United Kingdom) in New York on 12 Sept. 1951, Carl "Bobo" Olson (U.S.A.) in Chicago on 9 Dec. 1955, and Gene Fullmer (U.S.A.) in Chicago on 1 May 1957. The record number of title bouts in a career is 33 or 34 (at bantam and featherweight) by George Dixon (b. 29 July 1870, d. 6 Jan. 1909), *alias* Little Chocolate, of the U.S.A., between 1890 and 1901.

Greatest The only man to hold world titles at three weights
weight *simultaneously* was Henry ("Homicide Hank") Arm-
span strong (b. 12 Dec. 1912), now the Rev. Henry Jackson, of the U.S.A., at featherweight, lightweight and welterweight from August to December 1938.

Greatest The greatest "tonnage" recorded in any fight is
"tonnage" 700 lb. *317 kg* when Claude "Humphrey" McBride (Oklahoma) 340 lb. (24 st. 4 lb. [*154 kg*]) knocked out Jimmy Black (Houston, Texas), who weighed 360 lb.

(25 st. 10 lb. [*163 kg*]) in the third round at Oklahoma City on 1 June 1971. The greatest "tonnage" in a world title fight was 488¾ lb. (34 st. 12¾ lb. [*221 kg 69*]) when Carnera (then 259¼ lb. [*117 kg 59*]) fought Paolino Uzcuden (229½ lb. [*104 kg 09*]) of Spain in Rome on 22 Oct. 1933.

Smallest The smallest man to win any world title has been
champion Pascual Perez (b. Mendoza, Argentina, on 4 March 1926) who won the flyweight title in Tōkyō on 26 Nov. 1954 at 7 st. 9 lb. (107 lb. [*48 kg 5*]) and 4 ft 11½ in *1,51 m.* Jimmy Wilde (b. Merthyr Tydfil, 1892–1969) who held the flyweight title from 1916–23 was reputed never to have fought above 7 st. 10 lb. (108 lb. [*48 kg 9*]).

Most Vic Toweel (South Africa) knocked down Danny
knock- O'Sullivan of London 14 times in 10 rounds in their
downs in world bantamweight fight at Johannesburg on 2 Dec.
title fights 1950, before the latter retired.

ALL FIGHTS

Largest The greatest purse announced prior to any fight has
purse been the reportedly guaranteed £2,200,000 each to George Foreman (b. Marshall, Texas, U.S.A., 10 Jan. 1949) and Muhammad Ali for their world heavyweight title fight at Kinshasa, Zaire on 30 Oct. 1974.

Bare knuckle The largest stake ever fought for in this era was
stake $22,500 (*then £4,633*) in the 27-round fight between Jack Cooper and Wolf Bendoff at Port Elizabeth, South Africa on 29 July 1889.

Attendances The greatest paid attendance at any boxing fight has
Highest been 120,757 (with a ringside price of $27.50) for the Tunney *v.* Dempsey world heavyweight title fight at the Sesqui-centennial Stadium, Philadelphia, Pennsylvania, U.S.A., on 23 Sept. 1926. The indoor record is 37,321 at the Clay *v.* Ernie Terrell fight in the Astrodome, Houston, Texas, on 6 Feb. 1967.

The highest non-paying attendance is 135,132 at the Tony Zale *v.* Billy Pryor fight at Juneau Park, Milwaukee, Wisconsin, U.S.A., on 18 Aug. 1941.

Lowest The smallest attendance at a world heavyweight title fight was 2,434 at the Clay v. Liston fight at Lewiston, Maine, U.S.A., on 25 May 1965.

Highest earnings in career The largest known fortune ever made in a fighting career is an estimated $26½ million (£11½ million) amassed by Muhammad Ali to 1975. Including earnings for refereeing and promoting, Jack Dempsey had grossed over $10,000,000 to 1967.

Most knock-outs The greatest number of finishes classed by the rules prevailing as "knock-outs" in a career (1936 to 1963) is 141 by Archie Moore of the U.S.A. The record for consecutive K.O.'s is 44, set by Lamar Clark of Utah at Las Vegas, Nevada, U.S.A., on 11 Jan. 1960. He knocked out 6 in one night (5 in the first round) at Bingham, Utah, on 1 Dec. 1958.

Most fights The greatest recorded number of fights in a career is 1,309 by Abraham Hollandersky, alias Abe the Newsboy (U.S.A.), in the fourteen years from 1905 to 1918. He filled in the time with 387 wrestling bouts (1905–1916).

Most fights without loss Hal Bagwell, a lightweight, of Gloucester, England, was reputedly undefeated in 183 consecutive fights, of which only 5 were draws, between 15 Aug. 1938 and 29 Nov. 1948. His record of fights in the war-time period (1939–46), is however very sketchy. He never contested a British title. Of boxers with complete records Packey McFarland (1888–1936) had 97 fights in 1905–1915 without a defeat.

Greatest weight difference The greatest weight difference recorded in a major bout is 10 st. (140 lb. [63 kg]) between Bob Fitzsimmons (12 st. 4 lb. [78 kg]) and Ed Dunkhorst (22 st. 4 lb. [141 kg]) at Brooklyn, New York City, N.Y., U.S.A., on 30 April 1900. Fitzsimmons won in two rounds.

Longest career The heavyweight Jem Mace, known as "the gypsy" (b. Norwich, 8 April 1831), had a career lasting 35 years from 1855 to 1890, but there were several years in which he had only one fight. He died, aged 79, in Jarrow-on-Tyne, Tyne and Wear on 30 Nov., and was buried in Liverpool on 6 Dec. 1910. Walter Edgerton, the "Kentucky Rosebud", knocked out John Henry Johnson aged 45 in 4 rounds at the Broadway A.C., New York City, N.Y., U.S.A., on 4 Feb. 1916, when aged 63.

British titles The most defences of a British heavyweight title is 14 by "Bombardier" Billy Wells (b. 31 Aug. 1889–1967) from 1911 to 1919. The only British boxer to win three Lonsdale Belts outright has been Henry William Cooper, O.B.E. (b. Camberwell, London, 3 May 1934), heavyweight champion (1959–69, 1970–71). He retired on 16 Mar. 1971 having held the British heavyweight title from 12 Jan. 1959 to 28 May 1969 and from 24 Mar. 1970 until his retirement.

Most Olympic gold medals The only amateur boxer to win three Olympic gold medals is the southpaw László Papp (b. 25 Mar. 1926) (Hungary), who took the middleweight (1948) and the light-middleweight titles (1952 and 1956). The only man to win two titles in one celebration was Oliver L. Kirk (U.S.A.), who took both the bantam and featherweight titles in St. Louis, Missouri, U.S.A., in 1904, when the U.S. won all the titles. In 1908 Great Britain won all the titles. Harry W. Mallin (G.B.) was in 1924 the first boxer ever to defend successfully an Olympic title in retaining the middleweight title.

Oldest gold medallist Richard K. Gunn (b. 1870) (GB) won the Olympic featherweight gold medal on 27 Oct. 1908 in London aged 38.

A.B.A. TITLES

Most The greatest number of A.B.A. titles won by any boxer is 6 by Joseph Steers at middleweight and heavyweight between 1890 and 1893. Trevor Andrews (Battersea Club) has uniquely won 4 successive National Schools titles and two ABA Junior titles in 1972–73.

Longest span The greatest span of A.B.A. title-winning performances is that of the heavyweight H. Pat Floyd, who won in 1929 and gained his fourth title 17 years later in 1946.

Class	Instituted	Wins	Name	Years
Flyweight (8 st. [50 kg 800] or under)	1920	5	T. Pardoe	1929–33
Bantamweight (8 st. 7 lb. [54 kg] or under)	1884	4	W. W. Allen	1911–12, 1914, 1919
Featherweight (9 st. [57 kg] or under)	1884	5	G. R. Baker	1912–14, 1919, 1921
Lightweight (9 st. 7 lb. [60 kg] or under	1881	4	M. Wells	1904–7
		4	F. Grace	1909, 1913, 1919–20
Light-Welterweight (10 st. [63 kg 500] or under)	1951	2	D. Stone	1956–57
		2	R. Kane	1958–59
		2	L./Cpl. B. Brazier	1961–62
		2	R. McTaggart	1963, 1965
Welterweight (10 st. 8 lb. [67 kg] or under)	1920	3	N. Gargano	1954–55–56
		3	T. Waller	1970–73–74
Light-Middleweight (11 st. 2 lb. [70 kg] or under)	1951	2	B. Wells	1953–54
		2	B. Foster	1952, 1955
		2	S. Pearson	1958–59
		2	T. Imrie	1966, 1969
Middleweight (11 st. 11 lb. [74 kg] or under)	1881	5	R. C. Warnes	1899, 1901, 1903, 1907, 1910
		5	H. W. Mallin	1919–23
		5	F. Mallin	1928–32
Light-Heavyweight (12 st. 10 lb. [80 kg] or under)	1920	4	H. J. Mitchell	1922–25
Heavyweight (any weight)	1881	5	F. Parks	1899, 1901–02, 1905–06

BULLFIGHTING

The first renowned professional espada was Francisco Romero of Ronda, in Andalusia, Spain, who introduced the estoque and the red muleta c. 1700. Spain now has some 190 active matadors. Since 1700, 42 major matadors have died in the ring.

Largest stadiums The world's largest bullfighting ring is the Plaza, Mexico City, with a capacity of 48,000. The largest of Spain's 312 bullrings is Las Ventas, Madrid with a capacity of 28,000.

Most successful matadors The most successful matador measured by bulls killed was Lagartijo (1841–1900), born Rafael Molina, whose lifetime total was 4,867. The longest career of any 20th century espada was that of Juan Belmonte (1892–1962) of Spain who survived 29 seasons from 1909–1937, killing 3,000 bulls and being gored 50 times. In 1919 he took part in 109 corridas. Recent Spanish law requires compulsory retirement at 55 years of age. Currently Antonio Bienvenida is the doyen at 51.

Most kills in a day In 1884 Romano set a record by killing 18 bulls in a day in Seville and in 1949 El Litri (Miguel Báes) set a Spanish record with 114 novilladas in a season.

Highest paid The highest paid bullfighter in history is El Cordobés (b. Manuel Benítez Pérez, probably on 4 May 1936, Palma del Rio, Spain), who became a sterling millionaire in 1966, when he fought 111 *corridas* up to 4 October of that year. On 19 May 1968 he received £9,000 for a *corrida* in Madrid. In 1970 he received an estimated £750,000 for 121 fights.

The world's largest bullfighting ring is not in Spain. Mexico City's Plaza, which can accommodate 48,000 *aficionados* is the largest

Gerry Cranham

CANOEING

Origins The acknowledged pioneer of canoeing as a sport was John Macgregor, a British barrister, in 1865. The Canoe Club was formed on 26 July 1866.

DOWN STREAM CANOEING

River	Miles	Km			Date	
Rhine	714	*1 149*	Four Royal Marine 2-man crews	Chur, Switzerland to Willemstad, Neths.	9–18 Mar. 1974	10 days 11 hrs
Rhine	726	*1 168*	L.Cpl. Peter Salisbury Spr. Simon Chivers	Chur, to Hook of Holland with greater portages	17 Apr.–9 May 1972	21½ days
Murray	1,300	*2 100*	Philip Davis, 16, and Robert S. Lodge (15½ ft [*4,7 m*] canoe)	Albury, N.S.W. to Murray Bridge	27 Dec. 1970– 1 Feb. 1971	36 days
Murray	287	*461*	A. Powell (K.1)	Yarrawonga to Swan Hill	28 Dec. 1971– 1 Jan. 1972	33 hrs 49 min 37.8 sec.
Mississippi	2,250	*3 620*	Dr. Gerald Capers, Charles Saunders, Joseph Tagg	Lake Itasca, Minnesota	1937	49 days
Nile	4,000	*6 500*	John Goddard (U.S.), Jean Laporte and André Davy (France)	Kagera to the Delta	Nov. 1953–July 1954	9 months
Amazon	3,400	*5 470*	Stephen Z. Bezuk (U.S.) (Kayak)	Atalaya to Ponta do Céu	21 June–4 Nov. 1970	4½ months
Zaire (Congo)	2,600	*4 185*	John and Julie Batchelor (G.B.)	Moasampanga to Banana	8 May–12 Sept. 1974	128 days

Most Olympic gold medals Gert Fredriksson (b. 21 Nov. 1919) of Sweden has won most Olympic gold medals with 6: the 1,000 m Kayak singles in 1948, 1952 and 1956, the 10,000 m Kayak singles in 1948 and 1956 and the 1,000 m Kayak doubles in 1960.

Gert Fredriksson (Sweden) winner of the record number of 6 Olympic Canoeing Gold Medals. His first was in 1948 and his sixth 12 years later

Most World championships In addition to his 6 Olympic championships Gert Fredriksson has 3 other world titles in non-Olympic years: 1,000 m K.1 in 1950 and 1954 and 500 m K1 in 1954, for a record total of 9. The Olympic 1,000 m best performance of 3 min 8.71 sec by the 1972 Norwegian K4 represents an average speed of 11.85 m.p.h. *19,07 km/h* and a striking rate of about 125 strokes per min.

Most British titles The most British Open titles (instituted 1936) ever won is 27 by John Laurence Oliver (Lincoln Canoe Club) (b. 12 Jan. 1943) from 1966 to 1974 including 12 individual events. David Mitchel (Chester S. & C.C.) won 8 British slalom titles in 1963–68–70–71.

The only United Kingdom canoeists to win world titles have been Paul Farrant (died 18 April 1960) of Chalfont Park Canoe Club, who won the canoe slalom at Geneva, Switzerland, in August 1959, and Alan Emus, who won the canoe sailing at Hayling Island, Hampshire, in August 1961 and on the Boden See (Lake of Constance) in August 1965.

Longest journey The longest journey ever made by canoe is one of 7,165 miles *11 530 km* from New York City to Nome, Alaska on the North American river system by paddle and portage by Geoffrey Westbrook Pope aged 24 and Sheldon Penfield Taylor aged 25, from 24 Apr. 1936 to 11 Aug. 1937. The longest journey without portage is one of 6,102 miles *9 820 km* by Richard H. Grant and Ernest Lassy from Chicago to New Orleans from 22 Sept. 1930 to 15 Aug. 1931.

Cross-Channel The singles record for canoeing across the English Channel is 3 hr 36 min by David Shankland, aged 29, of Cardiff, in a home-made N.C.K.I. named "Jelly Roll" from Shakespeare Bay, Dover, to Cap Gris-Nez, France, on 21 June 1965. The doubles

253

record is 3 hr 20 min 30 sec by Capt. William Stanley Crook and the late Ronald Ernest Rhodes in their glass-fibre K.2 "Accord", from St. Margaret's Bay, Dover, to Cap Blanc Nez, France on 20 Sept. 1961.

The record for a double crossing is 14 hr 14 min in K.1 canoes by J. McCann, B. Cowburn, Mrs. J. Ledger and Mrs. G. Crow on 18–19 July 1971.

Devizes-Westminster The Senior Class record for the annual Devizes-Westminster Challenge Cup race (instituted officially 1949) over 125 miles *201 km* with 77 locks is 17 hrs

50 min 23 sec by B. Perrett (Leighton Park School) and B. Greenham (Royal Canoe Club) to win the 1975 race from 61 crews. The Junior Class record is 16 hr 6 min 7 sec by I. White and C. Gale (Sussex Police Cadets) to win the 1975 race from 66 crews. Junior crews have a compulsory night stop.

Eskimo rolls The record for Eskimo rolls is 1,004 in 107 min 12 sec by David Ansell, 19 at Bedford, England on 29 May 1972. A "hand-rolling" record of 100 rolls in 3 min 58.7 sec was set in the Bootham School Pool, York on 14 June 1975 by David A. Clapham, 15.

CAVING

Duration (trogging) The endurance record for staying in a cave is 463 days by Milutin Veljkovic (b. 1935) (Yugoslavia) in the Samar Cavern, Svrljig Mountains, northern Yugoslavia

from 24 June 1969 to 30 Sept. 1970. The British record is 130 days by David Lafferty, aged 27, of Hampstead, who stayed in Boulder Chamber, Goughs' Cave, Cheddar Gorge, Somerset, from 27 March to 4 Aug. 1966. He was alone until 1 Aug. when he thought it was 7 July.

PROGRESSIVE WORLD DEPTH RECORDS

ft	m	Cave	Cavers	Date
210	64	Lamb Lair, near West Harptree, Somerset	John Beaumont (explored)	c. 1676
454	138	Macocha, Moravia	Joseph Nagel	May 1748
742	226	Grotta di Padriciano, Trieste	Antonio Lindner Svetina	1839
1,079	328	Grotta di Trebiciano, Trieste	Antonio Lindner	6 April 1841
1,293	394	Nidlenloch, Switzerland	—	1909
1,433	436	Geldloch, Austria		1923
1,476	449	Abisso Bertarelli, Yugoslavia	R. Battelini, G. Cesca	24 Aug. 1925
1,491	454	Spluga della Preta, Venezia, Italy	*L. de Battisti	18 Sept. 1927
1,775	541	Antro di Corchia, Tuscany, Italy	E. Fiorentino Club	1934
1,980	603	Trou du Glaz, Isère, France	F. Petzl, C. Petit-Didier	4 May 1947
2,389	728	Gouffre de la Pierre Saint Martin, Basses-Pyrénées, France	*Georges Lépineux	15 Aug. 1953
2,428	740	Gouffre Berger, Sornin Plateau, Vercors, France	J. Cadoux, G. Garby	11 Sept. 1954
2,963	903	Gouffre Berger, Sornin Plateau, Vercors, France	*F. Petzl and 6 men	25 Sept. 1954
3,230	984	Gouffre Berger, Sornin Plateau, Vercors, France	L. Potié, G. Garby et al.	29 July 1955
>3,600	>1 100	Gouffre Berger, Sornin Plateau, Vercors, France	Jean Cadoux and 2 others	11 Aug. 1956
>3,600	>1 100	Gouffre Berger, Sornin Plateau, Vercors, France	*Frank Salt and 7 others	23 Aug. 1962
3,743	1 141	Gouffre Berger, Sornin Plateau, Vercors, France	Kenneth Pearce	4 Aug. 1963
3,842	1 171	Gouffre de la Pierre Saint Martin, Basses-Pyrénées, France	C. Queffélec and 3 others	Aug. 1966
3,842	1 171	Gouffre de la Pierre Saint Martin, Basses-Pyrénées, France	C. Queffélec and 10 others	Aug. 1968
3,842	1 171	Gouffre de la Pierre Saint Martin, Basses-Pyrénées, France	Ass. de Rech. Spéléo Internat.	8–11 Nov. 1969

*Leader

COURSING

Origins The sport of dogs chasing hares was probably of Egyptian origin in *c.* 3000 B.C. and brought to England by the Normans in 1067. The classic event is the annual Waterloo Cup, instituted at Altcar, Lancashire in 1836. A government bill to declare the sport illegal was "lost" owing to the dissolution of Parliament on 29 May 1970. The number of clubs in Britain has dwindled from 169 in 1873 to 25 in 1973.

Most successful dog The most successful Waterloo Cup dog recorded was Colonel North's *Fullerton*, sired by *Greentich*, who

tied for first in 1889 and then won outright in 1890–91–92. He died on 4 June 1899.

The only dogs to win the Victorian Waterloo Cup (instituted 1873) three times have been *Bulwark* in 1906–07–09, at which time it was known as the Australian Waterloo Cup, and *Byamee* in 1953–54–55.

Longest course The longest authenticated course is one of 4 min 10 sec, when Major C. Blundell's *Blackmore* beat *Boldon* in a Barbican Cup decider on 2 March 1934.

CRICKET

Earliest match The earliest evidence of the game of cricket is from a drawing depicting two men playing with a bat and ball dated *c.* 1250. The game was played in Guildford, Surrey, at least as early as 1550. The earliest major match of which the score survives was one in which a team representing England (40 and 70) was beaten by Kent (53 and 58 for 9) by one wicket at the Artillery Ground in Finsbury, London, on 18 June 1744. Cricket was played in Australia as early as 1803.

BATTING

Highest innings The highest recorded innings by any team was one of 1,107 runs by Victoria against New South Wales in an Australian inter-State match at Melbourne, Victoria, on 27–28 Dec. 1926.

England The highest innings made in England is 903 runs for 7 wickets declared, by England in the 5th Test against Australia at the Oval, London, on 20, 22 and 23 Aug. 1938. The highest innings in a county championship match is 887 by Yorkshire *versus* Warwickshire at Edgbaston on 7–8 May 1896.

Lowest The lowest recorded innings is 12 made by Oxford University *v.* the Marylebone Cricket Club (M.C.C.) at Oxford on 24 May 1877, and 12 by Northamptonshire *v.* Gloucestershire at Gloucester on 11 June 1907. On the occasion of the Oxford match, however, the University batted a man short. The lowest score in a Test innings is 26 by New Zealand *v.* England in the 2nd innings of the 2nd Test at Auckland on 28 Mar. 1955.

The lowest aggregate for two innings is 34 (16 in first and 18 in second) by Border v. Natal in the South African Currie Cup at East London on 19 and 21 Dec. 1959.

Greatest victory The greatest recorded margin of victory is an innings and 851 runs, when Pakistan Railways (910 for 6 wickets declared) beat Dera Ismail Khan (32 and 27) at Lahore on 2–4 Dec. 1964. The largest margin in England is one of an innings and 579 runs by England over Australia in the 5th Test at the Oval on 20–24 Aug. 1938 when Australia scored 201 and 123 with two men short in both innings. The most one-sided county match was when Surrey (698) defeated Sussex (114 and 99) by an innings and 485 runs at the Oval on 9–11 Aug. 1888.

FASTEST SCORING

The greatest number of runs scored in a day is 721 all out (10 wickets) in 5 hrs 48 min by the Australians v. Essex at Southchurch Park, Southend-on-Sea on the first day on 15 May 1948.

The Test record for runs in a day is 588 at Old Trafford on 27 July 1936 when England put on 398 and India were 190 for 0 in their second innings by the close.

Innings of 200 or more The fastest recorded exhibition of hitting occurred in a Kent v. Gloucestershire match at Dover on 20 Aug. 1937, when Kent scored 219 runs for 2 wickets in 71 min, at the rate of 156 runs for each 100 balls bowled.

Fastest 50 The fastest 50 ever hit was completed in 8 min (1.22 to 1.30 p.m.) and in 11 scoring strokes by Clive C. Inman (b. Colombo, Ceylon, 29 Jan. 1936) in an innings of 57 not out for Leicestershire v. Nottinghamshire at Trent Bridge, Nottingham on 20 Aug. 1965.

Century The fastest century ever hit was completed in 35 min by Percy George Herbert Fender (b. 22 Aug. 1892), when scoring 113 not out for Surrey v. Northamptonshire at Northampton on 26 Aug. 1920. The most prolific scorer of centuries in an hour or less was Gilbert Laird Jessop (1874–1955), with 11 between 1897 and 1913. The fastest Test century was one of 70 min by Jack Morrison Gregory (1895–1973) of New South Wales, for Australia v. South Africa in the 2nd Test at Johannesburg on 12 Nov. 1921. Edwin Boaler Alletson (1884–1963) scored 189 runs in 90 min for Nottinghamshire v. Sussex at Hove on 20 May 1911.

Double century The fastest double century was completed in 120 min by Gilbert Jessop (1874–1955) (286) for Gloucestershire v. Sussex at Hove on 1 June 1903.

Treble century The fastest treble century was completed in 181 min by Denis Charles Scott Compton, C.B.E. (b. Hendon, 23 May 1918) of Middlesex, who scored 300 for the M.C.C. v. North-Eastern Transvaal at Benoni on 3–4 Dec. 1948.

1,000 in May The most recent example of scoring 1,000 runs *in May* was by Charles Hallows (Lancashire) (1895–1972), who made precisely 1,000 between 5–31 May 1928. Dr. W. G. Grace (9–30 May 1895) and W. R. Hammond (7–31 May 1927) surpassed this feat with 1,016 and 1,042 runs. The greatest number of runs made *before the end of May* was by T. W. Hayward with 1,074 from 16 April to 31 May in 1900.

Slowest scoring The longest time a batsman has ever taken to open his scoring is 1 hr 37 min by Thomas Godfrey Evans (b. Finchley, 18 Aug. 1920) of Kent, who scored 10 not out for England v. Australia in the 4th Test at Adelaide on 5–6 Feb. 1947. Richard Gorton Barlow (1850–1919) utilized 2½ hrs to score 5 not out

A cartoon of Gilbert L. Jessop (1874–1955) still the most prolific scorer of century's in under 60 minutes— thirteen

Mary Evans

for Lancashire v. Nottinghamshire at Nottingham on 8 July 1882. During his innings his score remained unchanged for 80 min.

The slowest century on record was by Derrick John (Jackie) McGlew (b. 11 March 1929) of South Africa in the Third Test v. Australia at Durban on 25 and 27 Jan. 1958. He required 9 hrs 35 min for 105, reaching the 100 in 9 hrs 5 min. The slowest double century recorded is one of 10 hrs 8 min by Robert Baddeley Simpson (b. 3 Feb. 1936) of New South Wales, during an innings of 311, lasting 12 hrs 42 min, for Australia v. England in the Fourth Test at Old Trafford on 23, 24 and 25 July 1964.

Highest individual innings The highest individual innings recorded is 499 in 10 hrs 40 min by Hanif Muhammad (b. Junagadh, India, now Pakistan, 21 Dec. 1934) for Karachi v. Bahawalpur at Karachi, Pakistan, on 8, 9 and 11 Jan. 1959. The record for a Test match is 365 not out in 10 hrs 8 min by Sir Garfield St. Aubrun Sobers (b. Bridgetown, Barbados, 28 July 1936) playing for the West Indies in the Third Test against Pakistan at Sabina Park, Kingston, Jamaica, on 27 Feb.–1 March 1958. The England Test record is 364 by Sir Leonard Hutton (b. Fulneck, Pudsey, West Yorkshire, 23 June 1916) v. Australia in the 5th Test at the Oval on 20, 22 and 23 Aug. 1938. The highest score in England is 424 in 7 hr 50 min by Archibald Campbell MacLaren (1871–1944) for Lancashire v. Somerset at Taunton on 15–16 July 1895.

Longest innings The longest innings on record is one of 16 hrs 10 min for 337 runs by Hanif Muhammad (Pakistan) v. the West Indies in the 1st Test at Bridgetown, Barbados, on 20–23 Jan. 1958. The English record is 13 hrs 17 min by Hutton (see above).

Least runs in a career S. Clark the Somerset wicket-keeper, played five matches for his county in 1930, scoring no runs in each of his nine innings of which 7 were ducks.

Most runs off an over The first batsman to score the possible of 36 runs off a six-ball over was Sir Garfield Sobers (Nottinghamshire) off Malcolm Andrew Nash (Glamorgan) at Swansea on 31 Aug. 1968. The ball (recovered from the last hit from the road by a small boy) resides in Nottingham's Museum.

BIGGEST SCORERS

Season The greatest number of runs ever scored in a season is 3,816 in 50 innings (8 not out) by Denis Compton (Middlesex) in 1947. His batting average was 90.85.

Most runs in a career The greatest aggregate of runs in a career is 61,237 in 1,315 innings (106 not out) between 1905 and 1934 by Sir John (Jack) Berry Hobbs (1882–1963) of Surrey and England. His career average was 50.65.

Test matches The greatest number of runs scored in Test matches is 8,032 in 160 innings (21 not out) by Sir Garfield St. Aubrun Sobers of Barbados and Nottinghamshire playing for the West Indies between 1952–53 and 1973–74. His average is 57.78.

CENTURIES

Season The record for the greatest number of centuries in a season is also held by Compton with eighteen in 1947. With their restricted fixture list the Australian record is eight by Sir Donald George Bradman (b. 27 Aug. 1908) in only 12 innings in the 1947–48 season.

Career The most centuries in a career is 197 by Sir John Hobbs between 1905 and 1934. The Australian record is Sir Donald Bradman's 117 centuries between 1927 and 1949.

Test matches The greatest number of centuries scored in Test matches is 29 by Sir Donald Bradman (Australia) between 1928 and 1948. The English record is 22 by Walter Hammond (1903–65) of Gloucestershire, between 1927 and 1947, and 22 by Michael Colin Cowdrey, C.B.E. (Kent) between 1954–55 and 1974–5.

Highest averages The highest recorded seasonal batting average in England is 115.66 for 26 innings (2,429 runs) by Don Bradman (Australia) in England in 1938. The English record is 100.12 by Geoffrey Boycott (b. 21 Oct. 1940) of Yorkshire and England for 30 innings (2,503 runs) including 13 centuries and 5 times not out in 1971. The world record for a complete career is 95.14 for 338 innings (28,067 runs) by Bradman between 1927 and 1949. The record for Test matches is 99.94 in 80 innings (6,996 runs) by Bradman in 1928–48. The English career record is 56.37 for 500 innings (62 not out) by Kumar Shri Ranjitsinhji (1872–1933) later H. H. the Jam Saheb of Nawanagar, with 24,692 runs between 1893 and 1920.

Double centuries The only batsman to score double centuries in both innings is Arthur Edward Fagg (b. 18 June 1915), who made 244 and 202 not out for Kent v. Essex at Colchester on 13–15 July 1938.

Longest hit The longest measured drive is one of 175 yds *160 m* by Walter (later the Rev.) Fellows (1834–1901) of Christ Church, Oxford University, in a practice on their ground off Charles Rogers in 1856. J. E. C. Moore made a measured hit of 170 yds 1 ft 5 in *155,59 m* at Griffith, New South Wales, Australia, in February 1930. Peter Samuel Heine (b. 28 June 1929) of the Orange Free State is said to have driven a ball bowled by Hugh Joseph Tayfield (b. 30 Jan. 1929) of Natal for approximately 180 yds *164,5 m* at Bloemfontein on 3 Jan. 1955.

Percival Perrin, (Essex) who in 1904 scored an unrivalled 68 boundaries in a single innings

Press Association

Most sixes in an innings The highest number of sixes hit in an innings is 15 by John Richard Reid, O.B.E. (b. 3 June 1928), in an innings of 296, lasting 3 hrs 47 min, for Wellington v. Northern Districts in the Plunket Shield Tournament at Wellington, New Zealand, on 14–15 Jan. 1963. The Test record is 10 by Walter Hammond in an innings of 336 not out for England v. New Zealand at Auckland on 31 March and 1 April 1933.

Most sixes in a match The highest number of sixes in a match is 17 (10 in the first and 7 in the second innings) by William James Stewart (b. 31 Aug. 1934) for Warwickshire v. Lancashire at Blackpool on 29–31 July 1959. His two innings were of 155 and 125.

Most boundaries in an innings The highest number of boundaries in an innings was 68 (all in fours) by Percival Albert Perrin (1876–1945) in an innings of 343 not out for Essex v. Derbyshire at Chesterfield on 18–19 July 1904.

Most runs off a ball The most runs scored off a single hit is 10 by Samuel (later Sir) Hill-Wood (1872–1949) off Cuthbert James Burnup (1875–1960) in the Derbyshire v. M.C.C. match at Lord's, City of Westminster, Greater London, on 26 May 1900.

GREATEST PARTNERSHIP

World The record stand for any partnership is the fourth wicket stand of 577 by Gul Muhammad (b. 15 Oct. 1921), who scored 319, and Vijay Samuel Hazare (b. 11 March 1915) (288) in the Baroda v. Holkar match at Baroda, India, on 8–10 March 1947.

England The highest stand in English cricket, and the world record for a first wicket partnership, is 555 by Percy Holmes (1886–1971) (224 not out) and Herbert Sutcliffe (313) for Yorkshire v. Essex at Leyton on 15–16 June 1932.

Highest score by a No. 11 The highest score by a No. 11 batsman is 163 by Thomas Peter Bromly Smith (1908–67) for Essex v. Derbyshire at Chesterfield in August 1947.

BOWLING

Most wickets The largest number of wickets ever taken in a season is 304 by Alfred Percy ("Tich") Freeman (1888–1965) of Kent, in 1928. Freeman bowled 1,976.1 overs, of which 423 were maidens, with an average of 18.05 runs per wicket. The greatest wicket-taker in history is Wilfred Rhodes (1877–1973) who took 4,187 wickets for 69,993 runs (average 16.71 runs per wicket) between 1898 and 1930. The highest percentage of wickets gained unassisted is 73.50% (1,479 from 2,012) by Schofield Haigh (1871–1921), who played for Yorkshire from 1895 to 1913.

Tests The greatest number of wickets taken in Test matches is 307 for 6,625 runs (average 21.57) by Frederick Sewards Trueman (b. Scotch Springs, Yorkshire, 6 Feb. 1931), in 67 Tests between June 1952 and June 1965. The lowest bowling average in a Test career (minimum 15 wickets) is 112 wickets for 1,205 runs (10.75 runs per wicket) by George Alfred Lohmann (1865–1901) in 18 Tests for England between 1886 and 1896.

Fastest The highest measured speed for a ball bowled by any bowler is 93 m.p.h. *149 km/h* by Harold Larwood (b. Nuncargate, Notts., 14 Nov. 1904) in 1933. The fastest bowler of all time is regarded by many as Charles Jesse Kortright (1871–1952) who played for Essex from 1889 to 1907. Albert Cotter (1883–1917) of New South Wales, Australia, is reputed to have broken a stump more than 20 times. Wesley Winfield Hall (b. 12 Sept. 1937) of Barbados was timed to bowl at 91 m.p.h. *146 km/h* in practice in 1962–63, when playing for Queensland, Australia.

Most consecutive wickets No bowler in first class cricket has yet achieved five wickets with five consecutive balls. The nearest approach was that of Charles Warrington Leonard Parker (1884–1959) (Gloucestershire) in his own benefit match against Yorkshire at Bristol on 10 Aug. 1922, when he struck the stumps with five successive balls but the second was called as a no-ball. The only man to have taken 4 wickets with consecutive balls more than once is Robert James Crisp (b. 28 May 1911) for Western Province v. Griqualand West at Johannesburg on 23–24 Dec. 1931 and against Natal at Durban on 3 March 1934.

Most "hat tricks" The greatest number of "hat tricks" is seven by Douglas Vivian Parson Wright (b. 21 Sept. 1914) of Kent, on 3 and 29 July 1937, 18 May 1938, 13 Jan. and 1 July 1939, 11 Aug. 1947 and 1 Aug. 1949. In his own benefit match at Lord's on 22 May 1907, Albert Edwin Trott (Middlesex) took four Somerset wickets with four consecutive balls and then later in the same innings achieved a "hat trick".

Most wickets in an innings The taking of all ten wickets by a single bowler has been recorded many times but only one bowler has achieved this feat on three occasions—Alfred Percy Freeman of Kent, against Lancashire at Maidstone on 24 July 1929, against Essex at Southend on 13-14 Aug. 1930 and against Lancashire at Old Trafford on 27 May 1931. The fewest runs scored off a bowler taking all 10 wickets is 10, when Hedley Verity (1905–43) of Yorkshire dismissed (8 caught, 1 l.b.w., 1 stumped) every Nottinghamshire batsman in 118 balls at Leeds on 12 July 1932. The only bowler to have "clean bowled" a whole side out was John Wisden (1826–84) of Sussex, playing for the North v. the South at Lord's in 1850.

Most wickets in a match James Charles Laker (b. Frizinghall, West Yorkshire, 9 Feb. 1922) of Surrey took 19 wickets for 90 runs (9–37 and 10–53) for England v. Australia in the 4th Test at Old Trafford, Greater Manchester, on 26–31 July 1956. No other bowler has taken more than 17 wickets in a first class match. Henry Arkwright (1837–66) took 18 wickets for 96 runs in a 12-a-side match, M.C.C. v. Gentlemen of Kent, at Canterbury on 14–17 Aug. 1861. Alfred Percy Freeman (Kent) took ten or more wickets in a match on 140 occasions between 1914 and 1936.

Mary Evans

John Wisden (1826–84), editor of the cricket statisticians 'bible', who in 1850 clean bowled the entire South of England team

Most wickets in a day The greatest number of wickets taken in a day's play is 17 by Colin Blythe (1879–1917) for 48 runs, for Kent against Northamptonshire at Northampton on 1 June 1907; by Hedley Verity for 91 runs, for Yorkshire v. Essex at Leyton on 14 July 1933; and by Thomas William John Goddard (1900–66) for 106 runs, for Gloucestershire v. Kent at Bristol, Avon on 3 July 1939.

Most expensive bowling The greatest number of runs hit off one bowler in one innings is 362, scored off Arthur Alfred Mailey (1886–1967) in the New South Wales v. Victoria inter-State match at Melbourne on 24–28 Dec. 1926. The greatest number of runs ever conceded by a bowler in one match is 428 by C. S. Nayudu (b. 18 April 1914) in the Holkar v. Bombay match at Bombay on 4–9 March 1945, when he also made the record number of 917 deliveries.

Most maidens Hugh Joseph Tayfield bowled 16 consecutive 8-ball maiden overs (137 balls without conceding a run for) South Africa v. England at Durban on 25–27 Jan. 1957. The greatest number of consecutive 6-ball maiden overs bowled is 21 (130 balls) by Ragunath G. ("Bapu") Nadkarni (b. 4 April 1932) for India v. England at Madras on 12 Jan. 1964. The English record is 17 overs (105 balls) by Horace L. Hazell (b. 30 Sept. 1909) for Somerset v. Gloucestershire at Taunton on 4 June 1949, and 17 (104 balls) by Graham Anthony (Tony) Richard Lock (b. 5 July 1929) of Surrey, playing for the M.C.C. v. the Governor-General's XI at Karachi, Pakistan, on 31 Dec. 1955. Alfred Shaw (1842–1907) of Nottinghamshire bowled 23 consecutive 4-ball maiden overs (92 balls) for North v. the South at Nottingham in 1876.

Most balls The greatest number of balls sent down by any bowler in one season is 12,234 (651 maidens: 298 wickets) by Alfred Percy Freeman (Kent) in 1933. The most balls bowled in an innings is 588 (98 overs) by Sonny Ramadhin (b. 1 May 1930) of Trinidad, playing for the West Indies in the First Test v. England at Birmingham, West Midlands on 30 May and 1, 3 and 4 June 1957. He took 2 for 179.

Best average The lowest recorded bowling average for a season is one of 8.61 runs per wicket (177 wickets for 1,525 runs) by Alfred Shaw of Nottinghamshire in 1880.

FIELDING

Most catches in an innings The greatest number of catches in an innings is seven, by Michael James Stewart (b. 16 Sept. 1932) for Surrey v. Northamptonshire at Northampton on 7 June 1957, and by Anthony Stephen Brown (b. 24 June 1936) for Gloucestershire v. Nottinghamshire at Trent Bridge, Nottingham on 26 July 1966.

In a match Walter Reginald Hammond (1903–65) held a record total of 10 catches (4 in the first innings, 6 in the second) for Gloucestershire v. Surrey at Cheltenham, Gloucestershire on 16–17 Aug. 1928. The record for a wicket-keeper is 11.

In a season and in a career The greatest number of catches in a season is 78 by Walter Hammond (Gloucestershire) in 1928, and 77 by Michael James Stewart (Surrey) in 1957. The most catches in a career is 1,015 by Frank Edward Wooley (b. 27 May 1887) of Kent in 1906–1938. The Test record is 120 by Michael Colin Cowdrey between 1954–55 and 1974–5.

Longest throw The longest recorded throw of a cricket ball (5½ oz. [155 g]) is 140 yds 2 ft (422 ft [128,6 m]) by R. Percival on Durham Sands Racecourse on Easter Monday, 14 April 1884.

WICKET KEEPING

In an innings The most dismissals by a wicket-keeper in an innings is eight (all caught) by Arthur Theodore Wallace Grout (1927–68) for Queensland against Western Australia at Brisbane on 15 Feb. 1960. The most stumpings in an innings is six by Henry ("Hugo") Yarnold (1917–1974) for Worcestershire v. Scotland at Broughty Ferry, Tayside, on 2 July 1951. The Test record is six (all caught) by A. T. W. Grout (see above) for the First Australia v. South Africa Test at Johannesburg on 27–28 Dec. 1957; six (all caught) by Denis Lindsay (b. 4 Sept. 1939) of North-Eastern Transvaal, for South Africa v. Australia in the First Test at Johannesburg on 24 Dec. 1966; six (all caught) by John Thomas Murray (b. 1 April 1935) of Middlesex, for England v. India in the second Test at Lord's, on 22 June 1967.

In a match The greatest number of dismissals by a wicket-keeper in a match is 12 by Edward Pooley (1838–1907) (eight caught, four stumped) for Surrey v. Sussex at the Oval on 6–7 July 1868; nine caught, three stumped by Don Tallon (b. 17 Feb. 1916) of Australia for Queensland v. New South Wales at Sydney on 2–4 Jan. 1939; and also nine caught, three stumped by Hedley Brian Taber (b. 29 April 1940) of New South Wales against South Australia at Adelaide 17–19 Dec. 1968. The record for catches is 11 (seven in the first innings and four in the second) by Arnold Long

Alan Knott, the England wicket-keeper, who yielded not a single bye in 1,484 runs v. Australia in 1972

Associated Press

(b. 18 Dec. 1940), for Surrey v. Sussex at Hove, East Sussex on 18 and 21 July 1964. The most stumpings in a match is nine by Frederick Henry Huish (1872–1957) for Kent v. Surrey at the Oval on 21–23 Aug. 1911. The Test record for dismissals is 9 (eight caught, one stumped) by Gilbert Roche Andrews Langley of South Australia, playing for Australia v. England in the 2nd Test at Lord's, on 22–26 June 1956.

In a season The record number of dismissals for any wicket-keeper in a season is 127 (79 caught, 48 stumped) by Leslie Ethelbert George Ames, C.B.E. (b. 3 Dec. 1905) of Kent in 1929. The record for the number stumped is 64 by Ames in 1932. The record for catches is 96 by James Graham Binks (b. 5 Oct. 1935) of Yorkshire in 1960.

In a career The highest total of dismissals in a wicket-keeping career is 1,506 (a record 1,254 catches plus 252 stumpings) by John Thomas Murray (b. 1 April 1935) of Middlesex between 1952 and close of play on 1 Aug., 1975. The most stumpings in a career is 415 by Ames (1926–1951). The Test record is 219 dismissals in 91 matches by Godfrey Evans.

Least byes The best wicket keeping record for preventing byes is that of Archdale Palmer Wickham (1855–1935) when, keeping for Somerset v. Hampshire at Taunton on 20–22 July 1899, he did not concede a single bye in a total of 672 runs. The record for Test matches in one innings is no byes in 659 runs by Godfrey Evans for England in the 2nd Test v. Australia at Sydney, New South Wales, on 14, 16, 17 and 18 Dec. 1946. Alan Philip Eric Knott (b. 9 April 1946), in a Test series for England v. Australia in England in 1972, did not concede a single bye while Australia scored 1,484 runs between the 3rd and 5th Tests.

Most byes The records at the other extreme are those of Philip Harman Stewart-Brown (b. 30 April 1904) of Harlequins, who let through 46 byes in an Oxford University innings of only 188 on 21–23 May 1927 and 48 byes let through by Anthony William Catt of Kent in a Northamptonshire total of 374 at Northampton on 20–22 Aug. 1955.

TEST RECORDS

Most Test appearances The record number of Test appearances is 114 by Michael Colin Cowdrey (England) between 1954–55 and 1974–5. The highest number of Test captaincies is 41, including 35 consecutive games, by Peter Barker Howard May (b. 31 Dec. 1929) of Cambridge University and Surrey, who captained England from 1955 to 1961 and played in a total of 66 Tests. The most innings batted in Test matches is 188 in 114 Tests by Cowdrey of Kent, playing for England between 1954–55 and 1974–5. Sir Garfield Sobers (West Indies) holds the record for consecutive Tests, with 85 from April 1955 to April 1972.

Longest match The lengthiest recorded cricket match was the "time-less" Test between England and South Africa at Durban on 3–14 March 1939. It was abandoned after 10 days (8th day rained off) because the boat taking the England team home was due to leave. The lengthiest in England have been the 6-day 5th England v. Australia Test on 6–12 Aug. 1930, when rain prevented play on the fifth day and the 6-day 5th England v. Australia Test on 10–16 Aug. 1972, when play took place on all 6 days.

Largest crowds The greatest recorded attendance at a cricket match is 350,534 (receipts £30,124) for the Third Test between Australia and England at Melbourne on 1–7 Jan. 1937. For the whole series the figure was a record 933,513 (receipts £87,963). The greatest recorded attendance at a cricket match on one day was 90,800 on the second day of the Fifth Test between Australia and the West Indies at Melbourne on 11 Feb. 1961, when the receipts were £A13,132 (£10,484 sterling). The English record is 159,000 for the Fourth Test between England and Australia at Headingley, Leeds, West Yorkshire, on 22–27 July 1948, and the record for one day probably a capacity of 46,000 for a match between Lancashire and Yorkshire at Old Trafford on 2 Aug. 1926. The English record for a Test series is 549,650 (receipts £200,428) for the series against Australia in 1953.

Greatest receipts The world record for receipts from a match is £87,305, from the attendance paid by 95,530 at the Third Test between England and the West Indies at Lord's on 23–27 Aug, 1973. The Test series record is £261,283 paid by 294,845 for the five England v. Australia Tests of June–August 1972.

ENGLISH COUNTY CHAMPIONSHIP

The greatest number of victories has been secured by Yorkshire with 29 outright wins up to 1974, and one shared with Middlesex in 1949. The most "wooden spoons" have been won by Northamptonshire, with ten since 1923. They did not win a single match between May 1935 and May 1939. The record number of consecutive title wins is 7 by Surrey from 1952 to 1958. The greatest number of consecutive appearances for one county in county championship matches is 423 by Kenneth George Suttle (b. 25 Aug. 1928) of Sussex in 1954–69. James Graham Binks (b. 5 Oct. 1935) of Yorkshire played in every county championship match for his side between his debut in 1955 and his retirement in 1969—412 matches.

Oldest and youngest county cricketers The youngest player to represent his county was William Wade Fitzherbert Pullen (1866–1937), for Gloucestershire against Middlesex at Lord's on 5 June 1882, when aged 15 years 346 days. The oldest regular County players have been William George Quaife (1872–1951) of Sussex and Warwickshire, who played his full season last match for Warwickshire against Hampshire at Portsmouth on 27–30 Aug. 1927, when aged 55, and John Herbert King (1871–1946) of Leicestershire, who played his last match for his county against Yorkshire at Leicester on 5–7 Aug. 1925, when aged 54.

Highest benefit The highest "benefit" ever accorded a player is £21,109 for David John Brown (b. 30 Jan. 1942) of Warwickshire in 1973.

MINOR CRICKET RECORDS
(where excelling those in First Class Cricket)

Bowling Stephen Fleming bowling for Marlborough College "A" XI, New Zealand v. Bohally Intermediate at Blenheim, New Zealand in Dec. 1967 took 9 wickets in 9 consecutive balls. In February 1931 in a schools match in South Africa Paul Hugo also took 9 wickets with 9 consecutive balls for Smithfield School v. Aliwal North. In August 1917 Pte. J. Leake (9th Brigade Canadian Expeditionary Force) took all 10 wickets of the Canadian Army Service Corps all clean bowled in 12 balls.

In 1881 F. R. Spofforth in Australia clean bowled all 10 wickets in *both* innings. J. Bryant for Erskine v. Deaf Mutes in Melbourne on 15 and 22 Oct. 1887 repeated the feat. The most extreme double hat trick reported was by N. Stracy for the Belvine Club near Melbourne, Australia in late March 1903. All six deliveries struck the middle stump.

Highest individual innings In a Junior House match between Clarke's House and North Town, at Clifton College, Bristol, 22–23–26-7-8 June 1899, A. E. J. Collins (b. India, 1886—k. Flanders, Nov. 1914) scored an unprecedented 628 not

---

GILLETTE CUP, JOHN PLAYER LEAGUE AND BENSON & HEDGES CUP RECORDS

	Gillette Cup (Instituted 1963)	John Player League (Instituted 1969)	Benson and Hedges Cup (Instituted 1972)
Highest Individual Innings	177—C. G. Greenidge, Hants. v. Glams. Southampton 1975	155*—B. A. Richards, Hants v. Yorks. Hull, 1970	173*—C. G. Greenidge, Hants v. Minor Counties (South), Amersham, 1973
Best Individual Bowling	7–15—A. L. Dixon, Kent v. Surrey, Oval, 1967	8–26—K. D. Boyce, Essex v. Lancs, Old Trafford, 1971. *N.B.* A .Ward, Derby v. Sussex, Derby 1970 4 wickets in 4 balls	6–27—A. G. Nicholson, Yorks v. Minor Counties (North), Middlesbrough, 1972
Highest Innings Total	371 for 4 (off 60 overs), Hants. v. Glams. Southampton 1975	307 for 4 (off 38 overs) Worcs. v. Derbys. at Worcester, 1975	327 for 4 (off 55 overs), Leics. v. Warwicks, Coventry, 1972
Lowest Innings Total	41 (off 20 overs), Cambs. v. Bucks., Cambridge, 1972 41 (off 19.4 overs), Middlesex v. Essex, Westcliff, 1972 41 (off 36.1 overs), Shropshire v. Essex, Wellington, 1974	23 (off 19.4 overs), Middlesex v. Yorks., Headingley, 1974	62 (off 26.5 overs), Glos. v. Hants., Bristol, 1975
Highest Partnership	227 for 1st wicket—R. E. Marshall and B. L. Reed, Hants v. Beds, Goldington, 1968	182 for 3rd wicket—H. Pilling and C. H. Lloyd, Lancs v. Somerset, Old Trafford, 12 July 1970†	285* for 2nd wicket—C. G. Greenidge and D. R. Turner, Hants v. Minor Counties (South), Amersham, 1973

* Not Out
† 182 was equalled in Kent v. Somerset at Weston-super-Mare on 9 Aug. 1970 (M. H. Denness and B. W. Luckhurst—1st wicket) and again in Worcester v. Warwicks at Edgbaston 1972 (R. G. A. Headley and G. M. Turner—1st wicket).

259

out in 6 hrs 50 min, over five afternoons' batting, carrying his bat through the innings of 836. The scorer, E. W. Pegler, gave the score as "628—plus or minus 20, shall we say".

Fastest individual scoring S. K. Coen (South Africa) scored 50 runs (11 fours and 1 six) in 7 min for Gezira v. the R.A.F. in 1942, compared with the First Class record of 8 min. Cecil George Pepper hit a century in 24 min in a Services match in Palestine in 1943. Cedric Ivan James Smith hit 9 successive sixes for a Middlesex XI v. Harrow and District at Rayners' Lane, Harrow, Greater London in 1935. This feat was repeated by Arthur Dudley Nourse, Jr. in a South African XI v. Military Police match at Cairo in 1942–43. Nourse's feat included six sixes in one over.

Highest scoring rate In the match Royal Naval College, Dartmouth v. Seale Hayne Agricultural College in 1923, K. A. Sellar (now Cdr. "Monkey" Sellar, D.S.O., D.S.C., R.N.) and L. K. A. Block (now Judge Block, D.S.C.) were set to score 174 runs in 105 min but achieved this total in 33 min, so averaging 5.27 runs per min.

Lowest score There are at least 60 recorded instances of sides being dismissed for 0. A recent instance was in July 1970 when, in a 2nd XI House match at Brentwood School, Essex West dismissed North for 0 with 13 balls.

Greatest stand T. Patten and N. Rippon made a third wicket stand of 641 for Buffalo v. Whorouly at Gapsted, Victoria, Australia, on 19 March 1914.

Wicket-keeping In a Repton School match for Priory v. Mitre, the late H. W. P. Middleton caught one and stumped eight batsmen in one innings on 10 July 1930.

Fielding In a Wellington, New Zealand secondary schools 11-a-side competition match in 1973–74, Stephen Lane, 13, held 14 catches in the field (7 in each innings) for St. Patrick's College, Silverstream v. St. Bernard's College, Lower Hutt.

Longest Game A match under M.C.C. rules was played by 22 members of the Australian National University C.C. at Torrens, Canberra for 37 hrs 10 min on 25–27 Feb. 1975.

CROQUET

Earliest references Croquet, in its present-day form, originated as a country-house lawn game in Ireland in the 1830's when it was called "crokey". It was introduced to Hampshire 20 years later. The first club was formed in the Steyne Gardens, Worthing.

Most championships The greatest number of victories in the Open Croquet Championships (instituted at Evesham, Hereford and Worcester, 1867) is ten by John William Solomon (b. 1932) (1953, 1956, 1959, 1961, 1963 to 68). He has also won the Men's Championship on 10 occasions (1951, 1953, 1958 to 60, 1962, 1964–65, 1971 and 1972), the Open Doubles (with E. Patrick C. Cotter) on 10 occasions (1954–55, 1958–59, 1961 to 65 and 1969) and the Mixed Doubles once (with Mrs. N. Oddie) in 1954, making a total of 31 titles. Solomon has also won the President's Silver Cup (inst. 1934) on 9 occasions (1955, 1957 to 59, 1962 to 64, 1968 and 1971). He has also been Champion of Champions on all four occasions that this competition was run (1967–70).

Miss Dorothy D. Steel, fifteen times winner of the Women's Championship (1919 to 39), won the Open Croquet Championship four times (1925, 1933,

1935–36). She had also five Doubles and seven Mixed Doubles titles making a total of 31 titles.

International Trophy The MacRobertson International Shield (instituted 1925) has been played for 10 times. It has been won most often by Great Britain with 6 wins (in 1925, 1937, 1956, 1963, 1969 and 1974). The players to make 5 international appearances are J. C. Windsor (Australia) in 1925, 1928, 1930, 1935 and 1937 and John W. Solomon (G.B.) in 1951, 1956, 1963, 1969 and 1974.

Lowest handicap Historically the lowest playing handicap has been that of Humphrey O. Hicks (Devon) with minus 5½. In 1974 the limit was however fixed at minus 5. The player holding the lowest handicap is G. Nigel Aspinall with minus 4.

Largest club The largest number of courts at any one club is eleven, at the Sussex County (Brighton) Croquet and Lawn Tennis Club.

Most Protracted Game The longest croquet match on record is one of 86 hr 10 min by David Mattes, Jeremy D' Lemos, Stephen Jones and Peter Reynolds at Barnet, Herts. on 19–22 June 1975.

CROSS-COUNTRY RUNNING

International championships The earliest recorded international cross-country race took place over 14,5 km *9 miles 18 yds* from Ville d'Avray, outside Paris, on 20 March 1898, between England and France (England won by 21 points to 69). The inaugural International Cross-Country Championships took place at the Hamilton Park Racecourse, Glasgow, on 28 March 1903. The greatest margin of victory is 56 sec or 390 yds *356 m* by Jack T. Holden (England) at Ayr Racecourse, Scotland, on 24 March 1934. The narrowest win was that of Jean-Claude Fayolle (France) at Ostend, Belgium, on 20 March 1965, when the timekeepers were unable to separate his time from that of Melvyn Richard Batty (England), who was placed second.

The greatest team wins have been those of England, with a minimum of 21 points (the first six runners to finish) on two occasions, at Gosforth Park, Newcastle,

Gaston Roelants (Belgium) only the third athlete in the 72 year history of the annual cross-country international to win 4 times

Associated Press

Tyne and Wear, on 22 March 1924, and at the Hippodrome de Stockel, Brussels, Belgium, on 20 March 1932.

Most appearances The runners of participating countries with the largest number of international championship appearances are:

Belgium	20	M. Van de Wattyne, 1946–65
Wales	14	D. Phillips, 1922, 1924, 1926–37
England	12	J. T. Holden, 1929–39, 1946
Spain	12	A. L. Amoros, 1951–62
Scotland	12	A. H. Brown, 1955–56, 1958, 1960–68
France	11	A. Mimoun-o-Kacha, 1949–50, 1952, 1954, 1956, 1958–62, 1964

Most wins The greatest number of victories in the International Cross-Country Race is four by Jack Holden (England) in 1933–34–35–39 by Alain Mimoun-o-Kacha (France)

in 1949–52–54–56 and Gaston Roelants (Belgium) in 1962–67–69–72. England have won 43 times to 1975.

English championship The English Cross-Country Championship was inaugurated at Roehampton, Wandsworth, Greater London, in 1877. The greatest number of individual titles achieved is four by P. H. Stenning (Thames Hare and Hounds) in 1877–80 and Alfred E. Shrubb (1878–1964) (South London Harriers) in 1901–04. The most successful club in the team race has been Birchfield Harriers from Birmingham with 27 wins and one tie between 1880 and 1953.

Largest field The largest recorded field was one of 1,815 starters (1,020 completed the course) at Gosforth Park, Newcastle, Tyne and Wear in the summer of 1916. It was staged by the Northern Command of the Army and was won by Sapper G. Barber in 35 min 7.2 sec, by a margin of over 40 yd *36 m.*

CURLING

Origins The earliest illustration of the sport was in one of the Flemish painter Pieter Bruegel's winter scenes *c* 1560. The club with the earliest records, dating back to 1716, is that at Kilsyth, Stirlingshire which was resuscitated in 1954. The game was introduced into Canada in 1807. Organized administration began in 1838 with the formation of the Royal Caledonian

Curling Club, the international legislative body based in Edinburgh. The first indoor ice rink to introduce curling was at Southport, Merseyside in 1879.

The U.S.A. won the first Gordon International Medal series of matches, between Canada and the U.S.A., at Montreal in 1884. The first Strathcona Cup match between Canada and Scotland was won by Canada in 1903. Although demonstrated at the Winter Olympics

An early curling scene in Scotland dating from 3 years before the establishment there of the first international rules

Mansell Collection

of 1924, 1932 and 1964, curling has never been included in the official Olympic programme.

Most titles The record for international team matches for the Scotch Cup and Air Canada Silver Broom (instituted 1959) is 12 wins by Canada, in 1959–60–61–62–63–64–1966–68–69–70–71–72. The most Strathcona Cup wins is seven by Canada (1903–09–12–23–38–57–65) against Scotland.

Marathon The longest recorded curling match is one of 42 hr 4 min by 8 members of the South of Scotland Ice Rink Club, Lockerbie, Dumfriesshire with 252 ends on 11–13 Apr. 1974.

The duration record for two curlers in 14 hr 23 min by Timothy Moreton, 21 and Robert Maddock, 23 in

Toronto, Canada on 16–17 Apr. 1973. The weight handled was 10.8 tons each.

Most Durable Player In 1972 Howard "Pappy" Wood competed in his 65th consecutive annual bonspiel of the Manitoba Curling Association since 1908.

Largest Bonspiel The largest bonspiel in the world is the Alcan Employee's Bonspiel held in Arvida, Quebec, Canada. The tournament lasts 22 days, 396 games and involves 200 teams of 4 players.

Largest rink The world's largest curling rink is the Big Four Curling Rink, Calgary, Alberta, Canada opened in 1959 at a cost of \$Can. 2,250,000 *£867,050.* Each of the two floors has 48 sheets of ice, accommodating 96 teams and 384 players.

CYCLING

Earliest race The earliest recorded bicycle race was a velocipede race over 2 km *1.24 miles* at the Parc de St. Cloud, Paris, on 31 May 1868, won by James Moore (G.B.).

Slow cycling Slow bicycling records came to a virtual end in 1968 when Tsugunobu Mitsuishi, aged 39, of Tōkyō, Japan stayed stationary without support for 5 hr 25 min.

Highest speed The highest speed ever achieved on a bicycle is 140.5 m.p.h. *226,1 km/h* by Dr. Allan V. Abbott, 29, of San Bernadino, California, U.S.A., behind a windshield mounted on a 1955 Chevrolet over ¾ mile *1,2 km* at Bonneville Salt Flats, Utah, U.S.A. on 25 Aug. 1973. His speed over a mile *1,6 km* was 138.674 m.p.h. *223,174 km/h.* The first Mile a Minute was achieved by Charles Minthorne Murphy (b. 1872) behind a pacing locomotive on the Long Island

Railroad on 30 June 1899 in 57⅕ sec for an average of 62.28 m.p.h. *100,23 km/h*. Antonio Maspes (Italy) recorded an unofficial unpaced 10.6 sec for 200 m (42.20 m.p.h. [*67,93 km/h*]) at Milan on 28 Aug. 1962.

The greatest distance ever covered in one hour is 122,862 km *76 miles 604 yd* by Leon Vanderstuyft (Belgium) on the Montlhery Motor Circuit, France, on 30 Sept. 1928. This was achieved from a standing start paced by a motorcycle. The 24 hr record behind pace is 860 miles 367 yds *1 384,367 km* by Hubert Opperman in Australia in 1932.

Most world titles The greatest number of world titles for a particular event won since the institution of the amateur championships in 1893 and the professional championships in 1895 are:

Amateur Sprint	6	Daniel Morelon (France)	1966–67, 1969–71, 1973
Amateur 100 km Paced	7	Leon Meredith (U.K.)	1904–05, 1907–09, 1911, 1913
Amateur Road Race	2	Giuseppe Martano (Italy)	1930, 1932
	2	Gustave Schur (East Germany)	1958–59
Professional Sprint	7	Jeff Scherens (Belgium)	1932–37, 1947
	7	Antonio Maspes (Italy)	1955–56, 1959–62, 1964
Amateur Pursuit	3	G. Messina (Italy)	1947–48, 1953
	3	T. Groen (Netherlands)	1964–66
Professional Pursuit	4	Hugh Porter (U.K.)	1968, 1970, 1972–3
Professional 100 km Paced	6	Guillermo Timoner (Spain)	1955, 1959–60, 1962, 1964–65
Professional Road Race	3	Alfredo Binda (Italy)	1927, 1930, 1932
	3	Henri (Rik) Van Steenbergen (Belgium)	1949, 1956–57
Women's titles	7	Beryl Burton (U.K.)	1959–60–62–63–66 (pursuits) 1960–67 (Road)
	7	Yvonne Reynders Belgium)	1961–64–65 (pursuits) 1959–61–63–66 (Road)

Associated Press

An action shot of Pierre Trentin of France, who set the world 1 km unpaced standing start record at an average speed of 35.84 m.p.h. *57,69 km/h*

WORLD RECORDS   OPEN AIR TRACKS

MEN

Distance	hr min sec	Name and nationality	Place	Date
Professional unpaced standing start:				
1 km	1 07.5	Peder Pedersen (Denmark)	Rome	27 June. 1974
5 kms.	5 51.6	Ole Ritter (Denmark)	Mexico City	4 Oct. 1968
10 kms.	11 53.2	Eddy Merckx (Belgium)	Mexico City	25 Oct. 1972
20 kms.	24 06.8	Eddy Merckx (Belgium)	Mexico City	25 Oct. 1972
100 kms.	2 14 02.5	Ole Ritter (Denmark)	Mexico City	15 Nov. 1971
1 hour	30 miles 700 yd *49 km 432*	Eddie Merckx (Belgium)	Mexico City	25 Oct. 1972
Professional unpaced flying start:				
200 metres	10.8	Antonio Maspes (Italy)	Rome	21 July 1960
500 metres	28.8	Marino Morettini (Italy)	Milan	29 Aug. 1955
1,000 metres	1 02.6	Marino Morettini (Italy	Milan	26 July 1961
Professional motor-paced:				
100 kms.	1 03 40.0	Walter Lohmann (W. Germany)	Wuppertal	24 Oct. 1955
1 hour	58 miles 737 yd *94 km 015*	Walter Lohmann (W. Germany)	Wuppertal	24 Oct. 1955
Amateur unpaced standing start:				
1 km.	1 02.4⁴	Pierre Trentin (France)	Zürich	15 Nov. 1970
4 kms.	4 37.5⁴	Mogens Frey (Denmark)	Mexico City	17 Oct. 1968
5 kms.	6 01.6	Mogens Frey (Denmark)	Mexico City	5 Oct. 1969
10 kms.	12 23.8	Mogens Frey (Denmark)	Mexico City	5 Oct. 1969
20 kms.	25 00.5	Mogens Frey (Denmark)	Mexico City	5 Oct. 1969
100 kms.	2 18 43.6	Jorn Lund (Denmark)	Rome	19 Sept. 1971
1 hour	29 miles 933 yd *47 km 553*	Martinez Rodriguez (Colombia)	Mexico City	7 Oct. 1970
Amateur unpaced flying start:				
200 metres	10.61	Omari Phakadze (U.S.S.R.)	Mexico City	22 Oct. 1967
500 metres	27.85	Pierre Trentin (France)	Mexico City	21 Oct. 1967
1,000 metres	1 01.14	Luigi Borghetti (Italy)	Mexico City	21 Oct. 1967

WOMEN

Distance	hr min sec	Name and nationality	Place	Date
Amateur unpaced standing start:				
1 km.	1 15.1	Irena Kirichenko (U.S.S.R.)	Yervan	8 Oct. 1966
3 kms.	3 52.5	Tamara Garkushkina (U.S.S.R.)	Montreal	18 Aug. 1974
5 kms.	7 00.1	Maria Cressari (Italy)	Mexico City	24 Nov. 1972
10 kms.	14 19.9	Maria Cressari (Italy)	Mexico City	22 Nov. 1972
20 kms.	28 51.4	Maria Cressari (Italy)	Mexico City	22 Nov. 1972
100 kms.	2 44 54.8	R. Mykkanen (Finland)	Helsinki	23 Sept. 1971
1 hour	25 miles 1,354 yd *41 km 471*	Maria Cressari (Italy)	Mexico City	25 Nov. 1972
Amateur unpaced flying start:				
200 metres	12.3	Lyubov Razuvayeva (U.S.S.R.)	Irkutsk	17 July 1955
500 metres	32.5	Irena Kirichenko (U.S.S.R.)	Irkutsk	1967
1,000 metres	1 10.6	Irena Kirichenko (U.S.S.R.)	Irkutsk	1967

COVERED TRACKS

MEN

Distance		hr	min	sec	Name and nationality	Place	Date
Professional unpaced standing start:							
1 km.			1	07.3	Patrick Sercu (Belgium)	Zürich	2 Dec. 1972
5 kms.			6	05.6	Ferdinand Bracke (Belgium)	Brussels	5 Dec. 1964
10 kms.			12	26.8	Roger Riviére (France)	Paris	19 Oct. 1958
20 kms.			25	18.0	Siegfried Adler (W. Germany)	Zürich	2 Aug. 1968
1 hour	29 miles 162 yd 46 km 819				Siegfried Adler (W. Germany)	Zürich	2 Aug. 1968
Professional unpaced flying start:							
200 metres				10.99	Oscar Plattner (Switzerland)	Zürich	1 Dec. 1961
500 metres				28.6	Oscar Plattner (Switzerland)	Zürich	17 Aug. 1956
1,000 metres			1	01.23	Patrick Sercu (Belgium)	Antwerp	3 Feb. 1967
Professional motor-paced:							
100 kms.		1	23	59.8	Guillermo Timoner (Spain)	San Sebastian	12 Sept. 1965
1 hour	46 miles 669 yd 74 km 641				Guy Solente (France)	Paris	13 Feb 1955
Amateur unpaced standing start:							
1 km.			1	06.76	Patrick Sercu (Belgium)	Brussels	12 Dec. 1964
5 kms.			6	06.0	Xavier Kurmann (Switzerland)	Zürich	28 Nov. 1968
10 kms.			12	26.2	Xavier Krumann (Switzerland)	Zürich	1 Dec. 1968
20 kms.			25	14.6	Ole Ritter (Denmark)	Zürich	30 Oct. 1966
1 hour	28 miles 575 yd 45 km 587				Alfred Ruegg (Switzerland)	Zürich	16 Nov. 1958
Amateur unpaced flying start:							
200 metres				10.72	Daniel Morelon (France)	Zürich	4 Nov. 1967
500 metres				28.89	Pierre Trentin (France)	Zürich	4 Nov. 1967
1,000 metres			1	02.44	Pierre Trentin (France)	Zürich	15 Nov. 1970

WOMEN

Distance	hr	min	sec	Name and nationality	Place	Date
Amateur unpaced standing start:						
1,000 metres		1	15.5	Elizabeth Eicholz (Germany)	Berlin	4 Mar. 1964
Amateur unpaced flying start:						
200 metres			13.2	Karla Günther (Germany)	Berlin	7 Mar. 1964
500 metres			35.0	Karla Günther (Germany)	Berlin	7 Mar. 1964

ROAD CYCLING RECORDS
(British) as recognized by the Road Time Trials Council (out-and-home records)

Distance	hr	min	sec	Name	Course area	Date
MEN						
10 miles		20	36	Willi (sic) Moore	Tittensor, Staffordshire	29 July 1972
25 miles		51	00	Alf Engers	Catterick, North Yorkshire	30 Aug. 1969
30 miles	1	04	56	Dave Dungworth	Derby	10 June 1967
50 miles	1	43	46	John Watson	Boroughbridge North Yorks.	23 Aug. 1970
100 miles	3	46	37	Anthony Taylor	Boroughbridge, North Yorks.	31 Aug. 1969
12 hours	281.87 miles 453,62 km			John Watson	Blyth, Nottinghamshire	7 Sept. 1969
24 hours	507.00 miles 815,93 km			Roy Cromack	Cheshire	26–27 July 1969
WOMEN						
10 miles		21	25	Beryl Burton, O.B.E.	Blyth, Nottinghamshire	29 Apr. 1973
25 miles		54	44	Beryl Burton, O.B.E.	Boroughbridge, North Yorks.	22 July 1972
30 miles	1	12	20	Beryl Burton, O.B.E.	St. Neots, Cambridgshire	3 May 1969
50 miles	1	54	7	Beryl Burton, O.B.E.	Blyth, Nottinghamshire	8 July 1973
100 miles	3	55	5	Beryl Burton, O.B.E.	Essex	4 Aug. 1968
12 hours	277.25 miles 446,19 km			Beryl Burton, O.B.E.	Wetherby, West Yorkshire	17 Sept. 1967
24 hours	427.86 miles 688,57 km			Christine Minto (née Moody)	Cheshire	26–27 July 1969

ROAD RECORDS ASSOCIATION'S STRAIGHT-OUT DISTANCE RECORDS

Distance	days	hr	min	sec	Name	Date
25 miles			47	0	Peter Crofts	10 Oct. 1971
50 miles		1	35	45	David Lloyd	29 Oct. 1974
100 miles		3	28	40	Ray Booty	28 Sept. 1956
1,000 miles	2	10	40	0	Reg Randall	19–21 Aug. 1960
12 hours	276½ miles 444,9 km				Harry Earnshaw	4 July 1939
24 hours	475¾ miles 765,64 km				Ken Joy	26–27 July 1954

PLACE TO PLACE RECORDS
(British) as recognized by the Road Records Association

	days	hr	min	sec	Name	Date
London to Edinburgh (380 miles [610 km])		18	49	42	Cliff Smith	2 Nov. 1965
London to Bath and back (212 miles [341 km])		9	07	05	Les West	28 July 1973
London to York (197 miles [317 km])		7	41	13	Bob Addy	6 Aug. 1972
London to Brighton and back (107 miles [172 km])		4	18	18	Les West	3 Oct. 1970
Land's End to London (287 miles [461 km])		12	34	0	Robert Maitland	17 Sept. 1954
Land's End to John O'Groats (879 miles [1 414 km])	1	23	46	35	Richard W. E. Poole	18 June 1965

Most British Titles Beryl Burton, O.B.E. (b. 12 May 1937), 16 times British all-round time trial champion (1959–73) also holds 12 B.C.F. road race titles, 13 track pursuit titles and 48 R.T.T.C. titles. Mrs. Burton, won her 21st track title on 12 Aug. 1972, and has since collected a further two pursuit titles. Albert White won 12 individual National track championships from the ¼ mile to 25 miles in 1920–25. Granville Sydney (Huddersfield Star

Wheelers) (1941–74) won 6 R.T.T.C. national hill-climbing titles (1963–73) captaining his club to an 8th win in 1973.

Most Olympic titles Cycling has been on the Olympic programme since the revival of the Games in 1896. The greatest number of gold medals ever won is four by Marcus Hurley (U.S.A.) over the ¼, ⅓, ½ and 1 mile in 1904.

Tour de France The greatest number of wins in the Tour de France (inaugurated 1903) is five by Jacques Anquetil (b. 8 Jan. 1934) of France, who won in 1957, 1961, 1962, 1963 and 1964, and by Eddy Merckx (b. Belgium, 1945), who won in 1969, 1970, 1971, 1972 and 1974. The closest race ever was that of 1968 when after 2,898.7 miles *4 665 km* over the 25 days (27 June–21 July) Jan Janssen (Netherlands) (b. 1940) beat Herman van Springel (Belgium) in Paris by 38 sec.

The Land's End to John O'Groats (879 miles [*1 414 km*]) feminine record is 2 days 11 hr 7 min (average speed 14.75 m.p.h. [*23,73 km/h*]) by Mrs. Eileen Sheridan (b. 1925) on 9–11 June 1954. She continued to complete 1,000 miles *1 610 km* in 3 days 1 hr.

Roller cycling The greatest recorded distance registered in a 12 hr roller team cycling test is 544 miles 1,330 yd *876,7 km* by Torben Hjorth, Leon Ringbow, Erik Jensen and Peter Oreskov of Denmark at Slagelse, Denmark on 8 March 1975.

The eight-man 24 hr record is 1,199 miles *1 929 km* by the Fenland Clarion C.C. at Westgate, Cambridgeshire on 2–3 Nov. 1973.

Endurance The greatest endurance feat in cycling was by Tommy Godwin (G.B.) who in the 365 days of 1939 covered 75,065 miles *120 805 km* or an average of 205.65 miles *330,96 km* per day. He then completed 100,000 miles *160 934 km* in 500 days on 14 May 1940.

Trans-Continental Record The North American trans-continental record from San Francisco to New York City Hall is 13 days by Paul Cornish, 25, on 4–17 Mar. 1973.

Pennine Way Barry Davies of Holmfirth, West Yorkshire, cycled along the 270 mile *434,5 km* long Pennine Way from Edale, Derbyshire to Kirk Yetholm, Borders in 3 days, 3 hr 33 min on 14–17 June 1975.

Tandem Marathon David Martin (b. 3 Jan. 1957) and Scott Parcel (b. 16 Aug. 1957) set out from San Francisco, California on 4 Feb. 1973 and pedalled 4,837 miles *7 784 km* around the United States finishing in Washington, D.C. on 5 June 1973.

CYCLO-CROSS
The greatest number of world championships (inst. 1950) have been won by Eric de Vlaeminck (Belgium) who took the Open title in 1967 and the professional world titles in 1968–69–70–71–72–73. British titles (inst. 1955) have been won most often by John Atkins (Coventry R.C.) with 5 Amateur (1961–62–66–67–68) and 7 professional (1968–69, 1969–70, 1970–71, 1971–72, 1972–73, 1973–74 and 1974–75).

EQUESTRIAN SPORTS

Origins Evidence of horse-riding dates from an Anatolian statuette dated *c.* 1400 B.C. Pignatelli's academy of horsemanship at Naples dates from the 16th century. The earliest show jumping was in Paris in 1886. Equestrian events have been included in the Olympic Games since 1912.

Most Olympic medals The greatest number of Olympic gold medals is 5 by Hans-Günter Winkler (West Germany) (b. 24 July 1926) who won 4 team gold medals as captain in 1956, 1960, 1964 and 1972 and won the individual Grand Prix in 1956. The most team wins in the Prix des Nations is five by Germany in 1936, 1956, 1960, 1964 and 1972. The lowest score obtained by a winner was no faults by Frantisek Ventura on *Eliot* (Czechoslovakia) in 1928. Pierre Jonqueres d'Oriola (France) is the only two time winner of the individual gold medal in 1952 and 1964. Richard John Hannay Meade, O.B.E. (b. 4 Dec. 1938) (Great Britain) is the only 3 day event rider to win 3 gold medals—the individual in 1972 and the team in 1968 and 1972.

Jumping records The official *Fédération Equestre Internationale* high jump record is 8 ft 1¼ in *2,47 m* by *Huasó*, ridden by Capt. Alberto Larraguibel Morales (Chile) at Vina del Mar, Santiago, Chile, on 5 Feb. 1949, and 27 ft 2¾ in *8,30 m* for long jump over water by *Amado Mio* ridden by Lt.-Col. Lopez del Hierro (Spain), at Barcelona, Spain on 12 Nov. 1951. *Heatherbloom*, ridden by Dick Donnelly was reputed to have covered 37 ft *11,28 m* in clearing an 8 ft 3 in *2,51 m puissance* jump at Richmond, Virginia, U.S.A. in 1903. H. Plant on *Solid Gold* cleared 36 ft 3 in *11,05 m* over water at the Wagga Show, New South Wales, Australia in August 1936. The official Australian record is 32 ft 10 in *10,00 m* by *Monarch* in Brisbane in 1951. *Jerry M.* allegedly cleared 40 ft *12,19 m* over the water at Aintree in 1912.

At Cairns, Queensland, *Golden Meade* ridden by Jack Martin cleared an unofficially measured 8 ft 6 in *2,59 m* on 25 July 1946. *Ben Bolt* was credited with

clearing 9 ft 6 in *2,89 m* at the 1938 Royal Horse Show, Sydney, Australia. The Australian record is 8 ft 4 in *2,54 m* by *Flyaway* (Colin Russell) in 1939 and *Golden Meade* (A. L. Payne) in 1946. The world's unofficial best for a woman is 7 ft 5½ in *2,27 m* by Miss B. Perry (Australia) on *Plain Bill* at Cairns, Queensland, Australia in 1940. The greatest recorded height reached bareback is 6 ft 7 in *2,00 m* by *Silver Wood* at Heidelberg, Victoria, Australia, on 10 Dec. 1938.

The highest British performance is 7 ft 6¼ in *2,29 m* by the 16.2 hands *167 cm* bay gelding *Swank*, ridden by Donald Beard, at Olympia, Chelsea and Kensington, Greater London, on 25 June 1937. On the same day, the Lady Wright (*née* Margery Avis Bullows) set the best recorded height for a British equestrienne on her liver chestnut *Jimmy Brown* at 7 ft 4 in *2,23 m*. These records were over the now unused sloping poles. Harvey Smith on *O'Malley* cleared 7 ft 3 in *2,21 m* in Toronto, Canada in 1967.

Most titles The most B.S.J.A. men's championships won is five by Alan Oliver (1951–54–59–69–70). The only horses to have won twice are *Maguire* (Lt.-Col. Nathaniel Kindersley) in 1945 and 1947. *Sheila* (Hayes) in 1949–50 and *Red Admiral* (Oliver) in 1951 and 1954. The record for the Ladies' Championship is 8 by Miss Patricia Smythe (b. 22 Nov. 1928), now Mrs. Samuel Koechlin, O.B.E. (1952–53–55–57–58–59–61–62). She won on *Flanagan*, owned by Robert Hanson, C.B.E., in 1955, 1958 and 1962—the only three time winner.

George V Gold Cup and Queen Elizabeth II Cup Four men have thrice won this premier award (first held in 1911): the late Lt.-Col. J. A. Talbot-Ponsonby (1930–32–34), Lt.-Col. Harry M. Llewellyn, C.B.E. (1948–50–53 on *Foxhunter*), Piero d'Inzeo (Italy) (1957–61–62) and David Broome (b. 1 Mar. 1940) in 1960 on *Sunsalve*, 1966 on *Mister Softee* and 1972 on *Sportsman*. The Queen Elizabeth II Cup, (first held in 1949) the premier award for women, has been won outright twice by Miss Iris Kellett (Ireland) (1949, 1951) on *Rusty*, Miss Dawn Palethorpe (G.B.) 1955–56) on *Earlsrath Rambler*, Mrs. Marion

Harvey Smith (GB), who cleared 7 ft 3 in *2,21 m* in Toronto, Canada on *O'Malley* in 1967

Ed Lacey

Mould (*née* Coakes) (G.B.) (1965, 1971) on *Stroller* and Jean Davenport (*née* Goodwin) (G.B.) (1974–75) on *All Trumps* and *Hang On*. The only horse to win both these trophies is *Sunsalve* in 1960 and 1957 respectively.

World champions The men's world championships (ints. 1953) have been won twice by Hans Winkler (W. Germany) (1954–55) and Raimondo d'Inzeo (Italy) (1956 and 1960). The women's title (inst. 1965) has been won twice by Janov Tissot (*née* Lefebvre) (France) (1970 and 1974).

Three-day event The Badminton Three-Day Event (inst. 1949) has been won three times by Sheila Waddington (*née* Willcox) in 1957–59 and by Lt. (later Capt.) Mark Phillips in 1971–72 and 1974.

Driving The World Driving Championships have been held twice, 1972 and 1974. Great Britain has won the team gold medal on both occasions. The best individual performance by a Briton has been a silver medal won by Col. Sir John Miller in 1972.

Marathon The duration record in the saddle is 178 hr 8 min by Rani Kolbaba, 15, and Ethelyn Larsen, 14, of White Salmon, Washington State, U.S.A., from 14–21 June 1974. Marathons of this kind stipulate that mounts must be changed at least each 6 hours. Joseph Roberts, of Newport Pagnell, Bucks, rode at all paces (including jumping) for 48 hr 25 min at the Allerton Equitation Centre, Huntingdon on 20–22 Sept. 1974.

1,000 Mile Ride Gary Davies of Borehamwood, Hertfordshire rode his *Dandi* 1,000 miles *1 609 km* in 50 days from 1 July to 19 Aug. 1972 through 22 counties.

FENCING

Origins "Fencing" (fighting with single sticks) was practised as a sport in Egypt as early as *c*. 1360 B.C. The first governing body for fencing in Britain was the Corporation of Masters of Defence founded by Henry VIII before 1540 and fencing has been practised as sport, notably in prize fights, since that time. The foil was the practice weapon for the short court sword from the 17th century. The épée was established in the mid-19th century and the light sabre was introduced by the Italians in the late 19th century.

Most Olympic titles The greatest number of individual Olympic Gold Medals won is three by Ramón Fonst (Cuba) (b. 1883) in 1900 and 1904 (2) and by Nedo Nadi (Italy) (1894–1952) in 1912 and 1920 (2). Nadi also won three team gold medals in 1920 making a then unprecedented total of five gold medals at one celebration. Edoardo Mangiarotti (Italy) (b. 7 April 1919) with 6 gold, 5 silver and 2 bronze holds the record of 13 Olympic medals. He won them for foil and epée from 1936 to 1960. The women's record is 6 medals (2 gold, 3 silver, 1 bronze) by Ildikó Sagine-Retjö (formerly Ujlaki-Retjö) (Hungary) (b. 11 May 1937) from 1960 to 1972.

British Olympic records The only British fencer to win 3 Olympic medals has been Edgar Seligman with silver medals in the épée team event in 1906, 08 and 12. Allan Louis Neville Jay, M.B.E. (b. 30 June 1931) has competed most

Rudolf Kárpáti, the Hungarian sabreur, who won both individual and team Olympic gold medals in 1956 and 1960

Associated Press

often for Great Britain with 5 Olympic appearances (1952 to 1968).

Most World titles The greatest number of individual world titles won is 4 by d'Oriola (see details in table), but note that he also won 2 Individual Olympic titles. Of the three women

foilists with 3 world titles, Helène Mayer (Germany) (1929, 31, 37), Ellen Muller-Preiss (Austria) (1947, 49, 50) and Ilona Schachere-Elek (Hungary) (1934, 35, 51), only Elek won two individual Olympic titles (1936 and 1948).

MOST OLYMPIC AND MOST WORLD TITLES

Event	Olympic Gold Medals		World Championships (not held in Olympic years)	
Men's Foil, Individual	2	Christian d'Oriola (France) b. 3 Oct. 1928 (1952, 56)	4	Christian d'Oriola (France) b. 3 Oct. 1928 (1947, 49, 53, 54)
	2	Nedo Nadi (Italy) (1894–1952) 1912, 20		
Men's Foil, Team	5	France (1924, 32, 48, 52, 68)	12	Italy (1929–31, 33–35, 37, 38, 49, 50, 54, 55)
Men's Epée, Individual	2	Ramón Fonst (Cuba) (1883–1959) (1900, 04)	3	Georges Buchard (France) b. 21 Dec. 1893 (1927, 31, 33)
			3	Aleksey Nikanchikov (U.S.S.R.) b. 30 July 1940 (1966, 67, 70)
Men's Epée Team	6	Italy (1920, 28, 36, 52, 56, 60)	10	Italy (1931, 33, 37, 49, 50, 53–55, 57, 58)
Men's Sabre, Individual	2	Dr. Jenö Fuchs (Hungary) b. 29 Oct. 1882 (1908, 12)	3	Aladár Gerevich (Hungary) b. 16 Mar. 1910 (1935, 1951, 1955)
	2	Rudolf Kárpáti (Hungary) b. 17 July 1920 (1956, 60)	3	Jerzy Pawlowski (Poland) b. 25 Oct. 1932 (1957, 65, 66)
	2	Jean Georgiadis (Greece) b. 1874 (1896, 1906)	3	Yakov Rylsky (U.S.S.R.) (b. 25 Oct 1928 (1958, 1961, 1963)
Men's Sabre, Team	9	Hungary (1908, 12, 28, 32, 36, 48, 52, 56, 60)	14	Hungary (1930, 31, 33–35, 37, 51, 53–55, 57, 58, 66, 73)
Women's Foil, Individual	2	Ilona Schacherer-Elek (Hungary) b. 1907 (1936, 48)	3	Helène Mayer (Germany) 1910–53 (1929, 31, 37)
			3	Ilona Schacherer-Elek (Hungary) b. 17 May 1907 (1934, 35, 51)
			3	Ellen Muller-Preiss (Austria) b. 6 May 1912 (1947, 49, 50 (shared))
Women's Foil, Team	3	U.S.S.R. (1960, 68, 72)	11	Hungary (1933–35, 37, 53–55, 59, 62, 67, 73)

MOST AMATEUR FENCING ASSOCIATION TITLES

Foil	(Instituted 1898)	7	John Emrys Lloyd	1928, 1930–33, 1937–38
Epée	(Instituted 1904)	5	Robert Montgomerie	1905, 1907, 1909, 1912, 1914
Sabre	(Instituted 1898)	6	Dr. R. F. Tredgold	1937, 1939, 1947–49, 1955
Foil (Ladies)	(Instituted 1907)	10	Miss Gillian M. Sheen (now Mrs. R. G. Donaldson)	1949, 1951–58, 1960

FIVES

ETON FIVES

A handball game against the buttress of Eton College Chapel was recorded in 1825, but a court existed at Lord Weymouth's School (now Warminster School), Wiltshire, as early as 1773 and a handball game against the church wall at Babcary, Somerset, was recorded in June 1765. New courts were built at Eton in 1840, the rules were codified in 1877, rewritten laws were introduced in 1931 and the laws were last drawn up in 1950.

Most titles Only one pair have won the Amateur Championship (Kinnaird Cup) eight times—Anthony Hughes and Arthur James Gordon Campbell (1958, 1965–68, 1971, 1973 and 1975). Hughes was also in the winning pair in 1963 making nine titles in all.

RUGBY FIVES

As now known, this game dates from c. 1850 with the first inter-public school matches recorded in the early 1870s. The Oxford v. Cambridge contest was inaugurated in 1925 and the Rugby Fives Association was founded in the home of Dr. Cyriax, in Welbeck Street, City of Westminster, Greater London, on 29 Oct. 1927. The dimensions of the Standard Rugby Fives court were approved by the Association in 1931.

Most titles The greatest number of Amateur Singles Championships (instituted 1932) ever won is four by John Frederick Pretlove in 1953, 1955–56 and 1958, and by Eric Marsh in 1960–61–62–63. The record for the Amateur Doubles Championship (instituted 1925) is seven shared by Pretlove (1952–54–56–57–58–59–61) and David E. Gardner (1960–65–66–70–71–72–74).

FOOTBALL (ASSOCIATION)

Origins A game with some similarities termed *Tsu-chin* was played in China in the 3rd and 4th centuries B.C. The earliest clear representation of the game is an Edinburgh print dated 1672–73. It became standardized with the formation of the Football Association in England on 26 Oct. 1863. A 26-a-side game, however, existed in Florence, Italy, as early as 1530, for which rules were codified in *Discorsa Calcio* in 1580. The oldest club is Sheffield F.C., formed on 24 Oct. 1857. Eleven per side was standardized in 1870.

HIGHEST SCORES

Teams The highest score recorded in a British first-class match is 36. This occurred in the Scottish Cup match between Arbroath and Bon Accord on 5 Sept. 1885, when Arbroath won 36–0 on their home ground. But for the lack of nets and the consequent waste of retrieval time the score would have been even higher. The same day Dundee Harp beat Aberdeen Rovers 35–0.

Internationals The highest margin recorded in an international match is 17. This occurred in the England v. Australia match at Sydney on 30 June 1951, when England won 17–0. This match is not listed by England as a

full international. The highest in the British Isles was when England beat Ireland 13–0 at Belfast on 18 Feb. 1882.

F.A. Cup The highest score in an F.A. Cup match is 26, when Preston North End beat Hyde 26–0 at Deepdale, Lancashire on 15 Oct. 1887. This is also the highest score between English clubs. The biggest victory in a final tie is 6 when Bury beat Derby County 6–0 at Crystal Palace on 18 April 1903, in which year Bury did not concede a single goal in the five Cup matches.

League match The highest score by one side in Football League (Division I) match is 12 goals when West Bromwich Albion beat Darwen 12–0 at West Bromwich, West Midlands on 4 March 1892; when Nottingham Forest beat Leicester Fosse by the same score at Nottingham on 21 April 1909; and when Aston Villa beat Accrington 12–2 at Perry Barr, West Midlands on 12 March 1892.

League match aggregate The highest aggregate in League Football was 17 goals when Tranmere Rovers beat Oldham Athletic 13–4 in a 3rd Division (North) match at Prenton Park,

An artist's impression of mob football in a London street in the reign of Edward II (1307–1327)

Mansell Collection

Merseyside, on Boxing Day, 1935. The record margin in a League match has been 13 in the Newcastle United 13, Newport County 0 Division II match on 5 Oct. 1946 and in the Stockport County 13, Halifax 0 Division III (North) match on 6 Jan. 1934.

League season The highest number of goals by any British team in a professional league in a season is 142 in 34 matches by Raith Rovers (Scottish Division II) in the 1937–38 season. The English League record is 134 in 46 matches by Peterborough United (Division IV) in 1960–61.

Individuals The most scored by one player in a first-class match is 16 by Stains for Racing Club de Lens v. Aubry-Asturies, in Lens, France, on 13 Dec. 1942. The record for any British first-class match is 13 by John Petrie in the Arbroath v. Bon Accord Scottish Cup match in 1885 (see above). The record in League Football is 10 by Joe Payne (b. Bolsover, Derbyshire) for Luton Town v. Bristol Rovers in a 3rd Division (South) match at Luton on 13 April 1936. The English 1st Division record is 7 goals by Ted Drake (b. Southampton, Hampshire) for Arsenal v. Aston Villa at Birmingham on 14 Dec. 1935, and James Ross for Preston North End v. Stoke at Preston on 6 Oct. 1888. The Scottish 1st Division record is 8 goals by James McGrory for Celtic v. Dunfermline Athletic at Celtic Park, Glasgow, on 14 Jan. 1928.

The record number of goals scored by one player in an international match is 10 by Gottfried Fuchs for Germany who beat Russia 16–0 in the 1912 Olympic tournament (consolation event) in Sweden.

The record for individual goal-scoring in a British home international is 6 by Joe Bambrick for Ireland v. Wales at Belfast on 1 Feb. 1930.

Career Artur Friedenreich (b. 1892) is believed to have scored an undocumented 1,329 goals in Brazilian football, but the greatest total of goals scored in a specified period is 1,216 by Edson Arantes do Nascimento (b. Baurú, Brazil, 23 Oct. 1940), known as Pelé, the Brazilian inside left from 7 Sept. 1956 to 2 Oct. 1974 in 1,254 games. His best year was 1958 with 139 and the *milesimo* (1,000th) came in a penalty for his club Santos in the Maracaña Stadium, Rio de Janerio on 19 Nov. 1969 when playing his 909th first-class match. He came out of retirement in 1975

to add to his total with New York Cosmos. Franz ("Bimbo") Binder (b. 1911) scored 1,006 goals in 756 games in Austria and Germany between 1930 and 1950.

The best season League records are 60 goals in 39 League games by William Ralph ("Dixie") Dean (b. Birkenhead, Cheshire, 1906) for Everton (Division I) in 1927–28 and 66 goals in 38 games by Jim Smith for Ayr United (Scottish Division II) in the same season. With 3 more in Cup ties and 19 in representative matches Dean's total was 82.

The international career record for England is 49 goals by Robert ("Bobby") Charlton, O.B.E. (b. Ashington, Northumberland, 11 Oct. 1937). His first was v. Scotland in 1958 and his last on 20 May 1970 v. Colombia.

The greatest number of goals scored in British first-class football is 550 (410 in League matches) by James McGrory of Glasgow Celtic (1922–38). The most scored in League matches is 434, for West Bromwich Albion, Fulham, Leicester City and Shrewsbury Town, by George Arthur Rowley (b. Wolverhampton, West Midlands, 1926) between 1946 and April 1965. Rowley also scored 32 goals in the F.A. Cup and 1 for England "B".

Fastest Goals The fastest goal on record was one scored in 6 sec. by Albert Munday for Aldershot in a Fourth Division match v. Hartlepools United at Victoria Ground, Hartlepool, Cleveland on 25 Oct. 1958. The same time was recorded by Keith Smith of Crystal Palace in a Second Division match v. Derby County at Baseball Ground, Derby on 12 Dec. 1964. A goal 4 sec after the kick-off is claimed by Jim Fryatt of Bradford in a Fourth Division match against Tranmere Rovers at Park Avenue, Bradford, West Yorkshire on 25 April 1964. It is claimed that Maglioni scored 3 goals for Indipendienti v. Gimnasia y Esgrima de la Plata in 1 min 50 sec in Argentina on 18 Mar. 1973. John McIntyre (Blackburn Rovers) scored 4 goals in 5 min v. Everton at Ewood Park, Blackburn, Lancashire on 16 Sept. 1922. W. 'G.' (Ginger) Richardson (West Bromwich Albion) scored 4 goals in 5 min against West Ham United at Upton Park on 7 Nov. 1931. Frank Keetley scored 6 goals in 21 min in the 2nd half of the Lincoln City v .Halifax Town league match on 16 Jan. 1932.

267

The international record is 3 goals in $3\frac{1}{2}$ min by Willie Hall (Tottenham Hotspur) for England against Ireland on 16 Nov. 1938 at Old Trafford, Greater Manchester.

Goal-less streak In Oct.–Dec. 1919 Coventry played 11 successive games without scoring.

WORLD CUP

The *Fédération Internationale de Football* (F.I.F.A.) was founded in Paris on 21 May 1904 and instituted the World Cup Competition on 13 July 1930, in Montevideo, Uruguay.

The only country to win three times has been Brazil in 1958, 1962 and 1970. Brazil was also third in 1938 and second in 1950, and is the only one of the 45 participating countries to have played in all 10 competitions. Antonio Carbajal (b. 1923) played for Mexico in goal in the competitions of 1950–54–58–62 and 1966. The record goal scorer has been Just Fontaine (France) with 13 goals in 6 games in the final stages of the 1958 competition in Sweden. The most goals scored in a final is 3 by Geoffrey Hurst (b. Ashton-under-Lyne, Greater Manchester, 1941) (West Ham United) for England v. West Germany on 30 July 1966. Gerd Müller (West Germany) holds the aggregate record for goals scored in the World Cup Finals with 14 in 1970 and 1974.

WORLD CLUB CHAMPIONSHIP

This club tournament was started in 1960 between the winners of the European Cup and the Copa Libertadores, the South American equivalent. Three clubs have won it twice: Penarol, Uruguay in 1961, 1966; Santos, Brazil in 1962, 1963; and Inter-Milan in 1964, 1965.

F.A. CHALLENGE CUP

Wins The greatest number F.A. Cup wins is 7 by Aston Villa in 1887, 1895, 1897, 1905, 1913, 1920 and 1957 (nine final appearances). Of the 6-time winners Newcastle United have been in the final 11 times. The highest aggregate scores have been 6–1 in 1890, 6–0 in 1903 and 4–3 in 1953.

The greatest number of Scottish F.A. Cup wins is 24 by Celtic in 1892, 1899, 1900, 1904, 1907–08, 1911–12, 1914, 1923, 1925, 1927, 1931, 1933, 1937, 1951, 1954, 1965, 1967, 1969, 1971, 1972, 1974 and 1975.

Youngest player The youngest player in the F.A. Cup Final was Howard Kendall (b. 22 May 1946) of Preston North End, who played against West Ham United on 2 May 1964, 20 days before his 18th birthday. Note however, that Derek Johnstone (Rangers) (b. 4 Nov. 1953) was 16 years 11 months old when he played in the Scottish League Cup Final against Celtic on 24 Oct. 1970. The youngest goal scorer in the F.A. Cup Final was John Sissons (b. 30 Sept. 1945) who scored for West Ham United v. Preston North End on 2 May 1964.

Most medals Three players have won 5 F.A. Cup Winner's Medals: James Forrest (Blackburn Rovers) (1884–85–86–90–91); the Hon. Sir Arthur Fitzgerald Kinnaird K.T. (Wanderers) (1873–77–78) and Old Etonians (1879–82) and C. H. R. Wollaston (Wanderers) (1872–73–76–1877–78).

Longest tie The most protracted F.A. Cup tie in the competition proper was that between Stoke City and Bury in the 3rd round with Stoke winning 3–2 in the fifth meeting after 9 hours 22 min of play in January 1955. The matches were at Bury (1–1) on 8 January; Stoke on Trent 12 January (abandoned after 22 min of extra time with the score 1–1); Goodison Park (3–3) on 17 January; Anfield (2–2) on 19 January; and finally at Old Trafford on 24 January. In the 1972 final

Gerd Muller (West Germany) the top goal scorer in any World Cup series seen scoring against England in the quarter finals of 1970 tournament at Mexico City

Gerry Cranham

qualifying round Alvechurch beat Oxford City after five previous drawn games.

MOST LEAGUE CHAMPIONSHIPS

World The world record number of successive national League championships wins is 9 by Celtic (Scotland) 1966–74 and C.S.K.A., Sofia (Bulgaria) 1952–64.

English The greatest number of League Championships (Division I) is 8 jointly held by Arsenal in 1931, 1933, 1934, 1935, 1938, 1948, 1953 and 1971 and Liverpool in 1901, 1906, 1922, 1923, 1947, 1964, 1966, and 1973. The record number of points is in Division I 67 by Leeds United in 1969 while the lowest has been 8 by Doncaster Rovers (Division II) in 1904–5. Doncaster Rovers scored 72 points from 42 games in Division III (North) in 1947.

The only F.A. Cup and League Championship "doubles" are those of Preston North End in 1889, Aston Villa in 1897, Tottenham Hotspur in 1961 and Arsenal in 1971. Preston won the League without losing a match and the Cup without having a goal scored against them throughout the whole competition. Glasgow Rangers have won the Scottish League Championship 34 times between 1899 and 1975 and were joint champions on another occasion. Their 76 points in the Scottish 1st Division in 1921 represents a record in any division.

Closest win In 1923–24 Huddersfield won the Division I championship over Cardiff by 0.02 of a goal with a goal average of 1.81.

Most durable player The most durable player in League history has been Jimmy Dickinson (b. Alton, Hampshire, 1925) who made 764 appearances for Portsmouth F.C. between 1946 and 1965.

EUROPEAN CHAMPIONSHIP

The European equivalent of the World Cup started in 1958 and is staged every 4 years. Each tournament takes 2 years to run with the semi-finals and final in the same country. The U.S.S.R. won the first when they beat Yugoslavia 2–1 in Paris on 10 July 1960 followed by Spain (1964), Italy (1968) and West Germany (1972).

EUROPEAN CHAMPIONS CUP

The European Cup for the League champions of the respective nations was approved by F.I.F.A. on 8 May 1955 and was run by the European governing body U.E.F.A. (Union of European Football Associations) which came into being in the previous year. Real Madrid defeated Rheims 4–3 in the first final in 1956 and went on to win the Cup in the next 4 seasons and in 1966. They took part in all competitions, either as holders or Spanish champions up to and including 1969–70. Ajax, Amsterdam won the cup for three successive years 1971, 1972 and 1973.

Glasgow Celtic became the first British club to win the Cup when they beat Inter-Milan 2–1 in the National Stadium, Lisbon, Portugal, on 25 May 1967. At the same time they established the record of being the only British club to win the European Cup and the two senior domestic tournaments (League and Cup) in the same season.

EUROPEAN CUP WINNERS CUP

A tournament for the national Cup winners started in 1960–1 with 10 entries. Fiorentina beat Glasgow Rangers on 4–1 aggregate in a two-leg final in May 1961. Tottenham Hotspur were the first British club to win the trophy, beating Atletico Madrid 5–1 in Rotterdam in 1963 and were followed by West Ham United in 1965, Manchester City in 1970, Chelsea in 1971 and Glasgow Rangers in 1972.

U.E.F.A. CUP

Originally known as the International Inter-City Industrial Fairs Cup, this club tournament began in 1955. The first competition lasted 3 years, the second 2 years. In 1960–61 it became an annual tournament and since 1971–72 has been replaced by the U.E.F.A. Cup. The first British club to win the trophy were Leeds United in 1968 and were followed by Newcastle United in 1969, Arsenal in 1970, Leeds again in 1971, Tottenham Hotspur in 1972 and Liverpool in 1973.

MOST APPEARANCES

Robert Frederick ("Bobby") Moore, O.B.E. (b. Barking, Essex, 12 April 1941) of West Ham United and Fulham set up a new record of full international appearances by a British footballer by playing in his 108th game for England v. Italy on 14 Nov. 1973 at Wembley. His first appearance was v. Peru on 20 May 1962.

England The greatest number of appearances for England secured in the International Championship is 38 by William (Billy) Ambrose Wright C.B.E. (b. Ironbridge, Salop, 6 Feb. 1924) in 1946–1959.

Wales The record number of appearances for Wales in the International Championship is 48 by William (Billy) Meredith (Manchester City and United) in the longest international span of 26 years (1895–1920). This is a record for any of the four home countries. Ivor Allchurch, M.B.E. (born 29 Dec. 1929) of Swansea, Newcastle, Cardiff City and Worcester City played 68 times for Wales, including 37 times against the home countries, between 15 Nov. 1950 and Feb. 1968.

Scotland The Scottish record for International Championship matches is 30 by Alan Morton (Queen's Park and Glasgow Rangers) from 1920 to 1932. Morton also had a single foreign international making a total of 31 caps. Denis Law (Huddersfield Town, Manchester City (twice), Torino (Italy), Manchester United) has a record total of 55 appearances for Scotland between Oct. 1958 and June 1974.

Ireland The greatest number of appearances for Ireland is 59 by Terry Neill (b. Belfast) (Arsenal and Hull City) (1961 to 1973).

Scotland's most prolific winner of caps—Denis Law with 55 (1958–74)

Associated Press

Oldest cap The oldest cap has been William Henry (Billy) Meredith (1874–1958), who played outside right for Wales v. England at Highbury, Islington, Greater London, on 15 March 1920 when aged 45 years 229 days.

Youngest caps The youngest cap in the four home countries internationals has been Norman Kernoghan (Belfast Celtic) who played for Ireland v. Wales in 1936 aged 17 years 80 days. It is possible, however, that W. K. Gibson (Cliftonville) who played for Ireland v. Wales in 1894 at 17 was slightly younger. England's youngest home international was Duncan Edwards (b. Dudley, West Midlands, 1 Oct. 1936, d. 21 Feb. 1958, 15 days after the Munich air crash) the Manchester United left half, against Scotland at Wembley on 2 April 1955, aged 18 years 183 days. The youngest Welsh cap was John Charles (b. Swansea, 27 Dec. 1931) the Leeds United centre half, against Ireland at Wrexham on 8 March 1950, aged 18 years 71 days. Scotland's youngest international has been Denis Law (b. Aberdeen, 24 Feb. 1940) of Huddersfield Town, who played against Wales on 18 Oct. 1958, aged 18 years 236 days. Jackie Robinson played for England v. Finland in 1937 aged 17 years 9 months. Research remains to be completed on the date of birth of David Black of Hurlford, Ayrshire, who may have been 17 when he played for Scotland v. Ireland in 1889.

TRANSFER FEES

The world's highest transfer fee has been £922,300 paid by F.C. Barcelona, Spain to Ajax Amsterdam, Netherlands for Johan Cruyff announced on 20 Aug. 1973. On transfer (Sept. 1973) he received a record signing fee of c. £400,000. It is reported that Napoli, Italy paid Bologna, Italy around £1.4 m for centre-forward Giuseppe Savoldi on 11 July 1975. Two other players were included in this deal.

British transfer fee "records" have become of progressively less significance because fiscal and public relations considerations tend to distort published figures.

269

The British aggregate record is held by the centre forward Tony Hateley (b. Derby, 1942) who in six moves from July 1963 to 28 Oct. 1970 was reportedly valued at £393,500.

CROWD AND GATES

The greatest recorded crowd at any football match was 205,000 (199,854 paid) for the Brazil v. Uruguay World Cup match in the Maracaña Municipal Stadium, Rio de Janeiro, Brazil on 16 July 1950.

The record attendance for a European Cup match is 136,505 at the Glasgow Celtic v. Leeds United match at Hampden Park, Glasgow on 15 Apr. 1970.

The British record paid attendance is 149,547 at the Scotland v. England international at Hampden Park, Glasgow, on 17 April 1937. It is, however, probable that this total was exceeded (estimated 160,000) on the occasion of the F.A. Cup Final between Bolton Wanderers and West Ham United at Wembley Stadium on 28 April 1923, when the crowd broke in on the pitch and the start was delayed 40 min until the pitch was cleared. The counted admissions were 126,047.

The record attendance for a League match in Britain is 118,567 for Rangers v. Celtic at Ibrox Park, Glasgow on 2 Jan. 1939.

The Scottish Cup record attendance is an estimated 170,000 when Celtic played Aberdeen at Hampden Park on 24 April 1937.

Smallest The smallest crowd at a full home international was 4,946 for the Northern Ireland v. Wales match of 19 May 1973 at Goodison Park, Everton, Merseyside. The smallest crowd at a Football League fixture was for the Stockport County v. Leicester City match at Old Trafford, Greater Manchester, on 7 May 1921. Stockport's own ground was under suspension and the "crowd" numbered 13.

RECEIPTS

The record gross F.A. Cup receipts at Wembley, Brent, Greater London, is £303,000 (excluding radio and television fees) for the final on 3 May 1975.

The greatest receipts at any World Cup final were £204,805, from an attendance of 96,924 for England v. West Germany at the Empire Stadium, Wembley, on 30 July 1966.

The record for a British international match is £193,000 for the England v. Scotland match at Wembley on 19 May 1973 (attendance 100,000). The receipts for the Manchester United v. Benfica match at Wembley on 29 May 1968 were £118,000 (attendance 100,000).

Longest match The duration record for first class fixtures was set in the Copa Libertadores in Santos, Brazil, on 2–3 Aug. 1962, when Santos drew 3–3 with Penarol F.C. of Montevideo, Uruguay. The game lasted 3½ hours (with interruptions), from 9.30 p.m. to 1 a.m. It is claimed that a match between Dallas Tornado Soccer Club and Rochester Lancers lasted 3 hr 59 min (176 min playing time) in Sept. 1971.

The longest British match on record was one of 3 hours 23 min between Stockport County and Doncaster Rovers in the second leg of the 3rd Division (North) Cup at Edgeley Park, Stockport, Greater Manchester on 30 March 1946.

Most successful national coach The most successful national coach has been George Raynor (b. 1907) for Sweden. His teams won the 1948 Olympic competition and were 2nd in the 1958 World Cup and 3rd in both the 1950 World Cup and in the 1952 Olympic competition.

Brazil Embassy

The world's largest football stadium—the 205,000 capacity Maracaña Municipal Stadium, Rio de Janeiro, Brazil

Heaviest goalkeeper The biggest goalkeeper in representative football was the England international Willie J. "Fatty" Foulke (1874–1916), who stood 6 ft 3 in *1,90 m* and weighed 22 st. 3 lb. *141 kg*. His last games were for Bradford, by which time he was 26 st. *165 kg*. He once stopped a game by snapping the cross bar.

FOOTBALL (Amateur)

Most Olympic wins The only country to have won the Olympic football title 3 times is Hungary in 1952, 1964 and 1968. The United Kingdom won the unofficial tournament in 1900 and the official tournaments of 1908 and 1912. The highest Olympic score is Denmark 17 v. France "A" 1 in 1908.

Highest scores The highest aggregate score in a home Amateur International is 11 goals in the England v. Scotland match (8–3) at Dulwich on 11 March 1939. The foreign record was when England beat France 15–0 in Paris on 1 Nov. 1906.

The highest score in an F.A. Amateur Cup Final was 8, when Northern Nomads beat Stockton 7–1 at Sunderland, Tyne and Wear in 1926, and when Dulwich Hamlet beat Marine (Liverpool) by the same score at Upton Park in 1932.

In the match between Sandygate Youth Club v. 1st Burnley Boys' Brigade at Burnley, Lancashire on 10 Sept. 1955, the half time score was 27–0 and after 80 min play 53–0. Sandygate's top scorer was Roy Swift with 14 goals.

Individual The highest individual scores in amateur internationals are 6 by William Charles Jordan for England v. France (12–0) at Park Royal, Ealing, Greater London, on 23 March 1908; 6 by Vivian J. Woodward for England v. Holland (9–1) at Stamford Bridge, Hammersmith, Greater London, on 11 Dec. 1909; and 6 also by Harold A. Walden for Great Britain v. Hungary in Stockholm, Sweden, on 1 July 1912. Kim Barker, 11, of South Hobart, Tasmania, Australia scored 21 goals in his team's 25–0 win over Hutchins in the under-12 competition on 11 May 1974.

International Schoolboys The most prolific schoolboy international scorer has been Richard Smith Bell (England) who in the 1935–36 season scored 12 goals in three internationals: 3 v. Scotland, 3 v. Wales and 6 v. Ireland.

Most caps The record number of England amateur caps is held by Rod Haider, the Hendon captain and half-back, who made his 65th amateur international appearance for England v. Scotland on 5 Apr. 1974.

F.A. Amateur Cup wins The greatest number of F.A. Amateur Cup (instituted 1893) wins is 10 by Bishop Auckland who won in 1896, 1900, 1914, 1921–22, 1935, 1939, 1955, 1956 and 1957.

Largest crowd The highest attendances at amateur matches has been 100,000, first reached at the Cup Final between Pegasus and Bishop Auckland at Wembley on 21 April 1951. The amateur gate record is £39,500 at the final between Walton and Hersham and Slough Town on 14 April 1973.

Heading The highest recorded number of repetitions for heading a ball is 12,100 in 54 min 22 sec by Michael Helliwell, 17, of Elland on 14 Dec. 1973.

Most and Least Successful Teams The Lemington Comrades F.C. between 17 Sept. 1971 and 3 Feb. 1974 won 66 consecutive matches. They played 83 games without defeat up to Nov. 1974. The Nomads F.C. who participate in the Norwich Lads and Minor League lost 20 out of 20 matches in 1972–73 with a score of 11–431 (a goal average of minus 21.55) despite buying a new goalkeeper for 25p. The club was awarded the League's Best Sportsmen Cup.

Most Goals The greatest number of goals in a season reported for an individual player in junior league football is 96 by Tom Duffy, who played centre-forward professionally for Ardeer Thistle F.C., Ayrshire in the 1960–61 season. The highest season figure reported in any class of competitive football for an individual is 294 goals in 67 matches by centre forward Michael Jones for Afan Lido F.C., St. Joseph's School and Port Talbot Boys XI in 1972–73. His total (65 headers, 120 right boot and 109 left boot) included an 11, a 10 and 6 triple hat-tricks.

Fastest Own Goal The fastest own goal on record was one in 7 sec "scored" by Ascot Sports F.C. in the South Derbyshire Premier League in Sept. 1972. The feat was achieved by dint of two deft back passes. Hilton Athletic F.C. went on to cement this early bonus with a further 9 goals.

Longest ties The aggregate duration of ties in amateur soccer have not been collated but it is recorded that in the London F.A. Intermediate Cup first qualifying round Highfield F.C. Reserves had to meet Mansfield House F.C. on 19 and 26 Sept. and 3, 10 and 14 Oct. 1970 to get a decision after 9 hours 50 min play with scores of 0–0, 1–1, 1–1, 3–3, and 0–2.

In the Hertfordshire Intermediate Cup, London Colney beat Leavesden Hospital after 12 hours 41 min play and 7 ties on 6 Nov. to 17 Dec. 1971.

Most disciplined Coleridge F.C. of the Cambridgeshire F.A. completed 21 years without a single member having been cautioned, sent off or otherwise disciplined since its formation in 1954.

Most indisciplined In the local Cup match between Tongham Youth Club, Surrey and Hawley, Hampshire, England on

Michael Helliwell, the champion "header", in action

Halifax Courier

3 Nov. 1969 the referee booked all 22 players including one who went to hospital, and one of the linesmen. The match, won by Tongham 2–0, was described by a player as "A good, hard game". In a Dorset Junior Shield match at Chideock on 19 Dec. 1970 referee Douglas Chainey sent the entire R.A.O.C. team off. Glencraig United, Faifley, near Clydebank, had all 11 team members and two substitutes for their match against Goldenhill Boy's Club on 2 Feb. 1975 booked in the dressing room before a ball was kicked. The referee, Mr. Tarbet of Bearsden, took exception to the chant which greeted his arrival. It was not his first meeting with Glencraig. The teams drew 2–2.

Oldest Player Jack Whattam (b. 7 Jan. 1909) of Cleethorpes plays weekly for Burtons F.C. and Weelsby Rovers at the age of 66.

Longest marathons The longest recorded 11-a-side football match played under F.A. rules without substitutes has been one of 37 hrs by teams from Toccoa Falls, Georgia on 25–26 April 1975 and from Tenney H.S., Methuen, Mass., U.S.A., 7–8 June 1975.

The longest recorded authenticated 5-a-side games have been: outdoors: 55 hours by two teams (no substitutes) from R.A.F. Thorney Island, Hampshire on 18–20 Sept. 1974 and indoors: 67 hrs 42 min by two teams (no substitutes) from Middleton, Manchester on 23–25 May 1975.

FOOTBALL (GAELIC)

Earliest references The game developed from inter-parish "free for all" with no time-limit, no defined playing area nor specific rules. The formation of the Gaelic Athletic Association was in Thurles, Ireland, on 1 Nov. 1884.

Most titles The greatest number of All Ireland Championships ever won by one team is 22 by Ciarraidhe (Kerry) between 1903 and 1970. The greatest number of successive wins is four by Wexford (1915–18) and four by Kerry (1929–32).

Highest scores The highest score in an All-Ireland final was when Cork (3 goals, 17 points) beat Galway (2 goals, 13 points) in 1973. The highest combined score was also in this game. A goal equals 3 points.

Lowest scores In four All-Ireland finals the combined totals have been 7 points; 1893 Wexford (1 goal [till 1894 worth 5 points], 1 point) v. Cork (1 point); 1895 Tipperary (4 points) v. Meath (3 points); 1904 Kerry (5 points) v. Dublin (2 points); 1924 Kerry (4 points) v. Dublin (3 points).

Most appearances The most appearances in All-Ireland finals is ten by Dan O'Keeffe (Kerry) of which seven (a record) were on the winning side.

Individual score The highest recorded individual score in an All-Ireland final has been 2 goals, 5 points by Frank Stockwell (Galway) in the match against Cork in 1956.

Largest crowd The record crowd is 90,556 for the Down v. Offaly final at Croke Park, Dublin, in 1961.

Inter-provincials The province of Leinster has won most championships (Railway Cup) with 18 between 1928 and 1974. Sean O'Neill (Down) holds the record of 8 medals with Ulster (1960–71).

FOOTBALL (RUGBY LEAGUE)

Origins The Rugby League was formed originally in 1895 as "The Northern Rugby Football Union" by the secession of 22 clubs in Lancashire and Yorkshire from the parent Rugby Union. Though payment for loss of working time was a major cause of the breakaway the "Northern Union" did not itself embrace full professionalism until 1898. A reduction in the number of players per team from 15 to 13 took place in 1906 and the present title of "Rugby League" was adopted in 1922.

Most wins Under the one-league Championship system (1907–62 and 1965–71) the club with the most wins was Wigan with nine (1909, 1922, 1926, 1934, 1946, 1947, 1950, 1952 and 1960).

In the Rugby League Challenge Cup (inaugurated 1896–97) the club with the most wins is Leeds with 8 in 1910–23–32–36, 1941–42 (wartime), 1957 and 1968. Oldham is the only club to appear in four consecutive Cup Finals (1924–27).

Only three clubs have won all four major Rugby League trophies (Challenge Cup, League Championship, County Cup and County League) in one season: Hunslet in 1907–08, Huddersfield in 1914–15 and Swinton in 1927–28.

In addition to the three "All Four Cup clubs", on only five other occasions has a club taken the Cup and League honours in one season: Broughton Rangers (1902); Halifax (1903); Huddersfield (1913); Warrington (1954); and St. Helens (1966). In 1974 Warrington won the Cup and newly constituted Club championship.

World Cup The record aggregate score in a World Cup match is 72 points when Great Britain beat New Zealand at Hameau Stadium, Pau, France by 53 points to 19 on 4 Nov. 1972.

There have been six World Cup Competitions. Australia were winners in 1957, 1968 and 1970. Great Britain won in 1954, 1960 and 1972. The seventh competition will be decided in October 1975.

Senior match The highest aggregate score in Cup or League football in a game where a senior club has been concerned, was 121 points, when Huddersfield beat Swinton Park Rangers by 119 points (19 goals, 27 tries) to 2 points (one goal) in the first round of the Northern Union Cup on 28 Feb. 1914.

Cup Final The record aggregate in a Cup Final is 47 points when Featherstone Rovers beat Bradford Northern 33–14 at Wembley on 12 May 1973.

The greatest winning margin was 34 points when Huddersfield beat St. Helens 37–3 at Oldham on 1 May 1915.

Touring teams The record score for a British team touring the Commonwealth is 101 points by England v. South Australia (nil) at Adelaide in May 1914.

The record for a Commonwealth touring team in Britain is 92 points (10 goals, 24 tries) by Australia against Bramley's 7 points (2 goals, one try) at the Barley Mow Ground, Bramley, near Leeds, on 9 Nov. 1921.

Record crowds and receipts The greatest attendance at any Rugby League match is 102,569 for the Warrington v. Halifax Cup Final replay at Odsal Stadium, Bradford, on 5 May 1954.

The highest receipts for a match in the United Kingdom have been £140,732 45p for the Warrington v. Widnes Cup Final at Wembley on 10 May 1975.

Most international caps Test Matches between Great Britain (formerly England) and Australia are regarded as the highest distinction for an R.L. player in either hemisphere and Jim Sullivan (b. 2 Dec. 1903), the Wigan full-back and captain, holds a Test record for a British player with 15 appearances in these games between 1924 and 1933, though Mick Sullivan (no kin) of Huddersfield, Wigan, St. Helens and York, played in 16 G.B. v. Australia games in 1954–64, of which 13 were Tests and 3 World Cup matches.

In all Tests, including those against New Zealand and France, Mick Sullivan made the record number of 47 appearances and scored 43 tries.

Most Cup Finals Two players have appeared in seven Cup Finals: Alan Edwards (Salford, Dewsbury, and Bradford Northern) between 1938 and 1949, and Eric Batten (Leeds, Bradford Northern and Featherstone Rovers) between 1941 and 1952.

Eric Ashton, M.B.E. (b. 24 Jan. 1935), Wigan and Great Britain centre has the distinction of captaining Wigan at Wembley in six R.L. Cup Finals in nine years 1958–66, taking the trophy three times (1958, 1959 and 1965).

The youngest player in a Cup Final was Reg Lloyd (Keighley) who was 17 years 8 months when he played at Wembley on 8 May 1937.

Most goals The record number of goals in a season is 228 by David Watkins (Salford) (b. 5 Mar. 1942) in the 1972–1973 season. His total was made up of 221 in League, Cup, other competitions, and a Salford v. New Zealand match, plus 7 in two pre-season friendly fixtures.

Fast scoring David Watkins scored 13 points (3 tries, 2 conversions) in 5 min for Salford v. Barrow on 1 Dec. 1972.

MOST POINTS

Cup C. H. ("Tich") West of Hull Kingston Rovers scored 53 points (10 goals and 11 tries) in a 1st Round Challenge Cup-tie v. Brookland Rovers on 4 March 1905.

League Ernest Ward (Bradford Northern) scored 4 tries and 11 goals (34 points) against Liverpool Stanley on 20 Oct. 1945. Lionel Cooper of Huddersfield scored 10 tries and kicked two goals (34 points) against Keighley on 17 Nov. 1951.

Season The record number of points in a season was scored by B. Lewis Jones (Leeds) with 496 in season 1956–57 (he also scored 9 points in a friendly game). David Watkins (Salford) scored 493 points in season 1972–73 (he also scored 14 points in two friendly games).

Career Scores Jim Sullivan (Wigan) scored 6,192 points (2,955 goals and 94 tries) in a senior Rugby League career extending from 1921 to 1946.

Most Durable player David Watkins (Salford) played and scored in every club game during seasons 1972–3 and 1973–4—a total of 92 games contributing 41 tries and 403 goals—a total of 929 points. Together with seasons 1970–1 and 1971–2 he played 140 consecutive games.

Record transfer fees The highest R.L. transfer fee is £20,000 paid to Dewsbury for Michael Stephenson by Penrith, Australia on 17 July 1973. David Watkins (Welsh R.U.) received an £11,000 signing fee at a guaranteed £1,000 p.a. for 5 years from Salford in Oct. 1967.

Longest kick The longest claimed place kick was one of 80 yd *73 m* by H. H. (Dally) Messenger for Australia *v*. Hull in Hull, Humberside in 1908 but this was apparently only estimated. In April 1940 Martin Hodgson (Swinton) kicked a goal on the Rochdale ground later measured to be 77¾ yd *71 m*.

MOST TRIES

Season Albert Aaron Rosenfeld (Huddersfield), an Australian-born wing-threequarter, scored 80 tries in the 1913–14 season.

Career Brian Bevan, an Australian-born wing-threequarter, scored 834 tries in League, Cup, representative or charity games in the 18 seasons (16 with Warrington, 2 with Blackpool Borough) from 1946 to 1964.

Rugby League's top try scorer, Brian Bevan, with 834 in 18 seasons

John Mounfield, Warrington

HIGHEST SCORES

The highest aggregate scores in international Rugby League football are:

Match	Points	Score
Great Britain *v*. Australia (*Test Matches*)	62	Australia won 50–12 (Swinton, 9 Nov. 1963)
Great Britain *v*. New Zealand (*Test Matches*)	72	Great Britain won 52–20 (Wellington, 30 July 1910)
Great Britain *v*. France (*Test Matches*)	65	Great Britain won 50–15 (Leeds, 14 March 1959)
England *v*. Wales	63	England won 40–23 (Leeds, 18 Oct. 1969)
England *v*. France	55	France won 42–13 (Marseilles, 25 Nov. 1951)
England *v*. Other Nationalities	61	England won 34–27 (Workington, 30 March 1933)
Wales *v*. France	50	France won 29–21 (Bordeaux, 23 Nov. 1947)
Wales *v*. Other Nationalities	48	Other Nationalities won 27–21 (Swansea, 31 March 1951)
Australia *v*. Great Britain	76	Australia won 63–13 (Paris, 31 Dec. 1933)
Australia *v*. Wales	70	Australia won 51–19 (Wembley, 30 Dec. 1933)
Australia *v*. France (*Test Matches*)	62	Australia won 56–6 (Brisbane, 2 July 1960)
Australia *v*. New Zealand (*Test Matches*)	74	New Zealand won 49–25 (Brisbane, 28 June 1952)
New Zealand *v*. France (*Test Matches*)	53	France won 31–22 (Lyon, 15 Jan. 1956)

FOOTBALL (RUGBY UNION)

Records are determined in terms of present day scoring values, i.e. a try at four points; a dropped goal, penalty or goal from a mark at 3 points; and a conversion at 2 points. The actual score, in accordance with which ever of the 8 earlier systems was in force at the time, is also given, in brackets.

Origins The game is traditionally said to have originated from a breach of the rules of the football played in November 1823 at Rugby School by William Webb Ellis (later the Rev.) (*c.* 1807–72). This handling code of football evolved gradually and was known to have been played at Cambridge University by 1839. The Rugby Football Union was not founded until 1871.

HIGHEST TEAM SCORES

Inter-nationals The highest score in any full International was when France beat Romania by 72 points (7 goals, six tries and 2 penalty goals) to 3 (1 penalty goal) (59–3) in the Olympic Games at Colombes, Paris in May 1924.

The above aggregate score also equalled the International Championship record of 75 points when Wales beat France at Swansea in 1910 by 59 points (8 goals, 1 penalty goal, 2 tries) to 16 (1 goal, 2 penalty goals and 1 try) (49–14).

The highest aggregate score for any International match between the Four Home Unions is 69 when England beat Wales by 69 "points" (7 goals, 1 drop goal and six tries) to 0 at Blackheath, Greenwich, Greater London in 1881. (Note: no point scoring in 1881.)

The highest score by any Overseas side in an International in the British Isles is 53 points (7 goals, 1 drop goal and 2 tries) to 0 when South Africa beat Scotland at Murrayfield, on 24 Nov. 1951 (44–0).

Tour match The record score for any international tour match is 125–0 (17 goals, 5 tries and 1 penalty goal) (103–0) when New Zealand beat Northern New South Wales at Quirindi, Australia, on 30 May 1962.

Inter-Club L'Union Sportive Perpignanaise beat l'A.S. Carcasonne by 173 (19 goals, 14 tries and a drop goal) to 0 (141–0) in December 1922.

Schools Scores of over 200 points have been recorded in school matches, for example Radford School beat Hills Court 214 points (31 goals and 7 tries) to 0 (100–0) on 20 Nov. 1886.

Club Season Record The highest number of points accumulated in a season by an English club is 1,233 pts by Morley R.F.C., West Yorkshire in 1973–74. In 1970–71 Solihull R.U.F.C's 1st XV scored a record 247 tries.

HIGHEST INDIVIDUAL SCORES

Internationals The highest individual points score in any match between members of the International Board is 24 by W. Fergie McCormick—1 drop goal, 3 conversions and 5 penalty goals for New Zealand against Wales at Auckland on 14 June 1969.

Ian Scott Smith (Scotland) (1903–1972) has scored most consecutive tries in international matches with 6; 3 in the second half of Scotland v. France in 1925 and 3 in the first half against Wales two weeks later.

Career W. Fergie McCormick of Canterbury, New Zealand scored his 2,001st point on 21 Sept. 1974 in a 17 year career.

Senior Inter [Open] Club Chris Scotford (Solihull) contributed 41 points (7 tries, 1 penalty and 5 conversions) in a 48–7 win over Esher on 14 Dec. 1974.

Schools In a match in November 1963 between Stucley's and Darracott's in a junior house match at Bideford G.S., Devon the scrum-half, Alan McKenzie, 14, contributed 86 points (13 tries and 17 conversions) (73) to Sutcley's winning score.

Season Record The first class rugby scoring record for a season is 597 points (inc. 517 for his club in 49 games) by Robin John Williams (b. 11 Feb. 1950) of Pontypool R.F.C. in the 1974–75 season.

Sport & General

John Pullin (Bristol R.F.C.) winner of more caps (40) than any other of England's 1000 international players

County Championships The County Championships (instituted in 1889) have been won most often by Gloucestershire with 12 titles (1910, 1913, 1920–22, 1930–32, 1937, 1972, 1974 and 1975).

MOST CAPPED PLAYERS

The totals below are limited to matches between the seven member countries of the "International Rugby Football Board" and France. Including 17 appearances for the British Lions, Willie John McBride (63 times capped by Ireland) has played in 80 international matches.

Ireland	63	Willie John McBride, M.B.E.	1962–75
New Zealand	55	Colin Earl Meads	1957–71
France	50	Benoit Dauga	1964–72
Wales	44	Kenneth J. Jones, M.B.E.	1947–57
Australia	42	Peter G. Johnson	1958–72
Scotland	40	Hugh F. McLeod, O.B.E.	1954–62
	40	David M. D. Rollo	1959–68
	40	Alexander ('Sandy') B. Carmichael	1967–75
South Africa	38	Frik C. H. Du Preez	1960–71
England	40	John Vivian Pullin	1966–75

Most Olympic Gold Medals Rugby Football was included four times in the Olympic Games: 1900, 1908, 1920 and 1924. Four United States players, in the 1920 winning team won second gold medals in 1924: Charles W. Doe, John T. O'Neil, John C. Patrick and Rudolph J. Scholz. Daniel B. Carroll, who was in the winning Australian team in 1908, won a second gold medal in the 1920 U.S. team.

SEVEN-A-SIDES

First Seven-a-Sides Seven-a-Side rugby dates from 28 Apr. 1883 when Melrose R.F.C., Roxburghshire in order to alleviate the poverty of a club in such a small town staged a Seven-a-Side tournament. This idea was that of Ned Haig, the town's butcher. The bitter rivals Melrose and Galashiels tied in the final. In extra time, Melrose scored and absquatulated with the trophy declaring themselves to be the winners. Hence the present day tradition of "sudden death" extra-time.

Sport & General

Prop-forward Sandy Carmichael (West of Scotland), one of the three co-holders of the Scottish international caps record with 40 appearances

Middlesex Seven-a-Sides The Middlesex Seven-a-Sides were inaugurated in 1926. The most successful sides have been Harlequins with 7 wins (1926–27–28–29–33–35–67) and London Welsh (1930–31–56–68–71–72–73).

The only players to be in five winning "sevens" have been N. M. Hall (d. 1972) (St. Mary's Hospital 1944–1946 and Richmond 1951–53–55), and J. A. P. Shackleton and I. H. P. Laughland both of London Scottish (1960–61–62–63–65).

Highest posts The world's highest Rugby Union goal posts measure 93 ft 10½ in *28,61 m* and are made of metal. They are at the Municipal Grounds, Barberton, Transvaal, South Africa.

Longest kicks The longest recorded successful drop-goal is 90 yds *82 m* by Gerry Brand for South Africa *v.* England at Twickenham, Richmond upon Thames, Greater London, in 1932. This was taken 7 yd *6 m* inside the England "half" 55 yd *50 m* from the posts and dropped over the dead ball line.

The place kick record is reputed to be 100 yd *914 m* at Richmond Athletic Ground, Greater London, by D. F. T. Morkell in an unsuccessful penalty for South Africa *v.* Surrey on 19 Dec. 1906. This was not measured until 1932.

In the match Bridlington School 1st XV *v.* an Army XV at Bridlington, Humberside in 1944, Ernie Cooper, captaining the school, landed a penalty from a measured 81 yds *74 m* from the post with a kick which carried over the dead ball line.

Longest try The longest "try" ever executed is by 15 members of Chorley R.F.C., who scored at Twickenham R.U. Ground on 3 May 1975 from a "move" started 277.1 miles *445,9 km* away at their clubhouse on 1 May 1975. This superceded the 231 miles *371,7 km* try scored in Northern Ireland by 15 members of the Collegians R.F.C., Belfast between 16–18 Mar. 1974. There were no forward passes or knock-ons, and the ball was touched down between the posts in the prescribed manner (Law 12).

Greatest crowd The record paying attendance is 104,000 for Scotland *v.* Wales match at Murrayfield, Edinburgh, on 1 Mar. 1975. Scotland won 12 points to 10.

ALL TIME SCORING RECORDS — AGGREGATE and MARGIN of VICTORY in the ten annual matches in the "International Championship".

Note: Headnote on page 274 on Scoring systems

		Aggregate Record Present Day pts. value		Record Margin Present Day pts. value
England *v.* Scotland	Scotland (28) beat England (19) in 1931	57	England (19) beat Scotland (0) in 1924	21
			England (24) beat Scotland (5) in 1947	21
England *v.* Ireland	England (36) beat Ireland (14) in 1938	61	Ireland (22) beat England (0) in 1947	27
England *v.* Wales	England beat Wales by 7 goals, 1 drop goal and 6 tries to nil in 1881	69*	England beat Wales by 7 goals, 1 drop goal and 6 tries to nil in 1881	69
England *v.* France	England (49) beat France (15) in 1907	64	England (37) beat France (0) in 1911	44
Scotland *v.* Ireland	Scotland (29) beat Ireland (14) in 1913	51	Scotland beat Ireland by 6 goals and 2 tries to nil in 1877	44
Scotland *v.* Wales	Scotland (20) beat Wales (0) in 1887	56	Scotland (20) beat Wales (0) in 1887	56
Scotland *v.* France	Scotland (31) beat France (3) in 1912	41	Scotland (31) beat France (3) in 1912	33
Ireland *v.* Wales	Wales (28) beat Ireland (4) in 1920 and Wales (23) beat Ireland (9) in 1971 Wales (32) beat Ireland (4) in 1975	36 36 36	Wales (29) beat Ireland (0) in 1907	34
Ireland *v.* France	France (27) beat Ireland (6) in 1964	40	Ireland (24) beat France (0) in 1913	30
Wales *v.* France	Wales (49) beat France (14) in 1910	75	Wales (47) beat France (5) in 1909	52

* Point scoring was not introduced until 1886

FOX HUNTING

EARLIEST REFERENCES

Hunting the fox in Britain became prevalent only from the middle of the 17th century though there is a reference to a hunt staged as early as 28 Feb. 1557. Prior to that time hunting was confined principally to the deer or the hare with the fox being hunted only by mistake. It is now estimated that huntsmen account for 10,000 of the 50,000 foxes killed each year.

Pack Oldest The oldest pack of foxhounds in existence in England is the Sinnington (1680), but the old Charlton Hunt in West Sussex, now extinct, and the Mid-Devon and the Duke of Buckingham in the Bilsdale country, North Yorkshire, hunted foxes prior to that time.

Largest The pack with the greatest number of hounds has been the Duke of Beaufort's hounds maintained at Badminton, Avon, since *c.* 1780. At times hunting eight times a week, this pack had 120 couples.

HUNT

Longest The longest recorded hunt was one led by Squire Sandys which ran from Holmbank, northern Lanca-shire, to Ulpha, Cumbria, a total of nearly 80 miles *128 km* in reputedly only six hours, in January or February 1743. The longest hunt in Ireland is probably a run of 24 miles *38 km* made by the Scarteen Hunt, County Limerick, from Pallas to Knockoura in 1914. The longest duration hunt was one of 10 hours 5 min by the Charlton Hunt of West Sussex, which ran from East Dean Wood at 7.45 a.m. to kill over 24½ miles *39 km* away at 5.50 p.m. on 26 Jan. 1736.

Largest fox The largest fox ever killed by a hunt in England was a 23¾ lb. *10 kg 770* dog on Cross Fell, Cumbria, by an Ullswater Hunt in 1936. A fox weighing 28 lb. 2 oz. *12 kg 750* measuring 54 in *137 cm* from nose to the tip of the brush was shot on the Staffordshire-Worcester-shire border on 11 March 1956.

BEAGLING

The oldest beagle hunt is the Royal Rock Beagle Hunt, Wirral, Merseyside, whose first outing was on 28 March 1845. The Newcastle and District Beagles claim their origin from the municipally-supported Newcastle Harriers existing in 1787. The Royal Agricultural College beagle pack killed 75½ brace of hares in the 1966–67 season.

GAMBLING

World's biggest win The world's biggest gambling win was £954,583 for a bet of 2 cruzeiros (25p) in the Brazilian football pools Loteria Esportiva by Francisco Couto Portela, 25 of Salvador, Brazil on the results of 13 games on 17 Apr. 1974. He backed 3 "Zebras" (weak teams) to win. Some lotteries pay winners $1,000 a week for life. Carol Joyce, 23, won the Massachusetts State Lottery on 16 Aug. 1974 with an expectation of $2.8 million (£1¼ million).

World's biggest loss An unnamed Italian industrialist was reported to have lost £800,000 in 5 hours at roulette in Monte Carlo, Monaco on 6 Mar. 1974. A Saudi Arabian prince was reported to have lost more than $1 million in a single session at the Metro Club, Las Vegas, U.S.A. in December 1974.

Largest Casino The largest casino in the world is the Casino, Mar del Plata, Argentina with average daily attendances of 14,500 rising to 25,000 during carnivals. The Casino has more than 150 roulette tables running simultaneously.

BINGO

Origins Bingo is a lottery game which, as keno, was developed in the 1880s from lotto, whose origin is thought to be the 17th century Italian game *tumbule*. It has long been known in the British Army (called Housey-Housey) and the Royal Navy (called Tombola). The winner was the first to complete a random selection of numbers from 1–90. The U.S.A. version called Bingo differs in that the selection is from 1–75. There are 6 million players in the United Kingdom.

Largest house The largest 'house' in Bingo sessions was staged at the Empire Pool, Wembley, Brent, Greater London, on 25 April 1965 when 10,000 attended. A "Full House" call occurred on the 29th number by Mrs. H. A. Cotterall in the Women's Institute, Bulawayo, Rhodesia, on 7 Aug. 1974. At the Blackpool College of Technology and Art on 18 Jan. 1975, "House" was not called until the 78th number.

Largest prize Prizes have been controlled since 1 July 1970 by the Betting and Gaming Act 1968. Prior to limitation, prizes in linked games between more than 50 clubs reached £16,000. The largest in a single game was £5,000 won in the Mecca National Rally at the Empire Pool, Wembley on 29 March 1970.

Longest session A session of 73 hr (two callers) was held at King George Hospital, Ilford, Essex in March 1975 with Brian Butler and Chris Wiggins of Barkingside calling.

Most Cards The highest recorded number of cards played simultaneously (with a call rate of 31.7 secs per call) has been 346 by Robert A. Berg at Pacific Beach, California on 16 Nov. 1973.

FOOTBALL POOLS

The winning dividend paid out by Littlewoods Pools Ltd. in their first week in February 1923 was £2.12s.0d. In April 1937 a record £30,780 was paid to R. Levy of London on 4 away wins, and in April 1947 a record £64,450 for a 1d. points pool.

Progressive list of individual record winnings

Amount	Recipient	Date
£75,000	P.C. Frank H. Chivers, 54, Aldershot, Hampshire	6 April 1948
£91,832	George A. Borrett, Huyton Merseyside	26 Sept. 1950
£94,335	Thomas A. Wood, 42, Carlisle	10 Oct. 1950
£104,990	Mrs. Evelyn Knowlson, 43, Manchester	7 Nov. 1950
£75,000 (limit)	(45 limit winners)	from 20 Nov. 1951 to 10 Sept. 1957
£205,235	Mrs. Nellie McGrail (now Mrs. Albert Cooper), 37, of Reddish, Greater Manchester	5 Nov. 1957
£206,028	W. John Brockwell, 29, Epsom, Surrey	18 Feb. 1958
£209,079	Tom Riley, 58, of Horden, Co. Durham	1 April 1958
£209,837	Ronald Smith of Liverpool	23 Dec. 1958
£260,104	John Dunn, 45, of Chelsea, Greater London	27 Oct. 1959
£265,352	Arthur Webb, 70, of Scarborough, North Yorkshire	24 Nov. 1959
£301,739.45	Lawrence Freedman, 54, of Willesden, Brent, Greater London	8 Dec. 1964
£338,356.80	Percy Harrison, 52 of East Stockwith, Lincolnshire	30 Aug. 1966
£401,792	Albert Crocker, 54, of Dobwalls, Cornwall	17 April 1971
£512,683	Cyril Grimes, 62 of Liss, Hampshire	4 Mar. 1972
£542,252	James Wood, 56, of Bradford, West Yorkshire	28 Feb. 1973
£547,172	A London woman	3 Mar. 1973
£629,801	Colin Carruthers, 24, of Kirkintilloch, Strathclyde	17 Mar. 1973
£680,697	Mrs. Nell Fletcher, 32, of Furnace, Strathclyde	16 Feb. 1974

In order to earn £629,801 net of tax, a single man would have to have a 1973/74 salary of £2,499,819 but to earn £680,697 post tax in 1974/75 he would have to be paid £3,969,430.

The odds for selecting 8 draws (if there are 8 draws) from 54 matches for an all-correct line are 1,040,465,789 to 1 against.

Slot machines The world's biggest slot machine (or one armed bandit) is Super Bertha installed by Si Redd of Reno, Nevada, U.S.A. in Sept. 1973. Once in every 25,000 million plays it may yield $1 million for a $10 feed. The total gambling 'take' in 1973 in Nevada casinos was estimated at $804,200,000 (*£335 million*). The biggest beating handed to a "one-armed bandit" has been $65,093 (*£28,300*) to Frank W. Wahl, 66, at Harold's Club, Reno on 4 Sept. 1973. He estimated his losses since 1961 had been $60,000.

HORSE RACING

Highest ever odds The highest recorded odds ever secured were 665,000 to 1 by a backer from Preston, Lancashire on a 6 horse accumulator on 23 Mar. 1974. He was paid out £13,311 for a stake of 2p by Joe Coral at Moor Lane, Preston, Lancashire. The world record odds on a 'double' are 24,741 to 1 secured by Mr. Montague Harry Parker of Windsor, England, for a £1 each-way 'double' on *Ivernia* and *Golden Sparkle* with William Hill.

Biggest tote win The best recorded tote win was one of £341 2s 6d. to 2s. (£341.12½ to 10p) by Mrs. Catharine Unsworth of Blundellsands, Liverpool at Haydock Park on a race won by *Coole* on 30 Nov. 1929. The highest odds in Irish tote history were £184 7s. 6d. on a 2s. 6d. (£184.37½ on a 12½p) stake, *viz.* 1,475 to 1 on *Hillhead VI* at Baldoyle on 31 Jan. 1970.

Most complicated bet The most complicated bet is the Harlequin, a compound wager on 4 horses with 2,028 possible ways of winning. It was invented by Monty H. Preston of London who has been reputed to be the fastest settler of bets in the world. He once completed 3,000 bets in a 4½-hour test.

Largest bookmaker The world's largest bookmaker is Ladbroke's of London with a turnover which from mid 1972 to mid 1973 was estimated at £160 million. The largest chain of Betting Shops is Ladbroke's with 1,130 shops plus 12 credit offices in the United Kingdom.

Topmost tipster The only recorded instance of a racing correspondent forecasting 10 out of 10 winners on a race card was at Delaware Park, Wilmington, Delaware, U.S.A. on 28 July 1974 by Charles Lamb of the *Baltimore News American*.

Greatest pay-out The greatest published pay out on a single bet is £69,375 by Ladbroke's to the late Bernard Sunley on the Derby victory of *Santa Claus* in 1964. In 1944 it was said that a backer won £200,000 in an ante post bet on *Garden Path*, which won the 2,000 Guineas. The largest bet placed has been £5,000 at 200–1 by Frank Egerton with Henry Hallam of Nottingham in April 1975 that his political Centre party will win the next General Election.

ROULETTE

The longest run on an ungaffed (*i.e.* true) wheel reliably recorded is 6 successive coups (in No. 10) at El San Juan Hotel, Puerto Rico on 9 July 1959. The odds with a double zero were 1 in 38^6 or 3,010,936,383 to 1.

Longest Marathon The longest 'marathon' on record is one of 31 days from 10 April to 11 May 1970 at The Casino de Macao, to test the validity or invalidity of certain contentions in 20,000 spins.

ELECTIONS

Ladbroke's biggest turnover is on General Elections. The highest ever individual bet was £50,000 on Labour to win the 1964 Election by Sir Maxwell Joseph. He made £37,272 on the odds offered.

GLIDING

Emanuel Swedenborg (1688–1772) of Sweden made sketches of gliders *c.* 1714. (see under I.Q. levels, page 18).

The earliest man-carrying glider was designed by Sir George Cayley (1773–1857) and carried his coachman (possibly John Appleby) about 500 yd *460 m* across a valley near Brompton Hall, North Yorkshire in the summer of 1853. Gliders now attain speeds of 145 m.p.h. *233 km/h* and the Jastrzab aerobatic sailplane is designed to withstand vertical dives at up to 280 m.p.h. *450 km/h.*

Highest standard A Gold C with three diamonds (for goal flight, distance and height) is the highest standard in gliding. This has been gained by 46 British pilots up to June 1975.

Most Titles *World* World individual championships (inst. 1948) have been 5 times won by West Germans. The only two British wins have been by Philip A. Wills (1952) and H. C. N. Goodhart and F. Foster (2 seater, 1956).

British The British national championship (instituted 1939) has been won most often by Philip A. Wills (b. 26 May 1907), in 1948–49–50 and 1955. The first woman to win this title was Mrs. Anne Burns of Farnham, Surrey on 30 May 1966.

PARASAILING

The longest reported flight is 15 hr 3 min 50 sec by Bill Flewellyn (New Zealand) over Lake Bonney, Barmera, South Australia on 10 Jan. 1972.

HANG GLIDING

Duration *World* The longest reported flight is one of 10 hr 18 min by John Hughes and David Lane (U.S.A.) at Makapun, Oahu, Hawaii on 14 July 1974.

British The longest reported British flight is one of 8 hr 26 min by Brian Wood at Rhossili, Gower Peninsula on 19 Oct. 1974.

Descent The greatest vertical descent by a manned hang-glider is 4 007 m *13,146 ft* by Rudy Kishazy. He took off from Mont Blanc, France, glided 24 km *15 miles,* and landed at Servoz 35 min later.

The greatest altitude from which a hang-glider has descended is 17,100 ft *5 212 m* by Dennis Kulberg, 22, (U.S.A.) who was released from a balloon over Mt. Hamilton, San José, California, and landed 35 min. later 13½ miles *21,72 km* away on 22 Dec. 1974.

Sport & General

Mrs. Anne Burns, who in 1966 became first woman to win the British national gliding championship

Fox Photos

Rear-Admiral H. C. N. Goodhart, holder for over 16 years of the British Declared Goal flight record at 360 miles *579 km*

SELECTED WORLD RECORDS (Single-seaters)

Distance	907.7 miles *1 460,8 km*	Hans-Werner Grosse (W. Germany) in an ASW-12 on 25 Apr. 1972 from Lübeck to Biarritz
Declared Goal Flight	765.4 miles *1 231,8 km*	Hans-Werner Grosse (W. Germany) in an ASW-17 on 16 April 1974 from Lübeck to Marmande
Absolute Altitude	46,266 ft *14 102 m*	Paul F. Bikle, Jr. (U.S.A.) in a Schweizer SGS 1-23E over Mojave, California (released at 3,963 ft [*1 207 m*]) on 25 Feb. 1961 (also record altitude gain—42,303 ft [*12 894 m*])
Goal and Return	782 miles *1 260,44 km*	W. C. Holbrook (U.S.A.) in a Libelle 301 on 5 May 1973
Speed over Triangular Course 100 km	102.73 m.p.h. *165,34 km/h*	K. Briegleb (U.S.A.) in a Kestrel 17 over U.S.A. on 18 July 1974
300 km	95.95 m.p.h. *153,43 km/h*	Walter Neubert (W. Germany) in a Kestrel 604 over Kenya on 3 Mar. 1972
500 km[2]	87.19 m.p.h. *140,33 km/h*	Malcolm Jinks (Australia) in a Nimbus 2 over Australia on 31 Jan. 1975
750 km[2]	76.27 m.p.h. *122,75 km/h*	G. Eckle (W. Germany) in a Nimbus 2 over South Africa on 1 Jan. 1975

BRITISH NATIONAL RECORDS[1] (Single-seaters)

460.5 miles *741 km*	P. D. Lane in a Skylark 3F, Geilenkirchen to Hiersac, Germany on 1 June 1962
360 miles *579 km*	Rear Ad. H. C. N. Goodhart in a Skylark 3, Lasham, Hants to Portmoak, Scotland on 10 May 1959
42,814 ft *13 050 m*	Michael J. Field in a Skylark IV over Oxford—Swindon on 9 May 1972
437.1 miles *703,5 km*	Christopher Falkingbridge in a Standard Cirrus over S. Africa on 14 Dec. 1974
78.5 m.p.h. *126,4 km/h*	Edward P. Hodge in a Diamant 16.5 over Rhodesia on 1 Nov. 1970
81.33 m.p.h. *130,9 km/h*	Edward Pearson in a Standard Cirrus over South Africa on 1 Jan. 1972
75 m.p.h. *121 km/h*	J. Delafield in a Kestrel 19 over South Africa on 21 Dec. 1972

[1] British National Records may be set up by British pilots in any part of the world.
[2] Angela Smith (G.B.) holds the woman's world record for this event with 67.66 m.p.h. *108,9 km/h* in a Libelle 301 over South Africa on 28 Dec. 1972.

GOLF

Origins The earliest mention of golf occurs in a prohibiting law passed by the Scottish Parliament in March 1457 under which "golfe be utterly cryed downe". The Romans had a cognate game called *paganica* which may have been carried to Britain before A.D. 400. In February 1962 the Soviet newspaper *Izvestiya* claimed that the game was of 15th century Danish origin while the Chinese Nationalist Golf Association claim the game is of Chinese origin ("the ball hitting game") in the 3rd or 2nd century B.C. Gutta percha balls succeeded feather balls in 1848 and were in turn succeeded in 1902 by rubber-cored balls, invented in 1899 by Haskell (U.S.A). Steel shafts were authorized in 1929.

CLUBS

The oldest club of which there is written evidence is the Gentlemen Golfers (now the Honourable Company of Edinburgh Golfers) formed in March 1744—10 years prior to the institution of the Royal and Ancient Club at St. Andrews, Fife. The oldest existing club in North America is the Royal Montreal Club (1873).

Largest The only club in the world with 15 courses is the Eldorado Golf Club, California, U.S.A. The club with the highest membership in the British Isles is Wentworth Club, Virginia Water, Surrey, with 1,850 members. The Royal and Ancient Golf Club at St. Andrews, Fife, Scotland has 1,750 members and the largest in Ireland is Royal Portrush, Co. Antrim with 1,215 members.

COURSES

Highest The highest golf course in the world is the Tuctu Golf Club in Morococha, Peru, which is 4 369 m *14,335 ft* above sea-level at its lowest point. Golf has, however, been played in Tibet at an altitude of over 4 875 m *16,000 ft.*

The highest golf course in Great Britain is one of 9 holes at Leadhills, Strathclyde, 1,500 ft *457 m* above sea-level.

Lowest The lowest golf course in the world was that of the Sodom and Gomorrah Golfing Society at Kallia, on the north-eastern shores of the Dead Sea, 380 m *1,250 ft* below sea-level. The clubhouse was burnt down in 1948 but the game is now played on Kallia Hotel course.

Longest The longest hole in the world is the 17th hole (par 6) of 681 m *745 yd* at the Black Mountain Golf Club, North Carolina, U.S.A. It was opened in 1964. In August 1927 the 6th hole at Prescott Country Club in Arkansas, U.S.A., measured 766 m *838 yd.* The longest hole on a championship course in Great Britain is the sixth at Troon, Strathclyde, which stretches 580 yds *530 m.*

Largest green Probably the largest green in the world is the 5th green at Runaway Brook G.C., Bolton, Massachusetts, U.S.A. with an area greater than 2 600 m² *28,000 ft².*

Biggest bunker The world's biggest bunker (called a trap in the U.S.A.) is Hell's Half Acre on the seventh hole of the Pine Valley course, New Jersey, U.S.A., built in 1912 and generally regarded as the world's most trying course.

Longest "Course" Floyd Satterlee Rood used the United States as a course, when he played from the Pacific surf to the Atlantic surf from 14 Sept. 1963 to 3 Oct. 1964 in 114,737 strokes. He lost 3,511 balls on the 3,397.7 mile *5 468 km* trail.

Mansell Collection

An artist's impression of Mary, Queen of Scots, in 1563 playing golf on the links at St. Andrews, Fife

LOWEST SCORES

9 holes and 18 holes Men The lowest recorded score on any 18-hole course with a par score of 70 or more is 55 (15 under bogey) first achieved by A. E. Smith, the Woolacombe professional, on his home course on 1 Jan. 1936. The course measured 4,248 yd *3 884 m.* The detail was 4, 2, 3, 4, 2, 4, 3, 4, 3 = 29 out, and 2, 3, 3, 3, 3, 2, 5, 4, 1 = 26 in. Homero Blancas (b. 7 Mar. 1938, of Houston, Texas) also scored 55 (27 + 28) on a course of 4 592 m *5,002 yd* (par 70) in a tournament at the Premier Golf Course, Longview, Texas, U.S.A., on 19 Aug. 1962. The lowest recorded score on a long course (over 6,000 yd [*5 486 m*]) in Britain is 58 by Harry Weetman (1920–72) the British Ryder Cup golfer, for the 6,171 yd *5 642 m* Croham Hurst Course, Croydon, on 30 Jan. 1956.

Nine holes in 25 (4, 3, 3, 2, 3, 3, 1, 4, 2) was recorded by A. J. "Bill" Burke in a round in 57 (32 + 25) on the 5 842 m *6,389 yd* par 71 Normandie course St. Louis, Missouri, U.S.A. on 20 May 1970.

The United States P.G.A. tournament record for 18 holes is 60 by Al Brosch (30 + 30) in the Texas Open on 10 Feb. 1951; William Nary in the El Paso Open, Texas on 9 Feb. 1952; Ted Kroll (b. August 1919) in the Texas Open on 20 Feb. 1954; Wally Ulrich in the Virginia Beach Open on 11 June 1954; Tommy Bolt (b. 31 March 1918) in the Insurance City Open on 25 June 1954; Mike Souchak (b. May 1927) in the Texas Open on 17 Feb. 1955 and Samuel Jackson Snead (b. 27 May 1912) in the Dallas Open, Texas on 14 Sept. 1957. Two golfers have recorded 59 over 18 holes in non-P.G.A. tournaments; Sam Snead in the 3rd Round of the Sam Snead Festival at White Sulphur Springs, West Virginia, U.S.A. on 16 May 1959 and Gary Player (South Africa) (b. 1 Nov. 1936) in the 2nd round of the Brazilian Open in Rio de Janeiro on 29 Nov. 1974.

Women The lowest recorded score on an 18-hole course (over 6,000 yd *5 486 m*) for a woman is 62 (30 + 32) by Mary (Mickey) Kathryn Wright (b. 14 Feb. 1935) of Dallas, Texas, on the Hogan Park Course (5 747 m [*6,282 yds*]) at Midland, Texas, U.S.A., in November 1964. Miss Wanda Morgan recorded a score of 60 (31 + 29) on the Westgate-on-Sea and Birchington Golf Club over 18 holes (5,002 yd *4 573 m*) on 11 July 1929.

United Kingdom The British Tournament 9-hole record is 28 by John Panton (b. 1917) in the Swallow-Penfold Tournament at Harrogate, North Yorkshire, in 1952; by

Bernard John Hunt (b. 2 Feb. 1930) of Hartsbourne in the Spalding Tournament at Worthing, West Sussex, in August 1953; and by Lionel Platts (b. 10 Oct. 1934, Yorkshire), of Wanstead in the Ulster Open at Shandon Park, Belfast, on 11 Sept. 1965. The lowest score recorded in a first class professional tournament on a course of more than 6,000 yd *5 486 m* in Great Britain was set at 61 (29 + 32), by Thomas Bruce Haliburton (b. Scotland, 5 June 1915) of Wentworth G.C. in the Spalding Tournament at Worthing, West Sussex, in June 1952. Peter J. Butler (b. 25 Mar. 1932) equalled the 18-hole record with 61 (32 + 29) in the Bowmaker Tournament on the Old Course at Sunningdale, Berkshire, on 4 July 1967.

36 holes The record for 36 holes is 122 (59 + 63) by Snead in the 1959 Sam Snead Festival on 16–17 May 1959. Horton Smith (see below) scored 63 + 58 = 121 on a short course on 21 Dec. 1928. The lowest score by a British golfer has been 61 + 65 = 126 by Tom Haliburton (b. 5 June 1915).

72 holes The lowest recorded score on a first-class course is 257 (27 under par) by Mike Souchak (b. 10 May 1927) in the Texas Open at San Antonio in February 1955, made up of 60 (33 + 27), 68, 64, 65 (average 64.25 per round) exhibiting, as one critic said: "up and down" form.

Horton Smith (1908–1963), a U.S. Masters Champion, scored 245 (63, 58, 61 and 63) for 72 holes on the 4,700 yd *4 297 m* course (par 64) at Catalina Country Club, California, U.S.A., to win the Catalina Open on 21–23 Dec. 1928.

The lowest 72 holes in a national championship is 262 (67, 66, 66, 63) by Percy Alliss (G.B.) (1897–1975) in the 1932 Italian Open at San Remo, and by Liang Huan Lu (Taiwan) (b. 1936) in the 1971 French Open at Biarritz. The lowest for four rounds in a British first class tournament is 262 (66, 63, 66 and 67) by Bernard Hunt in the Piccadilly Stroke Play tournament on Wentworth East Course, Virginia Water, Surrey on 4–5 Oct. 1966. Kelvin D. G. Nagle (b. 21 Dec. 1920) of Australia shot 260 (64, 65, 66 and 65) in the Irish Hospitals Golf Tournament at Woodbrook Golf Club, near Bray, Ireland, on 21–23 July 1961.

Eclectic record The lowest recorded eclectic (from the Greek *eklektikos* = choosing) score, i.e. the sum of a player's all-time personal low scores for each hole, for a course of more than 6,000 yd *5 486 m* is 33 by the club professional Jack McKinnon on the 6,538 yd *1 992 m* Capilano Golf and Country Club course, Vancouver, British Columbia, Canada. This was compiled over the period 1937–1964 and reads 2-2-2-1-2-2-2-2-1 (= 16 out) and 2-1-2-2-1-2-2-2-3 (= 17 in) = 33. The British record is 39 by John W. Ellmore at Elsham Golf Club, Humberside (6,070 yd *5 550 m*). This is made up of 2, 3, 2, 2, 2, 2, 2, 3, 2 = 20 (out) and 3, 1, 2, 1, 2, 2, 3, 3, 2 = 19 (in).

Highest scores The highest score for a single hole in the British Open is 21 by a player in the inaugural meeting at Prestwick in 1860. Double figures have been recorded on the card of the winner only once, when Willie Fernie (1851–1924) scored a 10 at Musselburgh, Lothian, in 1883. Ray Ainsley of Ojai, California, took 19 strokes for the par-4 16th hole during the second round of the U.S. Open at Cherry Hills Country Club, Denver, Colorado, on 10 June 1938. Most of the strokes were used in trying to extricate the ball from a brook. Hans Merell of Mogadore, Ohio, took 19 strokes on the par-3 16th (222 yd [*202 m*]) during the third round of the Bing Crosby National Tournament at Cypress Point Club, Del Monte, California, U.S.A., on 17 Jan. 1959. It is recorded that Chevalier von Cittern went round 18 holes in 316, averaging 17.55 per hole, at Biarritz, France in 1888.

Gerry Cranham

Mr. Lu, of Taiwan, who is co-holder of the record for the lowest ever score (262) for any National title—the French Open Championship of 1971

Most shots for one hole A woman player in the qualifying round of the Shawnee Invitational for Ladies at Shawnee-on-Delaware, Pennsylvania, U.S.A., in *c.* 1912, took 166 strokes for the short 130 yd *118 m* 16th hole. Her tee shot went into the Binniekill River and the ball floated. She put out in a boat with her exemplary, but statistically minded husband at the oars. She eventually beached the ball 1½ miles *2,4 km* downstream but was not yet out of the wood. She had to play through one on the home run.

Fastest and slowest rounds With such variations in lengths of courses, speed records, even for rounds under par, are of little comparative value. Bob Williams at Eugene, Oregon, U.S.A., completed 18 holes (6,010 yd *5 495 m*)) in 27 min 48.2 sec in 1971 but this test permitted the striking of the ball whilst still moving. The record for a still ball is 31 min 22 sec by Len Richardson, the South African Olympic athlete at Mowbray, Cape Town (6,248 yd [*5 713 m*]) in Nov. 1931.

Fastest round Seventy-eight members of the Manukan Ladies Golf Club, Manurewa, Auckland, New Zealand completed the 18 hole 5,803 yd *5 358 m* course there in 10 min 32.5 sec on 6 March 1975.

Slowest round The slowest stroke play tournament round was one of 6 hours 45 min when South Africa won their first round of the 1972 World Cup at the Royal Melbourne G.C., Australia. This was a 4-ball medal round, everything holed out.

Seven Countries in one day The only golfers to have played 9 hole rounds in seven "countries" in a day are Dr. Gerry W. Donaldson of Newry and Edward S. "Skip" Wilson on 3 July 1974. They played on courses in Jersey, Channel Islands, Wales, England, Scotland, Isle of Man, Ireland and Northern Ireland.

Most rounds in a day The greatest number of rounds played in 24 hours is 22 rounds 5 holes (401 holes) on foot by Ian Colston, 35, at Bendigo G.C. Victoria (6,061 yd [*5 542 m*]) on 27–28 Nov. 1971. He covered more than 100 miles *160 km* in 23¾ hr play. Raymond A. Lasater, 44, played 1,530 holes (85 rounds) in 62 hr 20 min on the 6,155 yd *5 628 m* par-72 Hunter Point, Lebanon, Tennessee course on 19–21 June 1973. He used a golf cart and luminous balls.

Youngest and oldest champions The youngest winner of the British Open was Tom Morris, Jr. (born St. Andrew's 1850, died 25 Dec. 1875) at Prestwick, Ayrshire, in 1868 aged 18. The youngest winner of the British Amateur title was

John Charles Beharrel (born 2 May 1938) at Troon, Strathclyde, on 2 June 1956, aged 18 years 1 month. The oldest winner of the British Amateur was the Hon. Michael Scott at Hoylake, Merseyside in 1933, when 54. The oldest British Open Champion was "Old Tom" Morris (b. St Andrew's 16 June 1821), who was aged 46 when he won at Prestwick in 1867. In recent times the 1967 champion, Roberto de Vicenzo (b. Buenos Aires, Argentina, 14 April 1923) was aged 44 years 93 days. The oldest United States Amateur Champion was Jack Westland (b. 1905) at Seattle, Washington, in 1952 aged 47.

Longest drives In long-driving contests 330 yd *300 m* is rarely surpassed at sea level. The United States P.G.A. record is 341 yd *311 m* by Jack William Nicklaus (b. Columbus, Ohio, 21 Jan. 1940) in July 1963. Bill Calise, 32 won the McGregor contest at Wayne Country Club, New Jersey on 20 June 1954 with 365 yd *333 m*. The Irish Professional Golfers Association record is however 392 yd *358 m* by their amateur member William Thomas (Tommie) Campbell (Foxrock Golf Club) made at Dun Laoghaire, Co. Dublin, in July 1964. Under freak conditions of wind, slope, parched or frozen surfaces, or ricochet from a stone or flint, even greater distances are achieved. The greatest recorded drive is one of 445 yd *406 m* by Edward C. Bliss (1863–1917), a 12 handicap player, at the 9th hole of the Old Course, Herne Bay, Kent, in August 1913. Bliss, 6 ft *1,82 m* tall and over 13 st. *82 kg 500*, drove to the back of the green on the left-handed dog-leg. The drive was measured by a government surveyor, Capt. L. H. Lloyd, who also measured the drop from the tee to resting place as 57 ft *17 m*.

Other freak drives include the driving of the 483 yd *441 m* 13th at Westward Ho! by F. Lemarchand, backed by a gale; and to the edge of the 465 yd *425 m* downhill 9th on the East Devon Course, Budleigh Salterton, by T. H. V. Haydon in September 1934. Neither drive was accurately measured.

Perhaps the longest recorded drive on level ground was one of an estimated 430 yd *383 m* by Craig Ralph Wood (1901–1968) of the U.S.A. on the 530 yd *484 m* fifth hole at the Old Course, St. Andrews, Fife, in the Open Championship in June 1933. The ground was parched and there was a strong following wind.

Tony Jacklin, O.B.E. (b. Scunthorpe, Lincs., 7 July 1944) hit a ball from the roof of the Savoy Hotel (125 ft [*38 m*] above the pavement) 353 yd *322 m* to splash into the River Thames on 26 Nov. 1969. A drive of 2,640 yd *2 414 m* (1½ miles) across ice was achieved by an Australian meteorologist named Nils Lied at Mawson Base, Antarctica, in 1962. Arthur Lynskey claimed a drive of 200 yd *182 m* horizontal and 2 miles *3 200 m* vertical off Pikes Peak, Colorado (14,110 ft [*4 300 m*]) on 28 June 1968. On the Moon the energy expended on a mundane 300 yd *274 m* drive would achieve, craters permitting, a distance of a mile *1,6 km*.

Longest hitter The golfer regarded as the longest consistent hitter the game has ever known is the 6 ft 5 in *195 cm* tall, 17 st 2 lb *108 kg 86* George Bayer (U.S.A.), the 1957 Canadian Open Champion. His longest measured drive was one of 420 yd *384 m* at the fourth in the Las Vegas Invitational, Nevada, in 1953. It was measured as a precaution against litigation since the ball struck a spectator. Bayer also drove a ball pin high on a 426 yd *389 m* hole at Tucson, Arizona in 1955. Radar measurements show that an 87 m.p.h. *140 km/h* impact velocity for a golf ball falls to 46 m.p.h. *74 km/h* in 3.0 seconds.

Longest Putt The longest recorded holed putt in a major tournament was one of 86 ft *26 m* on the vast 13th green at the

Augusta National, Georgia by Cary Middlecoff (b. Jan. 1921) in the 1955 Master's Tournament.

The Open The Open Championship was inaugurated in 1860 at Prestwick, Strathclyde, Scotland. The lowest score for 9 holes is 29 by Tom Haliburton (Wentworth) and Peter W. Thomson, M.B.E. (Australia) (b. 23 Aug. 1929) in the first round of the Open on the Royal Lytham and St. Anne's course at Lytham St. Anne's, Lancashire on 10 July 1963 and by Tony Jacklin, O.B.E. in the first round of the Open at St. Andrews, Fife, on 8 July 1970.

The lowest rounds in The Open itself have been 65 by (Thomas) Henry Cotton, M.B.E. (b. Holmes Chapel, Cheshire, 26 Jan. 1907) at Royal St. George's, Sandwich, Kent in the 2nd round on 27 June 1934 to complete a 36-hole record of 132 (67 + 65); by Eric Chalmers Brown (b. 15 Feb. 1925) at Royal Lytham and St. Anne's, Lancashire in the third round on 3 July 1958; by Christy O'Connor (b. County Donegal, Ireland, 1925) (Royal Dublin) at Lytham in the 2nd round on 10 July 1969; by Neil C. Coles (b. 26 Sept. 1934) (Coombe Hill) on the Old Course, St. Andrews in the 1st round on 8 July 1970; by Nicklaus at Troon in the 4th round on 14 July 1973 and by Jack Newton (b. Sydney, Australia, 1950) at Carnoustie, Tayside in the 3rd round on 11 July 1975. The lowest 72-hole aggregate is 276 (71, 69, 67, 69) by Arnold Daniel Palmer (b. 10 Sept. 1929) of Latrobe, Pennsylvania, U.S.A., at Troon, Strathclyde, ending on 13 July 1962 and Tom Weiskopf (b. 9 Nov. 1942) of the United States also at Troon on 11–14 July 1973 (68, 67, 71, 70).

Gerry Cranham

Tom Weiskopf (U.S.A.) co-holder of the record low aggregate (276) for the Open, which he achieved in 1973

MOST TITLES

The most titles won in the world's major championships are as follows:

The Open	Harry Vardon (1870–1937)	6	1896–98–99, 1903–11–14
British Amateur	John Ball (1861–1940)	8	1888–90–92–94–99, 1907–10–12
U.S. Open	Willie Anderson (1880–1910)	4	1901–03–04–05
	Robert Tyre Jones, Jr. (1902–71)	4	1923–26–29–30
	Ben William Hogan (b. 13 Aug. 1912)	4	1948–50–51–53
U.S. Amateur	R. T. Jones, Jr. (1902–71)	5	1924–25–27–28–30
P.G.A. Championship (U.S.A.)	Walter Charles Hagen (1892–1969)	5	1921–24–25–26–27
Masters Championship (U.S.A.)	Jack William Nicklaus (b. 21 Jan. 1940)	5	1963–65–66–72–75
U.S. Women's Open	Miss Elizabeth (Betsy) Earle-Rawls (b. May 1928)	4	1951–53–57–60
	Miss "Mickey" Wright (b. 14 Feb. 1935)	4	1958–59–61–64
U.S. Women's Amateur	Mrs. Glenna C. Vare (née Collett) (b. 20 June 1903)	6	1922–25–28–29–30–35
British Women's	Miss Charlotte Cecilia Pitcairn Leitch (b. 13 Apr. 1891)	4	1914–20–21–26
	Miss Joyce Wethered (b. 17 Nov. 1901) (now Lady Heathcoat-Amory)	4	1922–24–25–29

Note: Nicklaus is the only golfer to have won 5 different major titles (the Open, U.S. Open, Masters, P.G.A. and U.S. Amateur titles) twice and a record 15 all told (1962–75).

Lee Trevino (U.S.A.), co-holder of the record low aggregate (69, 68, 69, 69 = 275) for the U.S. Open achieved in 1968

Gerry Cranham

British Amateur The lowest score for nine holes in the British Amateur Championship (inaugurated in 1885) is 29 by Richard Davol Chapman (born 23 March 1911) of the U.S.A. at Sandwich in 1948.

Michael Francis Bonallack, O.B.E. (b. 31 Dec. 1924) shot a 61 (32 + 29) on the par-71 6,905 yd *6 313 m* course at Ganton, North Yorkshire, on 27 July 1968 in the first 18 of the 36 holes in the final round of the English Amateur championship.

U.S. Open The United States Open Championship was inaugurated in 1894. The lowest 72-hole aggregate is 275 (71, 67, 72 and 65) by Jack Nicklaus on the Lower Course (6 414 m [*7,015 yd*]) at Baltusrol Country Club, Springfield, New Jersey, on 15–18 June 1967 and 275 (69, 68, 69 and 69) by Lee Trevino (born near Horizon City, Texas, 1 Dec. 1939) at Oak Hill Country Club, Rochester, N.Y., on 13–16 June 1968. The lowest score for 18 holes is 63 by John Miller (b. 29 Apr. 1947) on the 6,921 yd *6 328 m* par-71 Oakmont Country Club course, Pennsylvania on 17 June 1973.

U.S. Masters The lowest score in the U.S. Masters (instituted on the par-72 6 382 m *6,980 yd* Augusta National Golf Course, Georgia, in 1934) has been 271 by Jack Nicklaus in 1965. The lowest rounds have been 64 by Lloyd Mangrum (1914–1974) (1st round, 1940), Jack Nicklaus (3rd round, 1965), and Maurice Bembridge (G.B.) (b. 21 Feb. 1945) (4th round, 1974).

Richest prizes The greatest first place prize money was $100,000 (total purse $500,000 [£233,664]) in the World Open played at Pinehurst, North Carolina, U.S.A., over 144 holes on 8–17 Nov. 1973 won by Miller Barber, 42, of Texas, U.S.A., and in Britain £25,000 ($60,000) in the John Player Golf Classic at Hollinwell, Nottinghamshire, England on 3–6 Sept. 1970.

Highest earnings The all time professional money-winner is Jack Nicklaus who, up to Dec. 1974, has won $2,250,245 (£978,350). The record for a year is $353,000 (£153,475) by Johny Miller in 1974. The record career earnings for a woman is $554,781 (£241,200) by Kathy Whitworth (U.S.A.) (b. 27 Sept. 1938) up to June 1975. The British record for a year is £32,127 by Peter Oosterhuis in 1974.

Most tournament wins The record for winning tournaments in a single season is 19 (out of 31) by Byron Nelson (b. 4 Feb. 1912) of Fort Worth, Texas, in 1945. Of these 11 were consecutive, including the P.G.A., Canadian P.G.A. and Canadian Open, from 16 March to 15 August. He was a money prize winner in 113 consecutive tournaments. Miss Whitworth (see above) won 73 professional tournaments to June 1975.

Most club championships Ian Laughlin has won the Kerang Golf Club Championship, Victoria, Australia 24 times between 1947 and 1975. The British record for amateur club championships is 20 consecutive wins (1937–39 and 1946–62) by R. W. H. Taylor (d. 1974) at the Dyke Golf Club, Brighton, East Sussex, who retired unbeaten in July

281

1963, and by Edward Christopher Chapman (b. 9 April 1909), who won the Tunbridge Wells G.C. Scratch Championship 20 consecutive years from 1951 to 1971.

HOLES IN ONE

Longest The longest straight hole ever holed in one shot is the 10th (406 m [*444 yd*]) at Miracle Hills Golf Club, Omaha, Nebraska, U.S.A. Robert Mitera achieved a hole-in-one there on 7 Oct. 1965. Mitera, aged 21, stands 167 cm *5 ft 6 in* tall and weighs 165 lb. *74 kg 842* (11 st. 11 lb.). He is a two handicap player who can normally drive 245 yd *224 m*. A 50 m.p.h. *80 km/h* gust carried his shot over a 290 yd *265 m* drop-off. The longest "dog-leg" hole achieved in one is the 480 yd *438,9 m* 5th at Hope Country Club, Arkansas by L. Bruce on 15 Nov. 1962. The feminine record is 382 m *417 yd* by Mrs. A. Scott on the 18th hole of the Wittem course near Meerssen, the Netherlands on 7 May 1974. In 1974 *Golf Digest* magazine was notified of 24,699 "aces" indicating odds of 42,952 to 1 on any ace at a specific hole.

The longest hole in one performed in the British Isles is the 7th (393 yd [*359,3 m*]) at West Lancashire G.C. by Peter Parkinson in 1972.

Most The greatest number of holes-in-one in a career is 40 by Art Wall, Jr. (b. 23 Nov. 1923) between 1936 and 1973. The British record is 31 by Charles T. Chevalier (1902–1973) of Heaton Moor Golf Club, Stockport, Greater Manchester between 20 June 1918 and 1970. Douglas Porteous, 28, holed-in-one four times over 36 consecutive holes (3rd and 6th on 26 Sept.; 5th on 28 Sept. at Ruchill Golf Club, Glasgow; 6th at the Clydebank and District Golf Course on 30 Sept. 1974). Robert Taylor (Leicestershire) holed the 188 yd *171,9 m* 16th at Hunstanton, Norfolk on three successive days—31 May, 1 and 2 June 1974—in the Eastern Inter-Counties foursomes. Joe Lucius (U.S.A.), 59, holed the 138 yd *126 m* 15th at the Mohawk Golf Club, Tiffin, Ohio, in one for the eighth time on 16 Nov. 1974.

Consecutive Holes in One There is no recorded instance of a golfer performing three consecutive holes-in-one but there are at least 15 cases of "aces" being achieved in two consecutive holes of which the greatest was Norman L. Manley's unique "double albatross" on the par-4 301 m *330 yd* 7th and par-4 265 m *290 yd* 8th holes on the Del Valle Country Club Course, Saugus, California, on 2 Sept. 1964. Five examples by Britons have been:

Roger Game	7th & 8th	Walmer and Kingsdown	6 Feb.	1964
Charles Fairlie	15th & 16th	Gourock	June	1968
Dr. Robert Anderson	4th & 5th	Chorlton	27 Dec.	1969
John Hudson	11th & 12th	Royal Norwich	11 June	1971
Billy Taylor	1st & 2nd	Ladhope	9 Feb.	1975

Youngest and oldest The youngest golfer recorded to have shot a hole-in-one was Tommy Moore (6 years 36 days) of Hagerstown, Maryland on the 132 m *145 yd* 4th at the Woodbrier Golf Course, Martinsville, West Virginia, on 8 March 1968. The oldest golfers to have performed the feat are George Miller, 93 at the 11th at Anaheim G.C., California on 4 Dec. 1970 and Charles Youngman, 93 at the Tam O'Shanter Club, Toronto in 1971.

Shooting your age The record for scoring one's age in years over an 18-hole round is held by Weller Noble who between 1955 (scoring 64 aged 64) and 13 Dec. 1971 has amassed 644 "age scores" on the Claremont Country Club, Oakland, California par-68 course of 5 244 m *5,375 yds*. The course is provenly harder than many of 5 500 m *6,000 yds* or more on which to produce low scores.

The oldest player to score under his age is C. Arthur Thompson (1869–1975) of Victoria, British Columbia, Canada, who scored 103 on the Uplands course of 5 682 m *6,215 yd* aged 103 in 1973. He was reported to be still in action about twice a week until a few weeks

Robert Taylor, who holed the 16th at Hunstanton, Norfolk, England on three successive days

before his death. The youngest player to score his age is the professional Bob Hamilton (b. 10 Jan. 1916) who shot a 59 when aged 59 on his own 6,223 yd *5 690 m* course at Evansville, Kentucky, on 3 June 1975.

Record Tie The longest delayed result in any National Open Championship occurred in the 1931 U.S. Open at Toledo, Ohio. George von Elm and Billy Burke tied at 292, then tied the first replay at 149. Burke won the second replay by a single stroke after 72 extra holes.

Largest Tournament The annual *Daily Mirror* North of England Amateur (Match Play) Tournament in 1974 attracted a record 5,407 amateur competitors.

World Cup (formerly Canada Cup) The World Cup (instituted as the Canada Cup in 1953) has been won most often by the U.S.A., with twelve victories in 1955–1956–1960–1961–1962–1963–1964–1966–1967–1969–1971–1973. The only men to have been on six winning teams have been Arnold Palmer (1960, 62–64, 66–67) and Jack Nicklaus (1963–4, 66–67, 71 and 73). Only Nicklaus has taken the individual title 3 times (1963–64–71). The lowest aggregate score for 144 holes is 545 by Australia (Bruce Devlin [b. 10 Oct. 1937] and David Graham) at San Isidro, Buenos Aires, Argentina on 12–15 Nov. 1970. The lowest individual score has been 269 by Roberto de Vicenzo then 47 (Argentina) also in 1970.

Ryder Trophy The biennial Ryder Cup professional match between U.S.A. and the British Isles or Great Britain was instituted in 1927. The U.S.A. have won 14½ to 4½ to date. William Earl (Billy) Casper (b. San Diego, California, U.S.A., 24 June 1931) has the record of winning most singles with 11 wins in 1961–69. Christie O'Connor (G.B.) played in 10 matches up to 1973.

Walker Cup The U.S.A. *v.* G.B. series instituted in 1921 (for the Walker Cup since 1922 and now biennially) has been won by the U.S.A. 23½–2½ to date. Joseph Boynton Carr (G.B. & I) (b. Feb. 1922) has played in 10 contests (1947–67).

Throwing the golf ball The lowest recorded score for throwing a golf ball round 18 holes (over 5 500 m or *6,000 yds*) is 82 by Joe Flynn, 21, at the 6,228 yd *5 694 m* Port Royal Course, Bermuda, on 27 March 1975.

GREYHOUND RACING

Earliest meeting In Sept. 1876 a greyhound meeting was staged at Hendon, North London with a railed hare operated by a windlass. Modern greyhound racing originated with the perfecting of the mechanical hare by Owen P. Smith at Emeryville, California, U.S.A., in 1919. The earliest greyhound race behind a mechanical hare in the British Isles was at Belle Vue, Manchester, opened on 24 July 1926.

Derby The only two dogs to have won the English Greyhound Derby twice (held since 1928 over 525 yd *[480 m]* at the White City Stadium, London) are *Mick the Miller* (whelped in Ireland, June 1926 and died 1939) on 25 July 1929, when owned by Albert H. Williams, and on 28 June 1930 (owned by Mrs. Arundel H. Kempton) and *Patricias Hope* on 24 June 1972 (when owned by Gordon and Basil Marks and Brian Stanley) and 23 June 1973 (when owned by G. & B. Marks and J. O'Connor). The highest prize was £15,000 to *Tartan Khan* for the Derby on 28 June 1975. The only dogs to win the English, Scottish and Welsh Derby "triple" are *Trev's Perfection*, owned by Fred Trevillion in 1947, *Mile Bush Pride*, owned by Noel W. Purvis, in 1959, and *Patricias Hope* (see above) in 1972.

Grand National The only dog to have thrice won the Greyhound Grand National (instituted 1927) over 525 yd *480 m* and 4 flights is *Sherry's Prince*, a 75 lb. *32 kg* dog whelped in April 1967, owned by Mrs. Joyce Mathews of Sanderstead, Surrey. He won in 1970, 1971 (record 29.22 sec) and 1972 when he won by 6¼ lengths.

Fastest 525 yds timings The fastest *photo*-timing is 28.17 sec or 38.12 m.p.h. *61,34 km/h* by *Easy Investment* on 30 June 1973. The fastest *photo*-timing over 525 yds *480 m* hurdles is 29.10 sec (36.90 m.p.h. *[59,38 km/h]*) by *Sherry's Prince* on 8 May 1971.

Sporting Pictures

Westpark Mustard, holder of the record winning streak—20 consecutive wins during 1974

Winning streak *Westpark Mustard*, an Irish bitch, owned by Mr. & Mrs. Cyril Scotland, won a record 20 consecutive races in Britain between 7 Jan. and 28 Oct. 1974.

Fastest dog The highest speed at which any greyhound has been timed is 41.72 m.p.h. *67,14 km/h* (410 yd *[374 m]* in 20.1 sec) by *The Shoe* on the then straightaway track at Richmond, N.S.W., Australia on 25 Apr. 1968. It is estimated that he covered the last 100 yds *91,44 m* in 4.5 sec or at 45.45 m.p.h. *73,14 km/h*. The highest speed recorded for a greyhound in Great Britain is 39.13 m.p.h. *62,97 km/h* by *Beef Cutlet*, when covering a straight course of 500 yds *457 m* in 26.13 sec at Blackpool, Lancashire, on 13 May 1933.

GYMNASTICS

Earliest references Gymnastics were widely practised in Greece during the period of the ancient Olympic Games (776 B.C. to A.D. 393) but they were not revived until *c.* 1780.

World Championships The greatest number of individual titles won by a man in the World Championships is 10 by Boris Shakhlin (U.S.S.R.) between 1954 and 1964. He also won 3 team titles. The female record is 10 individual wins and 5 team titles by Larissa Semyonovna Latynina (born 1935, retired 1966) of the U.S.S.R., between 1956 and 1964.

Olympic Games Italy (1912, 20, 24 and 32) and Japan (1960, 64, 68 and 72) have won the men's team title most often. U.S.S.R. have won the women's title six times: 1952, 56, 60, 64, 68 and 72.

The only man to win six individual gold medals is Boris Shakhlin (U.S.S.R.), with one in 1956, four (two shared) in 1960 and one in 1964. He was also a member of the winning Combined Exercises team in 1956.

Vera Caslavska-Odlozil (Czechoslovakia), has won most individual Gold Medals with 7, three in 1964 and four (one shared) in 1968. Latynina won six individual Gold Medals and was in three winning teams in 1956–64 making 9 gold medals. She also won 5 silver and 4 bronze medals making 18 in all—an Olympic record for either sex in any sport.

British Championship The most times that the British Gymnastic Championship has been won is 10 by Arthur Whitford in 1928–36 and 1939. He was also in four winning Championship teams. The women's record is 8 wins by Miss Margaret Hirst (1947, 1949–50 and 1952–56). Miss Margaret Bell won the title five times in succession, 1965–69.

Rope climbing The United States Amateur Athletic Union records are tantamount to world records: 6 m *20 ft* hands alone—2.8 sec, Don Perry (U.S.A.) at Champaign, Illinois, U.S.A., on 3 April 1954; 7,6 m *25 ft* (hands alone). 4.7 sec, Garvin S. Smith at Los Angeles, California, U.S.A., on 19 April 1947.

Chinning the bar The greatest number of chin-ups (from a dead hang position) recorded is 106 by William D. Reed at the Weightman Hall, University of Pennsylvania, U.S.A. on 23 June 1969. The feminine record for one-handed chin-ups is 27 in Hermann's Gym, Philadelphia, Pennsylvania, U.S.A. in 1918 by Lillian Leitzel (Mrs. Alfredo Codona) (U.S.A), who was killed in Copenhagen, Denmark on 15 March 1931. Her total would be unmatched by any male but it is doubtful if they were achieved from a 'dead hang' position. It is believed that only one person in 100,000 can chin a bar one-handed. Francis Lewis (b. 1896) of Beatrice, Nebraska, U.S.A. in May 1914 achieved 7 consecutive chins using only the middle finger of his left hand. His bodyweight was 158 lb. *71 kg 667.*

Press-ups The greatest recorded number of consecutive press-ups is 6,006 in 3 hr 54 min by Chick Linster, aged 16, of Wilmette, Illinois, U.S.A. on 5 Oct. 1965. Father Leo Cook did 1,246 press-ups in 37 min in Everton Park, Brisbane, Queensland, Australia on 2 May 1975. Henry Marshall, 28, of San Antonio, Texas did 124 press-ups on his right arm in 61 sec. and 103 on his left in 65 sec on 12 Sept. 1974. James R. Ullrich (U.S.A.) did 140 finger tip press-ups in 80 sec on 11 March 1974.

Sit-ups The greatest recorded number of consecutive sit-ups on a hard surface without feet pinned down or knees bent is 25,222 in 11 hr 14 min by Richard John Knecht, aged 8, at the Idaho Fall High School Gymnasium, Idaho, on 23 Dec. 1972.

Jumping Jacks The greatest recorded numbers of side-straddle hops is 15,025 performed in 3 hr 32 min (better than 1 per sec) by Steven Welsher of Long Beach, California, U.S.A. on 27 July 1974.

Vertical Jumps The greatest height reached for a vertical jump (formerly known as Sargent [*sic*] Jumps) *i.e.* the differential between the height of the finger-tip reach static and in jumping is 42 in *100,6 cm* by David "Dr. D" Thompson (6ft 4in *1,93 m*) North Carolina, U.S.A. in 1972. Mary E. Peters (GB) is reported to have done 30 in *76,2 cm* in California in 1972.

Tumbling The only tumbler to have achieved a running triple back somersault on the ground is V. Bindler (U.S.S.R.), 16, from Minsk in Kiev in early March 1974. James Chelich (b. 12 Mar. 1957, Fairview, Alberta, Canada)

Ludmilla Tourischeva, member of the U.S.S.R. team which commanded a British record attendance of nearly 14,000 spectators at Earl's Court, London in 1973

Gerry Cranham

performed 8,450 forward rolls over 8.3 miles *13,35 km* on 21 Sept. 1974.

Hand-to-hand balancing The longest horizontal dive achieved in any hand-to-hand balancing act is 22 ft *6,7 m* by Harry Berry (top mounter) and the late Nelson Soule (understander) of the Bell-Thazer Brothers from Kentucky, U.S.A., who played at State fairs and vaudevilles from 1912 to 1918. Berry used a 10 ft *3 m* tower and trampoline for impetus.

Largest gymnasium The world's largest gymnasium is Yale University's Payne Whitney Gymnasium at New Haven, Connecticut, U.S.A., completed in 1932 and valued at $18,000,000 (*£7,500,000*). The building, known as the 'Cathedral of Muscle' has nine storeys with wings of five storeys each. It is equipped with four basketball courts, three rowing tanks, 28 squash courts, 12 handball courts, a roof jogging track and a 25 yds *22,8 m* by 42 ft *12,8 m* swimming pool on the first floor and a 55 yd *50,2 m* long pool on the third floor.

Largest crowd The largest recorded crowd was 13,922 at Earl's Court, Hammersmith, Greater London on 8–10 May 1973 who came to see the U.S.S.R. women's team which included Ludmilla Tourischeva and Olga Korbut, the Olympic Gold medallist.

HANDBALL (COURT)

Origins Handball played against walls or in a court is a game of ancient Celtic origin. In the early 19th century only a front wall was used but gradually side and back walls were added. The earliest international contest was in New York City, U.S.A., in 1887 between the champions of the U.S.A. and Ireland. The court is now a standardized 60 ft *18 m* by 30 ft *9 m* in Ireland, Ghana and Australia, and 40 ft *12 m* by 20 ft *6 m* in Canada, Mexico and the U.S.A. The game is played with both a hard and soft ball in Ireland and soft ball only in Australia, Canada, Ghana, Mexico and the U.S.A.

Championships World championships were inaugurated in New York in October 1964 with competitors from Australia, Canada, Ireland, Mexico and the U.S.A. The U.S.A. won in 1964; Canada and U.S.A. shared the title in 1967 and Ireland won in 1970.

Most titles In Ireland the most titles (instituted 1925) have been won as follows:

Hardball

Singles	John J. Gilmartin (Kilkenny)	
	10	1936–42, 1945–47
Doubles	John Ryan and John Doyle (Wexford)	
	6	1952, 1954–58

Softball

Singles	Paddy Perry (Roscommon)	
	8	1930–37
Doubles	James O'Brien and Patrick Downey (Kerry)	
	7	1955–56, 1960–64

The U.S. Championship 4 wall singles has been won 6 times by Jimmy Jacobs in 1955–56–57–60–64–65.

HANDBALL (FIELD)

Origins Handball, similar to association football, with hands substituted for feet, was first played *c.* 1895. It was introduced into the Olympic Games at Berlin in 1936 as an 11-a-side outdoor game with Germany winning, but in 1972 it was an indoor game with 7-a-side, the standard size of team since 1952.

By 1974 there were 54 countries affiliated to the International Handball Federation, a World Cup competition and an estimated 3 million participants. The earliest international match was when Sweden beat Denmark on 8 March 1935.

HOCKEY

Origins A representation of two hoop players with curved snagging sticks apparently in an orthodox "bully" position was found in Tomb No. 17 at Beni Hasan, Egypt and has been dated to *c.* 2050 B.C. There is a British reference to the game in Lincolnshire in 1277. The first country to form a national association was England with the first Hockey Association founded at Canon Street Hotel, City of London on 16 April 1875.

The oldest club with a continuous history is Teddington H.C. formed in the autumn of 1871. They played Richmond on 24 Oct. 1874 and used the first recorded circle *versus* Surbiton at Bushey Park on 9 Dec. 1876.

MEN

Earliest international The first international match was the Wales *v.* Ireland match at Rhyl on 26 Jan. 1895. Ireland won 3–0.

Highest international score The highest score in international hockey was when India defeated the United States 24–1 at Los Angeles, California, U.S.A., in the 1932 Olympic Games. The Indians were Olympic Champions from the re-inception of Olympic hockey in 1928 until 1960, when Pakistan beat them 1–0 at Rome. They had their seventh win in 1964. Of the six Indians who have won 3 Olympic team gold medals two have also won a silver medal—Leslie Walter Claudius (b. 25 Mar. 1927) in 1948, 1952, 1956 and 1960 (silver) and Udham Singh (b. 4 Aug. 1928) in 1952, 1956, 1964 and 1960 (silver). The greatest number of goals in a home international match was when England defeated France 16–0 at Beckenham on 25 March 1922. The World Cup was won by Pakistan at Barcelona in 1971, the Netherlands at Amsterdam in 1973 and India at Kuala Lumpur in 1975.

Most appearances The most by a home countries player is 106 by Harold A. Cahill (b. 9 June 1930) with 71 for Ireland and 35 for Great Britain won from 1953 to 1973.

England 66, Paul J. T. Svehlik (b. 15 April 1947) (1969–75)

Wales 73, D. Austen Savage (b. 1941) (1968–75)

Scotland 63, Frederick H. Scott (b. 29 Nov. 1932) (1955–70) and Dennis Hay (1964–74)

Ireland 100, H. David Judge (b. 19 Jan. 1936) (1957–75)

Great Britain 56, John W. Neill (England) (1959–68)

Greatest scoring feat M. C. Marckx (Bowdon 2nd XI) scored 19 goals against Brooklands 2nd XI (score 23–0) on 31 Dec. 1910. He was selected for England in March 1912 but declined due to business priorities.

Five brothers In the England *v.* Ireland match of 1904, the Irish team included five brothers, Jack, Cecil, Willie, Walter and Nick Peterson of the Palmerston Club. A sixth brother, Bertie, had played for Ireland *v.* Wales in 1900 and 1902.

Longest game The longest international game on record was one of 145 min (into the sixth period of extra time), when Netherlands beat Spain 1–0 in the Olympic tournament

Morley Pecher

Goalkeeper Austen Savage holder of the Welsh international caps record with 73 appearances since 1968

at Mexico City on 25 Oct. 1968. The longest club match on record was one of 175 min between Perth H.C. and Aberdeen G.S.F.P. at the North Inch, Perth in the Scottish Cup quarter-final on 24 Feb. 1973.

WOMEN

Origins The earliest women's club was East Molesey in Surrey, England formed in *c.* 1887. The first national association was the Irish Ladies' Hockey Union founded in 1894. The All England Womens' Hockey Association held its first formal meeting in Westminster Town Hall, London, on 23 Nov. 1895. The first international match was an England *v.* Ireland game in Dublin in 1896. Ireland won 2–0. In the 1971 World Tournament of 15 nations at Auckland, N.Z. the Netherlands were the only unbeaten team.

Highest international score The highest score in a women's international match occurred when England defeated France 23–0 at Merton, Greater London, on 3 Feb. 1923.

Most appearances The England records are 73 caps by Miss Hazell Feltwell (1965–73) and 17 seasons by Miss Mabel Bryant (1907–1929), who won 39 caps. The Irish record is 58 (46 full caps and 12 touring) by Mrs. Sean Kyle (born Maeve Esther Enid Shankey, 6 Oct. 1928) between November 1947 and 1966.

Highest attendance The highest attendance at a women's hockey match was 65,000 for the match between England and Wales at the Empire Stadium, Wembley, Brent, Greater London, on 8 March 1969.

HORSE RACING

Origins Horsemanship was an important part of the Hittite culture of Anatolia, Turkey dating from 1400 B.C. The 23rd ancient Olympic Games of 624 B.C. in Greece featured horse racing. The earliest horse race recorded in England was one held in about A.D. 210 at Netherby, North Yorkshire, among Arabians brought to Britain by Lucius Septimius Severus (A.D. 146–211), Emperor of Rome. The oldest race still being run annually is the Lanark Silver Bell, instituted in Scotland by William Lion (1165–1214).

The Jockey Club was formed in 1750–51 and the General Stud Book started in 1791. Racing colours (silks) became compulsory in 1889.

RACECOURSES

Largest The world's largest racecourse is the Newmarket course (founded 1636) on which the Beacon Course, the longest of the 19 courses, is 4 miles 397 yds *6,80 km* long and the Rowley Mile is 167 ft *50 m* wide. The border between Suffolk and Cambridgeshire runs through the Newmarket course. The world's largest grandstand is that opened in 1968 at Belmont Park, Elmont, Long Island, N.Y., U.S.A. at a cost of $30,700,000 (*£12.8 million*). It is 110 ft *33 m* tall, 440 yd *402 m* long and contains 908 mutuel windows. The highest seating capacity at any racetrack is 40,000 at Atlantic City Audit, New Jersey, U.S.A.

Smallest The world's smallest racecourse is the Lebong racecourse, Darjeeling, West Bengal, India (altitude 7,000 ft [*2 125 m*]), where the complete lap is 481 yd *439 m*. It was laid out *c.* 1885 and used as a parade ground.

HORSES

Greatest record The horse with the best recorded win-loss record was *Kincsem*, a Hungarian mare foaled in 1874, who was unbeaten in 54 races (1877–1880), including the Goodwood Cup of 1878. *Camarero* owned by Don José Coll Vidal of Puerto Rico, foaled in 1951, had a winning streak of 56 races from 19 April 1953 to 17 Aug. 1955. He died 'from a colic' on 26 Aug. 1956 the day after his 73rd win in 77 starts.

Tallest The tallest horse ever to race is *Fort d'Or*, owned by Lady Elizabeth (Eliza) Nugent (*née* Guinness) of Berkshire, England. He stands 18.2 hands *187 cm* and was foaled in County Wexford, Ireland in April 1963 out of *Golden Sunset*, who stood only 15.1 hands.

Highest price The highest price ever paid for a horse is $6,080,000 (*£2,533,000*) paid by Mrs. Helen "Penny" Tweedy (4 shares) and 28 other members of a $190,000 per unit syndicate in February 1973 for the 16.0½ hand chestnut *Secretariat*, foaled on 30 Mar. 1970. This price was equivalent to $345 (*£142*) per oz. or $12,166 *per kg* which is 8 times the official price of 22 carat gold. *Secretariat* duly became the U.S.'s ninth Triple Crown winner in taking the Belmont Stakes by an unprecedented 31 lengths in a world record dirt track time of 2 min 24.0 sec. He went to stud on 15 Nov. 1973.

Greatest winning The greatest amount ever won by a horse is $1,977,896 (*then £706,391*) by *Kelso* (foaled in 1957) in the U.S.A., between 1959 and his retirement on 10 March 1966. He is now the supreme status symbol of the hunt under Mrs. Richard C. du Pont. In 63 races he won 39, came second in 12 and third in 2. The most won by a filly is $1,316,135 (*£572,232*) by *Allez France* up to June 1975. In 16 starts she has won 12. The most won in a year is $860,404 (*£374,088*) by *Secretariat* in 1973. His total reached $1,176,781.

Largest prizes The richest race ever held is the All-American Futurity, a race for quarter-horses over 440 yds *402 m*

286

at Ruidoso Downs, New Mexico, U.S.A. The prizes in 1974 totalled $1,030,000 (*£447,826*). The richest first prize was 1,497,400 francs (*£166,370*) won by *Rheingold* in the 1973 *L'Arc de Triomphe* at Langchamps, Paris on 7 Oct.

JOCKEYS

The most successful jockey of all time has been Willie Shoemaker (b. weighing 2½ lb. [*1 kg 133*] on 19 Aug. 1931) now weighing 98 lb. *44 kg*, beating Johnny Longden's life-time record of 6,032 winners at Del Mar, California, U.S.A. on 7 Sept. 1970. Shoemaker, stands 4 ft 11½ in *151 cm* and rode his 6,624 winners from 19 Mar. 1949 to 31 Mar. 1974. His winnings have aggregated some $50 million. The highest number of wins on the North American turf in one year is 546 by Chris McCarron (U.S.A.), 19, in 1974.

The greatest amount ever won by any jockey in a year is $4,231,441 (*£1,839,750*) by Laffit Pincay Jr., in 1974. The oldest jockey was Levi Barlingame (U.S.A.), who rode his last race at Stafford, Kansas, in 1932 aged 80. The youngest jockey was Frank Wootton (English Champion jockey 1909–12), who rode his first winner in South Africa aged 9 years 10 months. The lightest recorded jockey was Kitchener (died 1872), who won the Chester Cup on *Red Deer* in 1844 at 3 st. 7 lb. *22 kg 226*. He was said to have weighed only 2 st. 12 lb. *18 kg 143* in 1840.

The greatest number of winners ridden on one card is 8 by Hubert S. Jones at Caliente, California, U.S.A. on 11 June 1944 of which 5 were photo-finishes. The longest winning streak is 12 by Sir Gordon Richards with 12 (last race at Nottingham on 3 Oct, 6 out of 6 at Chepstow on 4 Oct. and the first 5 races next day at Chepstow) in 1933. The greatest recorded age for a first win has been 67 years in the case of Mr. Victor Morley Lawson on *Ocean King* at Warwick on 16 Oct. 1973.

Trainers The greatest number of wins by a trainer in one year is 133 by Frank "Pancho" Martin (U.S.) in 1974.

Dead heats There is no recorded case in turf history of a quintuple dead heat. The nearest approach was in the Astley Stakes, at Lewes, England, in August 1880 when *Mazurka*, *Wandering Nun* and *Scobell* triple dead-heated for first place, just ahead of *Cumberland* and *Thora*, who dead-heated for fourth place. Each of the five jockeys thought he had won. The only two known examples of a quadruple dead heat were between *The Defaulter*, *Squire of Malton*, *Reindeer* and *Pulcherrima* in the Omnibus Stakes at The Hoo, Kent, England, on 26 April 1851, and between *Overeach*, *Lady Go-Lightly*, *Gamester* and *The Unexpected* at the Houghton Meeting at Newmarket on 22 Oct. 1855. The earliest recorded photo-finish dead heat in Britain was between *Phantom Bridge* and *Resistance* in the 5-furlong *1 005 m* Beechfield Handicap at Doncaster on 22 Oct. 1947.

Longest race The longest recorded horse race was one of 1,200 miles *1 925 km* in Portugal, won by a horse *Emir* bred from Egyptian-bred Blunt Arab stock. The holder of the world's record for long distance racing and speed is *Champion Crabbet*, who covered 300 miles *482 km* in 52 hr 33 min carrying 17½ st. *111 kg 130*, in 1920. In 1831 Squire George Osbaldeston (1787–1866), M.P. of East Retford covered 200 miles *321 km* in 8 hr 42 min at Newmarket, using 50 mounts, so averaging 22.99 m.p.h. *36,99 km/h*.

Shortest price The shortest odds ever quoted for any racehorse are 10,000 to 1 on for *Dragon Blood*, ridden by Lester Piggott (G.B.) in the Premio Naviglio in Milan, Italy on 1 June 1967. Odds of 100 to 1 on were quoted for the United States horse *Man o' War* (foaled 29 March 1917, died 1 Nov. 1947) on three separate occasions in 1920, and for the two British horses, *Ormonde*

Winner of the highest ever prize on the British Turf—*Grundy*, the 1975 Derby winner

Gerry Cranham

(Champion Stakes, 14 Oct. 1886 [three runners]), and *Sceptre* (Limekiln Stakes 27 Oct. 1903 [two runners]).

BRITISH TURF RECORDS

Most expensive horses The highest price ever put on a British-trained horse is "over £1,000,000" by a syndicate headed by Wing Cdr. Tim Vigors announced on 25 Oct. 1973 for *Rheingold* to stand at the Coolmore Stud, County Tipperary, Ireland.

Most successful horses Only fillies are eligible to win all five classics. *Sceptre* came closest in 1902 when she won the 1,000 Guineas, 2,000 Guineas, Oaks and St. Leger. In 1868 *Formosa* won the same four but dead-heated in the 2,000 Guineas. The most races won in a season is 23 by *Fisherman* in 1856. *Catherina* won 79 out of 174 races between 1833 and 1841. The only horse to win the same race in seven successive years was *Dr. Syntax*, who won the Preston Gold Cup (1815–21). The most successful sire was *Stockwell*, whose progeny won 1,153 races (1858–76) and in 1866 set a record of 132 races won. The first English-trained horse to win more than £300,000 in prize money was the U.S.-owned *Mill Reef* who won £300,191 in 1970 71–72 of which £135,937 was in France. The first English-trained horse to win over £300,000 on British racecourses was *Grundy* who during 1974 and 1975 won £312,122.

Most successful owners The greatest amount of stake money won is £1,025,592 from 784 races by H.H. Aga Khan III (1877–1957) from 1922 until his death. These included 35 classics, of which 17 were English classics. The record for a season was set by Charles W. Engelhard Jr (1916–1971) (U.S.A.), who surpassed the previous record of £120,924 by winning £182,059 in 1970. The most wins in a season is 115 by Mr. David Robinson in 1973. The most English classics won is 20 by the 4th Duke of Grafton, K.G. (1760–1844), from 1813 to 1831.

Most successful trainers Captain Sir Cecil Charles Boyd-Rochfort, K.C.V.O. (b. 16 April 1887) earned £1,651,514 (1,169 winners) between 1923 and 1968. The record for a season is £256,899 by Charles Francis Noel Murless (born Malpas, Cheshire, 24 Mar. 1910) in 1967. Noel Murless has also earned more than £2,500,000 in winning money and £3,000,000 counting place money for his patrons. The most classics won by a trainer is 40 or 41 by John Scott (1794–1871) including 16 St. Leger winners between 1827 and 1862. Alec Taylor of Manton, Wiltshire headed the trainers' lists for a record 12 seasons between 1907 and 1925. In 1867 John Barham Day won 146 races.

Most successful jockeys Sir Gordon Richards (b. Oakengates, Salop, 5 May 1904) retired in 1954, having won 4,870 races from 21,834 mounts since his first win at Leicester on 31 March 1921. In 1953, after 27 attempts, he won the Derby, six days after being knighted. In 1947 he won a record 269 races. The most classic races won by a jockey is 27 by Francis "Frank" Buckle (1766–1832), between 1792 and 1827.

Most runners The most horses in a race is 66 (a world record) in the Grand National of 22 March 1929. The record for the flat is 58 in the Lincolnshire Handicap on 13 March 1948. The most runners at a meeting were 214 (flat) in seven races at Newmarket on 15 June 1915 and 229 (National Hunt) in eight races at Worcester on 13 Jan. 1965.

THE DERBY

The greatest of England's five classic races, the Epsom Derby, was inaugurated on 4 May 1780 by the 12th Earl of Derby (1752–1834). It has been run over 1 mile 885 yds *2,418 km* since 1784 (1½ miles [*2,414 km*] since World War I) on Epsom Downs, Surrey, except for the two war periods, when it was run at Newmarket. Since 1884 the race has been for three-year-old colts carrying 9 st. *57 kg* and fillies carrying 8 st. 9 lb. *54 kg 884*.

Highest prize The highest Derby prize and the richest prize on British Turf was £106,465 50p for *Grundy* in the Derby on 4 June 1975.

287

Red Rum (right) on his way to shattering the Grand National record time in 1974

Ed Lacey

Most winning owners The only owner with five outright winners was the 3rd Earl of Egremont (1751–1837) with *Assassin* (1782), *Hannibal* (1804), *Cardinal Beaufort* (1805), *Election* (1807) and *Lapdog* (1826). H.H. Aga Khan III (1877–1957) had four winners in *Blenheim* (1930), *Bahram* (1935), *Mahmoud* (1936) and *Tulyar* (1952) and a half-share in *My Love* (1948).

Trainer The only two trainers with seven winners were John Porter with *Blue Gown* (1868), *Shotover* (1882), *St. Blaise* (1883), *Ormonde* (1886), *Sainfoin* (1890), *Common* (1891) and *Flying Fox* (1899), and Robert Robson with *Waxy* (1793), *Tyrant* (1802), *Pope* (1809), *Whalebone* (1810), *Whisker* (1815), *Azor* (1817), and *Emilius* (1823). Fred Darling had seven winners, including two in the war-time meetings at Newmarket (1940–41)—*Captain Cuttle* (1922), *Manna* (1925), *Coronach* (1926), *Cameronian* (1931), *Bois Roussel* (1938), *Pont l'Evique* (1940), and *Owen Tudor* (1941).

Jockey The most successful jockeys have been Jem Robinson (1794–1853) who won six times in 1817 1824–25, 1827–28 and 1836 and Lester Piggott, O.B.E., (1954–57–60–68–70–72). Steve Donoghue (1884–1945) rode six winners (1915–25) but the first two were war-time races not on the Epsom Course.

Record time The record time for the Derby is 2 min 33.8 sec (average speed 35.06 m.p.h. [*56,42 km/h*]) by *Mahmoud* ridden by Charles James William Smirke (b. 1906), owned by H.H. Aga Khan III, trained by Frank Butters (1878–1957), winning at 100 to 8 by three lengths from a field of 22 in 1936. The fastest time recorded over the Derby course is, however, the hand-timed 2 min 33.0 sec by the four-year-old *Apelle* in winning the 1928 Coronation Cup. The fastest mechanically timed run was 2 min 33.31 sec by *Bustino* in the Coronation Cup on 7 June 1975.

Dead heats The two instances of dead heats were in 1828, when *Cadland* beat *The Colonel* in the run off, and in 1884 between *Harvester* and *St. Gatien* (stakes divided).

Disqualifications The two disqualifications were of *Running Rein* (race awarded to *Orlando*) in 1844 and of *Craganour* (race awarded to *Aboyeur*) in the 'Suffragette Derby' on 4 June 1913, when Miss Emily Wilding Davison fatally injured herself by impeding King George V's horse *Anmer*.

Other records The only greys to have won were *Gustavus* (1821), *Tagalie* (1912), *Mahmoud* (1936) and *Airborne* (1946). Only two black horses have ever won—*Smolensko* (1813) and *Grand Parade* (1919). The longest odds quoted on a placed Derby horse were 200–1 against

for *Black Tommy*, second to *Blink Bonny* in 1857. The shortest priced winner was *Ladas* (1894) at 9–2 on and the highest priced winners were *Jeddah* (1898), *Signorinetta* (1908) and *Aboyeur* (1913), all at 100 to 1 against. The smallest field was four in 1794 and the largest 34 in 1862. The smallest winner was *Little Wonder* (14 hands 3½ in [*151,12 cm*]) in 1840.

Starter of most classics The only man to start more than 100 classics has been Alec Marsh, Senior Jockey Club starter who retired after his 101st classic start in 1972. His first was the 2,000 Guineas in 1952.

GRAND NATIONAL

Most wins Horse The first official Grand National Steeplechase may be regarded as the Grand Liverpool Steeplechase of 26 Feb. 1839 though the race was not so named until some years later. The first winner of the Grand Liverpool Steeplechase was Mr. Potts' *The Duke* in 1837. The race is for six-year-olds and over (since 1930) and is run over a course of 4 miles 856 yds *7,220 km*, with 30 jumps, at Aintree, near Liverpool. No horse has won three times but seven share the record of two wins:

Peter Simple	1849 and 1853	Manifesto	1897 and 1899
Abd-el-Kader	1850 and 1851	Reynoldstown	1935 and 1936
The Lamb	1868 and 1871	Red Rum	1973 and 1974
The Colonel	1869 and 1870		

Manifesto was entered eight times (1895–1904) and won twice, came third three times and fourth once. *Poethlyn* won in 1919 having won the war-time Gatwick race in 1918.

Jockey The only jockey to ride five winners was George Stevens on *Free Trader* (1856), *Emblem* (1863), *Emblematic* (1864) and *The Colonel* (1869–70).

Owner The only owners with three winners, since the race became a handicap in 1843, are Captain Machell with *Disturbance* (1873), *Reughy* (1874) and *Regal* (1876); and Sir Charles Assheton-Smith with *Cloister* (1893), *Jerry M.* (1912) and *Covertcoat* (1913).

Trainer The only trainer with four winners was the Hon. Aubrey Hastings with *Ascetic's Silver* (1906), *Ally Sloper* (1915), *Ballymacad* (1917, Gatwick) and *Master Robert* (1924).

Highest prize The highest prize was £38,005 won by *L'Escargot* on 5 April 1975.

Fastest time The record time is 9 min 1.9 sec set by *Red Rum* ridden by Brian Fletcher (b. 1947) owned by Noel Le Mare, 84 and trained by Donald McCain, 42 of Southport on 31 Mar. 1973. He won by ¾ length from

SPEED RECORDS

Distance	Time min sec	m.p.h.	km/h	Name	Course	Date
⅓ mile	20.8	43.26	69,62	*Big Racket* (U.S.A.)	Lomas de Sotelo, Mexico	5 Feb. 1945
⅓ mile	44.8	40.17	64,66	*Tamran's Jet* (U.S.A.)	Sunland, New Mexico, U.S.A.	22 Mar. 1968
⅝ mile	53.6	41.98	67,56	*Indigenous* (G.B.)	Epsom, Surrey	2 June 1960
¾ mile	1:07.4	40.06	64,47	*Zip Pocket* (U.S.A.)	Phoenix, Arizona, U.S.A.	6 Dec. 1966
	1:07.4	40.06	64,47	*Vale of Tears* (U.S.A.)	Ab Sar Ben, Omaha, Neb., U.S.A.	7 June 1969
	1:06.2	40.78	65,62	*Broken Tindril* (G.B.)	*Brighton, East Sussex	6 Aug. 1929
Mile	1:31.8	39.21	63,10	*Soueida* (G.B.)	*Brighton, East Sussex	19 Sept. 1963
	1:31.8	39.21	63,10	*Loose Cover* (G.B.)	*Brighton, East Sussex	9 June 1966
	1:32.2	39.04	62,82	*Dr. Fager* (U.S.A.)	Arlington, Ill., U.S.A.	24 Aug. 1968
1¼ miles	2:23.0	37.76	60,76	*Fiddle Isle* (U.S.A.)	Arcadia, Cal., U.S.A.	21 Mar. 1970
2 miles**	3:15.0	36.93	59,43	*Polazel* (G.B.)	Salisbury, Wiltshire	8 July 1924
3 miles	5:15.0	34.29	55,18	*Farragut* (Mexico)	Agua Caliente	9 Mar. 1941

* *Course downhill for two thirds of a mile.*
** *A more reliable modern record is 3 min 16.75 sec by Il Tempo (N.Z.) at Trentham, Wellington, New Zealand on 17 Jan. 1970.*

the joint favourite *Crisp*, which was earlier 20 lengths clear.

Highest jump The 15th jump, known as the 'Chair', is 5 ft 2 in *1,57 m* high and 3 ft 9 in *1,14 m* thick. The ditch on the take-off side is 6 ft *1,82 m* wide and the guard rail in front of the ditch is 1 ft 6 in *45 cm* in height.

STEEPLECHASING
Golden Miller won the Cheltenham Gold Cup on 14 March 1935 in very heavy conditions carrying 12 st. *76 kg* over 3 miles 3 furlongs *5,43 km* in 6 min 30 sec so averaging an unsurpassed 31.15 m.p.h. *50,13 km/h.*

Jockey The first National Hunt jockey to reach 1,000 wins is Stan Mellor, M.B.E. (b. Manchester, 10 Apr. 1937). This he achieved on *Ouzo* at Nottingham on 18 Dec. 1971 and retired on 18 June 1972 after 1,049 wins (incl. 14 abroad) in 20 years. He also won 3 flat races. Capt. Kenyon Goode owned, trained and rode 3 successive winners under National Hunt rules at Torquay, Devon on 7 Apr. 1931.

The record number of wins in a season is 125 by Ron Barry in 1972/73. The record number of National Hunt championships is 7 by Gerald Wilson (1903–68) from 1933–38 and 1941.

Ron Barry, who set a record for any National Hunt Season with 125 wins in 1972–73

Gerry Cranham

HURLING

Earliest reference A game of very ancient origin, hurling only became standardized with the formation of the Gaelic Athletic Association in Thurles, Ireland, on 1 Nov. 1884.

Most titles The greatest number of All-Ireland Championships won by one team is 22 by Tipperary in 1887, 1895–96, 1898–99–1900, 1906, 1908, 1916, 1925, 1930, 1937, 1945, 1949–50–51, 1958, 1961–62, 1964–65 and 1971. The greatest number of successive wins is the four by Cork (1941–44).

Highest score The highest score in an All-Ireland final was in 1896 when Tipperary (8 goals, 14 points) beat Dublin (no goals, 4 points). The record aggregate score was when Cork (6 goals, 21 points) defeated Wexford (5 goals, 10 points) in 1970. A goal equals 3 points.

Lowest score The lowest score in an All-Ireland final was when Tipperary (1 goal, 1 point) beat Galway (nil) in the first championship at Birr in 1887.

Most The most appearances in All-Ireland finals is ten shared by Christy Ring (Cork) and John Doyle (Tipperary). They also share the record of All-Ireland medals won with 8 each. Ring's appearances on the winning side were in 1941–42–43–44, 1946 and 1952–53–54, while Doyle's were in 1949–50–51, 1958, 1961–62 and 1964–65.

Individual score The highest recorded individual score was by Nick Rackard (Wexford), who scored 7 goals and 7 points against Antrim in the 1954 All-Ireland semi-finals.

John Doyle (Tipperary), co-holder of the record for All-Ireland hurling medals with 8

Hopkins Photo Agency

289

Largest crowd The largest crowd was 84,856 for the final between Cork and Wexford at Croke Park, Dublin, in 1954.

Inter-provincials Munster holds the greatest number of inter-provincial (Railway Cup) championships with 32 (1928–1970).

Christy Ring (Cork and Munster) played in a record 22 finals (1942–63) and was on the winning side 18 times.

Longest stroke The greatest distance for a "lift and stroke" is one of 129 yd *117 m* credited to Tom Murphy of Three Castles, Kilkenny, in a "long puck" contest in 1906. The record for the annual *An Poc Fada* (Long Puck) contest (instituted 1961) in the ravines of the Cooley Hills, north of Dundalk, County Louth, is 65 pucks (drives) plus 87 yd *79 m* over the course of 3 miles 320 yd *5,120 km* by Fionnbar O'Neill (Cork) in 1966. This represents an average of 84.8 yd *77,5 m* per drive.

ICE HOCKEY

Origins There is pictorial evidence that hockey was played on ice in the 17th century in The Netherlands. The game was probably first played in North America in 1860 at Kingston, Ontario, Canada, but Montreal and Halifax also lay claim to priority.

Olympic Games Canada has won the Olympic Championship six times (1920–24–28–32–48–52) and the world title 19 times, the last being at Geneva in 1961. The longest Olympic career is that of Richard Torriani (Switzerland) from 1928 to 1948. The most gold medals won by any player is three achieved by Vitaliy Davidov, Anatoliy Firssov, Viktor Kuzkin and Aleksandr Ragulin of the U.S.S.R. teams that won the Olympic titles in 1964–68 and 1972. Davidov and Ragulin had played in 9 World championship teams prior to the 1972 Games.

Stanley Cup The Stanley Cup, presented by the Governor-General Lord Stanley (original cost $48.67), became emblematic of world professional team supremacy several years after the first contest at Montreal in 1893. It has been won most often by the Montreal Canadiens [*sic*], with 18 wins in 1916, 1924, 1930, 1931, 1944, 1946, 1953, 1956, 1957, 1958, 1959, 1960, 1965, 1966, 1968, 1969, 1971 and 1973. Henri Richard (b. 1936) played in his eleventh finals in 1973.

Longest match The longest match was 2 hrs 56 min 30 sec when Detroit Red Wings eventually beat Montreal Maroons 1–0 in the sixth period of overtime at the Forum, Montreal, at 2.25 a.m. on 25 March 1936.

Most goals The greatest number of goals recorded in a world championship match has been 47–0 when Canada beat Denmark in 1947. The N.H.L. record is 21 goals when Montreal Canadiens beat Toronto St. Patrick's at Montreal, 14–7 on 10 Jan 1920.

Most National Hockey League goals in a season: 76 goals by Philip Anthony Esposito (b. 20 Feb. 1942) of the Boston Bruins in 1970–71. The most points in a season is 152 (76 goals and 76 assists) by Phil Esposito (Boston Bruins) also in 1970–71. The North American career record for goals is 786 by Gordie Howe (b. 31 Mar. 1928) (Detroit Red Wings) in 25 seasons ending in 1970–71. He has also collected 500 stitches in his face and on 27 Mar. 1975 became the first major league player to aggregate 2,000 pts. Two players have scored 1,000 goals in Great Britain—Chick Zamick (Nottingham Panthers and Wembley Lions) and George Beach (Wembley Monarchs and later Wembley Lions).

Fastest scoring Toronto scored 8 goals against the New York Americans in 4 min 52 sec on 19 March 1938. Bill Mosienko (Chicago) scored three goals in 21 sec against New York Rangers on 23 March 1952.

Most points one game The most points scored in one game is 10 (3 goals, 7 assists) by Jim Harrison (for Alberta, later Edmonton Oilers) in a W.H.A. match at Toronto on 30 Jan. 1973.

Most Shut-outs The most matches played by a goal minder without conceding a goal is 103 by Terry Sawchuk (b. 28 Dec.

Mary Evans

The 1932 Olympic Ice Hockey final at Lake Placid in which the Canadians (white jerseys) retained their title for a third time

1929) of Detroit Red Wings, Toronto Maple Leafs and Los Angeles Kings between 1950 and 1967.

Fastest player The highest speed measured for any player is 29.7 m.p.h. *47,7 km/h* for Bobby Hull (Chicago Black Hawks) (born 3 Jan. 1939). The highest puck speed is also attributed to Hull, whose left-handed slap shot has been measured at 118.3 m.p.h. *190,3 km/h.*

BRITISH LEAGUE

The highest score in a League match has been 23–0 when Durham Wasps beat Paisley Vikings on 31 Jan. 1967. The highest aggregate score has been 29 when Ayr Bruins beat Whitley Warriors 17–12 at Ayr on 24 Jan. 1971.

Most wins The British League championship (instituted 1934 but ended in 1960) has been won most often by the Wembley Lions with four victories in 1936–37, 1952 and 1957.

Fastest scoring Kenny Westman (Nottingham Panthers) scored a hat trick in 30 sec *v.* Brighton Tigers on 3 March 1955.

ICE SKATING

Origins The earliest reference to ice skating is in early Scandanavian literature referring to the 2nd century though its origins are believed, on archeological evidence, to be 10 centuries earlier still. The earliest English account of 1180 refers to skates made of bone. The earliest known illustration is a Dutch woodcut of 1498. The earliest skating club was the Edinburgh Skating Club formed in 1742. The earliest artificial ice rink in the world was the "Glaciarium" in Chelsea, Greater London, in 1876. The International Skating Union was founded in 1892.

FIGURE SKATING

Olympic The most Olympic gold medals won by a figure skater is three by Gillis Graftström (b. 7 June 1893) of Sweden in 1920, 1924 and 1928 (also silver medal in 1932); and by Sonja Henie (see below) in 1928, 1932 and 1936.

World The greatest number of world men's figure skating titles (instituted 1896) is ten by Ulrich Salchow (b. 7 Aug. 1877) of Sweden, in 1901–05 and 1907–11. The only British figure skater to win has been Henry Graham Sharp (b. 19 Dec. 1917) in Budapest on 18–19 Feb. 1939. The women's record (instituted 1906) is ten titles by Frk. Sonja Henie (b. 8 April 1912) of Norway, between 1927 and 1936. She died on 12 Oct. 1969.

Most pair titles (inst. 1908) have been won by Irena Rodnina (b. 12 Sept. 1949) (U.S.S.R.) with four with Aleksiy Ulanov (1969–72) and three with her husband Aleksandr Zaitsev (1973–75). Most ice dance titles (inst. 1950) won is five by Lawrence Demmy and Jean Westwood (G.B.) in 1951–55 and Aleksandr Gorshkov (b. 8 Dec. 1946) and Ludmilla Pakhomova (b. 31 Dec. 1946) (U.S.S.R.) 1970–74.

British The record number of British titles is 11 by Jack Page (Manchester S.C.) in 1922–31 and 1933, and six by Miss Cecilia Colledge (b. 28 Nov. 1920) (Park Lane F.S.C., London) in 1935–36–37(2)–38 and 1946.

Most Difficult Jump The triple Axel has been performed by only Gordon McKellen (b. 26 Sept. 1953), the 1973 and 1974 U.S. champion.

Longest race The longest race regularly held is the "Elfstedentocht" ("Tour of the Eleven Towns") in the Netherlands. It covers 200 km *124 miles 483 yds* and the fastest time is 7 hrs 35 min by Jeen van den Berg (b. 8 Jan. 1928) on 3 Feb. 1954.

Associated Press

Six times Olympic champion Lidia Skoblikova winning her 1964 1,500 metre titles at Innsbruck

Skating marathon The longest recorded skating marathon is one of 83 hr by Lynette Allen of Port Elizabeth, Cape Province, South Africa on 10–14 Jan. 1975. The fastest time to complete 100 miles *160 km* is 5 hr 34 min 1.45 sec by Kirt Barnes, 22, on 26 Feb. 1971 at Fuller Recreation Facility Ice Rink, Ann Arbor, Michigan, U.S.A.

Largest rink The world's largest indoor ice rink is the quadruple rink at Burnaby, British Columbia, Canada, completed in Dec. 1972, which has an ice area of 68,000 ft² *6 317 m²*. The largest artificial outdoor rink is the Fujikyu Highland Promenade Rink, Japan opened at a cost of £335,000 in 1967 and with an area of 165,750 ft² *15 400 m²* (3.8 acres [*1,5 ha*]).

SPEED SKATING

Olympic The most Olympic gold medals won in speed skating is six by Lidia Skoblikova (b. 8 March 1939) of Chelyaminsk, U.S.S.R., in 1960 (2) and 1964 (4). The male records are by Ivar Ballangrud (Norway) (b. 7

WORLD SPEED SKATING RECORDS

	Distance	min sec	Name and Nationality	Place	Date
MEN	500 metres*	37.00	Yeugeni Kulikov (U.S.S.R.)	Medeo, U.S.S.R.	29 Mar. 1975
	1,000 metres	1:16.92	Valeri Muratov (U.S.S.R.)	Medeo, U.S.S.R.	17 Mar. 1975
	1,500 metres	1:58.70	Ard Schenk (Netherlands)	Davos, Switzerland	15 Feb. 1971
	3,000 metres	4:08.30	Ard Schenk (Netherlands)	Inzell, West Germany	2 Mar. 1972
	5,000 metres	7:08.92	Yuri Kondatov (U.S.S.R.)	Medeo, U.S.S.R.	24 Mar. 1975
	10,000 metres	14:52.73	Victor Varlamov (U.S.S.R.)	Medeo, U.S.S.R.	25 Mar. 1975
WOMEN	500 metres	41.06	Tatiana Averina (U.S.S.R.)	Medeo, U.S.S.R.	29 Mar. 1975
	1,000 metres	1:23.46	Tatiana Averina (U.S.S.R.)	Medeo, U.S.S.R.	29 Mar. 1975
	1,500 metres	2:09.90	Tatiana Averina (U.S.S.R.)	Medeo, U.S.S.R.	11 Mar. 1975
	3,000 metres	4:44.69	Tamara Kuznetsova (U.S.S.R.)	Medeo, U.S.S.R.	17 Mar. 1975

BRITISH OUTDOOR RECORDS

	Distance	min sec	Name	Place	Date
MEN	500 metres	40.53	A. John Tipper	Madonna di Campilio, Italy	6 Jan. 1972
	1,000 metres	1:22.8	A. John Tipper	Davos, Switzerland	7 Jan. 1972
	1,500 metres	2:07.43	Peter R. Lake	Inzell, West Germany	10 Feb. 1974
	3,000 metres	4:34.70	John B. Blewitt	Cortina d'Ampezzo, Italy	16 Jan. 1968
	5,000 metres	7:51.2	John B. Blewitt	Davos, Switzerland	22 Jan. 1972
	10,000 metres	16:30.10	Terence A. Malkin	Oslo, Norway	19 Jan. 1964
WOMEN	500 metres	51.90	Patricia K. Tipper	Cortina d'Ampezzo, Italy	16 Jan. 1968
	1,000 metres	1:44.20	Patricia K. Tipper	Inzell, West Germany	7 Jan. 1968
	1,500 metres	2:42.80	Patricia K. Tipper	Cortina d'Ampezzo, Italy	17 Dec. 1967
	3,000 metres	5:39.40	Patricia K. Tipper	Cortina d'Ampezzo, Italy	16 Dec. 1967

* This represents a speed of 29.43 m.p.h. 47,36 km/h.   † *Awaiting ratification.*

March 1904) with 4 gold, 2 silver and 1 bronze medal
in 1928 32 36 and Clas Thunberg (b. 5 Apr. 1893)
(Finland) with 4 gold, 1 tied gold, 1 silver and 1 tied
bronze in 1924 28.

Most titles The greatest number of world speed skating titles
World (instituted 1893) won by any skater is five by Oscar

Mathisen (Norway) in 1908–09 and 1912–14, and
Clas Thunberg in 1923, 1925, 1928–29 and 1931. The
most titles won by a woman is four by Mrs. Inga
Voronina, *née* Artomonova (1936–66) of Moscow,
U.S.S.R., in 1957, 1958, 1962 and 1965 and Mrs.
Atje Keulen-Deelstra (b. 1938) (Netherlands) 1970–
72–73–74.

ICE AND SAND YACHTING

Origin The sport originated in the Low Countries from the
year 1600 (earliest patent granted) and along the
Baltic coast. The earliest authentic record is Dutch,
dating from 1768. Land or Sand yachts of Dutch
construction were first reported on beaches (now in
Belgium) in 1595. The earliest International
championship was staged in 1914.

Record The largest known ice yacht was *Icicle*, built for
Speeds Commodore John E. Roosevelt for racing on the
Ice Hudson River, New York, in *c.* 1870. It was 68 ft 11 in
21 m long and carried 1,070 ft² *99 m²* of canvas. The

highest speed officially recorded is 143 m.p.h. *230 km/h*
by John D. Buckstaff in a Class A stern-steerer on
Lake Winnebago, Wisconsin, U.S.A., in 1938. Such a
speed is possible in a wind of 72 m.p.h. *115 km/h.*

Sand The fastest recorded speed for a sand yacht is 57.69
m.p.h. *92,84 km/h* (measured mile in 62.4 sec) by
Coronation Year Mk. II owned by R. Millett Denning
and crewed by J. Halliday, Bob Harding, J. Glass-
brook and Cliff Martindale at Lytham St. Anne's,
Lancashire, England in 1956.

INDOOR PASTIMES

CHESS

Origins The name chess is derived from the Persian word *shah*
(a king or ruler). It is a descendant of the game
Chaturanga. The earliest reference is from the Middle
Persian Karnamak (*c.* A.D. 590 628), though there
are grounds for believing its origins are from A.D. 200
owing to the discovery, announced in December
1972, of two ivory chessmen in the Uzbek Soviet
Republic dateable to that century. It reached Britain in
c. 1255. The *Fédération Internationale des Échecs*
was established in 1924. There were an estimated
7,000,000 competitive players in the U.S.S.R. in 1973.

It has been calculated that the two opening moves by
each player can be made in 197,299 ways leading to
some 72,000 different positions. The approximate
number of different games possible is 2.5×10^{116}
a number astronomically much higher than the
number of atoms in the observable universe.

World World champions have been generally recognized
champions since 1886. The longest tenure was 27 years by
Dr. Emanuel Lasker (1868 1941) of Germany, from
1894 to 1921. The women's world championship has
been most often won by Vera Menchik-Stevenson in
1927, 1930 1, 1933 5, 1937 and 1939. Robert J.
Fischer (b. Chicago, U.S.A. 9 Mar. 1943) is reckoned
on the officially adopted Elo System to be the greatest
Grand Master of all-time. He has an I.Q. of 187
(Terman index) and became at 15 the youngest ever
International Grand Master.

Winning Robert J. Fischer won 20 games in succession in
streak Grand Master chess from 2 Dec. 1970 *v.* Jorge Rubinetti
(Argentine) to 30 Sept. 1971 *v.* Tigran Petrosian
(U.S.S.R.).

British Most British titles have been won by Dr. Jonathan
titles Penrose, O.B.E. (b. 1934) of East Finchley, London
with 10 titles in 1958 63, 1966 69. Mrs. Rowena M.
Bruce (b. 1919) of Plymouth won 11 titles in 1937 as
Miss Dew and in 1950 51 54 55 (shared) 59 60 62
63 67 (shared) and 1969 (shared).

Longest The most protracted chess match on record was one
games drawn on the 191st move between H. Pilnik (Argentina) and Moshe Czerniak (Israel) at Mar del Plata,
Argentina, in April 1950. The total playing time was
20 hrs. A game of 21½ hrs, but drawn on the 171st
move (average over 7½ min per move), was played
between Makagonov and Chekhover at Baku, U.S.S.R.,
in 1945.

Marathon The longest recorded session is one of 122 hours
between Mike Murphy and Leo Knoblauch both of
Whitehall, Ohio, U.S.A. ending 4 April 1975.

Slowest The slowest recorded move (before modern rules) was
one of 11 hours between Paul Morphy, the U.S.
Champion of 1852–62, and the chess master Louis
Paulsen.

Most Records by chess masters for numbers of opponents
opponents tackled simultaneously depend very much on whether
or not the opponents are replaced as defeated, are
in relays, or whether they are taken on in a simultaneous start. The greatest number tackled on a
replacement basis is 400 (379 defeated) by the Swedish
master Gideon Ståhlberg (died 26 May 1967) in 36 hrs
of play in Buenos Aires, Argentina, in 1940. The
greatest number of opponents tackled in a simultaneous start is 142 by G. J. Martin at Ilford High
School, Redbridge, Greater London in 1957. He won
130 with 11 draws and one loss in less than 4 hours
40 min. Georges Koltanowski (Belgium, now of
U.S.A.) tackled 56 opponents "blindfold" and won
50, drew 6, lost 0 in 9¾ hrs at Fairmont Hotel, San
Francisco, California, U.S.A., on 13 Dec. 1960.

CONTRACT BRIDGE

Earliest Bridge (a corruption of Biritch) is of Levantine origin,
references having been played in Greece in the early 1880s. The
game was known in London in 1886 under the title of
"Biritch" or Russian Whist.

Auction Bridge (highest bidder names trump) was
introduced in 1904 but was swamped by the Contract

game, which was devised by Harold S. Vanderbilt (U.S.A.) on a Caribbean voyage in November 1925. The new version became a world-wide craze after the U.S.A. v. Great Britain challenge match between Ely Culbertson (b. Romania, 1891) and Lt.-Col. Walter Thomas More Buller (1886–1938) at Almack's Club, London, on 15 Sept. 1930. The U.S.A. won the 54-hand match by 4,845 points.

World titles The World Championship (Bermuda Bowl) has been won most often by Italy's Blue Team (*Squadra Azzura*) (1957–58–59, 1961–62–63, 1965–66–67, 1969, 1973–75, whose team also won the Olympiad in 1964, 1968 and 1972. Giorgio Belladonna (b. 1923) was in 16 of these winning teams. The team retired in 1969 but came back to defeat the Dallas Aces (1970–71 World Champions) 338–254 in Las Vegas, Nevada in December 1971, and take the Olympiad in Miami, Florida in June 1972 followed by wins in the Bermuda Bowl at Guaruja, Brazil in 1973; at Venice, Italy in 1974 and at Bermuda in 1975.

Perfect deals The mathematical odds against dealing 13 cards of one suit are 158,753,389,899 to 1, while the odds against receiving a "perfect hand" consisting of all 13 spades are 635,013,559,599 to 1. The odds against each of the 4 players receiving a complete suit (a "perfect deal") are 2,235,197,406,895,366,368,301,559,999 to 1. Instances of this are reported frequently but the chances of it happening genuinely are extraordinarily remote—in fact if all the people in the world were grouped in bridge fours, and each four were dealt 120 hands a day, it would require 62×10^{12} years before one "perfect deal" should recur.

A "perfect" perfect deal with the dealer (South) with 13 clubs, round to East with 13 spades was the subject of affidavits by Mrs. E. F. Gyde (dealer), Mrs. Hennion, David Rex-Taylor and Mrs. P. Dawson at Richmond Community Centre, Greater London, on 25 Aug. 1964. This deal, 24 times more remote than a "perfect deal", the second of the rubber, was with a pack not used for the first deal. In view of the fact that there should be 31,201,794 deals with two perfect hands for each deal with four perfect hands and that reports of the latter far outnumber the former, it can be safely assumed that reported occurrences of perfect deals are almost without exception bogus.

Longest session The longest recorded session is one of 180 hr by 4 students at Edinburgh University on 21–28 April 1972.

Most master points In 1971 a new world ranking list based on Master Points was instituted. The leading male player in the world was Giorgio Belladonna (Italy) a member of the Blue team with 1,590 points as at June 1975, followed by five more Italians. The leading Briton is Boris Schapiro (b. 1911) in 16th place with 353 points. The world's leading woman player and only woman of Grand Master rank is Mrs. Rixi Markus (G.B.) with 229 points to June 1975. Britain had 4 more in the Top Ten.

HIGHEST POSSIBLE SCORES (excluding penalties)

Opponents bid 7 of any suit or No Trumps doubled and redoubled and vulnerable

	Opponents make no trick	
Above Line	1st undertrick	400
	12 subsequent undertricks at 600 each	7,200
	All Honours	150
		7,750

Bid 1 No Trump, double and redouble, vulnerable

Below Line	1st trick (40 × 4)	160
Above Line	6 over tricks (400 × 6)	2,400
	2nd game of 2-Game Rubber	*350
	All Honours	150
	Bonus for making redoubled contract	50
	(Highest Possible Positive Score)	3,110

* In Practice, the full bonus of 700 points is awarded after the completion of the second winning game rather than 350 after each game.

DARTS

Origins The origins of darts date from the use by archers of heavily weighted ten-inch throwing arrows for self-defence in close quarters fighting. The "dartes" were used in Ireland in the 16th century and darts was played on the *Mayflower* by the Plymouth pilgrims in 1620. Today there are an estimated 6,000,000 dart players in the British Isles—a higher participation than in any other sporting pastime. The National Darts Association of Great Britain (inst. 1953) is seeking to standardize the throwing distances and treble boards.

Lowest possible scores The lowest number of darts to achieve standard scores are: 201 four darts, 301 six darts, 501 nine darts, 1,001 seventeen darts. The four and six darts "possibles" have been many times achieved, the nine darts 501 occasionally but never the seventeen darts 1,001 which would require 15 treble 20's, a treble 17 and a 50. The lowest number of darts thrown for a score of 1,001 is 24 by Leighton Rees (123, 140, 140, 140, 140, 121, 100, 77) at Pontypridd, Mid-Glamorgan, in June 1975. The lowest even number which cannot be scored with three darts (ending on a double) is 162. The lowest odd number which cannot be scored with three darts (ending on a double) is 159.

Fastest match The fastest time taken for a match of three games of 301 is 2½ min by Jim Pike (1903–1960) at Broadcasting House, Broad Street, Birmingham, in 1952.

Fastest "round the board" The record time for going round the board in "doubles" at arm's length is 14.5 sec by Jim Pike at the Craven Club, Newmarket, in March 1944. The record for this feat at the nine-feet *2,7 m* throwing distance, retrieving own darts, is 2 min 13 sec by Bill Duddy at The Plough, Hornsey Road, Harringey, Greater London on 29 Oct. 1972.

Million and one up The shortest recorded time to score 1,000,001 up *on one board*, under the rules of darts, is 7 hr 36 min (scoring rate of 36.54 per sec) by eight players from

Bill Duddy, who has been "round the board" in doubles in 2 mins 13 sec, seen receiving his 1968 'News of the World' champions cup from Barbara Windsor

News of the World

the Fox and Grapes Inn, Wakefield, West Yorkshire. The back-up team consisted of 36 including 4 calculating machine operators and 6 dart extractors.

Longest unbeaten run The Ship Inn Dart Club, Southend-in-Sea, Essex were unbeaten in 106 successive games up to early 1972–73.

10 hour scores The record number of trebles scored in 10 hr is 2,150 (in 9,400 darts) for a percentage of 22.87 by E. Jacky Hughes at Heswall British Legion, Merseyside on 27 Sept. 1974. On 27 July 1973 Jacky Hughes scored a record 2,790 doubles (out of 9,984 darts) in 10 hr for a 27.94 percentage. The greatest score amassed in 10 hr is 337,079 by Ray Jacks and Terry Patton at the Moreton Social Club, Wirral, Merseyside on 23 May 1975.

Marathon record John Rodis, Bluey Scanlon, Brian and Ted Turnbull played non-stop for 554 hr at Great Western Hotel, Orange, N.S.W., Australia. They played on a shift system on 3–26 Oct. 1974.

Most titles Re-instituted in 1947, the annual *News of the World* England and Wales individual Championships consist of the best of 3 legs 501 up, "straight" start and finish on a double with an 8 ft *2,4 m* throwing distance. The only men to win twice are Tommy Gibbons (Ivanhoe Working Men's Club) of Conisbrough, South Yorkshire, in 1952 and 1958; Tom Reddington of New Inn, Stonebroom, Derbyshire in 1955 and of George Hotel, Alfreton, Derbyshire 1960; and Tom M. Barrett (Odco Sports Club, London) in 1964 and 1965.

The National Darts Association of Great Britain Individual title was won by Tom O'Regan of the Northern Star, New Southgate, Enfield, Greater London in 1970–71–72.

DOMINOES

Dominoes are known from 15th century China but remain unstandardised throughout the world. Though unknown in Europe in *c.* 1750, the game reached England *via* France *c.* 1795. The Eskimo game requires 148 pieces while that in Europe utilises only 28.

Toppling The greatest number of dominoes toppled is 13,832 by six students of Washington University at Seattle Centre, Washington, U.S.A., on 6 June 1975.

Marathon The longest sustained pairs game of dominoes is of 108 hr 4 min 20 sec maintained by 4 players from Thunderfield Venture Scout Unit, Horley, West Sussex on 28 Dec. 1972–1 Jan. 1973.

DRAUGHTS

Origins Draughts, known as checkers in North America, has origins earlier than chess. It was played in Egypt in the first millenium B.C. The earliest book on the game was by Antonio Torquemada of Valencia, Spain in 1547. The earliest U.S. *v.* Great Britain international was in 1905 and was won by the Scottish Masters, 73–34 with 284 draws. The U.S. won in 1927 in New York 96–20 with 364 draws.

The British Championship (biennial) was inaugurated in 1926. The only man to win 5 titles has been Mr. J. Marshall (Fife) in 1948–50–53–54–66. The longest tenure of invincibility in freestyle play was that of Melvin Pomeroy (U.S.), who was internationally undefeated from 1914 until his death in 1933.

Longest game In competition the prescribed rate of play is not less than 30 moves per hour with the average game lasting about 90 min. In 1958 a match between Dr. Marian Tinsley (U.S.) and Derek Oldbury (G.B.) lasted 7½ hours.

Most opponents Newell W. Banks (b. Detroit 10 Oct. 1887) played 140 games simultaneously winning 133 and drawing

7 in Chicago, Illinois in 1933. His playing time was 145 min so averaging about one move per sec.

MONOPOLY

Origins The patentee of Monopoly, the world's most popular proprietary board game of which Parker Bros. have sold 80,000,000 copies, was Charles Darrow (1889–1967). He invented the patented version of the game in 1933 while an unemployed heating engineer using the street names of Atlantic City, New Jersey where he spent his vacations. Claims the game derived from one called *The Landlord's Games*, devised during the period 1904–1923 by Elizabeth J. Magie later Mrs. Phillips, have been alleged.

Marathon The longest game by four players ratified by the Monopoly Marathon Records Documentation Committee is 264 hr by Ray Kessinger, Tom Lashbrook, Tony Stanaró and Kirk Hamiltons in Pinole, California, U.S.A., from 26 Dec. 1974 to 5 Jan. 1975. Thirty four high school students from Denver, Colorado, U.S.A. played for 1,008 hr ending on 30 July 1974.

SCRABBLE

Origins The crossword game was invented by Alfred M. Butts in 1931 and was developed, refined and trademarked as Scrabble ® Crossword Game by James Brunot in 1948.

U.S. Records Highest single turn score for a two handed game: 1,539 pts by Isaac Blech of Brooklyn, New York in June 1975. Highest single turn score for a solitary game: 1,572 pts by Daniel Pratt of Baltimore, Maryland in June 1975.

U.K. Record British National Championships were instituted in 1971. Miss Olive Behan won in 1972 and 1975. The highest British single turn score is 1,961 pts by Ronald E. Jerome of Bracknell, Berkshire in May 1961.

Marathon The longest Scrabble game on record is one of 100 hours set by Mike Borrello, Pat Edmond, Rick Varyas and Mike Wilson at Lakewood, California on 14–18 April 1973.

TABLE FOOTBALL

Bar The most protracted 2-a-side table football on record was one of 300 hours maintained by six members of the sixth form of Bournemouth School, Dorset, England on 25 June–7–July 1973.

An example of the verbal ingenuity of Ronald E. Jerome (G.B.) amassing 3,881 points in 32 moves at the word game Scrabble ®

Games and Puzzles

Subbuteo The longest recorded Subbuteo table soccer marathon was one of 227 hours by 6 boys (aged under 17) who sustained a continuous game at the City Hall, Johannesburg, South Africa on 19–28 Sept. 1974.

TIDDLY WINKS

Origins This game was only espoused by adults in 1955 when Cambridge University issued a challenge to Oxford.

Guinness Trophy England has remained unbeaten against Scotland, Ireland and Wales since the Trophy's inception on 7 May 1960. The closest result has been their 59½–52½ win over Wales at Warwick on 7 April 1968.

Silver Wink Trophy The *Silver Wink*, presented by H.R.H. The Duke of Edinburgh, for the British University championship has been won a record four times by Cambridge University.

Speed The record for potting 24 winks from 18 in *45 cm* is 21.8 sec by Stephen Williams (Altrincham Grammar School) in May 1966.

Four Pot Relay The greatest number of winks potted in 3 min by a relay of four is 29 by Paul Light, Paul Hoffman, Andrew James and Geoff Thorpe at "The Castle", Cambridge on 6 Dec. 1974.

Marathon Allen R. Astles (University of Wales) potted 10,000 winks in 3 hours 51 min 46 sec at Aberystwyth, Cardiganshire in February 1966. The most protracted game on record is one of 170 hrs by six players of Quinton Kynaston School, St. John's Wood, City of Westminster, Greater London, on 1–8 Jan. 1973.

WHIST

Whist, first referred to in 1529, was the world's premier card game until 1930. The rules were standardized in 1742.

Highest Score No collated records exist but the highest scores notified to the editors have been—for 24 hands—209 by Mrs. E. Heslop in the Shaldon Over 60 Club, Teignmouth, Devon on 5 Jan. 1973.

Perfect Hand Mrs. Ethel Annie Cliffe on 3 Dec. 1973 at the Lache Community Centre, Chester, Cheshire picked up 13 hearts.

JUDO

Origins Judo is a modern combat sport which developed out of an amalgam of several old Japanese fighting arts, the most popular of which was ju-jitsu (jiu-jitsu), which is thought to be of pre-Christian Chinese origin. Judo has greatly developed since 1882, when it was first devised by Dr. Jigoro Kano.

World and Olympic titles World championships were inaugurated in Tōkyō on 5 May 1956. The only man to have won 4 world titles is Wilhem Ruska (Netherlands), who won the 1967 Heavyweight, the 1971 Heavyweight and the 1972 Olympic Heavyweight and Open titles. In the European championships (instituted in 1951) only Great Britain (1957-58-59) and the U.S.S.R. (1972-73-74) have won 3 consecutive titles.

British titles The greatest number of titles (inst. 1966) won is nine by David Starbrook (b. 9 Aug. 1945) (5th dan) who won the middleweight title 1969–70, the light-heavyweight 1971–75 and the open division 1970–71. The

women's championships were instituted in 1971. Christine Child (4th dan) has won most titles with five wins: the heavyweight in 1971–74 and the open division in 1973.

Highest grade The efficiency grades in Judo are divided into pupil (*kyu*) and master (*dan*) grades. The highest awarded is the extremely rare red belt *Judan* (*10th dan*), given only to seven men so far. The Judo protocol provides for an *11th dan* (*Juichidan*) who also would wear a red belt and even a *12th dan* who would wear a white belt twice as wide as an ordinary belt, but these have never been bestowed. The highest British native Judo grade is *7th dan* by Trevor P. Leggett (b. 22 Aug. 1914,) Charles S. Palmer and Geoff Gleeson.

Marathon The longest recorded Judo marathon with continuous play by two of 6 Judoka in 5 min stints is 50 hr from the Dufftown and District Judo Club, Keith, Grampian, on 13–15 Sept. 1974.

KARATE

Origins Based on techniques devised from the 6th century Chinese art of *Chuan-fa* (Kempo), karate (empty hand) was developed by an unarmed populace on Okinawa as a weapon against armed Japanese oppressors *c.* 1500. Transmitted to Japan in the 1920's by Funakoshi Gichin, the founder of modern karate, this method of combat was further refined and organised into a sport with competitive rules. The five major styles of karate in Japan are: *Shotokan, Wado-ryu, Goju-ryu, Shito-ryu* and *Kyokushinkai*, each of which place different emphasis on speed and power etc. The military form of *Tae kwan-do* with 9 dans is a Korean equivalent of Karate. *Kung fu* is believed to have originated in Nepal or Tibet but was adopted within Chinese temples *via* India.

The Governing Body for the sport in Britain is the British Karate Control Commission on which the major karate styles in this country are represented.

Great Britain became the first country ever to defeat the Japanese in competition when they won in the World championships in Paris in 1972.

Most Titles The only winner of three All-Japanese titles has been Takeshi Oishi who won in 1969–70–71.

Keinosuke Enoeda, the Karate Union of Great Britain's 7th Dan instructor in action

Greatest force Considerably less emphasis is placed on *Tamashiwara* (wood breaking etc.) than is generally supposed. Most styles use it only for demonstration purposes. However, the force needed to break a brick with the abductor *digiti quinti* muscle of the hand is 130–140 lb. *59–63 kg force* up to a maximum of 196 lb. *88 kg f.* The greatest number of bricks reported broken in 3 hr is 3,773 by Harold Warden at White Oaks Mall, London, Ontario, Canada on 17 Nov. 1973.

Top exponents The highest dan among karatekas is Yamaguchi Gogen (b. 1907) a 10th dan of the *Goju-ryu* Karate Do. The leading exponents in the United Kingdom are Tatsuo Suzuki (7th dan, *Wado-ryu*), chief instructor to the United Kingdom Karate Federation; Keinosuke Enoeda (7th dan, *Shotokan*), resident instructor to the Karate Union of Great Britain and Steve Arneil (5th dan, *Kyokushinkai*) British national born in South Africa. David "Ticky" Donovan (4th Dan) won two successive All Britain Championships.

LACROSSE

Origin The game is of American Indian origin, derived from the inter-tribal game *baggataway*, and was played before 1492 by Iroquois Indians in lower Ontario, Canada and upper New York State, U.S.A. It was introduced into Great Britain in 1867. The English Lacrosse Union was formed in 1892. The Oxford *v.* Cambridge match was instituted in 1903 and the game was included in the Olympic Games of 1908 and featured as an exhibition sport in the 1928 and 1948 Games.

World championships The first World Tournament was held at Toronto, Canada in 1967 and the second in Melbourne, Australia in 1974. The United States won both championships.

Longest throw The longest recorded throw is 162.86 yds *148,91 m* by Barney Quinn of Ottawa on 10 Sept. 1892.

Most titles The English Club Championship (Iroquois Cup), instituted in 1890, has been won most often by Stockport with 15 wins between 1897 and 1934.

Highest scores The highest score in any international match was the United States' 26–15 win over Canada at Melbourne in 1974. England's highest score was their 19–11 win over Canada also at Melbourne in 1974. The highest score in the annual North of England *v.* South of England match has been 26–2 in 1927.

The record number of international representations for England is 21 by Michael Roberts, Tom Gare (both Urmston) and Roy Higson (Old Waconians) to 1974.

The record for women is 52 for Scotland by Caro Macintosh (1952–1969).

Caro Mackintosh, who won 52 Lacrosse caps for Scotland from 1952 to 1969

L. Middleton

LAWN TENNIS

Origins The modern game is generally agreed to have evolved as an outdoor form of the indoor game of Tennis (see separate entry). "Field Tennis" is mentioned in an English magazine—*Sporting Magazine*—of 29 Sept. 1793. The earliest club for such a game, variously called Pelota or Lawn Rackets, was the Leamington Club founded in 1872 by Major Harry Gem. The earliest attempt to commercialise the game was by Major Walter Clopton Wingfield, M.V.O. (1833–1912) who patented a form called "sphairistike" in February 1874. It soon became called Lawn Tennis. Amateur players were permitted to play with and against professionals in 'Open' tournaments in 1968.

ALL TIME RECORDS

Greatest Domination The grand slam is to win all four of the world's major championship singles: Wimbledon, the United States, Australian and French (on hard courts) championships. The first man to have won all four was Frederick John Perry (G.B.) (b. 18 May 1909) with the French title in 1935. The first man to hold all four championships simultaneously was John Donald Budge (U.S.A.) (b. 13 June 1915) with the French title

in 1938. The first man to achieve the grand slam twice was Rodney George Laver (Australia) (born 9 Aug. 1938) having won in 1962 as an amateur and again in 1969 when the titles were 'open' to professionals.

Only two women have achieved the grand slam: Maureen Catherine Connolly (U.S.A.) (1934–1969), later Mrs. Norman E. Brinker with the French title in 1953; and Mrs. Barrymore Court, M.B.E., (*née* Margaret Smith) (Australia) (b. 16 July 1942) in 1970.

Fastest service The fastest service ever *measured* was one of 154 m.p.h. *247 km/h* by Michael J. Sangster (U.K.) (b. 1940) in June 1963. Crossing the net the ball was travelling at 108 m.p.h. *173 km/h*. Some players consider the service of Robert Falkenburg (U.S.A.) (b. 29 Jan. 1926) the 1948 Wimbledon champion as the fastest ever produced.

Greatest crowd The greatest crowd at a tennis match was 30,472 at the Astrodome, Houston, Texas, on 20 Sept. 1973, when Mrs. Lawrence W. King (*née* Billie-Jean Moffitt) beat Robert Larimore Riggs, over a quarter of a century her senior. The record for an orthodox match is 25,578 at Sydney, N.S.W. on 27 Dec. 1954 in the Davis Cup Challenge Round (1st day) Australia v. U.S.A.

The greatest reward for playing one match is $500,000 (£217,400) won by Jimmy Connors (U.S.A.) (b. 2 Sept. 1952) when he beat John Newcombe (Australia) (b. 23 May 1944) in a challenge match at Caesars Palace, Las Vegas, U.S.A. on 26 Apr. 1975.

Lawn tennis marathons The longest recorded non-stop lawn tennis singles game is one of 30 hr 30 min by Sandy Goss and Rita Santarpia of Beltsville, Maryland, U.S.A. on 10–11 May 1975. The duration record for doubles is 58 hr by four players from Satellite High School, Florida, U.S.A. on 2–4 May 1975. Linford Stillson of Western Connecticut State College, Danbury, Conn., U.S.A. played singles against a number of opponents for 80 hr on 16–20 May 1975.

WIMBLEDON RECORDS

Youngest champions The youngest ever champion at Wimbledon was Miss Charlotte Dod (1871–1960), who was 15 years 8 months when she won in 1887. The youngest male singles champion was Wilfred Baddeley (b. 11 Jan. 1872 d. 1929) who won the Wimbledon title in 1891 at the age of 19.

Richard Dennis Ralston (b. 27 July 1942) of Bakersfield, California, U.S.A., was 25 days short of his 18th birthday when he won the men's doubles with Rafael H. Osuna (1938–69) of Mexico in 1960.

Most appearances Arthur Wentworth Gore (1868–1928) of the U.K. made 36 appearance at Wimbledon between 1888 and 1927, and was in 1909 at 41 years the oldest ever singles winner. In 1964, Jean Borotra (b. 13 Aug. 1898) of France made his 35th appearance since 1922. In 1975 he appeared in the Veteran's Doubles aged 76.

Most wins Miss Elizabeth Montague Ryan (U.S.A) (b. 1894) won her first title in 1914 and her 19th in 1934 (12 women's doubles [a record] with 5 different partners and 7 mixed doubles [a record] with 5 different partners). Her total of 19 Championships was equalled by the six time singles champion Mrs. Billie-Jean King (*née* Moffitt) (b. 22 Nov. 1943) (U.S.A.) who also won 9 women's doubles and four mixed doubles during the period 1961 to 1975.

Men The greatest number of wins by a man at Wimbledon has been 14 by William Charles Renshaw (1861–1904) (G.B.) who won 7 singles titles (1881–2–3–4–5–6–9) [a record for men] and 7 doubles (1880–1–4–5–6–8–9), partnered by his twin brother (James) Ernest.

Singles The greatest number of singles wins was eight by Mrs. F. S. Moody (*née* Helen N. Wills) (b. 6 Oct. 1905), now Mrs. Aiden Roark, of the U.S.A., who won in 1927, 1928, 1929, 1930, 1932, 1933, 1935 and 1938.

Doubles The greatest number of doubles wins by men was 8 by the brothers Reginald Frank (1872–1910) and Hugh Lawrence Doherty (1875–1919) (G.B.). They won each year from 1897 to 1905 except for 1902 (see above).

Mixed doubles The male record is four wins shared by Elias Victor Seixas (U.S.A) (b. 30 Aug. 1923) in 1953–54–55–56 and Kenneth N. Fletcher (Australia) (b. 15 June 1940) in 1963–65–66–68.

Attendance The record crowd for one day at Wimbledon is 37,290 on 27 June 1975. The record for the whole championship is 338,507 in 1975.

DAVIS CUP

Most victories The greatest number of wins in the Davis Cup (instituted 1900) has been (inclusive of 1974) the U.S.A., with 24 wins and Australasia/Australia with

Gerry Cranham

Chris Evert (U.S.), who set an all time feminine earnings record for a season $261,460 *(£113 678* in 1974

Press Association

Wimbledon's youngest male champion, the 17 year old Men's Doubles champion Dennis Ralston (U.S.), (with Osuna of Mexico) in 1960

23. The British Isles/Great Britain have won 9 times, in 1903–04–05–06, 1912, 1933–34–35–36.

Individual Performance Nicola Pietrangeli (Italy) played 164 rubbers, 1954 to 1972, winning 120. He played 110 singles (winning 78) and 54 doubles (winning 42). He took part in 66 ties.

OLYMPIC GAMES

Most Medals Lawn Tennis was part of the Olympic programme at the first eight celebrations of the Games (including the 1906 Games). The winner of most medals was Max Decugis (b. 24 Sept. 1882) (France) with six (four gold [a record], one silver and one bronze) in the 1900, 1906 and 1920 tournaments. The British male winners of most medals was Reginald F. Doherty (1872–1910) with four (three gold [a record] and one bronze) and Charles Percy Dixon (b. 1873) (one gold, one silver and two bronze).

Women The most medals won by a woman player is five by Miss Kitty McKane (later Mrs. L. A. Godfree) (G.B.), with one gold, two silver and two bronze in the 1920 and 1924 tournaments. Two gold medals is the record shared by Miss Charlotte Cooper (later Mrs. Alfred Sterry) (G.B.); Mrs. Edith M. Hannam (G.B.); Mlle. Suzanne Rachel Flore Lenglen (France); Mrs. Hazel Hotchkiss Wightman, C.B.E. (Hon.) (U.S.A.) and Miss Helen N. Wills (later Mrs. F. S. Moody and Mrs. A. Roark) (U.S.A.).

Nicola Pietrangeli, who represented Italy in a record 66 Davis Cup ties

Press Association

MARBLES

Origins Marbles was played by the Romans who are believed to have introduced it into Britain in the 1st Century A.D. It was organised as a competitive sport with the setting up of the British Marbles Board of Control at the Greyhound Hotel, Tinsley Green, Crawley, West Sussex in 1926.

The game is also played in Australia, Brazil (as *Gude*), Canada, China, France, Germany, India, Iran, New Zealand, Spain, Syria, Turkey and the United States.

Most championships The British Championship (established 1926) has been won most often by the Toucan Terribles with 20 consecutive titles (1956–75). Three founder members, Len Smith, Jack and Charlie Dempsey, have played in every title win. Len Smith (b. 13 Oct. 1917) has won the individual title 15 times (1957–64, 1966, 1968–73) but lost in 1974 to his son Alan.

The record for clearing the ring (between 5¾ and 6¼ ft [*1,75–1,90 m*] in diameter) of 49 marbles is 2 min 57 sec by the Toucan Terribles at Worthing, West Sussex in 1971.

MODERN PENTATHLON

Points scores in riding, fencing, cross country and hence overall scores have no comparative value between one competition and another. In shooting and swimming (300 m) the scores are of record significance.

The Modern Pentathlon (Riding, Fencing, Shooting, Swimming and Running) was inaugurated into the Olympic Games at Stockholm in 1912. The Modern Pentathlon Association of Great Britain was formed in 1922.

MOST TITLES

World The record number of world titles won is 6 by András Balczó (Hungary) in 1963, 1965, 1966, 1967 and 1969.

In Olympic year this title also rates as the world title, thus making Balczó sixth in 1972.

Olympic The greatest number of Olympic gold medals won is three by András Balczó (Hungary) a member of the winning team in 1960 and 1968 and the 1972 individual champion. Lars Hall (Sweden) has uniquely won two individual Championships (1952 and 1956). Balczó has won a record number of five medals (three gold and two silver). The best British performance is the fourth place gained by Sgt. Jeremy Robert Fox (b. 1941) at Munich in 1972.

British The pentathlete with most British titles is Sergeant Jeremy Robert Fox, M.B.E., with ten (1963, 65–68, 70–74).

MODERN PENTATHLON

	World			British		
Shooting	1,088	Mario Medda (Italy) Munich, W. Germany	29 Aug. 1972	1,066	Robert Lawson Phelps, Leipzig	21 Sept. 1965
Swimming	1,288	John Alexander (Canada) London, England	8 Sept. 1973	1,064	L/Cpl. Barry Lillywhite, San Antonio, Texas	13 Oct. 1971

MOTORCYCLING

EARLIEST RACES

The first motorcycle race was one from Paris to Dieppe, France, in 1897. The first closed circuit race was held at the Parc des Princes, Paris cycle track in 1903. The oldest motorcycle races in the world are the Auto-Cycle Union Tourist Trophy (T.T.) series, first held on the 15.81 mile *25,44 km* "Peel" ("St. John's") course in the Isle of Man on 28 May 1907, and still run in the island on the 37.73 mile *60,72 km* long "Mountain" circuit.

FASTEST CIRCUITS

World The highest average lap speed attained on any closed circuit is 182 m.p.h. *293 km/h* by a Kawasaki racer powered by a 748 c.c. three-cylinder two-stroke engine on a banked circuit in Tōkyō, Japan in December 1971.

The fastest road circuit is the Francorchamps circuit near Spa, Belgium. It is 8.761 miles *14,100 km* in length and was lapped in 3 min 52.2 sec (average speed 135.835 m.p.h. [*218,607 km/h*]) by Barry Sheene (b. Holborn, London, 11 Sept. 1950) on a 500 c.c. four-cylinder Suzuki during the 500 c.c. Belgian Grand Prix on 6 July 1975.

United The fastest circuit in the United Kingdom is the
Kingdom 10.000 mile *16,093 km* Portstewart-Coleraine-Portrush circuit in Londonderry, Northern Ireland. The lap record is 4 min 53.6 sec (average speed 122.616 m.p.h. [*197,331 km/h*]) by Michael Grant (b. Wakefield, Yorks., 10 July 1944) on a 750 c.c. three-cylinder Kawasaki, on lap 7 of the 750 c.c. event of the North-West 200, on 17 May 1975.

The lap record for the outer circuit (2.767 miles [*4,453 km*]) at the Brooklands Motor Course near Weybridge, Surrey (open between 1907 and 1939) was 80.0 sec (average speed 124.51 m.p.h. [*200,37 km/h*]) by Noel Baddow "Bill" Pope (later Major) (1909–1971) of the United Kingdom on a Brough Superior powered by a supercharged 996 c.c. V-twin "8-80" J.A.P. engine developing 110 b.h.p., on 4 July 1939. The race lap record for the outer circuit at Brooklands was 80.6 sec (average speed 123.588 m.p.h. [*198,895 km/h*]) by Eric Crudgington Fernihough (1905–1938) of the United Kingdom on a Brough Superior powered by an unsupercharged 996 c.c. V-twin J.A.P. engine, on 28 July 1935.

FASTEST RACES

World The fastest race in the world was held at Grenzland-ring, near Wegberg, W. Germany in 1939. It was won by Georg Meier (b. Germany, 1910) at an average speed of 134 m.p.h. *215 km/h* on a supercharged 495 c.c. flat-twin B.M.W.

The fastest road race is the 500 c.c. Belgian Grand Prix held on the Francorchamps Circuit. The record time for this 12-lap (105.136 mile [*169,200 km*]) race is 47 min 21.1 sec (average speed 133.219 m.p.h. [*214,396 km/h*]) by Philip William Read (b. Luton, Beds., 1 Jan. 1939) on a 500 c.c. four-cylinder M.V.-Agusta, on 6 July 1975.

United The fastest race in the United Kingdom is the 750 c.c.
Kingdom event of the North-West 200 held on the Londonderry circuit (see above). The record time for this 8-lap (80.00 mile [*128,75 km*]) race is 40 min 00.6 sec (average speed 119.970 m.p.h. [*193,073 km/h*]) by Michael Grant, on a 750 c.c. three-cylinder Kawasaki, on 17 May 1975.

MOST SUCCESSFUL RIDERS

Tourist The record number of victories in the Isle of Man T.T.
Trophy races is 12 by Stanley Michael Bailey Hailwood,

Phil Read, who in July 1975 set the record for the Belgian Grand Prix, the world's fastest road race on motorcycling's fastest circuit at Francorchamps at an average speed of 133.219 m.p.h.

Gerry Cranham

M.B.E., G.M. (b. Oxford, 2 April 1940) between 1961 and 1967. The first man to win three consecutive T.T. titles in two events was James A. Redman, M.B.E. (Rhodesia) (b. Hampstead, Camden, Greater London, 8 Nov. 1931). He won the 250 c.c. and 350 c.c. events in 1963–64–65. Mike Hailwood is the only man to win three events in one year, in 1961 and 1967.

World The most world championship titles (instituted by
champion- the *Fédération Internationale Motorcycliste* in 1949)
ships won are:

14 Giacomo Agostini (b. Lovere, Italy, 16 June 1942)
350 c.c. 1968, 69, 70, 71, 72, 73, 74.
500 c.c. 1966, 67, 68, 69, 70, 71, 72.

Giacomo Agostini is the only man to win two world championships in five consecutive years (350 and 500 c.c. titles in 1968–69–70–71–72).

Mike Hailwood is the youngest person to win a world championship. He was 21 when he won the 250 c.c. title in 1961. The oldest was Eric Staines Oliver (b. Crowborough, Sussex, 13 April 1911) who won the sidecar title in 1953 aged 42.

Giacomo Agostini won 120 races in the world championship series between 24 April 1965 and 27 July 1975, including a record 19 in 1970, also achieved by Mike Hailwood in 1966.

Trials Samuel Hamilton Miller (b. Belfast, Northern Ireland, 11 Nov. 1935) won eleven A.-C.U. Solo Trials Drivers' Stars in 1959–69.

Scrambles Jeffrey Vincent Smith, M.B.E. (b. Colne, Lancashire, 14 Oct. 1934) won nine A.-C.U. 500 c.c. Scrambles Stars in 1955–56, 1960–61–62–63–64–65 and 1967.

Joël Robert (b. Chatelet, Belgium, Nov. 1943) has won six 250 c.c. moto-cross world championships (1964, 1968–69–70–71–72). Between 25 April 1964 and 18 June 1972 he won a record fifty 250 c.c. Grands Prix. He became the youngest moto-cross world champion on 12 July 1964 when he won the 250 c.c. championship aged 20 years 8 months.

MOST SUCCESSFUL MACHINES

Italian M.V.-Agusta machines won 37 world championships between 1952 and 1973 and 272 world championship races between 1952 and 1974. Japanese Honda machines won 29 world championship races and five world championships in 1966.

SPEED RECORDS

The official world speed record (average speed for two runs over a 1 km [*1,093.6 yd*] course) is 224.569 m.p.h. *361,408 km/h* (average time 9.961 sec) by William A. "Bill" Johnson, aged 38, of Garden Grove, Los Angeles, California, U.S.A., riding a Triumph Bonneville T120 streamliner, with a 667.25 c.c. parallel twin-cylinder engine running on methanol and nitromethane and developing 75 to 80 b.h.p., at Bonneville Salt Flats, Tooele County, Utah, U.S.A., on 5 Sept. 1962. His machine was 17 ft *5 m* long and weighed 400 lb. *181 kg.* His first run was made in 9.847 sec (227.169 m.p.h. [*365,593 km/h*]).

Don Vesco (b. 1939) of El Cajon, Calif., U.S.A. recorded higher speeds over the measured mile *1,6 km* without F.I.M. observers, at Bonneville on 1 Oct. 1974 riding his 1,400 c.c. Yamaha Streamliner powered by two TZ700 four-cylinder engines. On the first run Vesco covered the mile *1,6 km* in 12,810 sec (281.030 m.p.h. [*452,274 km/h*]). On the second run his time was 12.749 sec (282.375 m.p.h. [*454,438 km/h*]). The average time for the two runs was 12.7795 sec (281.701 m.p.h. [*453,354 km/h*]). On the same day he covered a flying quarter mile in 3.130 sec (287.539 m.p.h. [*462,749 km/h*]). The highest speed ever achieved on a motorcycle.

The world record for two runs over 1 km *1,093.6 yd* from a standing start is 122.77 m.p.h. *197,57 km/h* (18.22 sec) by David John Hobbs (b. Woodford, Essex, 3 June 1947) on his supercharged Triumph *Olympus II* powered by two twin-cylinder 500 c.c. engines each developing 100 b.h.p. using methanol and nitromethane, at Elvington Airfield, North Yorkshire on 30 Sept. 1972.

The world record for two runs over 440 yd *402 m* from a standing start is 94.687 m.p.h. *152,384 km/h* (9.505 sec) by Keith Parnell (b. Newquay, Cornwall, 8 Oct. 1936) on his supercharged 750 c.c. Triumph *Rouge et Nois* at Elvington Airfield, North Yorkshire on 5 Oct. 1974. The faster run was made in 9.40 sec.

The fastest time for a single run over 440 yd *402 m* from a standing start is 8.201 sec (terminal velocity 173.74 m.p.h. [*279,61 km/h*]) by Joe Smith of West Covina, California, U.S.A., riding his supercharged twin-engined 3 500 c.c. Harley-Davidson, during the National Hot Rod Association's Supernationals at Ontario Motor Speedway, Ontario, California, U.S.A., on 13 Oct. 1974.

The highest terminal velocity recorded at the end of a 440 yd *402 m* run from a standing start is 180.13 m.p.h. *289,89 km/h* (elapsed time 9.35 sec) by Tom C. Christenson (b. 1943) of Kenosha, Wisconsin, U.S.A., riding his 1 490 c.c. *Hogslayer*, powered by two Norton Commando engines developing 150 b.h.p. each using nitromethane, at U.S. 30 Drag Strip, Gary, Indiana, U.S.A., in Aug. 1972.

MISCELLANEOUS

Longest race The longest race is the Liège 24 hours. The greatest distance ever covered is 2,523.26 miles *4 060,80 km* (average speed 105.136 m.p.h. [*169,200 km/h*]) by Jean-Claude Chemarin and Gerard Debrock, both of France, on a 860 c.c. four-cylinder Honda on the Francorchamps circuit on 17–18 Aug. 1974.

Non-stop The longest time a motorcycle has been kept in continuous motion is 24 hr 20 min by Michael Ayriss, Philip Freestone and Eric Tindall riding a 750 c.c. Mk II Norton Commando Fastback at Cadwell Park, Lincs., on 29–30 Sept. 1972. They covered 1,030 miles.

Longest circuit The 37.73 mile *60,72 km* "Mountain" circuit, over which the two main T.T. races have been run since 1911, has 264 curves and corners and is the longest used for any motorcycle race.

MOTOR RACING

EARLIEST RACES

The first automobile trial was one of 20 miles *32 km* from Paris to Versailles and back on 20 April 1887, won by Georges Bouton (1847–1938) of France in his steam quadricycle in 74 min, at an average speed of 16.22 m.p.h. *26,10 km/h.* The first "real" race was from Paris to Bordeaux and back (732 miles [*1 178 km*]) on 11–13 June 1895. The winner was Emile Levassor (d. 1897) (France) driving a Panhard-Levassor two-seater, with a 1,2 litre Daimler engine developing 3½ h.p. His time was 48 hr 47 min (average speed 15.01 m.p.h. [*24,15 km/h*]). The first closed circuit race was held at the Circuit du Sud-Ouest, Pau, France in 1900.

The oldest motor race in the world, still being regularly run, is the R.A.C. Tourist Trophy (38th race held in 1974), first staged on 14 Sept. 1905. in the Isle of Man The oldest continental race is the French Grand Prix (53rd in 1975), first held on 26–27 June 1906.

FASTEST CIRCUITS

World The highest average lap speed attained on any closed circuit is 217.854 m.p.h. *350,602 km/h* by Anthony Joseph "A. J." Foyt, Jr. (b. Houston, Texas, 16 Jan. 1935) who lapped the 2.66 mile *4,28 km*, 33-degree banked tri-oval at Alabama International Motor Speedway, Talladega, Alabama, U.S.A. in 43.956 sec, driving a 2,6 litre turbocharged Coyote Ford USAC car on 3 Aug. 1974.

The highest average race lap speed for a closed circuit is over 195 m.p.h. *313 km/h* by Richard Brickhouse

(U.S.A.) driving a 1969 Dodge Daytona Charger, powered by a 6 981 c.c. 600 b.h.p. V8 engine, during a 500 mile *804 km* race on the 2.66 mile *4,28 km*, 33-degree banked tri-oval at Alabama International Motor Speedway, Talladega, Alabama, U.S.A. on 14 Sept. 1969.

The fastest road circuit is the Francorchamps circuit near Spa, Belgium. It is 8.761 miles *14,100 km* in length and was lapped in 3 min 13.4 sec (average speed 163.086 m.p.h. [*262,461 km/h*]) on lap 7 of the Francorchamps 1000 km sports car race on 6 May 1973, by Henri Pescarolo (b. Paris, France, 25 Sept. 1942) driving a 2 993 c.c. V12 Matra-Simca MS670 Group 5 sports car. The practice lap record is 3 min 12.7 sec (average speed 163.678 m.p.h. [*263,414 km/h*]) by Jacques-Bernard "Jacky" Ickx (b. Brussels, Belgium, 1 Jan. 1945) driving a 2 998.5 c.c. flat-12 Ferrari 312P Group 5 sports car, on 4 May 1973.

United Kingdom The fastest circuit in the United Kingdom is the ex-aerodrome course of 2.927 miles *4,710 km* at Silverstone, Northamptonshire (opened 1948). The race lap record is 1 min 17.5 sec (average speed 135.964 m.p.h. [*218,812 km/h*]) by Bengt Ronald "Ronnie" Peterson (b. Orebro, Sweden, 14 Feb. 1944) driving a Formula One 2 993 c.c. Lotus 72 John Player Special-Cosworth V8 during the 25th *GKN/ Daily Express* International Trophy race on 8 April 1973. The practice lap record is 1 min 15.9 sec (138.830 m.p.h. [*223,425 km/h*]) by Albert François Cevert

The late François Cevert of France, co-holder with Jackie Stewart of the Silverstone lap record of 138.830 m.p.h. at practice

Gerry Cranham

(1944–1973) of France and John Young "Jackie" Stewart, O.B.E. (b. Milton, Dunbartonshire, 11 June 1939), both driving a Tyrrell-Cosworth V8, and Peterson in May 1973.

The lap record for the outer circuit (2.767 miles [*4,453 km*]) at the Brooklands Motor Course near Weybridge, Surrey (open between 1907 and 1939) was 1 min 9.44 sec (average speed 143.44 m.p.h. [*230,84 km/h*]) by John Rhodes Cobb (1899–1952) in his 3 ton *3,3 tonnes* 23 856 c.c. Napier-Railton, with a Napier *Lion* 12-cylinder aero-engine developing 450 b.h.p., on 7 Oct. 1935. His average speed over a km *0.6 mile* was 151.97 m.p.h. *244,57 km/h* (14.72 sec). The race lap record for the outer circuit at Brooklands was 1 min 9.6 sec (average speed 143.11 m.p.h. [*230,31 km/h*]) by Oliver Henry Julius Bertram (b. Kensington, Greater London, 26 Feb. 1910) driving a 7 963 c.c. Barnato-Hassan Special (Bentley engine), during the 7-lap "Dunlop Jubilee Cup" handicap race on 24 Sept. 1938.

The Motor Industry Research Association (MIRA) High Speed Circuit (2.82 mile [*4,53 km*] lap with 33-degree banking on the bends) at Lindley, Warwickshire, was lapped in 1 min 2.8 sec (average speed 161.655 m.p.h. [*260,158 km/h*]) by David Wishart Hobbs (b. Leamington, Warwickshire, 9 June 1939) driving a 4 994 c.c. V12 Jaguar XJ13 Group 6 prototype sports car in April 1967.

FASTEST RACES

World The fastest race in the world is the NASCAR Grand National 125 mile *201 km* event on the 2.50 mile *4,02 km*, 31-degree banked tri-oval at Daytona International Speedway, Daytona Beach, Florida, U.S.A. The record time for this race is 40 min 55 sec. (average speed 183.295 m.p.h. [*294,985 km/h*]) by William Caleb

"Cale" Yarborough (b. 27 March 1939) of Timmonsville, S. Carolina, U.S.A. driving a 1969 Mercury V8, on 19 Feb. 1970.

The fastest road race is the Francorchamps 1000 km sports car race held on the Francorchamps circuit (8.761 mile [*14,100 km*] lap) near Spa, Belgium. The record time for this 71-lap (622.055 mile [*1 001,100 km*]) race is 4 hr 1 min 9.7 sec (average speed 154.765 m.p.h. [*249,070 km/h*]) by Pedro Rodriguez (1940–1971) of Mexico and Keith Jack "Jackie" Oliver (b. Chadwell Heath, Essex, 14 Aug. 1942) driving a 4 998 c.c. flat-12 Porsche 917K Group 5 sports car, on 9 May 1971.

United Kingdom The fastest currently held race in the United Kingdom is the *Daily Express* International Trophy race. The record time for this 40-lap (117.08 mile [*188,42 km*]) race is 52 min 17.6 sec (average speed 134.334 m.p.h. [*216,190 km/h*]) by Niki Lauda (b. Vienna, Austria, 22 Feb. 1949), driving a Formula One 2 998.5 c.c. flat-12 Ferrari 312B3, at Silverstone, on 13 April 1975.

The fastest race ever held in the United Kingdom was the Broadcast Trophy Handicap held on the Brooklands outer circuit on 29 March 1937. The 29 mile *46 km* race was won by John Cobb driving his 23 970 c.c. 12-cylinder Napier-Railton at an average speed of 136.03 m.p.h. *218,91 km/h*.

TOUGHEST CIRCUITS

The Targa Florio (first run 9 May 1906) was widely acknowledged to be the most arduous race. Held on the Piccolo Madonie Circuit in Sicily, it covered eleven laps (492.126 miles [*792,000 km*]) and involved the negotiation of 9,350 corners, over severe mountain gradients, and narrow rough roads. The record time was 6 hr 27 min 48.0 sec (average speed 76.141 m.p.h. [*122,537 km/h*]) by Arturo Francesco Merzario (b.

301

Civenna, Italy, 11 March 1943) and Sandro Munari (Italy) driving a 2 995 c.c. flat-12 Ferrari 312P Group 5 sports car in the 56th race on 21 May 1972. The lap record was 33 min 36.0 sec (average speed 79.890 m.p.h. [128,570 km/h]) by Leo Juhani Kinnunen (b. Tampere, Finland, 5 Aug. 1943) on lap 11 of the 54th race on 3 May 1970 driving a 2 997 c.c. flat-8 Porsche 908/3 Spyder Group 6 prototype sports car. The race was last held on 13 May 1973.

The most difficult Grand Prix circuit is generally regarded to be that for the Monaco Grand Prix (first run on 14 April 1929), run round the streets and the harbour of Monte Carlo. It is 2.037 miles *3,278 km* in length and has eleven pronounced corners and several sharp changes of gradient. The race is run over 78 laps (158.875 miles [*255,68 km*]) and involves on average about 1,600 gear changes. The record time for the race is 1 hr 57 min 44.3 sec (average speed 80.963 m.p.h. [*130,297 km/h*]) by Jackie Stewart driving a 2 993 c.c. Tyrrell-Cosworth V8, on 3 June 1973. The race lap record is 1 min 27.9 sec (average speed 83.421 m.p.h. [*134,253 km/h*]) by Ronnie Peterson driving a 2 993 c.c. Lotus 72 John Player Special-Cosworth V8 during the race held on 26 May 1974. The practice lap record is 1 min 26.3 sec (average speed 84.967 m.p.h. [*136,742 km/h*]) by Niki Lauda driving a 2 998.5 c.c. flat-12 Ferrari 312B3 on 24 May 1974.

LE MANS

The world's most important race for sports cars is the 24 hour *Grand Prix d'Endurance* (first held on 26–27 May 1923) on the Sarthe circuit at Le Mans, France. The greatest distance ever covered is 3,315.210 miles *5 335,313 km* (average speed 138.134 m.p.h. [*222,305 km/h*]) by Dr. Helmut Marko (b. Graz, Austria, 27 April 1943) and Jonkheer Gijs van Lennep (b. Bloemendaal, Netherlands, 16 March 1942) driving a 4 907 c.c. flat-12 Porsche 917K Group 5 sports car, on 12–13 June 1971. The race lap record (8.369 mile [*13,469 km*] lap) is 3 min 18.7 sec (average speed 151.632 m.p.h. [*244,028 km/h*]) by Pedro Rodriguez (1940–1971) driving a 4 907 c.c. flat-12 Porsche 917L on 12 June 1971. The practice lap record is 3 min 13.6 sec (average speed 155.627 m.p.h. [*250,457 km/h*]) by Jackie Oliver driving a similar car on 18 April 1971. The pre-war record average speed was 86.85 m.p.h. *139,77 km/h* by a 3,3 litre Bugatti in 1939.

Most wins The race has been won by Ferrari cars nine times, in 1949, 1954, 1958 and 1960–61–62–63–64–65. The most wins by one man is four by Olivier Gendebien (b. 1924) (Belgium), who won in 1958 and 1960–61–62.

British wins The race has been won 12 times by British cars, thus: Bentley in 1924 and 1927–28–29–30, once by Lagonda in 1935, five times by Jaguar in 1951, 1953 and 1955–56–57 and once by Aston Martin in 1959.

INDIANAPOLIS 500

The Indianapolis 500 mile *804 km* race (200 laps) was inaugurated in the U.S.A. on 30 May 1911. The most successful drivers have been Warren Wilbur Shaw (1902–1954), who won in 1937, 1939 and 1940; Louis Meyer, who won in 1928, 1933 and 1936, and Anthony Joseph "A.J." Foyt, Jr., who won in 1961, 1964 and 1967. Mauri Rose won in 1947 and 1948 and was the co-driver with Floyd Davis in 1941. The record time is 3 hr 4 min 5.54 sec (average speed 162.962 m.p.h. [*262,261 km/h*]) by Mark Donohue (b. Summit, New Jersey, U.S.A., 18 March 1937) driving a 2 595 c.c. 900 b.h.p. turbocharged Sunoco McLaren M16B-Offenhauser on 27 May 1972. The record prize fund was $1,015,686.00 for the 58th race on 26 May 1974. The individual prize record is $271,697.72 by Al Unser (b. Albuquerque, New Mexico, U.S.A., 29 May 1939) on 30 May 1970. The race lap record is 47.02 sec (average speed 191.408 m.p.h. [*308,041 km/h*]) by Wally Dallenbach (b. 12 Dec. 1936) of E. Brunswick,

New Jersey, U.S.A., driving a 2,6 litre turbocharged Eagle-Offenhauser on lap 2 of the race held on 26 May 1974. The practice lap record is 45.21 sec (average speed 199.071 m.p.h. [*320,373 km/h*]) by Johnny Rutherford (b. 12 March 1938) of Fort Worth, Texas, U.S.A. driving a 2 595 c.c. 900 b.h.p. turbocharged Gulf McLaren M16B-Offenhauser on lap 3 of his 4-lap qualification run on 12 May 1973.

DRIVERS

Most successful Based on the World Drivers' Championship, inaugurated in 1950, the most successful driver is Juan-Manuel Fangio y Cia (b. Balcarce, Argentina, 24 June 1911) who won five times in 1951–54–55–56–57. He retired in 1958, after having won 24 Grand Prix races (2 shared). The most successful driver in terms of race wins is Richard Lee Petty (b. Randleman, N. Carolina, U.S.A., 2 July 1937) with 169 NASCAR Grand National wins from 1960 to April 1975.

The most Grand Prix victories is 27 by Jackie Stewart between 12 Sept. 1965 and 5 Aug. 1973. Jim Clark, O.B.E. (1936–1968) of Scotland holds the record for Grand Prix victories in one year with 7 in 1963. He won a record 61 Formula One and Formula Libre races between 1959 and 1968. The most Grand Prix starts is 176 (out of a possible 184) between 18 May 1958 and 26 Jan. 1975 by Norman Graham Hill, O.B.E. (b. Hampstead, Camden, Greater London, 15 Feb. 1929). Between 20 Nov. 1960 and 5 Oct. 1969 he took part in 90 consecutive Grands Prix.

Oldest and youngest world champions The youngest world champion was Emerson Fittipaldi (b. São Paulo, Brazil, 12 Dec. 1946) who won his first world championship on 10 Sept. 1972 aged 25 years 273 days. The oldest world champion was Juan-Manuel Fangio who won his last world championship on 18 Aug. 1957 aged 46 years 55 days.

Gerry Cranham
Graham Hill (G.B.), who between 1958 and 1975 started in 176 Grands Prix out of a possible 184.

Pollution Packer, which, powered by a hydrogen peroxide rocket, covered 440 yds standing start in 4.62 secs, passing the gate at 344.82 m.p.h.

John Roberg

Oldest and youngest G.P. winners and drivers The youngest Grand Prix winner was Bruce Leslie McLaren (1937–1970) of New Zealand, who won the United States Grand Prix at Sebring, Florida, U.S.A., on 12 Dec. 1959 aged 22 years 104 days. The oldest Grand Prix winner was Tazio Giorgio Nuvolari (1892–1953) of Italy, who won the Albi Grand Prix at Albi, France on 14 July 1946 aged 53 years 240 days. The oldest Grand Prix driver was Louis Alexandre Chiron, O. St-C., L.d'H., C.d'I (b. Monaco, 3 Aug. 1899), who finished 6th in the Monaco Grand Prix on 22 May 1955 aged 55 years 292 days. The youngest Grand Prix driver was Christopher Arthur Amon (b. Bulls, New Zealand, 20 July 1943), who took part in the Belgian Grand Prix at Spa on 9 June 1963 aged 19 years 324 days.

HILL CLIMBING

Pike's Peak race The Pike's Peak Auto Hill Climb, Colorado, U.S.A. (instituted 1916) has been won by Bobby Unser (b. Colorado Springs, Colorado, U.S.A., 20 Feb. 1934) 11 times between 1956 and 1969 (9 championship, 1 stock and 1 sports car title). On 30 June 1968, in the 46th race, he set a record time of 11 min 54.9 sec in his 5 506 c.c. Chevrolet championship car for the 12.42 mile *19,98 km* course rising from 9,402 ft to 14,110 ft *2 865–4 300 m* through 157 curves.

Most successful drivers The British National Hill Climb Championship (inaugurated in 1947) has been won six times by Anthony Ernest Marsh (b. Stourbridge, West Midlands, 20 July 1931), 1955–56–57, 1965–66–67. Raymond Mays (b. Bourne, Lincolnshire, 1 Aug. 1899) won the Shelsley Walsh hill climb, near Worcester, 19 times between 1923 and 1950.

RALLIES

Earliest The earliest long rally was promoted by the Parisian daily *Le Matin* in 1907 from Peking, China to Paris over a route of about 7,500 miles *12 000 km*. Five cars left Peking on 10 June. The winner, Prince Scipione Borghese, arrived in Paris on 10 Aug. 1907 in his 40 h.p. Itala.

Longest The world's longest ever rally was the £10,000 *Daily Mirror* World Cup Rally run over 16,243 miles *26 140 km* starting from Wembley, Brent, Greater London on 19 April 1970 to Mexico City *via* Sofia, Bulgaria and Buenos Aires, Argentina passing through 25 countries. It was won on 27 May 1970 by Hannu

Mikkola (b. Joensuu, Finland, 24 May 1942) and Gunnar Palm (b. Kristinehamn, Sweden, 25 Feb. 1937) in a 1 834 c.c. Ford Escort RS1600. The longest held annually is the East African Safari (first run 1953), run through Kenya, Tanzania and Uganda, which is up to 3,874 miles *6 234 km* long, as in the 17th Safari held between 8–12 April 1971. The smallest car to win the Monte Carlo Rally (founded 1911) was an 851 c.c. Saab driven by Erik Carlsson (b. Sweden, 1929) and Gunar Häggbom of Sweden on 25 Jan. 1962, and by Carlsson and Gunnar Palm on 24 Jan. 1963.

DRAGGING

Piston engined The lowest elapsed time recorded by a piston-engined dragster is 5.78 sec by Donald Glenn "Big Daddy" Garlits (b. 1932) of Seffner, Florida, U.S.A. driving his rear-engined AA/F dragster, powered by a 7 948 c.c. supercharged Dodge V8 engine, during the National Hot Rod Association's All Pro Supernationals at Ontario Motor Speedway, Ontario, California, U.S.A., on 25 Nov. 1973, (terminal velocity 244.56 m.p.h. *[393,56 km/h]*). He equalled this record during the American Hot Rod Association's Grand American No. 1 at Beeline Raceway, Phoenix, Arizona, U.S.A., in Feb. 1974 (terminal velocity 247.25 m.p.h. *[397,91 km/h]*). The highest terminal velocity is 250.50 m.p.h. *403,141 km/h* (elapsed time 6.13 sec) by Tommy Ivo (b. U.S. 1936) driving his rear-engined AA/F dragster powered by a 7 931 c.c. supercharged Dodge V8 engine, at Suffolk Raceway, Suffolk, Virginia in July 1975.

The world record for two runs over 440 yd *402 m* from a standing start is 134.328 m.p.h. *216,180 km/h* (6.70 sec) by Dennis Victor Priddle (b. 1945) of Yeovil, Somerset, driving his 6 424 c.c. supercharged Chrysler dragster developing 1,700 b.h.p. using nitromethane and methanol, at Elvington Airfield, North Yorkshire on 7 Oct. 1972. The faster run was made in 6.65 sec.

Rocket or jet-engined The highest terminal velocity recorded by any dragster is 377.754 m.p.h. *607,936 km/h* (elapsed time 4.65 sec) by Norman Craig Breedlove (b. 23 March 1938) of Los Angeles, Calif., U.S.A., in the rocket powered *English Leather Special* at Bonneville Salt Flats, Utah, U.S.A. in Sept. 1973. The lowest elapsed time recorded by any dragster is 4.62 sec (terminal velocity 344.82 m.p.h. *[554,934 km/h]*) by Dave Anderson of Minneapolis, Minnesota, U.S.A., in the hydrogen peroxide rocket powered *Pollution Packer* during the NHRA

303

U.S. Nationals at Indianapolis Raceway Park, Indiana, U.S.A., on 3 Sept. 1973.

Terminal velocity is the speed attained at the end of a 440 yd 402 m run made from a standing start and elapsed time is the time taken for the run.

LAND SPEED RECORDS

The highest speed ever recorded by a wheeled vehicle was achieved by Gary Gabelich (b. San Pedro, California, U.S.A., 29 Aug. 1940) at Bonneville Salt Flats, Utah, U.S.A., on 23 Oct. 1970. He drove the Reaction Dynamics *The Blue Flame*, weighing 4,950 lb. *2 245 kg* and measuring 37 ft *11 m* long, powered by a liquid natural gas–hydrogen peroxide rocket engine developing a maximum static thrust of 22,000 lb. *9 979 kg*. On his first run, at 11.23 a.m. (local time), he covered the measured km *0.6 miles* in 3.543 sec (average speed 631.367 m.p.h. [*1 016,086 km/h*]) and the mile *1,6 km* in 5.829 sec (617.602 m.p.h. [*993,934 km/h*]). On the second run, at 12.11 a.m., his times were 3.554 sec for the km *0.6 miles* (629.413 m.p.h. [*1 012,942 km/h*]) and 5.739 sec for the mile *1,6 km* (627.287 m.p.h. [*1 009,520 km/h*]). The average times for the two runs were 3.5485 sec for the km *0.6 miles* (630.388 m.p.h. [*1 014,511 km/h*]) and 5.784 sec for the mile *1,6 km* (622.407 m.p.h. [*1 001,666 km/h*]). During the attempt only 13,000 lb. *5 900 kg* s.t. was used and a peak speed of 650 m.p.h. *1 046 km/h* was momentarily attained.

The most successful land speed record breaker was Major Sir Malcolm Campbell (1885–1948) of the United Kingdom. He broke the official record nine times between 25 Sept. 1924, with 146.157 m.p.h. *235,216 km/h* in a Sunbeam, and 3 Sept. 1935, when he achieved 301.129 m.p.h. *480,620 km/h* in the Rolls-Royce engined *Bluebird*.

The world speed record for compression ignition engined cars is 190.344 m.p.h. *306,328 km/h* (average of two runs over measured mile [*1,6 km*]) by Robert Havemann of Eureka, California, U.S.A. driving his *Corsair* streamliner, powered by a turbocharged 6 981 c.c. 6-cylinder GMC 6-71 diesel engine developing 746 b.h.p., at Bonneville Salt Flats, Utah, U.S.A., in August 1971. The faster run was made at 210 m.p.h. *337 km/h*.

MISCELLANEOUS

Fastest pit stop Dick Simon (U.S.) took 7 sec to take on fuel on lap 44 of the Indianapolis 500 on 25 May 1975.

Duration record The greatest distance ever covered in one year is 400 000 km *248,548.5 miles* by François Lecot (1879–1949), an innkeeper from Rochetaillée, near Lyon, France, in a 1 900 c.c. 66 b.h.p. Citroën 11 sedan mainly between Paris and Monte Carlo, from 22 July 1935 to 26 July 1936. He drove on 363 of the 370 days allowed.

The world's duration record is 185,353 miles 1,741 yd *298 298 km* in 133 days 17 hr 37 min 38.64 sec (average speed 58.07 m.p.h. [*93,45 km/h*]) by Marchand, Presalé and six others in a Citroën on the Montlhéry track near Paris, France, during March-July 1933.

Go-kart circum-navigation The only recorded instance of a go-kart being driven round the world was a circumnavigation by Stan Mott, of New York, U.S.A., who drove a Lambretta engined 175 c.c. Italkart, with a ground clearance of 2 in *5 cm*, 23,300 land miles *37 500 km* through 28 countries from 15 Feb. 1961 to 5 June 1964, starting and finishing in New York, U.S.A.

MOUNTAINEERING

Origins Although bronze-age artifacts have been found on the summit of the Riffelhorn, Switzerland (9,605 ft [*2 927 m*]) mountaineering, as a sport, has a continuous history dating back only to 1854. Isolated instances of climbing for its own sake exist back to the 14th century. The Atacamenans built sacrificial platforms near the summit of Llullaillaco (22,058 ft [*6 723 m*]) in late pre-Columbian times *c.* 1490. The earliest recorded rock climb in the British Isles was of Stacna Biorrach, St. Kilda by Sir Robert Moray in 1698.

Mount Everest Mount Everest (29,028 ft [*8 847 m*]) was first climbed at 11.30 a.m. on 29 May 1953, when the summit was reached by Edmund Percival Hillary (born 20 July 1919), created K.B.E., of New Zealand, and the Sherpa, Tenzing Norgay (born, as Namgyal Wangdi, in Nepal in 1914, formerly called Tenzing Khumjung Bhutia), who was awarded the G.M. The successful expedition was led by Col. (later Hon. Brigadier) Henry Cecil John Hunt, C.B.E., D.S.O. (born 22 June 1910), who was created a Knight Bachelor in 1953 and a life Baron on 11 June 1966.

Greatest wall The highest final stage in any wall climb is that on the south face of Annapurna I (26,545 ft [*8 091 m*]). It was climbed by the British expedition led by Christian Bonington when from 2 Apr. to 27 May 1970, using 18,000 ft *5 500 m* of rope, Donald Whillans, 36 and Dougal Haston, 27 scaled to the summit. The longest wall climb is on the Rupal-Flanke from the base camp at 3 560 m *11,680 ft* to the South Point 8 042 m *26,384 ft* of Nanga Parbat—a vertical ascent of 4 482 m *14,704 ft*. This was scaled by the Austro-Germano-Italian Expedition led by Dr. Herrligkoffer in April 1970.

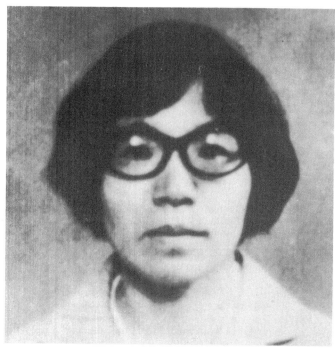

Popperfoto

Mrs. Junko Tabei, 35, mother of two, who became the 38th person and first woman to conquer Everest

Greatest Alpine Wall Europe's greatest wall is the 6,600 ft *2 000 m* North face of the Eigerwand (Ogre wall) first climbed on 20 Aug. 1932 by Hans Lauper, Alfred Zurcher, Alexander Graven and Josef Knubel. The first direct ascent was by Heinrich Harrar and Fritz Kasparek

Walter Bonatti (Italy) (*right*) being embraced after his 126 hour solo ordeal on the South West Pillar of the Dru in the Mont Blanc range

Associated Press

of Austria and Andreas Heckmair and Ludvig Vörg of Germany on 21–24 July 1938. The greatest alpine solo climb was that of Walter Bonatti (b. Bergamo, Italy, 22 June 1930) of the South West Pillar of the Dru, Montenvers now called the Bonatti Pillar with 5 bivouacs in 126 hr 7 min on 17–22 Aug. 1955.

The world's most demanding free climb is regarded as the Nabisco Wall in Yosemite, California on which two 100 foot pitches have special severity ratings of 5.10 and 5.11. It was first climbed by Jim Bridwell in 1973. Warren Harding and Dean Caldwell averaged 80 vertical feet (*24 m*) a day in their record 27 days on the wall of the Early Morning Light on Yosemite's El Capitan in November 1971.

MOUNTAIN RACING

Descent Rates It is recorded that John Ekema descended Mount Cameroun from the summit 13,350 ft *4 069 m* to Buea at 3,000 ft *914 m* in 99 min on 10 March 1973 achieving a vertical rate of 104 ft *31,8 m* per min.

In the much shorter Skiddaw Fell Race (3,053 to 250 ft [*930 to 107 m*]) a vertical descent rate of 128 ft *39 m* per min was achieved by Jeff Norman (Altrincham A.C.) in the 1972 race.

Ben Nevis The record time for the race from Fort William to the summit of Ben Nevis and return is 1 hr 29 min 38 sec by Harry Walker on 1 Sept. 1973. The feminine record is 1 hr 51 min for the ascent only, by Elizabeth Wilson-Smith on 14 Sept. 1909, and 3 hrs 2 min for the ascent and return by Kathleen Connachie, aged 16, on 3 Sept. 1965. The full course by the bridle path is about 14 miles *22 km* but distance can be saved by crossing the open hillside. The mountain was first climbed in about 1720 and the earliest race was in 1895.

The Lakeland 24-hour record is 72 peaks achieved by Joss Naylor (b. 10 Feb. 1936) of Wasdale on 22–23 June 1975. He covered 105 miles *168 km* with 40,000 ft *12 190 m* of ascents and descents in 23 hrs 11 min. Naylor has won every Ennerdale mountain race over 23 miles *37 km* since it was instituted in 1968 setting a record time of 3 hr 30 min 40 sec in 1972. The Yorkshire three peak record is 2 hr 29 min 53 sec by Jeff Norman on 28 April 1974.

The "Three Thousander" record over the 14 Welsh peaks of over 3,000 ft *914 m* is 4 hr 46 min with pacemakers by Naylor on 17 June 1973 despite misty conditions.

Three peaks record The Three Peaks run from sea level at Fort William, Inverness-shire, to sea level at Caernarvon, *via* the summits of Ben Nevis, Scafell Pike and Snowdon, was uniquely achieved by the late Eric Beard, 37 of Leeds Athletic Club, in 10 days in June 1969.

The motorised record, *under official R.A.C. or H.M. Forces observation*, sea level to sea level was set by Chris Ashton, Stuart Jackson, Alistair McDonald and John Lockwood (driver) in 16 hr 7 min 55 sec. (Car running time 9 hr 27 min 31 sec over 484.5 miles *779,7 km*.) on 21 June 1975. Thomas McClure Proudfoot, 38, holds the solo record with a time of 20 hrs 6 min (car running time 10 hr 8 min over 522 miles [*841 km*]) on 17–18 May 1975.

The Venture Scout record is 19 hr 59 min by four members of The Stourbridge District Venture Scout Unit of Stourbridge, West Midlands on 6–7 Sept. 1971.

Ten Peaks Record The Ten Peaks race is from Barnthwaite Farm, Wasdale Head, Cumbria to the top of Skiddaw *via* England's nine other highest mountains and tops: Great Gable, Sca Fell, Scafell Pike, Ill Crags, Broad Crag, Great End, Bow Fell, Helvellyn and Lower Man. The record time is 7 hr 20 min by Derek Southworth (b. 14 Mar. 1957) and Robert Neil Banks (b. 31 Dec. 1955) in a race organised by the Cumbrian Community Trust on 15 Sept. 1974.

PROGRESSIVE MOUNTAINEERING ALTITUDE RECORDS

ft	m	Mountain	Climbers	Date
9,605	2 927	Riffelhorn, Zermatt, Switzerland	—	Bronze Age
14,300	4 360	Kaoshan Pass, Hindu Kush	Alexander the Great's army	327 B.C.
12,388	3 775	Fuji, Japan	—	prior A.D. 806
17,887	5 452	Popocatépetl, Mexico	Francisco Montano	1521
18,400	5 608	Mana Pass, Zaskar Range	A. de Andrade, M. Morques	July 1624
18,096	5 515	On Chimborazo, Ecuador	Dr. A. Humboldt, Goujand (France) and C. Montufar	23 June 1802
19,411	5 916	On Leo Pargyal Range, Himalaya	Gerrard and Lloyd	1818
22,260	6 784	On E. Ibi Gamih, Garhwal Himalaya	A. & R. Schlagintweit	Aug. 1855
22,606	6 890	Pioneer Peak on Baltoro Kangri	W. M. Conway, M. Zurbriggen	23 Aug. 1892
22,834	6 959	Aconcagua, Andes	M. Zurbriggen	14 Jan. 1897
23,394	7 130	On Pyramid Peak, Karakoram	W. H. Workman, J. Petigax Snr. & Jnr., C. Savoie	12 Aug. 1903
23,787	7 250	On Gurla Mandhata, Tibet	T. G. Longstaff, A. & H. Brocherel	23 July 1905
c.23,900	c.7 285	On Kabru, Sikkim-Nepal	C. W. Rubenson and M. Aas	20 Oct. 1907
24,607	7 500	On Chogolisa, Karakoram	Duke of the Abruzzi, J. Petigax, H. &. E. Brocherel	18 July 1909
c.24,900	c.7 590	Camp V, Everest Tibet-Nepal	G. L. Mallory, E. F, Norton, T. H. Somervell, H. T. Morshead	20 May 1922
26,986	8 225	On Everest (North Face), Tibet	G. L. Mallory, E. F. Norton, T. H. Somervell	21 May 1922
c.27,300	c.8 320	On Everest (North Face), Tibet	G. I. Finch, J. G. Bruce	27 May 1922
28,125*	8 570*	On Everest (North Face), Tibet	E. F. Norton	4 June 1924
28,125*	8 570*	On Everest (North Face), Tibet	P. Wyn Harris, L. R. Wager	30 May 1933
28,125*	8 570*	On Everest (North Face), Tibet	F. S. Smythe	1 June 1933
28,215*	8 599*	South Shoulder on Everest, Nepal	R. Lambert, Tenzing Norkhay	28 May 1952
28,721	8 754	South Shoulder on Everest, Nepal	T. D. Bourdillon, R. C. Evans	26 May 1953
29,028	8 847	Everest, Nepal-Tibet	E. P. Hillary, Sherpa Tenzing Norkhay	29 May 1953

* Highest altitude attained without oxygen.

PROGRESSIVE LIST OF HIGHEST SUMMITS CLIMBED

The progressive list of highest summits climbed after Aconcagua in 1897 is as follows:

ft	m		Climbers	Date
23,360	7 120	Trusil, Garhwal Himalaya	T. G. Longstaff, A. & H. Brocherel, Karbir	12 June 1907
23,385*	7 127	Pauhunri, Sikkim Himalaya	A. M. Kellas, Sonam and another porter	16 June 1911
23,383	7 127	Pik Lenin, Trans-Alai Pamir	E. Allwein, K. Wien, E. Schneider	25 Sept. 1928
23,442	7 145	Nepal Peak, Sikkim-Nepal	E. Schneider	24 May 1930
23,344	7 417	Jongsong Peak, Nepal-Sikkim-Tibet	E. Schneider, H. Hoerlin	3 June 1930
25,447	7 756	Kamet, Garhwal Himalaya	F. S. Smythe, R. L. Holdsworth, E. E. Shipton, Lewa	21 June 1931
25,645	7 816	Nanda Devi, Garhwal Himalaya	N. E. Odell, H. W. Tilman	29 Aug. 1936
26,492	8 047	Annapurna I, Nepal	M. Herzog, L. Lachenal	3 June 1950
29,028	8 847	Mount Everest, Nepal-Tibet	E. P. Hillary, Tenzing Norgay	29 May 1953

(For subsequent ascents of Mount Everest, see above)

* Survey of India height now listed as 23,180 ft 7 065 m.

SUBSEQUENT ASCENTS OF MOUNT EVEREST BY ANOTHER 37 CLIMBERS

Climbers	Date	Climbers	Date
Ernst Schmidt, Jürg Marmet (Swiss)	23 May 1956	Capt. H. P. S. Ahluwalia, H. C. S. Rawat (India), Phu Dorji	29 May 1965
Hans Rudolf von Gunten, Adolf Reist (Swiss)	24 May 1956	Nomi Uemura, Tero Matsuura (Japan)	11 May 1970
*Wang Fu-chou, Chu Yin-hau (China), Konbu (Tibet)	25 May 1960	Katsutoshi Harabayashi (Japan), Sherpa Chotari	12 May 1970
James Warren Whittaker (U.S.), Sherpa Nawang Gombu	1 May 1963	Sgt. Mirko Minuzzo, Sgt. Rinaldo Carrel (Italy) with Lapka Tenzing and Sambu Tamang	5 May 1973
Barry C. Bishop (U.S.), Luther G. Jerstad (U.S.)	22 May 1963		
Dr. William F. Unsoeld (U.S.), Dr. Thomas F. Hornbein (U.S.)	22 May 1963	Capt. Fabrizio Innamorati, W. O. Virginio Epis and Sgt. Maj. Claudio Benedetti (Italy) with Sonam Gallien (Nepal)	7 May 1973
Capt. A. S. Cheema (India), Sherpa Nawang Gombu	20 May 1965	Hisashi Ishiguro, Yasuo Kato (Japan)	26 Oct. 1973
Sonam Gyaltso, Sonam Wangyal (India)	22 May 1965	Mrs. Junko Tabei, Ang Tserang	16 May 1975
C. P. Vohra (India), Sherpa Ang Kami	24 May 1965		

*Not internationally accepted as authentic.

Pennine Way The record for traversing the 271 mile *436 km* long Pennine Way is 3 days 4 hr 36 min by Joss Naylor (see above) on 22–25 June 1974.

Fell running Bill Teasdale, M.B.E., won the Guides' Race at the Grasmere Sports, Cumbria, for the eleventh time in 1966. It involves running to a turning point on Butter Crag (966 ft [*294 m*] above sea level) and back, a distance of about 1½ miles *2,4 km*. His time of 13 min 5.0 sec in 1965 constitutes the record time.

Greatest fall The greatest recorded fall survived by a mountaineer was when Christopher Timms (Christchurch University) slid 7,500 ft *2 300 m* down an ice face into a crevasse on Mt. Elie de Beaumont (10,200 ft [*3 100 m*]), New Zealand on 7 Dec. 1966. His companion was killed but he survived with concussion, bruises and a hand injury.

NETBALL

Origins The game was invented in the U.S.A. in 1891 and introduced into England in 1895 by Dr. Toles. The All England Women's Netball Association was formed in 1926. The oldest club in continuous existence, is the Polytechnic Netball Club of London founded in 1907.

World title World championships were inaugurated in August 1963 at Eastbourne, East Sussex and were won by Australia. The 1971 world championships at Kingston, Jamaica were also won by Australia. The record number of goals in the World Tournament is 402 by Mrs. Judith Heath (England) (b. 1942) in 1971.

Highest scores England has never been beaten in a home international. England's record score is 94 goals to 12 v. Wales in 1970 and 94 goals to 13 v. Northern Ireland in Jamaica in January 1971. The highest international score recorded was when New Zealand beat Northern Ireland 112–4 at Eastbourne, East Sussex on 2 Aug. 1963.

National Championships The National Championships (inst. 1968) have been won most often by Sudbury Netball Club with five titles (1968–70, 1971 (shared) and 1973).

County Titles Surrey have won the County Championships consecutively a record 18 times between 1948 and 1965.

Marathon An outdoor marathon netball match lasting 61 hr was played by 6 teams of 7 girls of the Napier Netball Association, New Zealand on 4–6 July 1975. An indoor marathon of 58 hr was sustained by 6 teams of 7 girls from Thornhill School, Sunderland, Tyne and Wear on 8–10 February 1975.

Most internationals The record number of internationals is 50 by Anne Miles (b. 9 April 1942) of England to 1974.

OLYMPIC GAMES

Note: These records now include the un-numbered Games held at Athens in 1906, which some authorities ignore. Although inserted between the regular III Games in 1904 and the IV Games in 1908, the 1906 Games, though unnumbered, were officially run by the International Olympic Committee and were of a higher standard than all three of those that preceded them.

Origins The earliest celebration of the ancient Olympic Games of which there is a certain record is that of July 776 B.C., when Koroibos, a cook from Elis, won a foot race, though their origin dates from *c.* 1370 B.C. The ancient Games were terminated by an order issued in Milan in A.D. 393 by Theodosius I, "the Great" (*c.* 346–395), Emperor of Rome. At the instigation of Pierre de Fredi, Baron de Coubertin (1863–1937), the Olympic Games of the modern era were inaugurated in Athens on 6 April 1896.

Largest crowd The largest crowd at any Olympic site was 150,000 at the 1952 ski-jumping at the Holmenkollen, outside Oslo, Norway. Estimates of the number of spectators of the marathon race through Tōkyō, Japan on 21 Oct. 1964 have ranged from 500,000 to 1,500,000.

MOST MEDALS

Individual gold In the ancient Olympic Games victors were given a chaplet of olive leaves. Milo (Milon of Krotōn) won 6 titles at *palaisma* (wrestling) 540–516 B.C. The most individual gold medals won by a male competitor in the modern Games is 10 by Raymond Clarence Ewry (U.S.A.) (b. 14 Oct. 1874 at Lafayette, Indiana d. 29 Sept. 1937) (see Track and Field Athletics). The female record is seven by Vera Caslavska-Odlozil (b. 3 May 1942) (see Gymnastics). The most won by a British competitor is four by Paul Radmilovic (1886–1968) in Water Polo in 1908, 1912 and 1920 and in the 800 m team swimming event in 1908. The Australian swimmer Ian Murray Rose, who won 4 gold medals, was born in Birmingham, England on 6 Jan. 1939. The sculler and oarsman Jack Beresford, C.B.E. (b. 1 Jan. 1899) won the three gold and two silver medals in the five Olympics from 1920 to 1936.

National The total figures for most medals and most gold medals for all Olympic events (including those now discontinued) for the summer (1896–1972) and Winter Games (1924–1972) and for the Art Competitions (1912–1948) are:

	Gold	Silver	Bronze	Total
1. U.S.A.	621*	473½	408½	1,503
2. U.S.S.R. (formerly Russia)	249*	208	201	658
3. G.B. (including Ireland to 1920)	161½	197½	173	532

* The A.A.U. (U.S.) reinstated James F. Thorpe (1888–1953) the disqualified highest scorer in the 1912 decathlon and pentathlon events on 12 Oct. 1973 but no issue of medals has yet been authorised by the I.O.C.

Oldest and youngest gold medallists The oldest recorded winner is Sir Eyre Massey Shaw, K.C.B. (G.B.) (1830–1908) who was over 70 and an amputee when he won the 2–3 ton class in the 1900 Yachting regatta on 25 May 1900 in *Ollé*. The youngest ever winner was a French boy (whose name is not recorded) who coxed the Netherlands pair in 1900. He was not more than 10 and may have been as young as 7. He substituted for Dr. Hermanus Brockmann, who coxed in the heats but proved too heavy.

The youngest-ever female gold medal winner is Miss Marjorie Gestring (U.S.A.) (b. 18 Nov. 1922, now Mrs. Bowman), aged 13 yr 9 months, in the 1936 women's springboard event.

Longest span The longest span of an Olympic competitor is 40 years by Dr. Ivan Osiier (Denmark), who competed as a fencer in 1908, 1912 (silver medal) 1920, 1924, 1928, 1932 and 1948, totalling seven celebrations. He refused to compete in the 1936 Games on the grounds that

Mary Evans

The one-legged Captain Sir Eyre Massey Shaw, who won an Olympic gold medal in 1900 after his 70th birthday

they were Nazi-dominated. The longest feminine span is 24 years (1932–1956) by the Austrian fencer Ellen Müller-Preiss. Janice Lee York Romary, the U.S. fencer, competed in all 6 Games from 1948 to 1968, and Lia Manoliu (Romania) competed from 1952 to 1972 winning the discus title in 1968. The longest span of any British competitor is 28 years by Enoch Jenkins who appeared in the 1924 and the 1952 Games in the clay pigeon shooting event, and by Mrs. Dorothy J. B. Tyler (*née* Odam), who high-jumped in 1936–48–52 and 56. The only Olympian to win 4 consecutive individual titles has been Alfred A. Oerter (b. 19 Sept. 1936, Astoria, N.Y.) of the U.S.A., who won the discus title in 1956–60–64–68.

Most Countries and participants The greatest number of competitors in any summer Olympic Games up to 1972 has been 7,147 (including 1,070 women) from a record 122 countries at Munich in 1972. The fewest was 285 competitors from 12 countries in 1896. In 1904 only 11 countries participated.

Ever present Five countries have never failed to be represented at the 21 Celebrations of the Games: Australia, Greece, Great Britain, Switzerland and the United States of America.

Largest team France entered 880 men and 4 women in the 1900 Games at Paris.

Modern celebrations have been voted for by the International Olympic Committee as follows. Dates indicate the span of Olympic competitions (excluding elimination contests). The first date is not necessarily that of the opening ceremony.

I	1896	Athens	6–15 April
II	1900	Paris	20 May–28 Oct.
III	1904	St. Louis	1 July–23 Nov.
*	1906	Athens	22 April–2 May
IV	1908	London	27 April–31 Oct.
V	1912	Stockholm	5 May–22 July
VI	1916	Berlin	not celebrated owing to war

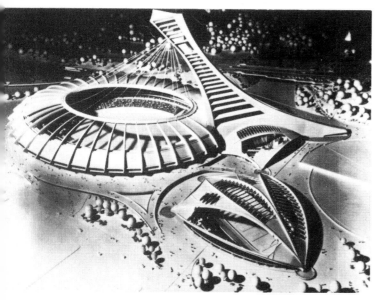

An artist's impression of the Olympic Stadium, Montreal, where the XXIst Games are due to open on 17 July 1976 (see book end papers for the Evolution of Olympic Records)

Mary Evans

The Averoff Stadium, Athens, where the Olympic Games were revived in 1896 after a lapse of more than 15 centuries

VII	1920	Antwerp	20 April–12 Sept.
VIII	1924	Paris	4 May–27 July
IX	1928	Amsterdam	17 May–12 Aug.
X	1932	Los Angeles	30 July–14 Aug.
XI	1936	Berlin	1–16 Aug.
XII	1940	Tokyo, then Helsinki	not celebrated owing to war
XIII	1944	London	not celebrated owing to war
XIV	1948	London	29 July–14 Aug.
XV	1952	Helsinki	19 July–3 Aug.
XVI	1956	Melbourne[1]	22 Nov.–8 Dec.
XVII	1960	Rome	25 Aug.–11 Sept.
XVIII	1964	Tokyo	10–24 Oct.
XIX	1968	Mexico	12–27 Oct.
XX	1972	Munich	26 Aug.–10 Sept.
XXI	1976	Montreal	17 July–1 Aug.
XXII	1980	Moscow	dates to be announced

* This celebration (to mark the 10th anniversary of the modern Games) was officially intercalated but is not numbered.
[1] The equestrian events were held in Stockholm 10–17 June 1956.

Separate Winter Olympics (there had been ice skating events in 1908 and 1920 and ice hockey in 1920) were inaugurated in 1924 and have been voted for as follows:

I	1924	Chamonix, France	25 Jan.–4 Feb.
II	1928	St. Moritz, Switzerland	11–19 Feb.
III	1932	Lake Placid, U.S.A.	4–15 Feb.
IV	1936	Garmisch-Partenkirchen, Germany	6–16 Feb.
V	1948	St. Moritz, Switzerland	30 Jan.–8 Feb.
VI	1952	Oslo, Norway	14–25 Feb.
VII	1956	Cortina d'Ampezzo, Italy	26 Jan.–5 Feb.
VIII	1960	Squaw Valley, California	18–28 Feb.
IX	1964	Innsbruck, Austria	29 Jan.–9 Feb.
X	1968	Grenoble, France	6–18 Feb.
XI	1972	Sapporo, Japan	3–13 Feb.
XII	1976	Innsbruck, Austria	4–15 Feb.

The first Winter Games in 1924 attracted 293 competitors from 16 nations.

ORIENTEERING

Origins Orienteering was invented by Major Ernst Killander in Sweden in 1918. World championships were inaugurated in 1966 and are held biennially. Annual British championships were instituted in 1967.

Most titles Sweden won the world men's relay titles in 1966–68–
World 72–74 and the women's relay in 1966–70–74 with Ulla Lindkvist (Sweden) winning the individual titles in both 1966 and 1968.

Britain The most successful British team has been Edinburgh Southern Orienteering Club which won the Senior Men's title in 1969 and 1970 and the Senior Ladies' title in 1970. Gordon Pirie won the men's individual title in 1967–68, Michael Wells-Cole in 1969–70 and Geoffrey Peck 1971–73. Carol McNeill won the women's title in 1967, 1969 and 1972.

Geoffrey Peck, twice British orienteering champion, in action

The Orienteer

308

PARACHUTING

Parachuting Origins Parachuting graduated from pure life saving, through stunt exhibitions to a regulated sport with the Institution of world championships at Lesce-Bled, Yugoslavia in 1951. A team title was introduced at the second Championships at Saint Yan, France in 1954 and women's events were included at the third Championships near Moscow, U.S.S.R. in 1956.

World Titles The U.S.S.R. won the men's team titles in 1954–58 60–66–72 and the women's team title in 1956–58–66–68–72. No individual has ever won a second world overall title.

Accuracy Records Kumbar (Czechoslovakia) scored nine consecutive dead centre strikes (10 cm disc) in the 11th World Championships at Tahlequah, U.S.A. in 1972.

British Mr. John Meacock (Peterborough) has thrice won the British title (1969–71–72).

Most Jumps The greatest number of jumps completed is 232 in 24 hr by Jean-Pierre Blanchet at St. Jean Chrysostome Airport, Quebec, Canada on 9–10 Sept. 1972.

The National Enquirer Free Fall team set a record for the world's largest human "star" over Florida, U.S.A.

National Enquirer

PELOTA VASCA (JAI ALAI)

Origins The game, which originated in Italy as *longue paume* and was introduced into France in the 13th century, is said to be the fastest of all ball games with speeds of up to 160 m.p.h. *257,5 km/h*. Gloves were introduced *c.* 1840 and the *chisterak* was invented *c.* 1860 by Gantchiki Dithurbide of Sainte Pée. The long *chistera* was invented by Melchior Curuchage of Buenos Aires, Argentina in 1888. The world's largest *fronton* (the playing court) is that built (opened July 1973) for $12,000,000 (now *£5.2 million*) at Macau, China with a seating capacity of 4,000 and a floor area of 34,000 m² *365,970 ft²*.

Longest Domination The longest domination as the world's No. 1 player was enjoyed by Chiquito de Cambo (*né* Joseph Apesteguy) (France), (1881–1955) from the beginning of the century until succeeded in 1938 by Jean Urruty (France) (b. 19 Oct. 1913).

Games played in a *fronton* are *Frontenis*, *pelote* and *paleta* with both leather and rubber balls. The sport is governed by the International Federation of Basque Pelote.

PIGEON RACING

Earliest references Pigeon Racing was the natural development of the use of homing pigeons for the carrying of messages—a quality utilized in the ancient Olympic Games (776 B.C.–A.D. 393). The sport originated in Belgium and came to Britain *c.* 1820. The earliest major long-distance race was from Crystal Palace, Bromley, Greater London, in 1871. The earliest recorded occasion on which 500 miles *800 km* was flown in a day was by "Motor" (owned by G. P. Pointer of

Alexander Park Racing Club) which was released from Thurso, Scotland, on 30 June 1896 and covered 501 miles *806 km* at an average speed of 1,454 yds *1 329 m* per min (49½ m.p.h. [*79,6 km/h*]).

Longest flights The greatest recorded homing flight by a pigeon was made by one owned by the 1st Duke of Wellington (1769–1852). Released from a sailing ship off the Ichabo Islands, West Africa, on 8 April, it dropped dead a mile from its loft at Nine Elms, Wandsworth, Greater London on 1 June 1845, 55 days later, having flown an airline route of 5,400 miles *8 700 km*, but an actual distance of possibly 7,000 miles *11 250 km* to avoid the Sahara Desert. It was reported on 27 Nov. 1971 that an exhausted pigeon bearing a Hanover label was found 10,000 miles *16 100 km* away at Cunnamulla, Queensland, Australia. The official British duration record (into Great Britain) is 1,141 miles *1 836 km* by A. Bruce's bird in the 1960 Barcelona Race which was liberated on 9 July and homed at Fraserburgh, Aberdeenshire, Scotland on 5 Aug.

Highest speeds In level flight in windless conditions it is very doubtful if any pigeon can exceed 60 m.p.h. *96 km/h*. The highest race speed recorded is one of 3,229 yds *2 952 m* per min (110.07 m.p.h. [*177,14 km/h*]) in the East Anglian Federation race from East Croydon on 8 May 1965 when the 1,428 birds were backed by a powerful south south-west wind. The winner was A. Vidgeon & Son.

The highest race speed recorded over a distance of more than 1 000 km *621.37 miles* is 2,432.70 yds *2 224,45 m* per min (82.93 m.p.h. [*133,46 km/h*]) by a hen pigeon in the Central Cumberland Combine race over 683 miles 147 yds *1 099,316 km* from Murray Bridge, South Australia to North Ryde, Sydney on 2 Oct. 1971. The world's longest reputed distance in 24 hrs is 803 miles *1 292 km* (velocity 1,525 yds [*1 394 m*] per min) by E. S. Peterson's winner of the 1941 San Antonio R.C. event Texas, U.S.A.

The best 24-hour performance into the United Kingdom is 686 miles *1 104 km* by A. R. Hill's winner of the 1952 race from Hanover, Germany to St. Just, Cornwall—average speed 1,300 yds *1 188 m* per min (44.31 m.p.h. [*71,31 km/h*]).

Lowest speed A pigeon *Blue Clip*, belonging to Harold Hart released in Renres, France arrived home in its loft in Leigh, Greater Manchester, on 29 Sept. 1974, 7 years and 2 months later. It had covered the distance of 370 miles *595 km* at an average speed of 0.00589 m.p.h. *0,00948 km/h* which is slower than the world's fastest snail (see page 46).

Highest Priced Bird The highest recorded price paid for a pigeon is £6,000 paid by Mr. Louis Massarella of Leicester on 29 March 1975 for the 12 year old *Motta*.

POLO

Earliest games Polo is usually regarded as being of Persian origin having been played as *Pula c.* 525 B.C. Other claims have come from Tibet and the Tang Dynasty of China A.D. 250 The earliest polo club of modern times was the Kachar Club (founded in 1859) in Assam, India. The game was introduced into England from India in 1869 by the 10th Hussars at Aldershot, Hampshire and the earliest match was one between the 9th Lancers and the 10th Hussars on Hounslow Heath, Greater London, in July 1871. The first all-Ireland Cup match was at Phoenix Park, Dublin, in 1878. The earliest international match between England and the U.S.A. was in 1886.

The game is played on the largest pitch of any ball game in the world. A ground measures 300 yd *274 m* long by 160 yd *146 m* wide with side boards, or 200 yd *182 m* wide without boards.

Highest handicap The highest handicap based on eight 7½-min "chukkas" is 10 goals introduced in the U.S.A. in 1891 and in the United Kingdom and in Argentina in 1910. The most recent additions to the select ranks of the 38 players ever to receive 10-goal handicaps are A. Heguy and A. Harriot of Argentina. The last (of six) 10-goal handicap players from Great Britain was G. Balding in 1939.

The highest handicap of any of the United Kingdom's 400 players is 8, by Julian Hipwood.

Highest score The highest aggregate number of goals scored in an international match is 30, when Argentina beat the U.S.A. 21–9 at Meadow Brook, Long Island, New York, U.S.A., in September 1936.

Most Olympic Medals Polo has been part of the Olympic programme on five occasions: 1900, 1908, 1920, 1924 and 1936. Of the 21 gold medallists, a 1920 winner, the Rt. Hon. Sir John Wodehouse, Bt., C.B.E., M.C., the 3rd Earl of Kimberly (b. 1883–k. 1941) uniquely also won a silver medal (1908).

Most internationals The greatest number of times any player has represented England is four in the case of Frederick M. Freake in 1900, 1902, 1909 and 1913. Thomas Hitchcock, Jr. (1900–44) played five times for the U.S.A. v. England (1921–24–27–30–39) and twice v. Argentina (1928–36).

Most expensive pony The highest price ever paid for a polo pony was $22,000 (now £7,857), paid by Stephen Sanford for Lewis Lacey's *Jupiter* after the U.S.A. v. Argentina international in 1928.

Largest trophy The world's largest trophy for a particular sport is the Bangalore Limited Handicap Polo Tournament Trophy. This massive cup standing on its plinth is 6 ft *1,83 m* tall and was presented in 1936 by the Raja of Kolanka.

Largest crowd World record crowds of more than 50,000 have watched floodlight matches at the Sydney Agricultural Show, Australia.

F. M. Freake, 4 times England international (1900–1913), alongside Lord Kimberly, gold and silver Olympic medal winner

POWER BOAT RACING

Origins The earliest application of the petrol engine to a boat was Gottlieb Daimler's experimental power boat on the River Seine, Paris, France, in 1887. The sport was given impetus by the presentation of an international championship cup by Sir Alfred Harmsworth in 1903, which was also the year of the first off-shore race from Calais to Dover.

Harmsworth Cup Of the 25 contests from 1903 to 1961, the United States has won 16, the United Kingdom 5, Canada 3 and France 1.

The greatest number of wins has been achieved by Commodore Garfield A. Wood (1881–1971) with eight (1920–21, 1926, 1928–29–30, 1932–33). The only

Aeromarine II driven by Sonny Kay averaging 93.1 m.p.h. *149,8 km/h* over the 63 mile *101,3 km* Lake Erie course in Ohio, U.S.A.

boat to win three times is *Miss Supertest III*, owned by James G. Thompson (Canada), in 1959–60–61. This boat also achieved the record speed of 115.972 m.p.h. *186,638 km/h* at Picton, Ontario, Canada in 1960.

Gold Cup The Gold Cup (instituted 1903) has been won five times by Bill Muncey (1956–57, 1961–62–72). The record speed is 120.356 m.p.h. *193,694 km/h* for a 3 mile *4,8 km* lap by Rolls-Royce-engined *Miss Exide*, owned by Milo Stoen, driven by Bill Brow at Seattle, Washington, U.S.A. on 4 Aug. 1965.

Highest speeds The highest speed attained is 93.1 m.p.h. *149,8 km/h* by Sonny Kay (U.S.) in his 36 ft *10,97 m Aeromarine II* powered by two 7,699 c.c. *600 h.p.* Kiekhaefer Aeromarine engines. This speed was recorded over the 63 statute miles *101,3 km* of the Cleveland Yachting Club's Fire cracker 50 race on Lake Erie, Ohio, U.S.A. on 30 June 1973. In the 1973 Tropheo Baleares race at Palma di Mallorca, Spain on 27 May 1973 a fastest British speed was set by Colonel Ronald Hoare of England, who recorded 80.9 m.p.h. *130,2 km/h* in his Don Shead designed, Aeromarine engined, *Unohoo*. The highest average race speed off British shores has been 71 m.p.h. *114 km/h* by Thomas Edward Brodie Sopwith (b. 1933) driving *Enfield Avenger* in the *Daily Telegraph/B.P.* International Off-Shore Race on 4 Sept. 1971 on the Solent-Bournemouth-Needles-Southsea (via South coast of Isle of Wight) route in 2 hr 35 min. The Countess of Arran drove her off-shore powerboat *Highland Fling* for a world's record of 85.63 m.p.h. *137,80 km/h* despite fuel trouble on the back-up run on Windermere on 21 Oct. 1971.

Longest races The longest race has been the Port Richborough London to Monte Carlo Marathon Off-Shore International event. The race extended over 2,947 miles *4 742 km* in 14 stages on 10–25 June 1972. It was won by H.T.S. (G.B.) driven by Mike Bellamy, Eddie Chater and Jim Brooks in 71 hrs 35 min 56 sec (average 41.15 m.p.h. [*66,24 km/h*]). The *Daily Telegraph and B.P.* Round Britain event was inaugurated on 26 July 1969 at Portsmouth with 1,403 miles *2 257 km* in 10 stages west—about England, Wales and across Northern Scotland *via* the Caledonian Canal. The 1969 race (26 July to 7 Aug.) was won by *Avenger Too* (Timo Makinen, Alan Pascoe Watson and Brian Hendicott) in 39 hrs 9 min 37.7 sec. Of the 42 starters, 24 finished.

Cowes-Torquay race The record average for the *Daily Express* International Off-Shore Race (instituted 1961) is 66.47 m.p.h. *106,97 km/h* by The Cigarette (Don Aronow) over the 236 mile *379 km* course from Cowes, Isle of Wight to Torquay, Devon and back in 3 hrs 33 min on 30 Aug. 1969. The only 3 time winner has been Tommy Sopwith in 1961, 1968 and 1970.

Dragsters The first drag boat to attain 200 m.p.h. *321 km/h* was Sam Kurtovich's *Crisis* which attained 200.44 m.p.h. *322,57 km/h* in California in Oct. 1969 at the end of a one-way run. *Climax* has since been reported to have attained 205.19 m.p.h. *330,22 km/h*.

Longest journey The Dane Hans Tholstrup, 25, circumnavigated Australia in a 17 ft Caribbean Cougar fibreglass runabout with a single 80 h.p. Mercury outboard motor from 11 May to 25 July 1971.

Longest Jump The longest jump achieved by a power boat has been 110 ft *32,5 m* by Jerry Comeaux, 29 in a Glastron GT-150 with a 135 h.p. Evinrude Starflite on an isolated waterway in Louisiana, U.S.A. in mid-Oct. 1972. The take off speed was 56 m.p.h. *90 km/h*. The jump was required for a sequence in the eighth Bond film *Live and Let Die*.

RACKETS

Origins There is record of the sale of a Racket Court at Southernhay, Exeter, Devon dated 12 Jan. 1798.

Earliest world champion The first world rackets champion was Robert Mackay, who claimed the title in London in 1820. The first closed court champion was Francis Erwood at Woolwich in 1860. The first new court built in Great Britain since 1914 was the Second Court opened at Harrow School in 1965.

Longest reign Of the 19 world champions since 1820 the longest reign is held by British-born U.S. resident Geoffrey W. T. Atkins (b. 1922) who has held the title since beating the professional James Dear in 1954 and retired after a fourth successful defence of it in April 1970.

Most Amateur titles Since the Amateur singles championship was instituted in 1888 the most titles won by an individual is nine by Edgar M. Baerlein (1879–1971) between 1903 and 1923. Since the institution of the Amateur doubles championship in 1890 the most shares in titles has been eleven by David Sumner Milford (b. 7 June 1905), between 1938 and 1959 and John R. Thompson between 1948 and 1966. Milford has also seven Amateur singles titles (1930–52), an open title (1936) and held the world title from 1937 to 1946. Thompson has additionally won an open singles title and 5 Amateur singles titles.

RODEO

Origins Rodeo came into being with the early days of the North American cattle industry. The earliest references to the sport are from Santa Fe, New Mexico, U.S.A., in 1847. Steer wrestling came in with Bill Pickett (Oklahoma) in 1903. The other events are calf roping, bull riding, saddle and bareback bronc riding.

The largest rodeo in the world is the Calgary Exhibition and Stampede at Calgary, Alberta, Canada. The record attendance has been 993,777 on 5–14 July 1973. The record for one day is 141,670 on 13 July 1974.

Most world titles The record number of all-round titles is six by Larry Mahan (U.S.A.) (b. 21 Nov. 1943) in 1966–67–68–69–70–73. The record figure for prize money in a single season is $66,929 (£29,099) by Tom Ferguson, the 1974 all round champion from Miami, Oklahoma, U.S.A.

Time records Records for timed events, such as calf-roping and steer-wrestling, are meaningless, because of the widely varying conditions due to the size of arenas and amount of start given the stock. The fastest time recorded for roping a calf is 7.5 sec by Junior Garrison of Marlow, Oklahoma, at Evergreen, Colorado, U.S.A. in 1967, and the fastest time for overcoming a steer was 2.4 sec by James Bynum of Waxahachie, Texas, at Marietta, Oklahoma, in 1955.

The standard required time to stay on in bareback, saddle bronc and bull riding events is 8 sec. In the now obsolete ride-to-a-finish events, rodeo riders have been recorded to have survived 90+ min, until the mount had not a buck left in it.

Champion bull The top bucking bull is *Tiger* a 7 year old 1,400 lb. *635 kg* brindle coloured cross-bred bull with horns owned by the Cervi Championship Rodeo Co. of Sterling, Colorado. He is seldom ridden but in 1974 Don Gay scored 94 points on him. The bull is notorious for "hooking" fallen cowboys.

Champion bronc Currently the greatest bronc is *Checkmate* a 10 year old stout animal weighing 1,200 lb. *544 kg*. He belongs to Christensen Bros. Rodeo Co., Eugene, Oregon, U.S.A. and during the 1974 season he threw 18 out of 24 of his riders including the 1974 world champion saddle bronc rider, John McBeth. He was voted "Bucking Horse of the Year" in 1974. Traditionally a bronc called *Midnight* owned by Jim McNab of Alberta, Canada was never ridden in 12 appearances at the Calgary Stampede.

ROLLER SKATING

Origins The first roller skate was devised by Joseph Merlin of Huy, Belgium, in 1760. Several "improved" versions appeared during the next century, but a really satisfactory roller skate did not materialize before 1866, when James L. Plimpton of New York produced the present four-wheeled type, patented it, and opened the first public rink in the world at Newport, Rhode Island, that year. The great boom periods were 1870–75, 1908–12 and 1948–54, each originating in the United States.

Largest rink The greatest indoor rink ever to operate was located in the Grand Hall, Olympia, Hammersmith, Greater London. It had an actual skating area of 68,000 ft² *6 300 m²*. It first opened in 1890, for one season, then again from 1909 to 1912.

Roller hockey Roller hockey (previously known as Rink Hockey in Europe) was first introduced in this country as Rink Polo, at the old Lava rink, Denmark Hill, Southwark/Lambeth, Greater London in the late 1870s. The Amateur Rink Hockey Association was formed in 1905, and in 1913 became the National Rink Hockey (now Roller Hockey) Association. Britain won the inaugural World Championship in 1936 since when Portugal has won most titles with 11 between 1947 and 1973.

Most titles Most world speed titles have been won by Miss A. Vianello (Italy) with 16 between 1953 and 1965. Most world pair titles have been taken by Dieter Fingerle (W. Germany) with four in 1959–65–66–67. The records for figure titles are 5 by Karl Heinz Losch in 1958–59–61–62–66 and 4 by Astrid Bader, also of West Germany, in 1965 to 1968. Leslie E. Woodley of Birmingham won 12 British national individual titles over the three regulation distances (880 yds [*804 m*], one mile [*1,6 km*] and five miles [*8 km*]) between 1957 and 1964. Chloe Ronaldson of London won 29 ladies' titles over 440 yds *800 m*, 880 yds *1 000 m* and 5,000 m in 1958–75.

Records The fastest speed put up in an official world record is 25.78 m.p.h. *41,48 km/h* when Giuseppe Cantarella (Italy) recorded 34.9 sec for 440 yds *402 m* on a road at Catania, Sicily on 28 Sept. 1963. The world mile record on a rink is 2 min 25.1 sec by Gianni Ferretti (Italy). The greatest distance skated in one hour on a rink by a woman is 20 miles 1,355 yds *33,407 km* by C. Patricia Barnett (G.B.) at Brixton, Lambeth,

Greater London on 24 June 1962. The men's record on a closed road circuit is 35,831 km *22 miles 465 yd* by Alberto Civolani (Italy) at Bologna, Italy on 15 Oct. 1967.

Marathon The longest recorded continuous roller skating mara-
record thon was one of 178 hours performed by Tammy Wilson and John Fowler at Skatehaven, Montgomery, Alabama, U.S.A., on 11–19 March 1975. The longest reported skate was by Clinton Shaw from Victoria, British Columbia to St. John's, Newfoundland (4,900 miles [*7 900 km*]) on the Trans-Canadian Highway *via* Montreal from 1 April to 11 Nov. 1967. On 20 July 1974 at Santa Monica, California he completed a coast to coast 3,100 miles *4 988 km* skate having started at New York on 4 May. His longest stint in a day was 106 miles *170 km* from Clines Corners to Laguna, New Mexico, U.S.A.

Clinton Shaw, who roller-skated 4,920 miles *7 900 km* across Canada from British Columbia to Newfoundland in 225 days

Jim England

ROWING

Oldest The earliest established sculling race is the Doggett's
race Coat and Badge, which was rowed on 1 Aug. 1716 over 5 miles *8 km* from London Bridge to Chelsea and is still being rowed every year over the same course, under the administration of the Fishmongers' Company. The first English regatta probably took place on the Thames by the Ranelagh Gardens, near Putney in 1775. Boating began at Eton in 1793, 72 years before the "song". The Leander Club was formed *c*. 1818.

OLYMPIC GAMES

Olympic Since 1900 there have been 105 Olympic finals of which
medals the U.S.A. have won 26, Germany (now West
most Germany) 15 and Great Britain 14.

Four oarsmen have won 3 gold medals: John B. Kelly (U.S.A.) (1889–1960), father of H.S.H. Princess Grace of Monaco, in the sculls (1920) and double sculls (1920 and 1924); his cousin Paul V. Costello (U.S.A.) (b. 27 Dec. 1899) in the double sculls (1920, 1924 and 1928); Jack Beresford, Jr., C.B.E. (G.B.) (b. 1 Jan. 1899) in the sculls (1924), coxless fours (1932) and double sculls (1936) and Vyacheslav Ivanov (U.S.S.R. (b. 30 July 1938) in the sculls (1956, 1960 and 1964).

BOAT RACE
The earliest University Boat Race, which Oxford won, was from Hambledon Lock to Henley Bridge on 10 June 1829. In the 120 races to 1975, Cambridge won 68 times, Oxford 52 times and there was a dead heat on 24 March 1877.

Record The race record time for the course of 4 miles 374
times yd *6,779 km* (Putney to Mortlake) is 17 min 35 sec by Oxford on 6 Apr. 1974. The smallest winning margin was Oxford's win by a canvas in 1952. The greatest margin (apart from sinking) was Cambridge's win by 20 lengths in 1900. The record for the distance (rowed on the ebb from Mortlake to Putney) is 17 min 24 sec by the Tideway Scullers School in the Head of the River Race on 21 March 1964.

Intermediate The record to the Mile Post is 3 min 47 sec (Oxford
times 1960 and 25 March 1967); Hammersmith Bridge 6 min 42 sec (Oxford 25 March 1967); Chiswick Steps 10 min 45 sec (Oxford 1965, in practice) and Barnes Bridge 14 min 39 sec (Oxford 19 March 1965, in practice.)

Oarsman The heaviest man ever to row in a University boat has
Heaviest been David L. Cruttenden (b. Hartlepool, 1947) the

No. 6 in the 1970 Cambridge boat at 16 st 0 lb *101 kg 604*. The 1972 Cambridge crew averaged a record 13 st 11⅛ lb *87 kg 600*.

Lightest The lightest oarsman was the 1882 Oxford Stroke, A. H. Higgins, at 9 st 6½ lb *60 kg 100*. The lightest cox was F. H. Archer (Oxford) in 1862 at 5 st 2 lb *32 kg 658*.

HENLEY ROYAL REGATTA
The annual regatta at Henley-on-Thames, Oxfordshire, was inaugurated on 26 March 1839.

Since 1839 the course, except in 1923, has been about 1 mile 550 yd *2 112 m* varying slightly according to the length of boat. In 1967 the shorter craft were "drawn up" so all bows start level. Prior to 1922 there were two slight angles.

Sculling The record number of wins in the Wingfield Sculls (instituted on the Thames 1830) is seven by Jack Beresford, Jr. (see Olympic Games), from 1920 to 1926. The fastest time (Putney to Mortlake) has been 21 min 11 sec by Leslie Southwood in 1933. The record number of world professional sculling titles (instituted 1831) won is seven by W. Beach (Australia) between 1884 and 1887. Stuart A. Mackenzie (Great Britain and Australia) performed the unique feat of winning the Diamond Sculls at Henley for the sixth consecutive occasion on 7 July 1962. In 1960 and 1962 he was in Leander colours.

Highest Speeds in tidal or flowing water are of no comparative
speed value. The highest recorded speed for 2,000 m *2,187 yd* by an eight is 5 min 32.54 sec (13.45 m.p.h. [*21,65 km/h*]) by East Germany in the European Championships in Copenhagen, Denmark on 21 Aug. 1971 and in the Olympic Games 5 min 54.02 sec

313

HENLEY ROYAL REGATTA—Classic Records (year in brackets indicates date the event was instituted)

			min sec	
Grand Challenge Cup (1839)	8 oars	Harvard University, U.S.A.	6:13	5 July 1975
	8 oars	Leander & Thames Tradesmen's R.C.	6:13	5 July 1975
Ladies' Challenge Plate (1845)	8 oars	University of London	6:30	5 July 1975
Thames Challenge Cup (1868)	8 oars	Princeton University, U.S.A.	6:33	5 July 1973
		University of Wisconsin, U.S.A.	6:33	6 July 1973
Princess Elizabeth Challenge Cup (1946)	8 oars	Ridley College, Canada	6:35	5 July 1975
Steward's Challenge Cup (1841)	4 oars	Potomac B.C., U.S.A.	6:50	6 July 1975
Visitor's Challenge Cup (1847)	4 oars	Hampton Grammar School	7:08	5 July 1975
Wyfold Challenge Cup (1855)	4 oars	Thames Tradesmen's R.C.	6:57	6 July 1975
Prince Phillip Challenge Cup (1963)	4 oars	North-eastern University, Rowing Association U.S.A.	7:00	6 July 1973
Britannia Challenge Cup (1969)	4 oars	Isis B.C.	7:15	5 July 1973
Silver Goblets (called Silver Wherries until 1850) (1845) and Nickalls' Challenge Cup (1895)	Pair oar	Peter Gorny and Gunther Bergau (ASK Vorwaerts Rostock, East Germany)	7:35	1 July 1965
Double Sculls Challenge Cup (1939)	Sculls	Michael J. Hart and Christopher L. Baillieu (Leander Club and Cambridge University)	6:59	6 July 1973
Diamond Challenge Sculls (1844)	Sculls	Sean Drea (Neptune R.C., Ireland)	7:40	5 July 1975

(12.64 m.p.h. [20,34 km/h]) by Germany at Toda, Japan, on 12 Oct. 1964.

Cross Channel The fastest row across the channel has been 3 hrs 50 min by Rev. Sidney Swann (b. 1862) in 1911.

Loch Ness Loch Ness, the longest stretch of inland water in Great Britain (22.7 miles [36,5 km]), was rowed by George G. Parsonage, 31, of Whitehill Secondary School, Glasgow in 2 hr 43 min 34.1 sec on 17 May 1975.

Oxford–London The fastest time registered between Folly Bridge, Oxford through 33 locks and 112 miles 180 km to Westminster Bridge, London is 14 hr 35 min 46 sec by an eight (no substitutes) of Guy's Hospital on 28 April 1974.

Circum-navigation of Ireland Ireland, the world's twentieth largest island, was first circumnavigated by an oarsman when Derek Paul King, 25, of Dartford, Kent, landed at Rosnowlagh, County Donegal on 3 Oct. 1971 having rowed Louise 1,500 miles 2 400 km in 108 days since 11 June.

Marathon Stephen Roll, 52, of Haberfield Rowing Club, Sydney, Australia rowed 100 miles 160 km in 16 hr 50 min on the Paramatta River on 30 Nov. 1974.

Whaler Pulling The Isle of Wight was circumnavigated in a 60 nautical mile 111 km pull in a 27 ft 8,22 m naval whaler by two crews from the Southampton City Fire Brigade in 12 hr 34 min on 9 June 1973.

Punting Punting was a sport with both amateur and professional championships instituted in the 1870's. Victorians

argued about the two styles of pole planting and running *versus* pricking. W. Haines won the Professional Championship of the Thames 8 times in the period 1897–1908. The longest recorded punt is one of 300 miles 482 km from Kingston upon Thames to Cambridge via Reading, Oxford, Northampton and Ely by Peter Stickland and Chris Hampson 10 Sept to 3 Oct. 1973.

Rowing Magazine

Christopher Baillieu (stroke) Michael Hart (bow), who set the Henley Double Sculls record in 6 min 59 secs

SHINTY

Shinty (from the Gaelic *sinteag*, a leap) was recorded in the West and Central Highlands c. 1790 when it was known as *lomain* (driving forward). Games were contested between whole clans or parishes without limit as to numbers or time until darkness stopped play among the walking wounded. The field of play was undelineated except by the occasional pail of *uisge-beatha* (whisky). In an inter-clan match a combatant who had failed to disable at least one opponent within a reasonable time had his curved stick (caman) confiscated as a punishment by the Chieftain so that he could only kick the ball (*cnaige*) or his opponents.

This ungovernable game was first given some rules in 1879 and the present governing body was set up by C. I. Macpherson of Balavil near Kingussie, Inverness-shire on 10 Oct. 1893.

Most titles The most successful club has been Newtonmore, Inverness-shire which has won the Camanachd Association Challenge Cup (instituted 1896) nineteen times (1907–1971).

Highest scores The highest Cup score was in 1909 when Newtonmore beat Furnace 11–3 at Glasgow. Dr. Johnnie Cattanach scored eight hails or goals.

SHOOTING

Earliest club A target shooting club in Geneva, Switzerland has records since 1474.

Olympic Games The record number of gold medals won is five by seven marksmen:—Carl Osburn (U.S.A.) (1912–1924);

Konrad Stäheli (Switz.) (1900 and 1906); Willis Lee (U.S.A.) (1920); Louis Richardet (Switz.) (1900 and 1906); Ole Andreas Lilloe-Olsen (Norway) (1920–1924); Alfred Lane (U.S.A.) (1912 and 1920) and Morris Fisher (U.S.A.) (1920 and 1924). Osburn also won 4 silver and 2 bronze medals to total 11. The only marksman to win 3 individual gold medals has been Gulbrandsen Skatteboe (Norway) (b. 18 July 1875) in 1906–08–1912.

Record heads The world's finest head is the 23-pointer stag head in the Maritzburg collection, Germany. The outside span is 75½ in *191 cm* the length 47½ in *120 cm* and the weight 41½ lb. *18 kg 824*. The greatest number of points is probably 33 (plus 29) on the stag shot in 1696 by Frederick III (1657–1713), the Elector of Brandenburg, later King Frederick I of Prussia.

The record head for a British Red Deer is a 47-pointer (length 33½ in [*85 cm*]) from the Great Warnham Deer Park, West Sussex in 1892. The record for a semi-feral stag is a 20-pointer with an antler length of 45¾ in *115 cm* from Endsleigh Wood, Devon, found in December 1950 and owned by G. Kenneth Whitehead.

Largest shoulder guns The largest bore shoulder guns made were 2 bores. Less than a dozen of these were made by two English wildfowl gunmakers *c.* 1885. Normally the largest guns made are double-barrelled 4-bore weighing up to 26 lb. *11 kg* which can be handled only by men of exceptional physique. Larger smooth-bore guns have been made, but these are for use as punt-guns.

Clay pigeon Most world titles have been won by S. De Lamniczer (Hungary) in 1929, 1933 and 1939. The only woman to win two world titles has been Gräfin von Soden (West Germany) in 1966–67. The record number of clay birds shot in an hour is 1,572 by Dave Berlet, 29 of New Knoxville, Ohio, U.S.A., at Camp Troy on 4 Sept. 1971. Using 5 guns and loaders he shot 1,000 in 38 min 30 sec.

BISLEY
The National Rifle Association was instituted in 1859. The Queen's (King's) Prize has been shot since 1860 and has only once been won by a woman—Miss Marjorie Elaine Foster, M.B.E. (1894–1974) (score 280) on 19 July 1930. Only Arthur G. Fulton, M.B.E. has won 3 times (1912, 1926, 1931).

The highest score (possible 300) is 293 by Richard P. Rosling (City R.C.) and A. Narcon (Canada) on 28–29 July 1972 and by Keith Martin Pilcher on 20–21 July 1973. The record for the Silver Medal, 150 (possible 150) by M. J. Brister (City Rifle Club) and the Lord Swansea on 24 July 1971. Brister won the tie shoot.

The world's hottest rifle shot, record-holder Gary Lee Anderson from Nebraska, U.S.A. in the 40 shot standing series

Bench rest shooting The smallest group on record at 1,000 yds *914 m* is 6.125 in *155 mm* by Kenneth A. Keefer, Jr., with a 7 mm 300 Remington Action in Williamstown, Pennsylvania, U.S.A., on 22 Sept. 1974.

Block tossing Using a pair of auto-loading Remington Nylon 66 0.22 calibre guns, Tom Frye (U.S.A.) tossed 100,010 blocks (2½ in [*6 cm*] pine cubes) and hit 100,004—his longest run was 32,860—on 5–17 Oct. 1959.

Biggest bag The largest animal ever shot by any big game hunter was a bull African elephant (*Loxodonta africana*) shot by J. J. Fénykövi (Hungary) 48 miles *77 km*

INDIVIDUAL WORLD RECORDS
(for Olympic Games programme events)
(as ratified by the International Shooting Union (U.I.T.) as at Dec. 1974)

			Possible—Score			
Free Rifle	300 m	3 × 40 shots	1,200—1,157	Gary L. Anderson (U.S.A.)	Mexico City, Mexico	23 Oct. 1968
Small bore Rifle	50 m	3 × 40 shots	1,200—1,167	Lones W. Wigger Jr. (U.S.A.)	Mexico City, Mexico	Oct. 1973
Small-bore Rifle	50 m	60 shots prone	600— 599	Ho Jun Li (North Korea)	Munich, West Germany	28 Aug. 1972
			600— 599	K. Bulan (Czech.)	Thun, Switzerland	Sept. 1974
			600— 599	M. Ilca (Romania)	Bucharest, Romania	July 1975
Free Pistol	50 m	60 shots	600— 572	Grigori Kossych (U.S.S.R.)	Pilsen, Czechoslovakia	1969
Rapid Fire Pistol	25 m	60 shots	600— 598	Giovanni Liverzani (Italy)	Phoenix, Arizona, U.S.A.	1970
Running (Boar) Target	50 m	60 shots "normal runs"	600— 577	H. Bellingradt (Colombia)	Thun, Switzerland	Sept. 1974
			600— 577	V. Postoianov (U.S.S.R.)	Thun, Switzerland	Sept. 1974
Trap	200 birds		200— 199	Angelo Scalzone (Italy)	Munich, W. Germany	29 Aug. 1972
			200— 199	Michel Carrega (France)	Thun, Switzerland	23 Sept. 1974
Skeet	200 birds		200— 200	Yevgeniy Petrov (U.S.S.R.)	Phoenix, Arizona, U.S.A.	1970
			200— 200	Yuri Tzuranov (U.S.S.R.)	Bologna, Italy	1971

The U.I.T. also ratifies 7 other men's events (including Air Rifle and Air Pistol) and 6 positional records for men and 7 events and 1 positional record for women and team events for all 29 world record events except women's trap and skeet. The nearest to a "possible" by a woman is 598/600 by E. Rolinska (Poland) for the Standard Rifle 50 metres 60 shots prone at Suhl, East Germany in 1971.

LARGEST BRITISH BAGS
Woodpigeon	550	1 gun	Major A. J. Coates, near Winchester, Hampshire	10 Jan.	1962
Pigeons	561	1 gun	K. Ransford, Salop-Powys	22 July	1970
Snipe	1,108	2 guns	Tiree, Inner Hebrides	25 Oct.–3 Nov.	1906
Hares	1,215	11 guns	Holkham, Norfolk	19 Dec.	1877
Woodcock	228	6 guns	Ashford, County Galway	28 Jan.	1910
Grouse	2,929	8 guns	Littledale and Abbeystead, Lancashire	12 Aug.	1915
Grouse	1,070	1 gun	Lord Walsingham in Yorkshire	30 Aug.	1888
Geese (Brent)	704[1]	32 punt-guns	Colonel Russell i/c, River Blackwater, Essex	*c.*	1860
Rabbits	6,943	5 guns	Blenheim, Oxfordshire	17 Oct.	1898
Partridges	2,015[2]	6 guns	Rothwell, Lincolnshire	12 Oct.	1952
Pheasants	3,937	7 guns[3]	Hall Barn, Beaconsfield, Buckinghamshire	18 Dec.	1913

[1] *Plus about 250 later picked up.*
[2] *Plus 104 later picked up.*
[3] *Including H.M. King George V.*

north-northwest of Macusso, Angola, on 13 Nov. 1955. It required 16 heavy calibre bullets from an 0.416 Rigby and weighed an estimated 24,000 lb. (10.7 tons [*10,87 tonnes*]), standing 13 ft 2 in *4,013 m* at the shoulders. In November 1965 Simon Fletcher, 28, a Kenyan farmer, claimed to have killed two elephants with one 0.458 bullet.

The greatest recorded lifetime bag is 556,000 birds, including 241,000 pheasants, by the 2nd Marquess of Ripon (1867–1923). He himself dropped dead on a grouse moor after shooting his 52nd bird on the morning of 22 Sept. 1923.

Revolver shooting The greatest rapid fire feat was that of Ed. McGivern (U.S.A.), who twice fired from 15 ft *4,5 m* 5 shots which could be covered by a silver half-dollar piece (diameter 1.205 in [*3,060 cm*]) in 0.45 sec at the Lead Club Range, South Dakota, U.S.A., on 20 Aug. 1932. On 13 Sept. 1932 at Lewiston, Montana, McGivern fired 10 shots in 1.2 sec from two guns at the same time double action (no draw) all 10 shots hitting two $2\frac{1}{4} \times 3\frac{1}{2}$ in *5,7 × 8,9 cm* playing cards at 15 ft *4,57 m.*

Small Bore The British team record (1966 target) is 1988 × 2000 by Lancashire in the Inter-County Association League, 1968–69. John Palin shot 600 × 600 prone .22 rifle in Switzerland in 1972. The record score for a round in the British School's Small Bore Rifle Association (B.S.S.R.A.) contest is a team possible of 500 × 500 by Gresham's School, Holt, Norfolk in Lent Term, 1972. S. J. Carter scored 500 × 500 in the 5 rounds in this .22 contest.

Air weapons The individual world record for air rifle (40 shots at 10 m) is 392 by Olegario Vazquez (Mexico) at Mexico City, 1973 and for Air Pistol (40 shots at 10 m) is 392 by Grigori Kossych (U.S.S.R.) at Linz, Austria in 1973.

Trick shooting The most renowned trick shot of all-time was Phoebe Anne Oakley Mozee (Annie Oakley) (1860–1926).

She demonstrated the ability to shoot 100 × 100 in trap shooting for 35 years aged between 27 and 62. At 30 paces she could split a playing card end-on, hit a dime in mid-air or shoot a cigarette from the lips of her husband—one Frank Butler.

SKIING

Origins The earliest dated skis found in Fenno—Scandian bogs have been dated to *c.* 2500 B.C. A rock carving of a skier at Rødøy, Tjøtta, North Norway, dates from 2000 B.C. The earliest recorded military competition was an isolated one in Oslo, Norway, in 1767. Skiing did not develop into a sport until 1843 at Tromsø, Norway. The Trysil Shooting and Skiing Club, founded in Norway in 1861, claims it is the world's oldest. Skiing was not introduced into the Alps until 1883, though there is some evidence of earlier use in the Carniola district. The earliest reference to skiing in Scotland dates from 1892. The earliest formal downhill race was staged at Montana, Switzerland in 1911. The first Slalom event was run at Mürren, Switzerland, on 6 Jan. 1921. The International Ski Federation (F.I.S.) was founded on 2 Feb. 1924. The Winter Olympics were inaugurated on 25 Jan 1924. The Ski Club of Great Britain was founded on 6 May 1903. The National Ski Federation of Great Britain was formed in 1964.

Most Olympic wins The most Olympic gold medals won by an individual for skiing is four (including one for a relay) by Sixten Jernberg (b. 6 Feb. 1929) of Sweden, in 1956–60–64. In addition, Jernberg has won three silver and two bronze medals. The only women to win three gold medals are Klavdiya Boyarskikh (b. 11 Nov. 1939) and Galina Koulakova, 30, both of the U.S.S.R., who each won the 5 km and 10 km and were members of the winning 3 × 5 km relay teams at Innsbruck, Austria and at Sapporo, Japan in 1964 and 1972 respectively. The most Olympic gold medals won in men's alpine skiing is three, by Anton ("Toni") Sailer (b. 17 Nov. 1935) in 1956 and Jean-Claude Killy (b. 30 Aug. 1943) in 1968.

Most world titles The world alpine championships were inaugurated at Mürren, Switzerland, in 1931. The greatest number of titles won is 12 by Christel Cranz (b. 1 July 1914) of Germany, with four Slalom (1934–37–38–39), three

Downhill (1935–37–39) and five Combined (1934–35–37–38–39). She also won the gold medal for the Combined in the 1936 Olympics. The most titles won by a man is seven by Anton ("Toni") Sailer who won all four in 1956 (Giant Slalom, Slalom, Downhill and the non-Olympic Alpine Combination) and the Downhill, Giant Slalom and Combined in 1958.

Triple Olympic gold medal winner in the Nordic events, Galina Koulakova

Associated Press

MOST OLYMPIC TITLES

Men Alpine	3	Anton (Toni) Sailer (Austria) (b. 17 Nov. 1935)	Downhill, slalom, giant slalom 1956
	3	Jean-Claude Killy (France) (b. 30 Aug. 1943)	Downhill, slalom, giant slalom 1968
Men Nordic	4[1]	Sixten Jernberg (Sweden) (b. 6 Feb. 1929)	50 km, 1956; 30 km, 1960; 50 km and 4 × 10 km, 1964
Women Alpine	2	Andrea Mead-Lawrence (U.S.A.) (b. 19 Apr. 1932)	Slalom, giant slalom, 1952
	2	Marielle Goitschel (France) (b. 28 Sept. 1945)	Giant slalom, 1964; Slalom, 1968
	2	Marie-Therese Nadig (Switz.) (b. 8 Mar. 1954)	Downhill, giant slalom, 1972
Women Nordic	3	Klavdiya Boyarskikh (U.S.S.R.) (b. 11 Nov. 1939)	5 km, 10 km and 3 × 5 km Relay, 1964
	3	Galina Koulakova (U.S.S.R.)	5 km, 10 km and 3 × 5 km Relay, 1972

[1] *Jernberg also won 3 silver and 2 bronze medals for a record 9 Olympic medals.*

Steve
McKinney
(U.S.) the
world's fastest
skier hitting
118.928 m.p.h.
191,396 km/h
so matching
the speed of a
free fall
parachutist

Associated Press

The world's
greatest off
piste downhill
skier Sylvain
Saudan, who
uniquely came
down Mount
Kinlay in
7 hours

In the Nordic events Sixten Jernberg (Sweden) won eight titles (four at 50 km, one at 30 km, and three in relays) in 1956–64. Johan Grøttumsbraaten (b. 24 Feb. 1899) of Norway won six individual titles (two at 18 km and four Combined) in 1926–32. The record for a jumper is five by Birger Ruud (b. 23 Aug. 1911) of Norway, in 1931–32 and 1935–36–37.

World The World Cup, instituted in 1967, has been won
Cup four times by Gustav Thöni (Italy) (b. 28 Feb. 1931) in 1971–72–73–75. The women's cup has been won five times by the 1,67 m *5 ft 6 in* 68 kg *150 lb.* Annemarie Moser *née* Proell (b. 27 March 1953) of Austria in 1971–72–73–74–75. In 1973 she completed a record sequence of 11 consecutive downhill wins.

Most The greatest number of British ski-running titles won
British is three by Leonard Dobbs (1921, 1923–24), William
titles R. Bracken (1929–31) and Jeremy Palmer-Tomkinson (1965–66–68). The most ladies titles is four by Miss Isobel M. Roe (1938–39, 1948–49) and Miss Gina Hathorn (b. 6 July 1946) (1966–68–69–70). The most wins in the British Ski-jumping championship (discontinued 1936) is three, by Colin Wyatt (1931, 1934, and 1936).

Highest The highest speed claimed for any skier is 118.928
speed m.p.h. *191,396 km/h* by Steve McKinney, 21, of Lexington, Kentucky, U.S.A. on the Kilometro Lanciato, Cervinia, Italy on 10 July 1975. The average speed in the 1968 Olympic downhill race on the Chamrousse course, Grenoble, France by Jean-Claude Killy (b. 30 Aug. 1943) of France was 86,79 km/h *53.93 m.p.h.*

Steepest The steepest descents in alpine skiing history, uniquely
Descents achieved, have been by Sylvain Saudan (b. Lausanne, Switzerland on 23 Sept. 1936). At the start of his descent from Mont Blanc on the north-east side down the Couloir Gervasutti from 4 248 m *13,937 ft* on 17 Oct. 1967 he skiied to gradients in excess of 60 degrees.

Duration The longest non-stop skiing marathon was one lasting 48 hr by Onni Savi, aged 35, of Padasjoki, Finland, who covered 305.9 km *190.1 miles* between noon on 19 April and noon on 21 April 1966.

Largest The world's greatest Nordic ski race is the "Vasa
entry Lopp", which commemorates an event of 1521 when Gustav Vasa (1496–1560), later King Gustavus Eriksson, skied 85 km *52.8 miles* from Mora to Sälen, Sweden. The re-enactment of this journey in reverse direction is now an annual event, with 9,397 starters on 4 March 1970. The record time is 4 hours 39 min 49 sec by Janne Stefansson on 3 March 1968.

Longest The longest ski-jump ever recorded is one of 169 m
jump *554 ft 6 in* by Heinz Wosipiwo (East Germany) at
World Oberstdorf, West Germany, on 9 March 1973. The record for a 70 m hill is 85,49 m *280 ft 6 in* by Tauno Käyhkö at Falun, Sweden on 19 Feb. 1973 when scoring 247.8 points for distance and style. The female record is 98 m *321 ft 5 in* jumped by Anita Wold at Okura, Sapporo, Japan on 14 Jan. 1975.

British The British record is 61 m *200.1 ft* by Guy John Nixon (b. 9 Jan. 1909) at Davos on 24 Feb. 1931. The record at Hampstead, Camden, Greater London, on artificial snow is 28 m *90.8 ft* by Reidar Anderson (b. 20 April 1911) of Norway on 24 March 1950.

Ski- The greatest recorded vertical descent in parachute
Parachuting ski-jumping is 2,300 ft *700 m* by Rick Sylvester, 29, (U.S.) who on 31 Jan. 1972 skied off the 3,200 ft *975 m* sheer face of El Capitan, Yosemite Valley, California. His parachute opened at 1,500 ft *460 m.*

Backflip The greatest number of skiers to perform a back layout flip while holding hands is 19 by members of the Sunset Sports Centre's "Hot Dog" team at the Grand Targhee Ski Resort, Wyoming, U.S.A. on 9 Feb. 1975.

Longest The longest all-downhill ski run in the world is the
run Weissfluhjoch-Küblis Parsenn course, near Davos, Switzerland, which measures 12,23 km *7.6 miles.* The run from the Aiguille du Midi top of the Chamonix lift (vertical lift 2 492 m [*8,176 ft*]) across the Vallée Blanche is 20,9 km *13 miles.*

Longest The longest chair lift in the world is the Alpine Way to
lift Kosciusko Châlet lift above Thredbo, near the Snowy

The one and only 19 man back flip by the Sunset Sports Centre's "Hot Dog" team

Gary McMillin

Mountains, New South Wales, Australia. It takes from 45 to 75 min to ascend the 3.5 miles *5,6 km*, according to the weather. The highest is at Chactaltaya, Bolivia, rising to 5 029 m *16,500 ft*.

Greatest descent The greatest reported aggregate elevation descended in 12 hr is 41 6,000 ft, *126 796 m* by Sarah Ludwig, Scott Ludwig and Timothy B. Gaffney at Mount Brighton, Brighton, Michigan, U.S.A. on 16 Feb. 1974.

Highest altitude Yuichiro Miura (Japan) skied 2,5 km *1.6 miles* down Mt. Everest starting from 26,200 ft *7 985 m*. In a run from a height of 24,418 ft *7 442 m* he reached speeds of 93.6 m.p.h. *150 km/h* on 6 May 1970. Sylvian Squdan (Switzerland) became the first man to ski down Mount McKinlay (20,320 ft [*6 193 m*]) on 10 June 1972. He took 7 hours to reach the 7,000 ft *2 133 m* level and made 2,700 jump turns on the 50–55° top slopes.

SKIJORING

The record speed reached in aircraft skijoring (being towed by an aircraft) is 175,78 km/h *109.23 m.p.h.* by Reto Pitsch on the Silsersee, St. Moritz, Switzerland, in 1956.

SKI-BOB

The ski-bob was invented by Mr. Stevens of Hartford, Connecticut, U.S.A., and patented (No. 47334) on 19 April 1892 as a "bicycle with ski-runners". The Fédération Internationale de Skibob was founded on 14 Jan. 1961 in Innsbruck, Austria and the first world championships were held at Bad Hofgastein, Austria in 1967. The Ski-Bob Association of Great Britain was registered on 23 Aug. 1967. The highest speed attained is 166 km/h *103,4 m.p.h.* by Erick Brenter (Austria) at Cervinia, north Italy, in 1964.

World Champion-ships The only ski-bobbers to retain a world championship are Alois Fischbauer (Austria) who won the men's title in 1973 and 1975, Gerhilde Schiffkorn (Austria) who won the women's title in 1967 and 1969 and Gertrude Geberth (Austria) who won in 1971 and 1973.

SNOWMOBILE

The world record speed for a snowmobile stood at 127.3 m.p.h. *204,8 km/h* by Yvon Duhamel on a Ski Doo XR-2 as at 10 Feb. 1973.

SNOOKER

Origins Research shows that snooker was originated by Field Marshal Sir Neville Chamberlain, G.C.B., G.C.S.I. (1820–1902) as a variation of "black pool", in the Ootacamund Club, Nilgiris, South India in the summer of 1875. It did not reach England until 1885, where the modern scoring system was adopted in 1891. Championships were not instituted until 1916. World Professional Championships were instituted in 1927.

Highest breaks It is possible if an opponent commits a foul with 15 reds on the table that his opponent can exercise an option of nominating a colour as a red and then pots this free ball and then goes on to pot the black with 15 reds still on the table, he can score 155. The official world record break of the maximum possible (excluding handicaps or penalties) of 147 was set by Joe Davis, O.B.E. (b. 15 April 1901) against Willie Smith at Leicester Square Hall, City of Westminster, Greater London on 22 Jan. 1955 and by Rex Williams (G.B.) against Manuel Francisco at Cape Town, South Africa, on 22 Dec. 1965. The official world amateur record break is 122 set by Ratan Bader (India) in the West Bengal Championships in 1964. Some 40 other "perfect" frames have been achieved under less rigorous conditions. The world professional champion Ray Reardon (b. Tredegar, Gwent, 1932) achieved a unique fifth "perfect" frame on 12 Apr. 1974. Three Canadian amateurs Leo Levitt (1948), Vic Kireluk (1968) and René Aubry (1973) have also made maximums. The first man to compile a 147 break was E. J. O'Donaghue (b. New Zealand, 1901) in 1934.

Marathon The most protracted snooker endurance record by 3 players (each resting for 1 frame in three) is one of 200 hr 28 min by Biran A. Parkin, John R. Charles and Robert G. Hamilton from the Royal Holloway College, Egham, Surrey on 22 Feb.–2 March 1975.

SOFTBALL

Origins Softball, the indoor derivative of baseball, was invented by George Hancock at the Parragut Boat Club of Chicago, Illinois in 1887. Rules were first codified in Minneapolis, Minnesota in 1895 as Kitten Ball International rules were set in 1933 when the name Softball was officially adopted and the ISF was formed in 1952 as governing body for both fast pitch and slow pitch (with a minimum of a 3 ft *1 m* arch in trajectory).

The world series for men was inaugurated in 1966 and for women in 1965.

Marathon The longest fast pitch marathon is one of 50 hours by two teams of 9 girls (with 2 substitutes per team) from North High School, Bakersfield, California, on 6–8 June 1975.

SPEEDWAY

Origins Motor cycle racing on large dirt track surfaces has been traced back to 1902 in the United States. The first organized "short track" races were at the West Maitland (New South Wales, Australia) Agricultural Show in November 1923. The sport evolved in Great Britain with small diameter track racing at Droylsden, Greater Manchester on 25 June 1927 and a cinder track event at High Beech, Essex, on 19 Feb. 1928. After three seasons of competition in Southern and Northern leagues, the National League was instituted in 1932. The best record is that of the Wembley Lions who won in 1932, 1946–47, 1949–53, making a record total of eight victories. Since the National Trophy knock-out competition was instituted in 1931, Belle Vue (Manchester) have been most successful with nine victories in 1933–34–35–36–37, 1946–47, 1949 and 1958. In 1965 the League was replaced by the British League in which Belle Vue have won three times in succession (1970–72).

Most world titles The world speedway championship was inaugurated at Wembley, Brent, Greater London in September 1936. The only five-time winner has been Ove Fundin (b. Tranås, 1933) (Sweden), who won in 1956, 1960, 1961, 1963 and 1967. Ivan Mauger (N.Z.) (b. Christchurch 1939) is the only rider to win three successive championships (1968–70). He also won in 1972. Barry Briggs (b. Christchurch, N.Z., 1934) made a record 17 consecutive appearances in the finals (1954–70) and won the world title in 1957–58–64–66.

Lap speed The fastest recorded speed on a British speedway track is 54.62 m.p.h. *87,90 km/h* on the 470 yd *429 m* 2nd Division track at Crewe by Barry Meeks. This track was shortened by 40 yd *36 m* in 1970 and the current fastest track record on a British circuit is an average of 52.46 m.p.h. *84,42 km/h* on the re-shaped Crewe track by Dave Morton on 12 Aug. 1974.

Ivan Mauger (New Zealand) the only rider to win three successive world championships (1968–70)

Associated Press

SQUASH RACKETS

(Note: "1973", for example, refers to the 1973–74 season.)

Earliest champion Although rackets (U.S. spelling racquets) with a soft ball was evolved *c.* 1850 at Harrow School, Greater London, there was no recognized champion of any country until John A. Miskey of Philadelphia won the American Amateur Singles Championship in 1906.

World title The inaugural Amateur International Federation championships were staged in Australia in August 1967 when Australia won the team title in Sydney and

Norman F. Borrett winning his fifth Amateur Squash title in 1950

Sport & General

Amateur Championship The most wins in the Amateur Championship is six by Abdel Fattah Amr Bey (b. Egypt, 1910) later appointed Ambassador in London, who won in 1931–32–33 and 1935–36–37. Norman F. Borrett of England won in 1946–47–48–49–50.

Professional Championship The most wins in the Professional Championship of Britain is 10 by J. H. Giles from 1954 to 1963. He relinquished the title in 1964 undefeated.

Longest championship match The longest recorded championship match was one of 2 hr 13 min in the final of the Open Championship of the British Isles at the Edgbaston-Priory Club, Birmingham in December 1969 when Jonah P. Barrington, M.B.E. (Ireland) (b. Cornwall, 1941) beat Geoffrey B. Hunt (b. Australia, 1947) 9–7, 3–9, 3–9, 9–4, 9–4 with the last game lasting 37 min.

Most international selections The record for international selection is held by D. M. Pratt with 51 for Ireland from 1956 to 1972. The record for England is 40 by J. G. A. Lyon from 1959 to 1968; O. L. Balfour (Scotland) with 45 between 1954 and 1968, and for Wales 44 by L. J. Verney between 1949 and 1965.

Longest span of internationals Mrs. Henry G. Macintosh (*née* Sheila Speight), the 1960 British Champion, played for England *v.* Wales in April 1949 and in Dec. 1971—a span of 22 years. Among men P. Harding-Edgar first played for Scotland in 1938 and last played 21 years later in 1959.

Most wins women The most wins in the Women's Squash Rackets Championship is 14 by Mrs. Heather McKay, M.B.E. (*née* Blundell) (b. Australia, 1941), 1961 to 1974.

Marathon record In squash marathons a rest interval of 1 min is allowed between games and 2 min between the 4th and 5th games with 5 min additional rest per hour. The rate of play must not exceed 11 games per hour. The longest recorded squash marathon (under these competition conditions) has been one of 72 hr 12 min by John Dean at the Essendon Squash Courts, Victoria, Australia on 13–16 June 1975. He played 526 games of which he won 262 against 145 opponents. The longest singles marathon by a pair is 67 hr 8 min by Philip Redmond and Robert Paterson at the Wootton Court Hotel and Country Club, Warwick on 22–25 May 1975.

Geoffrey B. Hunt (Victoria) took the individual title, both these titles being retained in 1969 and 1971.

MOST WINS

Open Championship The most wins in the Open Championship (amateurs or professionals), held annually in Britain, is seven by Hashim Khan (Pakistan) in 1950–51–52–53–54–55 and 1957.

SURFING

Origins The traditional Polynesian sport of surfing in a canoe (*ehorooe*) was first recorded by Captain James Cook, R.N., F.R.S. (1728–79) on this third voyage at Tahiti in December 1771. Surfing on a board (*Amo Amo iluna ka lau oka nalu*) was first described ("most perilous and extraordinary . . . altogether astonishing and is scarcely to be credited") by Lt. (later Capt.) James King, R.N., F.R.S. in March 1779 at Kealakekua Bay, Hawaii Island. A surfer was first depicted by this voyage's official artist John Webber.

The sport was revived at Waikiki by 1900. Australia's first body surfing events were run by the Bondi Surf Bathers Lifesaving Club, which was formed in February 1906. Australia's most successful champion has been Bob Newbiggin, who won the senior title in 1939–40–45–46–47 and the senior Belt Race in 1940. Hollow boards came in in 1929 and the light plastic foam type in 1956.

World Champions World Championships were inaugurated in 1964 at Sydney, Australia. The first surfer to win two titles has been Joyce Hoffman (U.S.) in 1965 and 1966.

Highest waves ridden Makaha Beach, Hawaii provides the reputedly highest consistently high waves often reaching the rideable limit of 30–35 ft *9–10 m*. The highest wave ever ridden was the *tsunami* of "perhaps 50 ft *15 m*", which struck Minole, Hawaii on 3 April 1868, and was ridden to save his life by a Hawaiian named Holua.

Longest ride *Sea wave* About 4 to 6 times each year rideable surfing waves break in Matanchen Bay near San Blas, Nayarit, Mexico which makes rides of *c.* 5,700 ft *1 700 m* possible.

River bore The longest recorded rides on a river bore have been set on the Severn bore, England. In 1968 local residents reported a ride of 4 to 6 miles *6–9 km* by Rodney Sumpter of Sussex. In September 1971 Mick Evans of Towyn Surfing Club, Gwyndd succeeded in making a run from Rea to Maisemore Weir a distance of 4 miles *6,4 km*.

Skid Boarding The sport in which a 15 lb. *7 kg* fibreglass coated plywood disc is substituted for a surfboard was introduced in 1967 on the coasts around Bournemouth, England. Speeds of 25 m.p.h. *40 km/h* and distances of 85 yds *77 m* have been achieved.

SWIMMING

Earliest references It is recorded that inter-school swimming contests in Japan were ordered by Imperial edict of Emperor Go-Yoozei as early as 1603. Sea water bathing was fashionable at Scarborough, North Yorkshire as early as 1660. In Great Britain competitive swimming originated in London *c.* 1837, at which time there were five or more pools, the earliest of which had been opened at St. George's Pier Head, Liverpool in 1828.

Largest pools The largest swimming pool in the world is the sea-water Orthlieb Pool in Casablanca, Morocco. It is 480 m *1,547 ft* long and 75 m *246 ft* wide, and has an area of 3.6 ha *8.9 acres*. The largest land-locked swimming pool with heated water was the Fleishhacker Pool on Sloat Boulevard, near Great Highway, San Francisco, California, U.S.A. It measures 1,000 × 150 ft *304,8 × 45,7 m* and up to 14 ft *4,26 m* deep and contains 7,500,000 U.S. gallons *28 390 hectolitres* of heated water. It was opened on 2 May 1925 but has now been abandoned to a few ducks. The world's largest competition pool is that at Osaka, Japan, which accommodates 25,000 spectators. The largest in the United Kingdom is the Royal Commonwealth Pool, Edinburgh, completed in 1970 with 2,000 permanent, and 400 temporary seats.

Fastest swimmer Excluding relay stages with their anticipatory starts, the highest speed reached by a swimmer is 5.05 m.p.h. *8,12 km/h* by David Holmes Edgar (U.S.A.), who recorded 20.23 sec for a heat of 50 yd *45,72 m* in a 25 yd *22,86 m* pool at Tuscaloosa, Alabama on 4 Mar. 1971. Andy Coan (U.S.)'s 100 m record of 51.11 sec required an average of 4.376 m.p.h. *7,042 km/h*.

Most world records Men, 32, Arne Borg (Sweden) (b. 1901), 1921–1929. Women, 42, Ragnhild Hveger (Denmark) (b. 10 Dec. 1920), 1936–1942.

OLYMPIC SWIMMING RECORDS

Most Olympic titles The greatest number of Olympic gold medals won is nine by Mark Andrew Spitz (U.S.A.) (b. 10 Feb. 1950):—

100 metres freestyle	1972
200 metres freestyle	1972
100 metres butterfly	1972
200 metres butterfly	1972
4 × 100 metres freestyle relay	1968 and 1972
4 × 200 metres freestyle relay	1968 and 1972
4 × 100 metres medley relay	1972

All but one of these performances (the 4 × 200 m relay of 1968) were also new world records.

Women The record number of gold medals won by a woman is four shared by Mrs. Patricia McCormick (née Keller) (U.S.A.) (b. 12 May 1930) with the High and Springboard Diving double in 1952 and 1956 (also the female record for individual golds) and by Dawn Fraser O.B.E. (now Mrs. Gary Ware) (b. Sydney, Australia, 4 Sept. 1937) with the 100 metres freestyle (1956–60–64) and the 4 × 100 metres freestyle relay (1956).

British The record number of gold medals won by a British swimmer (excluding Water Polo *q.v.*) is four by Henry Taylor (1885–1951) with the 400 metres freestyle (1908), 1,500 metres freestyle (1906 and 1908) and 4 × 200 metres relay (1908). None of the seven British women who have won a gold medal, won a second title.

Most Olympic medals The most medals won is 11 by Spitz, who in addition to his nine golds (see above), won a silver (100 m butterfly) and a bronze (100 m freestyle) both in 1968.

Women The most medals won by a woman is eight by Dawn Fraser, who in addition to her four golds (see above) won four silvers (400 metres freestyle 1956, 4 × 100 metres freestyle relay 1960 and 1964, 4 × 100 metres medley relay 1960).

Radio Times Hulton Picture Library
Capt. Webb, the centenary of whose pioneer Channel swim was celebrated in 1975.

British The British record is eight by Taylor who in addition to his four golds (see above) won a silver (400 m freestyle 1906) and three bronzes (4 × 200 m freestyle relay 1906, 1912, 1920). The most medals by a British woman is four by Margaret Joyce Cooper (now Mrs John Badcock) (b. 18 Apr. 1909) with one silver (4 × 100 m freestyle relay 1928) and three bronze (100 m freestyle 1928, 100 m backstroke 1928, 4 × 100 m freestyle relay 1932).

Most individual gold medals The record number of individual gold medals won is four by Charles M. Daniels (U.S.A.) (b. 12 July 1884) (100 m freestyle 1906 and 1908, 220 yd freestyle 1904, 440 yd freestyle 1904); Roland Matthes (E. Germany) (b. 17 Nov. 1950) with 100 m and 200 m backstroke 1968 and 1972 and Spitz (see above). The most individual golds by a British swimmer is three by Taylor (see above).

Closest Verdict The closest win in the Olympic Games was in the Munich 400 m individual medley final of 30 Aug. 1972 when Gunnar Larsson (Sweden) got the verdict over Tim McKee (U.S.A.) by 2/1,000th of a second in 4 min 31.98 sec—a margin of 3 mm or less than ⅛th of an inch or the length grown by a finger nail in 3 weeks.

Most difficult dives Those with the highest tariff (degree of difficulty 3.0) are the "3½ forward somersault in tuck position and the 1½ forward triple twisting somersault from the one metre board; the backward 2½ somersault piked; the reverse 2½ piked and the forward 3½ piked from the 10 m board". Joaquin Capilla of Mexico has performed a 4½ somersaults dive from a 10 m board, but this is not on the international tariff.

LONG DISTANCE SWIMMING

Longest Distance Ocean Swim The longest recorded ocean swim is one of 90¾ miles *146,0 km* by Walter Poenisch (U.S.A.) in the Florida Straits (in a shark cage) in 21 hr 18 min on 27–28 June 1972.

A unique achievement in long distance swimming was established in 1966 by the cross-Channel swimmer Mihir Sen of Calcutta, India. These were the Palk Strait from India to Ceylon (in 25 hr 36 min on 5–6 April); the Straits of Gibraltar (Europe to Africa in 8 hr 1 min on 24 August); the length of the Dardanelles (Gallipoli to Seddülbahir, Turkey) in 13 hr 55 min on 12 September) and the entire length of the Panama Canal in 34 hr 15 min on 29–31 October. He had earlier swum the English Channel in 14 hr 45 min on 27 Sept. 1958.

CHANNEL SWIMMING

Earliest Man The first man to swim across the English Channel (without a life jacket) was the Merchant Navy captain Matthew Webb (1848–83), who swam breaststroke from Dover, England, to Cap Gris-Nez, France, in 21 hrs 45 min from 12.56 p.m. to 10.41 a.m., 24–25 Aug. 1875. He swam an estimated 38 miles *61 km* to make the 21-mile *33 km* crossing. Paul Boyton (U.S.A.) had swum from Cap Gris-Nez to the South Foreland in his patent life-saving suit in 23 hrs 30 min on 28–29 May 1875. There is good evidence that Jean-Marie Saletti, a French soldier, escaped from a British prison hulk off Dover by swimming to Boulogne in July or August 1815. The first crossing from France to England was made by Enrique Tiraboschi, a wealthy Italian living in Argentina, who crossed in 16 hrs 33 min on 11 Aug. 1923, to win the *Daily Sketch* prize of £1,000.

Woman The first woman to succeed was Gertrude Ederle (U.S.A.) who swam from Cap Gris-Nez, France to Dover, England on 6 Aug. 1926, in the then overall record of 14 hrs 39 min. The first woman to swim from England to France was Florence Chadwick of California, U.S.A., in 16 hrs 19 min on 11 Sept. 1951. She repeated this on 4 Sept. 1953 and 12 Oct. 1955. The first Englishwoman to succeed was Ivy Gill on 14 Oct. 1927—the latest ever date in the year for any conquest.

Fastest The official Channel Swimming Association record is 9 hr 35 min by Barry Watson, aged 25, of Bingley, West Yorkshire, from Cap Gris-Nez, France, to St. Margaret's Bay, near Dover, on 15–16 Aug. 1964. The fastest feminine time is one minute slower by Lynne Cox, 16 (U.S.A.) which is also the fastest England to France time, made on 10 Aug. 1973. The fastest crossing by a relay team is one of 9 hr 29 min by Radcliffe Swimming Club of Lancashire, from Cap Gris-Nez to Walmer on 13 June 1966.

Slowest The slowest crossing was the third ever made, when Henry Sullivan (U.S.A.) swam from England to France in 26 hr 50 min on 5–6 Aug. 1923.

Earliest and latest The earliest date in the year on which the Channel has been swum is 6 June by Dorothy Perkins (England) aged 19, in 1961, and the latest is 14 October by Ivy Gill (England) in 1927. Both swims were from France to England.

Youngest The youngest conqueror is Abla Khairi (Egypt), who swam from Dover to Cap Griz Nez in 12 hrs 30 min on 18 Aug. 1974, when aged 13 years.

Andy Coan (U.S.A.) the fastest freestyle sprint swimmer in the world

Tony Duffy

Oldest The oldest swimmer to swim the Channel has been William E. (Ned) Barnie, aged 55, when he swam from France to England in 15 hrs 1 min on 16 Aug. 1951.

Double crossing First Antonio Abertondo (b. Buenos Aires, Argentina), aged 42, swam from England to France in 18 hrs 50 min (8.35 a.m. on 20 Sept. to 3.25 a.m. on 21 Sept. 1961) and after about 4 min rest returned to England in 24 hrs 16 min, landing at St. Margaret's Bay at 3.45 a.m. on 22 Sept. 1961, to complete the first "double crossing" in 43 hrs 10 min. Kevin Murphy, 21, completed the first double crossing by a Briton in 35 hrs 10 min on 6 Aug. 1970. The first swimmer to achieve a crossing both ways was Edward H. Temme (b. 1904) on 5 Aug. 1927 and 19 Aug. 1934.

Fastest The fastest double crossing, and the second to be achieved, was one of 30 hrs 3 min by Edward (Ted) Erikson, aged 37, a physiochemist from Chicago, Illinois, U.S.A. He left St. Margaret's Bay, near Dover, at 8.20 p.m. on 19 Sept. 1965 and landed at a beach

WORLD RECORDS
(at distances recognised by the *Fédération Internationale de Natation Amateur*

MEN

Distance	Time	Name and Nationality	Place	Date
FREESTYLE	min. sec.			
100 metres	51.11	Andrew Coan (U.S.A.)	Fort Lauderdale, Florida, U.S.A.	4 Aug. 1975
200 metres	1:50.89	Bruce Furniss (U.S.A.)	Long Beach, California, U.S.A.	18 June 1975
400 metres	3:53.95	Tim Shaw (U.S.A.)	Long Beach, California, U.S.A.	19 June 1975
800 metres	8:09.60	Tim Shaw (U.S.A.)	Mission Viejo, California, U.S.A.	12 July 1975
1,500 metres	15:20.91	Tim Shaw (U.S.A.)	Long Beach, California, U.S.A.	21 June 1975
BREASTSTROKE				
100 metres	1:03.88	John Hencken (U.S.A.)	Concord, California, U.S.A.	31 Aug. 1974
200 metres	2:18.21	John Hencken (U.S.A.)	Concord, California, U.S.A.	1 Sept. 1974
BUTTERFLY STROKE				
100 metres	54.27	Mark Andrew Spitz (U.S.A.)	Munich, West Germany	31 Aug. 1972
200 metres	2:00.70	Mark Andrew Spitz (U.S.A.)	Munich, West Germany	28 Aug. 1972
BACKSTROKE				
100 metres	56.3*	Roland Matthes (East Germany)	Moscow, U.S.S.R.	9 April 1972
100 metres	56.30†	Roland Matthes (East Germany)	Munich, W. Germany	4 Sept. 1972
200 metres	2:01.87	Roland Matthes (East Germany)	Belgrade, Yugoslavia	6 Sept. 1973
INDIVIDUAL MEDLEY				
200 metres	2:06.32	David Andrew Wilkie, M.B.E. (G.B.)	Vienna, Austria	24 Aug. 1974
200 metres	2:06.32	Steven Furniss (U.S.A.)	Concord, California, U.S.A.	1 Sept. 1974
400 metres	4:28.89	Andras Hargity, (Hungary)	Vienna, Austria	20 Aug. 1974
FREESTYLE RELAYS				
4 × 100 metres	3:24.85	United States (Bruce Furniss, James Montgomery, Andrew Coan, John Murphy)	Cali, Columbia	23 July 1975
4 × 200 metres	7:33.22	United States (Kurt Krumpholz, Robin Backhaus, Richard Klatt, James Montgomery)	Belgrade, Yugoslavia	7 Sept. 1973
MEDLEY RELAY				
4 × 100 metres	3:48.16	United States (Michael E. Stamm, Thomas E. Bruce, Mark Andrew Spitz, Jerry Heidenreich)	Munich, W. Germany	4 Sept. 1972

* *Timed to 1/10 sec.*
† *Achieved in a Medley Relay*

Rosemarie Kother (East Germany) holder of the world's 200 metre butterfly record in action

Associated Press

about a mile *1,6 km* west of Calais, after a swim of 14 hrs 15 min. After a rest of about 10 min he returned and landed at South Foreland Point, east of Dover, at 2.23 a.m. on 21 Sept. 1965.

Most conquests The greatest number of Channel conquests is 8 by Desmond Renford, 47 (Australia) from 1970 to 4 Aug. 1975. Greta Andersen-Sonnichsen (U.S.A.) made 5 crossings in 1957–1965.

Underwater The first underwater cross-Channel swim was achieved by Fred Baldasare (U.S.A.), aged 38, who completed the 42 mile *67,5 km* distance from France to England with Scuba in 18 hr 1 min on 10–11 July 1962. Simon Paterson, aged 20, a frogman from Egham, Surrey, travelled underwater from France to England with an air hose attached to his pilot boat in 14 hr 50 min on 28 July 1962.

Irish Channel The swimming of the 22 mile *35 km* wide Irish Channel from Donaghadee, Northern Ireland to Portpatrick, Scotland was first accomplished by Tom Blower of

Nottingham in 15 hr 26 min in 1947 and repeated by Kevin Murphy (b. Bushey Heath, Herts., 1949) in 1970 and 1971. The first Irish born swimmer to achieve the crossing was Ted Keenan on 11 Aug. 1973 in 52–56 °F water in 18 hr 27 min.

Bristol Channel The first person to achieve a double crossing of the Bristol Channel is Jenny James of Pontypridd, South Wales, who swam from Sully, South Glamorgan to Weston-super-Mare, Avon in 10 hr 2 min on 18 Sept. 1949 and the return course in 8 hr 21 min on 9 July 1950.

Solent The fastest time for swimming the Solent (Southsea to Ryde, Isle of Wight) has been 1 hr 22 min 57 sec by Keith Richards (Southsea) in 1970. The greatest number of crossings has been 21 single and 2 non-stop double crossings by Richard Glynn of Cheltenham.

Loch Ness The first person to swim the length of Great Britain's longest lake, the 22¾ mile *36,61 km* long Loch Ness,

WORLD RECORDS
(at distances recognized by the *Fédérationale de Natation Amateur*)

WOMEN

Distance	Time	Name and Nationality	Place	Date
FREESTYLE	Min. sec.			
100 metres	56.22	Kornelia Ender (East Germany)	Cali, Colombia	26 July 1975
200 metres	2:02.27	Kornelia Ender (East Germany)	Dresden, East Germany	15 Mar. 1975
400 metres	4:14.76	Shirley Babashoff (U.S.A.)	Long Beach, California, U.S.A.	20 June 1975
800 metres	8:43.48	Jenny Turrall (Australia)	Crystal Palace, London	31 Mar. 1975
1,500 metres	16:33.94	Jenny Turrall (Australia)	Concord, California, U.S.A.	25 Aug. 1974
BREASTSTROKE				
100 metres	1:12.28	Renate Vogel (East Germany)	Concord, California, U.S.A.	1 Sept. 1974
200 metres	2:34.99	Karla Linke (East Germany)	Vienna, Austria	19 Aug. 1974
BUTTERFLY STROKE				
100 metres	1:01.24	Kornelia Ender (East Germany)	Cali, Colombia	24 July 1975
200 metres	2:13.76	Rosemarie Kother (East Germany)	Belgrade, Yugoslavia	8 Sept. 1973
BACKSTROKE				
100 metres	1:02.98	Ulrike Richter (East Germany)	Vienna, Austria	18 Aug. 1974
200 metres	2:15.46	Birgit Treiber (East Germany)	Cali, Colombia	25 July 1975
INDIVIDUAL MEDLEY				
200 metres	2:18.83	Ulrike Tauber (East Germany)	Wittemberg, East Germany	10 June 1975
400 metres	4:52.20	Ulrike Tauber (East Germany)	Wittemberg, East Germany	7 June 1975
FREESTYLE RELAY				
4 × 100 metres	3:49.37	East Germany (Kornelia Ender, Barbara Krause, Claudia Hempel, Ute Bruckner)	Cali, Colombia	26 July 1975
MEDLEY RELAY				
4 × 100 metres	4:13.78	East Germany (Ulrike Richter, Renate Vogel, Rosemarie Kother, Kornelia Ender)	Vienna, Austria	24 Aug. 1974

Only performances set up in 50 m or 55 yd baths are recognized as World Records. F.I.N.A. no longer recognize any records made for distances over non-metric distances.

was Brenda Sherratt of West Bollington, Cheshire, aged 18, in 31 hr 27 min on 26–27 July 1966.

Round the Isle of Wight Kevin Murphy of Harrow achieved the first circumnavigation of the Isle of Wight covering the 55 miles *88 km* in 26 hr 51 min on 22–24 Sept. 1971.

Treading water The duration record (without any rest breaks) for treading water (vertical posture without touching the lane markers in an 8 ft *2,43 m* square) is 35 hr by Robert Olislagers, 20, (U.S.) at State University A & T College, Alfred, N.Y. on 2–3 Nov. 1974.

Ice swimming The coldest temperatures reported in voluntary ice swimming is 32 °F in the ice clogged Monongahela River, Pennsylvania, U.S.A., on 10 Feb. 1953 by the "Human Polar Bear" Gustave A. Brickner, (b. 1912). The air temperature was −18 °F, *−27,7 °C* and the wind speed 40 m.p.h. *64 km/h* with a −85 °F *−65° C* chill factor for his daily dip on 24 Jan. 1963.

Most dangerous One of the most dangerous swims on record was the unique crossing of the Potaro River in Guyana just above the 741 ft *226 m* high Kaieteur Falls by Private Robert Howatt (the Black Watch) on 17 April 1955. The river is 464 ft *141 m* wide at the lip of the falls.

Relays The longest recorded mileage in a 24 hr swim relay (team of 5) is 73 miles 245 yd *117,7 km* by St. James's Swimming Club, Dulwich at Peckham, Southwark, Greater London on 11–12 May 1974. The fastest time recorded for 100 miles *160 km* by a team of 20 swimmers is 25 hr 55 min 8.2 sec by Menzieshill High School in their short course bath in Dundee, Tayside, Scotland on 14–15 Dec. 1974.

Marathon relays In Buttermere, Cumbria on 18–28 July 1968 six boys, aged 13 to 15, covered 300 miles *482 km* in 230 hr 39 min.

Underground swimming The longest recorded underground swim is one of 3,402 yd *3 110 m* in 87 min by David Stanley Gale through the Dudley Old Canal Tunnel, West Midlands in August 1967.

Sponsored swimming The greatest amount of money raised in a sponsored swim is £17,454 45p. by the Lions Club of Jersey with 283 teams of six swimmers in a 40 hour marathon at the Fort Regent Pool, St. Helier, Jersey on 14–16 Feb. 1975.

BRITISH NATIONAL RECORDS

as ratified by the Amateur Swimming Association
(short course and record equalling performances are *not* recognised)   Times to only a tenth of a second are manually timed.

MEN

Distance	Time	Name	Place	Date
FREESTYLE	Min. sec.			
100 metres	53.4	Robert Bilsland McGregor, M.B.E.	Tokyo, Japan	29 Aug. 1967
200 metres	1:53.56	Brian Brinkley	Cali, Colombia	22 July 1975
400 metres	4:02.88	Gordon Downie	Cali, Colombia	24 July 1975
800 metres	8:32.13	David Parker	Cali, Colombia	26 July 1975
1,500 metres	15:54.78	James Carter	Vienna, Austria	25 Aug. 1974
BREASTSTROKE				
100 metres	1:04.26	David Andrew Wilkie, M.B.E.	Cali, Colombia	22 July 1975
200 metres	2:18.23	David Andrew Wilkie, M.B.E.	Cali, Colombia	24 July 1975
BUTTERFLY				
100 metres	56.68	Brian Brinkley	Cali, Colombia	26 July 1975
200 metres	2:02.47	Brian Brinkley	Cali, Colombia	24 July 1975
BACKSTROKE				
100 metres	59.82	Colin Cunningham	Vienna, Austria	25 Aug. 1974
200 metres	2:08.13	James Carter	Winnipeg, Canada	18 May 1975
INDIVIDUAL MEDLEY				
200 metres	2:06.32	David Andrew Wilkie, M.B.E.	Vienna, Austria	24 Aug. 1974
400 metres	4:36.29	Brian Brinkley	Coventry, Warwickshire	4 Aug. 1973

WOMEN

Distance	Time	Name	Place	Date
FREESTYLE	Min. sec.			
100 metres	1:00.3	Debbie Hill	Crystal Palace, London	7 June 1975
200 metres	2:09.42	Susan S. Edmondson	Vienna, Austria	28 Aug. 1974
400 metres	4:29.17	Diane Barclay Walker	Vienna, Austria	20 Aug. 1974
800 metres	9:17.41	Deborah Simpson	Christchurch, New Zealand	25 Jan. 1974
1,500 metres	18:43.2	Susan S. Edmondson	Coventry, Warwickshire	16 June 1973
BREASTSTROKE				
100 metres	1:15.82	Sandra Dickie	Leeds, Yorkshire	13 April 1974
200 metres	2:42.78	Margaret Mary Kelly	Cali, Colombia	25 July 1975
BUTTERFLY				
100 metres	1:05.26	Joanne Atkinson	Crystal Palace, London	25 May 1975
200 metres	2:21.15	Joanne Atkinson	Crystal Palace, London	24 May 1975
BACKSTROKE				
100 metres	1:08.55	Margaret Mary Kelly	Vienna, Austria	22 Aug. 1974
200 metres	2:26.2	Wendy Burrell	Barcelona, Spain	9 Sept. 1970
INDIVIDUAL MEDLEY				
200 metres	2:25.01	Anne Adams	Crystal Palace, London	25 May 1975
400 metres	5:06.71	Susan Richardson	Vienna, Austria	21 Aug. 1974

TABLE TENNIS

Earliest reference The earliest evidence relating to a game resembling table tennis has been found in the catalogues of London sports goods manufacturers in the 1880s. The old Ping Pong Association was formed in 1902 but the game proved only a temporary craze until resuscitated in 1921. The English Table Tennis Association was formed on 24 April 1927.

The highest total of English men's titles (instituted 1921) is 20 by G. Viktor Barna (1912–72). The women's record is 18 by Diane Rowe (b. 14 April 1933), now

Mrs. Eberhard Scholer. Her twin Rosalind (now Mrs. Cornett) has won 9 (two in singles).

Youngest international The youngest ever international (probably in any sport) was Joy Foster, aged 8, the 1958 Jamaican singles and mixed doubles champion.

Longest rally In the 1936 Swaythling Cup match in Prague between Alex Ehrlich (Poland) and Paneth Farcas (Romania) the opening rally lasted 2 hr 12 min. On 14 Apr. 1973 Nick Krajancie and Graham Lassen staged a 2 hr 31 min rally in Auckland, New Zealand.

Counter Hitting The record number of hits in 60 sec is 157 by Nicky Jarvis and Donald Parker at Barrow-in-Furness, Cumbria on 22 Apr. 1974.

Marathon records In the Swaythling Cup final match between Austria and Romania in Prague, Czechoslovakia, in 1936, the play lasted for 25 or 26 hours, spread over three nights.

The longest recorded time for a marathon singles match by two players is 85 hr 18 min 42 sec by Richard Lavigne and Bobby Laird at Fairfield Mall, Chicopee, Mass., U.S.A. on 3–6 June 1975.

The longest recorded marathon by 4 players maintaining continuous singles is 672 hours (28 days) by 4 players at the Fresno Fashion Fair, California, U.S.A. on 3–31 Aug. 1973. The longest doubles marathon by 4 players is 69 hr 1 min by four members of the Troon Youth Club, Troon, Cornwall on 11–14 July 1975.

Highest speed No conclusive measurements have been published but in a lecture M. Sklorz (West Germany) stated that a smashed ball had been measured at speeds up to 170 km/h *105.6 m.p.h.*

MOST WINS IN WORLD CHAMPIONSHIPS (Instituted 1926–27)

Event	Name and Nationality	Time	Years
Men's Singles (St. Bride's Vase)	G. Viktor Barna (Hungary)	5	1930, 1932–33–34–35
Women's Singles (G. Geist Prize)	Angelica Rozeanu (Romania)	6	1950–51–52–53–54–55
Men's Doubles	G. Viktor Barna (Hungary) with two different partners	8	1929–35, 1939
Women's Doubles	Maria Mednyanzsky (Hungary) with three different partners	7	1928, 1930–31–32–33–34–35
Mixed Doubles (Men)	Ferenc Sido (Hungary) with two different partners	4	1949–50, 1952–53
(Women)	Maria Mednyanszky (Hungary) with three different partners	6	1927–28, 1930–31, 1933–34

G. Viktor Barna gained a personal total of 15 world titles, while 18 have been won by Miss Maria Mednyanszky.
Note: With the staging of championships biennially the breaking of the above records would now be virtually impossible.

MOST TEAM TITLES

Event	Team	Times	Years
Men's Team (Swaythling Cup)	Hungary	11	1927–31, 1933–35, 1938, 1949, 1952
Women's Team (Marcel Carbillon Cup)	Japan	8	1952, 1954, 1957, 1959, 1961, 1963, 1967, 1971

MOST WINS IN ENGLISH OPEN CHAMPIONSHIPS (Instituted 1921)

Event	Name and Nationality	Times	Years
Men's Singles	Richard Bergmann (Austria, then G.B.)	6	1939–40, 1948, 1950, 1952, 1954
Women's Singles	Mrs. M. Alexandru (Romania)	6	1963–64, 1970–71–72–74
Men's Doubles	G. Viktor Barna (Hungary, then G.B.) with five different partners	7	1931, 1933–34–35, 1938–39, 1949
Women's Doubles	Miss Diane Rowe (G.B.) with four different partners	12	1950–56, 1960, 1962–65
Mixed Doubles (Men)	G. Viktor Barna (Hungary, then G.B.) with four different partners	8	1933–36, 1938, 1940, 1951, 1953
(Women)	Miss Diane Rowe (G.B.) (now Scholer) with three different partners	4	1952, 1954, 1956, 1960, 1969

TENNIS (REAL OR ROYAL)

Origins The game originated in French monasteries *c.* 1050.

Oldest court The oldest of the 17 surviving Tennis Courts in the British Isles is the Royal Tennis Court at Hampton Court Palace, which was built by order of King Henry VIII in 1529–30 and rebuilt by order of Charles II in 1660. The oldest court in the world is one built in Paris in 1496. There are estimated to be 3,000 players and 29 courts in the world.

World titles The first recorded World Tennis Champion was Clerge (France) *c.* 1740. Pierre Etchebaster (b. 1893) won the title at Prince's, Paris, in May 1928, last defended it in New York (winning 7–1) in December 1949 and retired undefeated in 1955, after 27 years. Etchebaster, a Basque, also holds the record for the greatest number of successful defences of his title with six.

British titles The Amateur Championship of the British Isles (instituted 1780) has been won 13 times by Edgar M. Baerlein (1879–1972) (1912 to 1930). The greatest number of international appearances has been 18 by Sir Clarance Napier Bruce, G.B.E., 3rd Baron Aberdare (1885–1957).

Pierre Etchebaster who was for 27 years the undefeated Peter Pan world champion tennis player until his retirement aged 62 in 1955

Sport and General

TRACK AND FIELD ATHLETICS

Earliest references Track and field athletics date from the ancient Olympic Games. The earliest accurately known Olympiad dates from 21 or 22 July 776 B.C., at which celebration Coroebus won the foot race. The oldest surviving measurements are a long jump of 7,05 m *23 ft 1½ in* by Chionis of Sparta in *c.* 656 B.C. and a discus throw of 100 cubits by Protesilaus.

Fastest runner Robert Lee Hayes (b. 20 Dec. 1942) of Jacksonville, Florida, U.S.A., was timed at the 60 (6.0 sec) and 75 yds (7.1 sec) marks in a 100 yard event at St. Louis, Missouri, on 21 June 1963, which indicates a speed of 27.89 m.p.h. *44,88 km/h* Wyomia Tyus (b. Griffin, Georgia, U.S.A., 29 Aug. 1945) was timed to touch 23.78 m.p.h. *38,27 km/h* in Kiev, U.S.S.R. on 31 July 1965.

Highest jumper There are several reported instances of high jumpers exceeding the official world record height of 7 ft 6½ in *2,30 m*. The earliest of these came from unsubstantiated reports of Tutsi tribesmen in Central Africa (see page 10) clearing up to 8 ft 2½ in *2,50 m*, definitely however, from inclined take-offs. The greatest height cleared above an athlete's own head is 18 in *45,7 cm* by Ron Livers (U.S.), who cleared 7 ft 3 in *2,21 m* despite a physical height of only 5 ft 9 in *1,75 m* at Provo, Utah on 7 June 1975. The greatest height cleared by a woman above her own head is 20 cm *7.87 in* by Rosemarie Witschas (now Ackermann) (East Germany) who stands 1,75 m *5 ft 8.9 in*, when she jumped 1,95 m *6 ft 5 in* at Rome, Italy on 8 Sept. 1974.

Most Olympic titles The most Olympic gold medals won is ten (an absolute Olympic record) by Ray C. Ewry (U.S.A.) (b. 14 Oct. 1873 d. 29 Sept. 1937) with:

Standing High Jump	1900, 1904, 1906, 1908
Standing Long Jump	1900, 1904, 1906, 1908
Standing Triple Jump	1900, 1904

Women The most gold medals won by a woman is four shared by Francina E. Blankers-Koen (Netherlands) (b. 26 April 1918) with (100 m, 200 m, 80 m hurdles and 4 × 100 m relay, 1948) and Betty Cuthbert (Australia) (b. 20 April 1938) with 100 m, 200 m, 4 × 100 m relay, 1956 and 400 m, 1964).

British The most gold medals won by a British athlete (excluding Tug of War and Walking *qq.v.*) is two by: Charles Bennett (1,500 m and 5,000 m team, 1900); Alfred Tysoe (800 m and 5,000 m team, 1900); John Rimmer (4,000 m steeplechase and 5,000 m team, 1900) Albert G. Hill (b. 24 March 1889) 800 m and 1,500 m, 1920 and Douglas Gordon Arthur Lowe (b. 7 Aug. 1902) 800 m 1924 and 1928).

Most Olympic medals The most medals won is 12 (9 gold and 3 silver) by Paavo Johannes Nurmi (Finland) (1897–1973):

1920 Gold: 10,000 m; Cross Country, Individual and Team; silver: 5,000 m.
1924 Gold: 1,500 m; 5,000 m; 3,000 m Team; Cross Country, Individual and Team.
1928 Gold: 10,000 m; silver: 5,000 m; 3,000 m steeplechase.

Women The most medals won by a woman athlete is seven by Shirley de la Hunty (*née* Strickland) (Australia) (b. 18 July 1925) with 3 gold, 1 silver and 3 bronze in the 1948, 1952 and 1956 Games.

British The most medals won by a British athlete is four by Guy M. Butler (b. 25 Aug. 1899) with a gold medal for the 4 × 400 m relay and a silver in the 400 m in 1920 and a bronze medal for each of these events in 1924. Two British women athletes have won three medals:

Dorothy Hyman, M.B.E. (b. 9 May 1941) with a silver (100 m, 1960) and bronze (200 m, 1960 and 4 × 100 m relay, 1964) and Mrs. Mary Denise Rand, M.B.E. (now Toomey, *née* Bignal), (b. 10 Feb. 1940) with a gold (Long Jump), a silver (Pentathlon) and a bronze 4 × 100 m relay) all in 1964.

Most wins at one Games The most gold medals at one celebration is five by Nurmi in 1924 (see above) and the most individual is four by Alvin C. Kraenzlein (U.S.A.) (1876–1928) in 1900, with 60 m, 110 m hurdles, 200 m hurdles and long jump.

Most national titles The greatest number of national A.A.A. titles (excluding those in tug of war events) won by one athlete is fourteen individual and two relay titles by Emmanuel McDonald Bailey (b. Williamsville, Trinidad 8 Dec. 1920), between 1946 and 1953.

The greatest number of consecutive title wins is seven by Denis Horgan (Ireland) in the shot putt (1893–99), Albert A. Cooper (2 miles walk, 1932–38), Donald Osborne Finlay, D.F.C., A.F.C. (1909–70) (120 yds hurdles, 1932–38), Harry Whittle (440 yds hurdles, 1947–1953) and Maurice Herriott (3,000 m steeplechase, 1961–67). The record for consecutive W.A.A.A. titles is eight by Mrs. Judy U. Farr (Trowbridge & District A.C.) (b. 24 Jan. 1942), who won the 1½ miles 2 500 m walk from 1962–69.

Earliest landmarks The first time 10 sec ("even time") was bettered for 100 yds under championship conditions was when John Owen recorded 9⅘ sec in the United States A.A.U. Championship at Analostan Island, Washington, D.C., U.S.A., on 11 Oct. 1890. The first recorded instance of 6 ft *1,83 m* being cleared in the high jump was when Marshall Jones Brooks jumped 6 ft 0⅛ in *1,832 m* at Marston, near Oxford, England, on 17 March 1876. The breaking of the "4-minute barrier" in the one mile *1 609,34 m* was first achieved by Sir Roger Gilbert Bannister, C.B.E. (b. Harrow, England 23 March 1929), when he recorded 3 min 59.4 sec on the Iffley Road track, Oxford, at 6.10 p.m. on 6 May 1954.

World record breakers
Oldest The greatest age at which anyone has broken a world athletics record in a standard Olympic event is 35 years 255 days in the case of Dana Zátopkova, *née* Ingrova (b. 19 Sept. 1922) of Czechoslovakia, who broke the women's javelin record with 182 ft 10 in *55,73 m* at Prague, Czechoslovakia, on 1 June 1958. On 20 June 1948 Mikko Hietanen (Finland) (b. 22 Sept. 1911) bettered his own world 30,000 m record with 1 hr 40 min 46.4 sec at Jyväskylä, Finland, when aged 36 years 272 days.

Youngest Ulrike Mayfarth (b. 4 May 1956) equalled the world record for the women's high jump with 1.92 m *6 ft 3½ in* in winning the gold medal on 4 Sept. 1972 at the Munich Olympics aged 16 years 4 months.

Most in a day Jesse Owens (U.S.A.) set six world records in 45 min at Ann Arbor, Michigan on 25 May 1935 with a 9.4 sec 100 yds (3.15 p.m.), a 26 ft 8¼ in *8,13 m* long jump (3.25 p.m.), a 20.3 sec 220 yds (and 200 m) at 3.45 p.m. and a 22.6 sec 220 yds low hurdles (and 200 m) at 4.0 p.m.

INTERNATIONALS

Most The greatest number of full Great Britain outdoor internationals won by a British male athlete is 61 by Andrew Howard Payne (b. 17 Apr. 1931). The feminine record is 52 full internationals by Brenda Bedford (*née* Sawyer) (b. 4 Sept. 1937, London) from 1961 to mid-Aug. 1975.

Oldest and youngest Of full Great Britain (outdoor) internationals the oldest have been Harold Whitlock (b. 16 Dec. 1903) at the 1952 Olympic Games, aged 48 years 218 days, and Mrs. Rosemary Payne (b. 19 May 1933) in the Great Britain versus Sweden match in September 1973, aged 40 years 4 months. The youngest have been William Land (b. 29 Nov. 1914) *versus* Italy in 1931, aged 16 years 271 days, and Janis Walsh (b. 28 Mar. 1960) *versus* Belgium (indoor) at 60 m and 4 × 200 m relay at Cosford on 15 Feb. 1975 41 days short of her 15th birthday.

24 hour record The greatest distance run in 24 hours is 161 miles 545 yd *259,60 km* by Ron Bentley, 43 at Walton-on-Thames, Surrey on 3–4 Nov. 1973. The fastest recorded time for 100 miles *160,934 km* is 11 hr 56 min 56 sec by D. Kay in Durban, South Africa on 6–7 Oct. 1972.

Mass relay records The record for 100 miles *160,9 km* by 100 runners belonging to one club is 8 hrs 5 min 24.8 sec by Sale Harriers at Crystal Palace, London on 29 June 1975. The best club time for a 100 × 400 metres relay is 1 hr 34 min 00.6 sec by the Tarnverein Länggasse Bern, Switzerland on 19 Apr. 1975.

Three-legged race The fastest recorded time for a 100 yds three-legged race is 11.0 sec by Harry L. Hillman (d. 9 Aug. 1945) and Lawson Robertson (b. 1883 Aberdeen d. 22 Jan. 1951) at Brooklyn, New York City, N.Y., U.S.A., on 24 April 1909.

Running Backwards The fastest time recorded for running the 100 yds backwards is 13.5 sec by Bill Robinson (1878–1949) in the U.S. early in the century.

End to End Barefoot On 5–9 Sept. 1971 a group of members of the International Budo Association ran from John O'Groats to Land's End, barefoot—891 miles *1 443 km*.

Greatest caber toss The weight and height of cabers (Gaelic *cabar*) vary considerably. Extreme values are 25 ft *7,62 m* and 280 lb. *127 kg*. The Braemar caber in Grampian, Scotland, was untossed (19 ft 3 in *5,86 m* and 120 lb. *54,4 kg*) from 1891 until 1951 when it was tossed by George Clark.

Associated Press

Steve Williams (U.S.A.), the most recent sub-10 sec 100 metre sprinter and claimant to the title of "World's Fastest Human"

WORLD RECORDS—MEN

This complete list of World Records for the 54 scheduled men's events (excluding the 6 walking records, see under WALKING) passed by the International Amateur Athletic Federation as at 1 Aug. 1975. Note: When a time is given to a hundredth of a second it represents the official electrically timed record, which is only applicable for the 7 metric events of up to 400 metres. Hand timings are only listed if faster than accepted electrical timings. * Denotes awaiting ratification.

RUNNING

Event	Min sec	Name and Nationality	Place	Date
100 yards	9.0	Ivory Crockett (U.S.A.)	Knoxville, Tennessee, U.S.A.	11 May 1974
	9.0*	Houston McTear (U.S.A.)	Long Beach, California, U.S.A.	4 May 1975
220 yards (straight)	19.5	Tommie C. Smith (U.S.A.)	San José, California, U.S.A.	7 May 1966
220 yards (turn)	19.9*	Donald O'Riley Quarrie (Jamaica)	Eugene, Oregon, U.S.A.	7 June 1975
	19.9*	Steven Williams (U.S.A.)	Eugene, Oregon, U.S.A.	7 June 1975
440 yards	44.5	John Smith (U.S.A.)	Eugene, Oregon, U.S.A.	26 June 1971
880 yards	1:44.1	Richard Wohlhuter (U.S.A.)	Eugene, Oregon, U.S.A.	8 June 1974
1 mile	3:49.4*	John Walker (N.Z.)	Göteborg, Sweden	12 Aug. 1975
2 miles	8:13.8	Brendan Foster (G.B.)	Crystal Palace, London	27 Aug. 1973
3 miles	12:47.8	Emiel Puttemans (Belgium)	Brussels, Belgium	20 Sept. 1972
6 miles	26:47.0	Ronald William Clarke, M.B.E. (Australia)	Oslo, Norway	14 July 1965
10 miles	46:04.2	Willy Polleunis (Belgium)	Brussels, Belgium	20 Sept. 1972
15 miles	1 hr 11: 52.6*	Pekka Päivärinta (Finland)	Oulu, Finland	15 May 1975
100 metres	9.9	James Ray Hines (U.S.A.)	Sacramento, California, U.S.A.	20 June 1968
	9.9	Ronald Ray Smith (U.S.A.)	Sacramento, California, U.S.A.	20 June 1968
	9.9	Charles Edward Greene (U.S.A.)	Sacramento, California, U.S.A.	20 June 1968
	9.95	James Ray Hines (U.S.A.)	Mexico City, Mexico	14 Oct. 1968
	9.9	Eddie Hart (U.S.A.)	Eugene, Oregon, U.S.A.	1 July 1972
	9.9	Reynaud Robinson (U.S.A.)	Eugene, Oregon, U.S.A.	1 July 1972
	9.9	Steven Williams (U.S.A.)	Los Angeles, California, U.S.A.	21 June 1974
	9.9*	Silvio Leonard (Cuba)	Ostrava, Czechoslovakia	5 June 1975
	9.9*	Steven Williams (U.S.A.)	Siena, Italy	16 July 1975
200 metres (straight)	19.5	Tommie C. Smith (U.S.A.)	San José, California, U.S.A.	7 May 1966
200 metres (turn)	19.83	Tommie C. Smith (U.S.A.)	Mexico City, Mexico	16 Oct. 1968
	19.81	Donald O'Riley Quarrie (Jamaica)	Cali, Colombia	3 Aug. 1971
	19.8*	Donald O'Riley Quarrie (Jamaica)	Eugene, Oregon, U.S.A.	7 June 1975
	19.8*	Steven Williams (U.S.A.)	Eugene, Oregon, U.S.A.	7 June 1975
400 metres	43.86	Lee Edward Evans (U.S.A.)	Mexico City, Mexico	18 Oct. 1968
800 metres	1:43.7	Marcello Fiasconaro (Italy)	Milan, Italy	27 June 1973
1,000 metres	2:13.9	Richard Wohlhuter (U.S.A.)	Oslo, Norway	30 July 1974
1,500 metres	3:32.2	Filbert Bayi (Tanzania)	Christchurch, New Zealand	2 Feb. 1974
2,000 metres	4:56.2	Michel Jazy (France)	St. Maur des Fosses, France	12 Oct. 1966
3,000 metres	7:13.2	Brendan Foster (G.B. & N.I.)	Gateshead, Tyne and Wear, England	3 Aug. 1974
5,000 metres	13:13.0	Emiel Puttemans (Belgium)	Brussels, Belgium	20 Sept. 1972
10,000 metres	27:30.8	David Colin Bedford (G.B. & N.I.)	Crystal Palace, London	13 July 1973
20,000 metres	57:44.4	Gaston Roelants (Belgium)	Brussels, Belgium	20 Sept. 1972
25,000 metres	1 hr 14:16.8*	Pekka Päivärinta (Finland)	Oulu, Finland	15 May 1975
30,000 metres	1 hr 31:30.4	James Noel Carroll Alder (G.B. & N.I.)	Crystal Palace, London	5 Sept. 1970
1 hour	12 miles 1,609 yd *20 784 m*	Gaston Roelants (Belgium)	Brussels, Belgium	20 Sept. 1972

HURDLING

120 yards (3′ 6″ [106,4 cm])	13.0	Rodney Milburn (U.S.A.)	Eugene, Oregon, U.S.A.	25 June 1971
	13.0	Rodney Milburn (U.S.A.)	Eugene, Oregon, U.S.A.	20 June 1973
220 yards (2′ 6″ [75,9 m]) (straight)	21.9	Donald Augustus Styron (U.S.A.)	Baton Rouge, Louisiana, U.S.A.	2 April 1960
440 yards (3′ 0″ [91,1 cm])	48.7	James Bolding (U.S.A.)	Turin, Italy	24 July 1974
110 metres (3′ 6″)	13.24	Rodney Milburn (U.S.A.)	Munich, West Germany	7 Sept. 1972
	13.1	Rodney Milburn (U.S.A.)	Zürich, Switzerland	6 July 1973
	13.1	Rodney Milburn (U.S.A.)	Sienna, Italy	21 July 1973
	13.1*	Guy Drut (France)	Paris, France	23 July 1975
200 metres (2′ 6″) (straight)	21.9	Donald Augustus Styron (U.S.A.)	Baton Rouge, Louisiana, U.S.A.	2 April 1960
200 metres (2′ 6″) (turn)	22.5	Karl Martin Lauer (West Germany)	Zürich, Switzerland	7 July 1959
	22.5	Glenn Ashby Davis (U.S.A.)	Bern, Switzerland	20 Aug. 1960
400 metres (3′ 0″)	47.82	John Akii-Bua (Uganda)	Munich, West Germany	2 Sept. 1972
3,000 metres Steeplechase	8:09.7*	Anders Garderud (Sweden)	Stockholm, Sweden	1 July 1975

MARATHON

There is no official marathon record because of the varying severity of courses. The best time over 26 miles 385 yards 42 km (standardised in 1924) is 2 hr 08 min 33.6 sec. (av. 12.24 m.p.h. [19,69 km/h]) by Derek Clayton (b. 1942, at Barrow-in-Furness, England) of Australia, at Antwerp, Belgium, on 30 May 1969.
The best time by a British international is 2 hr 9 min 12.0 sec by Ian Thompson (b. 16 Oct. 1949) at Christchurch, New Zealand, 1974.
The fastest time by a female is 2 hr 40 min 15 sec (av. 9.82 m.p.h. [15,80 km/h]) by Christa Vahlensiek (West Germany) at Dülmen, West Germany on 3 May 1975.

RELAYS

Event	Min sec	Team	Place	Date
4 × 110 yards (two turns)	38.6	University of Southern California, U.S.A. (Earl Ray McCullouch, Fred Kuller, Orenthal James Simpson, Lennox Miller [Jamaica])	Provo, Utah, U.S.A.	17 June 1967
4 × 220 yards	1:21.7†	Texas Agricultural & Mechanical College (Donald Rogers, Rockie Woods, Marvin Mills, Curtis Mills)	Des Moines, Iowa, U.S.A.	24 April 1970
4 × 440 yards	3:02.4	United States National Team Ronald Ray, Robert Taylor, Maurice Peoples, Stan Vinson	Durham, North Carolina, U.S.A.	July 1966
4 × 880 yards	7:10.4	University of Chicago Track Club (Tom Bach, Ken Sparks, Lowell Paul, Richard Wohlhuter)	Durham, North Carolina, U.S.A.	12 May 1973
4 × 1 mile	16:02.8	New Zealand Team (Kevin Ross, Anthony Polhill, Richard Taylor, Richard Quax)	Auckland New Zealand	3 Feb. 1972
4 × 100 metres (two turns)	38.19	United States National Team (Larry Black, Robert Taylor Gerald Tinker, Eddie Hart)	Munich, West Germany	10 Sept. 1972
4 × 200 metres	1:21.5	Italian Team (Franco Ossala, Pasqualino Abeti, Luigi Benedetti, Pietro Mennea)	Barletta, Italy	21 July 1972
4 × 400 metres	2:56.1	United States National Team (Vincent Matthews, Ronald Freeman, G. Lawrence James, Lee Edward Evans)	Mexico City, Mexico	20 Oct. 1968
4 × 800 metres	7:08.6	West Germany "A" Team (Manfred Kinder, Walter Adams, Dieter Bogatzki, Franz-Josef Kemper)	Wiesbaden, East Germany	13 Aug. 1966
4 × 1,500 metres	14:49.0	New Zealand (Anthony Polhill, John Walker, Rodney Dixon, Richard Quax)	Oslo, Norway	22 Aug. 1973

† The time of 1:20.7 achieved by University of Southern California (Edesel Garrison, Lee Brown, William Deckard and Donald O'Riley Quarrie) at Fresno, California U.S.A. 13 May 1972 is not eligible because Quarrie is a Jamaican national.

FIELD EVENTS

Event	ft	in	m	Name and Nationality	Place	Date	
High Jump	7	6½	2,30	Dwight Stones (U.S.A.)	Munich, West Germany	11 July	1973
Pole Vault	18	6½*	5,55	David Roberts (U.S.A.)	Gainsville, Florida, U.S.A.	28 May	1975
Long Jump	29	2½	8,90	Robert Beamon (U.S.A.)	Mexico City, Mexico	18 Oct.	1968
Triple Jump	57	2¾	17,44	Viktor Saneyev (U.S.S.R.)	Sukhumi, U.S.S.R.	17 Oct.	1972
Shot Putt	71	7	21,82	Allan Dean Feuerbach (U.S.A.)	San Jose, California, U.S.A.	5 May	1973
Discus Throw	226	8*	69,10	John Powell (U.S.A.)	Long Beach, California, U.S.A.	4 May	1975
Hammer Throw	260	2	79,29	Walter Schmidt (West Germany)	Frankfurt, West Germany	14 Aug.	1975
Javelin Throw	308	8	94,08	Klaus Wolfermann (West Germany)	Leverkusen, West Germany	5 May	1973

DECATHLON

8,454 points	Nikoliy Avilov (U.S.S.R.) (1st day: 100 m 11.0 sec, Long Jump 7,68 25′ 2½″, Shot Putt 14,36 47′ 1½″, High Jump 2,12 6′ 11½″ 400 m 48.5 sec	Munich, West Germany (2nd day: 110 m hurdles 14.31 sec, Discus 46,98 154′ 1½″, Pole Vault 4,55 14′ 11¼″, Javelin 61,66 202′ 3½″ 1,500 m 4:22.8 sec)	7–8 Sept. 1972

Note: Two professional performances are equal or superior to the I.A.A.F. marks but the same highly rigorous rules as to timing, measuring and weighing are not necessarily applied.

120 yard hurdles	13.0 sec		Rodney Milburn (U.S.A.)	El Paso, Texas, U.S.A.	10 May 1975
Shot Putt	75 ft 0 in	22,86 m	Brian Ray Oldfield (U.S.A.)	El Paso, Texas, U.S.A.	10 May 1975

Longest Career Duncan McLean (b. Gourock, Strathclyde, 3 Dec. 1884) won the South African 100 yard title in Feb. 1904 in 9.9 sec and was fifth in a heat in 13.2 sec in the Veterans' 100 metre handicap at Hurlingham, London on 7 Sept. 1974 more than 70 years later.

Blind 100 yards The fastest time recorded for a 100 yds by a blind man is 11.0 sec by Geoffrey Bull, aged 19, of Chippenham, Wiltshire, in a race at the Worcester College for the Blind, on 26 Oct. 1954.

Pancake race record The annual Housewives Pancake Race at Olney, Buckinghamshire, was first mentioned in 1445. The record for the winding 415 yd 380 m course (three tosses mandatory) is 61.0 sec, set by Sally Ann Faulkner, 16, on 26 Feb. 1974. The record for the counterpart race (inst. 1949) at Liberal, Kansas, U.S.A. is 59.1 sec by Kathleen West, 19, on 10 Feb. 1970.

Standing High Jump The best amateur standing high jump is 5 ft 9¼ in 1,76 m by Johan Christian Evandt (Norway) at Oslo on 4

Gerry Cranham

Steeplechaser Anders Garderud, Sweden's only reigning world record holder, whose 8 min 9.7 sec for the steeplechase is faster than the pre-war record for 3,000 metres *without* the 35 obstacles

Gerry Cranham

Jamaican-born Andrea Lynch, U.K. record-holder for the 100 metres and co-holder of the world's 60 metre record

WORLD RECORDS—WOMEN

The complete list of World Records for the 28 scheduled women's events passed by the International Amateur Athletic Federation as at 1 Aug. 1975. Those marked with an asterisk are awaiting ratification. The same stipulation about electrically timed events apply in the 7 metric events up to 400 metres as in the men's events.

RUNNING

Event	Min sec	Name and Nationality	Place	Date
100 yards	10.0	Chi Cheng (Taiwan, China)	Portland, Oregon, U.S.A.	13 June 1970
220 yards (turn)	22.6	Chi Cheng (Taiwan, China)	Westwood, Calif., U.S.A.	3 July 1970
440 yards	52.2	Kathleen Hammond (U.S.A.)	Urbana, Illinois, U.S.A.	12 Aug. 1972
	52.2	Debra Sapenter (U.S.A.)	Bakersfield, California, U.S.A.	29 June 1974
880 yards	2:01.0	Judith Florence Pollock (*née* Amoore) (Australia)	Helsinki, Finland	28 June 1967
1 mile	4:29.5	Paola Cacchi (*née* Pigni) (Italy)	Viareggio, Italy	8 Aug. 1973
60 metres	7.2	Betty Cuthbert (Australia)	Sydney, N.S.W. Australia	21 Feb. 1960
	7.2	Irina Robertovna Bochkaryova (*née* Turova) (U.S.S.R.)	Moscow, U.S.S.R.	28 Aug. 1960
	7.2	Andrea Joan Caron Lynch (U.K.)	London, England	22 June 1974
	7.2*	Lea Alaerts (Belgium)	Namour, Belgium	2 Aug. 1975
100 metres	10.8	Renate Stecher (*née* Meissner) (East Germany)	Dresden, East Germany	20 July 1973
	11.07	Wyomia Tyus (U.S.A.)	Mexico City, Mexico	15 Oct. 1968
	11.07	Renate Stecher (*née* Meissner) (East Germany)	Munich, West Germany	2 Sept. 1972
200 metres (turn)	22.1	Renate Stecher (*née* Meissner) (East Germany)	Dresden, East Germany	21 July 1973
	22.21	Irena Szewinska (*née* Kirszenstein) (Poland)	Potsdam, East Germany	13 June 1974
400 metres	49.9	Irena Szewinska (*née* Kirszenstein) (Poland)	Warsaw, Poland	22 June 1974
	50.14	Riitta Salin (Finland)	Rome, Italy	4 Sept. 1974
800 metres	1:57.5	Svetla Zlateva (Bulgaria)	Athens, Greece	24 Aug. 1973
1,500 metres	4:01.4	Lyudmila Bragina (U.S.S.R.)	Munich, West Germany	9 Sept. 1972
3,000 metres	8:46.8	Grete Andersen (Norway)	Oslo, Norway	24 June 1975

HURDLING

Event	sec	Name and Nationality	Place	Date
100 metres (2' 9" [83,7 cm])	12.3	Annelie Ehrhardt (East Germany)	Dresden, East Germany	22 July 1973
	12.59	Annelie Ehrhardt (East Germany)	Munich, West Germany	8 Sept. 1972
400 metres (2' 6" [76,2 cm])	56.51	Krystyna Kacperczyk (Poland)	Augsburg, West Germany	13 July 1974

March 1962. Joe Darby (1861–1937), the famous Victorian professional jumper reportedly cleared 6 ft *1,83 m* with ankles tied at Church Cricket Ground, Dudley, West Midlands on 11 June 1892.

Standing Long Jump Joe Darby, jumped a measured 12 ft 1½ in *3,69 m without* weights at Dudley Castle, on 28 May 1890. Evandt (see above) achieved 3,65 m *11 ft 11¾ in* as an amateur in Reykjavik, Iceland on 11 March 1962.

One legged High Jump One legged Anthony Willis, 18 (City of Plymouth A.C.) cleared 6 ft *1 m 83* at Plymouth, Devon, England in July 1973.

Throwing the 56 lb. weight for height The best authentic mark recorded is 15 ft 7 in *4,75 m* over a bar by W. Anderson at Lochearnhead, Central, Scotland in 1970 and also at Meadowbank, Edinburgh.

Ambidextrous Shot Putt The best recorded distance is 121 ft 6¾ in by Allan Feuerbach (U.S.A.) (left 51 ft 5 in *15,67 m*, right 70 ft 1¾ in *21,38 m*) at Malmo, Sweden in 1974.

329

FIELD EVENTS

Event	ft	in	m	Name and Nationality	Place	Date
High Jump	6	5*	1,95	Rosemarie Ackermann (née Witschas) (East Germany)	Rome, Italy	8 Sept. 1974
Long Jump	22	5¼	6,84	Heidemarie Rosendahl (West Germany)	Turin, Italy	3 Sept. 1970
Shot Putt	70	9¼	21,57	Helena Fibingerova (Czechoslovakia)	Gottwaldov, East Germany	21 Sept. 1974
Discus Throw	229	4	69,90	Faina Melnik (U.S.S.R.)	Prague, Czechoslovakia	27 May 1974
Javelin Throw	220	6	67,22	Ruth Fuchs (née Gamm) (East Germany)	Rome, Italy	3 Sept. 1974

PENTATHLON (1971 Scoring Tables)

4,932 points	Burglinde Pollak (East Germany) (100 m Hurdles 13.21 s; shot putt 52 ft 0 in 15,85 m; high jump 5 ft 10 in 1,78 m; long jump 21 ft 2½ in 6,47 m; 200 m 23.35 sec)	Bonn, West Germany · 22 Sept. 1973

RELAYS

Event	Min sec	Team	Place	Date
4 × 110 yards	44.07	West German National Team (Inge Heltea, Birgit Wilkes, Annegret Kroniger, Maren Gang)	Durham, North Carolina, U.S.A.	5 July 1975
4 × 220 yards	1:35.8	Australia (Marian R. Hoffman, Raelene Ann Boyle, Pamela Kilborn, Jennifer F. Lamy)	Brisbane, Australia	9 Nov. 1969
4 × 440 yards	3:30.3	West German National Team (Christiane Krause, Dagmar Jost, Erika Weinstein, Elke Barth)	Durham North Carolina, U.S.A.	July 1972
4 × 100 metres	42.51	East Germany (Doris Maletzki, Renate Stecher, Christina Heinich, Barbel Eckert)	Berlin	24 Aug. 1974
4 × 200 metres	1:33.8	United Kingdom National Team (Maureen Dorothy Tranter, Della P. James, Janet Mary Simpson, Valerie Peat [née Wild])	London (Crystal Palace)	24 Aug. 1968
4 × 400 metres	3:23.0	East German National Team (Dagmar Käsling, Rita Kühne, Helga Seidler, Monika Zehrt)	Munich, West Germany	10 Sept. 1972
4 × 800 metres	8:08.6	Bulgarian National Team (Svetla Zlateva, Lilyana Tomova, Tonka Petrova, Stefka Kordanova)	Sophia, Bulgaria	12 Aug. 1973

UNITED KINGDOM (NATIONAL) RECORDS—MEN

Since events in yards are so rarely run and never in championships these are now omitted with the exception of the one mile event. The adoption by the I.A.A.F. of separate lists for hand and for electrically timed metric events up to 400 metres has caused a re-examination of the credibility of some hand timed British records. Accordingly we now only list the best yet fully automatic electrically timed performances for these events.

Event	Min sec	Name	Place	Date	
100 metres	10.33	Brian William Green	London (Crystal Palace)	15 July	1972
200 metres (turn)	20.66	Richard Steane	Mexico City, Mexico	15 Oct.	1968
	20.66	David Andrew Jenkins	London (Crystal Palace)	27 Aug.	1973
400 metres	44.93	David Andrew Jenkins	Eugene, Oregon, U.S.A.	21 June	1975
800 metres	1:45.1	Andrew William Carter	London (Crystal Palace)	14 July	1973
1,000 metres	2:18.2	John Peter Boulter	London (Crystal Palace)	6 Sept.	1969
1,500 metres	3:37.4	Frank Clements	Stockholm Sweden	30 July	1974
1 mile	3:55.0*	Frank Clements	Stockholm Sweden	30 June	1975
2,000 metres	5:03.2	David Colin Bedford	London (Crystal Palace)	8 July	1972
3,000 metres	7:35.2	Brendan Foster	Gateshead, Tyne and Wear	3 Aug.	1974
5,000 metres	13:14.6	Brendan Foster	Christchurch, New Zealand	29 Jan.	1974
10,000 metres	27:30.8	David Colin Bedford	London (Crystal Palace)	13 July	1973
20,000 metres	58:39.0	Ronald Hill	Leicester	9 Nov.	1968
25,000 metres	1H15:22.6	Ronald Hill	Bolton, Lancashire	1 July	1965
30,000 metres	1H31:30.4	James Noel Carroll Alder	London (Crystal Palace)	25 Sept.	1970
1 hour	12 miles 1,268 yds 20 472 m	Ronald Hill	Leicester	9 Nov.	1968

HURDLING

Event	sec	Name	Place	Date	
110 metres	13.69	Berwyn Price	Moscow, U.S.S.R.	18 Aug.	1973
200 metres (turn)	23.0	Alan Peter Pascoe	Loughborough, Leicestershire	5 June	1969
200 metres (straight)	23.3	Peter Burke Hildreth	Imber Court, Surrey	27 Aug.	1955
400 metres	48.12	David Peter Hemery	Mexico City, Mexico	15 Oct.	1968
3,000 metres Steeplechase	8:22.6	John Davies	London (Crystal Palace)	13 Sept.	1974

FIELD EVENTS

Event	ft	in	m	Name	Place	Date	
High Jump	7	0¼	2,14	Angus McKenzie	London (Crystal Palace)	31 May	1975
	7	0¼	2,14	Michael Butterfield	London (Crystal Palace)	31 May	1975
Pole Vault	17	2¾	5,25	Michael Anthony Bull	London (Crystal Palace)	22 Sept.	1973
Long Jump	27	0	8,23	Lynn Davies, M.B.E.	Bern, Switzerland	30 June	1966
Triple Jump	54	0	16,46	Frederick John Alsop	Tokyo, Japan	16 Oct.	1964
Shot Putt	70	1½	21,37	Geoffrey Lewis Capes	London (Crystal Palace)	10 Aug.	1974
Discus Throw	213	0*	64,92	William Raymond Tancred	Loughborough	21 July	1974
Hammer Throw	233	9	71,26	Barry Williams	Edinburgh, Scotland	8 Sept.	1974
Javelin Throw	278	7	84,92	Charles Clover	Christchurch, New Zealand	2 Feb.	1974

DECATHLON (1962 Scoring Table)

7,903 (points)	Peter John Gabbett (1st day: 100 m 10.5 sec, Long Jump 24' 7¾" 7,51 m, Shot Putt 43' 8" 13,31 m, High Jump 6' 1¼" 1,85 m, 400 m 47.4 sec)	Kassel, West Germany · 5–6 June 1971 (2nd day: 110 m Hurdles 15.2 sec, Discus 151' 0" 46,02 m, Pole Vault 13' 9½" 4,20 m, Javelin 181' 10" 55,42 m, 1,500 m 4:39.8 sec)

RELAYS

Event	Min sec	Name	Place	Date
4 × 100 metres	39.33	United Kingdom National Team (Joseph William Speake, Ronald Jones, Ralph Banthorpe, Barrie Harrison Kelly)	Mexico City, Mexico	19 Oct. 1968
4 × 200 metres	1:24.1	Great Britain (Brian William Green, Roger Walters, Ralph Banthorpe, Martin Edward Reynolds)	Paris, France	2 Oct. 1971

* Awaiting Ratification

4 × 400 metres	3:00.5	United Kingdom National Team (Martin Edward Reynolds, Alan Peter Pascoe, David Peter Hemery, David Andrew Jenkins)	Munich, West Germany	10 Sept. 1972
4 × 800 metres	7:17.4	United Kingdom National Team (Martin Bilham, David Cropper, Michael John Maclean, Peter Miles Browne)	London (Crystal Palace)	5 Sept. 1970
4 × 1,500 metres	15:06.6	Great Britain (Roy C. Young, Walter Wilkinson, Ian Stewart, Adrian P. Weatherhead)	Paris, France	2 Oct. 1971

Gerry Cranham

Britain's two pioneer 7 foot high jumpers, Gus Mackenzie (left) and Michael Butterfield (right), who cleared *2,14 m* 7 ft 0¼ in within seconds of each other at Crystal Palace

UNITED KINGDOM (NATIONAL) RECORDS—WOMEN

Event	Min sec	Name	Place	Date
100 metres	11.16*	Andrea Joan Caron Lynch	London (Crystal Palace)	11 June 1975
200 metres	23.14	Helen Golden	Edinburgh, Scotland	7 Sept. 1973
400 metres	51.77	Donna-Marie Louise Murray	Stockholm, Sweden	30 July 1974
800 metres	2:00.2	Rosemary Olivia Sterling (now Mrs. T. Wright)	Munich, West Germany	3 Sept. 1972
1 mile	4:36.2	Joan Allison	London (Crystal Palace)	14 Sept. 1973
1500 metres	4:04.8	Sheila Janet Carey (*née* Taylor)	Munich, West Germany	9 Sept. 1972
3,000 metres	8:55.6	Joyce Smith (*née* Byatt)	London (Crystal Palace)	19 July 1974

HURDLING

Event	sec	Name	Place	Date
100 metres	13.2	Judith Ann Vernon (*née* Toeneboehn)	Helsinki, Finland	26 July 1971
	13.29	Mary Elizabeth Peters M.B.E.	Munich, West Germany	2 Sept. 1972
200 metres	26·7	Sharon Colyear	London (Crystal Palace)	16 July 1972
400 metres	58.86	Christine Anne Warden (*née* Howell)	London (Crystal Palace)	26 May 1974

FIELD EVENTS

Event	ft	in	m	Name	Place	Date
High Jump	6	1½	1,87	Barbara Jean Inkpen (now Mrs. Carl Lawton)	London (Crystal Palace)	22 Sept. 1973
Long Jump	22	2¼	6,76	Mary Denise Rand (now Toomey, *née* Bignal) M.B.E.	Tokyo, Japan	14 Oct. 1964
Shot Putt	53	6¼	16,31	Mary Elizabeth Peters M.B.E.	Belfast, Northern Ireland	1 June 1966
Discus Throw	190	4	58,02	Christine Rosemary Payne (*née* Charters)	Birmingham	3 June 1972
Javelin Throw	182	5	55,60	Susan Mary Platt	London (Chiswick)	15 June 1968

PENTATHLON

4,801 points (1971 Tables)	Mary Elizabeth Peters, M.B.E.	Munich, West Germany	2–3 Sept. 1972

RELAYS

Event	Min sec	Name	Place	Date
4 × 100 metres	43.71	United Kingdom National Team (Andrea Joan Caron Lynch, Della Patricia Pascoe [*née* James], Judith Ann Vernon [*née* Toeneboehm], Anita Doris Neil)	Munich, West Germany	10 Sept. 1972
4 × 200 metres	1:33.8	(for details see World record)		
4 × 400 metres	3:27.8*	United Kingdom National Team (Elizabeth Barnes, Gladys Taylor, Verona Marolin Elder [*née* Barnard], Donna-Marie Louise Murray)	Dresden, East Germany	22 June 1975
4 × 800 metres	8:23.8	Great Britain (Joan Florence Allison, Sheila Janet Carey [*née* Taylor], Patricia Barbara Lowe [now Cropper], Rosemary Olivia Stirling [now Wright])	Paris, France	2 Oct. 1971

* *Awaiting ratification*

TRAMPOLINING

Origins Trampolines were used in show business at least as early as "The Walloons" of the period 1910–12. The sport of trampolining (from the Spanish word *trampolín*, a springboard) dates from 1936, when the prototype "T" model trampoline was developed by George Nissen (U.S.A.).

Most difficult manoeuvres The most difficult manoeuvre yet achieved is the triple back somersault with a double twist ($\frac{1}{2}$ in $1\frac{1}{2}$ out triffis) known as a Luxon after the first trampolinist ever to achieve it—Paul Luxon (G.B.) the 1972 World Amateur and 1973 World Professional Champion, achieved at the University of South West Louisiana on 26 Feb. 1972. The most difficult for women is the Wills ($5\frac{1}{2}$ twisting back somersault), named after the five-time world champion Judy Wills (b. 1948) of the U.S.A., of which no analysable film exists.

Most titles The only men to win a world title (instituted 1964) twice have been Dave Jacobs (U.S.) the 1967–68 champion and Wayne Miller (U.S.), who won in 1966 and 1970. Judy Wills won the first 5 women's titles (1964–65–66–67–68). Both European men's titles (1969 and 1971) were won by Paul Luxon (G.B.), the 1972 world champion. Three United Kingdom titles have been won by David Curtis (1966–67–68) and Paul Luxon (1969–70–71), while Miss Jackie Allen (1960–61), Mary Hunkin (*née* Chamberlaine) (1963–64) and Lynda Ball (1965–66) have each won two British titles.

Marathon record The longest recorded trampoline bouncing marathon is one of 1,248 hr (52 days) set by a team of 6 members in Phoenix, Arizona, U.S.A. on 24 June to 15 Aug. 1974. The solo record is 72 hr (with 5 min breaks per hour permissible) shared by Darleen Blum and Sharyn Field each on separate trampolines at Matraville Youth Centre, Sydney, Australia ending on 19 Jan. 1975.

TROTTING AND PACING

Origins The trotting gait (the simultaneous use of the diagonally opposite legs) was first recorded in England in *c.* 1750. The sulky first appeared in harness-racing in 1829. Pacers thrust out their fore and hind legs simultaneously on one side.

Highest price The highest price paid for a trotter is $3,000,000 for *Nevele Pride* by the Stoner Creek Stud of Lexington, Kentucky from Louis Resnick and Nevele Acres in the autumn of 1969. The highest price ever paid for a pacer is $2,500,000 for *Albatross* in 1972.

Greatest winnings The greatest amount won by a trotting horse is $1,851,424 by *Une de Mai* up to retirement in 1973. The record for a pacing horse is $1,201,470 by *Albatross* which was retired to stud in December 1972.

Most Successful Driver The most successful sulky driver in North American harness racing history has been Herve Filion (b. 1 Feb. 1940) of Quebec, Canada who reached a record 5,147 wins at Roosevelt Raceway, New York after a record 637 wins in the 1974 season. Hans Fromming, 64 (West Germany) reached 5,202 wins in the 1974 season.

Troika Record The U.S.S.R. troika record for the standard 1 600 m (4 laps of 400 m) is 1 min 58.0 sec by a bay trio from Nolinsk, trained by Vladimir Kuznetsov in Moscow in Feb. 1974.

Canadian Herve Filion, the most successful sulky driver in North American harness racing history, with over 5,000 wins

U.S. Trotting Association

Records against time	Trotting				Pacing			
World (mile [*1 609,34 m*] track)	1:54.8	Nevele Pride (driver Stanley Dancer) (U.S.) Indianapolis, Indiana	31 Aug.	1969	1:52.0	Steady Star (driver Joe O'Brien (U.S.) Lexington, Kentucky	1 Oct.	1971
Australia	2:01.2	Gramel, Harold Park, Sydney		1964	1:57.3	Halwes, Harold Park, Sydney		1968
New Zealand	2:02.4	Control, Addington, Christchurch		1964	1:56.2	Cardigan Bay, Hutt Park, Wellington		1963
World race Record (mile)	1:55.6	Noble Victory (U.S.A.) at Du Quoin, Illinois	31 Aug.	1966	1:54.6	Albatross (U.S.A.) at Sportsman's Park, Cicero, Illinois	1 July	1972

TUG OF WAR

Tug of War is a competitive sport in 14 countries. The term was first recorded in 1876 in England. It became an Olympic event in 1900 in Paris and was dropped after 1920. In 1958 a separate governing body, the Tug-of-War Association, was formed to administer Britain's 800 clubs.

Most Olympic Medals The only three men to win two gold medals (1908 and 1920) (all also won a silver medal in 1912) were James Shepherd, Frederick H. Humphreys, and Edwin A. Mills (all G.B.).

Longest Pull The longest recorded pull is one of 2 hours 41 min between "H" Company and "E" Company of the 2nd Battalion of the Sherwood Foresters (Derbyshire

The most successful tug-of-war team in history—the 15 time A.A.A champion team from Wood Treatment, Cheshire. Left to right: John Hollinshead (Coach), Mike Eardley, Hilary (Jumbo) Brown, Ken Proudlove, Clem Ekin, Alec Brown (Trainer), Norman (Horse) Hyde, George Hickton, Peter Hirst, Barry Howson

Regiment) at Jubbulpore, India, on 12 Aug. 1889. "E" Company won.

The longest recorded pull under A.A.A. Rules (in which lying on the ground or entrenching the feet is not permitted) is one of 8 min 18.2 sec for the first pull between the R.A.S.C. (Feltham) and the Royal Marines (Portsmouth Division) at the Royal Tournament of June 1938.

Most A.A.A. titles Greatest team The catchweight Wood Treatment team (formerly the Bosley Farmers) of Cheshire, have represented and won for England every international against five countries since 1964. They have won 15 consecutive A.A.A. Championships since 1959. Hilary Brown, Mike Eardley, George Hicton, Peter Hirst and Norman Hyde have been in every team.

VOLLEYBALL

Origins The game was invented as *Minnonette* in 1895 by William G. Morgan at the Y.M.C.A. gymnasium at Holyoke, Massachusetts, U.S.A. The International Volleyball Association was formed in Paris in April 1947. The Amateur (now English) Volleyball Association of Great Britain was formed in May 1955. The ball travels at a speed of 70 m.p.h. *112,5 km/h* when smashed over the net, which measures 2.43 m (7 ft 11.6 in). In the women's game the net is 2.24 m *7 ft 4.1 in.*

World titles World Championships were instituted in 1949. The U.S.S.R. has won five men's titles (1949, 1952, 1960, 1962 and 1968). The U.S.S.R. won the women's championship in 1952, 1956, 1960, 1968, 1970 and 1973. The record crowd is 60,000 for the 1952 world title matches in Moscow, U.S.S.R.

Olympic The sport was introduced to the Olympic Games for both men and women in 1964. The only volleyball players of either sex to win three medals are Ludmila Bouldakova (U.S.S.R.) (b. 25 May 1938) and Inna Ryskal (U.S.S.R.) (b. 15 June 1944), who both won a silver medal in 1964 and golds in 1968 and 1972. The record for gold medals for men is shared by four members of the U.S.S.R.'s 1968 team who won a second gold medal in 1972: Eduard Sibiryakov, Yury Poyarkov, Yvan Bugayenkov and Georgy Mondzolevsky.

Marathon The longest recorded continuous volleyball marathon is one of 240 hr played by 4 teams of six girls from Porta High School, Petersburg, Illinois, U.S.A. on 31 May to 10 June 1974.

One Man Team Bob L. Schaffer, 50 of Suffern, New York specialises in taking on 6 men teams lone-handed. His latest reported life-time score is 1,865 wins since 16 Aug. 1963 and only three losses.

WALKING

Olympic Medals Most Walking races have been included in the Olympic events since 1906. The 20 kilometre event in Montreal in July 1976 will be the 25th Olympic race. The only walker to win three gold medals has been Ugo Frigerio (Italy) (b. 16 Sept. 1901) with the 3,000 m and 10,000 m in 1920 and the 10,000 m in 1924. He also holds the record of most medals with four (having additionally won the bronze medal in the 50,000 m in 1932) which total is shared with Vladimir Golubnitschyi (U.S.S.R.) (b. 2 June 1936), who won gold medals for the 20,000 m in 1960 and 1968, the silver in 1972 and the bronze in 1964.

The best British performance has been two gold medals by George E. Larner for the 3,500 m and the 10 miles in 1908, but Ernest J. Webb won three medals being twice runner up to Larner and finishing second in the 10,000 m in 1912.

Longest Desert Walk The longest desert walk (made in high summer daytime) ever recorded is one of 316 miles *508 km* by Bill Collins (b. 22 Oct. 1923) of Las Vegas through Death Valley, California in 10 days 10 hr on 28 July–6 Aug. 1972. The maximum daily shade temperatures varied between 122°F *50°C* and a low of 115°F *46,1°C* with ground temperatures at 4 p.m. of 195°F *90,6°C* to a low of 178°F *81,1°C*. The route took in Devil's Golf Course Badwater (282 ft *85 m* below sea level), 14 miles *22,5km* of Salt Flats hitherto untraversed, and Furnace Creek.

"End to end" The record for walking from John o'Groats to Land's End (route varies between 876 and 891 miles [*1 409 and 1 433 km*]) is 10 days 18 hr 20 min achieved by Johnnie Savile, 54 (one lung) and John Ryder, both of Battersea, Wandsworth, Greater London on 8–18 Aug. 1973. The feminine record is 17 days 7 hr by Miss Wendy Lewis ending on 15 March 1960. End to end and back has twice been achieved. Frederick E. Westcott, aged 31, finished on 18 Dec. 1966 and David Tremayne (Australia), aged 27, finished on 28 May 1971. The Irish "End to End" record over the 376 miles *605 km* from Mizen Head, Cork to Malin Head, Donegal is 7 days 22 hr 10 min, set by Tom Casey (b. 1930) on 1–9 July 1972.

London to Brighton The record time for the London to Brighton walk is 7 hr 35 min 12 sec by Donald James Thompson, M.B.E. (b. 20 Jan. 1933) on 14 Sept. 1957. The record time for London to Brighton and back is 18 hrs 5 min 51 sec by William Frederick Baker (b. 5 April 1889) of Queen's Park Harriers, London, on 18–19 June 1926.

24 hours The best performance for distance walked in 24 hours is 133 miles 21 yd *214,06 km* by Huw D. M. N. Neilson (England) at Walton-on-Thames, Surrey on 14–15 Oct. 1960.

Walking on crutches David Ryder, 21, a polio victim from Chigwell, Essex, arrived at Land's End from John o'Groats on 18 Aug. 1969 having completed the entire course on crutches. From 30 March to 14 Aug. 1970 he succeeded in walking on crutches 2,960 miles *4 763 km* across North America.

Road walking The world's best performances for the two Road Walking events on the programme of the last Olympic Games are: 20,000 m 1 hr 24 min 50.0 sec by Vincent Paul Nihill (G.B.) on the Isle of Man, 30 July 1972 and 50,000 m 3 hr 52 min 44.6 sec by Bernd Kannenberg (West Germany) 1972.

Most titles The greatest number of national titles won by a British walker is 26 by Nihill from 1963 to 1972. These are A.A.A. 2 miles/3 km 1965–70–71; 7 miles/ 10 km 1965–66–68–69 and R.W.A. 10 miles 1965–68– 69–72; 20 km 1965–66–68–69–71–72; 20 miles 1963– 64–65–68–69–71 and 50 km 1964–68–71.

Longest Annual Race The Strasbourg–Paris event (inst. 1926 in the reverse direction) over 504–554 km *313–344 miles* is the world's longest annual race walk. The record is 8,101 km/h *5.033 m.p.h.* (deducting the 4 hrs compulsory stops) by Robert Pinchard (Belgium) in 1973. Gilbert Roger (France) won 6 times (1949, 53, 54, 56, 58). The only Briton to have completed the course is Colin Young of Dagenham, Essex.

OFFICIAL WORLD RECORDS (Track Walking)

(As recognised by the International Amateur Athletic Federation)

Distance	Time hr min sec	Name and Nationality	Place	Date
20,000 metres	1 24 45	Bernd Kannenberg (West Germany)	Hamburg, West Germany	25 May 1974
30,000 metres	2 12 58	Bernd Kannenberg (West Germany)	Kassel, West Germany	11 May 1974
20 miles	2 30 38.6	Gerhard Weidner (West Germany)	Hamburg, West Germany	25 May 1974
30 miles	3 51 48.6	Gerhard Weidner (West Germany)	Hamburg, West Germany	8 Apr. 1973
50,000 metres	4 00 27.20	Gerhard Weidner (West Germany)	Hamburg, West Germany	8 Apr. 1973
2 hours	27 153 m *16 miles 1,534 yd*	Bernd Kannenberg (West Germany)	Kassel, West Germany	11 May 1974

WATER POLO

Origins Water Polo was developed in England as "Water Soccer" in 1869 and was first included in the Olympic Games in Paris in 1900.

Olympic Games Most medals Hungary has won the Olympic tournament most often with five wins in 1932, 1936, 1952, 1956 and 1964 Great Britain won in 1900, 1908, 1912 and 1920.

Five players share the record of three gold medals: George Wilkinson (b. 1880) in 1900–08–12; Paulo (Paul) Radmilovic (1886–1968), and Charles Sidney Smith (b. 1879) all G.B. in 1908–12–20; and the Hungarians Desző Gyarmati (b. 23 Oct. 1927) and György Kárpáti (b. 23 June 1935) in 1952–56–64.

Radmilovic (see above) also won a gold medal for the 4 × 200 m relay in 1908.

A.S.A. championships The club with the greatest number of Amateur Swimming Association titles is Plaistow United Swimming Club of Greater London, with eleven from 1928 to 1954.

Most goals The greatest number of goals scored by an individual in a home international is eleven by Terry C. Miller (Plaistow United), when England defeated Wales 13–3 at Newport, Gwent, in 1951.

Most caps The greatest number of internationals is 234 by Mirco Sandic (Partizan Club, Belgrade) for Yugoslavia. The British record is 101 by Murray Anderson (Scotland) in 1955–1975.

Marathon The longest match on record is one of 35 hr 2 min 27 sec between two teams of 15 from the Costa Mesa Aquatics Club, California, U.S.A. on 4–5 May 1974. Breaks and substitutions were in accordance with N.C.A.A. rules.

WATER SKIING

Origins The origins of water skiing lie in plank gliding or aquaplaning. A photograph exists of a "plank-riding" contest in a regatta won by a Mr. S. Storry at Scarborough, North Yorkshire on 15 July 1914. Competitors were towed on a *single* plank by a motor launch. The present day sport of water skiing was pioneered by Ralph W. Samuelson on Lake Pepin, Minnesota, U.S.A., on two curved pine boards in the summer of 1922, though claims have been made for the birth of the sport on Lake Annecy (Haute Savoie), France, in 1920. The first World Water Ski Organization was formed in Geneva on 27 July 1946. The British Water Ski Federation was founded in London in 1954.

Longest jumps The first recorded jump on water skis was made by Ralph Samuelson off a greased ramp, at Miami Beach, Florida, U.S.A. in 1928. The longest jump ever recorded is one of 180 ft *54,85 m* by Wayne Grimditch, (U.S.A.) at Callaway Gardens, Georgia, U.S.A. on 13 July 1975. The women's record is 125 ft *38,1 m* by Elizabeth Allen Shetter (U.S.) at Callaway Gadens, Georgia, U.S.A. on 25 Aug. 1974.

The British record is 48,55 m *159 ft 3 in* by Paul Seaton (b. 3 July 1975) at Hartbeespoort, South Africa, on 28 Sept. 1974. The Irish record is 134 ft *40,8 m* by Alan Dagg (Golden Falls W.S.C.) at Dublin on 25 Sept. 1971. Dagg, the six time Irish National Champion (1967–73) who also won two Irish Open titles in 1971–72. The women's record is 111 ft 11 in *34,1 m* by Karen Morse at Bogotá, Colombia on 16 Sept. 1973.

Slalom and Tricks The world record for slalom is 40 buoys (with the 75 ft *22 m* rope shortened by 36 ft *10 m*) by Kris La Point (U.S.A.) Horton Lake Open, U.S.A., in 1974. The record for figures is 5,740 points by Russ Stiffler (U.S.A.) at the Western Regional Championships in 1974. The British record for slalom is 38 buoys by Mike Hazelwood at Ruislip Lido on 15 July 1975 and by Paul Seaton at Princes Water Ski Club, Bedfont, Middlesex, on 20 July 1975. The British record for tricks is 4,850 pts. by Hazelwood at Biggleswade in July 1974.

Longest run The greatest distance travelled non-stop is 1,000 miles *1,609 km* by Ray de Fir of Portland, Oregon, U.S.A., in 33 hr 27 min on 22–23 Aug. 1958 over the Columbia River between Portland and Astoria, Oregon. The British record is 470.67 miles *757,46 km* (in 15 hr 1 min 53.2 sec) by Charles Phipps, 30, on Lake Windermere from 4.4 a.m. to 7.5 p.m. on 4 Oct. 1969.

Highest speed The water skiing speed record is 125.69 m.p.h. *202,27 km/h* by Danny Churchill at the Oakland Marine Stadium, California, U.S.A., in 1971. Sally Younger (b. 1953), set a feminine record of 105.14 m.p.h. *169,20 km/h* at Perris, California on 17 June 1970. The fastest recorded speed by a British skier over a measured kilometre is 81.535 m.p.h. *131,217*

km/h (average) on Lake Windermere, Cumbria on 18 Oct. 1973 by Billy Rixon, the 1973 European Ski-Racing Champion.

Water-ski racing The record for the 58 mile *93 km* Cross Channel race from Greatstone-on-Sea, near New Romney, England to Cap Gris-Nez, France and back is 1 hr 37 min 30 sec by Robin Manwaring of Kent on 13 Aug. 1972.

Most titles World overall championships (instituted 1949) have been won twice by Alfredo Mendoza (U.S.A.) in 1953–55, Mike Suyderhoud (U.S.A.) in 1967–69 and George Athans (Canada) in 1971 and 1973 and three times by Mrs. Willa McGuire (*née* Worthington) of the U.S.A., in 1949–50 and 1955. Mendoza won five championship events and McGuire and Elizabeth Allen-Shetter (U.S.A.) seven each. The most British overall titles (instituted 1953) ever won by a man is

The British tricks and slalom record holder Mike Hazelwood rounding one of a record 38 slalom buoys

four by Lance Callingham in 1959–60 and 1962–63, and Paul Seaton in 1971–73 and 1975; the most by a woman is five by Karen Morse in 1971–5.

Barefoot The barefoot duration record is 2 hrs 37 min by Paul McManus (Australia). The backward barefoot record is 39 min by McManus. A barefoot jump of 54 ft *16,45 m* was reported from Australia. The barefoot speed records are 98.9 m.p.h. *159,1 km/h* by Gordon Eppling at Long Beach California on 18 Aug. 1974 and 61 m.p.h. *98 km/h* by Miss Haidee Jones (Australia). The British duration record is 67 min 5 sec by John Doherty in October 1974. John Horder (G.B.) reached 57.36 m.p.h. *92,31 km/h* at Holme Pierrepoint, Nottinghamshire on 15 April 1975.

WEIGHTLIFTING

Origins Amateur weightlifting is of comparatively modern origin and the first world championship was staged at the Cafe Monico, Piccadilly, City of Westminster, Greater London, on 28 March 1891. Prior to that time, weightlifting consisted of professional exhibitions in which some of the advertised poundages were open to doubt. The first to raise 400 lb. *181 kg* was Charles Rigoulot (1903–62), a French professional, in Paris, with 402½ lb. *182 kg 570* on 1 Feb. 1929, but his barbell would not now be regarded as acceptable.

Greatest back lift The greatest weight ever raised by a human being is 6,270 lb. *2 844 kg* (2.80 tons [*2,84 tonnes*]) in a back

lift (weight raised off trestles) by the 26 st. *165 kg* Paul Anderson (U.S.A.) (born 1933), the 1956 Olympic heavyweight champion at Toccoa, Georgia, U.S.A., on 12 June 1957. The heaviest Rolls-Royce, the Phantom VI, weighs 5,600 lb. *2 540 kg* (2½ tons [*2,54 tonnes*]). The greatest lift by a woman is 3,564 lb. *1 616 kg* with a hip and harness lift by Mrs. Josephine Blatt *née* Schauer (1869–1923) at the Bijou Theatre, Hoboken, New Jersey, U.S.A., on 15 April 1895.

Greatest overhead lift The greatest overhead lifts made from the ground are the clean and jerks achieved by super-heavyweights which now exceed 4¾ cwt (532 lb.) *241,3 kg*. The greatest overhead lift ever made by a woman is 286 lb. *129 kg* in a continental jerk by Katie Sandwina, *née* Brummbach (Germany) (b. 21 Jan. 1884, d. as Mrs. Max Heymann in New York City, U.S.A., on 21 Jan. 1952) in *c.* 1911. This is equivalent to seven 40 lb. *18 kg* office typewriters. She stood 5 ft 11 in *1,80 m* tall, weighed 210 lb. *95 kg* (15 st 0 lb) and is reputed to have unofficially lifted 312½ lb *141 kg 747* and to have shouldered a cannon taken from the tailboard of a Barnum and Bailey circus wagon which allegedly weighed 1,200 lb *544 kg*.

Power lifts Paul Anderson, as a professional, has bench-pressed 627 lb *284 kg* and has achieved 1,200 lb *544 kg* in a squat so aggregating, with an 820 lb *371 kg* dead lift, a career total of 2,647 lb *1 200 kg*. The International Powerlifting Federation records in the Superheavyweight division are all set by Donald C. Reinhoudt (U.S.A.) in Chattanooga, Tennessee with Squat 914½ lb *415 kg* (27 Apr. 1974); bench press 601½ lb *272,5 kg*; deadlift 885½ lb *401,5 kg* and total 2,420 lb *1 097,5 kg* all on 3 May 1975. Britons hold the bantamweight total with Precious McKenzie MBE 1,180 lb *535,5 kg* at Harrisburg, Pennsylvania on 9 Nov. 1973 and middleweight Ronald Collins 1,655 lb *750,5 kg* in Liverpool on 15 Dec. 1973. With this lift Collins, weighing 165 lb *74,8 kg* became the first man in the world to lift a total ten times his own bodyweight.

The highest recorded two-handed dead lift is 882 lb. *400 kg* by John Kuc (U.S.A.). Hermann Gorner (Germany) performed a one-handed dead lift of 734½ lb. *333 kg 10* in Dresden on 20 July 1920. Peter B. Cortese (U.S.A.) achieved a one-armed dead lift of 370 lb. *167 kg i.e.* 22 lb. *9 kg 90* over triple his bodyweight at York, Pennsylvania on 4 Sept. 1954.

Gorner (see above) raised 24 men weighing 4,123 lb. *1 870 kg* on a plank on the soles of his feet in London on 12 Oct. 1927 and also carried on his back a 1,444 lb. *654 kg* piano for 52½ ft *4,8 m* on 3 June 1921.

The highest competitive two-handed dead lift by a woman is 394½ lb *178,9 kg* by Jan Suffolk Todd (U.S.) at Chattanooga, Tennessee on 3 May 1975.

It was reported that an hysterical 8 st. 11 lb. *55 kg 791* woman, Mrs. Maxwell Rogers, lifted one end of a 3,600 lb. *1 632 kg* (1.60 ton [*1,62 tonnes*]) station wagon which, after the collapsing of a jack, had fallen on top of her son at Tampa, Florida, U.S.A., on 24 April 1960. She cracked some vertebrae.

Brick Lifting Gorner (see above) is reputed to have lifted 14 bricks weighing 56 kg *123½* lb. horizontally using only lateral pressure.

Cue levering The only man ever to have levered six 16 oz. *453 g* billiard cues simultaneously by their tips through 90 degrees to the horizontal, is W. J. (Bill) Hunt of Darwen, Lancashire at the Unity Club, Great Harwood, Lancashire on 25 June 1954.

Olympic Games Most Gold Medals Of the 81 Olympic titles at stake the U.S.S.R. have won 21, the U.S.A. 15 and France 9. Eight lifters have succeeded in winning an Olympic gold medal in successive Games. Of these three have also won a silver medal:

Louis Hostin (France)	Gold, light-heavyweight 1932 and 1936; Silver 1928.
John Davis (U.S.A.)	Gold, heavyweight 1948 and 1952.
Tommy Kono (Hawaii/U.S.A.)	Gold, lightweight 1952; Gold, light-heavyweight 1956; Silver, middle-weight 1960.
Charles Vinci (U.S.A.)	Gold, bantamweight 1956 and 1960.
Arkady Vorobyev (U.S.S.R.)	Gold, middle-heavyweight 1956 and 1960.
Yoshinobu Miyake (Japan)	Gold, featherweight 1964 and 1968; Silver, bantamweight 1960.
Waldemar Baszanowski (Poland)	Gold, lightweight 1964 and 1968.
Leonid Zhabotinsky (U.S.S.R.)	Gold, heavyweight 1964 and 1968.

Most Medals The winner of most Olympic medals is Norbert Schemansky (U.S.A.) (b. 30 May 1924) with four: Gold, middle-heavyweight 1952; Silver, heavyweight 1948; Bronze, heavyweight 1960 and 1964. Schemansky achieved a world record—the heavyweight snatch at 361½ lb *163,75 kg* on 28 Apr. 1962 at Detroit—at the record age of 37 years and 10 months.

British The only British lifter to win an Olympic title has been Launceston Elliott the open one-handed lift champion in 1896 at Athens.

OFFICIAL WORLD WEIGHTLIFTING RECORDS (As at 1 August 1975)

Bodyweight Class	Lift	Lifted lb.	Lifted kg	Name and Nationality	Place	Date
Flyweight	Snatch	236¾	*107,5*	Alexander Voronin, (U.S.S.R.)	Meissen East Germany	12 Apr. 1975
(114½ lb. [*52 kg*])	Jerk	308½	*140*	Mohamed Nassiri (Iran)	Havana, Cuba	15 Sept. 1973
	Total	534¼	*242,5*	Alexander Voronin (U.S.S.R.)	Meissen, East Germany	12 Apr. 1975
Bantamweight	Snatch	259	*117,5*	Koji Miki (Japan)	Havana, Cuba	16 Sept. 1973
(123¼ lb. [*56 kg*])	Jerk	332¾	*151*	Mohamed Nassiri (Iran)	Sanandaj, Iran	2 Aug. 1973
	Total	573	*260*	Atanas Kirov (Bulgaria)	Burgas, Bulgaria	23 Feb. 1974
Featherweight	Snatch	281	*127,5*	Nurair Nurikyan, (Bulgaria)	Yambol, Bulgaria	27 June 1975
(132¼ lb. [*60 kg*])	Jerk	354¾	*161*	Nikolai Kolesnikov (U.S.S.R.)	Vilnus, U.S.S.R.	5 July 1975
	Total	617	*280*	Gyorgyi Todorov (Bulgaria)	Manila, Philippines	23 Sept. 1974
Lightweight	Snatch	304	*138*	Edward Dergachev	Vilnus, U.S.S.R.	6 July 1975
(148¾ lb. [*67,5 kg*])	Jerk	391¼	*177,5*	Murkharbi Kitzhinov (U.S.S.R.)	Munich, W. Germany	30 Aug. 1972
	Total	688¾	*312,5*	Murkharbi Kirzhinov (U.S.S.R.)	Munich, W. Germany	30 Aug. 1972
Middleweight	Snatch	336	*152,5*	Nedelcho Kolev (Bulgaria)	Paris, France	7 April 1974
(165¼ lb. [*75 kg*])	Jerk	418¾	*190*	Nedelcho Kolev (Bulgaria)	Havana, Cuba	19 Sept. 1973
	Total	749¼	*340*	Nedelcho Kolov (Bulgaria)	Verona, Italy	2 June 1974
Light-heavyweight	Snatch	364¾	*165,5*	Valeri Shary (U.S.S.R.)	Vilnus, U.S.S.R.	8 July 1975
(181¾ lb. [*82,5 kg*])	Jerk	448½	*203,5*	Valeri Shary (U.S.S.R.)	Vilnus, U.S.S.R.	8 July 1975
	Total	804¼	*365*	Valeri Shary (U.S.S.R.)	Vilnus, U.S.S.R.	8 July 1975
Middle-heavyweight	Snatch	392¼	*178*	David Rigert (U.S.S.R.)	Zaporozhe, U.S.S.R.	14 Dec. 1974
(198¼ lb. [*90 kg*])	Jerk	479½	*217,5*	David Rigert (U.S.S.R.)	Balashikha, U.S.S.R.	26 April 1975
	Total	870¾	*395*	David Rigert (U.S.S.R.)	Balashikha, U.S.S.R.	26 April 1975
Heavyweight	Snatch	392¼	*178*	Valentin Khristov (Bulgaria)	Marseille, France	12 July 1975
(242½ lb. [*110 kg*])	Jerk	507	*230*	Valentin Khristov (Bulgaria)	Marseille, France	12 July 1975
	Total	892¾	*405*	Valentin Khristov (Bulgaria)	Marseille, France	12 July 1975
Super-heavyweight	Snatch	424	*192,5*	Khristo Plachkov (Bulgaria)	Yambol, Bulgaria	29 June 1975
(Over 242½ lb. [*110 kg*])	Jerk	540	*245*	Vasili Alexeev (U.S.S.R.)	Vilnus, U.S.S.R.	11 July 1974
	Total	936¾	*425*	Vasili Alexeev (U.S.S.R.)	Manila, Philippines	29 Sept. 1974

Valentin Khristov, Bulgaria, is the only lifter to hold all the junior and senior world records in his class simultaneously. He set them all at the Junior World Championships in Marseille, France.

(As supplied by Mr. Oscar State, O.B.E., General Secretary of the International Weightlifting Federation.)

Most Successful British Lifter Louis George Martin, M.B.E., born Jamaica 1936, won four World and European mid-heavyweight titles in 1959–62–63–65. He won an Olympic silver medal in 1964 and a bronze in 1960 and also 3 Commonwealth gold medals in 1962–66–70. His total of British titles was 12.

Strand Pulling The International Steel Strandpullers' Association was founded by Gavin Pearson (Scotland) in 1940. The greatest ratified poundage to date is a super heavy-weight left arm push of 809 lb *366 kg 900* by John Randall of Staines, Surrey.

Harry Sawyer (Ashford Common) set a world 12 stone dislocation record of 353 lb *160 kg* in 1972 aged 55 and David Hoar (Ossett, Yorkshire) set a world 11 stone right arm push record of 601 lb *272,5 kg* aged 17.

WRESTLING

Earliest references The earliest depicting of wrestling holds and falls, are from the walls of the tomb of Ptahhotap so proving that wrestling dates from *c.* 2350 B.C. or earlier. It was introduced into the ancient Olympic Games in the 18th Olympiad in *c.* 704 B.C. The Greco-Roman style is of French origin and arose about 1860. The International Amateur Wrestling Federation (F.I.L.A.) was founded in 1912.

Most World Championships The greatest number of world championships won by a wrestler is eight by the freestyler Aleksandr Medved (U.S.S.R.), born 1937 with the Light-heavyweight titles in 1964 (Olympic) and 1966, the Heavyweight 1967 and 1968 (Olympic), and the Extra heavy weight in 1969-70-71-72 (Olympic). The only other wrestler to win world titles in 6 successive years has been Abdullah Movahad (Iran) in the lightweight division in 1965–70. The record for Greco-Roman titles is five shared by Roman Rurua (U.S.S.R.) with the featherweight 1966, 1967, 1968 (Olympic), 1969 and 1970 and Victor Igumenov (U.S.S.R.) with the Welterweight 1966, 1967, 1969, 1970 and 1971.

Most Olympic titles Three wrestlers have won three Olympic titles:

Carl Westergren (Sweden) (b. 13 Oct. 1895)
Greco-Roman Middleweight, 75 kg	1920
Greco-Roman Light Heavyweight, 82,5 kg	1924
Greco-Roman Heavyweight over 87 kg	1932

Ivar Johansson (Sweden) (b. 31 Jan. 1903)
Freestyle Middleweight, 79 kg	1932
Greco-Roman Welterweight, 72 kg	1932
Greco-Roman Middleweight, 79 kg	1936

Aleksandr Medved (U.S.S.R.) (b. 16 Sept. 1937)
Freestyle Light Heavyweight	1964
Freestyle Heavyweight	1968
Freestyle Extra Heavyweight	1972

The only wrestler with more medals is Imre Polyák (Hungary) who won the silver medal for the Greco-Roman featherweight class in 1952–56–60 and the gold in 1964.

Most wins Don Gable (U.S.A.) (b. 25 Oct. 1948) won 299 bouts with only 6 losses in 1963–73. He won the 1972 freestyle Olympic lightweight title.

Longest bout The longest recorded bout was one of 11 hrs 40 min between Martin Klein (Estonia representing Russia) and Armas Asikainen (Finland) in the Greco-Roman middleweight "A" event in the 1912 Olympic Games in Stockholm, Sweden.

Longest span The longest span for B.A.W.A. titles is 24 years by G. Mackenzie, who won his first title in 1909 and his last in 1933. Mackenzie, also jointly holds (see Fencing) the record of having represented Great Britain in five successive Olympiads from 1908 to 1928.

Heaviest heavyweight The heaviest heavyweight champion in British wrest-ling history was A. Dudgeon (Scotland), who won the 1936 and 1937 B.A.W.A. heavyweight titles, scaling 22 st. *139 kg.*

Cumberland wrestling The British Cumberland and Westmorland Champion-ships were established in 1904. The only 6 time champions have been J. Baddeley (Middleweight in 1905–06–08–09–10–12) and E. A. Bacon (Lightweight in 1919–21–22–23–28–29).

GREAT BRITAIN—MOST TITLES

Heavyweight	10	Ken Richmond, 1949–60
Middleweight	7	Thomas Albert Baldwin (b. 27 Sept. 1905), 1942, 1944–46, 1948, 1951–52 (also Welterweight in 1941)
Welterweight	9	Joe Feeney, 1957–60, 1962, 1964–66, 1968
Lightweight	8	Arthur Thompson, 1933–40
Featherweight	8	H. Hall, 1952–57, 1961, 1963 (also Light-weight 1958–59)
Bantamweight	6	Joe Reid, 1930–35

PROFESSIONAL WRESTLING

Professional wrestling dates from 1874 in U.S.A. Georges Karl Julius Hackenschmidt (b. Russia 1877 d. 1968) made no submissions in the period 1898–1908. The highest paid professional wrestler ever is Antonio ("Tony") Rocca, with $180,000 (*£75,000*) in 1958. The heaviest ever wrestler has been William J. Cobb of Macon, Georgia, U.S.A. (b. 1926), who was billed in 1962 as the 802 lb. *363 kg 781* (57 st. 4 lb.) "Happy" Humphrey. What he lacked in mobility he possessed in suffocating powers. By July 1965 he had reduced to a more modest 232 lb. *105 kg 233* (16 st. 8 lb.).

Most Successful Ed "Strangler" Lewis (1890–1966) *née* Robert H. Friedrich, fought 6,200 bouts in 44 years losing only 33 matches. He won world titles in 1920, 1922 and 1928. Jack Dempsey, the world heavyweight boxing champion, refused his challenge to a wrestling-boxing match.

Sumo wrestling The sport's origins in Japan certainly date from *c.* 200 A.D. The heaviest ever performer was probably Dewagatake, a wrestler of the 1920's who was 6 ft 5 in *195 cm* tall and weighed up to 30 st. *190 kg.* Weight is amassed by over alimentation with a high protein sea food stew called *chanko-rigori.* The tallest was probably Ozora, an early 19th century performer, who stood 7 ft 3 in *220 cm* tall. The most successful wrestler has been Koki Naya (b. 1940), *alias* Taiho ("Great Bird"), who won his 26th Emperor's Cup on 10–24 Sept. 1967. He was the youngest ever *Yokozuna* (Grand Champion) at the age of 21 in 1967. The highest *dan* is Makuuchi attained by Taiho in 1965.

YACHTING

Origins Yachting in England dates from the £100 stake race between Charles II and his brother James, Duke of York, on the Thames on 1 Sept. 1661 over 23 miles from Greenwich to Gravesend. The earliest club is the Royal Cork Yacht Club (formerly the Cork Harbour Water Club), established in Ireland in 1720.

The oldest yacht club in Britain which still is active is the Starcross Yacht Club at Powderham Point, Devon. Its first regatta was held in 1772. The word yacht is from the Dutch to hunt or chase.

Olympic Games The first sportsman ever to win individual gold medals in four successive Olympic Games was Paul B. Elvström (b. 25 Feb. 1928) (Denmark) in the Firefly class in 1948 and the Finn class in 1952, 1956 and 1960.

He has also won 8 other world titles in a total of 6 classes. The lowest number of penalty points by the winner of any class in an Olympic regatta is 3 points (6 wins [1 disqualified] and 1 second in 7 starts) by *Superdocius* of the Flying Dutchman class (Lt. Rodney Stuart Pattisson, M.B.E., R.N. (b. 5 Aug. 1943) and Iain Somerled Macdonald-Smith, M.B.E. (b. 3 July 1945)) at Acapulco Bay, Mexico in October 1968.

Great Britain The only British yacht to win two titles was *Scotia* in the Open class and Half-One Ton class at the 1900 Regatta with Lorne C. Currie, helmsman and crewed by J. H. Gretton and Linton Hope. The only British yachtsman to win two Olympic regattas is Rodney Pattisson in 1968 (see above) and again with *Superdoso* crewed by Christopher Davies (b. 29 June 1946) at Kiel, West Germany in 1972.

Admiral's Cup The ocean racing series to have attracted the largest number of participating nations (three boats allowed to each nation) is Admiral's Cup held by the Royal Ocean Racing Club in the English Channel in alternate years. In 1975 a record number of 18 nations competed. Up to 1975, Britain had won 6 times, U.S.A. twice and Australia and West Germany once.

Most numerous class The numerically largest class of sailing boat in the world is the "Sunfish" (U.S.). The total number is in excess of 140,000. The boat is a 14 ft *4,26 m* sailing surfboard with single sail and made of plastic. The numerically largest class of centreboard sailing dinghy is the International Optimist, a 7 ft 7 in *2,31 m* wooden or plastic boat for use by children. 105,000 are claimed by the class association. It is also the smallest in size and cheapest of any recognised international yachting class of boat.

24 Hour Dinghy Race The greatest distance covered in 24 hrs in the annual West Lancashire Yacht Club event at Southport is 112 nautical miles by a G.P. 14 from West Kirby Sailing Club on 11–12 Sept. 1968.

Highest Altitude The greatest altitude at which sailing has been conducted is 14,212 ft *4 331 m* on Lake Pomacocha, Peru by *Nusta* a 19 ft *5,79 m* Lightning dinghy owned by Jan Jacobi, reported in 1959.

Highest speed A speed of 30.95 knots (35,63 m.p.h.) was recorded by *Beowulf* in the World Multihull Championships at Los Angeles, California in 1974. The highest speed achieved in trials run in British waters has been 29.3 knots 33.73 m.p.h. *54,29 km/h* by the 55 ft *16,76 m* proa *Crossbow* (sail area 932 ft² [*86,58 m²*] designed by Rod McAlpine-Downie, with Timothy Colman as helmsman, off Portland, Dorset on 3 Oct. 1973. The U.S. Navy experimental hydrofoil craft *Monitor* is reported to have attained speeds close to 40 knots (46 m.p.h. [*74 km/h*]).

Most successful The most successful racing yacht in history was the Royal Yacht *Britannia* (1893–1935), owned by King Edward VII, when Prince of Wales and subsequently by King George V, which won 231 races in 625 starts.

America's Cup The America's Cup was originally won as an outright prize by the schooner *America* on 22 Aug. 1851 at Cowes and was later offered by the New York Yacht Club as a challenge trophy, On 8 Aug. 1870 J. Ashbury's *Cambria* (G.B.) failed to capture the trophy from the *Magic*, owned by F. Osgood (U.S.A.). Since then the Cup has been challenged by Great Britain in 15 contests, by Canada in two contests, and by Australia thrice, but the United States holders have never been defeated. The closest race ever was the fourth race of the 1962 series, when the 12 metre sloop *Weatherly* beat her Australian challenger *Gretel* by about three and a half lengths, a margin of only 26 sec on 22 Sept. 1962. The fastest time ever recorded by a 12 metre boat for the triangular course of 24 sea miles is 2 hr 46 min 58 sec by *Gretel* in 1962.

Peter Johnson

Two of the world's 140,000 Sunfishes—the most numerous of all classes of sailing boats

Little America's Cup The catamaran counterpart to the America's Cup was instituted in 1961 for International C-Class catamarans. The British entry won 8 times from 1961 to 1968.

Largest yacht The largest private yacht ever built was Mrs. Emily Roebling Cadwalader's *Savarona* of 5,100 gross tons, completed in Hamburg, Germany in Oct. 1931, at a cost of $4,000,000 (*now £1.66 million*). She (the yacht), with a 53 ft *16,15 m* beam and measuring 408 ft 6 in *124,50 m* overall, was sold to the Turkish government in March 1938. Operating expenses for a full crew of 107 men approached $500,000 (*now £200,000*) per annum. Currently she is a Turkish Navy training ship, once called "Gunes Dil", with a complement of 213. Currently the largest reported private yacht is *Apollo* 3,288 gross registered tons and 339.6 ft *103,51 m* overall built in Northern Ireland in 1936 and registered in Panama.

The largest private sailing yacht ever built was the full-rigged 350 ft *106 m* auxiliary barque *Sea Cloud* (formerly *Hussar*), owned by the oft-married Mrs. Marjorie Merriweather Post-Close-Hutton-Davies-May (1888–1973), one-time wife of the U.S. Ambassador in the U.S.S.R. Her four masts carried 30 sails with the total canvas area of 36,000 ft² *3 344 m²*.

Largest sail The largest sail ever made was a parachute spinnaker with an area of 18,000 ft² *1 672 m²* (more than two-fifths of an acre [*0,1 ha*]) for Vanderbilt's *Ranger* in 1937.

Most competitors The most competitors ever to start in a single race was 1,064 sailing boats in the Round Zealand (Denmark) race starting on 20 June 1975, over a course of 375 km *233 miles*. The greatest number to start in a race in Britain was 479 keeled yachts and multihulls on June 29 1974 from Cowes in the Annual Round-the-Island race.

STOP PRESS

CHAPTER 2—ANIMALS AND PLANTS

Page 53

Hay Fever A pollen count of 2,824 (av. pollen grains per cubic metre over 24 hours) was recorded at Aberystwyth on 29 June 1961. On 21 July 1971 the Asthma Research Unit at Penarth, Glamorgan, recorded a count of 161,037 for fungal spores.

CHAPTER 3—NATURAL WORLD

Page 60

Deepest Cave On 11 Aug. 1975 a depth of 4,166 ft *1 270 m* was attained by a French team in Gouffre de la Pierre Saint-Martin (see also page 254). Deepest Cave in Italy: Grotta di Monte Cucco, Appenines, 3,024 ft *922 m.*

Page 60

Highest Mountain On 25 July 1973 the Chinese News Agency announced that the height of Mount Everest, according to a new survey, was 29,029.24 ft. Since the official Government of India altitude since 1953 has been 29,028 ft or *8 847,7 m* (usually quoted as 8 848 m) the new metric height of *8 848,11 m* would entail no alteration. In practical terms the altitude could only be justified as 29,032 ft ± 25 ft or *8 841–8 856 m.*

Page 65

Progressive Temperature Extremes It was confirmed in July 1975 that the 139°F *59,4°C* temperature officially published for Insala, Algeria was misprinted and can be disregarded.

CHAPTER 4—UNIVERSE AND SPACE

Page 73

Ion Rockets Lewis Research Center, Cleveland, Ohio has announced that an ion thruster has been made operative for 9,715 hours (404 days 19 hours).

Oldest Man in Space Donald Kent "Deke" Slayton (b. Sparta, Wisconsin, U.S.A., 1 Mar. 1924), the 77th man in space, was aged 51 years 145 days when he landed from the Apollo-Soyuz mission on 24 July 1975.

CHAPTER 5—THE SCIENTIFIC WORLD

Page 74

Closest Approach to the Sun The research spacecraft *Helios* approached within 28 million miles *45 million km* of the Sun on 18 Mar. 1975. It carried both German and U.S. instrumentation.

Page 74

Progressive Rocket Altitude Kennedy Space Center, Cape Canaveral U.S. *Pioneer II* launch date 5 April 1973.

Page 77

Miniature Bottles The largest reported collection of unduplicated miniature bottles is one of 1,127 amassed over 21 years by G. H. White of Warminster, Wiltshire.

CHAPTER 6—ARTS AND ENTERTAINMENTS

Page 87

Most Expensive Sculpture A price of $750,000 (*£326,000*) was paid on 1 May 1974 at Sotheby Parke Bernet's salerooms Madison Avenue, New York City for Constantin Brancasi's polished bronze *Negresse Blonde* of 1926.

Page 88

Rarest Sound In the southern Bushman language !xo there is a click articulated with both lips, which is written ⊙.

Page 91

Shortest place names Sweden also has a place named Å in Vikholandet.

Page 93

Manuscript, highest priced A price of $250,000 (*£108,000*) was paid at Sotheby Parke Bernet on 2 May 1975 for the illuminated Iranian manuscript of Firdausis *Shah Nameh* (Book of Kings) dated Herat, August 1599.

Page 94

Best selling authors The publishers William Morrow & Co. Inc. of New York have estimated the world wide sales of the 131 fiction works of the late Earl Eric Stanley Gardner had by 1 Jan. 1975 exceeded 300,000,000 in 23 languages.

Page 95

Best Sellers The revised sales figures for *Valley of the Dolls* in June 1975 was 18,000,000 copies.

Page 95

Most Expensive Poem The U.S. Congress was revealed in June 1975 to have appropriated $5,500 to the poet, who wrote the poem "Lighght". Since this is not merely the title but also the entire poem, the cost to the unconsulted U.S. taxpayer was $785.71 per letter.

Page 95

Most Successful sloganeer Jack Gasneck was born 25 Mar. 1918.

Page 96

Map Least Informative The price of the sheet with a single line in May 1973 was 70c.

Page 97

Newspaper Most Expensive The selling price of *The Sunday Times*, when raised to 15p (3 shillings), surpassed the 2s 8d of *The London Gazette* of Nov. 1845.

Page 98

Advertising Rate A full page on The *Sunday Express* rate card for July 1975 was £12,992.

Page 98

Most Durable Organist Frederick Bell was appointed organist at All Saints Parish Church, Skelton, Cleveland, England in August 1902, and was still playing in 1975. His father Robert had been appointed in 1859.

STOP PRESS

Page 99

Organ Marathon Keith Rawlinson, 22, sustained a church organ recital at Rosegrove Methodist Church, Burnley for 86 hours on 21–25 July 1975. Vince Bull played an electric organ at the Oswald Hotel, Scunthorpe, Lincolnshire for 144 hours on 4–10 Aug. 1974.

Page 104

Most Successful Recording Artist The life-time sales of Bing Crosby on 179 labels reached 400,000,000 by July 1975. His new album "That's What Life is all About" is due for release in November 1975.

Page 105

Biggest Sellers For James E. Meyrs *read* James E. Myers.

Page 107

Most record requests Mrs. Jean Shrimpling of Grimsby, Humberside claimed an aggregate record 435 national and local radio requests by 1 June 1975, which figure was also reached by Mrs. Wain on 31 July 1975. Mrs. Hallgarth's claimed total up to 1 Aug. 1975 was 358.

Page 108

Most Durable Show Lawrence E. Speivak retired in 1975.

CHAPTER 7—THE WORLD'S STRUCTURES

Page 115

Sewage Works Largest In 1973 the average daily treatment rose to 835 million gallons per day of the tank capacity to 1,280,000 m³.

Page 117

Largest House It was reported in 1974 that 73 rooms had been demolished at Sandringham House.

Page 133

Colliery Deepest The depth of Bickershaw Colliery is now 3,690 ft *1 127 m.*

Page 133

Gold Mine Richest The Crown Mines aggregate yield is now 49.4 million ounces.

CHAPTER 8—MECHANICAL WORLD

Page 144

Fastest on British Rail A gas turbine powered A.P.T.E. (Advanced Passenger Train—Experimental) reached 149 m.p.h. on 27 July and 151 m.p.h. on 3 Aug. 1975 on the Swindon–Reading track.

Page 146

Rail Rover John Hobbs, Colin Best, Brian Pearson covered 9,783 miles *15 744 km* on a 7 day all-line British Rail Rover ticket, on 4–10 May 1975.

CHAPTER 9—BUSINESS WORLD

Pages 158–159

The greatest loss The greatest loss ever recorded by any enterprise in a year is £309,700,000 by the Post Office in the United Kingdom for 1974–75.

Page 165

Beer Mats The collection of Charles M. Schofield attained 14,293 by 1 May 1975.

Page 168

Medal The highest auction price paid for any British decoration was £9,500 at Sotheby's, London on 9 July 1975 for the K.T. (Knight of the Thistle) insignia of the 18th Earl of Erroll (1801–46) awarded in 1836.

Page 169

Table Cloth Largest A double damask table cloth of 219 yds *200 m* by 2 yds *1,7 m* made by John S. Brown & Sons Ltd. of Belfast to the order of a Royal Household in the Middle East was shipped in March 1975. There was a subsidiary order for matching napkins for 450 places.

Page 171

Sheep Shearing Mr. W. B. R. Davies of Maescar, Sennybridge, Brecon, Powys, sheared 609 sheep at Pentremenrig Farm, Llanwrsla, Dyfed in 9 working hours on 16 June 1975.

Page 172

Most Expensive Cheese Blue Cheshire Cheese was reported at 88p per pound in the late summer of 1975.

CHAPTER 10—THE HUMAN WORLD

Page 182

Oldest Head of State The date of birth of H.E. Hon. Mzee Jomo Kenyatta has not been established. In the current edition of "*Who's Who*", he states "born (approximately) 1889". This would make him at least more than 2 years older than Marshal Tito.

Page 203

Largest Sundae The estimated number of calories in the 3,956¾ lb. sundae was 2,121,306.

Page 205

Longest Telephone Call 765 hours from 15 February to 19 March 1975 between members of the Delta Gamma Sorority and Sigma Nu Fraternity, University of Nebraska.

Page 207

School— Most Expensive (World) The Oxford Academy, now located at Westbrook, Connecticut, U.S.A., charges annual tuition fees of $9,600 (£4,175).

CHAPTER 11—HUMAN ACHIEVEMENTS

Page 214

Most Travelled Man The mileage of J. Hart Rosdail as of 30 June 1975 grew to 1,482,729 miles *2 386 221 km.*

Page 217

Mountaineering For Junko Tabai read Junko Tabei.

Page 222

Coin Snatching A North American record of 65 "quarters" (25 cent pieces) was set by Gerry Berg of Vancouver, British Columbia, Canada on 18 June 1975.

Page 224

Disc Jockey A marathon of 800 hours was completed by Mark Gondelman at Woodstock, New York on 4 July to 7 Aug. 1975.

Page 228

Pogo Stick Jumping Scott Spencer, 13 of U.S.A. covered 6 miles in 6½ hours in September 1974.

Page 228

Potato Peeling A spud-bashing record for 60 minutes was established by a team of five from the 2nd Bletchley Company of The Boys' brigade in July 1975.

Page 229

Snakes and Ladders A marathon game of 168 hours was played by a team of 6 (4 always in play) from Airedale High School, Castleford, West Yorkshire on 11–18 July 1975.

Page 231
Tunnel of Fire Tim Macko of Illinois passed through a 6 ft 8 in square tunnel 157 ft 7 in *48,03 m* long on 20 July 1975.

Page 234
Cheese 16 oz. *509 g* in 3 min 17 sec by John Wharton at Swiss Colony Cheese Store, Aurora, Colorado, U.S.A. on 28 June 1975.

CHAPTER 12—SPORTS, GAMES AND PASTIMES

Page 241
Angling *Field & Stream* ratified a lake trout of 65 lb. *29,48 kg* caught by Larry Daunis at Great Bear Lake, N.W.T., Canada on 8 Aug. 1970.

Page 246
Basketball The longest recorded marathon played to F.I.B.A. rules (10 min half time intervals permitted) is 56 hrs 1 min by two teams of five players (no substitutes) from St. Mary's High School, Pennsylvania, U.S.A. on 24–26 June 1975.

Page 247
Bar Billiards A marathon of 262 hrs was played by 4 players from the "Five Bells", Colchester, Essex on 25 July–5 Aug. 1975.

Page 253
Canoeing Most British titles John L. Oliver has increased his total to 28.

Page 258
Cricket John Murray's total dismissals in a wicket keeping career reached 1,517 (a record 1,262 catches plus 255 stumpings) between 1952 and close of play on 12 Aug. 1975.

Page 259
Cricket The world record for receipts from a match is £119,500 from the Second Test between England and Australia at Lord's on 31 July–5 Aug. 1975.

Page 264
Roller Cycling A distance of 547 miles 410 yds *880,686 km* was achieved in 12 hours by the Schiffco Racing Team in London, Ontario, Canada on 5 Apr. 1975.

Page 271
Football The Fossa Youth Club, County Kerry, Ireland, played outdoor 5 a side football for 57 hours 1–3 Aug. 1975.

Page 276
Horse Racing Colin Turner, London Broadcasting's tipster, tipped 263 winners in the 74 days between February and May 1975.

Page 281
Golf Jack Nicklaus won his 16th title (U.S. P.G.A.) at Akron, Ohio, U.S.A. on 10 August 1975.

Page 291
Ice Skating Mark Losure and Steve Roberts completed 100 hrs at Ice Dome Rink, Indianapolis, Indiana on 1–5 Jan. 1975.

Page 292
Indoor Games Chess: Tony Deline and Ray Wood played Chess for 122 hrs at the Peterborough Holiday Inn, Ontario, Canada on 26–31 Dec. 1974.

Page 293
Darts The record low for 1,001 finishing on a "double" is 23 darts by Leighton Rees at Bettws, Glamorgan on 12 July 1975.

Page 317
Skiing Pino Meynet (Italy) recorded 120.784 m.p.h. *194,384 km/h* above Cervinia, Italy in July 1975.

Page 320
Squash Marathon 70 hours 12 minutes by Martyn Sayer and John Wilkinson at St. Bees School, St. Bees, Cumbria in July 1975.

Page 322
Double crossing Fastest double crossing of English Channel is 30 hours by Jon Erikson on 15 Aug. 1975.

Fastest relay Fastest crossing by a relay team is 8 hours 51 min by Hetzel's Volunteers in Aug. 1974.

Page 323
Swimming Richard Glynn has increased his total crossing, of the Solent to 27.

Page 324
Swimming Margaret Kelly, of Leeds, W. Yorkshire, swam 100 m breaststroke in 1 min 05.48 sec, a British record, on 15 Aug. 1975.

Pages 328–9
Track and Field Athletics Decathlon: 8,524 points, Bruce Jenner (U.S.A.) Eugene, Oregon 8–9 Aug. 1975. Women's Shot Putt: 70 ft 10½ in *21,60 m* Marianne Adam (East Germany) East Berlin 6 Aug. 1975. Mens 100 metres 9.9 sec. Reggie Jones, (U.S.A.) Boston, Mass. 26 July 1975.

The British record (women) 4 × 400 m relay is 3 min 26.6 sec, run by the Great Britain team at Nice, France, 17 Aug. 1975.

Page 334
Walking The oldest world record breaker is Gerhard Weidner (West Germany) (b. 15 Mar. 1933) who broke the world 20 mile track walking record at Hamburg, West Germany on 25 May 1974 when aged 41 years and 71 days.

Page 335
Water Skiing Paul Seaton (G.B.) jumped 167½ ft *53,75 m* in July 1975. The British barefoot jump record is 36 ft *11 m* by Dennis Akins at Northampton on 15 June 1975.

ADDITIONAL PHOTO CREDITS

Page 237 Rudyard Kipling *(The Mansell Collection)*
Page 240 Janet Lynn *(Associated Press)*
Page 246 The Harlem Globetrotters *(Gerry Cranham)*
Page 248 Nino Bibbia *(Gerry Cranham)*
Page 250 Pedlar Palmer *(Press Association)*
Page 251 Muhammad Ali and George Foreman *(Associated Press)*

ACKNOWLEDGEMENTS

J. W. Arblaster, Esq., A.I.M.; James Bond; British Airways; British Museum (Natural History); British Rail; British Travel; British Waterworks Association; A. W. Bulley, Esq.; Henry G. Button, Esq.; Kenneth H. Chandler, Esq.; Central Electricity Generating Board; Central Office of Information; Dr. A. J. C. Charig; Sq. Ldr. D. H. Clarke, D.F.C., A.F.C. Clerk of Dail Eireann; Fédération Aéronautique Internationale; Fédération Internationale de l'Automobile; Fédération Internationale des Hôpitaux; Frank L. Forster, Esq.; *Fortune*; Dr. Francis C. Fraser; General Post Office; *Greensboro Daily News*; A. Herbert, Esq. (New Zealand); Michael E. R. R. Herridge, Esq.; Dr. Arthur H. Hughes (Chairman Guinness Superlatives Ltd., 1954–1966); Derek Hurst, Esq.; Imperial War Museum; Institute of Strategic Studies; Erich Kamper; Kline Iron and Steel Company; Mr. Michael D. Lampen; The Library of Congress, Washington D.C.; *Lloyd's Register of Shipping*; London Transport Board; The late T. L. Marks, Esq. O.B.E., T.D.; (Chairman 1966–71); K. G. McWhirter, M.A., M.Sc.; Meteorological Office; Metropolitan Police; Alan Mitchell, Esq. B.A., B.Ag.(For); Music Research Bureau; National Aeronautics and Space Administration; National Geographic Society; National Maritime Museum; National Physical Laboratory; Mrs. Susann Palmer; E. T. Pugh, Editor; A. J. R. Purssell, Esq. (Chairman 1971–75); *Manned Spacecraft*; Jean Reville, Esq.; Royal Astronomical Society; Royal Botanic Gardens; Royal Geographic Society; Royal National Life-boat Institution; Dr. Albert Schwartz; John H. Stephens, Esq.; John W. R. Taylor, Esq.; Trinity House; U.N. Statistical Office; Juhani Virola; Gerry L. Wood, Esq., F.Z.S.; World Meteorological Organization; Francis Albert Young; Zoological Society of London.

Also to Mrs. Barbara Anderson, Mrs. Sally Bennett, Mrs. Christine Bethlehem, Mrs. Rosemary Bevan, D. Richard Bowen, Esq., Signa. Wendy Cirillo, Mrs. Pamela Croome, Miss Trudy Doyle, Mlle. Béatrice Frei, N. Gardner, Esq., Miss Amanda Griffin, Mrs. Susan Gullen, Harold C. Harlow, Esq., Peter H. Hathaway, Esq., Miss Tessa Hegley, E. C. Henniker, Esq., Mrs. Angela Hoaen, David F. Hoy, Esq., Miss Gillian Iddins, Mrs. Eileen Jackson, Mrs. Hilary Leavey, Mrs. Jane Mayo, G. M. Nutbrown, Esq., Mrs. Margaret Orr-Deas, Peter B. Page, Esq., John Rivers, Esq., Mrs. Judith Sleath, Mrs. Anne Symonds, Andrew Thomas, Esq. (Associate Editor 1964–68), Mrs. Winnie Ulrich, Mrs. Beverley Waites, Peter Whatley, Esq., Miss Diana Wilford.

An asterisk against a page reference indicates that there is a further reference in the Stop Press section

345

347

Indexing by

Gordon Robinson

CITIUS ALTIUS
EVOLUTION OF 80 YEARS OF
Athens 1896 to Montréal 1976

	1896–1912 Athens/Paris/St. Louis/ Athens/London/Stockholm	1920 Antwerp	1924 Paris/ Chamonix	1928 Amsterdam/ St. Moritz	1932 Los Angeles/ Lake Placid
CITIUS 100 metres sprint (men)	*11.8 T. Burke (USA) 1896; 10.8 F. W. Jarvis, J. W. B. Tewksbury (both USA) 1900; J. A. Rector (USA); R. E. Walker (SAF) 1908; *10.6 D. F. Lippincott (USA) 1912	—	10.6 sec H. M. Abrahams (GBR)	*10.6 sec P. Williams (CAN) R. MacAllister (USA) J. E. London (GBR)	10.3 sec E. Tolan (USA) R. H. Metcalfe (USA)
100 metres sprint (women)	not held	not held	not held	12.2 sec E. Robinson (USA)	11.9 sec S. Walasiewicz (POL) H. Strike (CAN)
Cycling 1,000 metres time trial (track conditions vary)	not held	not held	not held	1:14.4 W. Falck-Hansen (DEN)	1:13.0 E. Gray (AUS)
Swimming 100 metres free style (men)	1:22.2 A. Hajós (HUN) 1896; 1:13.4 C. M. Daniels (USA) 1906, and 1:05.6, 1908; *1:02.4 D. P. Kahanamoku (USA) 1912	*1:00.4 D. P. Kahanamoku (USA)	59.0 sec J. Weissmuller (USA)	58.6 sec J. Weissmuller (USA)	*58.0 sec Y. Miyazaki (JPN)
Swimming 100 metres free style (women)	*1:19.8 F. Durak (AUS/NZL) 1912	1:13.6 E. M. Bleibtrey (USA)	*1:12.2 M. Wehselau (USA)	1:11.0 A. Osipowick (USA)	1:06.8 H. Madison (USA)
Ice Speed Skating 500 metres (men)	not held	not held	44.0 sec C. Jewtraw (USA)	43.4 sec C. Thunberg (FIN) B. Evensen (NOR)	43.4 sec J. A. Shea (USA)
Ice Speed Skating 500 metres (women)	not held	not held	not held	not held	exhibition only
ALTIUS High Jumping (men)	5' 11" 1,81 m E. H. Clarke (USA) 1896; 6' 2¾" 1,90 m I. K. Baxter (USA) 1900; 6' 3" 1,905 m H. F. Porter (USA) 1908; 6' 4" 1,93 m A. W. Richards (USA) 1912	6' 4¼" 1,94 m R. W. Landon (USA)	6' 6" 1,98 m H. M. Osborn (USA)	—	—
High Jumping (women)	not held	not held	not held	5' 2½" 1,59 m E. Catherwood (CAN)	5' 5" 1,65 m J. M. Shiley (USA) M. Didrikson (USA)
Pole Vaulting (men)	10' 9¾" 3,30 m W. W. Hoyt, 1896 & I. K. Baxter, 1900. 11' 6" 3,50 m C. E. Dvorak 1904. E. T. Cooke & A. C. Gilbert 12' 2" 3,70 m 1908. 12' 11½" 3,95 m H. S. Babcock 1912 (all USA)	13' 5" 4,09 m F. K. Foss (USA)	—	13' 9¼" 4,20 m S. W. Carr (USA)	14' 1¾" 4,31 m W. W. Miller (USA)
FORTIUS Weight-lifting Two-handed Clean and Jerk	not held	253½ lb 115 kg F. Bottino (ITA) E. J. Jensen (DEN)	308½ lb 140 kg H. Tammer (EST)	330½ lb 150 kg A. Luhaäär (EST) J. Skobla (TCH)	336 lb 152,5 kg J. Skobla (TCH)

Abbreviations: The official Olympic Games abbreviations are used:
AUS—Australia; AUS/NZL—Australasia; CAN—Canada; DEN—Denmark; EST—Estonia; FIN—Finland; FRA—France; GBR—Great Britain; GDR—East Germany; GER—Germany or since 1968 West Germany; HOL—Netherlands; HUN—Hungary; ITA—Italy; JPN—Japan; NOR—Norway; POL—Poland; ROM—Romania; SAF—South Africa; TCH—Czecho-slovakia; USA—United States of America; URS—Soviet Union.